FINANCIAL ACCOUNTING

FINANCIAL

ACCOUNTING

FOURTH EDITION

ROBERT K. ESKEW
Professor of Accounting
Purdue University

DANIEL L. JENSEN
Ernst & Young Professor of Accounting
The Ohio State University

McGRAW-HILL, INC.

New York   St. Louis   San Francisco   Auckland   Bogotá   Caracas
Lisbon   London   Madrid   Mexico   Milan   Montreal   New Delhi
Paris   San Juan   Singapore   Sydney   Tokyo   Toronto

Financial Accounting

1   2   3   4   5   6   7   8   9   0   VNH VNH   9   0   9   8   7   6   5   4   3   2   1

ISBN 0-07-019616-8

This book was set in Times Roman by Progressive Typographers, Inc.
The editors were Johanna Schmid and Peggy Rehberger;
the production supervisor was Leroy A. Young.
The cover was designed by Wanda Siedlecka.
Von Hoffmann Press, Inc., was printer and binder.

Cover photo by André Baranowski.

Library of Congress Cataloging-in-Publication Data

Eskew, Robert K., (date).
   Financial accounting / Robert K. Eskew, Daniel L. Jensen. — 4th ed.
     p.   cm.
   Includes index.
   ISBN 0-07-019616-8
   1. Accounting.   I. Jensen, Daniel L.   II. Title.
HF5635.E85   1992
657—dc20   91-2884

ABOUT THE AUTHORS

ROBERT K. ESKEW is Professor of Accounting at Purdue University. He received his Ph.D. from Purdue University, has taught at the University of Iowa, has held a visiting assistant professorship at Stanford University, Graduate School of Business, and has been a staff member in the Office of the Chief Accountant, Securities and Exchange Commission. A contributor to *The Accounting Review* and the *Journal of Finance,* Professor Eskew's research interests are focused in financial accounting. He has coordinated the introductory financial accounting course at Purdue for fifteen years, where he frequently teaches two 450-student sections per semester. To date, 49,000 students have enrolled in introductory accounting during his administration.

DANIEL L. JENSEN is the Ernst & Young Professor of Accounting at The Ohio State University. He is co-author of *Advanced Accounting* (1988) and *Accounting for Changing Prices* (1984). Professor Jensen has served on many editorial boards and has just completed a three-year term as editor of *Issues in Accounting Education.* His research has been published in various journals, including *The Accounting Review,* the *Journal of Accounting Research,* the *Quarterly Review of Economics and Business,* the *Journal of Business Finance and Accounting,* and *Financial Management.* His national committee work includes service on the AICPA's Education Executive Committee and the Council and the Education Advisory Committee of the American Accounting Association. Professor Jensen has taught at the University of Illinois at Urbana-Champaign, at Purdue University, at Indiana University at Bloomington, and at the University of Minnesota. He received his Ph.D. from The Ohio State University. In 1991, Professor Jensen received the Outstanding Ohio Accounting Educator Award.

CONTENTS IN BRIEF

CONTENTS

PART **4** ACCOUNTING FOR LIABILITIES AND EQUITY 415

SUPPLEMENTARY TOPICS 789

PREFACE

Communication between teacher and student is perhaps the most critical element of the education process. Yet the ever-increasing number of students in our accounting classrooms makes it more and more difficult for teachers to reach their students. Students come to rely on texts more than on teachers, and teachers must spend increasing amounts of time explaining assigned texts, which leaves reduced amounts of time for discussion of what they view as really important. Recognizing this environment, we have endeavored to write a text that enables students to learn the fundamentals from the text, allowing the teacher to concentrate on particularly difficult areas and to elaborate on the basic material provided by the text. With the help of McGraw-Hill editors, we have made a special effort to present clearly understandable explanations of the fundamentals of financial accounting. We do not simply point to numerical examples and leave it at that. Rather, we explain basic issues thoroughly and demonstrate their applications. At the same time, we have tried to present the material in such a way as to communicate to the student the importance, pervasiveness, and dynamic nature of the financial accounting function.

Experience with the first three editions has confirmed our belief in this approach and has led to a significant number of refinements in the fourth edition. The principal changes are as follows:

- Every chapter and supplementary topic in the book has been edited for greater clarity and enhanced teaching effectiveness. Every effort has been made to use direct and simple wording, to provide concrete examples whenever possible, to define key accounting terms when first used, and to use terminology consistently from one chapter to another.

- A fifth supplementary topic, "Recognition and Measurement," has been added. It can be used in conjunction with Chapter 2 or later as a stand-alone topic.

- Account titles used in journal entries and related discussions have been standardized throughout the text and in exercises, problems, and solutions. A list of these account titles is presented in the Instructor's Resource Manual and as a supplement (see the Instructor Supplements section of this Preface). We believe that this standardization will help students understand accounting fundamentals by reducing one source of variation in terminology. However, we also believe that students should be prepared for the wide variation in terminology they will encounter in practice. Accordingly, alternative terminology is noted in discussions, and excerpts from real financial statements are presented without alteration.

- A new category of assignment materials, "Analytical Opportunities," has been added to every chapter. These additional assignment items, at least two of which are presented for each chapter, require students to prepare brief essays and analyses that address conceptual, institutional, and ethical issues related to the chapter.

- End-of-chapter materials have been significantly revised. Questions, exercises, and problems are each arranged in the order in which the related topics appear in the chapter.

SELF-TEACHING ASPECTS OF THE TEXTBOOK

Since the text and its accompanying materials must do much of the teaching in today's accounting classes, the text needs to contain examples and demonstrations that will assist the student when learning concepts and procedures. Furthermore, it should contain examples of the use of accounting concepts and procedures in decision settings. In this edition, as in the previous editions, our writing has been guided by the manner in which a good teacher thinks and talks in class. When users identified sections of the text with which students experienced difficulty, we attempted to rework the material to make it easier for students to digest. If the section was of fundamental importance, we worked with it until a more straightforward treatment could be found. If the section was an extension of a fundamental point, we considered relocating the section to a footnote, an appendix, an analysis section, or a separate Supplementary Topic. In some cases we deleted difficult technical material that was not of fundamental importance to an introductory course.

The ancillary materials for this text augment the self-teaching ability of the book, both in the small classroom and in the large-course setting. These materials have been thoroughly revised.

HELPING STUDENTS DEVELOP ACCOUNTING SKILLS

Beyond the self-teaching aspects of the book, we hope to meet another more general need of the students in the introductory accounting sequence. While the financial accounting function is an important and pervasive one, there is a tendency for introductory students not to appreciate its importance fully. For many students the course continues to be dull and without purpose. Our goal has been to present accounting as a dynamic field that performs important functions in our society and is a vital part of business activity. While the material covered in our text is primarily traditional, we present it in an issue-oriented atmosphere using the following tools:

- Analysis sections
- Conceptual framework for accounting procedures
- Examples from business environments
- Organizational and teaching flexibility
- Textual learning aids

Let us consider each of these tools in turn.

ANALYSIS SECTIONS

The analysis sections are discussions of factual situations that direct attention to issues that lie beyond the accounting concepts and procedures. Most chapters present three or four analysis sections to emphasize the interpretation of accounting issues in a decision-making environment, rather than the related calculations and procedures. Each analysis moves from a brief description of a business setting to a discussion of related issues of interest to an investor, lender, entrepreneur, manager, systems designer, or another user of accounting information. Some present judgments and inferences about the firm made by a user of accounting information. Others describe the organizational contexts in which accounting information arises. We have found that the analysis sections draw students into the chapter subject matter and stimulate them to think more carefully about its importance.

CONCEPTUAL FRAMEWORK FOR ACCOUNTING PROCEDURES

The discussion of accounting concepts is carefully woven into the fabric of the book. The conceptual framework for accounting is introduced gradually as the chapters unfold, and the discussion of concepts is integrated with the presentation of related accounting procedures. Chapter 1 describes the relationship between the conceptual framework for accounting and generally accepted accounting principles and procedures. Chapter 1 also presents the basic concepts of cost, asset, liability, and equity and demonstrates their interrelationship in the fundamental accounting model. The presentation of elements of financial

statements in Chapter 2 begins with a revised discussion of the concepts of the financing and operating cycles, periodicity, revenue recognition, and matching. A tabular summary of concepts is presented at the end of Chapters 1 and 2 to help students understand the conceptual framework. In a similar way, the accounting topics considered in subsequent chapters flow from a discussion of related aspects of the conceptual framework.

BUSINESS ENVIRONMENT

We attempt to make students feel comfortable with actual financial statements by introducing excerpts from carefully selected annual reports throughout the text. In each case we have chosen firms whose names and activities are familiar to students. For example, Chapter 2 presents a facsimile of the Wal-Mart Stores, Inc., financial statements to illustrate the form of financial statements and to provide a basis for a simple analysis of Wal-Mart's operating results and growth. In Chapter 15 we have reproduced the complete financial statements and accompanying notes for Compaq Computer Corporation as the basis for illustrating a variety of financial statement analyses. In this way, a student becomes increasingly at home with real-world financial statements and consequently more receptive to the accounting procedures and concepts on which they are built. In addition, we have drawn on the annual reports of many other companies to illustrate our discussions and to enhance further the students' awareness of current financial practices.

ORGANIZATIONAL AND TEACHING FLEXIBILITY

Recognizing that each instructor emphasizes different aspects of financial accounting, we have written our text with a high degree of organizational and teaching flexibility. For example, one instructor may emphasize students' understanding of financial statement content and organization; another instructor may stress accounting procedures. Chapters 2 through 5 are designed to accommodate both methods of teaching. In Chapter 2 we examine the content and organization of the income statement, balance sheet, and statement of changes in retained earnings with minimal attention to accounting procedures. In Chapters 3 through 5 we present the elements of the accounting cycle in three manageable increments. Chapter 3 examines the basic elements of the double-entry system and the recording of events. Chapter 4 is devoted exclusively to adjusting entries, and Chapter 5 discusses closing entries and the worksheet. In Chapters 3 through 5 we continue to emphasize the issues of financial statement content and organization. Instructors desiring a financial statement focus for their course can emphasize Chapter 2 and the financial statement portions of Chapters 3 through 5. Instructors who wish to emphasize accounting procedures can focus on the material describing elements of the accounting cycle presented in Chapters 3 through 5.

Another measure of flexibility is provided for teaching long-term liabilities. Chapter 10, "Current Liabilities, Contingent Liabilities, and the Time Value of Money," concludes with an optional section on the time value of money. If this section is not taught, students will go on to Chapter 11A, which teaches accounting for long-term liabilities using straight-line interest calculations. If the time value of money is covered, students will progress to Chapter 11B, which presents accounting for long-term liabilities using time-value-of-money calculations. In other words, students normally study *either* Chapter 11A or 11B, depending on whether or not the time-value-of-money section of Chapter 10 is covered.

Still more flexibility is provided for instructors who do not wish to give detailed consideration to topics such as the cash flow statement (Chapter 13) and long-term investments, consolidated financial statements, and business combinations (Chapter 14). To permit various levels of coverage for such topics, those chapters are divided into two parts. The first part presents basic issues. Subsequent parts present further development of these issues. Technical issues are reserved for appendixes. The first part of each chapter can be used alone to present the basic issues and, if additional coverage is required, subsequent parts and appendixes may be assigned as well. In addition, as mentioned earlier, the book concludes with five Supplementary Topics—nonbusiness entities, changing prices, international operations, personal income taxation, and recognition and measurement—which instructors may use to supplement and extend discussion in the main part of the text. The Instructor's Resource Manual accompanying this text offers a number of alternative syllabi from which the instructor may select the one best suited to his or her needs.

LEARNING AIDS

Textual Aids

Every effort has been made to produce a text that is easy for students to follow and to learn from. Particular attention has been given to the readability of the text and to the smooth flow and development of ideas and examples. The following features are worthy of note:

LEARNING OBJECTIVES. Each chapter begins with a list of learning objectives that previews the content of the chapter and stimulates the student to begin thinking about the material to come.

RUNNING GLOSSARY. Definitions of key terms are provided in the margins to facilitate retention and quick review. All these terms are compiled into a complete glossary, with chapter references, that appears at the end of the book.

NARRATIVE SUMMARIES. Chapter summaries highlight basic points and principles.

KEY-TERM REVIEW. Each chapter ends with a list of key terms, with page references, for quick review.

DISCUSSION QUESTIONS. Discussion questions are provided at the end of each chapter. These relate directly to the basic principles covered in the chapter and can be used for student review, class discussion, or homework assignments.

EXERCISES AND PROBLEMS. Exercises and problems are provided at the end of each chapter. Exercises are designed to illustrate basic issues in isolation, whereas problems are more comprehensive and more demanding. Each exercise and problem is labeled as to the topic it covers, making it easy for the instructor to select appropriate exercises and problems to address specific areas.

ANALYTICAL OPPORTUNITIES. At least two "analytical opportunities" are provided at the end of each chapter. These assignment items require students to prepare brief essays and analyses that address conceptual, institutional, and ethical issues related to the chapter.

DEMONSTRATION PROBLEMS. Many chapters contain demonstration problems, which are comprehensive recaps of the chapter's main points. These demonstration problems serve as model solutions for students to refer to when working on assignment material, and they are also excellent means of reviewing the chapter's most important topics.

Student Supplements

In addition to the learning aids contained in the text, the following supplements are also available to assist students in mastering concepts and procedures:

STUDENT MASTERY GUIDE—by Charles A. Neyhart, Jr., and Patrick S. Kemp (Oregon State University). Coordinated with the text, each chapter of this study guide contains review materials in the form of learning objectives, chapter reviews keyed to the learning objectives, and key-term review. Novel features are a diagnostic pre-test (with solutions) and a common errors section. Two post-tests (with solutions) provide students with additional opportunities to check their mastery of chapter content.

PRACTICE SET — by Nancy O. Tang (Portland State University). Based on financial data for Tang's Toys, a hypothetical retail store organized as a corporation, this supplement gives students hands-on experience in applying the accounting data processing cycle procedures to the development of financial statements.

WORKING PAPERS — by Richard S. Webster (Ohio State University). This supplement provides students with all the forms needed for solving the exercises and problems at the end of each chapter.

ASHCO, FOURTH EDITION, FOR THE IBM PC, XT, AND PS/2 — by Louis F. Biagioni (Indiana University). This revised package teaches the monthly accounting cycle of a corporation. Students generate financial reports by recording transactions in a general journal and a subsidiary ledger, with the option of using special journals. Two monthly cycles can be completed, one computerized, one manual. The program allows instructors and students to create their own accounts and also includes user-friendly HELP screens. This package is available for student purchase for use with the IBM PC, XT, and PS/2.

FINANCIAL ACCOUNTING TEMPLATES AND PROBLEMS FOR LOTUS 1-2-3, THIRD EDITION — by George F. Hanks and Paul W. Parkison (Ball State University). A set of spreadsheet templates to be used to solve problems and perform analyses for financial accounting using LOTUS 1-2-3. Available for student purchase for use with the IBM PC, XT, and PS/2 with LOTUS 1-2-3 software. Key features include a wide variety of problems, a flexible spreadsheet format that allows for "what-if" analysis, and the inclusion of a Lotus 1-2-3 tutorial. Problems in the text that are *similar to* those on the templates are designated by a computer icon (🖳) in the margin.

Instructor Supplements

A number of teaching aids are available to instructors as well. They are as follows:

INSTRUCTOR'S RESOURCE MANUAL — by Paul F. Williams and Kristine Lawyer (North Carolina State University) and Raymond J. Krasniewski (The Ohio State University). This manual offers recommendations on teaching the text. Chapter-by-chapter discussion includes suggestions on the presentation of difficult topics and alternative presentations of important issues. The manual also incorporates numerous large-type transparency masters designed for use with the text. This manual provides

an outline of each chapter and sample outlines for structuring a course around conceptual or procedural emphases and for organizing one-quarter, one-semester, and two-quarter courses. To help instructors enrich their lectures, conceptual and procedural extensions add depth to textual material. A long problem tied to a conceptual lecture topic is provided for each chapter.

SOLUTIONS MANUAL. Fully worked out solutions to all questions, exercises, problems, and analytical opportunities in the text are provided. The solutions are thoroughly explained and presented in a way that conveys the mental processes students go through in solving problems. The entire solutions manual is printed in large type to facilitate the production of transparencies. In addition, transparencies and transparency masters are available for exercises, problems, and analytical opportunities.

CHECK FIGURES. These are provided for end-of-chapter exercises and problems and are available (upon request) in quantity to instructors for distribution to their classes.

CHART OF ACCOUNTS. This list of account titles used throughout the text and in exercises, problems, and solutions is available (upon request) in quantity to instructors for distribution to their classes. It is also provided in the Instructor's Resource Manual.

TEST BANK — by Arnold Schneider (Georgia Institute of Technology). This balanced blend of conceptual and procedural questions has been thoroughly revised. Questions are coded by difficulty level and organized by chapter topic. The test bank now consists of over 1,400 multiple-choice questions and is available both in book form and in a computerized test-writing system.

COMPUTERIZED TEST BANK: RH TEST — The RH Test and MicroTest systems give access to a broad range of testmaking functions. With it, instructors can prepare tests quickly and easily. This powerful program allows instructors to view questions as they are selected for a test; scramble questions to create different versions of the test; add questions; edit questions; select questions by type (multiple-choice, true-false, matching, essay, or short answer), objective, and difficulty; and view and save a test. It includes all the questions available in the printed test bank. Available for the IBM PC/PC-XT and Macintosh and true compatibles.

OVERHEAD TRANSPARENCIES. These transparencies provide solutions to the end-of-chapter exercises and problems and many exhibits from the text.

ACKNOWLEDGMENTS

The text and its supplements have been enriched by the comments of many reviewers. We are indebted to each of them, particularly to the following educators who assisted us with the fourth edition: B. Michael Doran, *Iowa State University;* Susan R. Downs, *Babson College;* Dennis H. Ferguson, *Cornell University;* Donald P. Holman, *Weber State College;* Herbert G. Hunt, *University of Vermont;* Randy D. Johnston, *Pennsylvania State University;* Lawrence A. Ponemon, *State University of New York/Albany;* Paul F. Williams, *North Caroline State University;* and William T. Wrege, *Ball State University.*

We also wish to thank those who responded to our detailed questionnaire on the second and third editions: Helen Adams, *Northwestern University;* Jaime Agudelo, *University of the Pacific;* Teresa Anderson, *University of Texas/Dallas;* Gene Andrusco, *California State University/San Bernardino;* Stephen P. Baginski, *Florida State University;* Ben-Hsien Bao, *Georgia Institute of Technology;* Thomas M. Barton, *University of Georgia;* Lawrence D. Brown, *State University of New York/Buffalo;* Harold L. Cannon, *State University of New York/Albany;* Madeleine J. Carzin, *State University of New York;* Donald M. Cash, *Pittsburg State University;* Paul Chaney, *Vanderbilt University;* Robert C. Chang, *University of Bridgeport;* Mel Choate, *North Seattle Community College;* Roger A. Chope, *University of Oregon;* John W. Cook, *Georgia State University;* Arthur V. Corr, *University of Wisconsin/Parkside;* JoAnn Noe Cross, *University of Wisconsin/Oshkosh;* Janet Cunningham, *University of Oklahoma;* Srikant M. Datar, *Carnegie Mellon University;* Donald Davis, *Modesto Junior College;* Louis E. Dawkins, *Mississippi State University;* Ray D. Dillon, *Georgia State University;* Robert S. Doud, *Adelphi University;* James Douglas, *Temple University;* Allen R. Drebin, *Northwestern University;* John A. Elliot, *Cornell University;* Mary A. Flanigan, *Towson State University;* John C. Gardner, *University of Wisconsin/LaCross;* Thomas A. Gavin, *University of Tennessee;* Laverne Gebhard, *University of Wisconsin/Milwaukee;* David Gershater, *New York University;* Terry Gregson, *University of Texas/San Antonio;* John G. Hamer, *University of Lowell;* Al L. Hartgraves, Jr., *Emory University;* Robert L. Hines, *Humboldt State University;* J. Robert Jackson, *University of Wisconsin/Stevens Point;* Elizabeth Jenkins, *San Jose State University;* Kumen Jones, *Arizona State University;* Peter B. Kenyon, *Humboldt State University;* Marsha Kertz, *San Jose State University;* and William C. Kilpatrick, *Colorado State University.*

Likewise, we thank Glen McLaren, *Pittsburg State University;* Judy McLean, *Otago University;* Thomas I. Miller, *Murray State University;* John D. Minch, *Cabrillo College;* Thomas P. Moncado, *Eastern Illinois University;* Athar Murtuza, *Northern Arizona University;* Ralph M. Newkirk, Jr., *Rutgers University;* Terry J. Nunley, *University of North Caroline/Charleston;* Janes H. Ogburn, *University of North Carolina/Greensboro;* Guy W. Owings, *Pittsburg State University;* Lawrence M. Ozzello, *University of Wisconsin/Eau Claire;* William R. Pasewark, *University of Georgia;* Ernest J. Pavlock, *Virginia Polytechnic and State University;* Paul Plumer, *Towson State University;* Andrew J. Potts, *University of District of Columbia;* Mahmood A. Qureshi, *California State University/Northridge;* Steven C. Reimer, *University of Iowa;* Alan Reinstein, *Wayne State University;* Marilyn Rholl, *Lane Community College;* Michael Ruble, *University of Idaho;* Victoria S. Rymer, *Towson State University;* Clayton R. Sager, *University of Wisconsin/Whitewater;* Emanuel Schwartz, *San Francisco State University;* Wilbert H. Schwotzer, *Georgia State University;* W. Richard Sherman, *Rutgers University;* Philip Silverman, *Adelphi University;* Daniel T. Simon, *Indiana University Northwest;* L. Murphy Smith, *Texas A&M University;* Manuel A. Tipgos, *University of Kentucky;* Thomas S. Wetzel, *Oklahoma State University;* Neil Wilner, *North Texas State University;* Charles J. Woelfel, *University of North Caroline/Greensboro;* and Paul Zarowin, *New York University.*

We are especially grateful to Virginia Bidgood at the University of Nevada/Las Vegas and Marilyn Rholl at Lane Community College, who carefully reviewed each question, exercise, and problem for consistency with text discussions and painstakingly reworked our solutions, examining them for accuracy, completeness, and clarity of presentation. In addition to the benefit of reviewers' advice, this book has been improved by the hundreds of students around the country whose reactions have come to us either directly or through their teachers. In addition, this book has been improved by the assistance and encouragement of our colleagues, including Raymond J. Krasniewski, Richard S. Webster, and Melvin Greenball at The Ohio State University and John W. Hatcher at Purdue University. Finally, we wish to thank the editorial staff at McGraw-Hill, including June Smith, Johanna Schmid, Peggy Rehberger, and Judy Motto; designer, Wanda Siedlecka, and production manager, Leroy Young, all of whose skill and patience enabled us to refine the effectiveness of this text as a teaching instrument.

Robert K. Eskew

Daniel L. Jensen

PART **1**

INTRODUCTION

Careful study of this chapter will enable you to:

1. Identify different forms of business entities and business activities.

2. Describe the structure of the accounting profession.

3. State the purpose of generally accepted accounting principles and auditors' opinions.

4. Recognize the primary financial statements.

5. Explain the concepts of assets, liabilities, and equity.

6. Write the fundamental accounting model.

7. Explain the concepts of revenue and expense.

8. Describe the relationship of the statement of retained earnings to the income statement and balance sheet.

1 INTRODUCTION TO ACCOUNTING AND ACCOUNTANTS

Accounting is the process of identifying, measuring, recording, and communicating economic information to permit informed judgments and decisions by users of the information. Accounting is one of the most fundamental activities of modern society. Virtually every formal organization has an accounting system that gathers economic information about its activities and that summarizes the information and communicates it to interested parties.

Contemporary accounting can trace its beginnings to the earliest civilizations. Primitive accounting records have been found buried in the deserts of ancient Babylonia and inscribed on the walls of Egyptian ruins. Indeed, some historians speculate that the need to account for food and goods may have been the primary factor that led primitive societies to develop written language. (Exhibit 1–1 shows an example of an early accounting record.) The Phoenicians, Greeks, and Romans all developed effective accounting methods. In the fifteenth and sixteenth centuries, the extensive commercial and trading ventures of the European powers depended in part on accounting records. Accounting systems also played a crucial role in the Industrial Revolution that marked the eighteenth and nineteenth centuries.

From its origins, accounting has evolved into a highly adaptable system for recording and communicating the financial effects of activities undertaken by a wide variety of organizations. Accounting is not, however, an end in itself. It is a process that is intended to provide information for financial decision making, both inside and outside the organization. Although accounting systems are designed and operated by highly trained people, their value resides not in the systems themselves, but in the usefulness of the information they communicate. Consequently, accounting cannot be mastered merely by learning the procedural aspects of accounting systems and reports. One must also learn how to use accounting information in making judgments and decisions about the organization from which the information is derived. In this text, we will be concerned with both the preparation and the uses of accounting data.

The purposes of this chapter are to characterize accounting information, to describe the profession engaged in the production of such information, and to introduce some of the basic accounting concepts. The chapter is divided into three parts: The first describes the relationship between accounting information and business entities; the second introduces the idea of generally accepted accounting principles; and the third describes the general form in which accounting information is conveyed to users of the information.

ACCOUNTING: The identification, measurement, recording, and communication of economic information for use in financial decision making.

EXHIBIT 1-1   AN ANCIENT ACCOUNTING RECORD

A clay tablet from Susa, Iran, made prior to the development of written language (ca. 3200 B.C.). The single circular impression and the two linear impressions are symbols for 1 bushel, 2 pecks (or approximately equivalent measures) of grain. The other impressed motifs, some of which are animal forms, are signatures of temple administrators to record the receipt of offerings or the distribution of food or seed. (Photo: Département des Antiquités Orientales, Musée du Louvre, Paris, France. Courtesy Denise Schmandt-Besserat)

BUSINESS ENTITIES AND ACCOUNTING INFORMATION

ACCOUNTING ENTITY:
An organization that has an identity separate from that of its owners and managers and for which accounting records are kept and accounting reports are issued.

Accounting identifies, measures, records, and communicates economic information about organizations called *accounting entities.* An **accounting entity** is an organization that has an identity separate from that of its owners and managers and for which accounting records are kept and accounting reports are issued.

Accounting entities can be either business or nonbusiness entities. *Business entities* (which are also called *firms* or simply *businesses*) are established to sell goods or provide services at a profit, whereas the principal purpose of *nonbusiness entities* is to provide goods or services without regard to profitability. Business entities range from corporate giants like General Motors and General Electric to neighborhood grocery stores and restaurants. Some examples of nonbusiness entities are educational institutions, governments, religious organizations, charities, museums, and hospitals. Both business and nonbusiness entities use accounting systems to maintain detailed records of economic information and to issue accounting reports. Despite their similarities, the accounting systems of the two types of entity are different in many respects. For example, the measurement and reporting of profit are of central importance in the accounting systems of business entities, but these activities have a very limited role in nonbusiness entities. This book emphasizes accounting for business entities; however, the specialized accounting problems that pertain to nonbusiness entities are considered briefly in Supplementary Topic A, at the end of this book.

Each business entity has an identity of its own, distinct from the identities of the persons who own and manage the entity and distinct from other business entities. (For example, General Motors is distinct from any of its owners or creditors and also from General Electric.) In the gathering and reporting of information about a business entity, the affairs and resources of the entity must be distinguished from the personal affairs and resources of the owners, managers, and creditors as well as from the affairs and resources of other organizations.

FORMS OF BUSINESS ENTITY

Most business entities take one of three forms: (1) sole proprietorship, (2) partnership, or (3) corporation. A *sole proprietorship* is a business entity owned by one person. Many small retail and service businesses are sole proprietorships, and the owner and manager are frequently the same person. For accounting purposes, the sole proprietorship and its owner are separate accounting entities; under law, however, the two accounting entities are considered a single entity.

A *partnership* is a business entity owned jointly by two or more persons called *partners.* For example, law firms are generally organized as partnerships and are composed, in some cases, of many partners. For accounting purposes, the partnership is an entity distinct from any of its partners; however, a partnership is not legally separate from the personal activities of its partners. Thus partnerships are characterized by *unlimited liability,* which means that each partner has unlimited responsibility for the debts of the partnership as a whole. Therefore, if all other partners are unable to pay the partnership's debts, creditors may collect the entire amount from a single solvent partner, regardless of the extent of that partner's financial interest (or equity) in the partnership. Furthermore, a partner cannot withdraw from a partnership or sell his or her ownership interest unless the partnership is dissolved.

The third form of business entity is the *corporation,* an organization formed under state law by one or more owners called *stockholders.* At the formation of a corporation, stockholders transfer resources to the corporate entity in exchange for shares of stock, which represent units of ownership in the corporation. Like sole proprietorships and partnerships, corporations are accounting entities separate from their owners, but unlike sole proprietorships and partnerships, corporations are also legal entities separate from the legal identities of their owners. Accordingly, the liability of each stockholder is limited to the dollar amount of that stockholder's ownership interest. In addition, stockholders may sell their stock without disrupting the legal existence of the corporate entity.

Although corporations are owned by stockholders, they are run by managers whose job it is to make day-to-day decisions about corporate activities. Managerial decisions are subject to approval by a board of directors elected by the stockholders, but the board's review is necessarily restricted to matters of overwhelming importance. Consequently, management—particularly in large enterprises—is entrusted with far-reaching decision-making authority that normally is not subject to review by stockholders or directors. The separation between managers and stockholders is further increased by the ease with which ownership of shares can be transferred from one individual to another. The personal identity of a corporation's stockholders changes as its outstanding shares are bought and sold. Indeed, the stock of many corporations is bought and sold continuously in well-organized stock markets. In short, the modern corporation is characterized by a significant separation of corporate ownership from managerial control.

Most large business entities are organized as corporations, while many smaller business entities are sole proprietorships or partnerships. Because of its importance, we will emphasize the corporate form of organization in the illustrations throughout this book. As the following analysis shows, the selection of an organizational form requires careful evaluation of the relative benefits of the three available choices.

ANALYSIS
CHOICE OF
ORGANIZATIONAL
FORM

Joe Brooks, who is organizing a small retail business, is in the process of choosing among three organizational forms—sole proprietorship, partnership, and corporation. Brooks has sufficient personal capital to finance 40 percent of the undertaking, but he must secure the remaining 60 percent from other sources. The following are questions that Brooks must consider before deciding which form of entity to establish:

1. *What is the impact of organizational form on financing arrangements?*

Whichever type of organization Brooks chooses, the additional 60 percent of the financing could be borrowed from a financial institution. However, if it proves difficult to interest financial institutions in backing a new venture, partnerships and corporations offer advantages over sole proprietorships. The advantage resides in the ability to secure financing from a partner or through the issuance of stock.

2. *What is the impact of organizational form on control of the business?*

A sole proprietorship, of course, would offer Brooks complete control over the operations of the business, except for limitations imposed by lending institutions in order to protect their interests. A partnership would transfer a 60 percent controlling interest to the one or more partners who would join Brooks. Similarly, a corporation would transfer a 60 percent controlling interest to other stockholders. However, if the stock were widely dispersed among many investors, Brooks might retain effective control of operations.

3. *What is the impact of organizational form on the sharing of net income?*

In a sole proprietorship with financing from banks, Brooks would hold an interest in the entire net income after interest payments to banks. In a partnership, he would have an interest in 40 percent of net income, which includes no interest expense, and the 60 percent remainder would be held by his partner or partners. In a corporation, Brooks would hold an interest in 40 percent of net income, which includes no interest expense but does include income taxes expense. Although we have insufficient information to identify which of these three organizational forms would be most appropriate for Brooks, the foregoing discussion indicates the general structure that such analysis would take.

TYPES OF
BUSINESS
ACTIVITY

Business entities engage in three different types of activity: merchandising, manufacturing, and service. *Merchandising* is the selling of goods manufactured by other entities. Clothing stores and grocery stores are examples of merchandisers. *Manufacturing* is the making and selling of goods; a single entity both creates and sells a product. General Motors and General Electric are examples of large manufacturers. *Service* is the selling of services rather than goods. For example, banks, dry cleaners, and movie theaters are largely service businesses.

The type of business activity engaged in influences the form of a company's accounting system and accounting reports. For example, the accounting system of a merchandising entity gathers information about the acquisition, storage, and sale of goods. The accounting system of a manufacturing entity gathers information about the acquisition, storage, and use of raw materials and the conversion of those materials into salable goods. In contrast, the accounting system of a service entity gathers information about the performance of services rather than the acquisition and sale of goods. Although the accounting system is influenced by the type of business activity for which it accounts, all accounting systems for business entities rest on the same conceptual foundation.

MANAGERIAL AND FINANCIAL ACCOUNTING

FINANCIAL STATEMENTS: Summary reports on the economic performance and status of a business entity as a whole, prepared for all decision makers outside the entity.

FINANCIAL ACCOUNTING: The process by which financial statements are prepared.

MANAGERIAL ACCOUNTING: Preparation of financial information designed for use by managers and decision makers inside the business entity.

Accounting systems communicate information to decision makers both inside and outside the business entity (see Exhibit 1–2). Summary reports on the economic performance and status of the business entity as a whole are prepared for stockholders, creditors, and other interested parties outside the entity. Such reports are the **financial statements** (or financial reports) for the entity, and the process that underlies their preparation is **financial accounting.** The accounting reports intended for use by managers and other decision makers inside the business entity are managerial reports, and the process by which they are prepared is **managerial accounting.**

Although managerial accounting reports and financial statements flow from the same accounting system, they differ significantly from one another in their objectives. We have noted that managerial accounting reports reflect the informational needs of the decision makers inside the business entity: the board of directors, the president, the treasurer, various vice presidents, and the host of supporting managerial positions. The firm's accountants are usually able to tailor managerial reports to the needs of each type of internal user.

In contrast, the financial statements prepared for external users must reflect the information needs of a wide variety of decision makers — stockholders, creditors, and other interested parties — taken together. As a result, the objectives that guide the preparation of financial statements have caused much debate and discussion throughout the business community. Further, the preparation of financial statements is guided by rules and conventions known as *generally accepted accounting principles,* which need not be observed in the preparation of internal managerial reports. The subject matter of this book will be financial accounting and the preparation and use of financial statements for business entities.

THE ACCOUNTING PROFESSION

Accounting systems and the accountants who maintain them are absolutely essential to the functioning of business enterprises of all types and sizes, to governments at all levels (federal, state, and local), and to nonbusiness organizations, such as hospitals, museums, and academic institutions. In the United States, well over one million persons are currently employed as accountants, which makes accounting one of the largest single areas of employment. Several million more persons are employed in accounting-related computer and clerical positions. The accounting profession is organized into three major groups: (1) approximately 15 percent of accountants work in nonbusiness entities, (2) 60 percent are employed in business entities, and (3) 25 percent are in public practice.

EXHIBIT 1–2   **FINANCIAL STATEMENTS AND MANAGERIAL ACCOUNTING REPORTS**

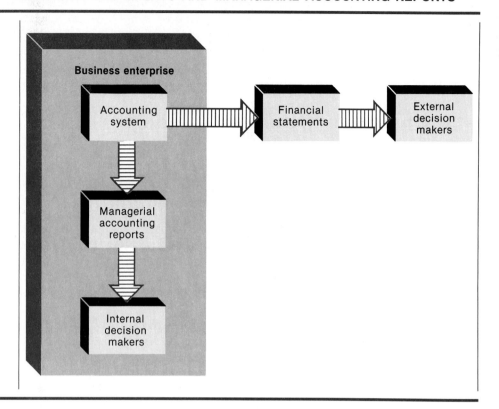

Accountants in Nonbusiness Entities

Nonbusiness entities are a diverse set of organizations, including educational institutions, governments, churches, charities, museums, and hospitals that are operated without regard to profit. In spite of their nonprofit basis, all nonbusiness organizations have accounting systems and most employ professional accountants who work with financial information reported to interested parties both inside and outside the organization. Two major groups of nonbusiness entities that employ accountants are educational institutions that employ accounting teachers and governments that employ accountants, auditors, and budgetary officers.

Accountants in Business Entities

Accountants in business entities are employed by individual enterprises (1) to gather and report the managerial accounting information needed for decision making inside the organization and (2) to prepare the financial statements required by stockholders, creditors, and others outside the enterprise.

Accountants in business entities are frequently called *managerial accountants* because they report to, and are part of, the entity's management. Managerial accountants provide accounting information for the business's income tax returns, budgeting, routine operating decisions, investment decisions, performance evaluation, and external financial reporting. Staff accounting positions in most businesses are under the direction of a *controller,* who is the chief accounting officer. Controllers are invariably trained as accountants and frequently have had prior experience in public accounting. Most corporate enterprises also designate a *treasurer,* who oversees financial resources and manages the cash of the organization. Treasurers frequently have an accounting background. *Internal auditors* are those management accountants who examine and evaluate the accounting systems of the enterprise to ensure their effectiveness and efficiency. Internal auditing, which is directed by management, differs from the auditing of financial statements, which is performed by accountants in public practice.

Accountants in Public Practice

Accountants who offer their professional services to the general public — much as many doctors and lawyers do — are referred to as *accountants in public practice.* The clients of public accountants include individuals, business enterprises, and nonbusiness entities. Public accounting organizations range in size from small single-accountant offices to large international firms. The largest public accounting firms in the United States have international operations, maintain offices in most major cities, and audit the financial statements of the majority of publicly held U.S. companies. Although in recent years the accounting profession has become increasingly concentrated in a relatively small number of large firms, the number of small public accounting firms nevertheless remains very large. Most accounting firms are organized as partnerships, although a few are incorporated. An accounting graduate who begins a career in public accounting enters as a staff accountant and from there progresses to senior accountant, to manager, and finally, to partner. Along this route, many senior accountants and managers accept positions in other enterprises, becoming, for example, corporate executives or managerial accountants.

Whether accounting is viewed from public practice or management, the financial statements are the focal point of the largest single segment of accounting activity. We turn now to the principles that guide the preparation of those statements.

GENERALLY ACCEPTED ACCOUNTING PRINCIPLES

GENERALLY ACCEPTED ACCOUNTING PRINCIPLES (GAAP): The basic set of rules and conventions for the accounting profession, consisting of both official pronouncements (standards) and uncodified practices and procedures.

Although financial statements are tailored to reflect the special circumstances of the individual business entity to which they apply, accountants in business entities and in public accounting firms are guided in the accounting process by a set of rules and conventions known as *generally accepted accounting principles.* **Generally accepted accounting principles (GAAP)** consist of (1) the official pronouncements (standards) of certain private-sector and governmental agencies and (2) the uncodified practices and procedures of the accounting profession. These two components of generally accepted accounting principles are of equal importance. Even though the volume of official pronouncements has increased in recent years, careful thought and research, supported by long experience, are still required in order to understand accounting systems and reports. Much of this accounting knowledge is not codified in the official pronouncements of rule-making agencies, yet it is widely used by accountants in practice and is evident in both professional and scholarly writings.

OFFICIAL PRONOUNCE-MENTS

FINANCIAL ACCOUNTING STANDARDS BOARD (FASB): The private-sector rule-making agency whose pronouncements are a primary source of generally accepted accounting principles.

The **Financial Accounting Standards Board (FASB)** is the main source of official pronouncements on generally accepted accounting principles. It is an independent rule-making agency created in the private sector and supported by various professional accounting organizations, including the American Institute of Certified Public Accountants (AICPA). The seven members of the FASB are highly qualified individuals drawn from public practice, industry, financial institutions, government, and education. The official pronouncements of the FASB are called *Statements of Financial Accounting Standards.* These also include the pronouncements of the Accounting Principles Board (APB), an earlier rule-making agency that was superseded by the FASB in 1973. The FASB statements are complex documents that must be studied by students embarking on careers in accounting. Although we will describe a few basic standards, thorough coverage is beyond the scope of an introductory text.

The FASB is designed to be responsive to both users and preparers of financial statements. The FASB is under the direction of the Financial Accounting Foundation, composed of representatives from government, law, academia, large and small businesses, large and small public accounting firms, investors, credit-granting agencies, and other users of accounting information. This group appoints members of both the FASB and the Financial Accounting Standards Advisory Council, which advises the FASB on its agenda and serves as a communication channel between the FASB and the diverse sets of persons and groups interested in financial statements. The FASB plays a critical role in the complex interactive process that leads to generally accepted accounting principles, a process in which the interests of reporting entities and the interests of the various groups requiring information about those entities are combined to reach mutually satisfactory results.

SECURITIES AND EX-CHANGE COMMISSION (SEC): The federal agency established by Congress to regulate securities markets and to ensure effective public disclosure of accounting information.

The FASB is also responsive to the **Securities and Exchange Commission (SEC),** an agency of the federal government that also issues pronouncements that become generally accepted accounting principles. The Securities and Exchange Commission was established by acts of Congress during the 1930s for the purpose of regulating the markets for common stock and other securities. An important objective of these securities acts was to ensure public disclosure of important financial information, and the SEC was empowered to prescribe accounting rules to achieve this objective. The SEC has used its broad powers to stimulate the private sector to undertake self-regulation of its accounting. The result is a growing body of accounting rules reflecting both the knowledge and understanding of practicing accountants and the demands for accounting information by users of financial statements.

THE CONCEPTUAL FRAMEWORK

CONCEPTUAL FRAME-WORK OF ACCOUNTING: General concepts that derive from the objectives of financial reporting and from which GAAP are derived.

Generally accepted accounting principles—whether official pronouncements (Financial Accounting Standards) or uncodified practices and procedures—rest on a **conceptual framework of accounting.** This framework, in turn, derives from the fundamental objective of financial reporting: to provide information that is useful in making business and economic decisions. The essential difference between an underlying concept and a principle is one of generality or breadth.[1]

[1] The FASB publishes *Statements of Financial Accounting Concepts,* which codify many important aspects of the conceptual framework of accounting. The scholarly and professional literatures of accounting also contain discussions of the conceptual framework, which is the subject of continuing debate.

CONCEPT: An idea or proposition that is broadly applicable to a variety of situations or contexts.

PRINCIPLE: A proposition or rule that applies to specific situations or contexts.

Concepts are broadly applicable in a variety of contexts, whereas **principles** are applicable only in fairly specific circumstances.

An example will further clarify the distinction between concepts and principles: The conceptual framework of accounting requires financial statements to report all assets of the entity, and it defines assets as "probable future economic benefits obtained or controlled by a particular entity." Certain "probable future benefits" very clearly satisfy the asset concept, but others are more difficult to assess. For example, most equipment that is owned and used by an entity clearly fits the definition of an asset. However, if the same equipment is rented by the entity, it may or may not fit the definition, depending on whether or not it meets certain additional tests. These additional tests are set forth in principles established by the Financial Accounting Standards Board. The FASB is guided in establishing the standards (or codified principles) for rented equipment by the general concept of an asset. The standards, in turn, provide additional guidance for the accountant who must reach a judgment as to whether or not a given type of rented equipment can be classified as an asset of a particular entity.

Although the designation of specific accounting propositions as either concepts or principles may be difficult and open to dispute, making the distinction between concepts and principles can help us understand the respective roles of individual practicing accountants and the accounting rule-making agencies. In particular, generally accepted accounting principles guide the practicing accountant in the preparation and evaluation of financial statements for an individual entity, whereas accounting concepts guide rule-making agencies in the formulation of explicit accounting principles or standards.

THE AUDITOR'S OPINION

AUDIT: An examination of financial statements and the underlying accounting system, conducted by a certified public accountant who issues a written opinion as to the fairness of the financial statements.

The preparation and auditing of financial statements requires accountants in business entities and independent public accountants to exercise skill and judgment within the framework of generally accepted accounting principles. Generally accepted accounting principles offer general guidance but do not completely specify the form and content of financial statements. Therefore, many difficult choices must be made both by the managerial accountants who prepare them and by the independent public accountants who audit these statements before they are issued to users. To assure that financial statements are reasonable representations of the resources and activities of the issuing entity, public accounting firms perform audits of the financial statements and the underlying accounting system. An **audit** is a detailed examination of an accounting system and requires that the public accounting firm express a written opinion as to the fairness of the financial statements under consideration. A favorable judgment is expressed in the following statement, which is part of the auditor's report accompanying the audited financial statements:

> In our opinion, the financial statements of XYZ Corporation present fairly, in all material respects, the financial position of XYZ Corporation at December 31, 19X3, 19X2, and 19X1, and the results of its operations and its cash flows for the years then ended in conformity with generally accepted accounting principles. These financial statements are the responsibility of the Company's management; our responsibility is to express an opinion on these financial statements based on our audits. We conducted our audits of these statements in accordance with generally accepted auditing standards, which require that we plan and perform the audit to obtain reason-

able assurance about whether the financial statements are free from material misstatement. An audit includes examining, on a test basis, evidence supporting principles used and significant estimates made by management, and evaluating the overall financial statement presentation. We believe that our audits provide a reasonable basis for the opinion expressed above.

If the financial statements violate generally accepted accounting principles or are not fairly presented, the language of the auditor's report must be altered to warn the reader. Of course, accounting is not an exact science; it involves many measurements based on judgment and estimation. Consequently, the auditor's opinion does not preclude minor or immaterial errors in the financial statements. The making of judgments and estimates and the correcting of errors are guided by a *materiality concept,* which states that financial statements need not be corrected for an error or report an item that is not large enough to influence an investor or decision maker.[2]

CERTIFIED PUBLIC AC-COUNTANT (CPA): A licensed public accountant trained to perform auditing, management consulting, and tax services.

Independent public accountants assume an important responsibility to the public when they express opinions on the financial statements of their clients. As a result, public accountants who perform auditing services are required by statute to be licensed as **certified public accountants (CPAs).** CPAs are trained to perform auditing, management consulting, and tax services and must be licensed by individual state boards of accountancy. Although examination and certification requirements vary somewhat from state to state (for example, some states require one year of professional experience for certification, while others require as many as three or four years), all states require that candidates pass a uniform examination administered by the American Institute of Certified Public Accountants. This three-day exam is given during May and November of each year in most major cities, and only about 10 percent of examinees pass all parts of the exam on their first attempt. Fewer than 20 percent of all accountants in the United States are CPAs, and about 40 percent of all CPAs in the United States are employed by the largest 25 public accounting firms.

FINANCIAL STATEMENTS

The typical business entity issues four primary financial statements:

1. The balance sheet
2. The income statement
3. The statement of changes in retained earnings
4. The statement of cash flows

These four statements are prepared and issued at the end of each year. They are frequently accompanied by a variety of supporting data and explanatory materials.

[2] Financial Accounting Standards Board, *Statement of Financial Accounting Concepts No. 2,* glossary and par. 123–32. In the interest of simplicity, we assume throughout this text that all amounts and errors are material unless the contrary is specifically stated.

The remainder of this chapter will describe the four primary financial statements and the relationships among them, with particular emphasis on the accounting concepts basic to each statement. A detailed discussion of the content and organization of financial statements will be presented in Chapter 2, and the relationship between the statements and their underlying data will be explained in Chapter 3.

THE BALANCE SHEET

BALANCE SHEET: The financial statement that provides information about an entity's economic resources (assets) and the claims against those resources by creditors and owners (liabilities and equity).

The **balance sheet** (see Exhibit 1–3) provides information about a business entity's economic resources and the claims against those resources by the creditors and owners of the entity.[3] The economic resources reported on the balance sheet are called *assets,* and they include such items as cash, accounts receivable, inventory, land, buildings, and equipment. Claims against the assets of an entity arise from outsiders—whether individuals or other entities—who expect payment from the entity. Claims against assets are called *liabilities* when the outside party is a creditor and *equity* when the outside party is an owner of the enterprise.[4] The balance sheet is, in effect, a pair of lists. The assets of a business are presented in one list, and the liabilities and equity are presented in the other. The two lists are arranged either side by side (with assets on the left and liabilities and equity on the right) or sequentially (with assets above liabilities and equity, as shown in Exhibit 1–3).

The balance sheet is a point-in-time measurement of the assets, liabilities, and equity of a business entity. It is prepared "as of" a particular date, which means the reported assets are owned or controlled by the entity on that date and also the reported claims against assets (liabilities and equity) are effective on that date. Because of its importance, this date must be included in the heading of the balance sheet.

Assets and Cost

ASSETS: Economic resources representing probable future economic benefits obtained or controlled by an entity (e.g., cash, accounts receivable, inventory, land, buildings, and equipment).

Assets, the economic resources reported on the balance sheet, are probable future economic benefits obtained or controlled by a particular entity. Most assets are *tangible resources,* whose value resides in the use of their physical substance. Examples include cash, inventory, land, buildings, and equipment. However, some assets, such as accounts receivable and patents, are *intangible resources.* The value of this type of asset resides in a legal claim for the future receipt of cash from customers (in the case of accounts receivable) or from use of an invention (in the case of patents).

The balance sheet provides two kinds of information about assets: (1) a description of the asset (cash, inventory, and so forth) and (2) its cost. For

---

[3] The balance sheet is also called the *statement of financial position* or, simply, the *position statement.* Although these alternatives are somewhat more descriptive of the statement, the term *balance sheet* is widely used and will be used throughout this book.

[4] The word *equity* is sometimes defined to include all claims against the assets of an entity. According to this definition, equity would include liabilities as well as the equity of owners. When the word *equity* is given this most inclusive definition, it is customary to refer to the equity of owners as *owners' equity.* We prefer here to define equity narrowly, encompassing only the equity of owners, because that definition is consistent with *Statement of Financial Accounting Concepts No. 6,* par. 49, and with prevailing use of the word in accounting.

EXHIBIT 1–3   THE BALANCE SHEET

MARSHALL'S LAUNDRY AND DRY CLEANERS, INC.
Balance Sheet
As of December 31, 19X8

ASSETS

Cash	$ 3,000
Accounts receivable	15,000
Supplies inventory, laundry and dry cleaning	6,000
Equipment (net)	8,000
Building (net)	42,000
Land	10,000
Total assets	$84,000

LIABILITIES

Accounts payable	$ 3,600
Income taxes payable	4,400
Notes payable	10,000
Total liabilities	$18,000

EQUITY

Capital stock (5,000 shares of stock)	$50,000	
Retained earnings	16,000	
Total equity		66,000
Total liabilities and equity		$84,000

example, land owned by Marshall's Laundry and Dry Cleaners, Inc., is listed among the assets on the balance sheet in Exhibit 1–3 as follows:

Land	$10,000

The cost ($10,000) of the asset (land) is the amount paid for it when it was acquired by Marshall's. Cost is not always measured by the amount of cash paid for an asset, however. When assets are acquired in exchange for assets other than cash, cost is measured by the cash value of the noncash assets given in exchange. For example, if an oil well that has a cash value of $850,000 is traded for a building, then the cost of the building is said to be $850,000. In still other cases, assets are acquired in exhange for liabilities, which represent promises to pay cash at a later time, or in exchange for equity, an ownership share in the business. In these situations, the cost of the asset is measured by the amount of the liability or equity. In summary, **cost** is the amount of cash expended or the cash value of noncash assets, liabilities, or equity given in exchange for an asset.

COST: The cash expended or the cash value of noncash assets, liabilities, or equity given in exchange for an asset. Cost is the basis for recording assets, liabilities, and equity.

Cost and Market Value

MARKET VALUE: The monetary worth attributed to an asset by the marketplace.

The **market value** of an asset is the monetary worth attributed to the asset by the marketplace. In other words, the market value is the agreed-upon (bargained or negotiated) price at which the asset changes hands. The marketplace pits buyer against seller, with the buyer seeking the lowest possible price and the seller seeking the highest. Provided that neither buyer nor seller is compelled to make the exchange, the agreed-upon price is a reasonable estimate of an asset's worth at the time of the exchange.

Although cost is a reasonable measure of an asset's worth at the time of its acquisition, market values of assets are unfortunately not stable over time. For a variety of reasons — including inflation and changes in demand and supply — the market value of an asset at a given time may differ markedly from its market value in another period. As a result, cost amounts can produce financial statements that are misleading. Suppose, for example, that you purchased a home 10 years ago at a cost of $50,000. Assume that, as a result of inflation and other factors, your home would now sell for $95,000. A balance sheet listing your home at its cost of $50,000 would materially understate the current market value of this asset. Although an entity's primary financial statements are prepared using the cost concept, generally accepted accounting principles also require that portions of the primary financial statements be supplemented with current market values. (These current market value concepts and measurements are discussed in later chapters.)

Liabilities

LIABILITIES: Probable future sacrifices of economic benefits (e.g., debts owed to creditors).

Liabilities, the creditors' claims against assets, are probable future sacrifices of economic benefits. Most liabilities are debts owed to creditors, representing an obligation to pay the creditor at some future time for cash, supplies, or other assets received from the creditor.

The liability *accounts payable* is an obligation to make a future payment for goods or services already delivered by the creditor. Usually, the creditor or supplier will require payment within 30 days of delivery. The liability *income taxes payable* is an obligation to make future payments to various taxing authorities. Income taxes are payable to federal, state, local, and foreign governments. The liability *notes payable* is an obligation to repay an amount borrowed plus interest and is usually evidenced by a formal document that gives the precise times and amounts of payment. The general definition of a liability admits many forms in addition to those explained here. (An extended discussion of liabilities is presented in Chapters 10, 11A, and 11B.)

Equity

EQUITY (OWNERS' EQUITY): The owners' claims against the assets of a business entity, which equal the residual interest in the assets that remains after deducting liabilities.

Equity, the third component of the balance sheet, represents the owner's claims against the assets and is sometimes called *owners' equity.* The conceptual framework defines equity as an amount determined by comparing assets and liabilities. Equity is the residual interest in the assets of a business entity that remains after deducting its liabilities from its assets. For example, in Exhibit 1 – 3 the amount of equity on the balance sheet for Marshall's Laundry and Dry Cleaning, Inc., is

$66,000, which can be calculated by deducting liabilities of $18,000 from assets of $84,000. Although liabilities are usually subject to external contractual arrangements that determine, or at least make estimable, both the amount of the claim and the future date on which the claim is to be paid, the owners of an entity can collectively control payments to themselves. The amount and timing of payments, however, depend on the company's profitability, on its expansion plans, and on numerous other considerations.

CAPITAL STOCK: The component of equity in a corporation contributed by owners of the entity.

RETAINED EARNINGS: The component of equity in a corporation representing accumulated profits in excess of losses and payments to owners.

Equity in a corporation arises from two sources: (1) the owners' contributions of cash or other assets to the business, called **capital stock,** and (2) the business's accumulated profits in excess of losses and payments to the owners, called **retained earnings.** The owners receive shares of stock in exchange for cash or other assets contributed to the business. Each share of stock is a legal document representing one unit of equity in the corporation. The number of shares held by any stockholder depends on the size of the stockholder's capital contribution. Although the number of shares held generally varies from one stockholder to another, each individual share represents an equal share of both capital stock and retained earnings. This equal-equity characteristic of stock shares simplifies transactions between corporations and their owners and makes it easier to transfer shares from one owner to another in securities markets.

The Fundamental Accounting Model

The three components of the balance sheet—assets, liabilities, and equity—exhibit a balancing relationship in the sense that the total dollar amount of assets must equal the total dollar amount of liabilities and equity (see Exhibit 1–4). This equality occurs because the two sides of the balance sheet simply represent different ways of describing the economic resources of the entity. The asset side describes the economic resources in terms of their identity and their costs to the entity. The liability-equity side describes the same resources in terms of the persons or organizations who can lay claim to them.

EXHIBIT 1–4   **THE BALANCE SHEET (AS OF A POINT IN TIME)**

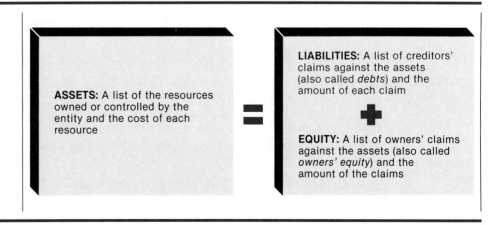

ASSETS: A list of the resources owned or controlled by the entity and the cost of each resource

=

LIABILITIES: A list of creditors' claims against the assets (also called *debts*) and the amount of each claim

+

EQUITY: A list of owners' claims against the assets (also called *owners' equity*) and the amount of the claims

The relationship among assets, liabilities, and equity on any balance sheet date can be written as an equation, which is sometimes called the *fundamental accounting model:*

ASSETS = LIABILITIES + EQUITY

This fundamental model is also called the *balance sheet equation.*[5] It is important to understand that within the framework of the balance sheet the relationship among these quantities is permanent. Nothing can happen to the entity to disrupt the equality. Although assets, liabilities, and equity change over time, they must change in ways that do not violate the equation. Consider a business with assets, liabilities, and equity of $100,000, $45,000, and $55,000, respectively. The fundamental accounting model would be written as follows:

ASSETS	LIABILITIES	EQUITY
$100,000 =	$45,000 +	$55,000

If the owner of the business invests an additional $20,000 cash, assets and equity each increase by $20,000, as shown below:

ASSETS	LIABILITIES	EQUITY
$100,000 =	$45,000 +	$55,000
+ 20,000	+	20,000
$120,000 =	$45,000 +	$75,000

The equality of the fundamental accounting model is maintained ($120,000 = $45,000 + $75,000). Such changes in the balance sheet are described by the three financial statements that remain to be discussed: the income statement, the statement of changes in retained earnings, and the statement of cash flows.

THE INCOME STATEMENT

INCOME STATE-MENT: The financial statement that reports the profitability of a business entity during a specific period of time.

Unlike the balance sheet, which is a point-in-time description of assets, liabilities, and equity, the **income statement** is a period-of-time description. Specifically, it is a report on the profitability of business operations during a specified period of time. Although income statements are usually prepared for the period of one year, they may be prepared quarterly or monthly as well. The 19X8 income statement for Marshall's Laundry and Dry Cleaners, Inc. (see Exhibit 1–5) illustrates the essential features of a typical income statement. The heading of Marshall's income statement includes the phrase "For the Year Ended December 31, 19X8," which indicates that the statement pertains to the year 19X8.

Business profitability is measured on the income statement as the difference between the *revenue* and *expense* of the period; the detailed revenues and ex-

---

[5] The equation can also be written in a way that emphasizes the residual nature of owners' interests: Assets − Liabilities = Equity. In this arrangement of terms, equity is shown to be the residual, or excess, of assets over liabilities.

EXHIBIT 1–5   **THE INCOME STATEMENT**

MARSHALL'S LAUNDRY AND DRY CLEANERS, INC.
Income Statement
For the Year Ended December 31, 19X8

Service revenue:		
Laundry		$100,000
Dry cleaning		40,000
Total service revenue		$140,000
Operating and financial expenses:		
Salaries	$60,000	
Supplies, laundry and dry cleaning	51,000	
Utilities	12,000	
Depreciation, equipment	2,000	
Depreciation, building	4,000	
Interest	1,000	
Total operating and financial expenses		130,000
Income before taxes		$ 10,000
Income taxes expense		3,400
Net income		$ 6,600
Earnings per share		$1.32

NET INCOME: The excess of an entity's revenue over its expense during a period of time.

NET LOSS: The excess of an entity's expense over its revenue during a period of time.

penses are itemized on the income statement. If revenue exceeds expense, the excess is called **net income.** If expense exceeds revenue, the difference is called **net loss** rather than net income.

It is customary to separate income taxes expense from other expenses, as shown on Marshall's income statement. The difference between revenue and operating and financial expenses is called *income before taxes.* Income taxes expense is subtracted from income before taxes to yield net income. It is also customary to report *earnings per share,* which is net income divided by the total number of shares held by all stockholders, at the end of the income statement. The balance sheet in Exhibit 1–3 shows that stockholders own 5,000 shares of Marshall's stock; thus Marshall's 19X8 earnings per share is $1.32 [$6,600/5,000 shares].

Revenue

REVENUE: The inflow of assets to an entity resulting from the sale of goods or services by the entity.

Revenue is the inflow of assets to an entity resulting from sales of goods or services by the entity. Marshall's, for example, has reported revenue from laundry services and from dry cleaning services. It is important to understand that the sale or delivery of goods or services by the seller need not occur at the same time as the payment to the seller by the customer. Frequently, for example, customers "charge" their purchases and pay for them at a later time. Consider a furniture store that sells a mattress for $300 in 19X8 and collects payment for it in 19X9. Since revenue is based on sales or deliveries, rather than collections, the selling price of $300 is included in 19X8 revenue. In other words, revenue of a period equals the total selling price of goods or services provided to customers during that period, without regard to the period in which the related cash is actually collected.

Expense

Expense, the second component of the income statement, is the outflow or other using up of assets by an entity in order to sell goods or services. Whereas revenue is measured in terms of the selling price of goods or services delivered, expense is measured in terms of the cost of goods or services delivered. Suppose that the mattress sold for $300 in 19X8 was acquired by the furniture store for $175 in 19X6 and paid for in 19X7; the $175 cost is included in the furniture store's expenses for 19X8, the year in which the mattress is sold to a customer.

Expense can occur in two ways: through the transfer of assets to customers or through the using up of assets. In most businesses that provide goods, the principal element of expense is the cost of merchandise transferred to customers. Even some service businesses transfer assets directly to their customers. For example, among the expenses in the income statement for Marshall's Laundry and Dry Cleaners, Inc. (Exhibit 1 – 5) is the cost of plastic bags, hangers, and other packaging supplies that are physically conveyed to customers. Other expenses are incurred as a result of using up assets within the business. For example, Marshall's expenses associated with salaries, utilities, equipment, and building represent the cost of assets consumed by the entity in its operations, not the cost of assets transferred to outside parties. Specifically, Marshall's two depreciation expense items ($2,000 and $4,000) represent that portion of the cost of its equipment and building assigned to 19X8.[6]

Accrual Basis versus Cash Basis

The concepts of revenue and expense used to construct the income statement are part of accrual-basis accounting, which is required by generally accepted accounting principles. Revenue and expense, like the other information reported in the financial statements, represent the accumulated effects of activities recorded in the accounting system. **Accrual-basis accounting** (also called **accrual accounting** or, simply, the *accrual basis*) is the method of recording these activities when they occur rather than when the related cash is received or paid. Thus accrual accounting recognizes revenue and expense when goods are sold or when services are performed, rather than when cash is received or paid. An alternative basis of accounting, called **cash-basis accounting,** records only cash receipts and payments and recognizes net income when cash is received and paid. Thus the $300 selling price of the mattress sold in 19X8 and not collected until 19X9 would be included in 19X8 revenue under accrual-basis accounting and in 19X9 revenue under cash-basis accounting. The $175 cost of the mattress, which was acquired in 19X6 and not paid until 19X7, would be included in 19X8 expenses under accrual-basis accounting and in 19X7 expenses under cash-basis accounting. In other words, cash-basis net income for a period is simply the difference between the period's cash receipts and cash payments related to sales of goods and performance of services.

[6] Depreciation expense is discussed in greater detail in later chapters. For the present, it is sufficient to understand that depreciation expense represents a portion of the cost of assets that are used for more than a single year. A portion of the cost of assets like equipment and buildings is recorded as expense in each year of their useful lives, reflecting the using up of the assets in the earning of revenue.

The accrual basis is superior to the cash basis for measuring the performance of a business because it ties income measurement to selling, the principal activity of the business entity. In contrast, cash-basis accounting for income is influenced by many factors that may have little to do with the performance of the entity. Although cash-basis accounting is not sanctioned by generally accepted accounting principles, income tax returns may be prepared on the cash basis under certain conditions, as the following analysis illustrates.

ANALYSIS

CASH-BASIS ACCOUNTING AND REVENUE RECOGNITION

Dr. Ronald Cruickshank, a nationally recognized expert on energy conservation, was retained as a consultant by the State of Ohio from September through November 19X1. He assisted in the design of the state's new energy conservation program and also conducted several one-day seminars in major metropolitan areas. At the end of his engagement, Dr. Cruickshank sent the state an invoice requesting compensation for 20 consulting days at the previously agreed upon rate of $1,000 per day. Owing to some unforeseen delays in processing his invoice, Cruickshank did not receive the state's check until January 7, 19X2. Cruickshank reports his income for tax purposes on a calendar-year basis.

1. *When will Dr. Cruickshank report the revenue from the consulting engagement on his income tax return?*

Most likely in 19X2. If Cruickshank is like the vast majority of Americans, he is a cash-basis taxpayer. Although government regulations require the use of the accrual basis in some circumstances (e.g., in the case of a taxpayer selling inventory), the cash basis is generally permitted for service providers like Cruickshank because they may not have sufficient "wherewithal to pay" their income taxes until they receive cash.

2. *If he is a cash-basis taxpayer, does Dr. Cruickshank have some control over when he reports his consulting revenue to the Internal Revenue Service?*

Absolutely. The cash basis affords him the ability to manipulate the timing of revenue recognition. If, for example, Cruickshank felt that his 19X1 taxable income was already fairly high (thereby causing any additional 19X1 income to be taxed in higher brackets) or if he expected the government to cut tax rates in 19X2, he could delay submitting his invoice to the state to ensure that he did not receive the cash in 19X1. Through careful timing of cash receipts and disbursements, most taxpayers can shift some income and deductions from one accounting period to another to maximize aftertax income.

3. *Would Cruickshank have the same amount of discretion over the timing of revenue recognition if he were an accrual-basis taxpayer?*

No. The accrual basis provides little if any flexibility. Revenue is reported on the tax return in the period in which it is earned. Using the accrual basis, Cruickshank's consulting revenue is taxable in 19X1, even though he did not receive cash until 19X2.

Although the accrual basis may not be advantageous in certain taxpaying situations, this lack of flexibility in determining when revenues and expenses are recognized is one of its most important strengths from a financial accounting standpoint. Readers of accrual accounting financial statements, which are required by generally accepted accounting principles, are assured that company management has not been able to change the amount of reported net income by manipulating the timing of cash receipts and disbursements.

EXHIBIT 1–6   THE STATEMENT OF CHANGES IN RETAINED EARNINGS

MARSHALL'S LAUNDRY AND DRY CLEANERS, INC.
Statement of Changes in Retained Earnings
For the Year Ended December 31, 19X8

Retained earnings, 12/31/X7	$ 9,900
Add: Net income for 19X8	6,600
	$16,500
Less: Dividends for 19X8	500
Retained earnings, 12/31/X8	$16,000

THE STATEMENT OF CHANGES IN RETAINED EARNINGS

STATEMENT OF CHANGES IN RETAINED EARNINGS: The financial statement that summarizes the factors that altered retained earnings during a given accounting period.

DIVIDENDS: Amounts paid periodically by a corporation to its stockholders as a return on their invested capital. Dividends represent distribution of net income, not expense.

We turn now to the third financial statement, the **statement of changes in retained earnings.** This document summarizes the factors that alter retained earnings during a given period of time.[7] Recall that retained earnings is the component of equity that represents the accumulated profits of the entity in excess of losses and payments to owners. Two important factors can change retained earnings: (1) net income and (2) amounts paid to owners, which are called **dividends** when paid by corporations. A dividend is an amount paid periodically by a corporation to its stockholders as a return on their invested capital. Dividends and net losses reduce retained earnings, whereas net income increases retained earnings. The 19X8 statement of changes in retained earnings for Marshall's Laundry and Dry Cleaners, Inc., is presented in Exhibit 1–6.

The first line of the statement lists retained earnings at the beginning of 19X8 ($9,900), an amount taken from Marshall's balance sheet as of December 31, 19X7 (which is shown on the left side of Exhibit 1–7). The final line of the statement lists retained earnings at the end of 19X8 ($16,000), which also appears on the balance sheet as of December 31, 19X8 (see Exhibits 1–3 and 1–7). Note that retained earnings at the end of each year is carried forward to become retained earnings at the beginning of the following year. The change in retained earnings is a $6,100 increase [$16,000 − $9,900], which arises from a net income of $6,600 less dividends of $500. In other words, the statement describes the change in retained earnings that occurs between two balance sheets, where the change derives from two sources—net income (or in certain cases, net loss) and dividends.

Exhibit 1–7 is a diagram of the relationship of the statement of changes in retained earnings to the balance sheet and the income statement. The starting point for the statement of changes in retained earnings is the beginning amount of retained earnings, which is taken from the balance sheet prepared at the end of the previous period. On the income statement, expenses are subtracted from revenues to yield net income (or net loss). Next, on the statement of changes in retained earnings, net income is added to the beginning-of-period retained earnings. (Of course, a net loss would be subtracted rather than added.) Then dividends are subtracted to yield the end-of-period retained earnings. The ending amount of retained earnings is then used to prepare the balance sheet at the end of the period. Thus the statement of changes in retained earnings is the essential link

[7] Information about changes in retained earnings is frequently included in a more comprehensive *statement of changes in stockholders' equity,* which describes the changes in all components of equity. Such statements are illustrated in Chapter 2 and elsewhere in this book.

EXHIBIT 1–7   **RELATIONSHIPS AMONG FINANCIAL STATEMENTS**

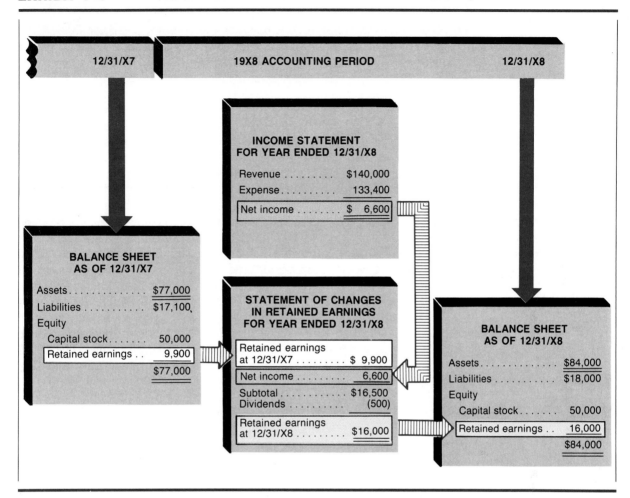

between the income statement for a period of time and the balance sheet at the end of that period. It also links the beginning and ending balance sheets by detailing the changes in the two retained earnings amounts.

Although the statement of changes in retained earnings is the essential link between income statements and successive balance sheets, the statement of changes in retained earnings contains little information (except for dividends) that is not duplicated in the income statements and balance sheets. Consequently, the statement of changes in retained earnings receives far less attention than the other financial statements.

THE STATEMENT OF CASH FLOWS

STATEMENT OF CASH FLOWS: The financial statement that describes the inflows (sources) and outflows (uses) of a firm's financial resources during a given period of time.

Like the income statement and the statement of changes in retained earnings, the **statement of cash flows** is a period-of-time statement. It describes changes in a single asset, cash. The statement of cash flows provides information about the financial, investment, and operating sources from which a firm secures its cash and other financial resources and about the uses made of those resources, including investment in assets, repayment of creditors, and payment of dividends to stockholders. This information is useful to creditors, stockholders, and others. Additional discussion of the statement of cash flows appears in Chapters 2 and 13.

The accounting information of a business entity is the responsibility of two groups of accountants. Managerial accountants gather information and prepare reports for users both inside and outside the entity. Certified public accountants (CPAs) audit the financial statements issued to outside users and express an opinion as to the fairness of the statements and their conformity with generally accepted accounting principles. Generally accepted accounting principles (GAAP), which guide the preparation of financial statements for external users, are the product of a complex interactive process that involves accountants, user groups, managers, and regulatory agencies. Although a thorough treatment of generally accepted accounting principles is beyond the scope of this book, the chapters that follow indicate the structure of these principles and the conceptual framework on which they are built. Nine basic accounting concepts that have been discussed in the foregoing chapter are summarized in Exhibit 1–8.

The financial statements prepared for users outside the business entity consist of four primary statements, which are usually accompanied by various explanatory footnotes and supporting data. These four basic statements are the balance sheet, the income statement, the statement of changes in retained earnings, and the statement of cash flows.

The balance sheet is a two-way description of the cost of economic resources available to the entity. The resources are described (1) in terms of various asset categories (cash, accounts receivable, inventory, land, equipment, and so forth) and (2) in terms of the claims against those assets by creditors (liabilities) and by owners of the entity (equity). The balance sheet "balances" in the sense that the total dollar amount of assets equals the total dollar amount of liabilities plus equity.

Unlike the balance sheet, which is a point-in-time description, the income statement is a period-of-time description. The income statement describes the company's profitability for a given period as the difference between the period's revenues and expenses. It is important to understand that revenue for a period is not necessarily the same as cash collected during the period and that the expense for a period is not necessarily the same as cash payments made during the period.

The statement of changes in retained earnings, which is also a period-of-time description, summarizes changes in an entity's equity, showing the amount of net income (or net loss), the amount of dividends (distributions to owners), and the effect of these items on the amount of retained earnings. In this sense, the statement of changes in retained earnings shows the manner in which the income statement for a period is connected with the balance sheets at the beginning and end of that period.

EXHIBIT 1–8   BASIC ACCOUNTING CONCEPTS

	PAGE
ACCOUNTING ENTITY: An organization that has an identity separate from that of its owners and managers and for which accounting records are kept and accounting reports are issued.	3
ASSETS: Economic resources representing probable future economic benefits obtained or controlled by an entity (e.g., cash, accounts receivable, inventory, land, buildings, and equipment).	12
LIABILITIES: Probable future sacrifices of economic benefits (e.g., debts owed to creditors).	14
EQUITY: The owners' claims against the assets of a business entity, which equal the residual interest in the assets that remains after deducting the liabilities.	14
COST: The cash expended or the cash value of noncash assets, liabilities, or equity given in exchange for an asset. Cost is the basis for recording assets, liabilities, and equity.	13
REVENUE: The inflow of assets to an entity resulting from the sale of goods or services by the entity.	17
EXPENSE: The outflow or other using up of assets by an entity in order to sell goods or services.	18
NET INCOME: The excess of an entity's revenue over its expense during a period of time.	17
ACCRUAL-BASIS ACCOUNTING: The method of recording the activities of a business entity when the activities occur rather than when the related cash is received and paid.	18

KEY TERMS

ACCOUNTING (p. 2)

ACCOUNTING ENTITY (p. 3)

ACCRUAL-BASIS ACCOUNTING (ACCRUAL ACCOUNTING) (p. 18)

ASSETS (p. 12)

AUDIT (p. 10)

BALANCE SHEET (p. 12)

CAPITAL STOCK (p. 15)

CASH-BASIS ACCOUNTING (p. 18)

CERTIFIED PUBLIC ACCOUNTANT (CPA) (p. 11)

CONCEPT (p. 10)

CONCEPTUAL FRAMEWORK OF ACCOUNTING (p. 9)

COST (p. 13)

DIVIDENDS (p. 20)

EQUITY (OWNERS' EQUITY) (p. 14)

EXPENSE (p. 18)

FINANCIAL ACCOUNTING (p. 6)

FINANCIAL ACCOUNTING STANDARDS BOARD (FASB) (p. 9)

FINANCIAL STATEMENTS (p. 6)

GENERALLY ACCEPTED ACCOUNTING PRINCIPLES (GAAP) (p. 8)

INCOME STATEMENT (p. 16)

LIABILITIES (p. 14)

MANAGERIAL ACCOUNTING (p. 6)

MARKET VALUE (p. 14)

NET INCOME (p. 17)

NET LOSS (p. 17)

PRINCIPLE (p. 10)

RETAINED EARNINGS (p. 15)

REVENUE (p. 17)

SECURITIES AND EXCHANGE COMMISSION (SEC) (p. 9)

STATEMENT OF CASH FLOWS (p. 21)

STATEMENT OF CHANGES IN RETAINED EARNINGS (p. 20)

QUESTIONS

Q1-1. What is an accounting entity? How do business and nonbusiness entities differ?

Q1-2. Name and describe the three different forms of business entity.

Q1-3. What does it mean to say that partnerships are characterized by unlimited liability? Does unlimited liability also characterize corporations? Explain.

Q1-4. Explain what is meant by the separation of ownership from control in reference to the modern corporation.

Q1-5. Name and describe the three types of business activity.

Q1-6. What is the difference between financial accounting and managerial accounting?

Q1-7. Identify the major occupational groups that constitute the accounting profession and briefly describe the employment of each group.

Q1-8. What are generally accepted accounting principles (GAAP)?

Q1-9. What are audits of financial statements? Why are they necessary?

Q1-10. What are certified public accountants? Why are they necessary?

Q1-11. Describe the Financial Accounting Standards Board (FASB). What is the relationship between the FASB and generally accepted accounting principles (GAAP)?

Q1-12. Describe the Securities and Exchange Commission (SEC). What is the relationship between the SEC and the FASB? What is the relationship between the SEC and generally accepted accounting principles (GAAP)?

Q1-13. What is the conceptual framework of accounting? How do concepts and principles differ?

Q1-14. Name and briefly describe the four primary financial statements.

Q1-15. Define the words *assets, liabilities,* and *equity.* How are the three words related?

Q1-16. Write the fundamental accounting model or equation. What is its significance?

Q1-17. What is point-in-time measurement? How does it differ from period-of-time measurement?

Q1-18. Define the word *revenue.* How does revenue differ from cash collections for a period?

Q1-19. How does accrual-basis net income differ from cash-basis net income?

Q1-20. How is the statement of changes in retained earnings related to balance sheets? How is the income statement related to the statement of changes in retained earnings?

EXERCISES

E1-21. BUSINESS ENTITIES AND BUSINESS ACTIVITY   For each of the three types of business entity, select as many of the definitions, examples, or descriptions as apply to that type of entity.

ENTITY	DEFINITION, EXAMPLE, OR DESCRIPTION
Sole proprietorship	**1.** Can sell goods (merchandising)
Partnership	**2.** Owned by one person and legally not separate from the owner
Corporation	**3.** Can make and sell goods (manufacturing)
	4. Jointly owned by two or more persons and legally not separate from the owners
	5. Owned by one or more persons and legally separate from the owner(s)
	6. Can provide and sell services
	7. K-mart
	8. A law firm owned by some of the employees, who are each liable for the financial obligations of the entity

E1-22. ACCOUNTING ENVIRONMENT   Match each of the terms listed below with the most closely related definition or example in the adjacent list. Your answer should pair each of the numbers from 1 through 8 with the appropriate letter.

TERM	DEFINITION OR EXAMPLE
1. CPA	a) The preparation of financial information for use inside a business
2. Managerial accounting	b) A business entity owned by one person
3. Audit	c) A private-sector organization formed to issue pronouncements on GAAP
4. Corporation	d) A business entity formed under state law by one or more owners called *stockholders*
5. Accounting	e) A public-sector organization that issues pronouncements on GAAP
6. FASB	f) A public accountant licensed by a state
7. SEC	g) The identification, measurement, recording, and communication of economic information for use in financial decision making
8. Sole proprietorship	h) An examination, conducted by a CPA, of financial statements and the underlying accounting system

E1-23. BUSINESS ENTITIES AND OWNERS' ACTIVITIES   Libby Vote owns and manages The Tennis Ball, a store selling tennis equipment and clothing. During 19X1 Libby engaged in the following activities:

a) Libby gave a tennis racket to Mary Jones as a birthday present. Libby had the business record the $80 cost of the racket as an addition to her salary expense.

b) While using The Tennis Ball's truck to make a delivery to a nearby tennis club, Libby paid $20 for gasoline for the truck from her personal funds. Libby had the store pay her the $20 and record that amount as an expense of the store.

c) Libby loaned $10,000 to The Tennis Ball last year. Libby had the store pay her $1,000 interest. The store recorded the payment of $1,000 as an interest expense.

REQUIRED:

Indicate whether or not each of these activities is properly recorded as an expense of the business. Explain your choices.

E1-24. THE FUNDAMENTAL ACCOUNTING MODEL   Compute the missing numbers in each of the three independent cases described below:

	ASSETS	LIABILITIES	EQUITY
a)	$107,000	$?	$51,000
b)	275,000	150,000	?
c)	?	15,000	65,000

E1-25. INCOME STATEMENT   Melody Radio, Inc., operates an FM radio station. During 19X2 Melody received revenue from commercials in the amount of $422,300. During the same year, Melody incurred rent expense of $208,000, wages expense of $113,200, utilities expense of $39,900, miscellaneous expense of $21,800, and income taxes expense of $7,800.

REQUIRED:

Prepare an income statement for Melody for 19X2.

E1-26. BALANCE SHEET   Abercrombie's Auto Service is a combination tune-up and body shop. At the close of business on December 31, 19X4, Abercrombie's had the following assets, liabilities, and equity:

Accounts payable	$ 5,000
Accounts receivable	7,000
Capital stock	12,000
Cash	2,000
Equipment	40,000
Income taxes payable	16,000
Note payable	9,000
Retained earnings	22,000
Supplies inventory	15,000

REQUIRED:

Prepare a balance sheet for Abercrombie's Auto Service as of the close of business on December 31, 19X4.

E1-27. RETAINED EARNINGS   At the end of 19X8, Sherwood Company had retained earnings of $21,240. During 19X9 Sherwood had revenues of $831,400 and expenses of $792,100, and paid cash dividends in the amount of $11,500.

REQUIRED:

Determine the amount of Sherwood's retained earnings at December 31, 19X9.

E1-28. CALCULATION OF REVENUE   Wallace Motors, which began business on December 31, 19X6, buys and sells used cars. All its sales are to other car dealers. Four cars were purchased during January and none were purchased during February. The cars were sold under the following terms:

a) Three of the four cars were sold to Russell Auto Sales for a total of $75,000; the cars were delivered to Russell on January 18. Russell paid Wallace $20,000 on January 18 and the remaining $55,000 on February 12.

b) The fourth car purchased during January was sold to Hastings Classics for $28,000; the car was delivered to Hastings on January 25. Hastings paid Wallace on January 30.

REQUIRED:

Calculate the monthly revenue for Wallace Motors for January and February 19X7.

E1-29. CALCULATION OF EXPENSE FROM BALANCE SHEET CHANGES   The following information is available for the month of November 19X3:

a) The only change in equity during November was net income.

b) During November assets increased by $10,000 and liabilities increased by $2,000.

c) Revenue for November was $20,000.

REQUIRED:

Determine the amount of expense for the month of November 19X3.

E1-30. CALCULATION OF DIVIDENDS FROM BALANCE SHEET CHANGES   The following information is available at the end of 19X2. Assume that no new stock was purchased by the owners during 19X2.

Total assets on 12/31/X1	$70,000
Total assets on 12/31/X2	78,000
Total liabilities on 12/31/X1	–0–
Total liabilities on 12/31/X2	–0–
Net income for 19X2	12,000

REQUIRED:

Calculate the amount of dividends reported on the statement of changes in retained earnings for 19X2.

E1-31. CASH-BASIS AND ACCRUAL-BASIS ACCOUNTING The records of Summers Lumber Company reveal the following information for 19X8:

a) Cash receipts during 19X8 (including $50,000 paid by stockholders in exchange for capital stock), $220,000.

b) Cash payments during 19X8 (including $8,000 of dividends paid to stockholders), $132,000.

c) Total selling price of goods delivered to customers during 19X8, $183,000.

d) Cost of goods delivered to customers during 19X8, $107,000.

e) Cost of assets used during 19X8 in the operation of the business, $42,000.

REQUIRED:

Calculate Summers Lumber's 19X8 net income on both an accrual basis and a cash basis.

E1-32. EFFECT OF EVENTS ON NET INCOME What *direct* effect does each of the following events have on the net income (revenues, expenses) of a firm? Ignore income taxes.

a) The firm provides services to a customer for cash.

b) The firm provides services to a customer on credit.

c) The firm collects cash from a credit customer.

d) The firm purchases office supplies on credit.

e) The office supplies purchased in **d** are used.

f) An owner of the firm invests additional cash in the firm.

g) The firm borrows cash from a bank.

E1-33. EFFECTS OF EVENTS ON ASSETS What *direct* effect does each of the following events have on the assets of a firm?

a) An owner invests cash in the firm.

b) The firm purchases equipment on credit.

c) The firm purchases equipment for cash.

d) The firm borrows cash from a bank.

E1-34. INFERRING EVENTS FROM BALANCE SHEET CHANGES Each of the following balance sheet changes is associated with a particular event:

a) Cash increases by $100,000 and capital stock increases by $100,000.

b) Cash decreases by $22,000 and land increases by $22,000.

c) Cash decreases by $9,000 and retained earnings decreases by $9,000.

d) Cash increases by $15,000 and notes payable increases by $15,000.

REQUIRED:

Describe the four events associated with the balance sheet changes listed above.

E1-35. CALCULATION OF INCOME FROM BALANCE SHEET DATA   During 19X5 Moore Corporation had no changes in its capital stock and paid $16,000 of dividends. Moore's assets and liabilities at the end of 19X4 and 19X5 were:

	12/31/X4	12/31/X5
Total assets	$149,200	$188,100
Total liabilities..................................	54,600	56,700

REQUIRED:

Using the information provided, compute Moore's net income for 19X5.

E1-36. REVENUE RECOGNITION   Volume Electronics sold a television to Sarah Merrifield on December 15, 19X3. Sarah paid $100 at the time of the purchase and agreed to pay $100 each month for five months beginning on January 15, 19X4. The television had been purchased by Volume Electronics in June 19X3 at a cost of $450. Volume had paid the $450 in August 19X3.

REQUIRED:

In what month or months should revenue from this sale be recorded by Volume Electronics to ensure proper application of accrual accounting?

E1-37. EXPENSE AND CASH PAYMENT   The following information is taken from the accrual accounting records of Kroger Sales Company:

a) During January 19X2, Kroger paid $8,500 for all the packing supplies to be used in sales to customers during the next two months (February and March) at a rate of $4,250 per month.

b) Kroger pays its employees at the end of each month for salaries earned during that month. Salaries paid at the end of February and March 19X2 amounted to $4,750 and $5,100, respectively.

c) Kroger placed an advertisement in the local newspaper during March 19X2 at a cost of $700. The ad promoted the annual prespring sale during the last week in March. Kroger did not pay for the newspaper ad until mid-April.

REQUIRED:

Calculate the amount of February expense and March expense associated with the information above.

E1-38. REVENUE AND CASH COLLECTION   McDonald Books sells used paperback books for $2.00 each. During the month of April, McDonald Books sold 21,200 books for cash and 7,300 books on credit. McDonald's cash collections in April included the $42,400 for the 21,200 books sold for cash, $11,800 for books sold on credit during the previous month, and $8,100 for books sold on credit during April.

REQUIRED:

1. Calculate the amount of revenue for the month of April.

2. For how many book sales did McDonald collect cash during April?

E1-39. CALCULATION OF REVENUE FROM CASH COLLECTION   Anderson Lawn Service provides mowing, weed control, and pest management services for a flat fee of $60 per lawn per month. During July Anderson collected $4,980 in cash from customers, which included $420 for lawn care provided in June. At the end of July Anderson had not collected from 11 customers who had promised to pay in August when they returned from vacation.

REQUIRED:

Calculate the amount of Anderson's revenue for July.

E1-40. CAPITAL STOCK AND EQUITY   On January 1, 19X9, Wiley Manufacturing has assets, liabilities, and equity of $1,000,000, $250,000, and $750,000, respectively. The following day, stockholders contribute cash and other assets totaling $450,000 to the business in exchange for newly issued shares of stock.

REQUIRED:

1. Calculate the total amounts of assets, liabilities, and equity immediately after this exchange.
2. If equity on January 1, 19X9, was composed of capital stock of $400,000 and retained earnings of $350,000, what is its composition immediately after the exchange?
3. Describe the two components of equity.

E1-41. ACCOUNTING CONCEPTS   A list of accounting concepts is presented below. Match each of the concepts with the corresponding definition or example by pairing each of the numbers from 1 through 9 with the appropriate letter.

CONCEPT	DEFINITION OR EXAMPLE
1. Revenue	a) An organization with an identity separate from its owners and managers and for which accounting records are kept and accounting reports are issued
2. Expense	
3. Accounting entity	
4. Equity	b) Capital stock and retained earnings
5. Asset	c) Income recognized when earned rather than when related cash is received and paid
6. Net income	d) Revenue minus expense
7. Accrual basis	e) Inflow to an entity from the sale of goods
8. Cost	f) Probable future economic benefit (economic resources) obtained or controlled by an entity
9. Liability	
	g) Outflow from an entity in order to sell goods
	h) Cash expended for an asset
	i) Probable future economic sacrifices represented by creditors' claims against an entity's assets

PROBLEMS

P1-42. APPLYING THE FUNDAMENTAL ACCOUNTING MODEL   At the beginning of 19X8 Huffer Corporation had total assets of $226,800, total liabilities of $84,200, capital stock of $80,000, and retained earnings of $62,600. During 19X8 Huffer had net income of $31,500, paid dividends of $11,900, and issued additional capital stock for $12,000. Huffer's total assets at the end of 19X8 were $278,200.

REQUIRED:

Calculate the amount of liabilities that Huffer must have at the end of 19X8 in order that the balance sheet equation balance.

P1-43. EQUITY, NET INCOME, AND DIVIDENDS   Compute the missing numbers in each of the four independent cases described below.

	EQUITY AT THE BEGINNING OF THE YEAR	DURING THE YEAR			EQUITY AT THE END OF THE YEAR
		INVESTMENT BY OWNERS	NET INCOME (NET LOSS)	DIVIDENDS	
a)	$150,000	$20,000	$ 7,000	$ 3,000	$?
b)	890,000	–0–	100,000	?	960,000
c)	?	–0–	250,000	60,000	1,300,000
d)	40,000	9,000	(6,200)	1,800	?

P1-44. ASSETS, LIABILITIES, AND EQUITY   The financial statements of Softspray Car Wash included the following amounts at the end of 19X4.

Accounts payable	$ 1,100
Accounts receivable	3,900
Building, car wash	34,000
Capital stock	40,000
Cash	800
Dividends	8,500
Equipment, car wash	85,000
Income taxes expense	7,000
Land	10,000
Miscellaneous expense	9,100
Notes payable, long-term	50,000
Retained earnings, 12/31/X3	29,700
Service revenue, car wash	230,800
Supplies inventory	4,200
Utilities expense	109,400
Wages expense	84,300
Wages payable	4,600

REQUIRED:

Using the amounts from the financial statements, calculate the total amounts of assets, liabilities, and equity at the end of 19X4.

P1-45. INCOME STATEMENT AND BALANCE SHEET RELATIONSHIPS   The table below presents data taken from the most recent financial statements of five different companies, designated A, B, C, D, and E. Each column presents information for a different company, with one or more items of data missing. Consider each column by itself. Use your understanding of the relationships among financial statements and financial statement items to find as many of the missing numbers as possible. Some may not be determinable. (Hint: Review Exhibit 1–7 and the related discussion.)

FINANCIAL STATEMENT ITEM	COMPANY				
	A	B	C	D	E
Total revenue	$100	$ 700	$	$2,900	$
Total expense	75		50		800
Net income (net loss)		150	15	(600)	(150)
Total assets	900	2,000		8,000	
Total liabilities	400		120	2,000	
Total equity		800	80		

P1-46. ARRANGEMENT OF THE INCOME STATEMENT   Powers Wrecking Service demolishes old buildings and other structures and sells the salvaged materials. During 19X3 Powers had $400,000 of revenue from demolition services and $137,000 of revenue from salvage sales. Powers also had $1,500 of interest revenue from investments. Powers incurred $240,000 of wages expense, $24,000 of depreciation expense, $50,000 of fuel expense, $84,000 of rent expense, $17,000 of miscellaneous expense, and $25,000 of income taxes expense.

REQUIRED:

Prepare an income statement for Powers Wrecking Service for 19X3.

P1-47. RETAINED EARNINGS RELATIONSHIPS Data from the financial statements of five different companies are presented in separate columns in the table below. Each column has one or more data items missing. Consider each column by itself.

FINANCIAL STATEMENT ITEM	COMPANY				
	V	W	X	Y	Z
Equity, 12/31/X1					
Capital stock	$50,000	$35,000	$40,000	$15,000	$80,000
Retained earnings	12,100	9,300	26,400	21,900	6,900
Total equity	$62,100	$44,300	$66,400	$36,900	$86,900
Net income (loss) for 19X2	$ 7,000	$ (1,800)	$ 6,000	$	$
Dividends during 19X2	$ 2,000	$ –0–	$	$ 1,400	$ –0–
Equity, 12/31/X2					
Capital stock	$50,000	$35,000	$55,000	$15,000	$80,000
Retained earnings				27,600	
Total equity	$	$	$84,500	$	$
Total assets, 12/31/X2	$92,500	$	$99,200	$	$
Total liabilities, 12/31/X2	$	$14,800	$	$10,700	$

REQUIRED:

Use your understanding of the relationships among the financial statement items to determine as many of the missing numbers as possible. Some may not be determinable. (Hint: Review Exhibit 1–7 and the related discussion.)

P1-48. ARRANGEMENT OF THE BALANCE SHEET Neil's Tracks sells CD recordings. At the close of business on December 31, 19X9, the following information is available.

Accounts payable	$ 23,200
Accounts receivable	82,500
Building	140,000
Capital stock	250,000
Cash	1,900
Equipment, store	25,000
Income taxes payable	18,000
Interest payable	3,000
Inventory, CDs	146,200
Long-term notes payable	60,000
Retained earnings	14,800
State sales tax payable	11,400
Wages payable	15,200

REQUIRED:

Prepare a balance sheet for Neil's Tracks as of the close of business on December 31, 19X9.

P1-49.   SEQUENTIAL RETAINED EARNINGS STATEMENTS   The table below presents the statements of retained earnings for Bass Corporation for three successive years. Certain numbers are missing.

	19X1	19X2	19X3
Retained earnings, beginning..............	$21,500	$?	$33,600
Add: Net income.......................	9,200	10,100	?
	$30,700	?	?
Less: Dividends........................	?	?	3,900
Retained earnings, ending	$27,200	$?	$41,200

REQUIRED:

Use your understanding of the relationship between successive statements of retained earnings to calculate the missing numbers.

P1-50.   CASH- AND ACCRUAL-BASIS INCOME   George Hathaway, an electrician, entered into an agreement with a real estate management company to perform all maintenance of basic electrical systems and air-conditioning equipment in the apartment buildings under the company's management. The agreement, which is subject to annual renewal, provides for the payment of a fixed fee of $6,000 on January 1 of each year plus amounts for parts and materials billed separately at the end of each month. Amounts billed at the end of one month are collected in the next month. During the first three months of 19X6, George makes the following additional billings and cash collections:

	ADDITIONAL BILLINGS FOR PARTS AND MATERIALS	CASH COLLECTED
January	$420	$6,110*
February	–0–	420
March	330	–0–

   * Including $110 for parts and materials billed in December 19X5.

REQUIRED:

1. Calculate the amount of cash-basis income reported for each of the first three months. Assume that cash payments for expenses by Hathaway total $300 per month.

2. Calculate the amount of accrual-basis income reported for each of the first three months. Assume that expenses total $300 per month.

P1-51.   CASH- AND ACCRUAL-BASIS INCOME   Martin Sharp, who repairs lawn mowers, collects cash from his customers when the repair services are completed. He maintains an inventory of repair parts that are purchased from a wholesale supplier. Martin's records show the following information for the first three months of 19X2:

	CASH COLLECTIONS FOR REPAIR WORK	COST OF REPAIR PARTS PURCHASED	CASH PAYMENTS TO WHOLESALER	COST OF PARTS USED IN REPAIRS
January	$2,100	$820	$710	$605
February	1,500	–0–	440	275
March	1,950	675	–0–	390

REQUIRED:

1. Ignoring expenses other than repair parts, calculate net income for each of the three months on a cash basis.

2. Ignoring expenses other than repair parts, calculate net income for each of the three months on an accrual basis.

P1-52. THE FUNDAMENTAL ACCOUNTING MODEL   Using the symbols defined below, write an equation that expresses the relationship requested in each of the requirements that follow. Assume that, except for dividends, the owners of the firm neither contribute amounts to the firm nor withdraw amounts from the firm during the year.

A = Total assets at the beginning of the period
A' = Total assets at the end of the period
L = Total liabilities at the beginning of the period
L' = Total liabilities at the end of the period
E = Equity at the beginning of the period
E' = Equity at the end of the period
D = Dividends for the period
I = Net income for the period
R = Revenue
X = Expense

REQUIRED:

1. Write an equation that expresses the relationship among amounts reported for assets, liabilities, and equity on a balance sheet.

2. Write an equation that expresses the relationship among amounts reported for revenue, expense, and net income on an income statement.

3. Write an equation that expresses the relationship between equity on the beginning-of-the-year balance sheet and equity on the end-of-the-year balance sheet.

ANALYTICAL OPPORTUNITIES

A1-53. COST OR MARKET VALUES   Randy Patterson, the president of Landco, is concerned about the way generally accepted accounting principles require his firm to present its assets. Landco specializes in the acquisition and resale of land that is used for shopping centers. Landco identifies the likely growth areas in Atlanta, Chicago, Seattle, and Phoenix. Landco then purchases land in these growth areas that it believes will be suitable for shopping centers. After holding the land for three to five years, Landco sells the land to shopping center developers. Because Landco purchases land prior to the time it is considered for use as a shopping center, the selling price is typically four to five times the price that Landco pays for the land.

Randy Patterson argues that the requirement that Landco state its assets at cost misleads users of the balance sheet. Randy notes that Landco has received bona fide offers to purchase nearly all the parcels of land that it holds for much more than their costs. Randy argues that Landco should be able to report its inventory of land in the balance sheet at market value rather than cost. Then, Randy argues, users of the balance sheet would be able to assess much more accurately the value of the firm.

REQUIRED:

Why do you suppose generally accepted accounting principles do not permit the kind of accounting Randy Patterson favors? (Hint: You might read paragraph 21 of FASB *Statement of Financial Accounting Concepts No. 1* and paragraph 17 of *APB Opinion 6* to help formulate your response.)

A1-54. CASH OR ACCRUAL ACCOUNTING   Katie Vote owns a small business that rents computers to students at the local university. Katie's typical rental contract requires the student to pay the year's rent of $900 ($100 per month) in advance. When Katie prepares financial statements at the end of December, her accountant requires that Katie spread the $900 over the nine months that a computer is rented. Therefore, Katie can recognize only $400 revenue (four months) from each computer rental contract in the year the cash is collected and must defer recognition of the remaining $500 (five months) to next year. Katie argues that getting students to agree to rent the computer is the most difficult part of the activity so she ought to be able to recognize all $900 as revenue when the cash is received from a student.

REQUIRED:

Why do you believe that generally accepted accounting principles require the use of accrual accounting rather than cash-basis accounting for transactions like the one described here? (Hint: You might read paragraphs 42–48 of FASB *Statement of Financial Accounting Concepts No. 1* to help you formulate your response.)

A1-55. ANALYSIS OF ACCOUNTING PERIODICALS The accounting profession is organized into three major groups: (1) accountants who work in nonbusiness entities, (2) accountants who work in business entities, and (3) accountants in public practice. The periodical literature of accounting includes monthly or quarterly journals that are written primarily for accountants within each of these groups.

REQUIRED:

1. Visit your library and identify one journal published for each of the three professional groups. Identify the publisher of each journal and describe its primary audience.
2. Choose two of the three audiences you have just described. Briefly explain how members of one audience would benefit by reading a journal published primarily for members of the other audience.

Careful study of this
chapter will enable you
to:

1. Define the financial
   and operating cy-
   cles.
2. Describe the rela-
   tionship between
   the periodicity con-
   cept and the length
   of accounting pe-
   riods.
3. Explain how the
   revenue and
   matching concepts
   guide the measure-
   ment of net income.
4. Differentiate be-
   tween product ex-
   penses and period
   expenses.
5. State the reason
   for separating
   current assets and
   liabilities from other
   assets and liabilities
   in the balance
   sheet.
6. Prepare classified
   income statements
   and balance sheets.
7. Examine and inter-
   pret simple financial
   statements.

Appendix 2–1
8. Separate the ef-
   fects of extraordi-
   nary items and dis-
   continued
   operations on the
   income statement.

2 THE CONTENT AND ORGANIZATION OF FINANCIAL STATEMENTS

Chapter 1 introduced financial statements and discussed the basic concepts that guide their preparation. In this chapter, we extend that discussion to include additional concepts and a detailed examination of the content and organization of the income statement and the balance sheet. A thorough knowledge of the content and organization of typical financial statements, including the proper location of particular statement items, is a prerequisite to understanding how the effects of business activities are represented in the financial statements.

As we know from Chapter 1, the purpose of financial accounting and of financial statements is to provide information to decision-making groups *outside* a business entity. In order to be useful for decision making, financial statements must present information that is both *relevant* to decision makers' needs and *reliable*. (As explained in Supplementary Topic E, sometimes it is necessary to sacrifice reliability to obtain relevant information.) In addition, information gains in usefulness if it can be compared with similar information about other entities and with similar information about the same entity from some other period or some other point in time. Thus, as discussed in the present chapter, the content and organization of financial statements should be consistent and uniform over time. Although the financial statements presented in this chapter are representative, some variation will be found in the content and organization of published financial statements.

One of the main objectives of this book is to help you develop the ability to interpret and analyze real financial statements. To begin this process, the chapter concludes with an analysis of the actual financial statements for Wal-Mart Stores, Inc. and Subsidiaries, the well-known chain of discount stores. Later in the text, an entire chapter (Chapter 15) is devoted to the methods used to secure information from financial statements.

CONCEPTS AFFECTING THE CONTENT AND ORGANIZATION OF FINANCIAL STATEMENTS

Before discussing the detailed content and organization of financial statements, we shall examine four important accounting concepts that influence their preparation and enable us to better understand their structure. The first, the *operating cycle concept,* calls attention to an important characteristic of business activity and specifies the placement of certain assets and liabilities in the balance sheet. The *periodicity concept* influences the length of the accounting period and therefore the frequency with which financial statements are prepared. The *revenue recognition* and *matching concepts* are closely related, and both direct the process of identifying accrual-basis income with the appropriate accounting period. We will discuss each of the four concepts in turn, beginning with the operating cycle concept. The remainder of this chapter will build on these concepts as the financial statements are explained in greater detail. Later chapters will introduce additional concepts as our discussion of financial statements unfolds.

THE CYCLICAL NATURE OF BUSINESS ACTIVITY

A business enterprise engages in a sequence of interconnected and regularly repeated key activities. Although these activities vary somewhat from one business to another, the typical business engages in the following five activities:

1. Receives financial resources (mainly cash) from owners (stockholders) and creditors (bankers and bondholders)
2. Purchases assets, including salable goods (or materials to produce salable goods or services), from outside suppliers
3. Sells goods or provides services to customers using purchased assets
4. Collects cash from customers for goods sold or services provided
5. Repays financial resources acquired from owners and creditors

Exhibit 2–1 shows the relationship among these five functions for a typical business selling goods to its customers. The business receives cash and other financial resources from owners and creditors. The cash is used to purchase various assets, including goods that will be held in inventory until sold to customers. The business sells all goods on credit, creating accounts receivable, and cash is not replenished until the receivables are collected. At regular intervals, dividends are paid to stockholders (owners) and interest is paid to creditors; ultimately, of course, the amount originally received from stockholders and creditors is repaid, although in the case of stockholders, it may not be repaid until the business is dissolved.

This cyclical view of business enterprise involves two related sequences of activities of quite different lengths. One activity sequence is called the *financing cycle,* and the other is called the *operating cycle.* The **financing cycle** begins with the receipt of financial resources from owners and creditors and ends with the repayment of the original amounts received. The length of the financing cycle varies with the type of financing used by the enterprise. Notes payable may pass

FINANCING CYCLE: The elapsed time between the receipt of financial resources from owners or creditors and the repayment of the original amount received.

EXHIBIT 2–1   THE FINANCING AND OPERATING CYCLES

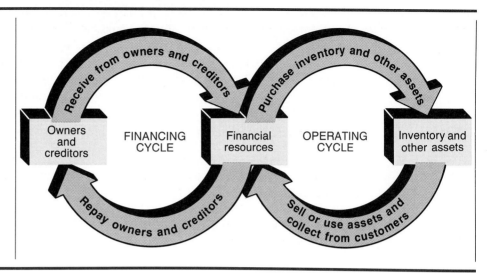

through the financing cycle in a year or less, whereas bonds payable may require 5 to 10 years or even longer. As noted above, the financing cycle for capital received from stockholders may be the entire lifetime of the business enterprise. In general, the financing cycle for most enterprises is likely to be many years.

In contrast, the operating cycle typically is a year or less. The **operating cycle** begins with the purchase of goods for inventory (or the purchase of materials to produce salable goods or services) and ends with the collection of cash from customers (presumably a larger amount of cash than was invested in the goods sold). The operating cycle varies in length from a week or less for perishable goods to many years for the production and sale of products such as timber. Let us illustrate the determination of an operating cycle: In 19X6 Skiles Furniture Store purchased furniture for resale costing $1,200,000. The furniture remained in inventory for an average of 3 months before being sold for $2,000,000. All furniture was sold on credit, and customers took an average of six months to pay for their purchases. Thus Skiles's operating cycle was nine months (three months to sell plus six months to collect), with the overall operating cycle representing an average of the specific operating cycles for each piece of furniture sold.

The operating cycle for a business enterprise is usually much shorter than its financing cycle. Indeed, it is the opportunity to use outside resources to finance multiple operating cycles that enables an enterprise to generate profit and pay interest and dividends. The operating cycle is an important way of characterizing the fundamental income-producing activities of a business entity. Accordingly, the operating cycle concept plays an important role in guiding the measurement of income, as we shall see when we discuss the periodicity and revenue recognition concepts. The length of the operating cycle also influences the classification of assets and liabilities on balance sheets, as shown later in this chapter. The length of the operating cycle also affects the amount of capital a firm needs and the prices it must obtain for the goods and services it sells, as the following analysis demonstrates.

OPERATING CYCLE: The elapsed time between the purchase of salable goods (or the purchase of materials used to produce salable goods or services) and the collection of cash from customers.

Assume that there are two firms, Short and Long, that sell on credit 1,000 units per month (12,000 units per year) of product A to similar customers at $10 per unit. Assume that each firm has 200 units of product A in inventory and that those units were purchased at a cost of $6 per unit (a total inventory of $1,200). Each firm has $1,000 in cash and no assets other than accounts receivable and inventory. Further, assume that Short collects its accounts receivable within one month, so that at any point in time one month's sales, or $10,000, are in Short's accounts receivable. Long, on the other hand, collects its accounts receivable three months after a sale and therefore at any given time has three months' sales, or $30,000, in accounts receivable. At present, the two firms have the following balance sheets:

Short		Long	
ASSETS		**ASSETS**	
Cash......................	$ 1,000	Cash......................	$ 1,000
Inventory	1,200	Inventory	1,200
Accounts receivable	10,000	Accounts receivable	30,000
Total assets..............	$12,200	Total assets..............	$32,200
LIABILITIES AND EQUITY		**LIABILITIES AND EQUITY**	
Equity	$12,200	Loans payable	$20,000
		Equity	12,200
Total liabilities and equity	$12,200	Total liabilities and equity	$32,200

1. *What is the effect of the difference in operating cycle on the capital requirements of Long and Short, respectively?*

A comparison of the two balance sheets shows that Long needs $20,000 more capital than Short, because of Long's longer operating cycle. The $20,000 needed is the difference between Short's $12,200 in assets and Long's $32,200 in assets.

2. *Assume that Long borrows the additional $20,000 on a long-term basis at 10 percent interest per year. The income statements for the two firms for the year immediately following the date of the above balance sheets are as follows:*

Short		Long	
Sales revenue	$120,000	Sales revenue	$120,000
Less: Cost of goods sold*...	72,000	Less: Cost of goods sold*...	72,000
Gross margin	$ 48,000	Gross margin	$ 48,000
Less: Operating expenses...	33,000	Less: Operating expenses...	33,000
Income from operations ...	$ 15,000	Income from operations....	$ 15,000
Less: Interest expense......	–0–	Less: Interest expense......	2,000
Income before taxes	$ 15,000	Income before taxes	$ 13,000
Less: Income taxes		Less: Income taxes	
expense (.20)	3,000	expense (.20)	2,600
Net income.............	$ 12,000	Net income.............	$ 10,400

* An expense representing the cost of the 12,000 units of product A that have been sold.

3. *What is the effect on profitability of the differences in the capital requirements of the two firms?*

Long's net income (the difference between revenue and expense) is less than Short's because the longer operating cycle for Long requires additional debt capital, which increases expenses. Thus, if Long wants the same net income as Short, it must sell enough extra units of product to earn the additional $1,600 after taxes. Had the additional capital been generated through increased stockholders' equity instead of a loan, additional cash dividend payments to stockholders would have been required of Long, again requiring additional sales in order to produce the additional cash for stockholder dividends.

We turn now to another concept related to a time interval — the periodicity concept, which influences the establishment of accounting periods.

THE PERIODICITY CONCEPT

PERIODICITY CONCEPT: The concept that financial statements should be issued sufficiently often to provide timely information, but not so often that the precision of the statements is seriously impaired.

The accounting period is the span of time for which financial statements are prepared. The **periodicity concept** requires that financial statements be prepared sufficiently often to provide timely information, but not so often that the precision of the statements is seriously impaired. One could argue, in the interest of precise income measurement, that the periodicity concept should require preparation of financial statements at the end of each operating cycle. However, different firms have different operating cycles, and a uniform accounting period is highly desirable. Fortunately, a year is a good approximation of many operating cycles. Consequently, the accounting period is usually defined to be one year in length, and annual financial statements are prepared and issued by virtually all companies.

We noted earlier that financial statements are prepared in order to provide information for interested decision makers outside the firm. Good decision making depends on the *timeliness* of the information available for use in the decision-making process. For example, assume that it is early December and that you are a banker considering a loan application from the owner of a local restaurant. The applicant wants to borrow $10,000 to remodel the restaurant kitchen. The loan is to be repaid at the end of six months, and the owner has provided you with a set of financial statements for the restaurant's fiscal year ending December 31 of the previous year. You realize that the restaurant's financial position and operating performance might have changed dramatically in the 11 months since the financial statements were prepared, and you therefore request more timely information. More recent financial statements indicating the continued profitability of the restaurant would support the restaurateur's loan application, but if profitability has declined, you would have reason to refuse the loan request.

In general, creditors and investors find that good decision making requires data on the performance and status of an entity to be available more often than once a year. Accountants and business organizations have responded to this need for more timely accounting information by preparing financial statements on a monthly or quarterly basis. Such statements are usually prepared in less detail than the annual statements. In short, although the principal accounting period is one year, the periodicity concept may lead an entity to supplement annual reporting with quarterly or monthly statements.[1]

We turn now to two concepts that influence the assignment of revenues and expenses to specific time periods for the purpose of measuring accrual-basis net income.

---

[1] Unless an alternative accounting period is stated, we shall assume throughout this book that the accounting period is one year in length, that it ends on December 31 of each year, and that financial statements are prepared and issued only once per year.

THE REVENUE RECOGNITION CONCEPT

REVENUE RECOGNITION: The process of identifying each dollar of revenue with a particular accounting period.

REVENUE RECOGNITION CONCEPT: The concept that revenue should be recognized as earned when the seller has put forth substantially all the effort required to sell the related goods or services and when the selling price is known.

Recall that revenue is the inflow of assets to an entity resulting from the sale of goods or services by the entity. **Revenue recognition** is the process of identifying each dollar of revenue with a particular accounting period. Under accrual accounting, which is required by generally accepted accounting principles, revenue is identified with the period in which it is *earned*. In Chapter 1, we noted that revenue is usually earned when the related goods or services are transferred to a customer; accordingly, revenue usually equals the total selling price of goods and services provided to customers during the period. Occasionally, however, revenue may be earned at some point in the operating cycle other than the point at which goods are transferred to customers. The revenue recognition concept guides accountants in identifying the point in the operating cycle at which revenue is earned and, thereby, the period in which revenue should be recognized. The **revenue recognition concept** says that revenue is earned when the seller has put forth substantially all the effort required to sell the related goods or services and when the selling price is known.

To illustrate the revenue recognition concept, let's assume that Barnes Electronics sells personal computers for $3,000 each. During 19X9 Barnes sells 20 computers to customers. Accordingly, Barnes recognizes revenue for 19X9 of $60,000 [($3,000)(20)]. The following argument, based on the revenue recognition concept, supports this treatment of revenues: By the time the computers are transferred to customers, most of the effort to earn the revenue has been put forth by Barnes. All that remains is to collect from the customers, which usually represents a relatively small part of the total effort to sell the product. In addition, the selling price of each computer is known to be $3,000. Prior to the transfer of goods or services, the selling price in many businesses is still open to negotiation, but such uncertainty is usually removed when the transfer takes place. Although the revenue recognition concept does not *require* recognition at the time of transfer of goods or performance of services, the generally accepted accounting principles that implement the concept assume that revenue will be recognized at the time of transfer unless exceptional circumstances are present.[2] Just as the revenue recognition concept guides the assignment of revenues to accounting periods, so the matching concept, to which we now turn, guides the assignment of expenses to accounting periods.

THE MATCHING CONCEPT

MATCHING: The process of identifying expense (the cost of assets that have been given up or used to earn revenue) with a particular accounting period.

MATCHING CONCEPT: The concept that the expense of a given accounting period is the cost of assets given up or used to earn the revenue recognized in that period.

Recall that expense is the cost of assets given up or used to earn revenue. **Matching** is the process of identifying expense with a particular accounting period. Under accrual-basis accounting, expenses are identified or "matched" with the period in which the related revenues are recognized. This process is influenced by the **matching concept,** which states that the expense of an accounting period is the cost of assets given up or used to earn the revenue recognized in that period. Thus expense for a given period should exclude the cost of assets used to earn revenues

[2] In the example above, we can imagine circumstances in which Barnes should not recognize revenue at the time computers are transferred, or sold, to customers. If, for example, Barnes sold computers on an installment basis that required significant collection efforts, then postponing recognition of revenue until the time of cash collection should be considered. Postponement would also be appropriate if a high proportion of Barnes's customers failed to pay their installment contracts, because, in that case, the revenue, which must be adjusted for such defaults, might be significantly less than $3,000 per computer and might be difficult to estimate at the time of sale. Later chapters consider certain circumstances in which revenues are recognized at times other than the sale of goods or the performance of services; however, a complete discussion of exceptions is deferred to intermediate accounting texts.

EXHIBIT 2–2 REVENUE RECOGNITION AND MATCHING: ESTABLISHING THE RELATIONSHIP BETWEEN INCOME AND THE ACCOUNTING PERIOD

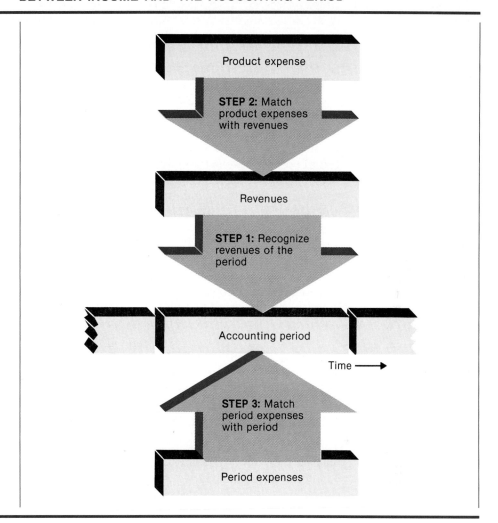

of earlier or later periods and should include all costs related to the revenue recognized in that period and that period only.

Expenses arising from assets that are physically transferred to customers are relatively easy to match with related revenues because the transfer of assets is a signal both to include the assets' selling price in revenue and to include the assets' cost in expense. For example, suppose that Barnes Electronics, which sold 20 computers at $3,000 each during 19X9, paid the manufacturer $2,200 for each computer. The sale of 20 computers in 19X9 contributes $60,000 [($3,000)(20)] to 19X9 revenue and $44,000 [($2,200)(20)] to 19X9 expense. The expense of $44,000 is clearly matched with the revenue of $60,000 in that both revenue and expense are associated with the 20 computers sold to customers. Expenses matched with revenues in this direct manner are **product expenses.** The recognition of revenue of the period and the matching of product expenses with that revenue are shown in Exhibit 2–2 (steps 1 and 2). Product expenses represent the cost of assets transferred to customers during a given period. Product expenses are

PRODUCT EXPENSES: The cost of assets sold to customers in a given period.

usually reported on the income statement as a single expense item called *cost of goods sold,* as explained below.

Unlike product expenses, expenses arising from assets that are used or consumed in operations — rather than physically transferred to customers — are frequently difficult to match with related revenues. As an example, let's consider the $60,000 annual salary of J. L. Barnes, president of Barnes Electronics. Although we may suspect that Barnes's activities are related to revenues in various years, we have no way of convincingly and efficiently measuring this relationship. Thus, the entire salary is taken as an expense in 19X9, the year in which Barnes worked to earn it. Period expenses also arise from the cost of assets used or consumed over several years. In such cases, a portion of the asset's cost is included in the expense of each year in which the asset is used or consumed. These practices do not perfectly match expense and revenue, but they are accepted as a necessary approximation to the matching concept. Expenses matched with revenues in this approximate way are called **period expenses.** In Exhibit 2–2, step 3 represents the matching of period expenses with the accounting period and thus with revenues of that period (which have already been recognized in the period by performing step 1). Period expenses represent the cost of assets included in the expenses for the period of their use or consumption.

PERIOD EXPENSES: The cost of assets assigned to the period of their use or consumption.

In the sections that follow, we discuss in detail the contents of the four major financial statements. The elements of these statements are the same for annual statements as for the more timely monthly or quarterly statements.

THE CLASSIFIED FINANCIAL STATEMENTS

The primary financial statements presented in the following sections are (1) the income statement, (2) the statement of changes in retained earnings, (3) the balance sheet, and (4) the statement of cash flows. The first three are described in detail. The discussion of the statement of cash flows is brief, however, because a more detailed coverage is given in Chapter 13 after its underlying accounting principles have been presented.

Before proceeding with our examination of the structure and content of the individual financial statements, we need to explain what is meant by *classified.* When used to describe an income statement, this term means simply that the revenues and expenses will be divided into categories — or classified — with subtotals provided after each classification. On a classified balance sheet, the assets, liabilities, and equity will be similarly categorized and subtotaled. Why do accountants prepare classified financial statements? Wouldn't it seem easier simply to list assets, liabilities, and equity on the balance sheet and revenues and expenses on the income statement without dividing them into categories? Reasons why classification helps financial statement users include:

1. Classifying the statement items makes it easier to locate necessary information quickly.

2. Classification clarifies and highlights important relationships among statement items.

3. Classification provides additional information about impending cash inflows (current assets) and impending cash outflows (current liabilities).

Unclassified income statements (but not balance sheets) are used in certain industries when there is only one source of revenues and all the expense items are necessary to produce revenues. In other words, there is no need to classify expenses when there is only one meaningful classification.

THE CLASSIFIED INCOME STATEMENT

As we know from Chapter 1, the income statement presents the results of the firm's operations (that is, the sales of goods and/or services) for a given accounting period. The long-term survival of a business depends on its ability to produce net income by earning revenue in excess of related expense. Income enables the firm to (1) pay for the capital it uses (dividends to stockholders and interest to the holders of debt); (2) pay higher wages to employees; (3) pay income taxes; and (4) attract new capital necessary for continued existence and growth. Since current and future income are so important to the firm, the income statement structure must indicate to statement users the sources and the amount of current income and must provide information that will help forecast the amount of future income for the firm. The classified income statement, therefore, is organized to aid in these determinations. A firm that sells goods would have a classified income statement organized as follows:

Sales revenue		$xx
Less: Cost of goods sold		xx
Gross margin		$xx
Less: Operating expenses:		
Selling	$xx	
Administrative	xx	xx
Income from operations		$xx
Plus: Other revenues and gains	$xx	
Less: Other expenses and losses	xx	xx
Income before taxes		$xx
Less: Income taxes expense		xx
Net income		$xx

In actual financial statements, the format above may be expanded to include many more subcategories, some of which appear in the income statement for McCool's Department Store (Exhibit 2–3).

Income Statement Classification

We turn now to an examination of the different kinds of economic activity represented by each of the major classifications in the income statement. Our discussion follows the order of the income statement shown in Exhibit 2–3.

SALES REVENUE: Revenue resulting from the sale of goods or services by a business.

   Sales revenue arises from the principal activity or activities of the business. In McCool's case, as in most businesses, the revenue recognition concept leads to the identification of sales revenue with the period in which the sale occurs. Thus sales revenue is the total of all sales made during the period. Revenue from other activities, such as interest on customers' credit purchases or investment revenue,

EXHIBIT 2-3   CLASSIFIED INCOME STATEMENT

McCOOL'S DEPARTMENT STORE
Income Statement
For the Year Ended December 31, 19X6

Gross sales revenue			$12,460,000
Less: Sales returns and allowances . . .			115,000
Net sales revenue			$12,345,000
Less: Cost of goods sold			7,410,000
Gross margin			$ 4,935,000
Less: Operating expenses:			
Selling expenses:			
Advertising	$1,075,000		
Wages, sales	1,185,000		
Salaries, sales	420,000		
Miscellaneous	110,000		
Total selling expenses		$2,790,000	
Administrative expenses:			
Salaries, administrative	$ 560,000		
Depreciation	20,000		
Insurance	15,000		
Property taxes	105,000		
Miscellaneous	20,000		
Total administrative expenses		720,000	
Total operating expenses . . .			3,510,000
Income from operations			$ 1,425,000
Other revenues and gains:			
Dividend revenue		$ 98,000	
Gain on sale of long-lived assets . . .		12,000	110,000
Other expenses and losses:			
Interest expense			(225,000)
Income before taxes			$ 1,310,000
Less: Income taxes expense			445,400
Net income			$ 864,600
Earnings per share			$8.65

appears later in the income statement. The selling price of returned merchandise and reductions in selling price for damaged or defective merchandise (sales returns and allowances) are subtracted from the gross sales revenue. A large number of sales returns and allowances may indicate serious operating problems, such as problems with the quality or handling of goods. McCool's sales returns and allowances are less than 1 percent of sales, a very reasonable ratio.

COST OF GOODS SOLD:
The purchase price of goods sold to customers during the accounting period plus the related cost of readying the goods for sale.

    Cost of goods sold is the sum of the purchase price and the other costs necessary to ready for sale the inventory sold during this accounting period. Cost of goods sold is the principal element of product expense for most businesses. In Chapters 6 and 7, we will discuss detailed procedures for determining cost of goods sold for firms that purchase and resell goods. A discussion of the procedures used to determine cost of goods sold for a firm that manufactures and then sells goods is deferred to a cost accounting or managerial accounting text.

GROSS MARGIN (GROSS PROFIT): Sales revenue minus cost of goods sold.

Gross margin, often called **gross profit,** is the first important subtotal on the income statement. Gross margin is the difference between the sales revenue, which represents the selling price of the goods sold, and the goods' cost to the firm:

SALES REVENUE – COST OF GOODS SOLD = GROSS MARGIN

The gross margin must be large enough to provide the business with the resources necessary to pay for operating expenses, financial expenses, and income taxes expense, and to provide profits for reinvestment and repayments to owners and creditors. The dollar amount of gross margin is affected by both the quantity of goods sold and the amount by which the selling price exceeds the cost of goods sold. Gross margin thus can be increased either by selling a larger quantity of goods at the same price or by selling the same quantity of goods for a higher price.[3] A careful reader of financial statements examines both the amount and the percentage of the gross margin in an attempt to determine the likely causes of the firm's current performance and thereby project its future performance. McCool's gross margin is $4,935,000, or almost 40 percent of sales.

OPERATING EXPENSES: The period expenses a business incurs in selling goods or providing services and in administering the entire range of its activities.

Operating expenses are the period expenses recognized in carrying out the most important activities of the business (selling goods or providing services). Since operating expenses are period expenses, they are usually listed separately from the cost of goods sold, which is a product expense. In addition, as shown in Exhibit 2–3, operating expenses are usually separated from nonoperating items (other revenues and gains, and other expenses and losses) and from income taxes expense. On the income statement, operating expenses are often divided into two subcategories: selling expenses and administrative expenses. **Selling expenses** are the costs of selling goods or selling and providing services. For example, selling expenses typically include such items as advertising expense and the salaries or wages that are paid to the company's salespersons. Note that the cost of goods sold is not included in selling expenses. **Administrative expenses** are the costs of managing and administering the firm's entire range of activities. Such expenses include salaries paid to managers and members of their staffs, depreciation on administrative buildings and equipment, and related amounts for insurance, utilities, property taxes, and repairs. The income statement in Exhibit 2–3 places selling expenses and administrative expenses in separate classifications.

SELLING EXPENSES: The costs of selling goods or selling and providing services.

ADMINISTRATIVE EXPENSES: The costs of managing and administering all activities of a business entity.

INCOME FROM OPERATIONS: Gross margin (gross profit) minus operating expenses.

Income from operations, another important subtotal, is the amount that remains after subtracting operating expenses from gross margin. It indicates the level and percentage of profit produced by the principal activities of the firm. Income from operations can be increased by increasing the gross margin or by reducing the level or percentage of operating expenses. Income from operations must be large enough to pay the firm's remaining expenses. Prudent external users scrutinize financial statements for changes in the level and percentage of income from operations as the firm's sales increase or decrease and as operating expenses respond to changes in prices.

[3] Increases of this sort assume that the cost per unit of the goods sold remains unchanged.

OTHER REVENUES AND GAINS: Revenues from activities not related to the firm's principal operations and gains from sales of assets that were not acquired for resale.

OTHER EXPENSES AND LOSSES: Expenses from activities not related to the firm's principal operations and losses from sales of assets that were not acquired for resale.

INCOME BEFORE TAXES: Income from operations plus the amount of other revenues and gains less the amount of other expenses and losses.

INCOME TAXES EXPENSE: The income tax paid or owed to federal or other governments that is related to income before taxes.

NET INCOME: Income before taxes minus income taxes expense.

EARNINGS PER SHARE: A corporation's net income divided by the number of shares of capital stock held by investors.

Other revenues and gains consist of revenues from activities not related to the firm's principal operations and gains from sales of assets that were not acquired for resale. McCool's had one item of other revenue, $98,000 of dividends received from its portfolio of marketable securities (see Exhibit 2–6), and one gain, $12,000 from the sale of store equipment.

Other expenses and losses are expenses from activities not related to the firm's principal operations and losses from sales of assets that were not acquired for resale. Normally one of the most important other expenses is interest on the firm's debt (formal borrowings). Debt (usually notes, loans, mortgages, bonds, and capital leases) is important to the financing of any firm because debt is frequently an inexpensive source of capital and because missed debt payments can cause bankruptcy. Interest expense may even be presented as a separate section in the income statement or, as in Exhibit 2–3, included with the rest of the other expenses and losses. McCool's had $225,000 of interest expense on its short-term notes payable, mortgage payable, and bonds payable (see Exhibit 2–6).

Income before taxes is the income from operations plus the amount of other revenues and gains less the amount of other expenses and losses. Note that the taxes referred to in the term *income before taxes* include only *income* taxes. Several other kinds of taxes are included among the firm's operating expenses and thus are subtracted from gross margin as part of the computation of income from operations. For example, property taxes assessed by city and county governments, local sales taxes, and payroll taxes (such as social security tax and state and federal unemployment taxes) are all included in operating expenses.

Income taxes expense is the income tax owed to federal and other governmental units that is related to income before taxes. Income taxes expense is one of the largest single expense items for many businesses. The differences in the amounts and percentages of income taxes expense among firms as well as differences across years for the same firm are informative to sophisticated readers of financial statements. A detailed discussion of corporate income taxes appears in Chapter 16.

Recall that net income is the excess of an entity's revenue over its expense during a given period of time. As computed on the income statement, **net income** is income before taxes less the income taxes expense. **Earnings per share** is net income divided by the number of shares of capital stock held by the firm's stockholders. Most readers of financial statements closely scrutinize the levels of, and changes in, the net income and earnings per share. The income statement for McCool's Department Store shows net income of $864,600. If we assume that the corporation's stockholders own 100,000 shares of capital stock, we can then calculate the earnings per share as $8.65 [$864,600/100,000].

The Classified Income Statement for a Service Business

Although we have been considering the income statement for a business that sells goods, many businesses provide services as their major activity. The income statement for a service business is quite similar to that for a firm that sells goods. The major difference is that two categories, cost of goods sold and gross margin, do not appear in the income statement for a firm that provides services. Normally there is no division of these expenses into selling and administrative cate-

EXHIBIT 2-4   CLASSIFIED INCOME STATEMENT: SERVICE BUSINESS

CLARENCE'S TELEVISION SERVICE
Income Statement
For the Year Ended December 31, 19X6

Gross service revenue		$575,000
Less: Allowances		3,000
Net service revenue		$572,000
Less: Operating expenses:		
Advertising	$ 13,000	
Depreciation, test equipment	11,000	
Depreciation, building	14,000	
Insurance	1,000	
Property taxes	3,000	
Supplies, repair parts	148,000	
Utilities	13,000	
Wages	264,000	
Miscellaneous	35,000	
Total operating expenses		502,000
Income from operations		$ 70,000
Other revenues and gains:		
Interest revenue		5,000
Other expenses and losses:		
Interest expense	$ 37,000	
Loss on sale of long-lived assets	2,000	(39,000)
Income before taxes		$ 36,000
Less: Income taxes expense		5,400
Net income		$ 30,600
Earnings per share		$6.12

ories because selling expenses are not usually large. These differences are illustrated in Exhibit 2-4, which shows a classified income statement for a service business.

Uses of the Income Statement

The income statement provides information of interest to persons both inside and outside the firm. Managers and employees are interested in net income because it is an indicator of the availability of resources for additional compensation. In some cases, part of the compensation of managers is tied directly to net income. Creditors and stockholders are interested in net income as an indicator of the availability of resources for interest and dividends. Net income is also an indicator of the firm's rate of growth, which, as the accompanying analysis demonstrates, is of interest to both present and potential stockholders of the firm. Growth in net income enhances the equity of stockholders and enables the firm to contemplate increases in dividends.

ANALYSIS

COMPARISON OF
INCOME STATEMENTS
FOR INVESTMENT
DECISION

As an example of the kind of information the classified income statement can provide, let's examine a simple illustration: Assume that you want to invest in one of two firms, either Growth, Inc., or Stagnation Company. Each firm pays out half its earnings to stockholders as dividends.

Your first step is to examine the current income statements of each firm:

Growth, Inc.		Stagnation Company	
Sales revenue	$1,000,000	Sales revenue	$1,000,000
Gross margin	400,000	Gross margin	400,000
Net income	50,000	Net income	50,000
Earnings per share	2.50	Earnings per share	5.00
Dividends per share*	1.25	Dividends per share*	2.50

* Total dividends divided by the number of shares of capital stock held by stockholders.

Next, you examine a five-year summary of sales revenue, net income, and earnings per share (EPS) for the two firms:

Growth, Inc.

	19X2	19X3	19X4	19X5	19X6
Sales revenue	$625,000	$700,000	$750,000	$875,000	$1,000,000
Net income	30,000	36,000	40,000	42,000	50,000
Earnings per share	1.50	1.80	2.00	2.10	2.50

Stagnation Company

	19X2	19X3	19X4	19X5	19X6
Sales revenue	$1,025,000	$975,000	$997,000	$950,000	$1,000,000
Net income	51,000	48,000	46,000	49,000	50,000
Earnings per share	5.10	4.80	4.60	4.90	5.00

For $50,000 you can purchase 10 percent of the capital stock of either firm: 2,000 shares of Growth or 1,000 shares of Stagnation. Astute investment decision making is a complex process. As an investor, you seek those investments that will provide the largest return at the lowest risk. One factor considered to be associated with large returns is growth. Accounting data are often helpful in judging growth potential. In assessing the expected growth potential for our two hypothetical companies, you should consider the following questions:

1. *Which firm has grown more during the past five years?*

Growth's sales have increased by an average of 12.5 percent per year; Stagnation's sales have decreased by an average of .6 percent per year. Growth's profits have increased by an average of 13.5 percent, while Stagnation's have declined by .5 percent.

2. *Which firm's dividends to stockholders have grown more during the past five years?*

Growth's dividends have increased more than have Stagnation's because Growth's earnings have grown more.

3. *Which investment of $50,000 would be expected to produce the larger return?*

While the future can never be predicted with certainty, the past five years' data suggest that the future dividends from Growth are likely to increase more rapidly than dividends from Stagnation if Growth continues to grow more rapidly than Stagnation. Thus the $50,000 invested in Growth would probably yield the larger return.

THE STATEMENT OF CHANGES IN RETAINED EARNINGS

The owners of a business contribute capital to a corporation in two ways: (1) directly, through purchases of capital stock from the corporation, and (2) indirectly, by allowing the corporation to retain some or all the net income earned each year (rather than paying it out in dividends). As we noted in Chapter 1, the income earned by a firm but not paid out in dividends is called *retained earnings*. One of the links between the income statement and the balance sheet is the statement of changes in retained earnings.

Once net income has been determined, the statement of changes in retained earnings can be prepared. The beginning retained earnings balance (ending retained earnings from the previous period) and the net income and dividends for this period are combined to produce the ending retained earnings balance for the current period (see Exhibit 2–5). Certain other items occasionally appear in statements of changes in retained earnings (principally, a type of correction called *prior period adjustments*). A discussion of such items is deferred until Chapter 12.

THE CLASSIFIED BALANCE SHEET

The balance sheet is a point-in-time description, whereas both the income statement and the statement of changes in retained earnings are period-of-time descriptions. The income statement describes the results of operations for one specific period. The statement of changes in retained earnings is also a period statement, but it describes the changes in only one item, retained earnings. The balance sheet is a list of the resources (assets) owned or controlled by the business, at their cost,[4] the obligations of the business to outsiders (liabilities), and the dollars of capital provided by the owners (equity), all as of the end of a specific

[4] A portion of the cost of most long-lived assets, such as buildings and equipment, is removed from the balance sheet each period and put on the income statement as depreciation expense. Therefore, for long-lived assets, only the unconsumed portion of their cost (that part not yet depreciated) is totaled among the assets on the balance sheet.

EXHIBIT 2–5   **STATEMENT OF CHANGES IN RETAINED EARNINGS**

McCOOL'S DEPARTMENT STORE
Statement of Changes in Retained Earnings
For the Year Ended December 31, 19X6

Retained earnings, 12/31/X5	$ 760,000
Add: Net income for 19X6	864,600
	$1,624,600
Less: Dividends for 19X6	400,000
Retained earnings, 12/31/X6	$1,224,600

accounting period. As the following diagram shows, the balance sheet provides a point-in-time measurement of a firm's financial position:

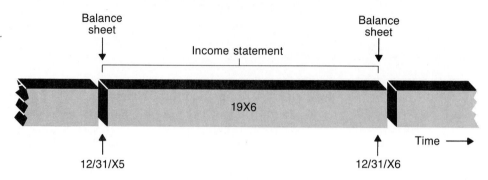

Historical Cost and Current Market Value

As noted in Chapter 1, when a business purchases goods and services, the cost of the item (also called its **historical cost**) is recorded in the firm's accounting records. Such costs are not altered to reflect increases in market value.[5] If all market prices were stable, the historical cost of assets would be very close to their current market value and the balance sheet would approximate the current market value of the firm. Market prices, however, are not stable, and even when the general price level for goods and services is stable, prices for specific items often change significantly. Thus the **current market value** — the monetary worth attributed to an asset by the marketplace at the present time — will differ significantly from the historical cost for some assets.

The assets of a healthy, ongoing firm are appropriately measured using both historical cost and current market value. If a firm will continue operations, then the firm can recover through normal operations the historical cost of assets already acquired and will replace those assets as they are used up or sold, paying their then current market values. A healthy, ongoing firm is said to satisfy the **going concern assumption.** A firm that faces discontinuance does not satisfy the going concern assumption. Such a firm will neither recover through normal operations the historical cost of assets currently held nor will it replace those assets. Consequently, historical cost measurements are of little interest to persons seeking information about such firms. When a firm faces discontinuance, current market values are of primary interest because the firm expects to dispose of its assets in the near future.

Balance Sheet Classifications

If it is not a statement of current values, what then is the balance sheet? To begin with, it is a statement made up of two lists: (1) a list of the company's assets at their historical costs and (2) a list of the sources on which the firm has drawn in order to purchase the assets. The contents of this second list are the firm's liabilities and equity. The balance sheet is organized, or classified, to help the user find the

---

[5] However, certain declines in value are recorded. These exceptions to the cost concept are called *lower-of-cost-or-market adjustments.* Such adjustments are consistent with the *conservatism convention,* which is discussed and illustrated in Chapter 7 and other later chapters.

necessary data quickly. The classifications clarify and add meaning by drawing attention to certain accounts and sets of accounts. A common structure for the classified balance sheet is as follows:

ASSETS	LIABILITIES
Current assets	Current liabilities
Long-term investments	Long-term liabilities
Property, plant, and equipment	
Intangible assets	**EQUITY**
Other assets	Capital stock
Deferred charges	Retained earnings

A typical classified balance sheet is presented in Exhibit 2–6 and is explained in the following section. Let us consider each of the major classifications on the balance sheet, beginning with current assets and current liabilities.

CURRENT ASSETS AND CURRENT LIABILITIES   Assets are held and liabilities are owed for varying lengths of time. For example, cash and inventories tend to turn over more frequently than land and buildings, and accounts payable turn over more frequently than notes payable. Balance sheets classify assets and liabilities into those of short duration — called *current assets and liabilities* — and those of long duration — called *long-lived assets* and *long-term liabilities.* In a typical business, it is reasonable to take one year as the dividing line between current and long-term assets and liabilities; however, if the operating cycle of a business is longer than one year (as it is for shipbuilders, for example), then accounts receivable, inventories, and accounts payable turn over much more slowly than for the typical business. In such cases, it is reasonable to extend the dividing line beyond one year to equal the length of the operating cycle. In other words, assets and liabilities that are expected to turn over within the next operating cycle or next year, whichever is longer, are identified on the balance sheet as current assets and current liabilities. This separation of current from long-term assets and liabilities is known as the **current asset and current liability concept.**

Following this concept, **current assets** consist of cash and all other assets that will be either converted into cash (as will short-term investments and accounts receivable) or used to provide goods or services (as will inventory and prepaid expenses) within one year or one operating cycle, whichever is longer. Similarly, **current liabilities** consist of obligations to outsiders that will require the firm to pay cash (as will accounts payable) or to provide goods or services (as will product warranties) within one year or one operating cycle, whichever is longer. Warranty obligations that are expected to require the firm to replace parts or products or to refund cash within the longer of one year or one operating cycle are usually considered current liabilities. Any portion of long-term debt due within the current period may also be considered a current liability, as are deposits and/or prepayments received from customers.

Current assets and current liabilities are usually listed in the balance sheet in the order of the time at which they will be received or paid in cash. Thus, among McCool's current assets, cash (which is already in the form of cash) is listed first, investments in marketable securities (which are virtually the same as cash) are listed second, accounts receivable (which may take several weeks or more to convert to cash) is listed third, and merchandise inventory (which may take months to convert into cash) is listed fourth. Prepaid expenses are advance

CURRENT ASSET AND CURRENT LIABILITY CONCEPT: The concept that assets and liabilities that are expected to turn over within the next operating cycle or next year, whichever is longer, should be identified on the balance sheet as current assets and current liabilities.

CURRENT ASSETS: Cash and other assets that will be either converted into cash or used to provide goods or services within one year or one operating cycle, whichever is longer.

CURRENT LIABILITIES: Obligations to outsiders that will require the firm to pay cash or provide goods or services within one year or one operating cycle, whichever is longer.

EXHIBIT 2–6   CLASSIFIED BALANCE SHEET

McCOOL'S DEPARTMENT STORE
Balance Sheet
As of December 31, 19X6

ASSETS

Current assets:

Cash.................................			$ 110,000
Short-term investments in marketable securities...............			200,000
Accounts receivable			1,090,000
Inventory, merchandise			1,630,000
Prepaid insurance			20,000
Total current assets..................			$3,050,000
Long-term investments in equity securities			105,000
Property, plant, and equipment:			
Land		$100,000	
Building.............................	$1,270,000		
Less: Accumulated depreciation.........	300,000	970,000	
Equipment, store.....................	$ 750,000		
Less: Accumulated depreciation.........	280,000	470,000	
Total property, plant, and equipment ..			1,540,000
Intangible assets:			
Trademark, store logo.................			15,000
Other assets:			
Land, held for future expansion			300,000
Deferred charges:			
Prepaid rent, equipment...............			75,000
Total assets....................			$5,085,000

payments for rent, insurance, and other services that will be used within one year or one operating cycle, whichever is longer. Although prepaid expenses are converted into services rather than cash, the services support a variety of cash-producing activities. Prepaid expenses are listed last among current assets because of their indirect relationship to the production of cash. Among current liabilities, accounts payable and wages and salaries payable (which are usually paid in a matter of weeks) are listed before short-term notes payable (which may not be paid for several months).

The excess of a firm's current assets over its current liabilities is called *working capital.* From Exhibit 2–6, for example, we can determine that McCool's working capital is $1,705,000 [$3,050,000–$1,345,000]. The amount of working capital is of interest to any outsiders (creditors, vendors, and taxing authorities) who are concerned about receiving cash in the near future from a business, because it helps to determine whether the cash necessary to pay the outsiders' claims will be available when the claims come due.

INVESTMENTS: A firm's holdings of shares of ownership or debt securities of other firms or of government securities.

SHORT-TERM AND LONG-TERM INVESTMENTS   **Investments** reflect the purchase by the business entity of shares of ownership or debt securities of other firms. Government securities are also investments. Investments may appear in two locations on the balance sheet. If the investing business (the investor) intends to dispose of the

LIABILITIES

Current liabilities:

Accounts payable	$ 160,000
Salaries payable	34,000
Wages payable	91,000
Notes payable, short-term	530,000
Income taxes payable	165,000
Property taxes payable	70,000
Mortgage payable, current portion	85,000
Estimated warranty liability, current portion	210,000
Total current liabilities	$1,345,000

Long-term liabilities:

Mortgage payable	$ 545,400	
Bonds payable, 10%, due 19X8	970,000	
Total long-term liabilities		1,515,400
Total liabilities		$2,860,400

STOCKHOLDERS' EQUITY

Capital stock	$1,000,000	
Retained earnings	1,224,600	
Total stockholders' equity		2,224,600
Total liabilities and stockholders' equity		$5,085,000

investment in the near future (within the longer of one year or the operating cycle), the investment is listed as a current asset. These short-term investments are often called *marketable securities.* If a longer holding period is anticipated, the investment is accounted for as a long-term investment and listed following current assets. Long-term investments include partial ownership in other businesses. Accounting for short-term investments is discussed in Chapter 8, and accounting for long-term investments is discussed in Chapter 14.

PROPERTY, PLANT, AND EQUIPMENT AND DEPRECIATION Those long-lived assets used by a business to produce revenues are normally called **property, plant, and equipment.** They include such assets as land, buildings, furniture, tools, and machinery. Property, plant, and equipment are *tangible operating assets* in the sense that they have a visible, physical presence. In contrast, a store logo is an *intangible operating asset* representing the recognition value of the store's insignia in the minds of its customers. Additional discussion of both tangible and intangible operating assets is presented in Chapter 9.

Since property, plant, and equipment are used to produce revenues, the matching concept requires that a portion of the cost of these assets be recognized as an expense in each period in which the assets are used (except for land, which is

PROPERTY, PLANT, AND EQUIPMENT: Tangible operating assets used by a business to produce revenues.

DEPRECIATION: The portion of the cost of tangible operating assets (other than land) recognized as expense for each period.

CONTRA ASSET: A balance sheet item that is subtracted from the cost of an asset (e.g., accumulated depreciation).

OTHER ASSETS: Any assets outside the standard categories, including assets no longer used and assets not yet in operation.

DEFERRED CHARGES: Usually, prepaid expenses scheduled to expire after one year or one operating cycle, whichever is longer.

LONG-TERM LIABILITIES: The firm's obligations to outsiders that will require payment beyond the next year or next operating cycle, whichever is longer.

STOCKHOLDERS' EQUITY: A title often used to identify the equity accounts on the balance sheets of corporations.

not consumed when earning revenue). This item of expense is called **depreciation** and represents the portion of the cost of tangible operating assets (other than land) recognized as expense for each period. *Accumulated depreciation* is simply the sum of the depreciation expense amounts recognized for an operating asset in all prior periods. In McCool's balance sheet, accumulated depreciation is $300,000 for the building and $280,000 for store equipment. Notice that accumulated depreciation is subtracted from the cost of the related assets on the balance sheet. Like accumulated depreciation, any balance sheet item that is subtracted from the cost of an asset is called a **contra asset.** Some firms do not show the amount of a contra asset separately on the balance sheet; instead, the cost of the related asset is reported as a single amount, net of the contra asset.

Each firm usually has a few assets that do not fit into any of the standard categories. These are grouped together as **other assets.** This classification includes operating assets no longer in use that have been retained for sale and operating assets that have not yet been placed in service (in McCool's balance sheet, for example, the land being held for expansion).

DEFERRED CHARGES **Deferred charges** are listed last among assets. For the most part, these deferred charges can be thought of as "long-term" prepaid expenses— expenditures already made for goods and services that will not be used until *after* the next year or the next operating cycle, whichever is longer. Remember that prepaid expenses are listed under current assets if they will be used *during* the longer of the next year or the next operating cycle. Prepaid expenses arise from cash payments for assets (such as insurance coverage or rent) made in advance of using the asset.

LONG-TERM LIABILITIES AND DEBT **Long-term liabilities** are those obligations of the business that will require payment beyond the next year or next operating cycle, whichever is longer. Common examples are bonds, notes, and mortgages. A portion of deferred federal income taxes payable (to be discussed in Chapter 10) is also a long-term liability, as are warranty obligations due *after* the longer of one year or one operating cycle.

The sum of the formal borrowings in current and long-term liabilities is the portion of the firm's capital that has been raised from creditors and is called *debt.* Debt is usually less expensive for a business than equity (funds acquired from stockholders). One reason is that creditors' interest payments are made on a fixed schedule and are given priority over dividends; another is that interest on debt is deductible for income tax purposes, whereas dividends on stock are not. If a firm should be short of cash, missing a debt payment can cause the firm to be declared bankrupt. Although there are exceptions, most stock does not require dividends to be paid at fixed times or in fixed amounts; consequently, most firms consider stock to be a less risky source of financing than debt. The prudent firm will try to balance the lower cost of debt against its higher risk in order to achieve reasonable proportions of debt and equity in its capital structure. McCool's Department Store has secured $2,860,400 of its capital from creditors ($1,345,000 from current creditors and $1,515,400 from long-term creditors); both the ratio of current debt to long-term debt and the ratio of all debt to equity seem appropriate for a department store of McCool's type and size.

STOCKHOLDERS' EQUITY The final major classification on the balance sheet is equity, which consists of capital stock and retained earnings. The balance sheets of corporations usually identify equity as **stockholders' equity.** Recall from Chapter 1 that equity arises from two sources: (1) the owners' contribution of cash or other assets to the business, called *capital stock,* and (2) the accumulated profits in excess of losses and payments to owners (dividends), called *retained earnings.* If a firm's operations have been profitable for many years and if its stockholders have been willing to forgo larger dividends, the firm's retained earnings may be a large segment of equity. For example, McCool's has $1,224,600 in retained earnings, over half of the $2,224,600 of equity. Capital stock can be further subdivided into categories that we shall study in Chapter 12.

Uses of the Balance Sheet

The balance sheet conveys important information about the structure of assets, liabilities, and equity to users of financial statements. Although the balance sheet reports assets at historical cost rather than current value, the historical cost can be used as a basis for estimating current values. Moreover, some large corporations disclose current value information for certain assets to supplement the balance sheet. The balance sheet is also used by lenders to assess the creditworthiness of prospective borrowers, as the following analysis shows.

ANALYSIS
ASSESSING THE
CREDITWORTHINESS
OF A PROSPECTIVE
BORROWER

Balance sheet data can be helpful in a variety of decision settings. Assume that you are the credit manager of Pioneer Stationery, a business equipment and products company. You have a request from the sales manager to evaluate the credit of Thin, Inc., a local health spa and reducing salon. Thin wants to purchase $5,000 of office equipment, for which it promises to pay the full amount plus 18 percent interest in three months. The sales manager wants to make this sale because he has been unable to sell to Thin before.

At your request, Thin provides you with the following balance sheet data:

CURRENT ASSETS		CURRENT LIABILITIES	
Cash	$10,000	Accounts payable.	$25,000
Accounts receivable.	60,000	Notes payable	20,000
Supplies inventory	4,000	Current portion of mortgage	
Total	$74,000	payable.	18,000
		Loans payable.	10,000
		Customer deposits	7,000
		Total.	$80,000

Granting short-term credit requires weighing the debtor's ability to repay the new credit out of the current assets available less any current liabilities that will come due before the new credit. The following are some questions that Pioneer, as a potential creditor, would ask to determine Thin's ability to repay short-term debt:

1. *What is the present relationship between Thin's current assets and current liabilities?*

Thin's current liabilities exceed current assets by $6,000.

2. *Is there likely to be any change in the relationship between current assets and current liabilities during the period of the loan?*

There is no evidence that Thin's liquidity problem will improve. Actually, it appears that Thin will have difficulty in paying its current liabilities as they come due. Thus it seems unrealistic for Thin to take on additional current liabilities at this time.

3. *What should Pioneer do?*

Unless Thin can demonstrate how it will pay its current short-term obligations as well as the additional funds that would be owed Pioneer, short-term credit should not be extended.

THE STATEMENT OF CASH FLOWS

The last of the major financial statements, the statement of cash flows, describes the company's cash receipts (cash inflows) and cash payments (cash outflows) and explains the change in a company's cash balance during the year. Cash flows can be organized into three categories: cash flow from operations, cash flow from investing, and cash flow from financing. Cash flow from operations includes cash sales and collections of accounts receivable less the amount of cash paid for the purchase of goods, services, wages, salaries, and interest. Cash flow from investing includes the cash received from sales of property, plant, and equipment, investments, and other long-lived assets less the cash spent to purchase those same items. Cash flow from financing is the cash received from creditors and owners less the amounts paid owners as dividends and the amounts spent to repay liabilities.

The relationship of the statement of cash flows to the other three financial statements for McCool's Department Store is shown in Exhibit 2–7. This exhibit extends the illustration of financial statement relationships presented in Exhibit 1–7 in Chapter 1. You should note that the statement of cash flows is more inclusive than the income statement. The cash flow statement includes the cash flow effects of operating, financing, and investment activities while the income statement is restricted to a report on revenues and expenses associated with operations.

Preparation and use of a statement of cash flows requires more than basic knowledge of the income statement and balance sheet. Therefore, we will defer further discussion of this statement until Chapter 13.

ANALYSIS OF THE CONSOLIDATED FINANCIAL STATEMENTS OF WAL-MART STORES, INC. AND SUBSIDIARIES

Although much remains to be learned about the analysis and construction of financial statements, by now you have developed a sufficient foundation to begin to interpret real statements. We will demonstrate this interpretation by presenting an analysis of the financial statements for an actual business—Wal-Mart Stores, Inc. and Subsidiaries. Wal-Mart operates discount stores throughout much of the United States and is one of the largest retailers in the country. We will develop answers to the following six questions by inspecting Wal-Mart's financial statements.

1. What happened to Wal-Mart's sales and profitability between 1989 and 1990 and between 1988 and 1989?
2. How does Wal-Mart's growth compare with the 4 to 7 percent growth in the general economy during the same periods?
3. What has Wal-Mart done with its net income?
4. Did Wal-Mart's assets grow between 1989 and 1990?
5. What is Wal-Mart's working capital (current assets − current liabilities)? Did working capital change between 1989 and 1990?
6. What is the ratio of Wal-Mart's total liabilities to total assets and of total liabilities to total equity for 1989 and 1990?

EXHIBIT 2–7   FINANCIAL STATEMENT RELATIONSHIPS

BALANCE SHEET, 12/31/X5

Assets:
Cash	$ 80,000
All other assets	4,550,000
Total	$4,630,000

Liabilities and Equity:
Liabilities	$2,970,000
Capital stock	900,000
Retained earnings	760,000
Total	$4,630,000

STATEMENT OF CASH FLOWS

Net cash flow from operations	$ 973,500
Net cash flow from investing	(1,188,900)
Net cash flow from financing	245,400
Net increase (decrease) in cash	$ 30,000
Beginning cash	80,000
Ending cash	$ 110,000

INCOME STATEMENT

Revenues	$12,443,000
Expenses	(11,578,400)
Net Income	$ 864,600

STATEMENT OF CHANGES IN RETAINED EARNINGS

Retained earnings, 12/31/X5	$ 760,000
Net income	864,600
Dividends	(400,000)
Retained earnings, 12/31/X6	$1,224,600

BALANCE SHEET, 12/31/X6

Assets:
Cash	$ 110,000
All other assets	4,975,000
Total	$5,085,000

Liabilities and Equity:
Liabilities	$2,860,400
Capital stock	1,000,000
Retained earnings	1,224,600
Total	$5,085,000

NEW ELEMENTS IN WAL-MART'S STATEMENTS

The financial statements of Wal-Mart were chosen because their content and organization are very similar to those discussed in the preceding pages. Some items in Wal-Mart's statements that we have not covered ("recoverable costs from sale/leaseback," "goodwill," and "deferred income taxes," for example) can simply be disregarded at this point. "Property under capital leases" is property that has been acquired using leases rather than more familiar forms of borrowing. "Obligations under capital leases" should be considered to be like other formal borrowings: notes, mortgages, and bonds payable. Wal-Mart's statements also have several characteristics not previously discussed that deserve a word of explanation.

Like most large business enterprises, Wal-Mart is composed of several interrelated corporations. When this situation occurs, the interrelated corporations form a single accounting entity. The accounting reports must combine or consolidate information gathered for the separate corporations into a single set of consolidated financial statements. In other words, **consolidated financial statements,** like those prepared for Wal-Mart, present combined information about several interrelated corporations that form a single entity.

CONSOLIDATED FINANCIAL STATEMENTS: Accounting reports presenting combined information about several interrelated corporations that form a single accounting entity.

Wal-Mart's statements differ in other minor respects from statements illustrated earlier. For example, information about changes in retained earnings is incorporated in a comprehensive statement of shareholders' equity; the data that would appear in a statement of changes in retained earnings are presented in the fourth column of this more comprehensive statement, which also includes columns showing changes in common stock (a form of capital stock) and changes in capital in excess of par value. Capital in excess of par value is a part of capital stock and will be discussed in Chapter 12. You should also note that Wal-Mart's statements present more than one year's data and that the most recent year's data are presented on the left in both the income statement and the balance sheet. We will use the same format when we consider multiple years' data in financial statements in our exhibits in later chapters.

THE INCOME STATEMENTS

Let us use Wal-Mart's income statements (Exhibit 2–8) to find answers to the first two analysis questions we posed. Wal-Mart's 1990 sales are 25.0 percent higher than its 1989 sales [($25,810,656 − $20,649,001)/$20,649,001] and 1989 sales are 29.4 percent higher than 1988 sales [($20,649,001 − $15,959,255)/$15,959,255].

Gross margin is not presented on the income statement but it can be computed from the amounts that are presented for sales and cost of goods sold (cost of sales):

	1990	1989	1988
Net sales	$25,810,656	$20,649,001	$15,959,255
Cost of sales	20,070,034	16,056,856	12,281,744
Gross margin	$ 5,740,622	$ 4,592,145	$ 3,677,511

Note: Dollar amounts are in thousands.

Between 1989 and 1990, Wal-Mart's gross margin grew by 25.0 percent [($5,740,622 − $4,592,145)/$4,592,145]. Between 1988 and 1989 gross margin grew by 24.9 percent. Gross margin growth for 1990 was the same as sales growth

EXHIBIT 2–8   **WAL-MART'S INCOME STATEMENTS**

Consolidated Statements of Income

Wal-Mart Stores, Inc. and Subsidiaries

(Amounts in thousands, except per share data)	Fiscal year ended January 31		
	1990	1989	1988
Revenue:			
Net sales	$25,810,656	$20,649,001	$15,959,255
Rentals from licensed departments	16,685	12,961	9,215
Other income—net	157,959	123,906	95,568
	25,985,300	20,785,868	16,064,038
Costs and expenses:			
Cost of sales	20,070,034	16,056,856	12,281,744
Operating, selling and general and administrative expenses	4,069,695	3,267,864	2,599,367
Interest costs:			
Debt...	20,346	36,286	25,262
Capital leases	117,725	99,395	88,995
	24,277,800	19,460,401	14,995,368
Income before income taxes	1,707,500	1,325,467	1,068,670
Provision for federal and state income taxes			
Current	608,912	474,016	432,133
Deferred	22,688	14,230	8,894
	631,600	488,246	441,027
Net income.......................................	$ 1,075,900	$ 837,221	$ 627,643
Net income per share	$ 1.90	$ 1.48	$ 1.11

but gross margin growth for 1989 was less than the corresponding growth in sales. Net income for 1990 increased by 28.5 percent [($1,075,900 − $837,221)/ $837,221] and 1989 net income increased by 33.4 percent, both of which are more than the rate of growth in gross margin. Growth in net income is larger than growth in gross margin largely because of relatively small increases in operating, selling and general and administrative expenses and total interest costs during a period in which sales and gross margin grew substantially. Obviously, Wal-Mart's growth in operating activities was much larger than the 4 to 7 percent growth in the general economy.

THE STATEMENTS OF CHANGES IN RETAINED EARNINGS   Let us use the retained earnings column of Exhibit 2–9, which represents the statements of changes in retained earnings, to find an answer to the third analysis question. The retained earnings column indicates that Wal-Mart paid just over 10 percent of its net income in dividends in all three years. The remainder of the income was retained in the business to provide part of the capital required for expansion.

EXHIBIT 2–9   WAL-MART'S STATEMENT OF CHANGES IN RETAINED EARNINGS

Consolidated Statements of Shareholders' Equity

Wal-Mart Stores, Inc. and Subsidiaries

(Amounts in thousands)	Number of shares	Common stock	Capital in excess of par value	Retained earnings	Total
Balance—January 31, 1987......	282,182	$28,218	$191,857	$1,470,418	$1,690,493
Net income				627,643	627,643
Cash dividends: ($.12 per share)..				(67,745)	(67,745)
Exercise of stock options........	37	4	452		456
100% common stock dividend...	282,219	28,222	(28,222)		
Exercise of stock options........	821	82	1,739		1,821
Tax benefit from stock options...			9,213		9,213
Other......................	(147)	(15)	(4,599)		(4,614)
Balance—January 31, 1988......	565,112	56,511	170,440	2,030,316	2,257,267
Net income				837,221	837,221
Cash dividends: ($.16 per share)..				(90,464)	(90,464)
Exercise of stock options........	609	61	2,974		3,035
Tax benefit from stock options...			4,778		4,778
Other......................	(130)	(13)	(3,915)		(3,928)
Balance—January 31, 1989......	565,591	56,559	174,277	2,777,073	3,007,909
Net income				1,075,900	1,075,900
Cash dividends: ($.22 per share)..				(124,491)	(124,491)
Exercise of stock options........	679	68	3,876		3,944
Tax benefit from stock options...			7,000		7,000
Other......................	(135)	(13)	(4,688)		(4,701)
Balance—January 31, 1990......	566,135	$56,614	$180,465	$3,728,482	$3,965,561

THE BALANCE SHEETS   The balance sheets (Exhibit 2–10) can be used to answer the last three analysis questions. Total assets grew between 1989 and 1990 by 28.9 percent [($8,198,484 − $6,359,668)/$6,359,668]. Working capital, the excess of current assets over current liabilities, grew by $302,223 (or 19.3 percent):

	1990	1989	CHANGE
Current assets	$4,712,616	$3,630,987	$1,081,629
Current liabilities	2,845,315	2,065,909	779,406
Working capital	$1,867,301	$1,565,078	$ 302,223

This sizable increase in working capital is largely the result of increases in inventories and accounts receivable offset by increases in notes payable, accounts payable, and accrued liabilities.

EXHIBIT 2–10   **WAL-MART'S BALANCE SHEETS**

Consolidated Balance Sheets

Wal-Mart Stores, Inc. and Subsidiaries

(Amounts in thousands)	January 31	
	1990	1989
ASSETS		
Current assets:		
Cash and cash equivalents	$ 12,790	$ 12,553
Receivables.	155,811	126,638
Recoverable costs from sale/leaseback	78,727	114,653
Inventories	4,428,073	3,351,367
Prepaid expenses	37,215	25,776
Total Current Assets	4,712,616	3,630,987
Property, plant and equipment, at cost:		
Land.	463,110	278,054
Buildings and improvements.	1,227,519	830,319
Fixtures and equipment	1,441,752	1,110,193
Transportation equipment.	57,215	58,818
	3,189,596	2,277,384
Less accumulated depreciation	711,763	520,318
Net property, plant and equipment	2,477,833	1,757,066
Property under capital leases.	1,212,169	1,114,034
Less accumulated amortization.	259,943	209,146
Net property under capital leases	952,226	904,888
Goodwill	37,493	41,036
Other assets and deferred charges	18,316	25,691
Total assets.	$8,198,484	$6,359,668
LIABILITIES AND SHAREHOLDERS' EQUITY		
Current liabilities:		
Notes payable.	$ 184,774	$ 19,000
Accounts payable.	1,826,720	1,389,730
Accrued liabilities:		
Salaries.	157,216	126,661
Taxes, other than income.	133,609	106,855
Other	340,068	281,156
Accrued federal and state income taxes.	179,049	121,158
Long-term debt due within one year	1,581	1,690
Obligations under capital leases due within one year	22,298	19,659
Total Current Liabilities	2,845,315	2,065,909
Long-term debt.	185,152	184,439
Long-term obligations under capital leases	1,087,403	1,009,046
Deferred income taxes	115,053	92,365
Common shareholders' equity:		
Common stock (shares outstanding, 566,135 in 1990 and 565,591 in 1989). .	56,614	56,559
Capital in excess of par value.	180,465	174,277
Retained earnings	3,728,482	2,777,073
Total Shareholders' Equity.	3,965,561	3,007,909
Total liabilities and shareholders' equity.	$8,198,484	$6,359,668

Total liabilities can be determined indirectly by subtracting total shareholders' (stockholders') equity from total liabilities and shareholders' equity.

	1990	1989
Total liabilities and shareholders' equity	$8,198,484	$6,359,668
Less: Total stockholders' equity	3,965,561	3,007,909
Total liabilities	$4,232,923	$3,351,759

Using this information, the ratios of liabilities to assets and of liabilities to shareholders' equity for 1989 and 1988 are as follows:

	1990	1989
Liabilities/Assets	51.6%	52.7%
Liabilities/Shareholders' equity	106.7	111.4

Liabilities decreased both as a percentage of assets and as a percentage of stockholders' equity. These decreases occurred because assets and stockholders' equity grew more rapidly than did liabilities. However, both owners and creditors provided substantial amounts of additional capital to Wal-Mart in 1990.

SUMMARY

This chapter began with a discussion of the cyclical nature of business activity and the important accounting concepts that guide the preparation and issuance of financial statements. The periodicity concept, which influences the frequency of financial statement preparation, requires that financial statements be issued sufficiently often to provide timely information, but not so often that the precision of the statements is seriously impaired. The revenue recognition concept and the matching concept guide the identification of revenue and expense with accounting periods.

The concepts just described are restated in Exhibit 2–11 along with three additional concepts related to the measurement of assets. As explained in Chapter 1, the cost concept requires that cost be used as the basis for recording assets. The historical cost concept is subject to several exceptions. For example, the going concern assumption sanctions the use of current disposal values instead of costs when evidence indicates that the firm is not a going concern. (Other exceptions to the cost concept are discussed in later chapters.) The current asset and current liability concept leads to separate balance sheet classifications for assets and liabilities that will turn over within the near future.

The remainder of this chapter examined the content and organization of each of the primary financial statements: the income statement, the statement of changes in retained earnings, the balance sheet, and the statement of cash flows. The discussion of each statement described the data contained and the meaning, classification, and placement of the various items.

At the end of the chapter, a set of financial statements for Wal-Mart Stores, Inc. and Subsidiaries was presented. These statements were analayzed to illustrate how decision makers draw information from financial statement data. The chapters that follow build on both the analysis and the knowledge of financial statement organization that have been introduced here.

EXHIBIT 2–11 **SELECTED ACCOUNTING CONCEPTS**

	PAGE
PERIODICITY: The concept that financial statements should be issued sufficiently often to provide timely information, but not so often that the precision of the statements is seriously impaired.	39
REVENUE RECOGNITION: The concept that revenue should be recognized as earned when the seller has put forth substantially all the effort required to sell the related goods or services and when the selling price is known.	40
MATCHING: The concept that the expense of a given accounting period is the cost of assets given up or used to earn the revenue recognized in that period.	40
HISTORICAL COST: The cash originally expended or the original cash value of noncash assets, liabilities, or equity given in exchange for an asset.	50
GOING CONCERN: The assumption that a firm is a healthy, ongoing enterprise that will recover through normal operations the cost of assets currently held and that will replace those assets as they are used up or sold.	50
CURRENT ASSET AND CURRENT LIABILITY: The concept that assets and liabilities that are expected to turn over within the next operating cycle or next year, whichever is longer, should be identified on the balance sheet as current assets and current liabilities. (The operating cycle is the elapsed time between purchase of salable goods or materials used to produce salable goods or services, and collection of cash from customers.)	51

APPENDIX 2–1
UNUSUAL INCOME ITEMS

Income statements occasionally include items that do not fit any of the general categories we have discussed thus far. These unusual items fall into two groups —*effects of discontinued operations* and *extraordinary items.* Effects of discontinued operations include gains and losses related to the sale or other disposition of a significant segment of the business. Although very few items qualify as "extraordinary" under current accounting rules, certain error corrections, tax effects, and adjustments related to foreign investments occasionally appear as extraordinary items. Effects of discontinued operations and extraordinary items appear at the bottom of the income statement, following *income from continuing operations,* as shown in the following partial income statement:

Income from operations		$xx
Plus: Other revenues and gains	$xx	
Less: Other expenses and losses	xx	xx
Income before taxes		$xx
Less: Income taxes expense		xx
Income from continuing operations		$xx
Effect of discontinued operations (net of tax)		xx
Income before extraordinary items		$xx
Extraordinary items (net of tax)		xx
Net income		$xx

Notice that these items are deducted from, or added to, income after the deduction of income taxes expense. Accordingly, these unusual items are reported net of related income taxes, and the tax effects of these items are excluded from the income taxes expense reported above.

Separating these items from income from continuing operations serves to emphasize their unusual character and encourages readers of the income statement to accord them special treatment. At the same time, this procedure follows the *comprehensive income concept,* which encourages the inclusion in net income of all changes in equity except those resulting from investments by owners and distributions to owners. The alternative procedure, which is not allowed by generally accepted accounting principles, would exclude such changes from net income, reporting them on the statement of changes in retained earnings.

The rules governing the recognition of unusual income items allow them to be reported separately, as shown above, only if complex requirements are met. When an unusual item does not meet these requirements, a company must report it as an element of income before taxes, probably as part of other revenues and gains or other expenses and losses.

KEY TERMS

ADMINISTRATIVE EXPENSES (p. 45)

CONSOLIDATED FINANCIAL
STATEMENTS (p. 58)

CONTRA ASSET (p. 54)

COST OF GOODS SOLD (p. 44)

CURRENT ASSET AND CURRENT LIABILITY
CONCEPT (p. 51)

CURRENT ASSETS (p. 51)

CURRENT LIABILITIES (p. 51)

CURRENT MARKET VALUE (p. 50)

DEFERRED CHARGES (p. 54)

DEPRECIATION (p. 54)

EARNINGS PER SHARE (p. 46)

FINANCING CYCLE (p. 36)

GOING CONCERN ASSUMPTION (p. 50)

GROSS MARGIN (GROSS PROFIT) (p. 45)

HISTORICAL COST (p. 50)

INCOME BEFORE TAXES (p. 46)

INCOME FROM OPERATIONS (p. 45)

INCOME TAXES EXPENSE (p. 46)

INVESTMENTS (p. 52)

LONG-TERM LIABILITIES (p. 54)

MATCHING (p. 40)

MATCHING CONCEPT (p. 40)

NET INCOME (p. 46)

OPERATING CYCLE (p. 37)

OPERATING EXPENSES (p. 45)

OTHER ASSETS (p. 54)

OTHER EXPENSES AND LOSSES (p. 46)

OTHER REVENUES AND GAINS (p. 46)

PERIOD EXPENSES (p. 42)

PERIODICITY CONCEPT (p. 39)

PRODUCT EXPENSES (p. 41)

PROPERTY, PLANT, AND EQUIPMENT (p. 53)

REVENUE RECOGNITION (p. 40)

REVENUE RECOGNITION CONCEPT (p. 40)

SALES REVENUE (p. 43)

SELLING EXPENSES (p. 45)

STOCKHOLDERS' EQUITY (p. 54)

QUESTIONS

Q2-1. Describe the operating cycle. Why are the operating cycles of some businesses longer than the operating cycles of others?

Q2-2. How are the operating and financing cycles related?

Q2-3. What are the effects of a longer operating cycle on a firm?

Q2-4. Why are financial statements usually organized in essentially the same way from period to period and from firm to firm?

Q2-5. Why are the primary financial statements prepared for the period of a year? Why are some financial statements prepared for a period of less than a year?

Q2-6. Describe the periodicity concept and its influence on the measurement of net income.

Q2-7. What is revenue recognition, and what does the revenue recognition concept say about it?

Q2-8. Why is revenue usually recognized at the time goods are transferred or services are performed?

Q2-9. What is matching, and what does the matching concept say about it?

Q2-10. How does the matching of product expenses differ from the matching of period expenses?

Q2-11. Why would a financial statement user prefer that revenues be recorded in the income statement according to the revenue recognition concept rather than as cash inflows occur? Why would the user also prefer that expenses be measured according to the matching concept rather than as cash outflows occur?

Q2-12. What kinds of expenses are reported on the classified income statement?

Q2-13. Define current assets and current liabilities. Why are current assets and current liabilities separated from long-lived assets and long-term liabilities on the balance sheet?

Q2-14. What are consolidated financial statements?

APPENDIX QUESTION

Q2-15. Name and describe the two groups of unusual income items presented separately at the end of the income statement.

EXERCISES

E2-16. OPERATING CYCLE   A list of businesses is presented below:

BUSINESS	OPERATING CYCLE DESCRIPTION
1. Appliance store	**a)** Very short—customers typically pay cash, and inventory is often held less than one day.
2. Clothing store	**b)** A few months—merchandise is typically on hand for several weeks, and some customers may accept credit.
3. Electric utility	
4. Evergreen nursery	**c)** More than one year—merchandise may be in inventory for several months, and most customers will pay for purchases over one or two years.
5. Fast-food restaurant	
	d) Several years—a number of years are required to make merchandise ready to sell. Customers probably pay cash for most items.
	e) Many years—customers pay monthly. However, the assets that are used to provide customer services are very costly and last for many years.

REQUIRED:

Match each business with a description of the operating cycle for that business.

E2-17. FINANCING AND OPERATING CYCLES   Which of the following activities belong to the operating cycle, and which belong to the financing cycle?

   a) Collection of cash from customers

   b) Payment of dividends to stockholders

   c) Acquisition of goods for resale

   d) Borrowing of cash from a bank

   e) Receipt of cash from owners in exchange for capital stock

   f) Performance of services for customers

   g) Acquisition of raw materials for manufacture of salable products

   h) Repayment to a lender of an amount borrowed

   i) Delivery of goods to customers

E2-18. REVENUE AND PRODUCT EXPENSES   Houston Hardware sold merchandise costing $253,000 for $387,000, received merchandise from suppliers that cost $262,000, paid $256,000 to merchandise suppliers, and collected cash from customers in the amount of $364,000.

REQUIRED:

Determine the amount of sales revenue and product expense (cost of goods sold) for Houston's income statement.

E2-19. REVENUE RECOGNITION AND MATCHING   P-Tronics, a seller of personal computers, sold 50 computers during 19X2. P-Tronics acquired and paid for 20 of the computers in 19X1 at a total cost of $24,000. Twenty-seven of the computers were acquired and paid for in 19X2 at a total cost of $46,000. The remaining 3 computers were acquired by P-Tronics in 19X2 at a total cost of $4,100 but were not paid for until 19X3. The selling price of each computer is $2,800. Salaries earned by sales personnel during 19X2 total $20,000. Other selling and administrative expenses related to assets used or consumed during 19X2 amount to $7,200.

REQUIRED:

   1. Calculate 19X2 revenue.

   2. Calculate 19X2 product expense (cost of goods sold)

   3. Calculate 19X2 period expense.

   4. Prepare the 19X2 income statement.

E2-20. PRODUCT AND PERIOD EXPENSE   The following list describes the acquisition, use, and disposition of assets during 19X6 by Morgenstern Furniture Stores:

   a) During 19X6 Morgenstern received from suppliers furniture with a total cost of $620,000. Morgenstern paid a total of $597,000 cash to suppliers during 19X6. Furniture costing $605,000 was delivered to customers during 19X6.

   b) Morgenstern paid $29,600 to employees for salaries earned during 19X6. An additional $6,100 was owed to employees at December 31, 19X6, for salaries earned during 19X6.

   c) Morgenstern paid $3,900 to utility companies during 19X6, including $650 for utility services taken in 19X5. No amounts were owed to utility companies at December 31, 19X6.

   d) Morgenstern rented store and warehouse facilities during 19X6 for $10,000, which was paid on December 15, 19X5. Rent for 19X7 in the amount of $11,500 was paid on December 15, 19X6.

REQUIRED:

Calculate the amount of 19X6 product expense and 19X6 period expense.

E2-21. RECOGNIZING EXPENSES   Treadway Athletic Shoes puts each pair of shoes purchased by customers in a paper bag with the store name and address imprinted on the bag. Treadway purchased 15,000 bags in October 19X2 for $3,000. The bags were delivered in November and paid for in December 19X2. Treadway began to use the bags in February 19X3. By the end of 19X3, 5,000 of the bags remain in inventory.

REQUIRED:

How much expense should be recorded for the 15,000 bags in 19X2, 19X3, and 19X4 in order to properly match expenses with revenues?

E2-22. RECEIVABLES, PAYABLES, INVENTORY, MATCHING, AND REVENUE RECOGNITION   Carrico Motors sells delivery vans. The following information describes Carrico's activities during 19X5:

a) At the beginning of 19X5, Carrico had 18 vans in inventory. Each van cost $10,000. During 19X5 Carrico purchased 136 additional vans from the manufacturer at $10,000 each. Van sales during 19X5 were 127 units at $15,000 each.

b) At the beginning of 19X5, Carrico owed the manufacturer for 14 vans purchased during 19X4. Carrico paid for those 14 vans and 120 of the 136 purchased during 19X5.

c) At the beginning of 19X5, Carrico's customers owed $45,000 for 3 vans purchased in 19X4. During 19X5 Carrico collected for those 3 vans and for 120 of the vans sold in 19X5.

d) Operating expenses for Carrico during 19X5 were $438,000, and interest expense was $146,000.

REQUIRED:

1. Calculate Carrico's 19X5 income before taxes.

2. Calculate the amount of Carrico's accounts receivable, accounts payable, and inventory at December 31, 19X5.

E2-23. REVENUE RECOGNITION AND OPERATING CYCLE   Identify the point in the operating cycle at which revenue recognition should occur for each of the following businesses:

a) A household appliance retailer will sell to anyone on an installment basis, even customers with questionable credit records. As a result, the firm encounters many customers who default on their payments and incurs substantial collection costs.

b) Most sales by a clothing store are made for cash or credit card receivables that pay cash within a few days.

c) A firm sells small-business computer systems and equipment on an installment basis. The firm runs a credit check on every customer and sells on an installment basis only to customers with very high credit ratings.

d) A firm manufactures special tools under a contract with the U.S. Department of Defense. The contract requires the firm to maintain an inventory of tools and obligates the Department of Defense to buy all the tools produced under specified production quotas at specified prices.

E2-24. IDENTIFYING CURRENT ASSETS AND LIABILITIES   Dunn Sporting Goods sells athletic clothing and footwear to retail customers. Dunn's accountant indicates that the firm's operating cycle averages six months. At December 31, 19X3, Dunn has the following assets and liabilities:

a) Prepaid rent in the amount of $16,000. Dunn's rent is $500 per month.

b) A $3,100 account payable due in 45 days.

c) Inventory in the amount of $44,230. Dunn expects to sell $38,000 of the inventory within three months. The remainder will be placed in storage until September 19X4. The items placed in storage should be sold by November 19X4.

d) An investment in marketable securities in the amount of $1,900. Dunn expects to sell $700 of the marketable securities in six months. The remainder are not expected to be sold until 19X6.

e) Cash in the amount of $350.

f) An equipment loan in the amount of $6,000 of which $1,000 is due in three months. The next $1,000 payment is due in March 19X5. Interest of $600 is also due with the $1,000 payment due in three months.

g) An account receivable from a local university in the amount of $2,850. The university has promised to pay the full amount in three months.

h) Store equipment at a cost of $8,500. Accumulated depreciation has been recorded on the store equipment in the amount of $1,250.

REQUIRED:

Prepare the current asset and current liability portions of Dunn's December 31, 19X3, balance sheet.

E2-25. CURRENT ASSETS AND CURRENT LIABILITIES   Hanson Construction has an operating cycle of 9 months. On December 31, 19X6, Hanson has the following assets and liabilities:

a) A note receivable in the amount of $1,000 to be collected in 6 months.

b) Cash totaling $600.

c) Accounts payable totaling $1,800, all of which will be paid within 2 months.

d) Accounts receivable totaling $12,000, including an account for $8,000 that will be paid in 2 months and an account for $4,000 that will be paid in 18 months.

e) An inventory of construction materials costing $9,200, all of which will be used in construction within the next 12 months. The inventory includes materials costing $6,720 that will be used within the next 9 months.

f) Construction equipment costing $60,000, on which depreciation of $22,400 has accumulated.

g) A note payable to the bank in the amount of $40,000, of which $7,000 is to be paid within the next year and the remainder in subsequent years.

REQUIRED:

Calculate the amounts of current assets and current liabilities reported on Hanson's balance sheet at December 31, 19X6.

E2-26. OPERATING CYCLE AND CURRENT RECEIVABLES   For each of the businesses described below, indicate the length of the operating cycle and the duration of the longest receivable that can be classified as current on the business's balance sheet.

a) Dither and Sly are attorneys-at-law who specialize in federal income tax law. They complete their typical case in six months or less and collect from the typical client within one additional month.

b) Johnston's Market specializes in fresh meat and fish. All merchandise must be sold within one week of purchase, and all business is cash and carry.

c) Mortondo's is a women's clothing store specializing in high-style merchandise. Merchandise spends an average of seven months on the rack following purchase. Most sales are on credit, and the typical customer pays within one month of sale.

d) Trees, Inc., grows Christmas trees and sells them to various Christmas tree lots for cash on delivery. It takes six years to grow a tree.

E2-27. DEPRECIATION   Swanson Products was organized as a new business on January 1, 19X1. On that date, Swanson acquired equipment at a cost of $400,000, which is depreciated at a rate of $40,000 per year.

REQUIRED:

1. Describe how equipment and related depreciation will be reported on the balance sheet at December 31, 19X1, and on the 19X1 income statement.

2. Describe how equipment and related depreciation will be reported on the balance sheet at December 31, 19X2, and on the 19X2 income statement.

E2-28. INCOME STATEMENT STRUCTURE   Organize the following items into a properly prepared classified income statement for a firm that sells goods to retail customers. Add subtotals where necessary. The items are salaries expense, administrative; advertising expense; cost of goods sold; depreciation expense, store equipment; depreciation expense, office equipment; interest expense; income taxes expense; sales revenue; sales returns and allowances; salaries expense, sales.

E2-29. BALANCE SHEET STRUCTURE   Organize the following items into a properly prepared classified balance sheet. Add subtotals where necessary. The items are accounts payable; accounts receivable; accumulated depreciation, building; accumulated depreciation, equipment; bonds payable; building; capital stock; cash; equipment; income taxes payable; inventory; mortgage payable; prepaid insurance; retained earnings; trademarks; wages payable.

E2-30. CLASSIFIED INCOME STATEMENT   The following information is available for Bergin Pastry Shop.

Gross margin.	$30,700
Income from operations	9,200
Income taxes expense (15% of income before taxes)	?
Interest expense.	1,800
Net sales	80,300
Sales returns and allowances	3,700

REQUIRED:

Prepare a classified income statement for Bergin for 19X3.

E2-31. CLASSIFIED INCOME STATEMENT   Prepare a classified income statement for the year ended December 31, 19X9, using the following information for Wright Auto Supply:

Cost of goods sold	$277,000
Depreciation expense, building	29,000
Income taxes expense (34% of income before taxes)	?
Interest expense.	2,700
Rent expense, equipment	18,000
Salaries, administrative	32,000
Sales returns and allowances	3,100
Sales revenue.	575,000
Wages expense, store	89,000

E2-32. CLASSIFIED INCOME STATEMENT WITH EARNINGS PER SHARE   ERS, Inc., maintains and repairs office equipment. The following income statement account balances are available for ERS at the end of 19X8.

Advertising expense.	$ 24,200
Depreciation expense, service van	17,500
Income taxes expense (28% of income before taxes)	?
Interest expense.	10,900
Rent expense, building	58,400
Rent expense, office equipment.	11,900
Salaries expense, administrative.	202,100
Service revenue	928,800
Supplies expense, repair parts	66,400
Wages expense, service support staff	38,600
Wages expense, service technicians	448,300

REQUIRED:

Prepare a classified income statement including earnings per share. Assume that ERS has 12,000 shares of capital stock outstanding.

E2-33. STOCKHOLDERS' EQUITY   On January 1, 19X1, Mulcahy Manufacturing, Inc., a newly formed corporation, issued 1,000 shares of capital stock in exchange for $150,000 cash. No other shares were issued during 19X1, and no shares were repurchased by the corporation. On November 1, 19X1, the corporation's major stockholder sold 300 shares to another stockholder for $60,000. The corporation reported net income of $22,300 for 19X1.

REQUIRED:

Prepare the stockholders' equity section of the corporation's balance sheet at December 31, 19X1.

E2-34. CLASSIFIED BALANCE SHEET   College Spirit sells sportswear with logos of major universities. At the end of 19X6 the following balance sheet account balances were available.

Accounts payable	$106,300
Accounts receivable	6,700
Accumulated depreciation, furniture and fixtures	21,700
Bonds payable	180,000
Capital stock	300,000
Cash	14,200
Furniture and fixtures	88,000
Income taxes payable	11,400
Inventory, sportswear	479,400
Long-term investment in equity securities	110,000
Note payable, short-term	50,000
Prepaid rent, building (current)	54,000
Retained earnings, 12/31/X6	82,900

REQUIRED:

Prepare a classified balance sheet for College Spirit.

E2-35. CLASSIFIED BALANCE SHEET   Jerrison Company operates a wholesale hardware business. The following balance sheet accounts and balances are available for Jerrison at December 31, 19X3.

Accounts payable	$ 62,100
Accounts receivable	96,300
Accumulated depreciation, data processing equipment	172,400
Accumulated depreciation, warehouse	216,800
Accumulated depreciation, warehouse operations equipment	31,200
Bonds payable (due 19X7)	200,000
Building, warehouse	419,500
Capital stock	250,000
Cash	8,400
Equipment, data processing	309,000
Equipment, warehouse operations	106,100
Income taxes payable	21,600
Interest payable	12,200
Inventory (merchandise)	187,900
Land	41,000
Long-term investments in equity securities	31,900
Notes payable (due June 1, 19X4)	50,000
Prepaid insurance (4 months)	5,700
Retained earnings, 12/31/X3	?
Salaries payable	14,400
Short-term investments in marketable securities	21,000

REQUIRED:

Prepare a classified balance sheet for Jerrison Company.

E2-36.   STATEMENT OF CASH FLOWS   Zachary Corporation's 12/31/X4 balance sheet included the following amounts:

Cash.	$ 23,400
Retained earnings.	107,600

Zachary's accountant provided the following data for 19X5:

Revenues	$673,900
Expenses	582,100
Dividends.	34,200
Cash inflow from operations	875,300
Cash outflow for investments.	(994,500)
Cash inflow from financing	156,600

REQUIRED:

Calculate the amount of cash and retained earnings at the end of 19X5.

E2-37.   THE OPERATING CYCLE   There are two retail stores in Millersburgh. One is a full-service store that typically sells on credit to its customers; the other is a discount store that usually sells for cash. Full-service stores typically charge higher prices than do discount stores for identical items. Does the operating cycle suggest some economic reason for a portion of this price difference? Explain your answer. Can you think of other reasons why a full-service store might charge more than a discount store for the same merchandise?

PROBLEMS

P2-38.   INCOME STATEMENT AND BALANCE SHEET   The following information for Rogers Enterprises is available at December 31, 19X9, and includes all of Rogers's financial statement amounts except retained earnings:

Accounts receivable.	$ 72,000
Capital stock (10,000 shares)	70,000
Cash	15,000
Income taxes expense	6,000
Income taxes payable	4,000
Interest expense.	16,000
Notes payable (due in 10 years).	25,000
Prepaid rent, building	30,000
Rent expense.	135,000
Retained earnings	?
Salaries expense.	235,000
Salaries payable.	15,000
Service revenue.	460,000
Supplies expense	36,000
Supplies inventory.	42,000

REQUIRED:

Prepare the 19X9 income statement, including earnings per share, and the balance sheet for the year ending December 31, 19X9, for Rogers Enterprises.

P2-39. REVENUES AND PRODUCT EXPENSES   Top Tunes sells only top-40 compact disks (CDs). Top Tunes purchases all its CDs for $8 each and sells them for $12 each. At the beginning of 19X2, Top Tunes owed manufacturers for 380 CDs purchased in 19X1, and customers owed Top Tunes for 620 CDs sold in 19X1. During 19X2, Top Tunes purchased 25,900 CDs, sold 25,200 CDs, paid for 24,500 CDs, and collected from customers for 24,980 CDs.

REQUIRED:

1. Compute 19X2 sales revenue for Top Tunes.

2. Compute Top Tunes' 19X2 product expense, cost of goods sold.

3. Compute 19X2 gross margin for Top Tunes.

P2-40. FINANCIAL STATEMENT PREPARATION   Ross Airport Auto Service provides parking and minor repair service at the local airport while customers are away on business or pleasure trips. The following account balances are available for Ross Airport Auto Service at December 31, 19X2.

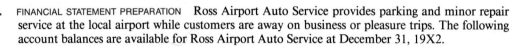

Accounts payable	$ 16,700
Accounts receivable	39,200
Accumulated depreciation, equipment	38,800
Capital stock (20,000 shares)	100,000
Cash	6,700
Depreciation expense, equipment	14,300
Dividends	6,300
Equipment	269,500
Income taxes expense	2,700
Income taxes payable	1,100
Interest expense	18,300
Interest payable	1,800
Interest revenue, long-term investments	4,100
Inventory, repair parts	4,900
Long-term investments in debt securities	35,000
Notes payable (due May 2, 19X9)	160,000
Prepaid rent (3 months)	27,300
Rent expense	103,500
Retained earnings, 12/31/X1	43,000
Service revenue, parking	224,600
Service revenue, repair	208,100
Supplies expense, repair parts	36,900
Wages expense	246,100
Wages payable	12,500

REQUIRED:

Prepare a classified income statement (including earnings per share), a statement of changes in retained earnings, and a classified balance sheet for Ross Airport Auto Service for the year ended December 31, 19X2.

P2-41. MEASURING SERVICE REVENUE   Millard Advisory Service advises individuals on how to structure transactions to minimize income taxes and assists those individuals in the preparation of their federal and state income tax returns. Millard bills its clients $120 per hour for its service. At the beginning of 19X7, customers owed Millard for 3,400 hours of tax advisory service provided during 19X6. During 19X7, Millard provided and billed clients for 29,200 hours of tax advisory service. At the end of 19X7, Millard had provided 1,600 hours of tax advisory service that would not be billed until 19X8. During 19X7, Millard collected $3,804,000 for 31,700 hours of service. The $3,804,000 included the December 31, 19X6, receivable.

REQUIRED:

Determine Millard's tax advisory service revenue for 19X7.

P2-42.   ACCOUNTING CONCEPTS   A list of accounting concepts is presented below. Match each concept with the corresponding statement or example, by pairing each of the numbers from 1 through 6 with the appropriate letter.

CONCEPT	STATEMENT
1. Matching	a) Typically, 120 days expire between the purchase of goods and the collection of cash from their sale.
2. Revenue recognition	
3. Operating cycle	b) A firm that cannot be expected to recover the cost of its assets through normal operations should report its assets at disposal values.
4. Historical cost	
5. Going concern	c) Financial statements should be issued sufficiently often to provide timely information.
6. Periodicity	
	d) The delivery of goods to customers is the usual point at which revenue is recorded.
	e) Most assets are recorded at an amount equal to the cash expended for them.
	f) The cost of assets given up or used to earn a period's revenue is called *expense.*

P2-43.   ACCOUNTING TERMINOLOGY   A list of accounting terms is presented below. Match each term with the corresponding example or statement, by pairing each of the numbers from 1 through 9 with the appropriate letter.

TERM	EXAMPLE OR STATEMENT
1. Depreciation	a) Property, plant, and equipment
2. Tangible operating assets	b) Income before income taxes and financial revenues and expenses
3. Contra asset	
4. Current assets	c) A clothing retailer's note payable due in three years
5. Current liability	
6. Period expense	d) A portion of the cost of equipment taken as expense
7. Product expense	
8. Income from operations	e) Cash, accounts receivable, and inventory
9. Long-term liability	f) A clothing retailer's obligation to pay $1,200 in two months' time
	g) Accumulated depreciation
	h) The cost of merchandise sold to customers during the accounting period
	i) Operating expenses

P2-44.   STATEMENT OF CHANGE IN RETAINED EARNINGS   Dittman Expositions has the following data available:

Dividends, 19X4	$ 8,500
Dividends, 19X5	9,900
Expenses, 19X4	386,500
Expenses, 19X5	410,600
Retained earnings, 12/31/X3	16,900
Revenues, 19X4	409,700
Revenues, 19X5	438,400

REQUIRED:

Prepare statements of changes in retained earnings for 19X4 and 19X5.

P2-45. CALCULATION OF INCOME FROM BALANCE SHEET DATA Carson Corporation reported the following amounts for assets and liabilities at the beginning and end of a recent year:

	BEGINNING OF YEAR	END OF YEAR
Assets	$390,000	$420,000
Liabilities	130,000	145,000

REQUIRED:

Calculate Carson's net income or net loss for the year in each of the following independent situations:

1. Carson declared no dividends, and its capital stock remained unchanged.
2. Carson declared no dividends and issued additional capital stock for $33,000 cash.
3. Carson declared dividends totaling $11,000, and its capital stock remained unchanged.
4. Carson declared dividends totaling $17,000 and issued additional capital stock for $29,000.

P2-46. CLASSIFIED INCOME STATEMENT, STATEMENT OF CHANGES IN RETAINED EARNINGS, AND CLASSIFIED BALANCE SHEET Using the following information for Ashton Appliances, prepare a properly classified income statement for 19X6, a statement of changes in retained earnings for 19X6, and a properly classified balance sheet as of December 31, 19X6:

Accounts payable	$ 18,000
Accounts receivable	70,000
Accumulated depreciation, building	100,000
Accumulated depreciation, fixtures	30,000
Bonds payable (due in 7 years)	192,000
Building	300,000
Capital stock	245,000
Cash	41,000
Cost of goods sold	510,000
Depreciation expense, building	10,000
Depreciation expense, fixtures	12,000
Furniture and fixtures	130,000
Interest expense	21,000
Income taxes expense	14,000
Income taxes payable	12,000
Insurance expense	36,000
Inventory	60,000
Other assets	93,000
Rent expense, store equipment	79,000
Retained earnings, 12/31/X5	54,000
Salaries expense, administrative	101,000
Salaries payable	7,000
Sales returns and allowances	19,000
Sales revenue	965,000
Wages expense, store	127,000

P2-47. INCOME STATEMENT, STATEMENT OF CHANGES IN RETAINED EARNINGS, AND BALANCE SHEET McDonald Marina provides docking and cleaning services for pleasure boats at its marina in southern Florida. The following account balances are available:

Accounts payable	$ 26,400
Accounts receivable	268,700

Accumulated depreciation, building.	64,500
Accumulated depreciation, docks.	950,400
Bonds payable (due 19X8)	2,000,000
Building	197,300
Capital stock (40,000 shares)	600,000
Cash.	22,300
Depreciation expense, building.	21,500
Depreciation expense, docks.	246,300
Dividends.	25,300
Equipment, docks.	2,490,000
Income taxes expense	21,700
Interest expense	236,000
Interest payable	18,000
Land.	875,000
Rent expense, office equipment	14,600
Rent payable, office equipment	2,400
Retained earnings, 12/31/X2	128,600
Service revenue, cleaning	472,300
Service revenue, docking	1,460,000
Supplies expense.	89,100
Supplies inventory	9,800
Utilities expense	239,400
Wages expense	987,200
Wages payable	21,600

REQUIRED:

Prepare a classified income statement (including earnings per share), a statement of changes in retained earnings, and a classified balance sheet for McDonald Marina for the year ended December 31, 19X3.

P2-48. CREDIT ANALYSIS   Saltzman Stereo Shops sells home and automobile stereo components and supplies. Sales have increased by 10 percent each year for the past four years, but net income has been declining by 5 percent per year over the same period. Total current assets and total current liabilities for Saltzman for the past four years are as follows:

	19X3	19X4	19X5	19X6
Current assets	$149,000	$168,000	$193,000	$219,000
Current liabilities	71,000	112,000	175,000	231,000

Saltzman wants to purchase 50 items of stereo equipment from your firm on credit. Saltzman says that it will pay for its purchase in 90 days. Would you sell the equipment to Saltzman on credit? Why, or why not?

P2-49. CREDIT ANALYSIS   Roberts' Rug Shop has been in business for 15 years. Sales during 5 consecutive years increased 8 to 10 percent each year, owing primarily to price increases resulting from inflation. Roberts' net income for each of the past 5 years is shown below:

	19X2	19X3	19X4	19X5	19X6
Net income	$94,000	$78,000	$83,000	$61,000	$72,000

Roberts' applies to your bank for a $250,000 loan, which it plans to use to remodel its store. Would you grant the loan? Why, or why not?

P2-50. CREDIT ANALYSIS (LONG-TERM)   Benninghove's Books sells college textbooks and supplies from a store near a major university. Benninghove's has lost its lease and is seeking financing for the purchase of a store building. You have the following financial data for Benninghove's Books for the past 3 years:

	19X4	19X5	19X6
Sales revenue	$873,000	$912,000	$1,075,000
Cost of goods sold	690,000	720,000	860,000
Gross margin	$183,000	$192,000	$ 215,000
Net income	$ 48,000	$ 53,000	$ 67,000

From other sources, you determine that the gross margin for college bookstores has averaged 15 percent of sales during the past 10 years and that the average gross margin percentage has been relatively stable during that period. Net income for bookstores has been approximately 4 percent of sales for the same period but has been below 4 percent of sales in each of the past 3 years. On the basis of this information and Benninghove's data, would you be inclined to lend Benninghove's Books the $400,000 necessary to purchase a new building? Why, or why not?

P2-51. STATEMENT OF CASH FLOWS   Henry Enterprises' accountant provided you with the following information:

Cash, 12/31/X7	$ 44,800
Cash, 12/31/X8	53,400
Retained earnings, 12/31/X7	246,300
Retained earnings, 12/31/X8	254,700
Net income, 19X8	88,100
Cash outflow for investments	(644,200)
Cash inflow from financing	240,000

REQUIRED:

Calculate 19X8 dividends and cash flow from operations for 19X8.

P2-52. FINANCIAL STATEMENTS FOR A FAILED FIRM   Berkshire Novelties sold toys to retail stores. For the past two years Berkshire has not been successful in identifying toys that would be in demand. Therefore, Berkshire has been unprofitable. The December 31, 19X4, historical cost balance sheet for Berkshire appears below.

ASSETS

Cash		$ 1,100
Accounts receivable		134,400
Inventory, toys		619,700
Prepaid rent		6,200
Total		$761,400

LIABILITIES AND EQUITY

Accounts payable		$196,400
Notes payable		150,000
Total liabilities		$346,400
Capital stock	$300,000	
Retained earnings	115,000	
Total equity		415,000
Total		$761,400

Because of its unprofitable operations, Berkshire must go out of business. Therefore, the historical cost balance sheet will have to be modified. Assume that in a "going out of business sale" accounts receivable can be sold for cash at 60 percent of historical cost and that inventory can be sold for cash at 10 percent of historical cost. None of the prepaid rent can be converted into cash.

REQUIRED:

Restate Berkshire's balance sheet to incorporate the reductions from cost to current disposal values. Where will you make changes among liabilities and equity?

P2-53. FINANCIAL ANALYSIS Reproduced below are portions of the president's letter to shareholders and selected income statement and balance sheet data for the Western Company. The Western Company provides services for existing oil wells and offshore contract oil well drilling services.

To Our Stockholders

In 1987 the worldwide oil and gas industry began to show some life. As oil prices rebounded and fluctuated between $15 and $20 per barrel following their disastrous plunge in 1986, it was generally perceived that a gradual recovery was in place. The increase in the number of drilling rigs operating domestically and improvements in worldwide utilization of offshore drilling rigs throughout the year translated into improved demand for Western's services. In fact, revenues for both our onshore and offshore segments improved in every quarter of 1987. Most importantly, the Company started generating cash from operations in the last half of the year, and the onshore segment returned to generating profits in the third quarter. . . .

With improved operating performance as the basis for negotiating a financial restructuring, the next critical step for Western is to satisfactorily restructure its obligations in order to insure that the Company can operate effectively in the future. With that in mind, a strategic decision, albeit a difficult one, was made in February 1988 — The Western Company of North America (WCNA) filed for reorganization under Chapter 11 of the U.S. Bankruptcy Code. . . .

	1987	1986	1985	1984	1983
			(in thousands)		
Revenues:					
Petroleum services. . . .	$ 141,343	$ 136,057	$354,246	$390,080	$337,871
Offshore drilling.	35,199	60,968	145,940	203,675	202,615
Total revenues	176,542	197,025	500,186	593,755	540,486
Operating income	(54,584)	(92,613)	(16,663)	52,137	39,527
Net income (loss).	$(182,647)	$(340,516)	$(67,269)	$(14,553)	$(22,461)
Current assets	$ 123,553	$ 134,009	$ 183,268	$ 193,943	$ 209,944
Total assets	542,523	678,846	1,068,509	1,180,484	1,263,922
Current liabilities.	698,583	641,645	542,640	129,369	120,960
Long-term debt	—	—	144,297	576,446	655,383
Stockholders' equity	(272,632)	(82,280)	265,686	335,088	357,155

REQUIRED:

1. What trends do you detect in revenues, operating income, and net income for the period 1983–1987?

2. What happened to the difference between current assets and current liabilities over the 1983–1987 period? To what do you attribute this result?

3. The price of Western Company stock declined steadily throughout the 1983–1987 period. Do you consider this decline to be a reasonable reaction to the financial results reported? Why, or why not?

ANALYTICAL OPPORTUNITIES

A2-54. REVENUE RECOGNITION Beth Rader purchased North Shore Health Club in June 19X3. Beth wanted to increase membership in the club by selling five-year memberships for $1,000, payable at the beginning of the membership period. The normal yearly membership fee is $300. Since few prospective members were expected to have $1,000, Beth arranged for a local finance company to provide a $1,000 installment loan to prospective members. By the end of 19X3, 250 people had purchased the five-year memberships using the loan provided by the finance company.

Beth prepared her income statement for 19X3 and included $250,000 as revenue because the Club had collected the entire amount in cash. Beth's accountant objected to including the entire $250,000. The accountant argued that the $250,000 should be recognized as revenue as the Club provides services for these members during the membership period. Beth countered with a quotation from a part of "Generally Accepted Accounting Principles," *Accounting Research Bulletin 43,* Chapter 1, section A, no. 1:

> "Profit is deemed to be realized when a sale in the ordinary course of business is effected, unless the circumstances are such that collection of the sale price is not reasonably assured."

Beth notes that the memberships have been sold and that collection of the selling price has occurred. Therefore, she argues that all $250,000 is revenue in 19X3.

REQUIRED:

Write a short statement supporting either Beth or the accountant in this dispute. (Hint: You might reread the section in this chapter titled "The Revenue Recognition Concept.")

A2-55. APPLYING THE MATCHING CONCEPT Newman Properties, Inc., completed construction of a new shopping center in July 19X9. During the first six months of 19X9, Newman Properties spent $450,000 for salaries, preparation of documents, travel, and other similar activities associated with securing tenants for the center. Newman Properties was successful, and the center will open on August 1 with all its stores rented on four-year leases. The rental revenue that Newman Properties expects to receive from the current tenants is $850,000 per year for four years. The leases will be renegotiated at the end of four years. The accountant for Newman Properties wonders whether the $450,000 should be a period expense in 19X9 or whether it should be matched against revenues over the four-year life of the leases that the tenants signed.

REQUIRED:

Write a short statement indicating why you support expensing the $450,000 in the current period or spreading the expense over the four-year life of the leases. (Hint: You might reread the section in this chapter titled "The Matching Concept.")

PART 2

THE ACCOUNTING CYCLE

Careful study of this
chapter will enable you
to:

1. Describe the char-
acteristics of trans-
actions that are
recorded in ac-
counting records.
2. Explain the three
key features of the
double-entry ac-
counting system.
3. Analyze transac-
tions and determine
their effect on the
entity.
4. Prepare journal en-
tries for transac-
tions.
5. Post journal entries
to ledger accounts.
6. Prepare trial bal-
ances and financial
statements from
ledger account bal-
ances.

ACCOUNTING CYCLE:
The procedures for pro-
cessing information about
the firm's economic activities in order to produce the
various financial state-
ments.

3 RECORDING ACCOUNTING DATA

The previous chapter provided a detailed description of the major financial statements of a business enterprise. In this chapter, we will begin our discussion of the procedures used for processing information about the firm's economic activities in order to produce the various financial statements. These procedures make up the **accounting cycle.** The discussion of this cycle will extend into the next two chapters, where adjusting entries, worksheets, and closing entries are explained. The accounting cycle is a simple and orderly process, based on a series of steps and conventions. The proper operation of the accounting cycle is essential if the financial statements are to present fairly the results of the firm's activities. Unless all the steps in the cycle are performed correctly, the financial statements can be seriously flawed.

You will find that the material here is significantly different in character from that studied in our first two chapters. Up to this point, we have been presenting *concepts* and *principles,* but we are now beginning to explain and illustrate *procedures.* Concepts can often be learned through reading and discussion, but procedures are usually best learned by doing. Your command of this chapter and the next two will be more complete if you work through the illustrations presented in the text as well as the exercises and problems assigned by your instructor.

This chapter begins with a characterization of the events recorded in an accounting system and moves on to describe the basic concepts and relationships that underlie an accounting system. We then consider an overview of the accounting cycle, to see how its steps interrelate and how the completion of each step moves the accounting system toward its end product — the financial statements. We conclude with a demonstration that illustrates the accounting cycle for a simple service business. In addition to reviewing the procedures presented in the chapter, this example is a useful reference section when solving the exercises and problems here and in subsequent chapters.

EVENTS AND TRANSACTIONS

Each day many events occur that affect the financial position and the operations of an accounting entity. Goods and services are bought and sold, employees are hired and fired, competitors introduce new products, governments act to encourage and discourage certain activities, equipment and facilities become obsolete, and so on. The objective of accounting is to measure the economic effects of these events and incorporate them into the accounting records and financial statements. Events that are recorded in the accounting records are called *transactions.* In other words, **transactions** are events or happenings of consequence to an entity that are recorded in its accounting system. Transactions include (1) exchanges with other entities and (2) certain nonexchange events that affect the entity. Transactions in the first category involve events in which entities both give and receive something of value, such as the purchase of merchandise on credit or the payment of wages in cash. Nonexchange transactions include such internal events as the use of office supplies or manufacturing equipment, as well as external events like floods, fires, and thefts.[1]

However, some events that affect the entity do not qualify as transactions and, therefore, are not recorded in the accounting system. To qualify as a transaction, the effect of the underlying events on the entity must be subject to reliable measurement. Events such as bad weather or changes in national economic policy are not recorded, because their effects on the firm cannot be measured reliably in dollars. On the other hand, the effects of events such as sales and purchases, which can be measured reliably, are recorded. A **reliable measurement** is a description in words and numbers that is reasonably free from error and bias and that is a faithful representation of what it purports to represent. Reliability is important because unreliable information can mislead decision makers who use it. Decision makers would find it extremely difficult, if not impossible, to use information that is subject to significant error or bias or information that fails to represent faithfully what it purports to represent.

TRANSACTIONS: Events or happenings of consequence to an entity that are recorded in its accounting system.

RELIABLE MEASUREMENT: A description in words and numbers that is reasonably free from error and bias and that is a faithful representation of what it purports to represent.

RECOGNITION OF EXCHANGE TRANSACTIONS

RECOGNITION: The act of recording transactions in the accounting system, which involves determinations of whether or not events qualify to be recorded and, if they do, when they should be recorded and how they should be measured.

The act of recording transactions in the accounting system is called **recognition.** Recognition involves determinations of whether or not events qualify to be recorded and, if they do, when they should be recorded and how they should be measured. Exchange transactions are usually recorded when at least one party to the transaction performs under the terms of the transaction. If at least one party has performed, the effect on the entity can usually be measured with reliability. For example, in purchases and sales of merchandise in exchange for cash, the seller performs by giving up the merchandise to the buyer, and the buyer performs by paying cash to the seller. If delivery by the seller or payment by the buyer has occurred—even if the exchange is not accompanied by a written contract—the selling price is known and accepted by both parties and the "deal" is likely to go through. Without knowledge of the selling price and reasonable assurance that the exchange will be completed, an entity could not reliably measure the effect of the exchange, as the following analysis section illustrates. The analysis section also illustrates recognition of an exchange in which performance involves activities in several accounting periods.

---

[1] In *Statement of Financial Accounting Concepts No. 6,* par. 137, the Financial Accounting Standards Board suggests that the term *transaction* be used only for exchanges of value between entities. Accounting practice, however, employs the broader definition used here.

ABC Security has a two-year contract with Bolton Airport Authority to provide security services at passenger gates. The contract was signed in April 19X4 and requires ABC to provide security services throughout 19X5 and 19X6. Under the terms of the contract, Bolton Airport Authority agrees to make 24 equal monthly payments to ABC beginning in October 19X4. ABC incurs significant training costs during the last three months of 19X4, before any security services are performed.

1. *When would ABC first record the contract in its accounting system?*

ABC would not record the contract in its accounting system in April 19X4 because neither party has performed under the terms of the contract. Bolton Airport Authority has not paid ABC, and ABC has not provided security services to Bolton. Although the price of the services is established by a written agreement, one of the parties to the contract could still act, perhaps with the assistance of a lawyer, to void the contract. Under generally accepted accounting principles, this uncertainty implies that the effects of the contract are not reasonably measurable. The contract cannot be recorded until one of the parties has performed, and then it is recorded only to the extent of that performance. Thus, ABC would not record the contract until October 19X4 when Bolton makes the first payment. At that time, ABC records an increase in cash in the amount of the payment and an equal increase in a liability to provide future services. Thus the contract is recorded in 19X4 only to the extent of the payments by Bolton.

2. *When would ABC recognize revenue related to the contract?*

ABC would not recognize any revenue related to the contract until 19X5 when services are performed. Recall that the revenue recognition concept discussed in Chapter 2 states that revenue is recognized as earned, that is, as the seller puts forth substantially all the effort required to sell the related goods or perform the related services. Since security services are not performed until 19X5, revenue related to those services should not be recognized before that time.

3. *When would ABC recognize the training expenses?*

Expenditures for training during 19X4 would be recorded as assets and would not affect expenses during 19X4. Recall that the matching concept requires expense in a year to be the cost of assets used to earn the revenue recognized in that year. Since the contract does not result in revenues in 19X4, the related expenses should not be recognized in that year. The expense arising from training cost should probably be divided equally between 19X5 and 19X6 to produce proper matching of revenues and expenses.

Thus reaching an agreement, even a written agreement, is not a sufficient reason for recognizing the agreement in the accounting records. Recognition of exchange transactions must wait until at least one party to the transaction performs. The analysis section also demonstrates that recognition of revenue is tied to performance by the seller and recognition of the related expense requires a matching of expense and revenue.

In some cases, the reliable measurement requirement delays the recording of an asset even if the asset has been delivered. Consider the following sequence of events:

1. On August 2, 19X4, a buyer agrees to pay cash to the seller of an asset within 30 days following its delivery, but the final selling price, which includes charges for custom work on the asset and for transportation costs, remains to be determined by the seller.

2. On August 20, 19X4, the buyer receives the asset but is unable to record the transaction because the seller has not communicated the final selling price to the buyer.

3. On August 22, 19X4, the buyer receives an invoice from the seller showing the final price of the asset. The buyer finds the price acceptable and records the purchase of the asset.

This sequence of events illustrates the way the reliable measurement requirement can delay the buyer's recording of an asset acquisition, even though the seller has "performed" by delivering the asset to the buyer. Such delays are rarely longer than a few days. Throughout this book, we will assume that the price is known to buyers upon delivery unless the contrary is specifically indicated.

RECOGNITION OF NONEXCHANGE TRANSACTIONS

The accounting system also records nonexchange transactions whose effects on the entity are reliably measurable. Some nonexchange transactions may involve internal use of assets, like supplies or machinery; the effects of most such transactions are reliably measurable when the use occurs. Thus office supplies are recorded as expense in the period in which they are used in the operation of the business, and a portion of the cost of manufacturing equipment is recorded as expense in each period in which the equipment is used. Other nonexchange transactions involve external events like floods, fires, thefts, and the imposition of taxes. Such nonexchange transactions are best considered on a case-by-case basis, because it is difficult to generalize about their recording. For example, losses resulting from a fire are recorded only after the fire has occurred and the amount of the loss is known. Income taxes, on the other hand, may be recorded as expense before the time at which they are assessed by the government.[2]

Accountants worldwide employ a double-entry system for recording and summarizing the effects of transactions. The concepts that underlie this system are discussed in the next section.

THE DOUBLE-ENTRY ACCOUNTING SYSTEM

The basic building blocks of the double-entry accounting system are the accounts themselves. As we have seen, financial statements contain five different categories of accounting items: Revenues and expenses appear on the income statement, and assets, liabilities, and equity appear on the balance sheet. Just as financial statements have separate lines for each kind of revenue, expense, asset, liability, and equity, there are also separate accounts for each. An **account** is a place in which all the changes in one of a firm's assets, liabilities, equity, revenues, or expenses are recorded. The amount in an account at any time is called the *balance* of the account. A transaction can either increase or decrease the balance of the account. For example, the purchase of supplies increases the balance of the

ACCOUNT: A place in which all the changes in one of the entity's assets, liabilities, equity, revenues, or expenses are recorded.

---

[2] Additional discussion of recognition criteria and their application to particular transactions is presented in Supplementary Topic E. It is best to postpone further consideration of the general recognition criteria until after you understand how to record the most common types of transactions including transactions related to inventory (Chapters 6 and 7).

supplies inventory account, whereas the use of supplies decreases its balance. Although an account can take a variety of forms, accounts are frequently shown in textbooks in the form of a T. A *T-account* is a two-column record in which increases in the account are shown under one arm of the T and decreases are shown under the other arm.

To illustrate recording increases and decreases in an account, we will use a supplies inventory account. The following transactions increase and decrease the account balance during January:

> January 5: Purchase supplies costing $350
> January 8: Use supplies costing $100
> January 20: Use supplies costing $160

These transactions would be recorded in the supplies inventory T-account as follows:

SUPPLIES INVENTORY

Increases		*Decreases*	
Supplies purchased, 1/5	350		
Balance, 1/5	350		
		Supplies used, 1/8	100
Balance, 1/8	250		
		Supplies used, 1/20	160
Balance, 1/20	90		

Observe that a new account balance can be computed after each transaction is recorded.

As explained in Chapter 1, the relationship among assets, liabilities, and equity on any balance sheet is given by the *fundamental accounting model* (or balance sheet equation):

ASSETS = LIABILITIES + EQUITY

Although transactions change the amounts of assets, liabilities, and equity over time, the two sides of the equation must remain equal. As a consequence, every transaction has a two-part, or double-entry, effect on the equation. One element of the equation cannot be altered without simultaneously altering another element. Let us consider the effect of several transactions on the equation. Assume, for example, that a firm purchases $1,000 of supplies on credit. (Supplies are received in exchange for a promise to pay cash later.) An asset, supplies inventory, is increased by $1,000, and accounts payable, a liability, is increased by the same amount.

ASSETS	=	LIABILITIES	+	EQUITY
Supplies inventory +$1,000		Accounts payable +$1,000		

The firm then borrows $3,000 cash from a bank. (A promise to pay the principal and interest at some later date is exchanged for cash.) In this case, an asset, cash, is increased by $3,000 and a liability, notes payable, is also increased by $3,000.

ASSETS	=	LIABILITIES	+	EQUITY
Cash +$3,000		Notes payable +$3,000		

Let's assume that our firm rents office space for six months, paying $2,400 in advance. (Cash is exchanged for the use of office space.) At the time of the transaction, prepaid rent, an asset, is increased and cash, also an asset, is decreased by $2,400.

ASSETS	=	LIABILITIES	+	EQUITY
Prepaid rent +$2,400				
Cash −$2,400				

DOUBLE-ENTRY SYSTEM: The system based on the fundamental accounting model that records a two-part effect for every transaction.

Within the fundamental accounting model, all transactions have this two-part effect. The system for recording such effects is called the **double-entry system.**

The fundamental accounting model ensures that the sum of all asset account balances will always equal the sum of all liability and equity account balances. Revenue and expense accounts are treated as special types of equity accounts. As you will recall from Chapter 1, revenues and expenses are the components of net income; net income is a part of retained earnings; and retained earnings, in turn, is an element of equity. Revenues represent transactions that increase retained earnings and, therefore, increase equity. Expenses represent transactions that decrease retained earnings and, therefore, decrease equity. In other words, revenues and expenses represent changes in equity that are singled out for special attention. Rather than being recorded directly in the appropriate equity account (retained earnings), revenues and expenses are recorded in separate accounts and transferred to the retained earnings account at the end of the accounting period.

In summary, then, the double-entry accounting system is based on three key features:

1. Every recorded transaction has a two-part, or double-entry, effect on the entity.
2. The effects of transactions are recorded in accounts.
3. Accounts are organized so that:
   a) Assets = Liabilities + Equity
   b) Equity is increased by revenues and decreased by expenses.

Now that the elements of the double-entry accounting system have been explained, we will examine the accounting cycle, the sequence of procedures that moves the system toward its end product—the financial statements.

STARTING THE ACCOUNTING CYCLE

The accounting cycle is a 10-step process. In this chapter, we discuss the first four steps in the accounting cycle: the procedures for collecting, analyzing, and entering the transactions into the accounting records (journalizing and posting). We will also discuss the preparation of the trial balance and the financial statements.

Once the accountant has identified the transactions to be recognized, the introductory portion of the accounting cycle begins. To complete the first two steps of the cycle, the accountant must secure documentation describing the transactions (data collection) and determine for each transaction the accounts and the amounts of the effects (transaction analysis). In the third and fourth steps (journalizing and posting), data on the accounts affected and the amounts of the effects are entered into the accounting system. These four steps in the accounting cycle are repeated regularly from the beginning to the end of any accounting period; only at the end of that period are the financial statements drawn up from the data in the accounting system. Other operations in the accounting cycle are performed at the end of an accounting period and will be discussed in Chapters 4 and 5.

DATA COLLECTION (STEP 1)

DATA COLLECTION: The identification of transactions affecting the firm and the gathering of all related documents in preparation for transaction analysis.

SOURCE DOCUMENTS: Those internally or externally prepared documents that describe a transaction and the monetary amount it involves.

Data collection is the identification of transactions affecting the firm and the gathering of all related documents in preparation for transaction analysis. For the majority of transactions recorded in the accounting system, there exist one or more internally or externally prepared **source documents** describing the transaction and the monetary amount involved. Common examples of source documents include purchase orders, cash register tapes, and invoices; in computerized accounting systems, source documents may take the form of electronic data-storage media (such as reels of magnetic computer tape) rather than paper. Source documents are the beginning of a "trail" of visible evidence that a transaction was processed by the accounting system. Most of the daily transactions that affect a business entity produce source documents that give clear indications of the accounts affected and the dollar amounts of those effects. Some transactions, however, have effects that are not so easily determined. If a transaction does not produce its own documentation, then some procedure must be developed that will measure the economic effect of the transaction so that it can be entered into the accounting system. For transactions of this type, the analysis step in the accounting cycle is particularly crucial.

TRANSACTION ANALYSIS (STEP 2)

TRANSACTION ANALYSIS: Examination of the source documents or other data for a transaction to determine the accounts affected, the monetary amount of each effect, and the resulting increases or decreases in the account balances.

Transaction analysis uses the source documents or other information secured in the data collection step to answer the following questions:

1. What accounts are affected?
2. What is the amount of the effect on each account?
3. Are the account balances increased or decreased?

Let us illustrate transaction analysis. Because an accounting entity ordinarily has no assets, liabilities, or equity at its inception, our illustration will begin at the time our example firm, Standard Printing Company, is formed. Let's assume that Standard engages in the following transactions:

1. Sells 10,000 shares of stock for $15 cash per share.
2. Borrows $15,000 from the Commercial National Bank on a one-year note payable.
3. Purchases printing supplies for $8,000 cash.

4. Purchases printing paper on credit for $13,000.

5. Sells printing services for $16,000 cash.

6. Sells printing services on credit in the amount of $17,000.

7. Pays in full the credit purchase of $13,000 in transaction 4.

8. Pays cash for wages in the amount of $18,000.

9. Collects $7,000 cash as partial payment of the credit sale in transaction 6.

10. Pays dividends in the amount of $10,000 in cash.

These ten transactions are analyzed in Exhibit 3–1. For each transaction, the exhibit identifies the accounts affected, the amount of each effect, and the direction of the effect (+ for increase or − for decrease). For example, the first transaction, sale of stock, causes both cash (an asset account) and capital stock (an equity account) to be increased by $150,000. Note that this transaction has increased both sides of the balance sheet equation by the same amount—$150,000—so the equation is still in balance. The second transaction, borrowing money from a bank, increases cash (an asset account) by $15,000 and increases notes payable (a liability account) by the same amount. Both sides of the balance sheet equation are increased by $15,000. The third transaction, purchase of supplies, increases one asset, supplies inventory, and decreases another asset, cash, both by $8,000. The net effect of purchasing the supplies is to change the balance in two asset accounts, which leaves total assets unchanged and produces no changes on the liability and equity side of the balance sheet equation. As you examine the remaining transactions in Exhibit 3–1, note that some transactions affect both sides of the balance sheet equation, while others affect only one side.

EXHIBIT 3–1   **TRANSACTION ANALYSIS**

STANDARD PRINTING COMPANY
Analysis of Transactions

TRANSACTION	ASSETS		=	LIABILITIES		+	EQUITY	
1. Sells stock	Cash	+ 150,000					Capital stock	+ 150,000
2. Borrows cash	Cash	+ 15,000		Notes payable	+ 15,000			
3. Purchases supplies for cash	Supplies inventory	+ 8,000						
	Cash	− 8,000						
4. Purchases supplies on credit	Supplies inventory	+ 13,000		Accounts payable	+ 13,000			
5. Sells services for cash	Cash	+ 16,000					Revenue	+ 16,000
6. Sells services on credit	Accounts receivable	+ 17,000					Revenue	+ 17,000
7. Pays a liability	Cash	− 13,000		Accounts payable	− 13,000			
8. Pays an expense	Cash	− 18,000					Wages expense	− 18,000
9. Collects a receivable	Cash	+ 7,000						
	Accounts receivable	− 7,000						
10. Pays dividends	Cash	− 10,000					Retained earnings	− 10,000
Totals		170,000 =			15,000 +			155,000

JOURNALIZING (STEP 3)

JOURNAL: A chronological record of the double-entry effects of transactions on an entity over a specific period of time.

JOURNALIZING: The process of entering the effects of transactions into a journal.

JOURNAL ENTRY: A double-entry change in accounts entered in a journal to record the effects of a transaction.

DEBIT: A change in an account representing an increase in an asset or a decrease in a liability or equity; debits are recorded on the left side of a T-account.

CREDIT: A change in an account representing a decrease in an asset or an increase in a liability or equity; credits are recorded on the right side of a T-account.

Once data from transactions have been collected and analyzed, the data can be entered in the journal. The journal is the first component of the formal accounting system to be altered by each transaction and, as such, is often called the *book of original entry.* A **journal** is a chronological record of the double-entry effects of transactions on an entity.[3] Data are recorded in the journal transaction by transaction, thereby establishing a complete, self-contained chronological record. The process of entering transactions into the journal is called **journalizing.** The effects of each transaction are recorded by a double-entry change in the accounts called a **journal entry.**

Exhibit 3–2 shows the journal entries for the first four transactions analyzed in Exhibit 3–1. Note that no plus or minus signs are used in Exhibit 3–2 to indicate which amounts are increases and which are decreases. Instead, the amounts are listed either in the column headed "debit" or in the column headed "credit." How do you know which are increases and which are decreases? Increases in assets and decreases in liabilities and equity are always listed as debits. Decreases in assets and increases in liabilities and equity are always listed as credits. The meaning of the terms **debit** and **credit** can be summarized as follows:

DEBITS	CREDITS
Increases in assets	Decreases in assets
Decreases in liabilities	Increases in liabilities
Decreases in equity	Increases in equity

Let us illustrate the use of debits and credits by examining the transactions presented in Exhibits 3–1 and 3–2. The first transaction involves a $150,000 increase in the asset account cash (which is a debit) and a $150,000 increase in the equity account capital stock (which is a credit). Notice that the debit equals the credit. The second transaction increases the asset account cash by $15,000 (a debit) and increases the liability account notes payable by $15,000 (a credit). Here too, the debit equals the credit. Consider the third transaction, which increases the asset account supplies inventory by $8,000 (a debit) and decreases the asset account cash by the same amount (a credit). Again, debit equals credit.

[3] William Paton and Robert Dixon in their text *Essentials of Accounting* describe the journal as a "diary." The journal is a systematic and selective diary in which only transactions are recorded.

EXHIBIT 3–2   JOURNAL ENTRIES

DATE	TRANSACTION	ACCOUNTS	DEBIT	CREDIT
6/1	1	Cash	150,000	
		Capital stock		150,000
6/5	2	Cash	15,000	
		Notes payable		15,000
6/11	3	Supplies inventory	8,000	
		Cash		8,000
6/18	4	Supplies inventory	13,000	
		Accounts payable		13,000

A similar analysis for each transaction would show that each journal entry has equal debits and credits. Remember that every transaction has a double-entry effect and that the two sides of the balance sheet equation must remain equal. Using the language of debits and credits, the requirements of the balance sheet equation can be reduced to this simple proposition: *The debits associated with each journal entry must equal the credits associated with that entry.*

If debits equal credits for *each* journal entry, then debits equal credits for *all* journal entries. This fact leads to a useful check on the journal entries. At the end of a period, the accuracy of entries in the accounts is checked simply by calculating the sum of all debits and the sum of all credits made during the period and determining if the two sums are the same. If total debits does not equal total credits for the period, then there must be one or more errors in the journal entries. For example, a debit may have been entered as a credit, or an incorrect amount may have been used for part of one or more entries. However, if the wrong amounts or the wrong accounts are used, debits can still equal credits yet the journal entries will be incorrect. A test for equal debits and credits will not detect errors of incorrect amounts or accounts.

Determining the sum of debits and the sum of credits is made easier by the convention of placing all debits on the left side of T-accounts and all credits on the right side of T-accounts:

Account	
Debits	Credits

Indeed, the word *debit* can also be defined as the left side of a T-account, and *credit* can be defined as the right side of a T-account. Total debits for a period, then, is simply the sum of all entries on the left side of T-accounts and total credits is simply the sum of all entries on the right side of T-accounts.

Recall that debits represent increases in asset accounts but decreases in liability and equity accounts. Similarly, credits represent decreases in asset accounts and increases in liability or equity accounts. As illustrated below, this convention means that increases in assets (debits) are recorded on the left (debit) side of asset accounts, whereas increases in liabilities and equity (credits) are recorded on the right (credit) side of liability and equity T-accounts. Similarly, decreases in assets (credits) are recorded on the right (credit) side of asset T-accounts, whereas decreases in liabilities and equity (debits) are recorded on the left (debit) side of liability and equity T-accounts.

ASSETS		=	LIABILITIES		+	EQUITY	
Debits	Credits		Debits	Credits		Debits	Credits
Increases	Decreases		Decreases	Increases		Decreases	Increases

The important point is that while debits are always on the left and credits on the right, the location of increases and decreases in an account depends on whether the account is an asset, a liability, or an equity.

A *normal balance* for any account is a positive balance. Thus a normal balance (positive balance) for an asset account is a debit balance, and a normal balance (positive balance) for a liability or equity account is a credit balance.

Recall that revenues and expenses are changes in the equity account retained earnings that are initially recorded in separate accounts. Revenues represent increases in retained earnings and expenses represent decreases in retained earnings, as the following T-accounts show:

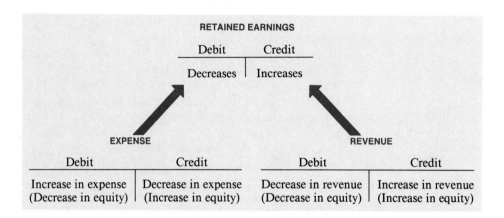

Since retained earnings is an equity account, it is increased by credits and decreased by debits. Because revenues increase net income, which then increases retained earnings, revenue increases are credits and revenue decreases are debits. To illustrate, consider the fifth transaction in Exhibit 3–1: Standard Printing Company sells printing services for $16,000. The transaction increases equity by increasing revenue in the amount of $16,000; the journal entry would include a credit of $16,000 to the revenue account. Since expenses decrease net income, which then decreases retained earnings, expense increases are debits and expense decreases are credits. In the eighth transaction in Exhibit 3–1, the company pays $18,000 in wages. This transaction decreases equity by increasing expense in the amount of $18,000; the journal entry would include an $18,000 debit to the expense account called "wages expense." A normal balance for a revenue account is a credit, and a normal balance for an expense account is a debit.

The following table summarizes the location of increases and decreases in each of the five major types of T-accounts:

ACCOUNT	INCREASE AND NORMAL BALANCE	DECREASE
Asset	Debit (left)	Credit (right)
Liability	Credit (right)	Debit (left)
Equity	Credit (right)	Debit (left)
Revenue	Credit (right)	Debit (left)
Expense	Debit (left)	Credit (right)

Journal entries recording debits and credits are usually made according to a specific format. The standard procedure for journalizing each transaction is to list the debit first. The credit follows and is indented to the right. The purpose of this standard format is to make it possible for anyone using the journal to identify debits and credits quickly and correctly. An explanation of an entry may appear beneath the credit.

DATE		DEBIT	CREDIT
6/5	Cash..	15,000	
	Notes payable.............................		15,000

Received $15,000 from the issuance of a one-year note.

The journal entry above indicates that the cash account is to be debited for $15,000 (add $15,000 to the left side of the cash T-account) and the notes payable account is to be credited for $15,000 (add $15,000 to the right side of the notes payable T-account). Since cash is an asset, the $15,000 debit is an increase. Since notes payable is a liability, the $15,000 credit is an increase. A single journal entry may require more than one debit or credit to completely capture the effects of the transaction, as illustrated below:

DATE		DEBIT	CREDIT
6/28	Machine	10,000	
	Supplies inventory	1,000	
	Cash.......................................		11,000

Machine and spare parts acquired for $11,000 cash.

We can now see why the use of a journal helps prevent the introduction of errors into the accounting system. Because all the parts of a transaction appear together, it is easy to see whether equal debits and credits have been entered. Each entry can also be examined to see if the accounts that appear together are logically appropriate. The following brief analysis shows how these checks for proper journalizing can work.

ANALYSIS
DETECTING JOURNAL
ENTRY ERRORS

You have been asked to inspect a delivery company's journal. Upon doing so, you find the following entry:

Equipment delivery truck............................		11,000	
Prepaid rent			11,000

You know that delivery trucks are not normally exchanged for prepaid rent, so you conclude that an error was made in preparing this journal entry. Had the same data been entered directly into the accounts, the error would have been much more difficult to detect and then correct.

DEMONSTRATION OF TRANSACTION ANALYSIS AND JOURNALIZING

Accurate analysis and the correct application of the debit and credit rules to the analyzed transactions are essential to the preparation of useful financial statements. Because you cannot meaningfully continue your study of the accounting cycle until you have thoroughly mastered these two steps, we examine here an illustration of analysis and journalizing for a series of typical transactions. Our hypothetical enterprise is Boonville Delivery Service, a firm that delivers small packages. Examine each transaction affecting Boonville and its representation in the journal. Then you should be able to perform your own analysis and prepare your own journal entries for the exercises and problems assigned by your instructor.

a) Sell Common Stock

TRANSACTION

Sold 1,000 shares of capital stock for $25 per share.

ANALYSIS

Cash, an asset, is increased by $25,000 [($25)(1,000 shares)]. Capital stock, an equity, is increased by $25,000.

ACCOUNT	TYPE	INCREASE OR DECREASE	DEBIT OR CREDIT	AMOUNT
Cash	Asset	Increase	Debit	$25,000
Capital stock	Equity	Increase	Credit	25,000

JOURNAL ENTRY

Cash 25,000
    Capital stock   25,000

EFFECT ON THE BALANCE SHEET EQUATION

$$\text{Assets} = \text{Liabilities} + \text{Equity}$$
$$+25,000 \qquad\qquad +25,000$$

b) Borrow Cash

TRANSACTION

Borrowed $40,000 by issuing a five-year note payable.

ANALYSIS

Cash, an asset, is increased by $40,000. Notes payable, a liability, is also increased by $40,000.

ACCOUNT	TYPE	INCREASE OR DECREASE	DEBIT OR CREDIT	AMOUNT
Cash	Asset	Increase	Debit	$40,000
Notes payable	Liability	Increase	Credit	40,000

JOURNAL ENTRY

Cash 40,000
    Notes payable   40,000

EFFECT ON THE BALANCE SHEET EQUATION

$$\text{Assets} = \text{Liabilities} + \text{Equity}$$
$$+40,000 \qquad +40,000$$

c) Purchase Assets for Cash

TRANSACTION

Purchased land and a building for $26,000 cash. The land was valued at $7,000 and the building at $19,000.

ANALYSIS

Land, an asset, is increased by $7,000. Buildings, an asset, is increased by $19,000. Cash, also an asset, is decreased by $26,000. (Note that a separate account is required for each asset acquired.)

ACCOUNT	TYPE	INCREASE OR DECREASE	DEBIT OR CREDIT	AMOUNT
Land	Asset	Increase	Debit	$ 7,000
Buildings	Asset	Increase	Debit	19,000
Cash	Asset	Decrease	Credit	26,000

JOURNAL ENTRY

```
Land.........................................    7,000
Buildings....................................   19,000
    Cash.....................................             26,000
```

EFFECT ON THE BALANCE SHEET EQUATION

Assets = Liabilities + Equity
+ 7,000
+19,000
−26,000

d) Purchase Assets on Credit

TRANSACTION

Purchased office furniture costing $12,000 by issuing a two-year note payable.

ANALYSIS

Furniture and fixtures, an asset, is increased by $12,000. Notes payable, a liability, is increased by $12,000. (In this chapter, we will ignore interest on liabilities.)

ACCOUNT	TYPE	INCREASE OR DECREASE	DEBIT OR CREDIT	AMOUNT
Furniture and fixtures	Asset	Increase	Debit	$12,000
Notes payable	Liability	Increase	Credit	12,000

JOURNAL ENTRY

```
Furniture and fixtures.......................   12,000
    Notes payable............................             12,000
```

EFFECT ON THE BALANCE SHEET EQUATION

Assets = Liabilities + Equity
+12,000   +12,000

e) Purchase Assets Using Cash and Credit

TRANSACTION

Purchased two delivery trucks for $9,300 each by paying $6,000 in cash and incurring a four-year installment loan of $12,600.

ANALYSIS

Equipment, an asset, is increased by $18,600 [($9,300)(2)]. Cash, also an asset, is decreased by $6,000. Installment notes payable, which is a liability, is increased by $12,600.

ACCOUNT	TYPE	INCREASE OR DECREASE	DEBIT OR CREDIT	AMOUNT
Equipment	Asset	Increase	Debit	$18,600
Cash	Asset	Decrease	Credit	6,000
Installment notes payable	Liability	Increase	Credit	12,600

JOURNAL ENTRY

```
Equipment ........................................  18,600
    Cash.........................................              6,000
    Installment notes payable...........................      12,600
```

EFFECT ON THE BALANCE SHEET EQUATION

```
    Assets = Liabilities + Equity
+ 18,600      + 12,600
−  6,000
```

f) Purchase Supplies on Credit

TRANSACTION

Purchased office supplies on credit for $1,180.

ANALYSIS

Office supplies inventory, an asset, is increased by $1,180. Accounts payable, a liability, is also increased by $1,180.

ACCOUNT	TYPE	INCREASE OR DECREASE	DEBIT OR CREDIT	AMOUNT
Office supplies inventory	Asset	Increase	Debit	$1,180
Accounts payable	Liability	Increase	Credit	1,180

JOURNAL ENTRY

```
Office supplies inventory ...........................  1,180
    Accounts payable..................................            1,180
```

EFFECT ON THE BALANCE SHEET EQUATION

```
    Assets = Liabilities + Equity
+ 1,180       + 1,180
```

g) Pay Account Payable

TRANSACTION

Paid $580 of the account payable arising from the purchase of office supplies in transaction **f**.

ANALYSIS

Accounts payable, a liability, is decreased by $580. Cash, an asset, is also decreased by $580.

ACCOUNT	TYPE	INCREASE OR DECREASE	DEBIT OR CREDIT	AMOUNT
Accounts payable	Liability	Decrease	Debit	$580
Cash	Asset	Decrease	Credit	580

JOURNAL ENTRY

```
Accounts payable....................................    580
    Cash............................................              580
```

EFFECT ON THE BALANCE SHEET EQUATION

$$\text{Assets} = \text{Liabilities} + \text{Equity}$$
$$-580 \qquad\quad -580$$

h) Perform Services for Cash

TRANSACTION

Performed delivery services for a customer who paid $3,400 cash.

ANALYSIS

Cash, an asset, is increased by $3,400. Service revenue is also increased by $3,400.

ACCOUNT	TYPE	INCREASE OR DECREASE	DEBIT OR CREDIT	AMOUNT
Cash	Asset	Increase	Debit	$3,400
Service revneue	Revenue	Increase	Credit	3,400

JOURNAL ENTRY

```
Cash............................................    3,400
    Service revenue................................              3,400
```

EFFECT ON THE BALANCE SHEET EQUATION

$$\text{Assets} = \text{Liabilities} + \text{Equity}$$
$$+3,400 \qquad\quad +3,400$$

(Remember that revenues become a part of equity through retained earnings.)

i) Perform Services on Credit

TRANSACTION

Performed $15,800 of delivery services on credit for a customer.

ANALYSIS

Accounts receivable, an asset, is increased by $15,800. Service revenue is also increased by $15,800. (Remember that revenues are recorded when sales are made or when services are performed, not when cash is collected.)

ACCOUNT	TYPE	INCREASE OR DECREASE	DEBIT OR CREDIT	AMOUNT
Accounts receivable	Asset	Increase	Debit	$15,800
Service revenue	Revenue	Increase	Credit	15,800

JOURNAL ENTRY

Accounts receivable................................. 15,800
    Service revenue....................................   15,800

EFFECT ON THE BALANCE SHEET EQUATION

Assets = Liabilities + Equity
+15,800   + 15,800

j) Collect Accounts Receivable

TRANSACTION

Collected $10,000 of the accounts receivable arising from the performance of the delivery services in transaction **i**.

ANALYSIS

Cash, an asset, is increased by $10,000. Accounts receivable, another asset, is decreased by $10,000. (Note that revenue is not recorded when the receivable is collected because revenue was recorded when the service was performed.)

ACCOUNT	TYPE	INCREASE OR DECREASE	DEBIT OR CREDIT	AMOUNT
Cash	Asset	Increase	Debit	$10,000
Accounts receivable	Asset	Decrease	Credit	10,000

JOURNAL ENTRY

Cash 10,000
    Accounts receivable...............................   10,000

EFFECT ON THE BALANCE SHEET EQUATION

Assets = Liabilities + Equity
+10,000
−10,000

k) Pay and Record an Expense

TRANSACTION

Paid $4,700 for local television advertising.

ANALYSIS

Advertising expense is increased by $4,700. Cash, an asset, is decreased by $4,700.

ACCOUNT	TYPE	INCREASE OR DECREASE	DEBIT OR CREDIT	AMOUNT
Advertising expense	Expense	Increase	Debit	$4,700
Cash	Asset	Decrease	Credit	4,700

JOURNAL ENTRY

Advertising expense.................................. 4,700
    Cash 4,700

EFFECT ON THE BALANCE SHEET EQUATION

$$\text{Assets} = \text{Liabilities} + \text{Equity}$$
$$-4,700 \qquad\qquad -4,700$$

(Expenses reduce net income, which in turn reduces retained earnings, an equity.)

l) Record an Expense Before Payment

TRANSACTION

Received a $790 bill from the firm's fuel supplier.

ANALYSIS

Fuel expense is increased by $790. Accounts payable, a liability, is also increased by $790. (Notice that the expense is recorded when the bill is received, which precedes payment for the expense.)

ACCOUNT	TYPE	INCREASE OR DECREASE	DEBIT OR CREDIT	AMOUNT
Fuel expense	Expense	Increase	Debit	$790
Accounts payable	Liability	Increase	Credit	790

JOURNAL ENTRY

Fuel expense 790
    Accounts payable................................. 790

EFFECT ON THE BALANCE SHEET EQUATION

$$\text{Assets} = \text{Liabilities} + \text{Equity}$$
$$+790 \qquad -790$$

m) Pay an Account Payable

TRANSACTION

Paid the $790 fuel bill received in transaction l.

ANALYSIS

Accounts payable, a liability, is decreased by $790. Cash, an asset, is also decreased by $790. (No expense is recorded when the bill is paid because the expense was recorded when the fuel bill was received.)

ACCOUNT	TYPE	INCREASE OR DECREASE	DEBIT OR CREDIT	AMOUNT
Accounts payable	Liability	Decrease	Debit	$790
Cash	Asset	Decrease	Credit	790

JOURNAL ENTRY

```
Accounts payable...................................     790
    Cash ..........................................              790
```

EFFECT ON THE BALANCE SHEET EQUATION

Assets = Liabilities + Equity
−790   −790

n) Declare a Dividend

TRANSACTION

Declared a dividend on the firm's capital stock in the amount of $1,800.

ANALYSIS

Dividends is a contra, or negative, equity account (like expenses, dividends decrease equity, but unlike expenses, they are not included in the calculation of net income). Dividends is increased by $1,800. Dividends payable, a liability, is also increased by $1,800. The equity reduction is recorded when the dividend is declared, even if the dividend is not paid until a later date.

ACCOUNT	TYPE	INCREASE OR DECREASE	DEBIT OR CREDIT	AMOUNT
Dividends	Equity	Decrease	Debit	$1,800
Dividends payable	Liability	Increase	Credit	1,800

JOURNAL ENTRY

```
Dividends .........................................   1,800
    Dividends payable ...............................            1,800
```

EFFECT ON THE BALANCE SHEET EQUATION

Assets = Liabilities + Equity
             +1,800   −1,800

o) **Pay a Declared Dividend**

TRANSACTION

Paid the $1,800 dividend declared in transaction **n**.

ANALYSIS

Dividends payable, a liability, is reduced by $1,800. Cash, an asset, is also reduced by $1,800. (When a dividend is declared, equity is reduced. At the time of payment, dividends payable is treated in the same way as any other liability.)

ACCOUNT	TYPE	INCREASE OR DECREASE	DEBIT OR CREDIT	AMOUNT
Dividends payable	Liability	Decrease	Debit	$1,800
Cash	Asset	Decrease	Credit	1,800

JOURNAL ENTRY

Dividends payable   1,800
    Cash   1,800

EFFECT ON THE BALANCE SHEET EQUATION

$$\text{Assets} = \text{Liabilities} + \text{Equity}$$
$$-1,800 \qquad -1,800$$

p) **Pay and Record an Expense**

TRANSACTION

Paid wages in the amount of $10,500 in cash.

ANALYSIS

Wages expense is increased by $10,500, and cash, an asset, is decreased by the same amount.

ACCOUNT	TYPE	INCREASE OR DECREASE	DEBIT OR CREDIT	AMOUNT
Wages expense	Expense	Increase	Debit	$10,500
Cash	Asset	Decrease	Credit	10,500

JOURNAL ENTRY

Wages expense   10,500
    Cash   10,500

EFFECT ON THE BALANCE SHEET EQUATION

$$\text{Assets} = \text{Liabilities} + \text{Equity}$$
$$-10,500 \qquad\qquad -10,500$$

(Again, remember that increases in expenses reduce net income, which in turn reduces retained earnings, an equity account.)

Sometimes transactions are analyzed and recorded in summary form. When similar transactions would cause the same entry to be made for each transaction, they may be recorded in a single summary entry to make the accounting system more efficient. For example, businesses rarely record each sale individually. Rather, all the sales that occur during a period of time—a week, a month, or even an entire year—are grouped together by underlying source documents and recorded in the accounts by a single summary entry. In keeping with our emphasis on the annual accounting period, many exercises and problems ask you to prepare journal entries to record revenue or expense transactions summarized for an entire year.

Now that we have thoroughly reviewed analysis and journalizing, we will turn to the next step in the accounting cycle: transferring of the data that have been collected, analyzed, and journalized from the journal into the accounts.

POSTING TO THE LEDGER (STEP 4)

LEDGER: The record containing the accounts of an entity.

The accounting record in which all the accounts of an entity are kept is called the **ledger.** When an entity is small and all accounting is performed by hand, the ledger is a book. Each page contains a separate account. As the entity grows, the ledger can be expanded to accommodate more accounts. Of course, ledgers can also be maintained using computers, which do away with the need for many paper records and documents. When computers are employed, the ledger is a reel of magnetic computer tape or some other high-density electronic storage medium.

During the discussion of financial statements in Chapters 1 and 2, you probably noticed that some businesses have a very large number of accounts, one for each type of asset, liability, equity, revenue, and expense. The accounting record that contains the accounts that appear in the financial statements is called the **general ledger.** In a large entity, the general ledger is usually supported by a number of *subsidiary ledgers.* The subsidiary ledgers provide a place for the individual subaccounts that provide supporting details for a specific general ledger account. For example, the J. C. Penney balance sheet contains one amount for accounts receivable. That amount is the sum of millions of subsidiary ledger account balances, one for each of Penney's customers. Subsidiary ledgers are normally maintained for such accounts as receivables, payables, inventory, and property, plant, and equipment. The general ledger account that contains the total of the subsidiary ledger account balances is called a *control account.* Subsidiary ledgers and control accounts are described in greater detail in Appendix 8–1.

GENERAL LEDGER: The accounting record that contains the accounts that appear in the financial statements.

CHART OF ACCOUNTS: A list of all accounts, with a specific block of numbers assigned to each category (e.g., liabilities all numbered in the 2000s).

When an accounting system contains many accounts, a **chart of accounts** is employed to help accountants locate the proper account. The chart of accounts assigns a number to each account, usually in ascending order from assets to liabilities to equity to revenues to expenses. Thus assets might be numbered 1000–1999, liabilities 2000–2999, equity 3000–3999, operating revenues 4000–4999, operating expenses 5000–5999, and other income statement accounts 6000–6999. Larger or smaller divisions are used when there are more or fewer accounts. We will employ account numbers throughout the remainder of this chapter to help you become accustomed to their use. In subsequent chapters, we will not use them, because the number of accounts in our demonstrations and problems is normally quite small.

POSTING: The process of transferring journalized transaction data to accounts in the ledger.

The process of transferring journalized transaction data to the ledger is called **posting.** Posting is accomplished by transferring into the ledger accounts the data recorded in journal entries. As we noted earlier, debits are added to the left side of accounts and credits are added to the right side. Computerized accounting systems may post data to the ledger automatically as soon as a journal

EXHIBIT 3-3   A LEDGER PAGE

		Item	Debit	Credit	Balance
					Cash *1010*
		Balance, 1/1			6200 00
		Collection of Receivable,			
		a. Smith	3400 00		9600 00
		Payment of Payable,			
		Joseph Company		3700 00	5900 00
		Sale of Common Stock	11000 00		16900 00
		Repayment of Loan,			
		Second National Bank		6500 00	10400 00
		Balance, 1/31			10400 00

entry is completed. The processes demonstrated here are the same as those accomplished by a computer in a computerized accounting system. However, to ensure that the process is illustrated clearly, we will describe posting as if it were being done by hand. We will use the T-account format to illustrate ledger accounts—even though in actual practice most accounting system ledgers do not use that format—because T-accounts enable us to present clear, simple diagrams of the posting process. (One ledger format that is commonly used in manual accounting systems is shown in Exhibit 3-3.)

Posting is accomplished by taking a single journal entry and debiting and crediting the accounts noted in the entry for the amounts indicated. As an illustration, assume that a firm purchases $3,500 of inventory for cash and prepares the following journal entry:

Inventory 3,500
   Cash   3,500

This entry would be posted to the ledger as follows:

	Cash	*1010*			Inventory	*1062*	
		3,500			3,500		

To illustrate posting more thoroughly, let's return to the Boonville Delivery Service example that we used earlier to illustrate analysis and journalizing. The journal entities are repeated in Exhibit 3-4. Exhibit 3-5 shows the ledger accounts after the entries have been posted, with letters to key each entry. For example, journal entry **a** has been posted with a $25,000 debit to cash and a $25,000 credit to capital stock. Examine Exhibits 3-4 and 3-5 carefully to see how each journal entry has been posted. Notice that each ledger account in Exhibit 3-5 has the account number from a chart of accounts to the right of the

EXHIBIT 3–4   JOURNAL ENTRIES

BOONVILLE DELIVERY SERVICE
Journal

a) Cash...	25,000	
Capital stock....................................		25,000
b) Cash...	40,000	
Notes payable.................................		40,000
c) Land	7,000	
Buildings..	19,000	
Cash...		26,000
d) Furniture and fixtures...........................	12,000	
Notes payable.................................		12,000
e) Equipment	18,600	
Cash...		6,000
Installment notes payable		12,600
f) Office supplies inventory	1,180	
Accounts payable		1,180
g) Accounts payable	580	
Cash...		580
h) Cash...	3,400	
Service revenue		3,400
i) Accounts receivable	15,800	
Service revenue		15,800
j) Cash...	10,000	
Accounts receivable		10,000
k) Advertising expense	4,700	
Cash...		4,700
l) Fuel expense....................................	790	
Accounts payable		790
m) Accounts payable	790	
Cash...		790
n) Dividends.......................................	1,800	
Dividends payable..............................		1,800
o) Dividends payable...............................	1,800	
Cash...		1,800
p) Wages expense..................................	10,500	
Cash...		10,500

EXHIBIT 3–5   **POSTED LEDGER ACCOUNTS**

BOONVILLE DELIVERY SERVICE
General Ledger Accounts

	Cash		*1010*			Accounts receivable		*1030*			Office supplies inventory	*1075*
(a)	25,000	26,000	(c)	(i)	15,800	10,000	(j)	(f)	1,180		
(b)	40,000	6,000	(e)								
(h)	3,400	580	(g)								
(j)	10,000	4,700	(k)								
		790	(m)								
		1,800	(o)								
		10,500	(p)								

	Land	*1210*		Buildings	*1220*		Equipment	*1230*
(c)	7,000		(c)	19,000		(e)	18,600	

	Furniture and fixtures		*1240*		Accounts payable		*2010*			Notes payable		*2020*
(d)	12,000			(g)	580	1,180	(f)			40,000	(b)	
				(m)	790	790	(l)			12,000	(d)	

	Dividends payable		*2400*		Installment notes payable	*2720*		Capital stock		*3000*
(o)	1,800	1,800	(n)		12,600	(e)		25,000	(a)	

	Dividends	*3810*		Service revenue		*4300*		Wages expense	*5110*
(n)	1,800			3,400	(h)	(p)	10,500		
				15,800	(i)				

	Fuel expense	*5260*		Advertising expense	*5710*
(l)	790		(k)	4,700	

account name. As you can see from this example, ledger accounts often have more than one entry.

DETERMINING AN ACCOUNT BALANCE At the end of the accounting period, the balance for an account is determined by comparing the sum of the debits to the sum of the credits. The smaller sum is subtracted from the larger sum, and the difference is entered on the side of the larger sum as the account balance. We use the cash account from Boonville Delivery Service's ledger to illustrate:

	Cash		*1010*
Beginning balance	–0–		
	25,000	26,000	
	40,000	6,000	
	3,400	580	
	10,000	4,700	
		790	
		1,800	
		10,500	
	78,400	50,370	

A line is drawn under the last item posted, and the debit and credit columns are summed. The sums are then entered under the rule. The sum of the debits (left side) is $78,400. The sum of the credits (right side) is $50,370. The smaller sum (credits) is subtracted from the larger sum (debits):

$$\$78,400 - \$50,370 = \$28,030$$

The balance of $28,030 is then placed on the debit side, the side with the larger sum, under a second rule. A double underline is sometimes placed under the ending account balance.

	Cash		1010
Beginning balance	-0-		
	25,000	26,000	
	40,000	6,000	
	3,400	580	
	10,000	4,700	
		790	
		1,800	
		10,500	
	78,400	50,370	
Ending balance	28,030		

At this point in the accounting cycle, we have progressed from the collection of data about transactions, through analysis and journalizing, to posting of ledger accounts and determining end-of-period ledger account balances. The next step in the accounting cycle is the organization of the ledger account balances into a trial balance. However, before we discuss the trial balance, let us review the first four steps in the accounting cycle, with an analysis of how electronic data processing technology can be incorporated into the accounting cycle.

ANALYSIS
ELECTRONIC DATA PROCESSING IN THE ACCOUNTING CYCLE

In a computerized accounting system, an entry of a single transaction often produces both a journal entry and the posting of the entry to the affected accounts. The completion of the entry is often a signal for the computer system to use the accounting data for other purposes as well. To illustrate how linking a cash register to a computerized accounting system can secure data for accounting transactions, let us follow a sample event from entry to posting. Our hypothetical business is C. H. Stereo, a retail store selling stereo equipment. Steve Student has just selected a $250 amplifier, to be purchased on credit.

a) The salesclerk presses a button on the cash register to signal that she is ready to enter a credit sales transaction.

b) The clerk types in the stock number of the stereo amplifier: SA-12-14-150. Often the stock number for an item contains the purchase price of the item as well as other identifying information. Let us assume that SA is the type of product (stereo amplifier), 12 is the brand identifier, 14 is the model designation, and 150 is C. H.'s cost for the item.

c) At this point, the computer may enter the sales price from data previously stored or it may request the clerk to do so. (Using previously stored price data provides more control but is unwieldy for an item whose selling price changes often.) Let's assume that the clerk enters the selling price of $250.

d) The computer now asks the clerk for Steve Student's account number.

e) The clerk enters Steve Student's account number.

f) The computer checks previously stored data to see whether Steve Student's credit is acceptable. If his credit is not good, the transaction is refused.

g) If the transaction is accepted, the computer has the cash register print the relevant information on a sales slip, a copy of which becomes a source document for the business after it has been signed by Steve Student. Another copy is given to Steve as a receipt.

h) The computer then prepares two journal entries:

Accounts receivable, Steve Student	250	
Sales revenue		250

Cost of goods sold....................................	150	
Inventory...		150

i) The journal entry is posted to the accounts by the computer. A subsidiary ledger account receivable for Steve Student is increased by $250, as is the control account for accounts receivable. The account balance for sales is increased by $250. Cost of goods sold is increased by $150. The inventory account for item SA-12-14-150 is decreased by $150.

j) The computer adds Steve Student to the list of individuals to whom bills (which the computer prepares, based on each account receivable balance) are sent. The computer also updates the information system that automatically informs the purchasing department when it is necessary to reorder items and indicates how many items should be reordered.

Note that the journal entry and account posting were accomplished without the involvement of the accounting department. In firms using computerized accounting systems, many routine transactions can be entered and posted by nonaccounting personnel from whom the computer elicits the necessary data. Still, as the remaining chapters in this text will illustrate, there is ample work for the accountants even when the nonaccounting staff and the computer perform many of the routine steps of the accounting cycle.

We will now continue our explanation of the accounting cycle with a discussion of the preparation of the trial balance.

PREPARATION OF THE TRIAL BALANCE

TRIAL BALANCE: An ordered list of all active accounts and their balances that shows whether total debit balances equal total credit balances.

The **trial balance** is an ordered list of all active accounts and each account's balance. Each account must have a debit, credit, or zero balance. The account balances are recorded in the trial balance in one of two columns, debit or credit; accounts with zero balances do not appear. The trial balance is prepared (1) to permit the accountant to determine whether the equality of debits and credits was preserved when journal entries were made and posted and (2) to organize the account balances to aid in the preparation of the financial statements. If journal entries were prepared or posted with unequal debits and credits, the trial balance total for debits will not equal the total for credits. The error or errors must be found and corrected before the financial statements are prepared. A word of caution is necessary here: The trial balance will *not* detect errors of analysis or amount. Sometimes the wrong account is selected for a journal entry or an incorrect amount is recorded for a transaction. So long as both the debit and the credit portions of the journal entry or posting reflect the misinformation, the debit and credit totals in the trial balance will be equal. Further, use of a trial balance will not detect the omission of an entire entry.

Normally, the trial balance is prepared with the balance sheet accounts listed first (assets, liabilities, and equity), followed by the income statement accounts (revenues and expenses). Within the balance sheet accounts, assets are followed by liabilities, which in turn are followed by equity accounts. The balance sheet accounts are listed in the order of their appearance on a classified balance sheet: assets in order of decreasing liquidity, liabilities from most to least current, and equity from capital stock to retained earnings. Revenue and expense accounts are listed in the order of their appearance on an income statement.

We can illustrate the preparation of a trial balance by using the ledger account balances developed after posting the journal entries for Boonville Delivery Service. The correct end-of-period balances for Boonville's accounts are

---

EXHIBIT 3–6   **LEDGER ACCOUNTS AFTER BALANCES ARE COMPUTED**

BOONVILLE DELIVERY SERVICE
General Ledger Accounts

Cash	1010		Accounts receivable	1030		Office supplies inventory	1075
25,000	26,000		15,800	10,000		1,180	
40,000	6,000		5,800				
3,400	580						
10,000	4,700						
	790						
	1,800						
	10,500						
78,400	50,370						
28,030							

Land	1210		Buildings	1220		Equipment	1230
7,000			19,000			18,600	

Furniture and fixtures	1240		Accounts payable	2010		Notes payable	2020
12,000			580	1,180			40,000
			790	790			12,000
			1,370	1,970			52,000
				600			

Dividends payable	2400		Installment notes payable	2720		Capital stock	3000
1,800	1,800			12,600			25,000
	–0–						

Dividends	3810		Service revenue	4300		Wages expense	5110
1,800				3,400		10,500	
				15,800			
				19,200			

Fuel expense	5260		Advertising expense	5710
790			4,700	

EXHIBIT 3-7   **TRIAL BALANCE**

BOONVILLE DELIVERY SERVICE
Trial Balance
As of December 31, 19X6

ACCOUNT NUMBER	ACCOUNT	DEBIT	CREDIT
1010	Cash.................................	$ 28,030	
1030	Accounts receivable	5,800	
1075	Office supplies inventory................	1,180	
1210	Land	7,000	
1220	Buildings.............................	19,000	
1230	Equipment............................	18,600	
1240	Furniture and fixtures	12,000	
2010	Accounts payable		$ 600
2020	Notes payable		52,000
2720	Installment notes payable		12,600
3000	Capital stock		25,000
3810	Dividends............................	1,800	
4300	Service revenue		19,200
5110	Wages expense........................	10,500	
5260	Fuel expense	790	
5710	Advertising expense	4,700	
	Totals	$109,400	$109,400

shown in Exhibit 3-6. The trial balance derived from Boonville's ledger accounts is shown in Exhibit 3-7.

PREPARATION OF FINANCIAL STATEMENTS

So far we have discussed how accounting data are collected and how transactions are analyzed. We have described how transactions are journalized and posted. We have shown how individual account balances are determined and organized into a trial balance. Now we will explain the preparation of financial statements, and that explanation will complete our discussion of the data entry portion of the accounting cycle. As you will recall from Chapter 2, the income statement is prepared first, then the statement of changes in retained earnings, and finally the balance sheet.

We will use the data from the trial balance for Boonville Delivery Service (Exhibit 3-7) to show how the financial statements are prepared. Remember that to simplify statement preparation, a trial balance is arranged with the accounts listed in the order in which they will appear in the financial statements. The income statement in Exhibit 3-8 is developed from the revenue and expense accounts (numbered 4300-5710) listed at the bottom of Boonville's trial balance. (To simplify the income statement in Exhibit 3-8, we have assumed that there is no income taxes expense.)

EXHIBIT 3–8 INCOME STATEMENT

BOONVILLE DELIVERY SERVICE
Income Statement
For the Year Ended December 31, 19X6

Service revenue		$19,200
Less: Operating expenses		
Wages.	$10,500	
Fuel	790	
Advertising	4,700	15,990
Net income		$ 3,210

EXHIBIT 3–9 STATEMENT OF CHANGES IN RETAINED EARNINGS

BOONVILLE DELIVERY SERVICE
Statement of Changes in Retained Earnings
For the Year Ended December 31, 19X6

Retained earnings, 12/31/X5.	$ –0–
Add: Net income.	3,210
	$3,210
Less: Dividends	1,800
Retained earnings, 12/31/X6.	$1,410

The statement of changes in retained earnings for Boonville Delivery Service, shown in Exhibit 3–9, is prepared by using a beginning retained earnings balance of $0 (remember that Boonville Delivery Service is a newly founded enterprise), the net income developed on the income statement, and the dividends of $1,800 (account 3810 on the trial balance).

Having computed ending retained earnings, we now have all the account balances necessary for preparation of the balance sheet shown in Exhibit 3–10. The balance sheet accounts are drawn from the asset, liability, and equity accounts (numbered in the 1000s, 2000s, and 3000s) listed in the top portion of Boonville's trial balance. Retained earnings is taken from the statement of changes in retained earnings. (For the sake of simplicity, the balance sheet in Exhibit 3–10 is not classified.)

The preparation of the financial statements from the trial balance completes our discussion of the six steps in the accounting cycle that are covered in this chapter. Exhibit 3–11 reviews each of these steps. The four remaining steps in the accounting cycle are discussed in the next two chapters.

Before we go on to examine the remaining steps in the accounting cycle, it is important to understand fully the procedures presented in this chapter. The demonstration that follows includes the activities that would typically occur during the operating cycle of a business enterprise. Careful study of this application will give you a thorough understanding of the steps in the accounting cycle that have been explained thus far.

EXHIBIT 3−10 **BALANCE SHEET**

BOONVILLE DELIVERY SERVICE
Balance Sheet
As of December 31, 19X6

ASSETS

Cash	$28,030
Accounts receivable	5,800
Office supplies inventory	1,180
Land	7,000
Buildings	19,000
Equipment	18,600
Furniture and fixtures	12,000
Total assets	$91,610

LIABILITIES

Accounts payable	$ 600
Notes payable	52,000
Installment notes payable	12,600
Total liabilities	$65,200

EQUITY

Capital stock	$25,000	
Retained earnings	1,410	
Total equity		26,410
Total liabilities and equity		$91,610

EXHIBIT 3−11   **THE ACCOUNTING CYCLE**

1. **DATA COLLECTION:** Transactions affecting the firm are identified, and data indicating their dollar effect on the firm are collected.
2. **TRANSACTION ANALYSIS:** The collected data are analyzed in order to determine the accounts affected, the monetary amount of each effect, and the resulting increases or decreases in the account balances.
3. **JOURNALIZING:** Journal entries are prepared from the analyzed data and entered chronologically in a journal.
4. **POSTING:** The journalized transaction data are transferred to ledger accounts.
5. **PREPARATION OF THE TRIAL BALANCE:** A list of balances for all active accounts is organized to aid in error detection and in preparing the financial statements.
6. **PREPARATION OF THE FINANCIAL STATEMENTS:** The income statement, statement of changes in retained earnings, and balance sheet are prepared from the account balances in the trial balance.

DEMONSTRATION OF THE ACCOUNTING CYCLE

Newburgh Advertising, Inc., an enterprise that has been in existence for several years, sells advertising services to local and national clients. Newburgh's accounting period is the calendar year. Assume that all transactions through December 9, 19X4, have been collected, analyzed, journalized, and posted. The accounts and account balances that reflect the results of these activities are presented in Exhibit 3–12.

DATA COLLECTION, TRANSACTION ANALYSIS, AND JOURNALIZING

The following transactions occur after December 9. The transactions are analyzed as described below. The resulting journal entries are shown in Exhibit 3–13.

a) TRANSACTION On December 10, Newburgh sells 500 shares of its capital stock to a present stockholder, Stephen Nienaber, for $12,000 ($24 per share).

ANALYSIS Cash, an asset, is increased by $12,000. Capital stock, an equity, is increased by $12,000.

b) TRANSACTION On December 12, Newburgh borrows $50,000 on a one-year note payable from the Warrick National Bank, to be repaid with 8 percent interest on December 12, 19X5.

ANALYSIS Cash, an asset, is increased by $50,000. A liability, notes payable, is increased by $50,000. (The interest owed on liabilities of this type is typically recorded at the end of an accounting period; we will discuss this procedure when we examine adjusting entries in Chapter 4. For now we will ignore the interest.)

c) TRANSACTION On December 12, Newburgh purchases blocks of commercial time on several local television stations for a total of $56,000 cash.

ANALYSIS Television commercial time, the purchased rights to show commercials at particular times, is increased by $56,000. Since commercial time can be sold to advertisers, it is an item of value and should be included among the firm's assets. Another asset, cash, is decreased by $56,000.

d) TRANSACTION On December 13, Newburgh buys several blocks of commercial time on local radio stations for an upcoming political campaign, at a total cost of $20,000. Newburgh agrees to pay for the time as it is used during January, February, and March.

ANALYSIS Radio commercial time, an asset, and accounts payable, a liability, are both increased by $20,000.

e) TRANSACTION On December 16, Newburgh purchases $7,000 worth of office equipment by paying $1,400 in cash and signing a one-year, 12 percent note payable for the balance.

ANALYSIS Furniture and fixtures, an asset, is increased by $7,000. Cash, another asset, is decreased by $1,400. Notes payable, a liability, is increased by $5,600.

EXHIBIT 3-12   **LEDGER ACCOUNTS WITH JOURNAL ENTRIES POSTED THROUGH DECEMBER 9**

NEWBURGH ADVERTISING, INC.
General Ledger Accounts

Cash 1010	Accounts receivable 1030	Supplies inventory 1070
12,200	38,000	9,000

Radio commercial time 1091	Television commercial time 1092	Equipment 1230
28,000	7,000	33,000

Accumulated depreciation, equipment 1231	Furniture and fixtures 1240	Accumulated depreciation, furniture and fixtures 1241
5,000	19,000	3,000

Accounts payable 2010	Notes payable 2020	Capital stock 3000
13,000	–0–	105,000

Retained earnings 3800	Service revenue 4300	Television commercial time expense 5031
31,000	507,700	156,000

Radio commercial time expense 5032	Salaries expense 5100	Wages expense 5110
98,000	187,000	37,500

Supplies expense 5210	Miscellaneous expense 5390
14,000	26,000

f) TRANSACTION On December 19, Newburgh pays $13,000 on an account payable to Chandler Art Supply.

ANALYSIS At some previous time, Newburgh had purchased supplies on credit (accounts payable) from Chandler Art Supply. This liability and cash are both reduced by $13,000 when Newburgh pays Chandler's bill.

g) TRANSACTION On December 20, Newburgh declares dividends of $.20 per share on its capital stock. The dividend is payable on December 26. There are 9,500 shares outstanding.

ANALYSIS A dividend of $.20 per share is declared and is payable to the owners of the capital stock. Dividends, a contra-equity account, is increased by $1,900 [($.20)(9,500 shares)]. Dividends payable, a liability, is also increased by $1,900.

h) TRANSACTION On December 26, the dividend declared on December 20 is paid.

ANALYSIS Dividends payable, a liability, is decreased by $1,900. Cash, an asset, is also decreased by $1,900.

i) TRANSACTION On December 26, Newburgh bills McBurger, a national restaurant chain, $40,000 for a series of local television and radio commercials run at McBurger's request. (Newburgh had previously prepared the commercials and had purchased and paid for the commercial time used.)

ANALYSIS Newburgh considers the work prepared for McBurger to be sufficiently complete so that recognition of revenue is appropriate. Service revenue and a corresponding asset, accounts receivable, are both increased by $40,000 when Newburgh bills McBurger.

j) TRANSACTION On December 27, Newburgh sells a newspaper ad layout to East Side Lumber Yard for $5,300 cash.

ANALYSIS An asset, cash, is increased by $5,300. Service revenue is also increased by the same amount.

k) TRANSACTION On December 28, McBurger pays the $40,000 bill submitted by Newburgh on December 26.

ANALYSIS When McBurger pays the bill submitted by Newburgh in transaction **i**, one kind of asset, cash, is received in exchange for another asset, accounts receivable.

l) TRANSACTION On December 28, Newburgh signs an agreement with Cord Motors, Inc., to create and run 50 minutes of commercials on local television and radio during the next 12 months. Newburgh expects to receive $400,000 of revenue for this contract, but the exact amount will depend on the cost of the commercials and the time slots in which they are run.

ANALYSIS This is an example of an important event that does not produce a journal entry at the time it occurs. Either Cord or Newburgh must begin to perform on its part of the contract before an exchange of benefits signals a transaction to be entered in Newburgh's accounting system.

m) TRANSACTION On December 29, Newburgh receives a bill of $1,500 from Mac's Catering for catering services performed at a party Newburgh held for its clients. (No previous entry has been made for this activity.)

ANALYSIS The $1,500 cost of entertainment (catering) is a miscellaneous expenditure incurred in the running of the business. Thus miscellaneous expense is increased by $1,500. Accounts payable, a liability, is also increased by $1,500.

n) TRANSACTION On December 31, Newburgh pays $1,600 cash in wages to its secretarial staff for the work period December 15 through 28.

ANALYSIS The services performed by Newburgh's secretarial staff were used in the generation of revenues. Therefore, wage expense is increased by $1,600 and cash is decreased by the same amount.

o) TRANSACTION On December 31, Newburgh's income taxes expense for 19X4 is determined to be $6,500.

ANALYSIS Income taxes expense and the associated income taxes payable are computed at the end of the period after all the other income statement amounts have been determined. Income taxes expense is increased $6,500. Income taxes payable, a liability, is also increased $6,500.

EXHBIT 3–13   **JOURNAL ENTRIES**

NEWBURGH ADVERTISING, INC.
Journal

a) Cash	12,000	
Capital stock		12,000
b) Cash	50,000	
Notes payable		50,000
c) Television commercial time	56,000	
Cash		56,000
d) Radio commercial time	20,000	
Accounts payable		20,000
e) Furniture and fixtures	7,000	
Cash		1,400
Notes payable		5,600
f) Accounts payable	13,000	
Cash		13,000
g) Dividends	1,900	
Dividends payable		1,900
h) Dividends payable	1,900	
Cash		1,900
i) Accounts receivable	40,000	
Service revenue		40,000
j) Cash	5,300	
Service revenue		5,300
k) Cash	40,000	
Accounts receivable		40,000
l) No entry		
m) Miscellaneous expense	1,500	
Accounts payable		1,500
n) Wages expense	1,600	
Cash		1,600
o) Income taxes expense	6,500	
Income taxes payable		6,500

EXHIBIT 3–14   LEDGER ACCOUNTS WITH JOURNAL ENTRIES POSTED THROUGH DECEMBER 31

NEWBURGH ADVERTISING, INC.
General Ledger Accounts

	Cash		1010			Accounts receivable		1030			Supplies inventory		1070
	12,200					38,000					9,000		
(a)	12,000	56,000	(c)		(i)	40,000	40,000	(k)					
(b)	50,000	1,400	(e)										
(j)	5,300	13,000	(f)										
(k)	40,000	1,900	(h)										
		1,600	(n)										
	119,500	73,900				78,000	40,000						
	45,600					38,000							

	Radio commercial time		1091			Television commercial time		1092			Equipment		1230
	28,000					7,000					33,000		
(d)	20,000				(c)	56,000							
	48,000					63,000							

	Accumulated depreciation, equipment		1231			Furniture and fixtures		1240			Accumulated depreciation, furniture and fixtures		1241
		5,000				19,000						3,000	
					(e)	7,000							
						26,000							

	Accounts payable		2010			Notes payable		2020			Income taxes payable		2210
		13,000					50,000	(b)				6,500	(o)
(f)	13,000	20,000	(d)				5,600	(e)					
		1,500	(m)										
	13,000	34,500					55,600						
		21,500											

POSTING   Once Newburgh's transactions have been analyzed and journalized, they are posted to the accounts in the ledger. The account balances are determined once all journal entries have been posted (Exhibit 3–14).

Dividends payable			2400
(h)	1,900	1,900	(g)
		–0–	

Dividends		3810
(g)	1,900	

Capital stock		3000
	105,000	
	12,000	(a)
	117,000	

Service revenue		4300
	507,700	
	40,000	(i)
	5,300	(j)
	553,000	

Retained earnings		3800
	31,000	

Television commercial time expense		5031
156,000		

Radio commercial time expense		5032
98,000		

Salaries expense		5100
187,000		

Wages expense		5110
	37,500	
(n)	1,600	
	39,100	

Supplies expense		5210
14,000		

Miscellaneous expense		5390
	26,000	
(m)	1,500	
	27,500	

Income taxes expense		5900
(o)	6,500	

PREPARATION OF THE TRIAL BALANCE The next step is to prepare the trial balance from the account balances (see Exhibit 3–15). Recall that the accounts are ordered in the trial balance so as to aid in financial statement preparation.

EXHIBIT 3-15   TRIAL BALANCE

NEWBURGH ADVERTISING, INC.
Trial Balance
As of December 31, 19X4

ACCOUNT NUMBER	ACCOUNT	DEBIT	CREDIT
1010	Cash.................................	$ 45,600	
1030	Accounts receivable....................	38,000	
1070	Supplies inventory.....................	9,000	
1091	Radio commercial time	48,000	
1092	Television commercial time.............	63,000	
1230	Equipment	33,000	
1231	Accumulated depreciation, equipment		$ 5,000
1240	Furniture and fixtures..................	26,000	
1241	Accumulated depreciation, furniture and fixtures.............................		3,000
2010	Accounts payable......................		21,500
2020	Notes payable.........................		55,600
2210	Income taxes payable		6,500
3000	Capital stock..........................		117,000
3800	Retained earnings		31,000
3810	Dividends	1,900	
4300	Service revenue........................		553,000
5031	Television commercial time expense	156,000	
5032	Radio commercial time expense..........	98,000	
5100	Salaries expense	187,000	
5110	Wages expense	39,100	
5210	Supplies expense	14,000	
5390	Miscellaneous expense	27,500	
5900	Income taxes expense	6,500	
	Totals............................	$792,600	$792,600

PREPARATION OF THE FINANCIAL STATEMENTS

Once the trial balance has been prepared, the financial statements can be prepared quite easily.

The Income Statement

The income statement for Newburgh Advertising (see Exhibit 3-16) is prepared from the income statement accounts (numbered in the 4000s and 5000s), which are arranged in sequential order at the bottom of the trial balance (Exhibit 3-15).

The Schedule of Changes in Retained Earnings

The beginning retained earnings balance, the net income just computed, and the dividends from the trial balance are combined in the statement of changes in retained earnings (see Exhibit 3-17) to determine the ending retained earnings balance for the balance sheet.

EXHIBIT 3–16   INCOME STATEMENT

NEWBURGH ADVERTISING, INC.
Income Statement
For the Year Ended December 31, 19X4

Revenues:		
Service revenue..................................		$553,000
Less: Operating expenses:		
Television commercial time.......................	$156,000	
Radio commercial time...........................	98,000	
Salaries.......................................	187,000	
Wages..	39,100	
Supplies......................................	14,000	
Miscellaneous.................................	27,500	521,600
Income before taxes...............................		$ 31,400
Less: Income taxes expense		6,500
Net income		$ 24,900
Earnings per share [$24,900/9,500 shares]		$2.62

EXHIBIT 3–17   STATEMENT OF CHANGES IN RETAINED EARNINGS

NEWBURGH ADVERTISING, INC.
Statement of Changes in Retained Earnings
For the Year Ended December 31, 19X4

Beginning retained earnings, 12/31/X3.............................	$31,000
Add: Net income...	24,900
	$55,900
Less: Dividends...	1,900
Ending retained earnings, 12/31/X4	$54,000

The Balance Sheet

The last statement, the balance sheet for Newburgh Advertising (see Exhibit 3–18), is prepared from the account balances included at the top of the trial balance (accounts numbered in the 1000s, 2000s, and 3000s) and the ending retained earnings balance that was computed in the statement of changes in retained earnings. This balance sheet completes our discussion of the data-entry portion of the accounting cycle.

EXHIBIT 3–18   **BALANCE SHEET**

NEWBURGH ADVERTISING, INC.
Balance Sheet
As of December 31, 19X4

ASSETS

Current assets:

Cash		$ 45,600
Accounts receivable		38,000
Supplies inventory		9,000
Radio commercial time............................		48,000
Television commercial time.......................		63,000
Total current assets		$203,600
Property, plant, and equipment:		
Equipment......................................	$ 33,000	
Less: Accumulated depreciation	5,000	28,000
Furniture and fixtures	$ 26,000	
Less: Accumulated depreciation	3,000	23,000
Total assets		$254,600

LIABILITIES

Current liabilities:

Accounts payable................................		$ 21,500
Notes payable		55,600
Income taxes payable.............................		6,500
Total current liabilities		$ 83,600

EQUITY

Capital stock	$117,000	
Retained earnings................................	54,000	
Total equity....................................		171,000
Total liabilities and equity		$254,600

SUMMARY

This chapter introduced the data-entry portion of the accounting cycle. These steps in the cycle measure, record, and then summarize the effects of transactions in the financial statements. The chapter began by discussing transactions and the need for reliable measurements of the transactions whose effects are recorded. Transactions are recorded in a double-entry accounting system that is based on three key features:

1. Every recorded transaction has a two-part, or double-entry, effect on the entity.

2. The effects of transactions are recorded in accounts.

3. Accounts are organized so that:
   a) Assets = Liabilities + Equity.
   b) Equity is increased by revenues and decreased by expenses.

In a double-entry system, the effects of transactions on asset, liability, equity, revenue, and expense accounts are described in terms of debits and credits. Debits are recorded on the left side of a T-account, and credits are recorded on the right side of a T-account. For asset and expense accounts, debits represent increases and credits represent decreases. For liability, equity, and revenue accounts, debits represent decreases and credits represent increases. These definitions of debit and credit, when combined with the fundamental accounting model, lead to the proposition that the debits associated with each journal entry must equal the credits associated with that entry.

The recording of transactions in the double-entry system follows an accounting cycle. The last section of the chapter provided an overview of the entire accounting cycle and described in detail the six steps of the cycle used to enter data into the accounting system:

1. Data collection

2. Transaction analysis

3. Journalizing

4. Posting

5. Preparation of the trial balance

6. Preparation of the financial statements

The accounting cycle also includes both adjustment procedures, which are described in Chapter 4, and closing activities, which are discussed in more detail in Chapter 5.

KEY TERMS

ACCOUNT (p. 83)

ACCOUNTING CYCLE (p. 80)

CHART OF ACCOUNTS (p. 100)

CREDIT (p. 88)

DATA COLLECTION (p. 86)

DEBIT (p. 88)

DOUBLE-ENTRY SYSTEM (p. 85)

GENERAL LEDGER (p. 100)

JOURNAL (p. 88)

JOURNAL ENTRY (p. 88)

JOURNALIZING (p. 88)

LEDGER (p. 100)

POSTING (p. 100)

RECOGNITION (p. 81)

RELIABLE MEASUREMENT (p. 81)

SOURCE DOCUMENTS (p. 86)

TRANSACTION ANALYSIS (p. 86)

TRANSACTIONS (p. 81)

TRIAL BALANCE (p. 105)

QUESTIONS

Q3-1. Of all the events that occur each day, how would you describe those that are recorded in a firm's accounting records?

Q3-2. In order for a transaction to be recorded in a business' accounting records, the effects of the transaction must be reliably measurable in dollars. What is reliable measurement and why is it important?

Q3-3. Why is the term *double-entry* an appropriate expression for decribing an accounting system?

Q3-4. What is the role in the accounting cycle of the fundamental accounting model (or the balance sheet equation)?

Q3-5. Why do revenues increase stockholders' equity? Why do expenses decrease stockholders' equity?

Q3-6. The words *debit* and *credit* are used in two ways in accounting: "to debit an account" and "a debit balance." Explain both usages of *debit* and *credit*.

Q3-7. What activities occur during the transaction analysis step in the accounting cycle?

Q3-8. When a journal entry is made, what must be equal? Why?

Q3-9. Describe the entry of accounting data into the journal and the ledger.

Q3-10. What kinds of errors will a trial balance detect? What kinds of errors will not be detectable by a trial balance?

Q3-11. Why is the order of accounts in a trial balance important?

EXERCISES

E3-12. EVENTS AND TRANSACTIONS Using the words "qualified" and "not qualified," indicate whether each of the following events would qualify as a transaction and be recognized and recorded in the accounting system for Norman's Grocery Store on the date indicated.

a) On February 15, 19X2, Norman's placed an order for a new cash register, for which $700 would be paid after delivery.

b) On February 17, 19X2, Norman's received a bill from the electric company indicating that it had used electric power during January 19X2 at a cost of $120; the bill need not be paid until February 25, 19X2.

c) On February 20, 19X2, Norman Jones, the sole owner of Norman's Grocery, purchased a new passenger car for $15,000 in cash. The car is entirely for personal use.

d) On February 21, 19X2, the cash register ordered on February 15, 19X2, was delivered to Norman's Grocery. Payment was not due until March.

e) On February 23, 19X2, Norman's paid $120 to the electric company.

f) On February 26, 19X2, Norman's signed a two-year extension of the lease on the store building occupied by Norman's Grocery. The new lease was effective on April 1, 19X2, and required an increase in the monthly rental from $750 to $900.

g) On March 1, 19X2, Norman's paid $750 to its landlord for March rent on the store building.

E3-13. EVENTS AND TRANSACTIONS Each of the following sequences of events describes the acquisition of an asset. For each sequence, indicate the letter corresponding to the event or events that would result in the recording of a transaction in the accounting records of the buyer.

Sequence 1:
a) Buyer agrees to pay seller within 30 days following delivery, but final selling price remains to be determined by seller.

b) Buyer receives asset from seller but does not yet know final selling price.

c) Buyer receives invoice from seller stating selling price, which the buyer finds acceptable.

d) Buyer pays cash to the seller.

Sequence 2:

a) Buyer agrees to pay seller within 30 days following delivery; a selling price of $2,000 is established, which includes a fixed amount to compensate the seller for transportation charges.

b) Buyer receives asset from seller.

c) Buyer receives invoice from seller stating the terms agreed to earlier.

d) Buyer pays $2,000 cash to seller.

Sequence 3:

a) Buyer agrees to pay seller half the selling price in advance of delivery; a selling price of $4,200 is established, which includes a fixed amount to compensate the seller for transportation charges.

b) Buyer pays $2,100 cash to the seller.

c) Buyer receives asset from seller.

d) Buyer receives invoice from seller stating that $2,100 remains to be paid.

e) Buyer pays $2,100 cash to the seller.

E3-14.   ACCOUNT BALANCE   Stony Brook Supply Company's accounts payable balance at March 1 was $6,400. During the month of March, Stony Brook engaged in the following transactions involving accounts payable:

a) Made payment on account, $3,500.

b) Purchased supplies on credit, $7,900.

c) Purchased materials on credit, $3,700.

d) Made payment on account, $2,900.

e) Made payment on account, $7,900.

f) Purchased computer on credit, $9,600.

g) Purchased furniture on credit, $2,100.

h) Made payment on account, $3,700.

REQUIRED:

Prepare a T-account for accounts payable, enter these transactions, and compute the ending balance in the account.

E3-15.   EFFECT OF TRANSACTIONS ON THE FUNDAMENTAL ACCOUNTING EQUATION   Goal Systems, a business consulting firm, engaged in the following transactions:

a) Sold capital stock for $50,000 cash.

b) Borrowed $20,000 from a bank.

c) Purchased equipment for $7,000 cash.

d) Prepaid rent on office space for six months in the amount of $6,600.

e) Performed consulting services in exchange for $4,300 cash.

f) Performed consulting services on credit in the amount of $16,000.

g) Incurred and paid wage expense of $7,500.

h) Collected $7,200 of the receivable arising from transaction f.

i) Purchased supplies for $1,100 on credit.

j) Used $800 of the supplies purchased in transaction i.

k) Paid for all of the supplies purchased in transaction i.

REQUIRED:

For each transaction described above, indicate the effects on assets, liabilities, and stockholders' equity. Use a format similar to the following:

TRANSACTION	ASSETS	=	LIABILITIES	+	EQUITY
a) Sold stock for cash	+50,000				+50,000

E3-16. TRANSACTION ANALYSIS   The accountant for Boatsman Products, Inc., received the following information:

a) Boatsman sent its customers a new price list. Prices were increased an average of 3 percent on all items.

b) Boatsman accepted an offer of $150,000 for land that it had purchased two years ago for $130,000. Cash and the deed for the property are to be exchanged in five days.

c) Boatsman accepted $150,000 cash and gave the purchaser the deed for the property described in item **b**.

d) Boatsman's president purchased 600 shares of the firm's capital stock from another stockholder. The president paid $15 per share. The former shareholder had purchased the stock from Boatsman for $4 per share.

e) Boatsman leases its delivery trucks from a local dealer. The dealer also performs maintenance on the trucks for Boatsman. Boatsman received a $1,254 bill for maintenance from the dealer.

REQUIRED:

Indicate whether or not each item should produce a journal entry. Explain your reasoning.

E3-17. OPERATING AND FINANCING CYCLES AND TRANSACTION ANALYSIS   The accountant for Compton Properties has collected the following information:

a) Compton purchased a tract of land from Jacobsen Real Estate for $860,000.

b) Compton issued 2,000 shares of its capital stock to George Micros in exchange for $120,000 cash.

c) Compton purchased a backhoe for $42,000 on credit.

d) Michael Rotunno paid Compton $8,000 cash for a building lot. The lot had been sold to Rotunno several months ago for a total price of $10,000 with a down payment of $2,000 cash.

e) Compton paid its monthly payroll by issuing checks totaling $38,000.

f) Compton declared and paid its annual dividend of $10,000 cash.

REQUIRED:

Indicate the accounts affected by the transactions listed above and the amount and direction of each effect. Also indicate whether the transaction is part of the financing or operating cycle and describe the portion of the cycle that is involved.

E3-18. TRANSACTION ANALYSIS   During December Cynthiana Refrigeration Service engaged in the following transactions:

a) On December 3, Cynthiana sold a one-year service contract to Jones Markets for $8,000 cash.

b) On December 10, Cynthiana repaired the refrigeration equipment of the Moonbeam Drive Inn. Moonbeam paid $800 in cash for the service call.

c) On December 10, Cynthiana purchased a new truck for business use. The truck cost $8,500. Cynthiana paid $2,500 down and signed a one-year note for the balance.

d) Cynthiana received an $8,000 order of repair parts from a supplier on December 19. The supplier is expected to submit a bill for $8,000 in a few days.

e) On December 23, Cynthiana purchased 20 turkeys from Jones Markets for $280 cash. Cynthiana gave the turkeys to its employees as a Christmas gift.

REQUIRED:

Indicate the accounts affected by each transaction and the amount and direction of the effect.

E3-19. DEBIT AND CREDIT EFFECTS OF TRANSACTIONS   Lincoln Corporation was involved in the following transactions during the current year:

a) The owners invested cash in the business in exchange for capital stock.

b) Lincoln borrowed cash from the local bank on a note payable.

c) Lincoln purchased operating assets on credit.

d) Lincoln purchased supplies inventory on credit.

e) Lincoln provided services in exchange for cash from the customer.

f) A customer secured services from Lincoln on credit.

g) The payable from transaction **d** was paid in full.

h) The receivable from transaction **f** was collected in full.

i) Lincoln paid wages in cash.

j) Lincoln used a portion of the supplies purchased in transaction **d**.

k) Lincoln paid dividends in cash.

REQUIRED:

In a table like the one below, enter debits and credits in the appropriate columns for each of the transactions. Transaction **a** is entered as an example.

TRANSACTION	ASSETS	=	LIABILITIES	+	EQUITY
a) Investment of cash by owners	Debit				Credit

E3-20. ANALYSIS, DEBITS, AND CREDITS   Jefferson Framers engaged in the following transactions:

a) Purchased land for $15,200 cash.

b) Purchased equipment for $23,600 in exchange for a one-year, 11 percent note payable.

c) Purchased office supplies on credit for $1,200.

d) Paid the $10,000 principal plus $700 interest on a note payable.

e) Paid an account payable in the amount of $2,600.

f) Provided $62,100 of services on credit.

g) Provided $11,400 of services for cash.

h) Collected $29,800 of accounts receivable.

i) Paid $13,300 of wages in cash.

j) Sold capital stock for $21,000 cash.

REQUIRED:

Using a table like the one below, enter the necessary information for each transaction:

TRANSACTION	ACCOUNT	INCREASE OR DECREASE	DEBIT OR CREDIT	AMOUNT

E3-21. ANALYSIS AND JOURNAL ENTRIES FOR A NEW BUSINESS   Pasta House, Inc., was organized in January of the current year. During the year, the following transactions occurred:

a) On January 14, Pasta House, Inc., sold Martin Halter, the firm's founder and sole owner, 10,000 shares of its capital stock for $7 per share.

b) On the same day, Ohio National Bank loaned Pasta House $30,000 on a 10-year note payable.

c) On February 22, Pasta House purchased a building and the land on which it stands from Frank Jakubek for $14,000 cash and a 5-year, $36,000 note payable. The land and building had appraised values of $10,000 and $40,000, respectively.

d) On March 1, Pasta House signed an $18,000 contract with Cosby Renovations to remodel the inside of the building. Pasta House paid $6,000 down and agreed to pay the remainder when Cosby completed its work.

e) On May 3, Cosby completed its work and submitted a bill to Pasta House for the remaining $12,000.

f) On May 20, Pasta House paid $12,000 to Cosby Renovations.

g) On June 4, Pasta House purchased restaurant supplies from Glidden Supply for $950 cash.

REQUIRED:

Analyze and journalize these transactions.

E3-22. ANALYSIS AND JOURNAL ENTRIES Remington Communications has been providing cellular phone service for several years. During the current year, the following transactions occurred:

a) Enrico Sales paid $3,400 on November 2 for October phone service.

b) On November 4, Remington paid $15,800 to First Eastern Bank in full settlement of a $15,000 note payable. The payment included interest expense of $800.

c) On November 10, Remington paid $4,250 to its hourly employees for their weekly wages.

d) Remington received and paid the following bills on November 15:

Equipment rent	$4,450
Electricity	3,140
Water and sewage	180

e) On November 21, Remington received a bill from Monticello Construction for $900 for repairs made to Remington's loading dock. Remington plans to pay the bill in early December, when it is due.

f) Remington paid the $900 to Monticello Construction on December 4.

REQUIRED:

Analyze and journalize these transactions.

E3-23. ANALYSIS AND JOURNAL ENTRIES Kauai Adventures rents surfboards and snorkeling and scuba equipment. During a recent month, Kauai engaged in the following transactions:

a) Received $34,200 cash from customers for rentals.

b) Purchased on credit five new surfboards for $110 each.

c) Paid wages to employees in the amount of $11,500.

d) Paid office rent for the month in the amount of $3,300.

e) Purchased a new truck for $9,800. Paid $1,000 down in cash and secured a loan from Princeville Bank for the $8,800 balance.

f) Collected a $650 account receivable.

g) Paid an account payable in the amount of $790.

h) Borrowed $10,000 on a six-month, 12 percent note payable.

i) Paid the monthly telephone bill of $345.

j) Paid a monthly advertising bill of $1,960.

REQUIRED:

Analyze these transactions and prepare journal entries.

E3-24. ANALYSIS, JOURNAL ENTRIES, AND POSTING Rosenthal Decorating, Inc., is a commercial painting and decorating contractor. During a recent year, the following transactions occurred:

a) On January 15, Rosenthal sold 500 shares of its capital stock to William Hensley for $10,000.

b) On February 20, Rosenthal paid $720 cash to Westwood Builders' Supply for painting supplies delivered on January 22. The invoice arrived on January 24, at which time Rosenthal recorded a $720 account payable.

c) On May 12, Rosenthal received $12,500 from Bultman Condominiums for painting and decorating performed during April. Upon completion of the work in April, Rosenthal recorded an account receivable of $12,500.

d) On June 5, Rosenthal sent Arlington Builders a $9,500 bill for a painting job completed on that day.

e) On June 24, Rosenthal paid wages for work performed during the preceding week in the amount of $6,700.

REQUIRED:

Analyze and journalize these transactions and post the journal entries to Rosenthal's ledger accounts.

E3-25. ANALYSIS, JOURNAL ENTRIES, AND POSTING   Bryant Scanning Systems has sold and serviced grocery store bar-code scanning systems for several years. Bryant engaged in the following transactions:

a) Foodplace had Bryant repair a scanning system. On January 11, the day repairs were completed, Foodplace secured a loan from Southern Bank for $1,500 and then paid Bryant the $1,500.

b) On January 15, Bryant purchased six new scanners from PCS for $14,000 each. Bryant agreed to pay for the scanners in four months or when sold, whichever was sooner.

c) On January 17, Bryant received and paid a bill for $475 from Richards Delivery Company for transportation of the six new scanners.

d) On January 21, Merit Grocery paid an outstanding $21,900 account receivable.

e) In order to take advantage of a special offer from a manufacturer, Bryant borrowed $30,000 from the Faneuli National Bank. The loan was effective on January 26. The amount of the loan plus $2,700 interest is to be repaid in eight months.

f) On January 31, Bryant paid for one of the scanning systems purchased in transaction **b**.

REQUIRED:

Analyze and journalize these transactions and post them to Bryant's ledger accounts.

E3-26. RULES FOR RECORDING ACCOUNTING DATA   The following accounts are available for Haubstadt Shoe Works:

Accounts payable
Accounts receivable
Accumulated depreciation, building
Accumulated depreciation, equipment
Building
Capital stock
Cash
Cost of goods sold
Depreciation expense, building

Depreciation expense, equipment
Equipment
General and administrative expense
Interest expense
Inventory
Long-term notes payable
Retained earnings
Sales revenue
Selling expense

REQUIRED:

Using a table like the one below, indicate whether each account normally has a debit or credit balance and indicate on which of the financial statements (income statement, statement of changes in retained earnings, or balance sheet) each account appears.

ACCOUNT	DEBIT	CREDIT	FINANCIAL STATEMENT

E3-27. TRIAL BALANCE PREPARATION   The following accounts and account balances are available for Badger Auto Parts store at December 31, 19X4:

Accounts payable	$ 9,200
Accounts receivable	41,100
Accumulated depreciation, furniture and fixtures	47,300
Capital stock	100,000
Cash	3,700
Cost of goods sold	189,000
Depreciation expense, furniture and fixtures	10,400
Furniture and fixtures	128,000
General and administrative expense	9,700
Income taxes expense	3,700
Income taxes payable	3,600
Interest expense	7,200
Interest payable	1,800
Inventory	60,500
Long-term notes payable	50,000
Prepaid rent	15,000
Retained earnings, 12/31/X3	15,900
Sales revenue	268,000
Selling expense	27,500

REQUIRED:

Prepare a trial balance with the accounts ordered so that the financial statements can be easily prepared. Assume that all accounts have normal balances (i.e., cash has a debit balance, and so on).

E3-28. TRIAL BALANCE PREPARATION   As of December 31, 19X9, the following accounts and account balances are available for Anderson Electronic Services:

Accounts payable	$ 10,900
Accounts receivable	19,200
Accumulated depreciation, building	30,000
Accumulated depreciation, testing equipment	256,000
Advertising expense	61,000
Building	170,000
Capital stock	140,000
Cash	1,200
Depreciation expense, building	15,000
Depreciation expense, testing equipment	92,000
Income taxes expense	13,500
Interest expense	12,000
Interest payable	4,000
Land	58,000
Long-term notes payable	120,000
Office expense	2,900
Office supplies inventory	12,700
Retained earnings, 12/31/X8	59,800
Service revenue	723,800
Testing equipment	420,000
Wages expense	467,000

REQUIRED:

Prepare a trial balance with the accounts ordered for easy preparation of financial statements. Assume that all accounts have normal balances.

E3-29. FINANCIAL STATEMENT PREPARATION   Using the trial balance you prepared for Exercise 3-27, prepare the 19X4 financial statements for Badger Auto Parts.

E3-30. FINANCIAL STATEMENT PREPARATION   Using the trial balance you prepared for Exercise 3-28, prepare the 19X9 financial statements for Anderson Electronic Services.

PROBLEMS

P3-31. EVENTS AND TRANSACTIONS   The following list contains events that occurred during January 19X1 and were of interest to Malcom Motors:

a) California Central University signed a contract to purchase a fleet of passenger cars from Malcom Motors at a total price of $200,000, payable to Malcom in two equal amounts — one on August 1, 19X1, and one on September 1, 19X1. The cars will be delivered to CCU during August 19X1.

b) The principal stockholder in Malcom Motors sold 10 percent of her stock in the company to John Lewis, the president of Malcom Motors, in exchange for $100,000 in cash.

c) Malcom Motors issued new stock to John Lewis in exchange for $50,000 in cash.

d) Malcom Motors owns the building it occupies; the company occupied the building during the entire month of January.

e) Malcom Motors owns land used for the storage of cars awaiting sale; the land was used by the company during the entire month of January.

f) Malcom Motors paid its lawyer $1,000 for services rendered in connection with the purchase agreement signed with California Central University.

g) Maintenance Management Company performed cleaning services for Malcom Motors during January under a contract that does not require payment for those services until March 1, 19X1.

REQUIRED:

1. Prepare a numbered list, using the words "qualified" and "not qualified," to indicate whether each event qualifies as a transaction and, therefore, is recognized and recorded in Malcom Motors' accounting system during January 19X1.

2. For each event that fails to qualify as a transaction, write a sentence in the list prepared in requirement 1 stating why it fails to qualify.

P3-32. EFFECTS OF TRANSACTIONS ON THE BALANCE SHEET EQUATION   Wiley Chemicals engaged in the following transactions:

a) Prepaid rent on office furniture for six months, $9,000.

b) Borrowed $25,000 on a nine-month, 12 percent note.

c) Provided services on credit, $35,000.

d) Purchased supplies on credit, $12,000.

e) Collected accounts receivable, $29,000.

f) Sold capital stock, $40,000.

g) Paid employee wages, $8,000.

h) Paid accounts payable, $10,000.

i) Provided services for cash, $11,000.

j) Paid utility bills, $2,000.

REQUIRED:

Analyze these transactions and determine their collective effect on assets, liabilities, and stockholders' equity. Use a format similar to the following:

ACCOUNT	ASSETS	=	LIABILITIES	+	EQUITY
a) Prepaid furniture rent	+9,000				
Cash	−9,000				

P3-33. THE DOUBLE-ENTRY ACCOUNTING SYSTEM   Monroe Company rents electronic equipment. Monroe engaged in the transactions described below:

a) Purchased a truck for cash.

b) Purchased electronic equipment on credit.

c) Purchased office supplies on credit.

d) Rented sound equipment and a crew to a traveling stage play. Monroe pays its crew on an hourly basis. The producer of the play paid for the service at the time it was provided.

e) Rented sound equipment and lights to a local student organization for a dance. The student organization will pay for services in 30 days.

f) Paid employee wages that have been earned and recorded as payable.

g) Collected the receivable from transaction **e**.

h) Borrowed cash from a bank on a three-year note payable.

i) Sold capital stock to new stockholders.

j) Paid cash dividends to stockholders.

REQUIRED:

Use a table like the one below to identify the accounts involved in the above transactions and the effect of these transactions on the fundamental accounting equation. Transaction **a** has been used to demonstrate the table entries.

ACCOUNT	ASSETS	=	LIABILITIES	+	EQUITY
a) Truck	+				
Cash	−				

P3-34. THE DEBIT AND CREDIT RULES   A list of accounts for Montgomery, Inc., appears below:

Accounts payable	Equipment	Prepaid rent
Accounts receivable	Income taxes expense	Retained earnings
Accumulated depreciation	Interest expense	Service revenue
Capital stock	Land	Supplies inventory
Cash	Long-term notes payable	Wages expense
Depreciation expense		

REQUIRED:

Complete a table like the one below for these accounts. The information for the first account has been entered as an example.

ACCOUNT	TYPE OF ACCOUNT	NORMAL BALANCE	INCREASE	DECREASE
Accounts payable	Liability	Credit	Credit	Debit

P3-35. TRANSACTION ANALYSIS, INCLUDING CARRYING VALUE CHANGES   Leonard Company rents, sells, and services motorcycles. During a recent month, the following information was provided to Leonard's accountant:

a) On August 1, Whittinghill Cycle Builders called and invited Leonard's president to Whittinghill's factory in January to view a new line of cycles for next year's selling season. Whittinghill will pay half the cost of the president's trip. The president has accepted the invitation.

b) Leonard received a purchase order from Speedy's Thrill Show for $1,400 for engine overhaul work on Speedy's motorcycles. Leonard will begin the overhaul later in the month.

c) Early in the month, Leonard reached an agreement with MBW Company to carry MBW cycles during the next season. The agreement permits Leonard to order 25 cycles at a cost of $800 each and to return to MBW, at no cost to Leonard, the unsold cycles at the end of the selling season. Cycles sold are to be paid for within 30 days of sale. Leonard plans to order all 25 cycles within three months.

d) John Ibsid returned a cycle rented from Leonard two weeks earlier. The cycle has $500 worth of damage, for which Ibsid refuses to pay. Leonard is considering legal action against Ibsid.

e) Five of Leonard's rental cycles were damaged when a roof collapsed during a severe thunderstorm. The cost of repairing the cycles is expected to total $1,900. Leonard does not have insurance for damage of this kind. The cycles will be repaired early next month.

REQUIRED:

Indicate whether or not each item should produce an entry in Leonard's journal. For those items that are to be recorded, prepare the journal entry.

P3-36. ANALYSIS, JOURNAL ENTRIES, AND POSTING   Cincinnati Painting Service, Inc., specializes in painting houses. During the month of June, Cincinnati Painting engaged in the following transactions:

a) Purchased painting supplies from River City Supply for $750 on credit.

b) Purchased a used van from Hamilton Used Car Sales for $6,500, paying $2,000 down and agreeing to pay the balance in six months.

c) Paid $3,200 to hourly employees.

d) Billed various customers a total of $8,700 for completed painting jobs.

e) Received $3,100 cash from James Eaton for a housepainting job completed and billed last month.

f) Collected $300 cash from Albert Montgomery on completion of a one-day painting job. This amount is not included in the bills mentioned in **d** above.

REQUIRED:

Analyze and journalize these transactions and post the journal entries to Cincinnati Painting's ledger accounts.

P3-37. TRANSACTION ANALYSIS   Frederick Company rents construction equipment. During April the following transactions occurred:

a) On April 1, a letter from Northwest Manufacturing arrived. The letter invited Frederick to purchase a new model of front loader for $35,000. This amount is $15,000 less than the regular price for the loader. Frederick's purchasing agent has decided to purchase the front loader.

b) Frederick received a written rental order from Scales Builders for a scaffold on April 6. The scaffold will be rented for May and June at $650 per month. Scales will pick the scaffold up on May 1 and will pay for the rental on June 30 when the scaffold is returned.

c) Frederick reached an agreement on April 10 with CEC, Inc., to carry a line of air hammers that is sold by CEC. Frederick has agreed to order 10 air hammers in July. CEC will permit Frederick to pay for the air hammers in December.

d) On April 15, Frederick received $3,600 from a customer for the use on that day of a bulldozer. The bulldozer was returned at the end of the day.

e) On April 20, a crane was returned that had been rented 10 days earlier. Ten days' rent on the crane is $4,000, and this amount is billed to the customer on April 20.

REQUIRED:

Indicate whether or not each transaction should be recorded in Frederick's journal in April. For those items that are to be recorded, indicate when the entry should be made. Justify your decisions.

P3-38. ANALYSIS, JOURNAL ENTRIES, AND POSTING   Findlay Testing, Inc., provides water testing and maintenance services for owners of hot tubs and swimming pools. During September the following transactions occurred:

a) Purchased chemicals for $2,750 cash.

b) Paid office rent for September, October, and November. The rent is $1,600 per month.

c) Paid $710 cash for office supplies purchased on credit in August.

d) Billed the city of Bellefontaine $4,200 for testing the water in the city's outdoor pools during the
summer swimming season that ended in early September. No previous recognition of this service
had been entered in Findlay's records.

e) Received $600 from Simon Kenton in response to a bill sent in August for testing his hot tub
water.

f) Received $300 from Alexander Blanchard upon completion of overhaul of his swimming pool
water circulation system. Since the job was completed and collected for on the same day, no bill is
sent to Blanchard.

g) Recorded and paid September salaries of $6,720.

REQUIRED:

Analyze and journalize these transactions and then post the journal entries to ledger accounts.

P3-39. ANALYSIS, JOURNAL ENTRIES, POSTING, AND TRIAL BALANCE   Karleen's Catering Service provides catered
meals to individuals and businesses. Karleen's purchases its food ready to serve from Mel's Restaurant. So that a realistic trial balance can be prepared, the events described below are aggregations of
many individual events.

a) During the year, Karleen's paid office rent of $11,500.

b) Telephone expenses incurred and paid were $950.

c) Wages of $67,400 were earned by employees and paid during the year.

d) During the year, Karleen's provided catering services:

On credit.	$142,100
For cash	21,700

e) Karleen's paid $62,100 for food and beverage supplies purchased.

f) Karleen's paid dividends in the amount of $4,000.

g) Karleen's collected accounts receivable in the amount of $134,200.

REQUIRED:

Analyze these 19X7 events, prepare journal entries, post the journal entries to ledger accounts, and
prepare a trial balance in proper order. Assume that all beginning account balances at January 1,
19X7, are zero.

P3-40. ANALYSIS, JOURNAL ENTRIES, POSTING, AND TRIAL BALANCE   Sweetwater Temporary Clerical Help
Service opened for business in June 19X5. From the opening until the end of the year, Sweetwater
engaged in the activities described below.

a) Sold 10,000 shares of capital stock for $3.50 per share.

b) Purchased office equipment for $14,200 cash.

c) Received $121,800 from clients for services provided.

d) Paid wages of $84,900.

e) Borrowed $15,000 from the Second Southern Bank on a three-year note payable.

f) Paid office rent of $17,500.

g) Purchased office supplies on credit for $1,300.

h) Paid $1,000 toward the payable established in transaction **g**.

i) Paid telephone charges incurred during the year of $910.

REQUIRED:

Analyze and journalize these transactions, post the journal entries to ledger accounts, and then prepare a trial balance in proper order.

P3-41. RECORDING DATA AND PREPARING STATEMENTS   Western Sound Studios records and masters audiotapes of popular artists in live concerts. The performers use the tapes to prepare "live" albums, cassettes, and compact disks. The following account balances were available at the beginning of 19X2:

Accounts payable	$ 11,900
Accounts receivable	384,000
Capital stock	165,000
Cash	16,300
Interest payable	11,200
Long-term notes payable	100,000
Rent payable, building	4,000
Rent payable, recording equipment	7,000
Retained earnings, 12/31/X1	101,200

During 19X2 the following transactions occurred:

a) Taping services in the amount of $994,000 were billed.

b) The accounts receivable at the beginning of the year were collected. In addition, cash for $983,000 of the services billed in transaction **a** was collected.

c) The rent payable for the building was paid. In addition, $48,000 of building rental costs was paid in cash. There was no rent payable or prepaid at year-end.

d) The equipment rent payable on January 1 was paid. In addition, $84,000 of equipment rental costs was paid in cash. There was no rent payable or prepaid at year-end.

e) Utilities expense of $56,000 was incurred and paid in 19X2.

f) Wages expense for the year was $287,000. All $287,000 was paid in 19X2.

g) Salaries expense of $415,000 was incurred and paid during the year.

h) The interest payable at January 1 was paid. During the year, an additional $11,000 of interest was paid. At year-end no interest was payable.

i) Income taxes for 19X2 in the amount of $19,700 were incurred and paid.

REQUIRED:

1. Establish a ledger for the accounts listed above and enter the beginning balances. Use a chart of accounts to order the ledger accounts.

2. Analyze each transaction. Journalize as appropriate. Post your journal entries to the ledger accounts. Add additional ledger accounts when needed.

3. Use the ending balances in the ledger accounts to prepare a trial balance in financial statement order.

4. Use the trial balance to prepare an income statement, a statement of changes in retained earnings, and a balance sheet.

P3-42. RECORDING DATA AND PREPARING STATEMENTS Mulberry Services sells electronic data processing services to firms too small to own their own computing equipment. Mulberry had the following accounts and account balances as of January 1, 19X8:

Accounts payable	$ 14,000
Accounts receivable	130,000
Capital stock	114,000
Cash	6,000
Interest payable	8,000
Long-term notes payable	80,000
Prepaid rent, computing equipment (short-term)	96,000
Retained earnings, 12/31/X7	16,000

During 19X8 the following transactions occurred:

a) During 19X8 Mulberry sold $690,000 of computing services, all on credit.

b) Mulberry collected $570,000 from the credit sales in transaction **a** and an additional $129,000 from the accounts receivable outstanding at the beginning of the year.

c) Mulberry paid the interest payable of $8,000.

d) Wages of $379,000 were paid in cash.

e) Administrative expenses of $90,000 were incurred and paid in 19X8.

f) The prepaid rent at the beginning of the year was used in 19X8. In addition, $28,000 of computer rental costs were incurred and paid. There is no prepaid rent or rent payable at year-end.

g) Mulberry purchased computer paper for $13,000 cash in late December. None of the paper was used by year-end.

h) Advertising expense of $26,000 was incurred and paid in 19X8.

i) Income tax of $10,300 was incurred in 19X8, all of which was paid in 19X8.

j) During 19X8 $10,000 of interest was paid on the long-term loan.

REQUIRED:

1. Prepare T-accounts and enter the January 1, 19X8, account balances.

2. Analyze and journalize the 19X8 transactions. Post the transactions to the T-accounts, adding any additional T-accounts you feel are necessary.

3. Prepare a trial balance.

4. From the trial balance, prepare an income statement and a statement of changes in retained earnings for 19X8 and a balance sheet as of December 31, 19X8.

P3-43. RECORDING TRANSACTIONS AND PREPARING STATEMENTS Complete Video rents videocassettes. At the beginning of the year, Complete's ledger included the following accounts and balances:

Accounts payable	$ 1,700
Capital stock	30,000
Cash	4,000
Long-term notes payable	15,000
Notes payable (short-term)	8,000
Office supplies inventory	1,600
Retained earnings, 12/31/X1	8,400
Equipment, videocassettes	57,500

During 19X2 Complete engaged in the following transactions:

a) Collected $264,100 cash from videocassette rentals.

b) Purchased new videocassettes on credit in the amount of $27,000.

c) Purchased office supplies on credit for $3,100.

d) Paid office rent in the amount of $71,400.

e) Paid employee wages in the amount of $134,700.

f) Used office supplies in the amount of $3,300.

g) Paid accounts payable in the amount of $31,000.

h) Paid short-term note payable plus interest of $500.

i) Paid interest of $1,200 on the long-term notes payable.

j) Incurred and paid income taxes of $8,000.

REQUIRED:

1. Establish a ledger for the accounts listed above and enter the beginning balances. Use a chart of accounts to order the ledger accounts.

2. Analyze each transaction. Journalize as appropriate. Post your journal entries to the ledger accounts. Add additional ledger accounts when needed.

3. Use the ending balances in the ledger accounts to prepare a trial balance in financial statement order.

4. Use the trial balance to prepare an income statement, a statement of changes in retained earnings, and a balance sheet.

P3-44. RECORDING TRANSACTIONS AND PREPARING STATEMENTS Highland Real Estate began business in January 19X4. The following transactions occurred in 19X4:

a) Mason Cleves purchased 800 shares of Highland's capital stock for $40,000 cash.

b) Highland borrowed $15,000 from Newton National Bank under a five-year note.

c) At the beginning of each month, Highland paid office rent of $1,000. (Consider the total $12,000 rent for the year as a single transaction.)

d) During the year, Highland's sales staff sold various properties with a total selling price of $4,500,000. As a result, Highland received in cash a commission of 6 percent of the selling price on all property sold.

e) As compensation for arranging sales during the year, Highland paid its sales staff a total of $150,000 cash.

f) Highland incurred and paid utilities expense of $2,800 during 19X4.

g) Highland incurred and paid advertising expense of $12,600 during 19X4.

h) Highland incurred and paid salaries of $15,000 during 19X4.

i) Highland incurred and paid income taxes of $11,600 during 19X4.

j) Highland declared and paid a $25,000 cash dividend to Mason Cleves, its only stockholder.

REQUIRED:

Analyze and journalize these transactions and post the journal entries to Highland's ledger accounts. Since the business began in January 19X4, the beginning balance for all accounts is zero. Prepare a trial balance in financial statement order. Use the trial balance to prepare an income statement, a statement of changes in retained earnings, and a balance sheet.

ANALYTICAL OPPORTUNITIES

A3-45. RECOGNITION OF SERVICE CONTRACT REVENUES Jackson Dunlap is president of New Miami Maintenance, Inc., which provides building maintenance services. On October 15, 19X6, Mr. Dunlap signed a service contract with Western College. Under the contract, New Miami will provide maintenance services for all Western's buildings for a period of two years, beginning on January 1, 19X7, and Western will pay New Miami on a monthly basis, beginning on January 31, 19X7. Although the same amount of maintenance services will be rendered in every month, the contract provides for higher monthly payments in the first year.

Initially, Mr. Dunlap proposed that some portion of the revenue from the contract should be recognized in 19X6; however, his accountant, Rita McGonigle, convinced him that this would be inappropriate. Then Mr. Dunlap proposed that the revenue should be recognized in an amount equal to the cash collected under the contract in 19X6. Again, Ms. McGonigle argued against his proposal, saying that generally accepted accounting principles required recognition of an equal amount of contract revenue each month.

REQUIRED:

1. Give a reason that might explain Mr. Dunlap's desire to recognize contract revenue earlier rather than later.

2. Put yourself in the position of Rita McGonigle. How would you convince Mr. Dunlap that his two proposals are unacceptable and that an equal amount of revenue should be recognized every month?

3. If Ms. McGonigle's proposal is adopted, how would the contract be reflected in the balance sheets at the end of 19X6 and at the end of 19X7?

A3-46. ANALYSIS OF THE OPERATION OF THE ACCOUNTING CYCLE Susan Eel wants to sell you her wholesale fish store and business. She shows you a balance sheet with total assets of $150,000 and total liabilities of $20,000. According to the income statement, last year's net income was $40,000.

When examining the accounting records, you notice that several accounts receivable in the $10,000 to $15,000 range are not supported by source documents. You also notice that there is no source documentation to support the $30,000 balance in the building account and the $10,000 balance in the equipment account. Susan tells you that she gave the building and refrigeration equipment to the business in exchange for stock. She also says that she has not had time to set up and monitor any paperwork for accounts receivable or accounts payable.

REQUIRED:

1. What requirements for transaction recognition appear to have been ignored when the accounts receivable, building, and equipment were recorded?

2. What would be the effect on the financial statements if the values appearing in the balance sheet for accounts receivable, building, and equipment were overstated? What would be the effect if the accounts payable were understated?

3. Assuming that you would like to purchase the business, what would you do to establish a reasonable purchase price?

A3-47. ANALYSIS OF THE EFFECTS OF USAGE ON ASSETS Refer to Problem 3-43, which presents information about Complete Video, a business that rents videocassettes. Note that Complete Video's balance sheet includes an asset representing its library of videocassettes.

REQUIRED:

1. How would you recommend that Complete Video account for wear and tear on its library of cassettes?

2. How would you recommend that Complete Video account for the fact that a typical cassette is rented frequently when it is first stocked but less and less frequently as it ages?

A3-48. ACCOUNTING FOR PARTIALLY COMPLETED EVENTS: A PRELUDE TO CHAPTER 4   Ehrlich Smith, the owner of The Shoe Box, has asked you to help him understand the proper way to account for certain accounting items as he prepares his 19X9 financial statements. Smith has provided the following information and observations:

a) A three-year fire insurance policy was purchased on May 1, 19X9, for $1,800. Smith believes that a part of the cost of the insurance policy should be allocated to each period that benefits from its coverage.

b) The store building was purchased for $60,000 in January 19X1. Smith expected then (as he does now) that the building will be serviceable as a shoe store for 20 years from the date of purchase. In 19X1 Smith estimated that he could sell the property for $6,000 at the end of its serviceable life. He feels that each period should bear some portion of the cost of this long-lived asset that is slowly being consumed.

c) The Shoe Box borrowed $20,000 on a one-year, 11 percent note that is due on September 1 next year. Smith notes that $22,200 cash will be required to repay the note at maturity. The $2,200 difference is, he feels, a cost for using the loaned funds and should be spread over the periods that benefit from the use of the loan funds.

REQUIRED:

1. Explain what Smith is trying to accomplish with the three preceding items. Are his objectives supported by the concepts that underlie accounting?

2. Describe how each of the three items should be reflected in the 19X9 income statement and the December 31, 19X9, balance sheet to accomplish Smith's objectives.

LEARNING
OBJECTIVES

Careful study of this
chapter will enable you
to:

1. Distinguish between
   discrete and contin-
   uous transactions.
2. Explain the pur-
   pose of adjusting
   entries.
3. Make adjustments
   for revenue earned
   before collection,
   expenses incurred
   before payment,
   revenue earned
   after collection, and
   expenses incurred
   after payment.
4. Compute amounts
   for depreciation
   and interest adjust-
   ments.
5. Describe the ef-
   fects of adjusting
   entries on the fi-
   nancial statements.

Appendix 4–1
6. Prepare adjust-
   ments for prepay-
   ments that were
   recorded in reve-
   nue and expense
   accounts.

4 ADJUSTING ENTRIES

The accounting cycle is a step-by-step procedure for processing information about an entity's transactions in order to produce its financial statements. In Chapter 3, we presented the steps of the cycle that enter the effects of transactions into the accounts. We then explained how the financial statements are prepared from the end-of-period account balances. The illustrations we used in Chapter 3 were not completely realistic, however, because they excluded transactions that are recorded by adjusting entries.

We begin this chapter by reviewing the accounting concepts that form the basis for adjusting entries. We next examine the actual preparation of adjusting entries. We describe a simple, but generally applicable, procedure for developing the data necessary for adjusting entries. Then we expand this procedure to cover two of the more involved adjustments: depreciation and interest. An analysis of the effects of adjusting entries on the financial statements completes the main part of the chapter. The chapter ends with an extended review problem showing the application of adjusting entries in a realistic situation that involves simple adjustments as well as the more involved computations for depreciation and interest. Throughout the discussion of adjusting entries in the chapter, we assume that prepayments are recorded in asset accounts and collections in advance are recorded in liability accounts. In Appendix 4–1, we discuss adjusting entries for situations in which prepayments and advance collections are recorded in expense and revenue accounts.

THE CONCEPTUAL BASIS FOR ADJUSTING ENTRIES

**DISCRETE TRANSAC-
TION:** A transaction that
occurs at a particular point
in time.

To understand adjusting entries, you must first recognize the distinction between discrete and continuous transactions. All transactions are either discrete or continuous. A **discrete transaction** is one that occurs at a particular point in time, such as the payment of cash or the delivery of goods. Discrete transactions are recorded in the accounts as they occur. Sometimes a separate journal entry is made for each individual transaction. As noted in Chapter 3, when discrete transactions of a given type occur frequently, it is often more efficient to record them with a single *summary entry* (say, daily, weekly, or monthly). For example, a firm that sells goods to five customers on a given day could use five separate journal entries to record the individual cash sales. Alternatively, the five sales could all be summarized and recorded at the end of the day in a single entry.

CONTINUOUS TRANSAC-TION: A transaction that is ongoing throughout a period of time.

A **continuous transaction** is a transaction that is ongoing throughout a period of time, like the use of operating assets, the use of rented facilities, or the accrual of interest.[1] The use of an operating asset is a continuous transaction that extends over the entire useful life of the asset. The use of borrowed money is a continuous transaction that extends over the entire life of a loan. Since journal entries are made at particular points in time rather than continuously, continuous transactions must be recorded periodically, often before the transactions are completed. For example, the interest expense that arises from the use of borrowed money during a particular accounting period is recorded at the end of that period. Recording continuous transactions requires a special class of journal entry called an *adjusting journal entry* or, simply, **adjusting entry.**

ADJUSTING ENTRY: A journal entry made at the end of an accounting period to record the completed portion of an incomplete continuous event.

Under accrual-basis accounting, we cannot wait until continuous transactions are completed before recording the related revenues and expenses. Nor can we record these transactions as though they had been completed in the current year if they won't in fact be completed until the next year or later. Instead, we must record revenue and expense amounts at year-end that appropriately reflect only those portions of the continuous transactions that were actually completed during the current year. Thus revenues must be adjusted at year-end to include only those amounts that reflect the completed portions of continuous revenue transactions. Similarly, expenses must be adjusted at year-end to include only those amounts that represent completed portions of continuous expense-producing activities. These changes to the revenue and expense accounts are accomplished by adjusting entries.

Every transaction can be identified as either discrete or continuous. In the analysis that follows, four transactions are classified as either discrete or continuous, and the implications of their classifications for data recording and for adjusting entries are discussed.

ANALYSIS
DISCRETE AND CONTINUOUS TRANSACTIONS IN THE DESIGN OF AN ACCOUNTING SYSTEM

Cromwell Cleaning, Inc., is a newly formed seller of cleaning supplies, equipment, and services. Jason Cromwell, the founder and principal stockholder in Cromwell Cleaning, has engaged an accountant to design an accounting system for the business. The accountant's report answered the following questions:

1. *How should Cromwell account for over-the-counter sales of supplies and equipment for cash?*

Over-the-counter sales of supplies and equipment for cash, which are discrete transactions, will be recorded as they occur at a cash register that determines total sales for each day. Daily cash register sales will be summarized on a monthly basis and recorded in the accounts at the end of each month. Since over-the-counter sales are discrete transactions, they are recorded by regular (summary) journal entries and do not require adjusting entries.

2. *How should Cromwell account for sales of supplies and equipment on credit?*

Sales of supplies and equipment on credit, which are also discrete transactions, will be recorded in a computer file when orders are received. When orders are shipped to

---

[1] The distinction between discrete and continuous transactions depends to some extent on our ability and willingness to keep track of discrete transactions. Discrete transactions may be so frequent or so difficult to measure individually that no record of individual transactions is maintained. In such cases, the sequence of discrete transactions becomes, for all intents and purposes, a continuous transaction. For example, the use of office supplies is often treated as a continuous transaction because it is too costly to maintain a record of the discrete uses of the supplies.

customers, the date of shipment and the total price of the order will be recorded in the computer file, a bill will be sent to the customer, and the sale will be recorded by entries to revenue and accounts receivable. Since the number of sales on credit is relatively small, this procedure will not result in an unduly large number of journal entries. If the number of credit sales grows as the business matures, consideration should be given to summarizing credit sale transactions and recording them on a weekly or daily basis. Credit sales, like over-the-counter sales, are discrete transactions that do not require adjusting entries; unlike over-the-counter sales, however, each credit sale is recorded by its own journal entry.

3. *How should Cromwell account for cleaning services provided?*

In contrast to both over-the-counter and credit sales of supplies and equipment, which are discrete transactions, provision of cleaning services is a continuous transaction defined by service contracts that may take months or even years to complete. At year-end, a portion of the revenue associated with incomplete service contracts should be recorded by an adjusting entry. Revenue should be recognized in proportion to the cleaning services performed.

4. *How should Cromwell account for the use of cleaning supplies?*

Use of supplies by the business, like sales of supplies and equipment, can be viewed as a sequence of discrete transactions. However, the preparation of documents required to keep track of these discrete transactions would be too costly. Instead, the use of supplies will be treated as a continuous transaction and recorded by an adjusting entry at year-end.

Let us use Cromwell Cleaning, Inc., to illustrate adjusting entries. Cromwell cleans the offices of the River City National Bank, billing the bank $6,000 on the 15th of each month for the completion of one month's cleaning services. Cromwell's fiscal year ends on December 31, which means that on December 31, 19X1, Cromwell has earned $3,000, half the $6,000 of cleaning service revenue that will be billed on January 15, 19X2. The revenue recognition concept provides that the revenue earned between December 16, 19X1, and January 15, 19X2, be split between the 19X1 and 19X2 accounting periods (years), so that $3,000 is recognized in each year. This split is accomplished by an adjusting entry. Another adjusting entry is required because Cromwell pays the supervisor of its cleaning crew on the 20th of each month. The supervisor will be paid $1,200 on January 20, 19X2, for the period December 21, 19X1, through January 20, 19X2. Since Cromwell's fiscal year ends on December 31, $400 (one-third of the month's wages) pertains to 19X1 and $800 (two-thirds of the month's wages) pertains to 19X2. In order to match expenses with the revenues earned in each year (the matching concept), $400 must be recognized as expense in 19X1 and $800 must be recognized as expense in 19X2. This split of wages is accomplished by a second adjusting entry.

FOUR CLASSES OF ADJUSTING ENTRIES

As suggested by the preceding example, every adjusting entry changes the balance of either a revenue account or an expense account and the balance of either an asset account or a liability account. In fact, some accountants say that the overall purpose of adjusting entries is to ensure that revenue, expense, asset, and liability account balances are properly stated at year-end.

Remember that accrual-basis accounting recognizes revenue when earned, regardless of when the related cash is received, and recognizes expenses when the related resources are sold or used in operations, not when cash is actually paid. This recognition process follows the revenue recognition, matching, and periodicity concepts discussed in the preceding chapters.

Adjusting entries related to revenues can be subdivided into two categories, according to whether the revenue is recognized before or after the related collection of cash. Adjusting entries that change expense account balances can also be subdivided into two categories, according to whether the expense is recognized before or after the related cash payment. In other words, every adjusting entry falls into one of these four categories:

1. Revenue recognized before collection

2. Expense recognized before payment

3. Revenue recognized after collection

4. Expense recognized after payment

ACCRUAL: An entry that recognizes revenue or expense and records the related noncash asset or liability.

Adjusting entries that fall into categories 1 and 2, in which revenue or expense is recognized *before* the related cash receipt or payment, are called accruals. An **accrual** is an entry that recognizes revenue or expense and records the related noncash asset or liability. Both of the adjusting entries in the Cromwell Cleaning example are accruals. The first adjusting entry recognizes the revenues for the last half of December 19X1, which will not be collected until 19X2. The entry increases revenue by $3,000 and increases accounts receivable (a noncash asset) by $3,000. The second adjusting entry recognizes the wages expense for Cromwell's supervisor during the last third of December 19X1, an expense that will not be paid until 19X2. The entry increases expense by $400 and increases wages payable (a liability) by $400.

DEFERRAL: An entry that records an asset or liability before the related expense or revenue is recognized. Deferrals frequently lead to subsequent adjusting entries.

On the other hand, if cash is received or paid before the related revenue or expense is recognized, the transaction is recorded as an increase to an asset or liability account. This kind of entry is called a deferral. A **deferral** is an entry that records an asset or liability before the related expense or revenue is recognized. Thus, the receipt or payment of cash is recorded as a liability or asset, but recognition of the revenue or expense is *deferred.* Subsequently, when the revenue is earned or the expense-related resources are sold or used in operations, an adjusting entry is required to update the account that received the deferral. Entries that update deferrals are the adjusting entries that fall into categories 3 and 4 of the list above. For example, insurance coverage is usually paid for in advance and recorded in an asset account called *prepaid insurance* (a deferred expense). At year-end, when all or part of the prepaid insurance has expired, an adjusting entry must be made to increase insurance expense and decrease prepaid insurance for the amount of the coverage expired during the period.

REVENUE RECOGNIZED BEFORE COLLECTION

Revenues arising from the performance of services, a continuous transaction, frequently require adjusting entries. The performance of revenue-producing services often extends over several days, weeks, or even months. The typical accounting system records service revenues during the year as service commitments are completed. Consequently, revenues associated with service commitments that are only partially completed at year-end represent unrecorded revenues. An adjusting entry (an accrual) is required to recognize these revenues and also to recognize the associated increase in the firm's assets (accounts receivable). Not every revenue earned prior to the related cash collection requires an adjusting entry. For example, revenues generated by the sale of goods are usually associated with discrete transactions (such as the delivery of goods to customers). Although such revenues may be recorded by summary journal entries on a daily, weekly, or even monthly basis, they are fully recorded by the end of the accounting period and thus do not require adjusting entries. An adjusting entry is necessary only if a continuous transaction has not been completed and revenue has not been recorded by the end of the accounting period.[2]

Common unrecorded revenues and their associated assets are:

REVENUE (INCOME STATEMENT ACCOUNT)	ASSOCIATED ASSET (BALANCE SHEET ACCOUNT)
Service revenue	Accounts receivable
Interest revenue	Interest receivable
Rent revenue	Rent receivable

EXPENSE RECOGNIZED BEFORE PAYMENT

Expenses arising from the use of services or performance of certain activities are continuous transactions and frequently require adjusting-entry accruals. Using rented assets (when rent is paid at the end of the rental period), using employees' services (when employees are paid after work is performed), borrowing money, and issuing product warranties are all examples of continuous transactions that frequently require such adjusting entries. A typical accounting system will not record a continuous transaction until it is complete. Consequently, expenses associated with partially completed transactions at year-end represent unrecorded expenses that must be accrued. An adjusting entry is required to recognize these expenses and also to recognize the associated liability. However, not every expense recognized prior to the related cash outflow requires an adjusting entry. An adjusting entry is necessary only if the transaction has not been completed and the related expense has not been recorded by the end of the accounting period. Common unrecorded expenses and their associated liabilities are:

EXPENSE (INCOME STATEMENT ACCOUNT)	ASSOCIATED LIABILITY (BALANCE SHEET ACCOUNT)
Rent expense	Rent payable
Wages expense	Wages payable
Interest expense	Interest payable
Warranty expense	Estimated warranty liability

---

[2] An important exception to the practice of recognizing a portion of the revenue from partially completed service commitments exists for services that end with a final act prior to which the commitment cannot be viewed as complete. In such cases, recognition of all related revenue must await the performance of the final act, and no adjusting entry is appropriate for the partially completed commitment. For example, a consulting firm responsible for the installation of a new computer system should probably wait to recognize any part of the related revenue until the system has been tested and "debugged." Additional discussion of this issue is presented in Supplementary Topic E.

REVENUE RECOGNIZED AFTER COLLECTION

Earlier we discussed adjustments for unrecorded revenue associated with partially completed transactions for which cash had not yet been received. Alternatively, a firm may collect payment for the sale of goods or services *before* it delivers those goods or services. When collected, these advances are frequently recorded (by a deferral) as a liability called *unearned revenue.* If, by the end of the accounting period, some portion of the revenue associated with the advance collection has been earned, an adjusting entry is required. This adjusting entry records as a revenue the portion of the advance that has been earned and leaves the remaining portion recorded (deferred) as an unearned revenue (a liability). Adjusting entries arising from advance collections of revenue alter the following pairs of accounts:

REVENUE (INCOME STATEMENT ACCOUNT)	ASSOCIATED LIABILITY (BALANCE SHEET ACCOUNT)
Rent revenue	Unearned rent revenue
Service revenue	Unearned service revenue

EXPENSE RECOGNIZED AFTER PAYMENT

We turn now to adjusting entries for expenses paid in advance of being recognized. When made, these *prepayments* are often recorded (by a deferral) as assets. If, by the end of the accounting period, some portion of the expense associated with the prepayment should be recognized, an adjusting entry is required. The adjusting entry records that portion of the prepayment as an expense and leaves the remainder (deferred) in the asset account. This is the most common type of adjusting entry. Resources that will eventually become expenses are often acquired (and recorded as assets) before they are needed. When an accounting period ends, the cost of the previously recorded items that have been used in operations or transferred to customers must be recorded as expenses. However, the portion still unused or on hand remains in the asset accounts (as deferred expenses). For example, depreciation expense associated with a delivery truck used in the selling function of the firm is recorded in this way. Use of the truck during its expected life represents a continuous transaction, part of which occurs in each of the accounting periods spanned by the truck's life. In a parallel way, part of the truck's cost is recorded as expense in each of those accounting periods by an adjusting entry that increases depreciation expense and reduces the carrying amount of the truck (by increasing accumulated depreciation). Similar examples of prepaid expenses are insurance, rent, and office supplies. Although the use of supplies is actually a series of discrete transactions, usually no attempt is made to record these transactions individually. Instead, the use of supplies is treated as a transaction that occurs continuously over the year and thus requires an adjusting entry at the end of each year. The adjusting entries following from such prepayments alter the following pairs of accounts:

EXPENSE (INCOME STATEMENT ACCOUNT)	ASSOCIATED ASSET (BALANCE SHEET ACCOUNT)
Depreciation expense	Accumulated depreciation
Insurance expense	Prepaid insurance
Rent expense	Prepaid rent
Supplies expense	Supplies inventory

We turn next to a general procedure for making all four types of adjusting entries and to more complete illustrations of each category.

PREPARATION OF ADJUSTING ENTRIES

The purpose of all adjusting entries is to alter the preadjustment balances in some of the revenue, expense, asset, and liability accounts so that those accounts will properly reflect revenues, expenses, assets, and liabilities as of the period's end. As the revenue and expense balances are altered (adjusted), asset and liability balances will be changed correspondingly because, as we have already noted, every adjusting entry pairs an income statement account (a revenue or an expense) with a balance sheet account (an asset or a liability). For instance, depreciation expense is paired with accumulated depreciation, interest revenue with interest receivable, wage expense with wages payable, rent revenue with unearned rent revenue, and so on. (Note, however, that equity accounts are not altered directly by adjusting entries; nor are the balances in the cash and long-term liability accounts normally affected by adjusting entries.)

The preparation of adjusting entries follows a four-step procedure:

1. Identify the pairs of income statement and balance sheet accounts that require adjustment, by conducting an examination of source documents and preadjustment balances.

2. Determine the preadjustment balances of each pair of accounts requiring adjustment.

3. Calculate the amount of the adjustment.

   a) For *adjustments that record accruals* (revenue recognized before collection or expense recognized before payment): Calculate the amount of the adjustment (the amount of revenue or expense to be accrued) directly from the source documents.

   ADJUSTED BALANCE:
   The postadjustment balance to which an account is changed by an adjusting entry.

   b) For *adjustments that update deferrals* (revenue recognized after collection or expense recognized after payment): Calculate the amount of the postadjustment balance (the **adjusted balance**) in one or both of the accounts, by analyzing the source documents, and then calculate the adjustment as the difference between the adjusted balance and the preadjustment balance.

4. Record the adjusting entry in the income statement and balance sheet accounts, using the information developed in step 3.

Exhibit 4–1 shows the relationship between the preadjustment and adjusted balances for both income statement and balance sheet accounts. Notice that the amount of the adjustment to the income statement account must equal the amount of the adjustment to the balance sheet account.

You will find the systematic application of the four steps just described extremely useful in making adjusting entries and in understanding this complex accounting process. To illustrate the application of this four-step procedure to each of the four categories of adjusting entry, our example will be Miller Equipment Company, an enterprise that rents construction equipment to contractors on a daily or monthly basis. A firm of this type would be likely to require many adjusting entries at year-end.

EXHIBIT 4-1   PREADJUSTMENT AND ADJUSTED BALANCES

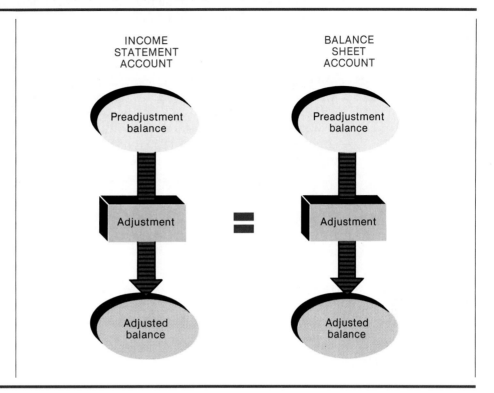

RECOGNIZING Miller Equipment Company has rented the following items to customers, but no
REVENUE BEFORE revenues have yet been recorded from these rentals:
COLLECTION

EQUIPMENT	DATE RENTED	RENT PER DAY
Air compressor	12/21	$50
Portable heater	12/26	35

Miller bills its customers 30 days after the equipment is rented or, for rental periods of less than 30 days, on return of the equipment. At December 31, the preadjustment balances in accounts receivable and rent revenue were $43,000 and $639,000, respectively.

Based on these data, the balance in both rent revenue and accounts receivable should be increased by $760 [(11 days)($50 per day) + (6 days)($35 per day)]. The general procedure for developing adjusting-entry data is often most easily followed when T-accounts are used to analyze the preadjustment and adjusted balances for the accounts being adjusted.

Accounts receivable			Rent revenue
43,000	Preadjustment balance		639,000
760	Adjusting entry		760
43,760	Adjusted balance		639,760

The following adjusting entry records this revenue earned in advance of collection:

Accounts receivable.....................................	760	
Rent revenue..		760

This adjusting entry, an accrual, increases accounts receivable by $760 and rent revenue by the same amount.

RECOGNIZING EXPENSE BEFORE PAYMENT

Miller Equipment Company pays its office staff every two weeks. December 31, Miller's fiscal year-end, is one week (halfway) into the two-week pay period. Therefore, at year-end one week's wages have been earned by the office staff without having been paid or recorded as an expense. The preadjustment balances in wages expense and wages payable are $33,000 and $0, respectively. Miller's accountant determines that $850 is owed the office staff for the one week's work that is unrecorded.

Wages expense			Wages payable
33,000		Preadjustment balance	–0–
850		Adjusting entry	850
33,850		Adjusted balance	850

The following adjusting entry records this expense incurred before payment:

Wages expense	850	
Wages payable.......................................		850

This entry, an accrual, increases the preadjustment balances in both wages expense and wages payable.

RECOGNIZING REVENUE COLLECTED IN ADVANCE

Miller rents 1,000 square feet of its warehouse to a contractor, Zimmerman Masonry, Inc., for equipment storage during the winter. The lease requires that Zimmerman pay half the four months' rent in advance. Thus, Zimmerman paid $2,000 (two months' rent) on November 15, and the entire amount of the $2,000 payment was credited to unearned revenue (a liability) on November 15. At December 31, when Miller's fiscal year ends, one and one-half months' rent ($1,500) has been earned. Thus, the rent revenue account should have an adjusted balance of $1,500. The preadjustment balances in the unearned revenue account and the rent revenue account are $2,000 and $0, respectively. The adjustment must increase rent revenue by $1,500 and decrease unearned revenue by the same amount.

Unearned revenue			Rent revenue
	2,000	Preadjustment balance	–0–
1,500		Adjusting entry	1,500
	500	Adjusted balance	1,500

The adjusting entry is as follows:

Unearned revenue	1,500	
Rent revenue.......................................		1,500

This adjustment removes dollars from a liability account and adds them to a revenue account, a typical procedure for a revenue collected in advance. The amount of the adjustment is the revenue earned between November 15 and December 31.[3] The adjustment updates the deferral of storage revenue collected in advance by recording the portion of the continuous revenue transaction that is complete at year-end.

RECOGNIZING EXPENSE PAID IN ADVANCE

At several times during the fiscal year, Miller purchased office supplies. The amount of each office supply purchase was debited to the office supplies inventory account when received. At the end of the fiscal year, the preadjustment balances in the office supplies inventory and office supplies expense accounts were $2,650 and $0, respectively. A count of the inventory after the close of business on December 31 indicated that $360 of office supplies remained unused. The adjusting entry must reduce office supplies inventory from $2,650 to $360. A credit to the office supplies inventory account of $2,290 [$2,650 − $360] will reduce the office supplies inventory account to its adjusted balance. The second half of this adjusting entry must be a debit of $2,290 to office supplies expense, which adjusts the office supplies expense account to its proper balance.

Office supplies inventory			Office supplies expense	
2,650		Preadjustment balance		−0−
	2,290	Adjusting entry	2,290	
360		Adjusted balance	2,290	

This adjusting entry, which is typical for an expense paid in advance, is as follows:

Office supplies expense 2,290
     Office supplies inventory. 2,290

The adjustment updates the deferral of supplies expense by recording the amount of supplies used during the year. (Although the use of supplies is technically a discrete transaction, the decision not to keep track of usage as it occurs makes the usage of supplies a continuous transaction that requires an adjusting entry.)[4]

[3] If the $2,000 had been credited to rent revenue on November 15, the adjusting entry would have decreased the revenue account and increased the liability account by $500, the amount still unearned at year-end. The appendix to this chapter discusses the adjusting entries for advance collections recorded in revenue accounts.

[4] If all purchases had been debited to the office supplies expense account, the adjusting entry would have decreased the expense account and increased the inventory account by $360, assuming a preadjustment inventory balance of zero. The appendix to this chapter discusses the adjusting entries for prepayments recorded as expenses.

PREPARATION OF ADJUSTING ENTRIES; SUMMARY

Using the four-step procedure for adjusting entries simplifies substantially the task of preparing adjusting entries, in part because this procedure works for any adjustment category. The procedure requires only that the accountant (1) determine what accounts require adjustment, (2) determine preadjustment balances in account pairs, (3) calculate the appropriate amount for the adjusting entry, and (4) record the adjusting entry. Knowledge of the four categories of adjusting entries helps accountants to perform efficiently and completely the first step in the four-step procedure: examining account balances to determine which account pairs require adjustment.

This section concludes our discussion of the conceptual basis for adjusting entries and the four-step procedure for determining the proper entries. We will now consider two other adjustments—depreciation and interest—that require more detailed analysis than those used to illustrate the adjusting process.

DEPRECIATION AND INTEREST

Depreciation and interest are important expense categories for many businesses. The borrowing of money, particularly for long periods of time, is one of the principal ways to finance the acquisition of property, plant, and equipment. This interaction between long-term debt and property, plant, and equipment is particularly apparent in the financial statements of electric utilities, as the following analysis shows.

ANALYSIS

DEPRECIATION AND INTEREST OF ELECTRIC UTILITIES

In the 1989 income statement of American Electric Power (AEP), interest and depreciation expenses total over $900 million, representing nearly 20 percent of sales revenue. The book value (cost less accumulated depreciation) of property, plant, and equipment represents approximately three-quarters of total assets, and the total of interest-bearing liabilities represents approximately 40 percent of total liabilities and equity as shown in the balance sheet on the facing page (from which explanatory notes have been omitted):

Electric utilities "mortgage" a high proportion of their costly plant and equipment by issuing long-term debt. Capital markets permit electric utilities to finance a high proportion of their assets through long-term debt, in part because of the stability and security of an electric utility's inflow of revenue. The importance of this distinctive characteristic of electric utilities is underscored by the placement of long-lived assets and long-term debt and equity at the "top" of the balance sheet.

1. *How is depreciation reported in the financial statements?*

Depreciation related to the generation, transmission, and distribution of electricity and to selling and administrative activities is reported as depreciation expense. Depreciation expense related to coal-mining operations is reported in combination with other costs of fuel for the production of electricity.

2. *How is interest reported in the financial statements?*

Interest expense is reported in a separate section of the income statement showing separate amounts for interest on long-term debt and interest on short-term debt. The amount of interest on long-term debt is over 20 times the interest on short-term debt, reflecting the fact that most of AEP's interest-bearing liabilities are in the form of long-term bonds.

Consolidated Balance Sheets

American Electric Power Company, Inc., and Subsidiary Companies

(in thousands, except share data)	December 31,	
	1989	1988
ASSETS		
Electric Utility Plant:		
Production	$ 7,922,653	$ 7,671,020
Transmission	2,853,530	2,773,107
Distribution	3,012,067	2,852,244
General *(includes mining plant and nuclear fuel)*	1,387,060	1,336,492
Construction Work in Progress	932,943	2,018,016
Total Electric Utility Plant	16,108,253	16,650,879
Accumulated Provisions for Depreciation and Amortization	5,265,047	4,948,086
Net Electric Utility Plant	10,843,206	11,702,793
Other Property and Investments	505,181	491,808
Current Assets:		
Cash and Cash Equivalents	1,104,840	229,793
Special Deposits—Restricted Funds	67,966	78,532
Accounts Receivable:		
Customers	444,397	344,352
Miscellaneous	54,149	56,816
Allowance for Uncollectible Accounts	(11,535)	(18,629)
Fuel—at average cost	288,093	342,818
Materials and Supplies—at average cost	155,757	133,408
Accrued Utility Revenues	180,110	145,511
Prepayments	76,884	73,754
Other	10,703	13,255
Total Current Assets	2,371,364	1,399,610
Deferred Debits:		
Deferred Income Taxes	374,296	95,224
Property Taxes	138,557	133,376
Deferred Depreciation and Return	131,879	148,840
Other	381,349	290,811
Total Deferred Debits	1,026,081	668,251
Total	$14,745,832	$14,262,462
CAPITALIZATION AND LIABILITIES		
Capitalization:		
Common Stock—Par Value $6.50:		
Shares Authorized—300,000,000		
Shares Outstanding—193,534,992	$ 1,257,977	$ 1,257,977
Paid-in Capital	1,904,777	1,905,862
Retained Earnings	1,231,512	1,062,136
Total Common Shareowners' Equity	4,394,266	4,225,975
Cumulative Preferred Stocks of Subsidiaries:		
Not Subject to Mandatory Redemption	551,596	555,398
Subject to Mandatory Redemption	149,454	190,497
Long-term Debt	4,515,960	5,422,014
Total Capitalization	9,611,276	10,393,884
Other Noncurrent Liabilities	360,447	360,313
Current Liabilities:		
Cumulative Preferred Stock Due Within One Year	20,449	2,419
Long-term Debt Due Within One Year	640,016	386,344
Notes Payable	67,075	44,300
Commercial Paper	65,973	45,075
Accounts Payable	259,668	240,094
Taxes Accrued	667,443	291,015
Interest Accrued	118,799	136,673
Obligations Under Capital Leases	68,792	73,607
Other	263,488	207,873
Total Current Liabilities	2,171,703	1,427,400
Deferred Credits:		
Deferred Income Taxes	1,412,525	1,472,918
Deferred Investment Tax Credits	595,131	538,499
Deferred Gains on Sale and Leaseback Transactions	503,720	4,305
Other	91,030	65,143
Total Deferred Credits	2,602,406	2,080,865
Commitments and Contingencies *(described in footnotes to financial statements)*		
Total	$14,745,832	$14,262,462

Both depreciation expense and interest expense are associated with continuous transactions that frequently require adjusting entries. Depreciation expense is associated with the use of buildings and equipment over the life of such assets. An adjusting entry at the end of every accounting period recognizes the amount of depreciation expense associated with the use of assets during that period. Similarly, interest expense is associated with the use of borrowed money over the term of the loan agreement. An adjusting entry at the end of every accounting period recognizes any portion of the period's interest expense that has not yet been paid. These adjustments are encountered so frequently that they cannot be omitted from this discussion, even though their computations are more involved than any we have illustrated thus far. Although we cannot explain here all forms of the depreciation and interest computations, we will provide a sufficient basis to enable you to understand their role in the accounting cycle. We will first discuss the adjustment for depreciation expense. The procedure explained here for the computation of depreciation expense will be used for all depreciation adjustments until we have described additional depreciation methods in Chapter 9. We will then describe the computation of interest revenue or interest expense accrued as of the end of an accounting period. The procedure described here will be used throughout the text whenever interest is to be determined for part or all of a single accounting period. (Interest for multiple periods will be taken up in Chapters 10 and 11.)

THE ADJUSTING ENTRIES FOR DEPRECIATION

When a firm acquires a long-lived asset, its cost is debited to an asset account. As a long-lived asset is used to produce revenues, accrual accounting requires that a portion of the asset's cost, corresponding to the portion of the asset consumed during a particular period, be recorded as an expense of that period. This expense is *depreciation expense* and is always recorded by an adjusting entry of the type that recognizes an expense paid in advance. The balance sheet half of the adjusting entry is a credit to accumulated depreciation, which is a *contra asset,* an account whose balance will be deducted from the balance of the related asset account. The balance in the accumulated depreciation account is the sum of the depreciation expenses recorded to date for a particular asset; thus it shows what portion of the cost of a long-lived asset has already been consumed in the production of revenues.

As you will learn in Chapter 9, there are a number of methods for computing depreciation expense. The method described here is *straight-line depreciation,* which is determined by dividing the expected life of an asset into the cost of the asset less its residual value:

$$\text{Depreciation expense} = \frac{\text{Cost of depreciable asset} - \text{Residual value}}{\text{Expected life of depreciable asset}}$$

Residual value (sometimes called *salvage value*) is the amount that the firm expects to receive when an asset is sold or traded in at the end of its expected life. The straight-line procedure takes its name from the fact that it allocates the same amount as an expense each year.

The computation of straight-line depreciation expense and the determination of end-of-period accumulated depreciation and book value are illustrated in the following example: Miller Equipment Company purchases a truck for $16,000. The truck has an expected life of five years and an expected residual value of $1,000. Thus

$$\text{Depreciation expense} = \frac{\$16,000 - \$1,000}{5 \text{ years}} = \$3,000 \text{ per year}$$

Each year, the adjusting entry for depreciation expense will be

Depreciation expense, truck............................	3,000	
Accumulated depreciation, truck		3,000

The depreciation expense, accumulated depreciation, and book value (cost minus accumulated depreciation) for each year during the five-year period are as follows:

YEAR	DEPRECIATION EXPENSE	ACCUMULATED DEPRECIATION	BOOK VALUE
1	$3,000	$ 3,000	$13,000
2	3,000	6,000	10,000
3	3,000	9,000	7,000
4	3,000	12,000	4,000
5	3,000	15,000	1,000

Thus this asset would appear on the Miller Company balance sheet at the end of the *third* year as follows:

Truck...	$16,000	
Less: Accumulated depreciation	9,000	$7,000

In the next section, we introduce the procedures used to compute the adjusting entries for interest revenue and interest expense.

THE ADJUSTING ENTRIES FOR INTEREST REVENUE AND INTEREST EXPENSE

Interest expense for notes payable and interest revenue from notes receivable are computed by multiplying the principal amount (the amount borrowed or loaned) times an annual interest rate times the fraction of the year for which the receivable or payable is outstanding:

Interest = (Principal)(Interest rate)(Fraction of year)

Although more fully developed interest calculations are described in Chapters 10 and 11, this simple formula enables us to illustrate adjusting entries for interest revenue and expense.

Adjusting for Accrued Interest

As with other partially completed continuous transactions, adjusting entries for borrowing and lending must be prepared at the end of a firm's fiscal year for unrecorded interest revenue and expense. Let us illustrate for both a payable and a receivable. On September 1, Miller Equipment Company borrowed $100,000 on a six-month, 12 percent note payable. On December 1, Miller loaned $6,000 on a four-month, 15 percent note to Pharris Construction Company. Miller Equipment Company closes its fiscal year on December 31. The borrowing and lending transactions and the end-of-period adjustments are recorded as follows:

NOTE PAYABLE (BORROWING)	NOTE RECEIVABLE (LENDING)
Miller borrows $100,000 on 9/1	*Miller lends $6,000 to Pharris on 12/1*
Cash.............. 100,000	Notes receivable 6,000
Notes payable.... 100,000	Cash 6,000
Interest expense at 12/31	*Interest revenue at 12/31*
($100,000)(.12)(4/12) = $4,000	($6,000)(.15)(1/12) = $75
Adjusting entry at 12/31	*Adjusting entry at 12/31*
Interest expense 4,000	Interest receivable....... 75
Interest payable .. 4,000	Interest revenue 75

In the next section, we discuss how to account for the completion of both borrowing and lending transactions in the period following the period in which adjusting entries for interest have been recorded.

Recording the Payment of a Note after Adjustment

When a note is paid at maturity in the period following an adjusting entry, the remaining interest on the note must be recorded, the payable or receivable accrued by the adjusting entry must be removed, the cash inflow or outflow must be recorded, and the principal amount of the note must be removed. The remaining interest is computed by the same interest formula that was used to determine the adjusting entry. The period, however, is from the date of the adjusting entry until the maturity date.

    The entries for notes payable and notes receivable at maturity can be illustrated by continuing the Miller Equipment Company example. Let's assume that the notes adjusted in the previous example are scheduled to mature in the next period. Look at the computations and entries shown below. The cash paid on the note payable ($106,000) is the face or principal amount of the note ($100,000) plus the current period's interest expense ($2,000) plus the interest expense recorded as an accrued payable with the adjusting entry ($4,000). The cash received at maturity for the note receivable ($6,300) is the principal or face amount of the note ($6,000) plus the interest revenue from the current period ($225) plus the interest accrued as a receivable in the previous period with the adjusting entry ($75).

NOTE PAYABLE (BORROWING)	NOTE RECEIVABLE (LENDING)
(Maturity two months after 12/31)	(Maturity three months after 12/31)

Interest expense for January and February

$$(\$100,000)(.12)(2/12) = \$2,000$$

Interest revenue for January, February, and March

$$(\$6,000)(.15)(3/12) = \$225$$

Payment to lender on 2/28

Notes payable	100,000	
Interest expense . . .	2,000	
Interest payable . . .	4,000	
Cash		106,000

Receipt of payment from borrower on 3/31

Cash	6,300	
Notes receivable		6,000
Interest revenue.		225
Interest receivable. . . .		75

With this discussion of depreciation and interest, we have completed our explanation of adjusting entries. In addition to knowing how to make adjustments, you will need to know what effects adjusting entries have on the income statement and the balance sheet in order to understand the adjusting process completely. In the next section, we will consider the effects of adjusting entries on the financial statements.

EFFECTS OF ADJUSTING ENTRIES ON THE FINANCIAL STATEMENTS

We have seen that the objective of adjusting entries is to update the balances in the revenue, expense, asset, and liability accounts to the proper amounts at the end of each accounting period. Since each adjusting entry directly affects one revenue or expense account and one asset or liability account, both the income statement and the balance sheet are affected when adjusting entries are recorded. Furthermore, adjustments to the revenue or expense accounts also affect the balance sheet *indirectly* because revenues and expenses alter the firm's net income or net loss for the period. The effect on net income will, in turn, alter the ending balance in retained earnings. To illustrate, let us consider Kelton Lawn Care Company. Assume first that Kelton has the following amounts of revenues, expenses, assets, liabilities, and equity before the effects of adjusting entries are considered. (We will also assume that there are no taxes, so that the effects of adjusting entries on the financial statements will stand out more clearly.)

REVENUES	−	EXPENSES	=	NET INCOME
$500,000	−	$475,000	=	$25,000

ASSETS	=	LIABILITIES	+	EQUITY
$390,000	=	$150,000	+	($215,000 + $25,000)

Note that the $25,000 of net income increases retained earnings and is a part of equity. (Net income is formally added to the retained earnings through the closing entries described in the next chapter.) To determine the effects of an adjusting entry, assume that Kelton has earned lawn care revenue of $3,000 that is unrecorded at December 31. The adjusting entry to record this revenue is

Accounts receivable 3,000
    Service revenue   3,000

The effect of this adjusting entry is to increase revenues (and, therefore, increase retained earnings) by $3,000 and to increase assets (accounts receivable) by $3,000.

	REVENUES	−	EXPENSES	=	NET INCOME
Preadjustment	$500,000	−	$475,000	=	$25,000
Adjustment	+3,000				+3,000
Adjusted	$503,000	−	$475,000	=	$28,000

	ASSETS	=	LIABILITIES	+	EQUITY
Preadjustment	$390,000	=	$150,000	+	($215,000 + $25,000)
Adjustment	+3,000				+3,000
Adjusted	$393,000	=	$150,000	+	($215,000 + $28,000)

The adjusting entry in this case involved revenue recognized before its collection. The effects on the financial statement of each category of adjusting entry are shown in Exhibit 4–2.

Another way to view adjusting entries is from the perspective of the financial statements. Adjusting entries remove understatements or overstatements from the income statement and balance sheet. An *overstated* account is too large relative to its correct balance. An *understated* account is too small relative to its correct balance. In the Kelton Lawn Care example, the unadjusted revenues, assets, and equity (retained earnings) had all been understated by $3,000. Exhibit 4–3 summarizes the preadjustment status of the financial statement accounts according to the type of adjusting entry.

This section ends our discussion of the development of adjusting entries and their effects on the financial statements. The next portion of the chapter presents a demonstration problem that reviews these concepts and procedures.

EXHIBIT 4–2   EFFECTS OF ADJUSTING ENTRIES ON FINANCIAL STATEMENTS

TYPE OF ADJUSTMENT	REVENUE	EXPENSE	ASSET	LIABILITY	EQUITY*
Revenue recognized before collection	Increase		Increase		Increase
Expense recognized before payment		Increase		Increase	Decrease
Revenue recognized after collection	Increase			Decrease	Increase
Expense recognized after payment		Increase	Decrease		Decrease

* Changes in equity are due to changes in retained earnings that arise from changes in net income as a result of adjustments to revenue or expense.

EXHIBIT 4–3   **PREADJUSTMENT STATUS OF FINANCIAL STATEMENT ACCOUNTS**

TYPE OF ADJUSTMENT	OVERSTATED PREADJUSTMENT BALANCE	UNDERSTATED PREADJUSTMENT BALANCE
Revenue recognized before collection	—	Revenues and assets
Expense recognized before payment	—	Expenses and liabilities
Revenue recognized after collection	Liabilities	Revenues
Expense recognized after payment	Assets	Expenses

REVIEW PROBLEM: ADJUSTING ENTRY CONCEPTS

The only way you will know if you understand the concepts and procedures presented in this chapter is by applying them to accounting situations in which adjustments may or may not be required. The review problem in this section is intended to reinforce our discussion of adjustments. You should follow the problem and its solution closely in order to review the concept of accrual accounting and its application through adjusting entries.

Our example business for this demonstration is Nicholson Orchards, a fruit grower. At the end of 19X3, Nicholson Orchards had preadjustment balances in its accounts as shown in Exhibit 4–4. An examination of account balances and supporting documents indicates that the following adjustments are required:

a) Jim Pokagon, a local physician, rents a portion of Nicholson's warehouses from October 1 to April 1 to store his pleasure boat. Pokagon's rent for the October 19X3 to April 19X4 period is $1,800 and is unpaid and unrecorded. Payment is expected in February 19X4.

b) A smaller orchard pays Nicholson to wash and pack its fruit. In September this orchard paid Nicholson $9,000 for washing and packing to be done during November, December, and January. Nicholson credited the payment to unearned revenue. By December 31, $7,000 of the $9,000 has been earned.

c) Administrative salaries in the amount of $1,500 are owed but unpaid and unrecorded.

d) Four months' interest at 10 percent on the notes payable (due in 19X9) is owed but unpaid and unrecorded.

e) The building has an expected life of 20 years and an expected residual value of $3,000.

f) The fruit processing equipment has an expected life of 5 years and an expected residual value of $3,000.

g) Income taxes expense of $5,200 is owed but unpaid and unrecorded.

EXHIBIT 4-4   UNADJUSTED TRIAL BALANCE

NICHOLSON ORCHARDS
Unadjusted Trial Balance
As of December 31, 19X3

ACCOUNT	DEBIT	CREDIT
Cash	$ 2,000	
Accounts receivable	13,000	
Inventory, 12/31/X3:*		
Apples	4,000	
Peaches	7,000	
Pears	1,000	
Plums	2,000	
Land	94,000	
Building	37,000	
Accumulated depreciation, building		$ 17,000
Equipment	23,000	
Accumulated depreciation, equipment		8,000
Accounts payable		4,000
Unearned revenue		9,000
Notes payable (due 19X9)		30,000
Capital stock		75,000
Retained earnings, 12/31/X2		18,000
Sales revenue		196,000
Cost of goods sold*	148,000	
Selling expense	13,000	
General and administrative expense	11,000	
Interest expense	2,000	
Totals	$357,000	$357,000

* Operating costs of the orchard are included in the cost of the inventory and cost of goods sold.

REQUIRED:

1. Prepare the adjusting entries for Nicholson Orchards.

2. Prepare an income statement for 19X3 and a balance sheet at December 31, 19X3, from the adjusted account balances.

3. Determine the effect of the adjusting entries on Nicholson's 19X3 financial statements.

SOLUTION:

1. The adjusting entries for Nicholson Orchards are as follows:

   a) At December 31, Pokagon owes rent for three months, $900. The adjusting entry is:

Rent receivable	900	
Rent revenue		900

b) The preadjustment balances in service revenue and unearned revenue are $0 and $9,000, respectively. At December 31, the adjusted balances should be $7,000 in service revenue and $2,000 in unearned revenue.

Unearned revenue			Service revenue	
	9,000	Preadjustment balance		–0–
7,000		Adjusting entry		7,000
	2,000	Adjusted balance		7,000

The adjusting entry is:

Unearned revenue	7,000	
Service revenue.		7,000

c) The unrecorded administrative salary expense is recorded by:

General and administrative expense.	1,500	
Salaries payable.		1,500

d) The unrecorded interest expense is:

Interest expense = ($30,000)(.10)(4/12) = $1,000

The adjusting entry is:

Interest expense	1,000	
Interest payable.		1,000

e) The depreciation expense for the building is:

$$\text{Depreciation expense} = \frac{\$37{,}000 - \$3{,}000}{20} = \$1{,}700$$

The adjusting entry is:

Depreciation expense, building	1,700	
Accumulated depreciation, building.		1,700

f) The depreciation expense for the processing equipment is:

$$\text{Depreciation expense} = \frac{\$23{,}000 - \$3{,}000}{5} = \$4{,}000$$

The adjusting entry is:

Depreciation expense, equipment.	4,000	
Accumulated depreciation, equipment.		4,000

g) The adjusting entry for income taxes expense is:

Income taxes expense	5,200	
Income taxes payable.		5,200

The next step is to determine the adjusted account balances needed for the preparation of the financial statements. To do this, we first list the adjusting entries alongside the original unadjusted trial balance (Exhibit 4–5), adding accounts as needed.

2. Using the unadjusted account balances and the adjusting entries presented together in Exhibit 4–5, the adjusted account balances can be determined and then used to prepare the financial statements for Nicholson Orchards (Exhibits 4–6, 4–7, and 4–8).

3. Using the tabular format illustrated earlier in the chapter, we see that the effects on the financial statements of the adjusting entries **a–g** are as follows:

	REVENUES	**–**	**EXPENSES**	**=**	**NET INCOME**
Preadjustment	$196,000	–	$174,000	=	$22,000
Adjustments	+7,900		+13,400		−5,500
Adjusted	$203,900	–	$187,400	=	$16,500

Revenue Adjustments	Expense Adjustments	Income Adjustments
+ 900 (a)	+ 1,500 (c)	+ 7,900 (revenues)
+7,000 (b)	+ 1,000 (d)	− 13,400 (expenses)
+7,900	+ 1,700 (e)	− 5,500
	+ 4,000 (f)	
	+ 5,200 (g)	
	+13,400	

	ASSETS	**=**	**LIABILITIES**	**+**	**EQUITY**
Preadjustment	$158,000	=	$43,000	+	($75,000 + $40,000)
Adjustments	−4,800		+700		−5,500
Adjusted	$153,200	=	$43,700	+	($75,000 + $34,500)

Asset Adjustments	Liability Adjustments	Equity Adjustment
+ 900 (a)	−7,000 (b)	−5,500 (net income)
−1,700 (e)	+1,500 (c)	
−4,000 (f)	+1,000 (d)	
−4,800	+5,200 (g)	
	+ 700	

Note that each of the adjusting entries altered the balance in one income statement account and one balance sheet account.

EXHIBIT 4–5   UNADJUSTED TRIAL BALANCE AND ADJUSTING ENTRIES

NICHOLSON ORCHARDS
Unadjusted Trial Balance and Adjusting Entries
As of December 31, 19X3

ACCOUNT	UNADJUSTED TRIAL BALANCE DEBIT	CREDIT	ADJUSTING ENTRIES DEBIT	CREDIT
Cash	$ 2,000			
Accounts receivable	13,000			
Rent receivable			(a) 900	
Inventory, 12/31/X3:				
Apples	4,000			
Peaches	7,000			
Pears	1,000			
Plums	2,000			
Land	94,000			
Building	37,000			
Accumulated depreciation, building		$ 17,000		(e) 1,700
Equipment	23,000			
Accumulated depreciation, equipment		8,000		(f) 4,000
Accounts payable		4,000		
Unearned revenue		9,000	(b) 7,000	
Salaries payable				(c) 1,500
Income taxes payable				(g) 5,200
Interest payable				(d) 1,000
Notes payable (due 19X9)		30,000		
Capital stock		75,000		
Retained earnings, 12/31/X2		18,000		
Sales revenue		196,000		
Service revenue				(b) 7,000
Rent revenue				(a) 900
Cost of goods sold	148,000			
Selling expense	13,000			
General and administrative expense	11,000		(c) 1,500	
Depreciation expense, building			(e) 1,700	
Depreciation expense, equipment			(f) 4,000	
Interest expense	2,000		(d) 1,000	
Income taxes expense			(g) 5,200	
Totals	$357,000	$357,000	$21,300	$21,300

EXHIBIT 4–6   **INCOME STATEMENT**

NICHOLSON ORCHARDS
Income Statement
For the Year Ended December 31, 19X3

Sales revenue		$196,000
Less: Cost of goods sold		148,000
Gross margin		$ 48,000
Less: Operating expenses:		
Selling	$13,000	
General and administrative	12,500	
Depreciation, building	1,700	
Depreciation, equipment	4,000	31,200
Income from operations		$ 16,800
Other revenues:		
Service revenue	$ 7,000	
Rent revenue	900	7,900
		$ 24,700
Other expenses:		
Interest expense		3,000
Income before taxes		$ 21,700
Less: Income taxes expense		5,200
Net income		$ 16,500

EXHIBIT 4–7   **STATEMENT OF CHANGES IN RETAINED EARNINGS**

NICHOLSON ORCHARDS
Statement of Changes in Retained Earnings
For the Year Ended December 31, 19X3

Retained earnings, 12/31/X2	$18,000
Add: Net income	16,500
	$34,500
Less: Dividends	–0–
Retained earnings, 12/31/X3	$34,500

This review problem concludes our discussion and illustration of adjusting entries. In the next chapter, we will conclude our examination of the accounting cycle as we discuss the closing process.

EXHIBIT 4−8   **BALANCE SHEET**

NICHOLSON ORCHARDS
Balance Sheet
As of December 31, 19X3

ASSETS

Current assets:

Cash		$ 2,000
Accounts receivable		13,000
Rent receivable............................		900
Inventory.................................		14,000
Total current assets		$ 29,900

Property, plant, and equipment:

Land.....................................		$94,000	
Building	$37,000		
Less: Accumulated depreciation	18,700	18,300	
Equipment................................	$23,000		
Less: Accumulated depreciation	12,000	11,000	123,300
Total assets			$153,200

LIABILITIES

Current liabilities:

Accounts payable		$ 4,000
Unearned revenue		2,000
Salaries payable............................		1,500
Interest payable............................		1,000
Income taxes payable.......................		5,200
Total current liabilities		$ 13,700

Long-term liabilities:

Notes payable		30,000
Total liabilities		$ 43,700

STOCKHOLDERS' EQUITY

Capital stock	$75,000	
Retained earnings............................	34,500	
Total stockholders' equity................		109,500
Total liabilities and stockholders' equity .		$153,200

SUMMARY

Adjusting entries are required at year-end to update accounts so that they reflect the effects of partially completed continuous transactions—events like the performance of services for customers, the renting of facilities, and the use of equipment. Without adjusting entries, continuous transactions would not be recorded until completed. Yet accrual-basis financial statements must incorporate the effects of transactions that are partially completed during the period for which the statements are prepared.

Each adjusting entry alters both balance sheet accounts and income statement accounts. To help identify accounts requiring adjustment, the following four categories of adjusting entries were established:

1. Revenues recognized before collection (requiring increases in revenue and asset accounts)
2. Expenses recognized before payment (requiring increases in expense and liability accounts)
3. Revenues recognized after collection (requiring adjustments to revenue and liability accounts)
4. Expenses recognized after payment (requiring adjustments to expense and asset accounts)

The data for adjusting entries must be developed in a systematic fashion from source documents and preadjustment account balances. Source documents determine either the amount of adjustment or the appropriate postadjustment balance (the adjusted balance). The difference between postadjustment and preadjustment balances then indicates the amount of the adjustment. The chapter illustrates this procedure for a variety of incomplete continuous transactions, including service engagements, use of rented property, use of owned operating assets (depreciation), and lending or borrowing of money (interest). In addition, the chapter presents a comprehensive illustration of adjustments and their effect on the financial statements. In Appendix 4–1, we will explain the link between the way prepayments are recorded and the subsequent adjusting entries.

With the discussion of adjusting entries presented in this chapter, we have explained all of the accounting cycle except the three steps associated with the closing process: preparing the worksheet, journalizing and posting closing entries, and preparing the postclosing trial balance. The next chapter will explain these remaining steps and, in addition, will provide opportunities to review adjusting entries and their effects on financial statements.

APPENDIX 4–1
AN ALTERNATIVE METHOD OF DEFERRING PREPAYMENTS AND ADVANCE COLLECTIONS

Both expenses recognized after payment and revenues recognized after collection require deferrals. These deferrals can occur in two ways. One method, which was used throughout the chapter, records prepayments and advance collections in balance sheet accounts. If rent is prepaid, for example, the prepayment is recorded as an asset, prepaid rent. An alternative method records prepayments and advance collections in income statement accounts. Using this method, if rent is prepaid, the prepayment is recorded as rent expense, an income statement account. Both methods require adjustments at the end of the period, and we will compare the adjusting entries for the two methods below.

A firm will usually select one or the other of these methods, based on cost and on the sophistication of its accounting staff. Many accountants feel that it is simpler and less costly to record prepayments and collections in advance directly in the income statement accounts. Since the majority of these entries involve transactions that will be completed in the short term, they reason, the effects of most prepayments and collections in advance will appear in the income statement accounts by year-end and relatively few adjusting entries will be required. On the other hand, other accountants consider the balance sheet to be the proper place for recording prepayments and advance collections, so many firms continue to enter them in the balance sheet accounts and make no attempt to educate their accounting staff about the potential cost savings of the other method.

Let us begin by reviewing the method used throughout the main part of the chapter. When balance sheet accounts are used for prepayments and collections in advance, the related expenses (e.g., rent or supplies) are temporarily recorded by debits to asset accounts (prepaid rent or supplies inventory). Similarly, collections from customers before revenue is recognized are temporarily recorded as liabilities (unearned revenue). To illustrate, consider two examples—a $600 advance from a customer and an $850 expenditure for office supplies. By the end of the accounting period in which these transactions are recorded, $200 of the $600 advance has been earned and $150 of the $850 office supplies purchase has been used. The journal entries used to record these two transactions in balance sheet accounts and the subsequent adjusting entries are as follows:

Entry to record advance from customer (using a liability account)

Cash.	600	
Unearned revenue (a liability)		600

Cash of $600 is received in advance and is recorded as a liability.

Adjusting entry

Unearned revenue (a liability)	200	
Revenue		200

Of the $600 received in advance, $200 has been earned.

Entry to record payment for office supplies purchased (using an asset account)

Office supplies inventory (an asset)	850	
Cash.		850

Office supplies are purchased for $850.

Adjusting entry

Office supplies expense.	150	
Office supplies inventory (an asset)		150

Of the $850 of office supplies, $150 has been used.

Since both these transactions are recorded in balance sheet accounts, the adjusting entries must, in effect, transfer dollars from the balance sheet to the income statement.

The other method of recording prepayments and advance collections uses income statement accounts, and the form of the required adjusting entries is altered. When prepayments and advance collections are recorded as expenses and revenues, it is likely that the amounts entered will be too large as of the end of an accounting period. For such situations, each adjusting entry would therefore *decrease* revenue or expense and *increase* the associated liability or asset. Thus the adjusting entries are, in effect, moving dollars from the income statement to the balance sheet, rather than the opposite. Using this method, the examples discussed above—a $600 advance from a customer and an $850 expenditure for office supplies—would be recorded in revenue and expense accounts as shown below. Notice how the subsequent adjusting entries move dollars from the income statement to the balance sheet:

Entry to record advance from customer (using a revenue account)

Cash.	600	
Revenue		600

Cash of $600 is received in advance and is recorded as a revenue.

Adjusting entry

Revenue	400	
Unearned revenue (a liability)		400

Only $200 of the $600 received in advance has been earned; therefore, $400 is transferred from the revenue account to the liability account.

Entry to record payment for office supplies purchased (using an expense account)

Office supplies expense.	850	
Cash.		850

Office supplies are purchased for $850 and are recorded as an expense.

Adjusting entry

Office supplies inventory (an asset)	700	
Office supplies expense.		700

Only $150 of the $850 of office supplies has been used; therefore, $700 is transferred from the expense account to the asset account.

Both the advance collection and the prepayment are recorded in income statement accounts, which means that the adjusting entries must transfer dollars from the income statement to the balance sheet.

Let us further illustrate adjustments that move dollars from the income statement to the balance sheet, using the four-step procedure for adjustments described in the chapter. (You should note that the four-step procedure is equally effective for these adjustments.) Our example firm, Kenny Properties, Inc., owns and manages commercial buildings. One of Kenny's buildings is rented to an office equipment company, from which Kenny collected six months' rent ($15,000) in advance on September 1. On that date, Kenny Properties credited the entire amount of the payment to rent revenue. Kenny ends its fiscal year on

December 31, by which time only four months' rent (September–December, $10,000) has been earned. An adjusting entry is therefore required to reduce rent revenue by $5,000 and to increase unearned revenue by $5,000.

Rent revenue				Unearned revenue
	15,000	Preadjustment balance		–0–
5,000		Adjusting entry		5,000
	10,000	Adjusted balance		5,000

On August 1, Kenny Properties also purchased a two-year insurance policy on the same office building for $3,600. At the time of this transaction, Kenny debited the full amount of the prepayment to insurance expense. At December 31, the end of Kenny Properties' fiscal year, 5 of the 24 months of insurance coverage ($750) have been used and 19 months' coverage ($2,850) remains unused. An adjusting entry is required to reduce insurance expense by $2,850 and to increase prepaid insurance by $2,850.

Insurance expense				Prepaid insurance	
3,600		Preadjustment balance		–0–	
	2,850	Adjusting entry		2,850	
750		Adjusted balance		2,850	

From these two illustrations, you can see the relationship between the way in which a prepayment or advance collection is recorded and the adjusting entry that must follow. The objective of all types of adjustments is the same: to produce balances for the revenue, expense, asset, and liability accounts that reflect the completed portion of the partially completed transactions at year-end.

KEY TERMS

ACCRUAL (p. 139)

ADJUSTED BALANCE (p. 142)

ADJUSTING ENTRY (p. 137)

CONTINUOUS TRANSACTION (p. 137)

DEFERRAL (p. 139)

DISCRETE TRANSACTION (p. 136)

QUESTIONS

Q4-1. Provide two examples of discrete transactions and two examples of continuous transactions.

Q4-2. Why are adjusting entries needed?

Q4-3. Describe the recording of discrete and continuous transactions by reference to summary entries and adjusting entries.

Q4-4. What accounting concepts require that adjusting entries be employed?

Q4-5. For each of the four categories of adjusting entries, describe the economic activity that produces circumstances requiring adjustment.

Q4-6. What is the difference between an *accrual* and a *deferral?*

Q4-7. Which types of adjusting entry will (a) increase both assets and revenues, (b) increase revenues and decrease liabilities, (c) increase expenses and decrease assets, and (d) increase both expenses and liabilities?

Q4-8. How is the amount for a depreciation expense adjusting entry determined?

Q4-9. How is the amount for an interest expense (or interest revenue) adjusting entry determined?

Q4-10. Describe the effect on the financial statements when an adjusting entry is prepared that records (a) revenue recognized before collection and (b) expense recognized before payment.

Q4-11. On the basis of what you have learned about adjusting entries, why do you think that adjusting entries are made on the last day of the accounting period rather than at several earlier times during the accounting period?

Q4-12. Why are interest and depreciation especially significant expense items for electric utilities?

EXERCISES

E4-13. IDENTIFICATION AND CLASSIFICATION OF ADJUSTING ENTRIES   Conklin Consulting Services prepares financial statements only once per year using an annual accounting period ending on December 31. Each of the following statements describes an entry made by Conklin Consulting Services on December 31 of a recent year.

a) On December 31, Conklin completed a service engagement begun in August and recorded the related revenue.

b) For a monthly fee billed seven working days after the end of every month, Conklin provides weekly service visits to check out and maintain various pieces of computer printing equipment. On December 31, Conklin recorded revenue for the visits completed during December for which cash will not be received until January.

c) Conklin's salaried employees are paid on the last day of every month. On December 31, Conklin recorded the payment of December salaries.

d) Conklin's hourly wage employees are paid every Friday. On December 31, Conklin recorded as payable the wages for the first three working days of the week in which the year ended.

e) On December 31, Conklin recorded the receipt of a shipment of office supplies to be paid for in January.

f) On December 31, Conklin recorded the estimated use of supplies for the year.

g) Early in December, Conklin was paid in advance by James Manufacturing for two months of weekly service visits. Conklin recorded the advance payment as a liability. On December 31, Conklin recorded revenue for the service visits to James Manufacturing that were completed during December.

h) On December 31, Conklin recorded depreciation expense on office equipment for the year.

REQUIRED:

Indicate whether each entry is an *adjusting entry* or a *regular journal entry,* and if it is an adjusting entry, identify it as one of the following types: (1) revenue recognized before collection, (2) expense recognized before payment, (3) revenue recognized after collection, or (4) expense recognized after payment.

E4-14. EFFECT OF ADJUSTMENTS ON THE FINANCIAL STATEMENTS   VanBrush Enterprises, a painting contractor, prepared the following adjusting entries at year-end:

a) Wages expense.   3,700

        Wages payable   3,700

b) Accounts receivable.   6,500

        Service revenue   6,500

REQUIRED:

Prepare tables that show the effects of these adjustments on (1) revenues, expenses, and net income and (2) assets, liabilities, and equity.

E4-15. EFFECT OF ADJUSTMENTS ON THE FINANCIAL STATEMENTS   The *Times Citizen,* a local newspaper, prepared the following adjusting entries:

a) Unearned revenue.   5,245
     Service revenue, advertising.   5,245

b) Rent expense.   3,820
     Prepaid rent.   3,820

REQUIRED:

Prepare tables that show the effects of these adjustments on (1) revenues, expenses, and net income and (2) assets, liabilities, and equity.

E4-16. REVENUE ADJUSTMENTS   Powers Building Services has the following items that require adjustment at year-end:

a) Cleaning service revenue of $6,920 is unrecorded.

b) For one cleaning contract, $14,000 cash was received in advance. The cash was credited to unearned revenue upon receipt. At year-end $3,750 of the service revenue was still unearned.

c) For a second cleaning contract, $9,500 cash was received in advance and credited to unearned revenue upon receipt. At year-end $4,300 of the services had been provided.

REQUIRED:

Prepare adjusting entries for these three items.

E4-17. REVENUE ADJUSTMENTS   Sentry Transport, Inc., of Atlanta provides in-town parcel delivery services in addition to a full range of passenger services. Sentry engaged in the following activities during the current year:

a) Sentry received $1,200 cash in advance from Goodwear Clothing for an estimated 200 deliveries during December of the current year and January and February of next year. The entire amount was recorded as unearned revenue when received. During December, 60 deliveries were made for Goodwear.

b) Sentry operates several small buses that take commuters from suburban communities to the central downtown area of Atlanta. The commuters purchase, in advance, tickets for 50 one-way trips. Each 50-ride ticket costs $180. At the time of purchase, Sentry credits the cash received to unearned revenue. At year-end, Sentry estimates that revenue from 1,800 one-way rides has been earned.

c) Sentry operates several buses that provide transportation for the clients of a social service agency in Atlanta. Sentry bills the agency quarterly at the end of January, April, July, and October for the service. The contract price is $900 per quarter. Sentry follows the practice of recognizing revenue from this contract in the period in which the service is performed.

d) On December 23, Mayhew Manufacturing chartered a bus to transport its marketing group to a meeting at a resort in West Virginia. The meeting will be held during the last week in January of next year, and Mayhew agrees to pay for the entire trip on the day the bus departs. At year-end, none of these arrangements have been recorded by Sentry.

REQUIRED:

Prepare adjusting entries at December 31 for these four activities.

E4-18. EXPENSE ADJUSTMENTS   Olney Company has the following items that require adjustment at year-end:

a) Wage expense of $3,180 is unrecorded and unpaid.

b) Cash for equipment rental in the amount of $4,200 was paid in advance. The $4,200 was debited to prepaid equipment rent when paid. At year-end $3,150 of the prepaid rent had been used.

c) Cash for building rent in the amount of $6,500 was paid in advance. The $6,500 was debited to prepaid building rent when paid. At year-end $1,300 of the prepaid rent was still unused.

REQUIRED:

Prepare adjusting entries for these three items.

E4-19. EXPENSE ADJUSTMENTS   Faraday Electronic Service repairs stereos and VCRs. During a recent year, Faraday engaged in the following activities:

a) On September 1, Faraday paid $1,860 to prepay its insurance for twelve months. The full amount of the prepayment was debited to prepaid insurance.

b) At December 31, Faraday estimates that utility costs that are unrecorded and unpaid amount to $830.

c) Faraday rents its testing equipment from VCR manufacturers. Equipment rent in the amount of $1,440 is unpaid and unrecorded at December 31.

d) In late October, Faraday agreed to become the sponsor for the sports segment of the evening news program on a local television station. The station billed Faraday $3,300 for three months' sponsorship—November, December, and January—in advance. When these payments were made, Faraday debited prepaid advertising expense. At December 31, two months' advertising expense has been used and one month remains unused.

REQUIRED:

Prepare adjusting entries at December 31 for these four activities.

E4-20. DETERMINATION OF REVENUE AND EXPENSE AMOUNTS   Allentown Services, Inc., is preparing adjusting entries for the year ending December 31, 19X4. The following data are available:

a) Interest is owed at December 31, 19X4, in connection with a six-month, 12 percent note on which Allentown borrowed $10,000 on September 1, 19X4.

b) Allentown Corporation provides daily building maintenance services to Asbury Manufacturing for a quarterly fee of $2,400, payable on the 15th of the month following the end of each quarter. No entries have been made for the services provided to Asbury during the quarter ended December 31, and the related bill will not be sent until January 15, 19X5.

c) At the beginning of 19X4, the cost of office supplies on hand was $1,220. During 19X4, office supplies with a total cost of $6,480 were purchased and debited to office supplies inventory. On December 31, 19X4, Allentown determined the cost of office supplies on hand to be $970.

d) On September 23, 19X4, Allentown received a $6,300 payment from Egg Harbor Products for nine months of maintenance services beginning on October 1, 19X4. The entire amount was credited to unearned revenue when received.

REQUIRED:

Compute the amount of 19X4 revenue or expense related to each of these items, and prepare the appropriate adjusting entries at December 31, 19X4.

E4-21. DETERMINATION OF REVENUE AND EXPENSE AMOUNTS   Reynolds Computer Service offers data processing services to retail clothing stores. The following data have been collected to aid in the preparation of adjusting entries for Reynolds Computer Service for 19X8:

a) Computer equipment was purchased in 19X5 at a cost of $540,000. Expected life is seven years and expected residual value is $32,500.

b) A fire insurance policy for a two-year period beginning September 1, 19X8, was purchased for $10,320 cash. The entire amount of the prepayment was debited to prepaid insurance. (Assume that the beginning balance of prepaid insurance was $0 and that there were no other debits or credits to that account during 19X8.)

c) Reynolds has a contract to perform the payroll accounting for Ron's Clothing Store. At the end of 19X8, $400 of services have been performed under this contract but are unbilled.

d) Reynolds rents 12 computer terminals for $20 per month per terminal from Equipment Leasing Company. At December 31, 19X8, Reynolds owes Equipment Leasing Company for half a month's rent on each terminal. The amount owed is unrecorded.

e) Perry's Tax Service prepays rent for time on Reynolds' computer. When payments are received from Perry's Tax Service, Reynolds credits unearned revenue. At December 31, 19X8, Reynolds has earned $1,430 for computer time used by Perry's Tax Service during December 19X8.

REQUIRED:

Prepare adjusting entries for each of these items after computing the proper amount of the revenues and expenses.

E4-22. DEPRECIATION   Lagarde Company has the following data for its depreciable assets:

ASSET	COST	ACQUISITION DATE	EXPECTED LIFE	EXPECTED RESIDUAL VALUE
Building	$410,000	1/1/X3	40 year	$24,000
Machine	61,000	1/1/X8	5 years	6,000
Truck	34,000	1/1/X9	4 years	2,600

REQUIRED:

1. Compute depreciation expense for one full year's use of each of the assets.
2. What are the accumulated depreciation and the book value of each asset at December 31, 19X9?

E4-23. DEPRECIATION EXPENSE   Complete Transportation rents automobiles, vans, trucks, and limousines. The following data are available for a portion of Complete's rental fleet at December 31, 19X5:

VEHICLE	COST	ACQUISITION DATE	EXPECTED LIFE	EXPECTED RESIDUAL VALUE
Car no. 161	$10,900	8/1/X4	24 months	$ 6,100
Van no. 205	16,400	4/1/X5	30 months	9,500
Truck no. 311	24,500	1/1/X3	60 months	8,000
Limo no. 402	38,400	7/1/X4	36 months	15,000

REQUIRED:

Compute depreciation expense for 19X5 for each of these vehicles.

E4-24. INTEREST-BEARING NOTE PAYABLE   Miller Theater Productions borrowed $330,000 from Valley National Bank on a one-year, 11 percent note payable. The loan was effective on August 1, 19X7, and is to be repaid July 31, 19X8.

REQUIRED:

1. Prepare the entry to record the borrowing in Miller's journal.
2. Compute interest expense from August 1 through December 31.
3. Prepare a December 31 adjusting entry for interest on the note for Miller's journal.
4. Determine interest expense on the note for 19X8.
5. Prepare the entry for Miller's journal to record payment of principal plus interest on the note at July 31, 19X8.

E4-25. INTEREST-BEARING NOTE RECEIVABLE   Clarey Financial Corporation loaned Elkhart Supply Company $180,000 on May 1, 19X8, on a one-year, 14 percent interest-bearing note.

REQUIRED:

1. Prepare the entry to record the loan for Clarey's journal.
2. Compute the interest revenue earned by Clarey from May 1 to December 31.
3. Prepare the adjusting entry to record interest on the note in Clarey's journal on December 31.
4. Determine the amount of the interest revenue earned in 19X9.
5. Prepare the entry to record the receipt of principal and interest from Elkhart on April 30, 19X9.

E4-26. FINANCIAL STATEMENT EFFECTS OF ADJUSTING ENTRIES   When adjusting entries were prepared at the end of 19X2, the accountant did not make adjustments for (1) $2,900 of wages that had been earned but were unpaid and (2) $3,750 of revenue that had been earned but was uncollected and unrecorded.

REQUIRED:

1. Identify the effects on the financial statements of the adjusting entries that were omitted (assume no taxes in your analysis).
2. Prepare the journal entries you would make in *January 19X3* to correct the balances in the accounts.

E4-27. ADJUSTMENT FOR SUPPLIES EXPENSE   Kittery Clothiers purchases large quantities of supplies, including plastic garment bags and paper bags and boxes, for use in its seven stores. At December 31, 19X5, the following information is available concerning supplies:

Supplies inventory, 1/1/X5	$ 4,150
Supplies inventory, 12/31/X5	5,220
Supplies purchased for cash during 19X5	15,700

All purchases of supplies during the year are debited to the supplies inventory.

REQUIRED:

1. What is the expense associated with the use of supplies during 19X5?
2. What is the proper adjusting entry at December 31, 19X5?

E4-28. THE EFFECT OF ESTIMATES OF LIFE AND RESIDUAL VALUE ON DEPRECIATION EXPENSE   Hattiesburg Manufacturing purchased a new computer-integrated manufacturing system to manufacture a group of fabricated metal and plastic products. The equipment was purchased from Bessemer Systems at a cost of $630,000. As a basis for determining annual depreciation, Hattiesburg's controller requests estimates of the expected life and residual value for the new equipment. The engineering and production departments submit the following divergent estimates:

	ENGINEERING DEPARTMENT ESTIMATES	PRODUCTION DEPARTMENT ESTIMATES
Expected life	9 years	7 years
Residual value	$90,000	–0–

Before considering depreciation expense for the new equipment, Hattiesburg Manufacturing has net income in the amount of $250,000.

REQUIRED:

1. Compute a full year's depreciation expense for the new equipment, using each of the two sets of estimates.

2. If the income tax rate is 34 percent, what will be the effect on net income of including a full year's depreciation expense based on the engineering estimates? Based on the production estimates?

3. If a firm has a significant investment in depreciable assets, the expected life and residual value estimates can materially affect depreciation expense and therefore net income. What might motivate management to use the highest or lowest estimates? How would cash outflows for income taxes be affected by the estimates?

APPENDIX EXERCISES

E4-29. PREPAYMENTS, COLLECTIONS IN ADVANCE, AND ADJUSTING ENTRIES   Greensboro Properties, Inc., owns buildings in which it leases office space to small businesses and professionals. During 19X6 Greensboro Properties engaged in the following transactions:

a) On March 1, Greensboro Properties paid $14,400 in advance to Patterson Account Services for billing services for the entire year beginning March 1, 19X6. The full amount of the prepayment was debited to rent expense.

b) On May 1, Greensboro Properties received $24,000 for one year's rent from Angela Cottrell, a lawyer and new tenant. Greensboro Properties credited rent revenue for the full amount collected from Cottrell.

c) On July 30, Greensboro Properties received $480,000 for six months' rent on an office building that is occupied by Newnan and Calhoun, a regional accounting firm. The rental period begins on August 1, 19X6. The full amount received was credited to rent revenue.

d) On November 1, Greensboro Properties paid $3,300 to La Grange Security for three months' security services beginning on that date. The entire amount was debited to other professional services expense.

REQUIRED:

1. Prepare journal entries for each of the transactions.

2. Prepare the adjusting entries you would make at December 31, 19X6, for each of these items.

E4-30. RECORDING PREPAYMENTS AND ADVANCE COLLECTIONS IN INCOME STATEMENT ACCOUNTS   Layhill Auto Service made the following two prepayments in 19X2. Layhill debits prepayments to expense accounts.

a) Paid $1,920 for a 12-month insurance policy on May 1, debiting insurance expense.

b) Paid $4,320 for office supplies, debiting the entire amount to office supplies expense. There was no inventory of office supplies on January 1.

Layhill received two advances from customers during 19X2. Layhill credits all advance collections to revenue accounts.

c) On November 1, Layhill received $450 for 6 months' preventive maintenance on a truck owned by the local cable television company. Service revenue was credited.

d) During December Layhill received $500 from customers who purchased books of gift certificates for car washes. Each car wash is priced at $2.50. Service revenue was credited.

At December 31, 19X2, there was $215 of office supplies on hand. During December Layhill redeemed 20 of the car wash gift certificates.

REQUIRED:

1. Prepare journal entries for each of these transactions.

2. Prepare adjusting entries for each of these items.

E4-31. PREPAYMENT OF EXPENSES   JDM, Inc., made the following prepayments for expense items during 19X8:

a) Prepaid building rent for one year on April 1. JDM paid $6,300, debiting rent expense for the amount of the prepayment.

b) Prepaid 6 months' insurance on October 1 by paying $870. Insurance expense was debited.

c) Purchased $3,750 of office supplies, debiting office supplies expense for the full amount. Office supplies costing $385 remain unused at December 31, 19X8.

d) Paid $2,880 for a 12-month service contract for maintenance on a computer. The contract begins November 1. The full amount of the payment was debited to maintenance expense.

REQUIRED:

1. Prepare journal entries to record the prepayments.

2. Prepare adjusting entries for the prepayments at December 31, 19X8.

PROBLEMS

P4-32. CONTINUOUS TRANSACTIONS AND ADJUSTING ENTRIES   Medina Motors is preparing adjusting entries for the year ended December 31, 19X7. The following items describe Medina's continuous transactions during 19X7:

a) Medina's salaried employees are paid on the last day of every month.

b) Medina's hourly employees are paid every other Friday for the preceding two weeks' work. The next payday falls on January 5, 19X8.

c) In November 19X7, Medina borrowed an amount of cash from a bank giving a note payable with interest in January 19X8. The note was properly recorded.

d) Medina rents its used car sales lot under a long-term lease that requires payment of rent six months in advance on April 1 and October 1 of each year. The October 1, 19X7, payment was made and recorded as prepaid rent.

e) Medina's service department recognizes the entire revenue on every auto service job when the job is complete. At December 31, several service jobs are in process.

f) Medina recognizes depreciation on shop equipment annually at the end of each year.

g) Medina acquires office supplies throughout the year, recording them in the office supplies inventory account. Supplies expense is calculated and recorded annually at the end of each year.

REQUIRED:

Indicate whether or not each item requires an adjusting entry at December 31, 19X7. If an item requires an adjusting entry, indicate which accounts are increased by the adjustment and which are decreased.

P4-33. EFFECTS OF ADJUSTING ENTRIES ON THE ACCOUNTING EQUATION   Four adjusting entries are shown below:

a) Wages expense.   2,490
      Wages payable   2,490
b) Accounts receivable.   3,350
      Service revenue   3,350
c) Rent expense.   1,760
      Prepaid rent.   1,760
d) Unearned service revenue   4,130
      Service revenue   4,130

REQUIRED:

Analyze the adjusting entries and identify their effects on the financial statement accounts. (Assume that there are no income tax effects for these adjustments.) Use the following format for your answer:

				BEGINNING			
TRANS- ACTION	ASSETS =	LIABILITIES +	CAPITAL STOCK +	RETAINED EARNINGS +	REVENUES −	EXPENSES −	DIVIDENDS

P4-34. PREPARATION OF ADJUSTING ENTRIES   Bartow Photographic Services takes wedding and graduation photographs. At December 31, the end of Bartow's accounting period, the following information is available:

a) All wedding photographs are paid for in advance, and all cash collected for them is credited to unearned revenue. Except for a year-end adjusting entry, no other entries are made for revenue from wedding photographs. During the year, Bartow received $42,600 for wedding photographs. At year-end $33,900 of the $42,600 had been earned. The beginning-of-the-year balance of unearned revenue was zero.

b) During December, Bartow photographed 60 members of the next year's graduating class of Fort Meade High School. The school has asked Bartow to print one copy of a photograph of each student for the school files; Bartow delivers these photographs on December 28 and will bill the school $5.00 per student in January of next year. Revenue from photographs ordered by students will be recorded as the orders are received during the early months of next year.

c) Developing and printing equipment rent of $18,000 for one year beginning on August 1 was paid on August 1. When made, the payment was debited to prepaid rent.

d) Depreciation on the firm's building is being recorded on a straight-line basis, using a 25-year expected life and a residual value of $15,000. The building cost $375,000.

e) Supplies inventory at the beginning of the year was $3,200. During the year, supplies costing $19,600 were purchased. When the purchases were made, their cost was debited to supplies inventory. At year-end a physical inventory indicated that supplies costing $4,100 were on hand.

REQUIRED:

Prepare the adjusting entries for each of these five items.

P4-35. PREPARATION OF ADJUSTING ENTRIES West Beach Resort operates a resort complex that specializes in hosting small business and professional meetings. West Beach closes its fiscal year on January 31, a time when it has few meetings under way. At January 31, 19X5, the following data are available:

a) A training meeting is under way for 16 persons. The organization employing the 16 people paid $1,500 in advance for each person attending the 10-day training session. The meeting began on January 27 and will end on February 5. West Beach credits collections in advance to unearned revenue.

b) Twenty-one people are attending a sales meeting. The daily fee for each person attending the meeting is $110 (charged for each night a person stays at the resort). The meeting began on January 29, and guests will depart on February 2. The participants' employer will be billed at the end of the meeting.

c) Depreciation on golf carts used to transport the guests' luggage to and from their rooms is recorded, assuming a three-year life with no residual value. West Beach owns four carts that cost $3,600 each and six that cost $3,900 each. All golf carts require a full year's depreciation.

d) At January 31, Fredereich Catering is owed $1,795 for food provided for guests through that date. This amount of food service expense is unrecorded.

e) Wages of $4,170 are owed but unpaid and unrecorded at January 31.

f) An examination indicates that the cost of office supplies on hand at January 31, 19X5, is $189. During the 19X4–19X5 fiscal year, $698 of office supplies was purchased. The cost of supplies purchased was debited to office supplies inventory. No office supplies were on hand on January 31, 19X4.

REQUIRED:

Prepare adjusting entries at January 31 for each of these items.

P4-36. PREPARATION OF ADJUSTING ENTRIES Libby Kueppers operates a large day-care center in South Orange, New Jersey. The day-care center serves several nearby businesses, as well as a number of individual families. The businesses pay $2,200 per child per year for day-care services for their employees' children. The businesses pay in advance on a yearly basis. For individual families, day-care services are provided monthly and billed at the beginning of the next month. At December 31, 19X8, the following transactions are partially complete:

a) Day-care service in the amount of $12,450 was provided to individual families, who will be billed in January 19X9.

b) At January 1, 19X8, the balance in unearned revenue was $105,100. During 19X8 the center collected $238,400 from businesses (crediting unearned revenue) for day-care services. At December 31, 19X8, $113,400 of service revenue is unearned.

c) The day-care center had prepaid insurance at January 1, 19X8, of $4,200. During the year, $15,600 was paid for insurance. An examination of insurance policies indicates that prepaid insurance at December 31, 19X8, is $5,200.

d) The day-care center owns a bus that it uses for field trips. The bus cost $24,800 and has an expected residual value of $3,400 and an expected life of eight years.

e) The day-care center has a five-year, $60,000, 11 percent note payable outstanding. Five months' interest on the note is unpaid and unrecorded at December 31.

f) Salaries of $8,320 are owed but unpaid and unrecorded at December 31.

g) The inventory of disposable diapers, on January 1, 19X8, is $1,400. During the year, disposable diapers were purchased at a cost of $16,700. The $16,700 cost was debited to supplies inventory. At the end of 19X8, the cost of diapers in inventory is $890.

REQUIRED:

Prepare adjusting entries for the day-care service at December 31, 19X8.

P4-37. THE EFFECT OF ADJUSTING ENTRIES ON THE FINANCIAL STATEMENTS   John Day, owner of several rental properties, has prepared his 19X8 financial statements. They are summarized as follows:

Revenues.	$370,000
Expenses	282,000
Net income	$ 88,000
Assets	$955,000
Liabilities	480,000
Equity	475,000

Your examination of the financial statements indicates that Mr. Day has overlooked several items that are likely to affect the accounts:

a) Depreciation is unrecorded for an apartment building with a cost of $140,000, an expected life of 20 years, and a residual value of $20,000.

b) Interest accrued on a $122,880, 12.5 percent note payable is unrecorded for the period August 1 through December 31.

c) Wage expense for December in the amount of $3,750 is unpaid and unrecorded at year-end.

d) Rent revenues in the amount of $12,700 were earned during December but were neither collected nor recorded at year-end.

e) Rent revenue in the amount of $6,770 were earned during December but was not recognized at year-end. The revenue was collected in advance and recorded as unearned revenue.

REQUIRED:

1. Prepare the omitted adjusting entries.

2. Determine the effect of these omitted adjusting entries on the income statement amounts (revenues, expenses, and net income) and on the balance sheet amounts (assets, liabilities, and equity).

P4-38. ADJUSTING ENTRIES AND THE INCOME STATEMENT   Garrett Products' accountant prepared the following income statement for 19X2:

GARRETT PRODUCTS
Income Statement
For the Year Ended December 31, 19X2

Sales revenue.	$968,500
Less: Cost of goods sold.	582,700
Gross margin.	$385,800
Less: Operating expenses	307,100
Income from operations	$ 78,700
Less: Interest expense	23,200
Income before taxes.	$ 55,500
Less: Income taxes expense	19,400
Net income	$ 36,100

After reviewing the accounting records, the accountant noticed that the following four items had been accounted for incorrectly when the 19X2 income statement was prepared:

a) 19X2 depreciation expense in the amount of $3,150 on a delivery truck was unrecorded.

b) Supplies inventory costing $2,470 was overlooked when the physical inventory was taken at December 31, 19X2.

c) An insurance policy that was purchased in 19X2 provided insurance coverage for 19X3 in the amount of $940. The full cost of the policy was recorded as an expense in 19X2.

d) Wages in the amount of $380 that were paid early in 19X2 and recorded as a 19X2 expense had actually been earned in 19X1.

REQUIRED:

Correct the affected income statement amounts and then revise the 19X2 income statement. (Assume that no tax effect results from these changes.)

P4-39. REVENUES, CASH FLOWS, AND ADJUSTING ENTRIES   Sack's Business Supply rents office copiers to small businesses. Some customers prepay their rentals, while others are billed by Sack's periodically for rent owed. The following data are available for rent revenues received in advance and for rent receivable at January 1 and December 31:

	1/1	12/31
Rent receivable	$9,100	$7,500
Unearned rent revenue	4,700	6,200

During the year, Sack's Business Supply received $88,600 in cash for copier rentals ($9,100 of which was for the January 1 receivable). Another $10,400 was from customers who prepay their copier rentals. During the year, the $4,700 of unearned rent revenue was earned, and $6,200 of the $10,400 was unearned at year-end.

REQUIRED:

1. Determine the amount of rent revenue earned during the year.

2. If the $88,600 of cash received for rentals is credited in full to unearned rent revenue, what is the necessary adjusting entry at December 31?

3. If $9,100 of the $88,600 is credited to rent receivable, $10,400 is credited to unearned rent revenue, and the remaining $69,100 is credited to rent revenue, what is the necessary adjusting entry at December 31?

P4-40. CASH FLOWS, REVENUES, AND EXPENSES   Sycamore Laundry and Dry Cleaners had the following account balances at December 31, 19X8, and December 31, 19X9:

	12/31/X8	12/31/X9
Supplies inventory, cleaning solvent	$2,100	$4,340
Supplies inventory, garment bags	295	230
Unearned revenue, dry cleaning	1,890	2,160
Unearned revenue, laundry	3,255	1,860

During 19X9 Sycamore recorded the following cash inflows and outflows. All amounts received were credited to unearned revenue accounts and all amounts paid were debited to inventory accounts.

Cleaning solvent purchases	$187,300
Garment bag purchases	1,390
Dry cleaning revenues received in advance	846,740
Laundry revenues received in advance	418,350

REQUIRED:

Determine the amount of cleaning solvent expense, garment bag expense, dry cleaning revenue, and laundry revenue for 19X9.

P4-41. INTEREST PAYMENTS, INTEREST EXPENSE, AND ADJUSTING ENTRIES Payette Farms, Inc., borrows small amounts of cash from local banks to purchase fertilizer and other supplies at times when prices are lowest. On January 1, 19X3, Payette owed $4,800 of interest on its outstanding loans. During 19X3, Payette paid interest in the amount of $16,230 (including the $4,800 owed on January 1, 19X3) and debited the entire amount to interest payable. On December 31, 19X3, Payette owed $6,220 of interest, none of which had been recorded.

REQUIRED:

1. What was the amount of 19X3 interest expense?

2. Prepare the journal entry to adjust the interest expense and interest payable accounts at December 31, 19X3.

P4-42. INTEREST REVENUE, COLLECTIONS OF CASH FOR INTEREST, AND ADJUSTING ENTRIES Aloma, Inc., often lends cash to its customers. At January 1, customers owed Aloma $7,000 of interest on outstanding notes. During the year, Aloma received $64,800 of interest, $7,000 of which was for the January 1 receivable. Aloma credited the entire amount received to interest receivable. At December 31, Aloma has interest receivable of $8,200, none of which has been recorded.

REQUIRED:

1. What was the amount of interest revenue for the year?

2. Prepare the journal entry to adjust the interest revenue and interest receivable accounts at December 31.

P4-43. INFERRING ADJUSTING ENTRIES FROM ACCOUNT BALANCE CHANGES The following schedule shows all the accounts of Fresno Travel Agency that received year-end adjusting entries:

ACCOUNT	UNADJUSTED TRIAL BALANCE	ADJUSTED TRIAL BALANCE
Prepaid insurance.....................	$ 23,270	$ 4,550
Prepaid rent	3,600	4,800
Accumulated depreciation	156,000	(1)
Wages payable	–0–	3,770
Unearned revenue, service	3,620	(2)
Service revenue	71,600	73,920
Insurance expense	–0–	(3)
Rent expense	29,700	(4)
Depreciation expense...................	–0–	16,000
Wages expense	44,200	(5)

REQUIRED:

1. Calculate the missing amounts identified by the numbers (1) through (5).

2. Prepare the five adjusting entries that must have been made to cause the account changes as indicated.

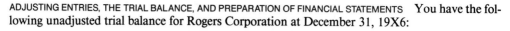

P4-44. ADJUSTING ENTRIES, THE TRIAL BALANCE, AND PREPARATION OF FINANCIAL STATEMENTS   You have the following unadjusted trial balance for Rogers Corporation at December 31, 19X6:

ROGERS CORPORATION
Unadjusted Trial Balance
As of December 31, 19X6

ACCOUNT	DEBIT	CREDIT
Cash.	$ 3,100	
Accounts receivable	15,900	
Office supplies inventory	4,200	
Prepaid rent	9,500	
Equipment.	625,000	
Accumulated depreciation, equipment.		$ 104,000
Other assets	60,900	
Accounts payable.		9,400
Unearned revenue		11,200
Note payable (due 19X9).		50,000
Capital stock		279,500
Retained earnings, 12/31/X5		37,000
Service revenue		598,000
Wages expense.	137,000	
Rent expense	229,000	
Interest expense	4,500	
Total	$1,089,100	$1,089,100

At year-end, you have the following data for adjusting entries:

a) An analysis indicates that prepaid rent on December 31 should be $7,900.

b) A physical inventory shows that $1,100 of office supplies is on hand.

c) The equipment is being depreciated over an expected life of seven years with a residual value of $30,000. Straight-line depreciation is used.

d) An analysis indicates that unearned revenue should be $8,400.

e) Wages in the amount of $2,800 are owed but unpaid and unrecorded at year-end.

f) Six months' interest at 12 percent on the note was paid on September 30. Interest for the period from October 1 to December 31 is unpaid and unrecorded.

g) Income taxes at 30 percent are owed but unrecorded and unpaid.

REQUIRED:

1. Prepare the adjusting entries.

2. Prepare an adjusted trial balance.

3. From the adjusted trial balance, prepare an income statement, a statement of changes in retained earnings, and a balance sheet.

P4-45. ADJUSTING ENTRIES, TRIAL BALANCE, AND FINANCIAL STATEMENT PREPARATION   The unadjusted trial balance for Mitchell Pharmacy appears below.

MITCHELL PHARMACY
Unadjusted Trial Balance
As of December 31, 19X7

ACCOUNT	DEBIT	CREDIT
Cash.	$ 3,400	
Accounts receivable	64,820	
Inventory.	583,400	
Prepaid insurance	11,200	
Building.	230,000	
Accumulated depreciation, building.		$ 44,000
Land	31,200	
Other assets	25,990	
Accounts payable.		47,810
Notes payable (due 19X9)		150,000
Capital stock		600,000
Retained earnings, 12/31/X6		41,200
Sales revenue		950,420
Cost of goods sold	573,180	
Wages expense.	298,240	
Interest expense	12,000	
Total	$1,833,430	$1,833,430

The following information is available at year-end for adjusting entries:

a) An analysis of insurance policies indicates that $1,400 of the prepaid insurance is coverage for 19X8.

b) The building is being depreciated on a straight-line basis over 25 years with an estimated residual value of $10,000.

c) Four months' interest at 12 percent is owed but unrecorded and unpaid on the note payable.

d) Wages of $4,410 are owed but unpaid and unrecorded at December 31.

e) Income taxes expense, computed at 30 percent of income before taxes, is owed but unrecorded and unpaid at December 31.

REQUIRED:

1. Prepare the adjusting entries.

2. Prepare an adjusted trial balance.

3. From the adjusted trial balance, prepare an income statement, a statement of changes in retained earnings, and a balance sheet.

APPENDIX PROBLEMS

P4-46. PREPAYMENTS FOR EXPENSES WITH BEGINNING BALANCES Bakersfield Products had the following balances in its prepaid rent and prepaid insurance accounts at January 1, 19X2:

Prepaid rent	$14,000
Prepaid insurance	10,800

The rent and insurance underlying the prepayments existing on January 1, 19X2, were used in the early months of 19X2. During 19X2, Bakersfield prepaid rent and insurance in the amounts and for the periods indicated below:

Rent (for the 12 months beginning March 1, 19X2)	$96,000
Insurance (for the 6 months beginning October 1, 19X2)	9,000

Bakersfield debits prepayments to expense accounts when the prepayments are made.

REQUIRED:

1. Determine the amount of rent and insurance expense for 19X2.

2. Prepare the adjusting entries necessary at December 31, 19X2.

P4-47. ADVANCE COLLECTIONS FOR REVENUES WITH BEGINNING BALANCES Popovich Enterprises rents small refrigerators to students for their rooms. Popovich's contracts are for 10 months at $5 per month (or $50 for the 10 months). Each contract is effective on August 1 and ends the following May 31. On January 1, 19X5, Popovich's unearned revenue account had a credit balance of $11,250. During 19X5 Popovich collected $26,750 in advance from customers for these 10-month contracts for the 19X5–19X6 school year. The entire $26,750 was credited to rent revenue.

REQUIRED:

1. What is the amount of 19X5 rent revenue for Popovich?

2. Prepare the adjusting entry necessary at December 31, 19X5.

P4-48. ADVANCE COLLECTIONS RECORDED IN INCOME STATEMENT ACCOUNTS Intercity Transportation rents buses to community groups for single- and multiple-day trips. Some groups pay in advance for these trips and some pay after. For 19X4 the following data were available:

	1/1/X4	12/31/X4
Accounts receivable	$48,100	$31,300
Unearned revenue	84,810	91,230

During 19X4 Intercity received $732,680 cash for transportation activities, crediting the entire amount to the revenue account. The cash received included $48,100 receivable at January 1 and the $91,230 that applies to 19X5 and is unearned at December 31, 19X4.

REQUIRED:

1. Determine the amount of revenue earned in 19X4.

2. Prepare the adjusting entry necessary to state properly the revenue, accounts receivable, and unearned revenue accounts.

ANALYTICAL OPPORTUNITIES

A4-49. ADJUSTING ENTRIES FOR REFUND COUPONS   Cal-Lite Products, Inc., manufactures a line of food products that appeals to persons interested in weight loss. To stimulate sales, Cal-Lite includes cash refund coupons in many of its products. Cal-Lite issues the purchaser a check when the coupon is returned to the company, which may be many months after the product is sold to stores and distributors. In addition, a significant number of coupons issued is never returned. As cash distributions are made to customers, they are recorded in an expense account.

REQUIRED:

1. Explain the conceptual basis for the determination of refund expense in each year. Describe the information and calculations required to estimate the amount of expense for each year.

2. Describe the year-end adjusting entry required at the end of the first year of the program's existence.

3. Describe the adjusting entry at the end of the second year of the program's existence.

A4-50. ADJUSTING ENTRIES FOR MOTION PICTURE REVENUES   Link Pictures, Inc., sells (licenses) the rights to exhibit motion pictures to theaters. Under the sales contract, the theater promises to pay a license fee equal to the larger of a guaranteed minimum or a percentage of the box office receipts. In addition, the contract requires the guaranteed minimum to be paid in advance. Consider the following contracts entered by Link during 19X2:

a) Contract A authorizes a group of theaters in Buffalo, New York, to exhibit a film called *Garage* for two weeks ending January 7, 19X3. Box office statistics indicate that first-week attendance has already generated licensing fees well in excess of the guaranteed minimum.

b) Contract B authorizes a chain of theaters in Miami, Florida, to exhibit a film called *Blue Denim* for a period of two weeks ending on January 20, 19X3. In most first-run cities, the film has attracted large crowds, and the percentage of box office receipts has far exceeded the minimum.

c) Contract C authorizes a chain of theaters in San Francisco to exhibit a film called *Toast Points* for a period of two weeks ending on January 5, 19X3. The film is a "dog," and the theaters stopped showing it after the first few days. All prints of the film were returned by December 31, 19X2.

The guaranteed minimum has been paid on all three contracts and recorded as unearned revenue. No other amounts have been received, and no revenue has been recorded for any of the contracts. Adjusting entries for 19X2 are just about to be made.

REQUIRED:

Describe the adjusting entry you would make at December 31, 19X2, to record revenue for each contract. Justify your entry by reference to generally accepted accounting principles. (Hint: In addition to general discussions of revenue recognition in the text, see paragraphs 3 and 4 of FASB Statement of Financial Accounting Standards No. 53.)

A4-51. THE EFFECT OF ADJUSTING ENTRIES ON THE FINANCIAL STATEMENTS (A CONCEPTUAL APPROACH)   Don Berthrong, the owner of a local bookstore, is wondering whether adjusting entries will affect his financial statements. Don's business has grown steadily for several years, and Don expects it to continue to grow for the next several years at a rate of 5 to 10 percent per year. Nearly all Don's sales are for cash. Other than cost of goods sold, which is not affected by adjusting entries, most of Don's expenses are for items that require regular cash outflows (e.g., rent on the building, wages, utilities, insurance).

REQUIRED:

1. Would Don's financial statement be affected significantly by adjusting entries?

2. Consider all businesses. What kinds of transactions would require adjustments that would have a significant effect on the financial statements? What kinds of businesses would be likely to require these kinds of adjustments?

5

COMPLETING THE ACCOUNTING CYCLE

The statement of changes in retained earnings links the income statement and successive balance sheets by describing the changes in the retained earnings account that occur during the accounting period, as shown in Exhibit 1–7 on page 21. These changes in retained earnings are recorded by special entries, called *closing entries,* as the next-to-the-last step in the accounting cycle. The last step in the accounting cycle is the preparation of the *postclosing trial balance,* which presents the debit and credit account balances after the closing entries have been made. These final steps in the accounting cycle are called the *closing process* and are discussed in the first section of the chapter.

After discussing the closing process, we introduce worksheet preparation, an optional but very useful step in the accounting cycle. The *worksheet* is a multicolumned schedule used to organize and summarize all the steps in the end-of-period portion of the accounting cycle, including adjusting entries and the closing process. Because it brings together these several steps, the worksheet provides a framework for illustrating the operation and ordering of this portion of the accounting cycle. Our discussion of the accounting cycle concludes with a comprehensive review of the complete cycle and a review problem that illustrates, in sequence, all the steps in the accounting cycle.

The performance of the final steps in the accounting cycle may lead to the discovery of errors in analysis, journalizing, or posting of transactions. In addition, the operations of accounting systems are governed by rules and procedures, called *internal controls,* that detect and prevent errors (whether accidental or intentional), encourage ethical behavior, and safeguard the firm's assets. The last two sections of the chapter consider these topics; the first illustrates the tracing and correcting of errors, and the second discusses internal controls.

The chapter concludes with an appendix that describes an optional but convenient record-keeping procedure called *reversing entries.* Reversing entries are made at the beginning of an accounting period and reverse the effects of adjusting entries for revenue earned before collection and expense incurred before payment.

THE CLOSING PROCESS

The closing process includes the last two steps in the accounting cycle—the preparation of closing entries and the preparation of the postclosing trial balance.

PREPARATION OF CLOSING ENTRIES

Net income or net loss is not recorded directly in the retained earnings account. Rather it is first recorded in the various revenue and expense accounts and is transferred (after being summarized in an income summary account) to retained earnings at the end of the accounting period. Similarly, dividends are not recorded directly in retained earnings, but are recorded first in a dividends account and transferred to retained earnings at the end of the accounting period. These year-end transfers involve a debit to each credit-balance account and a credit to each debit-balance account that reduce the corresponding balances to zero, preparing these accounts to receive next year's revenue, expense, and dividends.

Revenue, expense, and dividend accounts are called *temporary* (or *nominal*) *accounts* because revenue, expense, and dividend amounts reside in them only temporarily before being transferred to retained earnings, a balance sheet account. In contrast, the ending amounts in balance sheet accounts are carried forward from one period to the next; the ending balance of one period becomes the beginning balance of the next. Thus balance sheet accounts are called *permanent* (or *real*) *accounts.*

The transfers of revenue, expense, and dividends account balances at the end of the accounting period are accomplished by journal entries called **closing entries.** One closing entry transfers the balance of, or "closes," the dividends account directly to retained earnings; the entry simply credits the dividends account for the amount of its balance, reducing its balance to zero, and debits the same amount to retained earnings. Although closing entries may transfer revenues and expenses directly to retained earnings, we prefer a somewhat more elaborate closing procedure that uses an income summary account. **Income summary** is a temporary account to which all revenues and expenses are transferred or closed and which is itself closed to retained earnings. If revenues and expense are closed directly to retained earnings, then an income summary account is unnecessary; however, without the income summary account, the net income or net loss figure does not appear in the accounts. Since we believe it is useful to have the net income or net loss appear in the accounts, the income summary account is used in closing entries throughout this book.

CLOSING ENTRIES: Journal entries that transfer revenue, expense, and dividends account balances to retained earnings. The closing of revenue and expense accounts employs an income summary account as an intermediate step in the transfer.

INCOME SUMMARY: A temporary account to which all revenues and expenses are transferred or closed and which is itself closed to retained earnings.

PREPARATION OF THE POSTCLOSING TRIAL BALANCE

The final step in the accounting cycle is the preparation of a postclosing trial balance. A **postclosing trial balance** is a trial balance prepared from the account balances immediately after the closing entries have been posted. The process for preparing a postclosing trial balance is identical to the process used for an unadjusted trial balance: All the accounts with nonzero balances are listed in financial statement order with their net debit or credit balances. This trial balance provides a final opportunity to check the equality of debits and credits. Since the postclosing trial balance should contain only balance sheet accounts, it also allows the preparer to determine whether or not all the temporary accounts (revenues, expenses, income summary, and dividends) have been closed. The completion of the postclosing trial balance is a signal that the accounting cycle for the current period has been completed. The account balances it contains are the beginning balances for the next period.

POSTCLOSING TRIAL BALANCE: A trial balance prepared from the account balances immediately after the closing entries have been posted.

THE CLOSING PROCESS ILLUSTRATED

The closing process is a five-step procedure:

1. Establish a new account called *income summary.*
2. Close each revenue and expense account to income summary.
3. Close income summary to retained earnings.
4. Close dividends to retained earnings.
5. Prepare the postclosing trial balance.

Let us illustrate this five-step procedure by reference to an example. At the end of an accounting period and just prior to closing, Wheaton, Inc., has the balances in its revenue, expense, dividends, and retained earnings accounts that are shown in Exhibit 5–1.

We begin the closing process by establishing the income summary account. Since revenue accounts have credit balances, they are closed by entering debits equal to their respective credit balances. The corresponding credit is to income summary. Wheaton's revenue accounts are closed into the income summary account with the following journal entry:

Sales revenue	630,000	
Interest revenue	20,000	
Income summary.		650,000

Next, the expense accounts are closed into income summary. Since expense accounts have debit balances, they are closed by entering credits equal to their respective debit balances. The corresponding debit is to income summary. Wheaton's expense accounts are closed with the following journal entry:

Income summary.	635,000	
Cost of goods sold		310,000
Operating expenses, not detailed.		280,000
Interest expense		40,000
Income taxes expense		5,000

EXHIBIT 5–1   **PRECLOSING LEDGER ACCOUNTS**

Sales revenue	Interest revenue	Cost of goods sold
630,000	20,000	310,000

Operating expenses, not detailed	Interest expense	Income taxes expense
280,000	40,000	5,000

Dividends	Retained earnings
3,000	14,000

EXHIBIT 5-2 **LEDGER ACCOUNTS AFTER REVENUE AND EXPENSE ACCOUNTS HAVE BEEN CLOSED INTO INCOME SUMMARY**

Sales revenue		Interest revenue		Cost of goods sold	
(a) 630,000	630,000	(a) 20,000	20,000	310,000	310,000 (b)
	-0-		-0-	-0-	

Operating expenses, not detailed		Interest expense		Income taxes expense	
280,000	280,000 (b)	40,000	40,000 (b)	5,000	5,000 (b)
-0-		-0-		-0-	

Dividends		Retained earnings		Income summary	
3,000			14,000	(b) 635,000	650,000 (a)
					15,000

These entries complete step 2 of the closing process. After these closing entries are posted, the ledger accounts for Wheaton, Inc., have the balances shown in Exhibit 5-2. Note that debits have been entered in both revenue accounts that are equal to the previously recorded revenues. Also note that credits have been entered in the expense accounts that are equal to the previously recorded expenses. In the income summary account, a credit has been entered that is equal to the sum of the revenues ($650,000) and a debit has been entered that is equal to the sum of the expenses ($635,000).

At this point in the closing process, the balance in the income summary account is the net income or net loss for the period. This balance is transferred to retained earnings (step 3), thus closing the income summary account. When revenues exceed expenses, income summary has a credit balance (a net income situation) and is closed with a debit equal to that balance. The corresponding credit is to retained earnings. When expenses exceed revenues (a net loss situation), income summary has a debit balance and is closed with a credit equal to that balance. The corresponding debit is to retained earnings. In the Wheaton example, the $15,000 credit balance indicates that net income was $15,000. The following entry closes income summary:

Income summary................................... 15,000
  Retained earnings   15,000

The only account remaining to be closed is dividends (step 4). Recall that dividends are payments made to stockholders. These payments are not an expense; they are a distribution of income, which directly reduces stockholders' equity. The dividends account has a debit balance, so it is closed by entering a credit equal to that balance, with a corresponding debit to retained earnings. Therefore, Wheaton's dividends account is closed to retained earnings with the following entry:

Retained earnings 3,000
  Dividends   3,000

EXHIBIT 5–3   LEDGER ACCOUNTS AFTER COMPLETION OF THE CLOSING PROCESS

Sales revenue			Interest revenue			Cost of goods sold	
(a) 630,000	630,000		(a) 20,000	20,000		310,000	310,000 (b)
	–0–			–0–		–0–	

Operating expenses, not detailed			Interest expense			Income taxes expense	
280,000	280,000 (b)		40,000	40,000 (b)		5,000	5,000 (b)
–0–			–0–			–0–	

Dividends			Retained earnings			Income summary	
3,000	3,000 (d)			14,000		(b) 635,000	650,000 (a)
–0–			(d) 3,000	15,000 (c)			15,000
				26,000		(c) 15,000	
							–0–

When this final closing entry for the period has been posted, the retained earnings, dividends, and income statement accounts for Wheaton appear as shown in Exhibit 5–3. Note that the $15,000 net income that was developed in the income summary account has been added to retained earnings. The $3,000 in the dividends account has been deducted from retained earnings. Balances in the revenue, expense, dividends, and income summary accounts have all been returned to zero in preparation for recording the next period's activities.

The postclosing trial balance (step 5) would show retained earnings with its $26,000 balance in the credit column together with all other balance sheet accounts and their corresponding balances.

Thus, the closing process clears the revenue, expense, and dividends accounts, making them ready to receive next year's activity, and updates retained earnings for the current year's activities. The closing process also produces an income summary account that is a useful record of the balances that constitute the year's net income. Frequently, companies prepare monthly financial statements for internal use in addition to the annual financial statements issued to outsiders. The following analysis discusses the modifications to the accounting cycle required by the preparation of monthly financial statements.

ANALYSIS

MONTHLY FINANCIAL STATEMENTS AND THE CLOSING PROCESS

Monthly financial statements require monthly adjusting entries and monthly adjusted trial balances, but they do not require monthly closing entries. Monthly revenue, expense, and dividends amounts are calculated by subtracting the amount shown on the previous month's adjusted trial balance from the amount shown on the current month's trial balance. For example, wages expense for the month of April would be calculated by subtracting the adjusted balance of wages expense at the end of March (which includes wages expense for the three months January, February, and March) from the adjusted balance of wages expense at the end of April (which includes wages expense for the four months January, February, March, and April). These calculations can be summarized using a multicolumned schedule prepared at the end of each month; the schedule would show in parallel columns the previous month's adjusted trial balance, the current month's adjusted trial balance, and the differences in revenue, expense, and dividends balances between the two adjusted trial balances.

This subtraction process is not required to produce annual financial statements, because the revenue, expense, and dividends accounts are closed annually. Thus, the income statement and the statement of changes in retained earnings can be prepared using the balances of these accounts at closing. Although it is extremely unlikely to occur, monthly closing would remove the need for the subtraction process in the preparation of monthly statements but would require a summation of monthly revenue, expense, and dividends balances for the preparation of annual statements.

THE WORKSHEET

WORKSHEET: A schedule that summarizes the information generated in the performance of the end-of-period steps in the accounting cycle and enables the accountant to check this information for completeness and consistency.

The discussion of closing entries and the postclosing trial balance completes our presentation of the essential procedures that make up the accounting cycle. We are now ready to examine an informal, "scratch pad" tool or schedule, called a *worksheet,* that is outside the basic accounting system. Accountants use the term *schedule* to refer to any organized calculation or presentation of financial data. The worksheet is a schedule that helps accountants organize and prepare the data necessary to perform the end-of-period steps in the accounting cycle—namely, the preparation of adjusting entries, the adjusted trial balance, the financial statements, the closing entries, and the postclosing trial balance. The **worksheet** summarizes the information generated in the performance of these accounting cycle steps and enables the accountant to check this information for completeness and consistency.[1] We have deferred discussion of the worksheet until now, because its preparation and use require that you understand all the steps in the accounting cycle.

A typical completed worksheet is shown in Exhibit 5–4. Note that all the accounts are listed in a column at the left. Beginning at the top of that column, the balance sheet accounts appear first and are followed by the income statement accounts. (Recall that this is the same order in which the accounts appear on a trial balance.) Within each statement group, the accounts are listed in the order of their normal appearance in that statement (for example: current assets; property, plant, and equipment; other assets; current liabilities; and so forth).

Moving across the worksheet, there are six sets of debit and credit columns. The unadjusted trial balance is entered in the first set of columns, the adjusting entries in the second, and the adjusted trial balance in the third. The fourth pair of columns, which contains the income statement account balances, produces the income before taxes amount and the net income or net loss amount for the period. The fifth pair of columns shows the changes in retained earnings. The final set of columns contains the balance sheet accounts. The accounts and the amounts in the balance sheet columns are the postclosing trial balance accounts and their balances.

---

[1] Although a number of different worksheets are used by accountants to collect and present data, the schedule we describe here is generally referred to by the title "worksheet." You should be aware that other accounting schedules will often be identified as worksheets too, but they will normally carry an additional descriptor (such as statement of cash flows worksheet).

EXHIBIT 5–4   WORKSHEET

ELLEN'S EARTHENWARE EMPORIUM
Worksheet for the Year Ended December 31, 19X3

ACCOUNT TITLE	Part 1 UNADJUSTED TRIAL BALANCE Dr*	Cr	Part 2 ADJUSTING ENTRIES Dr	Cr	Part 3 ADJUSTED TRIAL BALANCE Dr	Cr	Part 4 INCOME STATEMENT Dr	Cr	Part 5 CHANGES IN RETAINED EARNINGS Dr	Cr	Part 6 BALANCE SHEET Dr	Cr
Cash	2,000				2,000						2,000	
Accounts receivable	20,000				20,000						20,000	
Inventory	16,000				16,000						16,000	
Prepaid insurance	2,000			(a) 1,600	400						400	
Building	90,000				90,000						90,000	
Accumulated depreciation, building		29,000		(b) 2,900		31,900						31,900
Land	15,000				15,000						15,000	
Other assets	6,000				6,000						6,000	
Accounts payable		10,000		(c) 1,500		11,500						11,500
Interest payable				(d) 1,000		1,000						1,000
Notes payable (due in 19X9)		24,000				24,000						24,000
Capital stock		40,000				40,000						40,000
Retained earnings, 12/31/X2		12,000				12,000				12,000		
Dividends	1,000				1,000				1,000			
Sales revenue		197,000				197,000		197,000				
Sales returns and allowances	4,000				4,000		4,000					
Cost of goods sold	102,000				102,000		102,000					
Operating expenses, not detailed	54,000		(c) 1,500		55,500		55,500					
Insurance expense			(a) 1,600		1,600		1,600					
Depreciation expense, building			(b) 2,900		2,900		2,900					
Interest expense			(d) 1,000		1,000		1,000					
Totals	312,000	312,000	7,000	7,000	317,400	317,400	167,000	197,000				
Income taxes expense			(e) 9,000		9,000		9,000					
Income taxes payable				(e) 9,000		9,000						9,000
Net income							(f) 21,000			(f) 21,000		
Totals							197,000	197,000	1,000	33,000		
Retained earnings, 12/31/X3									(g) 32,000			(g) 32,000
Totals									33,000	33,000	149,400	149,400

* On this and all worksheets in this text, *debit* and *credit* will be abbreviated as *Dr* and *Cr*, respectively.

186

The procedures for completing the worksheet correspond to six parts of the worksheet. To help you follow the process, the six parts of the worksheet in Exhibit 5–4 are shaded differently.

PART 1: UNADJUSTED TRIAL BALANCE

UNADJUSTED TRIAL BALANCE: A trial balance prepared immediately before the adjusting entries are posted.

An **unadjusted trial balance** is prepared immediately before the adjusting entries are posted. The data for this trial balance are the ledger account balances after all the regular transactions for the period have been journalized and posted, but before any adjusting entries have been recorded. If an unadjusted trial balance is prepared as a separate document, it is then reproduced in the first pair of columns on the worksheet. However, some accountants do not prepare a formal unadjusted trial balance. Instead, they use the ledger account balances to record the unadjusted trial balance directly in the first two columns of the worksheet.

PART 2: ADJUSTING ENTRIES

ADJUSTING ENTRY: A journal entry made at the end of an accounting period to record the completed portion of an incomplete continuous event.

An **adjusting entry** is a journal entry made at the end of an accounting period to record the completed portion of an incomplete continuous event. The adjusting entries necessary for the period, entries **a** through **e** on the worksheet in Exhibit 5–4, are first developed (as described in Chapter 4) and then entered into the second pair of columns. Remember that entering the adjusting entries onto the worksheet does *not* enter them into the journal. However, the entries on the worksheet do provide the data for the formal adjusting entries that must be journalized and posted. Adjusting entries are typically entered in the journal after the worksheet has been completed. The adjusting entries may be journalized and posted either before or after financial statements are prepared, but they must be entered into the accounting records before the closing entries are made. Adjusting entries often require the addition of accounts not included in the unadjusted trial balance. (See, for example, interest payable and the last three accounts above the first line of totals in Exhibit 5–4.) Space must be left for additions like these. As in Part 1, the trial balance format of the worksheet allows you to check the equality of debits and credits. Note, however, that income taxes expense and income taxes payable, entry **e**, appear separately at the bottom of the worksheet. This separation occurs because income taxes expense cannot be determined until the income before taxes amount has been developed. Thus the tax entry must be added later, after a portion of Part 4 (income statement) of the worksheet has been completed.

PART 3: ADJUSTED TRIAL BALANCE

ADJUSTED TRIAL BALANCE: A trial balance that incorporates the effects of adjusting entries on the unadjusted trial balance.

In this part of the worksheet, the adjustments entered in Part 2 are added to or subtracted from the unadjusted account balances entered in Part 1, and the resulting amounts are entered in the adjusted trial balance columns. An **adjusted trial balance** is simply a trial balance that incorporates the effects of adjusting entries on the unadjusted trial balance. For example, in Exhibit 5–4, accounts payable was increased from $10,000 to $11,500 by adding the $1,500 credit in the adjusting entry column to the unadjusted trial balance credit of $10,000. When there is no adjustment to an account, the unadjusted trial balance amount is simply transferred to the adjusted trial balance columns. In Exhibit 5–4, for example, the cash account debit balance of $2,000 is transferred unchanged from the unadjusted to the adjusted trial balance columns. The accounts and amounts appearing in the adjusted trial balance columns are the data that will be used in the income statement, changes in retained earnings, and balance sheet columns of the worksheet. Each account balance in the adjusted trial balance columns will be transferred to either the income statement, changes in retained earnings, or balance sheet columns of the worksheet.

PART 4: INCOME STATEMENT

This portion of the worksheet is completed in three steps. First, the income statement account balances are transferred from the adjusted trial balance columns to the income statement columns of the worksheet. These accounts contain all the revenue and revenue-related accounts and all the expense accounts except income taxes expense. The difference between the first debit and credit totals in the income statement columns is the amount of income before taxes. The first debit and credit totals in Exhibit 5–4 are $167,000 and $197,000, respectively. Therefore, the difference of $30,000 is income before taxes.

In the second step, the income tax rate (or rates) is applied to income before taxes to compute income taxes expense and income taxes payable. In this example, we assume a flat tax rate of 30 percent on all income. Income taxes expense and income taxes payable are thus $9,000 [(.30)($30,000)]. (Chapter 16 contains a more detailed discussion of the computation of income taxes expense.) The income taxes expense and income taxes payable are entered on the worksheet by recording adjustment **e** in the adjusting entry and adjusted trial balance columns, below the totals previously computed. The income taxes expense is also transferred to the income statement columns. At this point, all the data necessary to compute the firm's net income are available in the income statement columns of the worksheet. After income taxes expense is added to the debit column, the debit and credit columns totals are compared. If the total of the credits exceeds that of the debits, the difference is the net income for the period. If debits exceed credits in the income statement columns, then the debit excess is the net loss for the period. In Exhibit 5–4, the income statement credits exceed debits by $21,000 and that amount is net income for the period.

In the third step, the amount of net income for the period is entered in the debit column of the income statement and the credit column of the changes in retained earnings. (A net loss would be entered in the credit column of the income statement and the debit column of the changes in retained earnings.) This entry is made to equalize the income statement debit and credit column totals and to add net income to beginning retained earnings in the changes in retained earnings columns. In Exhibit 5–4, the net income of $21,000 is recorded as entry **f**.

PART 5: CHANGES IN RETAINED EARNINGS

This portion of the worksheet contains the data for the statement of changes in retained earnings and is completed in the same way as the bottom portion of the income statement. The amounts for beginning retained earnings and for dividends are transferred from the adjusted trial balance columns. The net income (or net loss) was entered when Part 4 was completed. The debit and credit columns are totaled at this intermediate point. In Exhibit 5–4, the debit and credit columns total $1,000 and $33,000, respectively, at this point. The difference between the column totals is the amount of ending retained earnings. If credits exceed debits, as they do in Exhibit 5–4, ending retained earnings is positive. However, if debits were to exceed credits at this intermediate point, then ending retained earnings would be negative. The amount of ending retained earnings, $32,000 in Exhibit 5–4, appears as entry **g** in the debit column of the changes in retained earnings columns and in the credit column of the balance sheet. An opposite entry, debiting the balance sheet and crediting the changes in retained earnings, would be made to record negative ending retained earnings.

PART 6: BALANCE SHEET The final portion of the worksheet is completed by transferring all the balance sheet account balances from the adjusted trial balance columns. At this point, all accounts have the correct balance sheet and postclosing trial balance amounts.

USING THE COMPLETED WORKSHEET The income statement, changes in retained earnings, and balance sheet columns of a completed worksheet provide all the information necessary to prepare the financial statements. The income statement is drawn from the income statement columns of the worksheet. Exhibit 5–5 shows how the income statement for Ellen's Earthenware Emporium is prepared from the worksheet. The statement of changes in retained earnings is prepared by using the data from the changes in retained earnings columns, as shown in Exhibit 5–6. Finally, the balance sheet (Exhibit 5–7) is prepared from the data in the balance sheet columns of the worksheet.

Once the financial statements have been prepared, the closing entries must be entered in the journal and posted. The data for closing entries involving revenues, expenses, and net income appear in the income statement columns. The changes in retained earnings columns contain the dividends data necessary

---

EXHIBIT 5–5   **USING THE WORKSHEET TO DEVELOP THE INCOME STATEMENT**

Income Statement Portion of the Worksheet	Dr	Cr	ELLEN'S EARTHENWARE EMPORIUM Income Statement For the Year Ended December 31, 19X3		
Sales revenue................		197,000	Sales revenue...............		$197,000
Sales returns and allowances ...	4,000		Less: Sales returns and		
Cost of goods sold	102,000		allowances................		4,000
Operating expenses, not			Net sales revenue		$193,000
detailed...................	55,500		Less: Cost of goods sold		102,000
Insurance expense	1,600		Gross margin		$ 91,000
Depreciation expense,			Less: Operating expenses		
building	2,900		Not detailed	$55,500	
Interest expense	1,000		Insurance.................	1,600	
Income taxes expense	9,000		Depreciation, building......	2,900	60,000
			Income from operations......		$ 31,000
			Less: Interest expense		1,000
			Income before taxes.........		$ 30,000
			Less: Income taxes expense ...		9,000
			Net income		$ 21,000

EXHIBIT 5–6   USING THE WORKSHEET TO DEVELOP THE STATEMENT OF CHANGES IN RETAINED EARNINGS

Statement of Changes in Retained Earnings Portion of the Worksheet

	Dr	Cr
Retained earnings, 12/31/X2		12,000
Dividends	1,000	
Net income		21,000
Retained earnings, 12/31/X3	32,000	

ELLEN'S EARTHENWARE EMPORIUM
Statement of Changes in Retained Earnings
For the Year Ended December 31, 19X3

Retained earnings, 12/31/X2	$12,000
Add: Net income	21,000
	$33,000
Less: Dividends	1,000
Retained earnings, 12/31/X3	$32,000

EXHIBIT 5–7   USING THE WORKSHEET TO DEVELOP THE BALANCE SHEET

Balance Sheet Portion of the Worksheet

	Dr	Cr
Cash	2,000	
Accounts receivable	20,000	
Inventory	16,000	
Prepaid insurance	400	
Building	90,000	
Accumulated depreciation, building		31,900
Land	15,000	
Other assets	6,000	
Accounts payable		11,500
Interest payable		1,000
Notes payable (due in 19X9)		24,000
Capital stock		40,000
Income taxes payable		9,000
Retained earnings, 12/31/X3		32,000

ELLEN'S EARTHENWARE EMPORIUM
Balance Sheet
As of December 31, 19X3

ASSETS

Current assets:

Cash		$ 2,000
Accounts receivable		20,000
Inventory		16,000
Prepaid insurance		400
Total current assets		$ 38,400

Property, plant, and equipment:

Building	$90,000	
Less: Accumulated depreciation, building	31,900	58,100
Land		15,000
Other assets		6,000
Total assets		$117,500

LIABILITIES

Current liabilities:

Accounts payable	$ 11,500
Interest payable	1,000
Income taxes payable	9,000
Total current liabilities	$ 21,500

Long-term liabilities

Notes payable (due in 19X9)	24,000
Total liabilities	$ 45,500

EQUITY

Capital stock	$40,000	
Retained earnings	32,000	72,000
Total liabilities and equity		$117,500

for the final closing entry. Next, the balance sheet columns of the worksheet can be used to prepare a formal postclosing trial balance.

Now reexamine the worksheet in Exhibit 5–4. Note how the data for all the end-of-period steps in the accounting cycle—adjusting entries, adjusted trial balance, financial statements, closing entries, and postclosing trial balance—appear on this one document.

This explanation of the worksheet completes the description of the accounting cycle that was begun in Chapter 3. The section that follows is a review of the entire accounting cycle.

REVIEW OF THE ACCOUNTING CYCLE

Now that we have completed our examination of the accounting cycle, let's briefly review all the steps covered in this and the previous two chapters. As you study the review, try to make sure that you understand each procedure and its position in the cycle.

The accounting cycle is made up of 10 steps. In the discussion that follows, the numbers in parentheses correspond to the numbered steps shown in Exhibit 5–8. The cycle begins with (1) the *collection of data* from transactions that affect the firm. The data are then (2) *analyzed* and those transactions for which formal recognition in the accounting system is appropriate are (3) *journalized.* The journal entries, which are based on the data collected and the analysis of those data, are then (4) *posted* to the ledger accounts. These four steps are repeated many times throughout the period.

The remaining six steps of the cycle are performed only at the end of the accounting period. After (5) an *unadjusted trial balance* has been prepared, (6) a *worksheet* may be compiled. If a worksheet is used, (7) the *adjusting entries* are entered on the worksheet and the adjusted trial balance on the worksheet is used to complete the worksheet. The adjusting entries are entered in the journal and posted to the ledger after the worksheet is completed. (If a worksheet is not used, the adjusting entries are computed directly from the ledger accounts; they are entered in the journal and posted to the ledger at this point in the cycle.) Next, (8) the *financial statements* are prepared from the data in the worksheet (or directly from the ledger accounts, if a worksheet is not used).[2] Then (9) the *closing entries* are journalized and posted, using data from the income statement columns of the worksheet (or from the ledger account balances, if a worksheet is not used). Finally, (10) the *postclosing trial balance* is prepared. At this point, the income statement accounts have all been closed to zero and the balance sheet accounts all contain the correct beginning balances for the start of the new accounting period. The 10-step cycle can begin again.

---

[2] Some accountants consider the worksheet to be a device to accelerate the preparation of financial statements. These accountants regard the determination of the adjusting entries to be a part of the preparation of the worksheet. In that case, steps 6, 7, and 8 of the accounting cycle are described as follows: (6) preparation of the worksheet, including determination of adjusting entries; (7) preparation of the financial statements; (8) journalizing and posting of the adjusting entries computed in step 6.

EXHIBIT 5–8 THE ACCOUNTING CYCLE

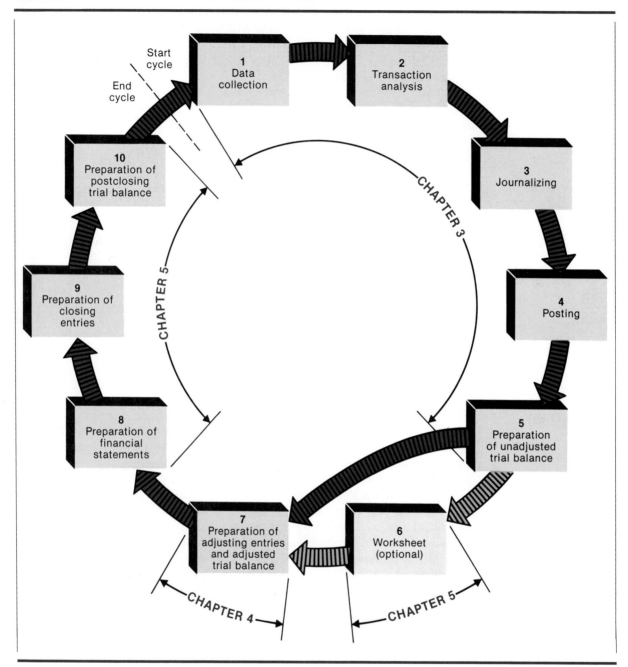

REVIEW PROBLEM The review problem that follows provides a review and illustration of the entire accounting cycle. To solve the problem, we will draw on our discussion of all 10 steps in the cycle, as presented in Chapters 3, 4, and 5. Our example firm is Hoosier Air Service, a commuter air carrier operating daily passenger and cargo

EXHIBIT 5-9   POSTCLOSING TRIAL BALANCE, DECEMBER 31, 19X5

HOOSIER AIR SERVICE
Trial Balance
As of December 31, 19X5

ACCOUNT	DEBIT	CREDIT
Cash..	$ 593,000	
Accounts receivable	2,200,000	
Supplies inventory, parts	240,000	
Supplies inventory, fuel	60,000	
Prepaid rent	130,000	
Equipment, aircraft..........................	9,820,000	
Accumulated depreciation, aircraft		$ 2,600,000
Equipment, ground...........................	130,000	
Accumulated depreciation, ground equipment		40,000
Equipment, office	80,000	
Accumulated depreciation, office equipment......		20,000
Accounts payable.............................		480,000
Salaries payable		183,000
Income taxes payable		450,000
Bonds payable (due in 19X9)		2,400,000
Capital stock.................................		2,600,000
Retained earnings		4,480,000
Totals..................................	$13,253,000	$13,253,000

flights from several Indiana and Illinois cities to O'Hare Airport in Chicago. Hoosier, which has been in business for several years, owns its own airplanes, ground equipment, and office equipment. Hangars, office space, and terminal space are rented. On December 31, 19X5, the postclosing trial balance shown in Exhibit 5-9 was prepared. During 19X6 the following events occurred:

a) Hoosier Air Service earned $9,400,000 of passenger revenue and $1,200,000 of cargo revenue. Of the total revenue, $8,050,000 was collected in cash. In addition to the $8,050,000 cash collection just described, the entire amount of the accounts receivable on January 1, 19X6, was collected during 19X6.

b) Two new aircraft were purchased for cash on July 1, 19X6, for $880,000 each. The aircraft were put into use immediately.

c) Salaries of $5,390,000 were paid during 19X6. The $5,390,000 includes the $183,000 of salaries payable on January 1, 19X6.

d) On June 30, 19X6, and December 31, 19X6, semiannual interest payments of $120,000 each were made on the bonds payable.

e) Rent payments of $1,690,000 were made during 19X6.

f) Fuel in the amount of $290,000 was purchased for cash during 19X6.

g) Repair parts costing $870,000 were purchased on credit during 19X6. Of the total amount, $400,000 was paid by the end of 19X6.

h) The accounts payable on January 1, 19X6, were all paid during 19X6.

i) The income taxes payable on January 1, 19X6, were paid during 19X6.

j) On December 1, 19X6, a large pharmaceutical manufacturer prepaid air cargo service for December 19X6 and January 19X7. The $130,000 cash receipt was credited to unearned cargo revenue.

k) During 19X6 dividends were declared and paid in the amount of $40,000.

The following information is available for adjusting entries:

l) Depreciation on the aircraft should be 10 percent of the December 31, 19X6, aircraft cost.

m) Depreciation on the ground equipment should be $20,000 per year.

n) Depreciation on the office equipment should be $10,000 per year.

o) As of December 31, 19X6, there is $50,000 of salaries payable to employees for services performed in 19X6.

p) An inventory indicates that there are $320,000 of parts and $60,000 of fuel on hand as of December 31, 19X6.

q) Prepaid rent as of December 19X6 is $80,000.

r) Unearned cargo revenue is $65,000 as of December 31, 19X6.

s) The income tax rate is 30 percent.

REQUIRED:

1. Using the data above, analyze transactions **a** through **k** and then prepare journal entries.

2. Update the December 31, 19X5, postclosing trial balance for the effects of the journal entries just prepared.

3. Using the information presented in items **l** through **s**, prepare the adjusting entries and enter them on the worksheet.

4. Complete the remainder of the worksheet.

5. Prepare an income statement for Hoosier Air Service for 19X6. Assume that there are 220,000 shares of capital stock outstanding.

6. Prepare a statement of changes in retained earnings for Hoosier Air Service for the year ended December 31, 19X6.

7. Prepare a balance sheet for Hoosier Air Service as of December 31, 19X6.

8. Prepare the closing entries for Hoosier Air Service at December 31, 19X6.

9. Prepare a postclosing trial balance for Hoosier Air Service as of December 31, 19X6.

SOLUTION:

1. The journal entries for transactions **a** through **k** are as follows:

a)	Cash	8,050,000	
	Accounts receivable	2,550,000	
	Service revenue, cargo		1,200,000
	Service revenue, passenger		9,400,000
	Cash	2,200,000	
	Accounts receivable		2,200,000
b)	Equipment, aircraft	1,760,000	
	Cash		1,760,000
c)	Salaries payable	183,000	
	Salaries expense	5,207,000	
	Cash		5,390,000
d)	Interest expense	240,000	
	Cash		240,000
e)	Rent expense	1,690,000	
	Cash		1,690,000
f)	Supplies inventory, fuel	290,000	
	Cash		290,000
g)	Supplies inventory, parts	870,000	
	Accounts payable		870,000
	Accounts payable	400,000	
	Cash		400,000
h)	Accounts payable	480,000	
	Cash		480,000
i)	Income taxes payable	450,000	
	Cash		450,000
j)	Cash	130,000	
	Unearned revenue		130,000
k)	Dividends	40,000	
	Dividends payable		40,000
	Dividends payable	40,000	
	Cash		40,000

EXHIBIT 5–10   WORKSHEET

HOOSIER AIR SERVICE
Worksheet for the Year Ended December 31, 19X6 (amounts in thousands)

ACCOUNT TITLE	UNADJUSTED TRIAL BALANCE Dr	Cr	ADJUSTING ENTRIES Dr	Cr	ADJUSTED TRIAL BALANCE Dr	Cr	INCOME STATEMENT Dr	Cr	CHANGES IN RETAINED EARNINGS Dr	Cr	BALANCE SHEET Dr	Cr
Cash	233				233						233	
Accounts receivable	2,550				2,550						2,550	
Supplies inventory, parts	1,110			(p) 790	320						320	
Supplies inventory, fuel	350			(p) 290	60						60	
Prepaid rent	130			(q) 50	80						80	
Equipment, aircraft	11,580				11,580						11,580	
Accumulated depreciation, aircraft		2,600		(l) 1,158		3,758						3,758
Equipment, ground	130				130						130	
Accumulated depreciation, ground equipment		40		(m) 20		60						60
Equipment, office	80				80						80	
Accumulated depreciation, office equipment		20		(n) 10		30						30
Accounts payable		470				470						470
Unearned revenue		130	(r) 65			65						65
Salaries payable				(o) 50		50						50
Bonds payable (due in 19X9)		2,400				2,400						2,400
Capital stock		2,600				2,600						2,600
Retained earnings, 12/31/X5		4,480				4,480				4,480		
Dividends	40				40				40			
Service revenue, passenger		9,400				9,400		9,400				
Service revenue, cargo		1,200		(r) 65		1,265		1,265				
Salaries expense	5,207		(o) 50		5,257		5,257					
Depreciation expense, aircraft			(l) 1,158		1,158		1,158					
Depreciation expense, ground equipment			(m) 20		20		20					
Depreciation expense, office equipment			(n) 10		10		10					
Rent expense	1,690		(q) 50		1,740		1,740					
Supplies expense, repair parts			(p) 790		790		790					
Supplies expense, fuel			(p) 290		290		290					
Interest expense	240				240		240					
Totals	23,340	23,340	2,433	2,433	24,578	24,578	9,505	10,665				
Income taxes expense			(s) 348		348		348					
Income taxes payable				(s) 348		348						348
Net income							(t) 812			(t) 812		
Totals			2,781	2,781	24,926	24,926	10,665	10,665				
Retained earnings, 12/31/X6									(u) 5,252			(u) 5,252
Totals									5,292	5,292	15,033	15,033

2. Updated postclosing trial balance: You can check your results against the amounts shown in the unadjusted trial balance columns in the worksheet in Exhibit 5–10.

3. Adjusting entries: The adjusting entries are shown in the adjusting entries columns on the worksheet in Exhibit 5–10.

4. Completed worksheet: The adjusted trial balance columns of the worksheet are completed by altering the unadjusted trial balance amounts for the amounts of the adjusting entries. The income statement and balance sheet accounts are then assigned to the appropriate columns, as described earlier in this chapter. Now that the worksheet has been completed, the adjusting entries from the worksheet can be entered in the journal and posted to the ledger accounts. It is also possible now to prepare the financial statements.

5. Income statement: From the income statement columns of the worksheet, the income statement for Hoosier Air Service (Exhibit 5–11) is prepared for the year 19X6.

6. Statement of changes in retained earnings: From the changes in retained earnings columns of the worksheet, the statement of changes in retained earnings for Hoosier Air Service (Exhibit 5–12) can be prepared.

EXHIBIT 5–11   **INCOME STATEMENT**

HOOSIER AIR SERVICE
Income Statement
For the Year Ended December 31, 19X6

Service revenue, passenger....................		$ 9,400,000
Service revenue, cargo.........................		1,265,000
Total revenue.............................		$10,665,000
Less: Operating expenses		
Salaries...................................	$5,257,000	
Depreciation, aircraft	1,158,000	
Depreciation, ground equipment	20,000	
Depreciation, office equipment................	10,000	
Rent......................................	1,740,000	
Supplies, repair parts........................	790,000	
Supplies, fuel	290,000	9,265,000
Income from operations.......................		$ 1,400,000
Less: Interest expense		240,000
Income before taxes		$ 1,160,000
Less: Income taxes expense		348,000
Net income...................................		$ 812,000
Earnings per share...........................		$3.69*

* $812,000/220,000 shares.

EXHIBIT 5–12   **STATEMENT OF CHANGES IN RETAINED EARNINGS**

HOOSIER AIR SERVICE

Statement of Changes in Retained Earnings
For the Year Ended December 31, 19X6

Retained earnings, 12/31/X5...................................	$4,480,000
Add: Net income..	812,000
	$5,292,000
Less Dividends...	40,000
Retained earnings, 12/31/X6.................................	$5,252,000

7. Balance sheet: From the balance sheet columns of the worksheet, data are collected for the preparation of the balance sheet as of December 31, 19X6 (Exhibit 5–13). Now we are ready to prepare the closing entries.

8. Closing entries: The data used to make the closing entries for the revenue and expense accounts are taken from the worksheet. First, revenues are closed into the income summary account:

Service revenue, passenger....................	9,400,000	
Service revenue, cargo	1,265,000	
Income summary		10,665,000

Next, the expenses are closed into income summary. (Note that this closing entry includes the effects of the adjustments on the income statement accounts.)

Income summary...........................	9,853,000	
Salaries expense		5,257,000
Depreciation expense, aircraft...............		1,158,000
Depreciation expense, ground equipment.....		20,000
Depreciation expense, office equipment		10,000
Rent expense..............................		1,740,000
Supplies expense, repair parts		790,000
Supplies expense, fuel.....................		290,000
Interest expense		240,000
Income taxes expense		348,000

The balance in income summary (an $812,000 credit) is closed into retained earnings:

Income summary	812,000	
Retained earnings		812,000

And finally, the dividends are closed into retained earnings:

Retained earnings	40,000	
Dividends.................................		40,000

EXHIBIT 5-13   **BALANCE SHEET**

HOOSIER AIR SERVICE
Balance Sheet
As of December 31, 19X6

ASSETS

Current assets:

Cash			$ 233,000
Accounts receivable			2,550,000
Supplies inventory, parts.........			320,000
Supplies inventory, fuel..........			60,000
Prepaid rent....................			80,000
Total current assets...........			$ 3,243,000

Property, plant, and equipment:

Aircraft.......................	$11,580,000		
Less: Accumulated depreciation ..	3,758,000	$7,822,000	
Ground equipment..............	$ 130,000		
Less Accumulated depreciation ...	60,000	70,000	
Office equipment	$ 80,000		
Less: Accumulated depreciation ..	30,000	50,000	
Total property, plant, and equipment			7,942,000
Total assets			$11,185,000

LIABILITIES

Current liabilities:

Accounts payable			$ 470,000
Unearned revenue			65,000
Salaries payable.................			50,000
Income taxes payable...........			348,000
Total current liabilities			$ 933,000

Long-term liabilities:

Bonds payable (due in 19X9).....			2,400,000
Total liabilities			$ 3,333,000

STOCKHOLDERS' EQUITY

Capital stock	$2,600,000		
Retained earnings................	5,252,000		
Total stockholders' equity....			7,852,000
Total liabilities and stockholders' equity			$11,185,000

9. Postclosing trial balance: From the balance sheet columns of the worksheet, the data are collected for the postclosing trial balance (Exhibit 5-14).

The Hoosier Air Service illustration has been used to review the 10 steps of the accounting cycle. If you had difficulty understanding any part of this demonstration, you should reread the discussion of that part of the cycle where relevant in Chapters 3, 4, or 5. Additional problems covering the entire cycle are included at the end of this chapter.

EXHIBIT 5–14   POSTCLOSING TRIAL BALANCE, DECEMBER 31, 19X6

HOOSIER AIR SERVICE
Postclosing Trial Balance
As of December 31, 19X6

ACCOUNT	DEBIT	CREDIT
Cash..	$ 233,000	
Accounts receivable	2,550,000	
Supplies inventory, parts	320,000	
Supplies inventory, fuel	60,000	
Prepaid rent	80,000	
Equipment, aircraft.............................	11,580,000	
Accumulated depreciation, aircraft		$ 3,758,000
Equipment, ground..............................	130,000	
Accumulated depreciation, ground equipment		60,000
Equipment, office	80,000	
Accumulated depreciation, office equipment......		30,000
Accounts payable...............................		470,000
Unearned revenue..............................		65,000
Salaries payable		50,000
Income taxes payable		348,000
Bonds payable (due in 19X9)		2,400,000
Capital stock..................................		2,600,000
Retained earnings		5,252,000
Totals....................................	$15,033,000	$15,033,000

ERROR EFFECTS AND ERROR CORRECTION

Accounting procedures are designed to help accountants record transactions properly. Occasionally, however, errors are made. Some errors are *self-correcting* in the sense that they produce misstated balances for only a limited number of periods even if not corrected. Suppose that the end-of-19X1 adjusting entry for salaries payable omits $7,500 owed to several managers. If the error is not corrected prior to closing, end-of-19X1 liabilities will be *understated* and 19X1 net income and end-of-19X1 retained earnings will be *overstated.* If the error is not detected in 19X2, the $7,500 omission will be recorded as part of 19X2 expense, with the result that 19X2 net income will be *understated;* however, end-of-19X2 retained earnings will be correctly stated because the 19X1 and 19X2 misstatements of net income counterbalance one another. Chapter 7 discusses self-correcting errors related to inventories. Of course, efforts should be made to discover and correct all errors at the earliest possible time and to avoid even temporary misstatements.

CORRECTING ENTRY: A journal entry that corrects erroneous account balances.

A **correcting entry** is a journal entry that corrects erroneous account balances. Correction of errors involves a procedure similar to that we recommended for analyzing some adjusting entries. First, identify the accounts that are misstated. Second, determine the correct balances for these accounts and calculate the amounts by which they are overstated or understated. Then prepare a correcting entry that changes the erroneous account balances to the correct ones.

Let us illustrate the correction of errors using an example. In December

19X3 the accountant for Magnaborg Products received a $9,700 invoice for repairs to delivery trucks. The repairs were performed during November 19X3. The transaction should have been recorded with a debit to maintenance expense and a credit to accounts payable. But the Magnaborg accountant was inattentive when recording this transaction and made the following erroneous entry:

Equipment, trucks	9,700	
Accounts payable		9,700

If uncorrected, the erroneous debit will cause 19X3 maintenance expense to be *understated* by $9,700, postclosing 19X3 retained earnings to be *overstated* by $9,700, and the postclosing 19X3 equipment, trucks account to be *overstated* by $9,700. For simplicity, we assume that there are no income taxes; hence, we need not consider the effect of the error on income taxes expense and related accruals. Further, we assume that the debit to the equipment, trucks account did not result in additional depreciation expense for 19X3. The form of the correcting entry depends on when the error is detected. We illustrate two cases—correction if the error is detected prior to the 19X3 closing and correction if the error is detected in 19X4.

If the Magnaborg accountant discovers the error prior to the 19X3 closing, then the following correcting entry would be made to avoid misstatements on the 19X3 financial statements:

Repair expense	9,700	
Equipment, trucks		9,700

The correcting entry removes the erroneous $9,700 debit from the equipment, trucks account and adds it to the repair expense account. Since the correction precedes closing, repair expense is correctly represented in the closing process and postclosing retained earnings is correctly stated.

On the other hand, if the Magnaborg accountant does not discover the error until 19X4, then the beginning-of-19X4 retained earnings balance is *overstated* by $9,700. Consequently, the correcting entry made in 19X4 takes the following form:

Retained earnings	9,700	
Equipment, trucks		9,700

Since error corrections qualify as *prior period adjustments,* as discussed in Chapter 12, the error correction is entered directly in the retained earnings account and would appear on the statement of changes in retained earnings.

INTERNAL CONTROL STRUCTURE

INTERNAL CONTROL STRUCTURE: All the policies and procedures established by an entity to achieve its objectives and the environment in which those policies and procedures are used.

The **internal control structure** is defined broadly to include all the policies and procedures established by an entity to achieve its objectives and the environment in which those policies and procedures are used. Thus the internal control structure includes many elements only indirectly related to the accounting system and financial statements. For example, policies and procedures concerning the extent and nature of research and development or advertising activities may have an important effect on the achievement of an entity's objectives but only an indirect effect on its accounting system and financial statements. The accounting system and financial statements are most directly affected by policies and procedures concerning the identification, measurement, recording, and communication of economic information.

The internal control structure of an entity involves the interaction of three major components — the accounting system, control procedures, and the control environment. Although these three components are useful concepts for purposes of discussion, the effectiveness of an entity's internal control structure depends on the successful integration of all three components.

CONTROL PROCEDURES

CONTROL PROCEDURES: The policies and procedures established by an entity to achieve its objectives.

Control procedures are the policies and procedures established by an entity to achieve its objectives. The control procedures most directly related to the accounting system and financial statements vary widely from one entity to another but generally can be associated with one of the following categories:

1. *Clearly defined authority and responsibility.* The *authority* to perform important duties should be delegated to specific individuals, and those individuals should be held *responsible* for the performance of those duties in the subsequent evaluation of their performance. Among the designated duties of an individual may be the authority to execute specified types of transactions for the entity or to authorize others to execute such transactions. (The clear delegation of authority and responsibility motivates individuals to perform well and facilitates corrective action if an employee fails to perform satisfactorily.)

2. *Segregation of duties.* The duties of record keeping should be segregated from the duties of administering related operations, transactions, or assets. In other words, accounting and administrative duties should be performed by different individuals, so that no one person prepares all the documents and records for a transaction. This segregation or separation of duties reduces the likelihood that records that will be used to conceal irregularities and increases the likelihood that irregularities will be discovered. The segregation of duties also reduces the likelihood that unintentional record-keeping errors will remain undiscovered.

3. *Adequate documents and records.* Accounting records are the basis for the financial statements and other reports prepared for interested parties both inside and outside the firm. Both summary records and their underlying documentation must provide information about specific transactions and facilitate the evaluation of individual performance. For example, prenumbered shipping documents provide a basis for monitoring shipments of goods to customers.

4. *Safeguards over assets and records.* Both assets and records must be secured against theft and destruction through such physical safeguards as fireproof vaults and locked storage facilities. Backup and access control systems must be provided for computer programs and data files, which are more fragile and susceptible to unauthorized access than manual or mechanical record-keeping systems.

5. *Checks on recorded amounts.* Recorded amounts should be checked by an independent party to determine that amounts are correct and that they correspond to properly authorized transactions. These procedures include clerical checks, reconciliations, comparisons of asset inspection reports with recorded amounts, computer-programmed controls, and management review of reports.

Designing and maintaining comprehensive systems of accounting-related control procedures are complex tasks that are never complete, because control is neither absolute nor permanent. The very fact that the authority to act and the responsibility for action are delegated by one person to another means that the delegating person's control over the action is not total or complete. Furthermore, even if control procedures are currently effective, the environment may change at any time, thereby creating new opportunities for error or misappropriation that must be eliminated by alterations in the procedures.

RELATIONSHIP BETWEEN CONTROL PROCEDURES AND ACCOUNTING SYSTEM

ACCOUNTING SYSTEM: The methods and records used to identify, measure, record, and communicate economic information about an entity.

The **accounting system** consists of the methods and records used to identify, measure, record, and communicate economic information about an entity. Although we distinguish between the accounting system and the control procedures, the two are really one integrated system designed to meet the needs of the particular entity. It is difficult to generalize about the relationship between control procedures and accounting systems because it depends so directly on the objectives and transaction details of the particular entity. Consequently, the relationship is best explored by reference to an example.

For our illustration of the relationship between control procedures and an accounting system, let us consider Hendrickson Theaters, Inc. Hendrickson operates 10 movie theaters in a single metropolitan area. All the theaters are rented, as are the projection equipment and concession facilities. Hendrickson's administrative offices are also rented. The following chart of accounts indicates the general structure of Hendrickson's simple accounting system:

Chart of Accounts for Hendrickson Theaters, Inc.

Assets
Cash
Supplies, concessions
Prepaid rent

Liabilities
Accounts payable
Salaries payable
Wages payable

Equity
Capital stock
Retained earnings

Revenues
Sales revenue, admissions
Sales revenue, concessions

Expenses
Salaries expense
Wages expense
Supplies, concessions
Rent expense, movies
Rent expense, theaters
Rent expense, equipment
Rent expense, office
Utilities expense
Advertising expense
Office supplies expense

Hendrickson uses a small computer and has purchased general-purpose accounting software to maintain its accounting records. Hendrickson's bookkeeper makes journal entries daily for revenues, biweekly for wages, and monthly for the other expenses. Because Hendrickson has a relatively small number of accounts, its accounting system is quite simple, yet a complete description would require many pages. Furthermore, a complete description is unnecessary to demonstrate the basic relationship between elements of the accounting system and control procedures. A portion of Hendrickson's accounting system related to revenues and the associated control procedures is described in Exhibit 5–15.

EXHIBIT 5–15   RELATIONSHIP BETWEEN ACCOUNTING SYSTEM AND CONTROL PROCEDURES

HENDRICKSON THEATERS, INC.
Illustrations from the Internal Control Structure for Revenue and Cash

ACCOUNTING SYSTEM

Entries: Admission and concession revenues are recorded daily by a debit to cash and a credit to the appropriate revenue account.

Documentation: The electronic cash register at each ticket booth and concession stand prepares a detailed list of cash transactions and a daily cash summary report. The daily summary reports are electronically transferred to the central office each night. These reports from each theater are automatically summarized upon receipt. Each morning a paper report is generated and revenue entries are made in the computerized general ledger.

Reports: A variety of revenue analyses are generated by the computer system, including analyses by theater, movie, day of the week, and month.

CONTROL PROCEDURES

Authority and responsibility: The central office accountant must authorize all general ledger entries. Each theater manager is responsible for the control of cash in his or her theater.

Segregation of duties: Maintenance of the general ledger is segregated from responsibility for local cash control. Ticket sellers and concession operators may assist in preparation of daily cash deposits but the manager must check and sign deposit documents.

Documentation: Prenumbered admission tickets are dispensed by machine at each theater. The machine also prepares a report of the numbers used each day, which is used by the theater manager to reconcile cash collected with the number of tickets sold.

Safeguards: The cash accumulates in each theater until the end of each day; when cash drawers reach a specified level, however, the cash register signals that a fixed amount of cash should be removed by the manager and placed in the theater's safe.

Checks: On an unannounced schedule, Hendrickson's accountant visits each theater and verifies cash receipts reported against the number of tickets used. On these same visits, concession revenues are checked against the amounts reported by inventorying concession supplies.

CONTROL ENVIRONMENT AND ETHICAL BEHAVIOR

CONTROL ENVIRONMENT: The collection of environmental factors that influence the effectiveness of control procedures.

Establishing and maintaining an internal control structure are responsibilities of management, working with internal accountants and external auditors and consultants. In addition to the accounting system and control procedures, the control structure includes the **control environment**—the collection of environmental factors that influence the effectiveness of control procedures. The control environment includes the philosophy and operating style of management, the personnel policies and practices of the entity, and the overall attitude, awareness, and actions of all persons in the entity concerning the importance of control procedures.

An important feature of this environment is the pursuit of individual goals that may differ from the goals of other individuals and the goals of the surrounding entity. The goals of managers are not always the same as the goals of stockholders. For example, managers anxious to maintain their positions may fight a takeover by another company that would be in the long-term interests of the stockholders. Similarly, the goals of factory workers do not always coincide with the goals of management.

Control procedures assume particular importance in the presence of conflicting goals, but they are not sufficient to prevent excesses of individual behavior. In addition, the entity must be able to rely on its members to behave ethically. The following analysis illustrates the way in which ethical dilemmas arise in internal control structures.

ANALYSIS
RESOLVING AN
ETHICAL DILEMMA

Donna Jones has just been hired as a junior-level accountant in a large manufacturing company. One of her jobs is to summarize invoices presented for payment by various creditors. Once the summary has been inspected by Ms. Adams, the assistant controller to whom Donna reports, Donna presents the summary to the controller for approval. The controller's approval requires a simple signature on the summary form. Mr. Stewart, of the controller's staff, then prepares and mails the checks. During Donna's second week on the job, Ms. Adams tells her that City Consulting Services, Inc., will make trouble for the company unless paid immediately and that Donna shouldn't bother to secure the controller's authorization for the day's invoices, in order to speed payment. "Old Stewart who prepares the checks is rarely at his desk and never looks at signatures anyway. It would cost us at least another day to get the controller's signature. Just put the unsigned summary on Stewart's desk, and the check will be in the mail by the end of the day," says Ms. Adams.

Donna knows that Ms. Adams will give her a low performance rating if she refuses to follow these instructions, and she wants to do well on her first job. Further, she is quite sure that Stewart will not notice the omitted control procedure, particularly if he doesn't see Donna leave the summary on his desk. On the other hand, Donna knows that the controller's approval is viewed as an important control procedure. Consider two possible endings for this story:

1. *Donna decides to go along with Ms. Adams.* Every month, Ms. Adams tells Donna the same story about City Consulting Services, and Donna places the unauthorized summary on Stewart's unoccupied desk. All goes well until the outside auditor runs a routine check on the credit ratings of the various entities with which the company does business and discovers that City Consulting Services is nothing more than a bank account established by Ms. Adams, the assistant controller. Ms. Adams is charged with fraud, and Donna's role in the fraud is exposed in the public trial that ensues. Donna is not charged in the case, but she loses her job and has great difficulty finding another comparable position.

2. *Donna refuses to go along with Ms. Adams.* Donna receives a negative review from Ms. Adams and is asked to leave the company. During an exit interview, Donna tells the controller why she believes that Ms. Adams gave her a negative review. In telling her friends about these events, Donna learns that several of her classmates also chose to do the "right thing" on their first job and, as a result, spent three or four months looking for a new position. Donna spends two months unsuccessfully looking for a new position when she receives a call from the controller of the former employer. "Although I wasn't very encouraging during your exit interview," says the controller, "your comments led me to ask internal auditing to investigate Ms. Adams' activities. As a result, we have uncovered her scheme to defraud the company, and would like you to return to the company with a promotion and a higher salary."

Like Donna Jones, most people in business face difficult ethical dilemmas from time to time. The "right thing to do" is an individual decision that must be approached thoughtfully and after careful consideration of the possible long-term as well as short-term consequences of the alternative actions the individual faces. The effectiveness of internal control structures depends on the ethical tone set by management and the ethical awareness of all company personnel.

SUMMARY

The discussion of the closing process—preparation of closing entries and the postclosing trial balance—completed our consideration of the 10-step accounting cycle, which began in Chapters 3 and 4. Closing entries are special journal entries that transfer revenue, expense, and dividends accounts to retained earnings. Revenue and expense accounts are transferred to retained earnings by way of an income summary account. By transferring revenue, expense, and dividends balances to retained earnings at the end of the period, closing entries update the balance of retained earnings and set next year's beginning balance to zero for each revenue, expense, and dividends account, preparing them to receive next year's activity. Thus the postclosing trial balance contains only balance sheet account balances. All other account balances have been reduced to zero. The postclosing trial balance provides a final check of the equality of debits and credits before the next accounting period begins.

The second section of the chapter introduced the worksheet, an optional but very useful multicolumned schedule used to organize and summarize all the steps in the end-of-period portion of the accounting cycle. In successive pairs of debit and credit columns, the worksheet presents the unadjusted trial balance, the adjusting entries, the adjusted trial balance, and information for the income statement, statement of changes in retained earnings, and balance sheet; the closing process is represented by a worksheet transfer from the income statement columns to the statement of changes in retained earnings columns.

The next section of the chapter presented a review of the entire accounting cycle, followed by a review problem that illustrated each of the 10 steps in the accounting cycle. The review and the review problem bring together the data-entry steps of the accounting cycle from Chapter 3, the adjusting-entry step from Chapter 4, and the end-of-period steps dscribed earlier in this chapter.

Accounting systems are subject to error. When errors in the analysis, journalizing, or posting of transactions are discovered, correcting entries are necessary. Of course, errors can also be prevented by control procedures and the varied policies, attitudes, and behaviors that make up the environment of the accounting system. Error correction and internal control structures are discussed in the last two sections of the chapter.

Control procedures vary widely from one entity to another but generally can be associated with one of the following categories:

1. Clearly defined authority and responsibility

2. Segregation of duties

3. Adequate documents and records

4. Safeguards over assets and records

5. Checks on recorded amounts

The effectiveness of the internal control structure depends on the adequacy and integration of its three components—the accounting system, control procedures, and the control environment, including the capacity of management and employees for ethical behavior.

In Appendix 5–1, we introduce reversing entries. When used, these entries are made after closing but before the beginning of the next accounting period. They reverse the adjustments made for revenue earned before collection and expense incurred before payment in order to simplify recording the completion of the transactions that required the adjustments.

APPENDIX 5-1
REVERSING ENTRIES

REVERSING ENTRIES:
Journal entries made at the beginning of an accounting period to reverse the preceding period's adjusting entries for revenue earned before collection or for expense incurred before payment.

To understand reversing entries, you need a thorough knowledge of all the steps of the accounting cycle and of the effects of various types of events on accounts and account balances. For that reason, we have deferred consideration of these entries until now. The purpose of reversing entries is to simplify the recording of subsequent parts of certain continuous transactions. **Reversing entries** are journal entries made at the beginning of an accounting period to reverse the preceding period's adjusting entries for revenue earned before collection or for expense incurred before payment. As you will remember from Chapter 4, the four categories of adjusting entries are (1) revenue earned before collection, (2) expense incurred before payment, (3) revenue earned after collection, and (4) expense incurred after payment. While not usually applicable to categories (3) and (4), reversing entries can be applied to adjustments for revenue earned before collection and expense incurred before payment.

As an illustration of a situation to which reversing entries can be applied, suppose that two days' wages in the amount of $12,000 have been earned by the employees of the Hudson Corporation at December 31, 19X2. These wages will not be paid until January 6, 19X3. The following adjusting entry is made on December 31, 19X2:

Wages expense	12,000	
Wages payable		12,000

When the wages are paid in the subsequent period, another entry is made. This entry records the income statement effect for the subsequent period and removes the balance sheet payable established by the adjusting entry. Thus on January 6, 19X3, if $30,000 of wages is paid to the employees of Hudson Corporation, $12,000 of that amount is the two days' wages earned in 19X2. The following entry records this event:

Wages expense	18,000	
Wages payable	12,000	
Cash		30,000

This entry in 19X3 leaves a zero balance in wages payable and an $18,000 balance in wages expense.

An alternative to the procedure just described would be to use a reversing entry at the beginning of the new accounting period. On January 1, 19X3, the reversing entry for the December 31, 19X2, $12,000 adjusting entry for wages expense and wages payable by the Hudson Corporation is:

Wages payable	12,000	
Wages expense		12,000

Note that this entry simply *reverses* the effects of the December 31, 19X2, adjusting entry. Then, when the $30,000 of wages is paid to Hudson's employees on January 6, 19X3, the following entry is made:

Wages expense	30,000	
Cash		30,000

Again, a zero balance is left in wages payable. And the combination of the reversing entry credit of $12,000 and the January 6, 19X3, debit of $30,000 to wages expense leaves an $18,000 balance in that account. Because the reversing entry removes the payable established by the adjusting entry, the accountant does not need to check to see if the wage payment transaction is part of an event that began in an earlier accounting period. The use of reversing entries thus enables the accountant to record all routine transactions in the same way. Because all routine transactions can be recorded without deviation from a standard format, fewer errors are likely to occur in analyzing, journalizing, and posting, and less highly skilled personnel can be used to operate the accounting system. All these factors can ultimately result in financial savings for the business. Reversing entries are optional and, if used, are the eleventh step in the accounting cycle. They involve no new accounting principles or procedures and, operationally, are simply a mechanical application of those concepts and procedures already discussed.

Let us consider two additional illustrations of reversing entries. The first illustrates the reversal of an adjusting entry made to record accrued interest expense. The second illustrates the reversal of an adjusting entry made to record accrued rent revenue.

Our first additional illustration of reversing entries involves borrowing funds in one period and repaying them with accrued interest in the next period. An adjusting entry is required at the end of the first period to account for unrecorded interest expense. On October 1, 19X2, Hudson Corporation borrowed $60,000 on a one-year, 15 percent note payable. The borrowing was recorded by the following entry on October 1, 19X2:

Cash	60,000	
Notes payable		60,000

The adjusting entry on December 31, 19X2, was:

Interest expense [($60,000)(.15)(3/12)]	2,250	
Interest payable		2,250

The difference in how the entries would be made with and without reversing entries is demonstrated in Exhibit 5–16.

Our second additional illustration is a revenue transaction that is unrecorded and partially complete at the end of the first accounting period. Hudson Corporation rented space in its building to Jones, Bayrnak, and Smith, an advertising agency, on November 1, 19X2. Jones, Bayrnak, and Smith are to pay rent

EXHIBIT 5–16   **MULTIPERIOD BORROWING TRANSACTIONS WITH AND WITHOUT REVERSING ENTRIES**

WITH REVERSING ENTRY	WITHOUT REVERSING ENTRY
Reversing entry, 1/1/X3	*1/1/X3*
Interest payable . . . . . 2,250 Interest expense . . . 2,250	No entry
Leaves a $0 balance in interest payable and a credit balance of $2,250 in interest expense.	Interest expense is $0, and interest payable has a credit balance of $2,250.
Repayment of borrowing, 9/30/X3	*Repayment of borrowing, 9/30/X3*

Notes payable.   60,000
 Interest expense   9,000
     Cash.   69,000
	Notes payable. 60,000
	 Interest expense 6,750
	 Interest payable 2,250
	     Cash. 69,000

Leaves a net debit balance of $6,750 in interest expense.	Leaves a $0 balance in interest payable and a debit balance of $6,750 in interest expense.

EXHIBIT 5–17   **MULTIPERIOD REVENUE TRANSACTIONS WITH AND WITHOUT REVERSING ENTRIES**

WITH REVERSING ENTRY	WITHOUT REVERSING ENTRY
Reversing entry, 1/1/X3	*1/1/X3*
Rent revenue. . . . . 3,000 Rent receivable. 3,000	No entry
Leaves a $0 balance in rent receivable and a debit balance of $3,000 in rent revenue.	Rent revenue is $0, and rent receivable has a debit balance of $3,000.
Rent payment received, 2/1/X3	*Rent payment received, 2/1/X3*

Cash   4,500
     Rent revenue   4,500
	Cash 4,500
	     Rent revenue 1,500
	     Rent receivable. 3,000

Leaves a net credit balance of $1,500 in rent revenue.	Leaves a $0 balance in rent receivable and a credit balance of $1,500 in rent revenue.

every three months, with the first payment due on February 1, 19X3. Rent is $1,500 per month.

The following adjusting entry is made in Hudson's journal on December 31, 19X2:

Rent receivable.   3,000
    Rent revenue   3,000

The accounting procedures for this transaction with and without reversing entries would differ as shown in Exhibit 5–17.

Because reversing entries are an optional step in the accounting cycle, the remainder of this text is written with the assumption that these entries are not used. However, we have included exercises and problems at the end of this chapter that offer you the opportunity to develop skill in using reversing entries. There are also problems in subsequent chapters that can be easily modified to assume the use of reversing entries.

KEY TERMS

ACCOUNTING SYSTEM (p. 203)

ADJUSTED TRIAL BALANCE (p. 187)

ADJUSTING ENTRY (p. 187)

CLOSING ENTRIES (p. 181)

CONTROL ENVIRONMENT (p. 204)

CONTROL PROCEDURES (p. 202)

CORRECTING ENTRY (p. 200)

INCOME SUMMARY (p. 181)

INTERNAL CONTROL STRUCTURE (p. 201)

POSTCLOSING TRIAL BALANCE (p. 181)

REVERSING ENTRIES (p. 207)

UNADJUSTED TRIAL BALANCE (p. 187)

WORKSHEET (p. 185)

QUESTIONS

Q5-1. What is the purpose of closing entries?

Q5-2. Describe the five steps in the closing process.

Q5-3. Identify each of the following categories of accounts as temporary or permanent: assets, liabilities, equity, revenues, expenses, and dividends. How is the distinction between temporary and permanent accounts related to the closing process?

Q5-4. Why do only balance sheet accounts appear in a postclosing trial balance?

Q5-5. How are revenue and expense amounts calculated for *monthly* income statements?

Q5-6. What is the relationship between the accounting cycle and the worksheet?

Q5-7. Describe the structure of a worksheet and the accounting information it contains.

Q5-8. Describe the procedure by which the adjusting entry for income taxes expense is determined and entered on the worksheet.

Q5-9. List the 10 steps in the accounting cycle in the order in which they occur. Assume that a worksheet is employed.

Q5-10. Why are some accounting errors self-correcting?

Q5-11. Describe the treatment for an error discovered after the period in which it was made.

Q5-12. What is the internal control structure, and what are its three major components?

Q5-13. Explain how each of the five categories of accounting-related control procedures helps a business protect against fraud and misrepresentation.

Q5-14. Why is ethical behavior an important component of the control environment?

APPENDIX QUESTIONS

Q5-15. What is the purpose of reversing entries?

Q5-16. Describe the types of adjusting entries that are the basis for reversing entries. Why are only these types of adjustments reversed?

EXERCISES

E5-17. INFERENCES FROM CLOSING ENTRIES   At the end of 19X6, Grand Rapids Consulting, Inc., made the following entries to close all revenue and expense accounts to the income summary account:

Service revenue	155,000	
Income summary		155,000
Income summary	122,400	
Salaries expense		83,000
Rent expense		15,000
Utilities expense		7,900
Office supplies expense		4,200
Income taxes expense		12,300

Grand Rapids Consulting began 19X6 with a retained earnings balance of $38,100. During 19X6, the company declared and paid dividends that total $16,400.

REQUIRED:

1. Prepare any additional closing entries made by Grand Rapids Consulting at the end of 19X6.

2. Prepare Grand Rapids Consulting's statement of changes in retained earnings for 19X6.

E5-18. EFFECT OF CLOSING ENTRIES   Hershel Transportation has the following summary data for 19X9:

Service revenue	$12,275,400
Operating expenses	10,380,150
Financial expenses	1,320,500
Income taxes expense	195,410
Dividends	230,000

REQUIRED:

1. Prepare the entries to close income summary and dividends into retained earnings.

2. How is retained earnings changed in 19X9?

E5-19. PREPARATION OF CLOSING ENTRIES   James and Susan Morley recently converted a large turn-of-the-century house into a hotel and incorporated the business as Saginaw Enterprises. Their accountant is inexperienced and has made the following closing entries at the end of Saginaw's first year of operations:

Income summary	210,000	
Service revenue		177,000
Accumulated depreciation		33,000
Depreciation expense	33,000	
Income taxes expense	8,200	
Utilities expense	12,700	
Wages expense	66,000	
Supplies expense	31,000	
Accounts payable	4,500	
Income summary		155,400
Income summary	54,600	
Retained earnings		54,600
Dividends	3,200	
Income summary		3,200

REQUIRED:

1. Indicate what is wrong with the closing entries above.

2. Prepare the correct closing entries. Assume that all necessary accounts are presented above and that the amounts given are correct.

E5-20. PREPARATION OF CLOSING ENTRIES   Herting Distributors has the following accounts and account balances at year-end:

Sales revenue	$24,500,700
Cost of goods sold	14,100,500
Depreciation expense, building	1,740,000
Depreciation expense, equipment	815,000
Utilities expense	243,200
Wages expense	7,136,800
Interest expense	45,000
Income taxes expense	225,200
Dividends	180,000

REQUIRED:

Prepare the journal entries to close the revenue and expense accounts into income summary and to close income summary and dividends into retained earnings.

E5-21. PREPARATION OF CLOSING ENTRIES AND AN INCOME STATEMENT   Port Austin Boat Sales and Service, Inc., has entered and posted its adjusting entries for 19X8. The following accounts and account balances were taken from the adjusted trial balance:

Sales revenue	$473,000
Service revenue	113,600
Accounts payable	8,330
Cost of goods sold	311,000
Inventory, boats, 12/31/X8	215,000
Supplies expense, repair parts	65,000
Supplies inventory, 12/31/X8	179,000
Prepaid rent	7,200
Rent expense	28,800
Wages expense	94,300
Wages payable	11,700
Utilities expense	14,000
Interest expense	9,500
Depreciation expense, equipment	20,000
Accumulated depreciation, equipment	75,000
Income taxes expense	12,300
Income taxes payable	8,300
Dividends	7,800

REQUIRED:

1. Using the accounts and balances above, prepare the closing entries for 19X8.

2. Prepare a classified income statement for Port Austin Boat Sales and Service, Inc.

E5-22. PREPARATION OF A WORKSHEET   The following adjusted trial balance has been prepared in a worksheet for Joe's Hairstyles at the end of 19X2:

ACCOUNT TITLE	ADJUSTED TRIAL BALANCE	
	Dr	Cr
Cash	1,600	
Accounts receivable	3,100	
Supplies inventory	2,400	
Prepaid rent, building	5,000	
Equipment	82,000	
Accumulated depreciation, equipment		8,000
Other assets	14,200	
Accounts payable		7,500
Salaries payable		13,800
Notes payable (due in 19X8)		20,000
Capital stock		25,000
Retained earnings		11,500
Dividends	3,000	
Service revenue		242,000
Salaries expense	154,300	
Rent expense, building	29,600	
Depreciation expense, equipment	6,000	
Supplies expense	11,900	
Utilities expense	12,300	
Interest expense	2,400	
Totals	327,800	327,800
Income taxes expense	7,500	
Income taxes payable		7,500
Totals	335,300	335,300

REQUIRED:

Complete the remaining six columns of the worksheet for Joe's Hairstyles.

E5-23. PREPARATION OF A WORKSHEET   The following unadjusted trial balance at December 31, 19X2, has been prepared for Rapisarda Company:

ACCOUNT	DEBIT	CREDIT
Cash	$ 2,000	
Accounts receivable	33,000	
Prepaid rent	26,000	
Equipment	211,000	
Accumulated depreciation, equipment		$ 75,000
Other assets	24,000	
Accounts payable		12,000
Note payable (due in ten years)		40,000
Capital stock		100,000
Retained earnings, 12/31/X1		11,000
Service revenue		243,000
Rent expense	84,000	
Wages expense	97,000	
Interest expense	4,000	
Totals	$481,000	$481,000

The following data are not yet recorded:

a) Depreciation on the equipment: Expected life is eight years and residual value is $11,000.

b) Unrecorded wages owed at December 31, 19X2: $2,000.

c) Prepaid rent at December 31, 19X2: $10,000.

d) Income tax rate: 30 percent.

REQUIRED:

Prepare a completed worksheet for Rapisarda Company.

E5-24. THE WORKSHEET AND FINANCIAL STATEMENTS Three pairs of columns from a worksheet for Barry's Campus Rentals appear below:

ACCOUNT TITLE	INCOME STATEMENT Dr	INCOME STATEMENT Cr	CHANGES IN RETAINED EARNINGS Dr	CHANGES IN RETAINED EARNINGS Cr	BALANCE SHEET Dr	BALANCE SHEET Cr
Cash					4,100	
Accounts receivable					13,200	
Prepaid insurance					4,800	
Office supplies inventory					600	
Rental assets					253,800	
Accumulated depreciation, rental assets						58,000
Other assets					15,400	
Accounts payable						5,700
Wages payable						2,900
Interest payable						1,200
Notes payable (due in 19X6)						40,000
Capital stock						150,000
Retained earnings, 12/31/X4				15,700		
Dividends			6,000			
Rent revenue		827,200				
Wages expense	346,300					
Rent expense, building	254,100					
Advertising expense	112,600					
Insurance expense	28,800					
Depreciation expense, rental assets	40,000					
Office supplies expense	1,500					
Utilities expense	14,700					
Interest expense	4,800					
Totals	802,800	827,200				
Income taxes expense	6,200					
Income taxes payable						6,200
Net income	(a) 18,200			(a) 18,200		
Totals			6,000	33,900		
Retained earnings, 12/31/X5			(b) 27,900			(b) 27,900
Totals	827,200	827,200	33,900	33,900	291,900	291,900

REQUIRED:

Prepare an income statement, a statement of changes in retained earnings, and a balance sheet for Barry's Campus Rentals at December 31, 19X5.

E5-25. USING A COMPLETED WORKSHEET   The worksheet on page 216 was completed for Potter Corporation at December 31, 19X7.

REQUIRED:

1. Prepare the adjusting entries made at the end of 19X7.
2. Prepare a classified income statement for 19X7.
3. Prepare a statement of changes in retained earnings for 19X7.
4. Prepare a balance sheet as of December 31, 19X7.
5. Prepare the closing entries made at the end of 19X7.
6. Prepare the postclosing trial balance as of December 31, 19X7.

E5-26. ERROR CORRECTION   The accountant for Merchant's Supply Company discovered that a $6,000 payment on an account payable was recorded earlier this year with the following journal entry:

Notes payable 6,000
  Cash   6,000

REQUIRED:

Prepare a journal entry to correct this error.

E5-27. FINANCIAL STATEMENT EFFECTS OF ERRORS AND ERROR CORRECTION   On December 20, 19X2, Henry's Pizza paid $1,150 for a six-month insurance policy for its delivery truck. The policy begins January 1, 19X3. Unfortunately, this transaction was recorded with the following erroneous entry:

Insurance expense. 1,150
  Cash   1,150

REQUIRED:

1. If this error is not corrected, how will the 19X2 financial statements be affected?
2. Prepare a journal entry to correct this error as of December 31, 19X2.

E5-28. INTERNAL CONTROL PROCEDURES FOR WAGES   Shortridge Construction Company resurfaces roads in all parts of Illinois. For each resurfacing job, Shortridge assigns one of its supervisors and several of its full-time equipment operators. The remaining labor necessary is hired for the duration of the job in the local area. Shortridge's accountant wants to establish internal control procedures that will help ensure that:

a) All employees put on the payroll locally actually exist.
b) Employees actually work the number of hours reported.

REQUIRED:

Propose some internal control procedures to help meet these objectives.

POTTER CORPORATION
Worksheet for the Year Ended December 31, 19X7

ACCOUNT TITLE	UNADJUSTED TRIAL BALANCE Dr	UNADJUSTED TRIAL BALANCE Cr	ADJUSTING ENTRIES Dr	ADJUSTING ENTRIES Cr	ADJUSTED TRIAL BALANCE Dr	ADJUSTED TRIAL BALANCE Cr	INCOME STATEMENT Dr	INCOME STATEMENT Cr	CHANGES IN RETAINED EARNINGS Dr	CHANGES IN RETAINED EARNINGS Cr	BALANCE SHEET Dr	BALANCE SHEET Cr
Cash	3,900				3,900						3,900	
Accounts receivable	14,600				14,600						14,600	
Supplies inventory	2,800			(d) 600	2,200						2,200	
Equipment	82,500				82,500						82,500	
Accumulated depreciation, equipment		16,400		(c) 18,600		35,000						35,000
Wages payable				(a) 1,600		1,600						1,600
Accounts payable		2,800		(b) 300		3,100						3,100
Interest payable				(e) 700		700						700
Notes payable (due in 19X9)		7,000				7,000						7,000
Capital stock		40,000				40,000						40,000
Retained earnings, 12/31/X6		10,700				10,700				10,700		
Dividends	2,400				2,400				2,400			
Sales revenue		48,000				48,000		48,000				
Wages expense	10,900		(a) 1,600		12,500		12,500					
Selling expense	7,800		(b) 300		8,100		8,100					
Depreciation expense, equipment			(c) 18,600		18,600		18,600					
Supplies expense			(d) 600		600		600					
Interest expense			(e) 700		700		700					
Totals	124,900	124,900	21,800	21,800	146,100	146,100	40,500	48,000				
Income taxes expense			(f) 1,900		1,900		1,900					
Income taxes payable				(f) 1,900		1,900						1,900
Net income							(g) 5,600			(g) 5,600		
Totals							48,000	48,000	2,400	16,300		
Retained earnings, 12/31/X7									(h) 13,900			(h) 13,900
Totals									16,300	16,300	103,200	103,200

E5-29. CLASSIFYING INTERNAL CONTROL PROCEDURES   Match each of the control procedures listed below with the most closely related control procedure type. Your answer should pair each of the numbers 1 through 10 with the appropriate letter.

CONTROL PROCEDURE TYPES
A. Clearly defined authority and responsibility
B. Segregation of duties
C. Adequate documents and records
D. Safeguards over assets and records
E. Checks on recorded amounts

CONTROL PROCEDURES
1. The controller is required to sign the daily summary of expenditures to authorize their payment.
2. Division managers are evaluated annually on the basis of their profitability.
3. Invoices received from outside suppliers are filed with purchase orders.
4. Employees with access to the accounting records are not permitted to open the mail, because it contains many payments by check from customers.
5. The extent of access to the many segments of the company's computer system is tightly controlled by individual identification cards and passwords that change at regular intervals.
6. Each shipment from inventory is recorded on a specially printed form bearing a sequential number; these forms are the basis for entries into the computer system, which makes entries to inventory records and produces periodic reports of shipments.
7. At regular intervals, internal auditing reviews a sample of expenditure transactions to determine that payment has been made to a bona fide supplier and that the related goods or services were received and appropriately used.
8. A construction company stores large steel girders in an open yard surrounded by a 5-foot fence and stores welding supplies in a controlled-access, tightly secured concrete building.
9. A grocery store uses cash registers that display to the customer the price of each item purchased as it is recorded and produce a customer receipt that describes each item and gives its price.
10. The person in the controller's office who prepares and mails checks to suppliers cannot make entries in the general ledger system.

E5-30. INTERNAL CONTROL PROCEDURES FOR INVENTORY AND COST OF GOODS SOLD   Malone's is a local grocery store. The store has two soft-drink machines, one inside and another outside, that produce approximately $100 per day per machine in revenues. It would be easier and less expensive if the store were to fill these two soft-drink machines from the store's inventory that is primarily intended for sale to customers. However, the store's accountant is concerned that using store inventories for this purpose will make it difficult to account accurately for cost of goods sold in the soft-drink area in the store and for revenue and costs associated with the soft-drink machines.

REQUIRED:

Propose some internal control procedures that could be used to mitigate the accountant's concerns.

E5-31. INTERNAL CONTROL PROCEDURES FOR CASH RECEIPTS   Corey and Dee Post are planning to open and operate a 24-hour convenience store near a university campus. Corey and Dee are concerned that part of the cash that customers pay for merchandise might be kept by some of the store's employees.

REQUIRED:

Identify some internal control procedures that could help ensure that all cash paid by customers is remitted to the business.

APPENDIX EXERCISES

E5-32. PREPARATION OF REVERSING ENTRIES The following data are available for adjusting entries for Caine Corporation at the end of 19X7:

Depreciation expense, truck	$3,300
Expiration of prepaid insurance	4,100
Interest on note payable (note due 1/31/X8)	1,600
Unrecorded rent revenue	4,800

REQUIRED:

1. Prepare adjusting entries for all four items.

2. Prepare reversing entries for those items for which reversing entries should be made.

E5-33. PREPARATION OF REVERSING ENTRIES When the adjusting entries were prepared at the end of 19X1, the accountant made adjustments for (1) $2,900 of wages that had been earned but were unpaid and (2) $3,750 of service revenue that had been earned but was uncollected and unrecorded.

REQUIRED:

1. Prepare reversing entries as of January 1, 19X2, for these two adjustments.

2. What is the effect on the financial statements of the reversing entries (e.g., the wages payable liability is decreased by $2,900)?

E5-34. PREPARATION OF REVERSING ENTRIES On September 1, 19X6, Livonia Enterprises borrowed $30,000 on a one-year, 14 percent note payable, with principal and interest payable on August 31, 19X7.

REQUIRED:

1. Prepare the adjusting entry for the note at December 31, 19X6.

2. Prepare a reversing entry at January 1, 19X7.

3. Assuming that the reversing entry was made on January 1, 19X7, record the repayment of the note principal and interest in 19X7.

4. Assume that the note described above is Livonia's only note payable and that the reversing entry was made on January 1, 19X7. Prepare a T-account showing the activity in interest expense during 19X7.

PROBLEMS

P5-35. INTERPRETING CLOSING ENTRIES Barnes Building Systems made the following closing entries at the end of a recent year:

a) Income summary	84,300	
Retained earnings		84,300
b) Retained earnings	35,000	
Dividends		35,000
c) Sales revenue	64,250,700	
Income summary		64,250,700
d) Income summary	104,100	
Interest expense		104,100

REQUIRED:

1. What was Barnes's net income?

2. By how much did Barnes's retained earnings change?

3. If the sales revenue identified in entry **c** was Barnes's only revenue, what was the total amount of Barnes's expenses?

P5-36. PREPARATION OF CLOSING ENTRIES   Round Grove Alarm Company provides security services to homes in northwestern Indiana. At year-end 19X2, after adjusting entries have been made, the following list of account balances is prepared:

Accounts receivable	$ 37,000
Accounts payable	23,000
Accumulated depreciation, equipment	124,000
Capital stock	150,000
Depreciation expense, equipment	42,000
Dividends	6,000
Equipment	409,500
Income taxes expense	24,300
Income taxes payable	24,300
Interest expense	4,800
Notes payable (due in 19X5)	34,000
Other assets	7,700
Prepaid rent	5,000
Rent expense	30,000
Retained earnings, 12/31/X1	29,400
Salaries payable	12,600
Salaries expense	144,000
Service revenue	605,500
Supplies expense	51,900
Supplies inventory	12,700
Utilities expense	48,800
Wages expense	186,500
Wages payable	7,400

REQUIRED:

Prepare closing entries for Round Grove Alarm Company.

P5-37. THE WORKSHEET, FINANCIAL STATEMENTS, AND CLOSING ENTRIES   Marsteller Properties, Inc., owns apartments that it rents to university students. At December 31, 19X7, the following unadjusted trial balance was prepared by Marsteller's accountant:

ACCOUNT	DEBIT	CREDIT
Cash	$ 4,600	
Rent receivable	32,500	
Supplies inventory	4,700	
Prepaid insurance	60,000	
Buildings	4,560,000	
Accumulated depreciation, buildings		$1,015,000
Land	274,000	
Other assets	26,100	
Accounts payable		17,300
Mortgage payable (due in 19X9)		2,000,000
Capital stock		1,500,000
Retained earnings, 12/31/X6		39,200
Rent revenue		660,000
Maintenance expense	33,200	
Rent expense	18,700	
Wages expense	84,300	
Utilities expense	3,400	
Interest expense	130,000	
Totals	$5,231,500	$5,231,500

The following information is available for adjusting entries:

a) An analysis of apartment rental contracts indicates that $3,800 of apartment rent is unbilled and unrecorded at year-end.

b) An inventory reveals that $1,400 of supplies are on hand at December 31, 19X7.

c) The buildings are being depreciated on a straight-line basis over 20 years, with an estimated residual value of $500,000.

d) An examination of insurance policies indicates that $12,000 of the prepaid insurance applies to coverage for 19X8.

e) Six months' interest at 13 percent is unrecorded and unpaid on the mortgage payable.

f) Wages in the amount of $6,100 are unpaid and unrecorded at December 31.

g) Utilities costs of $300 are unrecorded and unpaid at December 31.

h) Income taxes, 15 percent of income before taxes, is unrecorded and unpaid at December 31.

REQUIRED:

1. Prepare a worksheet for Marsteller Properties, Inc.

2. Prepare a classified income statement, a statement of changes in retained earnings, and a classified balance sheet for Marsteller Properties, Inc.

3. Prepare the closing entries.

P5-38. THE WORKSHEET, FINANCIAL STATEMENTS, CLOSING ENTRIES, AND POSTCLOSING TRIAL BALANCE   Flint, Inc., operates a cable television system. At December 31, 19X4, the following unadjusted trial balance was prepared:

ACCOUNT	DEBIT	CREDIT
Cash.	$ 2,000	
Accounts receivable	89,000	
Office supplies inventory	5,000	
Land	37,000	
Building.	209,000	
Accumulated depreciation, building.		$ 40,000
Equipment.	794,000	
Accumulated depreciation, equipment.		262,000
Other assets	19,700	
Accounts payable.		27,000
Notes payable (due in 19X8)		250,000
Capital stock		300,000
Retained earnings, 12/31/X3		14,700
Dividends	28,000	
Service revenue		985,000
Subscription expense	398,000	
Telephone expense.	3,000	
Utilities expense.	34,000	
Wages expense.	196,000	
Miscellaneous expense.	44,000	
Interest expense	20,000	
Totals.	$1,878,700	$1,878,700

The following data are available for adjusting entries:

a) At year-end $1,500 of office supplies remains unused.

b) The building is being depreciated over 10 years, with a residual value of $9,000.

c) The expected life of the equipment is 5 years. Residual value is $44,000.

d) The interest rate on the note is 12 percent. Four months' interest is unpaid and unrecorded at December 31, 19X4.

e) At December 31, 19X4, service revenue of $94,000 has been earned but is unbilled and unrecorded.

f) Utility bills of $2,800 are unpaid and unrecorded at December 31, 19X4.

g) The income tax rate is 25 percent.

REQUIRED:

1. Prepare a worksheet for Flint.
2. Prepare a classified income statement.
3. Prepare a statement of changes in retained earnings.
4. Prepare the closing entries.
5. Prepare a classified balance sheet.
6. Prepare a postclosing trial balance.

P5-39. THE WORKSHEET, FINANCIAL STATEMENTS, CLOSING ENTRIES, AND POSTCLOSING TRIAL BALANCE Tarkington Wholesalers sells merchandise to retail grocery stores in the Northeast. At the end of 19X2, the following unadjusted trial balance was prepared:

ACCOUNT	DEBIT	CREDIT
Cash.	$ 21,300	
Accounts receivable	317,500	
Inventory.	273,400	
Building, warehouse.	2,150,000	
Accumulated depreciation, warehouse		$ 280,000
Equipment, warehouse.	765,000	
Accumulated depreciation, warehouse equipment		580,000
Land	206,000	
Accounts payable.		147,800
Notes payable (due in 19X6)		900,000
Capital stock		1,400,000
Retained earnings, 12/31/X1		77,900
Dividends	25,000	
Sales revenue		4,256,700
Cost of goods sold	2,942,600	
Advertising expense	138,100	
Wages expense.	726,200	
Utilities expense.	14,300	
Interest expense	63,000	
Totals.	$7,642,400	$7,642,400

The following information is available for adjusting entries:

a) The warehouse has an expected life of 25 years and a residual value of $400,000.

b) The warehouse equipment has an expected life of five years and a residual value of $40,000.

c) Wages of $14,900 are unrecorded and unpaid at year-end.

d) Utilities costs of $1,600 are unrecorded and unpaid at year-end.

e) At year-end, five months' interest at 12 percent is unrecorded and unpaid on the notes payable.

f) Income taxes at an amount of 30 percent of income before taxes are unrecorded and unpaid at year-end.

REQUIRED:

1. Prepare a worksheet for Tarkington Wholesalers.

2. Prepare a classified income statement, a statement of changes in retained earnings, and a classified balance sheet for Tarkington Wholesalers.

3. Prepare the closing entries.

4. Prepare a postclosing trial balance.

P5-40. THE WORKSHEET, FINANCIAL STATEMENTS, CLOSING ENTRIES, AND POSTCLOSING TRIAL BALANCE   Wilburton Riding Stables provides stables, care for animals, and grounds for riding and showing horses. The postclosing trial balance for 19X2 was composed of the following accounts and account balances:

Cash	$ 2,200
Accounts receivable	4,400
Supplies inventory, feed	24,100
Supplies inventory, straw	3,700
Land	167,000
Buildings	115,000
Accumulated depreciation, buildings	36,000
Equipment, tack	57,000
Accumulated depreciation, tack	16,500
Accounts payable	23,700
Income taxes payable	15,100
Interest payable	4,200
Wages payable	14,200
Notes payable (due in 19X6)	60,000
Capital stock	150,000
Retained earnings	53,700

During 19X3 the following transactions occurred:

a) Wilburton provided animal care services, all on credit, for $210,300. Wilburton rented stables to customers who cared for their own animals and paid cash of $20,500. Wilburton rented its grounds to individual riders, groups, and show organizations for $41,800 cash.

b) Wilburton collected all the accounts receivable outstanding at December 31, 19X2. There remains $15,600 of accounts receivable to be collected at December 31, 19X3.

c) Feed in the amount of $62,900 was purchased on credit and debited to the supplies inventory, feed account.

d) Straw was purchased for $7,400 cash and debited to the supplies inventory, straw account.

e) Wages payable at the beginning of 19X3 were paid early in 19X3. Wages were earned and paid during 19X3 in the amount of $112,000.

f) The income taxes payable at the beginning of 19X3 were paid early in 19X3. The accounts payable at the beginning of the year were also paid during the year. There remains $13,600 of accounts payable unpaid at year-end.

g) One year's interest at 14 percent was paid on the note payable on July 1, 19X3.

h) During 19X3, Jon Wilburton, owner, purchased a horse for the use of his wife, Jennifer. The horse cost $7,000, and Wilburton used his personal credit to purchase it. The horse is stabled at the Wilburtons' home rather than at the riding stables.

i) Property taxes were paid on the land and buildings in the amount of $14,000.

j) Dividends were declared and paid in the amount of $7,200.

The following data are available for adjusting entries:

k) Feed in the amount of $26,000 remained unused at year-end. Straw in the amount of $4,400 remained unused at year-end.

l) The buildings are being depreciated over 15 years, with a residual value of $25,000.

m) The tack is being depreciated over 10 years, with a residual value of $2,000.

n) Wages of $4,000 were unrecorded and unpaid at year-end.

o) Interest for six months at 14 percent per year on the note is unpaid and unrecorded at year-end.

p) The income tax rate is 30 percent.

REQUIRED:

1. Prepare journal entries for transactions **a** through **j**. Post the amounts in the 19X2 postclosing trial balance and the journal entries for 19X3 to T-accounts. Then prepare the unadjusted trial balance portion of a worksheet using the T-account balances.
2. Prepare the adjusting entries and complete the worksheet.
3. Prepare a classified income statement.
4. Prepare a statement of changes in retained earnings.
5. Prepare closing entries.
6. Prepare a classified balance sheet.
7. Prepare a postclosing trial balance.
8. Did you include transaction **h** among Wilburton's 19X3 journal entries? Why or why not?

P5-41. MONTHLY FINANCIAL STATEMENTS   Wilmington Consulting Services, Inc., prepares monthly financial statements. The adjusted trial balance at the end of January 19X2 and the adjusted trial balance at the end of February 19X2 are as follows:

	ADJUSTED TRIAL BALANCES			
	JANUARY 31, 19X2		FEBRUARY 28, 19X2	
ACCOUNT	**DEBIT**	**CREDIT**	**DEBIT**	**CREDIT**
Cash......................	$ 2,500		$ 4,600	
Accounts receivable	5,600		11,100	
Prepaid rent	4,400		3,300	
Equipment....................	87,000		87,000	
Accumulated depreciation,				
equipment		$ 22,200		$ 22,800
Accounts payable..............		500		1,300
Income taxes payable...........		900		1,500
Capital stock		50,000		50,000
Retained earnings, 12/31/X1		23,800		25,900
Service revenue		31,300		58,900
Salaries expense	13,700		27,800	
Rent expense	1,100		2,200	
Depreciation expense...........	600		1,200	
Income taxes expense...........	900		1,500	
Other expense	12,900		21,700	
Totals.....................	$128,700	$128,700	$160,400	$160,400

REQUIRED:

1. Prepare the income statement for the month ended January 31, 19X2.
2. Prepare the income statement for the month ended February 28, 19X2.
3. Is it necessary to post monthly adjusting entries to the general ledger?

P5-42. CORRECTING ENTRIES AND SELF-CORRECTING ERRORS   Traverse City Properties purchased a one-year insurance policy for $12,000 on August 1, 19X3, with coverage beginning on the date of purchase. Traverse City's accountant credited cash for $12,000 and debited insurance expense for $12,000. Unfortunately, the accountant forgot to make the appropriate adjusting entry at the end of 19X3.

REQUIRED:

1. Assume that the accountant's error is discovered prior to making the 19X3 closing entries. Prepare the appropriate correcting entry.

2. Disregard the assumption and entry in (1) above, and assume that the accountant's error goes undiscovered until late in 19X4. Prepare the appropriate correcting entry.

3. Disregard the assumptions and entries in (1) and (2) above, and assume that the accountant's error goes undiscovered until late in 19X5. Prepare the appropriate correcting entry.

P5-43. FINANCIAL STATEMENT EFFECTS OF ERRORS AND ERROR CORRECTION   The accountant for Merchant's Supply Company discovered that a $1,600 purchase of office supplies on credit, made in 19X8, had been recorded incorrectly with the following entry:

Accounts payable	1,600	
Cash		1,600

Later, when the supplier submitted a $1,600 invoice, the $1,600 was paid. The $1,600 payment was recorded with the following entry:

Accounts payable	1,600	
Cash		1,600

REQUIRED:

1. If this error is not detected prior to the end of 19X8, how will the 19X8 financial statements be affected? Assume that there are no taxes.

2. Prepare a correcting entry as of December 31, 19X8.

P5-44. FINANCIAL STATEMENT EFFECTS OF ERRORS AND ERROR CORRECTION   Near the end of 19X4, the president of Thurber Products asked for a $20,000 advance on his 19X5 salary. The board of directors agreed to the advance and had the check issued. Thurber's accountant, unaware that the $20,000 was an expense of 19X5, made the following incorrect entry to record the $20,000 payment:

Accounts payable	20,000	
Cash		20,000

REQUIRED:

1. If this error is not detected in 19X4, how will the 19X4 financial statements be affected?

2. Prepare a journal entry to correct this error as of December 31, 19X4.

P5-45. INTERNAL CONTROLS FOR PURCHASES AND PAYABLES   Campus Supply Store purchases merchandise on credit from a large number of suppliers. During the past five years, Campus's annual sales have grown from $100,000 to $1,500,000. A recent article in the local newspaper disclosed that an employee of another firm had been arrested for embezzling funds from his employer by diverting payments for purchases to his own bank account. Because of that article, the accountant for Campus has decided to examine Campus's procedures for purchases and payables.

Currently three different employees are authorized to order merchandise for the store. These employees normally complete paperwork provided by the suppliers' sales representatives, keeping a copy for their records. When the ordered merchandise arrives, it is signed for by whomever the delivery person can locate. Bills are sent to the store by suppliers and are paid by Campus's accountant when due.

REQUIRED:

1. Indicate which general principles of internal control are violated by Campus's procedures for purchases and payables.

2. Recommend procedures that would incorporate the five general categories of internal control where possible.

P5-46. INTERNAL CONTROLS FOR DAMAGED MERCHANDISE   The Warehouse Store sells merchandise to retail customers, using a catalog and a showroom. The firm has a policy that merchandise that has been damaged is identified in each store and offered for sale at 35 percent of cost to employees of that store. Merchandise that is to be sold at the reduced price is identified by store stockroom employees when they notice the damage. Recently, the firm's accountant noticed that the quantity of merchandise that was being sold as damaged had increased substantially in one store. A quiet investigation was undertaken. The investigation revealed that most of the merchandise being sold as damaged was actually undamaged. The investigation also revealed that a small group of employees were buying much of the undamaged merchandise and reselling it at a profit to friends and relatives. In fact, some of these employees were using the firm's catalog to solicit orders for "damaged" merchandise.

REQUIRED:

Propose some internal control procedures that could be used to make it more difficult for employees to steal from the firm in this way.

P5-47. PREVENTING MISSTATEMENTS IN THE FINANCIAL STATEMENTS   Nutech Company provides data processing services for small and medium-size businesses. The president of Nutech has a compensation agreement that provides for a base salary plus 1 percent of Nutech's income before taxes for the year. During January 19X3, Nutech's auditors discovered that service revenues and, consequently, income before taxes had been overstated by $450,000 in the previous year. An investigation indicated that several adjusting entries had been made to record revenue earned but not collected. These entries had been requested by the president, based on information and documentation that he claimed to have for service contracts that he had sold and was supervising.

REQUIRED:

Recommend what the firm can do to make it less likely that the financial statements can be purposely misstated.

APPENDIX PROBLEMS

P5-48. PREPARATION OF REVERSING ENTRIES   Amplifications, Inc., rents sound systems to musical groups, political groups, and other organizations that use the equipment in mass meetings. Amplifications has entered into several long-term contracts with entertainers that require payment of the annual rental in advance. On November 1, 19X4, the Golden Lizards paid Amplifications $24,000 for one year's rental on an elaborate sound system that travels with the group. Upon receipt, Amplifications credited the entire advance payment to unearned revenue.

REQUIRED:

1. Prepare the adjusting entry made by Amplifications at the end of 19X4 for the prepayment by the Golden Lizards.

2. Prepare the reversing entry made by Amplifications on January 1, 19X5, and the entry to record renewal of the contract on November 1, 19X5, for $27,000.

3. Do reversing entries appear to be useful for transactions of this type? Why or why not?

P5-49. PREPARATION OF REVERSING ENTRIES   Harrison Equipment rents lights to universities for use at football games at stadiums that do not have permanent lighting. At the end of 19X5, Harrison had made adjusting entries to record the following:

Rent revenue, unbilled and unrecorded.	$85,900
Rent revenue, earned and previously recorded as unearned revenue	66,100
Wages expense, unbilled and unrecorded	31,200
Insurance expense, previously recorded as prepaid insurance	41,900

REQUIRED:

Prepare the reversing entries that are appropriate for these four adjustments as of January 31, 19X6.

P5-50. PREPARATION OF REVERSING ENTRIES   Tennyson Metal Works made adjusting entries for the following items on December 31, 19X2:

Unrecorded wages.	$14,950
Rent expense on computing equipment	12,100
Rent charges on copying machine.	985
Interest receivable	1,925

REQUIRED:

1. Prepare adjusting and reversing entries for each item.

2. Prepare subsequent entries, assuming the following:

    a) Wages paid on January 4, 19X3, are $29,870.

    b) Rent paid on computing equipment on January 15, 19X3, is $24,200.

    c) Rent paid on copying machines on March 15, 19X3, is $5,910.

    d) Interest received on April 15, 19X3, is $2,125.

3. Prepare the subsequent entries, assuming that the reversing entries were not made.

ANALYTICAL OPPORTUNITIES

A5-51. INTERNAL CONTROLS FOR COLLECTION OF RECEIVABLES   Carolyn Furniture Galleries sells traditional furniture from two stores in St. Louis. Carolyn's credit terms allow customers to pay for purchases over three months with no finance charges. Carolyn's accountant has been responsible for approving customers for credit, recording cash received from customers in the accounting records, depositing cash collections in the bank, and following up on customers who are behind in their payments. Each month the accountant has prepared a report for Carolyn's president, indicating the cash collected, outstanding receivables, and uncollectible accounts.

Carolyn's president has been concerned about a significant increase in uncollectible accounts that began about two years ago, shortly after the current accountant was hired. Recently, a personal friend of Carolyn's president called. The caller had moved from St. Louis to Denver about six months ago. A month ago, the caller's new bank had refused a loan because a credit rating bureau in St. Louis had indicated that the caller had left bills unpaid at Carolyn Furniture. Carolyn's president knew that the caller had paid his account before leaving the community.

Carolyn's president called a detective agency and arranged for an investigation. Two weeks later, Carolyn's president was informed that the accountant had been spending much more money than his salary would warrant. Carolyn then called its auditor and arranged to have the accounting records for receivables and uncollectible accounts examined. This examination indicated that about $100,000 of cash had been stolen from the firm by the accountant. The accountant had identified customers who had moved and had recorded cash sales to continuing customers as credit sales in the accounts of the relocated customers. Carolyn's accountant had kept the cash received from the cash sales and had eventually written off the fictitious credit sales as uncollectible accounts. Without the accountant's knowledge, one of Carolyn's new employees had sent the names of the customers who had apparently defaulted on their accounts to the credit bureau.

REQUIRED:

Identify the internal control weaknesses that permitted the accountant to steal the $100,000. Suggest internal control procedures that would make it difficult for someone else to repeat this theft.

A5-52.   RESOLVING AN ETHICAL DILEMMA   Suppose that you have just been hired as a part-time clerk in a large department store. Each week you work three evenings and all day Saturday. Without the income provided by this job you would be unable to stay in college. Charles Riley, the manager in the clothing department to which you are assigned, has worked for the store for many years. Managers receive both a salary and a commission on their sales. Late one afternoon, just as you begin work, Mr. Riley is ringing up a purchase by a man you know to be one of Mr. Riley's close friends. You observe that the purchase consists of two expensive suits, a coat, and several pairs of trousers and that the customer declines Mr. Riley's offer to have the store's tailor do the alterations. After the customer departs with his merchandise and as Mr. Riley is departing for the evening, you comment, "That's a great way to end the day, Chuck. See you tomorrow." Mr. Riley gives a brief, barely audible response and departs for the evening. As you return to the sales counter, you glance at the paper tape displayed through a small opening in the cash register that records all sales on an item-by-item basis. You have just completed the store course in register operation, so you are quite familiar with the register and the tape it produces. To your surprise, you note that the last sale consisted of just a single pair of trousers.

REQUIRED:

1. What do you conclude about this transaction?
2. What are the possible consequences for the store, for Mr. Riley, and for you personally of reporting your observations to Mr. Riley's superiors?
3. What are the possible consequences for the store, for Mr. Riley, and for you personally of *not* reporting your observations to Mr. Riley's superiors?
4. What would your decision be?

PART **3**

ACCOUNTING FOR ASSETS

LEARNING OBJECTIVES

Careful study of this chapter will enable you to:

1. Account for sales discounts, sales returns, and sales allowances.

2. Describe internal control procedures for sales of merchandise.

3. Determine amounts for uncollectible account expense and the allowance for uncollectible accounts, using two different methods.

4. Explain how the cost and matching concepts guide the measurement of cost of goods sold.

5. Distinguish between periodic and perpetual inventory methods.

6. Prepare a worksheet and adjusting entries for a merchandising business that uses a periodic inventory system and use the worksheet to develop financial statements and closing entries.

7. Explain the difference between purchases and net purchases in terms of discounts, returns, and transportation costs.

8. Calculate cost of goods sold, given beginning and ending inventory, purchases, purchase returns, and transportation-in.

6

SALES REVENUES AND COST OF GOODS SOLD

Inventory, which is classified as a current asset on the balance sheet, is of major importance in businesses that produce or purchase goods and then sell them. Both sales revenue and cost of goods sold—two important components of net income—are connected to the sale of inventory. Sales revenue and cost of goods sold represent, respectively, the inflow and outflow of resources caused by the sale of inventory. Thus gross margin (sales revenue − cost of goods sold) indicates the extent to which the resources generated by sales provide for operating expenses (expenses other than cost of goods sold) and net income. Since gross margin is such an important indicator of business performance, this chapter will focus on the importance and measurement of sales revenue and cost of goods sold. With a clear understanding of sales revenue and cost of goods sold, you will be able to appreciate how gross margin and net income are affected by the inventory accounting methods discussed in the next chapter.

Thus far we have assumed that revenues are amounts that are clearly and completely established at the time of a sale. However, sales revenues can be altered by transactions that occur at the time of the sale (sales discounts) as well as by transactions subsequent to a sale (sales returns and sales allowances). The first major section of this chapter describes sales discounts, sales returns, and sales allowances. The second major section considers uncollectible account expense, an estimate of the amount of sales revenue that will never be collected because of nonpayment by credit customers. Uncollectible accounts are treated not as revenue reductions, but as expense. We will examine two widely used methods of estimating this expense and the associated contra asset account, allowance for uncollectible accounts.

In the third major section of this chapter, we describe the process of accounting for cost of goods sold. We begin by examining the concepts and objectives of cost of goods sold determination. We then examine two questions that are central to accounting for cost of goods sold:

1. What *cost system* (perpetual or periodic) should be employed?

2. What costs should be included in the cost of goods acquired for resale (that is, in the *cost of purchases*)?

Once both the perpetual and periodic inventory accounting systems have been introduced and briefly described, subsequent discussion in this chapter and in Chapter 7 will assume that the periodic system is used. The effect of perpetual inventory procedures on accounting for cost of goods sold is described in Appendix 7–2. (This discussion comes at the end of Chapter 7, since it relies on the discussion of inventory costing methods presented in that chapter.)

ADJUSTMENTS TO SALES REVENUES

Up to this point in the text, our discussion of sales revenues has not allowed for the possibility that sellers might attempt to accommodate or entice potential purchasers by modifying the terms of a sale. In this section, we discuss three adjustments to sales revenues: discounts, returns, and allowances. Sales discounts are offered at the time of a sale to encourage the purchaser to pay promptly. Returns and allowances take place after the time of a sale. Let us begin our examination of these three revenue adjustments by discussing sales discounts.

SALES DISCOUNTS

SALES DISCOUNT: A price reduction (usually expressed as a percentage of the selling price) granted by the seller conditional on prompt payment by the purchaser; also called a *cash discount*.

When goods or services are sold by one business enterprise to another on credit, a **sales discount,** a reduction of the normal selling price, is often offered to encourage prompt payment by the purchaser. Some retail businesses also offer discounts for payment of cash at the time of a sale. (One major gasoline retailer in the Midwest offers a four-cents-per-gallon discount to customers who pay for purchases with cash rather than credit cards.) A discount for prompt payment is, in fact, attractive to both the seller and the purchaser because purchasers who pay promptly reduce the cost of acquiring goods and services. Sellers typically find that the longer a purchaser delays payment, the lower the probability that payment will ever be made. Furthermore, recall from Chapter 2 that the time required for the seller to collect cash from purchasers is a significant portion of the operating cycle for many firms. When receivables arising from sales are not paid promptly by the purchaser, the seller must secure capital from other sources to pay its suppliers and employees until cash is finally received from the purchaser; the cost of securing this additional capital affects net income.[1]

Sales invoices use a standard notation to state discount and credit terms. For example, the invoice of a seller who expects payment in 30 days and offers a 2 percent discount if payment is made in 10 days would bear the notation *2/10, n/30* (which is read "2 10, net 30"). The notation *n/30* indicates that the net amount of the invoice (the full prediscount amount) must be paid in 30 days. The notation *2/10* indicates that, if payment is made within the 10-day discount period, the amount owed is 2 percent less than the gross (prediscount) amount of the invoice. Of course, if payment is made within the 20 days following the end of the discount period, then the amount owed is equal to the gross (prediscount) amount of the invoice.

Recording Sales Discounts

There are two alternative methods for recording receivables when sales discounts are involved. The first method records a sale and the associated receivable at the gross (prediscount) amount of the invoice. When a discount is taken, the amount of the discount is recorded in a contra sales account called *sales discounts* and the associated receivable is reduced by that amount. If a firm expects that most of its customers will *not* pay within the discount period, then it is probably most efficient for the firm to record receivables and sales at the gross amount.

---

[1] Sales discounts should be distinguished from both trade discounts and quantity discounts. A *trade discount* is a reduction in the selling price granted by the seller to a particular class of customers, for example, to customers who purchase goods for resale rather than for use. A *quantity discount* is a reduction in the selling price granted by the seller because the large size of a purchase transaction incurs lower selling costs per unit than would a smaller transaction. For accounting purposes, the selling or invoice price is usually assumed to be the price after adjustment for trade and quantity discounts; accordingly, trade and quantity discounts are not recorded separately in the accounting records.

EXHIBIT 6–1   **RECORDING RECEIVABLE GROSS WITH SUBSEQUENT CASH COLLECTION**

Entry on the date of sale

Accounts receivable................	15,000	
Sales revenue....................		15,000

*Entry if payment received **within** the discount period*			*Entry if payment received **after** the discount period*		
Cash	14,700		Cash	15,000	
Sales discounts	300		Accounts receivable		15,000
Accounts receivable		15,000			

Let us illustrate recording receivables and sales at gross: Bolt Manufacturing Company sold merchandise with a gross (prediscount) price of $15,000 to Richardson's Wholesale Hardware. Bolt offered terms of 2/10, n/30. To record the sale, Bolt would make the first entry shown in Exhibit 6–1. To record the collection of cash, Bolt would make one of the two entries in the lower part of Exhibit 6–1.

When receivables are recorded at gross selling prices, sales discounts (if taken) are recorded at the time of cash receipt. The matching concept requires that discounts be applied against related sales revenues. If a sale and its related cash receipt occur within the same period, then the discount and the related sale are properly matched. However, if the cash receipt occurs within a period following the sale period, then discounts are not properly matched with related sales revenue.

The second method of accounting for sales discounts anticipates that the offered discount will be taken by most purchasers. Therefore, receivables and the associated sales revenue are recorded net of the discount (that is, they are recorded at the gross price less the available discount) at the time of the sale. If payment is received within the discount period, no adjustment is required. But if the payment is received after the discount period, then the discount not taken is recorded as sales discounts revenue at the time of collection.[2] Using the Bolt Manufacturing/Richardson's Wholesale Hardware example, Bolt would make the first entry shown in Exhibit 6–2 to record receivables and sales net of discounts. This collection of cash would be recorded with one of the two entries in the lower part of Exhibit 6–2.

When receivables are recorded net of discounts, the failure of a customer to take a discount is not recognized until the time of cash receipt. If the sale and the cash receipt occur in the same period, then the failure to take the discount is recognized in the correct period. However, if the cash receipt occurs in a period following the sale period, then a matching error occurs. The amount of the matching error is the total of sales discounts not taken on accounts receivable at the end of the period. Of course, if all discounts are taken, no matching error occurs.

Although both methods of recording receivables and the associated discounts on sales are acceptable, the gross method is more widely used — frequently

---

[2] Sales discounts revenue, which is also called *sales discounts lost,* is similar to interest revenue because, by delaying payment, the customer has effectively borrowed money from the seller.

EXHIBIT 6–2   **RECORDING RECEIVABLE NET WITH SUBSEQUENT CASH COLLECTION**

Entry on the date of sale

| Accounts receivable | 14,700 | |
| Sales revenue | | 14,700 |

*Entry if payment received **within** the discount period*		*Entry if payment received **after** the discount period*	
Cash	14,700	Cash	15,000
Accounts receivable	14,700	Accounts receivable	14,700
		Sales discount revenue	300

with an allowance procedure designed to correct for the matching error associated with the gross method.[3]

SALES RETURNS AND ALLOWANCES

Occasionally, a customer will return goods because they were found unsatisfactory. In other cases, a customer may agree to keep goods with minor defects if the seller is willing to make an "allowance" by reducing the selling price. The accounting for sales returns and allowances, which is described in the paragraphs that follow, has the effect of reversing all or part of a previously recorded sale.

SALES RETURNS:
Merchandise or goods returned by the purchaser to the seller.

Merchandise or goods returned by the purchaser to the seller are **sales returns.** A contra sales account called *sales returns* is used to record the selling price of returned goods. For example, Bolt Manufacturing sold $12,000 of house paint to Charlie's Hardware. Charlie's returned $4,000 of the paint because it had arrived after the painting season, as a result of a trucking strike. Bolt made the following entries to record these events:

Entry at the time of the sale

| Accounts receivable | 12,000 | |
| Sales | | 12,000 |

Entry at the time of the sales return

| Sales returns | 4,000 | |
| Accounts receivable | | 4,000 |

In an example such as the preceding, if the purchaser has already paid the account receivable, the seller might refund the purchase price and record a credit to cash. However, if the customer regularly purchases from the firm, the return can simply be applied as a credit to accounts receivable in anticipation of the customer's next purchase.

[3] Although the gross method is more widely used in practice, the net method has several advantages. First, failure to take reasonable discounts may indicate customers who are experiencing cash flow problems and therefore are potential credit risks; thus entries to sales discounts revenue may signal the need for a credit investigation. (Of course, failure of a large number of customers to take discounts may indicate that an increase in the discount percentage is called for.) Second, since the net method presents a smaller—and therefore more conservative—amount for receivables and sales, it is more consistent with conservative asset and revenue recognition guidelines. Finally, if most discounts are taken, the net method results in minimal mismatching of sales discounts and revenues. When most customers take discounts by paying within the discount period, then recording receivables net restricts the matching error to that relatively small component of sales on which discounts are forgone.

SALES ALLOWANCE: A price reduction granted by the seller when goods retained by the purchaser are slightly defective, are shipped late, or in some other way are rendered less valuable.

When goods are only slightly defective, are shipped late, or in some other way are rendered less valuable, a purchaser may be induced to keep them if a price reduction called a **sales allowance** is offered by the seller. Selling enterprises record such price reductions in a contra sales account called *sales allowances*. For example, Bolt Manufacturing sold several snowblowers for $9,800 to Johnson Home and Garden Store. The blowers shipped were larger than those Johnson had ordered and were therefore more difficult to sell. Bolt offered, and Johnson accepted, a $1,600 reduction in the total selling price as an allowance for the size difference. Bolt made the following accounting entries to record these events:

Entry at the time of the sale

Accounts receivable..................................	9,800	
Sales...		9,800

Entry when the allowance was accepted

Sales allowances.....................................	1,600	
Accounts receivable...............................		1,600

If the bill has already been paid, the firm can either refund a portion of the purchase price and record a credit to cash or apply the allowance against future purchases by the customer by recording a credit to accounts receivable.

On the income statement, as indicated in Chapter 2, sales returns and allowances are subtracted from gross sales revenue to produce net sales revenue, as shown here:

Gross sales revenue..	$752,000
Less: Sales returns and allowances..........................	5,600
Net sales revenue...	$746,400

In other words, sales returns and sales allowances are contra sales accounts. Presenting both gross sales revenue and sales returns and allowances rather than net sales revenue alone permits statement users to respond to unusual behavior in either account. Careful users of financial statements look for unusual behavior in both sales revenue and sales returns and allowances in the income statement. Often, significant changes in these accounts help to explain other changes in income statement or balance sheet accounts, as we illustrate in the following analysis.

ANALYSIS
SALES RETURNS
AND ALLOWANCES

Interplains, Inc., sells gears to heavy equipment manufacturers. Data for the past four years for sales revenue, sales returns and allowances, and net income are shown below.

	19X3	19X4	19X5	19X6
Sales revenue	$624,000	$653,000	$671,000	$887,000
Sales returns and allowances	6,100	6,400	6,300	14,800
Net income	30,000	29,000	31,500	12,200

The following questions raise issues that might provide some insight into the significant change in the relationship between sales revenue and sales returns and allowances in 19X6:

1. *Have there been any significant changes in other output-related data?*

Sales revenue, which had been relatively stable, increased by 32 percent in 19X6. Often, significant growth in output is accompanied by quality assurance problems, as might be indicated by the 135 percent growth in sales return and allowances. A check of production data might reveal the use of less highly trained workers or supervisors, or might indicate that the current work force is being worked heavily on overtime.

2. *Have there been any significant changes in the economic environment of the firm?*

The data indicate a significant profit decline despite the large increase in sales revenue. When a firm becomes significantly more or less profitable, the attitude of the employees toward their work can change, causing changes in the quality of output. Some key employees may leave a firm with declining profitability, thus causing quality difficulties.

INTERNAL CONTROL FOR SALES

Since sales revenues, sales returns, and sales allowances can have a significant effect on a firm's net income, internal control procedures must be established to ensure that the amounts reported for these items are correct. For sales revenues, these controls normally involve the following documents and procedures:

1. Accounting for a sale begins with the receipt of a purchase order or some similar document from a customer. The order document is necessary for the buyer to be obligated to accept and pay for the ordered goods.

2. Shipping and billing documents are prepared based on the order document. (Billing documents are usually called *invoices.*)

3. A sale and its associated receivable are recorded only when the order, shipping, and billing documents are all present.

When any of these three internal controls is not present, it is possible for valid sales to be unrecorded and for invalid sales to be recorded.

For sales returns and allowances, internal control procedures must be established that identify the conditions and documentation required before a sales return or a sales allowance can be recorded. These controls protect the firm from unwarranted reductions in revenues and receivables.

ACCOUNTING FOR UNCOLLECTIBLES

When sales revenues are reduced to reflect sales returns and allowances, the reductions are accomplished through contra revenue accounts. Although it might seem logical to reduce sales revenues in the same way when customers default on accounts receivable arising from credit sales, this treatment of *uncollectible account losses* (also called *bad debt losses*) is inappropriate. Deductions from revenues should be recorded only for transactions that result from actions of the seller, such as acceptance of returned merchandise (a sales return) or price reductions offered to purchasers (a sales allowance). Since uncollectible accounts or defaults on credit sales arise from actions of the purchaser rather than the seller, uncollectible accounts cannot be recorded as revenue reductions.

If uncollectible accounts are not treated as negative revenues, then they must be treated as expenses. And if they are expenses, the question then arises as to when the expense should be recorded. Consider two alternatives: (1) in the period of the sale and (2) in the period of default (which is most likely after the period of the sale). As you will remember, the matching concept requires that expenses be matched with the related revenues in the period in which the revenues are recognized on the income statement. Therefore, **uncollectible account expense** (also called *bad debt expense*) is properly matched with revenues only if it is recorded in the period of the sale. This expense must thus be estimated, since the exact amount of the uncollectible accounts will not be known until some subsequent accounting period.[4]

UNCOLLECTIBLE AC-COUNT EXPENSE: The amount of credit sales predicted to be uncollectible, estimated in the period of sale; also called *bad debt expense.*

When uncollectible account expense is estimated in the period of the sale, the recognition of the expense usually precedes the actual default of specific accounts receivable. Therefore, an account must be established to "store" the recorded uncollectible account expense until specific accounts have been determined to be uncollectible. This account is called **allowance for uncollectible accounts** (or *allowance for bad debts*). When uncollectible account expense is recognized, a corresponding credit (increase) is made to allowance for uncollectible accounts. The allowance account is a contra asset account that reduces accounts receivable to the amount estimated to be collectible. When specific accounts are determined to be uncollectible, they are *written off* by a debit to the allowance account and a credit to accounts receivable. Using the contra asset account solves the timing problem of uncollectible account expense by holding the expense as an estimate until actual losses are realized and accounts are written off. This process is called the *allowance procedure for uncollectible accounts.*

ALLOWANCE FOR UN-COLLECTIBLE AC-COUNTS: A contra asset account that reduces accounts receivable to the amount estimated to be collectible; also called *allowance for bad debts.*

Another method, the *direct write-off procedure,* is not accrual-based in that it does not match the expense of uncollectible accounts with the related revenues. Under the direct write-off procedure, uncollectible account expense is increased and accounts receivable decreased only at the time an account is determined to be uncollectible. Since accounts are often determined to be uncollectible in accounting periods subsequent to the sale period, direct write-off is inconsistent with the matching concept and should not be used.

Under the allowance procedure, two methods commonly used to estimate uncollectible account expense are the *credit sales method* and *aging method.*

THE CREDIT SALES METHOD

CREDIT SALES METHOD: A way of determining uncollectible account expense *directly* by multiplying an estimated uncollectible account percentage by the total dollar amount of credit sales for the period.

The simpler of the two methods for determining uncollectible account expense is the **credit sales method.** On the basis of previous experience (and on consideration by management about how the future may differ from the past), it is possible to estimate the percentage of credit sales of a given period that will eventually produce uncollectible accounts. This percentage, when multiplied by credit sales, yields directly the estimated uncollectible account expense for the period. The amount is then added to uncollectible account expense and to the allowance for uncollectible accounts by an adjusting entry. Suppose that Hawthorne Company has credit sales of $620,000 during 19X6 and estimates at the end of 19X6 that 1.43 percent of these credit sales will eventually default. The following adjusting

---

[4] The exact amount of an uncollectible account may not be known for several periods. The receivable may be one that is to be collected over several periods, or the debtor may not pay as scheduled and lengthy legal proceedings may be required to force full payment or a bankruptcy settlement.

entry would be made to record the uncollectible account expense and the addition to the allowance:

Uncollectible account expense [($620,000)(.0143)]. 8,866
  Allowance for uncollectible accounts   8,866

When a specific account is determined to be uncollectible, the amount of the account is deducted from accounts receivable and from allowance for uncollectible accounts. This procedure is called the *write-off of an uncollectible account.* Assume, for example, that Hawthorne determines that a $524 account owed by James Carmack is uncollectible. The following entry would be made:

Allowance for uncollectible accounts 524
  Accounts receivable   524

Suppose that Hawthorne had accounts receivable and allowance balances of $304,000 and $8,900 just before the $524 write-off. The following schedule shows that the $524 write-off does not affect the *net amount* of accounts receivable when the allowance procedure is used.

	BEFORE WRITE-OFF	AFTER WRITE-OFF
Accounts receivable	$304,000	$303,476
Allowance for uncollectible accounts	8,900	8,376
Net accounts receivable	$295,100	$295,100

  Occasionally, accounts receivable are written off and are later collected. Suppose that James Carmack pays Hawthorne $524 in full payment of the account that was written off earlier. Hawthorne would make the following entries:

Accounts receivable 524
  Allowance for uncollectible accounts   524

Cash 524
  Accounts receivable   524

Hawthorne's first entry reverses the write-off; it restores Carmack's account receivable balance and also restores the portion of the allowance written off with Carmack's account. The second entry records the cash collection from Carmack.
  To illustrate how a firm determines its uncollectible accounts percentage, suppose that Hawthorne Company has recorded the following amounts for credit sales and related uncollectible account losses during the past four years:

YEAR OF SALE	CREDIT SALES	UNCOLLECTIBLE ACCOUNT LOSSES	UNCOLLECTIBLE ACCOUNT RATE
19X2	$ 503,000	$ 7,042	1.40%
19X3	567,000	6,804	1.20
19X4	592,000	9,472	1.60
19X5	607,000	9,105	1.50
Total	$2,269,000	$32,423	1.43

The uncollectible account rate of 1.43 percent is a weighted average of the past uncollectible account rates and is developed by dividing the total uncollectible account losses for the four years by the total sales [$32,423/$2,269,000]. Hawthorne assumes that future defaults from credit sales are likely to be as frequent as those from past sales and therefore uses 1.43 percent to determine its 19X6 uncollectible account expense. If Hawthorne expected the loss rate to increase, it would use a percentage greater than the historical rate of 1.43 percent. If Hawthorne expected the loss rate to decrease, then it would use a lower percentage than the historical rate.

THE AGING METHOD

AGING METHOD: A way of determining uncollectible account expense *indirectly* by first multiplying estimated uncollectible accounts percentages by the dollar amount of accounts receivable in various age categories (to find the desired balance for the allowance for uncollectible accounts) and then computing the amount of adjustment necessary to bring the allowance to the desired balance; the amount of the adjustment is also the amount of the uncollectible account expense.

Under the **aging method,** uncollectible account expense is estimated by determining the collectibility of particular accounts or groups of accounts rather than by taking a percentage of total credit sales. At the end of each accounting period, the individual accounts receivable are categorized by age. Then an estimate is made of the amount expected to default in each age category. (Of course, the receivables at the end of the period would not include any accounts that had already been determined to be uncollectible and had been written off.) The total amount expected to default on year-end accounts receivable is the amount that should be the balance in the allowance for uncollectible accounts. The amount required to adjust the allowance for uncollectible accounts from its present (preadjustment) balance to the desired adjusted balance is then computed. Computing the adjustment also indirectly produces the appropriate amount for the uncollectible account expense. Once the amount of uncollectible account expense has been determined, the entries to record the expense and the eventual account write-offs are exactly the same as those illustrated for the credit sales method.

To illustrate the computation of uncollectible account expense using the aging method, let's assume that as of January 1, 19X6, Sullivan, Inc., has the following balances for accounts receivable and allowance for uncollectible accounts:

Accounts receivable. $224,000
Allowance for uncollectible accounts (a credit balance). 6,700

During 19X6 Sullivan had $3,100,000 of credit sales, collected $3,015,000 of accounts receivable, and wrote off $60,000 of accounts receivable as uncollectible. Therefore, on December 31, 19X6, the preadjustment balances in accounts receivable and allowance for uncollectible accounts are:

Accounts receivable			
Beginning balance	224,000		
Sales	3,100,000	3,015,000	Collections
		60,000	Write-offs
Preadjustment balance	249,000		

Allowance for uncollectible accounts			
		6,700	Beginning balance
Write-offs	60,000		
Preadjustment balance	53,300		

The accounts receivable are categorized by age, and an estimate (based on past experience and expectations about how the future may differ from the past) of the proportion of accounts in each category that are expected to default is multiplied by the dollar amount of the accounts in each category, as shown below:

ACCOUNTS RECEIVABLE AGE	AMOUNT	PROPORTION EXPECTED TO DEFAULT	AMOUNT EXPECTED TO DEFAULT
Less than 15 days	$190,000	.01	$1,900
16–30 days	40,000	.04	1,600
31–60 days	10,000	.10	1,000
Over 61 days	9,000	.30	2,700
	$249,000		$7,200

The sum of these products, $7,200, is the desired adjusted credit balance in the allowance for uncollectible accounts, and it is also the portion of accounts receivable as of December 31, 19X6, that is expected to default. The uncollectible account expense for 19X6 is the amount of the adjustment needed to change the allowance for uncollectible accounts from its preadjustment balance ($53,300 debit) to its desired adjusted balance ($7,200 credit). The adjustment needed is a $60,500 credit.

Allowance for uncollectible accounts

Preadjustment balance, 12/31/X6	53,300		
		60,500	Adjusting entry
		7,200	Adjusted balance

Uncollectible account expense

Adjusting entry	60,500	
Adjusted balance	60,500	

Uncollectible account expense is recorded by the following entry:

Uncollectible account expense. 60,500
    Allowance for uncollectible accounts.   60,500

Note that the $60,500 uncollectible account expense was developed by estimating the expected defaults on current accounts receivable and by including the effects of accounts already written off in the preadjustment balance of allowance for uncollectible accounts. Had more (or fewer) accounts been written off in 19X6, the preadjustment balance in the allowance for uncollectible accounts would have been a larger (or smaller) debit, necessitating a larger (or smaller) uncollectible account expense adjusting entry in order to reach the desired adjusted balance for the allowance account.

Although uncollectible accounts result from actions of the purchaser (nonpayment), the amount of uncollectible account expense is influenced by the credit policies of the seller, as the following analysis illustrates.

ANALYSIS
ARE BAD DEBTS
ALWAYS BAD?

"In God we trust. All others pay cash." Thus reads a sign prominently situated on the counter of Mt. Sterling Drug Company. For many years, Andy Forsythe, the owner of Mt. Sterling Drug, has been a pharmaceutical wholesaler. An outgoing and friendly individual who believes that the "personal touch" is an important ingredient in any successful business, Andy has always been very popular among pharmacists in the local community. However, recently Mt. Sterling Drug hasn't grown as much as Andy had hoped. He observes that the amount of sales to a group of longtime, loyal, and reliable customers has been steadily dwindling.

Andy has steadfastly maintained his "cash only" sales terms. "A bad debt [uncollectible account] is like money down the drain," he says. "Short of costly legal action, there's nothing you can do to recover your money. I refuse to have my company's future jeopardized by getting involved in bad debts."

Some of Andy's competitors, affiliates of large corporate conglomerates, have been attempting to lure business away from smaller wholesalers like Mt. Sterling by offering retail pharmacies various incentives. Among these are credit terms whereby a customer typically has 30 to 60 days to pay for a purchase and receives a 1 to 2 percent discount for prompt payment (usually within 10 days of sale). Although he is concerned about losing business to these larger companies, Andy fears uncollectible accounts even more.

Is Andy correct? Should uncollectible accounts be avoided at all costs?

There is no question that the inability to collect an account receivable is a serious problem. However, most wholesalers have come to accept uncollectible accounts as just another business expense. Certainly no company would grant credit knowing that the specific customer will never pay for the goods purchased. Nonetheless, granting credit is a "necessary evil" — something that must be done to generate repeat business and maintain a competitive position.

Andy's friendship with the local pharmacists does not guarantee that he will receive their business, especially if they can get a better deal elsewhere. Further, prudent screening of each customer's credit history should enable him to identify at least some of those who may have difficulty paying their accounts. Placing such restrictions as relatively low credit limits on these risky accounts or, in some cases, denying credit altogether should help Andy keep uncollectible accounts to a minimum. Suppose Mt. Sterling's gross margin is 30 percent of sales and that, as a result of the more liberal credit policy, sales increase by $100,000 and uncollectible accounts are limited to 3 percent of the new credit sales. Then Mt. Sterling's income from operations should increase by $27,000 (increased gross margin of $30,000 less uncollectible account expense of $3,000), rather than decreasing as Andy fears.

This section completes our examination of revenue modifications and uncollectible account expense. We turn now to an examination of the elements of cost of goods sold.

CONCEPTS UNDERLYING ACCOUNTING FOR COST OF GOODS SOLD

Although accounting for cost of goods sold is influenced by many accounting concepts, the cost concept and matching concept exert the greatest influence. The *cost concept* requires that inventories of goods acquired for resale, like other assets, be recorded at cost in the accounting records. To apply the cost concept to inventories, we must decide which costs to assign to goods acquired for resale. (For example, should expenditures for the transportation of goods or for interest on inventory-related loans be included in the cost of the goods?) Above all, however, it is important to recognize that accounting for the acquisition of inventory is fundamentally a matter of applying the cost concept to the specific circumstances of each particular good purchased.

The second concept, the *matching concept,* guides the calculation of the expense called *cost of goods sold.* In Chapter 2, cost of goods sold was defined as the purchase price of goods sold to customers during the accounting period plus the cost of readying the goods for sale. Taking the cost of goods as an expense in the period of their sale to customers matches that cost with revenues of that period. A firm that purchases and resells goods would calculate its cost of goods sold for a given period by first adding the cost of the items in its inventory at the beginning of the accounting period to the cost of items purchased. The resulting sum is the **cost of goods available for sale.** At the end of the period, all goods available for sale either remain in inventory or have been sold. Accordingly, when the cost of the ending inventory is subtracted from the cost of goods that were available for sale, the remainder is the **cost of goods sold.**

A simple example will illustrate the way in which the foregoing calculation yields the cost of goods sold expense. Bargain Shops began 19X8 with an inventory of $26,000. During 19X8 the firm purchased goods costing $411,000. At the end of 19X8, the cost of the unsold inventory was $38,000. From this information, the 19X8 cost of goods sold is computed as follows:

COST OF GOODS AVAILABLE FOR SALE: The cost of beginning inventory plus the cost of goods purchased during the accounting period.

COST OF GOODS SOLD: The purchase price of goods sold to customers during the accounting period plus the cost of readying the goods for sale. Cost of goods sold is calculated as the cost of goods available for sale minus the cost of the ending inventory.

Beginning inventory, 12/31/X7	$ 26,000
Add: 19X8 purchases	411,000
Cost of goods available for sale	$437,000
Less: Ending inventory, 12/31/X8	38,000
Cost of goods sold	$399,000

The general structure of this important calculation for cost of goods sold can be represented as follows:

Beginning inventory
Add: Purchases

Cost of goods available for sale
Less: Ending inventory

Cost of goods sold

Knowledge of this general structure should enhance your understanding of how the matching concept is applied to cost of goods sold.

PERIODIC AND PERPETUAL INVENTORY ACCOUNTING SYSTEMS

One of the most important influences on the cost of ending inventory and the cost of goods sold is the type of inventory accounting system employed. Most busi-

PERIODIC SYSTEM: An inventory accounting system that records the cost of purchases as they occur during the accounting period but records the cost of goods sold only at the end of the accounting period; the inventory account reflects the correct inventory balance only at the end of each accounting period.

PERPETUAL SYSTEM: An inventory accounting system that records both the cost of purchases and the cost of goods sold as purchases and sales occur during the accounting period; the inventory account reflects the correct inventory balance throughout the accounting period.

nesses use either a periodic or perpetual inventory system. A **periodic system** records the cost of purchases as they occur during the accounting period but records the cost of goods sold only at the end of each accounting period; the inventory account thus reflects the correct inventory balance only at the end of each accounting period. A **perpetual system** records both the cost of purchases and the cost of goods sold as purchases and sales occur during the accounting period; thus the inventory account reflects the correct inventory balance throughout the accounting period.

A simple example illustrates the structures of the alternative inventory accounting systems. On December 31, 19X3, Miami Valley Products has a $900 inventory. During 19X4, Miami Valley enters just four transactions, in the following order: (1) a $6,000 purchase, (2) a sale of goods costing $5,400, (3) a $2,200 purchase, and (4) a sale of goods costing $2,500. At December 31, 19X4, Miami Valley has a $1,200 inventory. Exhibit 6–3 shows the accounts used by the two systems to record these transactions. Under the periodic system, the two purchases ($6,000 and $2,200) are recorded in the purchases account as they occur during the year. However, cost of goods sold is not recorded piecemeal during the year; rather, it is calculated to be $7,900 and recorded only at the end of the year. Under the perpetual system, both purchases and cost of goods sold are recorded as they occur during the year. The cost of each purchase is recorded as an

EXHIBIT 6–3   **PERIODIC AND PERPETUAL INVENTORY SYSTEM ACCOUNTS**

MIAMI VALLEY PRODUCTS
Alternative Inventory Costing System Records for 19X4

PERIODIC

Inventory, 12/31/X3

Balance	900

Purchases

Purchase 1	6,000
Purchase 2	2,200
Balance	8,200

Year-end Calculation of Cost of Goods Sold

Inventory, 12/31/X3	$ 900
Purchases	8,200
Goods available for sale	$9,100
Inventory, 12/31/X4	1,200
Cost of goods sold	$7,900

PERPETUAL

Inventory				Cost of goods sold	
Balance	900				
Purchase 1	6,000				
Balance	6,900				
		5,400	Sale 1	Sale 1	5,400
Balance	1,500				
Purchase 2	2,200				
Balance	3,700				
		2,500	Sale 2	Sale 2	2,500
Balance	1,200			Balance	7,900

increase in the inventory account. The cost of each sale is recorded as an increase in the cost of goods sold account and a decrease in the inventory account. Thus the inventory account reflects the correct inventory balance throughout the accounting period — $6,900 after the first purchase, $1,500 after the first sale, and so forth.

Although the perpetual inventory system provides more information than the periodic system, both systems, if properly applied, will yield the correct amounts for ending inventory and cost of goods sold. The operations of the two systems are summarized below:

ACTIVITY	PERIODIC SYSTEM	PERPETUAL SYSTEM
Purchase	The costs of inventory purchases are recorded in a *purchases account.*	Inventory purchases are recorded in the *inventory account.*
Sale	When a sale is made, an entry is made to record the amount of sales revenue only. *No entry is made to reduce the balance in the inventory account or to increase the balance in the cost of goods sold account.*	When a sale is made, an entry is made to record the amount of sales revenue. *An addition to the cost of goods sold account is entered and a deduction from the inventory account is also entered.*
Costing ending inventory	*The amount of the ending inventory is determined at the end of the accounting period by taking a* **physical inventory,** a procedure in which all items in inventory on a given date are identified and counted. The costs of all inventory items are then summed to determine total cost of ending inventory.	At the end of the period, *the cost of ending inventory is the balance in the inventory account.* (The perpetual inventory record is verified by a physical inventory.)
Determining cost of goods sold	Cost of goods sold is determined only at the end of the period by *subtracting the cost of ending inventory from the cost of goods available for sale* (the sum of beginning inventory and purchases).	Cost of goods sold for the period is the *balance in the cost of goods sold account* at the end of the period.

PHYSICAL INVENTORY:
The process whereby all items in inventory on a given date are identified and counted.

The periodic system produces balances for the inventory and cost of goods sold accounts periodically (at the end of each accounting period). In contrast, the perpetual system constantly (perpetually) provides balances for inventory and cost of goods sold.

PERIODIC AND PERPETUAL JOURNAL ENTRIES Let us illustrate the entries for both the periodic and the perpetual systems with the example of Bateman Electronics. Data for Bateman's purchases and sales of televisions during 19X2 are shown in Exhibit 6–4. (Beginning inventory is

EXHIBIT 6–4   19X2 INVENTORY TRANSACTIONS FOR BATEMAN ELECTRONICS

DATE	ACTIVITY	PRICE PER UNIT	UNITS	PURCHASES	SALES
1/10/X2	Purchase	$400	5	$2,000	
3/20/X2	Sale	650	1		$ 650
5/5/X2	Sale	650	2		1,300
6/12/X2	Purchase	400	4	1,600	
8/4/X2	Sale	650	4		2,600
11/29/X2	Sale	650	1		650

EXHIBIT 6–5   JOURNAL ENTRIES TO RECORD 19X2 INVENTORY TRANSACTIONS FOR BATEMAN ELECTRONICS

ACTIVITY	PERIODIC SYSTEM			PERPETUAL SYSTEM		
Purchase, 1/10/X2	Purchases	2,000		Inventory	2,000	
	Cash		2,000	Cash		2,000
Sale, 3/20/X2	Cash	650		Cash	650	
	Sales revenue		650	Sales revenue		650
				Cost of goods sold	400	
				Inventory		400
Sale, 5/5/X2	Cash	1,300		Cash	1,300	
	Sales revenue		1,300	Sales revenue		1,300
				Cost of goods sold	800	
				Inventory		800
Purchase, 6/12/X2	Purchases	1,600		Inventory	1,600	
	Cash		1,600	Cash		1,600
Sale, 8/4/X2	Cash	2,600		Cash	2,600	
	Sales revenue		2,600	Sales revenue		2,600
				Cost of goods sold	1,600	
				Inventory		1,600
Sale, 11/29/X2	Cash	650		Cash	650	
	Sales revenue		650	Sales revenue		650
				Cost of goods sold	400	
				Inventory		400

composed of one unit at a cost of $400.) The journal entries that would be made under each system for the transactions listed in Exhibit 6–4 are illustrated in Exhibit 6–5.

The different inventory and cost of goods sold balances that result from using the two methods to record each purchase and sale are presented in Exhibit 6–6. At December 31, 19X2, the end of the accounting period, the account balances are as shown in Exhibit 6–7. Since the perpetual system produces the correct balances at the end of the accounting period, no adjusting entries are required (assuming that the physical inventory does not reveal any errors). Adjusting entries are required for the periodic system, however (even if no errors are made). These entries are described in the next section.

EXHIBIT 6–6   PERIODIC AND PERPETUAL SYSTEM ACCOUNT BALANCES

BATEMAN ELECTRONICS
Account Balances after Each Transaction

	PERIODIC SYSTEM		PERPETUAL SYSTEM	
DATE	INVENTORY	COST OF GOODS SOLD	INVENTORY	COST OF GOODS SOLD
1/1/X2	$400	–0–	$ 400	$–0–
1/10/X2	400	–0–	2,400	–0–
3/20/X2	400	–0–	2,000	400
5/5/X2	400	–0–	1,200	1,200
6/12/X2	400	–0–	2,800	1,200
8/4/X2	400	–0–	1,200	2,800
11/29/X2	400	–0–	800	3,200

EXHIBIT 6–7   DECEMBER 31 PREADJUSTMENT ACCOUNT BALANCES

BATEMAN ELECTRONICS
Preadjustment Account Balances at December 31, 19X2

PERIODIC SYSTEM		PERPETUAL SYSTEM	
ACCOUNT	BALANCE	ACCOUNT	BALANCE
Inventory, 12/31/X1	$ 400	Inventory, 12/31/X2	$ 800
Purchases	3,600	Purchases (account not used)	–0–
Sales revenue	5,200	Sales revenue	5,200
Cost of goods sold	–0–	Cost of goods sold	3,200

PERIODIC SYSTEM ADJUSTING ENTRIES   When a periodic system is used, adjusting entries must be made in order to divide the cost of goods available for sale (the cost of beginning inventory plus the cost of purchases) between ending inventory and cost of goods sold. In effect, this adjustment process closes the purchases account, replaces the beginning inventory with the ending inventory in the inventory account, and enters the correct amount in the cost of goods sold account.

The adjustment process for a periodic inventory system is accomplished with three adjusting entries, which are shown in Exhibit 6–8 for Bateman Electronics. The first entry transfers the cost of the beginning inventory from the inventory account to the cost of goods sold account. The effect of this entry, taken by itself, is to reduce the balance in the inventory account to zero and raise the balance in the cost of goods sold account to equal the cost of the beginning inventory ($400). The effect of the second entry is to reduce the purchases account to zero and raise the cost of goods sold account to equal the cost of goods available for sale ($4,000). The latter amount is the cost of the beginning inventory ($400) plus the cost of purchases ($3,600). As a result of the first two adjustments, the balance in the cost of goods sold account now exceeds the cost of goods sold by the amount of the ending inventory, and the inventory account

---

EXHIBIT 6–8   **PERIODIC SYSTEM ADJUSTING ENTRIES**

BATEMAN ELECTRONICS
Periodic System Adjusting Entries as of December 31, 19X2

Entry 1

Cost of goods sold	400	
Inventory		400

Adjusting entry to add the amount of beginning inventory to cost of goods sold and remove the amount of beginning inventory from the inventory account.

Entry 2

Cost of goods sold	3,600	
Purchases		3,600

Adjusting entry to transfer the cost of purchases to the cost of goods sold account from the purchases account.

Entry 3

Inventory	800	
Cost of goods sold		800

Adjusting entry to deduct the amount of the ending inventory from the current balance in the cost of goods sold account and add the amount of ending inventory to the inventory account.

contains a balance of zero. This situation is remedied by the third entry, which reduces cost of goods sold by the amount of the ending inventory (as determined by the physical inventory at year-end) and enters that amount in the inventory account.

These three adjusting entries divide the cost of goods available for sale between ending inventory and cost of goods sold. These three adjustments are, of course, not appropriate if a perpetual inventory system is employed. Indeed, since a perpetual system records both the cost of purchases and the cost of goods sold directly in the inventory accounts, no adjustments are required at the end of the period. The inventory and cost of goods sold accounts contain the appropriate balances throughout the accounting period. After inventory costing methods are described in Chapter 7, the operation of perpetual inventory systems will be described in detail in Appendix 7–2. We turn now to an evaluation of the respective merits of periodic and perpetual inventory systems.

MERITS OF THE PERPETUAL AND PERIODIC SYSTEMS

Since periodic and perpetual inventory systems each offer distinct benefits, the choice of one over the other must weigh advantages against operating costs. The perpetual system has the obvious advantage of making available continuously the correct balances for inventory and cost of goods sold, while the periodic system makes such balances available only at the end of each accounting period. Clearly, continuously available balances make possible more timely management of cost of goods sold, gross margin, and inventory, as well as greater protection of inventory against misappropriation or theft. In a periodic system, determination of the ending inventory rests solely on the physical inventory taken at the end of the accounting period. In a perpetual system, determination of the ending inventory depends on a physical inventory also, but with this system, the physical inventory is corroborated by the continuously available inventory balance.

The principal advantage of periodic systems is that they are relatively inexpensive to operate. In spite of its advantages, a perpetual system is likely to be significantly more expensive to operate than a periodic system because separate entries must be made to the inventory records for each purchase and sale transaction. (These entries must incorporate the effects of the inventory costing methods, which we will discuss in Chapter 7.) Although the use of electronic data processing equipment has considerably reduced the financial disadvantage of perpetual systems, they remain more costly than periodic systems. Thus continuously available inventory cost data may not be worth the cost of the perpetual system required to secure it. Evidently this is often the case, because most inventory systems in use by firms are periodic systems. Since all important elements of inventory acquisition and cost of goods sold accounting can be discussed and illustrated with the periodic system, the remainder of this chapter will assume its use. The comparative advantages of the two systems are illustrated by the following analysis.

Hart's Jewelry Store has two sales departments: One sells china and glassware, and the other sells jewelry and watches. In the past, Hart's has maintained a periodic inventory system for both departments, but the recent installation of an electronic cash register system coupled with a small computer makes feasible the use of a perpetual inventory system. At present the store's accounting records are maintained by Mr. Hart's niece, who spends one half of her time as a salesclerk and the other half working on the accounting records. If Mr. Hart institutes a perpetual system, his niece will be required to work full-time maintaining the accounting records, and a new half-time salesclerk will be needed.

1. *What benefits are associated with a conversion from a periodic to a perpetual inventory system?*

The periodic system gives Mr. Hart cost of goods sold and inventory cost data only once each year, when the year-end physical inventory is taken. The perpetual system would give him a continuous report of inventory and cost of goods sold. Under a perpetual system, Mr. Hart's niece could prepare a weekly or even daily report, indicating the store's realized gross margin and its investment in inventory.

2. *What costs are associated with a conversion from a periodic to a perpetual inventory system?*

The principal cost of converting to the perpetual system is probably the cost of the half-time clerk to replace Mr. Hart's niece at the sales counter. In addition, however, each salesclerk will probably be required to input more information at the cash register, including detailed stock numbers as well as dollar amounts, and this may require additional time and training of personnel. A perpetual system provides managers with "early warning" that inventory quantities are too low. The early warning system permits timely reorders of merchandise that may result in increasing the amount of inventory. Increased inventory would definitely require a larger investment and might also add to the interest costs to finance the larger investment. Of course, Mr. Hart might be able to trim the expense of the perpetual system by using it only on items that have substantial sales volume, leaving the remainder of his inventory on a periodic system.

**INVENTORIES AND
COST OF GOODS
SOLD ON THE
MERCHANDISING
WORKSHEET**

Let us continue our discussion of inventory and cost of goods sold by considering the preparation of the worksheet for a merchandising firm that uses a periodic inventory system. Periodic and perpetual systems require different worksheet procedures. In the worksheet introduced in Chapter 5 (Exhibit 5–4), correctly stated balances for ending inventory and cost of goods sold were presented in the unadjusted trial balance. In other words, that worksheet assumed that a perpetual system was used. In perpetual inventory accounting, the ending inventory and cost of goods sold accounts appear in the unadjusted trial balance. However, since we will be using the periodic system, the unadjusted trial balance will include only beginning inventory and purchases, leaving cost of goods sold and ending inventory to be developed in the adjusting process. The three adjusting entries for the periodic system (as described in Exhibit 6–8) have to be made on the worksheet.

To illustrate the relevant worksheet computations when a periodic system is used, assume that a firm has the following inventory and purchases data for a recent accounting period:

Beginning inventory	$ 10,000
Purchases	140,500
Ending inventory	14,000

Recall that cost of goods sold can be computed as follows:

BEGINNING INVENTORY $+$ PURCHASES $-$ ENDING INVENTORY $=$ COST OF GOODS SOLD
$10,000 $\quad+ $140,500 - \quad$ $14,000 \quad = \quad$ $136,500

On the worksheet, three adjusting entries perform the same cost of goods sold computation. They are as follows and also appear as entries **a** through **c** in the adjusting entries columns of Exhibit 6–9:

Entry a

Cost of goods sold	10,000	
Inventory		10,000

This entry removes the cost of beginning inventory from the inventory line on the worksheet and adds that amount to the cost of goods sold line.

Entry b

Cost of goods sold	140,500	
Purchases		140,500

This entry removes the cost of purchases from the purchases line and adds the amount to the cost of goods sold line.

Entry c

Inventory	14,000	
Cost of goods sold		14,000

This entry adds the cost of ending inventory on the inventory line and subtracts that amount on the cost of goods sold line.

After these adjustments are entered in the worksheet's adjusting entries columns (see Exhibit 6–9), only the cost of goods sold amount is carried to the income statement columns. The remainder of the worksheet is completed as described in Chapter 5.

Thus far in this chapter, we have examined the general relationships among the components of cost of goods sold. However, there is more that must be learned about these components if you wish to use financial statement data properly. In Chapter 7, we will discuss accounting for ending inventory (which becomes the next period's beginning inventory). In the next section of this chapter, we will consider in detail the largest single element of cost of goods sold — the purchases account.

EXHIBIT 6–9   PERIODIC SYSTEM WORKSHEET

THE CLOTHING SHOP
Worksheet for the Year Ended December 31, 19X1

ACCOUNT TITLE	UNADJUSTED TRIAL BALANCE Dr	Cr	ADJUSTING ENTRIES Dr	Cr	ADJUSTED TRIAL BALANCE Dr	Cr	INCOME STATEMENT Dr	Cr	CHANGES IN RETAINED EARNINGS Dr	Cr	BALANCE SHEET Dr	Cr
Cash	9,500				9,500						9,500	
Accounts receivable	40,000				40,000						40,000	
Allowance for uncollectible accounts		200		(d) 4,000		4,200						4,200
Prepaid rent	2,500			(e) 1,500	1,000						1,000	
Inventory	10,000		(c) 14,000	(a) 10,000	14,000						14,000	
Equipment	350,000				350,000						350,000	
Accumulated depreciation, equipment		100,000		(f) 25,000		125,000						125,000
Other assets	10,000				10,000						10,000	
Accounts payable		28,000		(g) 2,500		30,500						30,500
Interest payable				(h) 3,000		3,000						3,000
Notes payable (due in 19X8, 15%)		40,000				40,000						40,000
Capital stock		70,000				70,000						70,000
Retained earnings, 12/31/X0		58,800				58,800					58,800	
Dividends	7,000				7,000				7,000			
Sales revenue		387,000				387,000		387,000				
Sales returns and allowances	20,500				20,500		20,500					
Purchases	140,500			(b) 140,500								
Cost of goods sold			(a) 10,000 (b) 140,500	(c) 14,000	136,500		136,500					
Operating expenses (not detailed)	87,000		(g) 2,500		89,500		89,500					
Rent expense	4,000		(e) 1,500		5,500		5,500					
Uncollectible account expense			(d) 4,000		4,000		4,000					
Depreciation expense, equipment			(f) 25,000		25,000		25,000					
Interest expense	3,000		(h) 3,000		6,000		6,000					
Totals	684,000	684,000	200,500	200,500	718,500	718,500	287,000	387,000				
Income taxes expense			(i) 30,000		30,000		30,000					
Income taxes payable				(i) 30,000		30,000						30,000
Net income							(j) 70,000			(j) 70,000		
Totals			230,500	230,500			387,000	387,000	7,000	128,800		
Retained earnings, 12/31/X1									(k) 121,800			(k) 121,800
Totals					748,500	748,500			128,800	128,800	424,500	424,500

COST OF PURCHASES

PURCHASES: The cost of goods acquired for resale received from suppliers during the accounting period.

The word **purchases** refers to the cost of goods acquired for resale received from suppliers during the accounting period. Purchases accounting is based primarily on the application of the cost concept, which requires that all assets be recorded as the sum of the outflows required to ready them for resale or use. A number of factors affect the cost of purchases; the most important of these are purchase discounts, purchase returns, and transportation. The accounting treatment accorded these items affects not only the cost of purchases but also, in turn, the cost of goods sold and the cost of ending inventory. We will consider separately the effects of each of these factors on the cost of purchases and, in addition, the accounting for interest paid to finance purchases.

PURCHASE DISCOUNTS

PURCHASE DISCOUNT: A price reduction (usually expressed as a percentage of the purchase price) granted by the seller conditional on prompt payment by the purchaser; also called a *cash discount*.

As we noted earlier in this chapter, it is common for sellers to offer their customers sales discounts to encourage prompt payment. From the viewpoint of the customer or purchaser, such price reductions are called **purchase discounts.** Like sales subject to discounts, purchases subject to discounts can be recorded either gross or net of the discount. Let us use the Griggs Company, a small furniture retailer, to illustrate recording purchases when discounts are offered. Assume that Griggs Company purchases 200 folding tables and that the list price of the tables is $6,000. The seller offers Griggs terms of 2/10, n/30. Recording purchases gross, Griggs would make the entries shown in Exhibit 6–10. Recording purchases net, Griggs would make the entries shown in Exhibit 6–11. The account called

EXHIBIT 6–10   RECORDING PURCHASE GROSS WITH SUBSEQUENT CASH PAYMENT

Entry on the date of purchase

Purchases.............................	6,000	
Accounts payable....................		6,000

*Entry if payment made **within** the discount period*

Accounts payable..................	6,000	
Purchase discounts..............		120
Cash............................		5,880

*Entry if payment made **after** the discount period*

Accounts payable..................	6,000	
Cash............................		6,000

EXHIBIT 6–11   RECORDING PURCHASE NET WITH SUBSEQUENT CASH PAYMENT

Entry on the date of purchase

Purchases.............................	5,880	
Accounts payable....................		5,880

*Entry if payment made **within** the discount period*

Accounts payable..................	5,880	
Cash............................		5,880

*Entry if payment made **after** the discount period*

Accounts payable..................	5,880	
Purchase discounts lost.............	120	
Cash............................		6,000

purchase discounts lost is used when payment occurs after the discount period under the net recording method. Purchase discounts lost is considered to be an element of the firm's financing cost and is merged with interest expense on the income statement. The net method is more widely used for purchases because it highlights discounts lost. A significant balance in purchase discounts lost may indicate flaws in the internal control procedures governing the payment of invoices.

PURCHASE RETURNS

PURCHASE RETURNS: The cost of merchandise returned to suppliers during the accounting period.

Sometimes purchased merchandise must be returned. Perhaps it is the wrong merchandise, does not conform to specification, or has arrived too late at its destination. The cost of merchandise returned to suppliers during the accounting period is called **purchase returns.** The key to proper recording of purchase returns is that the entries must be consistent with the accounting to date for the affected purchase. Purchase returns reduce the amount of purchases, which ultimately reduces the cost of goods available for sale.

Let us illustrate accounting for purchase returns using the periodic system: Assume that the Dennis Department Store purchased 1,000 coats at $20 each. Assume also that 50 of the coats were defective and were returned. One of the following entries would be made to record this return:

Entry if payment was not made before the return

Accounts payable	1,000	
Purchase returns		1,000

Entry if payment was made before the return

Accounts receivable	1,000	
Purchase returns		1,000

In either case, purchase returns (a contra account to purchases) reduces the cost of purchases. Transportation expenditures, the subject of our next section, have the opposite effect, since they add to the cost of purchases.

TRANSPORTATION EXPENDITURES FOR PURCHASES

Transportation costs are expenditures made to move purchased inventory from the seller's premises to the buyer's premises. When the seller pays these costs, they typically become a part of the price charged by the seller. When the purchaser pays the transportation costs, they are added to the purchase price as a part of the cost of acquiring and readying the inventory for resale or use.

The terms of shipment stated on the sales invoice determine when the purchaser acquires title to the shipment and whether the purchaser or the seller is responsible for the transportation charges. If an invoice is marked "F.O.B. shipping point," then the goods become the property of the purchaser at the shipping point and the purchaser is responsible for the transportation charges. Thus, goods that have been shipped F.O.B. shipping point but are still in transit at the end of the period should be included in the purchaser's inventory. (Further, if the seller prepays the transportation charges in an F.O.B. shipping point transaction, then the purchaser must reimburse the seller; otherwise, the purchaser simply pays the carrier.) If an invoice is marked "F.O.B. destination," then the goods become the property of the purchaser at their destination and the seller is responsible for the transportation charges. *F.O.B.* is an abbreviation for "free on board," which is the traditional legal term used to describe goods up to the point at which they become the property of the purchaser.

To illustrate, consider a purchase of merchandise shipped F.O.B. shipping point. The invoice, which arrives with the shipment, shows a total price of $10,000, and the trucking company presents an additional bill for $800, which is due upon delivery. The purchaser makes the following entry:

Purchases...	10,000	
Transportation-in...................................	800	
Accounts payable.................................		10,000
Cash...		800

TRANSPORTATION-IN (FREIGHT-IN): The account debited for the cost to the purchaser of transporting goods from suppliers.

The account called **transportation-in** (also called **freight-in**) is debited for the cost to the purchaser of transporting goods from suppliers. Transportation-in is an adjunct purchases account. (An *adjunct account* accumulates additions to another account, in the same way that a contra account accumulates subtractions from another account.) The balance of transportation-in must be added to purchases in the calculation of cost of goods sold. It is also acceptable to debit transportation-in costs directly to the purchases account; however, a separate transportation-in account is usually justified by the increasing participation of purchasers in national and world markets and the resultant growth in the transportation costs as a component of purchase cost.[5]

INTEREST EXPENDITURES FOR PURCHASES

Although transportation and its associated cost are indispensable to readying purchases for use, interest outflows are not always necessary. A firm may elect to pay cash for purchases and thus avoid finance charges. However, many firms find it useful to borrow cash from banks and other lending sources to pay for purchases. The loan is then repaid when cash is collected from sales of the merchandise purchased. The interest expense associated with a particular borrowing to pay for purchases is combined with all other interest expense incurred by the firm and is thus not part of the cost of purchases.[6]

PURCHASES AND COST OF GOODS SOLD DETERMINATION

Now that we have expanded the purchases amount to include purchase discounts, purchase returns, and transportation costs, these elements must also be included in the computation of cost of goods sold. Earlier in the chapter, we indicated that cost of goods sold was computed by adding purchases to beginning inventory and then subtracting the cost of ending inventory. The introduction of

---

[5] The transportation-in account should not be confused with the transportation-out account, which records transportation costs on outbound shipments of goods to customers. Transportation-out is a selling expense.

[6] An exception to this general rule is the interest on money borrowed during the self-construction of long-lived assets. Interest expense on borrowings used to finance such construction is added to the cost of these assets only during the construction period, after which the interest again becomes a period expense.

purchase discounts, purchase returns, and transportation costs requires the following altered computation for cost of goods sold:

> Beginning inventory
> Add: Purchases
> Add: Transportation-in
> Less: Purchase discounts*
> Less: Purchase returns
> _____
> Cost of goods available for sale
> Less: Ending inventory
> _____
> Cost of goods sold
>
> *If purchases are recorded gross.

Of course, if transportation costs are charged directly to the purchases account, then transportation-in will not appear separately in the computation of cost of goods sold. Purchases plus transportation-in less purchase discounts and returns is usually called *net purchases.* Net purchases is sometimes calculated as a separate subtotal in the computation of cost of goods sold.

In summary, the cost of purchases differs from the total invoice price of goods received from suppliers during the accounting period. The cost concept requires that the cost of purchases include the transportation costs borne by the buyer; and in addition, the total cost of purchases must be reduced for the cost of purchases returned to suppliers.

REVIEW PROBLEM:
SALES AND PURCHASES

Salva, Inc., sells building materials to retailers in the Philadelphia area. Salva uses the gross method for recording sales, the net method of recording purchases, and the allowance procedure for uncollectible accounts. On December 30, 19X7, Salva engaged in the following transactions:

a) Sold $8,750 of plywood on terms 2/10, n/15.

b) Arranged a $400 sales allowance for a retailer with slow-selling merchandise purchased from Salva. The retailer had not yet paid for the goods.

c) Accepted a $1,100 sales return. The customer had paid for the goods.

d) Collected the gross amount of a $10,000 sale made earlier on terms 2/10, n/15.

e) Collected the net amount of a $6,200 sale made earlier on terms 2/10, n/15.

f) Purchased $15,400 of plumbing fixtures on terms 3/15, n/30.

g) Paid the net amount for a $3,700 purchase made earlier on terms 4/20, n/30.

h) Paid the gross amount for a $5,300 purchase made earlier on terms 1/5, n/30.

i) Returned $650 of defective wallboard purchased earlier. The purchase had not yet been paid for.

j) Paid $340 to Fleetwing Transportation for delivery of lumber shipped F.O.B. shipping point.

k) Received goods purchased from Johnson Hardware shipped F.O.B. destination; the invoice shows a total price of $1,250, after deduction of applicable sales discounts. Salva's accountant notes that the seller paid shipping charges of $60. No amount has been paid to Johnson.

l) Wrote off an uncollectible account of $465 from Mullins Company.

m) Collected $920 cash on an account receivable declared to be uncollectible earlier this year.

n) Estimated uncollectible account expense for the year to be $12,400; the preadjustment balance of uncollectible account expense is zero.

REQUIRED:

Prepare journal entries for the transactions described above.

SOLUTION:

a)	Accounts receivable.	8,750	
	Sales revenue		8,750
b)	Sales allowances.	400	
	Accounts receivable.		400
c)	Sales returns	1,100	
	Cash.		1,100
d)	Cash.	10,000	
	Accounts receivable.		10,000
e)	Cash.	6,076	
	Sales discounts	124	
	Accounts receivable.		6,200
f)	Purchases.	14,938	
	Accounts payable.		14,938
g)	Accounts payable.	3,552	
	Cash.		3,552
h)	Accounts payable.	5,247	
	Purchase discounts lost.	53	
	Cash.		5,300
i)	Accounts payable.	650	
	Purchase returns		650

j) Transportation-in	340	
Cash		340
k) Purchases	1,250	
Accounts payable		1,250
l) Allowance for uncollectible accounts	465	
Accounts receivable		465
m) Accounts receivable	920	
Allowance for uncollectible accounts		920
Cash	920	
Accounts receivable		920
n) Uncollectible account expense	12,400	
Allowance for uncollectible accounts		12,400

SUMMARY

Sales revenues and cost of goods sold frequently represent the largest revenue and expense amounts for businesses that produce or purchase and then sell merchandise. Adjustments to sales revenue are made for (1) discounts offered to encourage early payment, (2) returns of unwanted or defective merchandise, and (3) allowances to offset declines in usefulness to purchasers. Accounting for all three of these items results from actions initiated by the seller.

The second section of this chapter described uncollectible account expense. Because the computation of uncollectible account expense does depend on revenues and revenue modifications, it is included with the discussion of revenue adjustments. Our discussion of uncollectible accounts examined the two primary allowance methods of estimating uncollectible account expense: (1) the credit sales method and (2) the aging method. The credit sales method estimate is determined by multiplying an expected loss rate times the amount of credit sales. The aging method estimate is developed by first categorizing end-of-period receivables by age and then estimating the amount of each category's receivables that will default. The sum of the estimated defaults is compared with (added to or subtracted from) the current balance in the uncollectible account allowance to determine the uncollectible account expense.

Because cost of goods sold is an important expense the accounting concepts and accounting systems that are used to match the cost of goods sold with revenues are of particular importance. Two inventory accounting systems are available to accomplish these purposes: (1) a perpetual inventory system that records both the cost of purchases and the cost of sales as they occur and (2) a periodic inventory system that records the cost of purchases as they occur, but records the cost of sales only at the end of the year. Although the perpetual system provides more information about inventories, it is also more expensive to operate than the more widely used periodic system.

The final section of the chapter discussed the determination of the cost of purchases. Purchases are one of the major elements in the determination of cost of goods sold. The amount of purchases is affected by discounts offered, returns made, and transportation-in costs paid.

KEY TERMS

AGING METHOD (p. 238)

ALLOWANCE FOR UNCOLLECTIBLE ACCOUNTS (p. 236)

COST OF GOODS AVAILABLE FOR SALE (p. 241)

COST OF GOODS SOLD (p. 241)

CREDIT SALES METHOD (p. 236)

PERIODIC SYSTEM (p. 242)

PERPETUAL SYSTEM (p. 242)

PHYSICAL INVENTORY (p. 243)

PURCHASE DISCOUNT (p. 251)

PURCHASE RETURNS (p. 252)

PURCHASES (p. 251)

SALES ALLOWANCE (p. 234)

SALES DISCOUNT (p. 231)

SALES RETURNS (p. 233)

TRANSPORTATION-IN (FREIGHT-IN) (p. 253)

UNCOLLECTIBLE ACCOUNT EXPENSE (p. 236)

QUESTIONS

Q6-1. What is a sales discount? How can sales discounts be recorded?

Q6-2. What are trade discounts and quantity discounts? From an accounting viewpoint, how does the effect of trade and quantity discounts on selling (or invoice) price differ from the effect of sales discounts?

Q6-3. What are sales returns? Why do sales returns occur?

Q6-4. What are sales allowances? How do sales allowances differ from sales discounts?

Q6-5. Why do readers of financial statements prefer the separate disclosure of gross sales revenue and sales returns and allowances to the disclosure of a single net sales revenue amount?

Q6-6. Describe the documents that underlie the typical accounting system for sales. Give an example of a failure of internal control that might occur if these documents were not properly prepared.

Q6-7. Why does the accountant make an entry to record uncollectible account expense in the period of sale rather than in the period in which an account is determined to be uncollectible?

Q6-8. What kind of account is allowance for uncollectible accounts? What does it represent?

Q6-9. Why is the allowance procedure preferred over the direct write-off procedure for uncollectible accounts?

Q6-10. Name the two allowance methods used to compute uncollectible account expense. For each method, how is uncollectible account expense computed and what does the balance of the allowance for uncollectible accounts represent?

Q6-11. How do the periodic and perpetual inventory accounting systems differ from each other?

Q6-12. What are the components of cost of goods available for sale and of cost of goods sold? Assume that the firm uses the net method of recording purchase discounts.

Q6-13. Why are adjustments made to the gross purchase price of goods acquired for resale?

Q6-14. Describe the difference between "F.O.B. shipping point" and "F.O.B. destination."

Q6-15. Identify the accounting items for which adjustments are made to the purchase price of goods acquired for resale when determining the cost of purchases. Assume that the firm uses the net method of recording purchase discounts.

EXERCISES

E6-16.   EFFECTS OF SALES   Citron Mechanical Systems makes all sales on credit, with terms 2/10, n/30. During 19X9, the list price (prediscount) of goods sold was $498,500. Customers paid $350,000 (list price) of these sales within the discount period and the remaining $148,500 (list price) after the discount period. Citron records sales net.

REQUIRED:

1. Compute the amount of sales that Citron recorded for 19X9.
2. Compute the amount of cash that Citron collected from these sales.
3. Prepare a summary journal entry to record these sales and a second summary entry to record the cash collected.

E6-17.   SALES RECORDED NET   Nevada Company sold merchandise with a list price of $12,500 to Small Enterprises on terms 3/15, n/30. Nevada records sales *net* of discount.

REQUIRED:

1. Prepare the entries to record this sale in Nevada's journal.
2. Prepare the entry for Nevada's journal to record receipt of cash in payment for the sale *within* the discount period.
3. Prepare the entry for Nevada's journal to record receipt of cash in payment for the sale *after* the discount period.

E6-18.   SALES RECORDED GROSS   Using the data in Exercise 6-17, assume that Nevada records sales *gross.*

REQUIRED:

1. Prepare the entries to record this sale in Nevada's journal.
2. Prepare the entry for Nevada's journal to record receipt of cash for the sale *within* the discount period.
3. Prepare the entry for Nevada's journal to record receipt of cash for the sale *after* the discount period.

E6-19.   SALES, SALES RETURNS, AND SALES ALLOWANCES   Rubin Enterprises had the following sales-related transactions on a recent day:

a) List price of goods sold on credit was $14,700; terms 3/15, n/45.
b) Cash sales were $1,150.
c) Goods with a list price of $1,200 were returned. The goods had been sold last week on credit with terms 3/15, n/45, and the customer had not yet paid for the merchandise.
d) An allowance of $250 was provided on goods sold two weeks ago. The customer had paid cash at the time of the sale, and the allowance was paid in cash.

REQUIRED:

Prepare a journal entry for each of these transactions. Assume that Rubin records sales net of discounts.

E6-20.   SALES RETURNS   Swan and Bloom, Inc., is a wholesaler of novelty items to small stores. All sales are on credit with no discount offered. During March, Swan and Bloom accepted the following sales returns:

a) Johnson Company returned merchandise with a list price of $600. Johnson had not yet paid for the returned merchandise.

b) Becker Bargains returned merchandise with a list price of $750. Becker had paid for the merchandise.

c) Fifth Avenue Market returned merchandise with a list price of $200. The bill for the returned merchandise had been paid.

d) Thorn Catering returned merchandise with a list price of $600. Thorn had paid for the merchandise.

REQUIRED:

1. Record the returns, assuming that cash refunds are paid to customers who had paid for their purchases.

2. Record the returns, assuming that Swan and Bloom makes a credit to accounts receivable for all customers.

3. Under what circumstances might Swan and Bloom credit accounts receivable even though the customer has paid for the merchandise?

E6-21. INTERNAL CONTROL FOR SALES   Arrow Products is a mail-order computer software sales outlet. Most of Arrow's customers call on its toll-free phone line and order software, paying with a credit card.

REQUIRED:

Explain why the shipping and billing documents are important internal controls for Arrow.

E6-22. AVERAGE UNCOLLECTIBLE ACCOUNT LOSSES AND UNCOLLECTIBLE ACCOUNT EXPENSE   The accountant for Porile Company prepared the following data for sales and uncollectible account losses:

YEAR	CREDIT SALES	UNCOLLECTIBLE ACCOUNT LOSSES*
19X4	$514,000	$ 7,710
19X5	582,000	9,312
19X6	670,000	10,385
19X7	772,000	11,966

* Uncollectible account losses relate to sales of a year rather than write-offs of that year.

REQUIRED:

1. What is the weighted average percentage of uncollectible account losses for 19X4 through 19X7?

2. Assume that the credit sales for 19X8 are $874,000 and that the weighted average percentage calculated in (1) is used as an estimate of uncollectible account losses for 19X8 credit sales. Determine the uncollectible account expense for 19X8 using the credit sales method.

E6-23. UNCOLLECTIBLE ACCOUNT EXPENSE: CREDIT SALES METHOD   Gilmore Electronics had the following data for a recent year:

Cash sales . . . . $ 26,700
Credit sales 428,600
Accounts receivable determined to be uncollectible. 6,300

Gilmore uses the allowance procedure to record uncollectible account expense. The firm's estimated rate for uncollectible account losses is 2.15 percent.

REQUIRED:

1. Prepare the journal entry to write off the uncollectible accounts.

2. Prepare the journal entry to record uncollectible account expense.

E6-24. UNCOLLECTIBLE ACCOUNT EXPENSE: CREDIT SALES METHOD   Bradford Plumbing had the following data for a recent year:

Credit sales	$289,000
Allowance for uncollectible accounts, 1/1 (a credit balance)	950
Accounts receivable, 1/1	38,700
Collections on accounts receivable	291,000
Accounts receivable written off	4,620

Bradford estimates that 2.2 percent of credit sales will eventually default.

REQUIRED:

1. Compute uncollectible account expense for the year.

2. Determine the ending balances in accounts receivable and allowance for uncollectible accounts.

E6-25. AGING RECEIVABLES AND UNCOLLECTIBLE ACCOUNT EXPENSE   Perkinson Corporation sells paper products to a large number of retailers. Perkinson's accountant has prepared the following aging schedule for its accounts receivable at the end of the year.

ACCOUNTS RECEIVABLE CATEGORY	AMOUNT	PROPORTION EXPECTED TO DEFAULT
Within discount period	$384,500	.004
1–30 days past discount period	187,600	.015
31–60 days past discount period	41,800	.085
Over 60 days past discount period	21,400	.200

Before adjusting entries are entered, the balance in the allowance for uncollectible accounts is a *debit* of $7,213.

REQUIRED:

1. What is the desired postadjustment balance in Perkinson's allowance for uncollectible accounts?

2. Determine uncollectible account expense for the year.

E6-26. UNCOLLECTIBLE ACCOUNT EXPENSE: AGING METHOD   Glencoe Supply had the following accounts receivable aging schedule at the end of a recent year.

ACCOUNTS RECEIVABLE AGE	AMOUNT	PROPORTION EXPECTED TO DEFAULT	ALLOWANCE REQUIRED
Current	$310,500	.004	$ 1,242
1–30 days past due	47,500	.02	950
31–45 days past due	25,000	.08	2,000
46–90 days past due	12,800	.20	2,560
91–135 days past due	6,100	.25	1,525
Over 135 days past due	4,200	.60	2,520
			$10,797

The balance in Glencoe's allowance for uncollectible accounts at the beginning of the year was $9,620 (credit). During the year, accounts in the total amount of $51,232 were written off.

REQUIRED:

1. Determine uncollectible account expense.

2. Prepare the journal entry to record uncollectible account expense.

E6-27. ALLOWANCE FOR UNCOLLECTIBLE ACCOUNTS   At the beginning of the year, Kullerud Manufacturing had a credit balance in its allowance for uncollectible accounts of $6,307. During the year Kullerud made credit sales of $890,000, collected receivables in the amount of $812,000, wrote off receivables in the amount of $31,425, and recorded uncollectible account expense of $33,750.

REQUIRED:

Compute the ending balance in Kullerud's allowance for uncollectible accounts.

E6-28. CORRECTING AN ERRONEOUS WRITE-OFF   The new bookkeeper at Karlin Construction Company was asked to write off two accounts totaling $1,710 that had been determined to be uncollectible. Accordingly, he debited accounts receivable for $1,710 and credited uncollectible account expense for the same amount.

REQUIRED:

1. What was wrong with the bookkeeper's entry?
2. Give both the entry he should have made and the entry required to correct his error.

E6-29. ENDING INVENTORY AND COST OF GOODS SOLD   Hempstead Company has the following data for 19X9:

ITEM	UNITS	COST
Inventory, 12/31/X8	990	$11,200
Purchases	4,510	47,100
Inventory, 12/31/X9	720	?

REQUIRED:

1. Determine the cost of ending inventory.
2. Determine the number of units sold and the cost of goods sold.

E6-30. ENDING INVENTORY, COST OF GOODS SOLD, AND GROSS MARGIN   Wilson Company sells a single product. At the beginning of the year, Wilson had 120 units in stock at a cost of $8 each. During the year Wilson purchased 850 more units at a cost of $8 each and sold 210 units at $13 each, 250 units at $15 each, and 360 units at $14 each.

REQUIRED:

What is the amount of sales revenue, ending inventory, cost of goods sold, and gross margin for the year?

E6-31. USE OF THE WORKSHEET   For 19X4 CJ's Commercial Laundry has prepared the worksheet shown on the next page.

REQUIRED:

Using the worksheet data, prepare the adjusting entries, income statement, statement of changes in retained earnings, balance sheet, and closing entries for CJ's Commercial Laundry.

CJ'S COMMERCIAL LAUNDRY
Worksheet for the Year Ended December 31, 19X4

ACCOUNT TITLE	UNADJUSTED TRIAL BALANCE Dr	UNADJUSTED TRIAL BALANCE Cr	ADJUSTING ENTRIES Dr	ADJUSTING ENTRIES Cr	ADJUSTED TRIAL BALANCE Dr	ADJUSTED TRIAL BALANCE Cr	INCOME STATEMENT Dr	INCOME STATEMENT Cr	CHANGES IN RETAINED EARNINGS Dr	CHANGES IN RETAINED EARNINGS Cr	BALANCE SHEET Dr	BALANCE SHEET Cr
Cash	15,000				15,000						15,000	
Accounts receivable	38,000				38,000						38,000	
Allowance for uncollectible accounts		700		(f) 2,600		3,300						3,300
Prepaid rent	19,250			(g) 10,500	8,750						8,750	
Inventory	28,000		(c) 30,000	(a) 28,000	30,000						30,000	
Land	65,000				65,000						65,000	
Building	270,000				270,000						270,000	
Accumulated depreciation, building		85,000		(h) 5,000		90,000						90,000
Other assets	9,000				9,000						9,000	
Accounts payable		24,250		(i) 2,100		26,350						26,350
Interest payable				(j) 3,000		3,000						3,000
Note payable (due in 19X9, 18%)		50,000				50,000						50,000
Capital stock		190,000				190,000						190,000
Retained earnings, 12/31/X3		34,100				34,100				34,100		
Dividends	1,600				1,600				1,600			
Sales revenue		432,000				432,000		432,000				
Sales returns and allowances	2,100				2,100		2,100					
Purchases	245,000			(b) 245,000								
Purchase returns and allowances		2,000	(d) 2,000									
Transportation-in	9,100			(e) 9,100								
Cost of goods sold			(a) 28,000 (b) 245,000 (e) 9,100	(c) 30,000 (d) 2,000	250,100		250,100					
Operating expenses (not detailed)	110,000		(i) 2,100		112,100		112,100					
Rent expense			(g) 10,500		10,500		10,500					
Uncollectible account expense			(f) 2,600		2,600		2,600					
Depreciation expense, building			(h) 5,000		5,000		5,000					
Interest expense	6,000		(j) 3,000		9,000		9,000					
Totals	818,050	818,050	337,300	337,300	828,750	828,750	391,400	432,000				
Income taxes expense			(k) 10,000		10,000		10,000					
Income taxes payable				(k) 10,000		10,000						10,000
Net income							(l) 30,600			(l) 30,600		
Totals					838,750	838,750	432,000	432,000	1,600	64,700		
Retained earnings, 12/31/X4									(m) 63,100			(m) 63,100
Totals									64,700	64,700	435,750	435,750

E6-32. PREPARATION OF THE MERCHANDISING WORKSHEET   Jay Coat Company has prepared the following unadjusted trial balance as of December 31, 19X2:

ACCOUNT	DEBIT	CREDIT
Cash	$ 5,200	
Accounts receivable	38,400	
Inventory, 12/31/X1	31,500	
Land	36,400	
Building	309,000	
Accumulated depreciation, building		$ 42,000
Other assets	21,100	
Accounts payable		21,500
Notes payable (due in 10 years)		60,000
Capital stock		210,000
Dividends	1,000	
Retained earnings, 12/31/X1		26,000
Sales revenue		632,000
Purchases	301,000	
Operating expenses (not detailed)	243,000	
Interest expense	4,900	
Total	$991,500	$991,500

The following data are also available:

a) The building has an expected life of 20 years and a residual value of $29,000.

b) The cost of ending inventory is $24,200.

c) Unpaid wages are $1,800 at year-end.

d) Five months' interest at 14 percent on the note payable is unpaid and unrecorded at year-end.

e) Unpaid utility expense is $3,900 at year-end.

f) The income tax rate is 30 percent.

REQUIRED:

Enter the unadjusted trial balance in a worksheet, and complete the worksheet. Assume that Jay uses the periodic method of accounting for inventory.

E6-33. PURCHASES RECORDED NET   Clean Wheels Car Wash purchased $54,200 (list price) of soap for its car-washing machines. The seller offered credit terms of 2/10, n/20. Clean Wheels records purchases net of discounts.

REQUIRED:

1. Prepare the entry to record this purchase in Clean Wheels' journal.

2. Assume the payment for this purchase is made within 10 days. Prepare the journal entry to record the payment.

3. Assume the payment for this purchase is made after the end of the discount period. Prepare the journal entry to record the payment.

E6-34. PURCHASES RECORDED GROSS   Dawson Enterprises uses the periodic system and records purchases gross. On a recent day, Dawson engaged in the following three transactions:

a) Purchased merchandise on credit with a list price of $24,600 on terms 3/15, n/25.

b) Paid for a purchase made 9 days ago. The payment was for merchandise with a list price of $21,900 that had been purchased on terms 2/10, n/30.

c) Paid for a purchase made 29 days ago. The payment was for merchandise with a list price of $19,400 that had been purchased on terms 1/10, n/30.

REQUIRED:

Prepare journal entries for these three transactions.

E6-35. COST OF PURCHASES   Compass, Inc., purchased 1,000 bags of insulation from Glassco, Inc. The bags of insulation cost $4.25 each. Compass paid Turner Trucking $260 to have all 1,000 bags of insulation shipped to its warehouse. Compass returned 50 bags that were defective and paid for the remainder. Assume that Compass uses periodic inventory accounting.

REQUIRED:

1. Prepare a journal entry to record the purchase of the 1,000 bags of insulation.
2. Prepare the entry to record the payment for the shipping.
3. Prepare the entry for the return of the 50 defective bags.
4. Prepare the entry to record the payment for the 950 bags retained.
5. What is the total cost of this purchase?

E6-36. PURCHASES AND PURCHASE RETURNS   On November 6, Lubin Products purchased on credit 350 parts kits from Michaels Electronics for $38 per kit. Michaels paid $320 to have the kits shipped to Lubin. Lubin paid for the kits on December 1. On December 15, Lubin discovered that 4 kits were defective and returned them to Michaels for full credit against future purchases. Lubin uses the periodic method of accounting for inventory.

REQUIRED:

1. Prepare an entry for Lubin's journal to record the November 6 purchase.
2. Would Lubin record the cost of shipping paid by Michaels?
3. Prepare an entry for Lubin's journal to record the December 1 payment.
4. Prepare an entry for Lubin's journal to record the December 15 purchase return.

E6-37. COMPONENTS OF COST OF GOODS SOLD   Anna's Corner Store has the following data for a recent year:

Beginning inventory	$ 65,260
Purchases	1,275,000
Purchase returns	23,000
Transportation-in	9,200
Ending inventory	78,300

REQUIRED:

Prepare the adjusting and closing entries, assuming that Anna's uses periodic inventory accounting.

E6-38. PURCHASES, SALES, AND COST OF GOODS SOLD   Printer Supply Company sells computer printers and printer supplies. One of its products is toner cartridges for laser printers. At the beginning of 19X8 there were 200 cartridges on hand at a cost of $60 each. During 19X8 Printer Supply Company purchased 1,400 cartridges at $60 each, sold 800 cartridges at $95 each, and sold an additional 750 cartridges at $102 each after a mid-year selling price increase. Assume that Printer Supply Company uses the periodic system.

REQUIRED:

1. Prepare summary journal entries to record the purchases and the sales. Assume all purchases and sales are on credit but that no discounts were offered.

2. Prepare the adjusting entries necessary at year-end to produce the proper balance in the cost of goods sold account.

3. Prepare entries to close cost of goods sold and sales revenue.

E6-39. TERMS OF SHIPMENT AND ENDING INVENTORY   On December 31, Archive Products had two shipments of merchandise in transit from two different suppliers. The first shipment, which arrived on January 5, was shipped F.O.B. shipping point and had a total invoice price of $28,600. The second shipment, which arrived on January 7, was shipped F.O.B. destination and had a total invoice price of $16,300. The physical inventory taken on December 31 revealed that goods on hand on that date had a total cost of $177,500. Archive uses a periodic inventory system.

REQUIRED:

What amount should be reported for inventory on the company's balance sheet at December 31? Show the adjusting entry or entries to record the ending inventory.

E6-40. TERMS OF SHIPMENT AND RECORDING PURCHASES   On May 12, Digital Distributors received three shipments of merchandise. The first was shipped F.O.B. shipping point, had a total invoice price of $150,000, and was delivered by a trucking company that collected an additional $12,000 for transportation charges. The second was shipped F.O.B. shipping point and had a total invoice price of $89,000, including transportation charges of $6,200 that were prepaid by the seller. The third shipment was shipped F.O.B. destination and had an invoice price of $22,000, excluding transportation charges of $1,200 paid by the seller. Digital uses a periodic inventory system.

REQUIRED:

Prepare journal entries to record these purchases.

PROBLEMS

P6-41. EFFECTS OF DISCOUNTS ON SALES AND PURCHASES   Helmkamp Products sells golf clubs and accessories to pro shops. During 19X5, Helmkamp purchased merchandise with a list price of $628,500 on terms 2/10, n/30. Helmkamp paid for $555,000 (suppliers' list price) of the purchases within the discount period and the remaining $73,500 (suppliers' list price) after the discount period ended. Sales in 19X5 were $1,150,200 (Helmkamp's list price) on terms 3/15, n/45. Customers paid for $822,800 (Helmkamp's list price) of the merchandise within the discount period and the remaining $327,400 after the end of the discount period. Helmkamp records purchases and sales net of discounts.

REQUIRED:

1. Compute the amount of purchases.

2. Compute the amount of sales.

3. How much cash was expended for purchases?

4. How much cash was collected from sales?

P6-42. SALES AND PURCHASE DISCOUNTS   Sims Company regularly sells merchandise to Lauber Supply on terms 3/15, n/20. During a recent month, the two firms engaged in the following transactions:

a) Sims sold merchandise with a list price of $33,000.

b) Sims sold merchandise with a list price of $48,000.

c) Lauber paid for the purchase in transaction **a** *within* the discount period.

d) Lauber paid for the purchase in transaction **b** *after* the discount period.

REQUIRED:

1. Assume that Sims and Lauber both record transactions net of discounts. Prepare journal entries for both Sims and Lauber for these four transactions in parallel columns, as illustrated below:

Sims			*Lauber*		
Accounts receivable.	xxx		Purchases	xxx	
Sales revenue		xxx	Accounts payable.		xxx

2. Assume that Sims records the sales transactions gross. Assume that Lauber records the purchase transactions net of discounts. Prepare journal entries for both Sims and Lauber for these four transactions in parallel columns, as illustrated above.

P6-43. RECORDING SALES   Sullivan Company sells industrial cleaning supplies and equipment to other businesses. During the first quarter of 19X2, the following transactions occurred:

a) On January 10, Sullivan sold on credit 50 cases of paper towels to the WMT Manufacturing Company at a list price of $800 for the entire lot of 50 cases.

b) On January 14, West Side Mall Corporation purchased on credit two floor polishers at a list price of $150 each and 10 cases of nonskid wax at a list price of $50 per case.

c) On January 16, West Side Mall returned 4 cases of the wax purchased on January 14.

d) On January 24, WMT paid for its purchase of January 10.

e) Tom's Cleaning Service purchased on credit 3 cases of carpet shampoo at a list price of $64 per case on January 31.

f) On February 3, West Side Mall paid for its purchase less the wax returned on January 16.

g) Tom's Cleaning Service paid for its purchase of January 31 on February 10.

h) WMT returned a case of oversize paper towels on February 16. Sullivan credited WMT's account.

REQUIRED:

Prepare journal entries to record each of these transactions.

P6-44. SALES AND SALES RETURNS WITH DISCOUNTS   Fuente Office Supply sells all merchandise on credit with terms 2/10, n/30. Fuente engaged in the following transactions:

a) May 1: sold 50 staplers to Aaron Enterprises at a list price of $12 per stapler.

b) May 5: Fuente accepted 4 staplers returned by Aaron Enterprises.

c) May 10: Aaron paid for the 46 staplers retained.

d) May 11: Fuente sold 25 filing cabinets to Buckles Corporation at a list price of $70 per cabinet.

e) May 23: Buckles returned 5 filing cabinets that it did not need.

f) June 4: Buckles paid for the 20 filing cabinets retained.

REQUIRED:

Prepare journal entries for each of these transactions, assuming that Fuente records sales net.

P6-45. INTERNAL CONTROL FOR SALES Yancy's Hardware has three stores. Each store manager is paid a salary plus a bonus on the sales made by his or her store. On January 5, 19X6, Bill Slick, manager of one of the stores, resigned. Bill's store had doubled its expected December 19X5 sales, producing a bonus for Bill of $8,000 in December alone. Charles Brook, an assistant manager at another store, was assigned as manager of Bill Slick's store. Upon examination of the store's accounting records, Charles reports to Yancy that the store's records indicated sales returns and allowances of $110,000 in the first four days of January 19X6, an amount equal to about half of December 19X5 sales.

REQUIRED:

1. What does the large amount of sales returns and allowances suggest that Bill Slick might have done?

2. How could Yancy protect itself from a manager who behaved as Bill Slick did?

P6-46. UNCOLLECTIBLE ACCOUNT EXPENSE: CREDIT SALES METHOD The Glass House, a glass and china store, sells nearly half its merchandise on credit. During the past four years, the following data were developed for credit sales and uncollectible account losses:

YEAR OF SALE	CREDIT SALES	UNCOLLECTIBLE ACCOUNT LOSSES
19X2	$197,000	$12,608
19X3	202,000	13,299
19X4	212,000	13,285
19X5	273,000	22,274
Total	$884,000	$61,466

In 19X4 The Glass House expanded its line significantly and began to sell to new kinds of customers.

REQUIRED:

1. What is the loss rate for each year from 19X2 through 19X5?

2. Does there appear to be a significant change in the loss rate over time?

3. If credit sales for 19X6 are $392,000, what loss rate would you recommend to estimate uncollectible accounts?

4. Using the rate you recommend, record uncollectible account expense for 19X6.

P6-47. AGING METHOD UNCOLLECTIBLE ACCOUNT EXPENSE Cindy Bagnal, the manager of Cayce Printing Service, has provided you with the following aging schedule for Cayce's accounting receivable:

ACCOUNTS RECEIVABLE CATEGORY	AMOUNT	PROPORTION EXPECTED TO DEFAULT
0–20 days	$ 88,200	.02
21–40 days	21,500	.08
41–60 days	11,700	.15
Over 60 days	5,300	.30
	$126,700	

Cindy indicates that the $126,700 of accounts receivable identified in the table does not include $8,900 of receivables that should be written off.

REQUIRED:

1. Journalize the $8,900 write-off.

2. What is the desired postadjustment balance in allowance for uncollectible accounts?

3. If the balance in allowance for uncollectible accounts before the $8,900 write-off was a debit of $450, compute uncollectible account expense.

P6-48. DETERMINING UNCOLLECTIBLE ACCOUNT EXPENSE USING THE AGING METHOD   At the beginning of the year, Tennyson Auto Parts had an accounts receivable balance of $31,800 and a balance in the allowance for uncollectible accounts of $2,980 (credit). During the year Tennyson had credit sales of $624,300, collected accounts receivable in the amount of $602,700, wrote off $18,600 of accounts receivable, and had the following data for accounts receivable at the end of the period:

ACCOUNTS RECEIVABLE AGE	AMOUNT	PROPORTION EXPECTED TO DEFAULT
Current	$20,400	.01
1–15 days past due	5,300	.02
16–45 days past due	3,100	.08
46–90 days past due	3,600	.15
Over 90 days past due	2,400	.30
	$34,800	

REQUIRED:

1. Determine the desired postadjustment balance in allowance for uncollectible accounts.

2. Determine the balance in allowance for uncollectible accounts before the uncollectible account expense adjusting entry is posted.

3. Compute uncollectible account expense.

4. Prepare the adjusting entry to record uncollectible account expense.

P6-49. PREPARATION AND USE OF THE MERCHANDISING WORKSHEET   Sacramento Stores' unadjusted trial balance as of December 31, 19X2, appears below:

ACCOUNT	DEBIT	CREDIT
Cash	$ 3,700	
Accounts receivable	41,200	
Prepaid insurance	2,400	
Inventory	38,100	
Land	12,500	
Building	315,000	
Accumulated depreciation, building		$ 72,500
Other assets	7,900	
Accounts payable		20,300
Notes payable (due 19X5)		70,000
Capital stock		180,000
Dividends	28,800	
Retained earnings, 12/31/X1		39,600
Sales revenue		467,600
Sales returns	6,200	
Purchases	253,500	
Purchase returns		2,900
Transportation-in	16,400	
Operating expenses (not detailed)	122,300	
Interest expense	4,900	
Totals	$852,900	$852,900

The following information is also available for preparation of adjusting entries for Sacramento:

a) An electric bill in the amount of $1,100 is unrecorded and unpaid at year-end.

b) Three months' insurance at $200 per month applies to 19X3 (is prepaid) at December 31, 19X2.

c) Five months' interest at 12 percent is unpaid and unrecorded on a $70,000 note payable at year-end.

d) At the time of its purchase the building had an expected life of 20 years and expected residual value of $25,000.

e) Based on a physical inventory, the appropriate amount for merchandise inventory has been determined to be $41,800.

f) The income tax rate is 25 percent.

REQUIRED:

1. Prepare a 19X2 worksheet for Sacramento Stores.

2. Prepare an income statement for 19X2.

3. Prepare a statement of changes in retained earnings for 19X2.

4. Prepare a balance sheet as of December 31, 19X2.

5. Prepare adjusting entries for 19X2.

6. Prepare closing entries for 19X2.

P6-50. PREPARATION AND USE OF THE MERCHANDISING WORKSHEET   Michael's Hardware has the following unadjusted trial balance at the end of 19X3:

MICHAEL'S HARDWARE
Unadjusted Trial Balance
As of December 31, 19X3

ACCOUNT	DEBIT	CREDIT
Cash	$ 9,600	
Accounts receivable	42,700	
Prepaid insurance	2,000	
Inventory	81,500	
Building	172,000	
Accumulated depreciation, building		$ 73,500
Land	20,000	
Other assets	6,400	
Accounts payable		18,700
Notes payable (due in 19X9, 10%)		24,000
Capital stock		132,000
Dividends	4,000	
Retained earnings, 12/31/X2		37,600
Sales revenue		215,000
Sales returns	11,500	
Purchases	109,000	
Purchase returns		7,100
Transportation-in	3,100	
Operating expenses (not detailed)	42,000	
Insurance expense	2,800	
Interest expense	1,300	
Totals	$507,900	$507,900

The following data are also available for preparation of adjusting entries:

a) One month's insurance ($250) remains prepaid at December 31, 19X3.

b) The building had an expected life of 10 years and an expected residual value of $25,000 when purchased.

c) Six months' interest at 10 percent is unpaid and unrecorded on the note payable at year-end.

d) Based on a physical inventory, the appropriate ending balance for merchandise inventory is $74,400.

e) The income tax rate is 30 percent.

REQUIRED:

1. Enter the unadjusted trial balance data into a worksheet and then complete the worksheet.

2. Using the completed worksheet, prepare an income statement, a statement of changes in retained earnings, and a balance sheet.

3. Prepare the closing entries for 19X3.   *INCOME STATEMENT & DIVIDEND ACCOUNTS.*

4. Prepare a postclosing trial balance.

P6-51.   PURCHASES, SALES, AND COST OF GOODS SOLD   The following data were available for Jeans Only, a seller of denim clothing, at January 1 of a recent year:

Inventory	$42,200
Accounts receivable.	41,900
Allowance for uncollectible accounts (a credit balance).	2,900

Jeans Only records purchases and sales net of discounts. During the year, Jeans Only engaged in the following transactions:

a) Sold merchandise for $220,000 cash.

b) Sold merchandise on credit: list price $378,000; terms 3/10, n/20.

c) Granted a sales allowance on a credit sale in the amount of $2,400.

d) Collected cash from accounts receivable in the amount of $394,100. Of that amount, $30,000 was collected after the discount period ended. (Receivables underlying the $30,000 collected had been recorded at $29,100.)

e) Wrote off accounts receivable in the amount of $2,730.

f) Purchased merchandise at a list price of $371,500. Terms were 2/10, n/30.

g) Returned merchandise with a recorded cost of $1,650.

h) Paid the account payable in full with a cash payment of $364,470. Of the amount paid, $20,000 was for accounts paid after the discount period. (Payables underlying the $20,000 payment had been recorded at $19,600.)

i) Uncollectible account expense was estimated to be .009 of *net* credit sales.

REQUIRED:

1. Prepare journal entries for these transactions. Assume a periodic inventory system. (Hint: Uncollectible account expense will be affected by the amount of sales discounts and sales allowances.)

2. Compute cost of goods sold and gross margin. Assume that ending inventory was $30,000.

P6-52.   PURCHASES, TRANSPORTATION-IN, AND PURCHASE RETURNS   Alpharack Company sells a line of tennis equipment to retailers. Alpharack uses periodic inventory accounting. Alpharack engaged in the following transactions related to purchases during 19X6:

a) Purchased on credit 320 Wilbur T-100 tennis rackets. The rackets have a list price of $30 each.

b) Paid Barker Trucking $63 to transport a purchase of tennis rackets from a manufacturer to Alpharack's warehouse.

c) Paid an account payable for a purchase of tennis balls. The tennis balls had been purchased at a list price of $1,500.

d) Purchased $8,000 of tennis clothing from Designer Tennis Wear by issuing a three-month, 13 percent note.

e) Returned 10 defective equipment bags to the manufacturer. The bags had been purchased at a cost of $16 each. Alpharack has paid for the purchase.

f) Paid the note payable issued in transaction **d** plus accrued interest.

REQUIRED:

1. Prepare entries for each of the items described.

2. By how much did the cost of goods available for sale increase as a result of these activities?

P6-53. PURCHASES, PURCHASE RETURNS, AND PAYMENTS FOR PURCHASES   Jordan Footwear sells athletic shoes. During April Jordan made the following purchases on credit with terms 3/15, n/40:

ITEM	QUANTITY (PAIRS)	LIST PRICE (PER PAIR)
Basketball shoes	100	$84
Cross-training shoes	80	53
Running shoes	210	56
Tennis shoes	120	49
Walking shoes	60	47

Assume that Jordan uses the periodic system and records purchases net of discounts.

REQUIRED:

1. Prepare a summary journal entry for the purchase of all the shoes.

2. When the shoes arrived, Jordan discovered that five pairs of basketball shoes were defective. The defective shoes were returned. Assume that Jordan had not yet paid for the purchase. Prepare a journal entry to account for this return.

3. Jordan paid for the remaining shoes within the discount period. Prepare the necessary journal entry.

4. Assume that Jordan's sales staff discovered seven pairs of defective running shoes when fitting shoes for customers. These shoes were returned to the manufacturer after payment had been made. Jordan was given credit toward its next purchase by the manufacturer. Prepare a journal entry to record this return.

P6-54. A CLASSIFIED INCOME STATEMENT FOR A MERCHANDISING BUSINESS   For each of the cases presented below, compute the missing amounts:

	A	B	C	D
Gross sales revenue	$?	$34,000	$7,900	$?
Sales returns	100	?	300	700
Net sales revenue	?	33,500	?	41,400
Cost of goods sold	?	21,200	?	29,600
Gross margin	5,000	?	?	?
Operating expenses	3,000	?	?	?
Income from operations	?	5,700	1,100	?
Other expenses	400	?	200	1,200
Income before taxes	?	4,900	?	?
Income taxes expense	?	2,200	300	2,500
Net income	$ 1,200	$?	$?	$ 4,700
Beginning inventory	$ 3,500	$ 4,800	$?	$ 1,300
Purchases	?	26,300	2,900	31,900
Purchase returns	200	?	50	200
Transportation-in	1,100	1,600	430	?
Cost of goods available for sale	14,500	?	3,500	33,100
Ending inventory	3,700	10,900	800	?
Cost of goods sold	$?	$21,200	$?	$29,600

P6-55. PRESENTATION OF SALES REVENUE AND COST OF GOODS SOLD   The accountant for Sneva, Inc., collected the following data for 19X7:

Beginning inventory	$ 26,700
Ending inventory.	28,300
Purchases	186,100
Purchase discounts lost	1,800
Purchase returns	7,400
Transportation-in (purchases)	4,300
Transportation-out (sales)	6,700
Sales revenue.	309,100
Sales returns	6,600

REQUIRED:

Assume that Sneva uses the periodic system and records purchases net of discounts. Prepare an income statement through gross margin including a computation of cost of goods sold. (Hint: Some of the data may not be relevant.)

ANALYTICAL OPPORTUNITIES

A6-56. INCOME EFFECTS OF UNCOLLECTIBLE ACCOUNTS   The credit manager and the accountant for Goldsmith Company are attempting to assess the effect on net income of writing off $100,000 of receivables. Goldsmith uses the aging method of determining uncollectible account expense and has the following aging schedule for its accounts receivable at December 31, 19X4:

ACCOUNTS RECEIVABLE AGE	AMOUNT	PROPORTION EXPECTED TO DEFAULT
Current	$2,980,400	.004
1–30 days past due	722,600	.035
31–60 days past due	418,500	.095
Over 60 days past due	322,800	.250
	$4,444,300	

The receivables being considered for write-off are all over 60 days past due.

REQUIRED:

1. Assume that the tax rate is 30 percent. What will be the effect on net income if the $100,000 is written off?

2. What data would you examine to provide some assurance that a company was not holding uncollectible accounts in its accounts receivable rather than writing them off when they are determined to be uncollectible?

A6-57. ERRORS IN ENDING INVENTORY   From time to time, business newspapers report that the management of a company has misstated its profits by knowingly establishing an incorrect amount for its periodic system ending inventory.

REQUIRED:

1. Explain how a misstatement of ending inventory can affect profit.

2. Why would a manager intent on misstating profits choose ending inventory to achieve the desired effect?

7

INVENTORY COSTING

As explained in Chapter 6, cost of goods sold is the remainder when the cost of ending inventory is subtracted from the cost of goods available for sale. This chapter continues our discussion of cost of goods sold by describing various methods—called *inventory costing methods*—of determining the cost of the ending inventory. Each inventory costing method is based on a different assumption about the prices paid for the items that compose the ending inventory. Four inventory costing methods are discussed—first-in, first-out (FIFO); last-in, first-out (LIFO); weighted average; and specific identification. The discussion also shows the different effects the four methods have on cost of goods sold, gross margin, income before taxes, and income tax payments when prices are changing.

Inventory costing methods assume that the exact number of units and the cost per unit of each item in ending inventory are known. Even when this information is unavailable, the cost of the ending inventory can still be determined by using an *inventory estimation method.* The second section of this chapter considers one such method, called the gross margin method, which derives its name from its reliance on an estimate of the firm's gross margin. A second inventory estimation method, called the *retail inventory method,* is described in Appendix 7–1. The third section of the chapter examines two circumstances that require a departure from the cost concept when assigning a dollar amount to ending inventory—when the market value of inventory is lower than its cost and when specific price change disclosures are made. The final section of the chapter examines the effect of inventory costing errors on the financial statements. Appendix 7–2 describes the perpetual inventory system and the differences among perpetual inventory calculations under FIFO, LIFO, and weighted average costing methods.

INVENTORY COSTING METHODS

If the prices paid for goods remain stable over time, then cost of goods available for sale is quite simple to compute. Each unit of each type of goods has the same cost per unit. The ending inventory has the same cost whether it is composed of the oldest units available for sale, the newest units available for sale, or some mixture of old and new units. For example, if all 1,000 units of a single product available for sale during 19X6 were purchased for $24 each, then the cost of a 200-unit ending inventory is $4,800 [($24)(200 units)] and cost of goods sold is $19,200 [$24,000 − $4,800]. It makes no difference which of the 1,000 units remain in the ending inventory.

On the other hand, if the price paid for a good changes over time, then the cost of goods available for sale may include units with different costs per unit. In such cases, the question arises as to which prices should be assigned to the units sold and which assigned to the units in ending inventory. For example, if three units available for sale have unit costs of $10, $10, and $12, respectively, and if two units are sold, then cost of goods sold could be either $20 [$10 + $10] or $22 [$10 + $12], depending on whether the $12 unit is sold or remains in inventory. One way to resolve this problem is to identify the specific units sold and their respective costs. If units have serial numbers and are relatively small in number, such a procedure is feasible. In most cases, however, specific identification is not a practical means of determining the amounts of cost of goods sold and ending inventory. Instead of identifying the specific units sold and in inventory, businesses usually make an assumption about which unit costs are assigned to ending inventory and cost of goods sold.

Let us demonstrate three such assumptions by using inventory data for Debbie Wrightson, who opened a small stereo shop in January. During the year, Wrightson recorded the data shown in Exhibit 7–1 for one model of stereo receiver. Note that during the year Wrightson had eight receivers of this model available for sale—four that cost $150 each and four that cost $180 each—and that she sold six of the eight. Exhibit 7–2 shows the results of applying three different assumptions to the data in Exhibit 7–1. Assumption A is that Wrightson sold all four of the $150 receivers and two of the $180 receivers, leaving two of the $180 receivers ($360) in ending inventory. Assumption B is that Wrightson sold three of the $150 receivers and three of the $180 receivers, leaving one of each

EXHIBIT 7–1   **PURCHASE AND SALES DATA**

DATE	ACTIVITY	UNITS	COST PER UNIT	TOTAL SALES	TOTAL COST
1/15	Purchase	4	$150		$600
3/20	Sale	1		$ 250	
5/14	Purchase	4	180		720
7/19	Sale	1		250	
9/30	Sale	1		250	
11/2	Sale	1		250	
12/15	Sale	2		500	
				$1,500	

EXHIBIT 7–2 **IMPACT OF INVENTORY ASSUMPTIONS ON FINANCIAL STATEMENT DATA**

	ASSUMPTION A	ASSUMPTION B	ASSUMPTION C
Sales revenue	$1,500	$1,500	$1,500
Cost of goods sold	960	990	1,020
Gross margin	$ 540	$ 510	$ 480
Ending inventory	$ 360	$ 330	$ 300

($330) in ending inventory. Assumption C is that Wrightson sold two of the $150 receivers and four of the $180 receivers, leaving two of the $150 receivers ($300) in ending inventory. As shown in Exhibit 7–2, the assumption made by Wrightson can have a significant impact on the amount of ending inventory, which in turn affects cost of goods sold and gross margin. Assumption A produces the largest ending inventory, which also results in the smallest cost of goods sold and the largest gross margin; assumption C produces the smallest ending inventory, thus resulting in the largest cost of goods sold and the smallest gross margin.

Although the assumption about the composition of ending inventory and cost of goods sold could take many different forms—each leading to a different inventory costing method—accountants typically employ one of three standard assumptions. When we add specific identification, there are four **inventory costing methods:**

INVENTORY COSTING METHODS: Various systematic methods of determining the cost of the ending inventory (and hence the cost of goods sold), each based on a different assumption about the composition of the ending inventory in terms of the different prices paid for goods over time.

1. First-in, first-out (FIFO)

2. Last-in, first-out (LIFO)

3. Weighted average

4. Specific identification

Each costing method represents a different procedure for allocating the cost of goods available for sale between inventory and cost of goods sold. Only the last method, specific identification, allocates the cost of purchases according to the flow of specific units through the inventory. That is, it follows a *flow of goods* principle. In contrast, the first three methods—FIFO, LIFO, and weighted average—follow not a flow of goods principle but a *flow of cost* principle. When the FIFO, LIFO, or weighted average method is employed, the actual flow of goods into inventory and then out to customers is frequently unrelated to the flow of unit costs. We make this point here because students new to accounting might think that a cost flow assumption describes how a firm actually moves its goods. The four inventory costing methods are taken up next. We will discuss their conceptual bases and their effects on the financial statements. The data in Exhibit 7–3 will be used to illustrate all four methods.

EXHIBIT 7-3   INVENTORY COST DATA

	UNITS	COST PER UNIT	TOTAL COST	
Beginning inventory	10	$ 6		$ 60
Purchase 1	50	10	$500	
Purchase 2	60	12	720	
Purchase 3	40	15	600	
Total purchases	150			1,820
Goods available for sale	160			$1,880
Less: Ending inventory	20			
Units sold	140			

FIRST-IN, FIRST-OUT

FIRST-IN, FIRST-OUT (FIFO) METHOD: The method of allocating the cost of goods available for sale between ending inventory and cost of goods sold based on the assumption that the earliest purchases are sold first.

The **first-in, first-out (FIFO) method** is based on the assumption that costs move through an inventory as an unbroken stream, with costs entering and leaving the inventory in the same order. In other words, the earliest purchases (the first in) are assumed to be the first sold (the first out). Under the FIFO method, the earliest purchases making up the cost of goods available for sale are allocated to the cost of goods sold and the most recent purchases are allocated to the ending inventory. Using the data in Exhibit 7-3, the following computation shows how the costs of beginning inventory, purchase 1, purchase 2, and part of purchase 3 are allocated to cost of goods sold by the FIFO method:

FIFO cost of goods sold

Beginning inventory (10 units at $6 each).....................	$ 60
Purchase 1 (50 units at $10 each)............................	500
Purchase 2 (60 units at $12 each)............................	720
Part of purchase 3 (20 units at $15 each).....................	300
FIFO cost of goods sold (140 units)	$1,580

The remaining part of purchase 3, the most recent purchase, is allocated to the ending inventory:

FIFO cost of ending inventory

Part of purchase 3 (20 units at $15 each)......................	$ 300

Alternatively, FIFO cost of goods sold can be computed simply by subtracting the FIFO cost of ending inventory from the cost of goods available for sale:

FIFO cost of goods sold calculation

Beginning inventory (10 units at $6 each).....................	$ 60
Add: Purchases ($500 + $720 + $600)	1,820
Cost of goods available for sale (160 units)....................	$1,880
Less: FIFO ending inventory (20 units at $15 each)	300
FIFO cost of goods sold (140 units)	$1,580

Although it is possible to compute FIFO cost of goods sold directly by calculating the cost of the beginning inventory and purchases of which it is composed, it is usually easier to compute cost of goods sold as shown immediately above, by subtracting the cost of the ending inventory from the cost of goods available for sale.

When prices are rising, as they are in our example, the FIFO method produces the largest cost for ending inventory, the smallest cost of goods sold, and, therefore, the largest gross margin of the four methods. In contrast, the LIFO method, to which we now turn, produces the smallest cost for ending inventory, the largest cost of goods sold, and, therefore, the smallest gross margin of the four methods when prices are rising.

LAST-IN, FIRST-OUT

LAST-IN, FIRST-OUT (LIFO) METHOD: The method of allocating the cost of goods available for sale between ending inventory and cost of goods sold based on the assumption that the most recent purchases are sold first.

The **last-in, first-out (LIFO) method** allocates the cost of goods available for sale between ending inventory and cost of goods sold based on the assumption that the most recent purchases (the last in) are the first to be sold (the first out). Under the LIFO method, the most recent purchases (newest costs) are allocated to the cost of goods sold and the earliest purchases (oldest costs) are allocated to ending inventory. Using the data in Exhibit 7–3, the costs of the beginning inventory and 10 units of purchase 1 are allocated to the ending inventory by the LIFO method as follows:

LIFO cost of ending inventory

Beginning inventory (10 units at $6 each)	$ 60
Part of purchase 1 (10 units at $10 each)	100
LIFO cost of ending inventory (20 units)	$160

Notice that the LIFO inventory is composed of two layers of cost—one associated with the beginning inventory at a unit cost of $6 and a second associated with the first purchase at a unit cost of $10. The costs of the remaining 40 units of purchase 1, all of purchase 2, and all of purchase 3 are allocated to the LIFO cost of goods sold:

LIFO cost of goods sold

Part of purchase 1 (40 units at $10 each)	$ 400
Purchase 2 (60 units at $12 each)	720
Purchase 3 (40 units at $15 each)	600
LIFO cost of goods sold (140 units)	$1,720

Alternatively, LIFO cost of goods sold can be computed by subtracting the LIFO cost of ending inventory from the cost of goods available for sale:

LIFO cost of goods sold calculation

Beginning inventory (10 units at $6 each)	$ 60
Add: Purchases ($500 + $720 + $600)	1,820
Cost of goods available for sale (160 units)	$1,880
Less: LIFO ending inventory (10 units at $6 each + 10 units at $10 each)	160
LIFO cost of goods sold (140 units)	$1,720

This second calculation of LIFO cost of goods sold is usually easier than the direct calculation which sums the cost of individual purchases.

WEIGHTED AVERAGE

WEIGHTED AVERAGE METHOD: The method of allocating the cost of goods available for sale between ending inventory and cost of goods sold based on a single, weighted average cost per unit.

The **weighted average method** allocates the cost of goods available for sale between ending inventory and cost of goods sold based on a single, weighted average cost per unit. The weighted average cost per unit is calculated by dividing the cost of goods available for sale by the number of units available for sale. This weighted average cost per unit is then multiplied by the number of units sold to produce cost of goods sold and by the number of units in ending inventory to produce cost of ending inventory. Using the data in Exhibit 7–3, cost of goods sold and cost of ending inventory are computed as follows:

Weighted average cost per unit

$$\frac{\text{Cost of goods available for sale}}{\text{Units in goods available for sale}} = \frac{\$1,880}{160} = \$11.75 \text{ per unit}$$

Weighted average cost of goods sold

$$(\$11.75)(140 \text{ units sold}) = \underline{\underline{\$1,645}}$$

Weighted average cost of ending inventory

$$(\$11.75)(20 \text{ units}) = \underline{\underline{\$235}}$$

Notice that all units sold and in ending inventory are allocated the same unit cost ($11.75).

The weighted average cost of goods sold can also be calculated by subtracting the weighted average cost of ending inventory from the cost of goods available for sale:

Weighted average cost of goods sold calculation	
Beginning inventory (10 units at $6 each).....................	$ 60
Add: Purchases ($500 + $720 + $600)	1,820
Cost of goods available for sale (160 units)....................	$1,880
Less: Weighted average ending inventory	
(20 units at $11.75 each)...................................	235
Weighted average cost of goods sold (140 units)	$1,645

When prices are rising, the weighted average method results in an allocation to cost of goods sold that is between the low allocation produced by FIFO and the high allocation produced by LIFO.

SPECIFIC IDENTIFICATION

SPECIFIC IDENTIFICATION METHOD: The method of allocating the cost of goods available for sale between ending inventory and cost of goods sold based on an identification of the actual units sold and in inventory.

The **specific identification method** allocates the cost of goods available for sale between ending inventory and cost of goods sold based on an identification of the actual units sold and in inventory. In other words, the specific identification method allocates to cost of goods sold the cost of those specific units identified as having been sold and allocates to ending inventory the cost of the specific units unsold. This method is practical only for situations in which very few items are purchased and sold (for example, a used-car dealership). When many units are purchased and sold, it is too time-consuming (and therefore too costly) to keep track of exactly which units are sold. Using the data in Exhibit 7–3 and additional data indicating which units have been sold and which remain in ending inventory, we can determine cost of goods sold and cost of ending inventory by the specific identification method:

ITEM	UNITS SOLD	UNITS IN ENDING INVENTORY
Beginning inventory	10	—
Purchase 1	45	5
Purchase 2	55	5
Purchase 3	30	10
	140	20

Specific identification cost of goods sold

(10 units)($6 each) = $	60
(45 units)($10 each) =	450
(55 units)($12 each) =	660
(30 units)($15 each) =	450
	$1,620

Specific identification cost of ending inventory

(5 units)($10 each) = $	50
(5 units)($12 each) =	60
(10 units)($15 each) =	150
	$ 260

Since there are usually far fewer units in ending inventory than in cost of goods sold, it is easier to compute the cost of the ending inventory and then find the cost of goods sold by subtraction than to compute the cost of goods sold directly. This alternative to the direct calculation has the following familiar form:

Specific identification cost of goods sold calculation

Beginning inventory (10 units at $6 each).....................	$ 60
Add: Purchases ($500 + $720 + $600)	1,820
Cost of goods available for sale (160 units)....................	$1,880
Less: Specific identification ending inventory..................	260
Specific identification cost of goods sold (140 units)..........	$1,620

THE CONSISTENCY CONVENTION

CONSISTENCY: The convention that discourages changes in accounting methods from one period to another, even if acceptable alternative methods exist.

Although each of the four inventory costing methods is an acceptable accounting method, once a business adopts a particular costing method for an item,[1] it must continue to use it. Continuing to use an accounting policy once adopted is required by the consistency convention. The **consistency** convention discourages changes in accounting methods from one period to another, even if acceptable alternative methods exist. In rare cases, a change in accounting method may be made; however, the effects of the change must be fully disclosed. The consistency convention and the required disclosures of accounting changes permit readers of financial statements to assume that accounting methods do not change over time

[1] All items of inventory need not be accounted for by the same costing method. Many firms use LIFO for the portion of inventory for which prices are expected to rise and FIFO or weighted average for the portion of inventory for which prices are not expected to rise.

unless a change is specifically indicated. We turn now to several factors that influence the choice of inventory costing method.

MATCHING INVENTORY COSTS AND RELATED REVENUES

All four inventory costing methods represent applications of the cost concept in that they identify a historical cost for units sold and units in ending inventory. The four methods also represent applications of the matching concept in that they determine cost of goods sold—the amount of expense to be matched with revenue—based in part on the number of units sold. Some accountants object to this application of the historical cost concept and argue—particularly in periods of rapidly rising prices—that it leads to a misleading understatement of cost of goods sold and a consequent overstatement of gross margin and net income. They maintain that the matching concept should be extended to require matching the current cost of replacing the goods sold against the current revenues. Matching current cost prices against current sales prices, they argue, will exclude from income the amounts required to replace goods that have been sold. Recognizing that such a departure from the cost concept in the determination of net income is not permitted by generally accepted accounting principles, many of these accountants express a preference for LIFO, which closely approximates matching the current cost of goods sold against current revenues. Recall that LIFO allocates the cost of the most recent purchases to cost of goods sold, whereas FIFO allocates the cost of the earliest purchases to cost of goods sold. In its 1985 annual report, Bergen Brunswig Corporation used this argument to support its decision to change to LIFO for a portion of its inventory:

Change to LIFO Accounting

To match costs and related revenues more properly, the Corporation changed its method of valuing the Drug and Health Care and Medical/Surgical Supplies inventories to the LIFO method in the third quarter of 1985. The Consumer Electronic segment inventories ($41,090,000 at August 31, 1985) continue to be valued using the FIFO method because of the deflationary nature of this inventory.

The firm's selection of LIFO is supported by a conceptual argument concerning the nature of net income and the desire to base cost of goods sold on current costs. In addition, LIFO can be advantageous for tax purposes, as the next section illustrates.

INCOME TAX IMPLICATIONS OF FIFO AND LIFO

In periods of rising prices, the use of LIFO (as compared to FIFO) allocates the newer—and therefore higher—inventory purchase costs to cost of goods sold. Higher cost of goods sold produces lower gross margin, lower income before taxes, and therefore lower income tax payments. To illustrate this relationship, let's assume that there are two firms, one that uses FIFO and another that uses LIFO. At the beginning of the period, the two firms have the following balance sheets:

	FIFO FIRM	LIFO FIRM
Cash	$1,000	$1,000
Total assets	$1,000	$1,000
Capital stock	$1,000	$1,000
Total liabilities and equity	$1,000	$1,000

EXHIBIT 7–4   FIFO AND LIFO INCOME STATEMENTS

	FIFO FIRM	LIFO FIRM
Sales revenue	$800	$800
Cost of goods sold		
Beginning inventory	$–0–	$–0–
Purchases	650	650
Cost of goods available for sale	$650	$650
Less: Ending inventory	160*	100†
Cost of goods sold	490	550
Gross margin	$310	$250
Less: Operating expenses	200	200
Income before taxes	$110	$ 50
Less: Income taxes expense (.30)	33	15
Net income	$ 77	$ 35

* FIFO is used, so ending inventory is the cost of the newest 20 units [(20 units)($8 each) = $160].
† LIFO is used, so ending inventory is the cost of the oldest 20 units [(20 units)($5 each) = $100].

During the year, both firms make the same purchases of inventory:

	UNITS	COST PER UNIT	TOTAL COST
Purchase 1	50	$5	$250
Purchase 2	50	8	400
Goods available for sale	100		$650

Both firms sell 80 of the 100 units purchased for $10 cash per unit and incur $200 of operating expenses. Income taxes are incurred at a rate of 30 percent (.30) and are paid in cash. The two firms prepare the income statements shown in Exhibit 7–4. Assume that both firms pay their tax expenses in cash before the end of the period. At the end of the period, the balance sheets for the two firms are as shown in Exhibit 7–5.

EXHIBIT 7–5   BALANCE SHEET EFFECTS OF FIFO AND LIFO

	FIFO FIRM	LIFO FIRM
Cash*	$ 917	$ 935
Inventory (20 units)	160	100
Total assets	$1,077	$1,035
Capital stock	$1,000	$1,000
Retained earnings	77	35
Total liabilities and equity	$1,077	$1,035

* Cash at end of period = Beginning cash + Sales − Purchases − Operating expenses − Taxes
            = $1,000 + 800 − 650 − 200 − Taxes.

In periods of rising prices, the use of LIFO produces a lower gross margin, lower income before taxes, and smaller cash outflows for income taxes than would FIFO. The result in our illustration is that the LIFO firm has $935 in cash and 20 units of inventory at the end of the accounting period. The FIFO firm has $917 in cash and the same 20 units of inventory. Both firms have exactly the same inventory (the only asset other than cash in our example), but since the LIFO firm has retained $18 more cash than the FIFO firm, the LIFO firm is better off by $18, despite the fact that the income statement and the balance sheet indicate that the FIFO firm had higher income (and therefore more assets). Because of the inflation-produced price increases of the 1970s, many firms adopted the LIFO method in order to gain the substantial cash savings resulting from lower taxes.[2]

The following analysis uses data from the annual reports of actual corporations to estimate the amount of cash a sample of firms saved by using LIFO, thus providing an example of the economic consequences of accounting decisions.

ANALYSIS

DOES LIFO MAKE A DIFFERENCE?

Does LIFO in fact save cash by reducing outflows in the form of taxes? In recent years, relatively low corporate income tax rates coupled with inventory reductions and moderate inflation have reduced the tax advantage of LIFO. But look at the following data from the annual reports of 10 large corporations for 1990, and decide for yourself:

FIRM	INVENTORY AT LIFO	INVENTORY AT FIFO	ESTIMATED CASH SAVINGS*
Caterpillar	$2,105	$4,033	$656
Deere	678	1,799	381
Eli Lilly	673	716	15
General Mills	394	466	24
Gerber Products	73	119	16
Procter & Gamble	2,865	3,058	66
Rubbermaid	217	241	8
Walgreen's	828	1,113	97

Note: All amounts are in millions of dollars.
* Estimated cash savings are the excess of FIFO and LIFO times the estimated marginal federal income tax rate of 34 percent (.34).

The tax advantage of LIFO disappears in times of falling prices. In those periods, FIFO produces the lowest taxable income. Falling inventory quantities also foil the tax advantages of LIFO by releasing old costs from LIFO inventory to cost of goods sold, which results in higher taxable income.

---

[2] Of course, the tax savings may be temporary. If inventory levels fall, then old LIFO layers become part of cost of goods sold and the tax savings are no longer effective. Tax savings will also end if a firm changes from LIFO to FIFO; however, a firm cannot change to another inventory costing method without permission of the Internal Revenue Service. Furthermore, the consistency of financial reporting discourages changes in inventory costing methods.

ESTIMATING PERIODIC SYSTEM COST OF GOODS SOLD AND ENDING INVENTORY

The first section of this chapter described four inventory costing methods, each based on a different assumption concerning the flow of costs (FIFO, LIFO, and weighted average) or the flow of goods (specific identification). In addition to the cost of beginning inventory and purchases, each of these methods requires information about the exact numbers of units in the ending inventory and the corresponding unit costs. Sometimes, though, the exact numbers of units in the ending inventory are unknown. Athough businesses are required to take a physical inventory at least once a year, financial statements are also prepared on an *interim* basis (monthly or quarterly). If a perpetual inventory system is used, the interim inventories can be easily determined. When a periodic system is used, however, it may be too expensive and time-consuming to take a physical inventory more than once a year. In such cases, the ending inventory cost required for monthly or quarterly financial statements must be estimated. Estimation methods must also be used whenever it is impossible to take a physical inventory, as when an inventory has been destroyed by fire.

One widely used estimating procedure is called the *gross margin method.* The **gross margin method** is a procedure for estimating cost of goods sold and ending inventory. To use this estimating method, you need to know three things: the firm's estimated gross margin rate, the net sales revenue, and the cost of goods available for sale.

A firm's **gross margin rate** is simply the ratio of gross margin to its net sales revenue; in other words, gross margin expressed as a percentage of net sales revenue (gross margin/net sales revenue). Past experience and the use of cost-based pricing formulas enable most firms to establish their gross margin rates quite accurately, even without taking a physical inventory and calculating the actual cost of goods sold and gross margin.

Once you know the estimated gross margin rate, you can multiply the rate by net sales revenue to estimate gross margin:

$$\text{Estimated gross margin} = (\text{Estimated gross margin rate})(\text{Net sales revenue})$$

Estimated gross margin may then be used to estimate cost of goods sold:

$$\text{Estimated cost of goods sold} = \text{Net sales revenue} - \text{Estimated gross margin}$$

The estimation of cost of goods sold can also be expressed in a single, simplified equation, which is derived algebraically as follows:

$$
\begin{aligned}
\text{Estimated cost of goods sold} &= \text{Net sales revenue} - \text{Estimated gross margin} \\
&= \text{Net sales revenue} - \left(\begin{array}{c}\text{Estimated gross} \\ \text{margin rate}\end{array}\right)\left(\begin{array}{c}\text{Net sales} \\ \text{revenue}\end{array}\right) \\
&= (\text{Net sales revenue})(1.0 - \text{Estimated gross margin rate})
\end{aligned}
$$

GROSS MARGIN METHOD: A procedure for estimating cost of goods sold and ending inventory on the basis of the estimated gross margin rate, net sales revenue, and cost of goods available for sale.

GROSS MARGIN RATE: The ratio of gross margin to net sales revenue.

Once you have determined the estimated cost of goods sold, you can then estimate the cost of the ending inventory by subtracting the estimated cost of goods sold from the cost of goods available for sale:

> Estimated
> ending = Cost of goods available for sale − Estimated cost of goods sold
> inventory

The following example demonstrates a three-step procedure for estimating ending inventory using the equations developed above. Wextram Company, a wholesaler of jewelry and watches, uses the periodic system of accounting for inventories. On March 31, when Wextram was preparing its quarterly financial statements, its accounting records indicated the following:

Beginning inventory	$ 63,100
Net purchases, 1/1 through 3/31	394,500
Net sales revenue, 1/1 through 3/31	640,000

Wextram's estimated gross margin rate is 40 percent. Cost of goods sold and ending inventory are estimated as follows:

Step 1: Estimate cost of goods sold

$$\frac{\text{Estimated cost}}{\text{of goods sold}} = (\text{Net sales revenue})(1.0 - \text{Estimated gross margin rate})$$

$$\$384,000 = (\$640,000)(1.0 - .40)$$

Step 2: Calculate cost of goods available for sale

$$\text{Cost of goods available for sale} = \text{Beginning inventory} + \text{Net purchases}$$

$$\$457,600 = \$63,100 + \$394,500$$

Step 3: Estimate ending inventory

> Estimated
> ending = Cost of goods available for sale − Estimated cost of goods sold
> inventory

$$\$73,600 = \$457,600 - \$384,000$$

Note that the accuracy of the estimates of cost of goods sold and ending inventory is affected by the accuracy of the estimate of the gross margin rate. If the gross margin rate is overestimated (that is, if actual gross margin turns out to be smaller than estimated), then the estimate of ending inventory will be too large; if the gross margin rate is underestimated, then the estimated ending inventory will be too small. Consider the following analysis.

ANALYSIS

USING ESTIMATES OF
COST OF GOODS
SOLD

Arson Smith, owner of a furniture store, notified his insurance company that his store burned on March 31, 19X6, destroying all his inventory and the structure as well. Arson provides the data shown below for the period from January 1 through March 31, 19X6:

Net sales revenue	$3,500,000
Smith's estimate of the gross margin rate	.40

Smith's estimate of cost of goods sold

($3,500,000)(1.0 − .40)	$2,100,000

Smith's estimate of inventory destroyed

Beginning inventory	$ 305,000
Net purchases	2,618,000
Cost of goods available for sale	$2,923,000
Less: Estimated cost of goods sold	2,100,000
Estimated ending inventory	$ 823,000

Upon investigation, the insurance examiner discovers the accounting data shown below for Arson's furniture store:

	19X3	19X4	19X5
Net sales revenue	$10,800,000	$11,100,000	$12,000,000
Cost of goods sold	7,560,000	7,992,000	9,000,000
Gross margin	$3,240,000	$3,108,000	$3,000,000
Gross margin rate	.30	.28	.25

Since Smith can provide no explanation or documentation to support his use of the 40 percent gross margin rate, it appears that he may have overestimated it. Applying the actual gross margin rate observed in 19X5 (.25) to the 19X6 data, the insurance examiner obtains revised results as follows:

Net sales revenue	$3,500,000

Reestimated cost of goods sold

($3,500,000)(1.0 − .25)	$2,625,000

Reestimate of inventory destroyed

Cost of goods available for sale	$2,923,000
Less: Reestimated cost of goods sold	2,625,000
Reestimated ending inventory	$ 298,000

The reestimation of ending inventory prompts an investigation of Arson Smith's fire and loss claim. Upon discussing the situation with the fire department, the claims examiner discovers that there is evidence that very little inventory was in the building when it burned. When confronted with the new estimate of ending inventory and statements by the fire department, Smith confesses that he had sold the inventory, had personally pocketed the cash proceeds, and had then burned his store, hoping to inflate the insurance settlement by overestimating the inventory lost in the fire. The key to discovering that this situation was not as originally described was the examiner's analysis of the historical accounting data for Smith's Furniture Store.

The principal weakness of the gross margin method is that the estimated gross margin rate is based on the relationship between gross margin and revenue (or, equivalently, between cost and revenue) in past periods—a relationship that might not hold for the current period. A second inventory estimation method, called the *retail method*, uses only current period data (data related to goods available for sale in the current period) as a basis for estimating the relationship between cost and revenue. The retail method is described and illustrated in Appendix 7–1.

DEPARTURES FROM COST FOR INVENTORY

The inventory accounting procedures described thus far have followed the cost concept—inventory is recorded in the firm's records at cost. We turn now to departures from the cost concept that are permitted by accounting principles. The first is called the *lower-of-cost-or-market principle,* which requires that inventory be reduced from cost to its market value whenever the market value falls below cost. The second departure is called *accounting for changing prices,* which provides for optional disclosures in footnotes to the financial statements describing the impact of inflation and specific price changes on inventories.

INVENTORIES AT THE LOWER OF COST OR MARKET

LOWER-OF-COST-OR-MARKET PRINCIPLE: The principle requiring that assets be reduced from their original cost to their current market value when the market value falls below cost.

The value of some items of inventory may decline before the items can be sold because the goods have become obsolete or shopworn or have otherwise diminished in value. The decrease in value is in turn reflected in a decline in the price for which these items can be sold (that is, in their market value). The **lower-of-cost-or-market principle** requires that the amount recorded for such assets be reduced from cost to market value. This reduction of the carrying amount of inventory, when market value is lower than cost, is considered a prudent reaction to the apparent uncertainty associated with the income that will be realized from the inventory.

To apply the lower-of-cost-or-market principle to inventory, it is first necessary to establish the market value.[3] Then market value is compared with historical cost (usually on an item-by-item basis), and the lower of market value or historical cost is used as the cost for the inventory. This process is illustrated in Exhibit 7–6. Note in Exhibit 7–6 that market value for item A is greater than historical cost, but historical cost is greater than market value for items B and C. Thus only items B and C are reduced to market; item A remains at historical cost.

[3] Market value of inventory items is established by using the following procedure:

1. Establish as a *ceiling price* the net realizable value (the estimated price at which goods can be sold minus all direct costs of selling, such as transportation or sales commissions).
2. Establish as a *floor price* the net realizable value less a normal markup (the amount normally added to cost when determining the selling price).
3. Compare *replacement cost* (the current cost of purchasing goods for resale) with the ceiling and floor amounts:
   a) If replacement cost is greater than the ceiling, market equals ceiling.
   b) If replacement cost is between ceiling and floor, market equals replacement cost.
   c) If floor is greater than replacement cost, market equals floor.

Note that market value is the middle of the three amounts: replacement cost, net realizable value (ceiling), and net realizable value minus a normal markup (floor).

EXHIBIT 7–6   **DETERMINATION OF LOWER OF COST OR MARKET**

ITEM	MARKET VALUE	HISTORICAL COST	LOWER OF COST OR MARKET
A	$100	$85	$85
B	55	65	55
C	15	20	15

The analysis that follows describes a situation requiring the application of the lower-of-cost-or-market principle.

ANALYSIS
OVERVALUATION OF
INVENTORY

High Tech Electronics is a personal computer manufacturer. High Tech's product line is a single personal computer, the HTC1. High Tech has been profitable, and sales of the HTC1 have grown steadily for the two years it has been manufactured. On December 9, High Tech announces that a more powerful personal computer, the HTC2, will replace the HTC1 in the firm's product line. The announcement indicates that the first units of the new computer will be available in four months. In the six months before the announcement of the HTC2, sales of the HTC1 have averaged 1,200 units per month at a price of $1,500 per unit. During December, High Tech continues to offer the HTC1 for sale at the $1,500 price. Between the announcement of the HTC2 and December 31, sales of the HTC1 are nearly zero as dealers and retail customers defer purchases until the new model becomes available. On December 31, High Tech's physical inventory indicates that there are 3,150 HTC1 computers in stock. High Tech's accounting records indicate that the cost of the 3,150 computers is $3,228,750, which is about 20 percent of High Tech's total assets.

1. *At what amount should the HTC1 computer inventory be reported in High Tech's December 31 balance sheet?*

The lack of sales of the HTC1 at $1,500 since the announcement of the HTC2 suggests that few of the 3,150 units can ever be sold at that price. Therefore, the lower-of-cost-or-market procedure appears to be appropriate for determining the carrying value of the HTC1 inventory. There are few guidelines for determining the market value of discontinued products in the personal computer industry. Similar experiences at other firms indicate that the selling price may have to be decreased to as little as $500 to ensure that the HTC1s can be sold.

2. *What would be the effect of a $500-per-unit market value on the carrying value of the HTC1 inventory?*

At a selling price of $500, the 3,150-unit inventory has a market value of $1,575,000. That amount is $1,653,750 less than cost.

3. *How should High Tech report a $1,653,750 write-down of its HTC1 inventory?*

Small reductions from cost to market are frequently added (debited) to cost of goods sold. However, because of the size of this write-down, it would be more appropriate to identify it as a loss and present it separately on the income statement after income from operations and before income before taxes. The journal entry would be:

Loss from decline in value of inventory.   1,653,750
    Inventory.   1,653,750

Presenting these losses as separate items helps statement users recognize that they have occurred and can aid users in comparing the firm's routine operating performance from period to period.

LOWER-OF-COST-OR-MARKET AND CONSERVATISM

CONSERVATISM: The convention that leads accountants to select among acceptable accounting methods and procedures the one that results in the lowest (the most conservative) net income and net assets in the current period.

The lower-of-cost-or-market principle is an example of the conservatism convention. The **conservatism** convention leads accountants to select among acceptable accounting methods or procedures the one that results in the lowest (the most conservative) net income and net assets in the current period. This convention leads accountants to recognize expenses and losses as early as possible and to recognize gains and revenues as late as possible, while still following generally accepted accounting principles. The purpose of the conservatism convention is to avoid overstating the earnings and financial strength of a business. Such overstatements usually have far more serious negative consequences for persons who rely on financial statements than do understatements. Of course, accelerating recognition of expenses or losses and delaying recognition of revenues or gains does not prevent their recognition. It merely moves them to another period. Consequently, to the extent that conservatism leads to understatements of net income and net assets in the current period, it also leads to equal overstatements of net income and net assets in one or more later periods.

ACCOUNTING FOR CHANGING PRICES

Lower-of-cost-or-market valuation of ending inventory is not the only alternative to historical cost. Although the Financial Accounting Standards Board does not require companies to disclose the current cost of their inventories, it permits them to do so in footnotes to the financial statements. The current cost of inventory is the amount that would be required to replace the inventory at the balance sheet date. During periods of modest inflation, the difference between the historical cost and current cost of most inventories is likely to be immaterial. Thus many companies in recent years have not made such disclosures. The current cost basis of accounting for inventories and other financial statement items is discussed in Supplementary Topic B.

THE EFFECT OF PERIODIC SYSTEM INVENTORY ERRORS ON THE FINANCIAL STATEMENTS

The cost of the ending inventory is based on a physical inventory of the goods on hand at the end of the accounting period. Recall that a physical inventory is the process in which all items in inventory on a given data are identified and counted. When inventories contain thousands of different items, a physical inventory represents a formidable and costly task. The cost of the ending inventory is calculated by multiplying the quantity of each item in inventory by the appropriate unit cost and then summing these products (quantity times cost) for all the units in inventory. Even with the use of electronic data processing equipment, it is easy to make errors in the determination of the cost of ending inventory as a result of incorrect counts, mistakes in costing, or errors in identifying items. Because of the way ending inventory is used in the computation of cost of goods sold, inventory errors self-correct in two periods. However, the income statement for each of these two periods is incorrect and the balance sheet at the end of the first period is also incorrect.

The financial statements presented in Exhibit 7–7 illustrate the self-correcting character of an inventory error. (Income taxes have been omitted to simplify the illustration.) The "Correct" column shows the financial statements for 19X1 and 19X2 as they would appear if no error were made. The "Erroneous"

EXHIBIT 7–7 FINANCIAL STATEMENTS SHOWING
SELF-CORRECTING INVENTORY ERROR

		CORRECT	ERRONEOUS	ERROR*
19X1 FINANCIAL STATEMENTS	**INCOME STATEMENT**			
	Sales revenue...................	$500	$500	
	Cost of goods sold			
	Beginning inventory	$ 50	$ 50	
	Purchases....................	250	250	
	Cost of goods available for sale ..	$300	$300	
	Less: Ending inventory	60	45	−$15
	Cost of goods sold	240	255	+$15
	Gross margin...................	$260	$245	−$15
	Less: Operating expenses	200	200	
	Net income	$ 60	$ 45	−$15
	BALANCE SHEET			
	Inventory.....................	$ 60	$ 45	−$15
	Other assets...................	240	240	
	Total assets	$300	$285	−$15
	Liabilities.....................	$100	$100	
	Capital stock	100	100	
	Retained earnings...............	100	85	−$15
	Total liabilities and equity	$300	$285	−$15
19X2 FINANCIAL STATEMENTS	**INCOME STATEMENT**			
	Sales revenue...................	$600	$600	
	Cost of goods sold			
	Beginning inventory	$ 60	$ 45	−$15
	Purchases....................	290	290	
	Cost of goods available for sale ..	$350	$335	−$15
	Less: Ending inventory	50	50	
	Cost of goods sold	300	285	−$15
	Gross margin...................	$300	$315	+$15
	Less: Operating expenses	220	220	
	Net income	$ 80	$ 95	+$15
	BALANCE SHEET			
	Inventory.....................	$ 50	$ 50	
	Other assets...................	335	335	
	Total assets	$385	$385	
	Liabilities.....................	$105	$105	
	Capital stock	100	100	
	Retained earnings...............	180	180	
	Total liabilities and equity	$385	$385	

* A minus sign (−) indicates an *understatement* and a plus sign (+) indicates an *overstatement*.

column shows the financial statements for the two years as they would appear if the firm understates its inventory at December 31, 19X1, as a result of miscounting or in some other way undervaluing its inventory by $15. The "Error" column describes the effect of the error on each line of the statements. Note that the understatement of the 19X1 ending inventory causes an understatement of 19X1 net income and an overstatement of 19X2 net income, with the result that retained earnings at the end of 19X2 is correctly stated.

Even though an inventory error is self-correcting over two periods, it is still necessary to correct the error in order to produce properly stated financial statements for those periods. As we indicated in Chapter 5, the time at which an error is found and the error itself jointly determine how the error is corrected. If an inventory error is found before the closing entries are made for the first period, a correction made to cost of goods sold and ending inventory corrects the error. If the error from the first period is not detected until the second period, then correction requires that beginning inventory and retained earnings for the second period be changed and that the financial statements for the first period be restated. If the error is found after the end of the second period, then no entry is required because the inventory error will have self-corrected in two periods; however, the financial statements for both the error period and the subsequent year must be restated.

One procedure used by accountants to detect inventory errors is to prepare an estimate of the amount of ending inventory. When the estimate is compared with the amount determined by the physical inventory, a discrepancy between the two amounts may signal the existence of an error. The gross margin method, described earlier in this chapter, is often used to estimate ending inventory.

Before turning to the appendixes on the retail inventory method and perpetual inventory systems, it will be helpful to review the material on inventory costing and cost of goods sold. The problem in the next section reviews and integrates the determination of ending inventory and cost of goods sold, the systems of inventory accounting, and the four inventory costing methods. Most students find that a firm grasp of these important accounting procedures requires repeated exposure.

REVIEW PROBLEM:
INVENTORY COSTING METHODS

The manager of the Sagamore Shop, a retail clothing store, is preparing an accounting of the store's inventory. She has the following data:

a) Inventory at December 31, 19X5: 1,000 units at a cost of $15,410.

b) Purchases during 19X6:

	UNITS	COST PER UNIT	AMOUNT
Purchase 1	5,100	$16.00	$ 81,600
Purchase 2	3,700	17.00	62,900
Purchase 3	6,400	17.00	108,800
Purchase 4	5,600	18.00	100,800

c) Inventory at December 31, 19X6: 2,200 units.

REQUIRED:

1. Sagamore used the weighted average accounting method before 19X6. Using the FIFO, LIFO, and weighted average methods, determine the amount of ending inventory and cost of goods sold for 19X6.

2. Determine which inventory method Sagamore should use to minimize cash outflows for taxes for 19X6.

3. If the effective income tax rate is 30 percent (.30), determine how much cash would be saved in 19X6 by using the accounting method found to be best in requirement 2, compared with each of the other methods.

SOLUTION:

1. Using the FIFO, LIFO, and weighted average methods, the cost of ending inventory and cost of goods sold are computed as follows:

	UNITS	COST PER UNIT	TOTAL COST	
Beginning inventory	1,000	$15.41		$ 15,410
Purchase 1	5,100	16.00	$ 81,600	
Purchase 2	3,700	17.00	62,900	
Purchase 3	6,400	17.00	108,800	
Purchase 4	5,600	18.00	100,800	
Total purchases	20,800			354,100
Goods available for sale	21,800			$369,510

FIFO—COST OF ENDING INVENTORY AND COST OF GOODS SOLD

With the FIFO method, the cost of the newest 2,200 units is placed in ending inventory, and the cost of the oldest 19,600 units is allocated to cost of goods sold.

FIFO cost of goods sold calculation

Beginning inventory	$ 15,410
Add: Purchases..	354,100
Cost of goods available for sale	$369,510
Less: FIFO ending inventory (2,200 units at $18 each)	39,600
FIFO cost of goods sold (19,600 units)	$329,910

LIFO—COST OF ENDING INVENTORY AND COST OF GOODS SOLD

With the LIFO method, the cost of the oldest 2,200 units is placed in ending inventory, and the cost of the newest 19,600 units is allocated to cost of goods sold.

LIFO cost of goods sold calculation

Beginning inventory	$ 15,410
Add: Purchases..	354,100
Cost of goods available for sale	$369,510
Less: LIFO ending inventory (1,000 units at $15.41 each + 1,200 units at $16.00 each)	34,610
LIFO cost of goods sold (19,600 units)	$334,900

WEIGHTED AVERAGE—COST OF ENDING INVENTORY AND COST OF GOODS SOLD

With the weighted average method, the weighted average cost per unit of goods available for sale is allocated to both ending inventory and cost of goods sold.

Weighted average cost of goods sold calculation

Beginning inventory	$ 15,410
Add: Purchases.	354,100
Cost of goods available for sale	$369,510
Less: Weighted average ending inventory (2,200 units at $16.95 each*)	37,290
Weighted average cost of goods sold (19,600 units)	$332,220

* Weighted average cost per unit = $369,510/21,800 units = $16.95.

2. The inventory method that will minimize taxes is the one that produces the largest cost of goods sold:

	FIFO	LIFO	WEIGHTED AVERAGE
Cost of goods sold	$329,910	$334,900	$332,220

Thus LIFO should be selected.

3. Tax savings for the year 19X6 would be the income tax rate multiplied by the difference in the amounts for cost of goods sold:

	LIFO VS. FIFO	LIFO VS. WEIGHTED AVERAGE
LIFO cost of goods sold	$334,900	$334,900
FIFO cost of goods sold	329,910	—
Weighted average cost of goods sold	—	332,220
Cost of goods sold difference	$ 4,990	$ 2,680
Income tax rate	×.30	×.30
Income tax savings from LIFO	$ 1,497	$ 804

If FIFO is compared with the weighted average method, weighted average provides the larger cost of goods sold and the lower income taxes:

Income tax savings = ($332,220 − $329,910)(.30) = $693

SUMMARY

In all inventory accounting systems, the cost of goods available for sale must be allocated between goods sold and goods still in inventory. This allocation is generally accomplished by determining a cost for ending inventory and subtracting that cost from the cost of goods available for sale. Four inventory costing methods can be used to determine the cost of ending inventory: FIFO, LIFO, weighted average, and specific identification. The FIFO costing method assumes that the earliest purchases (the first in) are the first sold (the first out), whereas the LIFO method assumes that the most recent purchases (the last in) are the first to be sold (the first out). The weighted average method allocates the cost of goods available for sale on the basis of a single, weighted average cost per unit. The specific identification method, the most exacting method, allocates the cost of goods available for sale based on an identification of the precise units sold and in inventory.

Ending inventory cost can be estimated by the gross margin method. This method uses an estimate of the firm's gross margin rate and actual data for net sales revenue and the cost of goods available for sale to develop an estimate of the cost of ending inventory. Estimates of ending inventory are employed when a physical inventory would be too costly or impossible.

Although the cost concept requires that inventories be recorded at cost, it is occasionally necessary to follow the lower-of-cost-or-market principle and state the cost of ending inventory at market value. In addition, for some purposes, ending inventory cost is determined based on current costs to replace the inventory.

If an error is made in the determination of the cost of ending inventory, the current period's income will be overstated or understated because of the effect of the error on the determination of cost of goods sold. In addition, the income for the next period will be incorrect by exactly the same amount but in the opposite direction because the error in the ending inventory of one period becomes an error in beginning inventory of the subsequent period.

In Appendix 7–1, we examine the retail method of inventory costing that is used by many wholesale and retail businesses to estimate ending inventory and cost of goods sold. The detailed accounting procedures for perpetual inventory systems are discussed and illustrated in Appendix 7–2.

APPENDIX 7–1
THE RETAIL METHOD

When financial statements are prepared without a physical inventory, it is necessary to estimate the amount of the ending inventory. Like the gross margin method described earlier in this chapter, the retail method is an inventory estimation method. It receives its name from its widespread use by retailers, for whom neither perpetual inventory systems nor frequent physical inventories are feasible. Knowledge of interim inventories is extremely important to the management of retail businesses. Furthermore, retailers are usually more interested in the sales value (or retail price) of their inventories than in their cost; consequently, sales value rather than cost is the usual basis for inventory estimation. In fact, a physical inventory in a retail business is usually stated in terms of retail prices; that is, the inventory is taken by summing the retail prices marked on all items in stock. For purposes of financial reporting, this sales value information—whether estimated using the retail method or based on a physical inventory in terms of retail prices—must be converted into cost information.

EXHIBIT 7–8   **THE RETAIL METHOD**

	AT COST	AT RETAIL	COST RATIO
Beginning inventory	$ 23,000	$ 48,000	
Purchases	217,000	452,000	
Goods available for sale	$240,000	$500,000	.48*
Less: Net sales revenue (at retail)		460,000	
Estimated ending inventory (at retail)		$ 40,000	
Estimated ending inventory (at cost) [($40,000)(.48)]	$ 19,200		
Estimated cost of goods sold ($240,000 − $19,200)	$220,800		

* Cost ratio = $240,000/$500,000 = .48

RETAIL METHOD: A procedure for estimating cost of goods sold and ending inventory by using the sales value (retail price) of the ending inventory and the ratio of cost to retail for the goods available for sale during the current period.

The **retail method** estimates cost of goods sold and cost of ending inventory by using the sales value (retail price) of the ending inventory and the ratio of cost to retail for the goods available for sale during the current period. Calculations illustrating the retail method are presented in Exhibit 7–8. First, beginning inventory is added to purchases to find the goods available for sale, both at cost and at retail (sales value). Next, the cost ratio is computed—goods available for sale at cost is divided by goods available for sale at retail. Then net sales revenue is subtracted from cost of goods available for sale (at retail) to find the estimated ending inventory (at retail). Finally, estimated ending inventory at retail is multiplied by the cost ratio to find estimated ending inventory at cost, which is then used to compute estimated cost of goods sold.

In order for the retail method to produce accurate estimates of ending inventory and cost of goods sold, the mix of goods in the beginning inventory, purchases, and sales must be similar. It is not necessary that all goods be marked up by the same percentage, but the markup percentage should remain constant for the same goods throughout goods available for sale. When different markup percentages are applied to different categories of goods, the accuracy of the estimated inventory cost can be enhanced by applying the retail method separately to each category of goods.

APPENDIX 7–2
THE PERPETUAL SYSTEM FOR INVENTORY ACCOUNTING

Although the preceding two chapters discuss and illustrate the important elements of inventory and cost of goods sold in the context of the periodic inventory system, the perpetual inventory system is an important alternative. When a perpetual inventory accounting system is used, the accounting records provide the data to add to inventory for each purchase and to add to cost of goods sold while simultaneously reducing inventory for each sale. The additions to inventory for purchases should include transportation costs on a purchase-by-purchase basis. For example, Buchman Products purchased 100 units of merchandise at a list price of $4.90 per unit. The supplier billed Buchman an additional $75 to ship the merchandise. If Buchman uses a perpetual inventory system, the following entry would be made for this purchase:

Inventory..	565	
Accounts payable...................................		565

Returns of purchased merchandise are recorded as reductions in the inventory account based on the cost of the specific items returned. For example, assume that Buchman returned 4 of the 100 units of merchandise it purchased. Buchman would make the following entry to record this return:

Accounts payable....................................	19.60	
Inventory...		19.60

When the purchase cost of merchandise is not stable, the amount recorded at the time of the sale to reflect the addition to cost of goods sold depends upon an assumption about the way in which costs flow through the accounts—FIFO, LIFO, or weighted average. And for the perpetual system, this cost flow must be assumed for *each* sale and *each* purchase rather than only at the period's end (as the periodic system assumes).

The perpetual system requires that data about the components of inventory be maintained continuously. For every item of inventory, a perpetual inventory data record must be maintained either in an electronic data processing device or by hand. It is from the data in this record that the cost of goods sold addition and inventory reduction for each sale are determined. All the sale-by-sale data are then summed to determine cost of goods sold for the period. The cost of ending inventory is the ending amount for inventory in the perpetual inventory data record.

Let us now illustrate the use of the perpetual inventory accounting system for each of the three applicable cost flow methods: FIFO, LIFO, and weighted average. We will employ the same basic data for each method.

FIFO INVENTORY COSTING USING PERPETUAL PROCEDURES

In a perpetual inventory system, the FIFO costing method requires that the cost of the oldest units on hand be transferred from inventory to cost of goods sold each time a sale is made. The cost of the newer units is retained in inventory. To understand the use of a perpetual system, it helps to think of inventory as if it were a stack of separate layers, segregated by purchase price. Each time a purchase is made at a unit cost different from that of the previous purchase, a new layer of inventory cost is added to the top of the stack. Under FIFO inventory costing, each time a sale is made, the cost of the oldest units is removed from the *bottom* of the inventory stack (the first in) and transferred to cost of goods sold. For exam-

EXHIBIT 7–9   FIFO PERPETUAL INVENTORY DATA RECORD

DATE	PURCHASES			COST OF GOODS SOLD			INVENTORY		
	UNITS	COST PER UNIT	TOTAL COST	UNITS	COST PER UNIT	COST OF GOODS SOLD	UNITS	COST PER UNIT	TOTAL COST
Beginning inventory							50	10.00	500
3/5				30	10.00	300	20	10.00	200
6/14	100	12.40	1,240				100	12.40	
							20	10.00	1,440
7/8				20	10.00				
				40	12.40	696	60	12.40	744
8/21				40	12.40	496	20	12.40	248
10/9	80	16.00	1,280				80	16.00	
							20	12.40	1,528
12/28				20	12.40				
				50	16.00	1,048	30	16.00	480
Purchases			2,520						
Cost of goods sold						2,540			
Ending inventory									480

ple, consider the inventory record shown in Exhibit 7–9. On June 14, 20 units at $10.00 remain from beginning inventory. Another 100 units are purchased at a cost of $12.40 each, adding a new cost layer on top of the cost of the 20 units remaining from beginning inventory:

100 units at $12.40 each

20 units at $10.00 each

On July 8, 60 units are sold. The cost of the older layer (20 units at $10.00 each) and a portion of the newer layer (40 units at $12.40 each) are removed from the bottom of the stack and transferred to cost of goods sold. Remaining in inventory is a single layer of 60 units at $12.40 each:

60 units at $12.40 each

EXHIBIT 7–10   LIFO PERPETUAL INVENTORY DATA RECORD

DATE	PURCHASES			COST OF GOODS SOLD			INVENTORY		
	UNITS	COST PER UNIT	TOTAL COST	UNITS	COST PER UNIT	COST OF GOODS SOLD	UNITS	COST PER UNIT	TOTAL COST
Beginning inventory							50	10.00	500
3/5				30	10.00	300	20	10.00	200
6/14	100	12.40	1,240				100	12.40	
							20	10.00	1,440
7/8				60	12.40	744	40	12.40	
							20	10.00	696
8/21				40	12.40	496	20	10.00	200
10/9	80	16.00	1,280				80	16.00	
							20	10.00	1,480
12/28				70	16.00	1,120	10	16.00	
							20	10.00	360
Purchases			2,520						
Cost of goods sold						2,660			
Ending inventory									360

FIFO perpetual and FIFO periodic procedures will always produce the same amounts for cost of goods sold because the cost of ending inventory must contain the same units at the same cost. Adjustments to the FIFO perpetual amount may, however, be necessary to bring the ending inventory to the lower of cost or market, or to reflect any difference between the perpetual inventory record and a physical inventory.

LIFO INVENTORY COSTING USING PERPETUAL PROCEDURES

In a perpetual system, the LIFO costing method requires that the cost of the newest units on hand be transferred from inventory to cost of goods sold each time a sale is made. The cost of the older units remains in inventory. LIFO perpetual accounting also requires that cost layers be established in the inventory data record for each purchase, so LIFO perpetual accounting can also be thought of as a stack of cost layers. Each purchase adds a new cost layer at the top of the stack; since each sale removes the newest units, it removes layers from the *top* of the stack (the last in). For example, consider the inventory record in Exhibit 7–10. On October 9, 80 units of inventory are purchased at a cost of $16.00 per unit, adding a new cost layer above the previous cost layer of 20 units at $10.00 each:

80 units at $16.00 each

20 units at $10.00 each

On December 28, 70 units are sold. The cost of goods sold for the 70-unit sale is taken entirely from the cost of the purchase on October 9, the newest units on hand, leaving two layers of cost in inventory, one of 10 units at $16.00 each and a second, older layer of 20 units at $10.00 each.

10 units at $16.00 each
20 units at $10.00 each

It is highly unlikely that periodic and perpetual LIFO methods will both produce the same amounts for cost of goods sold and ending inventory. The perpetual procedures will allocate some of the older inventory costs to cost of goods sold when inventories are low during the period. The periodic procedure, unless inventories are low at the end of the period, will retain the older inventory costs in the inventory account. To illustrate, had the periodic system been used in Exhibit 7–10, ending inventory would have been one layer of 30 units at $10.00 each ($300), all from beginning inventory.

WEIGHTED AVERAGE INVENTORY COSTING USING PERPETUAL PROCEDURES

The perpetual weighted average method differs from the FIFO and LIFO methods in that it does not produce an additional layer of cost at the time of each purchase. Instead, each time there is a purchase, the costs of all units available are summed and divided by the number of units available to produce a weighted average cost per unit (a "moving" weighted average) that is used to cost inventory and the additions to cost of goods sold until the next purchase is made. For example, in the inventory record in Exhibit 7–11, the purchase on June 14 at $12.40 per unit requires that a new weighted average cost per unit be computed. The $12.00-per-unit average cost is then used until October 9, when 80 units are purchased at $16.00 each. Had the weighted average periodic method been used, the cost of goods sold and the cost of ending inventory would have been different from the amounts for these two items developed by the weighted average perpetual system, as is shown in Exhibit 7–12.

If we use the periodic weighted average data from Exhibit 7–11, the cost of ending inventory would be $393.90 [($13.13)(30)] and the cost of goods sold would be $2,626.10 [$3,020.00 − $393.90]. As we indicated, the periodic method amounts are significantly different from the amounts that were developed for the weighted average perpetual method in Exhibit 7–10 ($393.90 versus $456.00 and $2,626.10 versus $2,564.00).

A COMPARISON OF PERPETUAL AND PERIODIC INVENTORY PROCEDURES

Having discussed perpetual inventory accounting in detail, let us summarize the differences between periodic and perpetual procedures. Perpetual methods involve allocations of the cost of purchased goods to cost of goods sold each time a sale is made. Periodic methods allocate cost of purchases to cost of goods sold only at the end of the period. Because of the difference in the timing of the cost allocations, different amounts for cost of goods sold and for the cost of ending inventory nearly always result for the LIFO and weighted average methods. FIFO amounts, however, are always the same for both periodic and perpetual systems. In periods of rising prices, periodic LIFO will always produce a cost of goods sold

EXHIBIT 7–11   WEIGHTED AVERAGE PERPETUAL INVENTORY DATA RECORD

DATE	PURCHASES UNITS	COST PER UNIT	TOTAL COST	COST OF GOODS SOLD UNITS	COST PER UNIT	COST OF GOODS SOLD	INVENTORY UNITS	COST PER UNIT	TOTAL COST
Beginning inventory							50	10.00	500
3/5				30	10.00	300	20	10.00	200
6/14	100	12.40	1,240				120	12.00*	1,440
7/8				60	12.00	720	60	12.00	720
8/21				40	12.00	480	20	12.00	240
10/9	80	16.00	1,280				100	15.20†	1,520
12/28				70	15.20	1,064	30	15.20	456
Purchases			2,520						
Cost of goods sold						2,564			
Ending inventory									456

* Weighted average cost per unit = ($200 + $1,240)/120 = $12.00.
† Weighted average cost per unit = ($240 + $1,280)/100 = $15.20.

EXHIBIT 7–12   PERIODIC WEIGHTED AVERAGE DATA

	UNITS	COST	COST PER UNIT
Beginning inventory	50	$ 500	$10.00
Purchase 1	100	1,240	12.40
Purchase 2	80	1,280	16.00
Goods available for sale	230	$3,020	$13.13*

* Periodic weighted average cost per unit = ($3,020/230) = $13.13 (rounded to nearest $.01).

amount that is at least as large as, and usually larger than, the perpetual amount. Again, the difference results from the timing of the cost allocations.

Perpetual systems are obviously more expensive to operate than periodic systems because they necessitate entering and maintaining more data. In particular, there are substantial additional costs in operating a perpetual system for an entity with thousands of different items in inventory. Furthermore, under a perpetual LIFO system, increasing inventories regularly produce additional cost layers, which must be carried forward on each perpetual inventory data record. The benefits of using a perpetual system would be reflected in either increased revenues or decreased expenses. If these advantages exceed the cost of operation, then a perpetual method should be employed.

KEY TERMS

CONSERVATISM (p. 288)

CONSISTENCY (p. 279)

FIRST-IN, FIRST-OUT (FIFO) METHOD (p. 276)

GROSS MARGIN METHOD (p. 283)

GROSS MARGIN RATE (p. 283)

INVENTORY COSTING METHODS (p. 275)

LAST-IN, FIRST-OUT (LIFO) METHOD (p. 277)

LOWER-OF-COST-OR-MARKET
PRINCIPLE (p. 286)

RETAIL METHOD (p. 294)

SPECIFIC IDENTIFICATION METHOD (p. 278)

WEIGHTED AVERAGE METHOD (p. 278)

QUESTIONS

Q7-1. Why do the four inventory costing methods produce different amounts for the cost of ending inventory and cost of goods sold when prices are changing?

Q7-2. The costs of which units of inventory are allocated to ending inventory and cost of goods sold using the FIFO, LIFO, weighted average, and specific identification inventory costing methods?

Q7-3. If prices are rising, which inventory costing method should produce the smallest cash outflow for taxes? Why?

Q7-4. How would reported income differ if LIFO rather than FIFO were used when prices are rising? When falling?

Q7-5. How would the balance sheet accounts be affected if LIFO rather than FIFO were used when prices are rising? When falling?

Q7-6. Which data are required to estimate ending inventory using the gross margin method? Which of these data are usually estimates themselves?

Q7-7. When using the gross margin method, what is the effect on estimates of ending inventory if the cost of goods sold percentage is overestimated? What is the effect of underestimating this percentage?

Q7-8. Which data might an accountant use to check the reasonableness of an estimate of the cost of goods sold percentage?

Q7-9. In general, how do inventory costing methods differ from inventory estimation methods? How are they the same?

Q7-10. Why are inventories written down to the lower of cost or market?

Q7-11. How are the floor and ceiling determined as a part of the lower-of-cost-or-market procedure? (See footnote 3 on page 286 in this chapter.)

Q7-12. Explain how profit is moved from the current period to a future period when inventories are written down to the floor using the lower-of-cost-or-market procedure.

Q7-13. What is the effect on the income statement and the balance sheet when inventory is written down to market using the lower-of-cost-or-market procedure?

Q7-14. Why does an error in the determination of ending inventory affect the financial statements of two periods?

APPENDIX 7–1 QUESTIONS

Q7-15. Why do many retailers use the retail method for estimating inventories?

Q7-16. How does the retail method differ from the gross margin method?

APPENDIX 7–2 QUESTIONS

Q7-17. "For each inventory costing method, perpetual and periodic systems yield the same amounts for ending inventory and cost of goods sold." Do you agree or disagree with this statement? Explain.

Q7-18. Why are perpetual inventory systems more expensive to operate than periodic inventory systems? What conditions justify the additional cost of a perpetual inventory system?

EXERCISES

E7-19. FINANCIAL STATEMENT EFFECTS OF FIFO AND LIFO The chart below identifies which costs (older or newer) are in ending inventory and cost of goods sold for FIFO and LIFO:

FINANCIAL STATEMENT ITEM	FIFO	LIFO
Ending inventory	Newer	Older
Cost of goods sold	Older	Newer

When prices are rising, older costs will be lower and newer costs will be higher.

REQUIRED:

Beginning with the relationships identified in the table above, complete the table below by indicating whether the specified financial statement item is higher or lower with FIFO or LIFO. The ending inventory and cost of goods sold rows have been completed for you.

FINANCIAL STATEMENT ITEM	FIFO	LIFO
Ending inventory	Higher	Lower
Cost of goods sold	Lower	Higher
Gross margin		
Income before taxes		
Payments for income taxes		
Net income		

E7-20. INVENTORY COSTING METHODS Jackson Company had 200 units in beginning inventory at a cost of $24 each. Jackson's 19X6 purchases were:

DATE	PURCHASES
2/21	6,200 units at $28 each
7/15	5,500 units at $32 each
9/30	8,100 units at $34 each

Jackson uses a periodic system and sold 19,600 units at $45 each during 19X6.

REQUIRED:

Prepare income statements through gross margin using the FIFO, LIFO, weighted average, and specific identification methods. For the specific identification method, assume the ending inventory is 20 percent beginning inventory, 60 percent from the 2/21 purchase, and 20 percent for the 9/30 purchase.

E7-21. INVENTORY COSTING METHODS The inventory accounting records for Lee Enterprises contained the following data:

Beginning inventory	400 units at $12 each
Purchase 1, 2/26	2,300 units at $14 each
Sale, 3/9 ($27 each)	2,500 units
Purchase 2, 6/14	2,200 units at $15 each
Sale, 9/22 ($29 each)	2,100 units

Assume that Lee uses a periodic inventory accounting system.

REQUIRED:

Prepare income statements through gross margin using the FIFO, LIFO, weighted average, and specific identification methods. For the specific identification method, assume that the ending inventory is composed of 100 units from beginning inventory, 100 units from purchase 1, and 100 units from purchase 2.

E7-22. INVENTORY COSTING METHODS   Harrington Company had the following data for inventory during a recent year:

	UNITS	COST PER UNIT	TOTAL COST
Beginning inventory	500	$ 9.00	$ 4,500
Purchase 1, 1/28	1,600	9.60	$15,360
Purchase 2, 5/2	1,200	10.30	12,360
Purchase 3, 8/13	1,400	10.80	15,120
Purchase 4, 11/9	1,100	11.10	12,210
Total purchases	5,300		55,050
Goods available for sale	5,800		$59,550
Less: Sales	5,240		
Ending inventory	560		

Assume that Harrington uses a periodic inventory accounting system.

REQUIRED:

Using the FIFO, LIFO, and weighted average methods, compute the ending inventory and cost of goods sold.

E7-23. INVENTORY COSTING METHODS   Handel Pyrotechnics buys and resells fireworks. During 19X8 Handel purchased item 16A4 three times. The first purchase was 23,300 units at $7.25 per unit. The second purchase was 28,500 units at $8.15 per unit. The third purchase was 26,300 units at $8.40 per unit. Beginning inventory was 1,900 units at $7.20 each, and 19X8 sales were 75,600 units at $14.50 each. Handel uses the periodic method.

REQUIRED:

Using the FIFO, LIFO, and weighted average inventory costing methods, compute the cost of ending inventory, cost of goods sold, and gross margin.

E7-24. INVENTORY COSTING METHODS: COMPUTATIONS AND COMPARISONS   Neyman, Inc., has the following data for purchases:

DATE	UNITS	COST PER UNIT
2/24	110	$37
7/2	170	33
10/31	90	27

Beginning inventory was 22 units at $38, and ending inventory is 10 units. Assume that Neyman uses a periodic inventory accounting system.

REQUIRED:

1. Compute the cost of goods available for sale, cost of ending inventory, and cost of goods sold, using the FIFO, LIFO, and weighted average methods.
2. Why is the cost of goods sold lower with LIFO than with FIFO?

E7-25. SPECIFIC IDENTIFICATION   Relocation Services Company purchases homes from homeowners being relocated by corporate employers and then resells those homes. During 19X4 Relocation Service Company purchased the following 10 homes:

PURCHASE	PRICE	PURCHASE	PRICE	PURCHASE	PRICE
X4-1	$66,900	X4-5	$109,300	X4-8	$86,100
X4-2	97,300	X4-6	91,400	X4-9	99,200
X4-3	82,700	X4-7	58,500	X4-10	67,600
X4-4	78,800				

At the end of the year, Relocation Services Company's inventory contains purchases X4-1, X4-6, and X4-9.

REQUIRED:

Using the specific identification method, compute cost of ending inventory and cost of goods sold.

E7-26. EFFECTS OF FIFO AND LIFO   Roberts Sales began operations on January 1, 19X1. Purchases and sales of its single product during its first three years of operations were as follows:

	PURCHASES	SALES
19X1	4,000 units at $7	3,000 units
19X2	5,000 units at $9	5,000 units
19X3	6,000 units at $11	6,000 units

REQUIRED:

1. Prepare a schedule showing the amount of ending inventory and cost of goods sold for each of the three years, using FIFO and LIFO and assuming that Roberts uses a periodic inventory accounting system.
2. On the basis of your schedule, what can you conclude about the effects of FIFO and LIFO on the cost of ending inventory and the amount of net income?

E7-27. EFFECTS OF FIFO AND LIFO WITH INVENTORY REDUCTIONS   Sheepskin Company sells to colleges and universities a special paper that is used for diplomas. Sheepskin typically makes one purchase of the special paper each year. You have the following data for the three years ending in 19X5:

19X3

Beginning inventory......................	0 pages
Purchases...............................	10,000 pages at $1.60 per page
Sales...................................	8,500 pages

19X4

Beginning inventory......................	1,500 pages
Purchases...............................	16,200 pages at $2.00 per page
Sales...................................	15,000 pages

19X5

Beginning inventory......................	2,700 pages
Purchases...............................	18,000 pages at $2.50 per page
Sales...................................	20,100 pages

REQUIRED:

1. What would be ending inventory and cost of goods sold for each year if FIFO is used?
2. What would be ending inventory and cost of goods sold for each year if LIFO is used?
3. Explain the cause of the differences in cost of goods sold for each year between FIFO and LIFO.

E7-28. EFFECTS OF INVENTORY COSTING METHODS ON INCOME TAX PAYMENTS   Jefferson Enterprises has the following income statement data available for 19X9:

Sales revenue.	$737,200
Operating expenses	243,700
Interest expense.	39,500
Income tax rate	.34

Jefferson uses a periodic inventory accounting system and is considering continuing with the weighted average method or adopting FIFO or LIFO for inventory costing. Jefferson's accountant prepared the following data:

	IF WEIGHTED AVERAGE USED	IF FIFO USED	IF LIFO USED
Ending inventory	$ 56,400	$ 73,200	$ 41,700
Cost of goods sold	401,600	384,800	416,300

REQUIRED:

1. Compute income before taxes, income taxes expense, and net income for each of the three inventory costing methods.

2. Why are the cost of goods sold and ending inventory amounts different for each of the three methods?

E7-29. EFFECTS OF INVENTORY COSTING METHODS ON CASH OUTFLOWS FOR INCOME TAXES   Kennebeck Stores has the following inventory data:

ITEM	UNITS	COST PER UNIT	TOTAL COST
Beginning inventory	50	$ 7.40	$ 370
Purchase 1, 2/16	220	9.00	1,980
Purchase 2, 8/27	180	12.00	2,160
Purchase 3, 11/14	210	13.00	2,730
Goods available for sale	660		$7,240
Ending inventory	60		

Kennebeck has sales of $21,200, operating expenses of $11,800, and an income tax rate of 25 percent (.25). Kennebeck uses a periodic inventory accounting system.

REQUIRED:

1. Compute ending inventory and cost of goods sold using the FIFO, LIFO, and weighted average methods of inventory accounting.

2. By how much will cash outflows for income taxes differ among the three inventory methods?

E7-30. ESTIMATING ENDING INVENTORY   Annapolis Company is preparing its financial statements for the first quarter of the year. Rather than taking a physical inventory, Annapolis will estimate ending inventory. As of March 31, the following data are available:

Beginning inventory	$ 45,000
Sales revenue.	425,000
Sales returns	12,000
Purchases	257,000
Purchase returns	4,000
Transportation-in	2,000
Estimated gross margin rate.	.38

Assume that Annapolis uses a periodic inventory accounting system.

REQUIRED:

Estimate cost of goods sold and ending inventory.

E7-31. ESTIMATED ENDING INVENTORY   The owner of Charleston Furniture Gallery wants to estimate the cost of the firm's inventory that was lost when the store was completely destroyed by a hurricane in September 19X0. Since the firm's accounting records were maintained in duplicate on a computer tape stored in an undamaged bank vault, the following data are available:

Normal gross margin rate....................................	60 percent
19X0 sales	$2,456,800
Inventory, 1/1/X0...	103,200
19X0 purchases	1,005,300

REQUIRED:

Compute the cost of the inventory lost in the hurricane.

E7-32. LOWER OF COST OR MARKET   Meredith's Appliance Store has the following data for the items in its inventory at the end of the accounting period:

ITEM	NUMBER OF UNITS	HISTORICAL COST PER UNIT	MARKET VALUE PER UNIT
Window air conditioner	15	$194	$110
Dishwasher	34	240	380
Refrigerator	27	382	605
Microwave	19	215	180
Washer (clothing)	36	195	290
Dryer (clothing)	21	168	245

REQUIRED:

Compute the carrying amount of Meredith's ending inventory using the lower-of-cost-or-market procedure on an item-by-item basis.

E7-33. LOWER OF COST OR MARKET   Shaw Systems sells a limited line of specially made products, using television advertising campaigns in large cities. At year-end Shaw has the following data for its inventory:

ITEM	UNITS	HISTORICAL COST PER UNIT	MARKET VALUE PER UNIT
Phone	600	$ 24	$ 20
Stereo	180	177	190
Shaver	220	30	35
Defroster	430	26	25
Calculator	570	40	19

REQUIRED:

Compute the carrying value of the ending inventory, using the lower-of-cost-or-market procedure on an item-by-item basis.

E7-34. EFFECTS OF AN ERROR IN ENDING INVENTORY   Waymire Company prepared the partial income statements presented below for 19X8 and 19X7.

	19X8		19X7	
Sales revenue		$538,200		$483,700
Cost of goods sold				
Beginning inventory	$ 39,300		$ 32,100	
Purchases	343,200		292,700	
Cost of goods available for sale	$382,500		$324,800	
Ending inventory	46,800	335,700	39,300	285,500
Gross margin		$202,500		$198,200
Operating expenses		167,200		151,600
Income before taxes		$ 35,300		$ 46,600

During 19X9 Waymire's accountant discovered that ending inventory for 19X7 had been overstated by $7,900.

REQUIRED:

1. Prepare corrected income statements for 19X8 and 19X7.

2. Prepare a schedule showing each financial statement item affected by the error and the amount of the error for that item. Indicate whether each error is an overstatement (+) or an understatement (−).

E7-35. EFFECTS OF ERRORS IN ENDING INVENTORY   The 19X8 ending inventory for Ajax Enterprises was overstated by $3,400. Assume that there are no income taxes.

REQUIRED:

1. Determine the effect of this error on the 19X8 and 19X9 financial statements.

2. Prepare the journal entry to correct the error if it is found in 19X9 before closing entries are made.

APPENDIX 7–1 EXERCISES

E7-36. RETAIL METHOD   Klein's Department Store uses the retail method. For the first quarter, Klein's had the following data:

	AT COST	AT RETAIL
Beginning inventory	$134,970	$204,500
Purchases.....................................	559,680	848,000
Sales revenue..................................		904,300

REQUIRED:

Determine the ending inventory at the end of the quarter. Then use the estimated ending inventory to estimate cost of goods sold and gross margin for the quarter.

E7-37. RETAIL METHOD   Mary's Bargains has the following data available for a recent year:

	AT COST	AT RETAIL
Beginning inventory	$ 63,000	$ 86,000
Purchases.....................................	477,000	634,000
Cost of goods available for sale	$540,000	$720,000

Sales for the year were $640,000. Mary's Bargains uses the retail method.

REQUIRED:

1. Determine the cost ratio.
2. Determine the dollar amount of ending inventory at retail.
3. Determine the cost of ending inventory.
4. Determine cost of goods sold.

APPENDIX 7-2 EXERCISES

E7-38. PERPETUAL FIFO, LIFO, AND WEIGHTED AVERAGE METHODS   Crandall Distributors has the following data available for inventory, purchases, and sales for a recent year:

ACTIVITY	UNITS	AMOUNT PER UNIT
Beginning inventory	120	$5.90
Purchase 1, 1/18	550	6.00
Sale	330	8.80
Sale	280	9.00
Purchase 2, 3/10	650	6.20
Sale	270	9.00
Sale	290	9.50
Purchase 3, 9/30	250	6.30
Sale	240	9.90

REQUIRED:

Using the perpetual inventory system and the FIFO, LIFO, and weighted average inventory costing methods, compute the cost of ending inventory and cost of goods sold.

E7-39. PERPETUAL FIFO, LIFO, AND WEIGHTED AVERAGE METHODS   Welding Products Company purchased 1,000 cases of welding rods at a cost of $95 per case on April 17. On August 19, the firm purchased another 1,000 cases at a cost of $112 per case. (Assume that there was no beginning inventory.) Sales data for the welding rods are as follows:

DATE	CASES SOLD
May 2	200
June 29	600
July 2	50
September 4	500
October 31	420

REQUIRED:

Using the perpetual inventory system, compute the cost of ending inventory by the LIFO, FIFO, and weighted average costing methods.

PROBLEMS

P7-40. EFFECTS OF INVENTORY COSTING METHODS ON THE BALANCE SHEET   Berkshire Enterprises has used the weighted average costing method for its inventories for several years. At the end of 19X6 Berkshire's accountant prepared the following balance sheet using weighted average inventory costing.

ASSETS

Cash		$ 37,200
Accounts receivable		215,300
Inventory		127,600
Total current assets		$380,100
Property, plant, and equipment	$535,000	
Less: Accumulated depreciation	185,200	349,800
Other assets		25,100
Total assets		$755,000

LIABILITIES AND EQUITY

Accounts payable		$ 54,900
Short-term notes payable		30,000
Wages payable		4,300
Total current liabilities		$ 89,200
Long-term notes payable		200,000
Total liabilities		$289,200
Capital stock	$350,000	
Retained earnings	115,800	
Total stockholders' equity		465,800
Total liabilities and equity		$755,000

If Berkshire had used the LIFO rather than the weighted average method, 19X6 cost of goods sold would have been larger and ending inventory smaller by $42,500. Assume that Berkshire's tax rate is 34 percent and that income taxes saved if the LIFO method is used would be used to reduce short-term notes payable.

REQUIRED:

Restate Berkshire's balance sheet assuming that LIFO rather than weighted average is used for inventory costing.

P7-41. INVENTORY COSTING METHODS   Larsen, Inc., uses a periodic inventory system. At the end of a recent year, Larsen, Inc.'s accounting records had the following data for inventory:

Beginning inventory	200 units at $10 each
Purchase 1, 2/14	860 units at $16 each
Sale, 4/26 (at $28 each)	890 units
Purchase 2, 5/21	770 units at $18 each
Sale, 12/4 (at $27 each)	730 units

REQUIRED:

Compute cost of goods sold and ending inventory using the FIFO, LIFO, weighted average, and specific identification methods. For the specific identification method, assume that the ending inventory is composed of 65 units from the beginning inventory, 75 units from purchase 1, and 70 units from purchase 2.

P7-42. INVENTORY COSTING METHODS FOR TWO YEARS   Hartwell Products Company uses a periodic inventory system. For 19X1 and 19X2 Hartwell has the following data:

19X1	UNITS	COST PER UNIT
Beginning inventory	100	$45
Purchase X1-1	700	52
Purchase X1-2	800	56
Purchase X1-3	900	60
Ending inventory	180	?
19X2		
Beginning inventory	180	?
Purchase X2-1	1,400	66
Purchase X2-2	1,320	71
Ending inventory	260	?

REQUIRED:

1. Compute 19X1 cost of goods sold and ending inventory using the FIFO, LIFO, weighted average, and specific identification methods. For the specific identification method assume that ending inventory is composed of 50 units from beginning inventory, 60 units from purchase X1-2, and 70 units from purchase X1-3.

2. Compute 19X2 cost of goods sold and ending inventory using the FIFO, LIFO, weighted average, and specific identification methods. For the specific identification method assume that ending inventory is composed of 30 units from *19X1* beginning inventory, 40 units from purchase X1-2, 100 units from purchase X2-1, and 90 units from purchase X2-2.

P7-43. THE EFFECT OF REDUCTIONS IN INVENTORY QUANTITIES   The 1986 annual report for General Motors presented the following information in its inventory note:

> Inventories are stated generally at cost, which is not in excess of market. The cost of substantially all domestic inventories other than the inventories of GM Hughes Electronics Corporation (GMHE) is determined by the last-in, first-out (LIFO) method. If the first-in, first-out (FIFO) method of inventory valuation had been used for inventories valued at LIFO cost, such inventories would have been about $2,203.8 million higher at December 3, 1986, and $2,196.3 million higher at December 31, 1985. As a result of decreases in LIFO eligible U.S. inventories, certain LIFO inventory quantities carried at lower costs prevailing in prior years, as compared with the costs of current purchases, were liquidated in 1986 and 1985. These inventory adjustments favorably affected income before income taxes by approximately $38.2 million 1986 and $20.9 million in 1985.

REQUIRED:

1. Explain why the reduction in inventory quantities increased General Motors' net income.

2. If General Motors had used the FIFO inventory costing method, would the reduction in ending inventory quantities have increased net income?

P7-44. EFFECT OF INVENTORY COSTING METHODS ON TAXES   Elmwood Company sells lawn mowers to retail customers. Elmwood obtains the product directly from the manufacturer. Since lawn mowers are fairly bulky items, Elmwood had found it convenient to use the specific identification method of accounting. However, sales volume has increased and Elmwood is now considering a change in inventory method. Data for the current year, using the periodic system, are as follows:

	UNITS	COST PER UNIT	TOTAL COST
Beginning inventory	15	$108	$ 1,620
Purchase 1	45	120	5,400
Purchase 2	60	130	7,800
Purchase 3	80	140	11,200
Purchase 4	100	142	14,200
Goods available for sale	300		$40,220
Units sold	280		
Ending inventory	20		

REQUIRED:

1. Compute the cost of goods sold and the cost of ending inventory, using the FIFO, LIFO, and weighted average methods.

2. If Elmwood's tax rate is 30 percent (.30), how much cash would be saved in the current year by selecting the inventory method that produces the lowest gross margin relative to the other two methods?

P7-45. EFFECT OF PURCHASE TIMING WITH LIFO   Boston Oil Company sells heating oil to retail customers in New England. In December 19X2, Boston is considering whether to purchase 10,000,000 gallons of home heating oil that it expects to sell early in 19X3. Boston can make the purchase now or defer it until late January 19X3. Boston uses a periodic inventory system and the LIFO method of accounting for inventory. The following data are available:

HEATING OIL	GALLONS	COST PER UNIT	TOTAL COST
Beginning inventory	15,000,000	$ .70	$10,500,000
Purchase X2-1	10,000,000	.90	9,000,000
Purchase X2-2	12,000,000	1.05	12,600,000
Purchase X2-3	9,000,000	1.20	10,800,000
Goods available for sale	46,000,000		$42,900,000
Sales	(40,000,000)		
Ending inventory	6,000,000		

No further sales are expected for 19X2. If the 10,000,000-gallon purchase is made now or in January 19X3, the oil will cost $1.18 per gallon. Boston's income tax rate is 34 percent (.34).

REQUIRED:

1. Compute the ending inventory and cost of goods sold for 19X2 assuming that the oil purchase is not made.

2. Compute the ending inventory and cost of goods sold assuming the purchase is made.

3. Assume that storage and financing costs for the oil will be $645,000 larger if the purchase is made in December 19X2, rather than January 19X3. Do the tax savings arising from a December 19X2 purchase exceed the additional storage and financing costs?

P7-46. EFFECTS OF INVENTORY REDUCTIONS   Alexander Petroleum Supply sells gasoline to independent service stations. Alexander has used the LIFO method of accounting for its gasoline inventory for several years. You have the following data for the 19X9 beginning inventory:

	QUANTITY	COST PER UNIT	TOTAL COST
19X1 layer	130,000	$.40	$ 52,000
19X4 layer	206,000	.52	107,120
19X7 layer	148,000	.61	90,280
19X8 layer	179,000	.73	130,670
Total	663,000		$380,070

Near the end of 19X9, Alexander's gasoline supplier had a refinery breakdown. As a result, Alexander was unable to purchase enough gasoline to maintain its beginning inventory. In fact, Alexander had only 50,000 gallons on hand at December 31, 19X9. Had the refinery been in operation, Alexander would have purchased sufficient gasoline so that ending inventory would have been 700,000 gallons.

REQUIRED:

1. If Alexander had purchased gasoline during 19X9 at $.81 per gallon, what is the effect on cost of goods sold of this unintended decline in inventory quantity?
2. Would cost of goods sold have been affected by the inventory decline if FIFO had been in use?
3. If Alexander's income tax rate is 34 percent (.34), by how much have taxes changed because of the unintended decline in inventory?

P7-47. MULTIYEAR EFFECTS OF ALTERNATIVE INVENTORY COSTING METHODS   Coverly Supply Company has the following data for 19X5 and 19X6:

	UNITS	COST PER UNIT	TOTAL COST
Inventory, 12/31/X4	100	$48.75	$ 4,875
Purchases, 19X5	800	60.00	48,000
Inventory, 12/31/X5	120		
Purchases, 19X6	880	65.00	57,200
Inventory, 12/31/X6	150		

REQUIRED:

1. Compute ending inventory and cost of goods sold for 19X5 and 19X6, using the FIFO, LIFO, and weighted average methods.
2. If Coverly's tax rate is 25 percent (.25), how much cash is saved in 19X5 and 19X6 by using LIFO relative to FIFO and weighted average?
3. Why are the beginning inventory amounts for 19X6 different for each of the three methods?

P7-48. ESTIMATING ENDING INVENTORY   In October 19X9, Bayside Products lost its entire inventory when the firm's warehouse was destroyed in an earthquake. The warehouse was covered by insurance, but the inventory was not. Bayside was able to salvage its accounting records and has developed the following information:

19X9 sales revenue.	$10,850,300
Inventory, 1/1/X9.	1,073,500
19X9 purchases	6,297,100
19X9 purchase returns	94,200
19X9 transportation-in.	236,900

Bayside estimates that its 19X9 gross margin rate is 36 percent (.36).

REQUIRED:

Compute the amount of the loss.

P7-49. ESTIMATING ENDING INVENTORY   Truitt and Company operates a wholesale oil products company. Truitt believes that an employee and a customer are conspiring to steal gasoline. The employee records sales to this customer for less than the amount actually placed in the customer's tank truck. In order to confirm or refute his suspicions, Truitt has collected the following data for the past 10 working days:

ITEM	GALLONS OF GASOLINE	COST PER GALLON	TOTAL COST
Inventory, 9/1	220,000	1.45	$ 319,000
Purchases	1,560,000	1.45	2,262,000
Goods available for sale	1,780,000		$2,581,000

Truitt has had sales of $2,512,000 during this 10-day period. All sales have been made at $1.60 per gallon. A physical inventory indicates that there are 192,000 gallons of gasoline in inventory at the close of business on September 10.

REQUIRED:

1. Determine how much inventory should be present.
2. What is the cost of the missing inventory?
3. How could Truitt arrange the firm's procedures to make this kind of theft more difficult?

P7-50. LOWER OF COST OR MARKET   Roanoke Beverage Distributors' income statement for a recent year appears below. The ending inventory amount was determined from historical cost data.

Sales revenue....................................		$920,000
Cost of goods sold		
Beginning inventory...........................	$ 48,000	
Purchases.....................................	562,000	
Cost of goods available for sale....................	$610,000	
Ending inventory..............................	92,000	
Cost of goods sold............................		518,000
Gross margin...................................		$402,000
Operating expenses		328,000
Income before taxes.............................		$ 74,000

Assume that you discover that the historical cost of the ending inventory overstates its market value by $18,600.

REQUIRED:

Restate the income statement to reflect the market value of the inventory.

P7-51. LOWER OF COST OR MARKET   Sue Stone, the president of Tippecanoe Home Products, has prepared the following information for the firm's television inventory at year-end 19X5:

MODEL	QUANTITY	COST	EXPECTED SELLING PRICE	SALES COMMISSION
T-260	11	$250 each	$445 each	$50 each
S-256	24	325	490	55
R-193	18	210	230	40
Z-376	12	285	250	30

Sue notes that the 19X6 models that will replace these items will cost 4 percent more than the equivalent 19X5 models. The normal markup is 80 percent of cost.

REQUIRED:

Determine the carrying amount of the inventory of unsold televisions using the lower-of-cost-or-market procedure. (See footnote 3, page 286, in this chapter.)

P7-52. INCOME STATEMENT EFFECTS OF AN INVENTORY ERROR   The income statements for Graul Corporation for the three years ending in 19X7 appear below:

	19X7	19X6	19X5
Sales revenue	$4,643,200	$4,287,500	$3,647,900
Cost of goods sold	2,208,400	2,181,600	2,006,100
Gross margin	$2,168,100	$2,105,900	$1,641,800
Operating expense	1,548,600	1,428,400	1,152,800
Income from operations	$ 619,500	$ 677,500	$ 489,000
Other expenses, interest	137,300	123,600	112,900
Income before income taxes	$ 482,200	$ 553,900	$ 376,100
Income taxes expense (.34)	163,948	188,326	127,874
Net income	$ 318,252	$ 365,574	$ 248,226

During 19X7 Graul discovered that the 19X5 ending inventory had been understated by $85,000.

REQUIRED:

1. Prepare correct income statements for all three years.
2. Did the error in 19X5 affect cumulative net income for the three-year period? Explain your response.
3. Why was 19X7 net income unaffected?

P7-53. EFFECTS OF ERRORS IN ENDING INVENTORY   On December 31, Courtland Enterprises finished taking a physical inventory for its year-end financial statements. The cost of the items counted in the inventory was $106,500. Cost of goods sold for the year was $853,700. During the audit of the statements, the firm's CPA identified the following transactions that had been recorded incorrectly:

a) Inventory costing $3,200 was not counted during the inventory.

b) Inventory costing $6,300 that was set aside as a purchase return was included as ending inventory. These items should have been excluded from the $106,500.

c) A purchase return of $1,900 made on May 23 was credited to transportation-in rather than to purchase returns.

REQUIRED:

1. Make the journal entry to correct item c.
2. Determine the correct amount for ending inventory and cost of goods sold.

P7-54. INVENTORY COSTING METHODS AND MARKET VALUE   Ortman Enterprises sells fuel oil. On January 1, 19X8, Ortman had 5,000,000 gallons of fuel oil on hand, for which it had paid $.50 per gallon. During 19X8 Ortman made the following purchases:

DATE	GALLONS	COST PER GALLON	TOTAL COST
2/20	10,000,000	$.52	$ 5,200,000
5/15	25,000,000	.56	14,000,000
9/12	32,000,000	.60	19,200,000
	67,000,000		$38,400,000

During 19X8 Ortman sold 65,000,000 gallons at $.75 per gallon, leaving an ending inventory of 7,000,000 gallons. Ortman uses the lower of cost or market for its inventories, as required by generally accepted accounting principles.

REQUIRED:

1. Assume that the market value of fuel oil is $.76 per gallon on December 31, 19X8. Compute the cost of goods sold (adjusted for any required market adjustment) using FIFO, LIFO, and weighted average costing methods.

2. Assume that the market value of fuel oil is $.58 per gallon on December 31, 19X8. Compute the cost of goods sold (adjusted for any required market adjustment), using FIFO, LIFO, and weighted average costing methods.

P7-55. EFFECT OF YEAR-END PURCHASES   Palmquist Company has a periodic inventory system and uses LIFO. The following information is available for 19X8:

Beginning inventory	3,000 units at $6.50
Purchase 1, 2/25	12,000 units at $7.80
Purchase 2, 7/15	20,000 units at $9.00
Purchase 3, 12/20	10,000 units at $11.00

During 19X8, 31,000 units were sold at $16.00 per unit, resulting in an inventory at December 31, 19X8, of 14,000 units.

REQUIRED:

1. Compute the gross margin for 19X8.

2. Suppose that purchase 3 had been delayed until after January 3, 19X9. Recompute the amount of gross margin for 19X8.

3. Suppose that purchase 3 had been for 15,000 units at $11 on December 20 rather than 10,000 units at $11. Recompute the amount of gross margin for 19X8.

4. What do you conclude about the effect of purchases made late in the year on gross margin when LIFO is employed?

5. Assume that Palmquist uses FIFO rather than LIFO. Recompute the amount of gross margin under each of the conditions specified in requirements 1, 2, and 3 above. What do you conclude about the effect of purchases made late in the year on gross margin when FIFO is employed?

P7-56. EFFECTS OF PRICE AND QUANTITY ON INVENTORY COSTING DATA   Quicksilver, Inc., is considering its choice of inventory costing for one of the items in its merchandise inventory. Quicksilver's accountant has prepared the following data for that item:

	FIFO	LIFO	WEIGHTED AVERAGE
Beginning inventory	$ 50,400	$ 50,400	$ 50,400
Purchases	460,300	460,300	460,300
Goods available for sale	$510,700	$510,700	$510,700
Ending inventory	(72,600)	(54,200)	(60,900)
Cost of goods sold	$438,100	$456,500	$449,600

REQUIRED:

1. What do these data imply about the number of items in beginning and ending inventory?

2. Can you infer from these data whether the prices at which Quicksilver purchased increased or decreased? Explain your answer.

APPENDIX 7-1 PROBLEMS

P7-57. RETAIL METHOD MacArthur's Fabric Store had sales of $260,000 during a recent year. The following information is also available:

	AT COST	AT RETAIL
Beginning inventory	$ 10,900	$ 32,600
Purchases.	114,200	245,400

REQUIRED:

1. What is the cost ratio for beginning inventory and purchases?

2. Estimate MacArthur's ending inventory using the retail method.

3. What is the appropriate action if a physical inventory reveals that the retail price of inventory on hand at year-end is only $14,600?

4. Do you think the retail method could be applied if the cost ratio for purchases was different from the cost ratio for beginning inventory? If so, how should it be applied?

P7-58. RETAIL METHOD: CHANGING SALES MIX Shuford Stores has the following data for the current year:

	AT COST	AT RETAIL
Beginning inventory		
60% markup.	$ 10,000	$ 16,000
30% markup.	10,000	13,000
	$ 20,000	$ 29,000
Purchases		
60% markup.	200,000	320,000
30% markup.	100,000	130,000
Cost of goods available for sale	$320,000	$479,000

Shuford's accountant reports that sales were as follows:

CATEGORY	NET SALES REVENUE
30% markup	$ 91,000
60% markup	309,000
Total	$400,000

REQUIRED:

1. Compute the cost of the ending inventory and cost of goods sold by applying the retail method separately to each category of goods.

2. Compute the cost of ending inventory and cost of goods sold by applying the retail method to all goods without regard to markup category.

3. Which computation should be preferred? Explain.

APPENDIX 7-2 PROBLEMS

P7-59. PERPETUAL FIFO, LIFO, AND WEIGHTED AVERAGE METHODS   Anderson's Department Store has the following data for inventory, purchases, and sales of merchandise for December:

ACTIVITY	UNITS PURCHASED	COST PER UNIT	TOTAL COST	UNITS SOLD	TOTAL SALES
Purchase, 12/1	16	$6.00	$ 96		
Purchase, 12/5	20	7.00	140		
Sale, 12/7				13	$117
Sale, 12/10				7	63
Sale, 12/12				6	54
Purchase, 12/14	8	5.50	44		
Sale, 12/16				18	164

Inventory at December 1 was five units at a cost of $6.00 each.

REQUIRED:

Prepare the journal entries to record these transactions for the FIFO, LIFO, and weighted average costing methods, using perpetual accounting procedures for the month of December.

P7-60. PERPETUAL FIFO, LIFO, AND WEIGHTED AVERAGE METHODS   Edwards Company began operations in February 19X7. Edwards' accounting records provide the following data for the remainder of 19X7 for one of the items that the firm sells:

ACTIVITY	UNITS	COST PER UNIT	TOTAL COST
Purchase 1, 2/15	6	$100	$600
Sale	(2)	—	—
Sale	(3)	—	—
Purchase 2, 6/18	4	120	480
Sale	(3)	—	—
Inventory, 12/31/X7	2		

REQUIRED:

1. Using the perpetual FIFO procedure, compute cost of goods sold and the cost of ending inventory.

2. Using the perpetual LIFO procedure, compute cost of goods sold and the cost of ending inventory.

3. Using the perpetual weighted average procedure, compute cost of goods sold and the cost of ending inventory.

4. Which perpetual costing method would you adopt to minimize the cash outflow for taxes?

P7-61. PERPETUAL INVENTORY COSTING METHODS FOR TWO YEARS   Gavin Products uses a perpetual inventory system. For 19X1 and 19X2, Gavin has the following data:

	UNITS	COST PER UNIT
19X1		
Inventory, 1/1/X1	200	$ 9
Purchase, 2/15/X1	300	12
Sell, 3/10/X1	220	—
Purchase, 9/15/X1	500	10
Sell, 12/3/X1	240	—
19X2		
Sell, 4/4/X2	400	—
Purchase, 6/25/X2	200	11
Sell, 12/18/X2	150	—

REQUIRED:

1. Compute 19X1 cost of goods sold and ending inventory using the FIFO, LIFO, and weighted average methods.
2. Compute 19X2 cost of goods sold and ending inventory using the FIFO, LIFO, and weighted average methods.

ANALYTICAL OPPORTUNITIES

A7-62. INVENTORY COSTING WHEN BALANCE SHEET QUANTITIES ARE SMALL   A number of companies have adopted a "just in time" procedure for acquiring inventory. These companies have arrangements with their suppliers that require the supplier to deliver inventory just as the company needs the goods. As a result, just in time companies keep very little inventory on hand.

REQUIRED:

1. Should the inventory costing method (LIFO or FIFO) have a material effect on cost of goods sold when a company adopts the just in time procedure and reduces its inventory significantly?
2. Once a company has switched to the just in time procedure and has little inventory, should the inventory costing method (LIFO or FIFO) affect cost of goods sold?

A7-63. INVENTORY PURCHASE PRICE VOLATILITY   In 1988 Steel Technologies, Inc., changed from the LIFO to the FIFO method for its inventory costing. Steel Technologies' annual report indicated that this change had been instituted because the price at which the firm purchased steel was highly volatile.

REQUIRED:

Explain how FIFO cost of goods sold and ending inventory would be different from LIFO when prices are volatile.

LEARNING OBJECTIVES

Careful study of this chapter will enable you to:

1. Describe the concept of liquidity.

2. Explain why internal control is important for financial assets and describe related internal control procedures.

3. Account for cash transactions and describe the presentation of cash on the balance sheet.

4. Prepare a bank reconciliation.

5. Describe debit cards and the different types of credit cards and, for each, explain the accounting and cash flow implications for merchants.

6. Account for notes receivable from receipt to collection or default.

7. Account for short-term investments at acquisition, year-end, and sale.

Appendix 8 – 1

8. Account for a petty cash fund.

9. Prepare special journals and subsidiary ledgers.

8 FINANCIAL ASSETS: ACCOUNTING AND CONTROL

Financial assets include cash, receivables, short-term investments in securities, and other liquid assets. The **liquidity of an asset** is the ease with which the asset can be converted into cash, or currency. Assets such as cash, receivables, and short-term investments in securities are called *liquid assets* because they are easily converted into cash or are already cash. Short-term investments in securities are less liquid than cash because securities must be sold in order to produce cash. Receivables, in turn, are usually less liquid than short-term investments in securities because receivables must await the customer's payment, whereas an investment theoretically can be sold at any time. Since cash is required to pay obligations as they come due, liquid assets provide a buffer against temporary shortages of cash that can result from variations in the rate of cash inflow and outflow or from unforeseen needs for cash. The liquidity of an asset is different from the liquidity of an entire firm. The **liquidity of a firm** refers to its ability to meet its financial obligations as they come due.

This chapter describes transactions, financial reporting, and control issues involving liquid assets. (Controls and safeguards over liquid assets are important because these assets are particularly vulnerable to misappropriation.) We begin with a discussion of cash and follow with sections devoted to credit card receivables, accounts and notes receivable, and short-term investments.

ACCOUNTING FOR CASH

The asset cash has future economic benefit because of what it can buy. Cash can be exchanged for virtually any available good or service, or it can be held and exchanged for goods and services in the future. Cash includes coins, currency, money orders, checks, and funds on deposit with banks or savings institutions.[1]

When cash is received, a cash account is increased by a debit for the amount taken in; and when cash is paid out, a cash account is decreased by a credit for the amount disbursed. Frequently, receipt and payment of cash are accomplished by a check sent through the mail, a process that may require several days, and additional time may pass between receipt of the check and its deposit in the bank by the payee. Further time may pass before funds are transferred from the bank of the payer to that of the receiver, although modern electronic systems have greatly

LIQUIDITY OF AN ASSET: The ease with which an asset can be converted into cash.

LIQUIDITY OF A FIRM: The ability of a firm to meet its financial obligations as they come due.

[1] Cash does not include notes receivable, IOUs, or postage stamps. Notes receivable and IOUs are classified separately as receivables, and postage stamps are classified as supplies.

reduced this lag. Despite the fact that there may be a time lag between the issuance of a check and the actual transfer of funds, the accounting system treats payment by check in exactly the same way that it treats the transfer of currency. The receipt of either a check or currency is recorded by a debit to cash; and, conversely, either the issue of a check or the payment of currency is recorded by a credit to cash.

INTERNAL CONTROL OF CASH

The more liquid an asset, the more easily it can be misappropriated. For example, misappropriation of poorly controlled cash is usually easier than misappropriation of poorly controlled office equipment or production tools. Hence the controls over liquid assets must be designed with special care. The authority to collect, hold, and disburse cash must be clearly assigned to specific individuals. Whenever feasible, cash-handling activities and cash record-keeping activities should be assigned to *different* individuals. Moreover, cash records should be examined often by an objective party as a basis for evaluating the performance of cash-handling activities. These controls should be supported by an appropriately designed record-keeping system. Specialized records, examples of which are described in Appendix 8 – 1, make it possible to distribute record-keeping responsibility among individuals. In addition, cash should be safeguarded in vaults and banks. The accompanying analysis illustrates the application of internal control principles to a cash control problem.

ANALYSIS
INTERNAL CONTROL IN A STUDENT ORGANIZATION

Internal control is frequently a problem for collegiate student organizations (clubs, fraternities, sororities, etc.). Internal control is likely to be weak in such organizations. Usually one individual, the treasurer, is given the responsibility for collecting dues, depositing cash in the bank account, writing all checks, maintaining the accounting records, and preparing bank reconciliations and financial statements. This is a clear violation of the segregation of duties principle that underlies a strong internal control system. Although some members may recognize the internal control advantages of segregation of duties, student organizations frequently face the reality that segregation of duties is not nearly so important as simply finding someone willing to perform the treasurer's tasks.

What steps can be taken by a typical student organization to strengthen its internal control system? The following list contains seven questions that should be answered by the leaders of a student organization. A "no" answer to any question indicates a potential internal control weakness.

1. *Are invoices and supporting documentation obtained from vendors whenever a cash disbursement is made or a liability is incurred?* The use of appropriate documentation assures the proper payment of expenditures and facilitates the accrual of liabilities at year-end.

2. *Does each check signer cancel (e.g., by writing "Paid by check number 123, October 20, 19X6") every vendor invoice and all supporting documents at the time the check is written?* This action helps to assure that duplicate payments are not made.

3. *Does the organization's faculty adviser initial all checks written for amounts greater than some specified minimum (say, $50)?* This control reduces the possibility of unauthorized expenditures.

4. *Are receipts of members' fees and dues deposited promptly (at least once a week)?* Prompt deposits help avoid misplacing receipts and combining membership and personal funds.

5. *Does the organization have procedures to assist in the collection of membership dues?* Despite the mutual trust and friendship that are a part of a student organization, uncollectible accounts can be a serious problem. The treasurer may need the assistance of formal procedures in collecting delinquent dues (e.g., placing sanctions on people who fail to pay).

6. *Does the organization have an accounting policies and procedures manual?* Such a manual may be needed to prepare the year-end financial report in conformity with the university's (and/or a national governing body's) requirements.

7. *Are complete minutes of all officers' meetings maintained?* The minutes should include (a) a listing of all changes in membership and officers, including the names of all new members, (b) a schedule of dues that documents all financial obligations of members, (c) approval of expenditures, and (d) authorization of check signers. Including this information, along with descriptions of all important decisions of the organization's governing body, documents in one record all important activities of the organization.

CASH ACCOUNTS

A firm's balance sheet usually reports a single cash amount, listed as the first item in the current assets section of the statement.[2] But the firm may have quite a number of different cash accounts in its general ledger. Transactions that involve cash are entered into three types of balance sheet accounts: (1) *cash in bank accounts,* (2) *petty cash fund accounts,* and (3) *change fund accounts.* Cash in bank accounts represent cash held by banks in the firm's checking accounts; a separate cash in bank account is maintained for each of the firm's checking accounts. Petty cash fund accounts represent cash held within a firm to be used in making small expenditures for which issuing a check is viewed as unnecessarily burdensome (see Appendix 8–1). A change fund account represents cash that will be used as a supply of currency for cash registers. The amount of cash shown on the balance sheet is the total of all the cash accounts in the firm's general ledger. To simplify the illustrations in this chapter, we will assume that the general ledger contains a single cash account (called "cash") unless multiple cash accounts are specified.

Cash Over and Short

An effective internal control system requires that all cash not used for petty cash and change funds be deposited in a bank daily. At the end of each day, the amount of cash received during the day is debited to the cash in bank accounts to which it has been deposited. The amount deposited should equal the total of cash register tapes plus other documents supporting the receipt of cash. If it does not (and differences will occasionally occur even when cash-handling procedures are carefully designed and executed), the discrepancy is recorded in an account called **cash over and short.**

CASH OVER AND SHORT: The account in which a firm records the difference, or discrepancy, between cash actually taken in and cash reported as received by documents of receipt.

To illustrate the use of the cash over and short account, suppose that on a certain day a firm has prepared for deposit a total of $20,671.12. However, the total of cash register tapes and other documents supporting the receipt of cash on that day is $20,685.14, including collections of accounts receivable of $6,760.50.

[2] In addition, footnotes to the financial statements must disclose any restrictions on the availability of cash to pay company obligations. For example, banks may require firms to maintain minimum balances to compensate the banks for providing credit or other services to the firms. Such requirements, called *compensating balance requirements,* are of interest to financial statement readers because they reduce the liquidity of the firm.

The $14.02 difference is the amount of cash short, and the following journal entry records this amount along with the day's receipts:

Cash.	20,671.12	
Cash over and short	14.02	
Sales revenue ($20,685.14 − $6,760.50)		13,924.64
Accounts receivable		6,760.50

Observe that a cash *shortage* requires a debit to cash over and short, whereas a cash *overage* would require a credit.

One common source of cash over or short is errors in making change for cash sales. Significant amounts of cash over or short signal the need for a careful investigation of the causes and appropriate corrective action. Cash over and short is usually treated as an income statement account and is reported as a part of other expenses or other revenues.

Checking Accounts

Cash receipts are customarily deposited in *checking accounts.* Only those persons designated by the depositor may write checks to withdraw checking account funds. This authority is confirmed in the bank's files by signature cards, and the bank should not process a check for payment unless it bears at least one and sometimes several authorized signatures.

Periodically — usually once a month — the bank returns to the depositor all checks processed during the period, together with a detailed statement of the activity of the account. This document is a *bank statement,* which shows the individual deposits and withdrawals and the balance of cash in the account at the end of the period. A checking account is carried as a liability account in the records of the bank. Therefore, deposits and other events that increase the bank account are labeled "credits" on the bank statement, and withdrawals and other events that decrease the account are labeled "debits." Although the form of the bank statement varies from one bank to another, Exhibit 8–1 on page 323 illustrates its important general features.

Bank statements and other checking account information prepared by the bank exactly duplicate a portion of the cash records maintained by the firm. This duplication provides a useful check on the accuracy of cash records and also discourages misappropriation of cash. However, although the two sets of records reflect the same cash transactions, the transactions are not recorded simultaneously by the bank and the firm. Consequently, comparison requires a reconciliation procedure, to which we now turn.

RECONCILIATION OF LEDGER CASH ACCOUNT AND BANK ACCOUNT

BANK RECONCILIA- TION: A comparison of the bank statement with the firm's own cash account.

Cash accounts are especially susceptible to error and even misappropriation unless effective internal controls are exercised. One important internal control procedure for cash is the monthly **bank reconciliation,** a comparison of the bank statement with the organization's own general ledger cash account. Reconciliation of these separately maintained records serves two purposes: First, it serves a control function by identifying errors and providing an inspection of detailed records that deters misappropriation. Second, reconciliation serves a transaction detection function by identifying transactions performed by the bank, so the firm can make the necessary entries in its records.

Sources of Differences Between Cash Account and Bank Balances

In general, differences between the cash account balance and the bank balance develop from three sources: (1) transactions recorded by the firm but not yet recorded by the bank, (2) transactions recorded by the bank but not yet recorded by the firm, and (3) errors in recording transactions on either set of records. Let us consider examples of each source of difference.

OUTSTANDING CHECK: A check issued and recorded by the firm but not yet presented to the firm's bank for payment.

TRANSACTIONS RECORDED BY FIRM BUT NOT YET RECORDED BY BANK One type of transaction in this category is an **outstanding check.** This is a check issued and recorded by the firm but not yet presented to the bank for payment and, therefore, not yet recorded by the bank. Outstanding checks cause the bank balance to be larger than the balance in the firm's ledger cash account.

DEPOSIT IN TRANSIT: An amount received and recorded by the firm and transmitted to the bank but not yet recorded by the bank.

Another transaction in this category is a **deposit in transit,** which is an amount received and recorded by the firm that has been transmitted to the bank but has not yet been recorded by the bank. Deposits in transit cause the bank balance to be smaller than the firm's cash account balance. Deposits in transit arise because many banks post any deposit received after 2:00 or 3:00 P.M. into their records on the next business day and because businesses often make deposits on weekends or holidays when the bank is not open for business.

TRANSACTIONS RECORDED BY BANK BUT NOT YET RECORDED BY FIRM Several types of transactions fall within this category. Bank *service charges* are fees charged by the bank for checking account services. The amount of the fee is not known to the firm (and therefore cannot be recorded) until the bank statement is received. Bank service charges unrecorded by the firm at the end of a month cause the bank balance to be smaller than the firm's cash account balance. An *NSF check* is a check that has been returned to the depositor because funds in the issuer's account are not sufficient to pay the check. The amount of the check was added to the depositor's account when the check was deposited; since the check cannot be paid, the bank deducts the amount of the NSF check from the account. This deduction is recorded by the bank before it is recorded by the firm, so NSF checks cause the bank balance to be smaller than the cash account balance.

Debit and credit memos are also recorded by the bank before they are recorded by the firm. A debit memo might result, for example, if the bank makes a prearranged deduction from the firm's account to pay a utility bill. Debit memos recorded by the bank but not yet recorded by the firm cause the bank balance to be smaller than the cash account balance. A credit memo could result if the bank collected a note receivable for the firm and deposited the funds in the firm's account. Credit memos recorded by the bank but not recorded by the firm cause the bank balance to be larger than the cash account balance.

After the reconciliation process, the firm must make adjusting journal entries to record all the transactions that have been recorded by the bank but not yet recorded in the firm's ledger cash account.

ERRORS The foregoing sources of difference between ledger account and bank account balances are the result of time lags between the recording of a transaction by the firm and its recording by the bank, or vice versa. Errors in recording transactions represent yet another source of difference between a firm's cash account balance and the bank balance. For example, a check may be erroneously entered into the firm's cash account for $67.00 yet actually have been issued and paid for $76.00. Such errors are inevitable in any accounting system and should

EXHIBIT 8–1   BANK STATEMENT

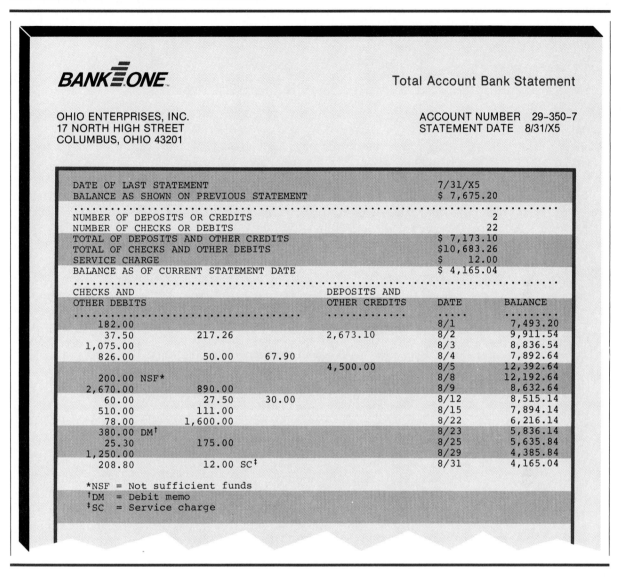

BANK ONE.   Total Account Bank Statement

OHIO ENTERPRISES, INC.   ACCOUNT NUMBER   29-350-7
17 NORTH HIGH STREET   STATEMENT DATE   8/31/X5
COLUMBUS, OHIO 43201

DATE OF LAST STATEMENT			7/31/X5	
BALANCE AS SHOWN ON PREVIOUS STATEMENT			$ 7,675.20	
NUMBER OF DEPOSITS OR CREDITS			2	
NUMBER OF CHECKS OR DEBITS			22	
TOTAL OF DEPOSITS AND OTHER CREDITS			$ 7,173.10	
TOTAL OF CHECKS AND OTHER DEBITS			$10,683.26	
SERVICE CHARGE			$ 12.00	
BALANCE AS OF CURRENT STATEMENT DATE			$ 4,165.04	

CHECKS AND OTHER DEBITS			DEPOSITS AND OTHER CREDITS	DATE	BALANCE
182.00				8/1	7,493.20
37.50	217.26		2,673.10	8/2	9,911.54
1,075.00				8/3	8,836.54
826.00	50.00	67.90		8/4	7,892.64
			4,500.00	8/5	12,392.64
				8/8	12,192.64
200.00 NSF*				8/9	8,632.64
2,670.00	890.00				
60.00	27.50	30.00		8/12	8,515.14
510.00	111.00			8/15	7,894.14
78.00	1,600.00			8/22	6,216.14
380.00 DM†				8/23	5,836.14
25.30	175.00			8/25	5,635.84
1,250.00				8/29	4,385.84
208.80	12.00 SC‡			8/31	4,165.04

*NSF = Not sufficient funds
†DM = Debit memo
‡SC = Service charge

be corrected as soon as discovered. In addition, an effort should be made to determine the cause of any error as a basis for corrective action. Obviously, an intentional error designed to hide misappropriation of funds calls for quite different corrective action than does an error resulting from human fatigue or machine failure.

Reconciliation Procedures

The sources of difference between ledger account and bank account balances are determined by a comparison of the accounting records and the bank statement. In general, this procedure has three parts: (1) comparison of beginning balances, (2) comparison of disbursements, and (3) comparison of receipts.

Let us illustrate the preparation of a bank reconciliation by using Ohio Enterprises, Inc., which received its bank statement for August during the second

EXHIBIT 8–2   **T-ACCOUNT FOR CASH**

OHIO ENTERPRISES, INC.
Prereconciliation Cash Account
For the Month Ended August 31, 19X5

Cash

Balance, 7/31	$6,200.94						

Date	Amount Deposited		Check Number	Check Amount	Check Number	Check Amount
8/1	$2,673.10		1886	$ 37.50	1896	$ 30.00
8/5	4,500.00		1887	826.00	1897	1,600.00
8/31	300.00‡		1888	50.00	1898	87.00†
			1889	2,670.00	1899	208.80
Total deposits	$7,473.10		1890	67.90	1900	1,250.00
			1891	890.00	1901	93.00*
			1892	27.50	1902	175.00
			1893	111.00	1903	25.30
			1894	60.00	1904	72.50*
			1895	510.00	1905	891.00*
					Total disbursements	$9,682.50

Balance, 8/31	$3,991.54					

* Outstanding check at 8/31. Determined by comparison of cash account with checks returned with bank statement.
† Recorded in error. Check 1898 was written for $78.00 to a local newspaper for advertising services. Error was discovered by comparison of cash account with checks accompanying bank statement.
‡ Deposit in transit at 8/31. Determined by comparison of cash account with deposits recorded on bank statement.

week of September (see Exhibit 8–1). Detailed data from the Ohio Enterprises cash account are shown in Exhibit 8–2, the *prereconciliation* cash account, which lists in T-account form all deposits taken to the bank and all checks issued by Ohio Enterprises during August. Notice that the prereconciliation cash account shows a balance of $3,991.54 at August 31, whereas the bank statement shows a balance of $4,165.04 for the same date. The three-part comparison performed by Ohio Enterprises, Inc., as a basis for the August 31 reconciliation is as follows.

COMPARISON OF BEGINNING BALANCES   For Ohio Enterprises, the difference between the cash account balance and bank balance at July 31 is accounted for on the bank reconciliation prepared at the end of the previous period (part of which is shown in Exhibit 8–3). Observe that the bank balance and cash account balance shown here also appear as the beginning balances for the August bank statement (Exhibit 8–1) and the August cash account (Exhibit 8–2), respectively. The checks that are outstanding at July 31 will more than likely be paid by the bank during August. However, any checks outstanding at July 31 that were not paid by the bank during August would also be listed as outstanding at August 31.

COMPARISON OF DETAILED DISBURSEMENTS   The list of August disbursements according to the firm's records is the list of all checks *issued* during August (shown on the right side in Exhibit 8–2), while the list of August disbursements according to the bank's records is the list of all checks *paid* by the bank (shown in the

EXHIBIT 8–3   **COMPARISON OF BEGINNING BALANCES**

OHIO ENTERPRISES, INC.

Reconciliation of Bank and Cash Account Balances

As of July 31, 19X5

Bank balance, 7/31		$7,675.20
Less: Outstanding checks		
1883	$ 182.00	
1884	217.26	
1885	1,075.00	1,474.26
Balance after adjustment, 7/31		$6,200.94

leftmost three columns in Exhibit 8–1). When the two lists are compared, any checks that appear on the firm's list of checks issued but not on the bank's list of checks paid are outstanding. There are three outstanding checks at the end of August—numbers 1901, 1904, and 1905; in Exhibit 8–2, these outstanding checks are indicated by asterisks. Exhibit 8–1 shows three other amounts that have been deducted by the bank but not yet recorded by the firm: an NSF check for $200.00, a debit memo (DM) for the automatic payment of a $380.00 electric bill, and service charges (SC) of $12.00.

COMPARISON OF DETAILED RECEIPTS   The list of August receipts in the firm's records is the list of all amounts *received* during August (shown on the left in Exhibit 8–2), while the list of August receipts according to bank records (Exhibit 8–1) is the list of all deposits *made* by the firm. Since most firms take deposits to the bank daily, the two lists are usually in agreement unless a deposit at the end of the period is not recorded by the bank until the following period. A comparison of the debits to the cash account (Exhibit 8–2) and the deposits added by the bank to Ohio's account (Exhibit 8–1) reveals that Ohio Enterprises has a $300.00 deposit in transit at August 31. In Exhibit 8–2, the deposit in transit is marked by a ‡ in the list of deposits. Comparing ledger receipts with bank receipts would also identify any existing credit memos. Credit memos would appear on the bank statement under "deposits and other credits," but there would be no corresponding entry in the firm's cash account. Ohio Enterprises' August bank statement does not show any credit memos.

The three-step reconciliation procedure will also reveal errors made by the firm or by the bank. The comparison of August disbursements in the ledger account with the list of checks paid on the bank statement reveals that the amount for check number 1898 (marked by a † in Exhibit 8–2) was incorrectly recorded in the Ohio Enterprises cash account as $87.00, instead of $78.00.[3]

The Bank Reconciliation Schedule

The various differences between the cash account balance and the bank balance are entered on a *bank reconciliation schedule,* a two-part calculation showing the various modifications to the cash account balance with a detailed explanation of

---

[3] The $9.00 error is called a *transposition error* because it is a result of transposing the digits 8 and 7, recording $87.00 rather than $78.00. The amount of a transposition error is exactly divisible by 9: $(87 - 78) = 9 = (9)(1); (53 - 35) = 18 = (9)(2)$. This fact makes transposition errors easier to locate.

EXHIBIT 8–4   **BANK RECONCILIATION SCHEDULE**

OHIO ENTERPRISES, INC.
Bank Reconciliation Schedule
As of August 31, 19X5

RECONCILIATION OF BANK AND CASH ACCOUNT BALANCES			ADJUSTMENTS TO CASH ACCOUNT BALANCE		
Bank balance, 8/31		$4,165.04	Cash account balance before modifications, 8/31		$3,991.54
Add: Deposit in transit		300.00	Add: Error in recording check 1898 for advertising services		9.00
		$4,465.04			$4,000.54
Less: Outstanding checks			Less:		
1901	$ 93.00		Service charge	$ 12.00	
1904	72.50		NSF check	200.00	
1905	891.00	1,056.50	Electric bill	380.00	592.00
Balance after adjustment, 8/31		$3,408.54	Balance after adjustment, 8/31		$3,408.54

the differences that required the modifications. Exhibit 8–4 shows a bank reconciliation schedule for Ohio Enterprises, Inc., which identifies the sources of difference between the ledger cash account balance and the bank balance on August 31.

The left side of a bank reconciliation modifies the end-of-period bank balance (1) for transactions recorded by the firm but not yet recorded by the bank, such as deposits in transit and outstanding checks, and (2) for errors made by the bank. In Exhibit 8–4, the bank balance is modified for one deposit in transit and three outstanding checks; there were no bank errors. The right side of the reconciliation modifies the end-of-period cash account balance (1) for transactions recorded by the bank but not yet recorded by the firm, such as service charges and NSF checks, and (2) for errors made by the firm. In Exhibit 8–4, the cash account balance is modified for an error made by the firm and for three transactions recorded by the bank that have not yet been recorded by the firm. The calculations on the right and left sides of the reconciliation must produce the same result, which is the correct cash account balance after modification for unrecorded transactions and errors (in Exhibit 8–4, $3,408.54).

Adjusting Entries Required by Reconciliation

The right side of the reconciliation for Ohio Enterprises shows the adjustments to the prereconciliation cash balance for transactions recorded by the bank but not yet recorded by the firm and for the firm's error in recording a transaction. All such adjustments require journal entries in the records of the firm. The adjusting entries required by Ohio Enterprises' reconciliation at August 31 are shown in Exhibit 8–5.

In summary, accounting for cash requires attention to both record-keeping and control issues. Record-keeping systems must separate cash held by banks in

EXHIBIT 8-5   **ADJUSTING ENTRIES**

OHIO ENTERPRISES, INC.
Journal Entries to Adjust Cash Account
To Agree with Bank Reconciliation
August 31, 19X5

Journal entry to correct error in recording check 1898

Cash..	9	
Advertising expense		9

Journal entry to record bank service charge expense

Bank service charge expense...............................	12	
Cash..		12

Journal entry to record NSF check returned by bank

Accounts receivable	200	
Cash..		200

Journal entry to record debit memo for payment of electric bill

Utilities expense, electricity................................	380	
Cash..		380

checking accounts from cash held by the firm in change and petty cash funds. The control system must prescribe cash-handling and recording procedures that recognize the differences in the nature of the various cash accounts. Control over cash in banks calls for bank reconciliations that make use of the duplicate records maintained by the firm and the bank. In contrast, petty cash funds require quite different control procedures, which are described in Appendix 8-1.

ACCOUNTING FOR CREDIT CARDS AND DEBIT CARDS

CREDIT CARD: A card that authorizes the holder to make purchases up to some limit from specified retail merchants.

Credit cards, sometimes collectively called "plastic money," are an alternative to cash and checks in retail sales. A **credit card** is a card that authorizes the holder to make purchases up to some limit from specified retail merchants. Over the past 20 years, the proportion of retail sales completed using cash or checks has decreased as the proportion of retail sales using credit cards has increased. From an accounting viewpoint, there are three types of credit cards:

1. Inside (in-house) credit cards

2. Bank credit cards

3. Outside-company credit cards

EXHIBIT 8–6   TYPES OF CREDIT CARDS

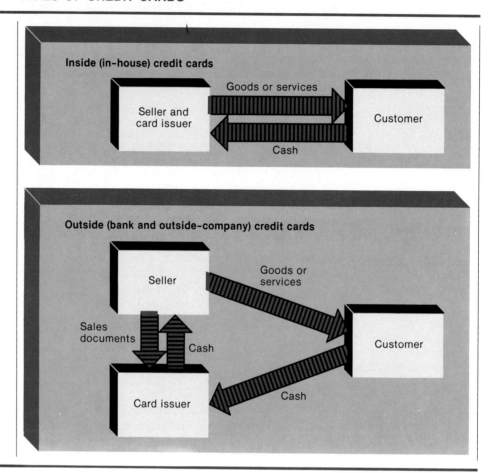

All three types are shown in Exhibit 8–6. An *inside (in-house) credit card* is issued by a seller directly to its customers and is used only in transactions between that seller and its customers. Large retail stores and petroleum companies issue inside credit cards. An *outside credit card* may be either a *bank credit card,* issued by a bank, or an *outside-company credit card,* issued by a nonbank financial services company. The issuer of an outside credit card pays a selling merchant the amount of each sale less a merchant's charge (or service charge) and then collects the full selling price from the customer. The merchant's charge compensates the card issuer for billing and collection services, as well as for uncollectible accounts. The amount of the merchant's charge is computed as a percentage of sales. Larger sellers are generally able to negotiate lower percentages. MasterCard and Visa are examples of bank credit cards. American Express, Diners Club, and Discover are examples of outside-company credit cards. The sections that follow describe the differences in the accounting used for the three types of credit cards.

INSIDE CREDIT CARDS   Sales made using inside credit cards are recorded in the same way as other credit sales. As an example, let's assume that a day's sales made by a department store with its inside credit cards totaled $3,670,910. These sales are recorded by the following general journal entry:

Accounts receivable	3,670,910	
Sales revenue		3,670,910

BANK CREDIT CARDS

Sales made using bank credit cards are virtually the same as cash sales because the bank pays the amounts generated by retail sales immediately upon deposit of the sales documents. The principal difference between a cash sale and a sale using a bank credit card is that the bank deducts a merchant's fee from the total amount of a sale made using a bank credit card. For example, on December 18, a leather goods shop makes sales totaling $2,680, including cash sales of $1,530 and bank credit card sales of $1,150. At the end of the day, the shopkeeper deposits all cash and bank credit card documents in the bank. The bank deducts a merchant's charge (or service charge) of 4 percent of the credit card sales. The following entry records these sales:

Cash [($1,530 + $1,150) − (.04)($1,150)]	2,634	
Credit card service charges [(.04)($1,150)]	46	
Sales revenue		2,680

Both cash sales and bank credit card sales (less the merchant's fee) are debited to cash.

OUTSIDE-COMPANY CREDIT CARDS

Unlike payments for amounts generated by sales with bank credit cards, payment for sales made using outside-company credit cards is not immediate.[4] Outside-company credit cards are issued by an entity other than a bank; that outside company pays merchants promptly, but not immediately, for card users' purchases, deducting a merchant's fee. Accordingly, sales under outside-company credit cards produce an account receivable from the card issuer. As an example, on March 16, the Ruffled Partridge restaurant had total sales of $9,670, including cash sales of $4,620 and outside-company credit card sales of $5,050 (all on American Express cards and subject to a 4 percent merchant's charge). The following entry records these sales:

Cash	4,620	
Accounts receivable [($5,050 − (0.04)($5,050)]	4,848	
Credit card service charges [(0.04)($5,050)]	202	
Sales revenue		9,670

Credit cards provide a variety of benefits to retail sellers. Outside credit cards enable the sellers to offer credit sales without maintaining costly accounts receivable records for individual customers. Inside credit cards require an accounts receivable record for each customer, but for large retail sellers such records may be less costly than the merchant's fee on outside credit cards. Moreover, inside

---

[4] As a service for their business customers, some banks accept major outside-company credit cards and credit the business's account for the amount of these credit card sales less the merchant's charge. The bank then submits the credit card receipts to the card issuer for payment to the bank.

credit cards can be designed and advertised to encourage customers to buy from the retailer issuing the card.[5]

ELECTRONIC CREDIT CARD PROCESSING

In recent years the major credit card companies and the banking system have developed the capability to electronically process sales transactions made with credit cards. To record a credit card sale electronically, a merchant uses an electronic terminal attached to a computer network operated by a bank or a credit card company. The merchant enters information about the goods sold (description, price, and quantity) and then passes the customer's credit card through a reader. The reader transfers the type of credit card and the customer name and account number to the network through the electronic terminal. If the customer's account is creditworthy, the transaction is accepted. The host computer for the credit card network then charges the customer's account for the amount of the sale and arranges to have the merchant paid the amount of the sale less the merchant's charge. The customer is given a printed receipt to sign, one copy of which is retained by the merchant and the other copy of which is given to the customer as a receipt. Otherwise, no paperwork is required to record this transaction by the merchant or the credit card company.

DEBIT CARDS

DEBIT CARD: A card that authorizes a bank to make an immediate electronic withdrawal (debit) from the holder's bank account.

As the capability and density of these point-of-sale electronic networks expand, banks and some large merchants are attempting to use debit cards and these networks to reduce the number of checks processed for retail sale transactions. A **debit card** authorizes a bank to make an immediate electronic withdrawal (debit) from the holder's bank account. The debit card is used like a credit card except that a bank electronically reduces (debits) the holder's bank account and increases (credits) the merchant's bank account for the amount of a sale made on a debit card.

While debit cards offer obvious advantages to banks and merchants in reduced check processing costs, they appear to be somewhat disadvantageous to the card holder, as transactions cannot be rescinded by stopping payment. Further, a purchase using a debit card causes an immediate reduction in a bank account balance, while a check written at the same time will require at least one or two days to clear, allowing the depositor to benefit from the additional money in the account until the check is presented at the bank for payment.

ACCOUNTING FOR RECEIVABLES

Although outside credit cards may be advantageous for some retail sellers, many businesses—particularly large retail sellers, nonretail sellers, and lenders—maintain accounts receivable records for individual customers. Recall that the receivables of a business are assets representing claims against an individual or another business, claims that remain to be settled at some future date. A business creates a receivable when it transfers cash, goods, or services to a customer. A

[5] Some financial institutions provide retailers with an entire inside credit card operation. For a fee, the financial institution approves credit applications, issues cards in the retailer's name, processes credit card transactions, bills customers, collects from customers, and absorbs the uncollectible account losses.

receivable is settled when the customer receiving the cash, goods, or services returns cash or other assets in payment. Between its creation and settlement, the receivable remains on the records of the business to which payment is due. In addition, of course, a corresponding payable remains on the records of the entity from which payment is due. In the sections that follow, we will consider two types of receivables: accounts receivable and notes receivable.

ACCOUNTS RECEIVABLE

ACCOUNT RECEIV-ABLE: Money due from another business or individual as payment for the performance of services or the sale of goods on credit.

TRADE RECEIVABLE: An account receivable due from a credit customer as a result of an ordinary business transaction.

An **account receivable** is money due from another business or individual as payment for the performance of services or the sale of goods on credit. The balance sheet entry for accounts receivable represents the total of all such amounts due to an entity. An account receivable due from a credit customer in the ordinary course of business is sometimes called a **trade receivable.** Accounts receivable due from employees or arising from other unusual transactions are called *special receivables* and are reported separately from trade receivables on the balance sheet. In Chapter 6, we discussed accounting for uncollectible accounts, as well as the effect of sales discounts on the reported amount of receivables.

In order to accelerate the inflow of cash, accounts receivable are occasionally sold to financial institutions. When receivables are sold, the buyer acquires the right to collect the funds due on the receivables. For example, in its 1989 annual report, Sears Merchandise Group reported on its sale of receivables:

> The Group's retail customer receivables at December 31, 1989 and 1988 have been reduced by $3.5 and $1.5 billion, respectively, of credit accounts that were securitized and sold . . . .

FACTORING: The sale of accounts receivable to a financial institution.

The sale of accounts receivable to a financial institution is called **factoring** and normally occurs at the date the receivable originates—when goods are sold or services are performed. A detailed discussion of the accounting and financial reporting issues for factoring is deferred to more advanced accounting courses.

NOTES RECEIVABLE

NOTE RECEIVABLE: A legal document given by a borrower to a lender stating the time of repayment and, directly or indirectly, the amount to be repaid.

A **note receivable** (also called simply a *note*) is a legal document given by a borrower (called the *maker* or the *payer* of the note) to a lender (called the *recipient* or the *payee* of the note) stating the time of repayment and the amount to be repaid.[6] A note is effective for a limited period that runs from the date the lender gives up cash or other assets in exchange for the note (the date of the note) to the date at which the borrower is to pay the note in full (the maturity date). Notes ordinarily specify the sum of money to be repaid indirectly, by stating the rate of interest and the principal amount. Consequently, it is usually necessary to calculate the amount of interest in order to determine the total amount to be repaid.[7] Our discussion here is limited to simple notes that specify the repayment of interest and principal in a single payment on a given day. (More complicated notes are described in Chapters 11A and 11B.)

[6] Sometimes notes are called *promissory notes* to emphasize the fact that they represent promises by one party to deliver cash to another at some future time.

[7] A note that indirectly specifies the sum to be repaid is called an *interest-bearing note* because it states an explicit interest rate. A note that directly specifies only the total amount to be repaid is called a *non-interest-bearing note* because it does not state an explicit rate of interest. However, it is important to understand that even a so-called non-interest-bearing note does bear interest in the sense that the amount borrowed (the principal amount) is less than the amount repaid (the maturity amount).

Calculation of Interest

The excess of the total amount of money paid to a lender over the amount borrowed is called **interest.** The amount borrowed is the **principal.** In other words, the total amount paid to the lender equals the sum of the interest and the principal for the note.

Interest can be considered as compensation paid to the lender for giving up the use of resources for the period of a note. The amount of interest on a note depends on the amount borrowed (the principal), the duration of the note, and the rate of interest. The dollar amount of interest on a note is determined in one of two ways: (1) as the excess of the amount repaid over the amount borrowed or (2) for notes of one year or less, as the product of the principal, the annual interest rate, and the period of the note (expressed as a fraction of a year). In other words:

$$\text{Interest} = (\text{Principal})(\text{Annual interest rate})(\text{Fraction of year})$$

Interest rates are usually expressed in annual terms; when calculating interest, it is therefore usually necessary to adjust the interest rate to reflect the duration of the note. Consider a three-month, $10,000 note bearing interest at an annual rate of 12 percent. The interest generated can be calculated as follows, using the formula given above:

$$\text{Interest} = (\$10,000)(.12)(3/12) = \$300$$

Recall from Chapter 2 that the matching concept and the revenue recognition concept require that expenses and revenues be identified with specific accounting periods. If only one month of the note receivable described above has expired by year-end, an adjusting entry is required to recognize interest revenue of $100 [(1/3)($300)]. Interest for the remaining two months ($200) is recognized in the following year.[8] We turn now to the application of these interest calculations to the accounting entries for notes receivable.

Recording Notes Receivable

Although a note receivable is usually taken in exchange for cash, it may also be taken in exchange for goods or services. This is often the case when the price of the goods or services represents an unusually large outlay for the buyer. Suppose, for example, that Schleswig, Inc., an equipment dealer, sells a $50,000 truck to Dover Electric Company in exchange for a three-month note bearing interest at 10 percent. The sale is recorded in Schleswig's journal by the following entry:

Notes receivable	50,000	
Sales revenue[9]		50,000

[8] Interest is, in fact, often computed in terms of days rather than months. Suppose, for example, that the three-month note illustrated above runs for 92 days (two 31-day months and one 30-day month). The total interest on the 92-day note would be $302.47 [($10,000)(.12)(92/365)], and the first 31-day month's interest would be $101.92 [($10,000)(.12)(31/365) or ($302.47)(31/92)]. Observe that daily interest complicates the arithmetic associated with interest calculations but does not alter the basic form of the calculations. To simplify interest computations, we will use monthly interest throughout this chapter.

[9] If the truck had been purchased on credit without interest, and if the note had been given sometime later to settle that account (as sometimes happens), then accounts receivable rather than sales revenue would receive the credit for $50,000.

When Dover pays the note three months later, Schleswig makes the following entry to record payment of the note plus three months' interest of $1,250 [($50,000)(.10)(3/12)]:

Cash	51,250	
Notes receivable		50,000
Interest revenue		1,250

If, at maturity, Dover had been unable to pay the note, the note would be said to be *dishonored* or *defaulted*. Schleswig would then make the following entry:

Accounts receivable, defaulted notes	51,250	
Notes receivable		50,000
Interest revenue		1,250

Despite the fact that the note was defaulted, this entry recognizes interest revenue earned to the maturity date. The entry also records the entire amount due (but unpaid) in accounts receivable, defaulted notes, on the assumption that the entire amount is collectible. If the amount of a defaulted note receivable is later determined to be uncollectible, it is then debited to allowance for uncollectible accounts.

Discounting Notes Receivable

Sometimes a lender will transfer a note to another party before maturity. Most notes are negotiable instruments in that they can be transferred from one party to another by endorsement. By endorsing the note, the endorser (or payee) can transfer his or her rights to receive payment for the note. Selling a note, rather than holding it to maturity, provides the seller with immediate access to the cash represented by the note. The buyer does not pay the full amount to be received at maturity, but instead pays the maturity amount less a discount. Hence, such sales of notes are called **discounting**. The discount is computed by using the following formula:

DISCOUNTING: The sale of a note receivable before maturity to a financial institution, such as a bank, at the note's maturity amount less a discount.

$$\text{Discount} = (\text{Maturity amount})(\text{Discount rate})(\text{Fraction of year})$$

The *discount rate* is the interest imposed by the buyer, expressed as an annual rate. It is important to note that the discount rate is applied to the maturity amount of a note, whereas the interest rate is applied to the principal.

    To illustrate, suppose that after one month Schleswig decides to discount the Dover note at a bank rather than wait the remaining two months for the payment of $51,250 at maturity. The bank charges a discount rate of 12 percent and computes the immediate payment to Schleswig as shown below. Observe that the discount is computed for two months, the time from the discount date to the maturity date.

Principal amount payable at maturity	$50,000
Interest payable at maturity [($50,000)(.10)(3/12)]	1,250
Maturity amount	$51,250
Discount withheld by bank [($51,250)(.12)(2/12)]	(1,025)
Proceeds, discounted note...............................	$50,225

Discounting the note requires the following journal entry by Schleswig:

Cash 50,225
    Notes receivable   50,000
    Interest revenue [$1,250 − $1,025]   225

Interest revenue of $225 is the excess of interest due at maturity over the discount withheld by the bank. When the discount exceeds the amount of interest due under the note, that excess is recorded as interest expense.

    Ordinarily, notes are endorsed *with recourse,* which means that the endorser retains responsibility for payment. If the maker of the note defaults, the endorser must pay the party to whom the note has been transferred. Occasionally, a note may be endorsed *without recourse.* In this case, the responsibility for collection in the event of default is transferred to the new holder of the note, leaving the endorser no longer liable for payment. The endorser of a note with recourse is said to be contingently liable for the amount due under the note. A **contingent liability** is an obligation that is dependent on the occurrence of future events to confirm the amount payable, the date of payment, the person to be paid, or the existence of the liability itself. In other words, a contingent liability is an obligation whose terms depend on future events. The amounts of contingent liabilities must be disclosed in the footnotes to a firm's financial statements.

CONTINGENT LIABILITY: An obligation whose amount, timing, or recipient depends on future events.

Notes Receivable in Financial Statements

The assets of financial institutions, such as banks and insurance companies, include substantial holdings of notes receivable. Specialized accounting standards guide the reporting of such notes receivable. The assets of nonfinancial institutions, such as retailers and manufacturers, also include notes receivable, but their notes usually represent a relatively small fraction of total assets.

    A note receivable held by a nonfinancial institution arising from a transaction with a customer is called a *trade note receivable.* A note receivable arising from a loan to an employee or from some other unusual loan is called a *special note receivable* and is usually listed separately and carefully explained in financial statements or the associated footnotes. Notes receivable also arise from transactions with financial institutions, governments, and other borrowers whose notes or notelike securities are held for investment purposes. We turn now to a discussion of short-term investments in securities, including investments in stocks and bonds as well as notes.

ACCOUNTING FOR SHORT-TERM INVESTMENTS

All securities held for investment can be classified as either short-term or long-term investments by applying two criteria: (1) marketability and (2) length of the intended holding period. *Marketability* refers to the ease with which a security can be sold and thereby converted into cash. A **marketable security** is one that has a determinable market value and is traded regularly in an active market. Accordingly, a marketable security is readily convertible into cash. The length of the intended holding period refers to the length of time the firm plans to hold the

MARKETABLE SECURITY: A security that has a determinable market value and is traded regularly in an active market.

security. If the firm intends to sell a marketable security within one year or the normal operating cycle of the business, whichever is longer, then the security is considered a *short-term investment.* If the firm anticipates holding the security for a longer time, then the security is said to be a *long-term investment.* A firm's short-term investments are reported among its current assets. Short-term investments must be marketable because nonmarketable securities may not be convertible into cash on short notice despite the intention of the firm to do so. Long-term investments and nonmarketable investments are reported among a firm's non-current assets.

Short-term and long-term investments require somewhat different accounting procedures, and in addition, accounting procedures differ for different types of securities. We conclude this chapter with an examination of accounting procedures for securities held as short-term investments. The accounting procedures for long-term investments are described in Chapter 14.

SHORT-TERM INVESTMENTS IN EQUITY SECURITIES

EQUITY SECURITIES: Ownership shares in another corporation in the form of capital stock.

Equity securities are shares of ownership in other corporations in the form of capital stock. The equity securities of most major corporations are marketable securities because they are regularly bought and sold (traded) on the New York Stock Exchange, the American Stock Exchange, or some other stock exchange. However, the equity securities of many small corporations and some large corporations are rarely traded. Such securities are nonmarketable and therefore cannot be classified as short-term investments. The following discussion illustrates accounting procedures for the acquisition, holding, and disposition of short-term investments in equity securities.

Accounting for the Cost of Equity Securities

Like other assets, investments in equity securities are recorded at cost when acquired. To illustrate, on August 1, Delphi Corporation acquired as a short-term investment 100 shares of Anderson Company's stock for $4,100 ($41 per share). The acquisition is recorded by the following entry:

Short-term investments.	4,100	
Cash		4,100

On September 30, Delphi Corporation received a cash dividend from Anderson Company of $.30 per share, which is recorded by the following entry:[10]

Cash	30	
Dividend income		30

On December 20, the market price of Anderson's stock had climbed to $49 per share, and Delphi decided to sell its entire holding. The following entry records the sale:

Cash	4,900	
Short-term investments.		4,100
Gain on sale of investments		800

[10] Dividend income should be recognized by investors at the dividend declaration date rather than the dividend payment date. When a cash dividend is declared in one year and paid in the following year, the investor should record the dividend declaration at year-end by a debit to dividends receivable and a credit to dividend income. In the following year, when the related cash is received, the investor should debit cash and credit dividends receivable.

The $800 gain will be included in Delphi Corporation's year-end net income, as will the $30 dividend received on September 30. In summary, this investment yielded two forms of income—dividends ($30) and a gain on sale ($800)—giving Delphi Corporation a profit of $830.

Lower-of-Cost-or-Market Adjustment

LOWER-OF-COST-OR-MARKET ADJUSTMENT: An adjusting entry that reduces the carrying amount of an asset from its cost to its lower market value and recognizes a corresponding loss on the income statement.

Although equity securities are recorded and carried at cost in the investment account, the account balance is adjusted when the end-of-period market value of the entire collection or portfolio of securities is below cost. This adjustment, which is called a **lower-of-cost-or-market adjustment,** reduces the asset account from cost to its lower market value and produces a corresponding loss on the income statement.

No adjustment is made if the market value of a portfolio has risen above cost. Although investors hope that the market value of their short-term portfolios will increase, the principal objective of short-term investments is to provide a return on funds that are temporarily available and may be needed at any time. In some cases, the cash needs of a firm may dictate the sale of short-term investments even though higher income might be produced by continuing to hold the portfolio. In this kind of decision environment, declines in market value assume a special importance because they reduce the amount of cash available on short notice. The lower-of-cost-or-market adjustment reflects the effects of such declines. This lower-of-cost-or-market adjustment is also an application of the conservatism convention.

To illustrate the lower-of-cost-or-market adjustment, first consider Delphi Corporation's short-term investment portfolio at December 31, 19X3. The acquisition dates, costs, and market values of the equity securities are as shown in Exhibit 8–7. Observe that the total market value of Delphi's portfolio at December 31, 19X3, is less than the total acquisition cost of the securities held on that date. The substantial increase in the market price of Ohio Foundry since its acquisition is more than offset by the substantial decrease in the market price of Indiana Enterprises, while the market price of Michigan Company is unchanged.

When the portfolio is viewed as a source of cash, the cost of Delphi's short-term investments overstates the amount of cash the portfolio could generate on December 31, 19X3. This deficiency of acquisition cost is accommodated by a lower-of-cost-or-market adjustment that allows Delphi Corporation to report short-term investments of $24,800 on its balance sheet at the end of 19X3, as shown in Exhibit 8–8.[11]

It is important to note that the amount of the lower-of-cost-or-market adjustment is calculated by using the portfolio's total market value and total cost. The rule is not applied on an item-by-item basis, as it is to inventories (see Chapter 7). Also note that the short-term investment account is not reduced directly. Rather, the $600 shortfall of market relative to cost [$25,400 − $24,800] is credited to a contra-asset account called *allowance to reduce short-term investments to market,* which is then subtracted from the investment account, as shown in Exhibit 8–8.

---

[11] The lower-of-cost-or-market adjustment described here follows financial accounting standards as set forth in *Statement of Financial Accounting Standards No. 12.*

EXHIBIT 8–7 INVESTMENT PORTFOLIO DATA

DELPHI CORPORATION
Short-Term Investment Portfolio
As of December 31, 19X3*

SECURITY	DATE OF ACQUISITION	ACQUISITION COST	MARKET VALUE AT 12/31/X3
Indiana Enterprises (100 shares)	6/20/X3	$ 6,700	$ 5,500
Michigan Company (100 shares)	3/3/X3	8,100	8,100
Ohio Foundry (100 shares)	11/20/X3	10,600	11,200
		$25,400	$24,800

* Anderson Company's stock is not included because it was sold on December 20, 19X3.

EXHIBIT 8–8 BALANCE SHEET PRESENTATION OF SHORT-TERM INVESTMENTS

DELPHI CORPORATION
Short-Term Investments
As of December 31, 19X3

Short-term investments (at cost).....................................	$25,400
Less: Allowance to reduce short-term investments to market...........	600
Short-term investments (at market).................................	$24,800*

* Alternatively, this information can be reported on a single line as:
Short-term investments at market (cost $25,400) $24,800

Adjustment of the Allowance

At the end of each period, the allowance account is adjusted upward or downward as needed to ensure that short-term investments are reported at the lower of cost or current market. When the current market value of the portfolio equals or exceeds the portfolio's cost, no allowance is required and the portfolio is reported at cost. In such cases, any allowance left over from the end of the previous period must be eliminated. When the current market value of the portfolio is below the portfolio's cost, the previously existing allowance (if any) must be adjusted upward or downward to equal the current excess of cost over market. Thus overstatements of the cash-generating potential of the portfolio are avoided by the lower-of-cost-or-market procedure, but understatements are not. Information about understatements is available to decision makers, however, since the current market value of the portfolio is disclosed in footnotes to the balance sheet.

UNREALIZED GAIN OR LOSS: A change in the market value of an investment that occurs prior to its sale.

Before sale, any potential loss or gain on investments, measured by changes in their market value relative to their cost, is said to be unrealized. An **unrealized gain or loss** on an investment is a change in the market value of the investment that occurs prior to its sale. The adjustment to the balance sheet allowance account at period-end gives rise to an income statement item called an *unrealized loss* (or a recovery of an unrealized loss). For example, Delphi Corporation makes the following adjusting entry at December 31, 19X3:

Unrealized loss on short-term investments	600	
Allowance to reduce short-term investments to market........		600

The adjustment is made for the entire year-end excess of cost over market ($600) because no allowance was established at the end of the previous year. If the allowance account had had a balance prior to the year-end adjustment (a balance carried forward from the previous year), then the amount of the adjustment would have to be altered accordingly. For example, had Delphi's allowance at December 31, 19X2, been $150 instead of zero, the December 31, 19X3, adjustment would have been $450 instead of $600. On the other hand, had Delphi's allowance at December 31, 19X2, been $720 instead of zero, then the December 31, 19X3, adjustment would have been as follows:

Allowance to reduce short-term investments to market	120	
Recovery of unrealized loss on short-term investments ..		120

In summary, if the existing allowance is larger than the allowance required at year-end or if an allowance exists but none is required at year-end, then the adjusting entry must reduce the existing allowance by a debit. In addition, the adjusting entry must recognize a recovery of unrealized loss, a credit that is reported as part of other income on the income statement.[12]

Realization of Gains and Losses

As we have noted, losses recognized under a lower-of-cost-or-market rule are unrealized; a gain or loss on securities is *realized* only when the related securities are sold. It is important to treat realized and unrealized gains and losses separately. Unrealized losses are calculated on the entire portfolio of securities held for investment and are recorded by the year-end adjustment procedure described above. Realized losses or gains on securities sold are measured by the difference between the cost and the selling price of those securities. Realized losses or gains are recorded without considering the balance in the allowance account.

Continuing our illustration, suppose that Delphi sells its entire portfolio in order to raise cash on January 20, 19X4. The sale brings $25,580 and is recorded with the following journal entry:

Cash	25,580	
Short-term investments.............................		25,400
Gain on sale of investments.........................		180

The realized gain of $180 is measured as the difference between the acquisition cost of Delphi's investments and the proceeds from the sale. The gain is recorded without regard to the unrealized loss of $600 recorded at December 31, 19X3.

---

[12] Notice that the amount recorded as a recovery of loss cannot exceed the existing balance of the allowance to reduce short-term investments to market. Recovery of any larger amount would not be merely a recovery of loss but would include recognition of an unrealized gain.

Since the unrealized loss never occurred and, assuming that the market value of any short-term investments held at December 31, 19X4, is not below cost, the following adjustment would be made at December 31, 19X4:

Allowance to reduce short-term investments to market   600
    Recovery of unrealized loss on short-term investments . .   600

To repeat, the recovery of an unrealized loss is not offset against the related realized gain. Rather, it is recorded in a separate recovery account that is reported as part of other income.

    The accounting procedures we have described for short-term investments in equity securities make up the cost method. The **cost method** is the method of accounting for investments that recognizes investment income as distributions (dividends and interest) are accrued and carries investments at cost, subject to a lower-of-cost-or-market adjustment. Since equity securities are subject to frequent and sometimes significant changes in market value, the lower-of-cost-or-market adjustment is of greater importance for equity securities than for debt securities, to which we now turn.

COST METHOD: The method of accounting for investments that recognizes investment income as distributions (dividends and interest) are accrued and carries investments at cost, subject to a lower-of-cost-or-market adjustment.

SHORT-TERM INVESTMENTS IN DEBT SECURITIES

DEBT SECURITIES: The interest-bearing debt of businesses and governments in the form of notes and bonds.

Debt securities represent the interest-bearing debt of businesses and governments in the form of notes and bonds. Investors purchase debt securities in order to receive interest income in addition to the repayment of the original amount or principal invested.

    A number of different debt securities may be purchased as short-term investments. *U.S. Treasury obligations* are the various interest-bearing notes, bonds, and bills issued by the federal government; *commercial paper* includes notes receivable issued by banks, insurance companies, savings institutions, and certain select industrial concerns; and *certificates of deposit* are negotiable certificates issued by commercial banks and savings institutions that promise a specified interest rate on funds held by the bank for a specified period. Although all these securities may be acquired at the date of their issuance and held until maturity, they are also regularly bought and resold by investors in well-organized securities markets.

    In general, all the securities described above are accounted for by the cost method and are recorded at acquisition cost. Under the cost method, interest income from short-term debt securities is recognized as the interest accrues to the investor. Since the market values of debt securities are usually less volatile than those of equity securities, financial accounting standards do not now require lower-of-cost-or-market adjustments for short-term investments in debt securities. Exercises and problems in this book will therefore not require lower-of-cost-or-market adjustments to short-term investments in debt securities. Chapter 14 describes additional aspects of accounting for short-term investments in corporate bonds.

SHORT-TERM INVESTMENTS AND CASH MANAGEMENT

Short-term investments are often an important part of a cash management program. Firms generally try to keep their bank cash balances to a minimum because most checking accounts earn only small amounts of interest; a larger return is usually available from short-term investments in securities. Accordingly, when cash balances exceed the minimum that is necessary and prudent for normal operations, firms usually invest the excess. If the cash surpluses are expected to be temporary, firms invest in securities and unrestricted savings accounts that are easily reconverted into cash. This use of short-term investments as a part of a cash management program is illustrated by the following analysis.

Ohio Wire is a medium-size manufacturer of cable and wire used in the construction of bridges and buildings. Since most basic construction occurs during the summer, the demand for Ohio Wire's products is seasonal. As a result, the firm tends to have surplus cash in the early months of each year. The company treasurer constructs a cash budget at the beginning of each year in an effort to determine in advance the periods in which cash will be available for short-term investment and the periods in which such investments will have to be liquidated. The budget shows that the treasurer anticipates the expenditure of cash at a steady rate of $300,000 per quarter. Budgeted cash receipts vary, however, according to the following schedule:

First quarter 19X6	$452,000
Second quarter 19X6	320,000
Third quarter 19X6	155,000
Fourth quarter 19X6	325,000
First quarter 19X7	527,000

Ohio Wire begins the year with a cash balance of $50,000, no short-term investments, and no short-term debt. The firm operates under the policy that the end-of-quarter cash balance should equal $50,000 plus the expected excess of disbursements over receipts, if any, during the next quarter. If receipts are expected to exceed disbursements during the next quarter, then the end-of-quarter cash balance should equal $50,000. The following questions might be asked concerning Ohio Wire's cash management policy:

1. *What addition to, or liquidation of, short-term investments should be made at the end of each quarter? Will short-term borrowing be necessary?*

Consider the calculation to be made at the beginning of the first quarter of 19X6: The cash balance on January 1 is $50,000, expected receipts for the first quarter are $452,000, and expected expenditures are $300,000, which will produce an end-of-first-quarter cash balance of $202,000 [$50,000 + $452,000 − $300,000]. Since receipts are expected to exceed expenditures during the second quarter, the end-of-first-quarter cash balance should equal $50,000. To reduce the cash balance to the desired level of $50,000, investments of $152,000 [$202,000 − $50,000] must be made during the first quarter. At the beginning of each quarter, the required investment, borrowing, or liquidation for the ensuing quarter is calculated in a similar way, as shown in the following schedule:

	FIRST QUARTER 19X6	SECOND QUARTER 19X6	THIRD QUARTER 19X6	FOURTH QUARTER 19X6
Calculation of ending balance before adjustment for investments, borrowings, or liquidations:				
Cash receipts	$452,000	$320,000	$155,000	$325,000
Cash disbursements	300,000	300,000	300,000	300,000
Excess (deficiency) of cash receipts	$152,000	$ 20,000	$(145,000)	$ 25,000
Beginning cash balance	50,000	50,000	195,000	50,000
Ending cash balance before adjustment	$202,000	$ 70,000	$ 50,000	$ 75,000
Calculation of required ending balance:				
Next quarter's deficiency of cash receipts	$ −0−	$145,000	$ −0−	$ −0−
Minimum cash balance	50,000	50,000	50,000	50,000
Required ending balance	$ 50,000	$195,000	$ 50,000	$ 50,000
Amount to invest (borrow or liquidate)	$152,000	$(125,000)	$ −0−	$ 25,000

In summary, the firm should plan to invest $152,000 in short-term securities during the first quarter, liquidate securities in the amount of $125,000 during the second quarter, neither buy nor sell securities during the third quarter, and invest $25,000 in securities during the fourth quarter. No short-term borrowing will be necessary. In some years, however, short-term investments may be insufficient to provide all the cash required, making short-term borrowing necessary. Such borrowing frequently takes place under a *line of credit,* an agreement between the company and its bank in which the bank promises to lend the company funds up to a specified limit and under specified terms.

2. *How did Ohio Wire determine its minimum cash balance to be $50,000?*

Formal decision-making techniques and models are available to assist in making such judgments, but it is also possible that Ohio Wire simply established the $50,000 minimum as a result of trial and error with a variety of cash management policies. Arrangements with banks also influence cash management policies. Banks sometimes require a minimum balance as compensation for service rendered to depositors; such *compensating balances* must be provided for in the formulation of a cash management policy and are usually disclosed in the footnotes to financial statements.

As we have shown, short-term investments are purchased with temporary surpluses of cash. The management of these investments must be coordinated with the management of cash and of the firm's other short-term assets and liabilities. Accordingly, the value and composition of short-term investment portfolios change continually in response to seasonal factors and other shifts in the business environment.

SUMMARY

Cash, receivables, and investments are financial assets that require both accurate accounting records and safeguards against misappropriation. Accuracy and security for such assets are aided by the system of internal control. Liquid assets are particularly vulnerable to misappropriation and error. In recognition of this fact, cash is usually kept in a bank account, which necessitates the periodic reconciliation of the firm's cash account and the bank account.

Credit cards and debit cards have replaced cash and checks in a large and growing number of retail sales transactions. Because cash collection and reimbursement practices differ among credit and debit cards, different accounting treatments are required. Notes receivable are financial assets that represent formal promises of borrowers to repay the amount borrowed at some future time. The lender is compensated by the inclusion of interest in the amount repaid. When a lender transfers a note to another party before its maturity, the note is said to be discounted. The calculation of interest for notes follows well-established rules, which are illustrated in the chapter.

Temporary accumulations of cash are frequently invested in securities that pay interest or dividends. Short-term investments in equity securities are recorded at cost but are subject to a lower-of-cost-or-market adjustment. Short-term investments in debt securities are also recorded at cost but usually do not require a lower-of-cost-or-market adjustment.

An appendix to the chapter describes petty cash accounts, special journals, and subsidiary ledgers—accounting devices that promote efficient record keeping and aid in the control of cash.

APPENDIX 8-1
THE STRUCTURE OF SPECIAL RECORDS AND CONTROL OF CASH

Accounting systems must provide controls that safeguard cash from misappropriation and erroneous representation in the records. As pointed out in the chapter, such controls are accomplished by carefully specifying each individual's authority and responsibility for cash and by providing records that enable managers to evaluate how employees handle cash. This appendix considers three special components of cash records that support the control of cash: petty cash accounts, subsidiary ledgers, and special journals.

PETTY CASH ACCOUNTS

Issuing checks to pay small bills is usually more costly than paying cash. To reduce such costs, an organization may establish a petty cash fund by issuing a check to a petty cash custodian, who then cashes the check and maintains a fund from which small claims are paid in cash. All expenditures from petty cash are recorded as they are made. When additional petty cash is required, the custodian presents a request for reimbursement to the organization, based on the expenditure record. Proper controls require that the request be accompanied by documents (invoices, sales slips, receipts, and so forth) to support every expenditure and that the documents be inspected by the organization before the custodian is reimbursed for petty cash expenditures.

The following illustration demonstrates the accounting for the establishment and replenishment of a petty cash fund: On January 1, Oregon Industries establishes a petty cash fund of $300 with Ms. Trout. Ms. Trout has been with the company for many years and has demonstrated an ability to maintain careful records. During January Ms. Trout makes the expenditures of petty cash shown in Exhibit 8-9. On January 31, Ms. Trout presents a record of all petty cash transactions for the month, together with related documents, and requests reimbursement. Company personnel (other than Ms. Trout) examine the documents to determine that they are authentic and that each transaction is supported by appropriate documentation. The company then issues a check to Ms. Trout for $260.90 to replenish the fund.

Oregon Industries makes the following journal entries pertaining to this petty cash fund:

Establishment of petty cash fund on January 1

Petty cash fund......................................	300.00	
Cash..		300.00

Replenishment of petty cash fund and recognition of expense on January 31

Office supplies expense ($30.00 + $28.70).................	58.70	
Postage expense ($7.00 + $8.20)........................	15.20	
Delivery expense	12.00	
Transportation-in.....................................	175.00	
Cash..		260.90

EXHIBIT 8–9   PETTY CASH EXPENDITURES DURING JANUARY

1/12	Hansen's Grocery (coffee)	$ 30.00
1/15	U.S. Postmaster (postage)	7.00
1/17	Northwest Taxi (parcel delivery)	12.00
1/19	Jorgensen Transit (transportation-in)	175.00
1/21	Mr. Washburn, Controller (reimbursement for postage)	8.20
1/25	Haugen Office Supply (special analysis paper)	28.70
	Total	$260.90

Although the expenditures of petty cash require entries in the records maintained by Ms. Trout, they are not recorded in Oregon Industries' accounting records until the fund is replenished. Also note that replenishment does not alter the balance of the petty cash fund on Oregon's records; the balance remains $300.00.

As an additional control measure, a company should periodically verify its petty cash balances by counting the cash in the hands of custodians. The amount of cash held by each custodian should equal the balance shown in the custodian's petty cash record.

SUBSIDIARY LEDGERS

SUBSIDIARY LEDGER: A ledger that provides supporting details for a specific account in the general ledger.

CONTROL ACCOUNT: An account in the general ledger that reports the total of the account balances of a subsidiary ledger.

Control accounts and subsidiary ledgers make record keeping easier when a large number of separate accounts form one financial statement account. For example, most firms that sell on credit have a large number of customers, each of which has a separate account with the firm. For each one of its customers, the firm maintains a separate account in a **subsidiary ledger;** a single **control account** in the general ledger reports the total of all the accounts in the subsidiary ledger. When a customer makes a purchase from the firm on credit, both the balance of the subsidiary ledger account for the customer and the balance of the control account are increased. Similarly, when a customer pays an outstanding account, both the balance in the subsidiary ledger account and the balance of the control account are decreased. The use of a subsidiary ledger and control account is illustrated in Exhibit 8–10, along with the credit sales journal, one of the special journals to which we now turn.

SPECIAL JOURNALS

Special journals represent another type of accounting record that supports both control objectives and record-keeping efficiency. A journal entry describes the effects of a transaction on the accounts of an entity. The journal entry names the accounts altered by the event and indicates the amount of the debit or credit to each account. The accounting equation, of course, requires that the debits in each entry must equal the credits.

Up to this point, we have assumed that each entity has a single general journal that lists each and every entry in chronological order. Although it is possible to maintain completely accurate accounts using a single general journal, it is usually inefficient to do so. The inefficiency is caused by the storage space consumed by the general journal and by the amount of posting activity that it requires. Many of the entries recorded in a firm's general journal will involve exactly the same accounts and will differ only in time and amount. When an entity has many entries that involve the same accounts, it is frequently possible to reduce the cost of record keeping by recording batches of similar entries in a

EXHIBIT 8–10   SPECIAL JOURNAL, GENERAL LEDGER, AND SUBSIDIARY LEDGER

WINDWORTH ENTERPRISES

Page 12

CREDIT SALES JOURNAL

DATE 19X4	CUSTOMER ACCOUNT NUMBER	CUSTOMER	TERMS	REF*	SALES INVOICE NUMBER	AMOUNT
January 3	78432	A. W. Jones	2/10, n/30	1	7822	1,760
January 3	65117	J. V. Lewis	1/15, n/25	2	6214	685
January 3	83998	H. T. Libby	3/10, n/40	2	6215	8,212
January 3	12471	C. B. James	net	1	7823	5,400
						16,057

GENERAL LEDGER

Accounts receivable		105
1/3	16,057	

Sales revenue		601
	1/3	16,057

SUBSIDIARY LEDGER, ACCOUNTS RECEIVABLE

12471—C. B. James	
1/3	5,400

65117—J. V. Lewis	
1/3	685

78432—A. W. Jones	
1/3	1,760

83998—H. T. Libby	
1/3	8,212

*"Ref" is an abbreviation for "reference." The Ref column is used here to indicate the cash register at which the sale was made.

special journal at regular intervals. Also at regular intervals (say, every month, week, or day), the special journal entries are collected and posted to the ledger accounts. The use of special journals not only reduces record-keeping and posting effort but also supports the system of internal control over cash and other assets.

Since the number of special journals used by a firm and the form of each journal depend on the firm's particular transactions, special journals vary considerably from one firm to another. Many businesses maintain the following special journals:

1. *Credit sales journal:* To record all entries that involve debits to customer accounts receivable

2. *Cash receipts journal:* To record all entries that involve debits to cash

3. *Credit purchases journal:* To record all entries that involve credits to accounts payable

4. *Cash payments journal:* To record all entries that involve credits to cash

EXHIBIT 8–11   CASH RECEIPTS JOURNAL

WINDWORTH ENTERPRISES

Page 48

				DEBITS		CREDITS			
							CREDIT CARD RECEIVABLES		
DATE 19X4	ACCOUNT TITLE	REF*	EXPLANATION	CASH	OTHER ACCOUNTS	IN-HOUSE	OUTSIDE-COMPANY	SALES REVENUE	OTHER ACCOUNTS
March 3	M. J. Stevens	1171	On account	300		285			
	Sales discount revenue	4210							15
March 3	American Express			1,750			1,750		
March 3	Sales revenue	4100	Per cash register	3,110				3,110	
March 3	Notes payable	2020	90-day note to Ohio Federal	4,000					4,000
				9,160		285	1,750	3,110	4,015

*"Ref" is an abbreviation for "reference." This column contains the number of the individual customer's account in the accounts receivable subsdiary ledger or the general ledger account number, depending on the type of transaction being recorded.

Let us examine the use of these four special journals by Windworth Enterprises. Windworth maintains a special journal to record credit sales (see Exhibit 8 – 10). This journal is posted to the general ledger at the end of each day. The total of daily credit sales ($16,057 for January 3) is debited to accounts receivable and credited to sales revenue. Instead of this single posting entry on January 3, four posting entries would be required if credit sales were recorded directly in the general journal. Note that each line in the special journal is also the basis for a debit to an individual customer account in the subsidiary ledger for accounts receivable. These entries are required whether credit sales are recorded in a special journal or in the general journal.

One advantage of the credit sales journal is that the four entries shown in Exhibit 8 – 10 require less space (fewer characters) to record than they would in a general journal. The special journal is also useful because it allows credit sales to be recorded separately from other transactions. An accounting system in which both credit sales and cash collections are recorded by a single person is vulnerable to the misappropriation of cash. However, when the two record-keeping functions are carried out by different individuals, it is considerably more difficult to conceal the misappropriation of cash by making false entries in accounts receivable and related subsidiary accounts.

A cash receipts journal is illustrated in Exhibit 8 – 11. This journal is set up for all entries that involve debits to cash, and special columns are provided for frequent credits to noncash accounts as well. These columns include credits to receivables under in-house and outside-company credit cards, sales revenue, and other receivables.

EXHIBIT 8–12   CREDIT PURCHASES JOURNAL

WINDWORTH ENTERPRISES

Page 17

CREDIT PURCHASES JOURNAL

DATE 19X4	SUPPLIER ACCOUNT NUMBER	SUPPLIER ACCOUNT CREDITED	TERMS	PURCHASE ORDER NUMBER	PURCHASES DEBITS/ ACCOUNTS PAYABLE CREDITS
May 1	63815	Clair Enterprises	2/10, n/30	3698	3,136
May 2	91081	Robert Products	1/15, n/25	3701	1,386
May 4	66092	Clifford, Inc.	3/10, n/40	3702	2,813
May 5	84121	Howard Services	2/15, n/35	3711	3,626
May 5	87738	Kenneth Company	net	3713	2,400
					13,361

At the end of the day on March 3, Windworth's cash receipts journal is the basis for the following entries in the general ledger:

A debit to cash of $9,160
A credit to accounts receivable, in-house credit cards of $285
A credit to accounts receivable, outside-company credit cards of $1,750
A credit to sales revenue of $3,110
A credit to sales discount revenue of $15
A credit to notes payable of $4,000

In addition, the March 3 cash receipts journal is the basis for a credit of $285 to the account of M. J. Stephens in the subsidiary ledger for in-house credit cards accounts receivable.

Windworth's credit purchases journal is illustrated in Exhibit 8–12. This journal is posted to the general ledger once each week. The total of the weekly purchases ($13,361 for the first week in May) is posted as a debit to purchases and a credit to accounts payable in the amount of $13,361. Each entry in this special journal is also posted to the individual supplier account in Windworth's subsidiary ledger for accounts payable.

Windworth's cash payments journal (see Exhibit 8–13) is posted to the general and subsidiary ledgers at the end of each day. This special journal provides the basis for debits to accounts payable as well as other asset, liability, or expense accounts. The total of debits to accounts payable and the total of credits to cash are posted to the general ledger. Some of the entries in this special journal are also posted to the accounts payable subsidiary ledger and other appropriate subsidiary ledgers.

Accounting records are costly to maintain, and every effort should be made to design records that gather accounting data as efficiently as possible. In addition, these records should be a part of the system of controls for the firm's assets. Frequently, the need to control assets and the need for information are compatible and are well served by the same set of records. In other cases, however, the need to control assets may require records that would otherwise be unnecessary. In such instances, a judgment must be made as to whether the value of the controls justifies the additional record-keeping cost.

EXHIBIT 8–13   **CASH PAYMENTS JOURNAL**

WINDWORTH ENTERPRISES

Page 115

CASH PAYMENTS JOURNAL

DATE 19X4	CHECK NUMBER	PAYEE	OTHER ACCOUNT DEBITED	REF*	DEBITS ACCOUNTS PAYABLE	DEBITS OTHER ACCOUNTS	CREDITS CASH
June 7	4362	Eugene Company		E144	3,430		3,430
June 7	4363	Curtis Insurance	Insurance expense	5230		7,300	7,300
June 7	4364	National Bank	Interest expense	6100		4,000	4,000
			Notes payable	2710		80,000	80,000
June 7	4365	Cee Machines	Equipment	1230		36,150	36,150
June 7	4366	Hebner Products		H088	7,350		7,350
					10,780		138,230

*"Ref" is an abbreviation for "reference." This column contains the number of the individual customer's account in the accounts payable subsidiary ledger or the general ledger account number, depending on the type of transaction being recorded.

KEY TERMS

ACCOUNT RECEIVABLE (p. 331)
BANK RECONCILIATION (p. 321)
CASH OVER AND SHORT (p. 320)
CONTINGENT LIABILITY (p. 334)
CONTROL ACCOUNT (p. 343)
COST METHOD (p. 339)
CREDIT CARD (p. 327)
DEBIT CARD (p. 330)
DEBT SECURITIES (p. 339)
DEPOSIT IN TRANSIT (p. 322)
DISCOUNTING (p. 333)
EQUITY SECURITIES (p. 335)
FACTORING (p. 331)

INTEREST (p. 332)
LIQUIDITY OF A FIRM (p. 318)
LIQUIDITY OF AN ASSET (p. 318)
LOWER-OF-COST-OR-MARKET ADJUSTMENT (p. 336)
MARKETABLE SECURITY (p. 334)
NOTE RECEIVABLE (p. 331)
OUTSTANDING CHECK (p. 322)
PRINCIPAL (p. 332)
SUBSIDIARY LEDGER (p. 343)
TRADE RECEIVABLE (p. 331)
UNREALIZED GAIN OR LOSS (p. 338)

QUESTIONS

Q8-1. How are the liquidity of an asset and the liquidity of a firm related?

Q8-2. Why does a firm give particular attention to internal controls for cash?

Q8-3. How does separation of duties support an effective system of internal control?

Q8-4. What items, in addition to currency and coins, are included in cash as reported on a balance sheet?

Q8-5. How is the cash over and short account used?

Q8-6. Explain how to prepare a reconciliation of a cash account and its associated bank account.

Q8-7. Describe the potential sources of difference between a cash account and its associated bank account.

Q8-8. What kinds of bank reconciliation items require the firm to prepare adjusting entries?

Q8-9. How does a merchant account for credit card sales?

Q8-10. How much interest will be due at maturity for each of the following interest-bearing notes?

	PRINCIPAL	MONTHS TO MATURITY	ANNUAL INTEREST RATE
a)	$10,000	2	12%
b)	42,000	5	14
c)	18,000	4	13
d)	37,000	6	11

Q8-11. A business borrows $1,000, giving a note that requires repayment of the amount borrowed in two payments of $600 each, one at the end of each of the next two 6-month periods. Calculate the total interest on the note. What is the principal amount of the note?

Q8-12. A business borrows $1,000, giving a note that requires an interest rate of 12 percent per year and repayment of principal plus interest in a single payment at the end of one year. Calculate the total interest on the note. What is the amount of the single payment?

Q8-13. "Non-interest-bearing notes do not bear interest." Is this statement correct? Why or why not?

Q8-14. What is the maturity amount of a note?

Q8-15. What is a defaulted note?

Q8-16. What is meant by discounting a note receivable?

Q8-17. What is the meaning of discounting a note receivable with recourse? What is the relationship between discounting with recourse and contingent liabilities?

Q8-18. Why do companies hold short-term investments?

Q8-19. Explain how to apply the lower-of-cost-or-market procedure to short-term investments in equity securities.

APPENDIX QUESTIONS

Q8-20. What is the purpose of a petty cash fund?

Q8-21. Explain how a subsidiary ledger and its associated control account are used.

Q8-22. Describe the difference between a general journal and a special journal.

EXERCISES

E8-23. LIQUIDITY Portions of the financial statements for Aaron Corporation and Zygmunt Enterprises are reproduced below. Aaron and Zygmunt sell similar products to similar customers.

	AARON CORPORATION	ZYGMUNT ENTERPRISES
Cash	$ 16,300	$ 6,950
Accounts receivable	487,810	613,220
Inventory	607,530	206,150
Short-term investments in marketable securities	6,900	311,830
Total current assets	$1,118,540	$1,138,150
Accounts payable	$ 639,750	$ 194,170
Rent payable	286,100	58,400
Interest payable	193,420	225,910
Total current liabilities	$1,119,270	$ 478,480
Long-term liabilities	$ 950,000	$1,200,000
Net income	$ 31,210	$ 257,300

REQUIRED:

Identify which of these two firms appears to have greater liquidity. Explain your choice.

E8-24. INTERNAL CONTROL OF CASH   Edward Thompson, a longtime employee of a small grocery wholesaler, is responsible for maintaining the company's cash records and for opening the daily mail, through which the company receives about 40 percent of its daily cash receipts. Virtually all cash received by mail is in the form of checks made payable to the company. Thompson is also responsible for preparing deposits of currency and checks for the bank at the end of each day.

REQUIRED:

1. Explain briefly how Thompson might be able to misappropriate some of the company's cash receipts.

2. What internal control procedures would you recommend to prevent this misappropriation?

E8-25. COMPONENTS OF CASH   The office manager for Bullock Products has accumulated the following information at the end of a recent year:

ITEM	AMOUNT
Accounts receivable.	$16,450
American Express receipts not yet transmitted to American Express	580
Change for cash registers (currency and coin)	2,500
Amount on deposit in checking account	9,280
Amount on deposit in savings account	25,000
Balance in petty cash.	300
Checks written by customers but not yet deposited in bank.	430
Checks written by Bullock but not yet presented at bank for payment.	670
Deposit in transit.	1,240
IOU from Gerry Bullock, company president	1,000
MasterCard receipts not yet deposited in bank	460
Notes receivable	10,000
NSF check written by Johnson Company	320
Prepaid postage.	250

REQUIRED:

Calculate the amount for cash in Bullock's balance sheet.

E8-26. CASH COLLECTIONS   Walker Department Store accepts cash payments on its in-house credit card at its service desk. On a recent day, the service desk cash register tape reported collections on accounts receivable in the amount of $2,247.63. Actual cash in the register (after deducting and removing the opening change amount of $50) was $2,238.48, which was deposited in the firm's bank account.

REQUIRED:

Prepare a journal entry to record these cash collections.

E8-27. CASH OVER AND SHORT   Miller Enterprises deposits all cash received during each day at the end of the day. Miller deposited $12,730 on October 3 and $15,610 on October 4. Cash register records and other documents supporting the deposits are summarized as follows:

	10/3	10/4
Cash sales	$ 4,072	$ 5,405
Collections on account	8,650	10,212
Total receipts.	$12,722	$15,617

REQUIRED:

1. Calculate the amount of cash over or cash short for each day.

2. Prepare the journal entry to record the receipt and deposit of cash on October 3.

3. Prepare the journal entry to record the receipt and deposit of cash on October 4.

E8-28. BANK RECONCILIATION   Johnson Corporation's bank statement for October reports an ending balance of $6,248, whereas Johnson's cash account shows a balance of $5,680 on October 31. The following additional information is available:

a) A $165 deposit made on October 31 was not recorded by the bank until November.

b) At the end of October, outstanding checks total $792.

c) The bank statement shows bank service charges of $20 not yet recorded by the company.

d) The company erroneously recorded for $397 a check actually written and paid by the bank for $379.

e) A $57 check from a customer, deposited by the company on October 29, was returned with the bank statement for lack of funds.

REQUIRED:

Prepare the October bank reconciliation for Johnson Corporation.

E8-29. BANK RECONCILIATION   The cash account for Fleming Company contains the following information for April:

Cash balance, 3/31		$ 3,500
Cash received during April		21,400
		$24,900
Cash disbursements during April:		
Check 7164	$11,000	
Check 7165	1,800	
Check 7166	3,900	
Check 7167	6,100	22,800
Cash balance, 4/30		$ 2,100

The bank statement for April contains the following information:

Bank balance, 3/31		$11,800
Add: Deposits during April		21,400
		$33,200
Less: Checks paid during April		
Check 7162	$ 5,200	
Check 7163	3,100	
Check 7164	11,000	
Check 7165	1,800	21,100
Bank balance, 4/30		$12,100

REQUIRED:

1. Identify the outstanding checks at April 30.

2. Prepare the reconciliation of the bank and cash account balances at April 30.

3. Identify the outstanding checks at March 31.

4. Prepare the reconciliation of the bank and cash account balances at March 31.

E8-30. BANK RECONCILIATION   Valentine Investigations has the following information for its cash account:

Balance, 1/31	$ 5,030
Deposits during February	93,160
Checks written during February	92,270

Valentine's bank statement for February contained the following information:

Balance per bank, 1/31		$ 6,730
Add: February deposits		90,190
		$96,920
Less: Checks paid in February.	$89,790	
Bank service charge	80	
Debit memo (electric bill).	630	90,500
Balance per bank, 2/28		$ 6,420

A comparison of company records with the bank statement provided the following data:

	AT 1/31	AT 2/28
Deposits in transit	$ 510	$3,480
Outstanding checks	2,210	4,690

REQUIRED:

1. Prepare a bank reconciliation.

2. Prepare adjusting entries for Valentine based on the information developed in the bank reconciliation.

E8-31.   ADJUSTING ENTRIES FROM A BANK RECONCILIATION   Cooper Advisory Services identified the following items on its October reconciliation that may require adjusting entries:

a) A deposit of $260 was recorded in Cooper's accounting records but not on the October 31 bank statement.

b) A check for $6,430 was outstanding at October 31.

c) Included with the bank statement was a check for $250 written by Hooper Advertising Services. The bank had, in error, deducted this check from Cooper's account.

d) Bank service charges were $120.

e) An NSF check written by one of Cooper's customers in the amount of $1,290 was returned by the bank with Cooper's bank statement.

REQUIRED:

For each of these five items, prepare an adjusting entry for Cooper's journal, if any is required.

E8-32.   RECORDING SALES TRANSACTIONS   Customers of Cheryl's Specialty Shops may pay for purchases with cash, national credit cards, and Cheryl's own credit card. On August 19, Cheryl's made sales as follows:

Cash sales	$20,540
Credit sales:	
American Express credit card	15,210
Cheryl's own credit card	47,380
Discover credit card.	4,250
Visa (bank credit card).	12,330
MasterCard (bank credit card).	10,970

Bank credit cards have a 4.3 percent merchant's charge. Outside-company credit cards have a 4 percent merchant's charge.

REQUIRED:

1. Prepare the journal entry to record sales for August 19.

2. From the viewpoint of Cheryl's Specialty Shops, what are the advantages and disadvantages of each of the three types of credit cards?

E8-33. ACCOUNTING FOR NOTES RECEIVABLE   Tucker Products sold a machine to Thomas, Inc., in exchange for a five-month, $39,000, 11 percent note receivable. After holding the note for two months, Tucker discounted the note (with recourse) at its bank. The bank used a discount rate of 12 percent. At the end of five months, Thomas paid the bank the maturity amount of the note.

REQUIRED:

Prepare the necessary entries for Tucker's journal to record the transactions described above.

E8-34. DISCOUNTING NOTES RECEIVABLE   On February 1, Anderson, Inc., accepts an eight-month, $12,000, 11 percent note from a customer in lieu of a $12,000 cash payment on an account receivable from the customer. Three months later, on May 1, Anderson discounts the note (with recourse) at its bank. The bank charges a discount rate of 13 percent.

REQUIRED:

1. Prepare the journal entry to record acceptance of the note on February 1.
2. Calculate the amount received from the bank on May 1.
3. Prepare the journal entry to record discounting the note with recourse.
4. What does the term *with recourse* mean in conjunction with the discounted note?

E8-35. RECORDING NOTES RECEIVABLE: ISSUANCE, PAYMENT, AND DEFAULT   Marydale Products permits its customers to defer payment by giving personal notes instead of cash. All the notes bear interest at a rate of 12 percent per year and require the customer to pay the entire note in a single payment six months after issuance. Consider the following transactions, which describe Marydale's experience with two such notes:

a) On January 31, Marydale accepts a six-month, 12 percent note from customer A in lieu of a $3,600 cash payment for merchandise delivered on that day.
b) On February 28, Marydale accepts a six-month, $2,400, 12 percent note from customer B in lieu of a $2,400 cash payment.
c) On July 31, customer A pays the entire note plus interest in cash.
d) On August 31, customer B is unable to pay and defaults on the note.

REQUIRED:

Prepare the journal entries required to record transactions **a** through **d** in Marydale's records.

E8-36. RECORDING TRANSACTIONS IN SHORT-TERM MARKETABLE SECURITIES   Morton Products had no investment in short-term marketable equity securities at January 1, 19X4. During 19X4 Morton engaged in the following marketable security transactions:

a) Purchased 400 shares of Sterling Company stock for $24 per share.
b) Purchased 600 shares of Burt Corporation stock for $32 per share.
c) Received a $2-per-share dividend on the Sterling stock.
d) Sold 250 shares of the Sterling stock for $27 per share.

At the end of 19X4, the Sterling stock had a market value of $26 per share, and the Burt stock had a market value of $29 per share.

REQUIRED:

1. Prepare journal entries for each of the four transactions.
2. If necessary, prepare a journal entry to recognize the December 31, 19X4, market values.
3. Assume that Morton sells the remaining Sterling stock for $25 per share and all the Burt stock for $30 per share early in 19X5. Prepare a journal entry to record this sale.

E8-37. CHANGING THE ALLOWANCE TO REDUCE SHORT-TERM INVESTMENT TO MARKET   Perry Corporation has the following information for its portfolio of short-term marketable equity securities at the end of the past four years:

DATE	PORTFOLIO COST	PORTFOLIO MARKET VALUE	ALLOWANCE NEEDED
12/31/X2	$162,300	$153,800	$8,500
12/31/X3	109,600	106,200	3,400
12/31/X4	148,900	151,300	–0–
12/31/X5	138,700	139,000	–0–

REQUIRED:

Prepare the journal entries, if necessary, to adjust the allowance account at the end of 19X3, 19X4, and 19X5.

E8-38. RECORDING INVESTMENTS IN SHORT-TERM DEBT SECURITIES   On September 1, 19X2, Chambers Corporation purchased a marketable debt security for $10,000 as a short-term investment of temporarily idle cash. The security earns interest at a rate of 15 percent per year and will pay all interest and principal on its maturity date, August 31, 19X3. On December 31, 19X2, the end of Chambers' accounting period, the security has a market value of $9,425. This security is held to maturity and is Chambers' only short-term investment.

REQUIRED:

1. Prepare Chambers' journal entries related to the security on September 1, 19X2; December 31, 19X2; and August 31, 19X3, respectively.
2. How would the security be presented in the financial statements issued for 19X2?

E8-39. ALLOWANCES FOR SHORT-TERM INVESTMENTS   McCarthy Corporation's allowance to reduce short-term investments to market is $7,200 on December 31, before the lower-of-cost-or-market adjustment. The cost and market value of the short-term investment portfolio at December 31 are $120,000 and $117,000, respectively.

REQUIRED:

Prepare the adjusting entry, if any, to adjust the allowance at year-end.

E8-40. COST METHOD FOR SHORT-TERM INVESTMENTS   Williams Corporation acquired the following equity securities during 19X5:

200 shares of Southwestern Company capital stock................... $14,600
500 shares of Montgomery Products capital stock................... 14,500

During 19X5, Southwestern paid a dividend of $1.20 per share, and Montgomery paid a dividend of $1.80 per share. At December 31, 19X5, the Southwestern stock has a market value of $75 per share, and the Montgomery stock has a market value of $25 per share.

REQUIRED:

1. Prepare entries for Williams's journal to record these two investments and the receipt of the dividends.
2. Calculate the market value of Williams's short-term investment portfolio at December 31, 19X5.
3. If a lower-of-cost-or-market adjustment is required at December 31, 19X5, prepare the necessary journal entry. If no adjustment is required, explain why.

E8-41.   USING THE COST METHOD FOR SHORT-TERM INVESTMENTS   Maxwell Company engaged in the following transactions involving short-term investments:

a) Purchased 200 shares of Bartco stock for $12,800.

b) Received a $1.60-per-share dividend on the Bartco stock.

c) Sold 40 shares of the Bartco stock for $61 per share.

d) Purchased 380 shares of Newton stock for $20,900.

e) Received a dividend of $1.00 per share on the Newton stock.

At December 31, the Bartco stock has a market value of $60 per share, and the Newton stock has a market value of $59 per share.

REQUIRED:

1. Prepare entries for Maxwell's journal to record these transactions.

2. Calculate the market value of Maxwell's short-term investment portfolio at December 31.

3. If a lower-of-cost-or-market adjustment is required at December 31, prepare the necessary journal entry. If no adjustment is required, explain why.

APPENDIX EXERCISES

E8-42.   RECORDING PETTY CASH ACCOUNT TRANSACTIONS   During March, Anderson Company engaged in the following transactions involving its petty cash fund:

a) On March 1, Anderson Company established the petty cash fund by issuing a check for $400 to the fund custodian.

b) On March 4, the custodian paid $176 out of petty cash for freight charges on new furniture.

c) On March 12, the custodian paid $87 out of petty cash for office supplies.

d) On March 22, the custodian paid $22 out of petty cash for express mail services for reports sent to the Environmental Protection Agency.

e) On March 25, the custodian filed a claim for reimbursement of petty cash expenditures during the month totaling $285.

f) On March 31, Anderson issued a check for $285 to the custodian, replenishing the fund for expenditures during the month.

REQUIRED:

Prepare the journal entries required to record the petty cash account transactions that occurred during the month of March.

E8-43.   CREDIT SALES JOURNAL   Efficient Products, a retailer of office furniture, records all credit sales in a special journal that summarizes credit sales and enables a single entry to be posted for each day. The following credit sales were made on April 12:

a) Invoice 8778: $2,110 (2/10, n/30) to Lotus Manufacturing (customer account number 935) on account.

b) Invoice 8779: $1,789 (net) to Taxus Supply (customer account number 734) on account.

c) Invoice 8780: $794 (2/10, n/30) to Henry Spencer (customer account number 235) on account.

REQUIRED:

Following the format illustrated in Appendix 8 – 1, prepare the credit sales journal for April 12. (Since Efficient Products has just one cash register, you may omit the reference column.)

E8-44. POSTING TO A SUBSIDIARY LEDGER   Using the procedures illustrated in Appendix 8–1 and the data from Exercise 8-43, prepare an accounts receivable subsidiary ledger and post the credit sales to accounts in both the subsidiary ledger and the general ledger.

PROBLEMS

P8-45. INTERNAL CONTROL FOR CASH   After comparing cash register tapes with inventory records, the accountant for Benning Convenience Stores is concerned that someone at one of the stores is not recording some of that store's cash sales and is stealing the cash from the unreported sales.

REQUIRED:

1. Explain why a comparison of sales and inventory records would reveal a situation in which cash sales are not being recorded and cash from those sales is being misappropriated.
2. Describe how an employee might be able to steal cash from sales.
3. What internal control procedure would you recommend be employed to make the theft you described in (2) more difficult?

P8-46. ACCOUNTING FOR CASH RECEIPTS   Pence Company had the following data from its cash registers for a recent day:

	CASH SALES PER REGISTER TAPE	CASH IN REGISTER*
Register 1	$12,656.12	$12,649.81
Register 2	11,429.57	11,432.16
Register 3	11,591.18	11,590.18

* After deducting and removing the $60 opening change amount for each register.

Pence deposits its cash receipts in its bank account daily.

REQUIRED:

Prepare a journal entry to record these cash sales.

P8-47. BANK RECONCILIATION   Shortly after July 31, Morse Corporation received a bank statement containing the following information:

DATE	CHECKS			DEPOSITS	BALANCE
6/30 Beginning balance					7,958
7/1				1,200	9,158
7/2	620	550	344	12,500	20,144
7/3	35	8,100			12,009
7/5	311	97	4,000	9,100	16,701
7/9	4,500	790	286		11,125
7/12	34	7,100			3,991
7/15	634	1,880		7,000	8,477
7/19	3,780	414			4,283
7/24	1,492	649			2,142
7/29	350	677*		4,620	5,735
7/31	575	18†			5,142

* NSF check.
† Bank service charge.

December cash transactions and balances on Morse's records are shown in the following T-account:

Cash

Balance, 6/60.	$ 7,609				

Date	Amount Deposited	Check Number	Check Amount	Check Number	Check Amount
7/1	$12,500	176	$8,100	186	$ 1,880
7/5	9,100	177	97	187	634
7/15	7,000	178	4,000	188	3,780
7/29	4,620	179	311	189	649
7/30	2,050	180	7,100	190	1,492
		181	4,500	191	37
Total deposits	$35,270	182	790	192	350
		183	34	193	575
		184	286	194	227
		185	414	195	1,123
				Total disbursements	$36,379

Balance, 7/31.	$ 6,500

REQUIRED:

1. Prepare a bank reconciliation for July.

2. Prepare the adjusting entries made by Morse Corporation as a result of this reconciliation process.

3. What amount is reported as cash on the balance sheet at July 31?

P8-48. BANK RECONCILIATION   Raymond Corporation received the bank statement shown at the top of page 357 for the month of October 19X3:

The cash in bank account of Raymond Corporation provides the following information:

Date	Item	Debit	Credit	Balance
10/1	Balance from 9/30			6,553.38
10/2	Check #1908		321.70	6,231.68
10/5	Check #1909		905.36	5,326.32
10/6	Check #1910		100.20	5,226.12
10/6	Check #1911		60.00	5,166.12
10/7	Check #1912		38.11	5,128.01
10/12	Deposit #411	4,000.00		9,128.01
10/15	Check #1913		516.11	8,611.90
10/16	Check #1914		309.24	8,302.66
10/17	Check #1915		431.15	7,871.51
10/17	Check #1916		21.72	7,849.79
10/18	Deposit #412	2,850.63		10,700.42
10/18	Check #1917		106.39	10,594.03
10/20	Check #1918		63.89	10,530.14
10/20	Check #1919		3,108.42	7,421.72
10/23	Check #1920		111.90	7,309.82
10/25	Check #1921		88.90	7,220.92
10/29	Check #1922		1,803.77	5,417.15
10/30	Check #1923		284.77	5,132.38
10/31	Check #1924		628.32	4,504.06
10/31	Deposit #413	3,408.20		7,912.26

Total Account Bank Statement

RAYMOND CORPORATION
1989 BRUIN WAY
CHICAGO, ILLINOIS 60601

ACCOUNT NUMBER 10-3894-6
STATEMENT DATE   10/31/X3

DATE OF LAST STATEMENT				9/30/X3	
BALANCE AS SHOWN ON PREVIOUS STATEMENT				$ 4,831.50	
NUMBER OF DEPOSITS OR CREDITS				3	
NUMBER OF CHECKS OR DEBITS				20	
TOTAL OF DEPOSITS AND OTHER CREDITS				$ 9,820.81	
TOTAL OF CHECKS AND OTHER DEBITS				$ 9,340.61	
SERVICE CHARGE				$ 20.00	
BALANCE AS OF CURRENT DATE				$ 5,311.70	

CHECKS AND OTHER DEPOSITS			DEPOSITS AND OTHER CREDITS	DATE	BALANCE
1,204.50			2,970.18	10/2	6,597.18
43.80	321.70			10/4	6,231.68
905.36				10/8	5,326.32
100.20	60.00	38.11		10/10	5,128.01
			4,000.00	10/13	9,128.01
290.45 NSF*				10/14	8,837.56
516.11	309.24			10/17	8,012.21
106.39	431.15	21.72	2,850.63	10/19	10,303.58
3,108.42				10/21	7,195.16
63.89				10/23	7,131.27
290.00 DM†	111.90			10/25	6,729.37
88.90				10/27	6,640.47
1,308.77				10/31	5,331.70
20.00 SC§					5,311.70

```
*NSF = Not sufficient funds
†DM  = Debit memo
§SC  = Service charge
```

The items on the bank statement are correct. The debit memo is for the payment by the bank of Raymond's office furniture rent for October.

REQUIRED:

1. Prepare a bank reconciliation. (Hint: There is one transposition error in the cash account.)

2. Prepare adjusting entries based on the bank reconciliation.

3. What amount is reported for cash in bank in the balance sheet at October 31?

P8-49. BANK RECONCILIATION   The cash account of Dixon Products reveals the following information:

Cash			
Balance, 4/30	11,800		
Deposits during May	37,600	Checks written during May	41,620

The bank statement for May contains the following information:

Bank balance, 4/30		$11,750
Add: Deposits during May.		37,250
		$49,000
Less: Checks paid during May.	$40,230	
Less: NSF check from Frolin, Inc..	190	
Less: Bank service charges.	40	40,460
Bank balance, 5/31		$ 8,540

A comparison of detailed company records with the bank statement indicates the following information:

	AT 4/30	AT 5/31
Deposit in transit	$800	$1,150
Outstanding checks	750	2,140

The bank amounts are determined to be correct.

REQUIRED:

1. Prepare a bank reconciliation for May.
2. Prepare the adjusting entries made by Dixon as a result of the reconciliation process.
3. What amount is reported for cash on the balance sheet at May 31?

P8-50. ACCOUNTING FOR SALES   Judy's College Shirts sells sweatshirts with imprinted college logos in Honey Creek Mall. At the end of a recent day, Judy's cash register included credit card documents for the following sales amounts:

MasterCard	$493.56
Visa	371.93
American Express	448.74

The merchant's charges are 3.5 percent for MasterCard and Visa and 3.8 percent for American Express. Judy's also had cash sales of $2,390.41 and $1,300.50 of sales on credit to Rampdan Services, a local business.

REQUIRED:

Prepare a journal entry to record these sales.

P8-51. ACCOUNTING FOR NOTES RECEIVABLE   Yarnell Electronics sells computer systems to small businesses. During 19X2 Yarnell engaged in the following activities involving notes receivable:

a) On February 1, Yarnell sold a $5,000 system to Ross Company. Ross gave Yarnell a six-month, 11 percent note as payment.

b) On March 1, Yarnell sold an $8,000 system to Searfoss, Inc. Searfoss gave Yarnell a nine-month, 10 percent note as payment.

c) On April 1, Yarnell discounted both the Ross and Searfoss notes with recourse at its bank. The bank used a 12 percent discount rate.

d) On August 1, Ross defaulted on its note. Yarnell paid its bank the maturity amount of the note and assumed responsibility for collection.

e) On August 15, Yarnell decided that the Ross note was uncollectible and wrote it off.

f) On December 1, Searfoss paid the amount due on its note to the bank.

REQUIRED:

Prepare entries for Yarnell Electronics' journal to record these transactions.

P8-52. NOTES RECEIVABLE AT YEAR-END   You have the following information for Douglas Corporation's notes receivable at December 31, 19X5:

MAKER OF NOTE	DATE ISSUED	MATURITY	AMOUNT	RATE	STATUS
Turner Company	7/1/X5	2/1/X6	$5,000	10.0%	Held by Douglas
Devito Products	8/1/X5	2/1/X6	4,000	10.5	Discounted with recourse
Stone, Inc.	8/1/X5	12/1/X5	6,000	11.0	Defaulted by Stone, held as a receivable by Douglas

REQUIRED:

Indicate how each of these notes should be presented in Douglas's December 31, 19X5, balance sheet.

P8-53. ALLOWANCES FOR SHORT-TERM INVESTMENTS   Prepare the adjusting entry required at year-end (if any) to adjust the allowance to reduce short-term investments to market for each of the cases described below. Assume that each case represents a different company.

	CASE 1	CASE 2	CASE 3	CASE 4
Allowance to reduce short-term investments to market (balance at 12/31 before adjustment)	$ –0–	$ –0–	$ 8,200	$ 1,100
Cost of short-term investment portfolio	9,000	23,700	45,200	66,100
Market value of short-term investment portfolio	8,050	21,500	46,500	64,200

P8-54. ACCOUNTING FOR INVESTMENTS IN STOCK   Amherst Corporation made its first purchase of marketable equity securities for its short-term investment portfolio in 19X5. The following data are available for that portfolio:

AS OF 12/31	PORTFOLIO COST	PORTFOLIO MARKET VALUE
19X5	$38,200	$40,100
19X6	31,500	29,200
19X7	37,100	36,700
19X8	41,700	42,800

REQUIRED:

1. Compute the amount of allowance to reduce short-term investments to market required, if any, at December 31 of each year.

2. Compute the amount of unrealized gain or loss, if any, on the short-term investment portfolio that should be recognized in the income statement each year.

P8-55. LOWER-OF-COST-OR-MARKET ADJUSTMENT FOR SHORT-TERM INVESTMENTS   Near the end of 19X5 Software Programming, Inc., purchased a portfolio of equity securities as a short-term investment. That portfolio had the following acquisition cost and market value data:

	SHARES	TOTAL ACQUISITION COST	MARKET VALUE, 12/31/X5
Gates Corporation	2,300	$184,000	$186,300
Microdata	1,200	54,000	56,400
Network Products	1,700	37,400	22,100
		$275,400	$264,800

During 19X6 Software Programming sold 500 shares of Microdata for $50 per share. At the end of 19X6, the market values of the three stocks were Gates, $88; Microdata, $49; and Network Products, $21.

REQUIRED:

1. Prepare the lower-of-cost-or-market adjustment, if any, for Software Programming at December 31, 19X5.

2. Show the presentation of short-term investments in Software Programming's 19X5 and 19X6 balance sheets.

3. Prepare the lower-of-cost-or-market adjustment, if any, for Software Programming at December 31, 19X6.

P8-56. SHORT-TERM INVESTMENTS   Cagney Products entered into the following investment transactions during a recent year:

a) On April 6, Cagney purchased the following securities for its short-term investment portfolio:

2,000 shares of Accessory Enterprises	$46,000
1,000 shares of Berner Manufacturing.	30,000
Total acquisition cost.	$76,000

b) On May 2, Cagney made a short-term investment by purchasing 500 shares of Image, Inc., for $32,000.

c) On June 29, Cagney sold 1,500 shares of Accessory for $39,000.

d) During November the following cash dividends were declared and paid:

Accessory Enterprises. . . . . $1.20 per share
Berner Manufacturing . . . . 1.25 per share
Image, Inc.. . . . . 1.10 per share

e) On December 31, the market values of the three stocks in Cagney's short-term investment portfolio were:

Accessory Enterprises . . . . $20 per share
Berner Manufacturing. . . . . 31 per share
Image, Inc. . . . . 59 per share

All investments held by Cagney at year-end were purchased by Cagney during the year.

REQUIRED:

1. Prepare the journal entries to record transactions **a** through **d**.

2. Prepare a schedule including each asset's name and its carrying amount for the balance sheet at December 31.

3. Prepare an adjusting entry, if necessary, at December 31 to establish the proper amount in Cagney's allowance to reduce short-term investments to market.

4. What is the amount of net income attributable to Cagney's short-term investments? (Ignore taxes.)

P8-57. CASH MANAGEMENT Each December Washington Growers' Association constructs a cash budget on a quarterly basis to assist in its program of cash management. The association anticipates cash receipts and expenditures for the next five quarters as follows:

	RECEIPTS	EXPENDITURES
First quarter 19X1	$200,000	$ 50,000
Second quarter 19X1	90,000	80,000
Third quarter 19X1	75,000	180,000
Fourth quarter 19X1	116,000	160,000
First quarter 19X2	250,000	54,000

On January 1, 19X1, the association has a cash balance of $20,000, no short-term investments, and no short-term debt. The association operates under the policy that the end-of-quarter cash balance should equal $20,000 plus the expected excess of expenditures over receipts, if any, during the next quarter. If receipts are expected to exceed disbursements, then the end-of-quarter cash balance should equal $20,000.

REQUIRED:

1. Prepare a schedule showing the cash balance required at the end of each quarter of 19X1.

2. What short-term borrowing or investment is anticipated for each quarter of 19X1?

P8-58. SHORT-TERM INVESTMENTS, SHORT-TERM DEBT, AND CASH REQUIREMENTS Ahrens Corporation has the following schedule for expected cash receipts and cash disbursements:

MONTH	EXPECTED CASH RECEIPTS	EXPECTED CASH DISBURSEMENTS
July	$210,000	$200,000
August	280,000	210,000
September	230,000	190,000
October	160,000	180,000

Ahrens begins July with a cash balance of $20,000, $15,000 of short-term debt, and no short-term investments. Ahrens uses the following cash management policy:

a) End-of-month cash should equal $20,000 plus the excess of disbursements over receipts for the next month.

b) If receipts are expected to exceed disbursements in the next month, the current month ending cash balance should be $20,000.

c) Excess funds should be invested in short-term instruments unless there is short-term debt, in which case excess funds should be used to reduce short-term debt.

d) Fund deficiencies are met first by liquidating short-term investments and, if additional funds are required, by incurring short-term debt.

REQUIRED:

1. Calculate the acquisition or liquidation of short-term investments or the incurrence or repayment of short-term debt at the end of July, August, and September.

2. Discuss the general considerations that help accountants develop a cash management policy.

APPENDIX PROBLEMS

P8-59. RECORDING PETTY CASH TRANSACTIONS SCB, Inc., had a balance of $600 in cash in its petty cash fund at the beginning of September. The following transactions took place in September:

a) On September 4, the custodian paid $34 out of petty cash for new stationery on which the company president's name appeared prominently.

b) On September 11, the custodian paid $167 out of petty cash for maintenance manuals for the firm's new jet aircraft.

c) On September 15, the custodian paid $37 out of petty cash for transportation-in.

d) On September 23, the custodian paid $46 out of petty cash to have documents delivered to the lawyers who were defending the firm in a lawsuit.

e) On September 27, the custodian paid $231 out of petty cash to reimburse the president for costs he had incurred when bad weather prevented the company jet from landing to pick him up after a meeting.

f) On September 30, the custodian submitted receipts for the above expenditures and a check was drawn for that amount to replenish the fund.

REQUIRED:

Prepare the journal entries made by the corporation to record these transactions.

P8-60. CASH RECEIPTS JOURNAL   Lowman Sales, a retailer of household appliances, records all cash receipts
in a special journal that serves as the basis for the daily posting of cash receipts to the general ledger
and as the basis for posting to various subsidiary ledgers. Lowman accepts outside-company credit
cards and credit sales from a small number of customers; separate subsidiary ledgers are maintained
for outside credit cards and credit customers. Lowman does not offer an in-house credit card. The
following cash was received on March 10:

a) Received $450 on account from J. P. Dillard (customer account number 289).

b) Received $4,722 on account from MasterCard (subsidiary account number 92).

c) Received $465 from a cash customer.

d) Received $7,000 from Franklinton Bank in exchange for a 90-day note; notes payable is account
number 45 in the general ledger.

e) Received $710 from a cash customer.

f) Received $150 on account from Joseph S. Jones (customer account number 111).

REQUIRED:

Adapt the format illustrated in Appendix 8–1 to prepare the cash receipts journal for March 10.

P8-61. POSTING TO SUBSIDIARY LEDGERS   Using the data from Problem 8-60, prepare the necessary subsidiary
ledgers and post the cash receipts to accounts in the subsidiary ledgers and to the general ledger.

ANALYTICAL OPPORTUNITIES

A8-62. SELLING NOTES RECEIVABLES WITH RECOURSE   Martenson Corporation builds small shopping centers
and then sells the centers to local investors. A typical sales transaction requires the shopping center
buyers to provide a very small down payment and a note for the balance. The buyers expect the cash
flows from rent on the shopping center to provide the cash necessary for the interest and principal
payments on the note. Martenson immediately sells the note to a local bank, promising the bank to
accept the note back if the buyers of the property default on the note.

REQUIRED:

1. Has Martenson really sold these notes? (Hint: Read paragraph 5 of *Statement of Financial
Accounting Standards No. 77.*)

2. If Martenson considers these notes sold, how should the contingent liability for these notes be
reported in its financial statements?

A8-63. SELLING MERCHANDISE WITH RIGHT OF RETURN   Jambox Corporation sells records, tapes, and CDs to
retail stores. The sales of Jambox's products are unpredictable. Therefore, Jambox has to agree to
accept unlimited returns for one year from retailers if the products do not sell.

REQUIRED:

Should Jambox record sales and receivables when products are shipped to retailers or should Jambox
wait to record sales and receivables until retailers are able to sell the products? (Hint: Read paragraphs 6 and 8 of *Statement of Financial Accounting Standards No. 48.*)

LEARNING OBJECTIVES

Careful study of this chapter will enable you to:

1. Measure the acquisition cost of operating assets.

2. Compute depreciation expense for property, plant, and equipment, using the straight-line, sum-of-the-years'-digits, declining balance, and usage methods.

3. Distinguish between postacquisition expenditures that are to be capitalized and those that are to be expensed.

4. Account for the disposition of operating assets.

5. Compute amortization for intangible assets.

6. Measure acquisition cost and depletion for natural resources.

Appendix 9–1

7. Account for both the acquisition and the disposition parts of trade-in transactions.

OPERATING ASSETS: Long-lived assets that remain on the business's records until used by the business in the course of operations.

SERVICE POTENTIAL CONCEPT: The view that an asset's cost should be allocated over its expected life to reflect the decline in its service potential.

9 OPERATING ASSETS

Once acquired by a business, an asset remains on the business's accounting records until the business transfers it to another party, collects it, or uses it. In Chapters 6 and 7, we saw that inventory remains on the business's records until it is transferred to customers and converted into the expense called *cost of goods sold.* As we discussed in Chapter 8, a receivable remains on the records until it is collected and converted into cash. We now turn to **operating assets,** which are the long-lived assets that remain on the business's records until used by the business in the course of operations. Operating assets are sometimes called *fixed assets, long-term assets,* or *plant assets.*

Unlike the goods and services that a business sells, operating assets are not transferred to customers. Instead, operating assets are used by the business in the course of operations; they are usually held by the business until they are no longer of service to the business or, in other words, until their *service potential* has been exhausted. The typical operating asset is used for a period of 4 to 10 years, although some are held for only 2 or 3 years and others for as long as 30 or 40 years. Operating assets are divided into three categories:

1. Property, plant, and equipment
2. Intangibles
3. Natural resources

Property, plant, and equipment are *tangible operating assets* and are often called simply *plant assets.* They include, among other things, land, buildings, machines, and motor vehicles. *Intangible operating assets* include patents, copyrights, trademarks, leaseholds, and goodwill. *Natural resources* are tangible operating assets to which special accounting procedures apply; natural resources include timberlands or deposits of natural resources such as coal, oil, and gravel.

Operating assets represent future economic benefits or service potential that will be used in the course of operations. At acquisition, an operating asset is recorded at its cost, including the cost of acquiring the asset and the cost of readying the asset for use (as required by the cost concept). As the service potential of an operating asset is consumed, the cost of the asset is allocated as an expense among the accounting periods in which the asset is used. This allocation is called *depreciation* for plant assets, *amortization* for intangible assets, and *depletion* for natural resources. The view that the cost of an asset should be allocated over its expected life to reflect the decline in the asset's service potential is the **service potential concept.**

Operating assets are often the most costly of the various types of assets acquired by an entity. For many firms, depreciation, amortization, and depletion are also among the largest items of periodic expense. In this chapter, we will discuss the measurement and reporting of operating assets from acquisition through use to disposition. We will address the following questions:

1. What is included in the acquisition cost of an operating asset?

2. How should the acquisition cost be allocated to expense?

3. How should expenditures subsequent to acquisition be treated?

4. How is retirement of an operating asset recorded?

The main concepts applied in accounting for operating assets are the cost concept, the service potential concept, and the matching concept. Following the cost concept, an operating asset is initially recorded at its cost. Following the service potential concept, that cost is then allocated as an expense over the asset's life. And following the matching concept, the allocation is matched with revenues.

We will now discuss the accounting process for each category of operating assets: (1) property, plant, and equipment; (2) intangibles; and (3) natural resources.

PROPERTY, PLANT, AND EQUIPMENT

TANGIBLE OPERATING ASSETS: Assets used in the operations of a firm that have a visible, physical presence in the firm (e.g., buildings, equipment, and land).

Tangible operating assets are used in the operations of a firm and include buildings, equipment, and land. These assets are tangible in the sense that they have a visible, physical presence in the firm. For many firms, tangible operating assets (or plant assets) represent the largest asset segment. Consequently, the financial statements are affected by the principles that guide accounting for these assets. The principles to which we now turn indicate how to determine acquisition cost for these assets, calculate their depreciation, and record their retirement from service.

ACQUISITION COST

ACQUISITION COST: The purchase price plus all costs necessary to ready an asset for use.

The **acquisition cost** of an operating asset is its purchase price plus all the costs necessary to ready the asset for use. As an example, the acquisition cost of a machine would be its purchase price (less any discount offered) plus sales taxes, freight, installation costs, and the cost of labor and materials for trial runs that check its performance.

Measuring and Recording Acquisition Cost

When cash is given in exchange for an asset, the amount of cash given is the purchase price of the acquired asset. However, when its purchase price is large, an operating asset may be purchased on credit. When an operating asset is purchased on credit, one might think that the interest paid should be added to the purchase price. However, except in rare situations, the interest on any particular borrowing is assumed to relate to the entire collection of assets owned by the business rather than to any specific asset.[1] In other words, the interest is viewed as resulting from the decision to finance rather than from the decision to acquire the asset. Interest on borrowed funds is therefore not normally added to the purchase price of an asset.

When a noncash consideration, such as land or other noncash assets, is given in exchange for an asset, the purchase price of the acquired asset is the fair value of the asset acquired. The **fair value** (or **fair market value**) of an asset is the estimated amount of cash that would be required to acquire the asset. This cash equivalent is inferred from information about similar assets in comparable transactions. Only if the fair value of the asset received cannot be accurately measured should the firm measure the purchase price at the fair value of the consideration given in exchange.

To illustrate the accounting procedures for the measurement and recording of the acquisition cost of an operating asset, we will examine an asset acquisition by Drew Company. Drew acquired a new automatic milling machine from Dayton, Inc. Drew paid $20,000 in cash and signed a one-year, 14 percent note for $80,000. Following the purchase, Drew incurred freight charges of $2,900 to ship the machine from Dayton's factory to Drew's plant. After the machine arrived, Drew paid J. B. Contractors $5,300 for installation. Drew also used $800 of materials and $1,500 of labor on trial runs. The total cost of the machine ($110,500) would be recorded as follows:

Equipment, milling machine	110,500	
Cash ($20,000 + $5,300)		25,300
Notes payable		80,000
Accounts payable (for freight charges)		2,900
Inventory, materials		800
Wages payable		1,500

The foregoing entry shows that freight ($2,900) and installation costs ($5,300 + $800 + $1,500) are included in the machine's cost. Interest on the note payable, however, is excluded from the machine's cost and is debited to interest expense when it accrues. Had Drew given 1,600 shares of its own stock, which was selling for $50 per share, instead of the 14 percent note, the acquisition would have been recorded as follows:

Equipment, milling machine	110,500	
Cash		25,300
Capital stock		80,000
Accounts payable		2,900
Inventory, materials		800
Wages payable		1,500

Since the fair value of the stock [($50)(1,600) = $80,000] equals the amount of the note, the acquisition cost is the same in both entries.

Basket Purchases

Occasionally, two or more assets are acquired in one transaction for a payment that does not indicate the separate price of each item purchased. Such a transac-

FAIR VALUE (FAIR MARKET VALUE): The estimated amount of cash required to acquire an asset.

---

[1] However, Financial Accounting Standards Board, *Statement of Financial Accounting Standards No. 34,* "Capitalization of Interest," permits the addition of interest to the acquisition cost of assets requiring a long period of preparation for use, such as ships or large plants or buildings.

BASKET PURCHASE:
The purchase of two or more assets together in a transaction that does not indicate the separate purchase price of each.

tion is called a **basket purchase.** One way to treat the "basket" would be a single asset in the entity's accounting records. However, this approach is inappropriate because each operating asset in a basket will normally have a different service life, and some of the items in the basket may not even be operating assets. Unless a separate cost is determined for each item, it is not possible to calculate the correct amount of depreciation and thereby properly match the cost of the items to the related revenues. The allocation of costs within a basket purchase is important because it ultimately affects the accounts and amounts presented in the current balance sheet and in future balance sheets and income statements (as the assets are used).

Accountants usually allocate the cost of a basket purchase according to the *relative fair value* of each component of the basket at acquisition. Fair values can be established from appraisals, tax assessments, or insurance policy valuations. The allocation procedure is applied by developing a ratio of the fair value of each item in the basket to the total fair value. Each ratio is then multiplied by the basket cost to determine the cost for each item. For example, Tecumseh Aggregates, Inc., purchased an operating sand and gravel pit for $632,000 cash. First, the fair values and expected lives of the items acquired were established from an insurance appraisal and internal evaluations. That information is shown in the following table:

ITEM	FAIR VALUE	EXPECTED LIFE
Gravel pit	$320,000	10 years
Sand pit	160,000	5 years
Electric shovel	128,000	20 years
Fuel inventory	32,000	*
Total	$640,000	

* Used in less than one year.

Next, the allocated cost of each item was determined as shown below, by developing the ratio of its fair value to the basket's total fair value and then multiplying this ratio by the basket's total cost of $632,000:

ITEM	FAIR VALUE	VALUE RATIO*	ALLOCATED COST†
Gravel pit	$320,000	.50	$316,000
Sand pit	160,000	.25	158,000
Electric shovel	128,000	.20	126,400
Fuel inventory	32,000	.05	31,600
Totals	$640,000	1.00	$632,000

* Ratio of fair value to total fair value of $640,000.
† Value ratio times total cost of $632,000.

The journal entry to record the acquisition is:

Gravel pit	316,000	
Sand pit	158,000	
Equipment, electric shovel	126,400	
Supplies inventory, fuel	31,600	
Cash		632,000

Thus, although Tecumseh's four assets were acquired in a basket purchase for a single price, the allocation procedure develops a separate cost for each asset.

Sometimes the purchase price of a basket may exceed the total fair value of the basket. In some cases, the assets are recorded at their individual fair values and the excess of the purchase price over the total fair value is written off as a loss. For example, if land and a building were acquired at a cost of $100,000, but the fair value was only $30,000 for the land and $65,000 for the building, the following entry would be made:

Land...	30,000	
Building..	65,000	
Loss on acquisition of assets	5,000	
Cash..		100,000

In other words, assets are recorded at acquisition at the lower of their cost or their fair value, in accordance with the conservatism convention. In other cases, especially if the purchased "basket" is an entire business, the excess of purchase price over total fair value is recorded as an intangible asset called *goodwill.* Accounting for goodwill is discussed later in this chapter.

DEPRECIATION

We observed earlier that the acquisition cost of plant assets represents the cost of future benefits or services to the firm. Over the life of each asset, these services are used or consumed in the operations of the firm. A firm can enjoy the services of land without decreasing its potential for future services, so land is not depreciated. However, the service potential of any item of property, plant, and equipment other than land is decreased by the consumption of its services. In addition, the service potential of an asset is decreased by obsolescence, wear and tear, the effects of environment, and the passage of time. Following the service potential concept, a portion of the asset's acquisition cost is assigned (as an expense) to the decrease in service potential that occurs in each period of the asset's life. Thus **depreciation** is the portion of the cost of a tangible operating asset (other than land) that is recognized as expense in each period of the asset's life.

DEPRECIATION: The portion of the cost of a tangible operating asset (other than land) that is recognized as expense in each period of the asset's life.

Matching Depreciation with Revenue

The service potential concept provides the conceptual basis for measuring the depreciation recognized as expense in each period of the asset's life. The matching concept provides the conceptual basis for measuring depreciation expense. Two situations complicate the matching of depreciation expense with related revenue: (1) the acquisition of assets at times other than the beginning of the accounting period and (2) the use of assets in manufacturing operations. Let us consider each situation in turn.

MID-YEAR ACQUISITIONS If a depreciable asset (an asset subject to depreciation) is acquired on the first day of the accounting period, then the years of the asset's life coincide with the annual accounting periods. Under this condition, depreciation for each year of the asset's life equals the depreciation expense for the corresponding accounting period. If, however, a depreciable asset is acquired during the accounting period, then the years of the asset's life do not coincide with the annual accounting period. Under this condition, the matching concept requires that depreciation for each year of the asset's life be divided between two accounting periods. To illustrate, consider an asset purchased on April 1,[2] 19X2, for which the first year's depreciation is $20,000 and the second year's depreciation is $16,000. The asset would contribute depreciation expense of $15,000 to 19X2 [($20,000)(9/12)] and $17,000 to 19X3 [($20,000)(3/12) + ($16,000)(9/12)]. For the sake of simplicity, most illustrations, exercises, and problems in this book assume that asset acquisitions occur at the beginning of the accounting period.

DEPRECIATION ON PLANT ASSETS USED IN MANUFACTURING The plant assets of most retail and service firms are usually associated with selling and administrative functions. Because the depreciation on a plant asset of this type is recognized as expense (matched with revenue) as the related service potential declines, it is a period expense. In contrast, the depreciation on a plant asset used in manufacturing operations is a part of the production costs incurred during the period and thus becomes part of the cost of goods produced in that period. Such depreciation is a component of cost of goods sold and is recognized as expense (matched with revenue) as products are sold. Thus depreciation on manufacturing equipment and facilities is a product expense. The accounting procedures used to match depreciation on manufacturing plant assets with revenues are described in courses on managerial and cost accounting. Accordingly, illustrations, exercises, and problems in this book are limited to those in which depreciation is treated as a period expense.

We begin our discussion of depreciation measurement by considering the basic elements of the depreciation calculation and then turn to the various depreciation methods.

Data Required for Measuring Depreciation

Three items of information are necessary in order to measure depreciation for a plant asset: (1) acquisition cost, (2) expected life, and (3) an estimate of residual value (salvage value) for the asset after its service potential has been consumed. We discussed the measurement of acquisition cost or installed cost at the beginning of this chapter. Here we will examine the other two items — expected life and estimates of residual value.

EXPECTED LIFE: The period of time over which a firm anticipates deriving benefit from the use of an asset.

EXPECTED LIFE ESTIMATION The **expected life** of an asset is the period of time over which the firm anticipates deriving benefit from the use of the asset.[3] The expected life of any plant asset reflects both the physical capacities of the asset and the firm's plans for its use. Many firms plan to dispose of assets before their entire service potential is exhausted. For example, major automobile rental companies typically use an automobile for only a part of its entire economic life before

---

[2] Although acquisitions may occur *during* a month, for purposes of simplifying depreciation calculations, many companies follow the policy of substituting the date of the nearer first of the month for the actual transaction date. Thus, acquisitions on March 25 or April 9 would be treated as acquisitions on April 1 for purposes of depreciation calculations. (Despite this simplification of depreciation calculations, of course, acquisitions and sales of assets are recorded on their actual transaction dates.)

[3] The expected life can be estimated in *service units* as well as in *units of time.* For example, an airline may choose to measure the expected life of its aircraft in hours of use rather than years.

disposing of it. Expected life is also influenced by technological change. Many assets lose their service potential through obsolescence long before the assets are physically inoperable.

RESIDUAL VALUE (SALVAGE VALUE): The amount of cash or trade-in consideration that a firm expects to recover on retiring a particular asset from service.

RESIDUAL VALUE ESTIMATION Residual value, like expected life, is an estimate dependent on future events. **Residual value** (also called **salvage value**) is the amount of cash or trade-in consideration that the firm expects to recover from the asset on retiring it from service. Accordingly, the residual value reflects the firm's plans for the asset and its expectations about the value of the asset to others once its expected life with the firm is over. A truck used for 2 years may have a substantial residual value, whereas the same truck used for 10 years may have minimal residual value. A relatively new computer may have little residual value after only a few months of use if the computer manufacturer brings out a newer model with superior features. As these examples indicate, residual value is based on projections of some of the same future events that are used to estimate an asset's expected life. Since depreciation depends on estimates of both expected life and residual value, depreciation itself is an estimate.

Depreciation and Acquisition Cost

Depreciation is the portion of an asset's acquisition cost assigned to the decrease in service potential that occurs during each period of the asset's expected life. Total depreciation over the entire expected life of an asset equals the excess of its acquisition cost over residual value. To illustrate, let's consider a machine acquired for $10,000 that has a 10-year expected life and a residual value of $2,000. The total depreciation over the entire expected life of the machine is $8,000. (In other words, the sum of the 10 annual depreciation amounts is $8,000.) The amount assigned to each year depends on the decrease in service potential that occurs during each year. If the machine's service potential declines by the same amount in each of the 10 years, then the depreciation is $800 in each year [$8,000/10]. Thus, the annual recognition of depreciation expense would require the following adjusting entry at each year-end:

```
Depreciation expense......................................  800
    Accumulated depreciation................................        800
```

However, service potential does not always decline at a uniform rate, and the various patterns of declining service potential thus give rise to different patterns of depreciation. The calculations required to determine periodic depreciation for each pattern of service potential decline are called *depreciation methods.* Of course, total depreciation over the entire expected life of an asset — the excess of acquisition cost over residual value — is the same for all depreciation methods.

ACCUMULATED DEPRE- CIATION: The total amount of depreciation that has been recorded for an asset as of any given time.

The total amount of depreciation that has been recorded for an asset as of any given time is called **accumulated depreciation** and is disclosed in the balance sheet. This information can provide useful insights into when a firm's plant assets will need to be replaced and how much cash may be required for that purpose. The analysis that follows illustrates the insights that can be derived by comparing the accumulated depreciation accounts on two balance sheets.

Assume that you are considering a major investment in one of two long-haul trucking companies. The two firms are about the same size and travel competitive routes. Their net incomes and earnings per share are also similar. However, your inspection of the balance sheets of both firms reveals a significant difference in the accumulated depreciation for the firms' trucks, as shown below.

	FIRM 1	FIRM 2
Trucks	$600,000	$550,000
Less: Accumulated depreciation, trucks...............	138,000	477,000
Book value.......................................	$462,000	$ 73,000

The following are questions that you might raise while investigating the significance of this difference in accumulated depreciation:

1. *Does the difference suggest that the timing of future cash outflows needed to replace fully depreciated trucks will be different for the two firms?*

Firm 2's trucks are nearly fully depreciated. Assuming that estimates of expected life are consistent with economic life, it would appear that firm 2 will have to spend more cash in the near future than firm 1 for truck replacement.

2. *Do these expected differences in future cash outflows for asset replacement have any implications for you as an investor?*

Firm 2 may have to find more cash in the near future than firm 1. To do so, firm 2 might cut dividends to provide the cash internally. It might secure the cash by issuing debt; interest on debt would reduce earnings and debt would also make firm 2 a more risky investment. Firm 2 might sell equity to raise the extra cash, but additional equity would reduce the present owners' claim on earnings and assets. Firm 2 might also sell some other assets to secure the cash; however, the amount and pattern of net income would likely be changed by a sale of assets.

Although more information is needed about firm 2 in order to know the precise impact of the impending replacement, the comparison of the two accumulated depreciation amounts leads us to the appropriate questions.

Although the recording of depreciation expense does not alter cash, accumulated depreciation signals the approaching future time for replacement of plant and equipment, which usually does require cash. We turn now to the calculation of depreciation using standard depreciation methods.

**DEPRECIATION
METHODS**

DEPRECIATION METH-
ODS: The standardized
calculations required to
determine periodic depre-
ciation for various patterns
of decline in the service
potential of assets.

The service potential of an asset is assumed to decline with each period of use, but the pattern of decline is not the same for all assets. Some assets decline at a constant rate each year; others decline sharply in the early years of use and then more gradually as time goes on; for still other assets, the pattern of decline depends on how much the asset is used in each period. **Depreciation methods** are the standardized calculations required to determine periodic depreciation for various patterns of decline in the service potential of assets. One of several patterns is used for most assets, and each pattern is associated with a particular depreciation method. Four primary depreciation methods will be described in the following discussion: (1) straight-line depreciation, (2) sum-of-the-years'-digits depreciation, (3) declining balance depreciation, and (4) usage depreciation. Each method produces a different pattern of expense over time. Sum-of-the-years'-digits depreciation and declining balance depreciation are commonly referred to as **accelerated depreciation** methods because they accelerate the assignment of an asset's cost to depreciation by allocating a larger amount of the asset's cost to the early years of its life. The method should be selected that best matches the pattern of decline in service potential over the life of the asset under consideration. Since decline in service potential cannot actually be observed, the best match for a particular asset is a matter of judgment. Some observers argue that managers may manipulate this judgment to overstate net income in the short run in an effort to deceive stockholders and creditors or to inflate executive compensation.

ACCELERATED DEPRE-CIATION: Depreciation computed using one of several depreciation methods that allocate a larger amount of an asset's cost to the early years of its life.

Straight-Line Method

As its name implies, **straight-line depreciation** allocates an equal amount of an asset's cost to each year of the asset's expected life. It is appropriate to apply this method to those assets for which an equal amount of service potential is considered to be consumed each period. The straight-line method is widely used in financial statements because it is simple to apply and is based on a pattern of service potential decline that is reasonable for many plant assets. The computation of straight-line depreciation is based on an asset's **depreciable cost,** which is the excess of the asset's acquisition cost over its residual value. An asset's depreciable cost is the portion of its acquisition cost that will be depreciated over the asset's life. Straight-line depreciation for each period is computed by subtracting the asset's residual value from its acquisition cost and then dividing that amount by the asset's expected life:

STRAIGHT-LINE DEPRE-CIATION: The depreciation method that allocates an equal amount of an asset's cost to each year of the asset's expected life.

DEPRECIABLE COST: The excess of an asset's acquisition cost over its residual value, which also equals the total depreciation over the life of the asset.

$$\text{Straight-line depreciation} = \frac{\text{Acquisition cost} - \text{Residual value}}{\text{Expected life}}$$

The straight-line depreciation equation can also be written as follows:

$$\text{Straight-line depreciation} = \left(\frac{1}{\text{Expected life}}\right)(\text{Acquisition cost} - \text{Residual value})$$

Restating the equation in this way does not alter the substance of the computation; it merely rearranges the terms of the equation. The first equation computes depreciation by *dividing* the depreciable cost by the expected life. The second equation computes depreciation by *multiplying* the depreciable cost by the fraction 1/Expected life (that is, the reciprocal of the expected life). The reciprocal of the expected life is called the *straight-line rate.* Using this new term, the second equation for straight-line depreciation can be written as follows:

$$\text{Straight-line depreciation} = (\text{Straight-line rate})(\text{Acquisition cost} - \text{Residual value})$$

EXHIBIT 9-1 CALCULATION OF STRAIGHT-LINE DEPRECIATION

DATA

Acquisition cost..	$5,000
Residual value...	500
Expected life..	5 years

COMPUTATION

$$\text{Straight-line depreciation} = \frac{\$5,000 - \$500}{5 \text{ years}} = \$900 \text{ per year}$$

END OF YEAR	DEPRECIATION EXPENSE	ACCUMULATED DEPRECIATION	BOOK VALUE
			$5,000
1	$ 900	$ 900	4,100
2	900	1,800	3,200
3	900	2,700	2,300
4	900	3,600	1,400
5	900	4,500	500
	$4,500		

Exhibit 9–1 uses the first equation to illustrate the calculation of straight-line depreciation. In this example, an asset that cost $5,000 and has a five-year expected life and a $500 residual value results in straight-line depreciation expense of $900 per year.[4] The contra-asset account accumulated depreciation rises at a constant rate of $900 per year until it equals the depreciable cost ($4,500). The **book value** of an item is the amount at which the item is currently carried in the accounting records. The book value of a depreciable asset is its cost less the accumulated depreciation that has been taken to date. In Exhibit 9–1, the book value of the asset falls by $900 per year, until it equals the residual value ($500) at the end of the asset's useful life.

BOOK VALUE: The amount at which an item is currently carried in the accounting records. In the case of depreciable assets, book value is cost less accumulated depreciation.

Sum-of-the-Years'-Digits Method

SUM-OF-THE-YEARS'-DIGITS DEPRECIATION: The accelerated depreciation method that calculates depreciation by multiplying depreciable cost by a declining ratio derived from the sum of the years in expected life.

Sum-of-the-year's-digits depreciation is the accelerated depreciation method that calculates depreciation by multiplying an asset's depreciable cost by a declining ratio derived from the sum of the number of years in the asset's expected life. The computations for sum-of-the-years'-digits depreciation are only slightly different from those for the straight-line method. As in the straight-line method, the asset's residual value is subtracted from its acquisition cost, to find the depreciable cost. This amount is then multiplied by the appropriate sum-of-the-

---

[4] If the asset had been acquired on September 1 (rather than January 1, as assumed in Exhibit 9–1), then the five-year life of the asset would cover six annual accounting periods. Depreciation expense for the first year would have been only $300 [($900)(4/12)]. Annual depreciation expense would have been $900 [($900)(8/12) + ($900)(4/12)] in the second, third, fourth, and fifth years, and $600 [($900)(8/12)] in the sixth year.

years'-digits ratio. Thus sum-of-the-years'-digits depreciation for a given asset for any given year of useful life is calculated as follows:

$$
\begin{array}{c}
\text{Sum-of-} \\
\text{the-years'-} \\
\text{digits} \\
\text{depreciation}
\end{array}
=
\left(
\begin{array}{c}
\text{Appropriate} \\
\text{sum-of-the-years'-} \\
\text{digits ratio}
\end{array}
\right)
(\text{Acquisition cost} - \text{Residual value})
$$

To arrive at the appropriate sum-of-the-years'-digits ratios for an asset's life, we first find the *sum* of the digits in the expected life. For example, the sum of the digits for an asset with a four-year expected life is $4 + 3 + 2 + 1 = 10$.[5] Then the number of years of expected life are taken successively in inverse order, and each year is divided by the sum of the digits. Since each of the years in the expected life is used in inverse order, with the largest (in this case, 4) in the first year and the smallest (in this case, 1) in the last depreciation year, the appropriate sum-of-the-years'-digits ratios and their corresponding years would be as follows:

YEAR	SUM-OF-THE-YEARS'-DIGITS RATIO
1	4/10
2	3/10
3	2/10
4	1/10

An example of depreciation computed using the sum-of-the-years'-digits method is shown in Exhibit 9–2. In this example, depreciation expense declines from $1,500 in the first year to $300 in the fifth year.[6] Accumulated depreciation rises each year, but at a decreasing rate. As with all depreciation methods, accumulated depreciation reaches the asset's depreciable cost ($4,500), and its book value reaches the residual value ($500) at the end of the expected life.

Declining Balance Method

DECLINING BALANCE DEPRECIATION: The accelerated depreciation method that calculates depreciation by multiplying the declining book value of an asset by a depreciation rate.

Declining balance depreciation is the accelerated depreciation method that calculates depreciation by multiplying the declining book value of an asset by a depreciation rate. Like sum-of-the-years'-digits depreciation, declining balance depreciation decreases in each successive year of the asset's life. But the calculation of declining balance depreciation differs in one important way from the calculation of straight-line and sum-of-the-years'-digits depreciation: Whereas both the straight-line and sum-of-the-years'-digits methods multiply a deprecia-

---

[5] A simple formula to compute the sum of the digits is (Expected life)(Expected life + 1)/2.

[6] If the asset had been acquired on September 1 (rather than January 1, as assumed in Exhibit 9–2), then the five-year life of the asset would cover six annual accounting periods. Depreciation expense would have been $500 [($1,500)(4/12)] for the first year, $1,400 [($1,500)(8/12) + ($1,200)(4/12)] for the second year, $1,100 [($1,200)(8/12) + ($900)(4/12)] for the third year, $800 [($900)(8/12) + ($600)(4/12)] for the fourth year, $500 [($600)(8/12) + ($300)(4/12)] for the fifth year, and $200 [($300)(8/12)] for the sixth year.

EXHIBIT 9-2   **CALCULATION OF SUM-OF-THE-YEARS'-DIGITS DEPRECIATION**

DATA

Acquisition cost. $5,000
Residual value 500
Expected life. . . . . 5 years
Sum of digits in expected life 15

COMPUTATION

Sum-of-the-years'-digits depreciation = (Appropriate sum-of-the-years'-digits ratio)($5,000 − $500)

END OF YEAR	DEPRECIATION EXPENSE	ACCUMULATED DEPRECIATION	BOOK VALUE
			$5,000
1	(5/15)($4,500) = $1,500	$1,500	3,500
2	(4/15)($4,500) = 1,200	2,700	2,300
3	(3/15)($4,500) = 900	3,600	1,400
4	(2/15)($4,500) = 600	4,200	800
5	(1/15)($4,500) = 300	4,500	500
	$4,500		

tion rate times *depreciable cost,* the declining balance method multiplies a depreciation rate times the *book value* of the asset.

The declining balance depreciation rate is some multiple (m) of the straight-line rate:

Declining balance rate = (m)(Straight-line rate)

The multiple (m) is often 2, in which case the declining balance method is called the *double declining balance method.* (In this text, a multiple of 2 is used for the declining balance method unless otherwise noted.) The declining balance rate can also be computed by using a more complicated formula that is described in later accounting courses.

Declining balance depreciation for each period of an asset's useful life equals the declining balance rate times the asset's book value (its acquisition cost minus accumulated depreciation) at the beginning of the period. Thus declining balance depreciation for each period is computed by using the following equation:

$$\text{Declining balance depreciation} = \left(\text{Declining balance rate}\right)\left(\text{Acquisition cost} - \text{Accumulated depreciation}\right)$$

EXHIBIT 9–3   CALCULATION OF DECLINING BALANCE DEPRECIATION

DATA

Acquisition cost.	$5,000
Residual value	500
Expected life.	5 years
Declining balance rate (twice the straight-line rate)	2/5

COMPUTATION

$$\text{Declining balance depreciation} = (2/5)(\text{Acquisition cost} - \text{Accumulated depreciation})$$

END OF YEAR	DEPRECIATION EXPENSE	ACCUMULATED DEPRECIATION	BOOK VALUE
			$5,000
1	(2/5)($5,000) = $2,000	$2,000	3,000
2	(2/5)($3,000) = 1,200	3,200	1,800
3	(2/5)($1,800) = 720	3,920	1,080
4	(2/5)($1,080) = 432	4,352	648
5	148*	4,500	500
	$4,500		

* Not [(2/5)($648) = $259], but the amount required to make book value equal residual value ($648 − $500 = $148).

Exhibit 9–3 presents an example of the calculation of declining balance depreciation. Note that depreciation expense in year 5 ($148) is less than two-fifths of the end-of-year-4 book value. The mathematics of the declining balance method can produce depreciation schedules that would reduce book value below residual value. When this occurs, the accountant must intervene and end depreciation when residual value is reached. Conversely, if the final year's depreciation does not reduce book value to residual value, then depreciation in excess of the computed amount must be recorded.

Usage Method

The three depreciation methods described so far yield periodic depreciation corresponding to three standarized patterns of service potential decline in an asset. Since the decline in service potential for most assets cannot be observed or measured, the pattern of decline in the service potential of most assets is usually known only in a most approximate way. In these cases, accountants, using such information as they have, assign one of the three standard patterns of service potential decline to assets and calculate depreciation accordingly.

However, when service potential decline is proportional to the usage of the asset and when asset usage can be measured, the service potential decline and the related periodic depreciation can be tailored to the asset. An automobile is an obvious example of an asset whose service potential usually declines with use, and automobile usage is readily measurable in terms of miles traveled. Such allocation of the depreciable cost of an asset to periods in direct proportion to actual use is called **usage depreciation.**

USAGE DEPRECIA-TION: The depreciation method that allocates the cost of an asset over its expected life in direct proportion to the actual use made of the asset.

EXHIBIT 9–4	CALCULATION OF USAGE DEPRECIATION

DATA

Acquisition cost	$5,000
Residual value...	500
Expected usage	135,000 miles

YEAR	ACTUAL USAGE* (IN MILES)
1	13,500
2	40,500
3	33,750
4	27,000
5	20,250

COMPUTATION

$$\frac{\text{Usage}}{\text{depreciation}} = (\text{Usage ratio})(\$5,000 - \$500)$$

END OF YEAR	USAGE RATIO	DEPRECIATION EXPENSE	ACCUMULATED DEPRECIATION	BOOK VALUE
				$5,000
1	.10†	$ 450	$ 450	4,550
2	.30	1,350	1,800	3,200
3	.25	1,125	2,925	2,075
4	.20	900	3,825	1,175
5	.15	675	4,500	500
	1.00	$4,500		

* Unlike expected usage, which is estimated in advance, actual usage is discovered year by year as the asset is used. When total actual usage differs from expected usage, depreciation in the last year is simply the remaining depreciable cost rather than the amount given by the usage depreciation equation.
† 13,500/135,000.

Usage depreciation is computed by multiplying an asset's depreciable cost by a usage ratio, as shown in the following equation:

Usage depreciation = (Usage ratio)(Acquisition cost − Residual value)

The usage ratio is the usage of the asset in the depreciation period divided by the total expected usage of the asset. For example, if a firm replaces its executive jet every 5,000 flight hours, the usage ratio for a year in which the jet was used for 1,000 hours would be .20 [1,000/5,000]. An example of automobile depreciation computed by the usage method is shown in Exhibit 9–4. Depending on the use of the asset during the year, usage depreciation can be accelerated, straight-line, decelerated, or erratic.

Because of the difficulty of predicting and measuring usage, usage depreciation is less widely used than the other three methods. The usage depreciation method does an excellent job of implementing the matching concept, particularly when usage varies widely and irregularly from period to period. However, the usage depreciation method is the most difficult to apply because it requires estimation of expected usage (which is more difficult than estimation of expected life in years) and the measurement of actual usage.

Now that all four depreciation methods have been introduced, let us summarize their attributes: Straight-line depreciation produces a constant amount of depreciation in each period of the asset's life and is consistent with a constant rate of decline in service potential. Sum-of-the-years'-digits depreciation and declining balance depreciation accelerate the assignment of an asset's cost to depreciation by allocating a larger amount of cost to the early years of an asset's life. These two methods are called accelerated depreciation methods and are consistent with a decreasing rate of decline in service potential and a decreasing depreciation charge. Usage depreciation is based on a measure of the asset's use in each period, and the periodic depreciation rises and falls with the asset's use. In this sense, usage depreciation is based not on a standardized pattern of service potential decline but on a pattern tailored to the individual asset and its use. Exhibit 9–5 shows the patterns of periodic depreciation over time created by straight-line, sum-of-the-years'-digits, and declining balance depreciation. The pattern created by usage depreciation is not shown, because it depends on the way a particular asset is used.

Tax Return Depreciation

The four depreciation methods discussed thus far are used to calculate depreciation expense for the financial statements prepared for stockholders and creditors. The choice among the four methods is guided by the service potential concept. In contrast, the depreciation calculations used when preparing a firm's tax return are specified by the federal income tax law. Tax depreciation rules are designed to stimulate investment in operating assets and, therefore, are not guided by the service potential concept. Tax depreciation rules provide for the rapid (accelerated) expensing of depreciable assets. By bringing forward the bulk of depreciation expense, tax depreciation rules enable firms to save cash by delaying the payment of taxes. Tax depreciation rules are described in greater detail in Chapter 16.

Impact of Depreciation Policy on Income

The measurement of periodic depreciation in a firm that owns hundreds of depreciable assets in dozens of different categories is a complex task calling for the exercise of careful judgment. Most large firms establish policies for depreciable assets that specify the measurement of acquisition cost, the estimation of expected lives and residual values, and the choice of depreciation methods. Since depreciation is a significant expense for many firms, net income may be quite sensitive to changes in depreciation policies and to differences in policies from one firm to another. For example, a change in the method of estimating expected lives that shortens estimates could significantly reduce net income. The following analysis demonstrates the importance of such changes to a bank loan officer.

EXHIBIT 9–5   DEPRECIATION PATTERNS OVER TIME

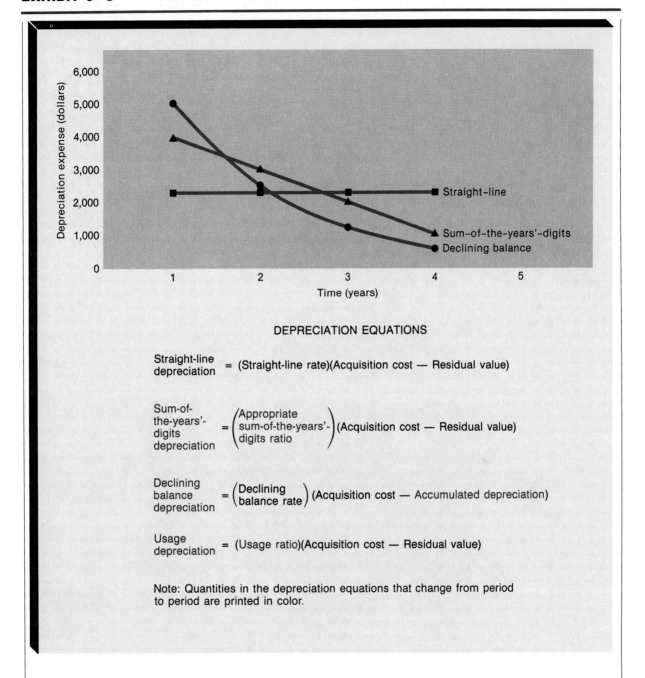

DEPRECIATION EQUATIONS

Straight-line
depreciation = (Straight-line rate)(Acquisition cost — Residual value)

Sum-of-
the-years'-
digits
depreciation = $\left(\begin{array}{l}\text{Appropriate} \\ \text{sum-of-the-years'-} \\ \text{digits ratio}\end{array}\right)$ (Acquisition cost — Residual value)

Declining
balance
depreciation = $\left(\begin{array}{l}\text{Declining} \\ \text{balance rate}\end{array}\right)$ (Acquisition cost — Accumulated depreciation)

Usage
depreciation = (Usage ratio)(Acquisition cost — Residual value)

Note: Quantities in the depreciation equations that change from period
to period are printed in color.

ANALYSIS
USE OF
DEPRECIATION
INFORMATION IN
BANK LOAN DECISION

Assume that you are a loan officer of the Prairie State Bank. The president of a ready-mix concrete company from a neighboring community, Concrete Transit Company, has applied for a five-year, $150,000 loan to finance his firm's expansion. You have examined Concrete's financial statements for the past three years and have summarized the following data:

	19X4	19X3	19X2
Sales revenue	$649,000	$613,000	$584,000
Cost of goods sold	317,000	304,000	287,000
Gross margin	$332,000	$309,000	$297,000
Operating expenses	288,000	263,000	249,000
Income from operations	$ 44,000	$ 46,000	$ 48,000
Financial expenses	25,000	23,000	20,000
Income before taxes	$ 19,000	$ 23,000	$ 28,000
Tax expense	4,000	6,000	7,000
Net income	$ 15,000	$ 17,000	$ 21,000
Plant assets	$470,000	$470,000	$470,000
Accumulated depreciation	(110,000)	(95,000)	(80,000)
Book value	$360,000	$375,000	$390,000
Depreciation expense*	$ 15,000	$ 15,000	$ 15,000

* Included in operating expenses.

Your analysis of the financial statements indicates that the statement amounts and the relationships among them are as you expect, except for the depreciation expense. Because you have another loan customer who is in the same business, you expected depreciation expense to be about 15 percent of the cost of the plant assets. Following are some questions you might ask in attempting to determine why the firm's annual depreciation expense is so much less than you expected:

1. *What variables can cause depreciation expense to differ from what is expected?*

Depreciation expense can be different from the expected amount because different methods are used from those expected or because estimates of expected life or residual value differ from those expected.

2. *You ascertain that Concrete Transit Company uses straight-line depreciation and that depreciation is, in fact, less than might be expected. In what direction do you think Concrete Transit has changed its estimate of expected life and residual value?*

Concrete Transit must be using much higher estimates of residual value or of expected life than do other firms in similar businesses.

3. *If you alter the firm's depreciation to 15 percent of the cost of the plant assets, what happens to net income for the years 19X2 through 19X4?*

Depreciation expense increases from $15,000 to $70,500 for each year. Net income is affected by the depreciation increase as follows:

	REPORTED	ADJUSTED
19X2	$21,000	($27,500)*
19X3	17,000	($32,500)
19X4	15,000	($36,500)

* In 19X2 operating expenses increase by $55,500 to $304,500. Income (loss) from operations is then ($7,500). Income (loss) before taxes becomes ($27,500). Since there are no taxes when income before taxes is negative, the adjusted net income for 19X2 is a net loss of $27,500. The amounts for 19X3 and 19X4 are determined similarly.

4. *Should your bank make the loan?*

The adjusted net income amounts suggest that the firm has been increasingly unprofitable. Since the principal and interest for the five-year loan would have to be repaid from cash provided by operations, the absence of profit suggests that the loan should not be made.

EXPENDITURES ON PLANT ASSETS AFTER ACQUISITION

CAPITAL EXPENDITURE: The original expenditure made to acquire a plant asset and any subsequent asset-related expenditure on which depreciation is taken. Such expenditures are said to be *capitalized* when added to an asset account.

REVENUE EXPENDITURE: An expenditure that is not subject to depreciation. Such expenditures are said to be *expensed* when added to an expense account.

Depreciation is not restricted to the acquisition cost of assets but is also applicable to certain subsequent expenditures related to assets. Both the original expenditure made to acquire a plant asset and any subsequent asset-related expenditures that are subject to depreciation are called **capital expenditures** and are *capitalized.* From a record-keeping perspective, capitalization means that the expenditure is debited to an asset account and is depreciated over a period of several years. When a firm invests in a new operating asset, all the expenditures made in acquiring and readying the asset for use are capitalized. In addition, expenditures for certain major one-time repairs or additions to assets are also capitalized and are therefore subject to depreciation. Such expenditures, which usually represent relatively large amounts, include the replacement of major components of machines, the complete overhaul of equipment, the remodeling of buildings, and additions made to buildings. An expenditure (whether or not it is asset-related) that is not subject to depreciation is called a **revenue expenditure** and is said to be *expensed,* meaning that the expenditure is debited directly to an expense account. Recurring and routine expenditures for the maintenance of equipment—as when machines are oiled and adjusted regularly and buildings are cleaned—are usually treated in this way.

The guide to selecting the proper accounting procedure for these expenditures is the service potential concept. (Recall that the service potential concept requires the cost of an asset to be expensed over its expected life to reflect the decline in its usefulness.) The services provided by a given expenditure may benefit the firm in the current period or may benefit both current and future periods. Expenditures that benefit only the current period should be expensed when made. Minor repairs that benefit future periods are often expensed as well, either because their amount is immaterial or because the amount spent for these repairs varies little from period to period. (When repair expenditures do not change significantly from period to period, it makes little difference in the financial statements whether the repairs are capitalized or expensed.) Expenditures for maintenance performed at regular intervals and for replacement of minor parts that wear out or become unserviceable are accumulated in a maintenance expense account or a repair expense account. For example, quarterly maintenance at a cost of $950 performed by a computer manufacturer's service department on Grey Company's computer would be recorded as follows:

Maintenance expense, computer	950	
Cash		950

Postacquisition expenditures for plant assets are capitalized if the expenditures are expected to benefit both current and future periods. In that case, expenses are recognized over the periods that benefit from the expenditure. Capital expenditures related to an existing asset are usually debited (added) to the account of the related asset. This procedure necessitates adjustment of the depreciation of the asset. To illustrate the accounting procedures used for making such adjustments, assume that Grey Company put a new machine into operation in January 19X3. At acquisition the following data were applicable for the machine:

Installed cost	$59,000
Residual value	5,000
Expected life	9 years

Straight-line depreciation of $6,000 per year was recorded in 19X3, 19X4, and 19X5. In January 19X6, the Grey Company spent $7,500 to replace the automatic control system on the machine. This expenditure enabled Grey to increase the output of the machine by 50 percent, extended the machine's expected life by two years, and increased its residual value by $500. The cost of the original automatic control system is included in the machine's acquisition cost; because such a cost normally cannot be separated from the asset's acquisition cost, it is therefore left in the asset account. The following journal entry can be made to record this capital expenditure:

Equipment	7,500	
Cash		7,500

Because of the effect this expenditure has on expected life, residual value, and expected future output, depreciation expense for the machine must be recomputed. The following procedure is applicable when straight-line depreciation is used:

Original installed cost	$59,000
Less: Accumulated depreciation	18,000
Book value	$41,000
Add: Capital expenditure	7,500
Revised book value	$48,500

The new amount to be depreciated is the revised book value ($48,500) less the revised residual value ($5,500). The new remaining life of the asset is the undepreciated portion of the original life (six years) plus the increment to the expected life (two years) resulting from the capital expenditure. The calculation of revised straight-line depreciation is as follows:

$$\frac{\text{Revised straight-line}}{\text{depreciation}} = \frac{\text{Revised book value} - \text{Revised residual value}}{\text{New remaining expected life}}$$

$$= \frac{\$48,500 - \$5,500}{8 \text{ years}} = \$5,375 \text{ per year}$$

In this case, the revised depreciation turns out to be less than the annual depreciation expense computed at acquisition. It could, however, have been the same as or even larger than the original depreciation. In other words, it should not be inferred from our example that prudent capital expenditures invariably decrease depreciation expense.

Although most capital expenditures related to an existing asset are debited to the account of the related asset, occasionally a capital expenditure for a plant asset causes the creation of a new asset that has an identity separate from that of the original asset. This happens when the effect of the expenditure on service potential cannot be represented by a simple adjustment to the depreciation of the original asset. For example, suppose a new roof is put on a building at a cost of

---

$150,000. The roof has an expected life of 20 years, but the building has a remaining life of 35 years. It would be incorrect to depreciate the roof over 35 years and equally incorrect to depreciate the building over 20 years. The proper procedure is to create a separate asset account for the roof and depreciate it over its own expected life. The new asset would be recorded as follows:

Building, roof	150,000	
Cash		150,000

The cost of the old roof would be removed from the accounts if it were in a separate account or if it could be separated from the acquisition cost of the building. We will next look at the accounting procedures for the retirement and disposal of plant assets.

RETIREMENT AND DISPOSITION OF PLANT ASSETS

VOLUNTARY RETIRE-MENT: Disposition of an asset by choice of the owner when the asset has reached the end of its usefulness to the owner.

INVOLUNTARY CONVERSION: Disposition of an asset as a result of theft, an act of nature, or an accident.

Although firms usually dispose of plant and equipment through voluntary retirement, involuntary conversion may also force disposition. **Voluntary retirement** occurs when the owner determines that an asset has reached the end of its usefulness to the owner. **Involuntary conversion** occurs when assets are lost or destroyed through theft, acts of nature, or accident. Voluntary retirement usually occurs at about the time predicted when the asset was acquired—at about the end of the asset's expected life. However, voluntary retirement may occur at earlier or later times as well. In some cases, obsolescence resulting from unforeseen technological developments may force the retirement of an asset before the end of its expected life; in others, an asset may be used beyond the end of its expected life because of intentional or unintentional delays in securing replacement equipment. In still other cases, equipment may be held beyond the end of its expected life for temporary use during periods of unusually heavy demand on newer facilities. (Retirement of the equipment from full-time use to "backup" status does not constitute disposition.)

The cost of an asset and the asset's related accumulated depreciation must remain in the firm's accounting records until the asset has been disposed of by sale or trade-in. At disposition, the asset's cost and related accumulated depreciation are removed from the asset accounts by entries that reflect the precise form of the disposition.

Recording Depreciation at Disposition

Depreciation on an asset disposed of before year-end must be recorded for that part of the year in which the asset was used before its retirement date. For example, Dickerson Corporation, which records annual depreciation at the end of each year, disposed of a punch press on August 1. The press had been depreciated on a straight-line basis at a rate of $7,200 per year. Thus, depreciation for the first seven months of the year in the amount of $4,200 [($7,200)(7/12)] must be recorded to bring the accumulated depreciation account up to date:

Depreciation expense	4,200	
Accumulated depreciation		4,200

This entry, made on August 1, records depreciation expense for the first seven months of the year. Once depreciation is recorded up to the date of disposition, the book value reflected in the accounts is used as a basis for computing the gain or loss on disposal.

Disposition by Sale

When plant assets are sold for cash, the gain or loss on the sale is computed and reported as part of the firm's net income. Once the final depreciation expense has been entered, any gain or loss on disposition can be computed by determining the difference between the book value of the asset (its acquisition cost less accumulated depreciation) and any proceeds from the sale of the asset.[7] Once the gain or loss has been computed, an entry is made to remove the asset and its accumulated depreciation from the ledger and to record the resulting gain or loss on disposition. For example, Khaki, Ltd., has a computer with an installed cost of $1,350,000 and accumulated depreciation of $1,280,000. Because the computer is no longer useful to Khaki, it has been sold to B&M Electronics for $85,000 cash. To determine its gain or loss on this disposition, Khaki would make the following computations:

Proceeds from sale............................		$85,000
Less: Book value of asset sold		
Acquisition cost...........................	$1,350,000	
Less: Accumulated depreciation	1,280,000	70,000
Gain on sale		$15,000

Khaki would then make the following entry to record the sale of its computer at a gain:

Accumulated depreciation, computer..............	1,280,000	
Cash...	85,000	
Equipment, computer		1,350,000
Gain on sale of plant assets.....................		15,000

Had B&M paid less than Khaki's book value ($63,000, for example), the following computation would have been made:

Proceeds from sale	$63,000
Less: Book value of asset sold...............................	70,000
Loss on sale	$ (7,000)

Khaki would then make the following entry to record the sale of its computer at a loss:

Accumulated depreciation, computer..............	1,280,000	
Cash...	63,000	
Loss on sale of plant assets	7,000	
Equipment, computer		1,350,000

Losses and gains on the disposition of plant assets are normally considered a part of "other expenses and losses" or "other revenues and gains," respectively, and appear immediately after income from operations on a classified income statement. However, when an entire segment of a business is sold—representing a separate line of business or class of customers—the resulting gain or loss must be

---

[7] The proceeds should be reduced for any costs of removal. If the firm pays to have an asset removed and receives no proceeds, then the sum of the book value and the removal payment is a loss on disposal.

reported (net of taxes) in a separate section of the income statement (called *discontinued operations*) following income taxes expense but preceding net income. The accounting procedures for sales of entire business segments are discussed in more advanced accounting courses.

Disposition by Trade-In

Rather than selling a used plant asset for cash, a firm may find it more advantageous to trade in the asset as part of a transaction to acquire another asset. A **trade-in** is an asset acquisition in which the consideration given includes previously used plant assets. A trade-in may or may not involve cash. A payment or receipt of cash that accompanies the exchange of plant assets is called **boot.**

An important aspect of accounting for trade-in transactions is the calculation of gains and losses on trade-ins and the recognition of these gains and losses in net income. When an old plant asset is sold for cash, the cash received measures the fair value of the old asset. (Recall that fair value is defined as the amount of cash required to acquire an asset.) However, when an old plant asset is traded in on another plant asset, the fair value of the old asset cannot be determined from the amount of cash received because the old asset is not being sold for cash. Thus the fair value of the old asset must be determined by using other information. For example, if other entities sell similar used assets for cash, then a cash price for the trade-in may be readily estimable. When the fair value of the old asset cannot otherwise be determined, then the fair value of the new asset acquired by trade-in may be used as a basis for estimating the fair value of the old asset.

The gain or loss on a trade-in transaction represents the difference between the fair value and the book value of the old asset. Following the conservatism convention, accounting principles require that all losses on trade-ins be included in net income of the trade-in period. Gains on trade-ins are treated somewhat differently from losses. If the trade-in involves the exchange of dissimilar assets (for example, a trade-in of land on the purchase of equipment), then the gain is included in net income of the trade-in period. On the other hand, if the trade-in replaces an old asset with a similar asset that performs approximately the same functions as the old one (as when an old company car is traded in for a new company car), then the gain is not included in net income of the trade-in period but is deferred. (Accounting procedures for recording both gains and losses on trade-in transactions are described in Appendix 9–1.)

TRADE-IN: An asset acquisition in which the consideration given includes previously used plant assets.

BOOT: A payment or receipt of cash that accompanies the exchange of plant assets in a trade-in.

INTANGIBLE ASSETS

INTANGIBLE OPERATING ASSETS: Assets used in the operations of a firm that have a legal rather than a physical substance (e.g., patents, trademarks, and copyrights).

Intangible operating assets, like tangible assets, represent future economic benefits to the firm, but, unlike tangible assets, they lack physical substance. Patents, copyrights, trademarks, leaseholds, organization costs, franchises, and goodwill are all examples of intangible assets. The economic benefits associated with most intangible assets are in the form of legal rights and privileges conferred on the owner of the asset. Thus the economic value of a patent, for example, is the legal right to restrict, control, or charge for the use of the idea or process covered by the patent.

An intangible operating asset has a limited life and rarely has any residual value at its end. The cost of an intangible asset, like the cost of a tangible asset, is allocated to accounting periods over the life of the asset to reflect the decline in service potential. However, intangible assets are said to be amortized rather than depreciated, and the cost allocated to each period of the asset's life is called **amortization** rather than *depreciation*.

Some intangible assets, such as goodwill and organization costs, confer benefits over many years. Indeed, some accountants argue that certain intangibles may have a life as long as the entity itself and should therefore not be subject to amortization. This argument has not been generally accepted, and accounting principles require that all intangibles with indefinite life be amortized over a period of 40 years or less.

AMORTIZATION: The portion of the cost of intangible operating assets recognized as an expense for each period.

TYPES OF INTANGIBLES

Accounting procedures, particularly those relating to amortization, are affected by the particular economic and legal attributes of intangible assets. Before examining the accounting procedures, we will look at the most important types of intangible assets.

PATENTS   The federal government grants patents for a period of 17 years. A patent provides its owner with the exclusive right to manufacture and sell the patented item during the period specified or to use the patented process in manufacturing during that period. Patents can be sold, or arrangements can be made under which the use of a patent by those other than the owners provides royalties to the owner.

The value of a patent consists of providing the owner with some economic advantage over competitors (such as lower production costs or higher product quality). Since technological progress often eliminates the economic advantage of a patent before the end of its legal life, amortization of the acquisition cost of a patent extends over the shorter of the patent's legal or expected economic life.

COPYRIGHTS   A copyright is a grant by the federal government giving an author, creator, or artist the right to publish, sell, or control a literary or artistic work for the lifetime of the author plus 50 years. A copyright can be sold outright or, as is frequently the case, used by others under a royalty arrangement. Copyrighted material normally has an economic life that is less than the legal life of the copyright, and the acquisition cost of a copyright is thus amortized over the shorter of the legal life or the expected economic life.

TRADEMARKS   A trademark is a distinctive name or symbol registered with the federal government. Once registered, the trademark's owner has exclusive rights to it for as long as it is used. Trademarks can be sold or assigned for use under royalty arrangements with the owner. The economic value of a trademark derives from the ability of its associated product to produce proportionally greater revenues from a higher sales volume or higher selling prices. The cost of developing or acquiring a trademark is amortized over its expected economic life.

LEASEHOLDS   A leasehold is an advance payment on a long-term lease. It is generally amortized on a straight-line basis over the life of the lease. Amortization of the leasehold is normally debited to the rent expense recorded for each period over the life of the lease. Leaseholds are most common in rentals of office, warehouse, or manufacturing space.

ORGANIZATION COSTS   The payments for legal fees, drawing up of the firm's charter and bylaws, and incorporation charges at the time of organization constitute organization costs. These expenditures are made under the assumption that their benefits will be reflected in future profits. Although organization costs benefit the enterprise over its entire life, they are normally amortized over a period of 5 to 40 years.

FRANCHISES   A fee paid by a business to some other entity for the exclusive right to conduct a certain type of business in some particular geographic area is a *franchise*. A franchise is normally granted for a specified period of time and has its acquisition cost amortized over the shorter of its economic or legal life. Many fast-food restaurants and motels are franchises.

GOODWILL   When an operating business is acquired, the purchase price frequently exceeds the sum of the fair value of the identifiable assets, such as land, buildings, equipment, accounts receivable, and the like. This excess, called *goodwill,* arises from the ability of the acquired business to produce a return on net assets that is greater than the returns for comparable businesses.[8] Goodwill arises from attributes such as customer satisfaction, quality products, skilled employees, and business location. When a business is purchased, the seller and the purchaser recognize that the tangible assets do not represent all the items of value conveyed in the purchase. Depending on the entity, goodwill can be a very large portion of the purchase price. Since the purchase of a business entity is recorded at cost, the portion of the purchase cost applicable to goodwill is recorded as an intangible asset. To illustrate, assume that Spirit Enterprises purchased Charlestown Dry Cleaners for $330,000 cash. The fair value of Charlestown's assets at the date of the purchase was $250,000 (land at $25,000, building at $130,000, equipment at $75,000, and supplies at $20,000). The difference between the purchase price and the fair value of the assets indicates that Spirit should record $80,000 of goodwill. The following entry would be made to record the purchase:

Supplies inventory	20,000	
Equipment	75,000	
Building	130,000	
Land	25,000	
Goodwill	80,000	
Cash		330,000

Accounting principles require that goodwill be amortized over the shorter of its expected life or 40 years.

There are special problems in accounting for intangibles. The benefits of intangibles are less obvious than those of tangibles and may therefore be difficult to measure. The expiration of such benefits can also be difficult to measure or may occur quite suddenly.

ACQUISITION OF INTANGIBLE ASSETS   Some intangible assets, like plant assets, are acquired by purchase from other enterprises. The acquisition cost of an intangible asset acquired from outside the entity is recorded in the same way as the acquisition cost of a plant asset. In other words, all the costs required to ready the intangible for use are capitalized. For example, the King Company purchased a patent from PNB, Inc., for $40,000.

[8] *Return* is defined as earnings divided by investment.

King would record the acquisition of this intangible asset with the following entry:

Patent.	40,000	
Cash		40,000

The primary element of the acquisition cost for externally acquired intangibles is the purchase price, as an intangible rarely requires installation or trial runs. Some intangible assets—particularly patents and trademarks—are developed within the organization. The acquisition costs of intangibles developed in this way are based on a careful accumulation of the costs necessary for their development. To illustrate, assume that the Dockworth Corporation developed a new trademark. Dockworth spent $33,400 for wages, used $1,200 of supplies, and spent $5,700 for legal services to verify the new trademark's uniqueness, debiting each amount to the appropriate expense account. Dockworth would record the development of this intangible as follows:

Trademark	40,300	
Wages expense		33,400
Supplies expense		1,200
Legal expense		5,700

Whether acquired piecemeal or intact, intangible assets are subject to amortization over their expected lives. In the next section, we will consider the procedures by which this allocation is accomplished.

AMORTIZATION OF INTANGIBLES

Although some intangibles appear to have a life as long as that of the entity (e.g., organization costs), generally accepted accounting principles require that all intangibles be amortized. The length of an intangible asset's life is determined either by the eventual expiration of the economic advantage offered by the asset or by the end of the intangible's legal life. Therefore, the cost of any intangible asset is to be allocated or amortized over the shorter of its economic or legal life. A patent, for example, has a legal life of 17 years from the date it is granted. From the viewpoint of the patent holder, the economic life of the patent cannot extend beyond 17 years because, thereafter, anyone can then use the patented idea or process with no restrictions. However, the economic advantage offered by a patent often expires before the end of its legal life as a result of new technological developments. Since the residual value of an intangible asset is nearly always zero by the end of its economic life, the entire cost of an intangible is usually subject to amortization.

The amortization of an intangible asset may be recorded in an accumulated amortization (contra-asset) account, as in our illustrations, but is more often credited directly to the asset account. Although any systematic method can be used to amortize the cost of the asset, the straight-line method is selected in most cases. To illustrate, Page Company estimated that a patent acquired for $60,000 had an economic life of 10 years. Page would record the following adjusting entry each year.

Amortization expense, patent	6,000	
Accumulated amortization, patent		6,000

Amortization expense, patent is an operating expense on the income statement. After one year's use, the patent could be reported as follows on the balance sheet:

Intangible assets:
Patent (cost $60,000 less accumulated amortization of $6,000) $54,000

Having described accounting for the acquisition and amortization of intangibles, we turn now to accounting for their retirement.

RETIREMENT OF INTANGIBLES

An intangible asset is usually retired at the end of the expected life established at its acquisition. Since zero residual value is normally assumed, the last entry to record amortization will reduce the book value of the intangible asset to zero. However, when an intangible asset is sold before the end of its expected life, a transaction similar to the retirement transaction for a plant asset is recorded. Proceeds from a sale greater than the book value produce gains, and proceeds smaller than the book value produce losses. For example, the King Company sold a patent that had a book value of $24,000 (acquisition cost of $32,000 less accumulated amortization of $8,000) for $28,000 cash. The journal entry to record the sale transaction is:

Cash	28,000	
Accumulated amortization, patent	8,000	
Patent		32,000
Gain on sale of patent		4,000

It is also possible for an intangible to lose its economic usefulness prior to the end of its expected life. A patent, as mentioned, may lose its value if newer and better technology is developed. If an intangible asset loses its total economic value before being completely amortized, the book value of the asset must be written off as a loss immediately. If the intangible asset loses only a portion of its value, the book value of the asset must be lowered to the new value. A loss is recorded for the decline in value, and a revised amortization schedule is developed. For example, one year ago the Carlton Corporation purchased a trademark for a brand of soup for $40,000. Carlton has been amortizing the trademark by the straight-line method, assuming an expected life of 10 years. Recently, a batch of the soup manufactured by the former owner of the trademark was found to cause botulism. As a result of the national publicity for the recall of the soup, Carlton has decided that the value of the trademark has declined from its book value of $36,000 ($40,000 less one year's amortization of $4,000) to only $3,000. Further, the expected economic life of the trademark is now only two years. At the time Carlton decided that the value of the trademark had been impaired, the following entry was made:

Loss from decline in value of trademark	33,000	
Accumulated amortization, trademark		33,000

Subsequently, Carlton will record an annual amortization of $1,500 for two years.

The accounting procedures for intangible operating assets are essentially the same as those for tangible operating assets. However, the application of these procedures to intangible operating assets is more difficult because they lack physical substance, as the accompanying analysis demonstrates.

ANALYSIS
MEASURING AND
ESTIMATING THE
DIMENSIONS OF A
PATENT

Marietta Corporation is a research-intensive firm engaged in the design and sale of ceramic products. For the past year, half of Marietta's research staff has been engaged in designing a process for coating iron and steel with a ceramic material for use in high-temperature areas of automobile engines. The firm has secured a patent for its process and is about to begin marketing equipment that uses the patented process. Accordingly, the firm's controller must establish the cost of developing the patent and formulate a procedure for its amortization.

1. *What considerations arise in measuring the cost of the patent?*

Clearly, the cost of the patent should include lawyers' fees and other similar costs incurred in securing the patent. In addition, the controller believes that half the year's cost of research activities should be assigned to the patent, including salaries paid to researchers and the costs of facilities and supplies used. However, accounting principles classify the expenditures for research activity as research and development costs and require that they be included in expense in the year in which they are incurred.

2. *What considerations arise in formulating an amortization procedure for the patent?*

Although the patent lasts for 17 years, Marietta expects the patented equipment to be a viable product for only five years. Moreover, 80 percent of the sales are expected to occur in the first two years following the introduction of the equipment. The firm expects to introduce an improved version of the equipment, which will be covered by another patent, within about four years. One of the assistant controllers argues, therefore, that the cost of this patent should be spread over the life of both the current equipment and its successor, with most of the cost amortized in the first two years following introduction of the current equipment. However, given the uncertainty of the projections on which the argument rests, the controller decides to amortize the entire cost of the patent over a five-year period, with 80 percent of the cost divided equally between years 1 and 2 and the remaining 20 percent divided equally among years 3 through 5. Of course, amortization will not begin until the equipment actually reaches the market. Until then, the cost of the patent is carried as an intangible asset on the balance sheet.

NATURAL RESOURCES

NATURAL RESOURCES: Operating assets that are physically consumed as they are used by the enterprise (e.g., coalfields, oil pools, and mineral deposits).

Like intangible operating assets, natural resources present formidable estimation and measurement problems. **Natural resources** (coalfields, oil pools, and mineral deposits, for example) differ from other operating assets in two important ways: First, unlike plant assets, natural resources are physically consumed as they are used by the enterprise. Second, natural resources can generally be replaced or restored only by an act of nature. (Timberlands are renewed by replanting and growth, but coalfields and most mineral deposits are not subject to renewal.)

The accounting for natural resources is quite similar to the accounting for intangible assets and plant assets. At acquisition, all the costs necessary to ready the natural resource for separation from the earth are capitalized, and the acqui-

DEPLETION: The portion of the cost of natural resources recognized as an expense for each period.

sition cost is then allocated to each unit of natural resource removed. This allocation process is called **depletion.** When the natural resource has been fully extracted, the asset representing the natural resource is removed from the accounting records. Any gain or loss is recognized upon disposition. Let us now consider, in turn, the accounting procedures for the acquisition, depletion, and disposition of natural resources.

ACQUISITION OF DEPLETABLE ASSETS

At the time a firm acquires the property on which a natural resource is located (or the property rights to the natural resource itself), only a small portion of the costs necessary to ready the asset for removal is likely to have been incurred. Costs such as sinking a shaft to an underground coalfield, drilling a well to an oil pool, or removing the earth over a mineral deposit can be several times greater than the cost of acquiring the property. Often, depreciable assets that are required to ready a natural resource for extraction are also used later, in the production process. Depreciation during the readying period is added to the acquisition cost of the natural resource. Once production has begun, however, the depreciation expense for these assets becomes an operating expense.

DEPLETION OF ACQUISITION COST

Recall that depletion is the portion of the cost of a natural resource allocated to each period in which the resource is used. Depletion is computed by using a procedure similar to that for usage depreciation. The first step in computing depletion is to determine the depletion rate. The *depletion rate* is the acquisition cost less residual value[9] divided by the total expected recoverable units of the natural resource at acquisition:

$$\text{Depletion rate} = \frac{\text{Acquisition cost} - \text{Residual value}}{\text{Recoverable units}}$$

Depletion is then calculated by multiplying the depletion rate by the number of units of the natural resource recovered during the period:

$$\text{Depletion} = (\text{Depletion rate})(\text{Units recovered})$$

To illustrate, in 19X4 the Miller Mining Company purchased a 4,000-acre tract of land in southern Indiana for $12,000,000, on which it developed an underground coal mine. Miller spent $26,000,000 to sink shafts to the coal seams. Elevators were installed at the beginning of 19X5 at a cost of $4,000,000. The elevators were used throughout 19X5 and 19X6 during the preparation of the mine for production; they had an expected life of 10 years and zero residual value. A building was constructed for the above-ground operations at a cost of $1,000,000. The building was occupied in January 19X5 and had zero residual value and an expected life of 10 years when completed. The building was also used for two years during the preparation of the mine for production. Miller estimates that there are 10,000,000 tons of recoverable coal and that the mine will

---

[9] Although natural resources do not usually have residual value, any associated equipment or land may. Laws requiring restoration of property after natural resources have been removed may result in a negative residual value if the costs of restoration exceed the positive elements of residual value. When residual value is negative, the amount subject to depletion exceds acquisition cost.

be fully depleted eight years after mining begins in early 19X7. The land has a residual value of $500,000.

In computing depletion, Miller first combines the cost of the land, depreciation on the elevators and buildings for two years, and the other development costs in order to determine the acquisition cost of the mine:

Cost of land...	$12,000,000
Depreciation, elevators (2 years).......................	800,000
Depreciation, building (2 years)........................	200,000
Preparation costs	26,000,000
Acquisition cost	$39,000,000

Knowing the acquisition cost, together with estimates of the residual value and the recoverable units, enables us to compute the depletion rate:

$$\text{Depletion rate} = \frac{\$39,000,000 - \$500,000}{10,000,000 \text{ tons}} = \$3.85 \text{ per ton}$$

If Miller mines 800,000 tons of coal in 19X7, then depletion for the year is calculated as follows:

$$\text{Depletion} = (\$3.85)(800,000) = \$3,080,000$$

Miller would make the following entry to record depletion for 19X7:

Depletion expense, coal mine....................	3,080,000	
Accumulated depletion, coal mine		3,080,000

For clarity, our illustrations record depletion in an accumulated depletion account; in practice, however, depletion is usually credited directly to the asset account. At December 31, 19X7, Miller could present the coal mine among its assets in the balance sheet as follows:

Operating assets:	
Coal mine (cost of $39,000,000 less accumulated depletion of $3,080,000).......................................	35,920,000

Alternatively, the accumulated depletion might be given on a separate line and subtracted from the cost of the mine.

DISPOSITION OF DEPLETABLE ASSETS

Although natural resources are consumed as used, salable land frequently remains after its resources have been removed. The sale of such land is treated like the sale of any other operating asset. A gain or loss is computed as the difference between the amount received from the sale and the book value of the land (acquisition cost less accumulated depletion), and the gain or loss is then included in net income of the disposition period.

Accounting for natural resources is plagued by difficult problems of estimation. The estimation of recoverable units is fraught with uncertainty, particularly in the early years of a resource's development. This uncertainty is transmitted to the treatment of related costs and can create difficult and sometimes controversial accounting issues. Such issues are treated in intermediate accounting texts.

REVIEW PROBLEM: ACCOUNTING FOR OPERATING ASSETS

In order to summarize the accounting differences associated with the various types of operating assets, it is useful to consider a comprehensive review problem. The Carroll Company manufactures a line of cranes, shovels, and hoists, all of which are electrically powered. During 19X4 the following transactions occurred:

a) On January 2, 19X4, land, an empty building, two used trucks, and an inventory of diesel fuel were acquired for $980,000, which Carroll paid in cash. An insurance appraisal provided the following data concerning these assets:

ITEM	FAIR VALUE	EXPECTED LIFE	EXPECTED RESIDUAL VALUE
Land	$247,500		
Building...................	702,900	30 years	$2,800
Truck A...................	9,900	3 years	1,000
Truck B...................	24,750	8 years	3,000
Diesel fuel................	4,950		
Total	$990,000		

b) Immediately after the acquisition, Carroll spent $2,200 on a new engine for truck A. After installing the engine, Carroll estimated that the truck had an expected life of 5 years and a residual value of $1,500.

c) In order to assure a coal supply for its heating plant, Carroll acquired a small operating coal mine for $2,100,000. Of the acquisition cost, $120,000 was allocated to depreciable assets with an expected life of 20 years and zero residual value. Carroll estimated that the recoverable coal reserves at acquisition were 495,000 tons. During 19X4 Carroll's mine produced 40,000 tons of coal.

d) Carroll owns a trademark that it purchased in 19X3 for $100,000. The trademark is being amortized over 8 years using straight-line amortization.

e) On July 2, 19X4, Carroll spent $16,000 to improve the efficiency of a metal press. Carroll estimated that, as a result of this expenditure, labor costs and scrap would be reduced by $8,000 per year for 6 years. The following data are available concerning the press:

Cost of press...	$40,000
Accumulated depreciation, 7/2/X4 (4½ years)..............	22,500
Old expected life	7 years
Old expected residual value............................	$ 5,000
Expected life from 7/2/X4	7 years
New expected residual value	$ 5,500

REQUIRED:

1. Allocate the $980,000 cost of the items purchased in transaction **a**. Make the necessary computations.

2. Compute and record a full year's depreciation for 19X4 on the building, using straight-line depreciation; on truck A, using sum-of-the-years'-digits depreciation; and on truck B, using double declining balance depreciation. Remember the major overhaul to truck A described in transaction **b**.

3. Compute and record 19X4 depletion for the coal mine.

4. Compute and record the amortization on the trademark for 19X4 on a straight-line basis.

5. Record the expenditure described in transaction **e**. Compute and record six months' straight-line depreciation on the improved press.

SOLUTIONS:

1. Allocation of the acquisition cost to the elements of a basket purchase:

ITEM	FAIR VALUE	VALUE RATIO*	ALLOCATED COST†
Land	$247,500	.250	$245,000
Building	702,900	.710	695,800
Truck A	9,900	.010	9,800
Truck B	24,750	.025	24,500
Diesel fuel	4,950	.005	4,900
Totals	$990,000	1.000	$980,000

* Fair value of each item divided by total fair value.
† Value ratio times cost ($980,000).

2. Depreciation on the items of property, plant, and equipment in the basket purchase:

STRAIGHT-LINE DEPRECIATION ON THE BUILDING

$$\text{Straight-line depreciation} = \frac{\text{Acquisition cost} - \text{Residual value}}{\text{Expected life}}$$

$$= \frac{\$695,800 - \$2,800}{30 \text{ years}} = \$23,100 \text{ per year}$$

Depreciation expense, building	23,100	
Accumulated depreciation, building		23,100

SUM-OF-THE-YEARS'-DIGITS DEPRECIATION FOR TRUCK A

$$\begin{pmatrix} \text{Sum-of-} \\ \text{the-years'-} \\ \text{digits} \\ \text{depreciation} \end{pmatrix} = \left(\begin{array}{c} \text{Appropriate} \\ \text{sum-of-the-years'-} \\ \text{digits ratio} \end{array} \right) \left(\begin{array}{c} \text{Acquisition} \\ \text{cost} \end{array} - \begin{array}{c} \text{Residual} \\ \text{value} \end{array} \right)$$

Acquisition cost = $9,800 + Overhaul cost
                 = $9,800 + $2,200 = $12,000

Residual value = $1,500

Sum of the digits = [(Expected life)(Expected life + 1)]/2
                  = [(5)(6)]/2 = 15

YEAR	DEPRECIATION EXPENSE	
19X4	(5/15)($12,000 − $1,500) =	$ 3,500
19X5	(4/15)($12,000 − $1,500) =	2,800
19X6	(3/15)($12,000 − $1,500) =	2,100
19X7	(2/15)($12,000 − $1,500) =	1,400
19X8	(1/15)($12,000 − $1,500) =	700
		$10,500

Depreciation expense, truck A	3,500	
Accumulated depreciation, truck A...................		3,500

DOUBLE DECLINING BALANCE DEPRECIATION FOR TRUCK B

$$\begin{pmatrix} \text{Declining} \\ \text{balance} \\ \text{depreciation} \end{pmatrix} = \left(\begin{array}{c} \text{Declining} \\ \text{balance rate} \end{array} \right) \left(\begin{array}{c} \text{Acquisition} \\ \text{cost} \end{array} - \begin{array}{c} \text{Accumulated} \\ \text{depreciation} \end{array} \right)$$

Acquisition cost = $24,500

$$\begin{array}{c} \text{Declining} \\ \text{balance rate} \end{array} = 2/8$$

YEAR	DEPRECIATION EXPENSE		ACCUMULATED DEPRECIATION	BOOK VALUE
Date of acquisition				$24,500
19X4	(2/8)($24,500) =	$ 6,125	$ 6,125	18,375
19X5	(2/8)($18,375) =	4,594	10,719	13,781
19X6	(2/8)($13,781) =	3,445	14,164	10,336
19X7	(2/8)($10,336) =	2,584	16,748	7,752
19X8	(2/8)($ 7,752) =	1,938	18,686	5,814
19X9	(2/8)($ 5,814) =	1,454	20,140	4,360
19Y0	(2/8)($ 4,360) =	1,090	21,230	3,270
19Y1		270*	21,500	3,000
		$21,500		

* The amount needed to achieve a $3,000 book value.

Depreciation expense, truck B	6,125	
Accumulated depreciation, truck B................		6,125

3. Depletion on the coal mine:

DEPLETION

$$\text{Depletion rate} = \frac{\text{Acquisition cost} - \text{Residual value}}{\text{Recoverable units}}$$

$$= \frac{\$1,980,000}{495,000 \text{ tons}} = \$4.00 \text{ per ton}$$

$$\text{Depletion} = (\text{Depletion rate})(\text{Units recovered})$$
$$= (\$4.00)(40,000) = \$160,000$$

Depletion expense, coal mine............................	160,000	
Accumulated depletion, coal mine		160,000

4. Amortization on the trademark (an intangible asset):

AMORTIZATION

$$\frac{\text{Straight-line}}{\text{depreciation}} = \frac{\text{Acquisition cost} - \text{Residual value}}{\text{Expected life}}$$

$$= \frac{\$100,000 - \$0}{8 \text{ years}} = \$12,500 \text{ per year}$$

Amortization expense, trademark....................	12,500	
Accumulated amortization, trademark.............		12,500

5. Recording a capital expenditure during use and recomputing depreciation after a capital expenditure:

JOURNAL ENTRY TO RECORD CAPITAL EXPENDITURE

Press	16,000	
Cash		16,000

REVISED ANNUAL AMOUNT OF STRAIGHT-LINE DEPRECIATION

Cost	$40,000
Less: Accumulated depreciation	22,500
Book value	$17,500
Add: Capital expenditure...................................	16,000
Revised book value	$33,500

$$\frac{\text{Revised straight-line}}{\text{depreciation}} = \frac{\text{Revised book value} - \text{Revised residual value}}{\text{New remaining expected life}}$$

$$= \frac{\$33,500 - \$5,500}{7 \text{ years}} = \$4,000 \text{ per year}$$

Six months' depreciation = (6/12)(4,000) = $2,000

JOURNAL ENTRY TO RECORD DEPRECIATION

Depreciation expense, press	2,000	
Accumulated depreciation, press..................		2,000

SUMMARY

There are three types of operating assets: plant (or tangible) assets, intangible assets, and natural resources. Operating assets are normally acquired for use by an enterprise for several accounting periods. At acquisition all the costs necessary to ready an operating asset for use are capitalized. This acquisition cost is then systematically allocated as expense to the periods in which the asset is used. This allocation is called *depreciation* for plant assets, *amortization* for intangible assets, and *depletion* for natural resources.

The four depreciation methods described and illustrated are the straight-line, declining balance, sum-of-the-years'-digits, and usage methods. The amortization of the acquisition cost of intangibles is normally performed on a straight-line basis. Depletion is a usage-based allocation procedure.

Once operating assets are in use, expenditures on those assets are classified as either expenses or capital expenditures. Expenses benefit only the firm's current reporting period. Capital expenditures provide benefits in both current and future periods and are subject to depreciation. Consequently, capital expenditures are added to an asset account and subsequently allocated to those periods in which the related benefit is derived.

Operating assets can be disposed of by sale or by trade-in. In each case, the old asset is removed from the accounting records. A loss on disposition is always included in net income of the asset's disposal period. A gain on disposition is included in net income of the disposition period unless the gain is associated with a trade-in involving similar assets (as explained in Appendix 9–1).

APPENDIX 9–1
ACCOUNTING FOR TRADE-INS

As we indicated when discussing trade-in transactions in the body of the chapter, several alternative computations and journal entries are used to record trade-in transactions. The presence of either gains or losses on the disposition of the old asset, together with the form of the exchange (for either similar or dissimilar assets), leads to four possible situations. The table below indicates the major elements of the accounting for each of those four situations.

GAIN OR LOSS ON OLD ASSET	TYPES OF ASSETS INVOLVED	DOLLAR AMOUNT FOR NEW ASSET	INCOME STATEMENT RECOGNITION OF GAIN OR LOSS
Gain	Similar	Book value of old asset plus boot	No
Loss	Similar	Fair value of old asset plus boot	Yes
Gain	Dissimilar	Fair value of old asset plus boot	Yes
Loss	Dissimilar	Fair value of old asset plus boot	Yes

Assume that a firm trades an old asset and pays boot of $35,000 cash for a new asset. The old asset originally cost $20,000; the accumulated depreciation on the old asset is $17,000, giving it a book value of $3,000. We will use this example, in each of the four possible situations, to illustrate the computation of cost for the new asset and the journal entries to record the trade.

DATA FOR TRADE-IN EXAMPLE

1. Old asset
   Cost.. $20,000
   Accumulated depreciation 17,000
   Book value... $ 3,000
2. Boot: $35,000 cash

GAIN ON DISPOSITION OF OLD ASSET, SIMILAR ASSETS INVOLVED

The first case listed in the table is that in which there is a gain on the disposition of the old asset and the assets involved in the trade-in transaction are similar. There is a gain on disposition of the old asset because its fair value exceeds its book value. Let us assume for this case that fair value for the old asset is $5,000. In this case, the cost of the new asset will be the sum of the book value of the old asset and the boot paid ($3,000 + $35,000 = $38,000). The journal entry to record this trade will be as follows:

New asset...	38,000	
Accumulated depreciation, old asset	17,000	
Old asset		20,000
Cash		35,000

Note that there is no recognition in an income statement account of the $2,000 gain ($5,000 fair value − $3,000 book value) arising from the disposition of the old asset. The amount of the gain has been incorporated into the cost of the new asset. In effect, it has been deferred and will be included in net income through reduced depreciation expense over the new asset's life.

LOSS ON DISPOSITION OF OLD ASSET, SIMILAR ASSETS INVOLVED

The second case described in the table is that in which there is a loss on the disposition of the old asset and the assets involved in the trade-in transaction are similar. Let us assume for this case that fair value for the old asset is $1,200. Because the book value of the old asset exceeds its fair value, there is a loss on disposition of the old asset. Therefore, the cost of the new asset will be the sum of the fair value of the old asset and the boot paid ($1,200 + $35,000 = $36,200). The journal entry to record this trade will be as follows:

New asset...	36,200	
Accumulated depreciation, old asset	17,000	
Loss on trade-in of plant asset*	1,800	
Old asset		20,000
Cash		35,000

* Fair value of $1,200 − Book value of $3,000.

Note that this journal entry includes recognition of the $1,800 loss ($1,200 fair value − $3,000 book value) arising from the disposition of the old asset. The cost of the new asset includes the fair value of all that was given to acquire it — cash of $35,000 and an asset worth $1,200.

GAIN ON DISPOSITION OF OLD ASSET, DISSIMILAR ASSETS INVOLVED

In the third type of trade-in transaction, there is a gain on the disposition of the old asset, and the assets are dissimilar. Let us assume that fair value for the old asset is $5,000. Fair value of the old asset exceeds its book value, resulting in a gain. Since the assets involved are dissimilar, accountants argue that the earnings process associated with activities using the old asset has ended and that it is now appropriate to record the gain on the disposition of the old asset. Therefore, the cost of the new asset will be the sum of the fair value of the old asset and the boot paid ($5,000 + $35,000 = $40,000). The journal entry to record this trade will be:

New asset...	40,000	
Accumulated depreciation, old asset	17,000	
Gain on trade-in of plant asset*		2,000
Old asset		20,000
Cash		35,000

* Fair value of $5,000 − Book value of $3,000.

This journal entry includes recognition of the $2,000 gain ($5,000 fair value − $3,000 book value) arising from the disposition of the old asset. The cost of the new asset includes the fair value of all that was given to acquire it—cash of $35,000 and an asset worth $5,000.

LOSS ON DISPOSITION OF OLD ASSET, DISSIMILAR ASSETS INVOLVED

In the fourth case identified in the table, there is a loss on the disposition of the old asset, and the assets involved in the trade-in transaction are dissimilar. Let us assume again that fair value for the old asset is $1,200. The book value of the old asset exceeds its fair value, resulting in a loss. Since the earnings process associated with activities using the old asset has ended and in order to adhere to the conservatism convention, the cost of the new asset will be the sum of the fair value of the old asset and the boot paid ($1,200 + $35,000 = $36,200). The journal entry to record this trade will be:

New asset...	36,200	
Accumulated depreciation, old asset	17,000	
Loss on trade-in of plant asset*........................	1,800	
Old asset		20,000
Cash		35,000

* Fair value of $1,200 − Book value of $3,000.

Note that the form of this journal entry is identical with that of the second case, including recognition of the $1,800 loss ($1,200 fair value − $3,000 book value) arising from the disposition of the old asset. The cost of the new asset again includes the fair value of all that was given to acquire it—cash of $35,000 and an asset worth $1,200.

A review of these four cases indicates that the accounting is similar for all trades except those involving similar assets when there is a "gain" on the disposition of the old asset. Only in this case is the new asset recorded at an amount other than the fair value of what was given to acquire it.

In rare instances, a business will trade in a plant asset and receive a new plant asset and cash in the exchange (in other words, boot is received rather than paid). Such a transaction implies that the fair value of the old plant asset exceeds the fair value of the new plant asset by the amount of the boot received. The recording of gains or losses in such cases involves computations and procedures that are discussed in intermediate accounting texts.

KEY TERMS

ACCELERATED DEPRECIATION (p. 372)

ACCUMULATED DEPRECIATION (p. 370)

ACQUISITION COST (p. 365)

AMORTIZATION (p. 386)

BASKET PURCHASE (p. 367)

BOOK VALUE (p. 373)

BOOT (p. 385)

CAPITAL EXPENDITURE (p. 381)

DECLINING BALANCE DEPRECIATION (p. 374)

DEPLETION (p. 391)

DEPRECIABLE COST (p. 372)

DEPRECIATION (p. 368)

DEPRECIATION METHODS (p. 371)

EXPECTED LIFE (p. 369)

FAIR VALUE (FAIR MARKET VALUE) (p. 366)

INTANGIBLE OPERATING ASSETS (p. 385)

INVOLUNTARY CONVERSION (p. 383)

NATURAL RESOURCES (p. 390)

OPERATING ASSETS (p. 364)

RESIDUAL VALUE (SALVAGE VALUE) (p. 370)

REVENUE EXPENDITURE (p. 381)

SERVICE POTENTIAL CONCEPT (p. 364)

STRAIGHT-LINE DEPRECIATION (p. 372)

SUM-OF-THE-YEARS'-DIGITS DEPRECIATION (p. 373)

TANGIBLE OPERATING ASSETS (p. 365)

TRADE-IN (p. 385)

USAGE DEPRECIATION (p. 376)

VOLUNTARY RETIREMENT (p. 383)

QUESTIONS

Q9-1. How do operating assets differ from nonoperating assets? What benefits do operating assets provide to the firm?

Q9-2. How are property, plant, and equipment; intangibles; and natural resources different from one another?

Q9-3. How do the cost concept and the matching concept affect accounting for operating assets?

Q9-4. How is the service potential concept applied over the useful life of an operating asset?

Q9-5. Why is a separate cost developed for each asset acquired in a basket purchase?

Q9-6. What objective should guide the selection of a depreciation method for financial reporting purposes?

Q9-7. What objective should be of primary importance in the selection of a depreciation method for income tax reporting?

Q9-8. How do accelerated and straight-line depreciation differ?

Q9-9. What accounting concepts should be considered when evaluating the accounting for expenditures that are made for an operating asset subsequent to acquisition?

Q9-10. Describe the benefits that intangible assets provide to an enterprise.

Q9-11. What factors should be considered when selecting the amortization period for an intangible asset?

Q9-12. What basis underlies the computation of depletion?

Q9-13. Explain how to account for depreciation on plant assets used in conjunction with natural resource assets.

APPENDIX QUESTIONS

Q9-14. How is the cost of the new asset determined in a trade-in transaction?

Q9-15. What circumstances determine whether a gain on a trade-in transaction is deferred (included in the cost of the new asset) or recognized in the income statement?

EXERCISES

E9-16. CHARACTERISTICS OF DEPRECIATION METHODS   Match one or more of the depreciation methods listed below with each characteristic in the list that follows. Your answer should list the numbers 1 through 8 and, opposite each number, the letters of the depreciation methods possessing the corresponding characteristic.

DEPRECIATION METHODS

A. Straight-line depreciation method

B. Sum-of-the-years'-digits depreciation method

C. Declining balance depreciation method

D. Usage depreciation method when actual usage increases over the life of the asset

CHARACTERISTICS

1. Allocates the same amount of cost to each period of a depreciable asset's life.

2. Results in depreciation expense that decreases over the life of the asset.

3. Results in depreciation expense that increases over the life of the asset.

4. Consistent with the service potential concept.

5. Calculated by multiplying a *changing* rate or ratio by depreciable cost.

6. Calculated by multiplying a *constant* rate or ratio by depreciable cost.

7. Calculated by applying a *constant* rate or ratio to the asset's book value at the beginning of the period.

8. Results in lowest income taxes in early years of the asset's life.

E9-17. ACQUISITION COSTS   Quick Stop, a convenience store, purchased a new soft-drink cooler. The cooler had a list price of $23,000. The manufacturer of the cooler offered Quick Stop terms of 3/15, n/30. Quick Stop paid cash for the cooler within the discount period and paid $730 to have the cooler shipped to its location. After the new cooler arrived, Quick Stop paid $2,410 to have the old cooler dismantled and removed. Quick Stop also paid $820 to a contractor to have new wiring and drains installed for the new cooler.

REQUIRED:

1. Prepare journal entries for the transactions described above.

2. Prepare the adjusting entry to record one year's straight-line depreciation on the new cooler. Assume an expected life of six years and residual value of $200.

E9-18. ACQUISITION COSTS IN A BASKET PURCHASE   Carthage Apartments purchased an apartment building and the land on which it stands for $490,000. In addition, Carthage paid closing costs and transfer taxes in the amount of $6,000. Immediately following acquisition, Carthage hired an appraisal firm to estimate the value of the land and building. The land was appraised at $125,000, and the building was appraised at $375,000. Shortly after the appraisal, Carthage spent $62,000 to renovate part of the building.

REQUIRED:

1. Compute the separate costs for the land and the building. Why is it necessary to separate the cost of the land from the cost of the building?

2. Prepare the journal entries to record the acquisition and the renovation.

E9-19. ACQUISITION AND REMODELING COSTS Mooney Sounds, a local stereo retailer, needed a new store because it had outgrown the leased space it had used for several years. Mooney acquired and remodeled a former grocery store. As a part of the acquisition, Mooney incurred the following costs:

Cost of grocery store	$350,000
Cost of land (on which the grocery store is located)	65,000
New roof for building	74,000
Lumber used for remodeling	23,200
Paint	515
Wire and electrical supplies	4,290
New doors	6,400
New windows	3,850
Labor (wages paid to Mooney employees who did the remodeling)	12,500
Additional inventory purchased for grand opening sale	45,300

REQUIRED:

Select the account to be used for recording each of these costs, and indicate the amount added to each account with these transactions.

E9-20. ACQUISITION COSTS Laurel Cleaners purchased an automatic dry cleaning machine from TGF Corporation on April 1, 19X1. The machine has a list price of $150,000. TGF typically offers cash customers a 10 percent discount from the list price. Laurel, however, paid $35,000 in cash and signed a five-year, 15 percent note for $100,000. Laurel will pay interest on the note each year on March 31, beginning in 19X2. A transfer tax of 4 percent on the purchase was paid by Laurel on April 30. Transportation charges of $3,500 for the machine were paid by Laurel. Laurel also paid $2,400 for the living expenses of the TGF installation crew. During installation one of the TGF employees inadvertently damaged Laurel's pants press. TGF paid $1,200 to repair the damage. Solvent costing $1,000 was acquired to supply the new machine, and $500 of the solvent was used to test and adjust the machine.

REQUIRED:

Compute the acquisition cost of the new dry cleaning machine. Indicate the disposition of any costs not included in the acquisition cost and explain why each is excluded.

E9-21. RECORDING AN ACQUISITION Colson Developing Service purchased a new enlarger on April 15. The list price of the enlarger was $13,400. The seller offered Colson terms of 3/10, n/15. Colson recorded the purchase net of discount and paid the list price in late May. During installation Colson incurred and paid in cash the following costs:

Rental of drill	$150
Electrical contractor	400
Plumbing contractor	190

Colson also paid $160 to replace a bracket on the enlarger that was damaged when one of Colson's employees dropped a box on it.

REQUIRED:

1. What should be done with the $402 discount that was not taken? Prepare the journal entry to record payment of the $13,400.

2. At what amount should the enlarger be recorded in Colson's ledger?

3. Why did you include or exclude the $160 bracket replacement cost?

E9-22. BASKET PURCHASE   Phyllis Sanchez has just purchased a small, successful frozen yogurt store from its previous owner. Phyllis paid $104,000 and acquired the items in the following list. The fair values were estimated so that adequate insurance could be obtained.

ITEM	FAIR VALUE
Land	$ 20,900
Building	68,200
Yogurt machines	8,305
Tables	3,300
Chairs	3,850
Cash register	1,925
Yogurt mix	825
Cones	275
Plastic dishes and spoons	1,870
Paper products	550
Total	$110,000

REQUIRED:

Allocate the total cost of the acquisition to the various assets acquired.

E9-23. DEPRECIATION METHODS   Berkshire Corporation purchased a copying machine for $9,800. The machine's residual value was $1,175 and its expected life was five years or 2,000,000 copies. Actual usage was 480,000 copies the first year and 440,000 the second year.

REQUIRED:

Compute straight-line, sum-of-the-years'-digits, double declining balance, and usage depreciation for the first two years for Berkshire's copying machine.

E9-24. DEPRECIATION AND MID-YEAR ACQUISITION   On April 1, 19X3, Cardiff Corporation purchased a large computer for $83,000 and placed it in service. The computer has an expected life of five years and a residual value of $23,000. The company records depreciation annually at the end of the year. Part-year depreciation is calculated using the nearest-whole-month convention.

REQUIRED:

1. Prepare the adjusting entries to be made at December 31, 19X3, and December 31, 19X4, to record depreciation expense on the machine using straight-line depreciation.

2. Prepare the adjusting entries to be made at December 31, 19X3, and December 31, 19X4, to record depreciation expense on the machine using sum-of-the-years'-digits depreciation.

E9-25. CHOICE AMONG DEPRECIATION METHODS   Walnut Ridge Printing, Inc., purchased a new computerized typesetting system at a cost of $370,000. The system has a residual value of $55,000 and an expected life of five years.

REQUIRED:

1. For the first three years of the computer's life, compute depreciation expense, accumulated depreciation, and book value, using the straight-line, sum-of-the-years'-digits, and double declining balance depreciation methods.

2. Which method would produce the largest income in the first, second, and third year, respectively, of the asset's life?

3. Why might the controller of Walnut Ridge Printing be interested in the effect of choosing a depreciation method? Evaluate the legitimacy of these interests.

E9-26. DEPRECIATION METHODS   Clearcopy, a printing company, acquired a new press this year. The press cost $171,600 and had an expected life of eight years or 4,500,000 pages and an expected residual value of $15,000. If Clearcopy printed 675,000 pages this year, what are straight-line, sum-of-the-years'-digits, double declining balance, and usage depreciation for a full year's use of the press?

E9-27. DEPRECIATION CALCULATIONS FOR FOUR YEARS   Campus Copy Shop provides its customers with access to computers attached to laser printers for word processing of term papers and résumés. Recently, Campus purchased a new computer for $5,700. The computer is expected to have a useful life of four years and a residual value of $400.

REQUIRED:

Compute depreciation expense for each of the four years, using the three methods shown in the following table, and enter your depreciation expense amounts in a table similar to the one that follows.

YEAR	STRAIGHT-LINE	SUM-OF-THE YEARS'-DIGITS	DOUBLE DECLINING BALANCE
1			
2			
3			
4			

E9-28. SUBSEQUENT EXPENDITURES   Roanoke Manufacturing replaced a robotic arm on a large assembly machine on October 1, 19X2. The following data are available:

Acquisition cost, assembly machine $750,000
Accumulated depreciation, 10/1/X2 480,000
Cost, robotic arm (installed) 210,000
Residual value (after arm replacement) 120,000
Expected life (after arm replacement) . . . . 6 years

REQUIRED:

Compute a full year's depreciation for the machine after installation of the new robotic arm.

E9-29. SUBSEQUENT EXPENDITURES AND DEPRECIATION   Eastern National Bank installed a telephone and data switch in January 19X2. The switch cost $120,000. At the time the switch was installed, Eastern estimated that it would have an expected life of eight years and a residual value of $10,000. By 19X5 the bank's business had expanded and modifications to the switch were necessary. At the end of 19X5, Eastern spent $45,000 on additional memory and software for the switch. The modified switch was put into service on the first business day of 19X6. Eastern estimates that the expected life of the switch from January 19X6 is six years and that the new residual value is $5,000. Had Eastern not modified the switch, it estimates that telephone and data transmission delays would have caused the bank to lose business that will provide a profit of at least $100,000 per year.

REQUIRED:

1. Compute the accumulated straight-line depreciation for the switch at the time the modifications were made (four years after acquisition).

2. What is the book value of the switch before and after the modification?

3. What will be annual straight-line depreciation for the switch after the modification?

4. The bank's president notes, "Since the after-modification depreciation exceeds the before-modification depreciation, this modification was a poor idea." Comment on the president's assertion.

E9-30. SALE OF PLANT ASSET AT YEAR-END   Perfect Auto Rentals sold one of its cars for $4,400 cash on July 1, 19X5. Perfect had acquired the car on February 1, 19X3, for $13,500. At acquisition Perfect assumed that the car would have an estimated life of 30 months and a residual value of $3,000. Assume that Perfect has recorded straight-line depreciation for 19X3 (11 months) and 19X4 (12 months).

REQUIRED:

1. Compute and record straight-line depreciation for the car for 19X5 (six months).

2. Prepare the journal entry to record the sale of the car.

E9-31. SALE OF PLANT ASSET AT YEAR-END   Pacifica Manufacturing retired a computerized metal stamping machine on December 31, 19X7. Pacifica transferred the particular stamping operations performed by the machine to another company and did not replace the machine. The following data are available for the machine:

Acquisition cost (installed), 1/1/X2 . . . . $920,000
Residual value expected on 1/1/X2   160,000
Expected life, 1/1/X2 . . . .   8 years

The machine was sold for $188,000 cash.

REQUIRED:

1. Compute accumulated depreciation on a straight-line basis at December 31, 19X7.

2. Prepare the journal entry to record straight-line depreciation for 19X7.

3. Prepare the journal entry to record the sale of the machine.

4. Explain how the sale would be reported on the 19X7 income statement.

E9-32. DEPLETION RATE   Oxford Quarries purchased 45 acres of land for $225,000. The land contained stone that Oxford will remove from the ground, finish, and then sell as facing material for buildings. After purchasing the land, Oxford spent $48,000 building a road, $30,000 removing topsoil from the rock deposit, and $60,000 constructing a building. The building was used for two years during the preparation of the site for quarrying and will be used for the remaining life of the quarry. Oxford estimates that the quarry contains 55,000 tons of usable stone and that it will require six years to remove all the usable stone once quarrying begins. Upon completion of quarrying, Oxford estimates that the land will have a residual value of $9,000 and that the building will be sold for $4,000 as scrap.

REQUIRED:

Compute the depletion rate per ton.

E9-33. DEPLETION OF TIMBER   Bedford Ridge Development purchased a 5,000-acre tract of forested land in southern Georgia. The tract contained about 1,500,000 pine trees that, when mature, can be used for utility poles. Bedford paid $900 per acre for the timberland. The land has a residual value of $180 per acre when all the trees are harvested. Bedford will spend a total of $600,000 over the next four years building logging roads and other facilities in preparation for harvesting the trees. Beginning in the fifth year following acquisition of the tract, Bedford expects to start harvesting trees.

REQUIRED:

1. Compute the depletion per tree.

2. Would your answer to requirement 1 change if the $600,000 expenditure over the next four years were for fire prevention and other normal operating expenditures rather than for depreciable roads and facilities? Explain, and if a different number results, recompute depletion per tree.

E9-34.   AMORTIZATION OF INTANGIBLES   Boulder Investments, Inc., acquired a franchise to operate a Burger Doodle restaurant. Boulder paid $160,000 for a 10-year franchise and incurred organization costs of $12,000. The cost of the franchise will be amortized over 10 years, and the organization costs will be amortized over 5 years.

REQUIRED:

1. Prepare the journal entry to record the payment with cash of the franchise fee and organization costs.

2. Prepare the journal entries to record the annual amortization at the end of the first year.

E9-35.   BALANCE SHEET PRESENTATION   Use the following data to prepare the property, plant, and equipment and intangible assets portions of a classified balance sheet for Westfield Semiconductors:

ASSET	ACQUISITION COST	EXPECTED LIFE	RESIDUAL VALUE	USED
Land..........	$104,300	Infinite	$100,000	10 years
Building.......	430,000	25 years	30,000	10 years
Machine.......	285,000	5 years	10,000	2 years
Test set........	114,000	3 years	6,000	2 years
Patent.........	80,000	10 years	–0–	3 years
Truck.........	21,000	100,000 miles	3,000	44,000 miles

APPENDIX EXERCISES

E9-36.   ASSET TRADE-IN   Lewis Company acquired a new asset by trading in an old asset and paying $19,350 cash. At the time of the trade, the old asset had an acquisition cost of $15,400 and accumulated depreciation of $13,700.

REQUIRED:

1. Prepare the trade-in journal entry if the fair value of the old asset is $2,000 and the assets are similar.

2. Prepare the trade-in journal entry if the fair value of the old asset is $2,000 and the assets are dissimilar.

3. Prepare the trade-in journal entry if the fair value of the old asset is $1,000 and the assets are similar.

4. Prepare the trade-in journal entry if the fair value of the old asset is $1,000 and the assets are dissimilar.

E9-37.   TRADE OF DISSIMILAR ASSETS   Woodside Paving Company purchased a paving machine five years ago. At acquisition the machine cost $144,000. Woodside has decided to end its paving business and become an installer of below-ground swimming pools. Therefore Woodside has just traded the paving machine for an air compressor. At the time of the trade, the paving machine had accumulated depreciation of $120,000. The trade-in transaction to acquire the air compressor also required Woodside to pay $24,000 cash. The fair value of the paving machine at the time of the trade was $35,000.

REQUIRED:

1. Prepare the entry to record the trade in Woodside's journal.

2. How would the entry have been different if the fair value of the paving machine at the time of the trade had been $19,000?

E9-38. TRADE OF SIMILAR ASSETS   Percival, a local rock band, decided to trade its sound and light control board for a newer, more capable board. Percival paid $27,300 cash and its old control board to acquire the new one. The following data are available for the old control board:

Cost. $15,400
Accumulated depreciation (as of date of trade)   10,200

REQUIRED:

1. Prepare the journal entry to record this trade if the fair value of the old control board is $5,800.
2. Prepare the journal entry to record this trade if the fair value of the old control board is $2,300.

PROBLEMS

P9-39. FINANCIAL STATEMENT PRESENTATION OF OPERATING ASSETS   Olympic Acquisitions, Inc., prepared the following postclosing trial balance at December 31, 19X7:

	DEBIT	CREDIT
Cash	$ 6,400	
Accounts receivable.	15,000	
Supplies inventory.	26,000	
Land	42,000	
Buildings	155,000	
Accumulated _____, buildings		$ 72,000
Equipment	279,000	
Accumulated _____, equipment.		102,000
Franchise.	62,000	
Accumulated _____, franchise		12,400
Goodwill	58,000	
Accumulated _____, goodwill.		29,500
Timber tract	285,000	
Accumulated _____, timber tract		91,000
Gravel pit	32,000	
Accumulated _____, gravel pit		16,300
Accounts payable.		4,100
Wages payable.		7,000
Interest payable		7,300
Income taxes payable.		12,000
Notes payable (due in 8 years)		190,000
Capital stock		300,000
Retained earnings		116,800
Totals.	$960,400	$960,400

REQUIRED:

Supply the missing words in the trial balance above, and prepare a classified balance sheet for Olympic Acquisitions at December 31, 19X7. Olympic reports the three categories of operating assets in separate subsections of assets. Intangibles and natural resources are reported net of the related contra-asset accounts, whose balances are not reported on the balance sheet; however, separate contra account balances are reported for plant assets:

P9-40. ACQUISITION OF USED AIRPLANES Baltimore Air Freight purchased three used airplanes for cash of $21,000,000. The aircraft were immediately overhauled and then put into service. Although the planes are similar, Baltimore decided to record them in separate accounts. The appraisal values, overhaul costs, remaining expected lives, and residual values of the three planes are presented in the following table:

	PLANE 1	PLANE 2	PLANE 3
Appraisal value	$7,717,500	$8,820,000	$5,512,500
Overhaul cost	1,400,000	900,000	1,800,000
Residual value	1,100,000	1,300,000	1,000,000
Expected life	5 years	5 years	4 years

REQUIRED:

1. Compute the acquisition cost of each aircraft.
2. Prepare the entry to record the acquisition in Baltimore's journal.
3. Prepare the journal entry to record the overhaul costs.
4. Write the journal entry to record one full year's straight-line depreciation for each of the planes.

P9-41. ACQUISITION COST Mist City Car Wash purchased a new brushless car-washing machine for one of its bays. The machine cost $31,800. Mist City borrowed the purchase price from its bank on a one-year, 12 percent note payable. Mist City incurred the following costs as a part of the installation:

Plumbing.	$2,700
Electrical	1,640
Water (for testing the machine)	35
Soap (for testing the machine)	18

During the testing process, one of the motors became defective when soap and water entered the motor because its cover had not been installed properly by Mist City's employees. The motor was replaced at a cost of $450.

REQUIRED:

Compute the cost of the car-washing machine.

P9-42. CONSTRUCTION OF AN APARTMENT BUILDING In early 19X2, Alice Ostanek purchased two large lots with old houses near a university for $340,000. Alice rented the houses to students for one year while she obtained zoning approvals for the apartment building she planned to build on the land. The students paid rent of $20,000, and Alice's expenses were $4,300 during that year. In January 19X3, Alice had the old houses torn down at a cost of $3,900. The following additional costs were incurred to construct the new apartment building:

Legal fees to secure zoning approval	$ 11,500
Architect's fees to design apartment building.	48,300
Cost of constructing apartment building	505,000
Cost of dirt required to level land for parking lot.	5,200
Cost of constructing parking lot.	38,100
Cost of landscaping (5-year life).	4,300

REQUIRED:

1. Compute the cost of the land.
2. Compute the cost of the apartment building.
3. Compute the costs of any other assets created.
4. Explain why each element of cost was allocated to the account you selected.

P9-43. BASKET PURCHASE   Vandalia Products, Inc., recently purchased Xenia Technology, a small manufacturing company, from the estate of the company's founder. Vandalia paid $1,800,000 cash for all the company's assets. Fair values for the acquired assets were established by an independent appraisal firm; book values were taken from Xenia's accounting records. The following assets were acquired:

	BOOK VALUE	FAIR VALUE
Land.....................................	$ 10,000	$ 250,000
Building	120,000	350,000
Equipment, manufacturing.....................	548,000	750,000
Furniture and fixtures.........................	38,000	80,000
Trademark	–0–	500,000
Inventory	70,000	70,000
Total.................................	$786,000	$2,000,000

REQUIRED:

1. Compute the cost to be recorded for each acquired asset, and prepare the journal entry to record the acquisition on Vandalia's records.

2. Justify your choice of fair value or book value as the basis for computing the cost of each acquired asset.

P9-44. DEPRECIATION METHODS   Hansen Supermarkets purchased an electronic code-scanning system for one of its stores at a cost of $150,000. Hansen determined that the system had an expected life of seven years and an expected residual value of $7,200.

REQUIRED:

1. Determine the amount of depreciation expense for the first and second years of the system's life, using the straight-line, double declining balance, and sum-of-the-years'-digits methods.

2. If the number of items scanned the first and second years were 7,200,000 and 8,150,000, respectively, compute usage depreciation for both years if the expected life of the system is 50,000,000 items scanned.

3. Prepare a table of book values for all four depreciation methods as of the end of the first and second years of the system's life.

P9-45. DEPRECIATION CALCULATIONS   Assume that a depreciable asset was put into service on January 1, 19X1. The following information is available for that asset:

Cash paid to acquire asset	$95,000
Installation costs	11,800
Estimated residual value	6,000
Expected life (in years)	8 years
Expected life (in usage)	16,000 hours
Actual usage for 19X1....................................	1,900 hours

REQUIRED:

1. Compute straight-line, sum-of-the-years'-digits, double declining balance, and usage depreciation for 19X1.

2. If usage is 2,050 hours in 19X2, compute straight-line, sum-of-the-years'-digits, double declining balance, and usage depreciation for 19X2.

3. Compute straight-line, sum-of-the-years'-digits, and double declining balance depreciation for 19X7 and 19X8.

P9-46. DEPRECIATION SCHEDULES   Wendt Corporation acquired a new depreciable asset for $80,000. The asset has a four-year expected life and a residual value of zero.

REQUIRED:

1. Prepare a depreciation schedule for four years for this asset, using straight-line depreciation.
2. Prepare a depreciation schedule for four years for this asset, using sum-of-the-years'-digits depreciation.
3. Prepare a depreciation schedule for four years for this asset, using double declining balance depreciation.

P9-47. MIDYEAR ACQUISITION AND SALE OF PLANT   On April 25, 19X3, Oxford Properties, Inc., purchased an apartment building for $490,000 cash, of which $30,000 was allocated to the land occupied by the building. Depreciation was calculated using an expected life of 15 years and a residual value of $100,000. On July 5, 19X6, Oxford Properties sold the land and the building for $420,000. For purposes of simplifying depreciation calculations, Oxford Properties substitutes the date of the nearer first of the month for actual acquisition and sale dates.

REQUIRED:

1. Prepare the journal entries to record the acquisition, annual depreciation, and sale of the building using straight-line depreciation.
2. Prepare the journal entries to record the acquisition, annual depreciation, and sale of the building using sum-of-the-years'-digits depreciation.

P9-48. CAPITAL VERSUS REVENUE EXPENDITURE   Warrick Water Company, a privately owned business, supplies water to several communities. Warrick has just performed an extensive overhaul on one of its water pumps. The overhaul is expected to extend the life of the pump by 10 years. The residual value of the pump is unchanged. You have been asked to determine which of the following costs should be capitalized as a part of this overhaul. Those costs not capitalized are to be expensed. Explain your classification of each cost.

ELEMENT OF COST	DISPOSITION AND EXPLANATION
New pump motor	
Repacking of bearings (performed monthly)	
New impeller	
Painting of pump housing (performed annually)	
Replacement of pump foundation	
New wiring (needed every five years)	
Installation labor, motor	
Installation labor, impeller	
Installation labor, wiring	
Paint labor	
Placement of fence around pump*	

* A new requirement of the Occupational Safety and Health Administration that will add to maintenance costs over the remaining life of the pump.

P9-49. SUBSEQUENT EXPENDITURES   Pasta, a restaurant specializing in fresh pasta, installed a pasta cooker in early 19X4 at a cost of $11,800. The cooker had an expected life of 5 years and a residual value of $600 when installed. As the restaurant's business increased, it became apparent that renovations were necessary so that the output of the cooker could be increased. In January 19X7, Pasta spent $8,200 to install new heating equipment and $4,100 to add pressure-cooking capability. After these renovations, Pasta estimated that the remaining useful life of the cooker was 10 years and that residual value was now $1,500.

REQUIRED:

1. Compute one year's straight-line depreciation on the cooker before the renovations.

2. Compute the capitalized cost of the cooker after the renovations were made.

3. Assume that three full years of straight-line depreciation had been recorded on the cooker before the renovations were made. Compute one year's straight-line depreciation on the renovated cooker.

P9-50. REPAIR DECISION   Clermont Transit operates a summer ferry service to islands in the Ohio River. Farmers use the ferry to move farming equipment to and from the islands. Clermont's ferry is in need of repair. A new engine and steering assembly must be installed, or the Coast Guard will not permit the ferry to be used. Because of competition, Clermont will not be able to raise its rates for ferry service if these repairs are made. Costs of providing the ferry service will not be decreased if the repairs are made.

REQUIRED:

1. Identify the factors that Clermont should consider when evaluating whether or not to make the repairs.

2. Since the revenue rate cannot be increased and expenses will not be decreased if the repairs are made, can the cost of the repairs be capitalized? Why?

P9-51. DISPOSITION OF A DAMAGED COMPUTER   The computer room of Pierce Systems, Inc., was flooded recently when a water pipe on the floor above broke during a weekend. The computer was running when the water flooded the area, and it was seriously damaged. Pierce's insurance company has agreed to pay Pierce $350,000 and take possession of the damaged computer. Pierce's accounting records include the following data for the computer:

Cost. $480,000
Accumulated depreciation (through date of damage).   120,000

REQUIRED:

Record the disposition of the computer in Pierce's journal.

P9-52. DISPOSITION OF OPERATING ASSETS   Salva Pest Control disposed of four assets recently. Salva's accounting records provided the following information about the assets at the time of their disposal:

ASSET	COST	ACCUMULATED DEPRECIATION
Pump	$ 5,900	$ 4,800
Truck	18,600	17,500
Office equipment.	4,200	4,000
Chemical testing apparatus	7,300	4,000

The truck was sold for $2,000 cash, and the chemical testing apparatus was donated to the local high school. Because the pump was contaminated with pesticides, $500 in cash was paid to a chemical disposal company to decontaminate the pump and dispose of it safely. The office equipment was taken to the local landfill.

REQUIRED:

Prepare a separate journal entry to record the disposition of each of these assets.

P9-53. SALE OF ASSETS   In order to provide capital for new hotel construction in other locations, Wilton Hotel Corporation has decided to sell its hotel in Pierre, South Dakota. Wilton auctions the hotel and its contents on October 1, 19X7, with the following results:

Land and building.	$720,000
Furniture and fixtures	120,000
Supplies.	25,000

An appraisal suggests that the land has a fair value of $600,000 and that the building has a fair value of $300,000. (Auction prices sometimes differ from fair value estimates because of variations in market conditions or imperfections in the auction market.) Wilton's accounting records reveal the following information about the assets sold:

ASSET	ACQUISITION COST	ACCUMULATED DEPRECIATION
Land.	$ 15,000	
Building	350,000	$295,000
Furniture and fixtures.	298,000	133,000
Supplies	48,000	

REQUIRED:

Prepare the journal entry to remove the assets sold from Wilton's accounting records. Record a separate gain or loss for each asset sold, and support your entry with appropriate computations.

P9-54. NATURAL RESOURCE AND INTANGIBLE ACCOUNTING   McLeansboro Oil Company acquired an operating oil well during a recent year. The following assets were acquired for $450,000 cash and 20,000 shares of McLeansboro's stock (with a fair value of $45 per share). Information about the assets at the time of their acquisition included the following:

ASSET	FAIR VALUE	EXPECTED LIFE
Oil well	$1,100,000	55,000 barrels
Land	85,000	Indefinite
Pump	65,000	550,000 barrels

REQUIRED:

1. Write the entry to record this acquisition in McLeansboro's journal. (Hint: Record the cost in excess of fair value as goodwill.)
2. If McLeansboro pumps and sells 11,000 barrels of oil in one year, compute the depletion.
3. Prepare journal entries to record depletion for the 11,000 barrels of oil pumped and sold and for one year's amortization of the goodwill. (Assume that goodwill is being amortized over the expected life of the well, 55,000 barrels.)
4. Why are the land and the pump capitalized separately from the oil well?

P9-55. DEPLETION OF NATURAL GAS FIELD   The Mudcat Gas Company owns an operational natural gas field in Oklahoma. When gas production began in 19X1, the gas field had a depletable cost of $156,217,500. Estimated recoverable gas was 104,145,000 cubic feet. In 19X8, Mudcat decided to increase production from this field by drilling two new wells into the field and by adopting a new recovery technique. The new technique should increase the amount of gas recoverable, and the additional wells will permit more gas to be recovered each year. During 19X8 the new wells were completed at a cost of $9,541,500. The equipment to employ the new gas recovery technique was also installed in 19X8 at a cost of $17,615,000. Increased production and use of the new recovery technique began in January 19X9. The following data are available:

Gas produced, 19X1–X8	20,150,000 cu. ft.
Gas recoverable, 1/1/X9	105,620,000 cu. ft.

REQUIRED:

1. What was the depletion rate when gas production began in 19X1?
2. What was the book value of the gas field at the end of 19X8 but before the addition of the cost of the new wells and the recovery technique?

3. What is the depletion rate for 19X9?

4. Record the 19X9 depletion if Mudcat produces 3,217,000 cubic feet of natural gas.

P9-56. GOODWILL   Brampton Corporation purchased the assets of London Products for $820,000 cash. The fair values of the assets acquired from London Products are as follows:

Land	$150,000
Building	340,000
Equipment	278,000
Supplies.	27,000

REQUIRED:

1. Prepare the journal entry by Brampton to record this acquisition of assets.

2. Brampton assumes that the goodwill has an expected life of 20 years. Prepare the entry to record one full year's amortization of goodwill.

P9-57. LEASEHOLD AMORTIZATION   The public accounting firm of Blackwell and Medford recently moved into a suite of offices in a new building. The lease required a payment of $75,000 in advance and monthly rental payments of $10,000. The lease has a term of 10 years and is renewable for another 10 years with another advance payment of $100,000. Monthly rental payments for the renewal will be based on the consumer price index at the time the lease is renewed.

REQUIRED:

1. Compute the rent expense for Blackwell and Medford for a full year's use of its new office.

2. Prepare the journal entry to record the amortization of the leasehold at the end of the first year's use of the new office.

3. Indicate how the leasehold would appear in the Blackwell and Medford balance sheet at the end of the first year.

P9-58. SUCCESSFUL DEFENSE OF PATENT   In 19X1, Technocraft, Inc., acquired a patent that was used for manufacturing semiconductor-based electronic circuitry. The patent was originally recorded in Technocraft's ledger at its cost of $1,796,000. Technocraft has been amortizing the patent over an expected economic life of 10 years. Residual value was assumed to be zero. In 19X8 Technocraft sued another firm for infringing on its patent. Technocraft spent $180,000 on this suit and won a judgment to recover the $180,000 plus damages of $500,000. The sued firm paid the $680,000.

REQUIRED:

1. Compute and record one year's amortization on the patent prior to the lawsuit.

2. Journalize the expenditure of $180,000 to defend the patent.

3. Journalize the award of $680,000.

4. Indicate the entry you would have made had Technocraft lost the suit. (Assume that the patent would be valueless if Technocraft had lost the suit.)

APPENDIX PROBLEMS

P9-59. TRADE-IN OF SIMILAR ASSETS WITH GAIN   Birch Dairy has decided to expand its retail milk and bakery products delivery. The trucks that Birch used for retail delivery are being traded in for a new model of refrigerated truck. The following data are available for the old trucks:

Cost.	$25,000
Accumulated depreciation.	18,600
Fair value	8,200

Acquisition of the new trucks required a cash payment of $28,400 plus the trade-in of the old trucks.

REQUIRED:

1. Should a gain be recorded on this trade-in transaction? Why?

2. Record the disposal of the old trucks and the acquisition of the new trucks.

P9-60. TRADE-IN OF DISSIMILAR ASSETS   Garrison Products traded some land that it had acquired several years ago for a conveyor system for its warehouse. The land had cost $30,000 and had a fair value when traded of $75,000. Garrison also paid the conveyor manufacturer $39,000.

REQUIRED:

1. Make the entry in Garrison's journal to record this transaction.

2. Did you record a gain on the disposal of the land? Why?

ANALYTICAL OPPORTUNITIES

A9-61. ETHICS, INTERNAL CONTROLS, AND THE CAPITALIZATION DECISION   James Sage, an assistant controller in a large company, has a friend and former classmate, Henry Cactus, who sells computers. Sage agrees to help Cactus get part of the business that has been going to a large national computer manufacturer for many years. Sage knows that the controller would not approve a shift away from the national supplier but believes that he can authorize a number of small orders for equipment that will escape the controller's notice. Company policy requires that all capital expenditures be approved by a management committee; however, expenditures under $2,000 are all expenses and are subject to much less scrutiny. The assistant controller orders four computers to be used in a distant branch office. In order to keep the size of the order down, he makes four separate orders over a period of several months.

REQUIRED:

1. What are the probable consequences of this behavior for the company? For the assistant controller?

2. Describe internal control procedures that would be effective in discouraging and detecting this kind of behavior.

A9-62. MANAGEMENT'S DEPRECIATION DECISION   Great Basin Enterprises, a large holding company, acquired North Spruce Manufacturing, a medium-sized manufacturing business, from its founder, who wishes to retire. Despite great potential for development, North Spruce's income has been dropping in recent years. Great Basin installs a new management group (including a new controller) at North Spruce and gives the group six years to expand and revitalize the operations; management compensation includes a bonus based on net income generated by the North Spruce operations. If North Spruce does not show considerable improvement by the end of the sixth year, Great Basin will consider selling it. The new management immediately makes significant investments in new equipment but finds that new revenues develop slowly. Most of the new equipment will be replaced in 8 to 10 years. To defer income taxes to the maximum extent, the controller uses accelerated depreciation methods and the minimum allowable "expected lives" for the new equipment, which average 5 years. In preparing financial statements, the controller uses straight-line depreciation and expected lives that average 12 years for the new equipment.

REQUIRED:

1. Why did the controller compute financial statement depreciation as he or she did?

2. What are the possible consequences of the controller's decision on financial statement depreciation if it goes unchallenged?

PART 4

ACCOUNTING FOR LIABILITIES AND EQUITY

LEARNING OBJECTIVES

Careful study of this chapter will enable you to:

Section A

1. Identify circumstances that give rise to current liabilities.

2. Compute and record current liabilities.

3. Record contingent liabilities for warranties and pensions.

4. Describe the circumstances that give rise to contingent liabilities and deferred income tax.

Section B

5. Explain how compound interest is computed.

6. Apply compound interest procedures to determine future amounts and present values.

7. Use tables of future amount and present value multiples to apply the compound interest procedures to accounting transactions.

10 CURRENT LIABILITIES, CONTINGENT LIABILITIES, AND THE TIME VALUE OF MONEY

While a firm's assets represent future economic benefits currently controlled by the firm, its liabilities and equity represent economic benefits that the firm will transfer to other entities (creditors and owners) at some future time. The four preceding chapters have examined the accounting principles pertaining to various assets: inventories (Chapters 6 and 7); other current assets and investments (Chapter 8); and operating assets (Chapter 9). This chapter begins an examination of the accounting concepts and principles that apply to liabilities and equity. The chapter is divided into two sections: Section A examines current liabilities, contingent liabilities, and deferred income tax liabilities. Section B describes time-value-of-money (or compound interest) calculations. These calculations are the basis for the effective interest approach to long-term liability accounting that is described in Chapter 11B. Coverage of Section B is not a prerequisite for Chapter 11A, which describes the straight-line approach to long-term liability accounting.

Because there are two widely accepted approaches to accounting for long-term liabilities, we have organized the discussion of liabilities so that material can be assigned in a way that is consistent with the approach taken in your course. For that reason, this chapter has been divided into two sections, and there are two separate chapters on long-term liabilities (Chapters 11A and 11B). If your course presents accounting for long-term liabilities using straight-line procedures, you will probably study Section A of this chapter, then skip Section B and go directly to Chapter 11A. If your course presents the effective interest approach for long-term liabilities, then Sections A and B of this chapter and Chapter 11B will likely be assigned. Generally instructors prefer to assign either Chapter 11A or 11B; however, some instructors will assign both chapters.

SECTION A
CURRENT LIABILITIES, CONTINGENT LIABILITIES, AND DEFERRED INCOME TAXES

Section A begins with a discussion of recognition and measurement concepts for liabilities and then turns to three specific types of liabilities—current liabilities, contingent liabilities, and deferred income tax liabilities. These three liabilities do not involve difficult interest computations. Long-term liabilities, which require more complex interest calculations, are discussed in Chapters 11A and 11B.

RECOGNITION AND MEASUREMENT OF LIABILITIES

LIABILITIES: Probable future sacrifices of economic benefits.

Liabilities are probable future sacrifices of economic benefits. These sacrifices arise from the present obligations of an entity to transfer assets or provide services to another entity in the future as a result of past transactions or events. Thus, for example, an account payable arises from the present obligation to pay cash to a creditor at some future date as a result of a past transaction in which goods or services were received from that creditor.

Within the general definition, liabilities exhibit a wide variety of characteristics. Although liabilities frequently require the payment of cash, some liabilities may require the transfer of noncash assets or the performance of services. Although the exact amount and timing of future payments are known for many liabilities, the amount and timing of payments for some liabilities are not known with certainty at the balance sheet date. Further, whereas many liabilities are legally enforceable claims, some may represent merely *probable* future payments. Finally, although liabilities usually identify the entity to be paid, the definition does not exclude liabilities to unknown recipients. Thus, the future economic sacrifice associated with a liability may or may not involve the payment of cash, may or may not be known with certainty, may or may not be legally enforceable, and may or may not be payable to a known recipient.

RECOGNITION OF LIABILITIES

Although most liabilities are recognized as part of the recording of exchange transactions involving the purchase of goods and services or the borrowing of money, liabilities are also recognized as part of the recording of nonexchange transactions. For example, deferred income tax liabilities are estimated and recorded as the related income is earned, and liabilities arising under lawsuits are recorded when the payment is estimable and judged to be probable (likely to occur).

When a liability depends on a future event, such as the outcome of a legal suit, recognition depends on how likely the occurrence of the event is. If the future payment is judged to be less than likely to occur, the related obligation should not be recognized but may require disclosure in footnotes to the financial statements, as explained later in this chapter.

MEASUREMENT OF LIABILITIES

Although liabilities represent economic sacrifices that will occur in the future, the amount reported for a liability in the balance sheet should be the *present value* of the future economic sacrifice. When the future sacrifice includes an amount of interest to compensate its recipient for waiting to receive payment, the present value equals the future payment less the interest yet to be accrued. For many current liabilities, such as accounts payable, the wait is short and the amount of such interest is negligible. Thus, accounts payable are recorded and reported at the total amount required to satisfy the account in the future. Of course, some current liabilities, such as notes payable, and many long-term liabilities accrue interest and are recorded and reported at present values less than the amount of the future payment.

CURRENT LIABILITIES

CURRENT LIABILITIES: Obligations to outsiders that will require the firm to pay cash or provide goods or services within one year or one operating cycle, whichever is longer.

Current liabilities were defined in Chapter 2 as the firm's obligations to outsiders that will require the firm to pay cash or to provide goods or services within one year or one operating cycle, whichever is longer. Since most firms have operating cycles shorter than one year, the one-year rule usually applies. Thus, amounts payable in six months are always classified as current liabilities, and amounts payable in two years are usually classified as long-term liabilities.

Current liabilities are usually reported in the balance sheet in the order in which they will require resource outflows. The current liabilities section of a balance sheet might have the following appearance:

	AS OF DECEMBER 31	
	19X2	19X1
Current liabilities:		
Accounts payable	$ 440.1	$ 427.5
Wages and salaries payable	72.3	70.9
Payroll tax payable	15.6	14.3
State sales tax payable	8.4	7.0
Property tax payable	119.3	114.8
Interest payable	12.7	9.2
Notes payable	130.0	95.0
Unearned revenue	56.5	58.6
Income taxes payable	199.8	172.4
Current portion of long-term liabilities	50.0	45.0
Other current liabilities	52.5	49.3
Total current liabilities	$1,157.2	$1,064.0

Note: Dollar amounts in thousands.

This current liabilities section lists the principal current liabilities that are considered in this chapter. In published annual reports, current liabilities are frequently summarized and presented in much less detail. We will now describe the principles that guide the reporting of the major types of current liabilities, beginning with accounts payable.

ACCOUNTS PAYABLE

ACCOUNT PAYABLE:
A current liability representing an amount owed by the entity for goods or services.

An **account payable** is a current liability representing an amount owed by the entity for goods or services. An account payable is recorded as part of the entry that records the purchase of goods or services. Credit terms generally require that the purchaser pay the account payable within a stated period, which may range from a few days to a month or more. Accounts payable are recorded and reported at the total amount required to satisfy the account, which equals the cost of the goods or services acquired. Accounts payable seldom require the payment of interest. When a discount is offered by the seller, the purchase and the account payable can each be recorded either gross or net of the discount, as illustrated in Chapter 6.

ACCRUED PAYABLES

ACCRUED PAYABLES:
Liabilities recorded by adjusting entries for expenses incurred but not paid—expenses associated with partially completed continuous events.

Unlike accounts payable, which are recorded when the related exchange transactions are completed, accrued payables are recorded by adjusting entries. **Accrued payables** are liabilities recorded by adjusting entries for expenses incurred but not paid—expenses associated with partially completed continuous events.

Wages, salaries, property taxes, and income taxes are common accrued, short-term payables. Wages and salaries payable arise at balance sheet dates when adjusting entries are made to record compensation earned by employees in the accounting period just ended, but not yet paid by the employer. Similarly, property tax payable reflects taxes levied by the local government but not yet paid. Since the total amount of income tax owed cannot be calculated until a firm's income for the period has been determined, an estimate of the tax is usually entered at the end of the period with an adjusting entry. Accruals for income taxes payable thus arise for the federal, state, and local taxes on income earned by an enterprise during the accounting period just ended. We turn now to the tax liabilities arising from taxes other than income and property taxes.

SALES AND PAYROLL TAXES

At the time of sale, many firms collect sales taxes, usage taxes, or excise taxes for various state, local, and federal taxing authorities. These taxes, though collected as part of the total selling price, are not additions to revenue; rather, they result in liabilities until they are paid to the taxing authority. Notice that these liabilities do not arise from either purchases or accruals.

Let us illustrate: Seiler Tire Company sold 50 tires to P. V. Construction Company at $40 each plus state sales tax of 4 percent. Included in the $40 price per tire was a $1.50-per-tire federal excise tax. This transaction would be recorded by Seiler as follows:

Accounts receivable	2,080	
Federal excise tax payable		75
State sales tax payable		80
Sales revenue		1,925

Note that the revenue is less than the receivable. The difference is the amount of the taxes to be collected as a part of the total selling price.

Businesses also withhold taxes from employees' earnings. These withholdings are liabilities until paid to the taxing authority. For example, if Seiler Tire

Company withholds taxes from its employees' wages, accrual and payment of a $50,000 payroll would be recorded as follows:

Wages expense	50,000	
Federal income tax withheld		11,500
FICA tax withheld		3,825
State income tax withheld		1,500
Wages payable		33,175
Wages payable	33,175	
Cash		33,175

Since they are frequently recorded at the same time, the two entries for accrual and payment of payroll may be combined in a single entry that omits the credit and debit to wages payable.

In addition to the taxes withheld from employees' earnings, an employer is required to pay various so-called payroll taxes. These taxes are an expense and are normally recorded at the time wage and salary expenses are accrued or paid. The most common payroll taxes are the employer's FICA tax (social security), federal unemployment tax, and state unemployment tax. Based on Seiler's $50,000 payroll, the following entry can be made to record Seiler's expense and liability for employer's payroll taxes:

Employer tax expense	5,355	
FICA tax payable		3,825
Federal unemployment tax payable		315
State unemployment tax payable		1,215

The current liabilities discussed thus far arise from the operating activities of the firm. We now turn to payables arising from the firm's financing activities.

NOTES PAYABLE

Notes create more formal obligations than many other current liabilities. Recall from our discussion of notes receivable in Chapter 8 that a *note* is a written, legal document given by a borrower (who is also called the *maker* or *payer* of the note) to a lender (who is also called the *recipient* or *payee* of the note) stating the amount to be repaid and the time of repayment. A **note payable** is the liability of a borrower arising from a note given to a lender. Short-term notes payable, like short-term notes receivable, are written in one of two forms—interest-bearing or non-interest-bearing. Let us consider the different accounting procedures applied to these two types of notes.

NOTE PAYABLE: The liability of a borrower arising from a note given to a lender.

Interest-Bearing Short-Term Notes

A note that indirectly specifies the amount to be repaid, by stating a principal amount and an interest rate, is called an *interest-bearing note* because it explicitly states an interest rate. The maturity amount of an interest-bearing note is not stated explicitly but is determined indirectly from the interest rate, the principal amount, and the maturity date. When an interest-bearing short-term note is issued, the lender transfers to the borrower cash, goods, or services whose value equals the principal amount of the note, or the lender discharges some other liability of the borrower (for example, the lender may replace an account payable

EXHIBIT 10–1   RECORDING NOTES PAYABLE

INTEREST-BEARING			NON-INTEREST-BEARING		
Entry to record issuance of interest-bearing note on December 1, 19X8:			*Entry to record issuance of non-interest-bearing note on December 1, 19X8:*		
Cash	12,000		Cash	12,000	
Notes payable		12,000	Discount on notes payable	600	
			Notes payable		12,600
Adjusting entry to record accrued interest expense at December 31, 19X8:			*Adjusting entry to record accrued interest expense at December 31, 19X8:*		
Interest expense	150		Interest expense	150	
Interest payable		150	Discount on notes payable		150
Entry to record accrued interest expense at March 31, 19X9:			*Entry to record accrued interest expense at March 31, 19X9:*		
Interest expense	450		Interest expense	450	
Interest payable		450	Discount on notes payable		450
Entry to record payment of note on March 31, 19X9:			*Entry to record payment of note on March 31, 19X9:*		
Notes payable	12,000		Notes payable	12,600	
Interest payable	600		Cash		12,600
Cash		12,600			

with a note payable). The borrower then records the liability at the principal amount. For example, assume that Paragon Stores borrows cash from a bank by issuing a four-month, 15 percent, $12,000, note payable on December 1, 19X8. Issuance of the note would be recorded by the first entry shown in the left-hand column of Exhibit 10–1.

If an accounting period ends while a note is outstanding, an adjusting entry is required to record the interest expense accrued as of the end of the accounting period. The interest expense for the entire four-month period of Paragon's note is $600, which is computed by multiplying the principal amount, the annual interest rate, and the fraction of the year covered by the note [$600 = ($12,000)(.15)(4/12)].[1] The total interest expense of $600 is divided between the two accounting periods on a straight-line basis ($150 per month). Accrued interest of $150 is recorded at December 31, 19X8, as shown by the second entry in the left-hand column of Exhibit 10–1. On the balance sheet at December 31, 19X8, the amount owed is reported in two separate liabilities, notes payable and interest payable, whose sum is $12,150. The third and fourth entries in this column of the exhibit would be made at maturity to record the interest expense for the first three months of 19X9 [($450 = $600 − $150) or

[1] Although practice varies, interest on short-term notes payable often begins on the day the note is issued; further, the maturity date of the note may also be counted as a day of interest. Of course, when interest is computed on a monthly basis, as is done throughout this book, the complexities of daily interest determination do not arise.

($450 = 3 \times $150)] and to record the payment of the notes payable and interest payable balances.

Non-Interest-Bearing Short-Term Notes

A note that directly specifies the amount to be repaid (stating only the sum to be repaid, including interest) is called a *non-interest-bearing note* because it does not explicitly state a rate of interest. For such notes, the rate of interest and the principal amount are determined indirectly from the value of the assets received. At issuance the lender transfers assets to the borrower (or discharges a liability of the borrower) valued at the principal amount of the note, which is less than the maturity amount. At maturity the borrower repays the maturity amount specified on the note document. The excess of the amount repaid (the maturity amount of the note) over the amount borrowed (the principal) is called the **discount on note** and is, in effect, the amount of interest on the note.

DISCOUNT ON NOTE:
The excess of the maturity amount of a non-interest-bearing note over the amount borrowed (the principal).

When a short-term note is issued, the borrower records the liability in two parts. To illustrate, suppose that Paragon Stores issued a $12,600, non-interest-bearing, four-month note in exchange for $12,000 cash. At issuance Paragon would make the first entry shown in the right-hand column of Exhibit 10–1. The $600 discount is debited to discount on notes payable, a contra-liability account. If a balance sheet were prepared on that date, the note would be reported as follows:

Notes payable..................................	$12,600	
Less: Discount on notes payable.................	600	$12,000

Notice that recording the issuance of the non-interest-bearing note results in the same net liability ($12,000) as recording the issuance of the equivalent interest-bearing note shown on the left-hand side of Exhibit 10–1. At December 31, 19X8, accrued interest of $150 for the month of December is recorded by the adjusting entry shown in the right-hand column of Exhibit 10–1. Unlike the adjusting entry for interest-bearing notes, the $150 credit is made to discount on notes payable rather than to interest payable. As a result, the note would be reported as follows on the December 31, 19X8, balance sheet:

Notes payable..................................	$12,600	
Less: Discount on notes payable.................	450	$12,150

Thus the amount of interest owed at December 31, 19X8 ($150), is included in the net liability ($12,150) reported for the non-interest-bearing note rather than being stated separately, as is done for interest-bearing notes.

The third and fourth entries in the right-hand column of Exhibit 10–1 would be made at maturity to record the remainder of the interest expense for the first three months of 19X9 ($450) and to record the payment of the maturity amount ($12,600).

Most financial institutions are required by law to disclose to borrowers the interest rate charged on each loan. Since non-interest-bearing notes do not explicitly state a rate of interest, their use is largely restricted to loans involving individuals or institutions not subject to such disclosure requirements.

Let us now turn to a different type of current liability—obligations arising from customer payments that precede the delivery of goods or services.

UNEARNED REVENUES

UNEARNED REVENUE:
A liability created by a customer paying for goods or services in advance of their delivery or performance.

Unearned revenue is the liability created by customers paying for goods or services in advance of their delivery or performance. Occasionally customers will pay for goods or services before the seller is able to deliver the merchandise or provide the services. In such instances, the seller has a liability to the purchaser in the amount of the prepayment. This liability is discharged either by providing the goods or services purchased (at which time the related revenue is recognized) or by refunding the amount of the prepayment.[2] Assume, for example, that Brown and Company sold six months of cleaning services to Southtown National Bank for $5,400. The bank paid in advance for the services, and Brown made the following entry at the time the services were sold:

Cash	5,400	
Unearned revenue		5,400

On completion of the services called for under the contract, Brown made the following entry:

Unearned revenue	5,400	
Service revenue		5,400

If the accounting period were to end before the contract was fulfilled, the portion of the service that had been provided would be removed from the liability unearned revenue, and added to service revenue. The remainder of the liability would be converted to revenue in the next period, when the contract had been fulfilled.

A similar *long-term* liability, called *customer deposits,* is recorded when customers make advance payments or security deposits that are not expected to be earned or returned soon enough to qualify as current liabilities. Upon receipt, the amounts of such deposits are credited to the customer deposits account. When deposits are repaid to customers or earned, the customer deposits account is debited. The current portion of customer deposits should be recorded as unearned revenue and reported as a current liability.

CURRENT PORTION OF LONG-TERM LIABILITIES

The current portion of long-term liabilities is the amount of a long-term liability to be paid within the longer of the next year or the next operating cycle. At the end of each accounting period, the current portion of long-term liabilities is reclassified as a current liability. In some cases, a long-term liability that is due within the current period will be paid with the proceeds of a new long-term liability. When such refinancing is expected, the maturing obligation is not transferred to the current liabilities section but is left as a long-term liability. Since the reclassification of most long-term liabilities as current does not usually change the accounts or amounts involved, a journal entry is not required.

Prudent users of financial statements examine the financial statements to determine when long-term liabilities will mature. This examination is assisted by the reclassification described here and by other information about liabilities reported in the financial statements. We conclude this section by analyzing current liability data from the perspective of a banker evaluating a short-term loan application.

[2] If the goods or services are not provided, the seller may also be liable for legal damages. The amount of such damages would be recorded as an expense.

Hydraulic Controls Company manufactures hydraulic clutch assemblies for compact foreign and domestic automobiles. The following data are available on Hydraulic's current liabilities, current assets, sales revenue, and net income (loss) for the past three years:

ITEM	19X3	19X2	19X1
Accounts payable	$ 174,000	$ 146,000	$ 104,000
Short-term notes payable	332,000	291,000	229,000
Income taxes payable	–0–	43,000	50,000
Total current liabilities	$ 506,000	$ 480,000	$ 383,000
Total current assets	$ 485,000	$ 546,000	$ 611,000
Sales revenue	$5,047,000	$5,293,000	$5,538,000
Net income (net loss)	$ (10,000)	$ 89,000	$ 130,000

Hydraulic Controls has asked its bank to increase its short-term notes payable by $100,000. Following are some questions the bank might ask Hydraulic's management:

1. *How will the short-term notes be repaid?*

The short-term notes would be repaid from current assets. The decline in the amount of current assets relative to current liabilities suggests that even the present amount of current liabilities may not be payable with the resources currently available.

2. *What might be causing the increases in current liabilities and the decreases in current assets?*

Because profitability is declining, the firm may not be able to secure capital from outside sources or from operations. Therefore, it may be drawing down current assets and increasing current liabilities to provide capital.

3. *Should the bank extend additional credit to Hydraulic?*

The decline in profitability, the trend in current assets and current liabilities, and the present excess of current liabilities over current assets suggest that it would be unwise to extend additional credit at this time.

Measurement of the liabilities described so far is not affected by uncertainties about the amount, timing, or recipient of the related future sacrifice of economic benefits. Such characteristics, however, are exhibited by the groups of liabilities we examine next.

CONTINGENT LIABILITIES

CONTINGENT LIABILITY:
An obligation whose amount, timing, or recipient depends on future events.

A **contingent liability** is an obligation whose amount, timing, or recipient depends on future events. For example, a firm may be contingently liable for damages under a lawsuit that has yet to be decided by the courts. When the courts reach a decision, the liability will be known, but until then the liability is contingent on that decision. A contingent liability does not qualify as a liability unless the event on which it is contingent is probable, that is, likely to occur. If the event is likely to occur, reliable measurement of the related liability is usually possible. Such is the case with contingent liabilities arising from product warranties and pensions. On the other hand, if the event is less than likely to occur, reliable measurement of the related obligation is usually impossible; therefore, the potential obligation is not recorded as a liability but may require disclosure in footnotes to the financial statements. Thus the required accounting treatment of contingent liabilities depends on the likelihood of events on which they are contingent, as indicated in the following table:

LIKELIHOOD OF CONTINGENT EVENT	REQUIRED ACCOUNTING TREATMENT
Probable, that is, likely to occur	Estimate the amount of the liability and record. (If a reasonable estimate of the amount cannot be made, then disclosure in a footnote to the financial statements is sufficient.)
Less than likely to occur, but occurrence is not remote	Do not record as a liability but disclose in a footnote to the financial statements.
Occurrence is remote	Neither record as a liability nor disclose in a footnote to the financial statements.

Of course, the likelihood of a contingent event may change as time goes on, and a contingent liability that should not be recorded or disclosed at one time may be recorded or disclosed appropriately at a later time. Contingent liabilities arising from litigation frequently have this character. However, contingent liabilities arising from warranties and pensions — to which we now turn — are usually viewed as probable and subject to reliable measurement.

WARRANTIES

WARRANTY: A guarantee given by a seller to a purchaser to repair or replace defective goods or parts of goods during a limited period following the sale.

When goods are sold, a manufacturing or a selling firm often provides the purchaser with a warranty against defects that might develop as the goods are used. A **warranty** usually guarantees the repair or replacement of defective goods or parts of goods during a limited period (ranging from a few days to several years) following the sale. The asset outflows to satisfy warranty claims may occur in the accounting period in which the sale is made, but they are more likely to occur in some subsequent accounting period. The matching concept requires that all expenses required to produce sales revenue for a given period be recorded in that period. Since warranty costs are sales-related, they must be recorded in the period of sale. And since these costs are not a directly calculable expense, they must be estimated.

The recognition of warranty expense and estimated warranty liability is normally recorded by an adjusting entry at the end of the accounting period. As warranty claims are paid to customers or related expenditures are made, this estimated liability is reduced. Assume, for example, that Crawford Computers offers a 12-month warranty on all its laptop computers. Crawford estimates that one computer of each 100 sold will require warranty service and that the average warranty claim will cost the firm $225. If we assume that Crawford sells 10,000 laptop computers in 19X2, the 19X2 warranty expense is $22,500 [(10,000/100)($225)]. Crawford would make the following warranty expense entry at the end of 19X2.

Warranty expense	22,500	
Estimated warranty liability..........................		22,500

During January 19X3, Crawford incurs costs of $7,700 to repair 35 computers. The entry to record these costs is as follows:

Estimated warranty liability...........................	7,700	
Cash		7,700

Actual warranty claims are unlikely to equal the firm's estimate exactly, and any small amount of overestimate or underestimate is usually combined with the next warranty estimate. However, large overestimates or underestimates must be recorded on the income statement as other income or other expenses as soon as they become apparent.

PENSIONS

Nearly all large firms, many small firms, and most governmental units have pension plans for their employees. Employees are compensated for their services by wages and salaries paid during the period of their employment and by pension benefits paid after their retirement. The Employee Retirement Income Security Act (ERISA), enacted by Congress in 1974, requires employers with pension plans to establish a fund with an independent agency to provide for the payment of future pension benefits. The pension fund is frequently held in trust and managed by an insurance company or a financial institution. The process of making payments to the fund by the employer is called **pension funding.** The amount of funding is influenced by the discretion of the employer, subject to the requirement of the pension plan (and ERISA), and by the cash requirements of the pension fund. The cash requirements of the pension fund, in turn, depend on the rate at which employees retire, their benefit schedules, the life expectancy of retired employees, and the income earned on invested pension funds.

PENSION FUNDING: The process of making payments to a pension fund established to provide for the future payment of pension benefits.

PENSION EXPENSE: The cost of pension benefits matched with a given period, which usually differs from both the amount of funding and the amount of benefits paid during the period.

PENSION LIABILITY: The liability of an employer for future payments to a pension fund.

Pension expense is the cost of pension benefits matched with a given period. Under accrual accounting, pension expense usually differs from both the amount of funding and the amount of pension benefits actually paid during the same period. The liability of an employer for future payments to a pension fund is called a **pension liability.** The pension liability represents the accumulated excess of pension expense over funding. For example, JWM, Inc., recorded a pension expense of $150,000 in 19X9 but contributed only $125,000 to its pension fund during that year. Thus, JWM's pension liability increased by $25,000 [$150,000 − $125,000], as shown in the following journal entry:

Pension expense.................................	150,000	
Cash...		125,000
Pension liability................................		25,000

Of course, if a firm's contribution to its pension fund exceeds the amount of pension expense, then the pension liability declines. The rules that direct the measurement of expenses and liabilities and the related financial statement disclosures for pensions, which are considered in more advanced accounting courses, are complex and controversial. For our purposes, it is sufficient to understand that pensions create a contingent liability—frequently a very large one—dependent on a complex fabric of future events.[3]

Now let us turn to a third type of liability, one that arises from differences between federal income tax rules and generally accepted accounting principles.

DEFERRED INCOME TAXES

State and federal income taxes create two types of liabilities for businesses organized as corporations—income taxes payable and deferred income tax liability.[4] Income taxes payable is the current liability for income taxes assessed on the tax return of the current period. The deferred income tax liability is the liability for income taxes to be assessed on future tax returns but related to net income reported on current and past years' income statements. Thus the deferred income tax liability is the result of differences between the rules and regulations for recognizing revenues and expenses for the tax return and the generally accepted accounting principles (GAAP) that guide the measurement of revenues and expenses for the income statement. In general, tax rules permit some revenues to be deferred to later accounting periods and allow many expenses to appear earlier, which produces temporary differences in the reporting of revenues and expenses. We mentioned in Chapter 9, for example, that most firms use an accelerated method to determine depreciation expense for the tax return and another method (usually straight-line) to determine depreciation for the financial statements. The use of accelerated depreciation for tax purposes increases the

---

[3] In addition to providing pension benefits, most large companies also cover a portion of the health care and insurance costs incurred by employees after their retirement. These postretirement health care and insurance benefits, like pension benefits, are earned over the employees' years of service. Application of the matching concept would suggest that the expense in each period should equal the cost of benefits earned in that period, as is the case for pension expense. Until recently, most companies simply recognized current payments for such benefits as expense and did not record or disclose the related liability. Effective in 1993, however, Financial Accounting Standard No. 106 requires most large companies to use accrual accounting for nonpension, postretirement benefits.

[4] As explained in Chapter 12, businesses organized as sole proprietorships and partnerships do not pay taxes on their income; rather, the taxes on such income are paid by the proprietors and partners as part of their personal income tax.

depreciation expense of an asset in the early years of its life. This causes before-tax income on the tax return to be lower than income before taxes on the income statement, and, as a result, the tax assessed on the tax return is less than the tax expense on the income statement. This difference between tax expense and tax assessed results in a deferred tax liability. In general, a **deferred tax liability** arises from the effects of temporary differences between the income statement and the tax return that will result in net taxable amounts in future years.

Exhibit 10–2 presents 19X4 revenue and expense data for Stewart Trucking Service, which we will use to illustrate the recording of a deferred tax liability. All revenues and expenses are the same on the tax return as on the income statement, except for depreciation. For its tax return, Stewart uses accelerated depreciation for its trucks; first-year tax return depreciation for the trucks is $15,000. On its income statement, Stewart uses straight-line depreciation for the trucks; first-year straight-line depreciation for the trucks, based on an acquisition cost of $100,000, residual value of $6,000, and expected life of eight years, is $11,750 [($100,000 − $6,000)/8]. The difference between Stewart Trucking's tax expense ($27,563) and the tax assessed ($26,750) is $813, which equals the difference between the tax return depreciation ($15,000) and the income statement depreciation ($11,750) times the tax rate (.25).

The effect of the depreciation difference is to defer the payment of income tax. The journal entry made by Stewart to record the tax expense, tax payable, and deferred tax liability is:[5]

Income taxes expense	27,563	
Income taxes payable		26,750
Deferred tax liability		813

The credit to the deferred tax liability provides for the inclusion in taxes expense of taxes that will not be assessed until future years. These taxes will be assessed during the later years of the assets' lives, when tax return depreciation will be lower than the depreciation expense on the income statement. The reversal of the relationship between the two depreciation amounts in later years will, taken by itself, cause income taxes assessed to exceed income taxes expense, resulting in debits to the deferred tax liability in those years. This process of deferring income taxes expense from one period to another by use of a deferred tax liability account is called **interperiod tax allocation.**

Although the deferred tax liability associated with each asset will eventually be reversed by debits, the deferred tax liability for all assets of a firm may not decline. If a firm's collection of depreciable assets continues to grow at a sufficiently rapid rate, then the deferred tax increases associated with newly acquired

DEFERRED TAX LIABILITY: A liability created when temporary differences between the income statement and the tax return produce net taxable amounts that will not be taxed until future years.

INTERPERIOD TAX ALLOCATION: The process of deferring income tax expense from one period to another by use of a deferred tax liability account.

---

[5] This journal entry to record taxes expense assumes that the tax liability for each year is paid in a single payment shortly after year-end. In practice, most corporations are required to pay taxes in advance of the date on which the final payment is due. For example, suppose that Stewart Trucking made three income tax payments during 19X4 of $6,200 each, recording each payment by a debit to prepaid income taxes and a credit to cash; under this assumption, the following year-end entry would be required:

Income taxes expense	27,563	
Prepaid income taxes		18,600
Income taxes payable		8,150
Deferred tax liability		813

EXHIBIT 10-2   TAX EXPENSE AND TAX ASSESSED

STEWART TRUCKING SERVICE
Income Statement and Tax Return Data
For the Year Ended December 31, 19X4

	INCOME STATEMENT		INCOME TAX RETURN*	
Service revenues		$780,000		$780,000
Less: Operating expenses:				
Wages	$379,000		$379,000	
Rent	184,000		184,000	
Depreciation	11,750		15,000	
Fuel	95,000	669,750	95,000	673,000
Income before taxes		$110,250		
Taxable income				$107,000
Income taxes *expense* (.25)		27,563		
Income taxes *assessed* (.25)				$ 26,750
Net income		$ 82,687		

* Our illustrations greatly simplify the calculation of taxable income, income taxes assessed, and income taxes expense. Realistic calculations are discussed in separate courses on income tax accounting.

assets may more than offset the deferred tax decreases associated with older assets in each year. As a result, the deferred tax account of a growing firm may not decline. This possibility has led some accountants to object to the practice of recording deferred income tax because it results in the creation of a liability that will not be paid unless the firm ceases to grow. These accountants argue that income tax expense for each period should equal the amount of tax assessed on that period's tax return. Although these views may be persuasive to some, generally accepted accounting principles require the use of deferred tax liabilities to match dollars of tax expense with related net income.

The portion of the deferred income tax liability representing tax payments to be made within the next year (or the next operating cycle if it is longer) is reported as a current liability; the remainder, which is usually the larger amount, is reported as a long-term liability. Additional discussion of the structure of the deferred tax liability is presented in Chapter 16.

Although liabilities represent *future* economic sacrifices, the amount reported for a liability on the balance sheet should be the *present* value of the future economic sacrifice. For most of the liabilities considered in the last few pages, the relationship between future economic sacrifice and present value is straightforward. In many cases, the present value is simply the sum of the future economic sacrifices (for example, accounts payable, wages payable, taxes payable, unearned revenue, customer deposits, deferred income taxes, and warranties). In other cases, the present value is less than the total future economic sacrifice by an amount determined by simple interest calculations (for example, with notes payable). For some interest-bearing liabilities, however, the relationship between future economic sacrifice and present value depends on fairly complex interest calculations. These time-value-of-money calculations are described in Section B, which follows.

SECTION B
TIME VALUE OF MONEY

TIME VALUE OF MONEY: A synonym for *interest.*

In transactions involving the borrowing and lending of money, it is customary for the borrower to compensate the lender by repaying a larger amount than is borrowed. The difference between the amount repaid and the amount borrowed is *interest.* For example, if a five-year loan of $1,800 is repaid in five installments of $500 at the end of each year, then interest on the loan is $700 [($500(5) − $1,800]. The amount of interest is determined by the duration of the loan and the interest rate agreed upon by the borrower and lender. Over the life of a loan, the liability balance increases by the amount of the interest that accrues with the passage of time and decreases by the amount of payments made to the lender. Interest, therefore, can be described as the **time value of money.**

Interest is not restricted to loans made to borrowers by financial institutions. It also arises on investments (notably, investments in debt securities and savings accounts); on installment sales or purchases (sales or purchases in which the buyer makes several payments over time rather than a one-time payment of the selling price); and on a variety of other contractual arrangements. In the case of investments, interest is paid by the borrower or security issuer to the investor. In the case of installment receivables, interest is paid by the installment customer to the seller. In all cases, the arrangement between the two parties (the note, security, or purchase agreement) creates an asset in the accounting records of one party and a corresponding liability in the accounting records of the other. All such assets and liabilities increase as interest is earned by the asset holder and decrease as payments are made by the liability holder. Our purpose here is to explain the basic interest (time-value-of-money) calculations that apply to the accounting for several simple financial arrangements. (Chapter 11B describes the application of time-value-of-money calculations to long-term debt.)

COMPOUND INTEREST CALCULATIONS

COMPOUND INTEREST: A method of computing interest and then adding interest to an account (representing money borrowed or loaned) at regular intervals.

INTEREST PERIOD: The time interval between interest calculations.

INTEREST RATE: The percentage multiplied by the beginning-of-period balance to yield the amount of interest for that period.

Time-value-of-money calculations are based on the principles of **compound interest,** which prescribe a method of computing interest and then adding interest to an account (representing money borrowed or loaned) at regular intervals. Whether the account represents an asset or a liability, the related interest calculations require careful specification of the interest period and the interest rate. The **interest period** is the time interval between interest calculations. For example, an annual interest period implies that interest is calculated at the end of each year, and a monthly interest period implies that interest is calculated at the end of each month. The **interest rate** is the percentage that is multiplied by the beginning-of-period balance to yield the amount of interest for that period. It is important that the interest rate be expressed in terms of the interest period. For example, if the interest period is one month, then the interest rate used to calculate interest must be stated as a percentage "per month."

When an interest rate is stated in terms of a time period that differs from the interest period, than the rate must be adjusted before interest can be calculated. Suppose, for example, that a bank advertises interest at a rate of 12 percent per year compounded monthly. The words *compounded monthly* indicate that the interest period is one month. Since there are 12 interest periods in one year, the interest rate for one month is one-twelfth of the annual rate, or 1 percent. In general, if the *rate statement period* differs from the *interest period,* the stated rate must be divided by the number of interest periods included in the rate statement period to obtain the interest rate to be used in interest calculations. Consider the following examples of stated rates and the corresponding adjusted rates required for interest computations:

STATED RATE	ADJUSTED RATE FOR COMPUTATIONS
18% per year compounded semiannually	9% per six-month period (18%/2)
18% per year compounded quarterly	4½% per quarter (18%/4)
18% per year compounded monthly	1½% per month (18%/12)

Whenever an interest rate is stated without reference to a rate statement period or an interest period, we assume that the unmentioned period is one year. For example, both "18 percent" and "18 percent per year" should be interpreted as 18 percent per year compounded annually.

COMPOUND INTEREST AND FUTURE AMOUNTS

Compound interest involves computing interest and then adding it to an account at regular intervals. The calculation of compound interest is based on three elements: (1) the initial amount of the account, (2) the interest period, and (3) the interest rate. The initial amount of the account is the original amount borrowed (or loaned) under a loan contract, the original amount invested under an investment arrangement, or the fair value of the assets transferred in an installment sale. As noted above, the interest period is the length of time (a year, six months, a quarter, a month, or even a day) between interest calculations. Interest is determined and added to the account balance at equal time intervals. The interest rate equals the dollar amount of interest for any interest period expressed as a percentage of the account balance at the beginning of that interest period. Conversely, the dollar amount of interest for any interest period is calculated by multiplying the interest rate times the account balance at the beginning of the interest period.

The following illustration presents a simple compound interest calculation: An investor deposits $4,000 in a savings account on January 1, 19X4. The bank determines interest at the end of each month at an interest rate of 1 percent per month. Activity in the investor's account is recorded in Exhibit 10–3. This schedule assumes that the $4,000 deposited on January 1, 19X4, remains in the bank without additional deposits or withdrawals during January, February, and

EXHIBIT 10–3   **INTEREST COMPOUNDING**

Account balance, 1/1/X4	$4,000.00
January interest [($4,000.00)(.01)]	40.00
Account balance, 1/31/X4	$4,040.00
February interest [($4,040.00)(.01)]	40.40
Account balance, 2/28/X4	$4,080.40
March interest [($4,080.40)(.01)]	40.80
Account balance, 3/31/X4	$4,121.20

EXHIBIT 10–4   INTEREST COMPOUNDING WITH ADDITIONS AND WITHDRAWALS

Account balance, 1/1/X1	$ 8,000.00
First quarter interest [($8,000.00)(.04)]	320.00
Subtotal	$ 8,320.00
Add: Additional deposit, 3/31/X1	2,000.00
Account balance, 3/31/X1	$10,320.00
Second quarter interest [($10,320.00)(.04)]	412.80
Subtotal	$10,732.80
Less: Withdrawal, 6/30/X1	6,000.00
Account balance, 6/30/X1	$ 4,732.80
Third quarter interest [($4,732.80)(.04)]	189.31
Account balance, 9/30/X1	$ 4,922.11

March. So long as the investor does not withdraw amounts from the savings account, the account balance continues to grow each month by an increasing amount of interest. The amount of monthly interest increases because interest is *compounded;* that is, interest is computed on accumulated interest as well as on principal. For example, February interest of $40.40 consists of $40 of interest on the $4,000 principal amount and $.40 of interest on the January interest [($40)(.01) = $.40].

In our illustration, interest is the only factor that alters the account balance after the initial deposit. In more complex illustrations, like the one shown in Exhibit 10–4, the account balance is changed by subsequent deposits and withdrawals as well as by interest. Withdrawals reduce the balance and therefore also reduce the amount of interest in subsequent periods. Additional deposits have the opposite effect, increasing the balance and increasing the amount of interest. Suppose that on January 1, 19X1, an investor deposits $8,000 in a bank. The bank determines interest at the end of each quarter at an interest rate of 4 percent per quarter. The investor deposits an additional $2,000 on March 31, 19X1, and withdraws $6,000 on June 30, 19X1. Notice that the additional deposit and the withdrawal both occurred on interest-determination dates. For the sake of simplicity, we shall assume that all transactions involving compound interest accounts occur on interest-determination dates.

FUTURE AMOUNT: The amount to which an account will grow by a specified future time when interest is compounded.

The amount to which an account will grow by a specified future time when interest is compounded is the **future amount** of the account. For example, at January 1, 19X4, the account in Exhibit 10–3 has a future amount associated with each end-of-month interest calculation. Specifically, the future amount at January 31, 19X4, is $4,040.00; the future amount at February 28, 19X4, is $4,080.40; and so on. (Later in this chapter, we will consider the use of tables as a shortcut for the calculation of future amounts.)

Time-value-of-money calculations can assume two fundamentally different forms: (1) calculations of future amounts and (2) calculations of present values. As illustrated, calculations of future amounts are projections of future balances based on past and future transactions. In contrast, calculations of present values, to which we now turn, are determinations of present amounts based on expected future transactions.

EXHIBIT 10-5   CASH FLOW DIAGRAM

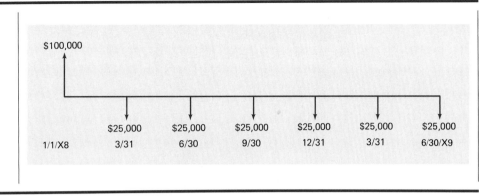

PRESENT VALUE OF FUTURE CASH FLOWS

Interest usually arises under contracts that specify the cash flows (transfers) between the parties to a loan, investment, or purchase transaction. When money is borrowed, an interest-bearing note specifies the amounts and times of repayment. When money is invested in debt securities, the security documents specify the amounts and times of payments by the borrower to the investor. When an asset is purchased on the installment basis, a sales contract specifies the amounts and times of payments by the purchaser to the seller. Each type of contract specifies a series of future cash payments or receipts, for which both amounts and time are given.

To illustrate, suppose that the Hilliard Corporation borrows $100,000 from the Citizens Bank of New Hope on January 1, 19X8. The note requires six $25,000 payments, one at the end of each of the ensuing six quarters, and hence provides for total interest of $50,000 [(6 × $25,000) − $100,000]. The cash flows for Hilliard are diagrammed in Exhibit 10-5. Cash flow diagrams that display both the amounts and the times of the cash flows specified by a contract are almost essential in the solution of time-value-of-money exercises and problems. It is customary in these diagrams to use a time line that runs from left to right; inflows are represented as arrows pointing upward and outflows as downward-pointing arrows.

Compound interest calculations establish the link between the amount borrowed (or loaned) under a note, borrowed (invested) under a debt security, or borrowed (loaned) under an installment contract and the future cash flows specified by the related contract. If compound interest is applied to the amount borrowed or invested, with appropriate additions and subtractions for all the specified cash flows, then the future amount on the last day of the contract should be zero. If on the last day of the contract the future amount is other than zero, the specified payments were either more or less than the amount required to pay off the note or to satisfy investment requirements at the interest rate established. For example, Putnam Corporation borrowed $10,000 from the Marietta National Bank on January 1, 19X6. The note specified that the loan was to be repaid in two equal payments of $5,607.69 each, on June 30, 19X6, and December 31, 19X6. The payments include interest computed at 16 percent per year compounded semiannually (8 percent per six-month period). The cash flow diagram and compound interest calculation in Exhibit 10-6 show the relationship between

EXHIBIT 10–6 CASH FLOW DIAGRAM AND COMPOUND INTEREST CALCULATIONS FOR A LIABILITY

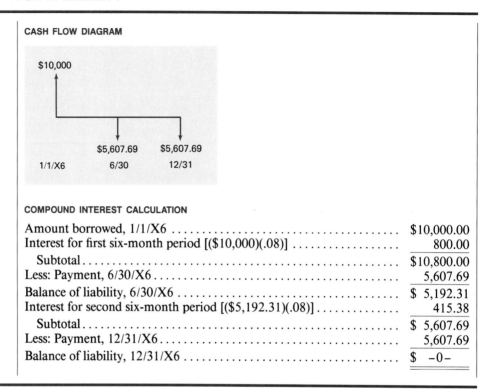

CASH FLOW DIAGRAM

$10,000

$5,607.69 $5,607.69

1/1/X6   6/30   12/31

COMPOUND INTEREST CALCULATION

Amount borrowed, 1/1/X6	$10,000.00
Interest for first six-month period [($10,000)(.08)]	800.00
Subtotal	$10,800.00
Less: Payment, 6/30/X6	5,607.69
Balance of liability, 6/30/X6	$ 5,192.31
Interest for second six-month period [($5,192.31)(.08)]	415.38
Subtotal	$ 5,607.69
Less: Payment, 12/31/X6	5,607.69
Balance of liability, 12/31/X6	$ –0–

the amount borrowed and the future payments required by the note, from the borrower's perspective. Observe that the compound interest calculation results in a zero balance after the last payment, indicating that the two payments of $5,607.69 exactly pay off the liability created by the note.

The compound interest calculation presented in Exhibit 10–6 is constructed from the borrower's viewpoint and traces the liability created by the note. A parallel cash flow diagram and calculation can be constructed from the lender's or investor's viewpoint to trace the asset created by the note (Exhibit 10–7). Observe that the numerical forms of both borrower and lender calculations are exactly the same, differing only in the interpretations of the numbers. The cash flow diagrams, which are also quite similar to one another, differ only in that the directions of the flows are exactly opposite for the borrower and lender.

Whenever a contract establishes a relationship of this form between the initial amount borrowed or loaned and one or more future cash flows, the initial amount borrowed or loaned is called the *present value of future cash flows*. The present value of future cash flows can be interpreted in two ways: From the borrower's viewpoint, it is the present liability balance that will be exactly paid off by the future payments. From the lender's viewpoint, it is the present receivable balance that will be exactly paid off by the future receipts. At inception the **present value** of a loan is the amount borrowed or loaned, which is usually known and need not be calculated.

In some transactions, however, the present value is not known and must be calculated using a schedule of future cash flows and an interest rate. Such a

PRESENT VALUE: The present liability balance that will be exactly paid off by the related future payments (or, from the lender's viewpoint, the present asset balance that will be exactly liquidated by the future cash receipts). More generally, the present value is the current value of future cash flows discounted at an appropriate interest rate.

EXHIBIT 10–7   **CASH FLOW DIAGRAM AND COMPOUND INTEREST CALCULATIONS FOR AN ASSET**

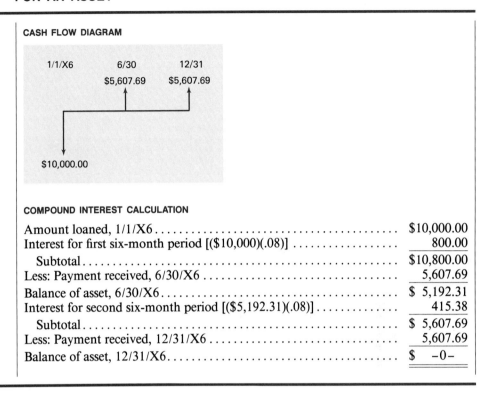

CASH FLOW DIAGRAM

1/1/X6	6/30	12/31
	$5,607.69	$5,607.69

$10,000.00

COMPOUND INTEREST CALCULATION

Amount loaned, 1/1/X6	$10,000.00
Interest for first six-month period [($10,000)(.08)]	800.00
Subtotal	$10,800.00
Less: Payment received, 6/30/X6	5,607.69
Balance of asset, 6/30/X6	$ 5,192.31
Interest for second six-month period [($5,192.31)(.08)]	415.38
Subtotal	$ 5,607.69
Less: Payment received, 12/31/X6	5,607.69
Balance of asset, 12/31/X6	$ –0–

calculation would be appropriate, for example, if a parcel of land were purchased under an installment contract that specified the number, amount, and time of future payments but did not specify the present value of the contract. Present value calculations are compound interest calculations in reverse, and since the reversal of compound interest calculations presents a burdensome and sometimes difficult algebraic problem, shortcut methods using tables have been developed. In the next section, we will examine the application of such methods to the calculation of both present values and future amounts.

FOUR BASIC TIME-VALUE-OF-MONEY PROBLEMS

The four problems presented here are called *basic* because every present value and future amount problem can be broken down into one or more of these basic problems. The basic problems can be solved with the aid of the present value and future amount tables presented at the end of this chapter (pages 466–469) and their solutions then combined to derive the solution to more complex problems. Before demonstrating how this is done, however, we will consider each of the four basic problems in turn.

EXHIBIT 10–8   FUTURE AMOUNT OF A SINGLE CASH FLOW: GENERAL FORM

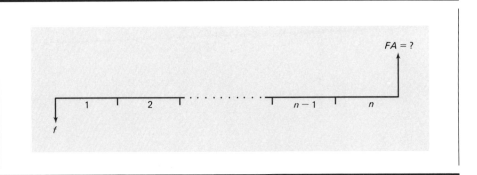

FUTURE AMOUNT OF A SINGLE CASH FLOW

The first basic problem is determining the future amount of a single cash flow. This problem is diagrammed from the lender's perspective, as shown in Exhibit 10–8. The problem has four symbolic elements: f represents the known cash flow, FA the unknown future amount, n the number of periods between the cash flow and the future amount, and i (not shown in the diagram) the interest rate per interest period. Problems of this form can be solved simply by establishing an account for f dollars and adding compound interest at i percent to that account for n periods. The balance of the account after n periods is the future amount. An alternative and easier solution technique makes use of the table shown in Exhibit 10–17 and the following formula:

$$FA = (f)(M_1)$$

where FA is the future amount, f is the cash flow, and M_1 is the multiple from Exhibit 10–17 corresponding to the appropriate values of n and i.

Every basic problem can be viewed from two perspectives—the lender's and the borrower's. By reversing the direction of each arrow in Exhibit 10–8, we could easily change the diagram from one perspective to the other. However, the change would not alter the relationship between f and FA, and both of the solution techniques just suggested can be used to calculate the future amount in either case.

The following example illustrates the two solution techniques: Suppose that a $10,000 loan earns interest at a rate of 10 percent per year compounded annually for four years. Finding the future amount (FA) at the end of the four years—the amount that will be repaid—is a basic problem, diagrammed in Exhibit 10–9. (We assume the lender's viewpoint.) Let us calculate the unknown future amount (FA) first by using a detailed compound interest calculation and then by the shortcut method using the table in Exhibit 10–17. The detailed compound interest calculation is as follows:

Initial cash flow (f)	$10,000
Interest for first year [($10,000)(.10)]	1,000
Balance at end of first year	$11,000
Interest for second year [($11,000)(.10)]	1,100
Balance at end of second year	$12,100
Interest for third year [($12,100)(.10)]	1,210
Balance at end of third year	$13,310
Interest for fourth year [($13,310)(.10)]	1,331
Balance at end of fourth year (FA)	$14,641

EXHIBIT 10–9   **FUTURE AMOUNT OF A SINGLE CASH FLOW: AN EXAMPLE**

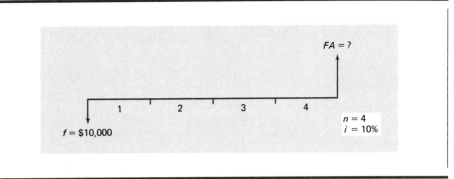

Observe that the amount of annual interest increases each year. This growth is the effect of computing interest for each year based on the beginning-of-year balance that includes the interest earned in prior years.

The shortcut calculation is made as follows:

$$FA = (f)(M_1)$$
$$= (\$10,000)(1.4641)$$
$$= \$14,641$$

The multiple 1.4641 is found at the intersection of the 10 percent column ($i = 10\%$) and the fourth row ($n = 4$) in Exhibit 10–17. The multiple can be interpreted as the future amount of $1 after having been borrowed (or invested) for four years at 10 percent interest. Consequently, the future amount of $10,000 is 10,000 times the multiple.

Interest and the Frequency of Compounding

The number of interest periods into which a given time-value-of-money problem is divided can make a significant difference in the amount of compound interest in a problem. To illustrate, assume that you are evaluating four 1-year investments, each of which requires a $10,000 investment at the beginning. All four investments earn interest at a rate of 12 percent per year, but they have different interest-compounding periods. The data in Exhibit 10–10 demonstrate the impact of the compounding frequency on the future amount. Observe that investment D, which offers monthly compounding, accumulates $68 more interest by the end of the year than investment A, which offers only annual compounding.

EXHIBIT 10–10   **EFFECT OF INTEREST PERIODS ON COMPOUND INTEREST**

INVESTMENT	INTEREST PERIOD	i	n	CALCULATION OF FUTURE AMOUNT IN ONE YEAR
A	1 year	12%	1	($10,000)(1.1200) = $11,200
B	6 months	6%	2	($10,000)(1.1236) = $11,236
C	1 quarter	3%	4	($10,000)(1.1255) = $11,255
D	1 month	1%	12	($10,000)(1.1268) = $11,268

EXHIBIT 10–11 PRESENT VALUE OF A SINGLE CASH FLOW: GENERAL FORM

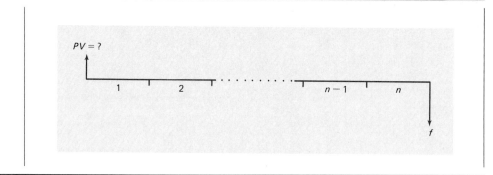

PRESENT VALUE OF A SINGLE CASH FLOW

The second basic problem is to find the present value of a single future cash flow. This problem is diagrammed from the borrower's viewpoint as shown in Exhibit 10–11. This problem also has four symbolic elements: f represents the known cash flow, PV the unknown present value, n the number of periods between the present time and the future cash flow, and i the interest rate per interest period. In present value problems, the interest rate is sometimes called the *discount rate*. Problems of this form must be solved by reverse compounding, which is most easily done by using the table in Exhibit 10–18 and the following formula:

$$PV = (f)(M_2)$$

where PV is the present value, f is the cash flow, and M_2 is the multiple from Exhibit 10–18 that corresponds to the appropriate values of n and i.

In the following example, this present value solution technique is applied to a single cash flow problem from a borrower's viewpoint. Suppose that a cash outflow of $1,728 will occur three years from now and that it includes interest earned at a rate of 20 percent per year compounded annually. Finding the present value (PV) of this future cash flow is a basic problem that is diagrammed in Exhibit 10–12. The present value can be calculated by using Exhibit 10–18 as follows:

$$PV = (f)(M_2)$$
$$= (\$1,728)(.5787)$$
$$= \$1,000$$

The multiple .5787 is found at the intersection of the 20 percent column ($i = 20\%$) and the third row ($n = 3$) in Exhibit 10–18. The multiple can be interpreted as the present value of $1 that will be a cash inflow or a cash outflow in three years at 20 percent. Thus the present value of $1,728 is 1,728 times as much as the multiple.

Although the compound interest calculation cannot be used to determine the present value, it can be used to verify that the present value calculated by using the table is correct. The following calculation demonstrates a proof for the present value problem at hand:

Calculated present value (PV)	$1,000.00
Interest for first year [($1,000.00)(.20)]	200.00
Balance at end of first year	$1,200.00
Interest for second year [($1,200.00)(.20)]	240.00
Balance at end of second year	$1,440.00
Interest for third year [($1,440.00)(.20)]	288.00
Balance at end of third year (f)	$1,728.00

EXHIBIT 10–12   PRESENT VALUE OF A SINGLE CASH FLOW: AN EXAMPLE

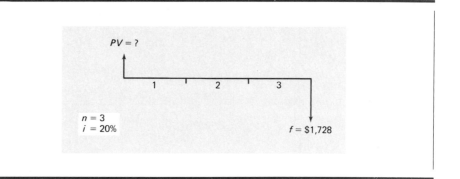

When interest is compounded on the calculated present value of $1,000, the present value calculation is reversed and we are returned to the future amount of $1,728. This reversal proves that $1,000 is the correct present value because only that amount leads us back to the future cash flow of $1,728. If interest were compounded on more than or less than $1,000, the balance at the end of the third year would have been more than or less than $1,728.

Both the first and the second basic problems involve a single cash flow. We turn now to problems with multiple cash flows, which are called *annuities*.

FUTURE AMOUNT OF AN ANNUITY

ANNUITY: A specified number of equal cash flows occurring one interest period apart.

The third and fourth basic problems involve series of cash flows called *annuities*. An **annuity** is a specified number of equal cash flows, occurring one interest period apart. For example, an investment in a security that pays $1,000 to an investor every December 31 for 10 consecutive years is an annuity. A loan repayment schedule that calls for a payment of $67.29 on the first day of each month can also be considered an annuity. (Although the number of days in a month varies from 28 to 31, the interest period is defined as one month without regard to the number of days in each month.)

Our third basic problem is to determine the future amount of an annuity. This problem is diagrammed in Exhibit 10–13 from an investor's viewpoint. In this problem, f represents the amount of each repeating cash flow, n represents the number of cash flows, FA the future amount immediately after the last (nth) of the cash flows, and i the interest rate per interest period. Note that the first period in Exhibit 10–13 is drawn with a dashed line. When using annuities, the

EXHIBIT 10–13   FUTURE AMOUNT OF AN ANNUITY: GENERAL FORM

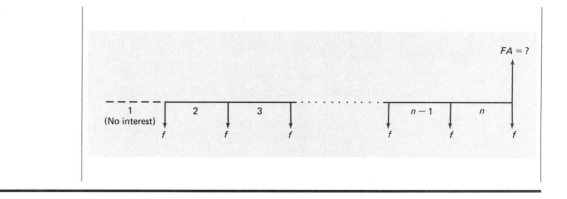

EXHIBIT 10–14   FUTURE AMOUNT OF AN ANNUITY: AN EXAMPLE

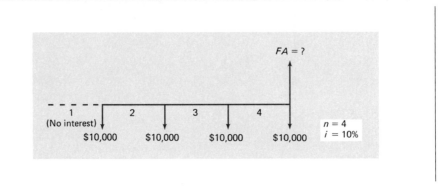

time-value-of-money model assumes that all cash flows occur at the end of a period. Therefore, the first cash flow in the future amount of an annuity occurs at the end of the first period. However, since interest cannot be earned until the first deposit has been made, the first period is also identified as a no-interest period. Problems of this form can be solved by compound interest calculations or by the use of the table in Exhibit 10–19 and the following formula:

$$FA = (f)(M_3)$$

where FA is the future amount, f is the amount of the repeating cash flow, and M_3 is the multiple from Exhibit 10–19 corresponding to the appropriate values of n and i. The tables and the formula for annuities are expressed in numbers of cash flows or numbers of periods. Therefore, when solving annuity problems by using the tables in Exhibits 10–19 and 10–20, remember that the first column, the number of periods, equals the number of annuity cash flows.

The following example demonstrates the computation of the future amount of an annuity. As for the other basic problems, the same solution techniques are applied to both the lender's and the borrower's perspectives. Consider an annuity of four cash flows of $10,000 each, where the interest rate is 10 percent per year compounded annually. Find the future amount of this annuity immediately after the fourth cash flow. This future amount problem is diagrammed in Exhibit 10–14 from the lender's perspective. Let us find the future amount (FA) first by using a detailed compound interest calculation and then with the shortcut method based on the table in Exhibit 10–19.

Our compound interest calculation is made as follows:

Interest for first period [($0)(.10)]	$ –0–
First cash flow..	10,000.00
Balance at end of first period	$10,000.00
Interest for second period [($10,000)(.10)].................	1,000.00
Second cash flow	10,000.00
Balance at end of second period	$21,000.00
Interest for third period [($21,000)(.10)]	2,100.00
Third cash flow.......................................	10,000.00
Balance at end of third period	$33,100.00
Interest for fourth period [($33,100)(.10)]	3,310.00
Fourth cash flow......................................	10,000.00
Balance at end of fourth period (FA)	$46,410.00

EXHIBIT 10–15   **PRESENT VALUE OF AN ANNUITY: GENERAL FORM**

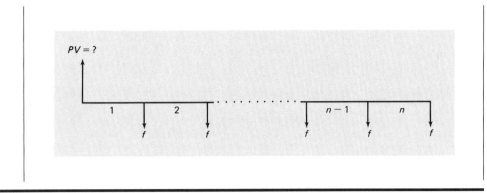

The compound interest calculation shows that the lender has accumulated a future amount (FA) of \$46,410 by the end of the fourth period, immediately after the fourth cash flow.

An easier means of computing the future amount, however, is by using the table shown in Exhibit 10–19, as follows:

$$FA = (f)(M_3)$$
$$= (\$10,000)(4.6410)$$
$$= \$46,410$$

The multiple 4.6410 is found at the intersection of the 10 percent column $(i = 10\%)$ and the fourth row $(n = 4)$ in Exhibit 10–19. The multiple can be interpreted as the future amount of an annuity of four cash flows of \$1 each at 10 percent. The future amount of an annuity \$10,000 cash flows is therefore 10,000 times the multiple. The table enables us to calculate the future amount of an annuity by a single multiplication, no matter how many cash flows are involved. Another table achieves a similar simplification for calculations of the present value of an annuity, as the next section explains.

PRESENT VALUE OF AN ANNUITY

The fourth and final basic problem is to find the present value of an annuity. This problem has the general form, from a borrower's perspective, shown in Exhibit 10–15. In this problem, f represents the amount of the repeating cash flow, n represents the number of cash flows and interest periods, PV the present value of the n future cash flows, and i the interest (or discount) rate per interest period. Problems of this form must be solved by reverse compounding, which is most easily done by using the table in Exhibit 10–20 in conjunction with the following formula:

$$PV = (f)(M_4)$$

where PV is the present value, f is the amount of the repeating cash flow, and M_4 is the multiple from Exhibit 10–20 corresponding to the appropriate values of n and i.

The following example illustrates the technique of reverse compounding. Bear in mind that the same solution techniques are applicable to both the lender's and borrower's perspectives. Consider an annuity of four cash flows of \$20,736 each, for which the interest rate is 20 percent per year compounded annually and

EXHIBIT 10–16   PRESENT VALUE OF AN ANNUITY: AN EXAMPLE

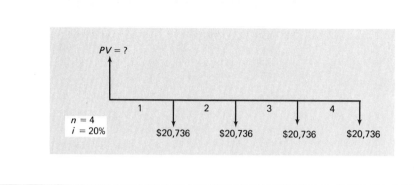

the first cash flow occurs one year from now. Determine the present value of this annuity. This problem, as diagrammed in Exhibit 10–16, assumes the borrower's perspective. The present value can be found by using the table in Exhibit 10–20, as follows:

$$PV = (f)(M_4)$$
$$= (\$20{,}736)(2.5887)$$
$$= \$53{,}679.28$$

The multiple 2.5887 is found at the intersection of the 20 percent column ($i = 20\%$) and the fourth row ($n = 4$) in Exhibit 10–20. The multiple can be interpreted as the present value of an annuity of four cash flows of $1 each at 20 percent. The present value of an annuity of four $20,736 cash flows is therefore 20,736 times the multiple.

Again, although the compound interest calculation is not used to determine the present value, it can be used to prove that the present value calculated by using the table is correct. The following calculation verifies the present value in the problem at hand:

Calculated present value (PV)	$53,679.28
Interest for first year [($53,679.28)(.20)]..................	10,735.86
Subtotal...	$64,415.14
Less: First cash flow	20,736.00
Balance at end of first year	$43,679.14
Interest for second year [($43,679.14)(.20)]	8,735.83
Subtotal...	$52,414.97
Less: Second cash flow....................................	20,736.00
Balance at end of second year............................	$31,678.97
Interest for third year [($31,678.97)(.20)]..................	6,335.79
Subtotal...	$38,014.76
Less: Third cash flow	20,736.00
Balance at end of third year	$17,278.76
Interest for fourth year [($17,278.76)(.20)]................	3,455.75
Subtotal...	$20,734.51
Less: Fourth cash flow	20,736.00
Balance at end of fourth year	$ (1.49)

This proof uses the compound interest calculation that was reversed in the present value formula. If the present value (PV) calculated with the formula is correct, then the proof should end with a balance of zero immediately after the last cash flow. This proof ends with a negative $1.49 because of rounding errors in the proof itself and in the multiple taken from the table in Exhibit 10–20.

Present value calculations are useful in more ways than those directly related to accounting for liabilities and assets subject to compound interest. For example, present value calculations can be useful to prospective buyers of a business, as the following analysis demonstrates.

ANALYSIS

DETERMINING THE VALUE OF A BUSINESS

In preparation for his retirement, Mr. R. J. Cole, founder and sole owner of Cole Manufacturing, has offered his company for sale. Mr. J. Elliot, a certified public accountant, has been engaged by a group of prospective buyers to advise them on various accounting and valuation issues concerning the proposed purchase.

With the assistance of appraisers and other experts, Mr. Elliot determines that the specific assets and liabilities listed on the records of Cole Manufacturing have a total current value of $3,000,000 and $1,400,000, respectively. Accordingly, the current value of stockholders' equity might be estimated at $1,600,000 [$3,000,000 − $1,400,000]. However, Mr. Cole has already rejected an offer of $1,600,000 on the grounds that the income-producing capability of the business is worth more than the current value of the specific net assets held. He argues that the business has built up goodwill over the years in the form of stable relationships with suppliers and customers and that this goodwill is an intangible asset of considerable value.

Cole Manufacturing is expected to generate a net cash flow (cash inflows from revenues less cash outflows for expenses) of approximately $450,000 per year for the next 20 years. Mr. Elliot believes that an interest rate of 20 percent is appropriate for valuing the expected cash flows of Cole Manufacturing. Mr. Elliot raises the questions listed below and performs the related analyses in order to assess the validity of Mr. Cole's arguments.

1. *What is the value of the expected cash flow to the prospective buyers?*

This question involves finding the present value of an annuity. The following cash flow diagram and solution assume the viewpoint of the prospective buyers of Cole Manufacturing:

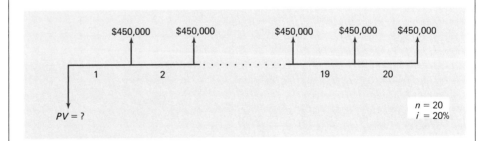

$$PV = (f)(M_4)$$
$$= (\$450,000)(4.8696)$$
$$= \$2,191,320$$

If we accept the assumptions on which this calculation is based, the present value of $2,191,320 supports Mr. Cole's contention by demonstrating that his company embodies unrecorded goodwill of approximately $591,320 [$2,191,320 − $1,600,000]. However, Mr. Elliot is inclined to question certain of the underlying assumptions.

2. *Mr. Elliot questions whether the cash flow can really be projected for 20 years. In his view, any projection beyond 10 years is apt to be so uncertain as to justify an estimate of zero cash flow.*

Mr. Elliot makes the following revised present value analysis, again from the perspective of the prospective buyers:

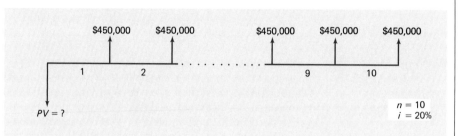

$$PV = (f)(M_4)$$
$$= (\$450,000)(4.1925)$$
$$= \$1,886,625$$

In this computation, the present value drops by \$304,695 [\$2,191,320 − \$1,886,625] but still exceeds the current value of equity by \$286,625 [\$1,886,625 − \$1,600,000]. In other words, the amount of the goodwill is surprisingly insensitive to the assumed duration of the cash flow stream. Notice that Mr. Elliot discarded the latter half of the cash flows and reduced the present value by only 14 percent [(\$2,191,320 − \$1,886,625)/\$2,191,320 = .139]. In general, the more distant a future cash flow, the less it contributes to the present value. Moreover, this effect is particularly strong for high interest rates. The higher the interest rate, the smaller the contribution of any given future cash flow to the present value. Higher interest rates require larger adjustments for interest in moving from future amounts to present values.

3. *Mr. Elliot also questions the estimated cash flow. He believes that \$400,000 would be a more reasonable estimate than \$450,000.*

Mr. Elliot revises the present value analysis as follows, continuing to use the 10-year duration:

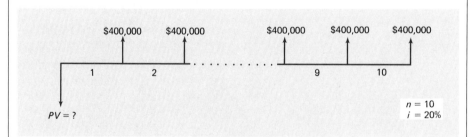

$$PV = (f)(M_4)$$
$$= (\$400,000)(4.1925)$$
$$= \$1,677,000$$

If this analysis is correct, then the present value of the goodwill is only \$77,000. It becomes apparent that the present value is somewhat more sensitive to an overstatement of the size of the repeating cash flow than it is to interest and the duration of the flow.

4. *Mr. Cole is asking $1,700,000 for his business. Using both revisions of the original analysis, what rate of interest does this price imply for the prospective buyers of the business, who wish to earn 22 percent on their investment?*

To answer this question, Mr. Elliot makes the following analysis (the problem here is to find the interest rate instead of the present value):

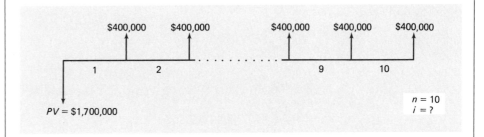

$$PV = (f)(M_4)$$
$$\$1,700,000 = (\$400,000)(M_4)$$
$$M_4 = 1,700,000/\$400,000$$
$$= 4.250$$

The multiple (M_4) for this problem turns out to be 4.250. If we look in the tenth row of the table in Exhibit 10–20, we do not find the exact multiple 4.250. However, 4.250 is between 18 percent and 20 percent, which means that the implied interest rate is somewhat less than 20 percent. This interest rate is less than the 22 percent that Mr. Elliot's clients want to earn on their investment. Accordingly, Mr. Elliot advises his clients to seek a price below $1,700,000 or to invest their money elsewhere.

ACCOUNTING APPLICATIONS OF TIME-VALUE-OF-MONEY ANALYSIS

Although time-value-of-money analysis has been discussed for transactions between borrowers and lenders, accounting for a variety of other transactions involving interest also requires the calculation of present values and future amounts. We now describe four typical situations in which such transactions arise. In each situation, time-value-of-money analysis is applied in order to determine the amounts required by the related accounting procedures.

CALCULATIONS FOR AN INVESTMENT IN MONEY MARKET SECURITIES
The Kitchner Company sells an unneeded northern factory site for $200,000 on July 1, 19X3. Kitchner expects to purchase another site in California in 18 months, to permit expansion into West Coast markets. Meanwhile, Kitchner decides to invest the $200,000 in a money market fund that is guaranteed to earn 16 percent per year compounded semiannually (8 percent per six-month period).

1. Draw a cash flow diagram for this investment from the investor's perspective.

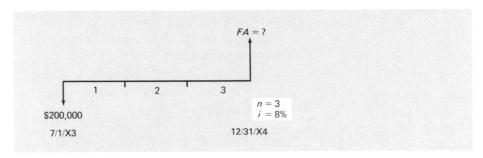

2. Write the journal entry to record this investment on July 1, 19X3.

Long-term investments............................ 200,000
    Cash....................................... 200,000

3. Calculate the number of dollars in the money market fund at December 31, 19X4.

$$FA = (f)(M_1)$$
$$= (\$200,000)(1.2597)$$
$$= \$251,940$$

4. Write the adjusting entries by Kitchner on December 31, 19X3, (1) to record the interest earned by the investment from July 1, 19X3, through December 31, 19X3, and (2) to reclassify the investment as short-term.

(1) Long-term investments......................... 16,000
    Interest revenue [($200,000)(.08)]............... 16,000

(2) Short-term investments......................... 216,000
    Long-term investments...................... 216,000

5. Write the entries by Kitchner at December 31, 19X4, (1) to record the interest earned in 19X4 and (2) to record the receipt of the maturity amount of the investment in cash.

(1) Short-term investments......................... 35,940
    Interest revenue ($251,940 − $216,000).......... 35,940

(2) Cash....................................... 251,940
    Short-term investments 251,940

Note that the interest earned by Kitchner in each six-month interest period is added to the investment account balance that existed at the beginning of that period to produce the ending balance. The ending balance becomes the beginning balance on which interest for the next period is computed.

CALCULATIONS FOR A PURCHASE OF EQUIPMENT WITH DEFERRED PAYMENT

On October 1, 19X1, Adelsman Manufacturing Company sold a new machine to Randell, Inc. The machine represented a new design that Randell was eager to place in service. Since Randell was unable to pay for the machine on the date of the purchase, Adelsman agreed to defer payment of $60,000 for 15 months. The appropriate rate of interest in such transactions is 16 percent per year compounded quarterly (4 percent per three-month period).

1. Draw the cash flow diagram for this deferred-payment purchase from Randell's perspective.

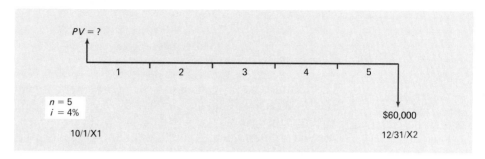

2. Calculate the cost of the machine as recorded by Randell.

$$PV = (f)(M_2)$$
$$= (\$60,000)(.8219)$$
$$= \$49,314$$

3. Write the journal entry made by Randell on October 1, 19X1.

Equipment....................................	49,314	
Accounts payable...............................		49,314

4. Write the adjusting entry made by Randell at December 31, 19X1.

Interest expense [($49,314)(.04)]	1,973	
Accounts payable...............................		1,973

Observe that the asset is recorded at the present value of the deferred payment. In other words, the cost of the new machine is $49,314 rather than $60,000 because the latter number includes interest charges of $10,686 [$60,000 − $49,314].

CALCULATIONS FOR ACCUMULATION OF A FUND

The Loeb Foundation has taken an option to purchase a tract of land for $1,000,000 for use by the city as a public park. The option must be exercised in five years. The Loeb Foundation plans to make five annual deposits of $150,000 each in a special fund that will earn 12 percent per year compounded annually.

1. Draw the cash flow diagram for the Loeb Foundation fund from the investor's perspective.

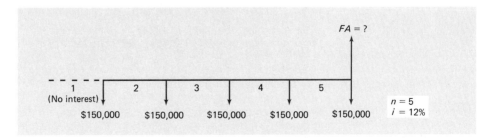

2. Calculate the future amount accumulated immediately after the fifth deposit.

$$FA = (f)(M_3)$$
$$= (\$150,000)(6.3528)$$
$$= \$952,920$$

3. Calculate the amount of the annual deposit required to accumulate exactly $1,000,000 in five annual deposits.

$$FA = (f)(M_3)$$
$$\$1,000,000 = (f)(6.3528)$$
$$f = \$1,000,000/6.3528$$
$$= \$157,411$$

The future amount calculation in requirement 2 shows that five deposits of $150,000 each will not accumulate the required $1,000,000. The calculation in requirement 3 shows that five deposits of $157,411 each are required to accumulate that amount. Note that requirement 3 uses the multiple from Exhibit 10–19 in a somewhat different way than has been done previously. In the examples thus far, the repeating cash flow f has been known, and the problem has been to find the future amount (FA). Accordingly, the repeating payment has been multiplied by the appropriate multiple. In this example, however, the future amount is known to be $1,000,000, and the problem is to find the repeating cash flow f. Thus, in this case, the future amount is divided by the multiple from Exhibit 10–19.

CALCULATIONS FOR THE PURCHASE OF LAND WITH AN INSTALLMENT NOTE

Bates Builders purchased a subdivision site from the Trust Department of Second National Bank and Trust Company on January 1, 19X4. The terms of the installment note were as follows: four annual payments of $100,000 each made on December 31 of each year beginning in 19X4, with interest computed at a rate of 15 percent per year compounded annually.

1. Draw the cash flow diagram for this purchase from Bates' perspective.

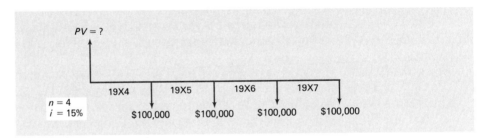

2. Calculate the cost of the land as recorded by Bates on January 1, 19X4.

$$PV = (f)(M_4)$$
$$= (\$100,000)(2.8550)$$
$$= \$285,500$$

3. Write the journal entry by Bates on January 1, 19X4, to record the purchase.

Land. 285,500
    Installment notes payable. 285,500

4. Write the journal entries by Bates (1) to record interest expense for 19X4 and (2) to record the payment of $100,000 at December 31, 19X4.

(1) Interest expense [($285,500)(.15)] 42,825
    Installment notes payable. 42,825

(2) Installment notes payable. 100,000
    Cash 100,000

5. Write the journal entries made by Bates (1) to record the interest expense for 19X5 and (2) to record the payment of $100,000 at December 31, 19X5.

(1) Interest expense [($285,500 + $42,825
  − $100,000)(.15)]   34,249
      Installment notes payable.   34,249

(2) Installment notes payable.   100,000
      Cash   100,000

The balance of the installment notes payable account continues to decline over the life of the note, as shown in the following schedule:

Installment notes payable, 1/1/X4	$285,500.00
Interest expense for 19X4 [($285,500.00)(.15)]	42,825.00
Subtotal	$328,325.00
Less: First payment	100,000.00
Installment notes payable, 12/31/X4	$228,325.00
Interest expense for 19X5 [($228,325.00)(.15)]	34,248.75
Subtotal	$262,573.75
Less: Second payment	100,000.00
Installment notes payable, 12/31/X5	$162,573.75
Interest expense for 19X6 [($162,573.75)(.15)]	24,386.06
Subtotal	$186,959.81
Less: Third payment	100,000.00
Installment notes payable, 12/31/X6	$ 86,959.81
Interest expense for 19X7 [($86,959.81)(.15)	13,043.97
Subtotal	$100,003.78
Less: Fourth payment	100,000.00
Installment notes payable, 12/31/X7	$ 3.78

Strictly speaking, the balance of the installment notes payable should decline to zero at December 31, 19X7. The $3.78 balance shown in the exhibit is the result of a rounding error in the table in Exhibit 10–20. The multiple 2.8550 used to compute the present value of the four payments is more precisely stated as 2.85498.

SUMMARY

Section A of this chapter deals with the measurement and reporting of three kinds of liabilities: (1) current liabilities, (2) contingent liabilities, and (3) the deferred income tax liability. Because they will be paid within a short time, most current liabilities are measured at the value of what was received or at the amount of the payment to be made. Current liabilities are usually reported in the balance sheet in the order in which they will be paid. Accounts payable may be measured either net or gross of discounts offered. Notes payable may be either interest-bearing or non-interest-bearing. Both types of notes require adjusting entries when the note is outstanding at the end of the accounting period. Accrued payables (wages or rent, for example) are also recorded with adjusting entries. Unearned revenues arise when customers pay for goods or services in advance.

Contingent liabilities arise when the firm has an obligation to outsiders for which the amount, timing, or recipient depends on future events. In such cases, the amount of the obligation must be estimated, and the required accounting depends on the likelihood of the related future events. Common examples of contingent liabilities are warranties and pensions.

A deferred income tax liability arises when there is a temporary difference that causes the revenues and expenses reported on the tax return to differ from those reported on the income statement. Normally, revenues appear later and expenses appear sooner on the tax return, resulting in a larger tax expense than is payable. This difference is reported on the balance sheet as a deferred tax liability.

Section B of the chapter presents the elements of time-value-of-money analysis, a measurement technique used to account for cash flows that extend over more than one period. Time-value-of-money analysis is based on a simple idea: A cash flow in the future is less valuable than a cash flow at the present. As discussed here, the time value of money is based on compound interest calculations. We explained four basic time-value-of-money problems: (1) the future amount of a single cash flow, (2) the present value of a single cash flow, (3) the future amount of an annuity, and (4) the present value of an annuity. We also demonstrated how to break complex problems into one or more of the four basic problems and how to use tables to solve the basic problems. We strongly recommend the use of cash flow diagrams for analyzing time-value-of-money problems.

KEY TERMS

ACCOUNT PAYABLE (p. 419)	INTERPERIOD TAX ALLOCATION (p. 428)
ACCRUED PAYABLES (p. 419)	LIABILITIES (p. 417)
ANNUITY (p. 439)	NOTE PAYABLE (p. 420)
COMPOUND INTEREST (p. 430)	PENSION EXPENSE (p. 426)
CONTINGENT LIABILITY (p. 424)	PENSION FUNDING (p. 426)
CURRENT LIABILITIES (p. 418)	PENSION LIABILITY (p. 426)
DEFERRED TAX LIABILITY (p. 428)	PRESENT VALUE (p. 434)
DISCOUNT ON NOTE (p. 422)	TIME VALUE OF MONEY (p. 430)
FUTURE AMOUNT (p. 432)	UNEARNED REVENUE (p. 423)
INTEREST PERIOD (p. 430)	WARRANTY (p. 425)
INTEREST RATE (p. 430)	

SECTION A QUESTIONS

Q10-1. What are liabilities? How is the amount of a liability measured?

Q10-2. Describe four liabilities. Each of the following characteristics should be illustrated by one or more of the liabilities you describe: (1) a liability that does not involve the payment of cash, (2) a liability that is not known with certainty, (3) a liability that is not legally enforceable, and (4) a liability payable to an unknown recipient.

Q10-3. List and describe the various types of current liabilities.

Q10-4. Describe the events that cause the recording of the following current liabilities, all of which require payments to taxing authorities: (1) sales tax on goods sold to customers, (2) federal income tax withheld from employees' wages, (3) employer's share of FICA tax.

Q10-5. How is interest computed on an interest-bearing short-term note? How is interest computed on a non-interest-bearing short-term note?

Q10-6. Why do unearned revenues and customer deposits qualify as liabilities?

Q10-7. What is the justification for classifying a portion of a long-term liability as a current liability?

Q10-8. Explain the concepts governing the recognition and measurement of liabilities that depend on future events. What are such liabilities called?

Q10-9. Why is the liability for warranties recognized when the related goods are sold rather than when the warranty services are performed?

Q10-10. Describe the entry to record payments by an employer into a pension fund? What is the meaning of a pension liability?

Q10-11. Explain the difference between income taxes payable and a deferred tax liability.

SECTION B QUESTIONS

Q10-12. Why does money have a time value?

Q10-13. Describe the four basic time-value-of-money problems.

Q10-14. How is compound interest computed? What is a future amount? What is a present value?

Q10-15. Define an annuity in general terms. Describe the cash flows related to an annuity from the viewpoint of the *lender* in terms of receipts and payments.

Q10-16. Explain how to use time-value-of-money calculations to estimate the value of a business.

SECTION A EXERCISES

E10-17. RECOGNITION AND REPORTING OF CONTINGENT LIABILITIES Match the appropriate accounting treatment with each of the potential liabilities listed below. Your answer should list the numbers 1 through 10 and, opposite each number, the letter of the appropriate accounting treatment.

ALTERNATIVE ACCOUNTING TREATMENTS

A. Estimate the amount of the liability and record.

B. Do not record as a liability but disclose in a footnote to the financial statements.

C. Neither record as a liability nor disclose in a footnote to the financial statements.

POTENTIAL CONTINGENT LIABILITIES

1. Income taxes related to net income of the current year and taxable income of a future year.

2. Income taxes related to net income and taxable income of a future year.

3. Estimated cost of future services under a product warranty related to past sales.

4. Estimated cost of future services under a product warranty related to future sales.

5. Estimated cost of pension benefits related to past employee services that has yet to be funded.

6. Loss from out-of-court settlement of lawsuit that is likely to occur toward the end of next year.

7. Potential loss on environmental cleanup suit against company; a court judgment against the company is considered less than probable but more than remotely likely.

8. Potential loss under class-action suit by a group of customers; during the current year, the likelihood of a judgment against the company has increased from remote to possible but less than probable.

9. Potential loss under an affirmative action suit by a former employee; the likelihood of a judgment against the company is considered to be remote.

10. Potential loss from a downturn in future economic activity.

E10-18. RECORDING VARIOUS LIABILITIES   Prepare the entry to record each of the following liabilities:

a) Purchase merchandise on credit for $20,000.

b) Record at year-end wages of $7,600 incurred, but not paid. Related federal income tax of $1,200, FICA tax at $280, and state income tax of $195 are withheld.

c) Record at year-end estimated income taxes payable but unpaid for the year in the amount of $21,300.

d) Sell merchandise on account for $872, including sales tax of $32.

e) Pay employees $11,226, which does not include previously recorded amounts for related federal income tax withheld of $2,300, related FICA tax withheld of $1,154, and related state income tax withheld of $410.

f) Record employer's share of FICA tax for the period, $1,154.

g) Borrow cash under a 90-day, non-interest-bearing note with a maturity amount of $9,000 and a discount of $820.

h) Borrow cash under a 90-day, 8 percent, interest-bearing note with a principal amount of $9,000.

E10-19. REPORTING LIABILITIES   Describe how each of the following items should be reported in the balance sheet:

a) A legally enforceable claim against the business to be paid in three months.

b) An excess of income taxes expense over income taxes assessed for a period.

c) A guarantee given by a seller to a purchaser to repair or replace defective goods during the first six months following sale.

d) An amount payable to a bank in 10 years.

e) An amount to be paid next year on a long-term note payable.

E10-20. ACCOUNTS PAYABLE   For Hammerton Autos, a used-car dealer, the following transactions occurred during the first 10 days of August:

a) Hammerton purchased on credit space for classified advertisements in the local newspaper for $245. The advertising was run the day the space was purchased.

b) Hammerton purchased office supplies on credit in the amount of $185.

c) One of Hammerton's salespeople sold a car. The salesperson's commission is $100. The commission will be paid September 10. (Concern yourself only with the commission.)

d) The electric bill for July was received. The bill is $239 and is due August 15.

e) A $390 bill from Carey Alignment services was received. Carey had aligned 10 cars for Hammerton in late July. The payment is due August 20.

REQUIRED:

Prepare journal entries for the above transactions. Assume that Hammerton prepares annual financial statements on December 31.

E10-21. PAYROLL ACCOUNTING   Blitzen Marketing Research paid its weekly and monthly payroll on January 31. The following information is available about the payroll:

ITEM	AMOUNT	EXPENSE CLASSIFICATION
Monthly salaries	$25,400	Administrative expense
Hourly wages.	79,600	Operating expense
FICA		
Employees' contribution	7.65%	
Employer's contribution	7.65%	Administrative expense
Withholding for federal income tax	$21,240	
Withholding for state income tax.	2,680	
Federal unemployment tax	1,200	Administrative expense
State unemployment tax	600	Administrative expense

Blitzen will pay both the employer's taxes and the taxes withheld on April 15.

REQUIRED:

Prepare the journal entry to record the payroll payment and the incurrence of the associated expenses and liabilities.

E10-22.   ACCOUNTING FOR INTEREST-BEARING NOTE   Rogers Machinery Company borrowed $140,000 on June 1 on a six-month, 12 percent, interest-bearing note.

REQUIRED:

1. Record the borrowing transaction in Rogers' journal.

2. Record the repayment transaction in Rogers' journal.

E10-23.   NON-INTEREST-BEARING NOTE   Webster Enterprises borrowed $262,400 on a 90-day, non-interest-bearing note on July 15, 19X8. The maturity amount of the note, $275,000, is to be repaid on October 12, 19X8.

REQUIRED:

1. Record the borrowing transaction in Webster's journal.

2. Record the repayment transaction in Webster's journal.

E10-24.   UNEARNED REVENUE   Irvine Pest Control signed a $2,100-per-month contract on November 1, 19X8, to provide pest control services to rental units owed by Garden Grove Properties. Irvine received three months' service fees in advance, on signing the contract.

REQUIRED:

1. Prepare Irvine's journal entry to record the $6,300 cash receipt.

2. Prepare Irvine's adjusting entry at December 31, 19X8.

3. How would the advance payment be reported in Irvine Pest Control's December 31, 19X8, balance sheet? How would the advance payment be reported in Garden Grove Properties' December 31, 19X8, balance sheet?

E10-25.   CUSTOMER DEPOSITS   Carrington Municipal Electric requires each new customer to pay a $600 "hookup fee" to offset the cost of extending service lines and installing meters. The fee is refundable when the customer moves to another location, dies, or discontinues service. Carrington is a small town in a rural region with a stable population.

REQUIRED:

1. On June 15, 1990, $600 is received from each of two new customers ($1,200 in total), Robert Nelson and Arnold Metz, and $600 is paid to the estate of Ernest Walton. Prepare the journal entries to record these cash transactions.

2. How should customer deposits be reported in the utility's balance sheet? The controller for the utility argues that these customer deposits are more like capital stock than long-term liabilities; do you agree with him?

E10-26.   WARRANTIES   Moon TV, Inc., sells television sets and other electronic sound and video equipment. Sales and expected warranty claims for the year are as follows:

ITEM	UNIT SALES	EXPECTED WARRANTY CLAIMS FOR WARRANTY PERIOD	COST PER CLAIM
Television set............	860	1 claim per 100 sold	$60
VCR	290	10 claims per 100 sold	38
Stereo	1,800	4 claims per 100 sold	42

REQUIRED:

Prepare the entry to record warranty expense for Moon TV for the year.

E10-27. DEFERRED INCOME TAX   Jergens, Inc., follows the tax law when computing depreciation expense on its tax return and uses straight-line depreciation to compute the depreciation expense for its income statement. For 19X7 the following data are available:

ITEM	INCOME TAX RETURN	INCOME STATEMENT
Income before taxes..........................	$826,000	$1,039,000
Tax rate.....................................	.34	.34

REQUIRED:

1. What is the amount of income taxes payable for 19X7?

2. What is the amount of income taxes expense for 19X7?

3. Prepare the journal entry to record income taxes for 19X7.

E10-28. CHANGES IN DEFERRED INCOME TAX LIABILITY   The deferred income tax liability reported by Stone Equipment Company is entirely the result of temporary differences related to depreciation expense. The following data are available for 19X4 and 19X5:

ITEM	19X4	19X5
Income taxes payable (at December 31)...............	$197,400	$260,300
Income taxes expense	211,000	248,500
Deferred income tax liability (at December 31).........	43,900	32,100

The tax liability for each year is paid in a single payment shortly after year-end.

REQUIRED:

1. Prepare the income tax entries for 19X4 and 19X5.

2. Explain why the deferred income tax liability declined between December 31, 19X4, and December 31, 19X5.

3. Explain in general terms the difference between income taxes payable and the deferred income tax liability.

SECTION B EXERCISES

E10-29. PRACTICE WITH TABLES   Using the appropriate tables in the text, determine:

a) The future amount of a single cash flow of $5,000 that earns 7 percent interest compounded annually for 10 years.

b) The future amount of an annual annuity of 10 cash flows of $500 each that earns 7 percent compounded annually.

c) The present value of $5,000 to be received 10 years from now, assuming that the interest (discount) rate is 7 percent per year.

d) The present value of an annuity of $500 per year for 10 years for which the interest (discount) rate is 7 percent per year and the first cash flow occurs 1 year from now.

E10-30. PRACTICE WITH TABLES   Using the appropriate tables in the text, determine:

a) The present value of $1,200 to be received in seven years, assuming that the interest (discount) rate is 12 percent per year.

b) The present value of an annuity of seven cash flows of $1,200 each (one at the end of each of the next seven years) for which the interest (discount) rate is 12 percent per year.

c) The future amount of a single cash flow of $1,200 that earns 12 percent per year for seven years.

d) The future amount of an annuity of seven cash flows of $1,200 each (one at the end of each of the next seven years), assuming that the interest rate is 12 percent per year.

E10-31. FUTURE AMOUNTS   Using the appropriate tables in the text, determine:

a) The future amount of a single deposit of $15,000 that earns compound interest for four years at an interest rate of 10 percent per year.

b) The annual interest rate that will produce a future amount of $14,963.20 in six years from a single deposit of $8,000.

c) The size of annual cash flows for an annuity of nine cash flows that will produce a future amount of $79,428.10 at an interest rate of 9 percent per year.

d) The number of periods required to produce a future amount of $25,459.50 from an initial deposit of $7,500 if the annual interest rate is 13 percent.

E10-32. FUTURE AMOUNTS AND ENTRIES FOR LONG-TERM INVESTMENTS   Pueblo Pottery, Inc., engaged in the following transactions during 19X2:

a) On January 1, 19X2, Pueblo deposited $12,000 in a certificate of deposit paying 10 percent interest compounded semiannually (5 percent per six-month period). The certificate will mature on December 31, 19X5.

b) On March 15, 19X2, Pueblo established an account with Durango Investment Management. Pueblo will make quarterly payments of $2,500 to Durango beginning on March 31, 19X2, and ending on December 31, 19X3. Durango guarantees an interest rate of 12 percent compounded quarterly (3 percent per three-month period).

REQUIRED:

1. Prepare the cash flow diagram for each of these two investments.

2. Calculate the amount to which each of these investments will accumulate at maturity.

3. Prepare the entries to record Pueblo's cash outflows in 19X2 and any necessary adjusting entries at December 31, 19X2.

E10-33. PRESENT VALUES   Using the appropriate tables in the text, determine:

a) The present value of a single $14,000 cash flow in seven years if the interest (discount) rate is 8 percent per year.

b) The number of periods for which $1,753 must be invested at an annual interest (discount) rate of 14 percent to produce an investment balance of $5,000.

c) The size of the annual cash flow for a 25-year annuity with a present value of $49,113 and an annual interest rate of 9 percent. One payment is made at the end of each year.

d) The annual interest rate at which an investment of $2,542 will provide for a single $4,000 cash flow in four years.

e) The annual interest rate earned by an annuity that costs $17,119 and provides 15 payments of $2,000 each, one at the end of each of the next 15 years.

E10-34. PRESENT VALUES   Ramon Company made the following two purchases on January 1, 19X3:

a) Purchased a new truck for $60,000, with payment deferred until December 31, 19X4. The appropriate interest rate is 9 percent compounded annually.

b) Purchased a small office complex from Wandrow Builders. The terms of the purchase require a $75,000 payment at the end of each quarter, beginning March 31, 19X3, and ending June 30, 19X5. The appropriate interest rate is 6 percent per quarter.

REQUIRED:

1. Prepare the cash flow diagrams for these two purchases.

2. Prepare the entries to record these purchases in Ramon's journal.

3. Prepare the cash payment and interest expense entries for purchase **b** at March 31, 19X3, and June 30, 19X3.

4. Prepare the adjusting entry for purchase **a** at December 31, 19X3.

E10-35. FUTURE AMOUNTS   On January 1, you make a single deposit of $8,000 in an investment account that earns 12 percent interest.

REQUIRED:

1. What will be the balance in the account in five years if the interest is compounded annually?
2. How much interest will be earned on the account in seven years if interest is compounded annually?
3. What will be the balance in the account in five years if the 12 percent interest is compounded quarterly?

E10-36. FUTURE AMOUNTS   Fargo Transit Company invested $70,000 in a tax-anticipation note on June 30, 19X4. The note earns 12 percent interest compounded monthly (1 percent per month) and matures on March 31, 19X5.

REQUIRED:

1. Prepare the cash flow diagram for this investment.
2. Determine the amount Fargo will receive when the note matures.
3. How much interest will Fargo earn on this investment from June 30, 19X4, through December 31, 19X4?
4. Prepare the adjusting entry to record the interest earned from June 30, 19X4, through December 31, 19X4.

E10-37. FUTURE AMOUNTS OF AN ANNUITY   On December 31, 19X1, you sign a contract to make annual deposits of $4,200 in an investment account that earns 10 percent. The first deposit is made on December 31, 19X1.

REQUIRED:

1. What will the balance in this investment account be just after the seventh deposit has been made if interest is compounded *annually*?
2. How much interest will have been earned on this investment account just after the seventh deposit has been made if interest is compounded *annually*?
3. How much interest will have been earned on this investment account just before the seventh deposit has been made if interest is compounded *annually*?
4. What will the balance in this investment account be just after the third deposit has been made if interest is compounded *semiannually*?

E10-38. FUTURE AMOUNT OF AN ANNUITY   Purdue Savings Bank pays 8 percent interest compounded weekly (.154 percent per week) on savings accounts. The bank has asked your help in preparing a table to show potential customers the number of dollars that will be available at the end of 10-, 20-, 30-, and 40-week periods during which there are weekly deposits of $1, $5, $10, or $50. The following data are available:

LENGTH OF ANNUITY	FUTURE AMOUNT OF ANNUITY AT AN INTEREST RATE OF .154% PER WEEK
10 weeks	10.0696
20 weeks	20.2953
30 weeks	30.6796
40 weeks	41.2250

REQUIRED:

Prepare and complete a table similar to the one below.

	AMOUNT OF EACH DEPOSIT			
NUMBER OF DEPOSITS	**$1**	**$5**	**$10**	**$50**
10				
20				
30				
40				

E10-39. FUTURE AMOUNT OF A SINGLE CASH FLOW   Shubert Products has just been paid $25,000 by Apex Enterprises, which had owed Shubert this amount for 30 months but had been unable to pay because of financial difficulties. Had it been able to invest this cash, Shubert assumes that it would have earned an interest rate of 15 percent compounded monthly (1 percent per month).

REQUIRED:

1. Prepare a cash flow diagram for the investment that could have been made if Apex had paid 30 months ago.

2. Determine how much Shubert has lost by not receiving the $25,000 when it was due 30 months ago.

3. Would Shubert make an entry to account for this loss? Why, or why not?

E10-40. PRESENT VALUES   You have an opportunity to purchase a government security that will pay $2,000 in five years.

REQUIRED:

1. What would you pay for the security if the appropriate interest (discount) rate is 10 percent compounded annually?

2. What would you pay for the security if the appropriate interest (discount) rate is 15 percent compounded annually?

3. What would you pay for the security if the appropriate interest (discount) rate is 10 percent compounded semiannually?

E10-41. INSTALLMENT SALE   Johnson Properties owns land on which natural gas wells are located. Columbus Gas Company has offered to buy this land from Johnson on January 1, 19X5, by paying Johnson $775,000 per year for 25 years. The first payment is to be made on December 31, 19X5. The appropriate interest rate is 9 percent compounded annually.

REQUIRED:

1. Prepare a diagram of the appropriate cash flows from Columbus Gas Company's perspective.

2. What is the present value of the payments?

3. What entry should Columbus Gas make at January 1, 19X5, if Johnson accepts the offer?

4. What entries should Columbus Gas make at December 31, 19X5, to record the 19X5 interest expense and the first $775,000 payment?

E10-42. INSTALLMENT SALE   Jeffery's Billiards sold a pool table to C. Cobbs on October 31, 19X2. The terms of the sale are no money down and payments of $50 per month for 30 months, with the first payment due on November 30, 19X2. The table that was sold to Cobbs cost Jeffery's $800. Jeffery's uses an interest rate of 12 percent compounded monthly (1 percent per month).

REQUIRED:

1. Prepare the cash flow diagram for this sale.

2. What amount of revenue should Jeffery's record on October 31, 19X2?

3. Prepare the entry to record the sale on October 31. Assume that Jeffery's records cost of goods sold at the time of the sale (perpetual inventory accounting).

4. How much interest revenue will Jeffery's record from October 31, 19X2, through December 31, 19X2?

5. By how much was 19X2 income before taxes increased by this sale?

SECTION A PROBLEMS

P10-43. SHORT-TERM BORROWING WITH RESTRICTIONS   Rocky Mountain Products has a line-of-credit agreement with its local bank that allows it to borrow up to $100,000 at any given time provided that Rocky Mountain's current assets always exceed its current liabilities by the principal amount of the outstanding loan. If this requirement is violated, the entire loan is payable immediately; thus Rocky Mountain is very careful to fulfill the requirement at all times. All loans under this line of credit are due in one month and bear interest at a rate of 1 percent per month. On January 1, 19X1, Rocky Mountain has current assets of $150,000 and current liabilities of $92,000; hence, the excess of current assets over current liabilities is $58,000. Rocky Mountain's current liabilities at January 1, 19X1, include a short-term loan under the line of credit of $35,000 due on February 1, 19X1.

REQUIRED:

1. Prepare the journal entry to record the borrowing of $35,000 on January 1, 19X1. By how much did this transaction increase or decrease the excess of current assets over current liabilities?

2. Assume that Rocky Mountain used the entire amount of the loan to purchase inventory for cash. Prepare the journal entry to record the purchase. By how much did this purchase increase or decrease the excess of current assets over current liabilities?

3. How much more would the loan restriction permit Rocky Mountain to borrow under its line of credit on January 1, 19X1, to invest in inventory? To invest in new equipment? Explain.

P10-44. ACCOUNTS PAYABLE   Richmond Company engaged in the following transactions during 19X3:

a) Purchased $16,000 of merchandise on February 16. The seller offered terms of 1/10, n/15.

b) Paid for the purchased merchandise (transaction a) on February 26.

c) Borrowed $140,000 on an eight-month, $155,000, non-interest-bearing note on April 30.

d) Purchased $28,000 of merchandise on June 4. The seller offered terms of 2/15, n/20.

e) Paid for the purchased merchandise (transaction d) on June 24.

f) Received from Haywood, Inc., on August 19 a $12,000 deposit against a total selling price of $120,000 for merchandise to be manufactured for Haywood.

g) Paid quarterly installments of FICA and individual federal income tax withholdings, as shown below, on October 15. The employer's share of FICA was recorded as an expense during the quarter.

FICA tax	$116,000
Federal income tax withheld	419,000

Assume that Richmond records purchases net of discounts offered.

REQUIRED:

1. Prepare journal entries for these transactions.

2. Prepare any adjusting entries necessary at December 31, 19X3.

P10-45. PAYROLL ACCOUNTING   Stadium Manufacturing has the following data available for its September 30, 19X8, payroll:

Wages earned.	$183,000*
Federal income tax withheld	45,900
State income tax withheld	4,300

* All subject to FICA matching and withholding at 7.65 percent.

Federal unemployment tax at .8 percent is payable on wages of $4,000, and state unemployment tax at 3.0 percent is payable on the same amount of wages.

REQUIRED:

Compute the amounts of taxes payable and the amount of wages that will be paid to employees. Then prepare the journal entries to record the wages earned and the payroll taxes.

P10-46. INTEREST-BEARING NOTE   Fairborne Company borrowed $240,000 on a five-month, 14 percent, interest-bearing note on November 1, 19X5. Fairborne ends its fiscal year on December 31. The note was paid with interest on March 31, 19X6.

REQUIRED:

1. Prepare the adjusting entry for this note on December 31, 19X5.

2. Indicate how the note and the accrued interest would appear in the balance sheet at December 31, 19X5.

3. Prepare the entry to record the repayment of the note on March 31, 19X6.

P10-47. NON-INTEREST-BEARING NOTE   Adler Discount Records borrowed $45,000 on a six-month, $49,900, non-interest-bearing note on December 1, 19X8. Adler's fiscal year ends on December 31. Before the note became due, Adler encountered financial difficulties. On June 1, 19X9, Adler exchanged the non-interest-bearing note for a four-month, $49,900, 14 percent interest-bearing note. This note was repaid with interest on October 1, 19X9.

REQUIRED:

1. Prepare the adjusting entry recorded on December 31, 19X8.

2. Indicate how the note and the unamortized discount would appear in Adler's balance sheet at December 31, 19X8.

3. Prepare the entry to record the exchange of notes on June 1, 19X9.

4. Prepare the entry to record the repayment of the note on October 1, 19X9.

P10-48. UNEARNED REVENUE AND CUSTOMER DEPOSITS   On November 20, 19X1, Green Bay Electronics agreed to manufacture and supply 500 electronic control units used by Wausau Heating Systems in large commercial and industrial installations. Wausau deposited $240,000 toward the purchase price upon signing the three-year purchase agreement, which set the selling price of each control unit at $1,500. No units were delivered during 19X1. During 19X2, 100 units were delivered, 150 units were delivered during 19X3, and the remaining units were delivered during 19X4.

REQUIRED:

1. Prepare the entry by Green Bay to record receipt of the deposit during 19X1. How would the deposit be reported in the financial statements at the end of 19X1?

2. Prepare the entry by Green Bay to record the delivery of 100 units during 19X2. How would the deposit be reported in the financial statements at the end of 19X2?

3. Prepare the entry by Green Bay to record the delivery of 150 units during 19X3. Wausau pays in cash upon delivery for units not covered by the deposit.

P10-49. RECOGNIZING LITIGATION LOSSES   In August 19X3, XTON Corporation was sued by a competitor for alleged violations of antitrust laws. The competitor claimed damages of $2,000,000. At the end of 19X3, XTON's lawyers believed that it was possible for the competitor to collect as much as $500,000 but that the competitor was less than likely to succeed in collecting anything. Litigation continued throughout 19X4. As a result of unfortunate press coverage and several unforeseen decisions in other antitrust cases, the proceedings turned against XTON; at the end of 19X4, XTON's lawyers believed that it was probable that the competitor would collect $1,000,000 from XTON. In March 19X5, the court awarded the competitor $1,200,000, payable immediately.

REQUIRED:

1. Prepare the entry, if any, to record XTON's liability under the antitrust suit at the end of 19X3. How would the contingent liability be disclosed in the financial statements?

2. Prepare the entry, if any, to record XTON's liability under the antitrust suit at the end of 19X4. How would the contingent liability be disclosed in the financial statements?

3. Prepare the entry to record the payment of $1,200,000 to its competitor in March 19X5.

P10-50. WARRANTIES   Mason Auto Repair specializes in the repair of foreign car transmissions. To encourage business, Mason offers a six-month warranty on all repairs. The following data are available for 19X9:

Estimated warranty liability, 1/1/X9	$1,100
Transmissions repaired, 19X9	2,430
Frequency of warranty claims	.07 per repair
Cost of each warranty claim	$21
Warranty claims, 19X9	181

Assume that warranty claims are paid in cash.

REQUIRED:

1. Compute the warranty expense for 19X9.

2. Prepare the entry to record the payment of the 19X9 warranty claims.

3. What is the December 31, 19X9, balance in the estimated warranty liability account? Why has the balance in the estimated warranty liability account changed from January 1, 19X9?

P10-51. TEMPORARY DIFFERENCES AND INCOME TAX LIABILITIES   Delray Manufacturing has the following income statement data available for 19X8:

Revenues.	$641,000
Less: Expenses*	488,000
Income before taxes.	$153,000

* Excluding income taxes expense.

Delray's expenses include straight-line depreciation of $67,400; depreciation deducted on the 19X8 tax return amounted to $95,000. All other revenues and expenses are the same on the tax return and the income statement. Delray's income tax rate is 34 percent.

The balance of income taxes payable was $7,400 on January 1, 19X8, representing the unpaid portion of 19X7 income taxes. This amount was paid during April 19X8. In addition, 19X8 taxes were prepaid at various times during 19X8 in the total amount of $36,500. The balance of the deferred income tax liability was $15,700 on January 1, 19X8.

REQUIRED:

1. Compute the income taxes expense for 19X8.

2. Compute the taxable income and the amount of income taxes assessed for 19X8.

3. Prepare the journal entries related to income taxes that would be recorded during 19X8.

P10-52. CHANGE IN DEFERRED INCOME TAX   Delta Sales Corporation had the following deferred income tax (credit) balances at the end of 19X5 and 19X6:

19X5...	$248,000
19X6...	281,000

The income tax rate is 34 percent.

REQUIRED:

Determine by how much 19X6 tax return (accelerated) depreciation must have exceeded income statement (straight-line) depreciation to cause deferred income tax to increase as it did between 19X5 and 19X6.

SECTION B PROBLEMS

P10-53. EVALUATING BONUS PLANS   James Archer is president of Newberry Products, Inc., a large manufacturer of household cleaning supplies. Mr. Archer has a choice of two executive bonus plans: (1) receive an immediate cash payment of $50,000 or (2) receive a payment of $75,000 in five years. Mr. Archer is able to earn 10 percent per year on his sizable investment portfolio.

REQUIRED:

1. Which of the two bonus plans will Mr. Archer prefer? Support your answer with appropriate calculations.

2. Suppose that Mr. Archer is able to earn only 7 percent per year on his investment portfolio. Would his evaluation of the two plans change? Explain the effect of the decrease in the interest rate from 10 to 7 percent.

P10-54. INTEREST RATES AND INVESTMENT VALUE   An investment broker offers you an opportunity to purchase an investment that pays $2,000 on December 31 of each of the next 10 years.

REQUIRED:

1. What would you pay for this investment if you require an interest (discount) rate of 8 percent per year?

2. What would you pay for this investment if you require an interest (discount) rate of 12 percent per year? Briefly explain the effect of this increase in the required interest rate on the present value of the investment.

3. How much would you be willing to pay if you require an interest (discount) rate of 8 percent per year but the payments are only $1,800 per year? Briefly explain the effect of this decrease in the amount of each payment on the present value of the investment.

P10-55. FINANCING AN ASSET PURCHASE   Andrea Bader, controller of SBP Corporation, has asked your advice regarding financing the purchase of a new truck. The following alternatives are available:

ALTERNATIVE	TERMS
A	A cash payment of $28,000 at the sale date.
B	A $3,000 down payment at the sale date and five annual payments of $7,100 each, with the first annual payment due 12 months after the sale.
C	No money down and four annual payments of $9,100 each, with the first annual payment due 12 months after the sale.

Assume that the appropriate interest (discount) rate is 12 percent compounded annually.

REQUIRED:

1. Compute the present value of the payments for each of the alternatives.

2. Indicate which alternative Andrea should select.

P10-56. DETERMINING THE SIZE OF INSTALLMENT PAYMENTS   You wish to determine the amount you will have to pay for an automobile loan. The car you wish to purchase will cost $10,400, and your bank requires that you pay 10 percent down. The remainder will be financed at 12 percent per year compounded monthly for 30 months.

REQUIRED:

1. What will the amount of your monthly payments be?

2. How much of the first payment is interest?

3. By how much would your payments change if the loan were to be repaid over 40 months?

P10-57. MORTGAGE PAYMENTS   You are trying to determine the amount of the mortgage payments that you would make if you purchased a new home. The home you like requires a 25-year, $85,000 mortgage at an interest rate of 15 percent compounded monthly (1.25 percent per month). The present value of an annuity of $1 for 300 periods at 1.25 percent is 78.0743.

REQUIRED:

1. Prepare the cash flow diagram for the mortgage.

2. What would be the amount of your monthly payments (rounded to the nearest dollar)?

3. By how much would you reduce the balance due on the mortgage in the first three months?

P10-58. ESTABLISHING A FUND OF SPECIFIED SIZE   On January 1, 19X6, Surfside Manufacturing borrowed $400,000 from a bank to pay for new equipment. The note requires that interest be paid annually and that the entire principal be paid in a single amount on December 31, 19X8. To provide for the final payment of principal and interest in the amount of $440,000, Surfside plans to make equal quarterly deposits in an investment fund that earns 8 percent per year compounded quarterly (2 percent per quarter). The first deposit will be made on June 30, 19X7, and the last on December 31, 19X8. How large must the quarterly deposits be to produce a fund of $440,000 on December 31, 19X8?

P10-59. CUSTOMER DEPOSITS WITH COMPOUND INTEREST   Indy Racing builds and sells racing versions of sports cars. Indy requires a $30,000 deposit to begin construction on a car. The construction period is six months. At the end of the construction period, Indy credits the buyer with the amount of the deposit plus compound interest.

REQUIRED:

1. What entry would Indy make upon receipt of a $30,000 deposit?

2. How much compound interest would Indy credit against the purchase price of a car during the six-month contruction period if 12 percent interest on the $30,000 deposit was compounded (a) semiannually, (b) quarterly, (c) monthly?

3. What entry would Indy make when construction is completed on a car and $30,000 plus semiannual compound interest at 12 percent (6 percent per six-month period) is credited against the $42,500 purchase price of a car?

P10-60. COMPARING INVESTMENTS   Max McPhee, a financial planner, is evaluating the following two investments for a client:

INVESTMENT	EXPECTED CASH FLOWS
A	Pays $4,200 every three months for five years and $40,000 at the end of the fifth year.
B	Pays $2,800 every three months for five years and $80,000 at the end of the fifth year.

REQUIRED:

1. Determine the present value of each investment if the client requires an interest (discount) rate of 16 percent compounded quarterly. Which investment should the financial planner recommend to the client?

2. Determine the present value of each investment if the client requires an interest (discount) rate of 12 percent compounded quarterly. Which investment should the financial planner recommend to the client?

3. What happens to the present value when the interest (discount) rate is decreased? Why does this occur?

4. Suppose that investment B is significantly riskier than investment A, and the client is known to be reluctant to assume additional risk. Would this affect the financial planner's recommendations to the client under either required interest rate above?

P10-61. RECORDING SALES WITH DELAYED PAYMENTS   On April 1, 19X6, Goldenrod Distributors sold an electronic air-cleaning system. The terms of the sale were $10,000 down and $20,000 payable in 18 months. The system cost Goldenrod $14,000 when purchased from the manufacturer.

REQUIRED:

1. Record this sale if Goldenrod uses a 12 percent interest rate compounded quarterly (3 percent per three-month period).

2. By how much would the selling price change if a 16 percent interest rate compounded quarterly (4 percent per three-month period) were used?

3. Prepare and complete a table similar to the one below.

	INTEREST RATES	
	12%	16%
19X6 Sales revenue Cost of goods sold Gross margin Interest revenue		
19X7 Interest revenue		
Total effect over both years on income before taxes		

4. Which interest rate do you think Goldenrod's management would prefer? Why?

P10-62. THE EFFECT OF INTEREST ON PRESENT VALUES   Bornholm Company purchased a new machine on January 1, 19X2. The terms of the purchase were $15,000 down and two payments of $25,000 on December 31, 19X2, and December 31, 19X3.

REQUIRED:

1. Determine the amount at which the machine should be recorded in Bornholm's ledger if an interest rate of 10 percent compounded annually is used.

2. What would be the appropriate acquisition cost for an interest rate of 15 percent compounded annually?

3. If the machine is to be depreciated on a straight-line basis over six years with no residual value, what is the amount of expense reported each year for depreciation and interest, using both the 10 percent and 15 percent interest rates?

4. Which interest rate do you suppose Bornholm would prefer to use? Why?

P10-63. EVALUATING AND RECORDING DEFERRED PAYMENT PURCHASES   The purchasing agent for your company has come to you for advice in selecting one of the following bids for the purchase of computer hardware:

a) $150,000 cash upon delivery of the hardware

b) $190,000 cash payable two years after delivery of the hardware

c) Three annual payments of $60,000 each, with the first payment due one year after delivery of the hardware

Your company pays 12 percent per year compounded annually for borrowed money.

REQUIRED:

1. Which bid do you recommend that the company accept? Explain your recommendation.

2. Give the journal entry to record the purchase under each of the three bids.

3. Would your recommendation to the purchasing agent change if the company pays 16 percent per year compounded annually for borrowed money?

ANALYTICAL OPPORTUNITIES

A10-64. CURRENT LIABILITIES AND CURRENT RATIO   The current ratio, which is discussed in Chapter 13, is one of the primary bases by which short-term creditors evaluate the ability of a company to pay its short-term obligations. The current ratio is computed by dividing current assets by current liabilities. Thus a company with current assets of $120,000 and current liabilities of $60,000 has a current ratio of "two to one." Everything else being the same, the higher the current ratio, the easier it will be to secure short-term credit; that is, more short-term credit will be available at lower interest rates.

Topeka Corporation is a small manufacturer whose annual financial statements for recent years (including the year just ended) indicate a current ratio of about 1.5 to 1. Topeka has been able to secure a limited amount of short-term credit, but bankers are cautious and charge a somewhat higher-than-average interest rate. At year-end, the auditors noted the following occurrences during their examination of the records of Topeka Corporation:

a) A large order, purchased on account, shipped F.O.B. shipping point just prior to year-end was not recorded at year-end but was recorded as a purchase in the following year.

b) A large payment of principal and interest due within the next year was not recorded as a current liability.

c) An effort was made at year-end to pay off current liabilities to the maximum extent possible.

REQUIRED:

1. What is the effect of each of the three occurrences on the current ratio? What factors might explain these three occurrences?

2. Do the three occurrences represent errors that must be corrected? Give reasons for your answers. If a correction is required, describe the correcting journal entry.

3. How would you recommend that bankers compute the current ratio?

A10-65. FOOTNOTE DISCLOSURES FOR CONTINGENT LIABILITY   During December 19X3, Benzonia Enterprises acquired Triple Duty Products, a small company that for many years had been careless in the use of hazardous materials in the manufacture of its products. Although no regulatory or legal actions were threatened or pending, Benzonia immediately instituted a long-term program to clean up the acquired manufacturing site.

During July 19X4, several residents of the community adjacent to Triple Duty's main manufacturing plant filed suit against the company under state and federal environmental protection statutes. The total amount of the suit was $3 million. Although company lawyers believed it was probable that the company would be required to make some payment significantly less than $3 million to settle the suit, they could not estimate the amount.

During 19X5, a regional water quality study conducted by the state's environmental protection agency revealed unexpectedly high levels of dangerous contaminants—some of which had been used many years before by Triple Duty. The results of the study, which were released in August 19X5, received a high level of attention in the press. Shortly after these events, residents of the community near the Triple Duty site increased their suit against the company from $3 million to $10 million. Company lawyers revised their earlier opinion stating in writing that a settlement of $8 million or more was only remotely likely, that a settlement of $4 million to $8 million was possible but less than likely, and that a settlement of about $2 million was probable.

During 19X6, Benzonia's cleanup program was completed. In December 19X6, company lawyers reaffirmed the opinion given at the end of 19X5 concerning the possible outcomes of the pending lawsuit.

In late February 19X7, before the issuance of Benzonia's 19X6 financial statements, the suit was settled for $2.7 million.

REQUIRED:

1. Benzonia's 19X3 consolidated financial statements include a brief footnote concerning the Triple Duty acquisition. What would the consequences be of including in that footnote a description of Triple Duty's reprehensible handling of hazardous materials? What would the consequences be of making no mention of the cleanup? What would you say about the cleanup in such a footnote?

2. How should the $3 million lawsuit be recorded or disclosed in the financial statements prepared at the end of 19X4? Draft a brief footnote that you believe would be appropriate for the end-of-19X4 financial statements. (For guidance, read paragraphs 8 and 10 of *FASB Statement No. 5*.)

3. How should the expanded lawsuit be recorded or disclosed in the financial statements prepared at the end of 19X5? Draft a brief footnote that you believe would be appropriate for the end-of-19X5 financial statements. (For guidance, read paragraph 10 of *FASB Statement No. 5*.)

4. How should the expanded lawsuit be recorded or disclosed in the financial statements prepared at the end of 19X6? Draft a brief footnote that you believe would be appropriate for the end-of-19X6 financial statements. (For guidance, read paragraph 11 of *FASB Statement No. 5*.)

A10-66. ERROR, MATERIALITY, AND PRESENT VALUE Consider the present value of a single future payment of $100,000 to be made in n years.

REQUIRED:

1. Prepare a graph with present value on the vertical axis (ranging from zero to $100,000) and n on the horizontal axis (ranging from zero to 30). Plot four curves on the graph—one showing the relationship between the present value of the $100,000 future payment and n when the interest rate is 5 percent, a second showing the relationship when the interest rate is 10 percent, a third showing the relationship when the interest rate is 15 percent, and a fourth showing the relationship when the interest rate is 20 percent.

2. What do you conclude about the effect of increasing distance to future payments (n) and increasing interest rates (i) on the present value of a future cash flow?

3. What do you conclude about the contribution of distant future cash flow requirements to the present value of related liabilities? Does your conclusion affect the way you think about the problem of estimating distant future cash flows?

4. Why are many current liabilities carried at face amount rather than present value?

EXHIBIT 10–17   FUTURE AMOUNT OF $1 ($M_1$)

NUMBER OF PERIODS	RATE OF INTEREST										
	1%	1.5%	2%	3%	4%	5%	6%	7%	8%	9%	10%
1	1.0100	1.0150	1.0200	1.0300	1.0400	1.0500	1.0600	1.0700	1.0800	1.0900	1.1000
2	1.0201	1.0302	1.0404	1.0609	1.0816	1.1025	1.1236	1.1449	1.1664	1.1881	1.2100
3	1.0303	1.0457	1.0612	1.0927	1.1249	1.1576	1.1910	1.2250	1.2597	1.2950	1.3310
4	1.0406	1.0614	1.0824	1.1255	1.1699	1.2155	1.2625	1.3108	1.3605	1.4116	1.4641
5	1.0510	1.0773	1.1041	1.1593	1.2167	1.2763	1.3882	1.4026	1.4693	1.5386	1.6105
6	1.0615	1.0934	1.1262	1.1941	1.2653	1.3401	1.4185	1.5007	1.5869	1.6771	1.7716
7	1.0721	1.1098	1.1487	1.2299	1.3159	1.4071	1.5036	1.6058	1.7138	1.8280	1.9487
8	1.0829	1.1265	1.1717	1.2668	1.3686	1.4775	1.5938	1.7182	1.8509	1.9926	2.1436
9	1.0937	1.1434	1.1951	1.3048	1.4233	1.5513	1.6895	1.8385	1.9990	2.1719	2.3579
10	1.1046	1.1605	1.2190	1.3439	1.4802	1.6289	1.7908	1.9672	2.1589	2.3674	2.5937
15	1.1610	1.2502	1.3459	1.5580	1.8009	2.0789	2.3966	2.7590	3.1722	3.6425	4.1772
20	1.2202	1.3469	1.4859	1.8061	2.1911	2.6533	3.2071	3.8697	4.6610	5.6044	6.7275
25	1.2824	1.4509	1.6406	2.0938	2.6658	3.3864	4.2919	5.4274	6.8485	6.6231	10.8347
30	1.3478	1.5631	1.8114	2.4273	3.2434	4.3219	5.7435	7.6123	10.0627	13.2677	17.4494
35	1.4166	1.6839	1.9999	2.8139	3.9461	5.5160	7.6861	10.6766	14.7853	20.4140	28.1024
40	1.4889	1.8140	2.2080	3.2620	4.8010	7.0400	10.2857	14.9745	21.7245	31.4094	45.2593

EXHIBIT 10–18   PRESENT VALUE OF $1 ($M_2$)

NUMBER OF PERIODS	RATE OF INTEREST										
	1%	1.5%	2%	3%	4%	5%	6%	7%	8%	9%	10%
1	.9901	.9852	.9804	.9709	.9615	.9524	.9434	.9346	.9259	.9174	.9091
2	.9803	.9707	.9612	.9426	.9246	.9070	.8900	.8734	.8573	.8417	.8264
3	.9706	.9563	.9423	.9151	.8890	.8638	.8396	.8163	.7938	.7722	.7513
4	.9610	.9422	.9238	.8885	.8548	.8227	.7921	.7629	.7350	.7084	.6830
5	.9515	.9283	.9057	.8626	.8219	.7835	.7473	.7130	.6806	.6499	.6209
6	.9420	.9145	.8880	.8375	.7903	.7462	.7050	.6663	.6302	.5963	.5645
7	.9327	.9010	.8706	.8131	.7599	.7107	.6651	.6227	.5835	.5470	.5132
8	.9235	.8877	.8535	.7894	.7307	.6768	.6274	.5820	.5403	.5019	.4665
9	.9143	.8746	.8368	.7664	.7026	.6446	.5919	.5439	.5002	.4604	.4241
10	.9053	.8617	.8203	.7441	.6756	.6139	.5584	.5083	.4632	.4224	.3855
15	.8613	.7999	.7430	.6419	.5553	.4810	.4173	.3624	.3152	.2745	.2394
20	.8195	.7425	.6730	.5537	.4564	.3769	.3118	.2584	.2145	.1784	.1486
25	.7798	.6892	.6095	.4776	.3751	.2953	.2330	.1842	.1460	.1160	.0923
30	.7419	.6398	.5521	.4120	.3083	.2314	.1741	.1314	.0994	.0754	.0573
35	.7059	.5939	.5000	.3554	.2534	.1813	.1301	.0937	.0676	.0490	.0356
40	.6717	.5513	.4529	.3066	.2083	.1420	.0972	.0668	.0460	.0318	.0221

$$FA = f(1 + i)^n$$

RATE OF INTEREST

NUMBER OF PERIODS	11%	12%	13%	14%	15%	16%	18%	20%	25%
1	1.1100	1.1200	1.1300	1.1400	1.1500	1.1600	1.1800	1.2000	1.2500
2	1.2321	1.2544	1.2769	1.2996	1.3225	1.3456	1.3924	1.4400	1.5625
3	1.3676	1.4049	1.4429	1.4815	1.5209	1.5609	1.6430	1.7280	1.9531
4	1.5181	1.5735	1.6305	1.6890	1.7490	1.8106	1.9388	2.0736	2.4414
5	1.6851	1.7623	1.8424	1.9254	2.0114	2.1003	2.2878	2.4883	3.0518
6	1.8704	1.9738	2.0820	2.1950	2.3131	2.4364	2.6996	2.9860	3.8147
7	2.0762	2.2107	2.3526	2.5023	2.6600	2.8262	3.1855	3.5832	4.7684
8	2.3045	2.4760	2.6584	2.8526	3.0590	3.2784	3.7589	4.2998	5.9605
9	2.5580	2.7731	3.0040	3.2519	3.5179	3.8030	4.4355	5.1598	7.4506
10	2.8394	3.1058	3.3946	3.7072	4.0456	4.4114	5.2338	6.1917	9.3132
15	4.7846	5.4736	6.2543	7.1379	8.1371	9.2655	11.9737	15.4070	28.4217
20	8.0623	9.6463	11.5231	13.7435	16.3665	19.4608	27.3930	38.3376	86.7362
25	13.5855	17.0001	21.2305	26.4619	32.9190	40.8742	62.6686	95.3962	264.6978
30	22.8923	29.9599	39.1159	50.9502	66.2118	85.8499	143.3706	237.3763	807.7936
35	38.5749	52.7996	72.0685	98.1002	133.1755	180.3141	327.9973	590.6682	2465.1903
40	63.0009	93.0510	132.7816	188.8835	267.8635	378.7212	750.3783	1469.7716	7523.1638

$$PV = \frac{f}{(1 + i)^n}$$

RATE OF INTEREST

NUMBER OF PERIODS	11%	12%	13%	14%	15%	16%	18%	20%	25%
1	.9009	.8929	.8850	.8772	.8696	.8621	.8475	.8333	.8000
2	.8116	.7972	.7831	.7695	.7561	.7432	.7182	.6944	.6400
3	.7312	.7118	.6931	.6750	.6575	.6407	.6086	.5787	.5120
4	.6587	.6355	.6133	.5921	.5718	.5523	.5158	.4823	.4096
5	.5935	.5674	.5428	.5194	.4972	.4761	.4371	.4019	.3277
6	.5346	.5066	.4803	.4556	.4323	.4104	.3704	.3349	.2621
7	.4817	.4523	.4251	.3996	.3759	.3538	.3139	.2791	.2097
8	.4339	.4039	.3762	.3506	.3269	.3050	.2660	.2236	.1678
9	.3909	.3606	.3329	.3075	.2843	.2630	.2255	.1938	.1342
10	.3522	.3220	.2946	.2697	.2472	.2267	.1911	.1615	.1074
15	.2090	.1827	.1599	.1401	.1229	.1079	.0835	.0649	.0352
20	.1240	.1037	.0868	.0728	.0611	.0514	.0365	.0261	.0115
25	.0736	.0588	.0471	.0378	.0304	.0245	.0160	.0105	.0038
30	.0437	.0334	.0256	.0196	.0151	.0116	.0070	.0042	.0012
35	.0259	.0189	.0139	.0102	.0075	.0055	.0030	.0017	.0004
40	.0154	.0107	.0075	.0053	.0037	.0026	.0013	.0007	.0001

EXHIBIT 10–19   FUTURE AMOUNT OF AN ANNUITY OF $1 ($M_3$)

NUMBER OF PERIODS	1%	1.5%	2%	3%	4%	5%	6%	7%	8%	9%	10%
					RATE OF INTEREST						
1	1.0000	1.0000	1.0000	1.0000	1.0000	1.0000	1.0000	1.0000	1.0000	1.0000	1.0000
2	2.0100	2.0150	2.0200	2.0300	2.0400	2.0500	2.0600	2.0700	2.0800	2.0900	2.1000
3	3.0301	3.0452	3.0604	3.0909	3.1216	3.1525	3.1836	3.2149	3.2464	3.2781	3.3100
4	4.0604	4.0909	4.1216	4.1836	4.2465	4.3101	4.3746	4.4399	4.5061	4.5731	4.6410
5	5.1010	5.1523	5.2040	5.3091	5.4163	5.5256	5.6371	5.7507	5.8666	5.9847	6.1051
6	6.1520	6.2296	6.3081	6.4684	6.6330	6.8019	6.9753	7.1533	7.3359	7.5233	7.7156
7	7.2135	7.3230	7.4343	7.6625	7.8983	8.1420	8.3938	8.6540	8.9228	9.2004	9.4872
8	8.2857	8.4328	8.5830	8.8923	9.2142	9.5491	9.8975	10.2598	10.6366	11.0285	11.4359
9	9.3685	9.5593	9.7546	10.1591	10.5828	11.0266	11.4913	11.9780	12.4876	13.0210	13.5795
10	10.4622	10.7027	10.9497	11.4639	12.0061	12.5779	13.1808	13.8164	14.4866	15.1929	15.9374
15	16.0969	16.6821	17.2934	18.5989	20.0236	21.5786	23.2760	25.1290	27.1521	29.3609	31.7725
20	22.0190	23.1237	24.2974	26.8704	29.7781	33.0660	36.7856	40.9955	45.7620	51.1601	57.2750
25	28.2432	30.0630	32.0303	36.4593	41.6459	47.7271	54.8645	63.2490	73.1059	84.7009	98.3471
30	34.7849	37.5387	40.5681	47.5754	56.0849	66.4388	79.0582	94.4608	113.2832	136.3075	164.4940
35	41.6603	45.5921	49.9945	60.4621	73.6522	90.3203	111.4348	138.2369	172.3168	215.7108	271.0244
40	48.8864	54.2679	60.4020	75.4013	95.0255	120.7998	154.7620	199.6351	259.0565	337.8824	442.5926

EXHIBIT 10–20   PRESENT VALUE OF AN ANNUITY OF $1 ($M_4$)

NUMBER OF PERIODS	1%	1.5%	2%	3%	4%	5%	6%	7%	8%	9%	10%
					RATE OF INTEREST						
1	.9901	.9852	.9804	.9709	.9615	.9524	.9434	.9346	.9259	.9174	.9091
2	1.9704	1.9559	1.9416	1.9135	1.8861	1.8594	1.8334	1.8080	1.7833	1.7591	1.7355
3	2.9410	2.9122	2.8839	2.8286	2.7751	2.7232	2.6730	2.6243	2.5771	2.5313	2.4869
4	3.9020	3.8544	3.8077	3.7171	3.6299	3.5460	3.4651	3.3872	3.3121	3.2397	3.1699
5	4.8534	4.7826	4.7135	4.5797	4.4518	4.3295	4.2124	4.1002	3.9927	3.8897	3.7908
6	5.7955	5.6972	5.6014	5.4172	5.2421	5.0757	4.9173	4.7665	4.6229	4.4859	4.3553
7	6.7282	6.5982	6.4720	6.2303	6.0021	5.7864	5.5824	5.3893	5.2064	5.0330	4.8684
8	7.6517	7.4859	7.3255	7.0197	6.7327	6.4632	6.2098	5.9713	5.7466	5.5348	5.3349
9	8.5660	8.3605	8.1622	7.7861	7.4353	7.1078	6.8017	6.5152	6.2469	5.9952	5.7590
10	9.4713	9.2222	8.9826	8.5302	8.1109	7.7217	7.3601	7.0236	6.7101	6.4177	6.1446
15	13.8651	13.3432	12.8493	11.9379	11.1184	10.3797	9.7122	9.1079	8.5595	8.0607	7.6061
20	18.0456	17.1686	16.3514	14.8775	13.5903	12.4622	11.4699	10.5940	9.8181	9.1285	8.5136
25	22.0232	20.7196	19.5235	17.4131	15.6221	14.0939	12.7834	11.6536	10.6748	9.8226	9.0770
30	25.8077	24.0158	22.3965	19.6004	17.2920	15.3725	13.7648	12.4090	11.2578	10.2737	9.4269
35	29.4086	27.0756	24.9986	21.4872	18.6646	16.3742	14.4982	12.9477	11.6546	10.5668	9.6442
40	32.8347	29.9158	27.3555	23.1148	19.7928	17.1591	15.0463	13.3317	11.9246	10.7574	9.7791

$$FA = [\,f\,]\left[\frac{(1+i)^n - 1}{i}\right]$$

RATE OF INTEREST

NUMBER OF PERIODS	11%	12%	13%	14%	15%	16%	18%	20%	25%
1	1.0000	1.0000	1.0000	1.0000	1.0000	1.0000	1.0000	1.0000	1.0000
2	2.1100	2.1200	2.1300	2.1400	2.1500	2.1600	2.1800	2.2000	2.2500
3	3.3421	3.3744	3.4069	3.4396	3.4725	3.5056	3.5724	3.6400	3.8125
4	4.7097	4.7793	4.8498	4.9211	4.9934	5.0665	5.2154	5.3680	5.7656
5	6.2278	6.3528	6.4803	6.6101	6.7424	6.8771	7.1542	7.4416	8.2070
6	7.9129	8.1152	8.3227	8.5355	8.7537	8.9775	9.4420	9.9299	11.2588
7	9.7833	10.0890	10.4047	10.7305	11.0668	11.4139	12.1415	12.9159	15.0735
8	11.8594	12.2997	12.7573	13.2328	13.7268	14.2401	15.3270	16.4991	19.8419
9	14.1640	14.7757	15.4157	16.0853	16.7858	17.5185	19.0859	20.7989	25.8023
10	16.7220	17.5487	18.4197	19.3373	20.3037	21.3215	23.5213	25.9587	33.2529
15	34.4054	37.2797	40.4175	43.8424	47.5804	51.6595	60.9653	72.0351	109.6868
20	64.2028	72.0524	80.9468	91.0249	102.4436	115.3797	146.6280	186.6680	342.9447
25	114.4133	133.3339	155.6196	181.8708	212.7930	249.2140	342.6035	471.9811	1054.7912
30	199.0209	241.3327	293.1992	356.7868	434.7451	530.3117	790.9480	1181.8816	3227.1743
35	341.5896	431.6635	546.6808	693.5727	881.1702	1120.7130	1816.6516	2948.3411	9856.7613
40	581.8261	767.0914	1013.7042	1342.0251	1779.0903	2360.7572	4163.2130	7343.8578	30088.6554

$$PV = [\,f\,]\left[\frac{1 - \dfrac{1}{(1+i)^n}}{i}\right]$$

RATE OF INTEREST

NUMBER OF PERIODS	11%	12%	13%	14%	15%	16%	18%	20%	25%
1	.9009	.8929	.8850	.8772	.8696	.8621	.8475	.8333	.8000
2	1.7125	1.6901	1.6681	1.6467	1.6257	1.6052	1.5656	1.5278	1.4400
3	2.4437	2.4018	2.3612	2.3216	2.2832	2.2459	2.1743	2.1065	1.9520
4	3.1024	3.0373	2.9745	2.9137	2.8550	2.7982	2.6901	2.5887	2.3616
5	3.6959	3.6048	3.5172	3.4331	3.3522	3.2743	3.1272	2.9906	2.6893
6	4.2305	4.1114	3.9975	3.8887	3.7845	3.6847	3.4976	3.3255	2.9514
7	4.7122	4.5638	4.4226	4.2883	4.1604	4.0386	3.8115	3.6046	3.1611
8	5.1461	4.9676	4.7988	4.6389	4.4873	4.3436	4.0776	3.8372	3.3289
9	5.5370	5.3282	5.1317	4.9464	4.7716	4.6065	4.3030	4.0130	3.4631
10	5.8892	5.6502	5.4262	5.2161	5.0188	4.8332	4.4941	4.1925	3.5705
15	7.1909	6.8109	6.4624	6.1422	5.8474	5.5755	5.0916	4.6755	3.8593
20	7.9633	7.4694	7.0248	6.6231	6.2593	5.9288	5.3527	4.8696	3.9539
25	8.4217	7.8431	7.3300	6.8729	6.4641	6.0971	5.4669	4.9476	3.9849
30	8.6938	8.0552	7.4957	7.0027	6.5660	6.1772	5.5168	4.9789	3.9950
35	8.8552	8.1755	7.5856	7.0700	6.6166	6.2153	5.5386	4.9915	3.9984
40	8.9511	8.2438	7.6344	7.1050	6.6418	6.2335	5.5482	4.9966	3.9995

LEARNING OBJECTIVES

Careful study of this chapter will enable you to:

1. Explain how interest on long-term liabilities is allocated under the straight-line interest amortization method.

2. Account for straight-line interest on long-term notes payable.

3. Record the issuance of bonds at par, at a discount, and at a premium.

4. Determine interest expense for bonds, using the straight-line interest amortization method.

5. Account for the retirement of bonds, both before and at maturity.

6. Determine the after-tax cost of financing with debt, and explain financial leverage.

7. Contrast the accounting for operating and capital leases.

Appendix 11A–1

8. Account for bonds sold during an accounting period or during an interest period.

INTEREST AMORTIZATION: The assignment of interest on a liability (or asset) to the interest periods that make up the term of the liability (or asset).

11A

LONG-TERM LIABILITIES: STRAIGHT-LINE INTEREST PROCEDURES

This chapter continues the discussion of long-term liabilities begun in Chapter 10, which described contingent liabilities and deferred tax liabilities. Long-term liabilities also include long-term notes and bonds payable and obligations associated with long-term capital leases.[1] Thus the long-term liabilities section of a typical balance sheet might appear as follows:

Long-term liabilities:	
Long-term notes payable	$ 12,500
Bonds payable	210,000
Capital lease liability	57,200
Pension liability	22,100
Estimated warranty liability	29,000
Deferred tax liability	77,540
Other long-term liabilities	8,200
Total long-term liabilities	$416,540

The cash flows or other economic sacrifices required to satisfy deferred tax liabilities and various contingent liabilities, such as the pension liability, usually must be estimated. In contrast, long-term notes, long-term bonds, and leases clearly specify the amount and timing of the future cash flows required to satisfy the related liability. These long-term liabilities also give rise to interest expense.

When a liability extends over several interest periods, the amount of interest associated with each period must be determined by a procedure called *interest amortization*. **Interest amortization** is the assignment of interest on a liability (or asset) to the interest periods that make up the term of the liability (or asset).[2] There are two methods of interest amortization. One method, *effective interest*

---

[1] As noted in Chapter 10, long-term liabilities that will be paid within the longer of the next year or the next operating cycle are not included in the long-term liability section of the balance sheet. Rather, they are reported in the current liability section. In the interest of simplifying our discussion of long-term liabilities, we will disregard calculations and entries for this reclassification throughout this chapter.

[2] The same interest amortization procedures used by borrowers to account for liabilities are also used by lenders to account for the corresponding assets.

amortization, is based on the time-value-of-money calculations presented in Section B of Chapter 10. The other method, *straight-line interest amortization,* represents a simple approximation to effective interest amortization. Although effective interest amortization is correct technically, straight-line interest amortization may be used if it produces approximately the same numerical results as the effective interest method. Frequently, the two methods do, in fact, produce quite similar results.

In this book, effective interest amortization and straight-line interest amortization are discussed in separate chapters. This chapter explains the measurement and reporting of long-term liabilities using straight-line amortization; application of the straight-line procedure is specifically illustrated for notes and bonds. Although the accounting for long-term liabilities arising from capital leases is normally based on effective interest amortization, the fundamentals of capital lease accounting are also reviewed here. Chapter 11B, which follows, discusses the measurement and reporting of long-term liabilities using effective interest amortization. In other words, Chapters 11A and 11B cover essentially the same material, but each uses a different interest amortization method. Most students will study either Chapter 11A or 11B, although some instructors will assign both.

STRAIGHT-LINE AMORTIZATION AND INTEREST EXPENSE

STRAIGHT-LINE INTER-EST AMORTIZATION: The assignment of an equal amount of interest to each interest period over the term of the related liability.

Recall that interest on a liability equals the excess of the amount paid to the lender over the amount borrowed. The accounting system must allocate this interest, sometimes called *total interest,* among the various accounting periods during which the liability exists.

The apportioning of total interest among accounting periods requires a two-stage allocation procedure. The first allocation, interest amortization, assigns total interest to the interest periods that make up the term of the liability. **Straight-line interest amortization** assigns an equal amount of interest to each interest period over the term of the related liability. A second allocation is frequently necessary for the determination of interest expense, in accordance with the matching concept. This allocation divides the interest assigned to a particular interest period proportionally between two accounting periods, each of which is partly overlapped by the interest period. If a six-month interest period to which $1,200 has been amortized overlaps the last four months of one annual accounting period and the first two months of the next accounting period, then $800 [(4/6)($1,200)] is allocated to interest expense in the first accounting period and $400 [(2/6)($1,200)] is allocated to interest expense in the second accounting period. Of course, if the interest period and the accounting period coincide, then the second-stage allocation is unnecessary. For example, if a note's interest period and the firm's accounting period are both one year, and if the note is issued at the beginning of an accounting period, then interest on the note does not require a second-stage allocation, because the interest expense for the accounting period is the same as the interest assigned to the interest period.

The second-stage allocation, the matching of periodic interest with accounting periods for expense determination, apportions dollars among periods on the basis of time. In contrast, the first-stage allocation of interest, the straight-line amortization of total interest among interest periods, apportions dollars among periods on the basis of new procedures, to which we now turn. We will illustrate straight-line interest amortization first for long-term notes and then for bonds.

LONG-TERM NOTES PAYABLE

LONG-TERM NOTES PAYABLE: Notes payable with terms that extend beyond the longer of one year or one operating cycle.

Long-term notes payable differ from short-term notes payable in that they require payments in one or more periods beyond the longer of one year or one operating cycle. Firms usually give long-term notes payable to financial institutions, such as banks and insurance companies, for periods of five years or less in exchange for cash. In some cases, long-term notes are secured by property, plant, or equipment specified in an agreement called a *mortgage.* If the borrower fails to pay the related note, the lender may seize the property in accordance with the provisions of the mortgage and various state laws. Although the mortgage and the note are usually separate documents, the liability arising from the note is frequently called a *mortgage payable* to indicate that the note is secured by a mortgage. As with short-term notes, there are two kinds of long-term notes: interest-bearing notes and non-interest-bearing notes. Both types are described in the sections below.

LONG-TERM INTEREST-BEARING NOTES

Some long-term interest-bearing notes require annual interest payments, with the final interest payment and the principal to be repaid at maturity. Other notes provide for repayment of the principal and the entire amount of interest in one lump sum at maturity. The measurement and reporting of both types of notes are taken up in turn in the discussions that follow.

Annual Interest Payments and Single Principal Repayment

To illustrate the accounting for this type of note, let us look at the case of the Kokomo Corporation. Assume that on September 1, 19X2, Kokomo borrows $12,000 on a three-year, 14 percent note. The note requires annual interest payments (each equal to 14 percent of $12,000) and repayment of the principal plus the final year's interest at the end of the third year. The following entry would be made to record the issuance of the note:

Issuance of note, 9/1/X2

Cash 12,000
    Notes payable 12,000

The annual interest payment is $1,680 [($12,000)(.14)], which is paid on August 31 of 19X3, 19X4, and 19X5. Thus the total amount of cash paid out over the life of the note is $17,040 [(3)($1,680) + $12,000], and the total interest on the note is $5,040 [$17,040 − $12,000]. Following straight-line procedures, the interest amortization to each interest period is $1,680 [$5,040/3], which is exactly the same as the interest payment in each period.[3]

Since Kokomo Corporation's note was issued on September 1, eight months into the annual accounting period, a second-stage allocation of interest is required to match interest expense with the appropriate accounting periods. Interest expense for the four-month period from September through December is $560 [(4/12)($1,680)], and interest expense for the eight-month period from January through August is $1,120 [(8/12)($1,680)]. The following entries record the recognition of interest expense and the payment of interest during the first two years and four months:

Adjusting entries to record interest, 12/31/X2, 12/31/X3, and 12/31/X4

Interest expense [($12,000)(.14)(4/12)]	560	
Interest payable		560

Interest payments, 8/31/X3 and 8/31/X4

Interest expense [($12,000)(.14)(8/12)]	1,120	
Interest payable (see adjusting entry)	560	
Cash		1,680

The interest amortization and the matching of interest to accounting periods are exactly the same for all three years of the note. The result is that the same adjusting entry is made on December 31, 19X2, December 31, 19X3, and December 31, 19X4. All three adjusting entries recognize interest expense of $560. In addition, all three entries to record the annual interest payments remove interest payable of $560 and record an interest payment of $1,680. The final interest payment, however, is accompanied by a $12,000 principal payment, as shown in the following entry:

Payment at maturity, 8/31/X5

Interest expense [($12,000)(.14)(8/12)]	1,120	
Interest payable (see adjusting entry)	560	
Notes payable	12,000	
Cash		13,680

Although Kokomo's note involves multiple payments extending over three years, the entries to record the note and its repayment are very similar to those made for short-term interest-bearing notes, as described in Chapters 4, 8, and 10. We turn now to the entries required to record a long-term note that requires a single payment of interest and principal at maturity.

Single Payment of Interest and Principal

Assume that on January 1, 19X6, Wayne Corporation borrows $10,000 on a two-year interest-bearing note at 15 percent, with the principal plus interest of

[3] When a note requires that exactly the amount of interest incurred in every interest period be paid at the end of every interest period, then the straight-line amortization for each interest period and the interest payment for that period are the same. However, when the payment at the end of every interest period does *not* equal the amount of interest for the period, then the straight-line amortization for each period does *not* equal the amount paid at the end of that period.

$3,000 payable in a single lump-sum payment on December 31, 19X7. The entries to record the issuance of the note, the recognition of interest expense, and the repayment of principal and interest are as follows:

Issuance of note, 1/1/X6

Cash	10,000	
Notes payable		10,000

Adjusting entry to record interest, 12/31/X6

Interest expense ($3,000/2)	1,500	
Interest payable		1,500

Payment at maturity, 12/31/X7

Interest expense	1,500	
Interest payable	1,500	
Notes payable	10,000	
Cash		13,000

Since the borrower makes no payments before the lump-sum payment on the maturity date, the amount of the liability rises by $1,500, the amount of the interest amortization, at the end of each period. The application of straight-line procedures results in the amortization of $1,500, or half the total interest [$3,000/2], in each of the two years. When notes of this type are issued anytime other than at the beginning of an accounting period, a second-stage allocation of periodic interest is required in order to match interest expense with the appropriate accounting period.[4] Non-interest-bearing notes, to which we now turn, employ similar straight-line amortization procedures.

LONG-TERM NON-INTEREST-BEARING NOTES

Interest accrues on both interest-bearing and non-interest-bearing notes. However, as we noted in Chapter 10, non-interest-bearing notes are distinctive in that the note document does not state an explicit interest rate. Instead, such notes merely specify the single amount to be paid by the borrower at maturity, without reference to the amount of interest or principal. Total interest on a non-interest-bearing note must be calculated as the excess of the total amount repaid by the borrower at maturity over the amount borrowed (the principal). When a non-interest-bearing note extends over several periods, the total interest must then be allocated among the periods. When interest is amortized by straight-line procedures, the total interest is allocated in an equal amount to each interest period.

Let us illustrate straight-line procedures for a two-year, single-payment, non-interest-bearing note. On January 1, 19X4, Kernford Company issued a two-year non-interest-bearing note with a maturity amount of $125,440 to the Second State Bank in exchange for $100,000 in cash. The note matures on

---

[4] For example, had this $10,000 note been issued on May 1, 19X6, the annual interest expense would be recorded as follows at the end of each accounting period:

19X6: (8/12)($1,500) = $1,000
19X7: (12/12)($1,500) = $1,500
19X8: (4/12)($1,500) = $ 500

December 31, 19X5. In other words, Kernford borrowed $100,000, which must be repaid at the end of two years by making a single payment of $125,440.

The maturity amount of a non-interest-bearing note—whether short-term (see Chapter 10) or long-term—is usually recorded in a separate liability account. Although the amount of Kernford's liability at issuance is only $100,000, the maturity amount of $125,440 is recorded in a notes payable account. The excess of the maturity amount of a note over the amount borrowed (the principal) is the *discount on the note.* The discount on Kernford's note is $25,440, the excess of its $125,440 maturity amount over its $100,000 principal amount. The discount is recorded in a contra-liability account called *discount on notes payable:*

Issuance of note, 1/1/X4

Discount on notes payable.	25,440	
Cash	100,000	
Notes payable		125,440

The contra-liability account reduces the maturity amount of the note to the amount of the liability. If Kernford were to prepare a balance sheet at January 1, 19X4 (the date of issue), it would report the note as follows:

Notes payable	$125,440	
Less: Discount on notes payable	25,440	$100,000

In other words, at issuance the note is reported at the amount of cash borrowed. The unamortized discount, which is the amount of the discount not yet added to interest expense, reduces the maturity amount of the note to the amount actually borrowed.

Since Kernford's obligation is a non-interest-bearing note, no interest rate is specified. However, the total amount of interest to be paid can be determined as follows:

Total cash paid by borrower	$125,440
Less: Total cash received by borrower	100,000
Total interest over two years	$ 25,440

CARRYING AMOUNT (BOOK VALUE): The recorded amount of a liability or asset after subtraction of contra accounts or addition of adjunct accounts.

The interest amortization for each of the two years, on a straight-line basis, would be $12,720 [$25,440/2]. Since the borrower makes no payments before maturity, the carrying amount of the liability should rise by the amount of the interest amortization ($12,720) at the end of each year. The **carrying amount** (or **book value**) is the recorded amount of a liability or asset after subtraction of contra accounts or addition of adjunct accounts. (Contra accounts accumulate reductions to another account, whereas adjunct accounts accumulate additions. Long-term non-interest-bearing notes give rise to contra accounts, but not to adjunct accounts.) The increase in the carrying amount at the end of each year is recorded by reducing the discount on the note payable, as shown in the following adjusting entries:

Adjusting entry to record interest, 12/31/X4

Interest expense	12,720	
Discount on notes payable..........................		12,720

Adjusting entry to record interest, 12/31/X5

Interest expense	12,720	
Discount on notes payable..........................		12,720

The balance sheet at December 31, 19X4 (one year after issuance of the note), reports Kernford's note as follows:

Notes payable	$125,440	
Less: Discount on notes payable	12,720	$112,720

The amount of the unamortized discount has declined by $12,720; the carrying amount of the liability has increased to reflect the accrued interest for 19X4. After the entry for interest and amortization of discount at December 31, 19X5, the entire discount has been amortized, and the carrying amount of the note has risen to equal its maturity amount of $125,440, which includes the amount borrowed plus interest accrued for 19X4 and 19X5. Thus, on December 31, 19X5, $125,440 in cash is paid to the Second State Bank, and Kernford makes the following entry:

Payment at maturity, 12/31/X5

Notes payable.....................................	125,440	
Cash...		125,440

The balances and calculations for Kernford's note are summarized in Exhibit 11A–1.

Occasionally, a firm finds that it is unable to make the interest or principal payments required by its long-term liabilities. If there is reason to expect that the

EXHIBIT 11A–1   NOTE LIABILITY TABLE

		KERNFORD COMPANY		
ANNUAL INTEREST PERIOD ENDED	**INTEREST EXPENSE* (DEBIT)**	**CASH PAYMENT (CREDIT)**	**CHANGE IN LIABILITY BALANCE†**	**LIABILITY BALANCE‡**
At issue				$100,000
12/31/X4	$12,720	–0–	+12,720	112,720
12/31/X5	12,720	$125,440	–112,720	–0–

* Interest expense = total interest/number of interest periods
$12,720 = $25,440/2.
† Change in liability balance = Interest expense − Cash payment.
‡ Liability balance = Beginning liability balance + Change in liability balance.

firm will eventually be able to secure enough cash to make part of or all the required payments, creditors may permit a restructuring of the cash payment schedule, as shown in the analysis that follows. The amount at which the liabilities are measured may or may not be changed by restructuring. In such cases, creditors must analyze the situation to ensure that they are better off than they would be if they forced bankruptcy.

ANALYSIS
LONG-TERM LIABILITY RESTRUCTURING

Metal Manufacturing, a supplier of machined metal parts to the automobile industry, has incurred substantial losses during the past two years as a consequence of decreased automobile production by one of its customers. The firm has secured wage concessions from its employees and has also recently won a contract to supply parts for a large order of military vehicles. This order should return Metal Manufacturing to profitability within a year. However, because of concerns that Metal Manufacturing may not have sufficient operating cash, a provision of the military vehicle contract requires that Metal Manufacturing secure an agreement with its creditors to restructure the principal and interest payment schedule on its long-term liabilities.

As of January 1, 19X6, prior to restructuring, Metal Manufacturing's long-term liabilities required the following payments for each of the next three years:

PERIOD	LONG-TERM LIABILITY	AMOUNT	
19X6	Bond interest....................	$ 60,000	
	Capital lease	20,000	
	Interest-bearing note	125,000	$ 205,000
19X7	Bond interest....................	$ 60,000	
	Capital lease	20,000	
	Non-interest-bearing note..........	200,000	280,000
19X8	Bond interest....................	$ 60,000	
	Capital lease	20,000	
	Bond principal	500,000	580,000
	Total.........................		$1,065,000

The following schedule indicates the cash generated by operations and by various nonoperating transactions that should be available for payments by Metal Manufacturing to long-term creditors over the next three years:

PERIOD	SOURCE OF CASH	AMOUNT	
19X6	Sale of investments	$ 40,000	
	Operations.....................	(15,000)	$ 25,000
19X7	Sale of surplus machinery.........	$ 90,000	
	Operations.....................	210,000	300,000
19X8	Issuance of capital stock	$100,000	
	Operations.....................	730,000	830,000
	Total........................		$1,155,000

Because liability payments exceed cash available in 19X6, Metal Manufacturing proposes to its creditors that all 19X6 payments be deferred until 19X7, that 19X7 payments be made in 19X8, and that 19X8 payments be made as scheduled in 19X8. Believing that it is to their advantage to help the firm secure the military parts order, the creditors agree. Since all cash owed the creditors will eventually be paid, there is no need for Metal Manufacturing to alter the recorded amounts of liabilities.* However, interest expense will increase because of the deferred payments. (Computing the amount of the increase in interest expense is beyond the scope of this text.)

* Financial Accounting Standards Board, "Accounting by Debtors and Creditors for Troubled Debt Restructurings," *Statement of Financial Accounting Standards No. 15.*

ACCOUNTING FOR BONDS

BOND ISSUE: A collection of bonds, all of which are issued or sold by an entity at the same time.

BOND: A formal promise by the issuer (borrower) to make specified future payments to discharge a liability.

FACE AMOUNT (PAR VALUE): A payment required by a bond on the maturity date of the bond.

STATED RATE (COUPON RATE, NOMINAL RATE, FACE RATE, OR CONTRACT RATE): The ratio of one year's total interest payments to the face amount of the bond.

When a firm requires capital for a period longer than the three- to five-year periods typical for credit extended by notes, the firm normally issues bonds. Unlike notes, which are issued singly, bonds are issued in groups. In other words, a **bond issue** is a collection of bonds, all of which are issued or sold by an entity at the same time. Bond issues are used to raise large amounts of capital and to provide for repayment of that capital over long periods of time. They are an important source of long-term capital for businesses and have also been the primary source of long-term capital for federal, state, and local governments. Bonds are attractive to corporations as a source of capital because of their low cost relative to the cost of capital secured from stock.

A **bond** is a formal promise by the issuer (borrower) to make specified future payments to discharge a liability. Like long-term notes, bonds may be either secured or unsecured; unsecured bonds are called *debenture bonds.* A bond is a document that specifies, among other things, the exact amount and time of the payments the issuer is required to make. In this way, a bond is similar to a non-interest-bearing note, but the form of payments required by a bond is subject to restrictions that are not imposed by a non-interest-bearing note. The payments required by a bond are of two kinds: interest payments and the face amount payment. Interest payments are made at regular intervals throughout a bond's life (semiannually, in many cases). Sometimes each interest payment is evidenced by a coupon that is detached from the bond by the bondholder (lender) and exchanged for cash. Such bonds are *coupon bonds,* and the required interest payments are *coupon payments.* The **face amount** (also called **par value**) is a payment required by a bond on the maturity date. Thus the face amount payment occurs on the same date as the last interest payment. The face amount of many bonds is $1,000, although bonds with face amounts of $5,000, $10,000, and $100,000 are also issued.

The amount of the recurring interest payment can be calculated from the face amount and the interest rate stated on the bond. This rate goes by various names, including *stated rate, coupon rate, nominal rate, face rate,* and *contract rate.* The **stated rate** is the ratio of one year's total interest payments to the face amount of the bond. To illustrate, consider a bond with a face amount of $1,000, a stated interest rate of 16 percent, and semiannual interest payments. The total amount of annual interest payments equals the stated interest rate times the face amount of the bond. The amount of each interest payment is obtained by dividing the annual total by the number of interest payments per year. For this $1,000 bond, the total amount of the annual interest payments is $160 [($1,000)(.16)], and the amount of each semiannual interest payment is $80 [$160/2].

The computations, journal entries, and financial statement presentation for bonds can be organized around four events in the life cycle of a bond:

1. Issuance
2. Recognition of interest expense and interest payment
3. Partial or complete redemption before maturity
4. Redemption at maturity

DISCOUNT AND PREMIUM ON BONDS PAYABLE

At issuance, bonds may sell at their face amount (at par), below their face amount (at a discount), or above their face amount (at a premium). When bonds sell at their face amount (at par), the amount received by the issuer (the proceeds or principal amount) equals the face amount, and there is neither discount nor premium. When bonds sell at a discount, the amount received by the issuer is less than the face amount, and that difference is called a *discount.* In other words, the **discount on bonds payable** is the excess of the total face amount of the bonds over the amount received from their sale. When bonds sell at a premium, the amount received by the issuer is greater than the face amount, and that difference is called a *premium.* In other words, the **premium on bonds payable** is the excess of the amount received from the sale of bonds over their total face amount.[5]

DISCOUNT ON BONDS PAYABLE: The excess of the total face amount of bonds over the amount received from their sale (proceeds).

PREMIUM ON BONDS PAYABLE: The excess of the amount received from the sale of bonds (proceeds) over their total face amount.

The issuance of bonds at a premium or a discount is frequently described by expressing the ratio of the proceeds to the face amount as a percentage. Hence, a $10,000 bond issued at a $100 premium is said to be issued at 101 percent of par [$10,100/$10,000], and a $10,000 bond issued at a $100 discount is said to be issued at 99 percent of par [$9,900/$10,000]. Although most firms try to design their bonds to sell at or near the face amount, changing credit market conditions and changing evaluations of firms by bondholders cause most bonds to sell at either a premium or a discount.

Over the life of a bond, the borrowing firm will pay its bondholders periodic interest payments plus the bond's face amount at maturity. These payments and the amount received by the firm when a bond is issued (the proceeds from the issue) determine the total interest expense over the life of the bond. Let us illustrate by examining what happens when the same 10-year, $100,000, 12 percent bond with semiannual interest payments is issued at a $1,000 discount (99 percent of par), at par, and at a $2,000 premium (102 percent of par). The computation of total interest expense is shown in Exhibit 11A–2.

For a bond issued at par (face amount), the total interest expense is equal to the sum of the cash interest payments. The interest expense will be greater than the cash interest payments for a bond issued at a discount. For the discount bond

[5] The bonds considered in this chapter provide for interest payments that are constant in amount throughout the bond's life and are approximately equal to interest expense. Some bonds do not exhibit these attributes. For example, some corporations issue non-interest-bearing bonds, called *deep-discount* or *zero-coupon bonds,* for which interest or coupon payments are either very small or zero. Further, some corporations issue *variable-rate bonds,* for which interest payments vary with market conditions. Accounting for such bonds is discussed in intermediate accounting texts.

EXHIBIT 11A–2   TOTAL BOND INTEREST EXPENSE

	BOND ISSUED AT DISCOUNT	BOND ISSUED AT PAR	BOND ISSUED AT PREMIUM
Face amount payment at maturity	$100,000	$100,000	$100,000
Interest payments (20 at $6,000 each)	120,000	120,000	120,000
Total payments to bondholders	$220,000	$220,000	$220,000
Less: Proceeds at issue	99,000	100,000	102,000
Total interest expense over life of bond	$121,000	$120,000	$118,000

in Exhibit 11A–2, total interest expense ($121,000) exceeds interest payments ($120,000) by $1,000. The interest expense will be less than the cash interest payments for a bond issued at a premium. For the premium bond in Exhibit 11A–2, total interest expense ($118,000) is $2,000 less than interest payments ($120,000).

Total interest expense must always be amortized over the life of the bond. The straight-line amortization of total interest allocates the same amount of interest to each interest period. The bonds illustrated in Exhibit 11A–2 require semiannual interest payments; this means that they have 2 six-month interest periods per year and that the 10-year term of the bonds contains 20 interest periods [(2 payments per year)(10 years)]. Straight-line amortization in each interest period equals the total interest expense divided by the number of interest periods contained in the term of the related bond.

For a bond issued at par, the total interest expense equals the total of cash interest payments, and the amortization in each interest period equals the cash interest payment at the end of that period. For example, the straight-line amortization of interest for the bond sold at par in Exhibit 11A–2 is $6,000 [$120,000/20], which equals the amount of the interest payment at the end of each period.

For a bond issued at a discount, the total interest expense exceeds the total of cash interest payments, and the interest amortized in each period exceeds the cash interest payment at the end of that period. For example, the straight-line amortization for the discount bond in Exhibit 11A–2 is $6,050 [$121,000/20], which exceeds the amount of the interest payment by $50 in each interest period. In other words, the payment at the end of each interest period repays $50 less than the amount of interest accrued in that period. Accordingly, the straight-line amortization can also be calculated as the interest payment plus 1/20 of the total discount: $6,000 + (1/20)($1,000) = $6,050.

Finally, when a bond is issued at a premium, the total interest expense is less than the total of cash interest payments, and the interest amortized in each period is less than the cash interest payment at the end of that period. In other words, the payment at the end of each interest period repays more than the amount of interest accrued in that period. For example, straight-line amortization for the bond sold at a premium in Exhibit 11A–2 is $5,900 [$118,000/20], which is $100 less than the interest payment ($6,000) for each period. Accordingly, the straight-line amortization can also be calculated as the interest payment minus 1/20 of the total premium: $6,000 − (1/20)($2,000) = $5,900.

To permit a simple but complete examination of the basic issues of bond accounting, in this chapter we assume the following:

1. Bonds are issued on the first day of the firm's fiscal year.

2. The first interest payment in each year is made halfway through the fiscal year.

3. The second interest payment in each year is made at the fiscal year-end.

4. Bonds are redeemed at a fiscal year-end.

We turn now to the accounting procedures for bonds issued under these assumptions. Appendix 11A–1 describes the computations and entries for bonds when these assumptions are relaxed.

ISSUANCE OF BONDS

Bonds are normally sold to individual investors through financial institutions known as *underwriters.* An underwriter negotiates with, or gives a bid to, the issuing entity for the right to sell a particular bond issue. In determining the price that is to be offered the issuer, underwriters examine the provisions of the bond issue, the credit standing of the issuing entity, and the current conditions in the credit markets. The underwriter's profit on a bond issue is generated either by offering a price that is slightly less than the expected market price of the issue (thereby producing a profit on resale) or simply by charging the issuer a fee. In either case, the issuer receives the proceeds from the underwriter. Both the underwriter and the issuing firm attempt to set an interest rate for bonds that will produce proceeds for the firm equal to the par value (face amount) of the bonds. When a bond is sold at par, equal debits and credits are made to cash and bonds payable. To illustrate, the following entry would be made for a $10,000,000 bond issue sold at par:

Cash	10,000,000	
Bonds payable.............................		10,000,000

However, as we have mentioned, most bonds sell at either a small premium or a small discount because (1) credit market conditions constantly change and (2) investors' perceptions of individual firms also change. When more than the face amount of a bond is received, the excess of proceeds over the face amount of the bond is recorded in an account called *premium on bonds payable.* For example, a $10,000,000 bond issue producing proceeds of $10,220,000 is recorded with the following entry:

Cash	10,220,000	
Bonds payable.............................		10,000,000
Premium on bonds payable		220,000

Conversely, a shortfall of proceeds below the face amount of the bond is recorded in a discount on bonds payable account. Thus if a $10,000,000 bond issue produces proceeds of $9,950,000, the following entry is made at issue:

Cash	9,950,000	
Discount on bonds payable....................	50,000	
Bonds payable.............................		10,000,000

Discounts and premiums are considered to be attached to individual bonds payable accounts. Discounts are contra liabilities and premiums are adjunct liabilities, respectively, because a discount reduces the carrying amount of a bond and a premium increases its carrying amount. In other words, discounts and premiums are subtracted from or added to the face amount of a bond liability to produce the net liability of the bond. Bonds appear among the long-term liabilities in the balance sheet at their carrying amount, as follows:

Long-term liabilities:		
Bonds payable:		
12.25% bonds, due in 20X5.........	$10,000,000	
Plus: Premium on bonds payable	220,000	$10,220,000
11.85% bonds, due in 19X9.........	$10,000,000	
Less: Discount on bonds payable	50,000	9,950,000

The issuance of bonds is an important activity for both the borrowing firm and the underwriter. The firm must secure as much cash as possible from the bond issue, and the underwriter must earn its profit from the sale of bonds to investors. The following analysis examines some of the considerations made by bond underwriters when deciding whether to bid on a proposed new bond issue.

ANALYSIS
ISSUING BONDS

Gutzwiller, Inc., has approached your firm to underwrite a 10-year bond issue of $10,000,000. Gutzwiller plans to use the proceeds to finance the construction of an addition to its plant and to purchase and install machinery in the plant addition. The following financial statement data for Gutzwiller are available:

	19X4	19X5	19X6
Sales revenue	$109,000,000	$122,000,000	$136,000,000
Net income	9,103,000	10,930,000	12,570,000
Current assets	7,100,000	7,300,000	7,900,000
Total assets	94,000,000	101,000,000	107,000,000
Current liabilities	3,500,000	3,750,000	3,825,000
Long-term liabilities	22,000,000	22,000,000	22,500,000

The following are questions that you might consider in determining whether to underwrite Gutzwiller's bond issue:

1. *From what source are the bonds to be repaid?*

Bonds are repaid from operating profits retained by the firm. (Recall that short-term liabilities are usually repaid from the normal cash inflows associated with current assets.)

2. *Is Gutzwiller likely to produce sufficient profits to repay the prospective issue?*

Gutzwiller is clearly profitable. Sales are growing (at an average of 11.7 percent per year), with profits growing faster than sales (at an average of 17.5 percent per year). This suggests that Gutzwiller should be able to repay the bond issue from profits.

3. *Does Gutzwiller have sufficient working capital to meet its currently maturing obligations?*

Current assets exceed current liabilities by $4,075,000. This excess has grown by $475,000 since 19X4. Thus Gutzwiller should be able to meet its current obligations.

4. *Is the ratio of Gutzwiller's liabilities to the sum of liabilities and equity appropriate?*

Gutzwiller's liabilities are now 24.6 percent of total liabilities and equity [($3,825,000 + $22,500,000)/$107,000,000], down from 27.1 percent in 19X4. Even after a $10,000,000 increase in liabilities and assets, Gutzwiller's liabilities will be only 31.0 percent of its total liabilities and equity [($3,825,000 + $22,500,000 + $10,000,000)/$117,000,000], which is a reasonable proportion for a firm with profits that are growing.

5. *Should you underwrite Gutzwiller's bond issue?*

Gutzwiller's bonds should sell well and should therefore be potentially profitable for the underwriter.

THE BOND MARKET

After being issued, bonds are often traded among investors at prices that fluctuate from day to day and from minute to minute. Exhibit 11A–3 shows a typical listing of prices and other data for the outstanding bonds of several companies at the close of a particular trading day. This kind of information is published daily in various newspapers including *The Wall Street Journal.* Immediately following the abbreviated company name (ArizP is Arizona Power, Motrla is Motorola, PierOn is Pier One, etc.) is either the stated or coupon rate (for example, 10⅝ percent for ArizP) or the designation of the bonds as zero-coupon (zr) or deep-discount (dc); this is followed by the last two digits of the maturity year (for example, "00" for the ArizP bonds maturing in the year 2000). Prices for traded bonds are usually quoted as percentages of par, which are determined by dividing the current selling price by the par value and then multiplying the result by 100. For example, the price of 85 reported in the "close" column for Pier One's deep-discount bonds indicates that they were selling at 85 percent of their par value at the close of trading on the preceding business day; the "net change" column indicates a half-percentage-point rise in the price over the preceding price report. The "volume" column gives the total par value of bonds traded in thousands of dollars, and the "current yield" column gives the ratio of the annual interest payment to the closing price. Current yields are not reported for zero-coupon or convertible bonds.

If the issuer of bonds defaults, the lender may not receive interest payments and some of or all the principal. Several long-established firms—including Stan-

---

EXHIBIT 11A–3   BOND MARKET DATA

DATA FOR SELECTED BOND ISSUES
As Reported in *The Wall Street Journal*

BONDS	CUR YLD	VOL	CLOSE	NET CHG
ArizP 10⅝00	10.6	12	100½	−½
Motrla zr 09		16	31	+⅜
PierOn dc11½03	13.5	5	85	+½
Zenith 6¼11	cv	116	28¾	+½

Abbreviations: **CUR YLD** = current yield; **VOL** = volume; **CLOSE** = closing price; **NET CHG** = net change; cv = convertible; dc = deep discount; and zr = zero coupon.

dard and Poors (a subsidiary of McGraw-Hill) and Moody's (a subsidiary of Dun and Bradstreet) — provide general evaluations or ratings of the creditworthiness of companies and the riskiness of their bonds and other financial instruments. Although the bond rating scale varies somewhat from rating firm to rating firm, most use combinations of the letters A, B, and C to indicate bond quality. For example, Standard and Poors' bond ratings from highest to lowest are AAA, AA, A, BBB, BB, B, CCC, CC, C, and D, where D is in default. Bonds with a BBB ("triple B") rating would be expected to promise a higher yield than otherwise equivalent bonds with a AAA ("triple A") rating to compensate investors for the additional risk. Bond ratings reflect confidential information made available by the rated companies to the bond rating firms.

The market for high-yield bonds with low ratings saw a significant bubble of activity during the 1980s. These high-yield, low-rating or *junk bonds* were used to finance a variety of high-risk ventures including acquisitions of one company by another. Junk bonds should be distinguished from so-called *fallen angels,* which are bonds whose yields rise to junk-bond levels as a result of declining bond prices reflecting the deteriorating fortunes of the issuing company.

Additional discussion of the institutional arrangements and technicalities surrounding corporate bonds occurs in corporate finance courses. We turn now to the accounting for interest expense and interest payments over the life of a bond.

BOND INTEREST EXPENSE AND INTEREST PAYMENTS

As has already been pointed out, a bond issue provides for regular interest payments plus a face amount payment at maturity. Over the life of the bond, the total interest expense is the difference between the payments the borrower makes and the proceeds received from the bond (as shown in Exhibit 11A–2 on p. 480).

For bonds sold at par, the interest expense for each period is equal to the cash payment to the bondholders. Assume, for example, that a firm has sold at par a five-year, $100,000, 12 percent bond. Every six months, the following entry would be made:

Interest expense 6,000
    Cash 6,000

When bonds are sold at a discount, the interest expense is the amount of the cash payment plus a portion of the discount that was recorded at issue. The *discount amortization* for each period is constant and equals the total discount divided by the number of interest periods:

$$\text{Periodic discount amortization} = \frac{\text{Total discount}}{\text{Number of interest periods}}$$

Adding discount amortization to the cash payment when calculating interest expense implies that the issuer of the bond is paying a higher rate of interest than the stated rate on which the cash payment is based.

The interest expense for bonds sold at a premium is the cash interest payment minus the period's *premium amortization,* which is calculated using the following formula:

$$\text{Periodic premium amortization} = \frac{\text{Total premium}}{\text{Number of interest periods}}$$

Subtracting premium amortization from the cash interest payment when calculating interest expense implies that the issuer of the bond is paying a lower rate of interest than the stated rate on which the cash payment is based. This lower rate of interest (or higher rate, in the case of discounts) is called the *effective interest rate* or *yield rate.* Since recalculating the discount and premium amortization amounts for each interest payment can be laborious, many accountants prepare bond liability tables that list interest expense, interest payments, the premium or discount amortization, and bond carrying amount. Such tables are not needed for bonds sold at par, because of the simplicity of these computations. The following sections illustrate how liability tables are used to determine the interest amortizations first for discount bonds and then for premium bonds.

Bonds Sold at Discount

Assume that a firm issues a five-year, $100,000, 12 percent bond for $99,000. The discount at issue is $1,000. The amounts relating to this bond over its life are shown in Exhibit 11A–4. Note that the amount of each period's interest expense for a discount bond is the sum of the interest paid in cash plus the discount amortization. Note also that, as the total discount of $1,000 is amortized over the life of the bond, the carrying amount increases by $100 each period. The liability balance is reduced to zero by the final payment of $106,000, which includes the last interest payment ($6,000) as well as the face amount payment ($100,000).

The journal entries to be made on interest payment dates can be developed from bond liability tables. Based on the data in Exhibit 11A–4 for a $100,000 bond sold at a discount, the interest expense and payment entry at the end of the first semiannual period is as follows:

Interest expense	6,100	
Discount on bonds payable		100
Cash		6,000

EXHIBIT 11A–4   **DISCOUNT BOND LIABILITY TABLE**

SEMIANNUAL PERIOD	INTEREST EXPENSE* (DEBIT)	CASH PAYMENT† (CREDIT)	CHANGE IN LIABILITY BALANCE‡	LIABILITY BALANCE§
At issue				$99,000
1	$ 6,100	$ 6,000	+100	99,100
2	6,100	6,000	+100	99,200
3	6,100	6,000	+100	99,300
4	6,100	6,000	+100	99,400
5	6,100	6,000	+100	99,500
6	6,100	6,000	+100	99,600
7	6,100	6,000	+100	99,700
8	6,100	6,000	+100	99,800
9	6,100	6,000	+100	99,900
10	6,100	106,000	−99,900	−0−
Total	$61,000	$160,000		

* Interest expense = Interest payment + Discount amortization.
† Interest payment = ($100,000)(.06) = $6,000.
‡ Change in liability balance = Interest expense − Cash payment.
§ New liability balance = Previous liability balance + Change in liability balance.

The entry to record the interest expense will be the same in each subsequent period; thus each entry will reduce the unamortized bond discount (the balance of the discount on bonds payable) by the same amount.

Bonds Sold at Premium

Next, assume that the firm also issues a five-year, $100,000, 12 percent bond for $100,500. The issue premium is $500. The amounts relating to this bond over its life are shown in Exhibit 11A–5. Note that each period's interest expense for the premium bond is less than the amount of the cash interest payment by the amount of the premium amortization. Note also that the bond's carrying amount decreases by $50 each period and is reduced to zero by the final payment of $106,000, which includes the last interest payment ($6,000) as well as the face amount payment ($100,000).

Based on the data in Exhibit 11A–5 for a $100,000 bond sold at a premium, the interest expense and payment entry at the end of the first period is as follows:

Interest expense	5,950	
Premium on bonds payable	50	
Cash		6,000

The entry to record interest expense will be the same in each subsequent period, thus reducing the unamortized bond premium (the balance of the premium on bonds payable) by the same amount in each period.

There are numerous complications in accounting for bonds. The interest expense and payment entries that are made when bonds are issued at times other than the beginning of a fiscal year are illustrated in Appendix 11A–1. These entries use a tabular summary of the liability similar to those presented here. However, the amounts for interest expense and for premium and discount amortization must also be allocated between consecutive accounting periods to achieve a proper matching of interest expense.

We have so far discussed two of the stages in the life cycle of a bond—issuance, and interest payment and expense. In the next sections, we will discuss the third and fourth stages—the redemption of all or a part of a bond issue before maturity and the redemption of all of an issue at maturity.

EARLY RETIREMENT OF BONDS

CALLABLE BONDS: Bonds that permit the issuer to repurchase or redeem the bonds at specified times by paying the bondholder a specified amount known as the *call price*.

Occasionally, interest rates will decline subsequent to a bond issue; or a firm may find that it has excess cash available. In such situations, it is often advantageous for the firm to retire all or part of a bond issue before maturity. If the issue consists of callable bonds, the firm can require bondholders to present their bonds for redemption at a specified price. **Callable bonds** provide that the issuer may repurchase or redeem the bonds at specified times by paying the bondholder a specified amount known as the *call price*. If the bonds are not callable, the firm may purchase the bonds from investors in the bond market and then retire the bonds.

In either case, the face amount of the bonds retired and any unamortized premium or discount applicable to the retired bonds are removed from the borrowing firm's accounting records. If the call price or the cash paid for the bonds exceeds the carrying amount of the bonds, an extraordinary loss on bond

EXHIBIT 11A–5   PREMIUM BOND LIABILITY TABLE

SEMIANNUAL PERIOD	INTEREST EXPENSE* (DEBIT)	CASH PAYMENT† (CREDIT)	CHANGE IN LIABILITY BALANCE‡	LIABILITY BALANCE§
At issue				$100,500
1	$ 5,950	$ 6,000	− 50	100,450
2	5,950	6,000	− 50	100,400
3	5,950	6,000	− 50	100,350
4	5,950	6,000	− 50	100,300
5	5,950	6,000	− 50	100,250
6	5,950	6,000	− 50	100,200
7	5,950	6,000	− 50	100,150
8	5,950	6,000	− 50	100,100
9	5,950	6,000	− 50	100,050
10	5,950	106,000	− 100,050	−0−
Total	$59,500	$160,000		

* Interest expense = Interest payment − Premium amortization.
† Interest payment = ($100,000)(.06) = $6,000.
‡ Change in liability balance = Interest expense − Cash payment.
§ New liability balance = Previous liability balance + Change in liability balance.

retirement is recorded for the amount of the excess. If the call price or the cash paid for the bonds is less than the carrying amount, an extraordinary gain on bond retirement is recorded for the amount of the deficiency. Extraordinary gains and losses are presented in a separate section of the income statement, just above net income and after all the other components of net income have been presented.

Bond liability tables provide the data necessary to compute the carrying amount of a bond (face amount plus unamortized premium or face amount less unamortized discount), as well as the other data necessary to develop the journal entry for early retirement. Exhibit 11A–6 presents a portion of a bond liability table for a 10-year, $1,000,000, 13 percent bond issue originally sold at a discount of $14,000. In this example, let's assume that just after the twelfth semiannual interest payment, $200,000 (20 percent) of the $1,000,000 face amount of the issue is retired for a $192,500 cash payment. Using the data in the table, we first determine the unamortized discount on the entire bond issue at the retirement point. The unamortized discount for the entire bond issue is the face amount less

EXHIBIT 11A–6   PARTIAL BOND LIABILITY TABLE

SEMIANNUAL PERIOD	INTEREST EXPENSE (DEBIT)	CASH PAYMENT (CREDIT)	CHANGE IN LIABILITY BALANCE	LIABILITY BALANCE
11	$65,700	$65,000	+ 700	$993,700
12	65,700	65,000	+ 700	994,400

the current carrying amount: $1,000,000 - \$994,400 = \$5,600$. The next step is to compute the unamortized discount for the bonds retired: $(\$5,600)(.20) = \$1,120$. The journal entry to record retirement of the bonds is:

Bonds payable	200,000	
Extraordinary gain on bond retirement..............		6,380
Discount on bonds payable		1,120
Cash..		192,500

In this case, there is an extraordinary gain because the cash paid ($192,500) is less than the carrying amount of the bonds retired [$200,000 - \$1,120 = \$198,880$]. After retirement of the $200,000 of bonds, there remains $800,000 of bonds with a carrying amount of $795,520, which is 80 percent of the amount shown in Exhibit 11A–6 [$(\$994,400)(.80) = \$795,520$]. Had the bonds been issued at a premium, similar computations would have been made, except that the premium for the retired bonds, rather than the discount, would have been computed. The journal entry would also have been similar, except that premium on bonds payable would have been debited as part of the retirement entry.

RETIREMENT OF BONDS AT MATURITY

Many bonds are not retired early but are held to maturity. At maturity the carrying amount of such bonds is the face amount. The final interest payment and interest expense entry amortizes the last portion of the unamortized premium or discount established when the bond was issued. The journal entry for retirement at maturity is made at the same time and is simply a debit to bonds payable and a credit to cash in the same amount. For example, a $500,000 bond issue would be retired at maturity with the following entry:

Bonds payable	500,000	
Cash..		500,000

Between them, the entry to record the final interest payment and any amortization of premium and the entry to retire the bonds remove from the balance sheet all traces of the retired bonds.[6]

---

[6] The foregoing paragraphs describe the accounting concepts and procedures for bonds used by *issuers* of bonds. Although the concepts and procedures used by *investors* in bonds are based on the same measurements and calculations, the reporting conventions are somewhat different. The most fundamental difference is that investors record bonds acquired as assets rather than liabilities and record the interest as revenue rather than expense. In addition, investors do not record premium or discount in a separate account; rather premium or discount is combined with the face amount and recorded in a single investment account. If the bonds are readily marketable and the investor intends to sell them within the longer of one year or one operating cycle, then the acquisition is recorded as a current asset in a short-term investment account. Otherwise, the bonds should be recorded in a long-term investment account. Premium and discount are amortized for bonds held as long-term investments in much the same way as for bond liabilities; amortization of premium reduces interest revenue and amortization of discount increases interest revenue. In contrast, premium and discount are not amortized for bonds held as short-term investments, because to do so would not result in a material change in the amount of interest revenue. Rather, interest revenue on bonds held as short-term investments is recorded as the amount of cash received. Further, as noted in Chapter 8, bonds held as short-term investments are not subject to the lower-of-cost-or-market adjustments made to the reported amount for other short-term investments in marketable securities.

EXHIBIT 11A-7   **EFFECTS OF FINANCING WITH BONDS**

	19X1		19X2	
	CARMEL COMPANY	NOBLESVILLE, INC.	CARMEL COMPANY	NOBLESVILLE, INC.
Balance sheet:*				
Assets	$3,000,000	$3,000,000	$3,000,000	$3,000,000
Bonds payable	1,000,000	–0–	1,000,000	–0–
Stockholders' equity	2,000,000	3,000,000	2,000,000	3,000,000
Number of capital stock shares	100,000	150,000	100,000	150,000
Income statement:				
Income from operations	$ 600,000	$ 600,000	$ 300,000	$ 300,000
Interest expense (.15)	150,000	–0–	150,000	–0–
Income before taxes	$ 450,000	$ 600,000	$ 150,000	$ 300,000
Income taxes expense (.30)	135,000	180,000	45,000	90,000
Net income	$ 315,000	$ 420,000	$ 105,000	$ 210,000
Earnings per share	$3.15	$2.80	$1.05	$1.40

* Annual averages (assume that current liabilities are negligible).

PROS AND CONS OF FINANCING WITH BONDS

A significant advantage of financing with bonds rather than stock is the fact that the interest expense on bonds is deductible for income tax purposes. To illustrate the effect of interest deductibility, consider the 19X1 financial statement information for Carmel Company shown in the first column of Exhibit 11A-7. Carmel issued $1,000,000 of 15 percent bonds that result in interest expense of $150,000 per year; however, the net cash outflow for the bonds is significantly less than $150,000. Since the interest is deductible in the calculation of taxable income, taxable income is $150,000 less than it would have been without the bond issue. Income taxes, which are computed at a rate of 30 percent of taxable income, are therefore reduced by $45,000 [($150,000)(.30)], making the net cash outflow for the bonds only $105,000 ($150,000 − $45,000). In other words, the cost of financing with bonds (or any other form of liability with tax-deductible interest payments) is the interest net of income taxes, which can be determined by using the following formula:

$$\text{Interest net of income taxes} = (1 - \text{Tax rate})(\text{Interest})$$
$$= (1 - .30)(\$150,000)$$
$$= \$105,000$$

The formula provides an efficient way of computing interest net of income taxes.

Another potential advantage of bonds is that they fix the amount of compensation to the lender. No matter how successful the firm is in using borrowed capital, its bondholders receive only the return specified in the bond agreement (interest and face amount). Thus, if the borrowed capital generates income in excess of the interest on the bonds, the stockholders of the borrowing firm benefit. The use of capital secured from creditors in the hope of producing more income than that needed to cover the interest on the related liability is called using **leverage** or **trading on equity.**

LEVERAGE (TRADING ON EQUITY): A firm's use of capital secured from creditors in the hope of producing more income than that needed to cover the interest on the related liability, with the excess income accruing to the stockholders.

Under the right conditions, using leverage has significant advantages; however, conditions also exist under which the use of leverage is disadvantageous. Exhibit 11A–7 illustrates both sets of conditions. Two companies—Carmel Company and Noblesville, Inc.—have identical financial data except that Carmel finances its operation with debt as well as stock whereas Noblesville finances its operations entirely with stock. Conditions in 19X1 create an advantage for Carmel's use of leverage. Carmel's stockholders earn $3.15 per share in 19X1, which includes an amount attributable to earnings in excess of the cost of borrowing. In contrast, Noblesville's stockholders earn only $2.80 per share in 19X1. However, income from operations falls in 19X2, with the result that Carmel's stockholders earn only $1.05 per share compared with $1.40 per share for Noblesville's stockholders. Just as the stockholders receive earnings in excess of the interest on debt, so the stockholders must bear the excess of the interest on debt over earnings.

A third advantage of financing with bonds is that in periods of inflation, bonds permit the borrowing entity to repay the lender in dollars of a smaller purchasing power. For instance, based on changes in the consumer price index (CPI), $1,000,000 borrowed in 1970 and repaid in 1990 provided the lender in 1990 with only 30 percent of the purchasing power of the amount loaned in 1970. Supplementary Topic B, at the back of this book, explains how to use price indexes to adjust accounting data for changes in purchasing power.

The primary negative attribute of bonds, as of most other forms of liabilities, is the inflexibility of the payment schedule. Bonds require specified payments to bondholders on specified dates. If a payment is not made as scheduled, the issuing entity can be declared bankrupt. This attribute of bonds causes them to be more risky than equity as a way of securing capital. The larger the proportion of liabilities an entity uses to finance its capital needs, the greater the risk of default for the firm and for the lenders. As risk increases (because of a higher proportion of liabilities), the cost of bond financing increases. At a certain point, however, the risk becomes so great that additional liabilities cannot be sold at any cost. For firms whose operational and competitive circumstances produce substantial fluctuations in earnings, even low levels of notes or bonds may be considered too risky. An entity must weigh both the negative and the positive aspects of bonds in deciding whether or not to obtain needed capital by issuing bonds. This extremely complex decision is treated more fully in finance courses.

We turn now to leases, which can serve as another means of financing asset acquisitions.

LEASES

LEASE: A document that enables its holder to use property without legally owning it.

During the past 25 years, leases have increasingly become an alternative to outright asset purchases for firms seeking to expand their operations. A **lease** enables a firm to use property without legally owning it. When leases first began to be used as sources of capital for asset acquisition, they generally were omitted from the liabilities of the entity. In 1976, however, the Financial Accounting Standards Board identified two kinds of lease obligations for lessees—operating leases and capital leases—and required that capital leases be included in a firm's assets and liabilities.[7] We will discuss both types of leases and their accounting procedures in the sections that follow.

ACCOUNTING FOR OPERATING LEASES

OPERATING LEASE: A lease in which the lessor retains the risks and obligations of ownership of the leased asset.

The most common form of lease is an **operating lease,** under which the lessor (the legal owner of the asset) retains the risks and obligations of ownership. The rental of automobiles, retail space, and office space is usually accomplished with an operating lease. All illustrations of rental arrangements considered earlier in this book have been operating leases. Under an operating lease, the leased asset does not appear in the records of the lessee, because the legal owner of the asset retains the risks and obligations of ownership. Rent paid in advance of the use of the asset is reported as prepaid rent, and rent expense is recognized in the period in which the leased asset is used. However, the sum of all payments required by noncancelable operating leases for the five years subsequent to the current accounting period must be disclosed in a footnote to the lessee's financial statements.

ACCOUNTING FOR CAPITAL LEASES

CAPITAL LEASE: A lease that is in substance a purchase of the asset leased.

A **capital lease** is a noncancelable agreement that is in substance a purchase of the asset leased. If a lease has any of the following characteristics, it is essentially a purchase and is therefore considered a capital lease:

1. A transfer of the leased property to the lessee at the end of the lease at no cost or at a "bargain price"
2. A term for the lease that is at least 75 percent of the economic life of the leased property
3. A present value of the lease payments that is at least 90 percent of the fair value of the leased property

At inception, the liability for a capital lease is recorded at the present value of the future lease payments. At this time, an asset is recorded in the same amount. During the life of the lease, the asset is depreciated, using an appropriate depreciation method, and the lease liability is reduced and interest expense is recorded as lease payments are made. To illustrate the computations and entries for capital leases, let's assume that on January 1, 19X6, the Rhea Company signed a five-year lease for data processing equipment. The current cash value (present value) of the future lease payments (and the fair value of the data processing equipment) is $600,000. The data processing equipment has an expected economic life of five years and no residual value. The terms of the capital lease require payments of $166,446 at the end of each year. On January 1, 19X6, Rhea would record the asset and the capital lease liability as follows:

Leased property	600,000	
Capital lease liability		600,000

Although the lessor remains the legal owner of the leased property, a capital lease transfers virtually all the benefits of ownership to the lessee; therefore, a capital

[7] Financial Accounting Standards Board, "Accounting for Leases," *Statement of Financial Accounting Standards No. 13.*

lease is appropriately shown among the lessee's assets and liabilities. The interest expense on the lease for the first year is $72,000 [($600,000)(.12)]. Thus at the end of the first year, Rhea would make the following entry for the capital lease:

Interest expense	72,000	
Capital lease liability	94,446	
Cash		166,446

Rhea would also make the following adjusting entry for depreciation expense for the leased property at the end of the first year:

Depreciation expense, leased property	120,000	
Accumulated depreciation, leased property		120,000

Thus the total expense for the property acquired with the capital lease for the first year is the sum of the interest expense and the depreciation expense: $72,000 + $120,000 = $192,000.

Depending on the terms, leases can be more or less attractive than borrowing as a means of financing asset acquisitions, as the following analysis demonstrates.

ANALYSIS

LEASING VERSUS BORROWING

The Ives Corporation plans to acquire five new trucks. If purchased, the trucks will cost $12,000 each. One truck dealer will allow Ives to pay 10 percent down ($6,000) and will finance the remaining $54,000 on a five-year, 10 percent interest-bearing note requiring annual interest payments of $5,400 and the principal payment of $54,000 at maturity. Another dealer will lease trucks of the same make to Ives on a capital lease requiring annual payments of $15,828 for five years. The leased trucks would become Ives' property at the end of the lease. Ives' accountant has asked you to help decide whether to lease or borrow in order to finance the truck acquisition. As a basis for making your decision, you develop the following data:

	LEASING	BORROWING
Cash payments:		
Year 1	$15,828	$11,400
Year 2	15,828	5,400
Year 3	15,828	5,400
Year 4	15,828	5,400
Year 5	15,828	59,400
Total for 5 years	$79,140	$87,000
Interest expense for 5 years	$19,140	$27,000

The leasing option promises a lower total cash outflow and a lower total interest expense. Does this mean that the company should lease rather than borrow and purchase?

Although the leasing option promises a lower total cash outflow and a lower total interest expense, its level payment schedule does not allow Ives to defer payment to the extent allowed by the borrowing option. The deferred payment advantage of borrowing may more than offset the cash flow and interest expense advantages of leasing.

In addition, the payment schedules shown above do not include the effects of the interest on income tax payments. Since the annual interest deduction declines more slowly under borrowing, the effects of interest on income tax payments enhance the deferred payment advantage of borrowing. Of course, the data presented here are insufficient to enable a final recommendation. A complete analysis of these options, which is explained in finance courses, would enable an evaluation of the amounts and timing of the payments required by the two options and the income tax effects of both interest and depreciation.

SUMMARY

Liabilities that represent economic sacrifices expected to occur beyond the longer of one year or one operating cycle are known as long-term liabilities. Long-term liabilities arise from transactions supported by a variety of legal documents, including notes, bonds, and capital leases. This chapter explains the accounting procedures for long-term liabilities, using straight-line amortization of interest.

Bond accounting is complicated by the fact that bonds are rarely sold at their par value (face amount) but are usually sold at a small premium or discount. A premium or discount affects the amount of interest expense associated with a bond. Bond accounting also involves recording extraordinary gains or losses on bonds that are retired before maturity.

This chapter also discusses the pros and cons of financing asset acquisitions with bonds, capital leases, and stock. Bonds are frequently a less expensive source of capital than stock (equity). In addition, leases represent an important alternative to bonds and equity as a means of acquiring assets. When a lease is in substance a purchase of leased facilities, it is known as a *capital lease;* an asset and a long-term liability are recorded for a capital lease. Since the ability of a firm to borrow by issuing bonds, capital leases, and other liabilities is usually limited, most firms are financed by a mixture of liabilities and equity. Equity as a source of long-term capital will be discussed in Chapter 12.

APPENDIX 11A–1
SOME TECHNICAL ISSUES IN ACCOUNTING FOR BONDS

To simplify the examples in this chapter, we made the assumption that bonds are sold only at the beginning of accounting and interest payment periods. In reality, however, bonds are often sold at times other than the beginning of an accounting period, and they can also be sold at times other than the beginning of an interest payment period. In those situations, more complicated computations and entries are necessary to match the interest amortization with the appropriate accounting periods. The following sections illustrate some of the complications, first in accounting for bonds sold at times other than the beginning of an accounting period, and then for bonds sold at times other than the beginning of an interest period.

BONDS SOLD AT TIMES OTHER THAN THE BEGINNING OF THE ACCOUNTING PERIOD

The Hadley Company issued a five-year, $200,000, 12 percent bond at a $3,000 discount on May 1, 19X6. Assume that the bond liability table in Exhibit 11A–8 was prepared for this issue. Since this bond was issued on May 1, 19X6, at the beginning of the first interest period, the first semiannual interest payment entry would be made on October 31, 19X6, as follows (using period 1 data from Exhibit 11A–8):

Interest expense	12,300	
Discount on bonds payable		300
Cash		12,000

The Hadley Company's fiscal year ends on December 31, 19X6. An adjusting entry is necessary to record the interest expense accrued from the date of the interest payment on October 31 through December 31. The data in Exhibit 11A–8 are used to allocate the period 2 interest expense between 19X6 and 19X7; the computations for the adjusting entry are as follows:

Interest expense, November and December 19X6
$(2/6)(\$12,300) = \$4,100$

Discount amortization, November and December 19X6
$(2/6)(\$300) = \$100$

Interest payable on December 31, 19X6
$(2/6)(12,000) = \$4,000$

EXHIBIT 11A–8   **BOND LIABILITY TABLE**

HADLEY COMPANY

SEMIANNUAL PERIOD	INTEREST EXPENSE (DEBIT)	CASH PAYMENT (CREDIT)	CHANGE IN LIABILITY BALANCE	LIABILITY BALANCE
At issue				$197,000
1	$ 12,300	$ 12,000	+300	197,300
2	12,300	12,000	+300	197,600
3	12,300	12,000	+300	197,900
4	12,300	12,000	+300	198,200
5	12,300	12,000	+300	198,500
6	12,300	12,000	+300	198,800
7	12,300	12,000	+300	199,100
8	12,300	12,000	+300	199,400
9	12,300	12,000	+300	199,700
10	12,300	212,000	−199,700	−0−
Total	$123,000	$320,000		

The following adjusting entry can now be made:

Interest expense	4,100	
Discount on bonds payable		100
Interest payable		4,000

On April 30, 19X7, when the next interest payment is due, the remainder of the period 2 discount amortization and interest expense must be recorded. The computations are as follows:

Interest expense, January 19X7 through April 19X7

$(4/6)(\$12,300) = \$8,200$

Discount amortization, January 19X7 through April 19X7

$(4/6)(\$300) = \$200$

The interest payment entry that follows an adjusting entry is then made, as follows:

Interest expense	8,200	
Interest payable	4,000	
Discount on bonds payable		200
Cash		12,000

Note that the interest payment entry removes the $4,000 interest payable established by the adjusting entry.

BONDS SOLD AFTER THE BEGINNING OF AN INTEREST PERIOD

Bonds normally are issued at the beginning of an interest period. Occasionally, however, difficulties in marketing a bond issue cause the initial sale to be delayed beyond the beginning of a semiannual interest period. When such a delay occurs, the amount the bondholders pay the issuer includes the interest from the beginning of the interest period to the date of sale. The issuer then makes a full six-month interest payment to the bondholders at the end of the interest period, thus repaying the interest paid by the bondholders at the sale date. Therefore, the issuer must allocate a portion of the proceeds to the interest that the bondholder will receive for the portion of the interest period that has already passed.

Assume that the Highland Corporation sold a 10-year, $100,000, 12 percent bond issue on September 1, 19X6, one month after the beginning of the interest period for the bonds. Highland received proceeds of $102,190 from the sale. Since the bonds have 119 months remaining until maturity, the entry to record the sale would be as follows:

Cash	102,190	
Bonds payable		100,000
Interest payable [($100,000)(.12)(1/12)]		1,000
Premium on bonds payable		1,190

A premium (or a discount) is a derived amount that is determined by subtracting the sum of the bond liability and interest payable from the proceeds:

$\$102,190 - (\$100,000 + \$1,000) = \$1,190$

EXHIBIT 11A–9   PARTIAL BOND LIABILITY TABLE

HIGHLAND CORPORATION

SEMIANNUAL PERIOD	INTEREST EXPENSE (DEBIT)	CASH PAYMENT (CREDIT)	CHANGE IN LIABILITY BALANCE	LIABILITY BALANCE
At issue				$101,190
1	$4,950*	$6,000*	−50*	101,140
2	5,940	6,000	−60	101,080

* There are 119 months from the issue point to maturity. Therefore, $10 of premium is amortized each month [$1,190/119 months = $10 per month]. In the first period, there are only five months of interest expense because the bond was sold one month after the interest period began. Six months' interest must still be paid to the bondholders. For each remaining period, six months' interest expense is recorded and paid.

In the case of a discount, the sum of the bond liability and the interest payable would exceed the proceeds.

The data for the entry at the time of sale and for the subsequent interest payment entries can be developed from the bond liability table that is made up when the bonds are sold (see Exhibit 11A–9). On the basis of these data and the sale entry, Highland would record the first interest payment with the following entry:

Interest expense	4,950	
Interest payable	1,000	
Premium on bonds payable	50	
Cash		6,000

Subsequent semiannual interest payment entries would follow the procedures described earlier in this chapter.

KEY TERMS

BOND (p. 478)

BOND ISSUE (p. 478)

CALLABLE BONDS (p. 486)

CAPITAL LEASE (p. 491)

CARRYING AMOUNT (BOOK VALUE) (p. 475)

DISCOUNT ON BONDS PAYABLE (p. 479)

FACE AMOUNT (PAR VALUE) (p. 478)

INTEREST AMORTIZATION (p. 470)

LEASE (p. 490)

LEVERAGE (TRADING ON EQUITY) (p. 489)

LONG-TERM NOTES PAYABLE (p. 472)

OPERATING LEASE (p. 491)

PREMIUM ON BONDS PAYABLE (p. 479)

STATED RATE (COUPON RATE, NOMINAL RATE, FACE RATE, OR CONTRACT RATE) (p. 478)

STRAIGHT-LINE INTEREST AMORTIZATION (p. 471)

QUESTIONS

Q11A-1. What is a long-term liability? Are all bonds classified as long-term liabilities?

Q11A-2. Name the long-term liabilities described in Chapter 10. How do they differ from the long-term liabilities described in the present chapter?

Q11A-3. How is total interest for a liability calculated?

Q11A-4. Describe the two-stage allocation procedure used to apportion the total interest associated with a liability among accounting periods. What is the relationship between this two-stage procedure and the matching concept?

Q11A-5. Name four long-term liabilities and describe the distinguishing features of each.

Q11A-6. How is the amount of discount computed on a single-payment non-interest-bearing note? What is the relationship between total discount and total interest on such a note?

Q11A-7. What is meant by restructuring a long-term liability? Why does restructuring occur?

Q11A-8. What are bond ratings, and how are they related to the cost of issuing debt? What are "junk bonds," and how do they differ from "fallen angels"?

Q11A-9. What is the face amount of a bond? How is the face amount related to the discount or premium on the bond?

Q11A-10. How do premiums and discounts on bonds affect interest expense?

Q11A-11. Describe the differences between the accounting for long-term bonds receivable by investors and the accounting for long-term bonds payable by issuers.

Q11A-12. How are premiums and discounts presented in the balance sheet?

Q11A-13. How does a firm "lever" its capital structure? When is leverage advantageous? When is it disadvantageous? Who receives the advantage or bears the disadvantage of leverage?

Q11A-14. Name and describe two kinds of leases.

Q11A-15. Which type of lease requires that a long-term liability and an asset be recorded at the inception of the lease?

EXERCISES

E11A-16. INTEREST EXPENSE AND ALTERNATIVE NOTES   Jacobi Corporation wishes to borrow $100,000 to finance the acquisition of new equipment during 19X1. Two alternative forms of the note are under consideration:

> *Note I:* Note I requires five annual interest payments of $10,000 each, beginning one year after issuance; the final interest payment is made in five years (at maturity), together with the $100,000 repayment of principal.

> *Note II:* Note II requires a single payment of $164,000 in five years (at maturity), which pays all interest and principal.

REQUIRED:

1. Assume that the note is issued and $100,000 cash received on January 1, 19X1. Calculate the amount of interest expense for note I and note II to be reported for 19X1 and 19X2.

2. Assume that the note is issued and $100,000 cash received on April 1, 19X1. Calculate the amount of interest expense to be reported for note I and note II for 19X1 and 19X2.

3. With reference to your calculations for note II, explain the two-stage amortization and matching of interest in 19X1 and 19X2 if the note is issued on April 1, 19X1. How does the two-stage process differ if note II is issued on January 1, 19X1?

E11A-17. INTEREST AMORTIZATION AND INTEREST MATCHING   Kerwin Company borrowed $10,000 on a two-year, 12 percent interest-bearing note. The note was issued on September 1, 19X7. Interest of $2,544 is to be paid in a lump sum at maturity on August 31, 19X9.

REQUIRED:

1. Allocate the interest of $2,544 to the two 1-year interest periods, using straight-line interest amortization.

2. Allocate the interest of $2,544 to the three calendar years in which the note is outstanding.

E11A-18. INTEREST-BEARING NOTE WITH ANNUAL INTEREST PAYMENTS   Kiwi Corporation issued a two-year, $150,000, 12 percent interest-bearing note on September 1, 19X7. Interest is paid annually on August 31. The principal and the final interest payment are due on August 31, 19X9.

REQUIRED:

1. Prepare the entry for Kiwi's journal to record the issuance of the note.

2. Prepare the adjusting entry for Kiwi's journal to record the interest expense from the date of issue through December 31, 19X7.

3. Prepare the entry for Kiwi's journal to record the first interest payment on August 31, 19X8.

E11A-19. SINGLE-PAYMENT INTEREST-BEARING NOTE   Lubeck Nursery issued a three-year, $75,000 interest-bearing note on March 1, 19X6. The principal plus $33,750 interest are to be repaid on February 28, 19X9.

REQUIRED:

1. Prepare the adjusting entry to record interest expense on December 31, 19X6.

2. Prepare the adjusting entry to record interest expense on December 31, 19X7.

3. Prepare the entry to record the 19X9 interest expense and the payment of the principal and interest on February 28, 19X9.

E11A-20. INTEREST-BEARING NOTE WITH LUMP-SUM PAYMENT   Johnson Company borrowed $90,000 on a two-year interest-bearing note on May 1, 19X7. The principal ($90,000) and interest ($24,840) are to be paid in a single payment on April 30, 19X9.

REQUIRED:

1. Prepare the entry for Johnson's journal to record issuance of the note.

2. Prepare the adjusting entry for Johnson's journal to record the interest expense from the date of issue through December 31, 19X7.

3. Prepare the adjusting entry at December 31, 19X8.

4. Prepare the entry to record the 19X9 interest expense and the repayment of the note and interest on April 30, 19X9.

E11A-21. NON-INTEREST-BEARING NOTE   Dodge City Products borrowed $100,000 cash by issuing an 18-month, $118,000 non-interest-bearing note on September 1, 19X7. The $118,000 face amount of the note is due on February 28, 19X9.

REQUIRED:

1. Prepare the entry for Dodge City's journal to record issuance of the note.

2. Prepare the adjusting entries for Dodge City's journal at December 31, 19X7, and December 31, 19X8.

3. Prepare the entry to record interest for January 1, 19X9, through February 28, 19X9, and the entry to record repayment of the note at maturity.

E11A-22. NON-INTEREST-BEARING NOTE   On April 1, 19X4, Saskatoon Lumber Company borrowed $58,000 by issuing a two-year, $72,400 non-interest-bearing note. The face amount of $72,400 is due on March 31, 19X6.

REQUIRED:

1. Prepare the entry for Saskatoon's journal to record issuance of the note.
2. Prepare the adjusting entries for Saskatoon's journal at December 31, 19X4, and December 31, 19X5.
3. Prepare the entry to record interest for January 1, 19X6, through March 31, 19X6, and the entry to record repayment of the note at maturity.
4. Why is Saskatoon's note described as "non-interest-bearing"?

E11A-23. JOURNAL ENTRIES FOR BOND PREMIUMS AND DISCOUNTS   Kartel Company is planning to issue 50 bonds, each having a face amount of $10,000.

REQUIRED:

1. Prepare the journal entry to record the sale of the bonds at par.
2. Prepare the journal entry to record the sale of the bonds at a premium of $34,000.
3. Prepare the journal entry to record the sale of the bonds at a discount of $41,000.

E11A-24. BOND INTEREST PAYMENTS AND INTEREST EXPENSE   On January 1, 19X8, Philips Corporation issued bonds with a total face amount of $800,000 and a stated (or coupon) rate of 12 percent.

REQUIRED:

1. Calculate the interest expense for 19X8 if the bonds were sold at par.
2. Calculate the interest expense for 19X8 if the bonds were sold at a premium and the premium amortization for 19X8 is $12,300.
3. Calculate the interest expense for 19X8 if the bonds were sold at a discount and the discount amortization for 19X8 is $9,700.

E11A-25. BOND PREMIUM AND DISCOUNT   Markway, Inc., is contemplating a bond issue to be composed of 150 bonds, each with a face amount of $2,000.

REQUIRED:

1. How much is Markway able to borrow if each bond is sold at a premium of $75?
2. How much is Markway able to borrow if each bond is sold at a discount of $85?
3. How much is Markway able to borrow if each bond is sold at 96 percent of par?
4. How much is Markway able to borrow if each bond is sold at 115 percent of par?
5. Assume that the bonds are sold for $1,975 each. Prepare the journal entry to record the issuance of the 150 bonds.
6. Assume that the bonds are sold for $2,019 each. Prepare the journal entry to record the issuance of the 150 bonds.

E11A-26. BOND INTEREST PAYMENTS AND INTEREST EXPENSE   Klamath Manufacturing sold a 10-year bond with a total face amount of $400,000 and a stated rate of 12 percent for $424,000 in cash. The bond was sold on April 1, 19X2, and pays interest quarterly.

REQUIRED:

1. Prepare the entry to record the sale of the bond.
2. Determine the amount of the quarterly interest payment required by the bond.
3. Prepare the journal entry made by Klamath at June 30, 19X2, to record the payment of three months' interest and the related interest expense.
4. Determine the amount of interest expense for 19X2 and for 19X3.

E11A-27. BOND INTEREST PAYMENTS AND INTEREST EXPENSE   On January 1, 19X6, Harrington Corporation sold for $96,000 a 10-year, $100,000 bond having semiannual interest payments and a stated rate of 12 percent.

REQUIRED:

1. Prepare the journal entry to record the sale of the bond.
2. Calculate the amount of the semiannual cash payment for interest.
3. Prepare the journal entry at June 30, 19X7, to record the payment of interest and the interest expense.
4. Calculate the annual interest expense for 19X6 and 19X7.

E11A-28. COMPLETING A BOND LIABILITY TABLE   Cagney Company sold a $200,000 bond issue on June 30, 19X5. A portion of the bond liability table appears below.

INTEREST PERIOD ENDING	INTEREST EXPENSE	CASH PAYMENT	CHANGE IN LIABILITY BALANCE	LIABILITY BALANCE
12/31/X6	$11,600	$11,000	+600	$194,600
6/30/X7	11,600	11,000	+600	195,200
12/31/X7	?	?	?	?

REQUIRED:

1. What is the stated interest rate on these bonds?
2. What are the interest expense and the discount amortization (change in liability balance) for the interest period ending December 31, 19X7?
3. What is the liability balance after the interest payment is recorded on December 31, 19X7?

E11A-29. USING A PREMIUM BOND LIABILITY TABLE   For Dingle Corporation, the following bond liability table was prepared when a five-year, $200,000, 14 percent bond issue was sold on January 1, 19X2, for $210,000:

INTEREST PERIOD ENDING	INTEREST EXPENSE	CASH PAYMENT	CHANGE IN LIABILITY BALANCE	LIABILITY BALANCE
At issue				$210,000
6/30/X2	$13,000	$ 14,000	−1,000	209,000
12/31/X2	13,000	14,000	−1,000	208,000
6/30/X3	13,000	14,000	−1,000	207,000
12/31/X3	13,000	14,000	−1,000	206,000
6/30/X4	13,000	14,000	−1,000	205,000
12/31/X4	13,000	14,000	−1,000	204,000
6/30/X5	13,000	14,000	−1,000	203,000
12/31/X5	13,000	14,000	−1,000	202,000
6/30/X6	13,000	14,000	−1,000	201,000
12/31/X6	13,000	214,000	−201,000	−0−

REQUIRED:

1. Prepare the entry to record the issuance of the bonds on January 1, 19X2.
2. Prepare the entry to record the first interest payment on June 30, 19X2.
3. What interest expense for this bond issue will Dingle report in its 19X3 income statement?
4. Indicate how this bond issue will appear in Dingle's December 31, 19X5, balance sheet.

E11A-30. USING A DISCOUNT BOND LIABILITY TABLE   Panamint Candy Company prepared the following bond liability table for $500,000 of five-year, 9.2 percent bonds issued and sold by Panamint on January 1, 19X3, for $472,000:

INTEREST PERIOD ENDING	INTEREST EXPENSE	CASH PAYMENT	CHANGE IN LIABILITY BALANCE	LIABILITY BALANCE
At issue				$472,000
6/30/X3	$25,800	$ 23,000	+2,800	474,800
12/31/X3	25,800	23,000	+2,800	477,600
6/30/X4	25,800	23,000	+2,800	480,400
12/31/X4	25,800	23,000	+2,800	483,200
6/30/X5	25,800	23,000	+2,800	486,000
12/31/X5	25,800	23,000	+2,800	488,800
6/30/X6	25,800	23,000	+2,800	491,600
12/31/X6	25,800	23,000	+2,800	494,400
6/30/X7	25,800	23,000	+2,800	497,200
12/31/X7	25,800	523,000	−497,200	−0−

REQUIRED:

1. Prepare the entry to record the issuance of the bonds on January 1, 19X3.
2. Prepare the entry to record the first interest payment on June 30, 19X3.
3. What interest expense for this bond issue will Panamint report on its 19X5 income statement?
4. Indicate how this bond issue will appear in Panamint's December 31, 19X5, balance sheet.

E11A-31. COMPLETING A BOND LIABILITY TABLE   Sondrini Corporation sold a $200,000 bond issue at a premium. A portion of the bond liability table appears below.

INTEREST PERIOD ENDING	INTEREST EXPENSE	CASH PAYMENT	CHANGE IN LIABILITY BALANCE	LIABILITY BALANCE
12/31/X1	$12,900	$13,000	−100	$201,400
6/30/X2	12,900	13,000	−100	201,300
12/31/X2	?	?	?	?

REQUIRED:

1. What is the stated annual interest rate on these bonds?
2. What is the carrying amount at December 31, 19X2?
3. When will the bonds mature?

E11A-32. EARLY RETIREMENT OF BONDS   On July 1, 19X1, O'Bryans Wholesale Distributors issued five-year, 12 percent bonds with a total face amount of $500,000 for $506,000 cash. The following is a portion of the bond liability table prepared at that time:

INTEREST PERIOD ENDING	INTEREST EXPENSE	CASH PAYMENT	CHANGE IN LIABILITY BALANCE	LIABILITY BALANCE
At issue				$506,000
12/31/X1	$29,400	$30,000	−600	505,400
6/30/X2	29,400	30,000	−600	504,800
12/31/X2	29,400	30,000	−600	504,200
6/30/X3	29,400	30,000	−600	503,600

On June 30, 19X3, O'Bryans redeemed all the bonds at their call price of 100.4 percent of the face amount, or $502,000.

REQUIRED:

1. Prepare the entry to record the interest expense for the period ended June 30, 19X3.
2. Prepare the bond retirement journal entry.

E11A-33. OPERATING LEASES AND CAPITAL LEASES   On January 1, 19X6, Moody Company leased a warehouse for $20,000 per year. The first annual payment is due December 31, 19X6. The present value of the lease payments, which is also the fair value of the warehouse, is $113,000.

REQUIRED:

1. Assume that the lease is an *operating* lease. Prepare the journal entries made by Moody during 19X6 and 19X7 for the lease.

2. Assume that the lease is a *capital* lease with an effective interest rate of 12 percent per year. Depreciate the cost of the leased warehouse on a straight-line basis over 10 years with zero residual value. Prepare the journal entries made by Moody only during 19X6 for the lease and the leased asset.

APPENDIX EXERCISES

E11A-34. BONDS SOLD AFTER THE BEGINNING OF THE YEAR   Haus Corporation sold a 10-year, $100,000, 12 percent bond issue on April 1, 19X6, at a $5,000 premium. Interest payments are to be made on September 30 and March 31 of each year. Haus's fiscal year ends December 31.

REQUIRED:

1. Prepare the entry to record the interest expense and payment on September 30, 19X6.

2. Prepare the adjusting entry for interest expense on December 31, 19X6.

3. Prepare the entry to record interest expense and payment on March 31, 19X7.

E11A-35. BONDS SOLD AFTER THE BEGINNING OF AN INTEREST PERIOD   Beckford Markets, a grocery chain, sold a five-year, $600,000, 12 percent bond issue on February 1, 19X2, one month after the interest period began. The interest payments are to be made June 30 and December 31 of each year. Beckford received $600,100, including $6,000 of interest for January, when the bonds were sold.

REQUIRED:

1. Prepare the journal entry to record the issuance of the bonds on February 1, 19X2.

2. Prepare the journal entry to record the interest expense and payment on June 30, 19X2.

3. Prepare the journal entry to record the interest expense and payment on December 31, 19X2.

PROBLEMS

P11A-36. REPORTING LONG-TERM LIABILITIES   Fridley Manufacturing's accounting records reveal the following account balances after adjusting entries at December 31, 19X2:

Accounts payable	$ 62,500
Bonds payable (7.8%, due in 19X7)	400,000
Bonds payable (9.4%, due in 19X9)	800,000
Current portion of long-term liabilities	70,000
Deferred tax liability	133,400
Discount on bonds payable (9.4%, due in 19X9)	12,600
Discount on notes payable (due in 19X3)	1,700
Income taxes payable	26,900
Interest payable	38,700
Capital lease liability	41,500
Long-term notes payable (due in 19X5)	50,000
Notes payable (due in 19X3)	25,000
Premium on bonds payable (7.8%, due in 19X7)	6,100

REQUIRED:

Prepare the classified liability section as it would appear on Fridley's balance sheet at December 31, 19X2.

P11A-37. USING ASSET VALUES TO ESTABLISH THE AMOUNT OF A LIABILITY   Micro Service Company acquired a new car for one of its service personnel. Because Micro is a good customer, the car dealer accepted a two-year non-interest-bearing note with a face amount of $12,951 as payment for the car. The car had a sticker price of $12,600, but the dealer would have accepted cash of $10,200 for the car.

REQUIRED:

1. Record this transaction in Micro's journal.
2. What is the amount of the addition to Micro's net liabilities?
3. What is the amount of the addition to Micro's assets?

P11A-38. ENTRIES FOR, AND STATEMENT PRESENTATION OF, INTEREST-BEARING NOTES   Perez Company borrowed $60,000 from the First National Bank on April 1, 19X6, on a three-year, 13.7 percent interest-bearing note payable. Interest is paid annually. The principal and the final interest payment will be made on March 31, 19X9.

REQUIRED:

1. Record this transaction in Perez's journal.
2. Prepare adjusting entries for December 31, 19X6, and December 31, 19X7.
3. Prepare the entry to record the first interest payment on March 31, 19X7.
4. Prepare the entry to record the repayment of the note and the last year's interest on March 31, 19X9.
5. Indicate how the note and associated interest would be presented in Perez's December 31, 19X6, balance sheet.

P11A-39. INTEREST-BEARING NOTES WITH LUMP-SUM INTEREST PAYMENT   On April 1, 19X1, Teresa Felix borrowed $80,000 to expand her business. Teresa secured a 24-month interest-bearing note requiring payment of principal plus interest of $25,800 on March 31, 19X3.

REQUIRED:

1. Record the issuance of the note in Teresa's journal.
2. Prepare the adjusting entries for Decembr 31, 19X1, and December 31, 19X2.
3. Prepare the journal entry to record the 19X3 interest expense and repayment of the note on March 31, 19X3.

P11A-40. PREPARING A LIABILITY TABLE FOR AN INTEREST-BEARING NOTE   On August 1, 19X3, Distel Company borrowed $15,000 on a three-year, 12 percent interest-bearing note. The note requires annual interest payments (each equal to 12 percent of $15,000) and repayment of the principal plus the final year's interest at the end of the third year.

REQUIRED:

Prepare a note liability table (similar to a bond liability table) for this note, using the following column headings:

INTEREST PERIOD ENDING	INTEREST EXPENSE	CASH PAYMENT	CHANGE IN LIABILITY BALANCE	LIABILITY BALANCE

P11A-41. PREPARING A LIABILITY TABLE FOR A NON-INTEREST-BEARING NOTE On March 1, 19X2, Georgetown Distributors borrowed $20,000 on a four-year non-interest-bearing note. The note requires a single payment of all interest and principal in the total amount of $26,620 at the end of the fourth year.

REQUIRED:

Prepare a note liability table (similar to a bond liability table) for this note, using the following column headings:

INTEREST PERIOD ENDING	INTEREST EXPENSE	CASH PAYMENT	CHANGE IN LIABILITY BALANCE	LIABILITY BALANCE

P11A-42. BOND COMPUTATIONS AND ENTRIES On January 1, 19X1, Sisek Company issued a 10-year, $500,000, 11.75 percent coupon bond, interest payable at 5.875 percent semiannually. Cash in the amount of $492,800 was received when the bond was issued.

REQUIRED:

1. Journalize the issuance of the bond.
2. Journalize the first interest payment on June 30, 19X1.
3. Journalize the second interest payment on December 31, 19X1.
4. What is the carrying amount of this bond at the end of the fifth year (December 31, 19X5)?

P11A-43. PREPARING A PREMIUM BOND LIABILITY TABLE Edmonston-Alston Corporation issued five-year, 9.5 percent bonds with a total face amount of $700,000 on January 1, 19X2, for $726,000. The bonds pay interest on June 30 and December 31 of each year.

REQUIRED:

1. Prepare a bond liability table.
2. Prepare the journal entries to record the issuance of the bonds and the interest payments made on June 30, 19X2, and December 31, 19X2.

P11A-44. PREPARING A DISCOUNT BOND LIABILITY TABLE St. Cloud Manufacturing, Inc., issued five-year, 11.2 percent bonds with a total face amount of $500,000 on January 1, 19X4, for $464,000. The bonds pay interest on June 30 and December 31 of each year.

REQUIRED:

1. Prepare a bond liability table.
2. Prepare the journal entries to record the issuance of the bonds and the interest payments made on June 30, 19X4, and December 31, 19X4.

P11A-45. PREPARING AND USING A BOND LIABILITY TABLE Girves Development Corporation has agreed to construct a plant in a new industrial park. To finance the construction, the county government has sold $5,000,000 of 10-year, 8.75 percent bonds for $4,875,000. Girves will pay the interest and principal on the bonds. When the bonds are repaid, Girves will receive title to the plant. In the interim, Girves will pay property taxes as if it owned the plant. This financing arrangement is attractive to Girves, as state and local government bonds are exempt from federal income taxation and thus carry a lower interest rate. The bonds are attractive to investors, as both Girves and the county are issuers. The bonds pay interest semiannually.

REQUIRED:

1. Prepare the first four lines of a bond liability table for these bonds.
2. Should Girves record the plant as an asset after it is constructed? Why?
3. Should Girves record the liability for these bonds?

P11A-46. RECORDING CAPITAL AND OPERATING LEASES Trippler Company has decided to lease its new office building. The following information is available for the lease:

Cost of building if purchased	$725,000
Length of lease	15 years
Terms	$100,000 per year*
Economic life of building	16 years
Appropriate interest rate	12 percent

* The first payment is due at the end of the first year of the lease.

REQUIRED:

1. Determine whether this is a capital lease or an operating lease.

2. Regardless of your answer to the preceding question, assume that this is a capital lease and that the present value of the lease payments is $725,000. Record the liability and corresponding asset for this acquisition.

3. Record the interest expense on the capital lease at the end of the first year. Also assume no residual value and a 15-year lease for the building. Record the first year's straight-line depreciation of the cost of the leased asset.

P11A-47. LEVERAGE Cook Corporation issued financial statements at December 31, 19X8, that include the following information:

Balance sheet at December 31, 19X8:	
Assets	$8,000,000
Liabilities	1,200,000
Stockholders' equity (300,000 shares)	6,800,000

Income statement for 19X8:	
Income from operations	$1,200,000
Less: Interest expense	100,000
Income before taxes	$1,100,000
Less: Income taxes expense (.30).............	330,000
Net income	$ 770,000

The levels of assets, liabilities, stockholders' equity, and operating income have been stable in recent years; however, Cook Corporation is planning a $1,800,000 expansion program that will increase income from operations by $500,000 to $1,700,000. Cook is planning to sell 12.5 percent bonds at par to finance the expansion.

REQUIRED:

1. What earnings per share does Cook report before the expansion?

2. What earnings per share will Cook report if the proposed expansion is undertaken? Would this use of leverage be advantageous to Cook's stockholders? Explain.

3. Suppose income from operations will increase by only $200,000. Would this use of leverage be advantageous to Cook's stockholders? Explain.

4. Suppose that income from operations will increase by $500,000 and that Cook could also raise the required $1,800,000 by issuing an additional 100,000 shares of capital stock. Which means of financing would stockholders prefer? Explain.

ANALYTICAL OPPORTUNITIES

A11A-48. BOND INFORMATION IN *THE WALL STREET JOURNAL* *The Wall Street Journal,* as currently published, is divided into three sections—a news section, a "Marketplace" section, and a "Money and Investing" section. The "Money and Investing" section contains a large amount of information concerning bonds.

REQUIRED:

1. Locate a recent copy of *The Wall Street Journal.* Prepare a list of the tables it contains that present information about bonds (or *debentures,* as unsecured bonds are called). For each table, write a sentence describing the bonds to which it pertains and information presented.

2. Write a brief paragraph that describes differences between the information presented about corporate bonds in corporate financial statements and the information presented about those bonds in *The Wall Street Journal.*

A11A-49. BOND COVENANTS AND FINANCIAL REPORTING STANDARDS Bondholders receive bond certificates, one for each bond, that describe the payments promised by the issuer of the bonds. In addition, the issuing corporation frequently enters a supplementary agreement, called a *bond indenture,* with a trustee who represents the bondholders. The provisions or covenants of the indenture may place restrictions on the issuer for the benefit of the bondholders. For example, an indenture may require that the issuer's ratio of total liabilities to total stockholders' equity never rise above a specified level or that periodic payments be made to the trustee who administers a "sinking fund" to provide for the retirement of bonds.

Consider Roswell Manufacturing's bond indenture, which requires Roswell's ratio of total liabilities to total stockholders' equity never to exceed 2:1. If Roswell violates this requirement, the bond indenture specifies very costly penalties, and if the violation continues, the entire bond issue must be retired at a disadvantageous price and refinanced. In recent years, Roswell's ratio has averaged about 1.5:1 ($15 million in total liabilities and $10 million in total stockholders' equity). However, Roswell has an opportunity to purchase one of its major competitors, Ashland Products. The acquisition will require $4.5 million in additional capital, but will double Roswell's net income. Roswell does not believe that a stock issue is feasible in the current environment. The Financial Accounting Standards Board has recently issued an exposure draft for a new standard concerning accounting for employee pension and retirement benefits, which is strongly supported by the Securities and Exchange Commission. Implementation of the new standard will add about $2 million to Roswell's long-term liabilities. Roswell's CEO, Martha Cooper, has written a strong letter of objection to the FASB. The FASB received similar letters from over 300 companies.

REQUIRED:

1. Write a paragraph presenting an analysis of the impact of the proposed standard on Roswell Manufacturing.

2. If you were a member of the FASB and met Martha Cooper at a professional meeting, how would you respond to her objection?

A11A-50. EVALUATING USE OF LEVERAGE Gearing Manufacturing, Inc., is planning a $1,000,000 expansion of its production facilities. The expansion could be financed by the issuance of $1,250,000 in 12 percent bonds or by the issuance of $1,250,000 in capital stock, which would raise the number of shares outstanding from 50,000 to 75,000. Gearing pays income taxes at a rate of 30 percent.

REQUIRED:

1. Suppose that income from operations is expected to be $550,000 per year for the duration of the proposed bond issue. Should Gearing finance with bonds or stock? Explain your answer.

2. Suppose that income from operations is expected to be $350,000 per year for the duration of the proposed bond issue. Should Gearing finance with bonds or stock? Explain your answer.

3. Suppose that income from operations varies from year to year but is expected to be above $450,000, 40 percent of the time and below $450,000, 60 percent of the time. Should Gearing finance with bonds or stock? Explain your answer.

4. As an investor, how would you use accounting information to evaluate the risk of excessive use of leverage? What additional information would be useful? Explain.

Careful study of this
chapter will enable
you to:

1. Explain how interest
on long-term liabili-
ties is allocated
under the effective
interest amortiza-
tion method.

2. Account for effec-
tive interest on
long-term notes
payable.

3. Record the issu-
ance of bonds at
par, at a discount,
and at a premium.

4. Determine interest
expense for bonds,
using the effective
interest amortiza-
tion method.

5. Account for the re-
tirement of bonds,
both before and at
maturity.

6. Determine the
after-tax cost of fi-
nancing with debt,
and explain finan-
cial leverage.

7. Contrast the
accounting for
operating and
capital leases.

Appendix 11B–1

8. Account for bonds
sold during an
accounting period
or during an inter-
est period.

Appendix 11B–2

9. Explain how inter-
est on long-term li-
abilities is allocated
under the straight-
line interest amorti-
zation method.

11B

LONG-TERM LIABILITIES: EFFECTIVE INTEREST PROCEDURES

This chapter continues the discussion of long-term liabilities begun in Chapter 10, which described contingent liabilities and deferred tax liabilities. Long-term liabilities also include long-term notes and bonds payable and obligations associated with long-term capital leases.[1] Thus the long-term liabilities section of a typical balance sheet might appear as follows:

Long-term liabilities:	
Long-term notes payable	$ 12,500
Bonds payable	210,000
Capital lease liability	57,200
Pension liability	22,100
Estimated warranty liability	29,000
Deferred tax liability	77,540
Other long-term liabilities	8,200
Total long-term liabilities	$416,540

The cash flows or other economic sacrifices required to satisfy deferred tax liabilities and the various contingent liabilities, such as the pension liability, usually must be estimated. In contrast, long-term notes, long-term bonds, and leases clearly specify the amount and timing of the future cash flows required to satisfy the related liability. These long-term liabilities also give rise to interest expense.

When a liability extends over several interest periods, the amount of interest associated with each interest period must be determined by a procedure called

[1] As noted in Chapter 10, long-term liabilities that will be paid within the longer of the next year or the next operating cycle are not included in the long-term liability section of the balance sheet. Rather, they are reported in the current liability section. In the interest of simplifying our discussion of long-term liabilities, we will disregard calculations and entries for this reclassification throughout this chapter.

interest amortization. **Interest amortization** is the assignment of interest on a liability (or asset) to the interest periods that make up the term of the liability (or asset).[2] There are two methods of interest amortization. One method, *effective interest amortization,* is based on the compound interest calculations presented in Section B of Chapter 10. The other method, *straight-line interest amortization,* represents a simple approximation to effective interest amortization. Although effective interest amortization is correct technically, straight-line interest amortization may be used if it produces approximately the same numerical results. Frequently, the two methods do, in fact, produce very similar results.

In this book, effective interest amortization and straight-line interest amortization are discussed in separate chapters. Chapter 11A, the preceding chapter, explains the measurement and reporting of long-term liabilities using straight-line amortization. In this chapter, we discuss the measurement and reporting of long-term liabilities using effective interest amortization. In other words, both chapters cover essentially the same material, but each uses a different interest amortization method. Most students will study either Chapter 11A or 11B, although some instructors will assign both. A discussion of straight-line interest amortization procedures applied to bonds is presented in Appendix 11B–2 for those who desire a brief comparison of straight-line and effective interest methods.

This chapter explains the application of effective interest procedures to long-term notes and bonds. In addition, the long-term liabilities arising from capital leases, which are normally accounted for using effective interest procedures, are discussed.

EFFECTIVE INTEREST AMORTIZATION AND INTEREST EXPENSE

Recall that interest on a liability equals the excess of the amount paid to the lender over the amount borrowed. The accounting system must therefore allocate this interest, sometimes called *total interest,* among the various accounting periods during which the liability exists.

The apportioning of total interest among accounting periods requires a two-stage allocation procedure. The first allocation, interest amortization, assigns total interest to the interest periods that make up the term of the liability. **Effective interest amortization** assigns interest to each interest period over the term of the liability in accordance with the principles of compound interest. A second allocation is frequently necessary for the determination of interest expense, in accordance with the matching concept. This allocation divides the interest assigned to a particular interest period proportionally between two accounting periods, each of which is partly overlapped by the interest period. If a six-month interest period to which $1,200 has been amortized overlaps the last four months of one annual accounting period and the first two months of the next accounting period, then $800 [(4/6)($1,200)] is allocated to interest expense in

[2] The same interest amortization procedures used by borrowers to account for liabilities are also used by lenders to account for the corresponding assets.

the first accounting period and $400 [(2/6)($1,200)] is allocated to interest expense in the second accounting period. Of course, if the interest period and the accounting period coincide, then the second-stage allocation is unnecessary. For example, if a note's interest period and the firm's accounting period are both one year and if the note is issued at the beginning of an accounting period, then interest on the note does not require a second-stage allocation because the interest expense is the same as the interest assigned to the interest period.

The second-stage allocation, the matching of periodic interest with accounting periods for expense determination, apportions dollars among periods on the basis of time. In contrast, the first-stage allocation of interest, the effective interest amortization of total interest among interest periods, apportions dollars among periods on the basis of compound interest principles, to which we now turn.

Effective interest amortization employs the time-value-of-money (compound interest) procedures that are discussed in Section B of Chapter 10. Interest on a liability is calculated at the end of each interest period and is added to the balance of the liability. The amount of interest equals the product of the interest rate and the balance of the liability at the beginning of the interest period. For example, suppose that a note with an annual interest period incurs interest at a rate of 15 percent per year. If the note was issued on January 1, 19X8, for $10,000, then the interest expense for 19X8 is $1,500 [($10,000)(.15)], which is also the effective interest amortization for 19X8. Thus interest expense for 19X8 is recorded by the following entry:

Interest expense	1,500	
Interest payable		1,500

Assuming that no repayments or additional borrowings are made during 19X8, the December 31, 19X8, balance of the liability would be $11,500 [$10,000 + $1,500]. If no repayments or additional borrowings are made during the following year, 19X9, then the interest expense for 19X9 would be $1,725 [($11,500)(.15)], which is also the effective interest amortization for 19X9. The December 31, 19X9, balance of the liability would be $13,225 [$11,500 + $1,725]. In other words, the effective interest amortization on a liability for any interest period is simply the product of the interest rate and the beginning-of-the-period liability balance, which (according to compound interest principles) includes both the balance of the liability account and the balance of the related interest payable account.

All liabilities, whether long-term or short-term, are originally entered in the accounting records at their present value. In other words, the initial or beginning balance equals the amount of cash (or the fair value of goods or services) received from a creditor. When the value of assets received is difficult to determine, the amount of a liability is measured by the estimated present value of the cash (or other asset) outflow that will be made to satisfy the liability. However, the present value of assets given or repaid establishes the initial amount of a liability only when the value received is not readily determinable.

Although the initial amount (beginning balance) of most liabilities is usually measured at the amount received rather than by the amount repaid, the amounts received and paid are related through time-value-of-money calculations. The initial amount of an interest-bearing liability must equal the present value of the amount or amounts to be repaid at an appropriate rate of interest. After incurrence, a long-term liability is carried on the balance sheet at an amount equal to the present value of the remaining outflows necessary to satisfy the liability. The determination of these present value balances and the amounts of interest expense are described below in separate sections on notes, bonds, and leases.

LONG-TERM NOTES PAYABLE

LONG-TERM NOTES PAY-ABLE: Notes payable with terms that extend beyond the longer of one year or one operating cycle.

Long-term notes payable differ from short-term notes payable in that they require payments in one or more periods beyond the longer of one year or one operating cycle. Firms usually give long-term notes payable to financial institutions, such as banks and insurance companies, for periods of five years or less in exchange for cash. In some cases, long-term notes are secured by property, plant, or equipment specified in an agreement called a *mortgage.* If the borrower fails to pay the note, the lender may seize the property in accordance with the provisions of the mortgage and various state laws. Although the mortgage and the note are usually separate documents, the liability arising from the note is frequently called a *mortgage payable* to indicate that the note is secured by a mortgage. As with short-term notes, there are two kinds of long-term notes: interest-bearing notes and non-interest-bearing notes. Both types are described in the sections below.

LONG-TERM INTEREST-BEARING NOTES

Some long-term interest-bearing notes require annual interest payments, with the final interest payment and the principal to be repaid at maturity. Other notes provide for repayment of the principal and the entire amount of interest in one lump sum at maturity. The measurement and reporting of both types of notes are taken up in turn in the discussions that follow.

Annual Interest Payments and Single Principal Repayment

To illustrate the accounting for this type of note, let us look at the case of the Dyer Corporation. Assume that on September 1, 19X2, Dyer borrows $12,000 on a three-year, 14 percent note. The note requires annual interest payments (each equal to 14 percent of $12,000) and repayment of the principal plus the final year's interest at the end of the third year. The following entry would be made to record the issuance of the note:

Issuance of note, 9/1/X2

Cash	12,000	
Notes payable		12,000

Dyer's note represents a liability equal to the amount borrowed (the principal) plus unpaid compound interest to date. Exhibit 11B–1 shows the changes in this liability over its three-year term. In each annual interest period, the liability increases by the amount of interest expense for the interest period and decreases by the amount of cash paid at the end of the interest period. Since the exact

EXHIBIT 11B–1   NOTE LIABILITY TABLE

DYER CORPORATION

ANNUAL INTEREST PERIOD ENDED	INTEREST EXPENSE* (DEBIT)	CASH PAYMENT (CREDIT)	CHANGE IN LIABILITY BALANCE†	LIABILITY BALANCE‡
At issue				$12,000
8/31/X3	$1,680	$ 1,680	–0–	12,000
8/31/X4	1,680	1,680	–0–	12,000
8/31/X5	1,680	13,680	–12,000	–0–

* Interest expense = (Beginning liability balance)(Interest rate) = ($12,000)(.14) = $1,680 per year.
† Change in liability balance = Interest expense − Cash payment.
‡ Liability balance = Beginning liability balance + Change in liability balance.

amount of interest expense is paid in cash at the end of each interest period, the balance of the liability returns to $12,000 at the end of each period. The amount of interest expense shown in Exhibit 11B-1 ($1,680 in each year) represents the effective interest amortization of interest for the note. Notice that the liability balance is reduced to zero by the final payment of $13,680, which includes the final interest payment ($1,680) as well as the repayment of principal ($12,000).

Although the initial liability equals the amount borrowed (the principal), the amount of the initial liability is also a present value that can be calculated from the amounts to be repaid, by using a time-value-of-money calculation of the type demonstrated in Section B of Chapter 10. The amounts to be repaid by the Dyer Corporation are shown in a cash flow diagram in Exhibit 11B-2. The present value of the three cash payments required by the note can be calculated by selecting the three multiples from Exhibit 10-18 (Present Value of $1, pages 466-467) that correspond to periods 1, 2, and 3, respectively, at an interest

EXHIBIT 11B–2   PRESENT VALUE OF DYER'S NOTE

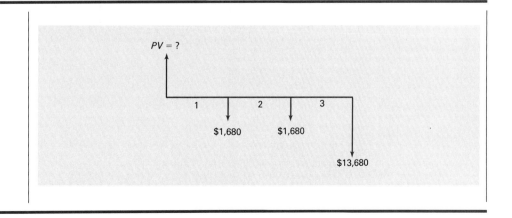

rate of 14 percent. Using these multiples, the present value is calculated as follows:

$$
\begin{aligned}
(\$1,680)(.8772) &= \$ \ 1,473.70 \\
(\$1,680)(.7695) &= \quad 1,292.76 \\
(\$13,680)(.6750) &= \quad 9,234.00 \\
\text{Present value} &= \$12,000.46
\end{aligned}
$$

The slight discrepancy between this computed present value and the correct, stated present value of $12,000 is due to rounding errors present in the multiples in Exhibit 10–18.

Present value calculations can also be used to measure the liability balance at the end of every interest period. For example, at August 31, 19X3, the $12,000 present value of Dyer Corporation's note represents the combined present values of the two payments remaining at that time ($1,680 on August 31, 19X4, and $13,680 on August 31, 19X5), calculated as follows:

$$
\begin{aligned}
(\$1,680)(.8772) &= \$ \ 1,473.70 \\
(\$13,680)(.7695) &= \quad 10,526.76 \\
\text{Present value} &= \$12,000.46
\end{aligned}
$$

Again, the slight discrepancy between this result and the correct present value of $12,000 could be avoided by using more precise present value multiples.

In summary, both the initial liability balance and the liability balance at the end of every interest period can be calculated in two ways: The liability balance can be calculated as the present value of the remaining future payments required by the liability, as demonstrated above. Or the liability balance can be calculated by applying compound interest to cash receipts and payments, as shown in Exhibit 11B–1. Both procedures produce the same liability balance at issue and at the end of each interest period.

Since Dyer Corporation's note was issued on September 1, eight months into the annual accounting period, a second-stage allocation of interest is required to match interest expense with the appropriate accounting periods. Interest expense for the last four months of 19X2 is $560 [(4/12)($1,680)], and interest expense for the first eight months of 19X3 is $1,120 [(8/12)($1,680)]. The following entries record the recognition of interest expense and the payment of interest during the first two years and four months:

Adjusting entries to record interest, 12/31/X2, 12/31/X3, and 12/31/X4

Interest expense [($12,000)(.14)(4/12)]   560
   Interest payable   560

Interest payments, 8/31/X3 and 8/31/X4

Interest expense [($12,000)(.14)(8/12)]   1,120
Interest payable (see adjusting entry)   560
   Cash   1,680

The interest amortization and the matching of interest to accounting periods are exactly the same for all three years of the note. The result is that the same adjusting entry is made on December 31, 19X2, December 31, 19X3, and December 31, 19X4. All three adjusting entries recognize interest expense of $560. In addition, all three entries to record the annual interest payments remove interest payable of $560 and record an interest payment of $1,680. The final interest payment, however, is accompanied by a $12,000 principal payment, as shown in the following entry:

Payment at maturity, 8/31/X5

Interest expense [($12,000)(.14)(8/12)].....................	1,120	
Interest payable (19X4 adjusting entry).................	560	
Notes payable.....................................	12,000	
Cash...		13,680

Although Dyer's note involves multiple payments extending over three years, the entries to record the note and its repayment are very similar to the entries made for short-term interest-bearing notes, as described in Chapters 4, 8, and 10. We now turn to the entries required to record a long-term note that requires a single payment of interest and principal at maturity.

Single Payment of Interest and Principal

Assume that on January 1, 19X6, the Cromer Corporation borrows $12,000 on a three-year, 14 percent interest-bearing note. The principal and interest compounded annually are payable in a single lump-sum payment on December 31, 19X8. The following entry would be made to record the issuance of the note:

Issuance of note, 1/1/X6

Cash...	12,000	
Notes payable.....................................		12,000

At issuance, the note represents a liability equal to the amount borrowed, which also equals the present value of the single lump-sum payment required by the note. Exhibit 11B–3 shows the changes in the liability represented by Cromer Corporation's note over its three-year term. The liability increases in each interest period by the amount of interest expense for the year. (Interest expense equals the beginning-of-period liability times the interest rate.) Accordingly, the liability rises to $17,778.53 immediately before the payment on December 31, 19X8, that reduces the liability to zero.

As before, each liability balance in Exhibit 11B–3 can be calculated as the present value of the remaining payment. The initial balance of $12,000 is the present value of the single payment on December 31, 19X8, which is calculated by using a multiple from the table in Exhibit 10–18 (Present Value of $1). The

EXHIBIT 11B–3   NOTE LIABILITY TABLE

CROMER CORPORATION

ANNUAL INTEREST PERIOD ENDED	INTEREST EXPENSE* (DEBIT)	CASH PAYMENT (CREDIT)	CHANGE IN LIABILITY BALANCE†	LIABILITY BALANCE‡
At issue				$12,000.00
12/31/X6	$1,680.00	–0–	+1,680.00	13,680.00
12/31/X7	1,915.20	–0–	+1,915.20	15,595.20
12/31/X8	2,183.33	$17,778.53	–15,595.20	–0–

* Interest expense = (Beginning liability balance)(Interest rate)
    $1,680.00 = ($12,000.00)(.14)
    $1,915.20 = ($13,680.00)(.14)
† Change in liability balance = Interest expense – Cash payment.
‡ Liability balance = Beginning liability balance + Change in liability balance.

multiple is for an interest rate of 14 percent and three periods. The present value is determined in the following manner:

$$PV = (\$17,778.53)(.6750)$$
$$= \$12,000.51$$

Again, the slight difference between this computed present value and the true present value of $12,000 is due to the rounded-off multiple taken from Exhibit 10–18.

The present value of subsequent liability balances can be obtained in a similar way. For example, on December 31, 19X6, the liability balance of $13,680.00 is the present value of the payment to be made on December 31, 19X8, calculated using the 14 percent, two-period multiple from Exhibit 10–18 in the following manner:

$$PV = (\$17,778.53)(.7695)$$
$$= \$13,680.58$$

Again, the slight divergence of this computation from the true present value of $13,680.00 is due to the rounded-off multiple taken from the present value table in Exhibit 10–18.

The liability associated with Cromer's note is reflected in the balances of two accounts. The first account is notes payable, which maintains a constant balance equal to the principal amount of the note ($12,000). The second account is interest payable, which rises by the amount of interest expense for each year. The following entries record interest expense and payments over the term of the note and the repayment of the note at maturity.

Adjusting entry to record interest, 12/31/X6

Interest expense [($12,000)(.14)].....................	1,680.00	
Interest payable...............................		1,680.00

Adjusting entry to record interest, 12/31/X7

Interest expense [($13,680)(.14)]....................	1,915.20	
Interest payable...............................		1,915.20

Adjusting entry to record interest, 12/31/X8

Interest expense [($15,595.20)(.14)]	2,183.33	
Interest payable...............................		2,183.33

Payment at maturity, 12/31/X8

Interest payable [($1,680 + $1,915.20 + $2,183.33)]	5,778.53	
Notes payable.................................	12,000.00	
Cash...		17,778.53

When notes of this type are issued any time other than at the beginning of an accounting period, a second-stage allocation of periodic interest is required in order to match interest expense with the appropriate accounting period.[3] Now let us turn to the accounting procedures for non-interest-bearing notes.

LONG-TERM NON-INTEREST-BEARING NOTES

Interest accrues on both interest-bearing and non-interest-bearing notes. However, as we noted in Chapter 10, non-interest-bearing notes are distinctive in that the note document does not state an explicit interest rate. Instead, such notes merely specify the single amount to be paid by the borrower at maturity, without reference to the amount of interest or principal. Total interest on non-interest-bearing notes must be calculated as the excess of the total amount repaid by the borrower at maturity over the amount borrowed (the principal). When a non-interest-bearing note extends over several periods, the total interest must then be allocated among the periods. In order to calculate the effective interest amortization of the total interest, we must first determine the interest rate implied by the non-interest-bearing note.

Let us illustrate this determination and the related accounting procedures: Assume that on January 1, 19X4, the Kernford Company issued a two-year, single-payment, non-interest-bearing note with a maturity amount of $125,440 to the Second State Bank in exchange for $100,000 in cash. The note matures on December 31, 19X5. In other words, Kernford borrowed $100,000, which must be repaid at the end of two years by making a single payment of $125,440.

---

[3] For example, if this $12,000 note had been issued on May 1, 19X6, the annual interest expense would be recorded as follows at the end of each accounting period:

19X6: (8/12)($1,680) = $1,120.00
19X7: (4/12)($1,680) + (8/12)($1,915.20) = $1,836.80
19X8: (4/12)($1,915.20) + (8/12)($2,183.33) = $2,093.95
19X9: (4/12)($2,183.33) = $727.78

EXHIBIT 11B-4   NOTE LIABILITY TABLE

		KERNFORD COMPANY		
ANNUAL INTEREST PERIOD ENDED	INTEREST EXPENSE* (DEBIT)	CASH PAYMENT (CREDIT)	CHANGE IN LIABILITY BALANCE†	LIABILITY BALANCE‡
At issue				$100,000
12/31/X4	$12,000	–0–	+ 12,000	112,000
12/31/X5	13,440	$125,440	– 112,000	–0–

* Interest expense = (Beginning liability balance)(Interest rate)
$12,000 = ($100,000)(.12)
$13,440 = ($112,000)(.12)
† Change in liability balance = Interest expense – Cash payment.
‡ Liability balance = Beginning liability balance + Change in liability balance.

Since the initial liability of $100,000 is the present value of the single future payment ($125,440), the two amounts are related by the following formula:

$$PV = (f)(M_2)$$
$$\$100,000 = (\$125,440)(M_2)$$

where M_2 is the multiple in the second row ($n = 2$) of the table in Exhibit 10–18 (Present Value of $1). M_2 can also be determined by dividing both sides of this equation by $125,440. The result is .7972, the same as the multiple in the 12 percent column and second row of the table in Exhibit 10–18. We can conclude that the non-interest-bearing note implies an interest rate of 12 percent and, on that basis, calculate the interest expense and liability balances shown in Exhibit 11B–4. The fact that the compound interest calculations underlying Exhibit 11B–4 result in a final liability balance of zero on December 31, 19X5, proves that 12 percent is indeed the correct implied interest rate.

The maturity amount of a non-interest-bearing note — whether short-term (see Chapter 10) or long-term — is usually recorded in a separate liability account. Although the amount of Kernford's liability at issuance is only $100,000, the maturity amount of $125,440 is recorded in a notes payable account. The excess of the maturity amount of a note over the amount borrowed (the principal) is the discount on the note. The discount on Kernford's note is $25,440, the excess of its $125,440 maturity amount over the $100,000 principal amount. The discount is recorded in a contra-liability account, called *discount on notes payable,* which reduces the maturity amount of the note to the amount of the liability:

Issuance of note, 1/1/X4

Discount on notes payable.............................	25,440	
Cash	100,000	
Notes payable		125,440

If Kernford were to prepare a balance sheet at January 1, 19X4 (the date of issue), it would report the note as follows:

Notes payable	$125,440	
Less: Discount on notes payable	25,440	$100,000

In other words, at issuance the note is reported at its present value, which is the amount of cash borrowed. The unamortized discount, which is the amount of the discount not yet added to interest expense, reduces the maturity amount of the note to the amount of the liability.

Since the borrower makes no payments before maturity, the carrying amount of the liability should rise by the amount of the interest amortization at the end of each year. The **carrying amount** (or **book value**) is the recorded amount of a liability or asset after subtraction of contra accounts or addition of adjunct accounts. (Contra accounts accumulate reductions to another account, whereas adjunct accounts accumulate additions. Long-term non-interest-bearing notes give rise to contra accounts, but not to adjunct accounts.) The increase in the carrying amount at the end of each year is recorded by reducing the discount on the note payable, as shown in the following adjusting entries:

CARRYING AMOUNT (BOOK VALUE): The recorded amount of a liability or asset after subtraction of contra accounts or addition of adjunct accounts.

Adjusting entry to record interest, 12/31/X4

Interest expense	12,000	
Discount on notes payable.........................		12,000

Adjusting entry to record interest, 12/31/X5

Interest expense	13,440	
Discount on notes payable.........................		13,440

At December 31, 19X4 (one year after issuance of the note), Kernford's balance sheet reports the note as follows:

Notes payable	$125,440	
Less: Discount on notes payable	13,440	$112,000

From the time of issuance until December 31, 19X4, the amount of the unamortized discount declined by $12,000, and the carrying amount of the liability increased to reflect the accrued interest for 19X4. After the entry for interest and amortization of discount is made at December 31, 19X5, the entire discount has been amortized, and the carrying amount of the note has risen to equal its maturity amount of $125,440, which includes the amount borrowed plus interest accrued for 19X4 and 19X5. On December 31, 19X5, $125,440 in cash is paid to the Second State Bank, and Kernford makes the following entry:

Payment at maturity, 12/31/X5

Notes payable.......................................	125,440	
Cash		125,440

If a non-interest-bearing note is issued at a time other than the beginning of an accounting period, the interest expense is allocated among the periods as described earlier for an interest-bearing note with a single payment of interest and principal.

Occasionally, a firm finds that it is unable to make the interest or principal payments required by its long-term liabilities. If there is reason to expect that the firm will eventually be able to secure enough cash to make part of or all the required payments, creditors may permit a restructuring of the cash payment schedule, as shown in the analysis that follows. The amount at which the liabilities are measured may or may not be changed by restructuring. In such cases, creditors must analyze the situation to ensure that they are better off than they would be if they forced bankruptcy.

ANALYSIS
LONG-TERM LIABILITY
RESTRUCTURING

Metal Manufacturing, a supplier of machined metal parts to the automobile industry, has incurred substantial losses during the past two years as a consequence of decreased automobile production by one of its customers. The firm has secured wage concessions from its employees and has also recently won a contract to supply parts for a large order of military vehicles. This order should return Metal Manufacturing to profitability within a year. However, because of concerns that Metal Manufacturing may not have sufficient operating cash, a provision of the military vehicle contract requires that Metal Manufacturing secure an agreement with its creditors to restructure the principal and interest payment schedule on its long-term liabilities.

As of January 1, 19X6, prior to restructuring, Metal Manufacturing's long-term liabilities required the following payments for each of the next three years:

PERIOD	LONG-TERM LIABILITY	AMOUNT	
19X6	Bond interest	$ 60,000	
	Capital lease	20,000	
	Interest-bearing note	125,000	$ 205,000
19X7	Bond interest	$ 60,000	
	Capital lease	20,000	
	Non-interest-bearing note	200,000	280,000
19X8	Bond interest	$ 60,000	
	Capital lease	20,000	
	Bond principal	500,000	580,000
	Total		$1,065,000

The following schedule indicates the cash generated by operations and by various nonoperating transactions that should be available for payments by Metal Manufacturing to long-term creditors over the next three years:

PERIOD	SOURCE OF CASH	AMOUNT	
19X6	Sale of investments	$ 40,000	
	Operations	(15,000)	$ 25,000
19X7	Sale of surplus machinery	$ 90,000	
	Operations	210,000	300,000
19X8	Issuance of capital stock	$100,000	
	Operations	730,000	830,000
	Total		$1,155,000

Because liability payments exceed cash available in 19X6, Metal Manufacturing proposes to its creditors that all 19X6 payments be deferred until 19X7, that 19X7 payments be made in 19X8, and that 19X8 payments be made as scheduled in 19X8. Believing that it is to their advantage to help the firm secure the military parts order, the creditors agree. Since all cash owed the creditors will eventually be paid, there is no need for Metal Manufacturing to alter the recorded amounts of liabilities.* However, interest expense will increase because of the deferred payments. (Computing the amount of the increase in interest expense is beyond the scope of this text.)

* Financial Accounting Standards Board, "Accounting by Debtors and Creditors for Troubled Debt Restructurings," *Statement of Financial Accounting Standards No. 15.*

ACCOUNTING FOR BONDS

BOND ISSUE: A collection of bonds, all of which are issued or sold by an entity at the same time.

When a firm requires capital for a period longer than the three- to five-year periods typical for credit extended by notes, the firm normally issues bonds. Unlike most notes, which are issued singly, bonds are issued in groups. In other words, a **bond issue** is a collection of bonds, all of which are issued or sold by an entity at the same time. Bond issues are used to raise large amounts of capital and to provide for repayment of that capital over long periods of time. They are an important source of long-term capital for businesses and have also been the primary source of long-term capital for federal, state, and local governments. Bonds are attractive to corporations as a source of capital because of their low cost relative to the cost of capital secured from stock.

BOND: A formal promise by the issuer (borrower) to make specified future payments to discharge a liability.

A **bond** is a formal promise by the issuer (borrower) to make specified future payments to discharge a liability. Like long-term notes, bonds may be either secured or unsecured; unsecured bonds are called *debenture bonds.* A bond is a document that specifies, among other things, the exact amount and time of the payments the issuer is required to make. In this way, a bond is similar to a non-interest-bearing note, but the form of payments required by a bond is subject to restrictions that are not imposed by a non-interest-bearing note. The payments required by a bond are of two kinds: interest payments and the face amount payment. Interest payments are made at regular intervals throughout the bond's life (semiannually, in many cases). Sometimes each interest payment is evidenced by a coupon that is detached from the bond by the bondholder (lender) and exchanged for cash. Such bonds are *coupon bonds,* and the required interest payments are *coupon payments.* The **face amount** (also called **par value**) is a payment required by a bond on the maturity date. Thus the face amount payment occurs on the same date as the last interest payment. The face amount of many bonds is $1,000, although bonds with face amounts of $5,000, $10,000, and $100,000 are also issued.

FACE AMOUNT (PAR VALUE): A payment required by a bond on the maturity date of the bond.

STATED RATE (COUPON RATE, NOMINAL RATE, FACE RATE, OR CONTRACT RATE): The ratio of one year's total interest payments to the face amount of the bond.

The amount of the recurring interest payment can be calculated from the face amount and the interest rate stated on the bond. This interest rate goes by various names, including *stated rate, coupon rate, nominal rate, face rate,* and *contract rate.* The **stated rate** is the ratio of one year's total interest payments to the face amount of the bond. To illustrate, consider a bond with a face amount of $1,000, a stated interest rate of 16 percent, and semiannual interest payments. The total amount of annual interest payments equals the stated interest rate times the face amount of the bond. The amount of each interest payment is obtained by dividing the annual total by the number of interest payments per year. For this $1,000 bond, the total amount of the annual interest payments is $160 [($1,000)(.16)], and the amount of each semiannual interest payment is $80 [$160/2].

The computations, journal entries, and financial statement presentation for bonds can be organized around four events in the life cycle of a bond:

1. Issuance
2. Recognition of interest expense and interest payment
3. Partial or complete redemption before maturity
4. Redemption at maturity

DISCOUNT AND PREMIUM ON BONDS PAYABLE

DISCOUNT ON BONDS PAYABLE: The excess of the total face amount of bonds over the amount received from their sale (proceeds).

PREMIUM ON BONDS PAYABLE: The excess of the amount received from the sale of bonds (proceeds) over their total face amount.

At issuance, bonds may sell at their face amount (at par), below the face amount (at a discount), or above the face amount (at a premium). When bonds sell at their face amount (at par), the amount received by the issuer (the proceeds or principal amount) equals the face amount, and there is neither discount nor premium. When bonds sell at a discount, the amount received by the issuer is less than the face amount, and that difference is called a *discount*. In other words, the **discount on bonds payable** is the excess of the total face amount of the bonds over the amount received from their sale. When bonds sell at a premium, the amount received by the issuer is greater than the face amount, and that difference is called a *premium*. In other words, the **premium on bonds payable** is the excess of the amount received from the sale of bonds over their total face amount.[4]

The issuance of bonds at a premium or a discount is frequently described by expressing the ratio of the proceeds to the face amount as a percentage. Hence, a $10,000 bond issued at a $100 premium is said to be issued at 101 percent of par [$10,100/$10,000], and a $10,000 bond issued at a $100 discount is said to be issued at 99 percent of par [$9,900/$10,000]. Although most firms try to design their bonds to sell at or near the face amount, changing credit market conditions and changing evaluations of firms by bondholders cause most bonds to sell at either a premium or a discount.

Over the life of a bond, the borrowing firm will pay its bondholders periodic interest payments plus the bond's face amount at maturity. These payments and the amount received by the firm when a bond is issued (the proceeds from the issue) determine the total interest expense over the life of the bond. Let us illustrate by examining what happens when the same five-year, $100,000, 12 percent bond with semiannual interest payments is issued at a $915 discount, at par, and at a $554 premium. The computation of total interest expense is shown in Exhibit 11B-5.

---

[4] The bonds considered in this chapter provide for interest payments that are constant in amount throughout the bond's life and are approximately equal to interest expense. Some bonds do not exhibit these attributes. For example, some corporations issue non-interest-bearing bonds, called *deep-discount* or *zero-coupon bonds,* for which interest or coupon payments are either very small or zero. Further, some corporations issue *variable-rate bonds,* for which interest payments vary with market conditions. Accounting for such bonds is discussed in intermediate accounting texts.

EXHIBIT 11B–5   **TOTAL BOND INTEREST EXPENSE**

	BOND ISSUED AT DISCOUNT	BOND ISSUED AT PAR	BOND ISSUED AT PREMIUM
Face amount payment at maturity	$100,000	$100,000	$100,000
Interest payments (10 at $6,000 each)	60,000	60,000	60,000
Total payments to bondholders	$160,000	$160,000	$160,000
Less: Proceeds at issue	99,085	100,000	100,554
Total interest expense over life of bond	$ 60,915	$ 60,000	$ 59,446

EFFECTIVE INTEREST RATE (YIELD RATE): The interest rate that, when used to compute the present value of the future cash payments specified by a bond, produces a present value equal to the amount borrowed.

For a bond issued at par (face amount), the total interest expense is equal to the sum of the cash interest payments. The interest expense will be greater than the cash interest payments for a bond issued at a discount. For the discount bond in Exhibit 11B–5, total interest expense ($60,915) exceeds interest payments ($60,000) by $915. The interest expense will be less than the cash interest payments for a bond issued at a premium. For the premium bond in Exhibit 11B–5, total interest expense ($59,446) is $554 less than interest payments ($60,000).

In order to calculate the effective interest amortization of the total interest owed, we need to know the interest rate implied by the bond. This rate is called the *effective interest rate* and is usually specified in the documents that describe the sale of the bond.[5] The **effective interest rate** (also known as the **yield rate**) is the interest rate that, when used to compute the present value of the future cash payments specified by a bond, produces a present value equal to the amount borrowed. The effective interest rate may be used in two ways: First, it may be used to compute the present value of the future cash payments specified by the bond at issue or at any subsequent time. Second, the effective interest rate may be used to compute the compound interest on the liability balance to determine interest expense in each interest period.

Let us illustrate both uses of the effective interest rate by referring to the bond issued at par in Exhibit 11B–5. Whenever bonds are sold at par, the effective interest rate equals the stated rate. The effective rate of the bond sold at par is thus 12 percent per year (6 percent per six-month interest period). In order to determine the present value of the future cash payments required by the bond, these payments can be represented as two present value problems—an annuity of 10 interest payments of $6,000 each (one at the end of each of 10 interest periods) and a single face amount payment at the end of the tenth interest period. The cash flow diagrams for these two problems and the related present value

[5] Although the effective interest rate is usually specified in the documents that describe the sale of bonds, it may be calculated from the amount borrowed and the amounts of interest and face amount payments required by the bond. The problem is to find the interest rate that makes the present value of interest and face amount payments equal to the amount borrowed. This problem can be solved by the use of tables of present value multiples and trial-and-error procedures. The effective interest rate can also be found by using the internal rate of return function in personal computer spreadsheet software. However, these solution techniques are beyond the scope of this introductory presentation.

EXHIBIT 11B–6   PRESENT VALUE OF BOND INTEREST AND FACE AMOUNT PAYMENTS

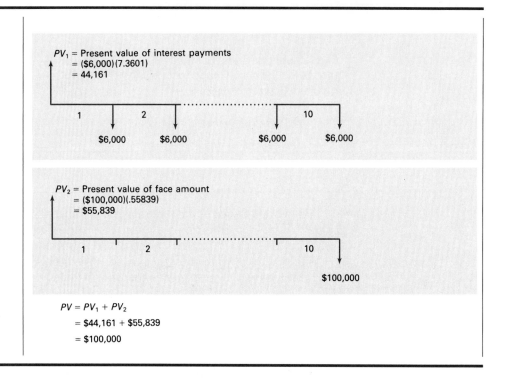

PV_1 = Present value of interest payments
  = ($6,000)(7.3601)
  = 44,161

PV_2 = Present value of face amount
  = ($100,000)(.55839)
  = $55,839

$PV = PV_1 + PV_2$
   = $44,161 + $55,839
   = $100,000

calculations are shown in Exhibit 11B–6. These calculations demonstrate that the present value of the interest and face amount payments, computed at the effective interest rate, equals the amount borrowed for the bond issued at par.

A similar demonstration can be made for bonds issued at a discount. For the discount bond in Exhibit 11B–5, the effective interest rate is 12.25 percent per year (6.125 percent per six-month interest period). The present value of interest and face amount payments at the effective interest rate equal the amount borrowed ($99,085). Notice that the effective interest rate for the discount bond is higher than the stated rate and results in a present value that is lower than the bond's $100,000 face amount. For the premium bond in Exhibit 11B–5, the effective rate is 11.85 percent per year (5.925 percent per six-month interest period). The present value of interest and face amount payments at this effective interest rate once again equal the amount borrowed ($100,554). Notice that the effective interest rate in the premium case is lower than the stated rate and results in a present value that is higher than the $100,000 face amount.

The effective interest rate is also used to compute compound interest on the amount borrowed, adjusted for subsequent repayments, in order to determine interest expense and liability balances. Exhibit 11B–7 summarizes these compound interest calculations for the $100,000 bond sold at par. In Exhibit 11B–7, observe that interest expense equals the cash payment in every period, with the result that the liability balance is $100,000 at the end of every interest period except the last. When bonds are sold at discounts or premiums, the related interest expense does not equal the recurring cash payment. (Exhibits will be

EXHIBIT 11B–7   LIABILITY ASSOCIATED WITH BONDS SOLD AT PAR

SEMIANNUAL PERIOD	INTEREST EXPENSE* (DEBIT)	CASH PAYMENT (CREDIT)	CHANGE IN LIABILITY BALANCE†	LIABILITY BALANCE‡
At issue				$100,000
1	$6,000	$ 6,000	–0–	100,000
2	6,000	6,000	–0–	100,000
3	6,000	6,000	–0–	100,000
4	6,000	6,000	–0–	100,000
5	6,000	6,000	–0–	100,000
6	6,000	6,000	–0–	100,000
7	6,000	6,000	–0–	100,000
8	6,000	6,000	–0–	100,000
9	6,000	6,000	–0–	100,000
10	6,000	106,000	– 100,000	–0–

* Interest expense = (Beginning liability balance)(Interest rate) = ($100,000)(.06) = $6,000.
† Change in liability balance = Interest expense − Cash payment.
‡ Liability balance = Beginning liability balance + Change in liability balance.

constructed for the discount and premium bonds, respectively, later in the chapter.)

To permit a simple but complete examination of the basics of bond accounting, in this chapter we assume the following:

1. Bonds are issued on the first day of the firm's fiscal year.

2. The first interest payment in each year is made halfway through the fiscal year.

3. The second interest payment in each year is made at the fiscal year-end.

4. Bonds are redeemed at a fiscal year-end.

We turn now to the accounting procedures for bonds issued under these assumptions. Appendix 11B–1 describes the computations and entries for bonds when these assumptions are relaxed.

ISSUANCE OF BONDS

Bonds are normally sold to individual investors through financial institutions known as *underwriters*. An underwriter negotiates with, or gives a bid to, the issuing entity for the right to sell a particular bond issue. In determining the price that is to be offered the issuer, underwriters examine the provisions of the bond issue, the credit standing of the issuing entity, and the current conditions in the credit markets. The underwriter's profit on a bond issue is generated either by offering a price that is slightly less than the expected market price of the issue (thereby producing a profit on resale) or simply by charging the issuer a fee. In either case, the issuer receives the proceeds from the underwriter. Both the underwriter and the issuing firm attempt to set an interest rate for bonds that will produce proceeds for the firm equal to the par value (face amount) of the bonds. When a bond is sold at par, equal debits and credits are made to cash and bonds payable. To illustrate, the following entry would be made for a $10,000,000 bond issue sold at par:

Cash	10,000,000	
Bonds payable.		10,000,000

However, as we have mentioned, most bonds sell at either a small premium or a small discount because (1) credit market conditions constantly change and (2) investors' perceptions of individual firms also change. When more than the face amount of a bond is received, the excess of proceeds over the face amount of the bond is recorded in an account called *premium on bonds payable.* For example, a $10,000,000 bond issue producing proceeds of $10,220,000 is recorded with the following entry:

Cash	10,220,000	
Bonds payable.		10,000,000
Premium on bonds payable		220,000

Conversely, a shortfall of proceeds below the face amount of the bond is recorded in a discount on bonds payable account. Thus if a $10,000,000 bond issue produces proceeds of $9,950,000, the following entry is made at issue:

Cash	9,950,000	
Discount on bonds payable.	50,000	
Bonds payable.		10,000,000

Discounts and premiums are considered to be attached to individual bonds payable accounts. Discounts are contra liabilities and premiums are adjunct liabilities, respectively, because a discount reduces the carrying amount of a bond and a premium increases its carrying amount. In other words, discounts and premiums are subtracted from or added to the face amount of a bond liability to produce the net liability of the bond. Bonds appear among the long-term liabilities in the balance sheet at their carrying amount, as follows:

Long-term liabilities:		
Bonds payable:		
12.25% bonds, due in 20X5	$10,000,000	
Plus: Premium on bonds payable	220,000	$10,220,000
11.85% bonds, due in 19X9	$10,000,000	
Less: Discount on bonds payable	50,000	9,950,000

The issuance of bonds is an important activity for both the borrowing firm and the underwriter. The firm must secure as much cash as possible from the bond issue, and the underwriter must earn its profit from the sale of bonds to investors. The following analysis examines some of the considerations made by bond underwriters when deciding whether to bid on a proposed new bond issue.

ANALYSIS
ISSUING BONDS

Gutzwiller, Inc., has approached your firm to underwrite a 10-year bond issue of $10,000,000. Gutzwiller plans to use the proceeds to finance the construction of an addition to its plant and to purchase and install machinery in the plant addition. The following financial statement data for Gutzwiller are available:

	19X4	19X5	19X6
Sales revenue	$109,000,000	$122,000,000	$136,000,000
Net income	9,103,000	10,930,000	12,570,000
Current assets	7,100,000	7,300,000	7,900,000
Total assets	94,000,000	101,000,000	107,000,000
Current liabilities	3,500,000	3,750,000	3,825,000
Long-term liabilities	22,000,000	22,000,000	22,500,000

The following are questions that you might consider in determining whether to underwrite Gutzwiller's bond issue:

1. *From what source are the bonds to be repaid?*

Bonds are repaid from operating profits retained by the firm. (Recall that short-term liabilities are normally repaid from the normal cash inflows associated with current assets.)

2. *Is Gutzwiller likely to produce sufficient profits to repay the prospective issue?*

Gutzwiller is clearly profitable. Sales are growing (at an average of 11.7 percent per year), with profits growing faster than sales (at an average of 17.5 percent per year). This suggests that Gutzwiller should be able to repay the bond issue from profits.

3. *Does Gutzwiller have sufficient working capital to meet its currently maturing obligations?*

Current assets exceed current liabilities by $4,075,000. This excess has grown by $475,000 since 19X4. Thus Gutzwiller should be able to meet its current obligations.

4. *Is the ratio of Gutzwiller's liabilities to the sum of liabilities and equity appropriate?*

Gutzwiller's liabilities are now 24.6 percent of total liabilities and equity [($3,825,000 + $22,500,000)/$107,000,000], down from 27.1 percent in 19X4. Even after a $10,000,000 increase in liabilities and assets, Gutzwiller's liabilities will be only 31.0 percent of its total liabilities and equity [($3,825,000 + $22,500,000 + $10,000,000)/$117,000,000], which is a reasonable proportion for a firm with profits that are growing.

5. *Should you underwrite Gutzwiller's bond issue?*

Gutzwiller's bonds should sell well and should therefore be potentially profitable for the underwriter.

THE BOND MARKET

After being issued, bonds are often traded among investors at prices that fluctuate from day to day and from minute to minute. Exhibit 11B–8 shows a typical listing of prices and other data for the outstanding bonds of several companies at the close of a particular trading day. This kind of information is published daily in various newspapers including *The Wall Street Journal*. Immediately following the abbreviated company name (ArizP is Arizona Power, Motrla is Motorola,

EXHIBIT 11B-8 BOND MARKET DATA

DATA FOR SELECTED BOND ISSUES
As Reported in *The Wall Street Journal*

BONDS	CUR YLD	VOL	CLOSE	NET CHG
ArizP 10⅝00	10.6	12	100½	−½
Motrla zr 09		16	31	+⅜
PierOn dc11½03	13.5	5	85	+½
Zenith 6¼11	cv	116	28¾	+½

Abbreviations: **CUR YLD** = current yield; **VOL** = volume; **CLOSE** = closing price; **NET CHG** = net change; cv = convertible; dc = deep discount; and zr = zero coupon.

PierOn is Pier One, etc.) is either the stated or coupon rate (for example, 10⅝ percent for ArizP) or the designation of the bonds as zero-coupon (zr) or deep-discount (dc); this is followed by the last two digits of the maturity year (for example, "00" for the ArizP bonds maturing in the year 2000). Prices for traded bonds are usually quoted as percentages of par, which are determined by dividing the current selling price by the par value and then multiplying the result by 100. For example, the price of 85 reported in the "close" column for Pier One's deep-discount bonds indicates that they were selling at 85 percent of their par value at the close of trading on the preceding business day; the "net change" column indicates a half-percentage-point rise in the price over the preceding price report. The "volume" column gives the total par value of bonds traded in thousands of dollars, and the "current yield" column gives the ratio of the annual interest payment to the closing price. Current yields are not reported for zero-coupon or convertible bonds.

If the issuer of bonds defaults, the lender may not receive interest payments and some or all of the principal. Several long-established firms—including Standard and Poors (a subsidiary of McGraw-Hill) and Moody's (a subsidiary of Dun and Bradstreet)—provide general evaluations or ratings of the creditworthiness of companies and the riskiness of their bonds and other financial instruments. Although the bond rating scale varies somewhat from rating firm to rating firm, most use combinations of the letters A, B, and C to indicate bond quality. For example, Standard and Poors' bond ratings from highest to lowest are AAA, AA, A, BBB, BB, B, CCC, CC, C, and D, where D is in default. Bonds with a BBB ("triple B") rating would be expected to promise a higher yield than otherwise equivalent bonds with a AAA ("triple A") rating to compensate investors for the additional risk. Bond ratings reflect confidential information made available by the rated companies to the bond rating firms.

The market for high-yield bonds with low ratings saw a significant bubble of activity during the 1980s. These high-yield, low-rating or *junk bonds* were used to finance a variety of high-risk ventures including acquisitions of one company by another. Junk bonds should be distinguished from so-called *fallen angels,* which are bonds whose yields rise to junk-bond levels as a result of declining bond prices reflecting the deteriorating fortunes of the issuing company.

Additional discussion of the institutional arrangements and technicalities surrounding corporate bonds occurs in corporate finance courses. We turn now to the accounting for interest expense and interest payments over the life of a bond.

BOND INTEREST EXPENSE AND INTEREST PAYMENTS

As has already been pointed out, the effective interest rate is used to compute compound interest on the amount borrowed, adjusted for subsequent repayments, in order to determine the interest expense and liability balances. The interest expense for a given interest period equals the effective interest rate times the liability balance at the beginning of the period. Interest expense increases the liability balance, and payments to the bondholders decrease the liability balance.

For bonds sold at par, the interest expense for each period is equal to the cash payment to bondholders. Assume, for example, that a firm sold at par a five-year, $100,000, 12 percent bond. Every six months, the following entry would be made:

Interest expense 6,000
    Cash 6,000

As a result, the liability balance at the end of each period (except the last) equals the par value, or face amount, of the bonds. However, when bonds are sold at a discount or a premium, the interest payment does not equal the accrued interest expense, and the liability balance changes from one period to the next. The following sections illustrate the calculations and accounting entries for bonds sold at a discount and at a premium, using as examples the discount and premium bonds described in Exhibit 11B–5 on page 521.

Bonds Sold at Discount

Assume that a firm issues a five-year, $100,000, 12 percent bond for $99,085, yielding an effective interest rate of 12.25 percent. The compound interest calculations leading to the interest expense and liability balances are summarized in Exhibit 11B–9. Note that the interest expense exceeds the $6,000 interest payment for each interest period. Since interest expense increases the liability and

EXHIBIT 11B–9   DISCOUNT BOND LIABILITY TABLE

SEMIANNUAL PERIOD	INTEREST EXPENSE* (DEBIT)	CASH PAYMENT† (CREDIT)	CHANGE IN LIABILITY BALANCE‡	LIABILITY BALANCE§
At issue				$99,085
1	$ 6,069	$ 6,000	+69	99,154
2	6,073	6,000	+73	99,227
3	6,078	6,000	+78	99,305
4	6,082	6,000	+82	99,387
5	6,087	6,000	+87	99,474
6	6,093	6,000	+93	99,567
7	6,098	6,000	+98	99,665
8	6,104	6,000	+104	99,769
9	6,111	6,000	+111	99,880
10	6,118	106,000	−99,882	(2)
Total	$60,913	$160,000		

* Interest expense = (Beginning liability balance)(.06125).
† Interest payment = ($100,000)(.06) = $6,000.
‡ Change in liability balance = Interest expense − Cash payment.
§ New liability balance = Beginning liability balance + Change in liability balance.

interest payment decreases the liability, this implies that the balance of a liability issued at a discount increases as it moves from one interest period to the next. For example, interest expense in the first period ($6,069) exceeds the cash payment at the end of that period by $69 [$6,069 − $6,000]. Consequently, the end-of-period liability balance of $99,154 exceeds the beginning-of-period liability balance of $99,085 by $69 [$99,154 − $99,085]. The increase in the liability balance over the term of the bond is just sufficient to offset the cash payments that pay off the bond (that is, except for rounding errors, it is just sufficient to produce a zero liability balance at the end of the tenth interest period).

The periodic increase in the liability balance or, equivalently, the excess of interest expense over the interest payment in each period is the *discount amortization*. The discount amortization, which is shown in a separate column in Exhibit 11B–9 (as the change in liability balance), is a component of the entry to record periodic interest expense. Recall that at issuance the face amount is recorded in a separate liability account and the discount is recorded in a related contra-liability account. The periodic increase in the liability balance is recorded by reducing the contra liability by the amount of the discount amortization. This reduction is recorded as part of the periodic entry to record interest. For example, the following entry is made at the end of the first interest period to record the interest expense, the interest payment, and the discount amortization for the first interest period:

Interest expense	6,069	
Discount on bonds payable		69
Cash		6,000

The same entry would be made at the end of each interest period, except that the discount amortization and interest expense amounts would change according to the amounts in Exhibit 11B–9.

Bonds Sold at Premium

Next, assume that the firm also issues a five-year, $100,000, 12 percent bond for $100,554, yielding an effective interest rate of 11.85 percent. The compound interest calculations leading to interest expense and liability balances are summarized in Exhibit 11B–10. Note that the interest expense is less than the $6,000 interest payment in each interest period. Since interest expense increases the liability and interest payment decreases the liability, this implies that the balance of a liability issued at a premium decreases as it moves from one interest period to the next. For example, the interest expense in the first period ($5,958) is less than the amount of the cash payment at the end of that period by $42 [$6,000 − $5,958]. Consequently, the end-of-period liability balance of $100,512 is less than the beginning-of-period liability balance ($100,554) by $42 [$100,554 − $100,512]. The decrease in the liability over the term of the bond is just sufficient to permit the cash payments to pay off the bond (that is, just sufficient to produce a zero liability at the end of the tenth interest period).

The decrease in the liability balance or, equivalently, the excess of the interest payment over interest expense in each period is known as *premium amortization*. The premium amortization, which is shown in a separate column in Exhibit 11B–10 (as the change in liability balance), is a component of the entry

EXHIBIT 11B–10   PREMIUM BOND LIABILITY TABLE

SEMIANNUAL PERIOD	INTEREST EXPENSE* (DEBIT)	CASH PAYMENT† (CREDIT)	CHANGE IN LIABILITY BALANCE‡	LIABILITY BALANCE§
At issue				$100,554
1	$ 5,958	$ 6,000	−42	100,512
2	5,955	6,000	−45	100,467
3	5,953	6,000	−47	100,420
4	5,950	6,000	−50	100,370
5	5,947	6,000	−53	100,317
6	5,944	6,000	−56	100,261
7	5,940	6,000	−60	100,201
8	5,937	6,000	−63	100,138
9	5,933	6,000	−67	100,071
10	5,929	106,000	−100,071	−0−
Total	$59,446	$160,000		

* Interest expense = (Beginning liability balance)(.05925).
† Interest payment = ($100,000)(.06) = $6,000.
‡ Change in liability balance = Interest expense − Cash payment.
§ New liability balance = Beginning liability balance + Change in liability balance.

to record periodic interest expense. Recall that at issuance, the bond's face amount is recorded in a separate liability account and the premium is recorded in an adjunct account. The periodic decrease in the liability balance is recorded by reducing the adjunct liability by the amount of the premium amortization. This reduction is recorded as part of the periodic entry to record interest. For example, the following entry is made at the end of the first interest period to record the interest expense, the interest payment, and the premium amortization for the first interest period:

Interest expense	5,958	
Premium on bonds payable	42	
Cash		6,000

The same entry would be made at the end of each interest period, except that the amount of premium amortization and interest expense would change according to the amounts in Exhibit 11B–10.

There are numerous complications in accounting for bonds. The interest expense and payment entries that are made when bonds are issued at times other than the beginning of an accounting period are illustrated in Appendix 11B–1. These entries use a tabular summary of the liability similar to those presented here. However, the amounts for interest expense and for premium and discount amortization must also be allocated between consecutive accounting periods to achieve a proper matching of interest expense. In Appendix 11B–2, we briefly illustrate how interest expense is determined when premiums and discounts are amortized by straight-line procedures instead of the effective interest procedures explained here. Straight-line procedures can be used only when the interest expense is not significantly different than it would be if determined by effective interest procedures.

We have so far discussed two of the stages in the life cycle of a bond—issuance, and interest payment and expense. In the next sections, we will discuss the third and fourth stages—the redemption of all or a part of a bond issue before maturity and the redemption of all of an issue at maturity.

EARLY RETIREMENT OF BONDS

CALLABLE BONDS:
Bonds that permit the issuer to repurchase or redeem the bonds at specified times by paying the bondholder a specified amount known as the *call price.*

Occasionally, interest rates will decline subsequent to a bond issue; or a firm may find that it has excess cash available. In such situations, the firm may find it advantageous to retire all or part of a bond issue before maturity. If the issue consists of callable bonds, the firm can require bondholders to present their bonds for redemption at a specified price. **Callable bonds** provide that the issuer may repurchase or redeem the bonds at specified times by paying the bondholder a specified amount known as the *call price.* If the bonds are not callable, the firm may purchase the bonds from investors in the bond market and then retire the bonds.

In either case, the face amount of the bonds retired and any unamortized premium or discount applicable to the retired bonds are removed from the borrowing firm's accounting records. If the call price or the cash paid for the bonds exceeds the carrying amount of the bonds, an extraordinary loss on bond retirement is recorded for the amount of the excess. If the call price or the cash paid for the bonds is less than the carrying amount, an extraordinary gain on bond retirement is recorded for the amount of the deficiency. Extraordinary gains and losses are presented in a separate section of the income statement, just above net income and after all the other components of net income have been presented.

Bond liability tables provide the data necessary to compute the carrying amount of a bond (face amount plus unamortized premium or face amount less unamortized discount), as well as the other data necessary to develop the journal entry for early retirement. Exhibit 11B–11 presents a portion of a bond liability table for a 10-year, $1,000,000, 13 percent bond issue that was sold at a discount. The effective interest rate for this bond is 13.25 percent. In this example, just after the twelfth semiannual interest payment, $200,000 (20 percent) of the $1,000,000 face amount of the issue is retired for a cash payment of $192,500. Using the data in the table, we first determine the unamortized discount on the entire bond issue at the retirement point. The unamortized discount for the entire bond issue is the face amount less the current carrying amount: $1,000,000 − $992,426 = $7,574. The next step is to compute the unamortized discount for the bonds retired: ($7,574)(.20) = $1,514.80. The journal entry to record retirement of the bonds is:

Bonds payable................................	200,000.00	
Extraordinary gain on bond retirement		5,985.20
Discount on bonds payable...................		1,514.80
Cash		192,500.00

In this case, there is an extraordinary gain. The amount of the gain is the excess of the carrying amount of the bonds retired [(.20)($992,426) = $198,485.20] over the cash paid ($192,500). After retirement of the $200,000 of bonds, there remains $800,000 of bonds with a carrying amount of $793,940.80, which is 80

EXHIBIT 11B-11   **PARTIAL BOND LIABILITY TABLE**

SEMIANNUAL PERIOD	INTEREST EXPENSE (DEBIT)	CASH PAYMENT (CREDIT)	CHANGE IN LIABILITY BALANCE	LIABILITY BALANCE
11	$65,658	$65,000	+658	$991,724
12	65,702	65,000	+702	992,426

percent of the carrying amount shown in Exhibit 11B-11 [($992,426)(.80) = $793,940.80]. Had the bonds been issued at a premium, similar computations would have been made, except that the premium for the retired bonds, rather than the discount, would have been computed. The journal entry would also have been similar, except that premium on bonds payable would have been debited as part of the retirement entry.

RETIREMENT OF BONDS AT MATURITY   Many bonds are not retired early but are held to maturity. At maturity the carrying amount of such bonds is the maturity or face amount. The final interest payment and interest expense entry amortizes the last portion of the unamortized premium or discount established when the bond was issued. The journal entry for retirement at maturity is made at the same time and is simply a debit to bonds payable and a credit to cash in the same amount. For example, a $500,000 bond issue would be retired at maturity with the following entry:

Bonds payable 500,000
    Cash   500,000

Between them, the entry to record the final interest payment and any amortization of premium or discount and the entry to retire the bonds remove from the balance sheet all traces of the retired bonds.[6]

---

[6] The foregoing paragraphs describe the accounting concepts and procedures for bonds used by issuers of bonds. Although the concepts and procedures used by investors in bonds are based on the same measurements and calculations, the reporting conventions are somewhat different. The most fundamental difference is that investors record bonds acquired as assets rather than liabilities and record the interest as revenue rather than expense. In addition, investors do not record premium or discount in a separate account; rather, premium or discount is combined with the face amount and recorded in a single investment account. If the bonds are readily marketable and the investor intends to sell them within the longer of one year or one operating cycle, then the acquisition is recorded as a current asset in a short-term investment account. Otherwise, the bonds should be recorded in a long-term investment account. Premium and discount are amortized for bonds held as long-term investments in much the same way as for bond liabilities; amortization of premium reduces interest revenue and amortization of discount increases interest revenue. In contrast, premium and discount are not amortized for bonds held as short-term investments, because to do so would not result in a material change in the amount of interest revenue. Rather, interest revenue on bonds held as short-term investments is recorded as the amount of cash received. Further, as noted in Chapter 8, bonds held as short-term investments are not subject to the lower-of-cost-or-market adjustments made to the reported amount for other short-term investments in marketable securities.

EXHIBIT 11B–12   EFFECTS OF FINANCING WITH BONDS

	19X1		19X2	
	CARMEL COMPANY	NOBLESVILLE, INC.	CARMEL COMPANY	NOBLESVILLE, INC.
Balance sheet:*				
Assets	$3,000,000	$3,000,000	$3,000,000	$3,000,000
Bonds payable	1,000,000	–0–	1,000,000	–0–
Stockholders' equity	2,000,000	3,000,000	2,000,000	3,000,000
Number of capital stock shares	100,000	150,000	100,000	150,000
Income statement:				
Income from operations	$ 600,000	$ 600,000	$ 300,000	$ 300,000
Interest expense (.15)	150,000	–0–	150,000	–0–
Income before taxes	$ 450,000	$ 600,000	$ 150,000	$ 300,000
Income taxes expense (.30)	135,000	180,000	45,000	90,000
Net income	$ 315,000	$ 420,000	$ 105,000	$ 210,000
Earnings per share	$3.15	$2.80	$1.05	$1.40

* Annual averages (assume that current liabilities are negligible).

PROS AND CONS OF FINANCING WITH BONDS

A significant advantage of financing with bonds rather than stock is the fact that the interest expense on bonds is deductible for income tax purposes. To illustrate the effect of interest deductibility, consider the 19X1 financial statement information for Carmel Company shown in the first column of Exhibit 11B–12. Carmel issued $1,000,000 of 15 percent bonds that result in interest expense of $150,000 per year; however, the net cash outflow for the bonds is significantly less than $150,000. Since the interest is deductible in the calculation of taxable income, taxable income is $150,000 less than it would have been without the bond issue. Income taxes, which are computed at a rate of 30 percent of taxable income, are therefore reduced by $45,000 [($150,000)(.30)], making the net cash outflow for the bonds only $105,000 ($150,000 − $45,000). In other words, the cost of financing with bonds (or any other form of liability with tax-deductible interest payments) is the interest net of income taxes, which can be determined by using the following formula:

$$\text{Interest net of income taxes} = (1 - \text{Tax rate})(\text{Interest})$$
$$= (1 - .30)(\$150,000)$$
$$= \$105,000$$

The formula provides an efficient way of computing interest net of income taxes.

    Another potential advantage of bonds is that they fix the amount of compensation to the lender. No matter how successful the firm is in using borrowed capital, its bondholders receive only the return specified in the bond agreement (interest and face amount). Thus, if the borrowed capital generates income in excess of the interest on the bonds, the stockholders of the borrowing firm benefit. The use of capital secured from creditors in the hope of producing more income than that needed to cover the interest on the related liability is called using **leverage** or **trading on equity.**

    Under the right conditions, using leverage has significant advantages; however, conditions also exist under which the use of leverage is disadvantageous.

LEVERAGE (TRADING ON EQUITY): A firm's use of capital secured from creditors in the hope of producing more income than that needed to cover the interest on the related liability, with the excess income accruing to the stockholders.

Exhibit 11B–12 illustrates both sets of conditions. Two companies—Carmel Company and Noblesville, Inc.—have identical financial data except that Carmel finances its operation with debt as well as stock whereas Noblesville finances its operations entirely with stock. Conditions in 19X1 create an advantage for Carmel's use of leverage. Carmel's stockholders earn $3.15 per share in 19X1, which includes an amount attributable to earnings in excess of the cost of borrowing. In contrast, Noblesville's stockholders earn only $2.80 per share in 19X1. However, income from operations falls in 19X2, with the result that Carmel's stockholders earn only $1.05 per share compared with $1.40 per share for Noblesville's stockholders. Just as the stockholders receive earnings in excess of the interest on debt, so the stockholders must bear the excess of the interest on debt over earnings.

A third advantage of financing with bonds is that in periods of inflation, bonds permit the borrowing entity to repay the lender in dollars of a smaller purchasing power. For instance, based on changes in the consumer price index (CPI), $1,000,000 borrowed in 1970 and repaid in 1990 provided the lender in 1990 with only 30 percent of the purchasing power of the amount loaned in 1970. Supplementary Topic B, at the back of this book, explains how to use price indexes to adjust accounting data for changes in purchasing power.

The primary negative attribute of bonds, as of most other liabilities, is the inflexibility of the payment schedule. Bonds require specified payments to bondholders on specified dates. If a payment is not made as scheduled, the issuing entity can be declared bankrupt. This attribute of bonds causes them to be more risky than equity as a way of securing capital. The larger the proportion of liabilities an entity uses to finance its capital needs, the greater the risk of default for the entity and for the lenders. As risk increases (because of a higher proportion of liabilities), the cost of bond financing increases. At a certain point, however, the risk becomes so great that additional liabilities cannot be sold at any cost. For firms whose operational and competitive circumstances produce substantial fluctuations in earnings, even low levels of notes or bonds may be considered too risky. An entity must weigh both the negative and the positive aspects of bonds in deciding whether or not to obtain needed capital by issuing bonds. This extremely complex decision is treated more fully in finance courses.

We turn now to leases as another means of financing asset acquisitions.

LEASES

LEASE: A document that enables its holder to use property without legally owning it.

During the past 25 years, leases have increasingly become an alternative to outright asset purchases for firms seeking to expand their operations. A **lease** enables a firm to use property without legally owning it. When leases first began to be used as sources of capital for asset acquisition, they generally were omitted from the liabilities of the entity. In 1976, however, the Financial Accounting Standards Board identified two kinds of lease obligations for lessees—operating leases and capital leases—and required that capital leases be included in a firm's assets and liabilities.[7] We will discuss both types of leases and their accounting procedures in the sections that follow.

[7] Financial Accounting Standards Board, "Accounting for Leases," *Statement of Financial Accounting Standards No. 13.*

ACCOUNTING FOR OPERATING LEASES

OPERATING LEASE: A lease in which the lessor retains the risks and obligations of ownership of the leased asset.

The most common form of lease is an **operating lease,** under which the lessor (the legal owner of the asset) retains the risks and obligations of ownership. The rental of automobiles, retail space, and office space is usually accomplished with an operating lease. All illustrations of rental arrangements considered earlier in this book have been operating leases. Under an operating lease, the leased asset does not appear among the assets of the lessee, because the legal owner of the asset retains the risks and obligations of ownership. Rent paid in advance of the use of the asset is reported as prepaid rent, and rent expense is recognized in the period in which the leased asset is used. However, the sum of all payments required by noncancelable operating leases for the five years subsequent to the current accounting period must be disclosed in a footnote to the lessee's financial statements.

ACCOUNTING FOR CAPITAL LEASES

CAPITAL LEASE: A lease that is in substance a purchase of the asset leased.

A **capital lease** is a noncancelable agreement that is in substance a purchase of the asset leased. If a lease has any of the following characteristics, it is essentially a purchase and is therefore considered a capital lease:

1. A transfer of the leased property to the lessee at the end of the lease at no cost or at a "bargain price"
2. A term for the lease that is at least 75 percent of the economic life of the leased property
3. A present value of the lease payments that is at least 90 percent of the fair value of the leased property

At inception, the liability for a capital lease is recorded at the present value of the future lease payments. At this time, an asset is recorded in the same amount. During the life of the lease, the asset is depreciated using an appropriate depreciation method, and the lease liability is reduced and interest expense is recorded as lease payments are made. To illustrate the computations and entries for capital leases, let's assume that Hatcher & Company, certified public accountants, has leased a computer from ES Leasing. The lease calls for 10 annual payments of $10,000 each, and the initial payment is at the end of the first year. At the end of the lease, ownership of the computer will transfer to Hatcher & Company. An appropriate interest rate for valuing the payments in the lease is 12 percent.

The first step is to determine the present value of the future payments required by the lease. The 10 future payments (f) of $10,000 each required by the lease represent an annuity whose present value (PV) is found by using Exhibit 10–20 (Present Value of an Annuity of $1, pages 468–469). The multiple (M_4) corresponding to an interest rate of 12 percent and 10 periods is 5.6502 and is substituted in the following formula for the present value:

$$PV = (f)(M_4)$$
$$= (\$10,000)(5.6502)$$
$$= \$56,502$$

The lease liability, which is the present value of the lease, is then recorded as follows:

Leased property	56,502	
Capital lease liability		56,502

Although the lessor remains the legal owner of the leased property, a capital lease transfers virtually all the benefits of ownership to the lessee; therefore, a captial lease is appropriately shown among the lessee's assets and liabilities. A lease liability table, similar to the bond liability table in Exhibit 11B–9, would be prepared and then used to develop the interest expense and the journal entries for the lease payments. The first lease payment is recorded as follows:

Interest expense [($56,502)(.12)]	6,780	
Capital lease liability ($10,000 − $6,780)	3,220	
Cash		10,000

Each payment reduces the lease liability by the amount of cash paid less the interest expense.

As noted, the recognition of the liability for a capital lease also requires that the leased property be recorded as an asset. This asset must be depreciated over its expected economic life. Depending on the terms, leases can be more or less attractive than borrowing as a means of financing asset acquisitions, as the following analysis demonstrates.

ANALYSIS

LEASING VERSUS BORROWING

The Ives Corporation plans to acquire five new trucks. If purchased, the trucks will cost $12,000 each. One truck dealer will allow Ives to pay 10 percent down ($6,000) and will finance the remaining $54,000 on a five-year, 10 percent interest-bearing note requiring annual interest payments of $5,400 and the principal payment of $54,000 at maturity. Another dealer will lease trucks of the same make to Ives on a capital lease requiring annual payments of $15,828 for five years. The leased trucks would become Ives' property at the end of the lease. Ives' accountant has asked you to help decide whether to lease or borrow in order to finance the truck acquisition. As a basis for making your decision, you develop the following data:

	LEASING	BORROWING
Cash payments:		
Year 1	$15,828	$11,400
Year 2	15,828	5,400
Year 3	15,828	5,400
Year 4	15,828	5,400
Year 5	15,828	59,400
Total for 5 years	$79,140	$87,000
Interest expense for 5 years	$19,140	$27,000

The leasing option promises a lower total cash outflow and a lower total interest expense. Does this mean that the company should lease rather than borrow and purchase?

Although the leasing option promises a lower total cash outflow and a lower total interest expense, its level payment schedule does not allow Ives to defer payment to the extent allowed by the borrowing option. The deferred payment advantages of borrowing may more than offset the cash flow and interest expense advantages of leasing.

In addition, the payment schedules shown above do not include the effects of the interest on income tax payments. Since the annual interest deduction declines more slowly under borrowing, the effects of interest on income tax payments enhance the deferred payment advantage of borrowing. Of course, the data presented here are insufficient to enable a final recommendation. A complete analysis of the options, which is explained in finance courses, would permit an evaluation of the amounts and timing of the payments required by the two options and the income tax effects of both interest and depreciation.

SUMMARY

Liabilities that represent economic sacrifices expected to occur beyond the longer of one year or one operating cycle are known as *long-term liabilities.* Long-term liabilities arise from transactions supported by a variety of legal documents, including notes, bonds, and capital leases. This chapter explains the accounting procedures for long-term liabilities, using effective interest amortization.

Bond accounting is complicated by the fact that bonds are rarely sold at their par value (face amount) but are usually sold at a small premium or discount. A premium or discount affects the amount of interest expense associated with a bond. Bond accounting also involves recording extraordinary gains or losses on bonds that are retired before maturity.

This chapter also discusses the pros and cons of financing asset acquisitions with bonds, capital leases, and stock. Bonds are frequently a less expensive source of capital than stock (equity). In addition, leases represent an important alternative to bonds and equity as a means of acquiring assets. When a lease is in substance a purchase of leased facilities, it is known as a *capital lease;* an asset and a long-term liability are recorded for a capital lease. Since the ability of a firm to borrow by issuing bonds, capital leases, and other liabilities is usually limited, most firms are financed by a mixture of liabilities and equity. Equity as a source of long-term capital is discussed in Chapter 12.

APPENDIX 11B–1
SOME TECHNICAL ISSUES IN ACCOUNTING FOR BONDS

To simplify the examples in this chapter, we made the assumption that bonds are sold only at the beginning of accounting and interest payment periods. In reality, however, bonds are often sold at times other than the beginning of an accounting period, and they can also be sold at times other than the beginning of an interest payment period. In these situations, more complicated computations and entries are necessary to match the interest amortization with the appropriate accounting periods. The following sections illustrate some of the complications, first in accounting for bonds sold at other than the beginning of an accounting period, and then for bonds sold at times other than the beginning of an interest period.

BONDS SOLD AT TIMES OTHER THAN THE BEGINNING OF THE ACCOUNTING PERIOD

The Webster Company issued a five-year, $200,000, 12 percent bond at a discount on May 1, 19X6. Assume that the bond liability table in Exhibit 11B–13 was prepared for this issue. Since this bond was issued on May 1, 19X6, at the beginning of the first interest period, the first semiannual interest payment entry would be made on October 31, 19X6, as follows (using period 1 data from Exhibit 11B–13):

Interest expense	12,138	
Discount on bonds payable		138
Cash		12,000

The Webster Company's fiscal year ends on December 31, 19X6. An adjusting entry is necessary to record the interest expense accrued from the date of the

EXHIBIT 11B-13   **BOND LIABILITY TABLE**

		WEBSTER COMPANY		
SEMIANNUAL PERIOD	INTEREST EXPENSE (DEBIT)	CASH PAYMENT (CREDIT)	CHANGE IN LIABILITY BALANCE	LIABILITY BALANCE
At issue				$198,171
1	$12,138	$ 12,000	+138	198,309
2	12,146	12,000	+146	198,455
3	12,155	12,000	+155	198,610
4	12,165	12,000	+165	198,775
5	12,175	12,000	+175	198,950
6	12,186	12,000	+186	199,136
7	12,197	12,000	+197	199,333
8	12,209	12,000	+209	199,542
8	12,222	12,000	+222	199,764
10	12,236	212,000	−199,764	−0−

interest payment on October 31 through December 31. The data from Exhibit 11B–13 are used to allocate the period 2 interest between 19X6 and 19X7; the computations for the adjusting entry are as follows:

Interest expense, November and December 19X6
(2/6)($12,146) = $4,049

Discount amortization, November and December 19X6
(2/6)($146) = $49

Interest payable on December 31, 19X6
(2/6)($12,000) = $4,000

The following adjusting entry can now be made:

Interest expense	4,049	
Discount on bonds payable		49
Interest payable		4,000

On April 30, 19X7, when the next interest payment is due, the remainder of the period 2 interest expense and discount amortization must be recorded. The computations (rounded to the nearest dollar) are as follows:

Interest expense, January through April 19X7
(4/6)($12,146) = $8,097

Discount amortization, January through April 19X7
(4/6)($146) = $97

The interest payment entry that follows an adjusting entry is then made, as follows:

Interest expense	8,097	
Interest payable	4,000	
Discount on bonds payable		97
Cash...		12,000

Note that the interest payment entry removes the $4,000 interest payable established by the adjusting entry.

BONDS SOLD AFTER THE BEGINNING OF AN INTEREST PERIOD

Bonds normally are issued at the beginning of an interest period. Occasionally, however, difficulties in marketing a bond issue cause the initial sale to be delayed beyond the beginning of a semiannual interest period. When such a delay occurs, the amount the bondholders pay the issuer includes the interest from the beginning of the interest period to the date of sale. The issuer then makes a full six-month interest payment to the bondholders at the end of the interest period, thus repaying the interest paid by the bondholders at the sale date. Therefore, the issuer must allocate a portion of the proceeds to the interest that the bondholder will receive for the portion of the interest period that has already passed.

Assume that the Ridgeway Corporation sold a 10-year, $100,000, 12 percent bond issue on September 1, 19X6, one month after the beginning of the interest period for the bonds. Ridgeway received proceeds from the sale of $102,441. Since the bonds have an effective interest rate of 11.75 percent, the entry to record the sale would be as follows:

Cash	102,441	
Bonds payable		100,000
Interest payable [($100,000)(.12)(1/12)]		1,000
Premium on bonds payable		1,441

A premium (or a discount) is a derived amount that is determined by subtracting the sum of the bond liability and the interest payable from the proceeds:

$$\$102,441 - (\$100,000 + \$1,000) = \$1,441$$

In the case of a discount, the sum of the bond liability and the interest payable would exceed the proceeds.

The data for the entry at the time of the sale and for the subsequent interest payment entries can be developed from the bond liability table that is made when the bonds are sold (see Exhibit 11B–14). On the basis of the data in Exhibit 11B–14 and the sale entry, Ridgeway would record the first interest payment with the following entry:

Interest expense [($101,441)(.05875)(5/6)]	4,966	
Interest payable	1,000	
Premium on bonds payable ($5,000 − $4,966)	34	
Cash		6,000

Subsequent semiannual interest payment entries would follow the procedure described earlier in this chapter.

BOND SINKING FUNDS

BOND SINKING FUND: A fund that will be used to redeem a bond issue at maturity.

Under certain circumstances, a firm and its bondholders establish an agreement requiring the firm to make regular payments to a fund that will be used to redeem its bond issue at maturity. Such a fund is called a **bond sinking fund.** Often the sinking fund is controlled by a trustee (usually a bank or an insurance company) to guarantee that the firm will not divert the fund to uses other than bond retirement. The amounts of the payments made by the company into a sinking fund are determined by dividing the required future amount by the appropriate

EXHIBIT 11B–14   PARTIAL BOND LIABILITY TABLE

RIDGEWAY CORPORATION

SEMIANNUAL PERIOD	INTEREST EXPENSE (DEBIT)	CASH PAYMENT (CREDIT)	CHANGE IN LIABILITY BALANCE	LIABILITY BALANCE
At issue				$101,441
1	$4,966*	$6,000†	−34†	101,407
2	5,958	6,000	−42	101,365

* The issue point is one month into the normal six-month interest period. Therefore, interest expense for the first period is computed by multiplying the effective semiannual interest rate by 5/6.

† The $6,000 cash payment is the sum of $5,000 owed the bondholders for the five months that the bonds are outstanding plus another $1,000 owed as interest payable from the issue transaction. Thus the change in liability balance is $34, the difference between $4,966 and $5,000.

multiple from Exhibit 10–19 (Future Amount of an Annuity of $1, pages 468–469). The multiple corresponds to the interest rate the fund will earn and the number of regular payments the company will make. For example, a bond issue of $600,000 maturing in 10 years would require that a company make 10 annual payments of $34,190.57 each into a sinking fund that earns 12 percent per year, with the first payment due at the end of the first year and the last payment due at the date the $600,000 issue matures. The 10 future payments (f) represent an annuity whose future amount (FA) is given by the following formula:

$$FA = (f)(M_3)$$

where M_3 is the appropriate multiple from Exhibit 10–19. The multiple for an interest rate of 12 percent and 10 annual payments is 17.5487. Accordingly, the formula is evaluated as follows:

$$\$600,000 = (f)(17.5487)$$
$$f = \$600,000/17.5487$$
$$f = \$34,190.57$$

In other words, 10 annual payments of $34,190.57 each (with the first payment made at the end of the first year) will provide the required $600,000 in 10 years. The assets of a sinking fund appear on the firm's balance sheet among the investments.

APPENDIX 11B–2
STRAIGHT-LINE ADJUSTMENT OF THE PREMIUM OR DISCOUNT FOR BONDS

In this chapter, we described how the effective interest method is used to determine interest expense and premium or discount amortization for long-term liabilities. As we indicated in the introduction to the chapter, straight-line procedures are also widely used. This appendix illustrates the use of straight-line procedures in accounting for bonds.

Interest expense over the life of a bond issue is the difference between the sum of the cash payments (semiannual interest plus principal) and the proceeds received from the bonds when issued. When the proceeds received from the issuance of bonds are more than the face amount, the excess is called *premium on bonds payable*. If bond proceeds are less than the face amount, the amount of the deficiency is called *discount on bonds payable*. For bonds issued for more or less than their face amount, the interest expense each period must amortize a portion of the premium or discount so that the interest expense over the life of the bonds will equal the difference between bond proceeds and the interest and principal payments. To illustrate, assume that Engerski Company issued two 5-year, $100,000, 14 percent bonds—one at a $200 premium and the other at a $300 discount. Interest expense over the life of the bonds is shown below:

	BOND ISSUED AT A PREMIUM	BOND ISSUED AT A DISCOUNT
Sum of the interest payments	$ 70,000	$ 70,000
Principal payment	100,000	100,000
Total payments to bondholders	$170,000	$170,000
Less: Proceeds at issue	100,200	99,700
Total interest expense over life of bond	$ 69,800	$ 70,300

Note that the total interest expense for the premium bond is less than the sum of the interest payments by $200, the amount of the premium. For the bond sold at a discount, interest expense is greater than the sum of the interest payments by $300, the amount of the discount.

When the straight-line amortization method is used, the interest expense is exactly the same in each period because an equal (straight-line) amount of premium or discount is amortized each period. For Engerski's premium bond with total interest expense of $69,800, the premium amortization in each period is $20 [$200/10 periods], and the interest expense in each period is $6,980 [$7,000 − $20]. The discount bond has discount amortization of $30 each period [$300/10 periods] and incurs straight-line interest expense of $7,030 [$7,000 + $30] each period.

A liability table for Engerski's $100,000 bond issued at a $200 premium is presented in Exhibit 11B–15. Note that the amount of each period's interest expense is the amount of the semiannual interest payment less the straight-line premium amortization. Also note that the carrying amount of the bond decreases by $20 each period as the total premium of $200 is amortized over the life of the bond on a straight-line basis.

The following entry is made at the end of the first semiannual interest period to record the interest payment, the amortization of the premium, and the interest expense:

Interest expense	6,980	
Premium on bonds payable	20	
Cash		7,000

The same entry would be made at the end of each interest period.

The liability table for the $100,000 bond issued at a $300 discount is presented in Exhibit 11B–16. Note that the amount of each period's interest

EXHIBIT 11B–15   **STRAIGHT-LINE PREMIUM BOND LIABILITY TABLE**

ENGERSKI COMPANY

SEMIANNUAL PERIOD	INTEREST EXPENSE (DEBIT)	CASH PAYMENT (CREDIT)	CHANGE IN LIABILITY BALANCE	LIABILITY BALANCE
At issue				$100,200
1	$6,980	$ 7,000	−20	100,180
2	6,980	7,000	−20	100,160
3	6,980	7,000	−20	100,140
4	6,980	7,000	−20	100,120
5	6,980	7,000	−20	100,100
6	6,980	7,000	−20	100,080
7	6,980	7,000	−20	100,060
8	6,980	7,000	−20	100,040
9	6,980	7,000	−20	100,020
10	6,980	107,000	−100,020	–0–

EXHIBIT 11B–16   **STRAIGHT-LINE DISCOUNT BOND LIABILITY TABLE**

ENGERSKI COMPANY

SEMIANNUAL PERIOD	INTEREST EXPENSE (DEBIT)	CASH PAYMENT (CREDIT)	CHANGE IN LIABILITY BALANCE	LIABILITY BALANCE
At issue				$99,700
1	$7,030	$ 7,000	+30	99,730
2	7,030	7,000	+30	99,760
3	7,030	7,000	+30	99,790
4	7,030	7,000	+30	99,820
5	7,030	7,000	+30	99,850
6	7,030	7,000	+30	99,880
7	7,030	7,000	+30	99,910
8	7,030	7,000	+30	99,940
9	7,030	7,000	+30	99,970
10	7,030	107,000	−99,970	–0–

expense is constant and is the amount of the semiannual interest payment plus the straight-line discount amortization of $30. The carrying amount of the discount bond increases by $30 each period as the total discount of $300 is amortized over the life of the bond.

The following entry is made at the end of the first semiannual interest period to record the interest payment, the amortization of the discount, and the interest expense:

Interest expense	7,030	
Discount on bonds payable		30
Cash		7,000

The same entry would be made at the end of each interest period.

When the amount of the premium or discount for a bond is small, the interest expense computed using the straight-line procedure is virtually the same as the interest expense determined using the effective interest procedure. For example, the $100,000 bond issued at a $300 discount has an effective interest rate of 7.043 percent. Using the effective interest procedure, interest expense for the bond for the first interest period is $7,022 [($99,700)(.07043)]. Using the straight-line procedure, interest expense is $7,030. The $8 difference between effective interest and straight-line interest expense is not material (.1 percent) relative to the size of the interest expense (over $7,000). When the difference between effective interest and straight-line amortization is not material, many firms use the straight-line procedure because its computations are easier.

KEY TERMS

BOND (p. 519)	FACE AMOUNT (PAR VALUE) (p. 519)
BOND ISSUE (p. 519)	INTEREST AMORTIZATION (p. 508)
BOND SINKING FUND (p. 538)	LEASE (p. 533)
CALLABLE BONDS (p. 530)	LEVERAGE (TRADING ON EQUITY) (p. 532)
CAPITAL LEASE (p. 534)	LONG-TERM NOTES PAYABLE (p. 510)
CARRYING AMOUNT (BOOK VALUE) (p. 517)	OPERATING LEASE (p. 534)
DISCOUNT ON BONDS PAYABLE (p. 520)	PREMIUM ON BONDS PAYABLE (p. 520)
EFFECTIVE INTEREST AMORTIZATION (p. 508)	STATED RATE (COUPON RATE, NOMINAL RATE, FACE RATE, OR CONTRACT RATE) (p. 519)
EFFECTIVE INTEREST RATE (YIELD RATE) (p. 521)	

QUESTIONS

Q11B-1. What is a long-term liability? Are all bonds classified as long-term liabilities?

Q11B-2. Name the long-term liabilities described in Chapter 10. How do they differ from the long-term liabilities described in the present chapter?

Q11B-3. Describe the two-stage allocation procedure used to apportion the total interest associated with a liability among accounting periods. What is the relationship between this two-stage procedure and the matching concept?

Q11B-4. Name four long-term liabilities and describe the distinguishing features of each.

Q11B-5. How is interest expense determined for an interest-bearing note? For a bond?

Q11B-6. What is meant by restructuring a long-term liability? Why does restructuring occur?

Q11B-7. What are bond ratings, and how are they related to the cost of issuing debt? What are "junk bonds," and how do they differ from "fallen angels"?

Q11B-8. What is the effective interest rate, and how is it used? What is the stated interest rate, and how is it used?

Q11B-9. What is the face amount of a bond? How is the face amount related to the discount or premium on the bond?

Q11B-10. How is the liability that is associated with a bond issue presented on the balance sheet?

Q11B-11. How do premiums and discounts on bonds affect interest expense?

Q11B-12. Describe the differences between the accounting for long-term bonds receivable by investors and the accounting for long-term bonds payable by issuers.

Q11B-13. How are premiums and discounts presented in the balance sheet?

Q11B-14. How does a firm "lever" its capital structure? When is leverage advantageous? When is it disadvantageous? Who receives the advantage or bears the disadvantage of leverage?

Q11B-15. Name and describe two kinds of leases.

Q11B-16. Which type of lease requires that a long-term liability and an asset be recorded at the inception of the lease?

Q11B-17. How is interest expense determined for a capital lease?

EXERCISES

E11B-18. INTEREST EXPENSE AND ALTERNATIVE NOTES Jacobi Corporation wishes to borrow $100,000 to finance the acquisition of new equipment during 19X1. Two alternative forms of the note are under consideration:

> *Note I:* Note I is a 10 percent interest-bearing note that requires five annual interest payments of $10,000 each, beginning one year after issuance; the final interest payment is made in five years (at maturity), together with the $100,000 repayment of principal.

> *Note II:* Note II is an 11 percent interest-bearing note that requires a single payment of $168,492 in five years (at maturity), which pays all interest and principal.

REQUIRED:

1. Assume that the note is issued and $100,000 cash received on January 1, 19X1. Calculate the amount of interest expense for note I and note II to be reported for 19X1 and 19X2.

2. Assume that the note is issued and $100,000 cash received on April 1, 19X1. Calculate the amount of interest expense to be reported for note I and note II for 19X1 and 19X2.

3. With reference to your calculations for note II, explain the two-stage amortization and matching of interest in 19X1 and 19X2 if the note is issued on April 1, 19X1. How does the two-stage process differ if note II is issued on January 1, 19X1?

E11B-19. INTEREST AMORTIZATION AND INTEREST MATCHING Kiwi Corporation borrowed $15,000 on a two-year, 14 percent interest-bearing note. The note was issued on September 1, 19X7. Interest is compounded annually on August 31. The face amount of the note plus two years' compound interest of $4,494 is due August 31, 19X9.

REQUIRED:

1. Allocate the interest of $4,494 to the two 1-year interest periods, using the effective interest method.

2. Allocate the interest of $4,494 to the three calendar years in which the note is outstanding.

E11B-20. INTEREST-BEARING NOTE WITH ANNUAL INTEREST PAYMENTS Sindy Nursery issued a three-year, $190,000, 12 percent interest-bearing note to the First National Bank. The note was issued April 1, 19X1, and interest is to be paid annually on March 31. The principal and the final interest payment are due March 31, 19X4.

REQUIRED:

1. Prepare the entry for Sindy's journal to record the issuance of the note.

2. Prepare the adjusting entry for Sindy's journal to record the interest expense from the date of issue through December 31, 19X1.

3. Prepare the entry for Sindy's journal to record the first interest payment on March 31, 19X2.

E11B-21. INTEREST-BEARING NOTE WITH ANNUAL INTEREST PAYMENTS Theil's Department Store borrowed $345,000 on a three-year, 11 percent interest-bearing note payable on September 1, 19X6. Assume that interest is compounded and paid annually.

REQUIRED:

1. Prepare the adjusting entry for Theil on December 31, 19X6.

2. Prepare the interest payment entry on August 31, 19X7.

3. Prepare the interest payment and note repayment entry on August 31, 19X9.

4. Compute the amount of compound interest that would be paid on August 31, 19X9, if interest were paid in a lump sum at maturity rather than annually.

E11B-22. INTEREST-BEARING NOTE WITH LUMP-SUM PAYMENT Able Products Company issued a two-year, $90,000, 13 percent interest-bearing note on May 1, 19X4. The principal and compound interest are to be paid April 30, 19X6.

REQUIRED:

1. Prepare the entry for Able's journal to record issuance of the note.

2. Prepare the adjusting entry for Able's journal to record the interest expense from the date of issue through December 31, 19X4.

3. Prepare the adjusting entry at December 31, 19X5. (Don't forget that the first year for the note ends on April 30, 19X5.)

4. Prepare the entry to record the 19X6 interest expense and the repayment of the note and compound interest on April 30, 19X6.

E11B-23. NON-INTEREST-BEARING NOTE Spool River Products borrowed $100,000 cash by issuing a two-year, $118,810 non-interest-bearing note on September 1, 19X7. The $118,810 face amount of the note is due on August 31, 19X9. The effective interest rate for the note is 9 percent per year. Spool River expects to refinance the debt at maturity by issuing a new note.

REQUIRED:

1. Prepare the entry for Spool River's journal to record issuance of the note.

2. Prepare the adjusting entries for Spool River's journal at December 31, 19X7, and December 31, 19X8.

3. Prepare the entries to record interest for the period January 1, 19X9, through August 31, 19X9, and to record payment of the note at maturity.

4. What is the accounting significance of Spool River's intention to refinance the debt at maturity?

E11B-24. NON-INTEREST-BEARING NOTE WITH RECLASSIFICATION On April 1, 19X4, Baraboo Lumber Company borrowed $70,000 by issuing a two-year non-interest-bearing note. The effective interest rate for the note is 12 percent per year compounded semiannually (6 percent per six-month period).

REQUIRED:

1. Compute the maturity (face) amount of this note.

2. Prepare the entry for Baraboo's jounal to record issuance of the note.

3. Prepare the adjusting entries for Baraboo's journal at December 31, 19X4, and December 31, 19X5.

4. Prepare the entry to record interest for January 1, 19X6, through March 31, 19X6, and the entry to record repayment of the note at maturity.

5. Why is Baraboo's note described as "non-interest-bearing"?

E11B-25. JOURNAL ENTRIES FOR BOND PREMIUMS AND DISCOUNTS   Kartel Company is planning to issue 50 bonds, each having a face amount of $10,000.

REQUIRED:

1. Prepare the journal entry to record the sale of the bonds at par.
2. Prepare the journal entry to record the sale of the bonds at a premium of $34,000.
3. Prepare the journal entry to record the sale of the bonds at a discount of $41,000.

E11B-26. BOND INTEREST PAYMENTS AND INTEREST EXPENSE   On January 1, 19X8, Philips Corporation issued bonds with a total face amount of $800,000 and a stated (or coupon) rate of 12 percent.

REQUIRED:

1. Calculate the interest expense for 19X8 if the bonds were sold at par.
2. Calculate the interest expense for 19X8 if the bonds were sold at a premium and the premium amortization for 19X8 is $1,230.
3. Calculate the interest expense for 19X8 if the bonds were sold at a discount and the discount amortization for 19X8 is $970.

E11B-27. BOND PREMIUM AND DISCOUNT   Wareham Manufacturing is contemplating a bond issue to be composed of 100 bonds, each with a face amount of $5,000.

REQUIRED:

1. How much is Wareham able to borrow if each bond is sold at a premium of $850?
2. How much is Wareham able to borrow if each bond is sold at a discount of $920?
3. How much is Wareham able to borrow if each bond is sold at 94 percent of par?
4. How much is Wareham able to borrow if each bond is sold at 104 percent of par?
5. Assume that the bonds are sold for $5,610 each. Prepare the journal entry to record the issuance of the 100 bonds.
6. Assume that the bonds are sold for $4,330 each. Prepare the journal entry to record the issuance of the 100 bonds.

E11B-28. BOND INTEREST PAYMENTS AND INTEREST EXPENSE   Cardinal Company sold a 10-year, $20,000, 14 percent bond for $20,430. The bond was sold July 1, 19X8, pays interest semiannually, and has an effective interest rate of 13.6 percent.

REQUIRED:

1. Prepare the entry to record the sale of the bond.
2. Determine the amount of the semiannual interest payments for the bond.
3. Prepare the entry for Cardinal's journal at December 31, 19X8, to record the payment of six months' interest and the related interest expense.
4. Determine interest expense for 19X9.

E11B-29. BOND INTEREST PAYMENTS AND INTEREST EXPENSE   On January 1, 19X1, Hawthorne Corporation sold for $13,994 cash a five-year, $15,000 bond with semiannual interest payments and a stated rate of 14 percent. The effective interest rate is 16 percent.

REQUIRED:

1. Prepare the journal entry to record the sale of the bond.
2. Calculate the amount of the semiannual cash payment for interest.
3. Prepare the journal entry at June 30, 19X2, to record the payment of interest and the interest expense.
4. Calculate the annual interest expense for 19X1 and for 19X2.

E11B-30. USING A PREMIUM BOND LIABILITY TABLE   For Ekelberry Corporation, the following bond liability table was prepared when a five-year, $400,000, 14.125 percent bond issue was sold on January 1, 19X2. (All amounts are rounded to the nearest dollar.)

INTEREST PERIOD ENDING	INTEREST EXPENSE	CASH PAYMENT	CHANGE IN LIABILITY BALANCE	LIABILITY BALANCE
At issue				$401,756
6/30/X2	$28,123	$ 28,250	−127	401,629
12/31/X2	28,114	28,250	−136	401,493
6/30/X3	28,104	28,250	−146	401,347
12/31/X3	28,095	28,250	−155	401,192
6/30/X4	28,083	28,250	−167	401,025
12/31/X4	28,072	28,250	−178	400,847
6/30/X5	28,059	28,250	−191	400,656
12/31/X5	28,046	28,250	−204	400,452
6/30/X6	28,032	28,250	−218	400,234
12/31/X6	28,016	428,250	−400,234	−0−

REQUIRED:

1. Prepare the entry to record the issuance of the bonds on January 1, 19X2.

2. Prepare the entry to record the first interest payment on June 30, 19X2.

3. What interest expense for this bond issue will Ekelberry report in its 19X3 income statement?

4. Indicate how this bond issue will appear in Ekelberry's December 31, 19X5, balance sheet.

E11B-31. USING A DISCOUNT BOND LIABILITY TABLE   Cottrell Corporation prepared the following bond liability table when five-year, 8.4 percent bonds with a total face amount of $500,000 were sold on January 1, 19X3. (All amounts are rounded to the nearest dollar.)

INTEREST PERIOD ENDING	INTEREST EXPENSE	CASH PAYMENT	CHANGE IN LIABILITY BALANCE	LIABILITY BALANCE
At issue				$484,252
6/30/X3	$22,276	$ 21,000	+1,276	485,528
12/31/X3	22,334	21,000	+1,334	486,862
6/30/X4	22,396	21,000	+1,396	488,258
12/31/X4	22,460	21,000	+1,460	489,717
6/30/X5	22,527	21,000	+1,527	491,244
12/31/X5	22,597	21,000	+1,597	492,842
6/30/X6	22,671	21,000	+1,671	494,512
12/31/X6	22,748	21,000	+1,748	496,260
6/30/X7	22,828	21,000	+1,828	498,088
12/31/X7	22,912	521,000	−498,088	−0−

REQUIRED:

1. Prepare the entry to record the issuance of the bonds on January 1, 19X3.

2. Prepare the entry to record the first interest payment on June 30, 19X3.

3. What amount of interest expense for this bond issue will Cottrell report in its 19X4 income statement?

4. Indicate how this bond issue will appear in Cottrell's December 31, 19X6, balance sheet.

E11B-32. COMPLETING A BOND LIABILITY TABLE   Cagney Company sold a $200,000 bond issue on June 30, 19X5. A portion of the bond liability table appears at the top of the facing page.

INTEREST PERIOD ENDING	INTEREST EXPENSE	CASH PAYMENT	CHANGE IN LIABILITY BALANCE	LIABILITY BALANCE
12/31/X6	$11,627	$11,000	+627	$194,417
6/30/X7	11,665	11,000	+665	195,082
12/31/X7	?	?	?	?

REQUIRED:

1. What is the stated interest rate on these bonds?

2. What is the effective annual interest rate on these bonds (rounded to the nearest 0.1 percent)?

3. What are the interest expense and discount amortization (change in liability balance) for the interest period ending December 31, 19X7?

4. What is the liability balance after the interest payment is recorded on December 31, 19X7?

E11B-33. COMPLETING A BOND LIABILITY TABLE   MacBride Enterprises sold a $200,000 bond issue on January 1, 19X2. A portion of the bond liability table appears below.

INTEREST PERIOD ENDING	INTEREST EXPENSE	CASH PAYMENT	CHANGE IN LIABILITY BALANCE	LIABILITY BALANCE
At issue				$224,333
6/30/X2	$8,973	$11,000	−2,027	222,306
12/31/X2	8,892	11,000	−2,108	220,198
6/30/X3	8,808	11,000	−2,192	218,006
12/31/X3	?	?	?	?

REQUIRED:

1. What is the stated annual interest rate on these bonds?

2. What is the effective annual interest rate on these bonds (rounded to the nearest 0.1 percent)?

3. What are the interest expense and premium amortization for the interest period ending December 31, 19X3?

4. When will the bonds mature?

E11B-34. EARLY RETIREMENT OF BONDS   Sunnyvale Manufacturing sold five-year, 10.8 percent bonds with a total face amount of $800,000 on July 1, 19X2. The effective interest rate was 11.2 percent per year, and interest payments were made semiannually. On the date of sale, Sunnyvale prepared the following bond liability table:

INTEREST PERIOD ENDING	INTEREST EXPENSE	CASH PAYMENT	CHANGE IN LIABILITY BALANCE	LIABILITY BALANCE
At issue				$787,997
12/31/X2	44,128	43,200	+928	788,925
6/30/X3	44,180	43,200	+980	789,905
12/31/X3	44,235	43,200	+1,035	790,940
6/30/X4	44,293	43,200	+1,093	792,032

On June 30, 19X4, Sunnyvale redeemed all the bonds at their call price of 100.6 percent of the face amount, or $804,800.

REQUIRED:

1. Prepare the entry to record the interest expense for the six-month period ending June 30, 19X4.

2. Prepare the journal entry to record the retirement of the bonds at June 30, 19X4.

E11B-35. OPERATING LEASES AND CAPITAL LEASES   Anderson Wholesale Distributors rents automobiles for its sales staff and warehouse space for its inventory. The vehicles are rented on operating leases from local automobile dealers, and the warehouse is leased under a capital lease from its owner. The following data are available regarding the leased assets:

Automobiles
19X9 payment to lessors $42,300

Warehouse
Present value of future lease payments, 1/1/X9 . . . . $123,716
Lease payments, 19X9.   30,000
Applicable interest rate 12%

REQUIRED:

1. Prepare journal entries to record the 19X9 payments for the operating and capital leases.

2. What total expense is reported in the 19X9 income statement for both leased automobiles and leased warehouse space?

E11B-36. OPERATING LEASES AND CAPITAL LEASES   On January 1, 19X6, Moody Company leased a warehouse for $20,000 per year. The first annual payment is due December 31, 19X6. The present value of the lease payments is $113,000, and the fair value of the warehouse is $113,000.

REQUIRED:

1. Assume that the lease is an *operating* lease. Prepare the journal entries made by Moody during 19X6 and 19X7 for the lease.

2. Assume that the lease is a *capital* lease with an effective interest rate of 12 percent per year. Depreciate the cost of the leased warehouse on a straight-line basis over 10 years with zero residual value. Prepare the journal entries made by Moody during 19X6 and 19X7 for the lease and the leased asset.

APPENDIX 11B–1 EXERCISES

E11B-37. ADJUSTING ENTRIES FOR BOND INTEREST   Vancouver Products, Inc., sold five-year, 12.6 percent bonds with a total face amount of $300,000 on April 1, 19X4. The bonds require interest payments on September 30 and March 31 of each year and were sold to yield an effective interest rate of 12 percent per year. Vancouver's fiscal year ends on December 31.

REQUIRED:

1. Prepare the entry to record interest expense and the payment of interest on September 30, 19X4.

2. Prepare the adjusting entry for interest expense on December 31, 19X4.

3. Prepare the entry to record interest expense and the payment of interest on March 31, 19X5.

E11B-38. BONDS SOLD AFTER THE BEGINNING OF AN INTEREST PERIOD   Beckford Markets, a retail grocery chain, issued a five-year, $600,000, 13.75 percent bond issue at an effective interest rate of 14 percent on February 1, 19X6, one month after the interest period began. Interest payments are due on June 30 and December 31 of each year. Beckford received $601,667, including $6,875 of interest for January, when the bonds were sold.

REQUIRED:

1. Prepare Beckford's journal entry to record the issuance of these bonds on February 1, 19X6.

2. Prepare the journal entry to record the interest expense and payment on June 30, 19X6.

3. Prepare the journal entry to record the interest expense and payment on December 31, 19X6.

E11B-39. BOND SINKING FUND Hendricks Corporation issued $650,000 of 10-year, 16 percent bonds at par. Hendricks wants to set up a sinking fund for repayment of the bond principal at maturity. Assume that Hendricks will make 10 annual payments to the fund trustee, with the first payment due at the end of 19X0 and the last payment due at the end of 19X9, when the bonds mature. The fund will earn 12 percent compounded annually.

REQUIRED:

1. Determine the amount of the annual payments.

2. How should the interest earned by the sinking fund be recorded in Hendrick's accounting records?

APPENDIX 11B–2 EXERCISES

E11B-40. USING A STRAIGHT-LINE BOND LIABILITY TABLE For Etter Corporation, the following bond liability table was prepared when $300,000 of five-year, 9.5 percent bonds were issued on Janaury 1, 19X2, for $302,000:

INTEREST PERIOD ENDING	INTEREST EXPENSE	CASH PAYMENT	CHANGE IN LIABILITY BALANCE	LIABILITY BALANCE
At issue				$302,000
6/30/X2	$14,050	$ 14,250	−200	301,800
12/31/X2	14,050	14,250	−200	301,600
6/30/X3	14,050	14,250	−200	301,400
12/31/X3	14,050	14,250	−200	301,200
6/30/X4	14,050	14,250	−200	301,000
12/31/X4	14,050	14,250	−200	300,800
6/30/X5	14,050	14,250	−200	300,600
12/31/X5	14,050	14,250	−200	300,400
6/30/X6	14,050	14,250	−200	300,200
12/31/X6	14,050	314,250	−300,200	−0−

REQUIRED:

1. Prepare the entry to record the issuance of the bonds on January 1, 19X2.

2. Prepare the entry to record the first interest payment on June 30, 19X2.

3. What interest expense for this bond issue will Etter report in its 19X3 income statement?

4. Indicate how this bond issue will appear in Etter's December 31, 19X5, balance sheet.

E11B-41. USING A DISCOUNT BOND LIABILITY TABLE Panamint Candy Company prepared the following bond liability table for $500,000 of five-year, 9.2 percent bonds issued and sold by Panamint on January 1, 19X3, for $472,000:

INTEREST PERIOD ENDING	INTEREST EXPENSE	CASH PAYMENT	CHANGE IN LIABILITY BALANCE	LIABILITY BALANCE
At issue				$472,000
6/30/X3	$25,800	$23,000	+2,800	474,800
12/31/X3	25,800	23,000	+2,800	477,600
6/30/X4	25,800	23,000	+2,800	480,400
12/31/X4	25,800	23,000	+2,800	483,200
6/30/X5	25,800	23,000	+2,800	486,000
12/31/X5	25,800	23,000	+2,800	488,800
6/30/X6	25,800	23,000	+2,800	491,600
12/31/X6	25,800	23,000	+2,800	494,400
6/30/X7	25,800	23,000	+2,800	497,200
12/31/X7	25,800	523,000	−497,200	−0−

REQUIRED:

1. Prepare the entry to record the issuance of the bonds on January 1, 19X3.

2. Prepare the entry to record the first interest payment on June 30, 19X3.

3. What interest expense for this bond issue will Panamint report on its 19X5 income statement?

4. Indicate how this bond issue will appear in Panamint's December 31, 19X5, balance sheet.

PROBLEMS

P11B-42. REPORTING LONG-TERM LIABILITIES   Fridley Manufacturing's accounting records reveal the following account balances after adjusting entries at December 31, 19X2:

Accounts payable	$ 62,500
Bonds payable (7.8%, due in 19X7)	400,000
Bonds payable (9.4%, due in 19X9)	800,000
Current portion of long-term liabilities	70,000
Deferred tax liability	133,400
Discount on bonds payable (9.4%, due in 19X9)	12,600
Discount on notes payable (due in 19X3)	1,700
Income taxes payable	26,900
Interest payable	38,700
Capital lease liability	41,500
Long-term notes payable (due in 19X5)	50,000
Notes payable (due in 19X3)	25,000
Premium on bonds payable (7.8%, due in 19X7)	6,100

REQUIRED:

Prepare the classified liability section as it would appear on Fridley's balance sheet at December 31, 19X2.

P11B-43. USING ASSET VALUES TO ESTABLISH THE AMOUNT OF A LIABILITY   Micro Service Company acquired a new car for one of its service personnel. Because Micro is a good customer, the car dealer accepted a two-year non-interest-bearing note with a face amount of $12,951 as payment for the car. The car had a sticker price of $12,600, but the dealer would have accepted cash of $10,200 for the car.

REQUIRED:

1. Record this transaction in Micro's journal.

2. What is the amount of the addition to Micro's net liabilities?

3. What is the amount of the addition to Micro's net assets?

P11B-44. USING THE PRESENT VALUE OF PAYMENTS TO DETERMINE LIABILITY AMOUNTS   Lufkin Development Company purchased a parcel of land in Arizona by issuing a note that requires payments of $200,000, $300,000, and $500,000 at one, two, and three years, respectively, from the date of purchase. The first appraisal of the land indicated a value of $675,000 and the second a value of $819,000. Because of the disparity between these appraisals, Lufkin's accountant has argued that the asset and the liability should be valued by computing the present value of the outflows required to satisfy the liability. Assume that the appropriate interest rate is 14 percent.

REQUIRED:

1. Compute the amount of the liability on the date of purchase.

2. Prepare the journal entry to record the liability and the land at the date of purchase.

P11B-45. INTEREST-BEARING NOTES WITH ANNUAL INTEREST PAYMENTS   Sagan Manufacturing borrowed $46,000 from First Third Bank of New York on June 1, 19X1, on a two-year, 12.7 percent interest-bearing note. Interest is to be paid annually.

REQUIRED:

1. Prepare Sagan's journal entry to record the issuance of the note.

2. Prepare Sagan's adjusting entries to be made on December 31, 19X1, and December 31, 19X2.

3. Prepare Sagan's journal entry to record the first interest payment on May 31, 19X2.

4. Prepare Sagan's journal entry to record the payment of the final interest payment and the repayment of the note on May 31, 19X3.

5. Indicate how the note and its associated interest would be presented in Sagan's December 31, 19X1, balance sheet.

P11B-46. PREPARING A LIABILITY TABLE FOR AN INTEREST-BEARING NOTE   On August 1, 19X7, Distel Company borrowed $15,000 on a three-year, 12 percent interest-bearing note. The note requires annual interest payments (each equal to 12 percent of $15,000) and repayment of the principal plus the final year's interest at the end of the third year.

REQUIRED:

Prepare a liability table for this note.

P11B-47. PREPARING A LIABILITY TABLE FOR A NON-INTEREST-BEARING NOTE   On March 1, 19X5, Georgetown Distributors borrowed $20,000 on a four-year, 10 percent non-interest bearing note. The note requires a single payment of all interest and principal at the end of the fourth year.

REQUIRED:

Prepare a liability table for this note.

P11B-48. BOND COMPUTATIONS AND ENTRIES   On December 31, 19X2, Sisek Company issued a 10-year, $500,000, 11.75 percent coupon bond, interest payable at 5.875 percent semiannually. The bond was sold at an effective interest rate of 6 percent per six months.

REQUIRED:

1. Journalize the issuance of the bond, using the effective interest method.

2. Journalize the first interest payment on June 30, 19X3.

3. Journalize the second interest payment on December 31, 19X3.

4. At the end of the fifth year (December 31, 19X7), what is the net present value of the future cash flows to be made on this bond?

P11B-49. BOND COMPUTATIONS AND ENTRIES   On June 30, 19X1, Spataro Company issued a 15-year, $700,000, 12.25 percent coupon bond, interest payable at 6.125 percent semiannually. The bond was sold at an effective interest rate of 6 percent per six months.

REQUIRED:

1. Journalize the issuance of the bond, using the effective interest method.

2. Journalize the first interest payment on December 31, 19X1.

3. Journalize the second interest payment on June 30, 19X2.

4. At the end of the fifth year (June 30, 19X6), what is the net present value of the future cash flows to be made on this bond?

P11B-50.   PREPARING A PREMIUM BOND LIABILITY TABLE   On January 1, 19X4, Powell Stores, Inc., issued five-year, 9 percent bonds with a total face amount of $50,000 and semiannual interest payments. The proceeds were $50,398, and the effective interest rate was 8.8 percent.

REQUIRED:

1. Prepare a bond liability table.

2. Prepare the journal entry to record the issuance of the bond on January 1, 19X4.

3. Prepare the journal entries to record interest expense and interest payments at June 30, 19X4, and December 31, 19X4.

P11B-51.   PREPARING A DISCOUNT BOND LIABILITY TABLE   Reynolds Manufacturing sold a 10-year, $60,000, 12.75 percent bond issue for $59,174. The effective interest rate was 13 percent.

REQUIRED:

1. Prepare the first five lines of the liability table for this bond issue. (Assume that the bonds were issued January 1, 19X6, and that interest payments are made on June 30 and December 31 of each year.)

2. Prepare the journal entries to record the issuance of the bonds and the December 31, 19X6, interest payment.

P11B-52.   DETERMINING THE EXISTENCE OF A LIABILITY   Alexander Glass, Inc., a producer of glass for the auto industry, agreed to construct a plant in a new industrial park. The county government sold 10-year, 7.6 percent bonds with a total face amount of $8,000,000 to finance the construction. The bonds were sold to yield an effective interest rate of 8 percent, and require semiannual interest payments to bondholders. Alexander will pay the interest and proceeds on the bonds; at the time of repayment, Alexander will receive title to the plant. In the interim, Alexander will pay property taxes as if it owned the plant. This financing arrangement is attractive to Alexander because state and local government bonds are exempt from federal income taxation and thus carry a lower rate of interest. Further, the bonds are attractive to investors because both Alexander and the county stand behind them.

REQUIRED:

1. Prepare a bond liability table for the first four interest periods.

2. Should Alexander record this asset and its associated liability?

P11B-53.   COMPUTING BOND PROCEEDS   Sunnyside Products is contemplating issuing bonds. Discussions with the underwriter have indicated that a 5-year, $850,000, 12 percent bond issue could be sold at effective interest rates of between 12.9 and 13.1 percent.

REQUIRED:

Compute the proceeds that Sunnyside would receive if the bond issue sold at 12.9 and 13.1 percent, respectively. Use the following time-value-of-money multiples:

Single Amount
10 periods at 6.45 percent 53523
10 periods at 6.55 percent 53023

Annuity
10 periods at 6.45 percent 7.20568
10 periods at 6.55 percent 7.17204

P11B-54.   EARLY RETIREMENT OF BONDS   Frederickson Corporation issued 10-year, 11.2 percent bonds on January 1, 19X3, with a total face amount of $750,000. The bonds were issued to yield an effective interest rate of 10.8 percent per year and make semiannual interest payments. The following information is taken from the bond liability table prepared on the date of issue:

INTEREST PERIOD ENDING	INTEREST EXPENSE	CASH PAYMENT	CHANGE IN LIABILITY BALANCE	LIABILITY BALANCE
At issue				$768,075
6/30/X3	$41,476	$42,000	−524	767,551
12/31/X3	41,448	42,000	−552	766,999
6/30/X4	41,418	42,000	−582	766,417
12/31/X4	41,387	42,000	−613	765,804
6/30/X5	41,353	42,000	−647	765,157

On June 30, 19X5, after recording interest for the six-month interest period ending on that date, Frederickson paid $224,400 to retire bonds with a total face amount of $225,000, which represented 30 percent of the bond issue.

REQUIRED:

1. Prepare the entry to record the interest for the six-month interest period ended on June 30, 19X5.

2. Compute the amount of unamortized premium for all the bonds at June 30, 19X5.

3. What is the unamortized premium applicable to the bonds that are being retired?

4. Prepare the journal entry to record the bond retirement.

P11B-55. RECORDING CAPITAL AND OPERATING LEASES   Trippler Company has decided to lease its new office building. The following information is available for the lease:

Cost of building if purchased	$725,000
Length of lease.	15 years
Terms	$100,000 per year*
Economic life of building.	20 years
Appropriate interest rate	12 percent

* The first payment is due at the end of the first year of the lease.

REQUIRED:

1. Determine whether this is a capital lease or an operating lease.

2. Regardless of your answer to the preceding question, assume that this is a capital lease. Record the liability and corresponding asset for this acquisition.

P11B-56. LEVERAGE   Cook Corporation issued financial statements at December 31, 19X8, that include the following information:

Balance sheet at December 31, 19X8:

Assets	$8,000,000
Liabilities	1,200,000
Stockholders' equity (300,000 shares)	6,800,000

Income statement for 19X8:

Income from operations	$1,200,000
Less: Interest expense	100,000
Income before taxes	$1,100,000
Less: Income taxes expense (.30).	330,000
Net income.	$ 770,000

The levels of assets, liabilities, stockholders' equity, and operating income have been stable in recent years; however, Cook Corporation is planning a $1,800,000 expansion program that will increase income from operations by $500,000 to $1,700,000. Cook is planning to sell 12.5 percent bonds at par to finance the expansion.

REQUIRED:

1. What earnings per share does Cook report before the expansion?

2. What earnings per share will Cook report if the proposed expansion is undertaken? Would this use of leverage be advantageous to Cook's stockholders? Explain.

3. Suppose income from operations will increase by only $200,000. Would this use of leverage be advantageous to Cook's stockholders? Explain.

4. Suppose that income from operations will increase by $500,000 and that Cook could also raise the required $1,800,000 by issuing an additional 100,000 shares of capital stock. Which means of financing would stockholders prefer? Explain.

P11B-57. CAPITAL VERSUS OPERATING LEASES   Stewart TV Rental plans to acquire 1,000 new television sets. The televisions will be leased from the manufacturer. Lease payments will be $122,000 per year for four years, with the first payment due one year after the lease is signed. The televisions have an expected life of four years and no residual value.

REQUIRED:

1. Assuming that this is a capital lease, determine the present value of the lease payments at an effective interest rate of 14 percent.

2. Prepare a capital lease amortization table, using the following column headings:

ANNUAL LEASE PERIOD ENDED	INTEREST EXPENSE	CASH PAYMENT	CHANGE IN LEASE LIABILITY	LEASE LIABILITY BALANCE

3. Determine the interest expense and straight-line depreciation expense for the first two years, assuming a capital lease.

4. By how much would the expense be changed in each of the first two years if the lease were considered to be an operating lease rather than a capital lease?

5. Why might a firm prefer a capital lease to an operating lease despite the larger reported expenses in the early years of the lease?

ANALYTICAL OPPORTUNITIES

A11B-58. BOND INFORMATION IN *THE WALL STREET JOURNAL*   *The Wall Street Journal,* as currently published, is divided into three sections—a news section, a "Marketplace" section, and a "Money and Investing" section. The "Money and Investing" section contains a large amount of information concerning bonds.

REQUIRED:

1. Locate a recent copy of *The Wall Street Journal.* Prepare a list of the tables it contains that present information about bonds (or *debentures,* as unsecured bonds are called). For each table, write a sentence describing the bonds to which it pertains and information presented.

2. Write a brief paragraph that describes differences between the information presented about corporate bonds in corporate financial statements and the information presented about those bonds in *The Wall Street Journal.*

A11B-59. BOND COVENANTS AND FINANCIAL REPORTING STANDARDS   Bondholders receive bond certificates, one for each bond, that describe the payments promised by the issuer of the bonds. In addition, the issuing corporation frequently enters a supplementary agreement, called a *bond indenture,* with a trustee who represents the bondholders. The provisions or covenants of the indenture may place restrictions on the issuer for the benefit of the bondholders. For example, an indenture may require that the issuer's ratio of total liabilities to total stockholders' equity never rise above a specified level or that periodic payments be made to the trustee who administers a "sinking fund" to provide for the retirement of bonds.

Consider Roswell Manufacturing's bond indenture, which requires Roswell's ratio of total liabilities to total stockholders' equity never to exceed 2 : 1. If Roswell violates this requirement, the bond indenture specifies very costly penalties, and if the violation continues, the entire bond issue must be retired at a disadvantageous price and refinanced. In recent years, Roswell's ratio has averaged about 1.5 : 1 ($15 million in total liabilities and $10 million in total stockholders' equity). However, Roswell has an opportunity to purchase one of its major competitors, Ashland Products. The acquisition will require $4.5 million in additional capital, but will double Roswell's net income. Roswell does not believe that a stock issue is feasible in the current environment. The Financial Accounting Standards Board has recently issued an exposure draft for a new standard concerning accounting for employee pension and retirement benefits, which is strongly supported by the Securities and Exchange Commission. Implementation of the new standard will add about $2 millon to Roswell's long-term liabilities. Roswell's CEO, Martha Cooper, has written a strong letter of objection to the FASB. The FASB received similar letters from over 300 companies.

REQUIRED:

1. Write a paragraph presenting an analysis of the impact of the proposed standard on Roswell Manufacturing.

2. If you were a member of the FASB and met Martha Cooper at a professional meeting, how would you respond to her objection?

A11B-60. EVALUATING USE OF LEVERAGE   Gearing Manufacturing, Inc., is planning a $1,000,000 expansion of its production facilities. The expansion could be financed by the issuance of $1,250,000 in 12 percent bonds or by the issuance of $1,250,000 in capital stock, which would raise the number of shares outstanding from 50,000 to 75,000. Gearing pays income taxes at a rate of 30 percent.

REQUIRED:

1. Suppose that income from operations is expected to be $550,000 per year for the duration of the proposed bond issue. Should Gearing finance with bonds or stock? Explain your answer.

2. Suppose that income from operations is expected to be $350,000 per year for the duration of the proposed bond issue. Should Gearing finance with bonds or stock? Explain your answer.

3. Suppose that income from operations varies from year to year but is expected to be above $450,000, 40 percent of the time and below $450,000, 60 percent of the time. Should Gearing finance with bonds or stock? Explain your answer.

4. As an investor, how would you use accounting information to evaluate the risk of excessive use of leverage? What additional information would be useful? Explain.

**LEARNING
OBJECTIVES**

Careful study of this
chapter will enable
you to:

1. List the various
   forms of equity and
   describe their use
   in raising capital.
2. Record sales of par
   and nopar stock.
3. State the effect of
   dividends on re-
   tained earnings and
   dividends payable.
4. Calculate preferred
   stock dividends.
5. Account for the
   purchase and sale
   of treasury stock.
6. Describe the differ-
   ences between
   cash dividends,
   stock dividends,
   and stock splits.
7. Prepare income
   statements and
   balance sheet
   equity sections for
   proprietorships and
   partnerships.

12 OWNERS' EQUITY

**EQUITY (OWNERS'
EQUITY):** The owners'
claims against the assets
of a business entity, which
equal the residual interest
in the assets that remains
after deducting liabilities.

As we have seen, liabilities—both current and noncurrent—represent the claims of creditors against the assets of a business entity, whereas equity, the subject of this chapter, represents the claims of a firm's owners against its assets. Current liabilities are claims that are satisfied within the longer of one year or one operating cycle, and long-term liabilities represent claims that are satisfied beyond the longer of one year or one operating cycle. Equity, in contrast, represents an assortment of claims held by owners of a firm, some of which will be paid as dividends and some of which will not be paid until the end of the entity's business life. Unlike liabilities, most equity items do not have a strict payment schedule but are paid at the discretion of the firm and its owners.

Equity, then (or **owners' equity,** as it is also called), is the owners' claims against the assets of a business entity, which equal the residual interest in the assets that remains after all liabilities have been deducted. Liabilities also represent interest in or claims against the assets of an entity, but unlike equity, liabilities usually arise from contracts that determine or make estimable both the amount of the claim and the date on which the claim is to be paid. Although the owners, as a body, can control the payment of their claims against the entity, the amount and timing of such payments also depend on the profitability of the firm, the firm's expansion plans, and numerous other considerations.

All business entities have owners' equity accounts that represent the claims of the owners against the assets of the entity. However, the structure of owners' equity accounts varies from one firm to another, depending on the form of the business entity. You will recall from Chapter 1 that business entities take three distinct forms: (1) corporations, (2) partnerships, and (3) sole proprietorships. Each form has a distinctive owners' equity account structure that reflects fundamental differences in the relationship between the entity and its owners. This chapter considers owners' equity accounting for all three forms of entity, but it emphasizes owners' equity accounting for corporations. The first two parts of the chapter explain owners' equity accounting for corporations, including accounting for capital stock (preferred and common), dividends, and retained earnings. The third part of the chapter describes owners' equity accounting for unincorporated business entities, including partnerships and sole proprietorships.

ACCOUNTING FOR CAPITAL STOCK

Our explanation of equity in corporations (which is called *stockholders' equity*) begins with a description of the legal basis for corporate equity and a discussion of the several forms of capital stock that are issued in exchange for capital contributions from stockholders. In addition, we will illustrate accounting procedures for various transactions between the entity and its stockholders.

CORPORATE CHARTERS AND STOCK

CHARTER (ARTICLES OF INCORPORATION): A document that authorizes the creation of a corporation, stating its name and purpose and the names of the incorporators and describing the stock the corporation is authorized to issue.

Corporations are authorized, or chartered, in accordance with the provisions of state laws that govern the structure and operation of corporations. Although the detailed provisions of incorporation laws vary from state to state, all states require persons who wish to form a corporation to apply to a prescribed state official for the issuance of a charter. The **charter,** which is sometimes called **articles of incorporation,** is a document that authorizes the creation of the corporation as a separate legal entity and sets forth the name and purpose of the corporation, the names of the persons creating the corporation (the incorporators), and a description of the stock the corporation is authorized to issue. (Under law, a corporation is an artificial person whose rights and duties are specified by law.)

A typical corporate charter contains provisions that describe how stock may be issued by the corporation. The following three provisions are of particular significance from an accounting viewpoint:

1. Authorization to issue stock in a limited number of classes
2. A maximum number of shares that a corporation may issue in each class
3. A minimum amount for which each share must be isssued

SHARE: One of a large number of equal units into which a firm's total equity is divided.

STOCK CERTIFICATE: A document that represents one or more shares of stock and is issued in exchange for cash or other assets.

STOCKHOLDER (SHAREHOLDER): The owner (holder) of one or more shares of a corporation's stock; an owner of the corporation.

The total equity of a corporation is divided into a large number of equal equity units called **shares.** Shares are represented by documents called **stock certificates;** a single certificate may represent one or more shares. Stock certificates are issued by a corporation in exchange for cash or other assets. The holders of stock certificates own the corporation and are called **stockholders** or **shareholders.** A stock certificate (illustrated in Exhibit 12–1) indicates the name of the issuing corporation, the name of the stockholder, the date of issuance by the corporation, the number of shares represented, and the class of stock. Stock certificates and their associated ownership rights can be transferred from one person to another without disrupting the operations of the corporation. (Gathering large amounts of capital and maintaining operations over long periods are much easier when ownership rights can be transferred in this way.) Individuals or organizations with capital are more willing to invest in a stable entity than in one that must be reorganized every time one of the owners wishes to withdraw his or her capital.

AUTHORIZED SHARES: The maximum number of shares of a given class of stock that a firm may legally issue (sell).

ISSUED SHARES: The number of shares of a given class of stock actually sold to stockholders.

OUTSTANDING SHARES: The number of issued shares actually in the hands of stockholders.

The corporation's charter limits the number of shares the entity may issue in each class of stock. This maximum is the number of **authorized shares,** as distinguished from the number of **issued shares,** which is the number of shares actually sold to stockholders. (A corporation rarely issues all the shares authorized.) The number of shares issued is further distinguished from the number of **outstanding shares,** which is the number of issued shares actually in the hands of stockholders. (When firms reacquire their own stock, the reacquired shares are not considered to be outstanding.) Accordingly, a firm's balance sheet usually reports the number of shares authorized, the number issued, and the number outstanding.

Separate capital stock accounts are established for each class of stock. Thus amounts contributed by stockholders in exchange for common stock and preferred stock, two forms of stock described later in this chapter, are recorded in different capital stock accounts. In addition, the amount contributed by stock-

EXHIBIT 12–1   STOCK CERTIFICATE

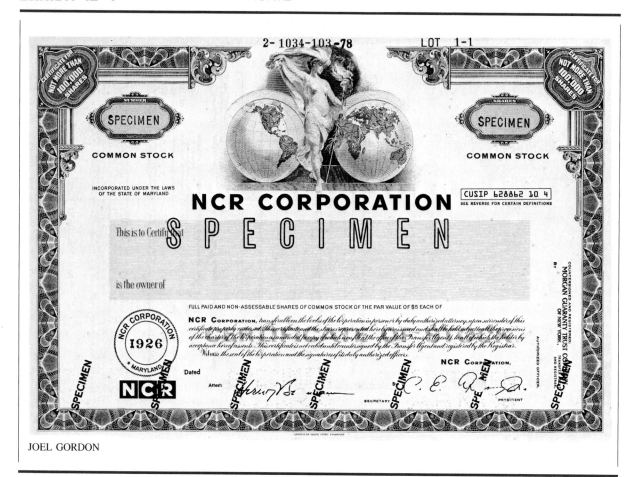

JOEL GORDON

holders in exchange for a single form of stock is often divided and recorded in two separate accounts, as explained in the next section.

PAR VALUE

PAR VALUE: A monetary amount assigned to, and printed on, each share of stock that establishes a minimum price for the stock when issued but does not determine the economic value of the stock.

PAID-IN CAPITAL IN EXCESS OF PAR: The excess of total paid-in capital over the total par value of common (or preferred) shares issued by a corporation.

In previous chapters, the contributions of stockholders in exchange for stock were recorded in a single account called *capital stock.* In practice, however, capital contributed, or paid in, by stockholders is usually divided between two accounts, on the basis of the par value of the stock. **Par value** is an arbitrary monetary amount printed on each share of stock that establishes a minimum price for the stock when issued but does not determine the market value of the stock. Although the par value of stock sold by the corporation should not exceed the owners' contribution, the par value is frequently less than the amount paid by owners. When par is less than the amount paid for the stock by owners, the capital contributed by stockholders is divided between a par value account, representing the par value times the number of shares sold, and an account called **paid-in capital in excess of par,** representing the excess of the proceeds over the par value of the shares sold.

To illustrate, consider TriCounty Corporation, which has a single class of common stock with a $10 par value. TriCounty has issued 8,000 shares. All 8,000 shares were issued 10 years ago for $12 per share. On December 31, 19X9, the equity section of TriCounty's balance sheet appears as follows:

Capital stock:	
Common stock, $10 par [($10)(8,000 shares)].	$ 80,000
Paid-in capital in excess of par [($12 − $10)(8,000 shares)]	16,000
Total capital stock.	$ 96,000
Retained earnings	31,000
Total equity	$127,000

The equity section is divided into two main subsections—one for capital contributed by stockholders, called *capital stock* (it is also often called *contributed capital* or *paid-in capital*), and another for accumulated income in excess of losses and payments to owners, called *retained earnings.* In the balance sheets shown in previous chapters, the capital stock subsection was represented by a single amount; here it is divided on the basis of par value. The $96,000 proceeds received from the sale of the stock was recorded in two separate accounts—$80,000 in common stock, $10 par, and $16,000 in paid-in capital in excess of par, common stock. (Note that it is possible to determine how many shares of stock have been sold by dividing the amount in the common stock account by the par value: $80,000/$10 = 8,000 shares.)

COMMON AND PREFERRED STOCK

COMMON STOCK: Shares of equity of a corporation that usually give stockholders both voting rights and a residual equity interest.

RESIDUAL EQUITY INTEREST: An interest in all retained earnings of a corporation that are not specifically reserved for parties other than common stockholders.

PREFERRED STOCK: Shares of equity of a corporation that usually do not give voting rights to the stockholders but grant a specified dividend subject to various guarantees or preferences.

All classes of stock are designated as either common stock or preferred stock. **Common stock** consists of shares of equity of a corporation that usually give stockholders both voting rights and a residual equity interest. Voting rights enable a stockholder to participate in electing the board of directors of the corporation. A **residual equity interest** is an interest in all retained earnings of the corporation that are not specifically reserved for parties other than common stockholders. In contrast, **preferred stock** consists of shares of equity of a corporation that usually do not give voting rights to the stockholders but grant specific dividends subject to various guarantees or preferences.

Some differences between preferred stock and common stock favor the preferred stockholder; other differences favor the common stockholder. Most differences between preferred and common stock are designated in the firm's corporate charter and take one or more of the following forms:

1. *Dividend preferences:* Many preferred stock issues require that the issuing corporation pay dividends to preferred stockholders before paying dividends to common stockholders. This means that common stockholders may be obliged to miss a dividend in order that preferred dividends be paid. In addition, preferred dividends may be cumulative and participating, as explained later in this chapter.

2. *Conversion privileges:* Under specified conditions, holders of convertible preferred stock have the option of exchanging their preferred shares for common shares. For example, the charter might provide that each share of preferred stock is convertible into a fixed number of common shares after a certain date.

3. *Liquidation preferences:* If and when a corporation is dissolved, liquidating distributions are made to stockholders. Corporate charters frequently require that the claims of preferred stockholders be satisfied before those of common stockholders. In addition, the charter may specify a liquidating amount for preferred shares.

4. *Call provisions:* The corporate charter may authorize or even require the corporation to repurchase any preferred shares that are sold. In such cases, the charter usually fixes the *call price* (the amount to be paid to the preferred stockholders) and specifies a date on or after which the shares may or must be repurchased.

5. *Denial of voting rights:* Most preferred stock does not confer voting rights, which means that preferred stockholders, unlike common stockholders, cannot vote at stockholders' meetings.

Observe that the first three characteristics of preferred stock are advantageous for preferred stockholders, whereas the last two characteristics usually work in the interest of common stockholders. We shall illustrate the distinctive character of preferred stock with two analysis sections. The first compares preferred and common stock as alternative means of raising expansion capital.

ANALYSIS
GOING PUBLIC

Georgian Manufacturing, Inc., is a successful small manufacturer of high-technology electronic components for computing equipment. Georgian wishes to double its scale of operations in order to meet both existing and expected demand for its products. Georgian is a *closed corporation,* which means that its stock is held by a small group of private investors and is not available for sale to the public. Various factors, including high interest rates and a shortage of loanable funds, preclude Georgian from borrowing the necessary expansion capital from financial institutions. Consequently, Georgian is forced to consider "going public," that is, issuing stock to the general public and making a transition from a closed corporation to an *open (public) corporation.* The corporation is considering issuing either preferred stock or common stock. A final decision as to the best means of financing the expansion has not been made, but the owners are discussing the following questions:

1. *What is the impact on corporate control and profit sharing of issuing common stock?*

The common stock issue required to double the size of operations would more than double the number of outstanding shares. Present stockholders would be unable to buy enough of the new shares to prevent control of the company from passing to the new stockholders. In other words, the new stockholder group would own more than 50 percent of the shares. If the new owners were sufficiently well organized and cohesive, they could elect a majority of directors and control the company. On the other hand, if the new shares were purchased by a large number of investors with no organized interest in controlling Georgian, then effective control would remain in the hands of the original owners. Of course, the risk of losing control at some future time would still exist. Furthermore, Georgian expects its expansion to be immensely profitable. The new common stock would transfer more than half of that profit to the new stockholders.

2. *What is the impact on control and profit sharing of securing the required capital by issuing preferred stock?*

Since preferred stock would not confer voting rights, control would remain in the hands of the original owners. However, in order to sell the required amount of preferred stock, the preferred dividend rate would have to be set at a very high level. Since preferred dividends must be paid before any dividends are paid to the common stockholders, there would be a severe reduction in common dividends during the early years of the expansion.

The following analysis illustrates the use of conversion privileges and call provisions — two important characteristics of many preferred stock issues.

ANALYSIS
FORCING
REDEMPTION OF
CONVERTIBLE
PREFERRED STOCK

Four years ago, Hansen Products Company issued at par 4,000 shares of 8 percent, $100 par, convertible preferred stock. The stock is callable at par. The conversion privilege normally allows the issuer to sell the convertible preferred stock with a lower dividend rate than would have been required for comparable stock without a conversion feature.

Each share of Hansen's convertible preferred stock can be exchanged for four shares of Hansen Products' common stock. Hansen's common stock is currently selling for $29 per share. Thus one share of convertible preferred stock can be exchanged for four shares of common stock that are selling for an aggregate price of $116 [(4) ($29)]. Dividends on the common stock are $1.00 per share per year. Hansen's controller suggests that the company notify owners of the convertible preferred stock that all 4,000 shares will be redeemed at par ($100) in 60 days if they are not converted into common stock.

1. *Is it wise for Hansen to force conversion or redemption of the convertible preferred stock?*

The prospective cash outflows for the convertible preferred and the equivalent common stock are as follows:

	PREFERRED STOCK	COMMON STOCK
Yearly dividend	$32,000*	$16,000†

* (.08) ($100) (4,000 shares) = $32,000
† Each preferred share is convertible into four shares of common stock, which totals 16,000 shares for the entire preferred stock issue. The dividend is $1.00 per share.

On the basis of these prospective cash outflows, Hansen should attempt to force conversion of the convertible preferred stock, because $16,000 of cash would be saved each year. Even if the common dividend is increased, so long as it stays below $2.00 per share, the annual cash savings would still be positive. If the common dividend exceeds $2.00 per share, owners of the convertible preferred stock are likely to request conversion, as dividends on four common shares would exceed the $8.00 per share preferred dividend.

However, another factor in Hansen's decision is the possibility that the common stock price will fall below $25 per share during the 60-day conversion period. When the common stock price is below $25 per share, owners of the convertible preferred stock could be better off by asking for the $100 redemption price. Redeeming the entire 4,000 shares would require a $400,000 cash outflow, a very undesirable outcome from Hansen's perspective.

Corporations are not restricted to issuing only one class of common or preferred stock. A corporation may be authorized by its charter to issue several classes of preferred stock, each with a different set of terms and provisions. Although most corporations issue only a single class of common stock, firms are sometimes authorized to issue several. For example, General Motors Corporation's capital stock consists of four classes of preferred stock and three classes of common stock:

GENERAL MOTORS CORPORATION
(Amounts in Millions of Dollars)

	1988	1987
Capital stock:		
Preferred stock, without par value, cumulative dividends:		
$5.00 series, stated value $100 per share, redeemable at Corporation option at $120 per share	$153.0	$153.0
$3.75 series, stated value $100 per share, redeemable at Corporation option at $100 per share	81.4	81.4
Preference stock, $0.10 par value:		
E series, convertible one for one at fixed dates into Class E common stock	1.0	1.0
H series, convertible one for two at fixed dates into Class H common stock	1.0	1.0
Common stock, $1⅔ par value	510.7	521.1
Class E common stock, $0.10 par value	5.1	5.2
Class H common stock, $0.10 par value	12.8	6.5
Total capital stock	$765.0	$769.2

When more than one class of common stock is issued, only one class of the stock represents the residual equity interest—the class without preferences or voting restrictions (GM's $1⅔ par value common in our example). When a corporation issues a single class of common stock, as is usually the case, the residual equity interest is vested in a single ownership group. That group receives all benefits not specifically assigned to preferred stockholders or to other holders of claims against the entity. However, that group also bears the ultimate responsibility for the losses of the corporation, because the residual equity interest is guaranteed neither dividends during the life of the corporation nor assets upon its liquidation.

So far, we have described the principal characteristics of common and preferred stock, including the legal basis for the issuance of stock and the various distinctions between preferred and common stock. We now turn to the accounting procedures for the issuance of stock.

ISSUANCE OF STOCK

The principal steps in the issuance of stock are the following:

1. The authorization of the stock in the corporation's charter
2. The issuance (sale) of shares
3. The collection of cash or other assets from stockholders

Stock is said to be issued, or sold, when the stockholder's name is entered on the corporation's record. Shares of stock are sold when a corporation is formed, and additional shares may be sold subsequently. Usually, a corporation does not sell all the shares of stock that it is authorized to issue, and a number of authorized but unissued shares are maintained to fulfill miscellaneous requirements. For example, a corporation with an employee stock purchase plan may prefer to issue new shares to the plan rather than buying back already outstanding shares for reissue. While it is possible to secure authorization to issue shares beyond the number specified in a corporation's original charter, the procedure is lengthy and complicated.

Although shares may be sold directly to individual stockholders, large corporations frequently delegate the actual selling of shares and collecting of proceeds to brokers or underwriters. In all illustrations, exercises, and problems in this book, the issuance of stock and the collection of the sale proceeds occur at the same time. However, in actual practice, cash collection may follow issuance by a few days or weeks. When collection follows the issuance of stock, the corporation must establish an account receivable in the interim.

Sale for Cash

Let us illustrate the accounting procedures for the sale of common and preferred stock. Assume that the newly organized Spectator Corporation is authorized by its charter from the State of Ohio to issue the following two classes of stock:

1. 50,000 shares of common stock with a $2 par value per share
2. 1,000 shares of preferred stock with a 9 percent dividend rate and a $20 par value per share

Four accounts are necessary to record the issuance of stock by Spectator: (1) common stock, par value, (2) paid-in capital in excess of par, common stock, (3) preferred stock, par value, and (4) paid-in capital in excess of par, preferred stock. In other words, two capital accounts are required to record the issuance of each class of stock, one for the par value and one for paid-in capital excess of par.

On January 1, 19X6, Spectator Corporation issues 200 shares of preferred stock at $22 per share and 20,000 shares of common stock at $2.50 per share. All shares are issued for cash, and the amounts of cash received for each issue are divided among the par and excess over par accounts as follows:

Preferred stock:

Par value [($20)(200 shares)]	$ 4,000	
Excess over par [($22 − $20)(200 shares)].	400	
Proceeds from preferred stock		
[($22)(200 shares)]		$ 4,400

Common stock:

Par value [($2)(20,000 shares)].	$40,000	
Excess over par [($2.50 − $2.00)(20,000 shares)]	10,000	
Proceeds from common stock		
[($2.50)(20,000 shares)]		50,000
Total proceeds		$54,400

The following entry records the issuance of these shares:

Cash	54,400	
Preferred stock		4,000
Paid-in capital in excess of par, preferred stock		400
Common stock		40,000
Paid-in capital in excess of par, common stock		10,000

A balance sheet prepared by Spectator immediately after the issuance of shares on January 1, 19X6, would contain the stockholders' equity section shown in Exhibit 12–2. (Note that retained earnings displays a zero balance because Spectator is a newly formed corporation.)

Sale for Noncash Assets

Stock may be sold for noncash assets as well as for cash, as an extension of our example shows. On February 1, 19X6, Spectator Corporation issues 4,000 addi-

---

EXHIBIT 12–2   STOCKHOLDERS' EQUITY

SPECTATOR CORPORATION
Stockholders' Equity
As of January 1, 19X6

Capital stock:
  Preferred stock, 9 percent, $20 par, 1,000 shares authorized,
    200 shares issued and outstanding . . . . $ 4,000
  Common stock, $2 par, 50,000 shares authorized,
    20,000 shares issued and outstanding 40,000
  Paid-in capital in excess of par:
    Preferred stock. 400
    Common stock 10,000
      Total capital stock. $54,400
Retained earnings . . . . –0–
      Total stockholders' equity $54,400

tional shares of common stock in exchange for a parcel of land valued at $11,000. The transaction is recorded by the following entry:

Land..	11,000	
Common stock [($2)(4,000)]..........................		8,000
Paid-in capital in excess of par, common stock		
($11,000 − $8,000).................................		3,000

The value of the land ($11,000) suggests that the stock exchanged for it is worth $2.75 per share [$11,000/4,000 shares]. Thus the value of Spectator's stock seems to have increased by $.25 per share [$2.75 − $2.50] since January 1, 19X6, when it was first issued. If there were reason to believe that the stock was still worth only $2.50 per share (as there would be if the stock were being bought and sold at $2.50 on a stock exchange), then this might suggest that the land was worth $10,000 [($2.50)(4,000 shares)], rather than $11,000. If the land were worth only $10,000, then Spectator would record $10,000 for land, $8,000 for common stock, and only $2,000 for paid-in capital in excess of par.

Nopar Stock

The stock issued by Spectator Corporation carried a par value that represents the stated capital of the corporation. **Stated capital (legal capital)** is the amount of capital that, under law, cannot be returned to the corporation's owners unless the corporation is liquidated. Even when state law permits the issuance of **nopar stock** (stock without a par value), it frequently requires that nopar stock have a stated (legal) value set by the corporation in order to establish the corporation's stated or legal capital. Stated value, like par value, is recorded in a separate equity account called *common* (or *preferred*) *stock, nopar.* Any excess paid for the stock over its stated value is recorded in an equity account called *paid-in capital in excess of stated value.* To illustrate, 1,000 shares of nopar common stock with a stated value of $20 per share, issued for $22,400 cash, would be recorded by the following entry:

Cash	22,400	
Common stock, nopar ($20 stated value)		20,000
Paid-in capital in excess of stated value...............		2,400

In this instance, the stated value of stock functions exactly as does the par value of stock to identify the legal capital portion of total paid-in or contributed capital (capital stock). However, some state laws define stated (legal) capital as the entire paid-in capital associated with nopar stock. In those cases, the entire paid-in capital amount is credited to a single common (or preferred) stock account.

TRANSFERS OF SHARES AMONG STOCKHOLDERS

In general, the purchase or sale of stock after it is first issued does not alter the equity accounts of the issuing corporation unless that corporation is itself the purchaser or the seller. Each corporation maintains a list of its stockholders that includes the quantity and serial numbers of the shares held. When shares are sold by one stockholder to another, the stockholder list of the issuing corporation must be updated. (Of course, such sales do not alter the amounts recorded in the equity accounts; nor do they cause any additional journal entries on the records of the corporation whose shares are traded.) Large corporations usually retain an independent *stock transfer agent* to maintain their stockholder lists. Stock transfer agents also arrange for the transfer of certificates among stockholders and the issuance of new certificates to stockholders. Although the sale or purchase of shares among stockholders does not affect the equity accounts of the issuing entity, such sales or purchases obviously require entries into the accounts of the buyers and sellers of the shares. These transactions are investments, as explained in Chapter 8 and 14.

PURCHASES AND SALES OF TREASURY STOCK

When a corporation purchases its own previously issued stock, the stock that it buys is called **treasury stock.** Corporations purchase treasury stock for many reasons:

TREASURY STOCK: Previously issued stock that is repurchased by the issuing corporation.

1. To buy out the ownership interest of one or more stockholders
2. To reduce the size of corporate operations
3. To reduce the number of outstanding shares of stock in an attempt to increase earnings per share and market value per share
4. To acquire shares to be transferred to employees under stock bonus, stock option, or stock purchase plans
5. To satisfy the terms of a business combination in which the corporation must give a quantity of shares of its stock as part of the acquisition of another business
6. To reduce vulnerability to an unfriendly takeover

If the objective of acquiring treasury stock is to reduce the size of corporate operations, the treasury shares are likely to be retired after purchase. More frequently, however, repurchased stock is held in the corporation's treasury until circumstances favor its resale to stockholders or until it is used to meet the various obligations of the corporation that must be satisfied with shares of stock.

At first thought, one might consider recording the acquisition of treasury stock as an exchange of cash for an investment in stock (an exchange of one asset for another). However, that approach fails to recognize that the treasury stock is already represented by amounts in the corporation's own equity accounts. Although the shares would represent an asset to another entity that acquired them, they cannot represent an asset to the entity that issued them. Thus the purchase of treasury stock is a temporary reduction of equity rather than the acquisition of an investment. In other words, instead of requiring a debit to an investment account, the acquisition of treasury stock requires a debit to a contra-equity account, treasury stock. This interpretation is consistent with the provisions of most state incorporation laws, which preclude the payment of dividends on treasury shares.

The illustration that follows demonstrates the appropriate accounting for the purchase and sale of treasury stock and shows the impact of treasury stock transactions on the equity section of the balance sheet.[1] On June 30, 19X2, the balance sheet of Tyrrell, Inc., includes the information shown in Exhibit 12–3.

---

[1] Actually, generally accepted accounting principles allow two alternative methods of accounting for treasury stock. The first, the *cost method,* is demonstrated here. The second is the *par value method,* which is described in intermediate accounting courses.

EXHIBIT 12–3 **EQUITY ACCOUNTS IN THE BALANCE SHEET**

TYRRELL, INC.
Balance Sheet
As of June 30, 19X2

ASSETS

Cash	$ 30,000
Other assets	140,000
Total assets	$170,000

LIABILITIES

Liabilities	$ 50,000

EQUITY

Capital stock:

Common stock, $10 par, 10,000 shares authorized,		
6,000 shares issued and outstanding	$60,000	
Paid-in capital in excess of par	24,000	
Total capital stock	$84,000	
Retained earnings	36,000	
Total equity		120,000
Total liabilities and equity		$170,000

On the next day, July 1, 19X2, Tyrrell purchases 500 outstanding shares of its own common stock for $22 cash per share. The acquisition of these treasury shares is recorded as follows:

Treasury stock	11,000	
Cash		11,000

Since treasury stock is a contra-equity account, this entry reduces both assets and equity by $11,000. If a balance sheet were prepared on July 1, 19X2, stockholders' equity would be presented as follows:

Capital stock:

Common stock, $10 par, 10,000 shares authorized,	
6,000 shares issued, 5,500 shares outstanding	$ 60,000
Paid-in capital in excess of par	24,000
Total capital stock	$ 84,000
Retained earnings	36,000
	$120,000
Less: Treasury stock (500 shares at cost)	11,000
Total equity	$109,000

Notice in the description of common stock that the number of outstanding common shares has been reduced by the purchase of the 500 treasury shares.

On July 2, 19X2, Tyrrell sells 200 of its treasury shares for $25 cash per share. This sale is recorded by the following entry:

Cash	5,000	
Treasury stock (at cost, $22 per share)		4,400
Paid-in capital from treasury stock transactions		
[($25 − $22)(200)]		600

The $600 excess of proceeds over the cost of the 200 treasury shares is recorded as a credit to a special paid-in capital account. This $600 is not a gain, because a corporation cannot generate income by buying and selling its own stock. Accordingly, this sale of treasury stock does not alter Tyrrell's retained earnings.[2]

Assuming that the purchase and sale of treasury stock are Tyrrell's only transactions on July 1 and July 2, the balance sheet on July 2, 19X2, would be as shown in Exhibit 12–4. Transactions involving treasury stock do not alter the amounts recorded for the original quantity of stock issued. Thus Tyrrell's common stock and paid-in capital in excess of par remain at $60,000 and $24,000, respectively. These original amounts are unaltered because the entire cost of the treasury shares is recorded in a contra-equity account, which then is subtracted as the final item in the stockholders' equity section of the balance sheet. Of course, if the appropriate legal action were taken to permanently retire treasury shares, then both the treasury stock and the common stock accounts would have to be reduced.

Although the balances of common stock and paid-in capital are not altered by treasury stock transactions, the description of the common stock balance must be changed to reflect the decrease in the number of common shares outstanding. Before the treasury stock purchase and sale, 6,000 shares of common stock were issued and outstanding; after the treasury stock purchase and sale, 6,000 shares remain issued but only 5,700 shares (6,000 − 500 + 200) are outstanding, with 300 held as treasury shares. Thus the number of shares issued is not altered by these transactions.

In summary, accounting procedures for capital stock provide for the recording of the temporary purchase of the firm's own stock as well as the issuance and retirement of stock. Issuance and retirement of shares alter the balances of the capital stock accounts directly, but the purchase of treasury shares is recorded in a contra-equity account, leaving the capital stock balances unaltered.

DIVIDENDS AND RETAINED EARNINGS

Recall that equity consists of two parts—capital stock and retained earnings. Capital stock is recorded in accounts that are separate from the retained earnings and dividends accounts to which we now turn. Retained earnings is the accumulation of net income from corporate operations less distributions of that income in the form of dividends. Retained earnings may be altered to reflect certain adjustments to the firm's prior period earnings or to establish "reserve" accounts

---

[2] When proceeds from the sale of treasury stock fall short of the cost of the treasury stock, the difference is recorded as a debit to paid-in capital from treasury stock transactions. If the balance of that paid-in capital account is not large enough to absorb the entire debit, then the unabsorbed debit reduces retained earnings.

EXHIBIT 12–4   BALANCE SHEET WITH TREASURY STOCK DATA

TYRRELL, INC.
Balance Sheet
As of July 2, 19X2

ASSETS

Cash	$ 24,000
Other assets	140,000
Total assets	$164,000

LIABILITIES

Liabilities	$ 50,000

EQUITY

Capital stock:

Common stock, $10 par, 10,000 shares authorized, 6,000 shares issued, 5,700 outstanding	$ 60,000	
Paid-in capital in excess of par	24,000	
Paid-in capital from treasury stock transactions	600	
Total capital stock	$ 84,600	
Retained earnings	36,000	
	$120,600	
Less: Treasury stock (300 shares at cost)	6,600	
Total equity		114,000
Total liabilities and equity		$164,000

for those segments of retained earnings that may not be paid out as dividends. The sections that follow discuss the accounting and reporting procedures related to retained earnings. Among these are accounting for common and preferred dividends, accounting for stock dividends and stock splits, accounting for prior period adjustments and reserves, and preparing the statement of changes in retained earnings. The corporation's record of retained earnings provides important information for those who must decide on dividend policy; in addition, the retained earnings record is of considerable interest to stockholders because it is a major element in determining their relative shares of equity in the corporation.

CASH DIVIDENDS Recall from Chapter 1 that a dividend is an amount paid periodically by a corporation to a stockholder as a return on invested capital. Dividends represent distributions of accumulated net income, and they may be paid as cash, as noncash assets, or even as additional shares of a corporation's own stock. All dividends, whatever their form, reduce retained earnings.

Let us begin by considering accounting for cash dividends, which are by far the most common form of dividend. The payment of a cash dividend is preceded by an official announcement or declaration by the firm's board of directors of the intention to pay a dividend. The dividend declaration specifies four things:

DECLARATION DATE: The date on which a corporation announces its intention to pay a dividend on capital stock.

DATE OF RECORD: The date on which a stockholder must have owned one or more shares of stock in order to receive the dividend.

PAYMENT DATE: The date on which a dividend is actually paid.

1. The **declaration date,** the date on which a corporation announces its intention to pay a dividend on capital stock

2. The dollar amount of the dividend, usually stated as the number of dollars per share

3. The **date of record,** the date on which a stockholder must have owned one or more shares of stock in order to receive the dividend

4. The **payment date,** the date on which a dividend is actually paid

Since the stock of most corporations is continually changing hands, it is necessary to establish a date at which ownership of one or more shares entitles the owner to receive a dividend. If a share of stock is sold between the date of record and the dividend payment date, the former owner of the share, rather than the new owner, is entitled to the dividend. On the other hand, if a share of stock is sold between the declaration date and the date of record, the new owner, rather than the former owner, is entitled to the dividend. As we have already mentioned, when stock is widely traded, an independent stock transfer agent usually maintains the corporation's stockholder list and determines who holds outstanding shares on the date of record for each dividend.

The following illustration demonstrates the complete sequence of accounting events related to the declaration and payment of cash dividends: The Kingsmill Corporation has issued 3,000 shares of common stock, all of the same class; 2,800 shares are outstanding and 200 shares are held as treasury stock. (Remember that dividends are not paid on treasury stock.) On November 15, 19X9, Kingsmill's board of directors declares a cash dividend of $2.00 per share payable on December 15, 19X9, to stockholders of record on December 1, 19X9. The dividend declaration requires the following entry on November 15, 19X9:

Dividends [($2)(2,800 shares)]	5,600	
Dividends payable		5,600

No correcting entry is required on December 1, 19X9 (the date of record). Since the exact number of outstanding shares is usually known on the date of declaration, the declaration date entry generally records the correct amount of the dividend.

On December 15, 19X9, the payment date of Kingsmill's dividend, the following entry is required:

Dividends payable	5,600	
Cash		5,600

Payment of the dividend merely removes the dividend liability from Kingsmill's records, since the dividend (a reduction in retained earnings) was recorded on its declaration date.

At the end of the accounting period, the dividends account is closed into Kingsmill's retained earnings account. Thus the declaration and payment of cash dividends reduces both total assets (cash) and total equity (retained earnings).

If the dates of declaration, record, and payment are assumed to occur on the same day, the preparation of the journal entries and related discussions are simplified. Unless otherwise noted, this assumption will be used in all illustrations, exercises, and problems in this text. This simplification permits the declaration and payment of dividends to be recorded in a single entry of the following form:

Dividends.	xxx	
Cash		xxx

A corporation's policy on payment of dividends to stockholders is established by the corporation's board of directors. However, the dividend policy is subject to the limitations set by the incorporation laws of the state in which the entity is incorporated. The laws of most states specify that dividends paid by a corporation cannot reduce equity below the corporation's stated (or legal) capital.[3] Such reduction constitutes *liquidation* of the corporation which, under the law, may precipitate dissolution of the organization. In other words, equity may not fall below legal capital without endangering the continuance of the corporation. Legal capital thus restricts the payment of dividends on all classes of stock, including preferred as well as common stock. The next section considers additional restrictions on the payment of dividends that may be imposed by the terms of preferred stock issues.

PREFERRED STOCK DIVIDEND PREFERENCES

While dividends on common stock are set by the corporation's board of directors, dividends on preferred stock are usually established as one of the terms of the preferred stock issue. Most preferred stock issues fix their dividend rate as a percentage of the par value. For example, an 8 percent preferred share with a $100 par value has an annual dividend of $8. Of course, both preferred and common dividends are subject to various restrictions imposed by statute, by the corporate charter, by the terms of preferred stock issues, and by contracts with bondholders and others.

Although preferred stockholders have no voting rights, they are "preferred" in the sense that corporations are required to pay dividends to them before paying dividends to common stockholders. Such dividend preferences can take three forms: (1) current dividend preference, (2) cumulative dividend preference, and (3) participating dividend preference. Most preferred stock issues grant a current dividend preference, and some preferred stock issues also grant one or both of the other preferences, thereby further enhancing the likelihood of dividend payments. The following sections will describe and illustrate the current dividend preference, first alone and then in combination with the cumulative and participating dividend preferences.

Current Dividend Preference

CURRENT DIVIDEND PREFERENCE: The provision that stockholders of preferred shares are to be paid current dividends before any dividends are paid to common stockholders.

Current dividend preference provides that current dividends must be paid to preferred stockholders before any dividends are paid to common stockholders. Although this means that common stockholders might not receive a dividend in a year in which preferred stockholders do receive a dividend, the current dividend preference does not guarantee payment of preferred dividends. In lean years, both common and preferred stockholders may fail to receive dividends.

[3] As pointed out earlier, stated (legal) capital is measured differently in different states. In many states, it is defined as the total par value of shares issued to stockholders. However, in states that permit the issuance of nopar stock, stated (legal) capital may be defined as either (1) the total value of all nopar shares, based on the per-share value established by the corporation, or (2) the amount for which all nopar stock was issued by the corporation.

The following illustration demonstrates the impact of the current dividend preference: During the period 19X6 through 19X9, Cook Corporation's capital stock maintained the following structure:

Capital stock:	
Preferred stock, 8 percent, $10 par, 5,000 shares authorized, 4,000 shares issued and outstanding.....................	$ 40,000
Common stock, $5 par, 50,000 shares authorized, 30,000 shares issued and outstanding.........................	150,000
Paid-in capital in excess of par, common stock.............	60,000
Total capital stock....................................	$250,000

Cook's board of directors determined the total dollar amount available for preferred and common dividends in each year from 19X6 through 19X9 as shown in the second column of the following schedule:

YEAR	AMOUNT AVAILABLE FOR DIVIDENDS	DIVIDEND TO PREFERRED	DIVIDEND TO COMMON
19X6	$12,200	$3,200*	$9,000†
19X7	7,000	3,200	3,800
19X8	2,000	2,000	–0–
19X9	–0–	–0–	–0–

* (.08)($40,000) = $3,200.
† ($12,200 − $3,200) = $9,000.

This schedule shows that the common dividend is any positive amount remaining after the full preferred dividend has been paid. If the total amount available for dividends is less than the full preferred dividend, the entire amount available is paid to preferred stockholders.

Cumulative Dividend Preference

CUMULATIVE DIVIDEND PREFERENCE: The provision that stockholders of cumulative preferred shares are to be paid both dividends in arrears and current dividends before dividends are paid to common stockholders.

Most preferred stock is cumulative. The **cumulative dividend preference** requires the eventual payment of all preferred dividends, both dividends in arrears and current dividends, before any dividends are paid to common stockholders. (Preferred stock dividends remaining unpaid for one or more years are considered to be in arrears.) In other words, no dividends can be paid to common stockholders until all prior preferred dividends and all current dividends have been paid. The cumulative dividend preference thus includes the current dividend preference.

The impact of the cumulative dividend preference is demonstrated in the following illustration: Jefferson Manufacturing has a single class of common stock and a single class of cumulative preferred stock. The cumulative preferred stock requires the corporation to pay an annual dividend of $6,500 to preferred stockholders. On January 1, 19X4, Jefferson's preferred dividends are one year in arrears, which means that Jefferson declared neither preferred nor common dividends in 19X3. During the three years 19X4–19X6, Jefferson's board of directors determined the total dollar amount available for dividends to be as shown in the second column of the following schedule:

YEAR	AMOUNT AVAILABLE FOR DIVIDENDS	DIVIDEND TO PREFERRED	DIVIDEND TO COMMON
19X4	$ 9,000	$ 9,000	$ –0–
19X5	12,000	10,500	1,500
19X6	15,000	6,500	8,500

This schedule also shows the required payments to preferred and common stockholders. The $9,000 dividend paid to preferred stockholders in 19X4 removes the $6,500 arrearage from 19X3, but it leaves dividends in arrears at January 1, 19X5, of $4,000, the excess of preferred dividends for 19X3 and 19X4 over the amount paid in 19X4 [(2)($6,500) − $9,000 = $4,000]. The $10,500 dividend to preferred stockholders in 19X5 pays the current preferred dividend ($6,500), removes the $4,000 arrearage, and leaves $1,500 to be paid to common stockholders [$12,000 − $6,500 − $4,000 = $1,500].

Dividends do not become a liability of a corporation until they have been declared by the board of directors. If preferred dividends in arrears have not been declared, they are not recorded as liabilities, but they are disclosed in a footnote to the financial statements.

Participating Dividend Preference

PARTICIPATING DIVIDEND PREFERENCE: The provision that stockholders of participating preferred shares receive a share of amounts available for dividends to other classes of stock in addition to the stated dividend on the preferred stock.

For some classes of preferred stock, dividends are not restricted to a fixed rate. Preferred stock that pays dividends in excess of its stated dividend rate is called *participating preferred stock.* (Preferred stock that cannot pay dividends in excess of the current dividend preference plus cumulative dividends in arrears, if any, is called *nonparticipating preferred stock.*) The **participating dividend preference** provides that stockholders of participating preferred shares receive, in addition to the stated dividend, a share of amounts available for distribution as dividends to other classes of stock. Participating preferred stock may be either fully participating or partially participating. Fully participating preferred stock receives a share of *all* amounts available for dividends. Common stock is allocated a dividend at the same rate on par as the current dividend preference, and any remainder is divided between preferred and common stockholders, usually in proportion to the total par value of the two classes of stock. Assume that $26,000 is available for dividends, the total par value of the 8 percent preferred is $50,000, and the total common par value is $150,000. First, the preferred stockholders are allocated $4,000, using the preferred dividend rate [(.08)($50,000)]. Second, the common stockholders are allocated $12,000, also using the preferred dividend rate [(.08)($150,000)]. Finally, the $10,000 remainder [$26,000 − $4,000 − $12,000] is allocated—$2,500 to preferred [($50,000/$200,000)($10,000)] and $7,500 to common [($150,000/$200,000)($10,000)]. Partially participating preferred stock also receives a share of amounts available for dividends, but the share is limited to a specified percentage of preferred par value.

The following analysis illustrates the impact that preferred stock dividend preferences and other factors can have on the formulation of dividend policy for common stock.

ANALYSIS
DIVIDEND POLICY

The balance sheet of Edwardian Products, Inc., has the following equity section:

Capital stock:
  Preferred stock, 12 percent, $100 par, 1,000 shares authorized, issued,
    and outstanding $100,000
  Common stock, $20 par, 10,000 shares authorized, issued, and
    outstanding   200,000
  Paid-in capital in excess of par, common stock   60,000
Retained earnings   120,000
    Total equity $480,000

Edwardian's preferred stock is cumulative, but nonparticipating. Preferred dividends of $6,000 are in arrears. An agreement with bondholders precludes $75,000 of retained earnings from serving as a basis for dividend declaration. Edwardian is in the process of formulating its cash dividend policy for the current year. The questions that follow bear on Edwardian's decision:

1. *How much cash is available for the payment of current dividends?*

The board of directors has examined the requirements for cash in coming years and has determined that current cash dividends to holders of preferred and common shares cannot exceed $33,000. In determining the limitation, the board considered its plans for growth as well as its expectations for cash requirements arising from normal operations.

2. *What limitation is imposed on the current dividend by the availability of retained earnings?*

The retained earnings balance is $120,000, but only $45,000 is available to support current dividends because of the $75,000 restriction imposed by bondholders. Edwardian's directors believe, however, that it would be imprudent to pay dividends up to the limit of available retained earnings. Moreover, the retained earnings limitation is not the most immediate limitation on dividends, since the cash limitation is less.

3. *How is the dividend divided between preferred and common stockholders?*

The board decides that it will pay a total current dividend of $33,000. The preferred stockholders must be paid $18,000, $12,000 to satisfy the current dividend [(.12)($100,000)] plus the $6,000 arrearage. Since the preferred stock is nonparticipating, the $15,000 remainder is allocated to common stockholders. Accordingly, common stockholders receive $15,000 of the $33,000 and preferred stockholders receive $18,000.

STOCK DIVIDENDS

STOCK DIVIDEND: A dividend paid to stockholders in the form of additional shares of stock (instead of cash).

When a cash divided is paid, a corporation transfers cash to stockholders. In contrast, when a corporation pays a **stock dividend,** the corporation transfers additional shares of its own stock to stockholders. While a cash dividend reduces both total assets and total equity, a stock dividend alters neither total assets nor total equity. A stock dividend merely rearranges the equity section of the balance sheet. For each share outstanding, a fixed number of new shares is issued, and an amount of retained earnings is transferred to capital stock accounts in a process known as *capitalization of retained earnings.* The amount of retained earnings capitalized for each new share depends on the size of the stock dividend. Small stock dividends increase the number of outstanding shares by less than 20 to 25 percent; they are capitalized by using the stock's market value just before the dividend. On the other hand, large stock dividends increase the number of outstanding shares by more than 20 to 25 percent; they are capitalized by using the stock's par value.

The following illustration demonstrates accounting for a small stock dividend: Arlington Corporation has 6,000 shares of outstanding common stock at a par value of $10 per share. Arlington's common stock is selling at $12 per share when the corporation declares and pays a 5 percent stock dividend. This means that the outstanding common shares increase in number by 5 percent, so that one new common share is issued for each 20 shares of outstanding common stock. Thus an investor holding 100 shares of Arlington's common stock would receive

5 additional shares [(.05)(100 shares), or 100 shares/20] upon payment of the 5 percent stock dividend. In total, Arlington's 5 percent stock dividend requires the issuance of 300 new shares [(.05)(6,000) or 6,000/20]. Declaration and payment of the stock dividend are summarized in the following journal entry:

Retained earnings [($12)(300 shares)]	3,600	
Common stock [($10)(300 shares)]		3,000
Paid-in capital in excess of par, common stock		600

Note that the stock dividend merely transfers $3,600 of equity from retained earnings to the capital stock accounts. Since this is a small stock dividend, the amount of transferred equity is based on the current market price of the stock.

Although a stock dividend increases the number of shares held by each stockholder, it does not alter the proportion of shares held by each stockholder. For example, if an investor held 1,500 out of 6,000 outstanding shares before a 10 percent stock dividend, the investor would hold 1,650 out of 6,600 outstanding shares after the dividend. Thus the investor would hold 25 percent of the outstanding shares both before and after the stock dividend [(1,500/6,000) = (1,650/6,600) = .25] and would have a 25 percent claim on earnings and stockholders' equity before and after the stock dividend.

Stock dividends neither enhance the wealth of investors nor alter the proportionate ownership shares in the corporation. They merely notify stockholders that a portion of retained earnings has been capitalized (transferred to capital stock) and thus is no longer available to support the payment of dividends.

STOCK SPLITS

STOCK SPLIT: A stock issue by a corporation that increases the number of outstanding shares without changing the balance of any of its equity accounts.

A stock split, like a stock dividend, increases the number of outstanding shares without altering the proportionate ownership interest of a stockholder. Unlike a stock dividend, however, a stock split involves a decrease in the per-share par value (or stated value), with no capitalization of retained earnings. In other words, a **stock split** is a stock issue by a corporation that increases the number of outstanding shares without changing the balance of any of its equity accounts. Let's consider a corporation that has 10,000 outstanding common shares with a par value of $30 per share. In a two-for-one stock split, stockholders will exchange each of the 10,000 original shares for two new shares; the number of outstanding shares will rise from 10,000 to 20,000; and the par value of each share will be reduced to $15 per share. The total par value of all the stock remains $300,000 [($30)(10,000 shares) = ($15)(20,000 shares)], but the split has the effect of distributing that par value over a larger number of shares. No entry is required to record a stock split because no account balance changes. The changes in the par value and the number of outstanding shares are merely noted in the corporation's records.

Stock splits are used to reduce the per-share price of the stock. If nothing else changes, a two-for-one split should cut the market price of the stock in half. A corporation may reduce the per-share price to facilitate trading of the stock, under the assumption that a higher per-share price is an obstacle to purchases and sales of stock, particularly for small investors.

STATEMENT OF CHANGES IN RETAINED EARNINGS

Dividends are reported in the firm's statement of changes in retained earnings. Recall from Chapter 1 that this statement links the income statement and the balance sheet by showing net income as one of the factors that causes retained earnings to change. Net income is not the only factor that causes retained earnings to change. We have just seen that cash dividends and stock dividends alter retained earnings. Retained earnings may also be altered by a group of items known as prior period adjustments. Furthermore, certain restrictions on dividends may require the establishment of special retained earnings accounts that are described in footnotes to the statement of changes in retained earnings. These topics are discussed in the sections that follow.

Error Corrections and Prior Period Adjustments

PRIOR PERIOD ADJUST-MENT: Correction of an error made in the financial statements of a prior period that is entered as a direct adjustment to retained earnings.

Errors in recording transactions can distort the financial statements. If errors are discovered and corrected before the closing process described in Chapter 5, then no great harm is done. However, if errors go undetected, then flawed financial statements are issued. No matter when they are discovered, errors should be corrected. If an error resulted in a misstatement of net income, then correction may require a direct adjustment to retained earnings called a **prior period adjustment.** To illustrate, let us suppose that Byrnes Corporation uses a computer program to calculate depreciation expense. In 19X8 a programming error caused the 19X8 depreciation expense to be understated by $16,000. The error was not discovered until August 19X9; consequently, 19X8 net income after income taxes (which are paid at a rate of 25 percent) was overstated by $12,000 [$16,000 $(1 - .25)$]. The following correcting entry is appropriate in 19X9:

Tax refund receivable	4,000	
Retained earnings	12,000	
Accumulated depreciation		16,000

In addition, Byrnes Corporation's statement of changes in retained earnings (shown in Exhibit 12–5) includes a $12,000 prior period adjustment resulting from the depreciation error. Notice that the adjustment is deducted from the beginning balance of retained earnings to produce an adjusted beginning balance.

Financial accounting standards define prior period adjustments in a way that specifically excludes adjustments arising from estimation errors and changes

---

EXHIBIT 12–5   **PRIOR PERIOD ADJUSTMENT**

BYRNES CORPORATION
Statement of Changes in Retained Earnings
For the Year Ended December 31, 19X9

Retained earnings, 12/31/X8		$157,000
Less: Prior period adjustment:		
Correction of error in calculation of 19X8 depreciation		
expense (net of tax).		12,000
Retained earnings as adjusted, 12/31/X8		$145,000
Add: Net income for 19X9		65,000
		$210,000
Less: Dividends declared in 19X9:		
Cash dividend, preferred stock	$ 4,000	
Stock dividend, common stock	20,000	24,000
Retained earnings, 12/31/X9		$186,000

from one accounting principle to another. These errors are corrected by adjusting the related income accounts for the period in which they are discovered. Because of the FASB's strict definition, relatively few corrections qualify for treatment as prior period adjustments. The definition of prior period adjustments is restrictive because of the view that adjustments reported on the statement of changes in retained earnings are not as visible to the readers of financial statements as adjustments reported as part of net income.

Restrictions on Retained Earnings

The reporting of retained earnings is also complicated by legal restrictions on the payment of dividends. For example, under most corporate charters, the balance of a corporation's retained earnings represents an upper limit to the entity's ability to pay dividends. (Dividends cannot reduce retained earnings below zero.) A corporation's capacity to pay dividends may be further restricted by agreements with lenders, by the corporation's board of directors, and by various provisions of state law, as the following examples indicate:

1. An agreement between the corporation and bondholders may require that retained earnings never fall below a specified level so long as the bonds are outstanding.

2. The firm's board of directors may set aside a portion of retained earnings and declare it unavailable for the payment of dividends. Such action may be used to communicate to stockholders changes in dividend policy made necessary by expansion programs or other decisions of the board.

3. State law may require that dividends not reduce retained earnings below the cost of treasury stock.

Restrictions of this sort are usually disclosed in footnotes to the statement of changes in retained earnings. In some cases, however, a separate "reserve" account is established for the restricted portion of retained earnings. The reserve account is called either *restricted earnings* or *appropriation of retained earnings*. The account title frequently indicates quite specifically the nature of the restriction or appropriation, as, for example, "restricted retained earnings under agreements with bondholders" or "appropriation of retained earnings for plant expansion." When reserve accounts are used, retained earnings is reported on two or more lines in the equity section of the balance sheet, with one line for each restriction and one for "unrestricted retained earnings" or "unappropriated retained earnings."

This completes our discussion of equity accounting for corporations. We turn now to equity accounting for unincorporated entities and a comparison of the equity structures exhibited by the three forms of business entity.

EQUITY IN UNINCORPORATED ENTITIES

Accounting for owners' equity is not restricted to corporations. Although the largest share of business activity is conducted by corporations, the actual number of unincorporated businesses—sole proprietorships and partnerships—is greater. Unlike the equity of corporations, the equity of unincorporated business entities is not divided into equal equity units or shares. Instead, varying amounts of equity are identified with the proprietor or with particular partners. Like the equity of a stockholder, the equity of a proprietor or partner can be sold and transferred to another individual. But unlike the transfer of corporate stock, the transfer of a proprietor's or partner's equity must be negotiated with great care and attention to the unique character of the equity interest. The existence of equal equity units or shares makes the sale and transfer of corporate equity interests much easier than the transfer of equity in sole proprietorships and partnerships.

STRUCTURE OF EQUITY ACCOUNTS

In sole proprietorships and partnerships, the identification of equity interest with particular persons influences both the structure of the equity accounts and the calculation of net income. A separate equity account is established to record the equity interest of each proprietor or partner, and salaries paid to proprietors or partners are treated as income distributions rather than as expenses.

Although the equity of any business entity can be divided into paid-in, or contributed, capital and retained earnings, not all entities record the two sources of equity in separate accounts. Corporations record capital stock and retained earnings in separate accounts, but sole proprietorships and partnerships usually combine the two sources of equity. Sole proprietorships usually maintain a single equity account that represents the entire equity of the owner. Partnerships usually maintain a separate equity account for each partner.

Exhibit 12–6 shows the different account structures for equity accounts in sole proprietorships, partnerships, and corporations. All three types of business entity record net income in temporary accounts before transferring it to the permanent equity or retained earnings accounts. All three maintain an income summary account, and all three maintain one or more accounts to record distributions to owners. In a corporation, distributions to owners are recorded as dividends. In sole proprietorships and partnerships, distributions to owners are recorded as *drawings;* in partnerships a separate drawings account is maintained for each partner. As shown in Exhibit 12–6, all temporary equity accounts are closed into permanent equity accounts.

INCOME AND CLOSING ENTRIES

Accounting for the income of sole proprietorships and partnerships differs from accounting for the income of corporations in two important respects: First, salaries paid by a corporation to employees who are also stockholders of the corporation are treated as expenses and, like any salary expense, are subtracted in the calculation of net income. In contrast, salaries paid by a proprietorship or partnership to owners of the entity are treated as drawings rather than expenses and are not subtracted in the determination of net income. In other words, salaries paid to owners of sole proprietorships and partnerships are regarded as distributions of income and are treated in the same manner as dividends.

Income tax laws are responsible for a second source of difference between accounting for the income of incorporated and unincorporated business entities. Corporations and their owners must pay taxes twice on corporate income. When corporate income is reported, the corporation pays a tax based on the amount reported; when dividends are distributed to stockholders, stockholders in turn pay a personal tax on dividends received. In contrast, the income of sole proprietorships and partnerships is taxed only once. A proprietor pays tax on reported

EXHIBIT 12–6 THREE EQUITY ACCOUNT STRUCTURES

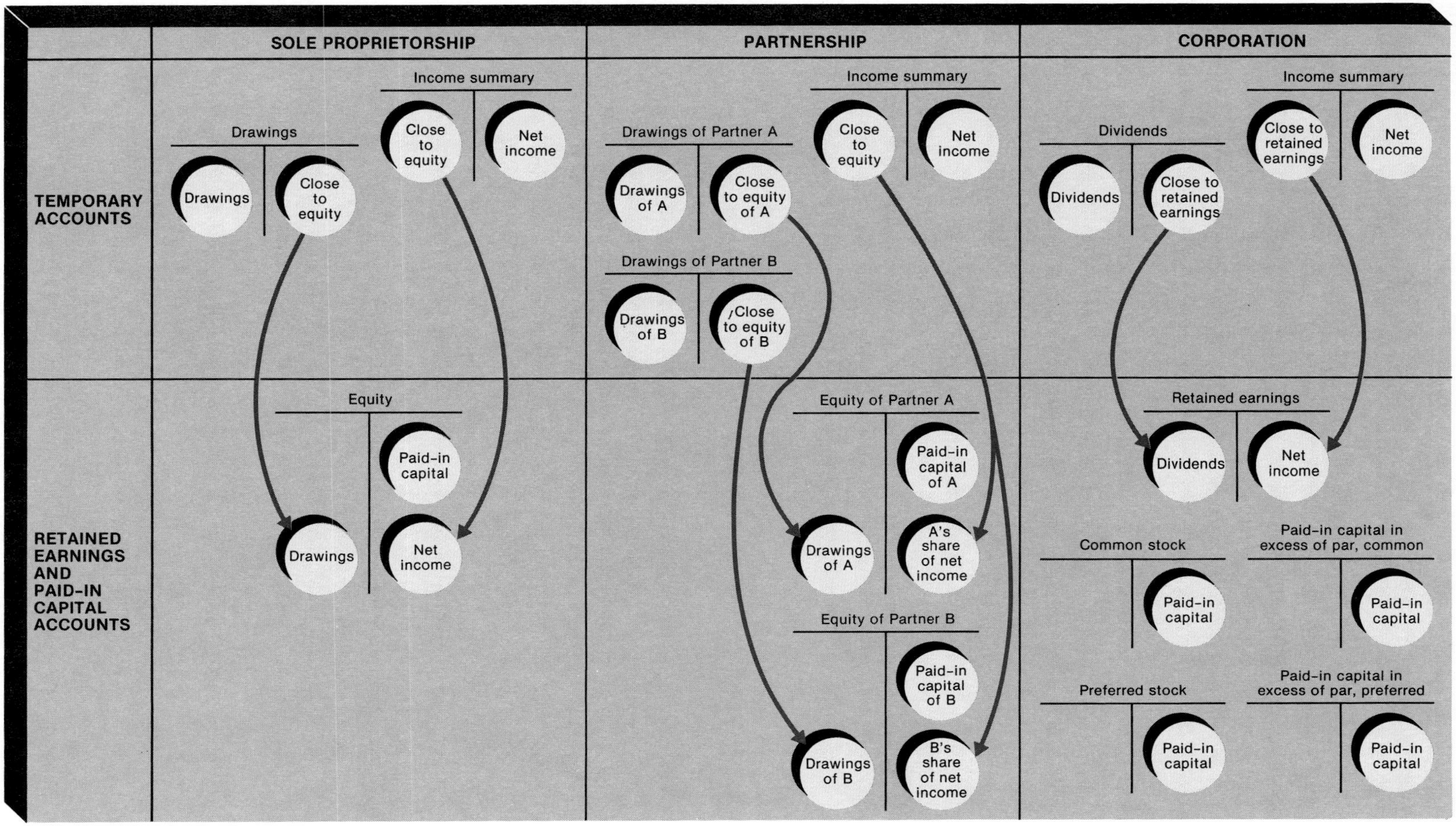

EXHIBIT 12–7 **EQUITY AT JANUARY 1, 19X9**

	SOLE PROPRIETORSHIP	PARTNERSHIP	CORPORATION
Paid-in capital	$220,000	$220,000	$220,000
Retained earnings	80,000	80,000	62,000*
Total equity	$300,000	$300,000	$282,000

* Differs from proprietorship and partnership retained earnings because corporate income is taxed directly.

proprietorship income as part of the tax on his or her total personal income. A member of a partnership also pays tax on his or her share of partnership income as part of the tax on total personal income.

The following illustration demonstrates the differences between the incomes of incorporated and unincorporated business entities. In addition, this example demonstrates the income distribution and closing entries for sole proprietorships and partnerships that were shown diagrammatically in Exhibit 12–6. Consider three business entities that are virtually identical except that the first is a sole proprietorship, the second is a partnership, and the third is a corporation. Except for differences arising from income taxes, these three organizations have the same financial transactions, the same assets, the same liabilities, and the same distribution of income to the owner or owners. As shown in Exhibit 12–7, the owners have contributed the same amount of paid-in capital ($220,000) and have permitted the same amount of pretax income to be retained ($80,000).[4]

The sole proprietor, one partner, and one stockholder are employed by their respective organizations, and each is paid an annual salary of $20,000. Additional distributions to owners total $6,000. Condensed 19X9 income statements for the three organizations are shown in Exhibit 12–8. Observe that both the sole proprietorship and the partnership report net income of $35,000, while the corporation reports a net income of only $12,000. The $23,000 difference stems from two sources: (1) The owner's $20,000 salary is included in the corporation's salary expense but will be a distribution of net income for the sole proprietorship and the partnership, and (2) taxes of $3,000 on corporate income were paid by the corporation and included in other expenses.

Each of the three business entities differs from the other two in still another way: As shown in Exhibit 12–9, each entity uses distinctive income distribution and closing entries. The sole proprietorship records income-related cash distributions to the owner in a drawings account; both the income summary account and the drawings account are closed into an equity account. The partnership entries are based on two additional pieces of information: (1) Total drawings of $6,000 include $3,000 drawn by partner A and $3,000 drawn by partner B, and

[4] Note that the amount of retained earnings for the corporation is $18,000 less than the amount of retained earnings for either the sole proprietorship or the partnership. This difference is the accumulated result of differing income tax assessments since the inception of the organizations. (Recall that corporations pay taxes on income, whereas sole proprietorships and partnerships do not. Of course, taxes on the earnings of proprietorships and partnerships are levied on the personal tax returns of the proprietors or partners.)

EXHIBIT 12–8   THREE ENTITIES' 19X9 INCOME STATEMENTS

SOLE PROPRIETORSHIP		PARTNERSHIP		CORPORATION	
Revenue	$100,000	Revenue	$100,000	Revenue	$100,000
Salary expense	(30,000)	Salary expense	(30,000)	Salary expense	(50,000)
Other expenses	(35,000)	Other expenses	(35,000)	Other expenses	(38,000)
Net income	$ 35,000	Net income	$ 35,000	Net income	$ 12,000

EXHIBIT 12–9   INCOME DISTRIBUTION AND CLOSING ENTRIES FOR THREE ENTITIES

	SOLE PROPRIETORSHIP	PARTNERSHIP	CORPORATION

INCOME DISTRIBUTION	Drawings. 20,000
	  Cash 20,000
	Entry to record salary to owner
	
	Drawings. 6,000
	  Cash 6,000
	Entry to record other drawings by owner
		Drawings of A. 20,000
		  Cash 20,000
		Entry to record salary to partner A
		
		Drawings of A. 3,000
		Drawings of B. 3,000
		  Cash 6,000
		Entry to record other drawings by partners
			The corporation records the $20,000 salary paid to a stockholder as an expense rather than as an income distribution.
			
			Dividends 6,000
			  Cash 6,000
			Entry to record dividend payment to stockholders

CLOSING ENTRIES	Income summary 35,000
	  Equity 35,000
	Entry to close income summary to equity
	
	Equity. 26,000
	  Drawings. 26,000
	Entry to close drawings account to equity
		Income summary 35,000
		  Equity of A (80%) . . . 28,000
		  Equity of B (20%) . . . 7,000
		Entry to close income summary to equity and to distribute income between partners
		
		Equity of A 23,000
		Equity of B 3,000
		  Drawings of A 23,000
		  Drawings of B 3,000
		Entry to close drawings to equity accounts
			Income summary 12,000
			  Retained earnings . . . 12,000
			Entry to close income summary to retained earnings
			
			Retained earnings 6,000
			  Dividends 6,000
			Entry to close dividends to retained earnings

(2) under the terms of the partnership agreement, partner A's equity account is credited with 80 percent of partnership net income and partner B's equity account is credited with the remaining 20 percent.

The partnership records income-related cash distributions to partners in the drawings accounts of the two partners, and the drawings account balances are closed into the respective partners' equity accounts. Finally, the corporation records income-related cash distributions to stockholders in a dividends account; like the income summary, the dividends account is closed into the retained earnings account.

The 19X9 statements of changes in equity or retained earnings for the three organizations are as shown in Exhibit 12–10. While corporations prepare statements of changes in retained earnings, sole proprietorships and partnerships

EXHIBIT 12–10   THREE ENTITIES' 19X9 SUMMARY STATEMENTS OF CHANGES IN EQUITY OR RETAINED EARNINGS

SOLE PROPRIETORSHIP		PARTNERSHIP		CORPORATION	
Equity, 12/31/X8	$300,000	Equity, 23/31/X8	$300,000	Retained earnings, 12/31/X8	$62,000
Net income	35,000	Net income	35,000	Net income	12,000
	$335,000		$335,000		$74,000
Owner's salary	(20,000)	Partner's salary	(20,000)		
Other drawings	(6,000)	Other drawings	(6,000)	Dividends	(6,000)
Equity, 12/31/X9	$309,000	Equity, 12/31/X9	$309,000	Retained earnings, 12/31/X9	$68,000

prepare statements of changes in equity that include both paid-in capital and retained earnings.

SUMMARY

Equity represents the claims of owners against the assets of a business entity. The first part of the chapter discussed the characteristics of two forms of equity — common and preferred stock. Common stockholders control the corporation, while preferred stockholders have the right to receive dividends before dividends are paid to common stockholders. The next part of the chapter examined the entries necessary to record the issuance of par, nopar, and stated value common and preferred stock. When stock is issued at amounts in excess of par or stated value, the excess is recorded in a separate capital stock account. The par and excess over par received from stockholders at issuance are both components of capital stock. Stock may be reacquired by the firm after issuance. Reacquired stock is called *treasury stock* and is recorded in a contra-equity account that is subtracted from the total of stockholders' equity. Sale of treasury stock above cost produces a credit to the paid-in capital from treasury stock account. Sale of treasury stock below cost reduces the paid-in capital account and may reduce retained earnings.

The next section of the chapter discussed dividends. Dividends reduce retained earnings. Corporations pay both cash and stock dividends. Cash dividends require that cash be transferred to stockholders. Stock dividends require the transfer of additional stock to stockholders. Entries for dividends are required on the dates of declaration and payment. A list of the persons to whom dividends are paid is compiled between declaration and payment on the date of record. Preferred dividends may be cumulative (i.e., dividends in arrears must be paid before common stockholders are paid any dividends), participating (i.e., preferred stockholders share with common stockholders in all amounts available for dividends), or both.

The next section of the chapter examined the statement of changes in retained earnings. In addition to net income (or net loss) and dividends, retained earnings may be altered for prior period adjustments to correct errors in previous financial statements or for certain types of restrictions on dividends.

The final section of the chapter explained equity accounting in unincorporated entities (proprietorships and partnerships). The major differences between equity accounting in corporations and unincorporated entities are (1) the use of capital stock and retained earnings accounts to record the equity of all owners in corporations versus a separate equity account for each owner in unincorporated entities and (2) the terminology used for payments to owners.

KEY TERMS

AUTHORIZED SHARES (p. 557)

CHARTER (ARTICLES OF INCORPORATION) (p. 557)

COMMON STOCK (p. 559)

CUMULATIVE DIVIDEND PREFERENCE (p. 572)

CURRENT DIVIDEND PREFERENCE (p. 571)

DATE OF RECORD (p. 570)

DECLARATION DATE (p. 570)

EQUITY (OWNERS' EQUITY) (p. 556)

ISSUED SHARES (p. 557)

NOPAR STOCK (p. 565)

OUTSTANDING SHARES (p. 557)

PAID-IN CAPITAL IN EXCESS OF PAR (p. 558)

PARTICIPATING DIVIDEND PREFERENCE (p. 573)

PAR VALUE (p. 558)

PAYMENT DATE (p. 570)

PREFERRED STOCK (p. 559)

PRIOR PERIOD ADJUSTMENT (p. 576)

RESIDUAL EQUITY INTEREST (p. 559)

SHARE (p. 557)

STATED CAPITAL (LEGAL CAPITAL) (p. 565)

STOCK CERTIFICATE (p. 557)

STOCK DIVIDEND (p. 574)

STOCKHOLDER (SHAREHOLDER) (p. 557)

STOCK SPLIT (p. 575)

TREASURY STOCK (p. 566)

QUESTIONS

Q12-1. What is the purpose of a corporate charter?

Q12-2. Describe the difference between authorized, issued, and outstanding shares.

Q12-3. What is the difference between a closed corporation and an open corporation?

Q12-4. How do common and preferred stock differ?

Q12-5. What is the difference between par value and stated value?

Q12-6. When are paid-in capital (capital stock) and legal capital different?

Q12-7. How is treasury stock presented in the balance sheet?

Q12-8. Why is it not appropriate to report treasury stock as an asset?

Q12-9. What entries are made (if any) at the declaration date, date of record, and date of payment for cash dividends?

Q12-10. Name and describe the four items of information specified by a cash dividend declaration on common stock. What is the significance of each of these items from the viewpoint of the accounting system of the corporation that declares the dividend?

Q12-11. Are dividends in arrears reported among the liabilities of the dividend-paying firm? If not, how are they reported, and why?

Q12-12. How is a stock dividend different from a cash dividend?

Q12-13. What is the effect of a stock dividend on the wealth of a stockholder receiving such a dividend?

Q12-14. What is the effect of a stock split on stockholders' equity account balances?

Q12-15. When are prior period adjustments used?

Q12-16. How does equity accounting differ among sole proprietorships, partnerships, and corporations?

Q12-17. In what way are corporations subject to double taxation?

EXERCISES

E12-18.   CAPITAL STOCK   Renee Corporation has the following stockholders' equity information:

	$10 PAR COMMON	$50 PAR PREFERRED
Paid-in capital in excess of par	$750,000	$30,000
Shares:		
Authorized	1,000,000	100,000
Issued	250,000	15,000
Outstanding	246,500	15,000

Retained earnings is $109,400, and the cost of treasury shares is $42,000.

REQUIRED:

Prepare the stockholders' equity portion of Renee's 19X1 balance sheet.

E12-19.   PRESENTING COMMON STOCKHOLDERS' EQUITY   At the time of its incorporation seven years ago, LaFontain Enterprises issued 14,320 shares of $5 par common stock for $16.50 per share. At December 31, 19X9, LaFontain has $11,300 of retained earnings.

REQUIRED:

Prepare the stockholders' equity portion of LaFontain's December 31, 19X9, balance sheet.

E12-20.   ISSUING COMMON STOCK   Thoman Products, Inc., sold 21,250 shares of common stock to stockholders at the time of its incorporation. Thoman received $24.40 per share for the stock.

REQUIRED:

1. Assume that the stock has a $20 par value per share. Prepare the journal entry to record the sale and issue of the stock.
2. Assume that the stock has a $15 stated value per share. Prepare the journal entry to record the sale and issue of the stock.
3. Assume that the stock has no par value and no stated value. Prepare the journal entry to record the sale and issue of the stock.

E12-21.   ISSUING PREFERRED STOCK   Saddlebrook Enterprises sold 2,100 shares of its $50 par value preferred stock for $111,300.

REQUIRED:

Prepare the journal entry to record the sale and issuance of this stock.

E12-22.   ACCOUNTING FOR SHARES   Kress Products' corporate charter authorizes the firm to sell 800,000 shares of $10 par common stock. At the beginning of 19X7, Kress had sold 243,000 shares and had reacquired 1,650 of those shares. The reacquired shares were held as treasury stock. During 19X7 Kress sold an additional 16,300 shares and purchased 3,100 more treasury shares.

REQUIRED:

Determine the number of authorized, issued, and outstanding shares at December 31, 19X7.

E12-23.   EXCHANGE OF STOCK FOR EQUIPMENT   Grace Metallurgy acquired a new furnace by exchanging 1,250 shares of its $10 par common stock for the furnace.

REQUIRED:

1. Assume that the stock is not actively traded and that the furnace has a fair value of $31,300. Prepare the journal entry to record the exchange.
2. Assume that the stock is traded actively at a price of $27 per share and that the fair value of equipment is unknown. Prepare the journal entry to record the exchange.
3. Assume that the equipment is appraised at $34,200 and that Grace's stock is actively traded at $26 per share. Prepare the journal entry to record the exchange.

E12-24. TREASURY STOCK TRANSACTIONS   Dennison Service Corporation had no treasury stock at the beginning of 19X4. During January 19X4, Dennison purchased 7,600 shares of treasury stock at $21 per share. In April 19X4, Dennison sold 4,100 of the treasury shares for $25 per share. In August 19X4, Dennison sold the remaining treasury shares for $20 per share.

REQUIRED:

Prepare journal entries for the January, April, and August treasury stock transactions.

E12-25. PRESENTATION OF STOCKHOLDERS' EQUITY   Rehberger Corporation has the following stockholders' equity information at the end of 19X4:

Common stock, $10 par, 100,000 shares authorized, 60,000 shares issued, 59,400 shares outstanding.

Preferred stock, $100 par, 10,000 shares authorized, 1,200 shares issued and outstanding.

Paid-in capital in excess of par:

Common	$420,000
Preferred	2,400
Retained earnings	173,800
Treasury stock	9,000

REQUIRED:

Prepare the stockholders' equity portion of Rehberger's balance sheet.

E12-26. ANALYSIS OF STOCKHOLDERS' EQUITY   Gilbert Systems' December 31, 19X5, balance sheet includes the following stockholders' equity section:

Capital stock:	
Common stock, $10 par, 25,000 shares authorized	$180,000
Paid-in capital in excess of par	198,000
Paid-in capital from treasury stock transactions	3,600
Total capital stock	$381,600
Retained earnings	38,910
	$420,510
Less: Treasury stock (1,100 shares at cost)	38,500
Total stockholders' equity	$382,010

REQUIRED:

1. How many shares of common stock have been issued?

2. How many shares of common stock are outstanding?

3. What does the item "paid-in capital from treasury stock transactions" represent? Explain briefly.

E12-27. ACCOUNTING FOR EQUITY CHANGES   Fiberglass Products prepared the following statement of stockholders' equity at December 31, 19X7:

Capital stock:	
Preferred stock, 9 percent, $40 par	$ 240,000
Common stock, $10 par	1,630,000
Paid-in capital in excess of par:	
Preferred stock	12,000
Common stock	1,793,000
Paid-in capital from treasury stock transactions	7,000
Total capital stock	$3,682,000
Retained earnings	437,000
Treasury stock	(75,000)
Total stockholders' equity	$4,044,000

During 19X8, Fiberglass sold 21,000 shares of common stock for $31 per share, purchased 1,200 shares of common stock for the treasury at a cost of $25 each, and sold 1,000 of the treasury shares purchased during 19X8 for $27 per share. 19X8 net income and dividends were $238,100 and $92,000, respectively.

REQUIRED:

Prepare the stockholders' equity portion of Fiberglass' December 31, 19X8, balance sheet.

E12-28. CASH DIVIDENDS ON COMMON STOCK   Berkwild Company is authorized to issue 1,000,000 shares of common stock. At the beginning of 19X3, Berkwild had 338,000 issued and outstanding shares. On July 2, 19X3, Berkwild purchased 1,310 shares of common stock for its treasury. On March 1 and September 1, Berkwild declared a cash dividend of $1.10 per share. The dividends were paid on April 1 and October 1.

REQUIRED:

1. Prepare the entries to record the declaration of the two cash dividends.
2. Prepare the entries to record the payment of the two dividends.
3. Why are the amounts of the two dividends different?

E12-29. PREFERRED DIVIDENDS   Nathan Products' equity includes 10.8 percent, $100 par preferred stock. There are 100,000 shares authorized and 20,000 shares outstanding. Assume that Nathan Products declares and pays preferred dividends quarterly.

REQUIRED:

1. Prepare the journal entry to record declaration of one quarterly dividend.
2. Prepare the journal entry to record payment of the one quarterly dividend.

E12-30. CUMULATIVE PARTICIPATING PREFERRED DIVIDENDS   Capital stock of Barr Company includes:

> Capital stock:
> Common stock, $10 par, 150,000 shares outstanding $1,500,000
> Preferred stock, 12 percent, $100 par, 5,000 shares outstanding   500,000

As of December 31, 19X4, three years' dividends are in arrears on the preferred stock. During 19X5 Barr plans to pay dividends that total $460,000.

REQUIRED:

1. Determine the amount of dividends that will be paid to Barr's common and preferred stockholders in 19X5.
2. If Barr paid $280,000 of dividends, determine how much each group of stockholders would receive.

E12-31. STOCK DIVIDENDS   Crystal Corporation has the following information regarding its common stock:

> Its common stock is $20 par, with 300,000 shares authorized, 132,000 shares issued, and 130,600 shares outstanding.

> In August 19X6 Crystal declared and paid a 15 percent stock dividend when the market price of the common was $28 per share.

REQUIRED:

Prepare the journal entry to record declaration and payment of this stock dividend.

E12-32. STOCK DIVIDENDS AND STOCK SPLITS   The balance sheet of Castle Corporation includes the following equity section:

Capital stock:	
Common stock, $2 par, 50,000 shares authorized, 30,000 shares issued and outstanding	$ 60,000
Paid-in capital in excess of par	71,800
Total capital stock	$131,800
Retained earnings	73,000
Total equity	$204,800

REQUIRED:

1. Assume that Castle issued 30,000 shares for cash at the inception of the corporation and that no new shares have been issued since. How much cash was received for the shares issued at inception?

2. Assume that Castle issued 15,000 shares for cash at the inception of the corporation and subsequently declared a two-for-one stock split. How much cash was received for the shares issued at inception?

3. Assume that Castle issued 25,000 shares for cash at the inception of the corporation and that the remaining 5,000 shares issued are the result of stock dividends that capitalized retained earnings of $21,600. How much cash was received for the shares issued at inception?

E12-33. STATEMENT OF CHANGES IN RETAINED EARNINGS   At the end of 19X6, Wadsworth Corporation reported retained earnings of $317,200. During 19X7 Wadsworth had net income of $63,100, declared and paid cash dividends of $21,500, and declared and paid a 10 percent stock dividend in the amount of $14,200. In addition, Wadsworth determined that an error had caused its 19X4 income tax expense to be understated by $44,900.

REQUIRED:

Prepare a statement of changes in retained earnings for Wadsworth for 19X7.

E12-34. RESTRICTIONS ON RETAINED EARNINGS   At December 31, 19X7, Longfellow Clothing had $107,300 of retained earnings, all unrestricted. During 19X8 Longfellow earned net income of $39,500 and declared and paid cash dividends on common stock of $12,400. During 19X8 Longfellow sold a bond issue with a covenant that required Longfellow to transfer from retained earnings to restricted retained earnings an amount equal to the principal of the bond issue, $40,000. At December 31, 19X8, Longfellow has 10,000 shares of $10 par common stock issued and outstanding. Paid-in capital in excess of par on the common stock is $142,500.

REQUIRED:

Prepare the stockholders' equity portion of Longfellow's December 31, 19X8, balance sheet.

E12-35. PROPRIETORSHIP EQUITY ACCOUNTING   Chris Brandon operates an organ repair business as a proprietorship. At the beginning of 19X2, Chris' capital account balance was $34,150. During 19X2, the proprietorship net income was $51,280, and Chris withdrew $3,100 for living expenses each month.

REQUIRED:

1. Prepare the journal entries to record one month's drawings.

2. Prepare the journal entries to close the income summary and the year's drawings account.

3. What is Chris' capital balance after closing at the end of 19X2?

E12-36. PARTNERSHIP EQUITY ACCOUNTING   Teresa Felix and Laura Bramer operate a small accounting practice as a partnership. For 19X4 the following data are available for Teresa and Laura:

	TERESA FELIX	LAURA BRAMER
Equity, 1/1/X4	$75,000	$56,800
Drawings	62,400	55,200

19X4 partnership net income was $149,400. The partnership agreement requires that 50 percent of income or losses be divided equally and that the other 50 percent be divided according to the partners' equity, with equity being defined as beginning equity less half of drawings.

REQUIRED:

1. Prepare the journal entries to record each partner's drawings.

2. Determine the division of partnership net income, and then prepare a journal entry to close the partnership income summary account.

3. What is each partner's end-of-period equity account balance?

PROBLEMS

P12-37. PRESENTATION OF STOCKHOLDERS' EQUITY   Yeager Corporation was organized in January 19X4. During 19X4 Yeager engaged in the following stockholders' equity activities:

a) Secured approval for a corporate charter that authorizes Yeager to sell 500,000 $10 par common shares and 40,000 $100 par preferred shares.

b) Sold 60,000 of the common shares for $16 per share.

c) Sold 2,000 of the preferred shares for $102 per share.

d) Purchased 550 of the common shares for the treasury at a cost of $18 each.

e) Earned net income of $31,300.

f) Paid dividends of $6,000.

REQUIRED:

Prepare the stockholders' equity portion of Yeager's balance sheet.

P12-38. PRESENTING COMMON STOCKHOLDERS' EQUITY   Harrison Properties was incorporated at the beginning of 19X2. During 19X2 Harrison had an initial public offering of 14,000 shares of $20 par common stock at a price of $32.60 per share. All 14,000 shares were sold. Harrison had net income for the year of $4,150 and declared and paid a $.10 per share cash dividend.

REQUIRED:

Prepare the stockholders' equity portion of Harrison's December 31, 19X2, balance sheet.

P12-39. ISSUING COMMON AND PREFERRED STOCK   G. R. Clark, Inc., engaged in the following transactions during a recent year:

a) Sold 8,500 shares of $5 par common stock for $28.60 per share.

b) Sold 180 shares of 11 percent, $100 par preferred stock for $104 per share.

c) Exchanged 8,000 shares of $10 par common stock for six months' rent on 10,000 square feet of retail space. (The retail space normally rents for $4 per square foot per month.)

d) Exchanged 115 shares of the 11 percent, $100 par preferred stock for a truck that had been owned by the firm's president. The preferred stock was selling for $101 per share at the time of the exchange.

REQUIRED:

Prepare a journal entry for each of these transactions.

P12-40. ISSUING COMMON AND PREFERRED STOCK   Klaus Herrmann, a biochemistry professor, organized Bio-products, Inc., early this year. The firm will manufacture antibiotics using gene splicing technology. Bioproducts' charter authorizes the firm to issue 5,000 shares of 12 percent, $50 par preferred stock and 100,000 shares of $10 par common stock. During the year the firm engaged in the following transactions:

a) Issued 25,000 common shares to Klaus Herrmann in exchange for $275,000 cash.

b) Sold 10,000 common shares to a potential customer for $11 per share.

c) Issued 3,000 shares of preferred stock to a venture capital firm for $52 per share.

d) Gave 75 shares of common stock to Margaret Robb, a local attorney, in exchange for Margaret's work in arranging for the firm's incorporation. Margaret usually charges $900 for an incorporation.

REQUIRED:

Prepare a journal entry for each of these transactions.

P12-41. TREASURY STOCK TRANSACTIONS   Hansen, Inc., engaged in the following transactions during the current year:

a) Purchased 4,000 shares of its own $20 par common stock for $26 per share on January 14.

b) Sold 2,400 of the treasury shares to employees for $20 per share on January 31.

c) Purchased 2,000 common shares for the treasury at a cost of $27 each on July 24.

d) Sold the remaining 1,600 shares from the January 14 purchase and 1,500 of the shares from the July 24 purchase to employees for $22 per share on August 1.

REQUIRED:

1. Prepare journal entries for each of these transactions.

2. What is the effect on total stockholders' equity of each of the four transactions?

P12-42. SALES OF TREASURY STOCK   The balance sheet of Amdahl Printing, Inc., on December 31, 19X2, shows the following equity section:

Common stock, $20 par, 10,000 shares issued and outstanding.	$200,000
Paid-in capital in excess of par	84,000
Retained earnings	132,000
Total equity.	$416,000

REQUIRED:

1. On January 1, 19X3, the company reacquired 300 shares of its stock for cash of $35 per share. Prepare the journal entry to record the acquisition, and prepare the equity section of the balance sheet immediately after the acquisition.

2. On March 20, 19X3, the company sold 100 shares of treasury stock for $37 per share. Give the journal entry to record the sale.

3. On June 10, 19X3, the company sold the remaining 200 shares of treasury stock for $33.50 per share. Prepare the journal entry to record the sale.

P12-43. STATEMENT OF STOCKHOLDERS' EQUITY   At the end of 19X4, Jeffco, Inc., had the following equity accounts and balances:

Common stock, $20 par	$410,000
Paid-in capital in excess of par, common stock	381,400
Retained earnings	102,470

During 19X5 Jeffco engaged in the following transactions involving its equity accounts:

a) Sold 2,900 shares of common stock for $41 per share.

b) Sold 1,500 shares of 12 percent, $100 par preferred stock at $102 per share.

c) Declared and paid cash dividends of $11,500.

d) Purchased 1,000 shares of treasury stock (common) for $45 per share.

e) Sold 600 of the treasury shares for $43 per share.

REQUIRED:

Assume that 19X5 net income was $51,300. Prepare a statement of stockholders' equity at December 31, 19X5.

P12-44. CHANGES IN EQUITY   Duncan Data Systems engaged in the following transactions this year:

a) Sold 21,000 shares of $5 par common stock for $8 per share.

b) Declared a $14,300 cash dividend.

c) Paid the $14,300 cash dividend.

d) Declared and paid in one transaction a 10 percent stock dividend. At the time of the dividend, there were 50,000 shares of $5 par common stock outstanding. The market price of the stock was $9 per share when the dividend was declared and paid.

e) Purchased 4,200 shares of stock (common) for the treasury at a cost of $11 per share.

f) Sold 2,200 shares of the treasury stock for $13 per share.

g) Sold the remaining 2,000 treasury shares for $10 per share.

REQUIRED:

For each of these transactions, indicate the effect on capital stock, retained earnings, and total stockholders' equity.

P12-45. COMMON DIVIDENDS   Papke Payroll Service began 19X2 with 1,000,000 authorized and 225,000 issued and outstanding $10 par common shares. During 19X2 Papke entered into the following transactions:

a) Declared a $.40 per share cash dividend on March 10.

b) Paid the $.40 per share dividend on April 10.

c) Purchased 8,000 common shares for the treasury at a cost of $24 each on May 2.

d) Sold 3,000 unissued common shares for $26 per share on June 9.

e) Declared a $.55 per share cash dividend on August 10.

f) Paid the $.55 per share dividend on September 10.

g) Declared and paid a 10 percent stock dividend on October 15 when the market price of the common stock was $28 per share.

h) Declared a $.60 per share cash dividend on November 10.

i) Paid the $.60 per share dividend on December 10.

REQUIRED:

1. Prepare journal entries for each of these transactions.

2. What is the total amount of dividends (cash and stock) for the year?

3. What was the effect on total assets and total stockholders' equity of these dividend transactions?

P12-46. COMMON DIVIDENDS   At December 31, 19X0, Skelton Food Products' stockholders' equity included retained earnings of $20,470 and 60,000 outstanding shares of $2 par common stock. In May 19X1, Skelton declared and paid a cash dividend of $.30 per share.

REQUIRED:

1. What is the effect of the cash dividend on Skelton's retained earnings?

2. Skelton's controller has asked you to indicate whether Skelton could legally declare and pay a 4 percent stock dividend on December 31, 19X1. The market price of Skelton's stock is $5 per share. The controller informs you that Skelton expects net income for the year to be $15,000.

P12-47. PREFERRED DIVIDENDS   California Produce Company had outstanding 1,000 shares of 10 percent, $40 par preferred stock at the end of 19X6. Preferred dividends are one year in arrears at that date. California Produce plans to pay $20,000 in dividends in 19X7.

REQUIRED:

1. How much of the dividend will go to common stockholders if the preferred stock is noncumulative and nonparticipating?

2. How much of the dividend will go to common stockholders if the preferred stock is cumulative and nonparticipating?

3. Assume that there are 12,000 shares of $5 par common stock outstanding. How much of the dividend will go to common stockholders if the preferred stock is cumulative and participating?

P12-48. PREFERRED DIVIDENDS   Magic Conglomerates had the following preferred stock outstanding at the end of a recent year:

$25 par, 10 percent....................................	6,000 shares
$40 par, 8 percent, cumulative	11,000 shares
$50 par, 12 percent, cumulative, convertible...................	2,000 shares
$80 par, 11 percent, nonparticipating........................	15,000 shares

REQUIRED:

1. Determine the amount of annual dividends on each issue of preferred stock and the total annual dividend on all four issues.

2. What would be the amount of dividends in arrears if the dividends were omitted for one year?

P12-49. PROPRIETORSHIP EQUITY   Rich Nardone sells a line of pumps on consignment for a large manufacturer. Rich has organized his business as a proprietorship. At the beginning of 19X4 Rich's equity account had a $24,200 balance. During 19X4, Rich invested $11,500 additional capital from his savings and withdrew $34,200 for living expenses. The proprietorship net income for 19X4 was $39,830.

REQUIRED:

1. Prepare the journal entries to record the proprietorship equity transactions described above.

2. Prepare a statement of changes in proprietorship equity for 19X4.

P12-50. PARTNERSHIP   Darrell Jones, Darrell Newton, and Larry Brown operate an income tax advisory service as a partnership. The tax advisory service was formed in early 19X2, at which time each partner invested $25,000. Drawings and partnership income for the years 19X2 through 19X5 are:

		DRAWINGS		
	PARTNERSHIP INCOME	DARRELL JONES	DARRELL NEWTON	LARRY BROWN
19X2	$63,000	$11,000	$12,000	$10,000
19X3	72,000	16,000	18,000	14,000
19X4	81,000	20,000	22,000	21,000
19X5	96,000	24,000	23,000	26,000

The partners share income and losses equally.

REQUIRED:

1. Prepare journal entries to record 19X5 drawings and the division of 19X5 partnership net income.

2. Prepare a journal entry to record closing the 19X5 drawings accounts.

3. Prepare a statement of changes in partners' equity for 19X5.

P12-51. LEVERAGE Enrietto Aquatic Products' offer to acquire Fiberglass Products for $2,000,000 cash has been accepted. Enrietto has $1,000,000 of liquid assets that can be converted into cash and plans to either sell common stock or issue bonds to raise the remaining $1,000,000. Before this acquisition, Enrietto's condensed balance sheet and condensed income statement were as follows:

ENRIETTO AQUATIC PRODUCTS
Preacquisition Condensed Balance Sheet

ASSETS		LIABILITIES AND EQUITY	
Assets	$20,000,000	Liabilities	$ 8,000,000
		Common stock, $10 par	6,000,000
		Retained earnings	6,000,000
			$20,000,000

ENRIETTO AQUATIC PRODUCTS
Preacquisition Condensed Income Statement

Income from operations.	$6,000,000
Less: Interest expense	1,000,000
Income before taxes	$5,000,000
Less: Income taxes expense (.34)	1,700,000
Net income.	$3,300,000

Enrietto's policy is to pay 60 percent of net income to stockholders as dividends. Enrietto expects to be able to raise the $1,000,000 it needs for the acquisition by selling 50,000 shares of common stock at $20 each or by issuing $1,000,000 of 20-year, 12 percent bonds. Enrietto expects income from operations to grow by $700,000 after Fiberglass Products has been acquired. (Interest expense will increase if debt is used to finance the acquisition.)

REQUIRED:

1. Determine the return on equity (net income/total equity) before the acquisition and for both financing alternatives.
2. If Enrietto sells additional stock, what will be the cash outflow for dividends?
3. If Enrietto sells bonds, what will be the net cash outflows for new interest and for all dividends? (Remember that interest is tax-deductible.)
4. Assume that Enrietto sells stock and that none of the preacquisition stockholders buy any of the 50,000 new shares. What total amount of dividends will the preacquisition stockholders receive after the acquisition? How does this amount compare with the dividends they receive before the acquisition?
5. Which alternative is better for Enrietto's preacquisition stockholders?

P12-52. COMMON AND PREFERRED STOCK Expansion Company now has $2,500,000 of equity (100,000 common shares). Current income is $400,000 and Expansion Company needs $500,000 of additional capital. The firm's bankers insist that this capital be acquired by selling either common or preferred stock. If Expansion sells common stock, the ownership share of the current stockholders will be diluted by 16.7 percent (20,000 more shares will be sold). If preferred stock is sold, the dividend rate will be 15 percent of the $500,000. Furthermore, the preferred stock will have to be cumulative, participating, and convertible into 20,000 shares of common.

REQUIRED:

Indicate whether Expansion should sell additional common or preferred stock, and explain the reasons for your choice.

P12-53. STOCK DIVIDENDS AND STOCK SPLITS   Lance Products' balance sheet includes total assets of $320,000 and the following equity account balances at December 31, 19X3:

Capital stock:	
Common stock, $5 par, 20,000 shares issued and outstanding........	$100,000
Paid-in capital in excess of par...............................	44,000
Total capital stock	$144,000
Retained earnings	53,600
Total stockholders' equity...............................	$197,600

Lance's common stock is selling for $24 per share on December 31, 19X3.

REQUIRED:

1. How much would Lance Products have reported for total assets and retained earnings on December 31, 19X3, if the firm had declared and paid a $10,000 cash dividend on December 31, 19X3? Provide the journal entry for this cash dividend.

2. How much would Lance have reported for total assets and retained earnings on December 31, 19X3, if the firm had issued a 10 percent stock dividend on December 31, 19X3? Provide the journal entry for this stock dividend.

3. How much would Lance have reported for total assets and retained earnings on December 31, 19X3, if the firm had affected a two-for-one stock split on December 31, 19X3? Is a journal entry needed to record the stock split? Why, or why not?

P12-54. THREE EQUITY ACCOUNTING SYSTEMS   Assume that there are three firms engaged in the same business. One business is organized as a proprietorship, the second is organized as a partnership, and the third is organized as a corporation. The three businesses were all formed on January 1, 19X4. Each business had beginning equity of $500,000 that was contributed by the owner or owners. For 19X4 the following data are available:

	PROPRIETORSHIP AND PARTNERSHIP	CORPORATION
Revenues	$820,000	$820,000
Salary paid to owner(s)*	30,000	30,000
Other operating expenses*	700,000	700,000
Financial expenses	50,000	50,000
Income taxes expense†	—	6,000

* Not included in other operating expenses.
† Proprietorship and partnership are not taxed directly.

Additional distributions to owners are $10,000.

REQUIRED:

1. Calculate 19X4 net income for each of the three businesses.

2. Prepare a statement of changes in equity or retained earnings for 19X4 for each business.

P12-55. CLOSING ENTRIES FOR THREE ORGANIZATIONS   Each of the following companies makes closing entries annually at December 31:

a) Company A is a sole proprietorship owned by Grabner and is financed in part by a $40,000 note payable to Kim. The company has preclosing balances at the end of 19X8 as follows: drawings, $15,000 debit; equity, $85,000 credit; income summary, $24,000 credit.

b) Company B is a partnership formed by Blain and Patton. The company has preclosing balances at the end of 19X8 as follows: drawings of Blaine, $15,000 debit; drawings of Patton, $5,000 debit; equity of Blain, $85,000 credit; equity of Patton, $40,000 credit; income summary, $29,000 credit. Net income is distributed equally between the partners.

c) Company C is a corporation, with Buser and Cole as the only stockholders. The company has preclosing balances at the end of 19X8 as follows: dividends, $12,000 debit; income summary, $16,700 credit; common stock (par), $80,000 credit; paid-in capital in excess of par, $32,000 credit; retained earnings, $18,000 credit.

REQUIRED:

1. Prepare closing entries at December 31, 19X8, for the three companies.

2. Prepare the equity section of each company's balance sheet at December 31, 19X8.

ANALYTICAL OPPORTUNITIES

A12-56.   SELLING COMMON STOCK WITH A PUT   Isaacson Corporation needs to raise $15,000,000 to expand its operations into Florida and Georgia. Isaacson considered acquiring the $15,000,000 by selling long-term bonds, but the firm's existing agreement with its creditors requires the firm to pay off all $20,000,000 existing long-term debt before additional debt is sold. Isaacson also considered selling common stock but discovered that 1,500,000 additional common shares would have to be sold to raise the $15,000,000. If 1,500,000 shares are sold, then existing shareholders would lose control of the firm to the new owners.

Isaacson's investment banker analyzed the situation and recommended that the firm sell common stock with a put. These shares could be sold for a much higher price ($50 each) than normal shares ($10 each) because the shareholders can require Isaacson to repurchase the shares after five years at 160 percent of their selling price. Because these shares can be sold for a higher price, the $15,000,000 can be raised by selling only 300,000 shares and control of the company will not pass to the new shareholders.

REQUIRED:

Is stock sold with a put really a sale of equity? (Hint: Read paragraphs 28–33 and 43–49 of *Statement of Financial Accounting Concepts No. 3.*)

A12-57.   ARRANGING FOR PRIOR PERIOD ADJUSTMENTS   Beth Rader, one of the junior accountants for Microbox, Inc., is concerned about the firm's most recent financial statements. Beth was responsible for developing the information for the firm's cost of goods sold calculation. As a part of that work, Beth supervised the physical inventory and is confident that the amount she developed, $2,355,000, was reasonable. However, when Beth received a copy of the financial statements, she notes that the ending inventory is reported at $3,255,000 and that cost of goods sold is $900,000 lower than the amount she calculated. This change in cost of goods sold caused Microbox to report a substantial profit rather than a small loss for the year.

Beth approaches the controller with her concern. The controller advises Beth that he will look into the matter. Several weeks later he advises Beth that Microbox's financial vice president claimed that he had transposed Beth's numbers. The controller wonders whether the transposition was inadvertent. At the time that the financial statements were released with this error, Microbox's stock price had been badly depressed. The financial vice president said that he would authorize a prior period adjustment to correct this error. Coincidentally, the market price of the Microbox stock is no longer depressed.

REQUIRED:

1. If this was an inadvertent error, is a prior period adjustment the proper way to correct the mistake? (Hint: Read paragraph 13 of *Accounting Principles Board Opinion No. 20.*)

2. Why might the financial vice president think that a prior period adjustment reducing retained earnings by $900,000 (less the applicable income taxes) would be less visible than a $900,000 expense?

PART 5

ADDITIONAL
DIMENSIONS
OF
FINANCIAL
REPORTING

LEARNING OBJECTIVES

Careful study of this chapter will enable you to:

1. Identify the important types of business activity that produce cash inflows and require cash outflows.

2. Classify cash inflows and outflows into three categories: operations, investing, and financing.

3. Compute cash flow from operations, using both the direct and the indirect methods.

4. Prepare statements of cash flows from beginning and ending balance sheets, an income statement, and data about cash transactions.

5. Compare a series of consecutive statements of cash flows.

Appendix 13–1

6. Use a worksheet to prepare a statement of cash flows.

13

THE STATEMENT OF CASH FLOWS

Although most financial statement users are primarily interested in the accrual-basis financial statements—income statement, balance sheet, and statement of changes in retained earnings—they are also interested in the amounts, timing, and uncertainties of the cash flows. Investors are interested in the ability of the stock issuer to pay cash dividends, lenders are interested in the ability of the borrower to make payments of interest and principal, employees are interested in the ability of the employer to pay salaries and fringe benefits, and suppliers are interested in the ability of purchasers to pay for goods purchased on credit. The statement of cash flows helps meet this need for information.

Like the income statement, the balance sheet, and the statement of changes in retained earnings, the statement of cash flows is one of the primary financial statements.[1] The objective of the statement of cash flows is to provide financial statement users with an organized report that shows sources from which the firm has acquired its cash (inflows) and the uses to which cash has been applied (outflows). The report should help statement users to (1) assess a business's ability to produce future net cash inflows, (2) assess its ability to meet its obligations and pay dividends and its needs for external financing, (3) understand the reasons for differences between net income on the one hand and cash receipts and payments on the other, and (4) evaluate the effects on the firm's financial position of cash and noncash investing and financing transactions.

The chapter begins with a description of the principal components of the statement of cash flows, followed by a conceptual discussion of the relationship between the statement of cash flows and other financial statements. The remainder of the chapter illustrates the preparation of the statement of cash flows, including two methods of reporting cash flows from operations, and considers how a statement of cash flows can be used in financial analysis.

---

[1] For a number of years, the inflows and outflows of financial resources were reported in a financial statement called the *statement of changes in financial position.* Companies could prepare this "statement of changes" either in terms of cash flows, as is currently required, or in terms of working capital flows, defined as increases and decreases in the excess of current assets over current liabilities. When the requirement to issue a statement of changes was first imposed in 1971, most companies chose to issue a statement based on working capital flows. However, as investors and creditors indicated their strong preference for a statement based on cash flows, firms gradually shifted toward a cash flow statement. Beginning with the 1988 financial statements, the Financial Accounting Standards Board (in *Statement of Financial Accounting Standards No. 95,* "The Statement of Cash Flows") required companies to issue a statement of cash flows.

COMPONENTS OF CASH FLOW

At the beginning of an accounting period, a firm prepares a balance sheet that reports the firm's assets, liabilities, and equity. During the accounting period, the firm engages in *operating activities* that result in the recognition of the revenues and expenses presented on the income statement. The operating activities that produce revenues and expenses also result in inflows and outflows of cash. For example, sales on credit increase receivables that, when collected, increase cash. Expenses may decrease cash directly; increase liabilities that, when paid, decrease cash; or decrease other assets like inventory whose acquisition requires the use of cash. In addition, firms engage in *nonoperating activities* that result in inflows and outflows of cash. For example, the sale of stock and the issuance of debt usually result in the inflow of cash, and the payment of dividends and the acquisition of operating assets usually result in the outflow of cash. Thus the activities of a business entity can be described in terms of inflows and outflows of cash.

STATEMENT OF CASH FLOWS: The financial statement that describes the inflows (or sources) and outflows (or uses) of cash for a business entity during a given period of time.

The **statement of cash flows** is the financial statement that describes the inflows (or sources) and outflows (or uses) of cash for a business entity during a given period of time. Recall from Chapter 8 that *cash* was defined as anything that is accepted by a bank for deposit and immediate payment to the account of a depositor, including currency and checks on hand and funds on deposit with banks and savings institutions. In some cases, cash may also include readily marketable short-term securities that are considered to be cash equivalents. Of course, the same definition of cash must be observed in the preparation of both the balance sheet and the statement of cash flows.

The statement of cash flows, like the income statement, is a period-of-time description. The income statement describes the contribution of a firm's activities to its retained earnings during a given period of time in terms of revenue inflows and expense outflows. The statement of cash flows, as shown in Exhibit 13–1 at the top of the next page, describes the effects of a firm's activities on its cash balance during a given period of time in terms of the sources of cash secured during the period and the uses to which that cash was put during the period.

The statement of cash flows is organized around three types of activities in which every business is involved: operations, investing, and financing. The cash flows associated with each activity are presented in a separate section of the statement.

OPERATIONS

For merchandising and manufacturing entities, operations include the purchase or production, the sale, and the delivery of goods. For service entities, operations include the activities necessary for the sale and performance of services. Examples of cash inflows from operations include cash sales, cash received from services provided, and collections of accounts receivable that arose from goods sold or services provided. In addition, cash inflows also include cash received for dividends or interest on investment securities and notes payable. Cash outflows for operations include payments for goods or services purchased, payments for wages and salaries, payments for property and income taxes, and payments for interest on borrowed funds.

EXHIBIT 13-1 THE STATEMENT OF CASH FLOWS

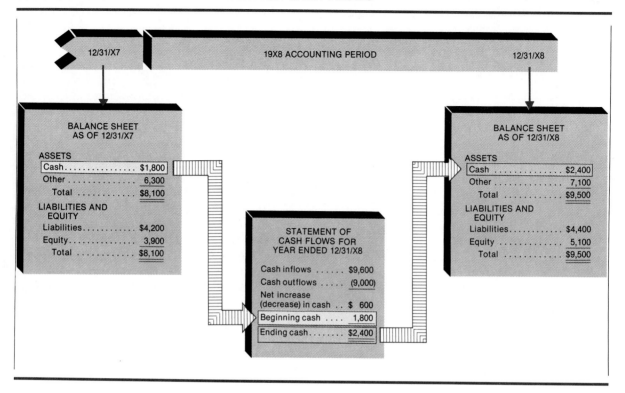

In general, operating cash flows correspond in *type* to items on the income statement. Of course, operating cash flows do not correspond in *amount* to income statement items, because the income statement is an accrual-basis statement whereas the cash flow statement is a cash-basis statement. Thus operating cash inflows and outflows arise from activities that produce revenues and expenses recognized in previous, current, or future periods.

INVESTING Investing activities include transactions involving long-term assets, as well as the lending of funds and the acquisition or sale of securities. Examples of cash inflows from investing include proceeds from the sale of long-lived assets, receipt of principal payments from borrowers, sales of loans made by the firm, and the sale of debt or equity securities of other firms. (Remember that cash inflows from interest or dividends are revenues and are thus cash inflows from operations.) Cash outflows for investment may include payments made to acquire long-lived assets, receipt of payments to acquire debt or equity securities of other firms, and loans made or purchased by the firm.

FINANCING Financing includes obtaining cash from creditors and owners as well as the associated repayments of cash. Cash inflows from financing may include the proceeds from issuing equity securities, bonds, mortgages, notes, and other short- or long-term financial instruments. Examples of cash outflows for financing include the payment of dividends, outlays for purchases of the firm's own stock,

EXHIBIT 13–2   **FINANCIAL RESOURCE FLOWS**

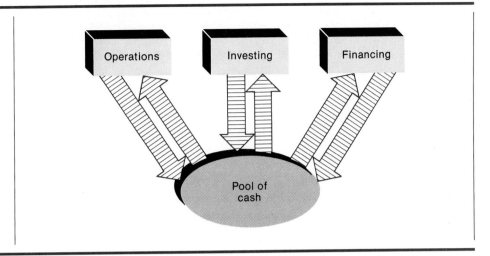

and payments on principal amounts of loans. (Remember that cash paid for interest is an expense and is thus a cash outflow for operations.)

A helpful approach is to think of each type of activity as producing both contributions to and deductions from the firm's pool of cash, as we illustrate in Exhibit 13–2. The following analysis indicates the types of questions an investor or bondholder might raise relative to the cash flows of a retailer in a troubled market.

ANALYSIS

CASH FLOWS AND INCOME

Five years ago, Nester Corporation was a very successful regional clothing retailer with 20 stores built gradually over a period of 40 years. Nester began as a family business, but as it grew, control gradually passed to parties outside the family. About five years ago, a new management team undertook an aggressive program of expansion financed by the issuance of long-term, high-interest-rate bonds. The expansion program increased the number of Nester Corporation stores from 20 to 70. The expansion was accomplished by acquiring several other regional clothing chains and a large national retailer selling through both stores and catalogs. At first, Nester had difficulty meeting its interest payments, but the retail clothing market was growing and Nester was able to hold its share of the total market. In addition, the highly competitive character of clothing manufacturing, the tremendous growth in Pacific Rim clothing manufacturing, and a strong U.S. dollar held Nester's cost of goods sold down. After a few years, Nester was able to retire 20 percent of its debt, but interest expense was still 40 percent of gross margin. Recently, the U.S. dollar has weakened, causing the cost of merchandise from Pacific Rim clothing manufacturers to increase. Further, an economic downturn has contracted the retail clothing market and intensified price competition among retailers. Thus the gross margins of retailers have fallen. Nester, however, has been able to maintain approximately the same level of net income as in preceding years.

1. *What questions concerning the cash flows from operations might an investor or bondholder raise about Nester?*

Does the statement of cash flows indicate impending problems for Nester despite the maintenance of net income? Did company operations generate enough cash last year to pay the interest on its debt and provide a dividend? If the cash flow from operations was not sufficient to pay interest and dividends, how did the company make up the difference? Did it reduce dividends, increase liabilities, or dispose of assets? Does the company's cash position appear to be stable?

2. *What questions concerning the investing cash flows might an investor or bondholder raise about Nester?*

Did the company sell any investments during the period to cover a cash shortage? If not, is it likely to do so in the future? How large a cash cushion do these investments provide?

3. *What questions concerning the financing of cash flows might an investor or bondholder raise about Nester?*

Has the company been retiring its debt at the same rate as in prior years? If debt retirement has slowed, has the company been able to refinance outstanding debt? Did the company borrow additional amounts to cover a cash shortage? If not, is the company likely to be able to borrow additional amounts in the future?

Of course, such questions cannot be answered by analyzing the statement of cash flows alone. Answers must be developed by examining all available information, including accrual-basis financial statements, supplementary disclosures, and information reported in the financial press. We turn now to a conceptual discussion of the relationship between statements of cash flows and accrual-basis financial statements.

STOCKS, FLOWS, AND FINANCIAL STATEMENTS

STOCKS: Account balances that measure the dollar amount of an asset, a liability, or an equity at a given time.

FLOWS: Measurements of changes in account balances (stocks) that occur during a given period of time.

The recording of transactions in accounts creates two types of financial measurements—*stocks* and *flows*. **Stocks** are account balances that measure the dollar amount of an asset, liability, or equity at a given time. **Flows** measure the changes in account balances that occur during a period of time. (In other words, flows measure the dollar effect on an asset, liability, or an equity of all transactions that occur during a particular period.) As an example, consider the following T-account, which summarizes a firm's accounts receivable transactions during 19X2:

Accounts receivable			
Balance, 12/31/X1	11,000		
Credit sales	90,000	92,000	Cash collections
Balance, 12/31/X2	9,000		

The T-account shows two stocks and two flows. The beginning and ending balances ($11,000 and $9,000) are stocks that measure the amounts receivable on December 31 of 19X1 and 19X2, respectively. The credit sales ($90,000) and cash collections ($92,000) are flows that measure the effect of selling goods and collecting cash, respectively. (As noted in Chapter 3, transactions of a given type may be summarized and recorded at the end of the period in a single entry; thus the amounts recorded by such summary entries are flows.)

EXHIBIT 13–3   STOCK AND FLOW SCHEDULE

McCORD'S CANDY STORE
Schedule of Stocks and Flows
For the Year Ended December 31, 19X6

	BALANCE SHEET 12/31/X6 (STOCKS)	DEBITS (FLOWS)		CREDITS (FLOWS)		BALANCE SHEET 12/31/X5 (STOCKS)
		DESCRIPTION	AMOUNT	DESCRIPTION	AMOUNT	
Cash	$ 14	(a) Cash sales	100	(d) Other expenses	6	$ 20
				(e) Dividends	12	
				(f) Payments on account	81	
				(g) New display case	7	
Inventory	57	(h) Purchases	72	(b) Cost of goods sold	60	45
Equipment	72	(g) New display case	7	(c) Depreciation expense	15	80
	$143					$145
Accounts payable	$ 9	(f) Payments on account	81	(h) Purchases	72	$ 18
Common stock	100					100
Retained earnings	34	(b) Cost of goods sold	60	(a) Cash sales	100	27
		(c) Depreciation expense	15			
		(d) Other expenses	6			
		(e) Dividends	12			
	$143					$145

Like accounts receivable in the example above, every balance sheet account can be described in terms of stocks and flows. Let us consider the stocks and flows associated with all the balance sheet accounts for a simple business. McCord's Candy Store makes all sales for cash and purchases all merchandise on credit. The stocks and flows that are associated with 19X6 are summarized in Exhibit 13–3. Each row of the schedule summarizes the activity in a different balance sheet account. For example, the inventory row shows that the inventory account changed from $45 on December 31, 19X5 (see balance sheet column on right), to $57 on December 31, 19X6 (see balance sheet column on left), as a result of purchases of $72 and cost of goods sold of $60 [$45 + $72 − $60 = $57].

The schedule of stocks and flows includes all the information reported in the financial statements. Although rarely prepared in practice, the schedule of stocks and flows is useful to students because it shows the relationships among the financial statements in a single schedule. All the 19X6 financial statements for McCord's Candy Store could be prepared from the schedule of stocks and flows. The beginning and ending balance sheets in Exhibit 13–4 could be prepared from the balance sheet columns of Exhibit 13–3. The 19X6 income statement in Exhibit 13–5 could be prepared from the portion of Exhibit 13–3 that explains the changes in the retained earnings balance. Note that the income statement includes all the flows affecting retained earnings except dividends. Dividends are incorporated into the statement of changes in retained earnings (see Exhibit 13–6), which summarizes the stocks and flows associated with retained earnings. The statement of cash flows could also be prepared from the schedule of stocks and flows, as the next section will demonstrate.

EXHIBIT 13–4   BALANCE SHEETS

McCORD'S CANDY STORE
Balance Sheets
As of December 31, 19X6 and 19X5

ASSETS	12/31/X6	12/31/X5
Cash	$ 14	$ 20
Inventory	57	45
Equipment	72	80
Total assets	$143	$145

LIABILITIES AND EQUITY		
Accounts payable	$ 9	$ 18
Common stock	100	100
Retained earnings	34	27
Total liabilities and equity	$143	$145

EXHIBIT 13–5   INCOME STATEMENT

McCORD'S CANDY STORE
Income Statement
For the Year Ended December 31, 19X6

Sales revenue		$100
Cost of goods sold	$60	
Depreciation expense	15	
Other expenses	6	81
Net income		$ 19

EXHIBIT 13–6   STATEMENT OF CHANGES IN RETAINED EARNINGS

McCORD'S CANDY STORE
Statement of Changes in Retained Earnings
For the Year Ended December 31, 19X6

Retained earnings, 12/31/X5	$27
Add: Net income	19
	$46
Less: Dividends	12
Retained earnings, 12/31/X6	$34

MEASURING CHANGES IN FINANCIAL RESOURCES   On the statement of cash flows, inflows and outflows from operations are presented first, followed by inflows and outflows from investing, and then by inflows and outflows from financing. Thus, before a statement of cash flows can be prepared, the inflows and outflows of cash shown in McCord's schedule of stocks and flows have to be divided by type of activity. Exhibit 13-3 indicates that McCord's cash flows from operating activities include one inflow, cash sales of $100, and two outflows, payments for other expenses of $6 and payments on account of $81. McCord's cash flows from operating activities would be presented as follows:

Cash flows from operating activities:		
Cash collected from customers......................		$100
Less: Cash paid to suppliers and others:		
Accounts payable	$81	
Other expenses..................................	6	87
Net cash provided by operating activities...........		$ 13

The schedule of stocks and flows also indicates that McCord's has one cash flow for investing activities, the $7 outflow for the purchase of a new display case, and one cash flow for financing activities, the $12 outflow for dividends. This information can be combined with the information about cash flows from operating activities to prepare the complete statement of cash flows shown in Exhibit 13-7.

EXHIBIT 13-7   STATEMENT OF CASH FLOWS

McCORD'S CANDY STORE
Statement of Cash Flows
For the Year Ended December 31, 19X6

Cash flows from operating activities:		
Cash collected from customers		$100
Less: Cash paid to suppliers and others:		
Accounts payable.....................................	$ 81	
Other expenses	6	87
Net cash provided by operating activities.................		$ 13
Cash flows from investing activities:		
Purchase of display case	$ (7)	
Net cash used by investing activities.....................		(7)
Cash flows from financing activities:		
Payment of dividends	$(12)	
Net cash used by financing activities		(12)
Net decrease in cash......................................		$ (6)
Cash at beginning of year		20
Cash at end of year.......................................		$ 14

THE ALL-RESOURCES CONCEPT

Usually, the acquisition of operating assets, the payment of long-term liabilities, and the repurchase of capital stock result in a reduction in cash. Similarly, the sale of operating assets and the issuance of long-term liabilities or capital stock usually increase cash. Occasionally, however, there may be transactions in securities; property, plant, and equipment; long-term liabilities; or capital stock that do not alter cash. For example, suppose that a firm wishes to finance the acquisition of property, plant, and equipment by issuing bonds. If the firm issues the bonds for cash and then, in a separate transaction, acquires the property, plant, and equipment for cash, the issuance of bonds is reported as a financing inflow and the equipment acquisition as an investment outflow. However, if the firm acquires the property, plant, and equipment directly in exchange for the issuance of bonds, then the cash account is not altered by the transaction. Such a transaction is called a *noncash investing and financing activity.* The **all-resources concept** requires that the financial statements disclose information about all acquisitions and sales of assets, all issues and repayments of debt, and all issues and repurchases of capital stock, regardless of whether or not they affect cash. Thus noncash investing and financing activities must be reported in a supplementary schedule that is either shown as a part of the statement of cash flows or clearly referenced in that statement.

ALL-RESOURCES CONCEPT: The concept that requires that financial statements disclose information about all acquisitions and sales of assets, all issues and repayments of debt, and all issues and repurchases of capital stock, regardless of whether or not they affect cash.

DATA NECESSARY FOR STATEMENT PREPARATION

As we have seen, the statement of cash flows is derived in part from information contained in the other financial statements. To prepare a cash flow statement, we need two balance sheets, the intervening income statement, and transactions data from the firm's cash account. In addition, we need data for any transactions that used or produced financial resources but that did not flow through the cash account. To find investment and financing inflows and outflows, it is often necessary to look for changes in balance sheet accounts other than cash. Exhibit 13–8 indicates the various types of changes in balance sheet accounts that could indicate investment and financing inflows and outflows. Suppose that, during the past year, a firm sold a piece of manufacturing equipment that it no longer needed. An examination of the firm's balance sheet accounts would show that an asset account, equipment, had decreased. This change suggests that there may have been a cash inflow from investment activities. Conversely, an increase in the equipment account could indicate that there had been an outflow for investment. In a sense, Exhibit 13–8 represents a "road map" that directs the search for financing and investment cash flows. The remainder of this chapter will illustrate the analytical procedures that underlie the search for investment and financing cash flows and, finally, the preparation of the statement of cash flows itself.

EXHIBIT 13–8   **INVESTMENT AND FINANCING CASH FLOWS AND BALANCE SHEET CHANGES OTHER THAN CASH**

INFLOWS	OUTFLOWS
Investment: Asset *decrease*	Investment: Asset *increase*
Financing: Liability *increase*	Financing: Liability *decrease*
Financing: Equity *increase*	Financing: Equity *decrease*

THE STATEMENT OF CASH FLOWS

Accrual accounting systems record activities when they occur, rather than when cash is received or paid. Accrual accounting systems also record cash receipts and payments for these activities. Thus, accrual accounting systems provide the basis for both accrual-basis financial statements and a cash flow statement. The purpose of this section is to review the cash effects of representative transactions and to illustrate the preparation of the statement of cash flows, including two methods of reporting cash flows from operations.

Exhibit 13–9 demonstrates how several types of transactions affect cash. Let us consider each of these transactions, beginning with the acquisition of equipment on credit (transaction 1). The acquisition of equipment on credit does not alter cash, and therefore the transaction is neither an outflow nor an inflow of cash. The outflow of cash occurs when the firm makes the subsequent payment of accounts payable (transaction 2). Like the acquisition of equipment on credit, the purchase of merchandise on credit (transaction 3) does not alter cash and is thus neither an outflow nor an inflow of cash. Similarly, since sales of merchandise on credit (transaction 4) do not constitute inflows of cash, the inflow of cash occurs when the firm collects the associated accounts receivable (transaction 5). The issuance of stock for cash and the repayment of long-term debt with cash (transactions 6 and 7) do constitute an inflow and an outflow of cash, respectively. The recording of depreciation expense (transaction 8) represents neither an inflow nor an outflow of cash. In general, only transactions that change the cash balance are designated as inflows and outflows of cash.

EXHIBIT 13–9   **EFFECTS OF SELECTED TRANSACTIONS ON CASH**

			EFFECT ON CASH	
TRANSACTION	ACCOUNT	AMOUNT	AMOUNT	INFLOW OR OUTFLOW
1. Acquisition of equipment on credit, $8,000	Equipment Accounts payable	+8,000 +8,000	–0–	Neither
2. Payment on account, $8,000	Cash Accounts payable	–8,000 –8,000	8,000	Outflow
3. Purchase of merchandise on credit, $4,000	Inventory Accounts payable	+4,000 +4,000	–0–	Neither
4. Sale of merchandise on credit, $2,200 (cost, $1,500)	Inventory Accounts receivable Retained earnings	–1,500 +2,200 +700	–0–	Neither
5. Collection from credit customers on account, $1,100	Cash Accounts receivable	+1,100 –1,100	1,100	Inflow
6. Issuance of common stock for $10,000 cash	Cash Common stock	+10,000 +10,000	10,000	Inflow
7. Repayment of long-term debt (bonds), $6,000	Cash Bonds payable	–6,000 –6,000	6,000	Outflow
8. Depreciation expense, $3,000	Accumulated depreciation Retained earnings	+3,000 –3,000	–0–	Neither

EXHIBIT 13–10   BALANCE SHEETS

BROOKE, INC.
Balance Sheets
As of December 31, 19X8 and 19X7

ASSETS		19X8		19X7
Current assets:				
Cash		$ 15,000		$ 13,000
Accounts receivable (net)		53,000		46,000
Prepaid insurance..............		1,000		2,000
Inventory....................		63,000		51,000
Total current assets		$132,000		$112,000
Property, plant, and equipment:				
Land.......................	$ 50,000		$ 50,000	
Building	275,000		275,000	
Equipment[1]	243,000		210,000	
	$568,000		$535,000	
Accumulated depreciation	(178,000)		(150,000)	
Net property		390,000		385,000
Investments[2]		53,000		41,000
Total assets		$575,000		$538,000
LIABILITIES				
Current liabilities:				
Accounts payable..............		$ 13,000		$ 17,000
Notes payable[3]		24,000		15,000
Wages payable.................		3,500		2,000
Interest payable...............		1,500		1,000
Income taxes payable...........		3,000		6,000
Total current liabilities		$ 45,000		$ 41,000
Long-term liabilities:				
Mortgage payable[4]		85,000		100,000
Total liabilities		$130,000		$141,000
EQUITY				
Common stock[5]	$165,000		$151,000	
Retained earnings...............	280,000		246,000	
Total stockholders' equity...		445,000		397,000
Total liabilities and equity		$575,000		$538,000

[1] Equipment with a cost of $20,000 and accumulated depreciation of $12,000 was sold for $2,000 cash in 19X8. Equipment was purchased for $53,000 cash.

[2] Long-term investments with a cost of $16,000 were sold for $31,000 cash. Additional long-term investments were purchased for $28,000 cash.

[3] Notes payable in the amount of $20,000 were repaid, and new notes payable in the amount of $29,000 were issued for cash during 19X8.

[4] A principal payment of $15,000 was made on the mortgage in 19X8.

[5] Common stock was issued for $14,000 cash in 19X8.

In order to provide different kinds of businesses the flexibility needed to characterize their cash flows adequately, the operations section of the statement of cash flows may be prepared using either a direct method or an indirect method. When the direct method is used, the operating cash inflows and cash outflows are identified by source and their amounts totaled to produce net cash flow from operations. When the indirect method is used, the cash flows from operations section begins with net income, followed by a series of adjustments that are added to or subtracted from net income to produce net cash flow from operations. In the sections that follow, we will illustrate both methods, using the financial statements for Brooke, Inc., that are presented in Exhibits 13–10, 13–11, and 13–12.

EXHIBIT 13–11   **INCOME STATEMENT**

BROOKE, INC.
Income Statement
For the Year Ended December 31, 19X8

Sales revenue		$472,000
Less: Cost of goods sold		232,000
Gross margin		$240,000
Less: Operating expenses:		
Wages	$142,000	
Insurance	15,000	
Depreciation	40,000	197,000
Income from operations		$ 43,000
Other income:		
Loss on sale of equipment	$ (6,000)	
Gain on sale of long-term investment	15,000	9,000
		$ 52,000
Less: Interest expense		5,000
Income before taxes		$ 47,000
Less: Income taxes expense		8,000
Net income		$ 39,000

EXHIBIT 13–12   **STATEMENT OF CHANGES IN RETAINED EARNINGS**

BROOKE, INC.
Statement of Changes in Retained Earnings
For the Year Ended December 31, 19X8

Retained earnings, 12/31/X7	$246,000
Add: Net income	39,000
	$285,000
Less: Dividends	5,000
Retained earnings, 12/31/X8	$280,000

DIRECT METHOD OF REPORTING CASH FLOWS FROM OPERATIONS

Using the direct method, major operating inflows and outflows of cash are reported in the statement of cash flows for the following categories:

1. Cash collected from customers
2. Cash paid to suppliers of merchandise
3. Cash paid to employees and other suppliers of goods and services
4. Cash paid for interest
5. Income taxes paid

Let us develop the data for each of these categories from the Brooke, Inc., financial statements in Exhibits 13–10, 13–11, and 13–12.

Cash Collected from Customers

When accrual accounting is used, the balance of the sales revenue account includes both cash sales and credit sales. Cash collected from customers includes a part of this balance—the cash sales—plus the cash collected from accounts receivable during the period. The amount of cash collected from both cash and credit customers can be developed by analyzing T-accounts for sales revenue and accounts receivable:

Sales revenue		Accounts receivable	
	Cash sales	Balance, 12/31/X7	
	Credit sales	Credit sales	Cash collections from accounts receivable
	Total sales revenue for 19X8		
		Balance, 12/31/X8	

To compute the amount of cash collected from customers, we start with sales revenue (which includes both cash sales and credit sales during the period) and then add the beginning balance in accounts receivable and subtract the ending receivables balance. For Brooke, Inc., cash collected from customers is computed as follows:

Sales revenue	$472,000
Plus: Accounts receivable, 12/31/X7	46,000
Amount available to be collected from customers.............	$518,000
Less: Accounts receivable, 12/31/X8	53,000
Cash collected from customers	$465,000

The beginning accounts receivable balance is added to sales revenue because it represents amounts from the previous year's sales available to be collected this year. The ending accounts receivable balance is subtracted because it represents sales that will not produce cash inflows until a future period.

Cash Payments to Suppliers of Merchandise

Under accrual accounting, cost of goods sold includes only the cost of merchandise sold during the year. To determine how much cash was actually paid to suppliers of merchandise requires the analysis of two T-accounts — merchandise inventory and accounts payable:

Inventory	
Balance, 12/31/X7	
Cost of goods purchased	Cost of goods sold
Balance, 12/31/X8	

The cost of goods purchased can be computed as cost of goods sold plus the ending inventory balance less the cost of beginning inventory. The cost of goods purchased can be used with the beginning and ending accounts payable balances to determine the cost of payments to suppliers of merchandise.

Accounts payable	
	Balance, 12/31/X7
Cash payments	Cost of goods purchased
	Balance, 12/31/X8

The amount of cash payments to suppliers of merchandise is the cost of goods purchased plus the beginning balance in accounts payable less the ending payables balance. If these two T-account analyses are combined with the data from Exhibits 13–10 and 13–11, the amount of cash Brooke, Inc., paid to suppliers can be computed as follows:

Cost of goods sold	$232,000
Plus: Inventory, 12/31/X8	63,000
Cost of goods available for sale	$295,000
Less: Inventory, 12/31/X7	(51,000)
Cost of goods purchased	$244,000
Plus: Accounts payable, 12/31/X7	17,000
Amount payable to suppliers of merchandise	$261,000
Less: Accounts payable, 12/31/X8	(13,000)
Cash payments to suppliers of merchandise	$248,000

Notice that Brooke, Inc.'s cash payments to suppliers of merchandise are $16,000 more than its cost of goods sold. The $16,000 excess was produced by a $12,000 increase in inventory and a $4,000 decrease in accounts payable.

Cash Payments to Employees and Other Suppliers of Goods and Services

Recall that under accrual accounting, expenses are recognized when incurred, not when cash is paid. Therefore, the expense amounts reported on the income statement may not equal the amount of cash actually paid to employees and other suppliers during the period. To determine the amount of cash payments to employees and other suppliers of goods and services (such as advertising, insurance, or supplies), it is necessary to look for changes in the balance sheet accounts that reveal accrued expenses. Let us illustrate with the wages expense and insurance expense accounts for Brooke, Inc., using data from Exhibits 13–10 and 13–11.

In order to determine the amount of cash payments to employees, we must take the wages expense amount and adjust it to reflect any changes during the year in the amount of wages accrued but not paid. Since accrued wages are recorded in the wages payable account, cash payments to employees can be determined as follows:

Wages expense	$142,000
Plus: Wages payable, 12/31/X7	2,000
Less: Wages payable, 12/31/X8	(3,500)
Cash payments to employees	$140,500

Notice that the adjustment adds $2,000—the amount of cash that was paid in 19X8 for wages actually earned in 19X7—and subtracts $3,500—the amount of wages accrued in 19X8, for which no cash has been paid out. Thus, in other words, cash payments to employees is the amount of wages expense less a $1,500 increase in wages payable.

Similarly, cash paid to suppliers of insurance is the amount of the insurance expense adjusted for the change in prepaid insurance, computed as follows:

Insurance expense	$15,000
Plus: Prepaid insurance, 12/31/X8	1,000
Less: Prepaid insurance, 12/31/X7	(2,000)
Cash payments for insurance	$14,000

The adjustment adds $1,000—the amount of cash paid in 19X8 for insurance coverage that will not be included in insurance expense until it is used in the following year—and subtracts $2,000—the cost of insurance coverage used in 19X8 for which the cash was prepaid in 19X7. Thus, cash payments to suppliers of insurance is the insurance expense less a $1,000 decrease in prepaid insurance.

An examination of the adjustments to wages expense and insurance expense leads to the following rule for adjusting income statement expense amounts to cash outflows:

> Cash outflow for an expense equals the income statment expense amount **plus** increases in associated assets and decreases in associated payables **less** decreases in associated assets and increases in associated payables.

Cash Paid for Interest

Interest expense can be adjusted to cash paid for interest by using the rule stated above and the data for Brooke, Inc., from Exhibits 13–10 and 13–11 as follows:

Interest expense	$5,000
Less: Increase in interest payable	(500)
Cash paid for interest	$4,500

Cash paid for interest is less than the 19X8 interest expense because interest payable increased by $500, indicating that less cash was paid for interest than was recorded as an expense.

Income Taxes Paid

The cash outflow for income taxes can be developed in a similar fashion, by using income taxes expense, the change in income taxes payable, and the expense adjustment rule. Using data from Exhibits 13–10 and 13–11, we compute income taxes paid as follows:

Income taxes expense	$ 8,000
Plus: Decrease in income taxes payable	3,000
Income taxes paid	$11,000

Cash outflow for income taxes was $3,000 more than income taxes expense because the income taxes payable account was reduced by paying cash of $3,000 more than was recorded as an expense.

Net Cash Flow from Operating Activities

Now that the components have all been computed, the net cash flow from operations can be prepared. Exhibit 13–13 illustrates the direct presentation of net cash flow from operations for Brooke, Inc.

INDIRECT METHOD OF REPORTING CASH FLOWS FROM OPERATIONS

Under the indirect method, net income is adjusted to net cash flow from operating activities. Adjustments to net income are required for (1) changes in the balance of operating current asset and current liability accounts that adjust revenues and expenses to cash received and cash paid[2] and (2) the effects of income statement items that do not affect cash flows in the current period (such as depreciation and losses or gains on sales of assets).

[2] Formally, these adjustments are referred to as the effects of deferrals of past operating cash receipts and payments and the effects of accruals for expected operating cash receipts and payments.

EXHIBIT 13–13   DIRECT METHOD OF DETERMINING NET CASH FLOW FROM OPERATIONS

BROOKE, INC.
Net Cash Flow from Operations
For the Year Ended December 31, 19X8

Cash flows from operating activities:	
Cash collected from customers	$465,000
Cash paid to suppliers of merchandise	(248,000)
Cash paid to employees and other suppliers of goods and services[1]	(154,500)
Cash paid for interest	(4,500)
Income taxes paid	(11,000)
Net cash provided by operating activities	$ 47,000

[1] Includes $140,500 to employees and $14,000 for insurance.

Operating current asset and current liability accounts include inventory, receivables, payables, and prepaid items but exclude short-term debt and other current accounts that relate to investing or financing activities. Adjustments to net income for changes in the current asset and current liability accounts are made according to the following rule:

> An adjustment to net income is **positive** for decreases in operating current assets and increases in operating current liabilities, **negative** for increases in operating current assets and decreases in operating current liabilities.

The second type of adjustment to net income is for those income statement items that do not provide or require cash flows in the current period. Depreciation, depletion, and amortization are expenses that do not require an outflow of cash in the current period; they are, therefore, added to net income when adjusting to cash flow from operations. Because losses on sales of long-lived assets reduce net income but do not require an outflow of cash, they also require a positive adjustment to net income. Conversely, gains increase the amount of net income but do not provide an equivalent amount of cash, so they must be subtracted. The proceeds from sales of property, plant, and equipment and other long-lived assets are included among the cash flows from investing activities, as the next section explains, rather than among the operating cash flows.

An example of an indirect determination of the cash flow from operations is

---

EXHIBIT 13–14   **INDIRECT METHOD OF DETERMINING NET CASH FLOW FROM OPERATIONS**

BROOKE, INC.
Net Cash Flow from Operations
For the Year Ended December 31, 19X8

Cash flows from operating activities:

Net income		$39,000
Adjustments to reconcile net income to net cash provided by operating activities:		
Increase in accounts receivable	$ (7,000)	
Decrease in prepaid insurance	1,000	
Increase in inventory	(12,000)	
Decrease in accounts payable	(4,000)	
Increase in wages payable	1,500	
Increase in interest payable	500	
Decrease in income taxes payable	(3,000)	
Depreciation expense	40,000	
Loss on sale of equipment	6,000	
Gain on sale of long-term investment	(15,000)	
Total adjustments		8,000
Net cash provided by operating activities		$47,000

illustrated in Exhibit 13–14 and is based on the Brooke, Inc., balance sheet and income statement data in Exhibits 13–10 and 13–11. Note that the net cash provided by operating activities is exactly the same amount as determined by the direct method in Exhibit 13–13.

CASH FLOWS FROM INVESTING ACTIVITIES

The second major section of the statement of cash flows reports the net cash flows from investing activities. Investing activities include acquisition and disposal of property, plant, and equipment or other long-lived assets; purchase and sale of debt and equity instruments of other companies; and receipt of interest or dividends from investments in debt or equity instruments of other firms. (An exception is made for banks and other financial institutions, allowing them to classify loans made and loan principal repayments received as cash flows from investing activities and to report interest received on loans as an operating cash flow.) Recall that short-term investments that are readily marketable are cash equivalents. Since such short-term investments are a component of cash, transactions in these investments are neither inflows nor outflows of cash.

Data for the investing activities portion of the statement of cash flows are secured from the changes in the investment and property, plant, and equipment accounts. Since all these accounts are assets, increases that were financed by cash payments would be investment outflows and decreases that produced cash receipts would be investment inflows. Although the beginning and ending balance sheets are useful sources for identifying changes in these accounts, one must refer to transactions data to determine the actual amount of cash inflows and outflows. For example, a firm might purchase capital stock in another firm at a cost of $200,000 and, during the same accounting period, sell another investment that had cost $145,000. If only the beginning and ending balance sheets are examined, one would erroneously conclude that there had been a cash outflow for investments of $55,000.

An examination of the balance sheets for Brooke, Inc. (see Exhibit 13–10) indicates that there were investment transactions in the equipment account and in the investments account during the year. The first footnote to the balance sheet explains that equipment costing $20,000 with accumulated depreciation of $12,000 was sold for $2,000 cash. That footnote also explains that equipment was purchased for $53,000 cash. The second footnote to the balance sheet explains that long-term investments that had cost $16,000 were sold for $31,000 cash and that there was a cash outflow of $28,000 for the purchase of additional investments. The cash flows from investing activities section of the statement of cash flows for Brooke, Inc., would report this information as follows:

Cash flows from investing activities:	
Cash received from sale of equipment.	$ 2,000
Purchase of equipment.	(53,000)
Cash received from sale of long-term investments	31,000
Purchase of long-term investments	(28,000)
Net cash used by investing activities	$(48,000)

Note that the loss on the sale of equipment and the gain on the sale of the investment are not included here. Only the proceeds from selling these assets are included.

CASH FLOWS FROM FINANCING ACTIVITIES

The intent of the financing activities section of the statement of cash flows is to identify for statement users the inflows and outflows of cash that arise from financing activities. Financing activities include borrowing, repayment of borrowing (except for interest expense, which is an operating cash flow), sale of common or preferred stock, payments of cash dividends, and the purchase and sale of treasury stock.

Data for financing activities are secured from changes in the short- and long-term debt, capital stock (common and preferred stock and associated paid-in capital in excess of par or stated value), and treasury stock accounts. These accounts are all liabilities or equity. Therefore (except for treasury stock), increases in these accounts suggest that cash has been received and decreases suggest that cash has been paid. (Treasury stock is a contra-equity account. Therefore, increases indicate outflows of cash and decreases indicate inflows of cash.)

The beginning and ending balance sheets are again a useful source of indications of changes in the financing accounts. However, one must refer to transactions data to determine actual cash inflows and outflows. For example, during one accounting period, a firm might borrow $150,000 on a new short-term loan and repay a previous short-term loan of $120,000. If only the beginning and ending balance sheets were examined, the $30,000 net increase in short-term loans would be identified. But the implications of a new borrowing of $150,000 and a repayment of $120,000 are quite different from those of a new borrowing of $30,000 with no repayment.

An examination of the balance sheets and statement of changes in retained earnings for Brooke, Inc. (see Exhibits 13–10 and 13–12) indicates that there were five financing transactions: new short-term borrowing, repayment of short-term borrowing, repayment of mortgage principal, sale of common stock, and payment of dividends. The third footnote to the balance sheets explains that short-term notes payable with a face amount of $20,000 were repaid during 19X8 and that new notes in the amount of $29,000 were issued. The fourth footnote explains that the decrease in the mortgage account was the result of a $15,000 cash payment. The fifth footnote explains that the increase in the common stock account resulted from the sale of stock for $14,000 cash. The statement of changes in retained earnings indicates that dividends of $5,000 were paid. The cash flows from financing activities section of the statement of cash flows for Brooke, Inc., would report this information as follows:

Cash flows from financing activities:
Cash received from issuance of short-term debt	$29,000
Principal payments on short-term debt	(20,000)
Principal payments on mortgage	(15,000)
Proceeds from issuance of common stock	14,000
Payment of dividends	(5,000)
Net cash provided by financing activities	$ 3,000

STATEMENT OF CASH FLOWS

A complete statement of cash flows for Brooke, Inc., is presented in Exhibit 13–15. This exhibit presents cash flows from operating activities using the direct method (from Exhibit 13–13) as well as the cash flows from investing activities and cash flows from financing activities that were developed as those sections of the statement of cash flows were described. A statement of cash flows using the

EXHIBIT 13-15   **STATEMENT OF CASH FLOWS**

BROOKE, INC.

Statement of Cash Flows

For the Year Ended December 31, 19X8

Cash flows from operating activities:		
Cash collected from customers.	$465,000	
Cash paid to suppliers of merchandise	(248,000)	
Cash paid to employees and other suppliers of goods and services	(154,500)	
Cash paid for interest.	(4,500)	
Income taxes paid.	(11,000)	
Net cash provided by operating activities.		$47,000
Cash flows from investing activities:		
Cash received from sale of equipment	$ 2,000	
Purchase of equipment	(53,000)	
Cash received from sale of long-term investments	31,000	
Purchase of long-term investments	(28,000)	
Net cash used by investing activities		(48,000)
Cash flows from financing activities:		
Cash received from issuance of short-term debt	$ 29,000	
Principal payments on short-term debt	(20,000)	
Principal payments on mortgage	(15,000)	
Proceeds from issuance of common stock	14,000	
Payment of dividends	(5,000)	
Net cash provided by financing activities.		3,000
Net increase in cash and cash equivalents		$ 2,000
Cash and cash equivalents at beginning of year		13,000
Cash and cash equivalents at end of year.		$15,000

indirect method of determining cash flows from operations would differ only in that the operating activities portion of Exhibit 13–15 would be replaced by the schedule shown in Exhibit 13–14.

Now that we have described the preparation of the statement of cash flows, let us explain how it can be used.

USING THE STATEMENT OF CASH FLOWS

Effective analysis of a statement of cash flows requires (1) an examination of the statement itself, (2) a comparison of the current statement's data with data from earlier statements of cash flows for the same firm, and (3) a comparison of data from the firm's own statement of cash flows with data from statements of cash flows for other similar firms. This section discusses facts and considerations that should guide statement analysis.

A number of determinations can be made by an inspection of the current period's statement of cash flows. One of the most important factors in statement analysis is to discover how long cash outflows will be tied up before they can be recovered. Most uses of cash are either long-term (such as investments in property, plant, and equipment) or permanent (such as payments of dividends or repayments of debt). Investments in property, plant, and equipment are likely to require several years of successful operation by the firm before the cash invested can be recovered by selling at a profit the goods or services produced. Therefore, prudent management will seek long-term or permanent sources of cash, such as long-term debt or equity, which need not be repaid before the original investment has been recovered through cash generated by operations.

The sources most frequently used to provide permanent or long-term cash inflows are operations, the issue of long-term liabilities, and the sale of equity. Of these three, operations is considered the least risky or the most controllable. The sale of debt or equity requires that investors or creditors make sizable resource commitments to the firm. Cash inflows from operations also require an outsider (the customer) to make a commitment, but the size and timing of a customer's cash commitments are such that it is likely that the firm can produce cash inflows from customers on a regular basis. Because inflows from operations are more controllable than inflows from debt or equity, most firms attempt to secure from two-thirds to three-fourths of their total cash inflows from operations. Because the cost of selling large debt or equity issues in the public capital markets is high, most large businesses sell debt or equity in relatively large amounts. Small amounts of long-term debt, however, are often issued by large firms directly to banks, to insurance companies, and to other financial intermediaries more than once a year. Sales of small amounts of stock to employees through stock options and stock bonus plans are also made continually.

An analysis of the statement of cash flows also requires a comparison of the firm's current statement with earlier statements. When a series of statements of cash flows is examined, the analysis should focus on a period of several consecutive years in order to determine trends in inflows and outflows. The following questions may be helpful in beginning the analysis of a series of statements of cash flows:

1. What proportions of cash have come from operations, financing, and investing, respectively?
2. Are there discernable trends in these proportions?
3. What proportions of long-term applications of cash are financed by long-term sources?
4. How has the firm financed any permanent increases in current assets?
5. Has the firm begun any investment programs that are likely to require significant cash outflows in the future?
6. What are the probable sources for the cash inflows likely to be needed in the near future?
7. Are these projected sources likely to be both able and willing to provide the amounts of cash needed?
8. If the firm were to be unable to secure the cash necessary, could outflows be restricted to the available supply of cash without seriously affecting operations?

Finally, the analysis of the statement of cash flows requires comparing data from other similar firms. Such comparisons often provide reference points for the data of the firm being analyzed because similar firms generally secure cash from similar sources and are likely to expend cash for similar activities. Comparative analysis can reveal significant deviations in (1) the amounts of cash inflows, (2) the source of those inflows, and (3) the types of activities to which cash is applied. When significant differences among similar firms are found, an explanation is sought in the other financial statements, in the notes accompanying the statements, or from management.

The analysis that follows examines statements of cash flows for Toys "R" Us for the period 1985–1990.

ANALYSIS COMPARISON OVER TIME OF STATEMENTS OF CASH FLOW	Toys "R" Us is engaged primarily in operating retail toy and children's clothing stores that are located in major metropolitan areas in the United States, Canada, and Europe. Summarized cash flow data for Toys "R" Us for the six-year period 1985–1990 follow: [3]

TOYS "R" US, INC.
Summarized Cash Flow Data
For the Years Ended

IN THOUSANDS	1/28/90	1/29/89	1/31/88	2/1/87	2/2/86	2/3/85
Cash flows from operations:						
Net earnings	$321,080	$268,024	$203,922	$152,217	$119,774	$111,424
Adjustments:						
Depreciation	65,839	54,564	43,716	33,288	26,074	18,378
Receivables	14,932	(5,886)	(24,642)	(11,531)	(2,564)	(5,498)
Inventory	(299,274)	(158,287)	(243,894)	(115,446)	(15,580)	(133,721)
Payables	92,316	158,802	144,364	102,382	(153)	97,843
Other	6,181	11,097	10,206	13,864	8,454	7,266
Net cash from operations	201,074	328,314	133,672	174,774	136,005	95,692
Cash flows from investment:						
Additions to property (net)	(371,851)	(327,010)	(314,827)	(259,388)	(221,794)	(164,201)
Other	(5,114)	4,463	15,137	10,952	11,053	(13,802)
Cash used for investment	(376,965)	(322,547)	(299,690)	(248,436)	(210,741)	(178,003)
Cash flows from financing:						
Short-term borrowing (net)	129,380	58,476	17,663	(1,136)	(19,118)	20,113
Long-term borrowing	–0–	693	96,611	–0–	2,493	36,080
Repayment, long term borrowing	(1,199)	(3,899)	(1,860)	(2,027)	(3,819)	(2,851)
Sale of equity (stock options)	19,861	52,429	15,221	25,033	16,072	8,410
Repurchase of equity (treasury stock)	(54,168)	(36,550)	–0–	–0–	–0–	–0–
Cash flow from financing	93,874	71,149	127,635	21,870	(4,372)	61,752
Increase (decrease) in cash	(82,017)	76,916	(38,383)	(51,792)	(79,108)	(20,559)
Beginning of year	122,912	45,996	84,379	136,171	215,279	235,838
End of year	$ 40,895	$122,912	$ 45,996	$ 84,379	$136,171	$215,279

[3] Because the statement of cash flows was not required until 1988, it was not possible to present data from actual cash flow statements for years before 1988. These data were taken from the Toys "R" Us statements of changes in financial position and reformatted by the authors into statements of cash flows.

To help detect trends, the annual data on cash flows for Toys "R" Us are further summarized by major inflow or outflow category. During the six-year period, Toys "R" Us secured cash and applied cash in the amounts and proportions that follow:

	TOTAL SIX-YEAR AMOUNT*	PERCENTAGE OF TOTAL INFLOWS OR OUTFLOWS
Inflows of cash:		
Operations	$1,069,531	68.1
Long-term and short-term borrowing	341,255	21.7
Sale of equity (stock options)	137,026	8.7
Other inflows	22,689	1.5
Total inflows	$1,570,501	100.0
Outflows of cash:		
Repayment of long-term borrowing	$ 15,655	0.9
Investment in property	1,659,071	94.0
Repurchase of equity (treasury stock)	90,718	5.1
Total outflows	$1,765,444	100.0
Excess of outflows over inflows	$ 194,943	

* Amounts in thousands.

On the basis of the annual statements of cash flows and the six-year summary of inflows and outflows, the following issues can be addressed when analyzing the financial results for Toys "R" Us:

1. *What cash sources has Toys "R" Us employed?*

Operations has been the most significant source of cash for Toys "R" Us over this six-year period; it represents 68.1 percent of total cash inflows. Long-term borrowing and the sale of equity have also produced sizable cash inflows. In recent years, short-term borrowing has also provided a significant amount of cash.

2. *What have been the major uses of cash?*

Investment in property has been by far the largest use of cash. Cash also also been used to repay long-term borrowings and, in recent years, to purchase treasury stock.

3. *Has Toys "R" Us matched the time commitment of cash inflows and outflows?*

Toys "R" Us appears to have matched the time commitment of inflows and outflows adequately. Nearly all the firm's outflows have been for investments in property, a long-term use of cash. Inflows (primarily from operations, long-term borrowing, and the sale of equity) are sources of cash that will be invested in the firm permanently or for the long term.

4. *Are debt and equity likely to be available as inflows of cash in the near future?*

Because Toys "R" Us has been growing rapidly, considerable amounts of cash have been invested in property during the past six years. During that same six-year period, as noted above, operations have provided 68.1 percent of the cash inflows. Although Toys "R" Us has borrowed and has sold equity, those two sources have not been overused and should continue to provide 20 percent or more of the firm's total cash needs. Another important factor in a firm's ability to secure cash from creditors is profitability. Toys "R" Us has been highly profitable, so one would expect that potential owners and creditors would continue to be willing to invest cash in the firm.

5. *What are the trends in inflows and outflows?*

The annual cash inflow from operations has grown over the six-year period, although not in every year. In several years, the cash flow from operations has been down due to an increase in inventories. The proportion of cash provided by financing has also varied from year to year, tending to rise when cash flows from operations have been low. The annual investment in property has increased in each of the six years, indicating a strong commitment to a growth strategy.

6. *What projections would you make regarding inflows and outflows in the near future?*

So long as operations continue to provide a substantial portion of the cash needed for investment in property, Toys "R" Us is likely to continue to grow. Should profitability decline, however, the firm may find it difficult to secure cash from creditors and owners. If cash should become scarce, Toys "R" Us may have to postpone its expansion into new markets. However, it does appear that Toys "R" Us has invested wisely and has operated efficiently. Therefore, one would expect that satisfactory profitability will continue.

Thus the cash flow statement can be used as a basis for answering important questions raised by investors, creditors, and others interested in the activities of a business.

SUMMARY

The statement of cash flows is designed to measure a business' inflows (sources) and outflows (uses) of cash during a period of time. The statement is useful to creditors, stockholders, and others who seek information about the sources from which a firm derives cash, about the rate at which the firm recovers cash invested in operating assets, and about the rate at which the firm returns that cash to the parties from which it was obtained.

The statement of cash flows is developed from data contained in the balance sheets and income statement and from transactions data involving the cash account. The statement is organized into three sections: cash flows from operations, cash flows from financing activities, and cash flows from investing activities. The cash flows from operations section can be prepared by using a direct method or an indirect method. The direct method presents cash inflows from sales and deducts cash outflows for expenses to arrive at cash flows from operations. The indirect method begins with net income and employs a series of adjustments to transform net income into cash flows from operations. Both the direct and the indirect methods produce the same number for cash flows from operations.

Appendix 13–1 describes the rudiments of a worksheet procedure for the preparation of a statement of cash flows.

APPENDIX 13–1
USING A WORKSHEET TO DEVELOP DATA FOR THE STATEMENT OF CASH FLOWS

As we have seen, the changes in the balance sheet accounts from the beginning to the end of a period include amounts that appear in a statement of cash flows. The worksheet technique for the preparation of the statement of cash flows provides a means of systematically analyzing these balance sheet changes, along with income statement and cash account transactions data, to determine the amounts of cash inflows and cash outflows. The analysis produces worksheet entries (which are recorded only on the worksheet) that simultaneously reconstruct and explain the changes in the balance sheet accounts and indicate the inflows and outflows of cash.

Every worksheet entry reconstructs in summary form the debit-and-credit effect of the transaction that changes the balance sheet account under consideration. Thus each worksheet entry adjusts both the balance sheet account under consideration and the statement of cash flows section of the worksheet *or* another balance sheet account (other than cash). The chart in Exhibit 13–16 indicates the effects that various types of balance sheet account changes have on the statement of cash flows. Note that all inflows in the statement of cash flows worksheet will be recorded as debits and that outflows will be recorded as credits.

To illustrate the worksheet technique, we will use a worksheet to prepare a statement of cash flows for Solar Systems Company. The income statement, statement of changes in retained earnings, and balance sheets for Solar Systems are presented in Exhibits 13–17, 13–18, and 13–19. To simplify the presentation of the data and the development of the statement of cash flows, we will use the indirect method for presenting cash flows from operations.[4]

[4] Using the direct method would require a worksheet that is considerably more involved than the one presented here. The direct method worksheet is, therefore, deferred to intermediate accounting texts.

EXHIBIT 13–16   **BALANCE SHEET CHANGES IN THE STATEMENT OF CASH FLOWS WORKSHEET**

BALANCE SHEET CHANGE		STATEMENT OF CASH FLOWS	
TYPE OF CHANGE	HOW RECORDED	FLOW CLASSIFICATION	HOW RECORDED
Asset increase	Debit	Outflow	Credit
Liability increase	Credit	Inflow	Debit
Equity increase	Credit	Inflow	Debit
Asset decrease	Credit	Inflow	Debit
Liability decrease	Debit	Outflow	Credit
Equity decrease	Debit	Outflow	Credit

EXHIBIT 13-17   INCOME STATEMENT

SOLAR SYSTEMS COMPANY
Income Statement
For the Year Ended December 31, 19X2

Sales revenue		$1,339,000
Less: Cost of goods sold		908,000
Gross margin		$ 431,000
Less: Operating expenses:		
Salaries	$230,000	
Depreciation	24,000	
Rent	96,000	
Utilities	7,000	
Other operating expenses	9,000	366,000
Income from operations		$ 65,000
Other income:		
Gain on sale of equipment	$ 3,000	
Loss on sale of long-term investment	(4,000)	(1,000)
		$ 64,000
Less: Interest expense		14,000
Income before taxes		$ 50,000
Less: Income taxes expense		12,000
Net income		$ 38,000

EXHIBIT 13-18   STATEMENT OF CHANGES IN RETAINED EARNINGS

SOLAR SYSTEMS COMPANY
Statement of Changes in Retained Earnings
For the Year Ended December 31, 19X2

Retained earnings, 12/31/X1	$ 7,000
Add: Net income	38,000
	$45,000
Less: Dividends	15,000
Retained earnings, 12/31/X2	$30,000

The worksheet shown in Exhibit 13-20 lists the balance sheet accounts in the upper portion, with debit and credit columns for worksheet adjustments. Note that credit balances appear in parentheses. Also note that the ending balances appear in the left column and the beginning balances in the far-right column. The data for the statement of cash flows are entered in the lower portion of the worksheet.

EXHIBIT 13-19   BALANCE SHEETS

SOLAR SYSTEMS COMPANY
Balance Sheets
As of December 31, 19X2 and 19X1

ASSETS		19X2		19X1
Current assets:				
Cash		$ 17,000		$ 15,000
Accounts receivable		123,000		107,000
Prepaid expenses.		10,000		9,000
Inventory		52,000		46,000
Total current assets		$202,000		$177,000
Property, plant, and equipment:				
Equipment[1]	$270,000		$262,000	
Accumulated depreciation	(118,000)		(109,000)	
Net property		152,000		153,000
Investments[2]		39,000		32,000
Total assets		$393,000		$362,000
LIABILITIES				
Current liabilities:				
Accounts payable		$ 18,000		$ 11,000
Short-term notes payable[3].		40,000		50,000
Salaries payable.		5,000		9,000
Income taxes payable.		7,000		5,000
Total current liabilities		$ 70,000		$ 75,000
Long-term liabilities:				
Bonds payable.		80,000		80,000
Total liabilities		$150,000		$155,000
EQUITY				
Common stock[4]	$213,000		$200,000	
Retained earnings.	30,000		7,000	
Total stockholders' equity...		243,000		207,000
Total liabilities and equity		$393,000		$362,000

[1] Equipment with a cost of $24,000 and accumulated depreciation of $15,000 was sold for $12,000 cash in 19X2. Equipment was purchased for $32,000 cash.

[2] Long-term investments with a cost of $17,000 were sold for $13,000 cash. Additional long-term investments were purchased for $24,000 cash.

[3] Short-term notes payable in the amount of $10,000 were repaid, and no new notes payable were issued.

[4] Common stock was issued for $13,000 cash in 19X2.

EXHIBIT 13–20   STATEMENT OF CASH FLOWS WORKSHEET

SOLAR SYSTEMS COMPANY
Statement of Cash Flows Worksheet

BALANCE SHEET ACCOUNT	12/31/X2 BALANCE SHEET	WORKSHEET ENTRIES DEBIT	WORKSHEET ENTRIES CREDIT	12/31/X1 BALANCE SHEET
Cash	$ 17,000	(p) 2,000		$ 15,000
Accounts receivable	123,000	(b) 16,000		107,000
Prepaid expenses	10,000	(c) 1,000		9,000
Inventory	52,000	(d) 6,000		46,000
Equipment	270,000	(k) 32,000	(i) 24,000	262,000
Accumulated depreciation	(118,000)	(i) 15,000	(h) 24,000	(109,000)
Investments	39,000	(l) 24,000	(j) 17,000	32,000
	$ 393,000			$ 362,000
Accounts payable	$ (18,000)		(e) 7,000	$ (11,000)
Short-term loans payable	(40,000)	(n) 10,000		(50,000)
Salaries payable	(5,000)	(f) 4,000		(9,000)
Income taxes payable	(7,000)		(g) 2,000	(5,000)
Bonds payable	(80,000)			(80,000)
Common stock	(213,000)		(m) 13,000	(200,000)
Retained earnings	(30,000)	(o) 15,000	(a) 38,000	(7,000)
	$(393,000)			$(362,000)

STATEMENT OF CASH FLOWS				
Operations:				
Net income		(a) 38,000		
Increase in accounts receivable			(b) 16,000	
Increase in prepaid expenses			(c) 1,000	
Increase in inventory			(d) 6,000	
Increase in accounts payable		(e) 7,000		
Decrease in salaries payable			(f) 4,000	
Increase in income taxes payable		(g) 2,000		
Depreciation expense		(h) 24,000		
Gain on sale of equipment			(i) 3,000	
Loss on sale of investments		(j) 4,000		
Investing:				
Purchase of equipment			(k) 32,000	
Sale of equipment		(i) 12,000		
Purchase of investments			(l) 24,000	
Sale of investments		(j) 13,000		
Financing:				
Sale of common stock		(m) 13,000		
Repayment of notes payable			(n) 10,000	
Payment of dividends			(o) 15,000	
Increase in cash			(p) 2,000	

First, let us demonstrate how the debit-and-credit effect of transactions related to the change in accounts receivable is analyzed and adjusted. As explained in the chapter, the change in accounts receivable is an element of the reconciliation between net income and net cash provided by operations—a reconciliation that appears on the statement of cash flows. Thus the $16,000 increase in Solar Systems Company's accounts receivable shown in Exhibit 13–19 leads to a $16,000 debit worksheet entry to accounts receivable and a $16,000 credit worksheet entry to net income on the statement of cash flows. The adjustment is shown as entry **b** in Exhibit 13–20, which places a $16,000 debit in the accounts receivable row of the balance sheet section and enters a $16,000 credit in the statement of cash flows section, a negative adjustment that reduces net income by the amount of the increase in accounts receivable.

The following list provides an explanation for each of the entries in both the balance sheet and the statement of cash flows portions of the worksheet:

WORKSHEET ENTRY	EXPLANATION
a	The net income of $38,000 requires a credit entry to retained earnings and a corresponding positive (debit) entry in the cash flows portion of the worksheet.
b	The $16,000 increase in accounts receivable requires a debit entry to accounts receivable and a negative (credit) adjustment to net income in determining cash flows from operations.
c	The $1,000 increase in prepaid expenses requires a debit entry to prepaid expense and a negative (credit) adjustment to net income in determining cash flows from operations.
d	The $6,000 increase in inventory requires a debit entry to inventory and a negative (credit) adjustment to net income in determining cash flows from operations.
e	The $7,000 increase in accounts payable requires a credit entry to accounts payable and a positive (debit) adjustment to net income in determining cash flows from operations.
f	The $4,000 decrease in salaries payable requires a debit entry to salaries payable and a negative (credit) adjustment to net income in determining cash flows from operations.
g	The $2,000 increase in income taxes payable requires a credit entry to income taxes payable and a positive (debit) adjustment to net income in determining cash flows from operations.
h	Depreciation expense is $24,000 and is credited to accumulated depreciation in the balance sheet portion of the worksheet. The corresponding debit in the statement of cash flows portion of the worksheet indicates a positive adjustment to net income to remove the effects of an expense that does not consume cash.
i	This worksheet entry records the balance sheet and statement of cash flows effects of the sale of the

WORKSHEET ENTRY	EXPLANATION
	equipment. The $12,000 cash inflow from the sale of the equipment is recorded in the statement of cash flows with a debit. The removal of the accumulated depreciation for the equipment sold is recorded on the balance sheet with a $15,000 debit. The cost of the equipment sold is removed from the equipment account with a $24,000 credit. Finally, the gain on the sale of the equipment is recorded with a $3,000 credit on the statement of cash flows and is a negative adjustment to net income because the gain increases net income but does not provide additional cash. All the cash received was already recorded with the $12,000 debit.
j	The $13,000 inflow from the sale of the investment is recorded with a debit on the statement of cash flows. The $17,000 cost of the investments sold is removed from the balance sheet with a debit. The $4,000 loss is recorded as a debit on the statement of cash flows and is a positive adjustment to net income because the loss reduces net income but does not consume cash.
k	The $32,000 outflow for the purchase of equipment is entered on the worksheet with a debit on the equipment line of the balance sheet and with a credit in the investment section of the statement of cash flows.
l	The $24,000 outflow for the purchase of long-term investments is recorded on the worksheet with a debit on the investments line on the balance sheet and with a credit in the investment section of the statement of cash flows.
m	The $13,000 inflow from the sale of common stock is recorded on the worksheet with a debit in the financing section of the statement of cash flows and a credit on the common stock line on the balance sheet.
n	The $10,000 outflow for repayment of the short-term loan is entered on the worksheet with a debit on the short-term loans payable line in the balance sheet and with a credit in the financing section of the statement of cash flows.
o	The $15,000 outflow for dividends is recorded on the worksheet with a debit on the retained earnings line of the balance sheet and with a credit in the financing section of the statement of cash flows.
p	This entry reconciles the increase in the cash account and balances the debits and credits on the statement of cash flows.

The statement of cash flows can be prepared from the data developed in the statement of cash flows portion of the worksheet. A statement of cash flows for Solar Systems Company is presented in Exhibit 13–21 shown at the top of the next page.

EXHIBIT 13–21   STATEMENT OF CASH FLOWS

SOLAR SYSTEMS COMPANY
Statement of Cash Flows
For the Year Ended December 31, 19X2

Cash flows from operating activities:		
Net income		$38,000
Adjustments to reconcile net income to net cash		
provided by operating activities:		
Increase in accounts receivable	$(16,000)	
Increase in prepaid expenses	(1,000)	
Increase in inventory	(6,000)	
Increase in accounts payable	7,000	
Decrease in salaries payable	(4,000)	
Increase in income taxes payable	2,000	
Depreciation expense	24,000	
Gain on sale of equipment	(3,000)	
Loss on sale of investment	4,000	
Total adjustments		7,000
Net cash provided by operating activities		$45,000
Cash flows from investing activities:		
Purchase of equipment	$(32,000)	
Cash received from sale of equipment	12,000	
Purchase of long-term investments	(24,000)	
Cash received from sale of long-term investments	13,000	
Net cash used by investing activities		(31,000)
Cash flows from financing activities:		
Cash received from sale of common stock	$ 13,000	
Principal payments on short-term notes	(10,000)	
Payment of dividends	(15,000)	
Net cash used by financing activities		(12,000)
Net increase in cash and cash equivalents		$ 2,000
Cash and cash equivalents at beginning of year		15,000
Cash and cash equivalents at end of year		$17,000

KEY TERMS

ALL-RESOURCES CONCEPT (p. 604)	STATEMENT OF CASH FLOWS (p. 597)
FLOWS (p. 600)	STOCKS (p. 600)

QUESTIONS

Q13-1.   What does the statement of cash flows report?

Q13-2.   How is a statement of cash flows different from an income statement?

Q13-3.   What are the three categories into which inflows and outflows of cash are divided?

Q13-4.   Which items usually constitute the largest components of cash provided by operations?

Q13-5.   Why are depreciation, depletion, and amortization added to net income when the indirect method is used to develop net cash flows from operations?

Q13-6. What are the most common sources of cash inflows from financing and investment?

Q13-7. Which items appear most frequently as outflows in statements of cash flows?

Q13-8. Why are direct exchanges of long-term debt for operating assets included in supplementary information for statements of cash flows even though the exchanges do not affect cash?

Q13-9. From what source(s) should most firms secure the majority of cash inflows? Why?

Q13-10. Why should firms attempt to secure cash for investment in operating assets from long-term or permanent sources?

Q13-11. Why might a firm that reports a net loss have a cash outflow (rather than a cash inflow) from operations?

Q13-12. What balance sheet account changes might you expect to find for a firm that must draw on sources other than operations to fund its cash outflows?

Q13-13. Where do the components of the changes in retained earnings appear in the statement of cash flows?

Q13-14. Does the fact that the cash flow from operations is normally positive imply that cash and cash equivalents usually increase each year?

EXERCISES

E13-15. CLASSIFICATION OF CASH FLOWS   The controller of Newstrom Software, Inc., provides the following information as the basis for a statement of cash flows:

Cash collected from customers	$794,000
Cash paid for interest.	22,100
Cash paid to employees and other suppliers of goods and services	215,000
Cash paid to suppliers of merchandise.	388,000
Cash received from the issuance of short-term debt.	12,700
Cash received from sale of equipment	44,000
Cash received from sale of long-term investments.	71,400
Income taxes paid	58,300
Payment of dividends	24,000
Principal payments on mortgage payable	50,000
Principal payments on short-term debt	15,000
Proceeds from issuance of common stock	85,000
Purchase of equipment	120,000
Purchase of long-term investments	83,000

REQUIRED:

1. Using the information provided above, calculate the net cash provided (used) by operations.

2. Using the information provided above, calculate the net cash provided (used) by investing activities.

3. Using the information provided above, calculate the net cash provided (used) by financing activities.

E13-16. DIRECT DETERMINATION OF CASH FLOWS FROM OPERATIONS   Casey Company engaged in the following transactions:

a) Made credit sales of $600,000. The cost of the merchandise sold was $410,000.

b) Collected accounts receivable in the amount of $580,000.

c) Purchased goods on credit in the amount of $425,000.

d) Paid accounts payable in the amount of $392,000.

REQUIRED:

Determine the effect of each transaction on cash inflows or cash outflows.

E13-17. INDIRECT DETERMINATION OF CASH FLOWS FROM OPERATIONS For Cornelius, Inc., you have the following data:

INCOME STATEMENT ITEM	AMOUNT
Depreciation expense	$11,000
Net income	38,000

BALANCE SHEET ITEM	ENDING	BEGINNING
Accounts receivable	$27,000	$21,000
Inventory (using perpetual inventory accounting).........	43,000	47,000
Accounts payable	32,000	24,000

REQUIRED:

Determine the net cash flow provided by operations.

E13-18. STATEMENTS FROM STOCKS AND FLOWS Wayne Sales, Inc., is a retailer of drinking water filtration systems. The accompanying schedule of stocks and flows represents a comprehensive description of Wayne's financial activities during 19X2. All sales by Wayne are credit sales, and all purchases of merchandise are on account. All expenses other than cost of goods sold and depreciation expense are paid in cash.

REQUIRED:

1. Prepare the income statement for 19X2.
2. Prepare the statement of changes in retained earnings for 19X2.
3. Prepare the statement of cash flows for 19X2.

WAYNE SALES, INC.
Statement of Stocks and Flows
For the Year Ended December 31, 19X2

	BALANCE SHEET 12/31/X2 (STOCKS)	DEBITS (FLOWS) DESCRIPTION	AMOUNT	CREDITS (FLOWS) DESCRIPTION	AMOUNT	BALANCE SHEET 12/31/X1 (STOCKS)
Cash	$ 620	(f) Collections from customers	21,940	(d) Other expenses	2,600	$ 190
				(e) Dividends	1,100	
		(j) Borrowing	1,500	(h) Equipment acquisition	5,000	
		(l) Stock issue	2,000	(i) Payments on account	14,910	
				(k) Repayment of note	1,400	
Accounts receivable	1,700	(a) Revenues	22,500	(f) Collections from customers	21,940	1,140
Inventory	2,450	(g) Purchases	16,100	(b) Cost of goods sold	15,600	1,950
Building and equipment (net)	18,300	(h) Equipment acquisition	5,000	(c) Depreciation expense	1,800	15,100
	$23,070					$18,380
Accounts payable	$ 1,910	(i) Payments on account	14,910	(g) Purchases	16,100	$ 720
Notes payable	3,660	(k) Repayment of note	1,400	(j) Borrowing	1,500	3,560
Common stock	10,000			(l) Stock issue	2,000	8,000
Retained earnings	7,500	(b) Cost of goods sold	15,600	(a) Revenues	22,500	6,100
		(c) Depreciation expense	1,800			
		(d) Other expenses	2,600			
		(e) Dividends	1,100			
	$23,070					$18,380

E13-19. EFFECT OF TRANSACTIONS ON CASH FLOWS The accompanying schedule describes 16 transactions that characterize the activities of Summit Sales, Inc., for 19X7:

SUMMIT SALES, INC.
Schedule of Effects on Accounts and Cash Flows
For the Year Ended December 31, 19X7

| | EFFECTS ON ACCOUNTS | | | | | EFFECTS ON CASH FLOWS |
| | ASSETS | | LIABILITIES AND EQUITY | | | |
TRANSACTION	CURRENT	NON-CURRENT	CURRENT LIABILITIES	NON-CURRENT LIABILITIES	EQUITY	
a) Purchased supplies on credit, $30,000						
b) Paid $22,600 cash toward the $30,000 purchase in transaction **a**						
c) Provided services to customers on credit, $37,800						
d) Collected $47,000 cash from accounts receivable						
e) Recorded depreciation expense, $7,350						
f) Employees earned salaries, $9,200						
g) Paid $9,200 cash to employees for salaries earned						
h) Incurred interest expense on long-term liabilities, $2,400						
i) Paid $15,000 on long-term liabilities, including interest of $2,400 from transaction **h**						
j) Paid $1,850 cash for one year's insurance coverage in advance						
k) Incurred insurance expense, $950						
l) Sold old equipment for its book value of $3,900						
m) Declared and paid cash dividend, $5,000						
n) Purchased new equipment, $14,300						
o) Issued capital stock, $20,000 cash						
p) Used $28,100 of supplies to produce revenues						

REQUIRED:

1. Indicate in the five asset, liability, and equity columns the effect of each transaction on the corresponding account. If the transaction increases an account corresponding to the column, write the amount of the increase preceded by a plus sign (+). If the transaction decreases an

account corresponding to the column, write the amount of the decrease preceded by a minus sign (−). If the transaction increases one account and decreases another, with both accounts corresponding to the same column, then write the amounts of both effects preceded by the appropriate signs.

2. Indicate in the cash flows column the effect of each transaction on cash. If the event is an inflow of cash, write the word *inflow* and the amount of the inflow. If the transaction is an outflow of cash, write the word *outflow* and the amount of the outflow.

3. Prepare a statement of cash flows, using the direct method to determine cash flows from operations.

E13-20. CASH FLOWS FROM OPERATIONS, INDIRECT METHOD   Service Company had net income during 19X3 of $111,000. The following data are available for balance sheet account changes during 19X3:

Accounts receivable.	$20,000 increase
Inventory	25,000 increase
Accounts payable	16,000 decrease
Interest payable	9,000 increase
Accumulated depreciation, equipment*	27,000 increase
Accumulated depreciation, building	12,000 increase
Retained earnings†	75,000 increase

* Equipment with accumulated depreciation of $15,000 was sold during 19X3.
† Includes net income of $111,000 and cash dividends paid of $36,000.

REQUIRED:

Prepare the cash flows from operations section of the statement of cash flows, using the indirect method.

E13-21. REFORMATTING A STATEMENT OF CASH FLOWS   Rolling Meadows Country Club, Inc., is a privately owned corporation that operates a golf club. The corporation's statement of cash flows appears below.

ROLLING MEADOWS COUNTRY CLUB, INC.
Statement of Cash Flows
For the Year Ended November 30, 19X6

INFLOWS OF CASH

Net income	$106,000	
Decrease in accounts receivable, dues	4,000	
Increase in accounts payable	11,400	
Increase in income taxes payable	7,500	
Proceeds from issue of short-term note payable	35,000	
Cash received from sale of used golf carts	7,000	
Cash received from issuance of common stock	40,000	
Depreciation expense, buildings.	49,000	
Depreciation expense, golf carts.	23,000	
Total inflows of cash		$282,900

OUTFLOWS OF CASH

Increase in pro shop inventory.	$ 28,600	
Increase in prepaid insurance	15,800	
Decrease in wages payable	11,400	
Payment of cash dividends	40,000	
Payment on mortgage payable.	45,000	
Cash paid for new golf carts.	123,000	
Total outflows of cash		263,800
Net increase in cash		$ 19,100

REQUIRED:

Prepare a properly formatted statement of cash flows.

E13-22. CASH FLOWS FROM OPERATIONS, DIRECT METHOD   Colassard Industries has the following data available for preparation of its statement of cash flows:

Sales revenue.	$345,000
Cost of goods sold	182,500
Wages expense	34,400
Insurance expense	12,000
Interest expense.	20,800
Income taxes expense	16,200
Accounts receivable, decrease	14,300
Inventory, increase	9,700
Prepaid insurance, increase	6,100
Accounts payable, increase	11,600
Short-term notes payable, increase	32,000
Interest payable, increase.	5,000
Wages payable, decrease	8,400

REQUIRED:

Prepare the cash flows from operations section of the statement of cash flows, using the direct method.

E13-23. CASH FLOWS FROM OPERATIONS, INDIRECT METHOD   The following data are available for Bernard Corporation for a recent year:

Net income	$206,000
Accounts receivable, decrease	4,900
Inventory, increase	15,300
Prepaid rent, decrease	2,100
Salaries payable, increase.	14,400
Income taxes payable, increase	11,200
Short-term notes payable, increase	20,000
Depreciation expense	42,000
Amortization expense, goodwill.	5,000

REQUIRED:

Prepare the cash flows from operations portion of the statement of cash flows, using the indirect method.

E13-24. PREPARATION OF A STATEMENT OF CASH FLOWS   For the year ended December 31, 19X2, Beckwith Products Company has the following data available:

Sales revenue.	$481,000
Cost of goods sold	329,000
Expenses (wages and services)	71,000
Interest expense.	12,000
Income taxes expense	17,000
Accounts receivable, decrease	15,000
Inventory, increase	9,300
Accounts payable, increase	2,100
Interest payable, increase.	5,500
Wages payable, decrease	4,900
Short-term notes payable (cash proceeds from issuance of note)	20,000
Long-term notes payable (cash payment on principal).	35,000
Common stock (cash proceeds from stock sold)	40,000
Dividends (cash paid)	16,000
Equipment (cash paid for items purchased).	58,000

REQUIRED:

Prepare a statement of cash flows for Beckwith Products for 19X2.

E13-25. REFORMATTING A STATEMENT OF CASH FLOWS   Boeke Company has prepared the following statement of cash flows for 19X7:

BOEKE COMPANY
Statement of Cash Flows
For the Year Ended December 31, 19X7

INFLOWS OF CASH

Cash collections from sales	$511,400	
Cash proceeds from sale of equipment...............	6,100	
Cash received from issuance of short-term notes payable..	30,000	
Cash received from sale of common stock............	50,000	
Total inflows of cash		$597,500

OUTFLOWS OF CASH

Cash payments for cost of goods sold................	$302,000	
Cash payments for operating expenses...............	83,400	
Cash payments for interest expense.................	13,100	
Cash payments for income taxes expense.............	22,300	
Cash paid for purchase of equipment................	136,100	
Payment of cash dividends	20,000	
Cash paid on mortgage	15,000	
Total outflows of cash		591,900
Net increase in cash		$ 5,600

REQUIRED:

Recast the Boeke statement into a properly prepared statement of cash flows.

E13-26. DETERMINING CASH FLOWS INVOLVING EQUIPMENT   Burns Company's 19X9 and 19X8 balance sheets presented the following data for equipment:

	12/31/X9	12/31/X8
Equipment	$260,000	$225,000
Accumulated depreciation.........................	115,000	92,000
Book value	$145,000	$133,000

During 19X9 equipment costing $35,000 with accumulated depreciation of $30,000 was sold for cash, producing a $4,400 gain.

REQUIRED:

1. What was the amount of depreciation expense for 19X9?

2. What was the amount of cash spent for equipment during 19X9?

3. What amount should be included as a cash inflow from the sale of the equipment?

E13-27. DETERMINING CASH FLOWS FOR INVESTMENT   Airco owns several aircraft, which it leases to businesses. Airco's balance sheet indicated the following amounts for its aircraft accounts at the end of 19X3 and 19X2:

	12/31/X3	12/31/X2
Equipment, aircraft	$28,500,000	$21,750,000
Accumulated depreciation	11,900,000	10,100,000
Book value................................	$16,600,000	$11,650,000

REQUIRED:

1. Assume that Airco did not sell any aircraft during 19X3. What was the amount of depreciation expense for 19X3, and what was the cash spent for aircraft purchases in 19X3?

2. If Airco sold for cash aircraft that cost $4,100,000 with accumulated depreciation of $3,500,000, producing a gain of $300,000, what were the amounts of depreciation expense and cash paid for aircraft purchases in 19X3?

3. Refer to requirement 2. Determine the amount of the cash inflow from the sale of aircraft.

E13-28. PREPARING A STATEMENT OF CASH FLOWS   Financial statements for Cincinnati Health Club, Inc., appear below:

CINCINNATI HEALTH CLUB, INC.
Balance Sheets
As of December 31, 19X9 and 19X8

ASSETS	19X9		19X8	
Current assets:				
Cash..........................		$ 5,300		$ 9,200
Accounts receivable, dues		10,500		8,900
Supplies inventory...............		19,800		18,600
Total current assets		$ 35,600		$ 36,700
Property, plant, and equipment:				
Land	$ 40,000		$ 40,000	
Building......................	450,000		450,000	
Equipment[1]	280,000		270,000	
	$770,000		$760,000	
Accumulated depreciation[2]	(148,000)		(120,000)	
Net property, plant, and equipment		622,000		640,000
Total assets		$657,600		$676,700
LIABILITIES				
Current liabilities:				
Accounts payable................		$ 55,300		$ 36,100
Wages payable		9,500		11,700
Income taxes payable.............		1,100		9,900
Total current liabilities...........		$ 65,900		$ 57,700
Long-term liabilities:				
Mortgage payable[3]		350,000		400,000
Total liabilities		$415,900		$457,700
EQUITY				
Common stock	$180,000		$150,000	
Retained earnings	61,700		69,000	
Total equity		241,700		219,000
Total liabilities and equity.....		$657,600		$676,700

[1] No equipment was sold in 19X8. Equipment was purchased for $10,000 cash.
[2] Depreciation expense for 19X8 was $28,000.
[3] A principal payment of $50,000 was made on the mortgage during 19X8, as required by its loan agreement.

Due to adverse temporary local economic conditions, Cincinnati Health Club had a net loss in 19X8 of $7,300. Cincinnati Health Club paid no dividends during 19X8. To help the firm through the temporary downturn, owners provided the corporation $30,000 cash by purchasing common stock.

REQUIRED:

Prepare a statement of cash flows for Cincinnati Health Club for 19X8, using the indirect method to determine cash flows from operations.

E13-29. PREPARING A STATEMENT OF CASH FLOWS Financial statements for Rowe Publishing Company appear below and on the next page:

ROWE PUBLISHING COMPANY
Balance Sheets
As of December 31, 19X5 and 19X4

ASSETS		19X5		19X4
Current assets:				
Cash..........................		$ 85,000		$ 66,000
Accounts receivable..............		240,000		231,000
Inventory.....................		190,000		170,000
Total current assets		$515,000		$467,000
Property, plant, and equipment:				
Land	$ 30,000		$ 30,000	
Building......................	370,000		370,000	
Equipment[1]	155,000		130,000	
	$555,000		$530,000	
Accumulated depreciation	(375,000)		(350,000)	
Net property, plant, and equipment .		180,000		180,000
Total assets		$695,000		$647,000
LIABILITIES				
Current liabilities:				
Accounts payable................		$133,000		$121,000
Notes payable[2]...................		115,000		150,000
Salaries payable		15,000		11,000
Income taxes payable.............		10,000		17,000
Total current liabilities...........		$273,000		$299,000
Long-term liabilities:				
Bonds payable[3]		50,000		–0–
Total liabilities		$323,000		$299,000
EQUITY				
Common stock	$300,000		$300,000	
Retained earnings	72,000		48,000	
Total equity		372,000		348,000
Total liabilities and				
equity		$695,000		$647,000

[1] No equipment was sold in 19X5. Equipment was purchased for $25,000 cash.
[2] Short-term notes payable in the amount of $35,000 were repaid during 19X5.
[3] Bonds payable were issued for $50,000 cash.

ROWE PUBLISHING COMPANY
Income Statement
For the Year Ended December 31, 19X5

Sales revenue		$1,051,000
Less: Cost of goods sold		578,000
Gross margin		$ 473,000
Less: Operating expenses		
Salaries	$351,000	
Depreciation	25,000	376,000
Income from operations		$ 97,000
Less: Interest expense		16,000
Income before taxes		$ 81,000
Less: Income taxes expense		22,000
Net income		$ 59,000

ROWE PUBLISHING COMPANY
Statement of Changes in Retained Earnings
For the Year Ended December 31, 19X5

Retained earnings, 12/31/X4	$ 48,000
Add: Net income	59,000
	$107,000
Less: Dividends	35,000
Retained earnings, 12/31/X5	$ 72,000

REQUIRED:

Prepare a statement of cash flows for 19X5, using the direct method to determine cash flows from operations.

E13-30. PREPARING A PROSPECTIVE STATEMENT OF CASH FLOWS   Jane and Harvey Wentland have decided to open a retail athletic supply store, Fitness Outfitters, Inc. They will stock clothing, shoes, and supplies used in running, swimming, bicycling, weight lifting, and other exercise and athletic activities. During their first year of operations, 19X3, they expect the following results. (Subsequent years are expected to be more successful.)

Sales revenue	$629,000
Less: Cost of goods sold	291,000
Gross margin	$338,000
Less: Operating expenses	355,000
Net loss	$ (17,000)

By the end of 19X3, Fitness Outfitters needs to have a cash balance of $5,000 and is expected to have the following partial balance sheet:

ASSETS

Inventory		$ 53,000
Store equipment	$97,000	
Accumulated depreciation, store equipment	15,000	82,000

LIABILITIES AND EQUITY

Accounts payable	$ 37,000
Common stock	100,000
Retained earnings	(17,000)

Assume that all sales will be for cash and that store equipment will be acquired for cash.

REQUIRED:

1. Prepare as much of the statement of cash flows for 19X3 as you can. Use the direct method to determine cash flows from operations.

2. In the statement that you prepared for requirement 1, by how much does the prospective cash balance exceed or fall short of the desired cash balance? If a shortfall occurs, where would you suggest that Jane and Harvey seek additional cash?

3. Does the preparation of a prospective statement of cash flows seem worthwhile for an ongoing business? Why?

PROBLEMS

P13-31. NET INCOME, CASH FLOWS, AND DIVIDENDS   Granville Consulting, Inc., included the following income statements in its 19X9 annual report:

	19X9	19X8
Service revenue	$4,200,000	$3,750,000
Salaries expense.	(1,720,000)	(1,450,000)
Administrative expense	(851,000)	(802,000)
Uncollectible account expense.	(156,000)	(144,000)
Depreciation expense.	(610,000)	(597,000)
Other expense	(255,000)	(229,000)
Net income	$ 608,000	$ 528,000

During 19X8 the balance of accounts receivable decreased by $1,600,000. During 19X9 the balance of accounts receivable increased by $900,000, and a $1,000,000 long-term note was paid off. No accounts were written off during either year. All other noncash current asset, and all current liability, balances remained fairly constant throughout this two-year period.

REQUIRED:

1. Calculate the approximate amount of cash provided by operations during 19X8 and 19X9.

2. Although the customary dividend was paid in 19X8, no dividend was paid in 19X9. Several angry stockholders at the annual stockholders' meeting ask why no dividend was paid when income increased by 15 percent. How would you answer them?

P13-32. DIRECT DEVELOPMENT OF A STATEMENT OF CASH FLOWS   According to Laurie Bond, controller for Transworld Export, the firm engaged in the following transactions during a recent year:

a) Made credit sales of $1,007,000.

b) Collected receivables in the amount of $978,000.

c) Purchased merchandise on credit at a cost of $672,000.

d) Paid accounts payable in the amount of $657,000.

e) Incurred operating and financial expenses in the amount of $307,000. All operating and financial expenses were paid in cash when incurred.

f) Incurred depreciation expense (not included in transaction e) in the amount of $17,000.

g) Repaid a long-term note payable at maturity in the amount of $10,000.

h) Paid dividends in the amount of $7,000.

i) Purchased new equipment for cash in the amount of $37,000.

j) Sold common stock for $25,000 cash.

REQUIRED:

Prepare a statement of cash flows, using the direct method to determine cash flows from operations.

P13-33. PREPARATION OF A STATEMENT OF CASH FLOWS FROM BALANCE SHEET DATA   Jane Bahr, controller of Endicott & Thurston Associates, prepared the following balance sheets at the end of 19X4 and 19X3:

ENDICOTT & THURSTON ASSOCIATES
Balance Sheets
As of December 31, 19X4 and 19X3

ASSETS	19X4		19X3	
Current assets:				
Cash.........................		$ 2,000		$ 17,000
Accounts receivable..............		78,000		219,000
Prepaid rent....................		29,000		104,000
Total current assets		$109,000		$340,000
Property, plant, and equipment:				
Equipment, computing[1]............	$488,000		$362,000	
Equipment, office furniture[2]........	400,000		365,000	
	$888,000		$727,000	
Accumulated depreciation[3]	(366,000)		(554,000)	
Net property..................		522,000		173,000
Long-term investments[4]		51,000		40,000
Total assets		$682,000		$553,000
LIABILITIES				
Current liabilities:				
Accounts payable................		$ 56,000		$ 58,000
Salaries payable		89,000		105,000
Total current liabilities...........		$145,000		$163,000
Long-term liabilities:				
Long-term note payable[5]		80,000		105,000
Equipment mortgage payable[6]		140,000		–0–
Total liabilities		$365,000		$268,000
EQUITY				
Common stock	$225,000		$225,000	
Retained earnings[7]..................	92,000		60,000	
Total equity		317,000		285,000
Total liabilities and equity.....		$682,000		$553,000

[1] Computing equipment with a cost of $250,000 and accumulated depreciation of $230,000 was sold for $5,000. New computing equipment was purchased for $376,000.
[2] New office furniture was purchased at a cost of $35,000.
[3] Depreciation expense for 19X4 was $42,000.
[4] Investments costing $20,000 were sold for cash at a loss of $2,000. Additional investments were purchased for $31,000 cash.
[5] A $25,000 principal payment on the long-term note was made during 19X4.
[6] A portion of the cash needed to purchase computing equipment was secured by issuing a mortgage for $140,000 cash.
[7] Net income for 19X4 was $70,000 and dividends paid were $38,000.

REQUIRED:

Prepare a statement of cash flows, using the indirect method to determine cash flows from operations.

P13-34. PREPARATION OF A STATEMENT OF CASH FLOWS   Yogurt Plus, a restaurant, collected the following data on inflows and outflows for 19X9:

INFLOWS

Sales (all for cash)	$379,000
Cash received from sale of common stock	50,000
Proceeds from issuance of new long-term notes payable	40,000
Proceeds from sale of used restaurant fixtures	13,000
Proceeds from issuance of short-term note payable	35,000
Bonds payable issued in exchange for kitchen equipment	30,000
Total inflows	$547,000

OUTFLOWS

Cash payments for merchandise sold	$203,000
Cash payments for operating expenses	125,000
Cash payments for interest	22,000
Cash payments for income taxes	8,000
Purchase of restaurant fixtures for cash	105,000
Principal payment on mortgage	35,000
Payment of dividends	6,000
Cost of kitchen equipment acquired in exchange for bonds payable	30,000
Total outflows	$534,000

REQUIRED:

Prepare a statement of cash flows, using the direct method to determine cash flows from operations.

P13-35. PREPARATION AND ANALYSIS OF A STATEMENT OF CASH FLOWS   SDPS, Inc., provides airport transportation services in Southern California. An income statement for 19X6 and balance sheets for 19X6 and 19X5 appear below and on the next page:

SDPS, INC.
Income Statement
For the Year Ended December 31, 19X6

Service revenue		$937,000
Less: Operating expenses:		
Wages	$278,000	
Rent	229,000	
Fuel	83,000	
Maintenance	138,000	
Depreciation	215,000	943,000
Income (loss) from operation		$ (6,000)
Less: Loss on sale of vehicles		(3,000)
Less: Interest expense		(14,000)
Net loss		$ (23,000)

SDPS, INC.
Balance Sheets
As of December 31, 19X6 and 19X5

ASSETS	19X6		19X5	
Current assets:				
Cash.		$ 40,000		$ 82,000
Accounts receivable.		126,000		109,000
Inventory, fuel.		11,000		25,000
Total current assets		$177,000		$216,000
Property, plant, and equipment:				
Equipment, vehicles[1]	$524,000		$409,000	
Less: Accumulated depreciation.	(174,000)		(136,000)	
Net property.		350,000		273,000
Total assets		$527,000		$489,000
LIABILITIES				
Current liabilities:				
Accounts payable.		$103,000		$ 58,000
Wages payable		22,000		29,000
Maintenance service payable		41,000		34,000
Rent payable		92,000		51,000
Total current liabilities.		$258,000		$172,000
Long-term liabilities:				
Long-term note payable[2]		100,000		125,000
Total liabilities		$358,000		$297,000
EQUITY				
Common stock	$150,000		$150,000	
Retained earnings[3].	19,000		42,000	
Total equity		169,000		192,000
Total liabilities and equity.		$527,000		$489,000

[1] Vehicles with a cost of $310,000 and accumulated depreciation of $177,000 were sold for $130,000 cash. New vehicles were purchased for $425,000 cash.
[2] A $25,000 principal payment on the long-term note was made during 19X6.
[3] No dividends were paid during 19X6.

REQUIRED:

1. Prepare a statement of cash flows for 19X6, using the direct method to determine cash flows from operations.

2. What has been responsible for the decrease in cash?

3. Does an examination of the changes in the current liability accounts suggest how SDPS financed its increases in net property during a period in which it had a substantial net loss?

P13-36. THE STATEMENT OF CASH FLOWS AND CREDIT ANALYSIS June's Camera Shop sells cameras and photographic supplies of all types to retail customers. June's also repairs cameras and develops and prints color and black-and-white film. To compete with the camera departments of discount stores, June's offers fast, efficient, and effective repairs and film processing. For fiscal 19X9 and 19X8, June's accountant prepared the following statement of cash flows:

JUNE'S CAMERA SHOP
Statements of Cash Flows
For the Years Ended January 31, 19X9 and 19X8

	19X9		19X8	
Cash flows from operating activities:				
Net income.....................		$ 87,000		$ 63,000
Adjustments to reconcile net income to net cash provided by operating activities:				
Increase in accounts receivable	$(17,000)		$(12,000)	
Increase in inventory............	(19,000)		(11,000)	
Increase in accounts payable	15,000		14,000	
Increase in wages payable	11,000		5,000	
Increase in income taxes payable...	6,000		3,000	
Depreciation expense............	41,000		37,000	
Total adjustments		37,000		36,000
Net cash provided by operating activities		$124,000		$ 99,000
Cash flows from investing activities:				
Purchase of long-term investments ...	$(15,000)		$(10,000)	
Purchase of equipment	(45,000)		(40,000)	
Net cash used by investing activities		(60,000)		(50,000)
Cash flows from financing activities:				
Principal payments on mortgage.....	$(15,000)		$(15,000)	
Payment of dividends	(12,000)		(10,000)	
Net cash used by financing activities		(27,000)		(25,000)
Net increase in cash and cash equivalents		$ 37,000		$ 24,000
Cash and cash equivalents at beginning of year........................		158,000		134,000
Cash and cash equivalents at end of year		$195,000		$158,000

REQUIRED:

1. Does June's Camera Shop appear to have grown in size during the past two years?

2. June's president, June Smith, would like to open a second store. Smith believes that $225,000 is needed to equip the facility properly. The business has $100,000 of cash and liquid investments to apply toward the $225,000 required. Do the data in the 19X9 and 19X8 statements of cash flows suggest whether or not June's Camera Shop is likely to be able to secure a loan for the remaining $125,000 needed for the expansion?

3. How long should it take June's Camera Shop to pay back the $125,000?

P13-37. PROFITABILITY DECLINES AND THE STATEMENT OF CASH FLOWS   The Bookbarn, Inc., is a retail seller of new books in a moderate-sized city. Although initially very successful, The Bookbarn's sales volume has declined since the opening of two competing bookstores two years ago. The accountant for The Bookbarn prepared the following statement of cash flows at the end of the current year:

THE BOOKBARN, INC.
Statement of Cash Flows
For the Year Ended December 31, 19X5

Cash flows from operating activities:		
Net income		$26,500
Adjustments to reconcile net income to net cash		
provided by operating activities:		
Depreciation expense	$ 38,500	
Loss on sale of equipment....................	2,100	
Increase in accounts receivable	(1,200)	
Increase in inventory	(3,800)	
Increase in accounts payable..................	6,700	
Decrease in wages payable	(1,200)	
Total adjustments		41,100
Net cash provided by operating activities.......		$67,600
Cash flows from investing activities:		
Equipment purchase..........................	$(12,000)	
Proceeds from sale of equipment	2,300	
Net cash used by investing activities		(9,700)
Cash flows from financing activities:		
Payment of dividends.........................	$ (4,000)	
Repayment of mortgage.......................	(10,000)	
Net cash used by financing activities		(14,000)
Net increase in cash.............................		$43,900

Your analysis suggests that The Bookbarn's net income will continue to decline by $8,000 per year to $18,500 as sales continue to fall. Thereafter, you expect sales to stabilize.

REQUIRED:

1. What will happen to the amount of cash provided by operations as net income decreases?

2. Assume that equipment is nearly fully depreciated but that it will be fully serviceable for several years. What will happen to cash flows from operations as depreciation declines?

3. Do the operations of businesses experiencing declining sales volumes always consume cash? Explain your answer.

4. Can current assets and current liabilities buffer operating cash flows against the impact of declines in sales volume in the short run? In the long run? Explain your answer.

P13-38. ACCRUED LIABILITY CHANGES AND THE STATEMENT OF CASH FLOWS   Rod Bucher, the accountant for Green's Appliance Stores, has asked you how to account for warranty expense and the change in the estimated warranty liability (a current liability) in the statement of cash flows. Rod provides you with the following data:

ESTIMATED WARRANTY LIABILITY

Beginning balance.	$ 20,000
Less: Warranty claims paid in cash	43,000
	$(23,000)
Plus: Warranty expense.	52,000
Ending balance	$ 29,000

REQUIRED:

1. Should the amount of warranty expense be a positive adjustment to net income in the indirect method of determining cash flows from operations (as are depreciation, depletion, and amortization)?

2. How would you account for $52,000 of warranty expense and the $9,000 increase in the estimated warranty liability?

P13-39. USING FINANCIAL STATEMENTS AND TRANSACTIONS DATA TO PREPARE A STATEMENT OF CASH FLOWS   Erie Company has the following data for 19X7:

BALANCE SHEET ACCOUNT	CHANGE
Cash	$21,200 increase
Accounts receivable.	8,000 increase
Inventory	2,000 increase
Prepaid rent	4,000 decrease
Equipment[1]	12,000 increase
Accumulated depreciation, equipment[2]	5,400 increase
Long-term investments[3]	14,200 decrease
Accounts payable	1,100 decrease
Salaries payable.	2,500 increase
Interest payable.	1,300 decrease
Income taxes payable	1,900 increase
Long-term notes payable[4]	25,000 decrease
Common stock[5]	30,000 increase
Retained earnings[6]	12,600 increase

[1] Equipment with a cost of $15,000 and accumulated depreciation of $13,500 was sold for $3,800 cash. New equipment was purchased for $27,000 cash.
[2] Depreciation expense was $18,900.
[3] Long-term investments with a cost of $35,000 were sold for cash at a gain of $4,100. Additional long-term investments were purchased for $20,800 cash.
[4] A principal payment of $25,000 was made on long-term notes.
[5] Common stock was sold for $30,000 cash.
[6] Net income was $20,500, and dividends paid were $7,900.

REQUIRED:

Prepare a statement of cash flows for Erie, using the indirect method to compute cash flows from operations.

P13-40. REORGANIZING A STATEMENT OF CASH FLOWS Befuddled Corporation prepared the following statement of cash flows for 19X2:

BEFUDDLED CORPORATION
Statement of Cash Flows
For the Year Ended December 31, 19X2

INFLOWS OF CASH

Cash collections from sales	$941,500	
Cash proceeds from sale of equipment.	7,000	
Cash received from issuance of bonds payable.	50,000	
Total inflows of cash		$ 998,500

OUTFLOWS OF CASH

Cash payments for cost of goods sold.	$523,900	
Cash payments for operating expenses.	173,200	
Cash payments for interest expense	38,600	
Cash payments for income taxes	41,300	
Cash payments for purchase of equipment	209,000	
Repayment of short-term notes payable.	15,000	
Payment of cash dividends	48,000	
Total outflows of cash		1,049,000
Net decrease in cash		$ (50,500)

REQUIRED:

Prepare a properly formatted statement of cash flows for Befuddled for 19X2, using the direct method to determine cash flows from operations.

P13-41. PREPARING A STATEMENT OF CASH FLOWS The income statement for 19X9 and balance sheets for 19X9 and 19X8 for Monon Cable Television Company follow:

MONON CABLE TELEVISION COMPANY
Income Statement
For the Year Ended December 31, 19X9

Service revenue		$519,000
Less: Operating expenses:		
Royalty expense.	$240,000	
Wages	26,000	
Utilities	83,000	
Supplies	13,000	
Rent, poles.	17,000	
Rent, building	62,000	
Depreciation	28,000	469,000
Income from operations		$ 50,000
Other income:		
Gain on sale of antenna.		800
		$ 50,800
Less: Interest expense		1,800
Income before taxes.		$ 49,000
Less: Income taxes expense		9,000
Net income		$ 40,000

MONON CABLE TELEVISION COMPANY
Balance Sheets
As of December 31, 19X9 And 19X8

ASSETS		19X9		19X8
Current assets:				
Cash.........................		$ 2,000		$ 3,000
Accounts receivable..............		11,300		11,000
Supplies inventory...............		1,200		1,700
Total current assets		$ 14,500		$ 15,700
Property, plant, and equipment:				
Antenna[1]......................	$ 60,000		$ 35,000	
Equipment[2]....................	210,000		190,000	
Cable system[3]..................	81,000		75,000	
	$351,000		$300,000	
Accumulated depreciation[4]	(125,000)		(131,000)	
Net property..................		226,000		169,000
Total assets		$240,500		$184,700
LIABILITIES				
Current liabilities:				
Accounts payable................		$ 6,500		$ 8,000
Rent payable, poles		2,900		2,600
Royalties payable................		3,300		3,100
Rent payable, building............		2,000		11,000
Total current liabilities...........		$ 14,700		$ 24,700
Long-term liabilities:				
Long-term note payable[5]		40,000		–0–
Total liabilities		$ 54,700		$ 24,700
EQUITY				
Common stock	$100,000		$100,000	
Retained earnings[6].................	85,800		60,000	
Total equity		185,800		160,000
Total liabilities and equity.....		$240,500		$184,700

[1] The old antenna with a cost of $35,000 and accumulated depreciation of $34,000 was taken down and sold as scrap for $1,800 cash during 19X9. A new antenna was purchased for cash at an installed cost of $60,000.
[2] Additional equipment was purchased for $20,000 cash.
[3] Wiring for 300 additional homes was purchased for $6,000 cash.
[4] Depreciation expense for 19X9 was $28,000.
[5] A long-term note payable was issued for $40,000 cash.
[6] Dividends of $14,200 were paid during 19X9.

REQUIRED:

Prepare a statement of cash flows, using the direct method to determine cash flows from operations.

P13-42. FIRST-YEAR STATEMENT OF CASH FLOWS   Fleet Limousine Service, Inc., began operations in late March 19X6. At the end of 19X6, the following balance sheet was prepared for Fleet:

FLEET LIMOUSINE SERVICE, INC.
Balance Sheet
As of December 31, 19X6

ASSETS

Current assets:

Cash		$ 7,200
Accounts receivable......................		15,900
Supplies inventory.......................		3,100
Total current assets		$ 26,200

Property, plant, and equipment:[1]

Land	$ 11,000	
Building	175,000	
Equipment	233,400	
	$419,400	
Less: Accumulated depreciation[2].................	35,500	
Net property		383,900
Total assets................................		$410,100

LIABILITIES

Current liabilities:

Accounts payable		$ 12,700
Unearned revenue...........................		21,800
Wages payable............................		4,600
Rent payable.............................		8,200
Total current liabilities......................		$ 47,300

Long-term liabilities:

Long-term notes payable[3]		95,000
Total liabilities............................		$142,300

EQUITY

Common stock[4]	$300,000	
Retained earnings[5]	(32,200)	
Total equity		267,800
Total liabilities and equity		$410,100

[1] During 19X6, land was purchased for $11,000, a building was purchased for $175,000, and equipment was purchased for $233,400.
[2] Depreciation expense for 19X6 was $35,500.
[3] The long-term note was issued for $100,000, and a principal payment of $5,000 was made during 19X6.
[4] Common stock was issued for $300,000 cash during 19X6.
[5] During 19X6, there was a net loss of $32,200, and no dividends were paid.

REQUIRED:

1. Prepare a statement of cash flows for Fleet Limousine, using the indirect method to determine cash from operations.

2. Does Fleet Limousine appear to have matched the timing of inflows and outflows of cash?

ANALYTICAL OPPORTUNITIES

A13-43. DISSENTING VIEWS AND THE CASH FLOW STATEMENT   The preparation of cash flow statements is required by *Statement of Financial Accounting Standards No. 95,* "The Statement of Cash Flows," adopted by a four-to-three vote of the FASB. Several members of the Board took exception to various aspects of the statement, including (1) the classification of interest and dividends received and interest paid as cash flows from operations and (2) the use of the indirect method.

REQUIRED:

1. How did dissenting members of the FASB prefer that interest and dividends received and interest paid be classified? (See the section following paragraph 34 of the full text of *Statement No. 95.*) How did the FASB justify classifying these items as cash flows from operations? (See paragraph 90 of *Statement No. 95.*)

2. Why did dissenting members of the FASB take exception to the indirect method? (See the section following paragraph 34 of the full text of *Statement No. 95.*) How did the FASB justify permitting use of the indirect method? (See paragraphs 108, 109, and 119 of *Statement No. 95.*)

A13-44. INTERPRETING STATEMENTS OF CASH FLOWS   Visit your library and locate the financial statements for the last four years for a company of your choice.

REQUIRED:

1. Prepare a comparative statement of cash flows for the most recent four years. (Use a format similar to that used for the Toys "R" Us analysis in the chapter; of course, if your company uses the direct method, the presentation of operating cash flows will differ from that of Toys "R" Us.)

2. Describe the major sources of cash employed by the company.

3. Describe the major uses of cash by the company.

4. Are the time commitments of inflows and outflows well matched by the company?

5. Are debt and equity likely to be available as inflows of cash in the near future?

6. What are the trends in inflows and outflows?

7. What projections would you make regarding inflows and outflows in the near future?

A13-45. INCOME, CASH FLOW, AND FUTURE LOSSES   On January 1, 19X1, Cermack National Bank loaned $5,000,000 under a two-year, non-interest-bearing note to a real estate developer. The bank recognized interest revenue on this note of approximately $400,000 per year. Due to an economic downturn, the developer was unable to pay the $5,800,000 maturity amount on December 31, 19X2. The bank convinced the developer to pay $800,000 on December 31, 19X2, and agreed to extend $5,000,000 credit to the developer despite the gloomy economic outlook for the next several years. Thus, on December 31, 19X2, the bank issued a new two-year, non-interest-bearing note to the developer to mature on December 31, 19X4 for $6,000,000. The bank recognized interest revenue on this note of approximately $500,000 per year.

The bank's external auditor insisted that the riskiness of the new loan be recognized by increasing the allowance for uncollectible notes by $1,500,000 on December 31, 19X2, and $2,000,000 on December 31, 19X3. On December 31, 19X4, the bank received $1,200,000 from the developer and learned that the developer is in bankruptcy and that no additional amounts would be recovered.

REQUIRED:

1. Prepare a schedule showing annual cash flows for the two notes in each of the four years.

2. Prepare a schedule showing the effect of the notes on net income in each of the four years.

3. Which figure, net income or net cash flow, does the better job of telling the bank's stockholders about the effect of these notes on the bank? Explain by reference to the schedules prepared in requirements 1 and 2.

4. A commonly used method for predicting future cash flows is to predict future income and adjust it for anticipated differences between net income and net cash flow. Does the Cermack National Bank case shed any light on the justification for using net income in this way rather than simply predicting future cash flows by reference to past cash flows?

LEARNING OBJECTIVES

Careful study of this chapter will enable you to:

1. Decide whether to use the cost method or the equity method for various long-term investments.

2. Describe the differences between the cost and equity methods.

3. Construct a consolidated balance sheet.

4. Distinguish between the purchase method and the pooling-of-interests method for business combinations.

Appendix 14–1

5. Account for the parent's share of its subsidiary's net income under the equity method.

6. Construct a consolidated income statement.

Appendix 14–2

7. Account for a business combination by the pooling-of-interests method.

14 LONG-TERM INVESTMENTS, CONSOLIDATED FINANCIAL STATEMENTS, AND BUSINESS COMBINATIONS

As we explained in Chapter 8, short-term investments are used when the firm temporarily has excess cash. The management of these investments must be coordinated with the management of cash and the firm's other short-term assets and liabilities. Accordingly, the value and composition of short-term investment portfolios change continually in response to seasonal factors and other factors in the business environment. In contrast, long-term investments are used when the firm intends to maintain the investment for a lengthy period. For example, a firm may purchase the stock of another firm that manufactures products it uses or sells in order to assure a long-term business relationship. Indeed, many long-term investments are motivated by the desire of the *investor* to gain a degree of influence or control over the operations of the *investee,* the corporation whose stock is held by the investor.

Long-term investments include both equity and debt securities that management intends to hold for a period extending beyond the normal operating cycle (usually one year). Securities that are not readily marketable are also automatically classified as long-term investments, since a long period may be required to sell them. Long-term investments are classified as noncurrent assets on the balance sheet, usually immediately following current assets. Although both debt and equity securities may be classified as long-term investments, the discussion in this chapter will emphasize investments in common stock.

The cost method, which is used for short-term investments, is also applied to long-term investments in preferred stock and debt securities. Long-term investments in preferred stock are recorded at their cost to the investor and, if marketable and redeemable, are subject to a lower-of-cost-or-market adjustment. Preferred dividends are recorded as income by the investor when they are received. Accounting for long-term investments in debt securities closely parallels accounting for long-term liabilities, which is discussed in Chapters 11A and 11B. Long-term investments in debt securities are carried at their cost to the investor, and interest revenue is recognized as it accrues.

This chapter begins with a discussion of accounting for long-term investments in common stock using the cost and equity methods. The second section of the chapter considers consolidated financial statements, which are required when an investment is large enough to permit the investor to control the company whose securities are held. The chapter concludes with a section on business combinations, including a discussion of the purchase and pooling-of-interests combination methods. Appendix 14–1 discusses consolidated net income and Appendix 14–2 illustrates a pooling-of-interests business combination.

ACCOUNTING FOR LONG-TERM INVESTMENTS IN COMMON STOCK

Long-term investments in common stock are accounted for by either the cost method or the equity method, depending on the ability of the investor to influence the operations of the investee. An investment in common stock entitles the investor to vote in elections of the investee's directors. When the investment is small (less than 20 percent ownership), the investor usually cannot significantly influence the elections, and the investor uses the cost method. On the other hand, when an investment represents a sufficiently large ownership share (20 percent or higher), the investor may be able to influence the elections and thereby the operations of the investee. In those cases, the equity method is used. We now turn to a discussion of the cost and equity methods.

COST METHOD FOR LONG-TERM INVESTMENTS IN COMMON STOCK

COST METHOD: The method of accounting for investments that recognizes investment income as distributions are accrued and carries investments at cost, subject to a lower-of-cost-or-market adjustment.

When a long-term investment in the voting stock of another corporation gives an investor only a low level of influence over the investee, the investment should be accounted for by the **cost method.** Under this method, the investment is recorded at its acquisition cost (the market price of the stock plus commissions and other fees directly related to the transaction). For example, assume that Portland Corporation acquired 10 percent (200 shares) of the outstanding stock of Eugene Products for $38,000 cash ($190 per share) on January 1, 19X1. Portland would make the following entry to record the investment:

Long-term investments in equity securities. 38,000
   Cash 38,000

If a common stock investment is accounted for using the cost method, income is recognized when dividends are declared by the investee. Assume that Eugene Products declared and paid a $7.20 per share dividend on its common stock during 19X1. Portland would make the following entry:

Cash 1,440
   Dividend income 1,440

The entire collection of a firm's long-term investments in common and preferred stock accounted for by the cost method is called the firm's long-term *portfolio* of equity securities.[1] Following acquisition, investments are carried at

[1] For the sake of simplicity, we shall assume that all equity securities included in a portfolio are marketable unless we specifically indicate the contrary.

acquisition cost unless the market value of the entity's entire long-term portfolio falls below the portfolio's cost. In the event that market is less than cost at the end of an accounting period, a lower-of-cost-or-market adjustment is calculated on the basis of the total value of all long-term equity investments and is recorded as an adjusting entry to reduce the portfolio to market value. Let us illustrate: Assume that Portland Corporation's only investment is the 200 shares of Eugene Products' stock with a cost of $38,000. At December 31, 19X1, the market value of the Eugene Products stock is $181 per share. Therefore, the market value of Portland's portfolio is $1,800 below cost [(190 − $181)(200 shares)]. Portland would make the following adjusting entry to reduce the carrying value of the portfolio to market value:

Unrealized loss on long-term investments................	1,800	
Allowance to reduce long-term investments to market...		1,800

The allowance to reduce long-term investments to market is a contra account to the cost of Portland's investments in equity securities. The unrealized loss on long-term investments is reported in the equity section of the balance sheet, and its balance always equals the balance of the allowance account. The use of an unrealized loss account permits the investment portfolio to be reported at the lower of cost or market on the balance sheet without altering net income. Recall that, in contrast, applying the lower-of-cost-or-market rule to short-term equity investments results in reporting such losses (or loss recoveries) as part of net income. Although declines in the current market value of long-term investments are of interest to readers of balance sheets, their effects are not included in net income because these effects will not be realized in the short run.

A gain or loss on long-term equity securities (the difference between the acquisition cost and the selling price of the securities) is included in net income when the securities are sold. Assume that Portland sold 80 shares of Eugene Products' stock for $192 per share on March 15, 19X2. Portland would make the following entry:

Cash [($192 per share)(80 shares)]........................	15,360	
Long-term investments in equity securities		
[($190 per share)(80 shares)].........................		15,200
Gain on sale of long-term investments................		160

Let us continue the Portland Corporation example to illustrate an additional element of the lower-of-cost-or-market procedure. By the end of 19X2, assume that the market price of Eugene Products' stock has declined from the $192 that applied on March 15 to $189. A market value of $189 per share requires an allowance of $120 [($190 − $189)(120 shares)] at December 31, 19X2. In order to establish a $120 allowance, the end-of-19X1 allowance of $1,800 must be reduced by $1,680 [$1,800 − $1,680 = $120]. Portland would make the following entry to adjust the allowance account from $1,800 to $120:

Allowance to reduce long-term investments to market.....	1,680	
Unrealized loss on long-term investments.............		1,680

This entry reduces both the allowance account and the temporary equity account. Again, if the portfolio contains several securities, the amount of the allowance is the excess of cost over market for the entire portfolio. In such cases, the market price of some securities in the portfolio may be above cost.

Observe that Portland's income from its investment in each year equals the cash dividend received from the investee.[2] The decline in the market price of Eugene Products' stock during 19X1 results in a lower-of-cost-or-market adjustment of $1,800 at December 31, 19X1. The lower-of-cost-or-market adjustment for Portland Corporation establishes an $1,800 allowance, which is subtracted from the investment account on the balance sheet, and an $1,800 unrealized loss, which is reported as part of the stockholders' equity on the balance sheet. In other words, the adjustment has no effect on the income statement. The sale of 80 shares on March 15, 19X2, requires the recognition of a $160 gain on the 80 shares sold (which is determined relative to the acquisition cost and is unaffected by the lower-of-cost-or-market adjustment made on December 31, 19X1). The balance sheets of Portland Corporation will report the investment net of the allowance, as shown below:

	12/31/X2	12/31/X1
Long-term investment in equity securities (cost)...	$22,800	$38,000
Less: Allowance to reduce long-term investments to market.................................	120	1,800
Net long-term investment in equity securities ...	$22,680	$36,200

In addition, the stockholders' equity section of the balance sheet will include an unrealized loss on long-term investments in the amount of $1,800 at December 31, 19X1, and $120 at December 31, 19X2.

EQUITY METHOD FOR LONG-TERM INVESTMENTS IN COMMON STOCK

EQUITY METHOD: The method of accounting for long-term investments in equity securities that recognizes investment income as it is reported by the investee, causing investments to be carried at acquisition cost plus the investor's share of investee net income less the investor's share of investee dividends.

Under the cost method, the investor does not recognize income from investments until the investee declares a cash dividend. This income-recognition rule is appropriate for investors who own only a small fraction of the investee's common stock because such investors have little influence over the distribution of investee dividends or over the other operating and financial policies of the investee. In contrast, when an investor owns more than 20 percent of the investee's stock, the investor can usually exercise significant influence over the investee's operating and financial policies. The presence of significant influence over the investee requires that the investor employ the *equity method,* a different procedure for the recognition of income and dividends from investments.

The **equity method** requires the investor to recognize income when it is reported as earned by the investee, causing investments to be carried at acquisition cost plus the investor's share of investee income less the investor's share of investee dividends. The equity method thus prevents an investor from manipulating its own income by exerting influence over an investee's dividend policy, as the following analysis indicates:

[2] Strictly speaking (as noted in Chapter 8), dividend income is recognized by investors at the dividend declaration date rather than at the dividend payment date. When a cash dividend is declared in one year and paid in the following year, the investor should recognize the dividend declaration by a debit to dividends receivable, a current asset account, and a credit to dividend income, an income statement account. In the following year, when the related cash is received, the investor should debit cash and credit dividends receivable.

ANALYSIS

INCOME
MANIPULATION BY
INVESTOR

As a result of competition and technological change, the net incomes of both Sacramento Electronics and its 40 percent-owned investee, Hayward Manufacturing, have been depressed in recent years. Although Hayward's net income has been depressed, the sale at a loss of several unprofitable real estate investments has provided the company with a large reserve of liquid assets. Sacramento does not control Hayward's board of directors, but certain directors loyal to Sacramento are in a position to exercise significant influence over Hayward's dividend policy.

1. *How might Sacramento's influence over Hayward lead to income manipulation if Sacramento's investment in Hayward were accounted for by the cost method?*

Sacramento might encourage certain Hayward directors to press for a substantial increase in Hayward's cash dividend. Under the cost method, the increase in dividends would increase Sacramento's net income.

2. *How does the requirement that the equity method be used for Sacramento's investment in Hayward thwart possible income manipulation?*

The equity method forces Sacramento to recognize 40 percent of Hayward's reported net income, an amount that is not influenced by Hayward's dividend policy.

Let us illustrate the application of the equity method: On January 1, 19X8, Williamette Company acquired 25 percent of the outstanding common stock (400 of 1,600 outstanding shares) of Seattle Manufacturing for $80,000 ($200 per share). Williamette would record its investment in Seattle with the following entry:

Long-term investment in Seattle Manufacturing	80,000	
Cash		80,000

As with the cost method, the equity method requires the initial investment to be recorded at acquisition cost ($80,000), using the first entry shown in Exhibit 14–1.

On December 31, 19X8, Seattle Manufacturing reported net income of $26,000 and declared and paid cash dividends of $18,000 ($11.25 per share).

EXHIBIT 14–1   **COST AND EQUITY METHODS FOR LONG-TERM INVESTMENTS IN EQUITY SECURITIES**

COST METHOD		EQUITY METHOD	
Investor acquires stock for cash			
Long-term investment xxx		Long-term investment xxx	
Cash....................	xxx	Cash..................	xxx
Investor receives notice of investee net income for the period			
No entry		Long-term investment xxx	
		Income from investment .	xxx
Investee declares and pays dividend			
Cash..................... xxx		Cash.................... xxx	
Dividend income	xxx	Long-term investment ...	xxx

Williamette's share of Seattle's net income and dividends is $6,500 and $4,500, respectively [(.25)($26,000) and (.25)($18,000)]. Williamette would record its equity in Seattle's net income with the following entry:

Long-term investment in Seattle Manufacturing	6,500	
Income from investment in Seattle Manufacturing		6,500

Unlike the cost method, the equity method recognizes income not when a cash dividend is declared and paid, but when income is earned by the investee, using the second equity-method entry shown in Exhibit 14–1. Accordingly, Williamette recognizes $6,500 of income from its investment in Seattle, representing 25 percent of Seattle's 19X8 net income [(.25)($26,000)]. Notice that the $6,500 credit to the income account is accompanied by an equal debit to the investment account.

Williamette would record the declaration and payment of its share of Seattle's dividends with the following entry:

Cash	4,500	
Long-term investment in Seattle Manufacturing		4,500

The receipt of dividends from Seattle reduces Williamette's investment. Accordingly, Williamette credits the investment account for $4,500 and debits cash for an equal amount upon receipt of the dividend. While dividend distributions under the cost method cause the recognition of investment income, dividend distributions under the equity method cause reductions in the investment account, as shown in the third equity-method entry in Exhibit 14–1.

Assume that Seattle neither declares nor pays a cash dividend during 19X9 and reports a net loss of $6,000 on December 31, 19X9. Williamette would make the following entry to record its equity in Seattle's 19X9 net loss:

Loss from investment in Seattle Manufacturing [(.25)($6,000)]	1,500	
Long-term investment in Seattle Manufacturing		1,500

When an investee reports a net loss, the investor recognizes its share of the loss by debiting an income statement account and reducing the investment account.

As a consequence of the 19X8 and 19X9 journal entries, Williamette's December 31, 19X9, balance sheet will show an investment balance of $80,500, which is $500 more than the acquisition cost of the investment. The additional $500 represents the excess of Williamette's share of Seattle's 19X8 net income [(.25)($26,000) = $6,500] over Williamette's share of Seattle's 19X8 dividend [(.25)($18,000) = $4,500] and Seattle's 19X9 net loss [(.25)($6,000) = $1,500]. Williamette's 19X8 income statement will include income from its investment in Seattle of $6,500, representing its share of Seattle's reported net income. Williamette's 19X9 income statement will include a loss from its investment in Seattle of $1,500. The equity method does not require a lower-of-cost-or-market adjustment for short-term changes in the market value of the investment.

Exhibit 14–2 presents a summary of accounting for long-term investments. Notice that the accounting procedures for investments in common stock depend on the degree to which the investor can influence the operations of the investee and that the degree of influence depends, in turn, on the size of the investment. Thus the cost method is used for investments representing less than 20 percent

EXHIBIT 14–2   **SUMMARY OF ACCOUNTING FOR LONG-TERM INVESTMENTS**

Common stock:	
Low influence: less than 20% ownership	Cost method*
Significant influence: 20%–50% ownership	Equity method
Control: more than 50% ownership	Equity method plus consolidation
Preferred stock	Cost method*
Debt securities	Cost method*

* When the cost method is applied to long-term investments in marketable securities, then a lower-of-cost-or-market adjustment is required (except that such adjustments are not made for long-term investments in debt securities). Recall that lower-of-cost-or-market adjustments for short-term investments are debited to an income account; in contrast, such adjustments for long-term investments are debited to a contra-equity account.

ownership, and the equity method is used for investments representing ownership of 20 percent or more. Investments representing more than 50 percent ownership enable an investor effectively to control the operations of the investee and require additional accounting procedures discussed in the next section. Although the percentage thresholds shown in Exhibit 14–2 are usually reliable indicators of the degree of potential influence, accountants must be alert for special circumstances in which another conclusion is warranted.[3]

So far in this chapter, we have assumed that the acquisition cost of an investment requiring the equity method equals the investor's share of the book value of the investee's stockholders' equity. If the acquisition cost does not equal this book value, then the equity method requires additional depreciation and amortization. These additional expenses result from a revaluation of the investee's assets caused by a difference between acquisition cost and book value. (They are explained in the section that follows.)

CONSOLIDATED FINANCIAL STATEMENTS

When an investment in common stock gives an investor complete or nearly complete control over an investee, the operating assets of both corporations are under the common control of the investor corporation and the two corporations are no longer separate accounting entities. Under these circumstances, the investor corporation is required to prepare a special set of financial statements, called **consolidated financial statements,** that present combined information about the interrelated corporations as if they were a single accounting entity. These consolidated financial statements are provided to the stockholders of the investor corporation and to other interested parties. Of course, the single accounting entity is nevertheless represented by two legal entities, two corporations, each of which maintains separate accounting records as a basis for its own corporate financial statements. Furthermore, on the basis of these records, each corporation will

CONSOLIDATED FINAN-CIAL STATEMENTS: Accounting reports presenting combined information about several interrelated corporations that form a single accounting entity.

[3] If, for example, Company A sold a single product manufactured only by Company B and Company B provided substantial amounts of long-term debt financing to Company A, one could argue that Company B has at least significant influence if not control over Company A even if it owns none of Company A's common stock.

frequently prepare separate (nonconsolidated) corporate financial statements. Thus the investor corporation will frequently prepare both separate financial statements (using the equity method for its investment in the investee corporation) and consolidated financial statements.

CONTROL AND CONSOLIDATION

PARENT: An entity whose investment in the stock of another firm enables it to control the other firm.

SUBSIDIARY: A firm whose operations are controlled by another entity through that entity's investment in the firm's stock.

Usually an investor can control an investee when the investor owns more than 50 percent of the outstanding voting stock of the investee. In rare cases, an investor may be unable to control an investee even if the investor owns more than 50 percent of the investee (when, for example, the investee is located in a foreign country whose government restricts the exercise of such control). However, the 50 percent rule is appropriate in the majority of cases and is applied throughout this book. When an investor controls an investee, the investor is called the **parent** and the investee, the **subsidiary.** Many large companies for which consolidated financial statements must be prepared involve numerous separate corporations that are interrelated in a complex network of parent-subsidiary relationships. However, for the sake of simplicity, this chapter is restricted to simple two-corporation structures involving one parent and one subsidiary.

Consolidated financial statements are prepared from information contained in the separate corporate financial statements of both the parent and the subsidiary. The consolidated balance sheet is essentially the same as the parent's corporate balance sheet, except that the parent's investment in subsidiary account is replaced by the detailed assets and liabilities of the subsidiary. The consolidated income statement is essentially the same as the parent's corporate income statement, except that the parent's income from investment in subsidiary account is replaced by the detailed revenues and expenses of the subsidiary. The next section illustrates the preparation of a consolidated balance sheet. Consolidated income statements are discussed in Appendix 14–1.

To illustrate the preparation of consolidated balance sheets, let us look at a situation in which a parent acquires all the outstanding stock of its subsidiary. On January 1, 19X4, Tucson, Inc., purchased all the outstanding common shares of Canyon Corporation in exchange for $400,000 cash. The cash was paid directly to the stockholders of Canyon, who surrendered their shares to Tucson. Just before Tucson's acquisition of stock, the balance sheets of the two corporations were as shown in the preacquisition column in Exhibit 14–3.

RECORDING THE ACQUISITION OF STOCK

The acquisition of Canyon's stock by Tucson is recorded on Tucson, Inc.'s accounting records by the following entry:

Long-term investment in Canyon.	400,000	
Cash		400,000

The effects of the acquisition on the parent corporation and on its subsidiary can be seen if we compare the preacquisition and postacquisition balance sheets of the two firms shown in Exhibit 14–3. The acquisition is accomplished by a transaction between Tucson, Inc., and the stockholders of Canyon as individuals; Canyon Corporation, the subsidiary, is not a party to the transaction. Observe that Tucson's ownership of Canyon is reflected in the investment account on Tucson's postcombination balance sheet. Since Tucson is Canyon's only stock-

EXHIBIT 14–3   **INDIVIDUAL CORPORATION BALANCE SHEETS BEFORE AND AFTER ACQUISITION OF CANYON BY TUCSON**

TUCSON, INC.

ASSETS	PREACQUISITION	POSTACQUISITION
Cash..	$1,200,000	$ 800,000
Long-term investment in Canyon............	–0–	400,000
Equipment.................................	6,800,000	6,800,000
Total assets	$8,000,000	$8,000,000

LIABILITIES AND EQUITY		
Liabilities	$1,000,000	$1,000,000
Common stock.............................	4,000,000	4,000,000
Retained earnings.........................	3,000,000	3,000,000
Total liabilities and equity	$8,000,000	$8,000,000

CANYON CORPORATION

ASSETS	PREACQUISITION	POSTACQUISITION
Cash	$ 70,000	$ 70,000
Equipment.................................	230,000	230,000
Total assets	$300,000	$300,000

LIABILITIES AND EQUITY		
Liabilities..................................	$ 25,000	$ 25,000
Common stock.............................	100,000	100,000
Retained earnings.........................	175,000	175,000
Total liabilities and equity	$300,000	$300,000

holder, Canyon is effectively controlled by Tucson; the two firms thus represent a single accounting entity. Canyon, nevertheless, retains its identity as a separate legal entity or corporation. In other words, three distinct accounting entities are now identifiable: (1) the corporate entity of Tucson (the parent), (2) the corporate entity of Canyon (the subsidiary), and (3) the consolidated entity of Tucson and Canyon.

The financial statements for the separate corporate entities (the corporate financial statements of Tucson and Canyon) are prepared directly from the corporate accounting records of the two firms. However, the preparation of consolidated financial statements requires a special worksheet procedure in which the financial statements of the separate corporate entities are added together or, to put it more accurately, consolidated. A *consolidation* is based on a careful analysis of the parent and subsidiary (corporate) financial statements and particularly on analysis of the difference between the cost of the acquired stock of the subsidiary and its book value on the records of the subsidiary. We will begin by considering the form of this analysis and then turn to the related worksheet procedure that produces the consolidated financial statements.

EXHBIT 14–4   ANALYSIS OF VALUATION DIFFERENTIAL

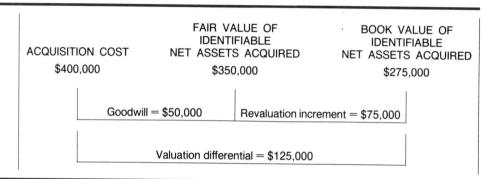

ANALYSIS OF THE VALUATION DIFFERENTIAL

VALUATION DIFFEREN-TIAL: The difference between the acquisition cost of stock to a long-term investor and the book value of the stock (equity) on the financial statements of the acquired firm.

REVALUATION INCRE-MENT: The portion of the valuation differential applicable to specific assets.

GOODWILL: The portion of the valuation differential in excess of the revaluation increment.

When one firm acquires the stock of another, the acquisition cost usually does not equal the book value of the stock (equity) recorded on the financial statements of the acquired firm. This difference between the acquisition cost and the book value of the stock acquired is the **valuation differential.** To illustrate, assume that one firm acquires all the outstanding stock of another firm for $200,000 cash, and that the balance sheet of the latter firm reports equity of $160,000. The valuation differential in this case is $40,000 [$200,000 − $160,000] and is evidence that one or more assets of the acquired corporation (subsidiary) are carried in its accounting records at an amount below fair value (which is not unusual, since accounting records are based on historical cost). In the financial statements of the consolidated entity, the individual assets of the acquired firm should be reported at their fair value because the fair value represents the amount given up to acquire those assets. Accordingly, the valuation differential must be attributed to the assets to which it is related. The portion of the valuation differential applicable to specific assets is called the **revaluation increment.** Any unattributed remainder is identified as an intangible asset called **goodwill.**[4] Goodwill represents assets that cannot be specifically identified, such as well-known brand names and reputations for quality products.

To return to our original illustration, when Tucson, Inc., acquired Canyon Corporation, Canyon's stock had a book value (equity) of $275,000: assets of $300,000 − liabilities of $25,000. In the purchase transaction, Tucson gave up cash of $400,000. Accordingly, the valuation differential associated with the acquisition was $125,000: acquisition cost of $400,000 − book value of $275,000 (see Exhibit 14–4). This valuation differential implies that Canyon's assets are undervalued by $125,000. Let us suppose that Canyon's equipment has a fair value of $305,000 and that Canyon's liabilities are reported at fair value. The fair value of Canyon's net assets (assets minus liabilities) then is $350,000: cash of $70,000 + equipment of $305,000 − liabilities of $25,000. This information enables us to divide the valuation differential into two parts: (1) a revaluation increment of $75,000 that is attributed entirely to equipment [$305,000 − $230,000] and (2) goodwill of $50,000 that cannot be attributed to identifiable assets [$125,000 − $75,000].

---

[4] The unattributed remainder of the valuation differential is sometimes called *excess of acquisition cost over fair value acquired.* Although a better description of the remainder, this term is cumbersome and thus the shorter label is used here.

The two-way breakdown of the valuation differential in the Tucson-Canyon illustration is summarized in Exhibit 14–4. Observe that the amount of goodwill ($50,000) can be calculated in two ways: (1) as the portion of the valuation differential that cannot be attributed to the identifiable assets [$125,000 − $75,000] and (2) as the excess of acquisition cost over the fair value of identifiable assets acquired [$400,000 − $350,000]. The $75,000 revaluation increment can also be computed in two ways: (1) as the portion of the valuation differential attributable to identifiable net assets [$350,000 − $275,000] and (2) as the excess of the fair value over the book value of identifiable net assets [$305,000 − $230,000]. Valuation differential analysis provides important data for the consolidation of balance sheets, to which we now turn.

CONSOLIDATION OF BALANCE SHEETS AT ACQUISITION

As we have seen, the acquisition of a subsidiary's stock creates an investment account on the records of the parent. The amount in the investment account is the appropriate amount for the acquired net assets. But on the consolidated entity's balance sheet, that amount must be divided and appropriately classified among the assets and liabilities of the subsidiary. Thus the consolidated balance sheet reports all the assets of both the parent and its subsidiary as if the two were one entity. The consolidated entity's balance sheet must be constructed from information contained in the corporate statements of both the parent and its subsidiary. This construction procedure, which is called the *consolidation of balance sheets,* in effect substitutes the detailed assets and liabilities of the subsidiary for the investment account of the parent. The substitution procedure converts the balance sheet of the parent into the balance sheet of the combined entity, which is called a *consolidated balance sheet.*

Consolidation Worksheet

CONSOLIDATION WORK-SHEET: A schedule on which adjustments are made that transform corporate financial statements of a parent and its subsidiary into consolidated financial statements.

To convert the corporate balance sheets of a parent and its subsidiary into a consolidated balance sheet, we use a consolidation worksheet. A **consolidation worksheet** is a schedule on which adjustments are made that transform corporate financial statements of a parent and its subsidiary into consolidated financial statements. The worksheet procedure for balance sheets simplifies the consolidation calculations. Exhibit 14–5 shows the worksheet that would be used to prepare the consolidated balance sheet for Tucson and Canyon. The corporate balance sheets for the parent and subsidiary are listed in the left-hand columns of the worksheet; consolidation adjustments are entered in the center columns of the worksheet; and then these adjustments are taken into account, as items from the corporate balance sheets are added across the worksheet to produce the consolidated balance sheet in the right-hand column.

Consolidation of these two balance sheets involves two adjustments: The first adjustment eliminates the stockholders' equity (book value) of the acquired corporation, and the second adjustment reclassifies the valuation differential into the appropriate asset accounts. It is important to understand that these worksheet adjustments are not entered on the accounting records of either the parent or the subsidiary.

In Exhibit 14–5, worksheet adjustment **a** eliminates the portion of the investment account that corresponds to the book value of the stock acquired, and it also eliminates the book value of the subsidiary's stockholders' equity. If

EXHIBIT 14-5   CONSOLIDATION WORKSHEET

TUCSON, INC., AND CANYON CORPORATION
Worksheet Consolidation of Balance Sheets

	CORPORATE BALANCE SHEETS		CONSOLIDATION ADJUSTMENTS		CONSOLIDATED BALANCE SHEET
	TUCSON	CANYON	DR	CR	
Cash	$ 800,000	$ 70,000			$ 870,000
Long-term investment in Canyon	400,000			(a) 275,000 (b) 125,000	–0–
Equipment	6,800,000	230,000	(b) 75,000		7,105,000
Goodwill			(b) 50,000		50,000
Total assets	$8,000,000	$300,000			$8,025,000
Liabilities	$1,000,000	$ 25,000			$1,025,000
Common stock	4,000,000	100,000	(a) 100,000		4,000,000
Retained earnings	3,000,000	175,000	(a) 175,000		3,000,000
Total liabilities and equity	$8,000,000	$300,000	400,000	400,000	$8,025,000

written as a journal entry, this worksheet adjustment would have the following form:

Common stock	100,000	
Retained earnings	175,000	
Long-term investment in Canyon		275,000

Worksheet adjustment to eliminate the book value of the equity (net assets) acquired.

If the book value of the stock acquired were not eliminated from both the investment account and the stockholders' equity accounts, the worksheet would produce a consolidated balance sheet that reports the stock of that entity as an asset, an outcome that is clearly inappropriate.

Worksheet adjustment **b** in Exhibit 14–5 reclassifies the portion of the investment account that corresponds to the valuation differential. It would have the following journal entry form:

Equipment	75,000	
Goodwill	50,000	
Long-term investment in Canyon		125,000

Worksheet adjustment to reclassify valuation differential.

The information for this reclassification adjustment is obtained by analyzing the valuation differential, as described earlier.

In more realistic consolidation problems, additional worksheet adjustments will be required. For example, when a parent lends money to its subsidiary, a worksheet adjustment is required to eliminate the liability of the subsidiary and the asset of the parent. Similarly, when a subsidiary lends money to its parent, a worksheet adjustment is required to eliminate the receivable of the subsidiary and the liability of the parent. Additional adjustments are required for intercorporate transfers of merchandise and other assets. These complications are explained in advanced accounting courses.

Minority Interest

The consolidation procedures demonstrated above are appropriate when the parent acquires 100 percent of the subsidiary's outstanding common stock. Consolidations are also required when a parent acquires between 50 and 100 percent of the subsidiary's stock. Despite the fact that a minority (less than half) of the subsidiary's stock is not acquired by the parent, the parent is able to control the subsidiary because it owns more than half the subsidiary's shares. The equity associated with subsidiary stock not held by the parent (that is, shares held by minority shareholders) is called the **minority interest.**

MINORITY INTEREST:
The portion of a subsidiary's stockholders' equity that corresponds to shares held by minority stockholders.

Minority interest is usually listed on the balance sheet between long-term liabilities and stockholders' equity. For example, the consolidated balance sheet of United Technologies Corporation at December 31, 1988, reports minority interest among its liabilities and equity as follows:

UNITED TECHNOLOGIES CORPORATION

In Millions of Dollars	DECEMBER 31	
	1988	1987
LIABILITIES AND SHAREOWNERS' EQUITY		
Short-term borrowings	$ 323.8	$ 702.0
Accounts payable	1,545.8	1,577.8
Accrued salaries, wages, and employee benefits	688.8	644.1
Other accrued liabilities	1,201.5	1,154.1
Long-term debt, currently due	261.7	71.3
Income taxes currently payable	351.3	241.3
Advances on sales contracts	575.2	500.0
Total Current Liabilities	$ 4,948.1	$ 4,890.6
Deferred income taxes	$ 371.0	$ 602.1
Long-term debt	$ 1,642.8	$ 2,229.6
Other long-term liabilities	$ 726.7	$ 636.2
Commitments and contingent liabilities	—	—
Minority interest in subsidiary companies	$ 236.3	$ 222.4
Shareowners' Equity		
Capital stock:		
Preferred stock, $1 par value (Authorized— 250,000,000 shares) Outstanding—9,053 and 14,772 shares, respectively	$ .9	$ 1.5
Common stock, $5 par value (Authorized— 500,000,000 shares) Outstanding— 130,764,424 and 130,413,308 shares, respectively	1,720.5	1,710.8
Deferred foreign currency translation adjustments	(14.0)	(79.6)
Retained earnings	3,116.0	2,659.9
Total Shareowners' Equity	$ 4,823.4	$ 4,292.6
Total Liabilities and Shareowners' Equity	$12,748.3	$12,873.5

From a conceptual point of view, minority interest is not appropriately classified as a liability and is probably best viewed as an element of equity. However, most published balance sheets place minority interest in an unlabeled category between long-term liabilities and equity, to differentiate it from the equity of the parent's stockholders.

BUSINESS COMBINATIONS

Consolidated financial statements describe parent and subsidiary corporations as if they were a single accounting entity. The acquisition by a parent of a controlling interest in a subsidiary's stock, like Tucson's acquisition of Canyon's stock, brings the operations and assets of the two corporations under the control of the parent and prevents the subsidiary from exercising independent control over its operations and assets. Any transaction or set of transactions that brings together two or more previously separate business entities to form a single accounting entity is called a *business combination.* Business combinations take many forms. Some, like Tucson-Canyon, involve the acquisition of stock in exchange for cash; others involve the acquisition of one corporation's assets in exchange for cash; and still others involve the exchange of one corporation's stock for another's. In this section, we consider two accounting methods applied to business combinations. One method, called the **purchase method,** uses the fair value of the consideration given to determine the acquisition cost. The second method, called the **pooling-of-interests method,** is employed only when there is a stock-for-stock exchange and uses the book value of the investee's stockholders' equity as the investor's acquisition cost.

PURCHASE METHOD: A method of accounting for business combinations that uses the fair value of the consideration given to determine the acquisition cost.

POOLING-OF-INTERESTS METHOD: A method of accounting for business combinations that uses the book value of the investee's stockholders' equity as the investor's acquisition cost; applies only to a stock-for-stock exchange.

The investor uses the purchase method to record combinations accomplished by exchanging cash for assets or cash for stock. The purchase method employs the concepts and procedures described earlier in this chapter. Such combinations frequently require the preparation of consolidated financial statements to replace the investment account with the assets and liabilities acquired.

When the investor exchanges its stock for the stock of the investee, it may be possible to use the pooling-of-interests method. This method is appropriate for combinations that do not constitute the purchase of one company by another. For example, a combination accomplished by exchanging stock for stock may simply "pool" the stockholders of two separate corporations so that the stockholders of the single resulting entity are the same investors who held stock in the previously separate entries. When companies are pooled, there is no need to revalue assets to their fair value. Thus, pooling-of-interest accounting frequently produces smaller postacquisition depreciation expense than does purchase accounting. Consequently, pooling tends to produce a larger net income, which gives managers an incentive to use this method.

In order to qualify for the pooling-of-interests method, a business combination must meet rather stringent conditions established by the Accounting Principles Board in 1970. The conditions identify aspects of a combination that are considered to alter the stockholdings of investors in the previously separate entities and that thereby make the combination a purchase rather than a pooling. In other words, strictly interpreted, the pooling-of-interests method should be reserved for those rare combinations that leave ownership interests unaltered.

Unfortunately, such combinations are difficult to identify. Despite the elaborate rules established by the Accounting Principles Board, many business combinations that significantly alter ownership interests—including combinations of banks and other financial institutions—are recorded as poolings of interests. Appendix 14–2 illustrates the pooling-of-interests method.

BUSINESS COMBINATIONS FROM VARIOUS VIEWPOINTS

The significance of any business combination depends on the perspective from which it is viewed. Owners are interested in the impact of the combination on the value and income-producing capability of their investment, while creditors are interested in its effect on the security of their obligations. Managers are interested in a business combination's effect on the quality of their managerial positions, and customers are interested in its effect on the level of prices and the quality of goods and services produced. In addition, regulatory agencies hold distinctive viewpoints respecting business combinations.[5]

In the analysis that follows, we examine a business combination from the perspective of the stockholders and management of the acquired firm and the management of the acquiring firm.

ANALYSIS
EXPANSION BY ACQUISITION OR INTERNAL GROWTH

The Bristol Corporation is a manufacturer of sophisticated electronic production equipment. Recent advances in engineering technology make possible the creation of highly versatile robots applicable to a variety of manufacturing operations, and Bristol's management has decided to expand its operations to include the manufacture of such robots. Bristol is considering two alternative expansion plans:

Plan 1: Assemble the required research and engineering staff to build and equip the required manufacturing facility.

Plan 2: Negotiate a business combination with Robotec, Inc., a smaller company that has already pioneered in the field of robot technology.

Let us consider the viewpoints of Bristol and Robotec as the two firms face the prospect of a business combination.

1. *What factors regarding the proposed expansion should be considered by the management of Bristol?*

Undoubtedly, Bristol's management will first undertake detailed studies of the probable impact of each of the expansion plans on company profitability. Bristol predicts that both expansion plans will produce about the same amount of additional annual revenue ($60 million), although Plan 2, the business combination, will produce the expected increase about a year and a half earlier than Plan 1, the internal expansion. Hence Plan 2 has a $90 million revenue advantage [(1.5)($60 million)] over Plan 1. Bristol's management also predicts that the cost of new facilities under Plan 1 is about the same as the cost of acquiring Robotec's existing facilities. Moreover, the existing facilities will have about the same useful life and annual operating costs as the new

---

[5] When carried to an extreme within a given industry, business combinations weaken competitive market structures by concentrating market power in the hands of one or a small number of entities. The Sherman Act (1890), the Clayton Act (1914), and the Federal Trade Commission Act (1914) form the legal basis for federal regulatory efforts intended to prevent excessive concentrations of market power. These acts are administered by the Federal Trade Commission (FTC) and enforced by the Antitrust Division of the Justice Department. Depending on the judgment of these policymakers, business combinations may be actively discouraged, mildly discouraged, weakly discouraged, or passively encouraged.

facilities. However, Plan 1 will require significant outlays for assembling the required research and production staff and for a program of product research and development. Under Plan 2, Bristol believes that most of these costs can be avoided by a carefully considered program to integrate Robotec's personnel into the organization. In short, Bristol's economic projections favor the business combination.

2. *What factors regarding the proposed combination should be considered by the stockholders of Robotec?*

Robotec's stockholders believe that they will be unable to sustain their highly profitable operations of recent years without the assistance of a larger organization, since the next round of technological development will probably require capital and skills that Robotec is unable to provide on its own. In short, economic considerations suggest that the time is right for a combination.

3. *What factors regarding the proposed combination should be considered by the management of Robotec?*

Although economic arguments seem to favor combination, the management of Robotec has serious misgivings about the impact of combination on managerial positions and on the performance of production and development personnel. (If the combination occurs, several of the senior managers plan to seek positions with other firms.)

SUMMARY

Long-term investments in debt and equity securities, like short-term investments, are accounted for by the cost method, except for long-term investments in equity securities that give the investor significant influence over the investee. When a long-term investment in equity securities represents 20 percent or more of the investee's outstanding voting shares, then the investor must account for its investment using the equity method rather than the cost method. The equity method recognizes investment income when the investee reports its net income, while the cost method recognizes investment income when the investee distributes income to investors in the form of dividends or interest.

A long-term investment in equity securities that represents more than 50 percent of the investee's outstanding stock enables the investor (called the *parent*) to control the investee (called the *subsidiary*). (Of course, the parent must use the equity method to account for its investment in the subsidiary.) The parent must issue consolidated financial statements that substitute the detailed assets and liabilities of the subsidiary for the investment account.

Any transaction or set of transactions that brings together two or more previously separate business entities to form a single accounting entity is called a *business combination*. Business combinations are accounted for by either the purchase method or the pooling-of-interests method, depending on the form of the combination transaction. The purchase method, which must be applied to most business combinations, records the assets and liabilities of the acquired company at their current or fair value when the combination occurs. The pooling-of-interests method, which is applicable to some stock-for-stock exchanges, records the assets and liabilities of the combining companies at their book values as of the date of the combination.

Appendix 14–1 describes the consolidation procedures that produce income statements for combined entities in both purchases and poolings of interests. Appendix 14–2 illustrates the application of the pooling-of-interests method to the balance sheet accounts in a business combination.

APPENDIX 14–1
CONSOLIDATED INCOME STATEMENTS

The treatment of business combinations in the text of this chapter is limited to accounting for business combinations on the date of acquisition. Accordingly, the related consolidation procedures in the chapter are limited to the date-of-acquisition balance sheet. We turn now to consolidation procedures required subsequent to the date of acquisition. Postacquisition consolidation procedures include the consolidation of parent and subsidiary income statements and statements of changes in retained earnings, the amortization of valuation differential, and various adjustments necessitated by operating transactions between the parent and its subsidiary. Although a comprehensive treatment of these problems is reserved for advanced accounting textbooks, this appendix presents the rudiments of preparing consolidated income statements.

More precisely, our purpose here is to explain the difference between the consolidated income statement and the income statement of the parent corporation. The consolidation procedures for income statements discussed here assume that the parent firm uses the equity method to account for its investment in its subsidiary. Accordingly, we begin with a brief review of the equity method for investments.

USE OF THE EQUITY METHOD BY THE PARENT CORPORATION

Since parent corporations hold over 50 percent of their respective subsidiaries' stock, parents must apply the equity method of accounting for their subsidiaries when issuing separate parent company financial statements.

Let us use the combination of Tucson, Inc., and Canyon Corporation from the chapter to demonstrate the application of the equity method to the preparation of financial statements. To reiterate the facts of the original transaction, on January 1, 19X4, Tucson, Inc., purchased all the outstanding shares of Canyon Corporation in exchange for $400,000 cash. On that date, Canyon reported net assets of $275,000, which had a fair value of $350,000, as shown in the analysis of the valuation differential presented in Exhibit 14–6. Observe that the entire revaluation increment is attributable to the difference between fair value and book value of the equipment: $305,000 − $230,000 = $75,000. The remaining $50,000 of the valuation differential is attributable to goodwill.

Recall that the equity method specifies how investors record investment income. Hence, in order to demonstrate the equity method, our example must be extended to include information about the income and dividends of the investee (the Canyon Corporation) and about Tucson's plan for amortization of the valuation differential. During 19X4, the first year of Tucson's ownership, Canyon reports net income of $60,000 and declares cash dividends of $25,000, all of

EXHIBIT 14–6   ANALYSIS OF VALUATION DIFFERENTIAL

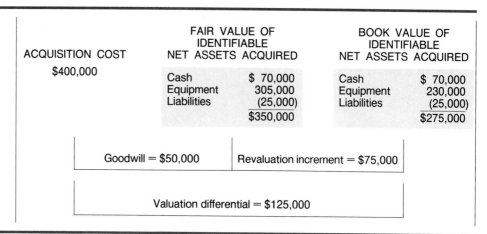

	ACQUISITION COST $400,000	FAIR VALUE OF IDENTIFIABLE NET ASSETS ACQUIRED	BOOK VALUE OF IDENTIFIABLE NET ASSETS ACQUIRED
		Cash	$ 70,000	Cash	$ 70,000
		Equipment	305,000	Equipment	230,000
		Liabilities	(25,000)	Liabilities	(25,000)
			$350,000		$275,000

Goodwill = $50,000 | Revaluation increment = $75,000

Valuation differential = $125,000

EXHIBIT 14–7   SEPARATE CORPORATE INCOME STATEMENTS

TUCSON, INC., AND CANYON CORPORATION
Separate Corporate Income Statements

		TUCSON		CANYON
Revenue		$900,000		$200,000
Less: Cost of goods sold		320,000		95,000
Gross margin		$580,000		$105,000
Less: Operating expenses:				
Depreciation	$210,000		$23,000	
Miscellaneous	160,000	370,000	22,000	45,000
Income from operations		$210,000		$ 60,000
Income from investment in Canyon .		40,000		–0–
Net income		$250,000		$ 60,000

which are declared and paid on November 20, 19X4. (The detailed income statements for Tucson and Canyon are presented in Exhibit 14–7.) The undervalued equipment that gives rise to the $75,000 revaluation increment has a remaining useful life of five years on January 1, 19X4. Tucson amortizes all goodwill over a 10-year period.

The equity method requires an investor (in this case, the parent, Tucson, Inc.) to recognize investment income as it is earned by the investee (the subsidiary, Canyon). Accordingly, Tucson must recognize $60,000 — 100 percent of the income reported by Canyon—as the 19X4 income from its investment. In addition, Tucson must recognize that its subsidiary computes income on the basis of book values that do not reflect the higher acquisition cost incurred by Tucson. In particular, Canyon computes equipment depreciation expense based on a book value of $230,000, whereas the cost to Tucson of acquiring Canyon's

EXHIBIT 14–8   EQUITY METHOD CALCULATION OF INCOME FROM SUBSIDIARY

Net income reported by subsidiary		$60,000
Multiplied by parent's ownership proportion		100%
Parent's share of reported net income.		$60,000
Less: Adjustments for amortization of valuation differential:		
Additional depreciation on equipment.	$15,000	
Amortization of goodwill	5,000	20,000
Income from investment in subsidiary.		$40,000

EXHIBIT 14–9   EQUITY METHOD JOURNAL ENTRIES

TUCSON, INC.

Journal Entries for Long-Term Investment in Canyon

1/1/X4	Long-term investment in Canyon	400,000	
	Cash		400,000

Journal entry by Tucson to record acquisition of 100 percent of Canyon's outstanding common stock.

11/20/X4	Cash	25,000	
	Long-term investment in Canyon		25,000

Journal entry by Tucson to record declaration and payment of cash dividend by Canyon.

12/31/X4	Long-term investment in Canyon	40,000	
	Income from investment in Canyon.		40,000

Journal entry by Tucson to record income from investment.

stock includes $305,000 for the equipment. Accordingly, Tucson must adjust the income reported by Canyon for additional equipment depreciation of $15,000 [(1/5)($305,000 − $230,000) = (1/5)($75,000)]. Similarly, Tucson paid $50,000 for goodwill, representing unidentifiable assets of Canyon, that is subject to amortization over 10 years and requires an additional adjustment (reduction) of net income in the amount of $5,000 [(1/10)($50,000)].

The calculation of Tucson's income from its investment in Canyon is summarized in Exhibit 14–8. When using the equity method, an investor whose ownership percentage of an entity is less than 100 percent recognizes only its ownership percentage of the investee's reported net income. Thus, since Tucson owns 100 percent of Canyon, Tucson recognizes 100 percent of Canyon's net income (before adjustment for amortization of the valuation differential).

The calculation of the parent's income from its subsidiary, the cost of the investment ($400,000), and the amount of the dividend ($25,000) are the basis for the parent's equity-method entries, as shown in Exhibit 14–9. Observe that the third entry records the investment income by a credit to an income statement account (income from investment in Canyon) and a debit to the investment account. As a result of these entries, the investment account appears as shown in the T-account that follows:

Long-term investment in Canyon			
Acquisition cost	400,000		
Investment income	40,000	25,000	Dividend
Balance, 12/31/X4	415,000		

In other words, the parent's investment account is increased for its share of the subsidiary's net income (adjusted for amortization of the valuation differential) and is decreased for subsidiary dividends paid to the parent (which represent a liquidation of income previously recorded in the investment account).

CONSOLIDATED AND PARENT COMPANY INCOME STATEMENTS

We turn now to the consolidation of the parent's equity method income statement with the income statement of the subsidiary. You will recall that consolidated balance sheets present the financial position of parent and subsidiary as if the two entities were a single entity. In much the same way, a consolidated income statement presents the income of parent and subsidiary as if the two were a single entity. And like the consolidation of balance sheets, the consolidation of income statements requires a consolidation procedure. The procedure for balance sheets uses a worksheet to substitute the detailed assets and liabilities of the subsidiary for the investment account of the parent. In a similar way, the consolidation procedure for income statements uses a worksheet to substitute the detailed revenues and expenses of the subsidiary for the related investment income on the parent's income statement. Exhibit 14–10 presents the worksheet that is used to prepare the consolidated income statement for the combination of Tucson and Canyon.

The preconsolidation income statements for the parent and the subsidiary are shown in the first two columns of Exhibit 14–10. Note that the income statements are presented in an artificial form, with net income listed among the debits in order to effect a balance between debits and credits. The use of the balancing form permits us to present the consolidation of only the income statements (otherwise we would have to present a worksheet that included the balance sheet as well).

The amounts for the consolidated income statement are determined by adding corresponding statement items from the parent and subsidiary income statements and by making the following consolidation adjustments:

a) Amortization of valuation differential 20,000
      Income from investment in Canyon................ 20,000

    Consolidation worksheet adjustment to reclassify amortization of valuation differential.

b) Income from investment in Canyon.................. 60,000
      Net income 60,000

    Consolidation worksheet adjustment to eliminate parent's share of subsidiary net income.

EXHIBIT 14–10   **CONSOLIDATION WORKSHEET**

TUCSON, INC., AND CANYON CORPORATION
Worksheet Consolidation of Income Statements

	CORPORATE INCOME STATEMENTS		CONSOLIDATION ADJUSTMENTS		CONSOLIDATED INCOME STATEMENT
	TUCSON	CANYON	DR	CR	
CREDITS					
Revenue	$900,000	$200,000			$1,100,000
Income from investment in Canyon	40,000		(b) 60,000	(a) 20,000	–0–
Total credits	$940,000	$200,000			$1,100,000
DEBITS					
Cost of goods sold	$320,000	$ 95,000			$ 415,000
Depreciation expense	210,000	22,000			232,000
Other expenses	160,000	23,000			183,000
Amortization of valuation differential	–0–	–0–	(a) 20,000		20,000
Net income	250,000	60,000		(b) 60,000	250,000
Total debits	$940,000	$200,000			$1,100,000

These two adjustments (which are strictly worksheet adjustments and are not entered in either the parent's or the subsidiary's journal) perform two functions: The first adjustment reclassifies the amortization of the valuation differential ($20,000). The amortization of the valuation differential reduced the amount of income from Tucson's investment in Canyon from $60,000 to $40,000 when Tucson recorded its share of Canyon's income. Worksheet adjustment **a** temporarily restores Tucson's share of Canyon's income to $60,000 on the worksheet. The debit half of this entry sets up a separate line for the amortization in the worksheet. The second adjustment eliminates the parent's share of the subsidiary's net income, which was just reestablished at $60,000. Since subsidiary net income of $60,000 is represented in both the subsidiary's income statement and the parent's income from investment account, the elimination of $60,000 prevents double counting of that income when parent and subsidiary income statements are added together on the worksheet.

Note that on the worksheet in Exhibit 14–10 consolidated net income is $250,000, which is exactly the same as the parent's corporate net income. From the parent's viewpoint, the consolidation procedure does not change the amount of net income reported, but merely alters the composition of revenues and expenses on which that income is based. In other words, the consolidated income statement reports the revenues and expenses of the subsidiary combined with the corresponding revenues and expenses of the parent. Such a presentation is consistent with the fact that the two corporations are a single accounting entity.

APPENDIX 14–2
COMBINATION BY EXCHANGE OF STOCK: A POOLING OF INTERESTS

To illustrate the pooling-of-interests method, we will look at a combination accomplished by the exchange of stock. A combination agreement negotiated by Mason, Inc., and the Wolfe Corporation requires that on January 1, 19X6, Mason issue 60,000 shares of its common stock to the stockholders of Wolfe in exchange for all their Wolfe Corporation common shares.[6] Just before the combination, the two firms had the balance sheets shown in Exhibit 14–11.

While the newly issued shares of Mason have a total current market value of $1,000,000, the pooling of Mason and Wolfe is recorded without incorporating the $1,000,000 fair value by the following entry in Mason's journal:

Long-term investment in Wolfe..................	900,000	
Common stock (60,000 shares at $10 par)........		600,000
Retained earnings.............................		300,000

To record acquisition of Wolfe's stock.

This journal entry by Mason records the issuance of its shares and the acquisition of the Wolfe shares as an investment. No entry is made in the accounting records of Wolfe Corporation, because the combination was accomplished by an exchange of shares between Mason and the stockholders of Wolfe. Wolfe itself was not a party to the combination transaction.

Mason's journal entry illustrates two important differences between pooling-of-interests and purchase combinations. First, the investment in Wolfe, instead of being recorded at its fair value ($1,000,000, the current market value of the newly issued stock) is recorded at its book value to Wolfe: $900,000 = assets of $1,100,000 − liabilities of $200,000 = common stock of $600,000 + retained earnings of $300,000. (If the combination had been a purchase rather than a pooling, the investment in Wolfe would have been recorded at its fair value.) The second difference between poolings and purchases is that equity accounts of the investor are increased by the corresponding equity account balances of the corporation whose stock is acquired. The journal entry by Mason increased its common stock by the amount of Wolfe's common stock balance, $600,000, and increased its retained earnings by the amount of Wolfe's retained earnings balance, $300,000.[7] To illustrate this distinction, had the combination been a pur-

---

[6] Technically speaking, this illustration does not provide enough information to determine whether the business combination transaction is a pooling or a purchase under generally accepted accounting principles. As explained earlier in this chapter, the identification of poolings requires the application of technical criteria to determine whether or not ownership interests have changed. We will assume that this illustration satisfies the criteria.

[7] Observe that the total par value of the new shares issued by Mason equals the total par value of the shares surrendered by Wolfe's stockholders [($10)(60,000) = ($5)(120,000) = $600,000]. When the newly created par value does not equal the par value of the surrendered shares, the issuing firm's entry to equity accounts must reclassify some elements of equity. Such complications are discussed in more advanced accounting texts.

EXHIBIT 14–11   **PRECOMBINATION BALANCE SHEETS**

	MASON, INC.		WOLFE CORPORATION	
Cash	$1,600,000	Cash	$ 100,000	
Equipment (net)	8,200,000	Equipment (net)	1,000,000	
Total assets	$9,800,000	Total assets	$1,100,000	
Liabilities	$3,000,000	Liabilities	$ 200,000	
Common stock ($10 par)	4,000,000	Common stock ($5 par) .	600,000	
Retained earnings	2,800,000	Retained earnings	300,000	
Total liabilities and equity	$9,800,000	Total liabilities and equity	$1,100,000	

chase rather than a pooling, the following entry would have been made in Mason's journal:

Long-term investment in Wolfe	1,000,000	
Common stock		600,000
Paid-in capital in excess of par		400,000

Observe that Mason's entry to record the purchase combination does not alter retained earnings but adds the entire excess of the investment's current value over the par of stock given to paid-in capital in excess of par. No entry is made by Wolfe, regardless of whether the combination is a pooling or a purchase.

In summary, when the acquiring firm issues new stock in exchange for the outstanding stock of the acquired firm, the acquiring firm records its investment at the book value of the acquired equity if the combination is a pooling and at the acquisition cost of the acquired equity if the combination is a purchase. Accordingly, the postcombination balance sheets for poolings, to which we now turn, differ from those for purchases.

POSTCOMBINATION BALANCE SHEETS FOR POOLINGS

Three postcombination balance sheets require our attention: the separate corporate balance sheets of the acquiring and acquired firms and the consolidated balance sheet. Let us begin by examining the corporate balance sheets of the acquiring and acquired firms and then consider their consolidation.

Immediately following the exchange of shares, the balance sheets of Mason and Wolfe are as shown in Exhibit 14–12. Observe that when compared with the precombination balance sheets in Exhibit 14–11, Wolfe's balance sheet is unaltered by the combination. However, Mason's balance sheet now includes a $900,000 investment account, and $600,000 and $300,000 have been added to common stock and retained earnings, respectively, as a result of the pooling.

Mason's postcombination balance sheet reflects the net assets acquired from Wolfe in an investment account ($900,000). Consequently, the consolidation procedure shown in Exhibit 14–13 is required to produce the balance sheet for the combined entity. Here again, the procedure substitutes the detailed net assets of Wolfe for the investment account carried on Mason's records. Since

EXHIBIT 14–12   POSTPOOLING BALANCE SHEETS

MASON, INC.		WOLFE CORPORATION	
Cash.................	$ 1,600,000	Cash...................	$ 100,000
Long-term investment		Equipment (net)	1,000,000
in Wolfe	900,000		
Equipment (net)	8,200,000		
Total assets..........	$10,700,000	Total assets...........	$1,100,000
Liabilities	$ 3,000,000	Liabilities	$ 200,000
Common stock ($10 par).	4,600,000	Common stock ($5 par)...	600,000
Retained earnings.......	3,100,000	Retained earnings........	300,000
Total liabilities		Total liabilities	
and equity	$10,700,000	and equity...........	$1,100,000

EXHIBIT 14–13   CONSOLIDATION WORKSHEET FOR POOLING

MASON, INC., AND WOLFE CORPORATION
Worksheet Consolidation of Balance Sheets

	CORPORATE BALANCE SHEETS		CONSOLIDATION ADJUSTMENTS		CONSOLIDATED BALANCE SHEET
	MASON	**WOLFE**	**DR**	**CR**	
Cash	$1,600,000	$ 100,000			$ 1,700,000
Long-term investment in Wolfe	900,000			(a) 900,000	–0–
Equipment	8,200,000	1,000,000			9,200,000
Total assets	$10,700,000	$1,100,000			$10,900,000
Liabilities	$ 3,000,000	$ 200,000			$ 3,200,000
Common stock	4,600,000	600,000	(a) 600,000		4,600,000
Retained earnings	3,100,000	300,000	(a) 300,000		3,100,000
Total liabilities and equity	$10,700,000	$1,100,000	900,000	900,000	$10,900,000

poolings of interests are recorded at net book value rather than at acquisition cost, adjustment **a**, which eliminates the net book value, is the only consolidation adjustment required. The consolidation adjustment that reclassifies the valuation differential is not required in consolidations following poolings because the valuation differential in poolings is always zero.

KEY TERMS

CONSOLIDATED FINANCIAL
STATEMENTS (p. 653)

CONSOLIDATION WORKSHEET (p. 657)

COST METHOD (p. 648)

EQUITY METHOD (p. 650)

GOODWILL (p. 656)

MINORITY INTEREST (p. 659)

PARENT (p. 654)

POOLING-OF-INTERESTS METHOD (p. 660)

PURCHASE METHOD (p. 660)

REVALUATION INCREMENT (p. 656)

SUBSIDIARY (p. 654)

VALUATION DIFFERENTIAL (p. 656)

QUESTIONS

Q14-1. How do long-term investments differ from short-term investments? Where do long-term investments appear on the balance sheet?

Q14-2. Describe the accounting methods used for long-term investments in preferred stock and debt securities.

Q14-3. Under what circumstances should the equity method be used for long-term investments in common stock? Under what circumstances should the cost method be used for such investments?

Q14-4. What event triggers the recognition of investment income under the cost method? What event triggers the recognition of investment income under the equity method?

Q14-5. Describe the equity method of accounting for long-term investments in common stock.

Q14-6. Describe the cost method of accounting for long-term investments in common stock.

Q14-7. How does the equity method discourage the manipulation of net income by investors?

Q14-8. Define the terms *parent* and *subsidiary.*

Q14-9. How does the consolidated balance sheet differ from the corporate balance sheet of the parent?

Q14-10. What is a business combination? Name three ways in which a business combination can be achieved.

Q14-11. Describe the interests and concerns of the owners and managers of a corporation that is acquired in a business combination.

Q14-12. Explain why some business combinations do not require the preparation of consolidated financial statements.

Q14-13. Preparation of the consolidated balance sheet for a parent and its subsidiary requires an analysis of the valuation differential. What is the valuation differential, and what are its two principal components?

Q14-14. Where is goodwill reported on the consolidated balance sheet, and how should it be interpreted?

Q14-15. Explain the differences between the purchase method and the pooling-of-interests method for recording business combinations.

Q14-16. Under what circumstances will a consolidated balance sheet show an account called *long-term investments in equity securities?*

Q14-17. Where is minority interest reported on the consolidated balance sheet, and how should it be interpreted?

Q14-18. Describe the lower-of-cost-or-market adjustments made for long-term investments in common stock. How do such adjustments differ from those made for short-term investments in common stock?

APPENDIX 14-1 QUESTIONS

Q14-19. What is the relationship between the corporate net income of a parent and consolidated net income?

Q14-20. Describe the function of the consolidation worksheet for income statements.

Q14-21. How does analysis of the valuation differential affect the application of the equity method? How does analysis of the valuation differential affect the consolidation of financial statements?

APPENDIX 14-2 QUESTIONS

Q14-22. Describe the effect of a pooling of interests, accomplished by an exchange of common shares, on the equity of the *acquiring* company.

Q14-23. Describe the effect of a pooling of interests, accomplished by an exchange of common shares, on the equity of the *acquired* company.

EXERCISES

E14-24. COST AND EQUITY FINANCIAL STATEMENT EFFECTS   At the beginning of 19X4, Pacaoli Corporation has $10,000 that it wants to use to acquire a partial ownership interest in either Sequoya Company or Spruce Enterprises. If Pacaoli spends $10,000, it will be able to acquire a 15 percent interest in Sequoya or a 25 percent interest in Spruce. Pacaoli's accountant expects that Sequoya and Spruce will have the following financial results for 19X4:

	SEQUOYA COMPANY	SPRUCE ENTERPRISES
Net income	$18,000	$14,000
Dividends (declared and paid)	2,000	8,000

REQUIRED:

1. What will be the effect on 19X4 net income (ignoring income taxes) of the two alternative investments?

2. What will be the effect on 19X4 total assets (again ignoring income taxes) of the two alternative investments?

E14-25. COST AND EQUITY METHOD JOURNAL ENTRIES   Smith Corporation acquired a long-term interest in Virgil, Inc., on January 1, 19X9, for $100,000 cash. During 19X9 Virgil declared and paid cash dividends to Smith in the amount of $8,000. The portion of Virgil's 19X9 net income corresponding to Smith's ownership of Virgil is $12,400. The market price of Virgil's stock increased by 20 percent during 19X9.

REQUIRED:

1. Assume that Smith uses the *cost method* for its investment in Virgil. Write the journal entries made by Smith during 19X9 relative to this investment.

2. Assume that Smith uses the *equity method* for its investment in Virgil. Write the journal entries made by Smith during 19X9 relative to this investment.

E14-26. COST METHOD FOR LONG-TERM INVESTMENTS IN COMMON STOCK   On January 1, 19X7, Reduction Products, Inc., acquired 15 percent of the outstanding common stock (1,500 of 10,000 outstanding shares) of Tupper Corporation for $24,000 ($16 per share, including commissions). This investment is Reduction's only long-term investment in equity securities. On October 1, 19X7, Tupper declared and paid a cash dividend of $2 per share. On November 15, 19X7, Reduction sold 300 shares of Tupper for $5,000. Tupper reported 19X7 net income of $36,000. Tupper's stock sold for $15 per share on December 31, 19X7.

REQUIRED:

1. Write the journal entries made by Reduction Products to record the transactions related to its investment in Tupper.

2. Give the title and amount of each item (except cash) on the December 31, 19X7, balance sheet related to the investment. Name the balance sheet section in which each item appears.

E14-27. EQUITY METHOD FOR LONG-TERM INVESTMENTS IN COMMON STOCK   On January 1, 19X3, Hill Corporation acquired 40 percent of the outstanding common stock (400 of 1,000 outstanding shares) of Valley Manufacturing, Inc., for $60,000 ($150 per share, including commissions). On December 31, 19X3, Valley Manufacturing reported net income of $30,000 and declared and paid a cash dividend of $11,500 ($4,600 to Hill). Assume that the acquisition cost of an investment requiring the equity method equals the book value of the related stockholders' equity on the investee's books.

REQUIRED:

1. Write the journal entries made by Hill Corporation to record the transactions related to its investment in Valley Manufacturing.
2. Give the title and amount of each item (except cash) on the December 31, 19X3, balance sheet related to the investment. Name the balance sheet section in which each item appears.

E14-28. MATCHING ACCOUNTING METHODS AND INVESTMENTS   Consider the following accounting methods for long-term investments:

a) Cost method
b) Equity method
c) Consolidation of parent and subsidiary financial statements

REQUIRED:

Match one or more of these methods with each of the long-term investments described below:

1. Mueller, Inc., owns 75 percent of Johnston Corporation's outstanding voting stock.
2. Anderson, Inc., owns 25 percent of Peterson Corporation's outstanding voting stock.
3. Wixon Corporation owns 12 percent of the outstanding voting stock of Gilman, Inc.
4. Kohler Corporation owns 50 percent of the outstanding nonvoting preferred stock of Bennett, Inc.

E14-29. ACCOUNTING FOR LONG-TERM INVESTMENTS IN COMMON STOCK   On January 1, 19X6, Stern Corporation purchased 100 shares of common stock issued by Milstein, Inc. (representing 12 percent of the total shares outstanding) for $6,000 cash, and 500 shares of Heifetz, Inc. (representing 25 percent of the total shares outstanding) for $20,000 cash. Assume that the acquisition cost of each investment equals the book value of the related stockholders' equity on the records of the investee. These investments are the only long-term investments in securities held by Stern. During 19X6 Milstein declared and paid cash dividends to Stern of $500, and Heifetz declared and paid paid cash dividends to Stern of $1,700. Milstein reported 19X6 net income of $12,000, and Heifetz reported 19X6 net income of $15,000. Assume that no change occurred during 19X6 in the market price of either stock.

REQUIRED:

On your own paper, list the answers to complete the following table, which raises questions about the investor's accounting for the two investments:

QUESTION	INVESTMENT IN MILSTEIN	INVESTMENT IN HEIFETZ
1. Which accounting method is applicable to the investment?		
2. What amount is recorded in the investment account on the date of acquisition?		
3. What amount is included in Stern's net income from the investment?		
4. What amount is reported for the investment on the balance sheet at December 31, 19X6?		

E14-30. ANALYSIS OF VALUATION DIFFERENTIAL   Pindar Corporation acquired all the outstanding stock of Strauss Company for $23,000 cash. The book value of Strauss's equity (assets minus liabilities) at the date of the acquisition of its stock was $17,800. All Strauss's assets and liabilities have book values equal to their fair value except for equipment, which has a book value of $6,300 and fair value of $10,700.

REQUIRED:

1. Calculate the amount of the valuation differential.

2. Prepare a diagrammatic analysis of the valuation differential similar to that presented in Exhibit 14–4.

E14-31. CONSOLIDATION WORKSHEET ADJUSTMENTS   Patrick, Inc., acquired all the common stock of Staple Products Company for $33,100 cash. On the date of the acquisition, Staple's equity consisted of common stock of $23,000 and retained earnings of $4,700. All Staple's assets and liabilities have book values that are equal to their fair values except for land, which is undervalued by $3,600.

REQUIRED:

1. Prepare a diagrammatic analysis of the valuation differential similar to that presented in Exhibit 14–4.

2. Write the consolidation worksheet adjusting entries required for the preparation of a consolidated balance sheet immediately after the acquisition of Staple's stock.

E14-32. CORPORATE VERSUS CONSOLIDATED BALANCE SHEETS   Lawton Corporation is the wholly owned subsidiary of Gilbert, Inc. Immediately after the acquisition of Lawton, Gilbert has the following corporate and consolidated balance sheets:

	CONSOLIDATED BALANCE SHEET	GILBERT BALANCE SHEET	CONSOLIDATED MINUS GILBERT
Cash	$ 1,600	$ 900	$ 700
Long-term investment in Lawton	–0–	1,750	(1,750)
Equipment (net)	9,770	8,600	1,170
Goodwill	80	–0–	80
Total assets	$11,450	$11,250	$ 200
Liabilities	$ 850	$ 650	$ 200
Common stock	7,000	7,000	–0–
Retained earnings	3,600	3,600	–0–
Total liabilities and equity	$11,450	$11,250	$ 200

Gilbert purchased all of Lawton's outstanding common stock for $1,750, which exceeds Lawton's book value by $330. The $330 valuation differential consists of goodwill of $80 and a revaluation increment on equipment of $250.

REQUIRED:

1. Briefly explain the following differences between the corporate and consolidated balance sheets shown above:

a) The $700 difference in cash

    b) The $1,170 difference in equipment (net)

    c) The $80 difference in goodwill

    d) The $200 difference in liabilities

    e) The $1,750 difference in investment

2. Prepare the balance sheet of Lawton immediately after the combination.

3. Why are the consolidated equity accounts the same as Gilbert's equity accounts?

E14-33. ALTERNATIVE COMBINATION OF TWO CORPORATIONS   Paine Company is evaluating a potential business combination transaction with Slater Corporation. If the combination transaction is effected, Paine will become Slater's sole stockholder. Slater's current stockholders have no preference between receiving $27,000 in cash or 2,000 shares of newly issued Paine stock. Before the combination, Paine has 1,800 shares of common stock outstanding. If Paine acquires the stock for cash, it will have to borrow nearly all the $27,000.

REQUIRED:

Discuss the advantages and disadvantages from Paine's perspective in the two ways that Paine could acquire all Slater's stock.

E14-34. CORPORATE VIEWPOINTS IN BUSINESS COMBINATIONS   Porter Enterprises is considering acquiring all the stock of Sullivan Corporation so that it can immediately expand its operations into the Northeast. Both corporations produce dairy products for retail grocery stores.

REQUIRED:

1. From Porter's perspective, compare the potential benefits of acquiring facilities through a business combination with the benefits of constructing new processing facilities.

2. From Porter's perspective, identify the potential risks or disadvantages of acquiring facilities versus those of contructing new ones.

3. What concerns might the management of Sullivan have about a combination?

4. Why might the management of Sullivan regard a business combination as more desirable than continued existence as a separate enterprise?

APPENDIX 14–1 EXERCISE

E14-35. EQUITY METHOD AND VALUATION DIFFERENTIAL   On January 1, 19X8, Delilah, Inc., acquired all the outstanding stock of Samson Corporation for $400,000 cash ($50 per share, including commissions). On that date, Samson's stockholders' equity totaled $381,000. All Samson's assets and liabilities are reported at their current fair values except for a building that is undervalued by $12,000. The building has a remaining life of 10 years, and straight-line depreciation is used. Goodwill is amortized on a straight-line basis over a 20-year period. On December 31, 19X8, Samson reported net income of $64,000 and declared and paid a cash dividend of $32,000.

REQUIRED:

1. Prepare a diagrammatic analysis of the valuation differential similar to that demonstrated in Exhibit 14–6.

2. Prepare a schedule showing Delilah's calculation of income from its subsidiary, Samson (see Exhibit 14–8).

3. Write the journal entries made by Delilah, Inc., to record the events related to its investment in Samson Corporation.

4. Give the title and amount of each item (except cash) on the December 31, 19X8, balance sheet related to the investment. Name the balance sheet section in which each item appears.

APPENDIX 14-2 EXERCISE

E14-36. JOURNAL ENTRIES FOR PURCHASE OR POOLING   Pear Company and Straw Corporation enter into a business combination in which Pear acquires all the outstanding common stock of Straw in exchange for newly issued shares of Pear. Immediately before the business combination, the two corporations have the following balance sheets:

PEAR COMPANY		STRAW CORPORATION	
Total assets	$8,000	Total assets	$1,000
Liabilities.	$2,200	Liabilities.	$ 300
Common stock ($10 par).	5,000	Common stock ($5 par).	600
Retained earnings.	800	Retained earnings.	100
Total liabilities and equity. . . .	$8,000	Total liabilities and equity. . . .	$1,000

The business combination requires Pear to issue 60 new shares of its common stock to the stockholders of Straw in exchange for all the Straw shares. The newly issued shares of Pear have a market value of $800.

REQUIRED:

1. Write the journal entries required for the two corporations to record the combination as a pooling of interests.

2. Write the journal entries required for the two corporations to record the combination as a purchase combination.

PROBLEMS

P14-37. FINANCIAL STATEMENT EFFECTS OF INVESTMENTS   Percival Corporation held the following investments for all of 19X4:

1,000 shares of Abigail Company. During 19X4 Abigail has 8,000 shares of common stock outstanding, has net income of $4,200, and declares and pays $1,200 in dividends.

2,500 shares of Meredith Enterprises. During 19X4 Meredith has 6,250 shares of common stock outstanding, earns $6,500 of net income, and declares and pays $2,000 in dividends.

1,500 shares of Zecher Products. During 19X4 Zecher has 10,000 shares of common stock outstanding, has $3,400 of net income, and declares and pays $1,800 in dividends.

REQUIRED:

1. What is the effect on Percival's net income (ignoring income taxes) of each of these investments?

2. By how much has Percival's investment account changed for each of these investments during 19X4?

P14-38. COST METHOD FOR LONG-TERM INVESTMENTS IN COMMON STOCK   On January 1, 19X4, Braddock Corporation acquired 15 percent of the outstanding common stock (3,000 of 20,000 outstanding shares) of Nathan, Inc., for $90,000 cash ($30 per share, including commissions). The investment is the only long-term investment in equity securities held by Braddock. Nathan declares and pays dividends on August 31 of each year—$4 per share on August 31, 19X4, and $5 per share on August 31, 19X5. On June 1, 19X5, Braddock sold 600 shares of its investment in Nathan for $33 per share. On December 31, 19X4, Nathan's stock was selling for $27 per share; one year later, on December 31, 19X5, Nathan's stock was selling for $29 per share.

REQUIRED:

1. Write the journal entries made by Braddock Corporation to record the events related to its investment in Nathan.

2. Give the title and amount of each item (except cash) on the December 31, 19X5, balance sheet related to the investment. Name the balance sheet section in which each item appears.

P14-39. EQUITY METHOD FOR LONG-TERM INVESTMENTS IN COMMON STOCK   On January 1, 19X2, Boulder, Inc., acquired 25 percent of the outstanding stock (2,000 of 8,000 outstanding shares) of Colorado Corporation for $100,000 ($50 per share, including commissions). Colorado declares and pays an annual cash dividend on September 30 of each year—$1 per share on September 30, 19X2, and $2.50 per share on September 30, 19X3. Colorado reported a *net loss* of $16,000 for 19X2 and *net income* of $40,000 for 19X3. Assume that the acquisition cost of the investment equals the book value of the related stockholders' equity on the investee's books.

REQUIRED:

1. Write the journal entries made by Boulder, Inc., to record the events related to its investment in Colorado Corporation.

2. Give the title and amount of each item (except cash) on the December 31, 19X3, balance sheet related to the investment. Name the balance sheet section in which each item appears.

P14-40. COST METHOD FOR LONG-TERM INVESTMENTS IN COMMON STOCK   On January 1, 19X6, Stanton, Inc., acquired 12 percent of the outstanding common stock (2,400 of 20,000 outstanding shares) of Calamity Corporation for $84,000 cash ($35 per share, including commissions). This is the only long-term investment in equity securities held by Stanton. Calamity declares and pays dividends on November 1 of each year—$3 per share on November 1, 19X6, and $3.50 per share on November 1, 19X7. On April 1, 19X7, Stanton sold 800 shares of its investment in Calamity for $31 per share. On December 31, 19X6, Calamity's stock was selling for $32 per share; one year later, on December 31, 19X7, Calamity's stock was selling for $33.50 per share.

REQUIRED:

1. Write the journal entries made by Stanton, Inc., to record the events related to its investment in Calamity.

2. Give the title and amount of each item (except cash) on the December 31, 19X7, balance sheet related to the investment. Name the balance sheet section in which each item appears.

P14-41. COST METHOD FOR A TWO-STOCK PORTFOLIO   During January 19X9, Edwards Corporation purchased the following shares of common stock as long-term investments:

a) 100 shares of Hermanson, Inc. (100 out of 1,000 outstanding shares) for $12 per share.

b) 200 shares of Salmonson, Inc. (200 out of 2,000 outstanding shares) for $8 per share.

These are the only long-term investments in securities held by Edwards. Hermanson reported net income for 19X9 of $1,500; on August 20, 19X9, Hermanson declared and paid cash dividends totaling $900 (including $90 paid to Edwards). Salmonson reported net income for 19X9 of $1,000; on September 15, 19X9, Salmonson declared and paid cash dividends totaling $600 (including $60 paid to Edwards). On December 31, 19X9, the market price of Hermanson's stock was $10.20 per share, and the market price of Salmonson's stock was $8.50 per share.

REQUIRED:

1. Write the journal entries made by Edwards Corporation to record the events during 19X9 related to its investments in Hermanson, Inc., and Salmonson, Inc.

2. Give the title and amount of each item (except cash) on the December 31, 19X9, balance sheet related to the investment. Name the balance sheet section in which each item appears.

P14-42. CONSOLIDATED BALANCE SHEET   Peachtree Corporation acquired 100 percent of the outstanding common stock of Standard Company in a business combination transaction accounted for as a purchase. Immediately before the business combination, the two businesses had the following balance sheets:

PEACHTREE CORPORATION		STANDARD COMPANY	
Cash	$ 3,100	Cash	$ 180
Equipment (net)	9,500	Equipment (net)	930
Total assets	$12,600	Total assets	$1,110
Common stock	$ 9,100	Common stock	$ 700
Retained earnings	3,500	Retained earnings	410
Total liabilities and equity . .	$12,600	Total liabilities and equity . .	$1,110

In the business combination transaction, Peachtree agreed to give Standard's shareholders $1,500 cash in exchange for all their Standard Company common shares. Standard's equipment has a fair value of $1,100.

REQUIRED:

1. Write the journal entries (if any) for Peachtree and Standard to record the business combination.

2. Prepare the balance sheet of Peachtree immediately after the business combination transaction.

3. Prepare the balance sheet of Standard immediately after the business combination transaction.

4. Prepare a diagrammatic analysis of the valuation differential similar to that presented in Exhibit 14–4.

5. Prepare a consolidation balance sheet worksheet immediately after the business combination transaction.

6. Prepare a consolidated balance sheet for the combined entity immediately after the business combination transaction.

APPENDIX 14–1 PROBLEMS

P14-43.   CONSOLIDATED INCOME STATEMENT   Johnson, Inc., is the wholly owned subsidiary of Stuart Corporation. The 19X1 income statements for the two corporations are as follows:

STUART CORPORATION			JOHNSON, INC.		
Revenue		$3,200	Revenue		$500
Income from investment in Johnson		?			
		$?			
Cost of goods sold	$920		Cost of goods sold	$160	
Depreciation expense . . .	410		Depreciation expense . . .	95	
Other expenses	680	2,010	Other expenses	135	390
Net income		$?	Net income		$110

The acquisition cost of Stuart's 100 percent ownership interest in Johnson exceeded the book value of the interest on Johnson's records; the excess represents a valuation differential associated with equipment and goodwill. The revaluation increment is amortized at a rate of $22 per year, and goodwill is amortized at a rate of $9 per year. During 19X1 Johnson pays a cash dividend of $25 to Stuart.

REQUIRED:

1. Calculate the income from investment in Johnson as reported on Stuart's income statement.

2. Write the journal entries required by Stuart to record income and dividends from Johnson during 19X1.

3. Calculate the 19X1 net income reported by Stuart on its parent company income statement.

4. Prepare a worksheet to consolidate the parent and subsidiary income statements for 19X1.

5. Prepare the 19X1 consolidated income statement for Stuart and Johnson.

P14-44. PARENT COMPANY AND CONSOLIDATED INCOME STATEMENTS Subwalk Company is the 100 percent-owned subsidiary of Principal, Inc. Principal acquired all the outstanding stock of Subwalk on January 1, 19X4. Principal issued the following consolidated and corporate income statements for 19X4:

	CONSOLIDATED INCOME STATEMENT	PRINCIPAL INCOME STATEMENT	CONSOLIDATED MINUS PRINCIPAL
Sales revenue	$ 2,700	$ 2,150	$ 550
Income from investment in subsidiary	-0-	100	(100)
Total	$ 2,700	$ 2,250	$ 450
Cost of goods sold	(1,570)	(1,240)	(330)
Depreciation expense	(250)	(210)	(40)
Other expenses	(520)	(490)	(30)
Amortization of valuation differential	(50)	-0-	(50)
Net income	$ 310	$ 310	$ -0-

REQUIRED:

1. Briefly explain the following differences between the separate and consolidated income statements shown above:
a) The $550 difference in sales revenue.
b) The $330 difference in cost of goods sold.
c) The $40 difference in depreciation expense.
d) The $30 difference in the amortization of the valuation differential.
e) The $100 difference in income from investment in subsidiary.

2. Prepare a separate income statement for Subwalk.

3. Explain why Subwalk's net income is different from the amount Principal reports for income from investment in subsidiary.

4. Why does the consolidated net income equal Principal's net income?

APPENDIX 14–2 PROBLEM

P14-45. POOLING OF INTERESTS WITH CONSOLIDATION Puritan Company and Sturgis, Inc., enter into a business combination that is to be accounted for as a pooling of interests. The balance sheets of the two firms immediately before the pooling are as follows:

PURITAN COMPANY		**STURGIS, INC.**	
Cash	$ 410	Cash	$ 250
Equipment (net)	8,950	Equipment (net)	2,630
Total assets.	$9,360	Total assets.	$2,880
Liabilities.	$1,850	Liabilities.	$ 810
Common stock ($20 par).	6,500	Common stock ($5 par).	1,800
Retained earnings	1,010	Retained earnings	270
Total liabilities and equity . .	$9,360	Total liabilities and equity . .	$2,880

In the business combination transaction, Puritan agreed to give Sturgis's shareholders 90 shares of newly issued Puritan common stock in exchange for all their Sturgis common shares. Puritan's 90 shares of newly issued common stock have a fair value of $2,500.

REQUIRED:

1. Calculate the total par value of the newly issued shares of Puritan.

2. Prepare journal entries (if any) required for Puritan and Sturgis to record the business combination.

3. Prepare the balance sheet of Puritan immediately after the business combination transaction.

4. Prepare the balance sheet of Sturgis immediately after the business combination transaction.

5. Prepare the consolidated balance sheet for the combined entity immediately after the business combination transaction. (First prepare the consolidation worksheet. Then use the worksheet to prepare the consolidated balance sheet.)

6. Does the consolidation procedure for Puritan and Sturgis make use of the fact that the newly issued Puritan stock has a fair value of $2,500? Explain briefly.

7. Prepare the journal entry Puritan would make to record the business combination as a purchase combination rather than a pooling of interests.

ANALYTICAL OPPORTUNITIES

A14-46. POOLING VERSUS PURCHASE INCOME STATEMENTS   The text indicates that a pooling-of-interests business combination transfers the book values of subsidiary assets to the consolidated balance sheet while a purchase combination transfers subsidiary assets to the consolidated balance sheet at fair value. A purchased combination may also involve creation of consolidated goodwill, while a pooling does not.

REQUIRED:

1. What will be the effects on net income in the period of the business combination and on future income statements of the purchase-pooling differences for recording assets and goodwill?

2. If management of the parent can cause a business combination to be either a purchase or a pooling, which do you think they would prefer? Briefly explain your answer.

A14-47. CONSOLIDATING DIFFERENT KINDS OF BUSINESSES   Pinafore Manufacturing Company has decided that competitive conditions require that it offer financing to its customers. Since Pinafore's management has no experience in operating a financial institution, it is considering acquiring in a business combination transaction all the stock of Staley Credit Corporation, a company that has specialized in providing credit to customers of manufacturers like Pinafore. If Staley is acquired, Pinafore will operate Staley as a subsidiary and consolidated financial statements will have to be prepared.

Edgar Hemmer, the president of Pinafore, observes (correctly) that the kinds and quantities of assets, liabilities, revenues, and expenses are quite different for Pinafore and Staley Credit Company. Edgar wonders whether it is wise to prepare consolidated financial statements when the two businesses are so different.

REQUIRED:

Explain why it is appropriate for consolidated financial statements to include the balance sheets and income statements of all majority-owned businesses, regardless of the differences in their assets and liabilities and in the nature of their operating activities. (*Hint:* Read *FASB Statement No. 94,* Paragraphs 28–33.)

15 FINANCIAL STATEMENT ANALYSIS

Careful study of this chapter will enable you to:

1. Explain how financial statements are used by creditors, investors, and other interested businesses and individuals.

2. Identify the information that can be extracted from comparative financial statements.

3. Prepare and use comparative component percentage statements.

4. Compute and interpret 19 important financial ratios.

5. Use comparative financial statements, component percentage statements, and financial ratios to analyze the performance and financial position of businesses.

Throughout this book, we have tried to demonstrate how financial statements can be useful to persons interested in the firm for which the statements are prepared. Analysis sections included throughout the text have illustrated various uses of financial statement data. In this chapter, we take a closer look at the role of financial statements in the decision-making process. Various types of decision making are examined, including that of creditors, investors, customers, suppliers, and employees. In addition, we present general techniques for extracting information from financial statements and indicate the impact that different accounting methods can have on the analysis of financial statements. The chapter concludes with a comprehensive demonstration of these general techniques, using the financial statements of Compaq Computer Corporation.

USE OF FINANCIAL STATEMENTS IN MAKING DECISIONS

Financial statements are frequently the basis for judgments and predictions about a firm that serve, in turn, as the foundation for decisions by creditors, investors, and others. In general terms, a *decision* is a choice among alternatives that is made on the basis of available information. In this context, the role of financial statements is to provide information that will help decision makers select the best action. Financial statements provide important information for a wide variety of decisions. Creditors, investors, customers, suppliers, and employees all use financial statement data to make decisions, but each group uses the accounting information differently. In the sections that follow, we examine briefly the decisions made by each of these groups and the financial statement data that are commonly used.

CREDIT DECISIONS

An individual or an organization that is considering making a loan to another enterprise obviously needs to know whether the borrower is likely to be able to repay the loan and its interest. For short-term loans (those of one year or less), the principal and interest will be repaid from cash on hand and cash that can be secured by selling inventory and collecting accounts receivable (in other words, from current assets). A short-term lender, then, is most interested in the borrowing firm's working capital (the excess of current assets over current liabilities).

The principal and interest for a long-term loan will be repaid from cash provided by profits earned over the period of the loan. A long-term lender, then, is most interested in estimating (1) the future profits of the enterprise and (2) the amount of other claims against those profits, such as dividends to stockholders, payments to other lenders, and future investments by the firm.

Whether contemplating short-term or long-term loans, creditors draw useful information from the financial statements of prospective borrowers. Analysis of the balance sheet can provide information about the current liquidity of the borrower. Profitability data developed from current and previous income statements are often helpful in forecasting future profitability. The sources and uses of cash presented in the statement of cash flows are helpful in estimating the amount and timing of future claims against profits.

INVESTMENT DECISIONS

Investors, too, draw useful information from the financial statements of the firms in whose securities they contemplate investing. Investors who consider acquiring total or partial ownership of an enterprise expect to secure returns on their investments from (1) dividends and (2) an increase in the value of the investment (a capital gain). Both dividends and increases in the value of a share of ownership depend on the future profitability of the enterprise. The larger the profits of an enterprise, the more resources it has available for payment of dividends and for investment in new assets that will be used to create additional profits. Although investors are interested in future rather than past profitability, past income and dividend data are used to forecast future returns from dividends and increases in stock prices.

CUSTOMER DECISIONS

Financial statements also convey useful information to potential customers. Customers of firms that sell goods or provide services want to purchase from organizations that will (1) produce goods or provide services in the current period, (2) produce goods or provide services as needed in the future, and (3) provide repair or warranty service if required.[1] The financial statements contain data describing the profitability and efficiency of a firm's operations; these data are used by customers to estimate the likelihood that a potential supplier will be able to deliver goods or services as contracted.

SUPPLIER DECISIONS

An organization that is considering selling goods or providing services to another enterprise is concerned about whether its customer will (1) pay for the purchase as agreed and (2) be able to continue to purchase and pay for goods and services. In the short term, a supplier is actually a short-term creditor and is thus concerned about the resources available to pay for items purchased as well as other claims against those resources. In the long term, a supplier is much like a long-term creditor or investor in that the long-term supplier must make an investment in the resources necessary to produce goods for or provide services to the customer.

---

[1] Because of difficulties in securing parts and services, most customers prefer not to purchase goods produced by a manufacturer that has ceased to do business or is likely to do so.

Balance sheet data are used by a supplier to estimate the likelihood that a customer will be able to pay for current purchases, and income statement data are used to analyze whether a customer will be able to continue purchasing and paying for goods or services in the future.

EMPLOYMENT DECISIONS

When making employment decisions, an individual wants to be sure that a prospective employer will provide (1) competitive salary and benefits, (2) experiences that will prepare the employee to assume increased responsibility, and (3) a secure position for the foreseeable future. Employees also make an investment in an organization. In the short term, they realize returns from the same resources used to satisfy the claims of short-term creditors — the excess of the firm's current assets over the claims against those assets. In the long term, salary and advancement will develop from the profit and growth of the organization, the same factors considered by creditors, investors, customers, and suppliers. Income statement data can help a prospective employee assess the likelihood that an organization will provide the growth and profits necessary for a successful career.

Frequently, the contents of the financial statements do not directly indicate to a decision maker the course of action that should be selected. Instead, financial statement data usually must be analyzed and then used as the basis for a judgment or prediction. We will now consider a variety of analytical techniques used by decision makers to reach judgments or predictions on the basis of financial statement data.

TECHNIQUES FOR EXTRACTING INFORMATION FROM FINANCIAL STATEMENTS

Financial analysts use three general analysis techniques to extract information from financial statements: (1) examination of comparative financial statements, (2) examination of comparative component percentage statements, and (3) ratio analysis. Each of these techniques is based on comparison. Some analysis techniques compare a firm's performance in one time period with its performance in different time periods, while other techniques compare the performance of one firm with the performances of similar firms in either current or past periods. Very few analysis techniques involve comparison with an absolute standard that can be applied to a large cross section of firms for many periods.

COMPARATIVE FINANCIAL STATEMENTS

COMPARATIVE FINANCIAL STATEMENTS: Side-by-side presentations of consecutive financial statements of the same type.

Comparative financial statements are side-by-side presentations of consecutive financial statements of the same type (balance sheets, income statements, and so forth). Comparative statements permit interperiod comparisons of important accounts and account groups. Comparative income statements (like those shown in Exhibit 15–1) frequently present revenues, expenses, and net income for two or more consecutive periods of the firm's activity in parallel columns. Comparative balance sheets (as shown in Exhibit 15–3) present assets, liabilities, and equity for two or more consecutive year-ends in parallel columns. A 5-year or 10-year summary of the financial statements is often presented in a separate section of the financial report.

Comparative financial statements help decision makers identify the causes of changes in a firm's income or financial position. Knowing the causes of these changes is helpful in forecasting a firm's future financial position.

We shall illustrate how comparative financial statements are used by referring to the financial statements of The Limited, Inc., a large retailer. Exhibits 15–1, 15–2, and 15–3 present The Limited's comparative financial statements for the three years ended February 3, 1990, January 28, 1989, and January 30, 1988. In addition, Exhibit 15–4 presents a five-year summary of selected financial data for The Limited for the fiscal years 1985–1989. The Limited's statements are both comparative and consolidated—comparative in that they include more than one year's data and consolidated because The Limited has combined its affairs with those of its subsidiaries and produced a single set of comparative financial statements for the entire group of affiliated companies.

Let us first examine the comparative income statements in Exhibit 15–1 ("Consolidated Statements of Income") in conjunction with the five-year summary in Exhibit 15–4 ("Financial Summary"). These data indicate steady growth in revenues and net income for all five years, with the largest increase in revenues in 1986 and net income in 1989. The various expense catagories and

---

EXHIBIT 15–1   **COMPARATIVE INCOME STATEMENTS**

The Limited, Inc.
CONSOLIDATED STATEMENTS OF INCOME
(thousands, except per share amounts)

	1989	1988	1987
Net Sales	$4,647,916	$4,070,777	$3,527,941
Cost of Goods Sold, Occupancy and Buying Costs	3,201,281	2,856,074	2,535,166
Gross Income	1,446,635	1,214,703	992,775
General, Administrative and Store Operating Expenses	821,381	747,285	583,903
Operating Income	625,254	467,418	408,872
Interest Expense	(58,059)	(63,418)	(40,322)
Other Income (Expense), Net	6,731	(7,864)	9,638
Income Before Income Taxes	573,926	396,136	378,188
Provision for Income Taxes	227,000	151,000	143,000
Net Income	$ 346,926	$ 245,136	$ 235,188
Net Income per Share	$ 1.92	$ 1.36	$ 1.25
Weighted Average Shares Outstanding	180,644	180,093	188,313

EXHIBIT 15-2   COMPARATIVE STATEMENTS OF CHANGES IN RETAINED EARNINGS

The Limited, Inc.
CONSOLIDATED STATEMENTS OF RETAINED EARNINGS
(thousands)

	Retained Earnings
Balance, January 31, 1987	$ 487,720
Net Income	235,188
Cash Dividends	(44,724)
Other	(952)
Balance, January 30, 1988	677,232
Net Income	245,136
Cash Dividends	(42,982)
Balance, January 28, 1989	879,386
Net Income	346,926
Cash Dividends	(57,470)
Balance, February 3, 1990	$1,168,842

income subtotals appear to have increased in proportion with the revenue increases, except for interest expense, which decreased in 1989. The comparative statements of changes in retained earnings and the five-year summary indicate that dividends per share increased each year except 1988. Note that dividends per share are the same in 1988 and 1987 but that total dollar dividends are smaller in 1988 than 1987 because fewer shares are outstanding in 1988 than 1987.

The comparative balance sheets in Exhibit 15-3 ("Consolidated Balance Sheets") and the five-year summary in Exhibit 15-4 indicate that the major asset categories (receivables, inventory, and property and equipment) and total assets have increased steadily each year. Total liabilities decreased in 1988 and 1989 primarily because of the large decreases in long-term debt each year. Shareholders' (stockholders') equity increased substantially each year due to large increases in retained earnings. Paid-in capital actually decreased each year. Note also the large amounts of treasury stock held at the end of each year.

As our brief analysis indicates, large dollar changes between periods in accounts or groups of accounts can be detected by examining comparative financial statements. These changes may indicate that the firm is changing or that the conditions under which the firm operates are changing.

EXHIBIT 15–3   COMPARATIVE BALANCE SHEETS

The Limited, Inc.
CONSOLIDATED BALANCE SHEETS
(thousands)

Assets	Feb 3, 1990	Jan 28, 1989	Jan 30, 1988
Current Assets			
Cash and Equivalents	$ 21,734	$ 15,276	$ 47,953
Accounts Receivable	596,171	531,461	514,101
Inventories	482,136	407,006	353,693
Other	63,703	69,851	47,906
Total Current Assets	1,163,744	1,023,594	963,653
Property and Equipment, Net	1,172,688	1,066,646	889,155
Other Assets	82,054	55,266	76,669
Total Assets	$2,418,486	$2,145,506	$1,929,477
Liabilities and Shareholders' Equity			
Current Liabilities			
Accounts Payable	$ 175,319	$ 189,184	$ 153,528
Accrued Expenses	239,921	189,579	131,602
Income Taxes	62,980	77,192	48,740
Total Current Liabilities	478,220	455,955	333,870
Long-Term Debt	445,674	517,952	681,000
Deferred Income Taxes	214,858	198,893	174,209
Other Long-Term Liabilities	39,280	26,499	11,227
Shareholders' Equity			
Common Stock	94,863	94,863	94,837
Paid-In Capital	196,232	203,693	205,328
Retained Earnings	1,168,842	879,386	677,232
Unrealized Loss on Marketable Equity Securities	—	—	(8,219)
	1,459,937	1,177,942	969,178
Less Treasury Stock at Cost	(219,483)	(231,735)	(240,007)
Total Shareholders' Equity	1,240,454	946,207	729,171
Total Liabilities and Shareholders' Equity	$2,418,486	$2,145,506	$1,929,477

EXHIBIT 15-4   FIVE-YEAR SUMMARY

The Limited, Inc.
FINANCIAL SUMMARY
(thousands, except per share amounts)

Fiscal Year	1989	1988	1987	1986	1985
Operations					
Net Sales	$4,647,916	$4,070,777	$3,527,941	$3,142,696	$2,387,110
Net Income	346,926	245,136	235,188	227,780	145,317
Net Income per Share	$1.92	$1.36	$1.25	$1.21	$ .80
Dividends per Share	.32	.24	.24	.16	.107
Balance Sheet					
Total Assets	$2,418,486	$2,145,506	$1,929,477	$1,726,544	$1,494,313
Working Capital	685,524	567,639	629,783	586,827	419,706
Long-Term Debt	445,674	517,952	681,000	417,420	670,744
Shareholders' Equity	1,240,454	946,207	729,171	781,542	404,075

COMPARATIVE COMPONENT PERCENTAGE FINANCIAL STATEMENTS

COMPONENT PERCENTAGE STATEMENTS: Financial statements in which the statement items are expressed as percentages of the largest statement amount.

COMPARATIVE COMPONENT PERCENTAGE STATEMENTS: The side-by-side presentation of consecutive component percentage statements.

While comparative financial statements help statement users detect changes in the amounts of financial statement items, analysts also prepare component percentage statements to help them detect changes in the relative importance of financial statement items. **Component percentage statements** are financial statements in which the statement items are expressed as percentages of the largest statement amount. On a component percentage income statement, for example, all amounts are restated as percentages of revenues, and on a component percentage balance sheet, all amounts are restated as percentages of total assets. The side-by-side presentation of consecutive component percentage statements produces **comparative component percentage statements.**

Comparative component percentage statements help statement analysts distinguish between changes in account balances that are a result of growth and changes that are likely to have arisen from other causes. Identifying nongrowth changes and their causes can help analysts forecast a firm's future level of profitability or its future financial position. Component percentage statements are usually prepared from comparative financial statement data to help evaluate change in the accounts and the relationship among the accounts.

We will illustrate the preparation and use of component percentage statements using The Limited, Inc., income statements and balance sheets presented in Exhibits 15-1 and 15-3. An evaluation of comparative component percentage income statements helps an analyst understand the sources of year-to-year profit changes. The Limited's comparative component percentage income statements (see Exhibit 15-5) indicate that the cost of sales component percentage has declined each year, that both the general and administrative expenses and the

EXHIBIT 15–5   COMPARATIVE COMPONENT PERCENTAGE INCOME STATEMENTS

THE LIMITED, INC.
Comparative Component Percentage Statements of Income

(dollar amounts in thousands)

	1989 AMOUNT	1989 %	1988 AMOUNT	1988 %	1987 AMOUNT	1987 %
Net sales..........................	$4,647,916	100.0	$4,070,777	100.0	$3,527,941	100.0
Cost of sales......................	3,201,281	68.9	2,856,074	70.2	2,535,166	71.9
Gross income	$1,446,635	31.1	$1,214,703	29.8	$ 992,775	28.1
General and administrative expenses .	821,381	17.7	747,285	18.3	583,903	16.5
Operating income..................	$ 625,254	13.4	$ 467,418	11.5	$ 408,872	11.6
Interest expense	(58,059)	(1.2)	(63,418)	(1.6)	(40,322)	(1.1)
Other income (expense), net.........	6,731	.1	(7,864)	(.2)	9,638	.2
Income before income taxes.........	$ 573,926	12.3	$ 396,136	9.7	$ 378,188	10.7
Provision for income taxes..........	227,000	4.9	151,000	3.7	143,000	4.0
Net income	$ 346,926	7.4	$ 245,136	6.0	$ 235,188	6.7

interest expense component percentages increased in 1988 and declined in 1989 but are still above 1987 levels, and that the provision for income tax component percentage declined in 1988 and increased in 1989. As we noted earlier, The Limited's revenues grew substantially each year. Revenue growth is normally accompanied by increases of about the same percentage in cost of sales and general and administrative expenses. However, The Limited has been able to keep the growth in cost of sales below the growth in revenues. As a result cost of sales decreased to 68.9 percent of revenues in 1989. The overall effect of the changes in cost of sales and general and administrative expenses was to cause the operating income component percentage to decrease by a small amount in 1988 and increase substantially in 1989. The net income component percentage decreased in 1988 and increased in 1989 by an amount that is larger than the 1988 decrease. Thus, the dollar amount of The Limited's 1989 net income is larger than one would expect based on the 1987 net income and the growth in revenues from 1987 to 1989.

By examining component percentage balance sheets, we can detect shifts in the composition of assets, liabilities, and equity. The Limited's component percentage balance sheets (see Exhibit 15–6) indicate that the proportions of current assets (48.1, 47.7, and 49.9 percent in 1989, 1988, and 1987, respectively) and long-lived assets (48.5, 49.7, and 46.1 percent in 1989, 1988, and 1987, respectively) changed very little over the three years. The component percentages among the current assets have also been relatively stable.

The mixture of liabilities and equity that a firm uses to finance its assets is often referred to as its *capital structure.* The Limited's proportion of liabilities declined steadily (62.2, 55.9, and 48.7 percent in 1987, 1988, and 1989, respectively), while the proportion of equity increased (37.8, 44.1, and 51.3 percent in 1987, 1988, and 1989, respectively). The major factors in these changes are the decrease each year in the dollar amount and component percentage of long-term debt accompanied by increases in the dollar amounts and component percentages for retained earnings. The retained earnings increases were achieved even though The Limited paid substantial cash dividends in each of the three years (see

EXHIBIT 15–6   COMPARATIVE COMPONENT PERCENTAGE BALANCE SHEETS

THE LIMITED, INC.
Comparative Component Percentage Balance Sheets

(dollar amounts in thousands)	YEAR					
	1989		1988		1987	
ASSETS	AMOUNT	%	AMOUNT	%	AMOUNT	%
Current assets:						
Cash and equivalents	$ 21,734	.9	$ 15,276	.7	$ 47,953	2.5
Accounts receivable.	596,171	24.7	531,461	24.8	514,101	26.6
Inventories	482,136	19.9	407,006	19.0	353,693	18.3
Other	63,703	2.6	69,851	3.2	47,906	2.5
Total current assets	$1,163,744	48.1	$1,023,594	47.7	$ 963,653	49.9
Property and equipment, net.	1,172,688	48.5	1,066,646	49.7	889,155	46.1
Other assets.	82,054	3.4	55,266	2.6	76,669	4.0
Total assets	$2,418,486	100.0	$2,145,506	100.0	$1,929,477	100.0
LIABILITIES AND EQUITY						
Current liabilities:						
Accounts payable.	$ 175,319	7.3	$ 189,184	8.8	$ 153,528	8.0
Accrued expenses.	239,921	9.9	189,579	8.8	131,602	6.8
Income taxes.	62,980	2.6	77,192	3.6	48,740	2.5
Total current liabilities	$ 478,220	19.8	$ 455,955	21.3	$ 333,870	17.3
Long-term debt	445,674	18.4	517,952	24.1	681,000	35.3
Deferred income taxes	214,858	8.9	198,893	9.3	174,209	9.0
Other long-term liabilities	39,280	1.6	26,499	1.2	11,227	.6
Total liabilities	$1,178,032	48.7	$1,199,299	55.9	$1,200,306	62.2
Shareholders' equity:						
Common stock.	$ 94,863	3.9	$ 94,863	4.4	$ 94,837	4.9
Paid-in capital	196,232	8.1	203,693	9.5	205,328	10.6
Retained earnings	1,168,842	48.3	879,386	41.0	677,232	35.1
Unrealized loss on marketable equity securities	—	—	—	—	(8,219)	(.4)
	$1,459,937	60.3	$1,177,942	54.9	$ 969,178	50.2
Less: Treasury stock at cost	(219,483)	(9.0)	(231,735)	(10.8)	(240,007)	(12.4)
Total shareholders' equity	$1,240,454	51.3	$ 946,207	44.1	$ 729,171	37.8
Total liabilities and equity . . .	$2,418,486	100.0	$2,145,506	100.0	$1,929,477	100.0

Note: Percentages do not always add to subtotals and totals because of rounding.

the comparative statements of changes in retained earnings in Exhibit 15–2 and the five-year summary in Exhibit 15–4). The component percentages for the individual current liabilities are relatively constant.

The component percentage data for The Limited illustrate how the causes of changes in profitability, in the composition of assets, and in capital structure can be identified. A careful analyst uses component percentage data as a starting point for an inquiry into the causes of these changes, with the eventual objective of developing an appropriate forecast for the firm's next set of financial statements.

Next we turn to ratio analysis, the third of the general analysis techniques presented in this chapter.

RATIO ANALYSIS

Ratio analysis is the examination of financial statements for decision-making information by preparing and evaluating a series of ratios developed from the statement data. *Ratios* (or *financial ratios*), like other financial analysis data, normally provide meaningful information only when compared with previous ratios for the same firm or similar firms. Ratios help analysts make meaningful comparisons of one firm with another by removing most of the effects of size differences. When financial statement amounts are used directly in analysis, size differences between firms may make a meaningful comparison impossible. However, properly constructed financial ratios permit the performance and status of firms of quite different sizes to be compared. For example, an analyst might want to compare Reebok International Ltd. and L.A. Gear, two manufacturers of athletic footwear. If revenue is used as the basis for comparison, Reebok appears to be the stronger firm, because Reebok's revenue for a recent year is nearly three times as large as L.A. Gear's ($1,822,100,000 versus $617,100,000 for the same year). If a ratio measuring profitability is constructed for the same year, say, a ratio of net income to total assets, then the following comparative data result:

FIRM	NET INCOME TO TOTAL ASSETS
Reebok	15.7%
L.A. Gear	27.9

When the ratio of net income to total assets is used to compare the firms, L.A. Gear appears to be stronger than Reebok.

Financial ratios can be classified into five categories: *Short-term liquidity ratios* are helpful to short-term creditors. *Debt-management ratios* and *profitability ratios* provide information for long-term creditors and stockholders. *Operating ratios* help management operate the firm and indicate to outsiders the efficiency with which certain of the firm's activities are performed. *Stockholder ratios* are of interest to a firm's stockholders.

We will use the data in The Limited, Inc., financial statements to illustrate each type of financial statement ratio. We turn first to an examination of the ratios in each category. After all the ratios have been explained, we will provide a summary exhibit.

Short-Term Liquidity Ratios

Short-term creditors must be able to assess the likelihood that a firm to which they plan to extend credit will be able to pay its current obligations as they come due. The cash necessary to pay liabilities as they mature will come from the firm's available cash and from assets that can be converted into cash readily. Receivables, marketable securities, and inventory can all be converted into cash relatively quickly. Property, plant, and equipment and other long-lived assets are much more difficult to turn into cash quickly and are not likely to provide resources that can be used to meet current liabilities. **Short-term liquidity ratios** measure a firm's ability to meet its short-term obligations as they mature.

Two ratios are typically used to measure a firm's short-term liquidity: the *current ratio* and the *quick ratio*. Both focus on the relationship between current assets and current liabilities. They differ only in that the quick ratio is based on a more conservative measure of liquidity.

CURRENT RATIO   Since a firm will have to meet its current obligations primarily by using its current assets, the current ratio should be especially useful to short-term creditors. The **current ratio** is an assessment of the firm's short-term liquidity that

EXHIBIT 15–7   **CURRENT RATIOS FOR THE LIMITED, INC.**

(dollar amounts in thousands)	1989	1988
Total current assets.	$1,163,744	$1,023,594
Total current liabilities.	478,220	455,955
Current ratio	**2.43**	**2.24**

is computed by dividing current assets by current liabilities. Expressed as an equation, this ratio is

$$\text{Current ratio} = \frac{\text{Current assets}}{\text{Current liabilities}}$$

The current ratios for The Limited for 1989 and 1988 are shown in Exhibit 15–7. The Limited's current ratio increased in 1989 because the increases in accounts receivable and inventory were greater than the increase in accrued expenses.

QUICK RATIO   Some analysts believe that the current ratio overstates short-term liquidity. They argue that prepaid expenses (expenses for which payments are made before consumption) often cannot be converted into cash. Further, inventories must be sold, which can require a lengthy period before producing receivables that may in turn remain outstanding for a period of time before cash is produced. It is argued that only those current assets that can be turned into cash almost immediately should be used to measure short-term liquidity. This second measure of short-term liquidity is characterized as the ratio of *quick assets* (usually cash, receivables, and marketable securities) to current liabilities. The **quick ratio** (or *acid test ratio,* as it is sometimes called) is a conservative measure of short-term liquidity, since it includes only the most liquid current asset accounts. The quick ratio is expressed in equation form as

QUICK RATIO: A conservative assessment of a firm's short-term liquidity, computed by dividing quick assets (cash, receivables, and marketable securities) by current liabilities.

$$\text{Quick ratio} = \frac{\text{Quick assets}}{\text{Current liabilities}}$$

In Exhibit 15–8, The Limited's quick assets are identified among its current assets for 1989 and 1988. Then the quick ratios are developed. The quick ratios

EXHIBIT 15–8   **QUICK RATIOS FOR THE LIMITED, INC**

(dollar amounts in thousands)	1989		1988	
Current assets				
Cash and equivalents	$ 21,734		$ 15,276	
Accounts receivable	596,171		531,461	
Inventories	482,136		407,006	
Other	63,703		69,851	
Total current assets	$1,163,744		$1,023,594	
Quick assets		$617,905		$546,737
Total current liabilities		$478,220		$455,955
Quick ratio		**1.29**		**1.20**

indicate that The Limited should have little difficulty in meeting its current obligations, as the quick assets are larger than current liabilities. Both the quick and the current ratios increased in 1989, indicating The Limited's short-term liquidity improved.

Because both the quick ratio and the current ratio measure short-term liquidity, they often change in the same direction at the same time, as in our example. There are no absolute standards for any ratios, but reasonably good guidelines exist for the quick ratio and the current ratio. A quick ratio of 1.0 is considered to indicate adequate liquidity. At 1.0 there are just enough liquid assets available to satisfy the current liabilities. Since some of the current assets cannot be converted into cash quickly (e.g., inventory or prepaid expenses), a current ratio of 2.0 is thought to indicate sufficient liquidity. Creditors typically prefer that both these measures of short-term liquidity be as large as possible. However, because investments in current assets (especially cash and receivables) earn very small returns compared with the returns that can be earned from investments in long-lived assets, management must minimize the proportion of capital invested in current assets if it is to maximize its profit.

Debt-Management Ratios

DEBT-MANAGEMENT RATIOS: Measurements of a firm's ability to meet obligations involving debt.

While short-term creditors expect to be repaid from current assets, long-term creditors expect to be repaid from a firm's profits rather than from the cash or other liquid assets on hand when credit is granted. Recall that interest and principal payments on debt must be made as scheduled; for this reason, the larger the proportion of capital provided by creditors, the more likely it is that a firm will have difficulty meeting these payments should it be unprofitable for one or more periods. **Debt-management ratios** measure the ability of a firm to meet obligations involving debt. In general, debt-management ratios measure either (1) the excess of earnings over interest or (2) the proportion of debt in the firm's liabilities and equity.

TIMES INTEREST EARNED RATIO: Measurement of the excess of income available for interest payments over the amount of interest payments.

TIMES INTEREST EARNED RATIO   As we indicated in Chapters 10, 11A, and 11B, the rigidity of the payment schedules for a firm's obligations varies widely. Some liabilities, like accounts payable, have flexible payment schedules that can be modified when necessary. Other liabilities, primarily short-term and long-term debt, have specific payment schedules that must be met. The cash used to make the payments required by these debt obligations over their lives must come from profits. Therefore, analysts use the **times interest earned ratio** to indicate the excess of net income over interest. The larger the excess of net income over interest, the greater the probability that a firm will be able to meet the interest payments on current or contemplated obligations.

The amount of income available to cover interest is derived by adding interest and taxes to net income. Taxes are added to net income because they are paid after interest payments. (In other words, if income were just large enough to cover interest payments, taxes would be zero.) The equation used to calculate the times interest earned ratio is:

$$\text{Times interest earned ratio} = \frac{\text{Net income} + \text{Interest} + \text{Taxes}}{\text{Interest}}$$

Based on data from the 1989 and 1988 financial statements, The Limited's times interest earned ratio is developed in Exhibit 15–9. The Limited had suffi-

EXHIBIT 15–9   TIMES INTEREST EARNED RATIOS FOR THE LIMITED, INC.

(dollar amounts in thousands)	1989	1988
Net income	$346,926	$245,136
Interest	58,059	63,418
Taxes	227,000	151,000
Net income + interest + taxes	$631,985	$459,554
Times interest earned	**10.89**	**7.25**

cient income to cover its interest payments 10.89 times in 1989 and 7.25 times in 1988. Times interest earned increased in 1989 because income increased and interest decreased.

Now let us turn to the second type of debt-management ratio and consider four different ways of measuring the proportion of debt within a firm's capital structure.

DEBT: The sum of long-term debt and the debtlike obligations in current liabilities (notes or short-term loans).

DEBT TO EQUITY RATIO **Debt** is usually defined as the sum of long-term debt and the debtlike obligations in current liabilities (notes or short-term loans). Occasionally, debt is defined as the sum of long-term debt and current liabilities. We prefer the first definition and use it to demonstrate the computation of debt-based ratios.

Compared with equity, debt is a less expensive source of capital. (This is because interest payments are tax-deductible, whereas dividends to stockholders are not.) Debt, however, is riskier than equity because unless the interest and principal payments are made to creditors when due, the firm may fall into bankruptcy. In most firms, management attempts to achieve an appropriate balance between the cost advantage of debt and its extra risk. Although the appropriate amount of debt (both short-term and long-term) varies from firm to firm, in general, the greater a firm's use of *leverage* (i.e., the higher the proportion of total debt to a firm's total capital), the greater the likelihood that the firm will have difficulty meeting its obligations in some future period. Chapters 11A and 11B contain additional discussion of leverage.

DEBT TO EQUITY RATIO: Measurement of the proportion of capital provided by creditors relative to that provided by stockholders.

The **debt to equity ratio** measures the proportion of capital provided by creditors relative to that provided by stockholders. The equation used in calculating this ratio is

$$\text{Debt to equity ratio} = \frac{\text{Total debt}}{\text{Total equity}}$$

DEBT TO TOTAL ASSETS RATIO: Measurement of the proportion of total capital provided by creditors; most useful when equity is small or subject to substantial changes.

DEBT TO TOTAL ASSETS RATIO The proportion of total capital provided by creditors is also shown by the **debt to total assets ratio.** This ratio is most useful when equity is small or subject to substantial changes. The ratio is computed as the sum of long-term and short-term debt divided by total assets (or by total liabilities plus equity):

$$\text{Debt to total assets ratio} = \frac{\text{Total debt}}{\text{Total assets}}$$

EXHIBIT 15–10   DEBT RATIOS FOR THE LIMITED, INC.

(dollar amounts in thousands)	1989	1988
Long-term debt (A).............................	$ 445,674	$ 517,952
Debt in current liabilities.........................	–0–	–0–
Total debt (B)	$ 445,674	$ 517,952
Total shareholders' equity (C).....................	$1,240,454	$ 946,207
Total assets (D).................................	$2,418,486	$2,145,506
Debt to equity ratio (B/C)........................	.36	.55
Debt to total assets ratio (B/D)	.18	.24
Long-term debt to equity ratio (A/C)...............	.36	.55
Long-term debt to total assets ratio (A/D)...........	.18	.24

LONG-TERM DEBT TO EQUITY RATIO: Measurement of the proportion of capital provided by long-term creditors relative to that provided by stockholders; most useful when there is little permanent short-term debt.

LONG-TERM DEBT TO EQUITY RATIO   In some firms, the debt in current liabilities is not permanently outstanding. (Debt is not permanently outstanding if the firm does not intend always to have short-term debt outstanding. Thus, there will be times when there is short-term debt outstanding and other times when the short-term debt has been repaid and none is outstanding.) For these firms, the debt to equity ratio overstates the firm's actual debt burden. A more appropriate debt-management measure, when there is little permanent short-term debt, is the **long-term debt to equity ratio,** which measures the proportion of capital provided by long-term creditors relative to that provided by stockholders. The equation used to calculate the long-term debt to equity ratio is

$$\text{Long-term debt to equity ratio} = \frac{\text{Long-term debt}}{\text{Total equity}}$$

LONG-TERM DEBT TO TOTAL ASSETS RATIO: Measurement of the proportion of total capital provided by long-term creditors; most useful when there is little short-term debt and when equity is small or subject to substantial changes.

LONG-TERM DEBT TO TOTAL ASSETS RATIO   When there is little equity or when equity changes significantly from period to period, the long-term debt to equity ratio may not be indicative of the firm's debt burden. Therefore, analysts often construct the **long-term debt to total assets ratio** as a measure of the proportion of total capital provided by long-term creditors.

$$\text{Long-term debt to total assets ratio} = \frac{\text{Long-term debt}}{\text{Total assets}}$$

The four debt-based ratios are developed for The Limited in Exhibit 15–10. All four ratios indicate that The Limited employs a moderate amount of debt in its capital structure and that all the debt is long-term. Since long-term debt is normally somewhat less expensive than short-term debt, the absence of short-term debt seems prudent. The ratios also indicate that the proportion of debt in the capital structure declined in 1989.

Let us now examine another group of ratios, those that measure the efficiency with which a firm's operations are conducted. While long-term debt ratios are intended primarily for long-term creditors, the operating ratios discussed in the next section provide information for many different decision makers.

EXHIBIT 15–11   OPERATING RATIOS FOR THE LIMITED, INC.

(dollar amounts in thousands)	1989	1988
Revenues	$4,647,916	$4,070,777
Average accounts receivable*	563,816	522,781
Accounts receivable turnover ratio	**8.24**	**7.79**
Days receivables outstanding (365/receivables turnover ratio)	44	47
* (Beginning receivables + Ending receivables)/2		
Cost of sales	$3,201,281	$2,856,074
Average inventory*	444,571	380,350
Inventory turnover ratio	**7.20**	**7.51**
Days inventory on hand (365/inventory turnover ratio)	51	49
* (Beginning inventory + Ending inventory)/2		
Revenues	$4,647,916	$4,070,777
Average total assets*	2,281,996	2,037,492
Asset turnover ratio	**2.04**	**2.00**
* (Beginning total assets + Ending total assets)/2.		

Operating Ratios

OPERATING RATIOS (EFFICIENCY RATIOS): Measurements of a firm's intensity of use of its assets (e.g., receivables, inventory, or total assets).

Operating ratios (efficiency ratios) are measurements of a firm's intensity of use of its assets (such as receivables, inventory, or total assets). The principal operating ratios are measures of **turnover,** the average length of time required for assets to be consumed or replaced. These ratios provide managers and other users of a firm's financial statements with easily interpreted measures of the time required to turn receivables into cash, inventory into cost of goods sold, or total assets into sales. The less time required to turn over these assets, the more efficiently the firm is operating. Since well-managed, efficiently operated firms are usually among the most profitable, and since profits are the source of cash from which long-term creditors receive their interest and principal payments, creditors seek information about the firm's profit prospects from operating ratios. Stockholders find that larger profits are usually followed by increased dividends and higher stock prices, so they too are concerned with indicators of efficiency. Three different turnover measures are illustrated in Exhibit 15–11. Let us explain the receivables turnover ratio first.

TURNOVER: The average length of time required for assets to be consumed or replaced.

ACCOUNTS RECEIVABLE TURNOVER RATIO   The length of time required to record and collect payment for a credit sale is the time required to turn over accounts receivable. The **accounts receivable turnover ratio** indicates how many times accounts receivable is turned over each year. The more times accounts receivable turns over each year, the more efficient are the credit-granting and credit-collection activities of a firm.

ACCOUNTS RECEIVABLE TURNOVER RATIO: Measurement of the number of times accounts receivable is turned over each year.

The receivables turnover is computed by dividing net credit sales (credit sales less sales returns and allowances) by the average receivables balance:

$$\text{Accounts receivable turnover ratio} = \frac{\text{Net credit sales}}{\text{Average accounts receivable}}$$

For all ratios requiring an average balance for some statement item, the average is most frequently developed by taking half the sum of the beginning and ending balances. Average receivables, then, is the sum of beginning and ending receivables divided by 2.

Careful analysts examine quarterly or monthly financial statements, when available, to determine whether the amount of receivables recorded in the annual statements is representative of the receivables carried during the entire year. For example, retailers often have much larger receivables for some months after the Christmas selling season than during other parts of the year.

INVENTORY TURNOVER RATIO   Inventory turnover is the length of time required to record a purchase and then sell the purchased goods to customers. The **inventory turnover ratio** indicates the number of times inventory is turned over each year. The more efficient a firm, the more times inventory will be turned over each year. The inventory turnover ratio is computed by dividing the cost of goods sold by the average inventory. Average inventory is beginning inventory plus ending inventory divided by 2.

INVENTORY TURNOVER RATIO: Measurement of the number of times inventory is turned over each year.

$$\text{Inventory turnover ratio} = \frac{\text{Cost of goods sold}}{\text{Average inventory}}$$

As with the receivables turnover, careful analysts inspect quarterly and monthly statements to determine whether the annual financial statement amounts for inventory are representative of the amounts carried throughout the year. Businesses with strong seasonal fluctuations in sales often have substantial inventory fluctuations as well.

ASSET TURNOVER RATIO   The more sales dollars produced by each dollar invested in assets, the more efficiently a firm is considered to be operating. Thus another measure of the efficiency of a firm's operations is the asset turnover ratio. The **asset turnover ratio** is a measure of the intensity with which a firm's assets are used to produce sales revenues. The ratio is computed by dividing net sales by average total assets (beginning total assets plus ending total assets divided by 2):

ASSET TURNOVER RATIO: Measurement of the intensity with which a firm's assets are used to produce sales revenues.

$$\text{Asset turnover ratio} = \frac{\text{Net sales}}{\text{Average total assets}}$$

Operating ratios for The Limited for 1989 and 1988 are computed in Exhibit 15–11. For accounts receivable and inventory turnover, the ratios are also presented in days. Days receivables outstanding and days inventory on hand are developed by dividing the number of days per year by the turnover ratios.

A firm's ability to increase its receivables turnover ratio is limited by competitive considerations. If competitors allow customers a lengthy period before payment is expected, then the firm must offer similar credit terms or lose customers. In periods of high interest rates, the cost of carrying customers' receivables should not be underestimated. For example, a firm with credit sales of $5,000 per day that collects in 30 rather than 90 days would save $54,000 per year if it must pay 18 percent to borrow the funds to finance the increased receivables [(60 days)($5,000 sales per day)(.18)]. The data in Exhibit 15–11 indicate that The Limited's 1989 receivables turn over 8.24 times per year or are collected in an average of 44 days.

A firm's ability to increase its inventory turnover ratio is also partially affected by its competition. For example, if competitors stock large quantities of inventory, a firm must do the same or risk losing customers because of the unavailability of goods. Data in Exhibit 15–11 indicate that The Limited turned its inventory over 7.2 times per year in 1989 or that there was, on average, 51 days' sales of inventory on hand.

Now that we have examined both receivables and inventory turnover, let us combine these measurements to approximate the length of the operating cycle (the length of time required for an investment in inventory to produce cash). The Limited's 1989 operating cycle can be estimated by summing the number of days needed to turn over both receivables and inventory. Data in Exhibit 15–11 indicate that The Limited's operating cycle was 95 days (51 days for inventory to turn over and 44 days for receivables to be collected). The longer the operating cycle, the larger the investment necessary in receivables and inventory. When assets are larger, more liabilities and equity are required to finance the assets. Large amounts of capital negatively affect net income and cash flows for dividends as capital suppliers are paid. Therefore, firms attempt to maintain as short an operating cycle as possible. The Limited's operating cycle is relatively short, suggesting a well-managed business.

Care must be exercised when evaluating the asset turnover ratio. Some industries (such as electric utilities and farming) require a substantially larger investment in assets in order to produce a sales dollar than do other industries (such as fast-food restaurants, consumer products, and meat packing). Obviously, a firm's total assets turn over much more slowly than its inventories and receivables. The data in Exhibit 15–11 indicate that in 1989 The Limited's assets turned over slightly more than two times per year.

Operating ratios measure the efficiency of a firm's operations—a factor ultimately related to the firm's profits. Let us now examine some direct measures of a business's profitability.

Profitability Ratios

PROFITABILITY RATIOS: Measurements of (1) the contribution of the elements of operations to a firm's profit or (2) the relationship of profit to total investment and stockholder investment.

Profitability ratios measure two different aspects of a firm's profits: (1) the elements of operations that contribute to profit or (2) the relationship of profit to total investment and to investment of stockholders. The first group of profitability ratios (gross margin ratio, operating income ratio, and net income ratio) expresses income statement elements as percentages of total revenues. The second group of profitability ratios (return on assets and return on equity) divides measures of income by measures of investment required to produce income. All the profitability ratios are illustrated in Exhibit 15–12. Let us explain the gross margin ratio first.

GROSS MARGIN RATIO: Measurement of the proportion of each sales dollar that is gross margin.

GROSS MARGIN RATIO   You will recall from Chapter 2 that the gross margin is the excess of the selling price over the cost of the merchandise sold. The **gross margin ratio** (or gross margin rate), which is a measurement of the proportion of each sales dollar that is gross margin, indicates the effectiveness of pricing, marketing, purchasing, and production decisions and is determined by dividing gross margin by net sales:

$$\text{Gross margin ratio} = \frac{\text{Gross margin}}{\text{Net sales}}$$

In evaluating the gross margin ratio, the amount of gross margin must be examined as well. Although the gross margin ratio can be increased by increasing the selling price of merchandise, this action may decrease the amount of the gross margin if sales are decreased by the higher prices.

OPERATING INCOME RATIO: Measurement of the profitability of a firm's operations per sales dollar.

OPERATING INCOME RATIO   The **operating income ratio** (or *operating income rate*) indicates the profitability of a firm's operations per sales dollar. All operating revenues and expenses are included in operating income, but expenses, revenues, gains, and losses that are unrelated to operations are excluded. (For example, a retailer would exclude from operating income interest revenues produced by its credit activities.) The operating income ratio is expressed as follows:

$$\text{Operating income ratio} = \frac{\text{Operating income}}{\text{Net sales}}$$

The objective of this ratio is to measure the profitability of a firm's most significant operations. The higher the operating income ratio, the more profit the firm's operations produced per dollar of sales, an indication of effective and efficient management.

NET INCOME RATIO: Measurement of the proportion of each sales dollar that is profit; sometimes called the *profit margin.*

NET INCOME RATIO   The **net income ratio** (or *net income rate*) measures the proportion of each sales dollar that is profit; it is sometimes called the *profit margin.* This ratio is determined by dividing net income by net sales:

$$\text{Net income ratio} = \frac{\text{Net income}}{\text{Net sales}}$$

When evaluating the net income ratio, it is important to recognize that there is substantial variation from industry to industry in the profit per sales dollar. (For example, retail grocery stores have a very small amount of profit per sales dollar, whereas pharmaceutical manufacturers usually have a large profit per sales dollar.) Since net income is the result of many factors, changes in the net income ratio from period to period must be investigated to determine their cause if the ratio is to be informative to statement users.

Now let us examine two profitability measures that are based on income per dollar of investment.

RETURN ON ASSETS RATIO: Measurement of the profit earned by a firm through the use of all its capital.

RETURN ON ASSETS RATIO   The **return on assets ratio** measures the profit earned by a firm through the use of all its capital (or the total of the investment by both creditors and owners). Profit, or return, is determined for this ratio by adding interest net of tax to net income. As we indicated in Chapters 11A and 11B, interest net of tax = $(1 - \text{Tax rate})(\text{Interest})$. Interest is added to net income because it is a return to creditors for their capital contributions. The actual capital contribution made by creditors is included in the denominator (average total assets), and thus the numerator must be computed on a comparable basis. Average total assets is half the sum of the beginning and ending total assets. The equation for return on assets is

$$\text{Return on assets ratio} = \frac{\text{Net income} + \text{Interest (net of tax)}}{\text{Average total assets}}$$

Appropriate values for this ratio vary from industry to industry because of differences in risk factors. For instance, the return on assets for an electric utility ought to be smaller than the return on assets for a firm in the home appliance industry; firms in the home appliance industry have a much larger variability of net income because their operations are more sensitive to economic conditions.

RETURN ON EQUITY RATIO: Measurement of the profit earned by a firm through the use of capital supplied by stockholders.

RETURN ON EQUITY RATIO   The **return on equity ratio** measures the profit earned by a firm through the use of capital supplied by stockholders. Return on equity is similar to return on assets, except that the payments to creditors are removed from the numerator and the creditor's capital contributions are removed from the denominator. Therefore, return on equity is simply net income divided by average equity (beginning equity plus ending equity divided by 2):

$$\text{Return on equity ratio} = \frac{\text{Net income}}{\text{Average equity}}$$

One of the primary objectives of the management of a firm is to maximize the returns for its stockholders. Although there is no direct link between a firm's net income and the dividends and share price increases from which stockholders derive their return, the return on equity ratio is still an effective measure of management's performance for the stockholders. As is the case with return on assets, firms often differ in return on equity because of differences in risk. (For example, the return on equity for an electric utility should be lower than for a retail department store because of the lower sensitivity to economic conditions.)

The five profitability ratios for The Limited are developed in Exhibit 15–12. Note in the top panel of Exhibit 15–12 that the gross margin ratio, the operating income ratio, and the net income ratio are really component percentages from the income statement. In 1989 all three revenue-related ratios indicate increased profitability. This result suggests that The Limited has been able to keep the rate of growth in costs below the rate of growth in revenues.

The remaining two profitability measures, the return on assets ratio and the return on equity ratio, are based on income per dollar of investment. The return on assets ratio indicates the firm's profitability as a percentage of investment made by all suppliers of capital. The return on equity measure indicates the firm's profitability as a percentage of the investment by suppliers of equity capital. The Limited's return on assets and return on equity ratios were adequate in both years, though the return on equity ratio is clearly much better than the return on assets ratio. Note that return on assets is lower than the return on equity. Recall our discussion of leverage in Chapters 11A and 11B. When assets earn a higher return than is required to pay interest supplied by creditors, the excess return accrues to the stockholders and levers upward their return. For The Limited the return on equity exceeded the return on assets by 15.0 percent in 1989 and 15.3 percent in 1988. Therefore the average aftertax interest rate paid on The Limited's liabilities is considerably lower than the 16.7 or 14.0 percent earned on all assets. In part, the low average interest rate results from the fact that no interest is paid on many liabilities (for example, on accounts payable, accrued expenses, and deferred income taxes). In addition, The Limited's debt that does require interest is a deductible expense for income tax purposes and therefore carries an aftertax interest rate that is reduced by the tax rates of just less than 40 percent.

EXHIBIT 15–12   PROFITABILITY RATIOS FOR THE LIMITED, INC.

(dollar amounts in thousands)	1989		1988	
	AMOUNT	PERCENT OF SALES	AMOUNT	PERCENT OF SALES
Net sales	$4,647,916		$4,070,777	
Cost of goods sold	3,201,281		2,856,074	
Gross margin (and ratio)	$1,446,635	**31.1**	$1,214,703	**29.8**
General, administrative, and store operating expenses	821,381		747,285	
Operating income (and ratio).	$ 625,254	**13.4**	$ 467,418	**11.5**
Interest expense	(58,059)		(63,418)	
Other income (expense)	6,731		(7,864)	
Income before taxes	$ 573,926		$ 396,136	
Provision for income taxes	227,000		151,000	
Net income (and ratio)	$ 346,926	**7.5**	$ 245,136	**6.0**
Provision for income taxes	$ 227,000		$ 151,000	
Income before taxes	573,926		396,136	
Income tax rate (Provision for income taxes/ income before taxes)	39.6%		38.1%	
Interest net of tax [(1 − Tax rate)(Interest)]	$ 35,068		$ 39,256	
Net income	346,926		245,136	
Net income + Interest (net of tax)	$ 381,994		$ 284,392	
Average total assets (Exhibit 15–11)	2,281,996		$2,037,492	
Return on assets ratio		**16.7%**		**14.0%**
Net income	$ 346,926		$ 245,136	
Average stockholders' equity*	1,093,331		837,689	
Return on equity ratio		**31.7%**		**29.3%**

* (Beginning equity + Ending equity)/2.

We now turn to the last ratio category, those ratios that provide information primarily to stockholders.

Stockholder Ratios

Stockholder ratios (such as earnings per share, dividend yield, dividend payout, and price earnings) provide investors with measures of a firm's performance and stock returns that are relevant to investors' decisions. As we have seen, stockholders earn returns from stock ownership in two ways—from dividends and from increases in the market price of their stock. The relationships among financial statement data, dividends, and changes in stock prices constitute an area of

EXHIBIT 15–13   STOCKHOLDER RATIOS FOR THE LIMITED, INC.

	1989	1988
Net income	$346,926,000	$245,136,000
Weighted average shares outstanding (Exhibit 15–1)	180,644,000	180,093,000
Earnings per share ratio (EPS)	**1.92**	**1.36**
Dividends per share (Exhibit 15–4)	$.32	$.24
Market price per share:		
High	39⅞	27⅞
Low	25¼	16⅜
Dividend yield ratio (range)	**.8% to 1.3%**	**.9% to 1.5%**
Dividends per share	$.32	$.24
Earnings per share	1.92	1.36
Dividend payout ratio	**16.7%**	**17.6%**
Market price per share:		
High	39⅞	27⅞
Low	25¼	16⅜
Earnings per share	1.92	1.36
Price earnings ratio (P/E)	**13.2 to 20.8**	**12.0 to 20.5**

continuing accounting research.[2] Still, it is widely accepted that generally there are positive relationships of some form between net income and dividends and between net income and stock prices. The stockholder ratios presented here (and illustrated in Exhibit 15–13) should give investors information that will be helpful when deciding whether to buy or sell stock. Let us first examine the earnings per share ratio.

EARNINGS PER SHARE RATIO (EPS): Measurement of the income available for common stockholders on a per-share basis.

EARNINGS PER SHARE RATIO   **Earnings per share ratio, or EPS,** is a measurement of the income available for common stockholders on a per-share basis. EPS is one data item that is examined by nearly all statement users. EPS is conceptually very simple: net income less preferred dividends divided by the average number of common shares outstanding.[3] Remember that treasury shares are not considered to be outstanding. Preferred dividends are subtracted from net income because those payments are a return to holders of shares other than common stock. (Net

[2] For a discussion of accounting and its relationships to security prices, see George Foster, *Financial Statement Analysis,* 2d ed. (Englewood Cliffs, N.J.: Prentice-Hall, 1986), and William Beaver, *Financial Reporting: An Accounting Revolution,* 2d ed. (Englewood Cliffs, N.J.: Prentice-Hall, 1989).

[3] The Accounting Principles Board developed a lengthy set of rules by which earnings per share is computed. These rules are presented in *Accounting Principles Board Opinion No. 15.* For some firms, significant adjustments are made to both the numerator and the denominator of the ratio before determining earnings per share. We defer a discussion of these adjustments to later accounting courses.

income less preferred dividends is often called *income available for common.*) The equation for the earnings per share ratio is

$$\text{Earnings per share ratio} = \frac{\text{Net income} - \text{Preferred dividends}}{\text{Average number of common shares outstanding}}$$

DIVIDEND YIELD RATIO: Measurement of the rate at which dividends provide a return for the stockholder.

DIVIDEND YIELD RATIO The **dividend yield ratio** measures the rate at which dividends provide a return for the stockholder, by comparing dividends with the market price of a share of stock. The market price of the stock is the investors' current investment cost. In other words, the dividend paid per share is divided by the market price of each share:

$$\text{Dividend yield ratio} = \frac{\text{Dividends per share}}{\text{Market price per share}}$$

This ratio is affected by both the dividend policy of the firm and the behavior of the firm's stock price. Thus, because stock prices often change by substantial amounts over short periods, the dividend yield ratio is not stable. In fact, when a firm's stock is traded regularly, the market price is likely to change many times each day. For this reason, some analysts compute dividend yield based on the average stock price for a given period. Others use the highest and the lowest prices for a period and present the dividend yield as a range.

DIVIDEND PAYOUT RATIO: Measurement of the proportion of a firm's profits that are returned to stockholders immediately as dividends.

DIVIDEND PAYOUT RATIO The **dividend payout ratio** measures the proportion of a firm's profits that are returned to the stockholders immediately as dividends. To calculate this ratio, dividends per share are divided by earnings per share:

$$\text{Dividend payout ratio} = \frac{\text{Dividends per share}}{\text{Earnings per share}}$$

This ratio varies from firm to firm, even within a given industry. Most firms attempt to pay some stable proportion of earnings as dividends over time, and firms also are generally reluctant to reduce dividends unless absolutely necessary. The result of these two tendencies is that dividends per share are usually increased only when the firm is confident that higher earnings per share can be sustained. An increase in the dividend payout ratio is usually a signal to statement users that management is confident that future net income will be larger and sustainable.

Next, let us examine a stockholder ratio that reports on the stock market's assessment of a firm's future prospects relative to its current income—the price earnings ratio.

PRICE EARNINGS RATIO (P/E): Measurement of the market's risk assessment and growth expectations for a firm's net income.

PRICE EARNINGS RATIO The **price earnings ratio,** or **P/E,** measures the market's expectations regarding both risk and the future growth of the firm's net income. P/E is the market price per share of common stock divided by the earnings per share:

$$\text{Price earnings ratio} = \frac{\text{Market price per share}}{\text{Earnings per share}}$$

Firms whose net income is expected to grow substantially often have a high price earnings ratio. (The stock of such firms is often referred to as a *growth stock*). Firms that are thought to be risky investments usually have a lower price earnings ratio than consideration of the earnings growth factor alone would suggest. The difficulty mentioned earlier in selecting a market price for the dividend yield ratio also occurs with the price earnings ratio. The amount of earnings represents the results of operations for a given period. A stock price, on the other hand, is applicable only for some particular point in time. Thus some analysts use averages, and others use the stock price that is observed on the day earnings are reported.

The four stockholder ratios for The Limited are computed in Exhibit 15–13. For the two ratios that require the stock price, we have used the high and low prices for the year. Earnings per share increased significantly because of the large increase in net income while shares outstanding were nearly unchanged. The dividend yield ratio is nearly unchanged because the 33 percent increase in dividends per share was matched by an equivalent percentage increase in stock price. The dividend payout ratio declined somewhat because earnings per share grew more rapidly than dividends (41 percent versus 33 percent). The price earnings ratio range is essentially unchanged because stock price increased at about the same rate as earnings per share.

Two of the stockholder ratios, dividend yield and price earnings, are often reported in the daily stock exchange listings in business newspapers or the business section of many daily newspapers. They typically appear in a table like the one below.

| 365-day | | | | Div. | | Sales | | | | Net |
High	Low	Name	Div.	Yield	P/E	(100s)	High	Low	Last	Chg.
25½	11¾	Limited Inc	.24	1.7	14	3766	14¾	14¼	14¼	− ½

In the two left-most columns, the high and low price for the past year are listed. The next two columns contain the name of the company, followed by the current annual dividend. The fifth column contains the dividend yield ratio, followed by the price earnings ratio. The seventh column indicates the day's sales of the firm's stock, in 100s. The next three columns indicate the high, low, and last prices at which the stock traded. The right-most column indicates the change in the closing (last) price from the previous day.

In Exhibit 15–14, we summarize the financial ratios presented in this chapter. This summary should be a useful reference in solving problems and exercises that require the computation of ratios. In more advanced accounting texts, you may be presented with additional ratios; however, those introduced here are among the most widely used. Important steps in ratio analysis are developing data for comparisons and interpreting the effect of accounting alternatives on financial statement data (and thereby the ratios). In the next section, we discuss these topics.

EXHIBIT 15–14   THE FINANCIAL RATIOS

SHORT-TERM LIQUIDITY RATIOS

1. Current ratio $= \dfrac{\text{Current assets}}{\text{Current liabilities}}$

2. Quick ratio $= \dfrac{\text{Quick assets}}{\text{Current liabilities}}$

DEBT-MANAGEMENT RATIOS

3. Times interest earned ratio $= \dfrac{\text{Net income} + \text{Interest} + \text{Taxes}}{\text{Interest payments}}$

4. Debt to equity ratio $= \dfrac{\text{Total debt}}{\text{Total equity}}$

5. Debt to total assets ratio $= \dfrac{\text{Total debt}}{\text{Total assets}}$

6. Long-term debt to equity ratio $= \dfrac{\text{Long-term debt}}{\text{Total equity}}$

7. Long-term debt to total assets ratio $= \dfrac{\text{Long-term debt}}{\text{Total assets}}$

OPERATING RATIOS

8. Accounts receivables turnover ratio $= \dfrac{\text{Net credit sales}}{\text{Average accounts receivable}}$

9. Inventory turnover ratio $= \dfrac{\text{Cost of goods sold}}{\text{Average inventory}}$

10. Asset turnover ratio $= \dfrac{\text{Net sales}}{\text{Average total assets}}$

DATA FOR RATIO COMPARISONS

As pointed out earlier in the chapter, developing information from financial ratios requires that comparisons be made (1) among ratios of the same firm over time, (2) among ratios of similar firms over time, and (3) among ratios of similar firms at the present time. To fulfill their needs for a broad range of ratio and other financial statement data for individual firms and for groups of firms, classified by industry, analysts rely on several sources. Data for individual firms by industry are provided in *Industry Surveys,* which is published by Standard and Poors. The *Almanac of Business Industrial Ratios* (published by Prentice-Hall) provides 24 financial ratios for industry groups and for firms within those industries, on the basis of asset size. The Robert Morris Association publishes *Financial Statement Studies,* an extensive collection of aggregate financial statement ratios and other financial statement data by industry. Finally, Dun and Bradstreet, Inc., prepares a set of publications that includes financial ratios by industry.

PROFITABILITY RATIOS

11. Gross margin ratio $= \dfrac{\text{Gross margin}}{\text{Net sales}}$

12. Operating income ratio $= \dfrac{\text{Operating income}}{\text{Net sales}}$

13. Net income ratio $= \dfrac{\text{Net income}}{\text{Net sales}}$

14. Return on assets ratio $= \dfrac{\text{Net income} + \text{Interest (net of tax)}}{\text{Average total assets}}$

15. Return on equity ratio $= \dfrac{\text{Net income}}{\text{Average equity}}$

STOCKHOLDER RATIOS

16. Earnings per share ratio $= \dfrac{\text{Net income} - \text{Preferred dividends}}{\text{Average number of common shares outstanding}}$

17. Dividend yield ratio $= \dfrac{\text{Dividends per share}}{\text{Market price per share}}$

18. Dividend payout ratio $= \dfrac{\text{Dividends per share}}{\text{Earnings per share}}$

19. Price earnings ratio $= \dfrac{\text{Market price per share}}{\text{Earnings per share}}$

To illustrate how the information provided by financial ratios is analyzed, we will use data from Standard and Poors' *Stock Report* to show how comparisons of ratio data for similar firms for a series of years can indicate whether or not there are substantial performance differences among the firms. One group identified by Standard and Poors is the food processing industry. One of the ratios reported by Standard and Poors is the return on assets ratio. The return on assets ratio for several firms in the food processing industry for the years 1985–1989 are presented in Exhibit 15–15.

An examination of the return on assets ratios in Exhibit 15–15 indicates several things. First, the ratios taken together suggest that there was a small general increase in the ratio through 1987 and that there was a decline in 1988 and 1989. The data also indicate that Wrigley's return on assets was substantially larger than any of the other firms and that Kellogg's was a distant second. If one

EXHIBIT 15–15 **COMPARATIVE RATIOS**

FOOD PROCESSING INDUSTRY
Return on Assets Ratios, 1985–1989

	1989	1988	1987	1986	1985
Campbell Soup Company	.3	7.2	8.5	8.6	8.5
Hershey Foods	9.6	8.5	9.9	10.4	10.4
Kellogg Company	12.6	16.1	16.6	16.7	16.6
Quaker Oats	6.6	8.2	7.0	9.0	8.6
Ralston Purina	8.3	9.2	13.0	7.7	11.0
Sara Lee	7.1	7.1	6.9	6.7	6.8
Wm. Wrigley	22.6	20.6	17.5	14.4	13.2

were to rank the remaining five firms on the basis of their return on assets each year, no one firm would consistently outperform the others.

These firms have shown varying capacities to earn returns on their assets, and careful investors and creditors would incorporate these differences into their evaluations of the firms when considering whether or not or how to invest or lend.

When comparing financial analysis data across firms, analysts must know how the accounting numbers were developed. Often, differences in accounting estimates or accounting policies are responsible for what seem to be significant performance differences between firms. In the next section, we discuss some of the items that can cause these differences.

ACCOUNTING ALTERNATIVES AND FINANCIAL STATEMENT ANALYSIS

We indicated early in the text that many accounting amounts are not precise statements of a firm's assets, liabilities, equity, revenues, and expenses. In many cases, the amounts are estimates. Other amounts are determined largely by the accounting policies adopted by a firm's management. Certain portions of the financial statements contain more accounting items that can be substantially affected by accounting policy choices or estimates than other portions do. Careful analysts examine these statement items very closely, noting the particular accounting policies and estimates that underlie the data. Following is a list of statement items that analysts are most likely to consider:

REVENUES

1. *The policy employed for recognizing revenues on installment sales:* Are revenues recognized at the time of the sale, or are they recognized over the collection period?

2. *The tax component of sales revenue:* Are sales, value-added, excise, or producers' taxes included in revenues?

3. *Interest revenues:* Are customers' finance charges included as a revenue, or are they an offset against interest expense or some other expense?

EXPENSES

1. *Inventory accounting policy:* Is inventory valued on a FIFO, LIFO, or weighted-average basis?

2. *Depreciation:* What are the estimates used for expected life and residual value? What depreciation method is used?

3. *Depletion:* Are the estimates of recoverable reserves reasonable?

4. *Uncollectible accounts:* What method is used? Are the estimates appropriate?

5. *Warranties:* Do provisions cover actual expenditures?

6. *Pensions:* Does the firm expense the minimum or maximum amount for pensions?

7. *Postretirement benefits:* How does the firm account for the cost of postretirement benefits?

BALANCE SHEET

1. *Receivables:* Is the allowance for uncollectible accounts large enough?

2. *Inventories:* What inventory method is used? Are obsolete or unmarketable items written off as soon as the value decline is apparent?

3. *Property, plant, and equipment:* Will these assets provide future services that are sufficient to recover the undepreciated cost?

4. *Intangibles:* Do the intangible assets represent real economic advantages that justify the unamortized cost?

5. *Liabilities:* Are all the liabilities reported? Are they properly classified? Are estimated liabilities large enough?

Most firms assist statement users in identifying statement items that are affected by accounting policy choices by including as the first note to financial statements a list of the firm's important policy choices. In the following analysis, we will illustrate how the effects of accounting policies can be analyzed.

ANALYSIS
EVALUATION OF THE
EFFECTS OF USING
LIFO RATHER THAN
FIFO

The accounting policies note for K mart Corporation indicates that the firm uses the LIFO method to account for its inventory. The notes to the financial statements also indicate the FIFO cost of the inventory. Using these data, an analyst could construct the following table (dollar amounts in thousands):

	AS REPORTED USING LIFO	PROSPECTIVE AMOUNTS USING FIFO
Beginning inventory	$ 5,671,000	$ 6,569,000
Ending inventory	6,933,000	7,921,000
Cost of sales	21,745,000	21,655,000
Current ratio	1.86	2.09
Gross margin ratio	26.4%	26.7%

The data in the table indicate that FIFO beginning and ending inventories are larger than corresponding LIFO amounts, while LIFO cost of sales is larger than FIFO cost of sales. The current ratios are derived in part from these data. The FIFO-based ratio is, as you would expect, much larger than the LIFO-based ratio. However, the FIFO gross margin ratio is increased only slightly by the accounting policy choice.

The effects that this accounting policy choice have on the financial statements are representative of the kinds of effects that other similar accounting policy choices can have. Some analysts recast financial statements to a comparable accounting policy basis before evaluating comparative financial statements, comparative component percentage statements, or financial ratios.

In the next section, we will review the preparation and analysis of comparative financial statements, comparative component percentage statements, and financial ratios. Although the three general analysis techniques presented in this chapter are straightforward, the use of the techniques to develop information to help decision makers select from alternative courses of action is not at all straightforward. The review problem that follows is intended to provide additional insight into both the straightforward and the involved aspects of financial statement analysis.

REVIEW PROBLEM: FINANCIAL STATEMENT ANALYSIS TECHNIQUES

This review problem is based on the financial statements of Compaq Computer Corporation, a manufacturer of personal computers and workstations. The 1989 financial statements and associated notes for Compaq are reproduced on pages 709–725 as Exhibit 15–16. We selected Compaq because its growth has caused changes in its financial statements that should be revealed through financial statement analysis. You should examine the statements and the notes carefully before you continue with this review problem.

EXHIBIT 15–16   COMPAQ COMPUTER CORPORATION FINANCIAL STATEMENTS

REPORT OF INDEPENDENT ACCOUNTANTS

Price Waterhouse

To the Stockholders and Board of Directors of
Compaq Computer Corporation

In our opinion, the accompanying consolidated balance sheet and the related consolidated statements of income,
of cash flows and of stockholders' equity present fairly, in all material respects, the financial position of Compaq
Computer Corporation and its subsidiaries at December 31, 1989 and 1988, and the results of their operations and
their cash flows for each of the three years in the period ended December 31, 1989, in conformity with generally
accepted accounting principles. These financial statements are the responsibility of the Company's management;
our responsibility is to express an opinion on these financial statements based on our audits. We conducted our
audits of these statements in accordance with generally accepted auditing standards which require that we plan and
perform the audit to obtain reasonable assurance about whether the financial statements are free of material misstatement. An audit includes examining, on a test basis, evidence supporting the amounts and disclosures in the
financial statements, assessing the accounting principles used and significant estimates made by management, and
evaluating the overall financial statement presentation. We believe that our audits provide a reasonable basis for the
opinion expressed above.

Price Waterhouse

Houston, Texas
February 1, 1990

Compaq Computer Corporation
CONSOLIDATED BALANCE SHEET

	December 31, 1989	December 31, 1988
	(in thousands)	
ASSETS		
Current assets:		
Cash and short-term investments	$ 161,313	$ 281,179
Accounts receivable, less allowance		
of $11,467,000 and $14,368,000	530,228	428,338
Inventories	559,042	386,973
Prepaid expenses	61,916	18,152
Total current assets	1,312,499	1,114,642
Investment in affiliated company	58,673	35,731
Property, plant and equipment, less		
accumulated depreciation	705,475	428,937
Other assets	13,742	10,687
	$2,090,389	$1,589,997
LIABILITIES AND STOCKHOLDERS' EQUITY		
Current liabilities:		
Notes payable	$ 30,000	
Accounts payable	253,909	$ 238,634
Income taxes payable	20,100	23,135
Other current liabilities	259,439	218,078
Total current liabilities	563,448	479,847
Long-term debt	274,434	274,930
Deferred income taxes	80,872	20,666
Commitments and contingencies		
Stockholders' equity:-		
Preferred stock: $.01 par value; 10,000,000 shares		
authorized; none outstanding		
Common stock: $.01 par value; 150,000,000 shares		
authorized; 39,272,904 shares and 38,549,221		
shares issued and outstanding	393	385
Capital in excess of par value	363,973	340,200
Retained earnings	807,269	473,969
Total stockholders' equity	1,171,635	814,554
	$2,090,389	$1,589,997

The accompanying notes are an integral part of these financial statements.

Compaq Computer Corporation
CONSOLIDATED STATEMENT OF INCOME

| | Year ended December 31, | | |
	1989	1988	1987
	(in thousands, except per share amounts)		
Sales	$2,876,062	$2,065,562	$1,224,067
Cost of sales	1,715,243	1,233,283	717,336
	1,160,819	832,279	506,731
Research and development costs	132,474	74,859	47,104
Marketing and sales expense	332,592	235,035	142,774
General and administrative expense	206,129	162,328	83,222
Unrealized gain on investment in affiliated company	(13,691)	(9,683)	(4,468)
Other income and expense, net	18,776	2,893	10,034
	676,280	465,432	278,666
Income from consolidated companies before provision for income taxes	484,539	366,847	228,065
Provision for income taxes	165,010	119,296	92,709
Income from consolidated companies	319,529	247,551	135,356
Equity in net income of affiliated company	13,771	7,691	911
Net income	$ 333,300	$ 255,242	$ 136,267
Per common and common equivalent share:			
Net income	$ 7.77	$ 6.30	$ 3.59
Assuming full dilution	$ 7.76	$ 6.27	$ 3.57

The accompanying notes are an integral part of these financial statements.

Compaq Computer Corporation
CONSOLIDATED STATEMENT OF CASH FLOWS

	Year ended December 31,		
	1989	1988	1987
	(in thousands)		
Cash flows from operating activities:			
Cash received from customers	$2,771,724	$1,883,647	$1,094,414
Cash paid to suppliers and employees	(2,433,833)	(1,636,486)	(961,684)
Interest received	22,269	14,164	11,067
Interest paid	(38,898)	(19,596)	(12,070)
Income taxes paid	(134,619)	(98,094)	(84,795)
Net cash provided by operating activities	186,643	143,635	46,932
Cash flows from investing activities:			
Purchases of property, plant and equipment	(367,645)	(273,477)	(104,393)
Proceeds from sale of equipment	494	816	1,287
Purchases of other assets	(3,886)	(1,762)	(1,033)
Proceeds from sale of stock of affiliated company	10,815		
Net cash used in investing activities	(360,222)	(274,423)	(104,139)
Cash flows from financing activities:			
Proceeds from issuance of long-term debt		270,210	145,461
Proceeds from issuance of notes payable	30,000		
Proceeds from sale of equity securities	14,820	5,485	4,889
Repayment of borrowings	(444)	(143)	(73)
Net cash provided by financing activities	44,376	275,552	150,277
Effect of exchange rate changes on cash	9,337	4,139	(17,927)
Net increase (decrease) in cash	(119,866)	148,903	75,143
Cash and short-term investments at beginning of year	281,179	132,276	57,133
Cash and short-term investments at end of year	$ 161,313	$ 281,179	$ 132,276
Reconciliation of net income to net cash provided by operating activities:			
Net income	$ 333,300	$ 255,242	$ 136,267
Depreciation and amortization	84,575	49,006	22,438
Provision for bad debts	1,014	3,607	4,285
Equity in net income of affiliated company	(13,771)	(7,691)	(911)
Unrealized gain on investment in affiliated company	(13,691)	(9,683)	(4,468)
Realized gain on investment in affiliated company	(7,621)		
Deferred income taxes	29,315	13,017	(4,256)
Loss on disposal of assets	1,235	487	97
Exchange rate effect	5,727	(7,289)	7,625
Net change in net current assets excluding notes payable	(233,440)	(153,061)	(114,145)
Net cash provided by operating activities	$ 186,643	$ 143,635	$ 46,932

The accompanying notes are an integral part of these financial statements.

Compaq Computer Corporation
CONSOLIDATED STATEMENT OF STOCKHOLDERS' EQUITY

	Common stock		Capital in excess of par value	Retained earnings	Total
	Shares	Par value			
	(in thousands, except for shares)				
Balance, December 31, 1986	27,044,628	$270	$100,572	$ 82,460	$ 183,302
Issuance pursuant to stock option plans	772,408	8	4,881		4,889
Issuance on conversion of convertible subordinated debentures	6,352,431	64	72,042		72,106
Compensation expense associated with grant of nonqualified stock options			237		237
Tax benefit associated with stock options			2,731		2,731
Net income				136,267	136,267
Balance, December 31, 1987	34,169,467	342	180,463	218,727	399,532
Issuance pursuant to stock option plans	625,802	6	5,479		5,485
Issuance on conversion of convertible subordinated debentures	3,753,952	37	148,082		148,119
Compensation expense associated with grant of nonqualified stock options			205		205
Tax benefit associated with stock options			5,971		5,971
Net income				255,242	255,242
Balance, December 31, 1988	38,549,221	385	340,200	473,969	814,554
Issuance pursuant to stock option plans	722,886	8	14,812		14,820
Issuance on conversion of convertible subordinated debentures	797		52		52
Compensation expense associated with grant of nonqualified stock options			204		204
Tax benefit associated with stock options			8,705		8,705
Net income				333,300	333,300
Balance, December 31, 1989	39,272,904	$393	$363,973	$807,269	$1,171,635

The accompanying notes are an integral part of these financial statements.

Compaq Computer Corporation
NOTES TO CONSOLIDATED FINANCIAL STATEMENTS

NOTE 1 — SIGNIFICANT ACCOUNTING POLICIES:

The Company has adopted accounting policies which are generally accepted in the industry in which it operates. Set forth below are the Company's more significant accounting policies.

Principles of consolidation—

The consolidated financial statements include the accounts of Compaq Computer Corporation and its wholly-owned subsidiaries. The investment in Conner Peripherals, Inc., which represents a less than majority interest, is accounted for under the equity method. All significant intercompany transactions have been eliminated.

Inventories—

Inventories are stated at the lower of cost or market, cost being determined on a first-in, first-out basis.

Property, plant and equipment—

Property, plant and equipment are stated at cost. Major renewals and improvements are capitalized; minor replacements, maintenance and repairs are charged to current operations. Depreciation is computed applying the straight-line method over the estimated useful lives of the related assets, which are 30 years for buildings and range from three to ten years for equipment. Leasehold improvements are amortized over the shorter of the useful life of the improvement or the life of the related lease.

Intangible assets—

Licenses and trademarks are carried at cost less accumulated amortization, which is being provided on a straight-line basis over the economic lives of the respective assets.

Warranty expense—

The Company provides currently for the estimated cost which may be incurred under product warranties.

Revenue recognition—

The Company recognizes revenue at the time products are shipped to its dealers. Provision is made currently for estimated product returns which may occur under programs the Company has with its dealers and dealer finance companies.

Foreign currency translation—

Foreign operations are measured in U.S. dollars. Financial statements of the Company's foreign subsidiaries are translated to U.S. dollars for consolidation purposes using current rates of exchange for monetary assets and liabilities and historical rates of exchange for nonmonetary assets and related elements of expense; revenue and other expense elements are translated at the rates in effect on the transaction dates. Gains or losses resulting from this process are included in operations.

The Company hedges certain portions of its exposure to foreign currency fluctuations, principally through forward exchange contracts. Gains and losses associated with currency rate changes on such contracts are recorded currently, while the interest element is recognized over the life of each contract.

Income taxes—

The provision for income taxes is computed based on the pretax income included in the consolidated statement of income. Deferred taxes result from differences in the timing of recognition of revenue and expenses for tax and financial reporting purposes. Research and development tax credits are recorded to the extent allowable as a reduction of the provision for federal income taxes in the year the qualified research and development expenditures are incurred.

The Financial Accounting Standards Board has promulgated standards which will change the method of determining reported income tax expense. The effective date of such standards has been delayed until 1992. These standards, as currently set forth, will not have a significant impact on the Company's reported income tax expense when adopted.

NOTE 2 — SHORT-TERM INVESTMENTS:

The Company held the following short-term investments:

	December 31, 1989	December 31, 1988
	(in thousands)	
Money market instruments	$152,976	$163,067
Commercial paper		98,827
	$152,976	$261,894

All such investments are carried at cost plus accrued interest, which approximates market, and are considered as cash equivalents for purposes of reporting cash flows.

NOTE 3 — INVENTORIES:

Inventories consisted of the following components:

	December 31, 1989	December 31, 1988
	(in thousands)	
Raw material	$361,052	$220,243
Work-in-process	29,528	77,480
Finished goods	168,462	89,250
	$559,042	$386,973

NOTE 4 — PROPERTY, PLANT AND EQUIPMENT:

Property, plant and equipment are summarized below:

	December 31, 1989	December 31, 1988
	(in thousands)	
Land	$ 61,894	$ 31,511
Buildings	265,748	179,644
Machinery and equipment	377,318	223,922
Furniture and fixtures	35,069	20,945
Leasehold improvements	17,184	10,398
Construction-in-progress	120,873	56,650
	878,086	523,070
Less-accumulated depreciation	172,611	94,133
	$705,475	$428,937

NOTE 5 — INVESTMENT IN CONNER PERIPHERALS, INC.:

In 1986 the Company invested $12 million in Conner Peripherals, Inc. (Conner), which at that time was a development stage company. Net income for each of the years 1989, 1988 and 1987 includes pretax gains of $13.7 million, $9.7 million and $4.5 million, respectively, resulting from increases in the carrying value of the Company's investment in Conner. In each instance, the gain resulted from Conner's issuance of additional equity securities at prices higher than the per share carrying value of the Company's interest in Conner. Additionally, the Company realized a pretax gain of approximately $7.6 million in 1989 through the sale of one million of its Conner shares.

The market value of the Company's investment in Conner was approximately $150 million at December 31, 1989 as measured by the closing bid price of Conner's common stock in the NASDAQ National Market System. It is likely, however, that if the Company were to liquidate some or all of its investment in Conner, it would receive a substantial discount from the quoted market price. The aggregate, cumulative amount of Conner's undistributed earnings included in the Company's consolidated retained earnings was approximately $21 million at December 31, 1989. Conner is currently prohibited by certain contractual arrangements from paying dividends on its common stock.

In February 1989 Conner issued $75 million principal amount of convertible subordinated debentures due 2014. The debentures are convertible to Conner common stock at a price of $9.85 per share. In the event that all of such debentures were exchanged for common stock, the Company's percentage ownership of Conner would be reduced by 5%.

The Company made disk drive purchases from Conner during 1989 and 1988 of approximately $204 million and $122 million, and at December 31, 1989 and 1988 had balances owing to Conner of $22 million and $18 million, respectively. While the Company controls approximately 31% of the equity securities of Conner, the Company believes that purchases from Conner are made at market prices.

NOTE 6 — CREDIT AGREEMENT:

At December 31, 1989 the Company had an unsecured line of credit from a consortium of banks for $200 million, of which $170 million was available and unused. Borrowings under this credit agreement bear interest at either the base rate (10.5% at December 31, 1989), an interbank offered rate plus ⅜% or a market auction rate. The agreement provides for payment of commitment fees and requires maintenance of specified levels of working capital, stockholders' equity and tangible net worth to debt.

At December 31, 1989 the Company had outstanding borrowings under the agreement of $30 million, bearing interest at 9.18%. Fees paid and accrued under credit agreements aggregated $475,000, $612,000 and $449,000 in 1989, 1988 and 1987, respectively.

NOTE 7 — LONG-TERM DEBT:

At December 31, 1987 the Company had outstanding $149 million of 5¼% convertible subordinated debentures due 2012. During 1988 substantially all of the debentures were converted to 3,753,952 shares of the common stock of the Company. Similarly in 1987, $74 million of convertible subordinated debentures were converted to 6,352,431 shares of common stock. Deferred debt issuance costs of $4.3 million in 1988 and $2.3 million in 1987 were charged to capital in excess of par value as a result of the conversion of debentures.

On May 4, 1988 the Company issued $200 million of 6½% convertible subordinated debentures due in May 2013. The debentures are convertible any time prior to maturity into common stock of the Company at $65 per share, subject to adjustment in certain events. Substantially all of the debentures remained outstanding at December 31, 1989 and, at that date, 3,076,126 shares of common stock were reserved for issuance upon conversion of the outstanding debentures. The debentures are not redeemable by the Company prior to May 1, 1991, unless the closing price of the common stock of the Company shall have equaled or exceeded 150% of the then effective conversion price for a specified period of 20 trading days. Beginning May 1, 1999, the Company is required to make annual sinking fund payments of $10 million to retire the debentures. The debentures are subordinate to all other indebtedness for borrowed money. The Company incurred costs of approximately $3.9 million in connection with the issuance of the debentures. Such costs, which are included in other assets, are being amortized over the 25 year term of the debentures.

In October 1988 the Company concluded an agreement with a lender providing for the issuance of $150 million of ten-year mortgage notes. The notes are collateralized by land and buildings located in Houston, Texas having a net book value of approximately $148 million. Concurrent with the consummation of this agreement, the Company issued a note for $75 million, which bears interest at 9.77%. The interest rate on the outstanding note is to be reset at a market rate in October 1993. While the Company is currently making nominal principal payments on the note, $68 million of principal becomes due in 1998. The agreement provides the Company with an option for a period of two years from the date of the agreement to issue the remaining $75 million of notes, subject to certain conditions, for which the Company is paying a commitment fee of ¼%. The agreement requires specified levels of net worth and debt to total capitalization. Principal amounts due in each of the next five years are as follows:

Year	Amount
	(in thousands)
1990	$490
1991	540
1992	595
1993	656
1994	723

NOTE 8 — OTHER INCOME AND EXPENSE:

Other income and expense consisted of the following components:

| | Year ended December 31, | | |
	1989	1988	1987
	(in thousands)		
Interest and dividend income	($21,289)	($13,705)	($11,062)
Interest expense	40,388	22,757	12,466
Realized gain on investment in affiliated company	(7,621)		
Currency exchange (gains) losses, net	5,727	(7,289)	7,625
Loss on disposition of assets, net	1,235	487	97
Other, net	336	643	908
	$18,776	$ 2,893	$10,034

Interest aggregating approximately $6.4 million, $4.9 million and $1.7 million was capitalized and added to the cost of the Company's fixed assets in 1989, 1988 and 1987, respectively.

NOTE 9 — INCOME TAXES:

Domestic income from consolidated companies before provision for income taxes was $346 million, $245 million and $182 million in 1989, 1988 and 1987 while the foreign component of income before provision for income taxes was $139 million, $122 million and $46 million, respectively. The components of related income taxes were as follows:

| | Year ended December 31, | | |
	1989	1988	1987
	(in thousands)		
U. S. federal income tax:			
Current	$100,377	$ 70,100	$74,746
Deferred	28,738	15,641	(2,764)
Foreign income taxes:			
Current	31,467	33,143	18,886
Deferred	577	(2,624)	(1,492)
State income taxes	3,851	3,036	3,333
	$165,010	$119,296	$92,709

The principal items which cause the Company's effective tax rates to be less than the United States statutory tax rates are research and development tax credits and certain exempt income associated with export sales through the Company's Foreign Sales Corporation. Offsetting these items are state income taxes and the provision for taxes on the equity in net income of Conner. Additional factors contributing to a lower effective tax rate in 1988 were benefits associated with previously unutilized foreign tax credits and the effect of applying the reduced 1988 United States statutory tax rate to the cumulative unremitted earnings of offshore subsidiaries.

Deferred and prepaid taxes result from differences in the timing of revenue and expenses for tax and financial reporting purposes. Some of the more significant items resulting in deferred and prepaid taxes include unremitted earnings of international subsidiaries, intercompany profits which are not included in income for financial reporting purposes, reserves for inventory obsolescence, royalty payments and income associated with the Company's investment in Conner.

NOTE 10 — EARNINGS PER SHARE:

Earnings per common and common equivalent share and earnings per common and common equivalent share—assuming full dilution in all years were computed using the weighted average number of shares outstanding adjusted for the incremental shares attributed to outstanding options to purchase common stock and assuming conversion of outstanding convertible subordinated debentures at the beginning of the year or date of issuance, if later.

NOTE 11 — STOCKHOLDERS' EQUITY AND EMPLOYEE BENEFIT PLANS:

Equity incentive plans—

At December 31, 1989 there were 9,067,387 shares of common stock reserved by the Board of Directors for issuance under the Company's employee stock option plans. Pursuant to these plans, options are generally granted to all employees of the Company at the fair market value of the common stock at the date of grant and generally vest over four to five years. In limited circumstances, options may be granted at prices less than fair market value and may vest immediately. Vested options may not be exercised until the holder has been a full-time employee of the Company for one year. Options granted under the plans must be exercised not later than ten years from the date of grant. Options on 1,912,923 shares were exercisable at December 31, 1989. The following table summarizes activity under the plans for each of the three years ended December 31, 1989:

	Shares	Price per share
Options outstanding, December 31, 1986	3,184,359	
Options granted	1,924,338	$10.50-$55.38
Options lapsed or canceled	(155,535)	
Options exercised	(772,408)	.51-19.75
Options outstanding, December 31, 1987	4,180,754	
Options granted	1,818,717	47.38-65.13
Options lapsed or canceled	(124,223)	
Options exercised	(625,802)	.53-50.13
Options outstanding, December 31, 1988	5,249,446	
Options granted	1,467,735	67.63-105.50
Options lapsed or canceled	(122,373)	
Options exercised	(712,886)	.53-65.13
Options outstanding, December 31, 1989	5,881,922	

There were 3,185,465; 430,827 and 125,321 shares available for grants under the plans at December 31, 1989, 1988 and 1987, respectively.

In 1987 the stockholders approved a plan providing for the grant to all non-employee directors of the Company appointed after September 1, 1986 of an option to purchase 10,000 shares of the Company's common stock. The plan authorizes an aggregate of 100,000 shares to be issued. Grants of options under the plan are made at a price equal to the fair market value of the Company's common stock at the date of the director's initial appointment and are exercisable during the period beginning one year from such appointment and ending not more than ten years after such appointment. During 1987 options on 20,000 shares were granted at an average price of $22.00 per share. In 1988 options on 10,000 shares were granted at a price of $49.25. During 1989 no options were granted and options on 10,000 shares having an average exercise price of $28.75 were exercised. At December 31, 1989 options on the remaining 20,000 shares having an average exercise price of $32.25 per share were outstanding and exercisable.

Pursuant to a plan adopted by the Board of Directors in 1986, the Company granted to selected officers and key employees options on shares of Conner stock owned by the Company. Such options, which were granted at $.09 per share, vest ratably over four years and expire ten years from the date of grant. During 1989 options on 393,970 shares were exercised and options on 6,335 shares lapsed or were canceled. At December 31, 1989 options on 827,512 shares of Conner common stock were outstanding of which 654,944 were exercisable.

Compaq Computer Corporation Investment Plan—

The Company has an Investment Plan available to all domestic employees and intended to qualify as a deferred compensation plan under Section 401(k) of the Internal Revenue Code of 1986. Employees may contribute to the plan up to 14% of their salary with a maximum of $7,627 in 1989 ($7,979 in 1990). The Company will match employee contributions for an amount up to 6% of each employee's base salary. Contributions are invested at the direction of the employee in one or more funds or can be directed to purchase common stock of the Company at fair market value. Company contributions generally vest over three years although Company contributions for those employees having five years of service vest immediately. Company contributions are charged to expense in accordance with their vesting. Amounts charged to expense were $5.3 million, $4.2 million and $1.6 million in 1989, 1988 and 1987, respectively.

Stockholder Rights Plan—

The Board of Directors adopted a Stockholder Rights Plan in May 1989 which in certain limited circumstances would permit stockholders to purchase securities at prices which would be substantially below market value.

NOTE 12 — CERTAIN MARKET AND GEOGRAPHIC DATA:

Compaq Computer Corporation designs, develops, manufactures and markets personal computers for business and professional users. The Company has subsidiaries in various foreign countries which manufacture and sell the Company's products in their respective geographic areas. Summary information respecting the Company's geographic operations in 1989, 1988 and 1987 follows:

	United States and Canada	Europe	Other countries	Eliminations	Consolidated
			(in thousands)		
1989					
Sales to dealers	$1,569,611	$1,201,638	$104,813		$2,876,062
Intercompany transfers	796,944	31,220	250,354	($1,078,518)	
	$2,366,555	$1,232,858	$355,167	($1,078,518)	$2,876,062
Income from operations	$ 402,316	$ 85,476	$ 71,521	($ 32,123)	$ 527,190
Corporate expenses, net					42,651
Pretax income					$ 484,539
Identifiable assets	$1,352,086	$ 510,214	$ 90,472	($ 23,696)	$1,929,076
General corporate assets					161,313
Total assets					$2,090,389
1988					
Sales to dealers	$1,269,036	$ 734,502	$ 62,024		$2,065,562
Intercompany transfers	540,880	13,108	156,560	($ 710,548)	
	$1,809,916	$ 747,610	$218,584	($ 710,548)	$2,065,562
Income from operations	$ 291,497	$ 81,009	$ 42,820	($ 19,790)	$ 395,536
Corporate expenses, net					28,689
Pretax income					$ 366,847
Identifiable assets	$ 936,894	$ 348,366	$ 62,244	($ 38,686)	$1,308,818
General corporate assets					281,179
Total assets					$1,589,997
1987					
Sales to dealers	$ 905,317	$ 291,750	$ 27,000		$1,224,067
Intercompany transfers	253,043	329	39,880	($ 293,252)	
	$1,158,360	$ 292,079	$ 66,880	($ 293,252)	$1,224,067
Income from operations	$ 226,369	$ 16,045	$ 6,659	($ 13,395)	$ 235,678
Corporate expenses, net					7,613
Pretax income					$ 228,065
Identifiable assets	$ 620,708	$ 145,542	$ 24,580	($ 22,076)	$ 768,754
General corporate assets					132,276
Total assets					$ 901,030

In each year, the Company's hedging activities substantially offset the effects of changes in the value of the United States dollar relative to the currencies of those countries where the Company's foreign subsidiaries operate.

Products are transferred between countries at prices which are intended to approximate those that would be charged to unaffiliated customers in the respective countries. Transactions with one of the Company's Authorized Dealers accounted for 11%, 13% and 15% of consolidated sales in 1989, 1988 and 1987, respectively.

NOTE 13 — COMMITMENTS AND CONTINGENCIES:

The Company is subject to legal proceedings and claims which arise in the ordinary course of its business. Management does not believe that the outcome of any of those matters will have a material adverse effect on the Company's financial condition.

The Company leases certain manufacturing and office facilities under noncancelable operating leases with terms from one to 30 years. Certain of the leases contain renewal options at escalated rental rates. Rent expense for 1989, 1988 and 1987 was $24.9 million, $16.9 million and $10.4 million, respectively.

The Company's minimum rental commitments under all noncancelable operating leases at December 31, 1989 were as follows:

Year	Amount
	(in thousands)
1990	$ 23,112
1991	18,740
1992	13,028
1993	9,173
1994	7,531
Thereafter	33,822
	$ 105,406

NOTE 14 — SELECTED QUARTERLY FINANCIAL DATA (NOT COVERED BY REPORT OF INDEPENDENT ACCOUNTANTS):

The table below sets forth selected financial information for each quarter of the last two years.

	1st quarter	2nd quarter	3rd quarter	4th quarter
	(in thousands, except per share amounts)			
1989				
Sales	$682,863	$722,076	$682,980	$788,143
Gross profit	276,702	290,977	277,853	315,287
Net income	83,201	83,940	87,107	79,052
Net income per share:				
Net income	1.96	1.96	2.02	1.84
Assuming full dilution	1.95	1.95	2.02	1.84
1988				
Sales	439,471	456,790	501,634	667,667
Gross profit	176,367	183,040	200,726	272,146
Net income	46,846	58,621	57,870	91,905
Net income per share:				
Net income	1.21	1.46	1.40	2.18
Assuming full dilution	1.21	1.45	1.40	2.18

Through the first nine months of both 1989 and 1988, the Company estimated that its effective tax rate would be 35%. The actual effective tax rates were 34.1% and 32.5% in 1989 and 1988, respectively. The full benefit of the lower rate was recorded in the fourth quarter of each year. The inclusion of that portion of the benefit attributable to the first nine months had the effect of increasing fourth quarter earnings per share by $.08 in 1989 and $.14 in 1988.

There were no other unusual or infrequently occurring items or adjustments, other than normal recurring adjustments, in any of the quarters presented.

Compaq Computer Corporation
SELECTED CONSOLIDATED FINANCIAL DATA

	Year ended December 31,				
	1989	1988	1987	1986	1985
	(in thousands, except per share amounts and ratios)				
Sales	$2,876,062	$2,065,562	$1,224,067	$625,243	$503,880
Cost of sales	1,715,243	1,233,283	717,336	360,698	325,804
	1,160,819	832,279	506,731	264,545	178,076
Research and development costs	132,474	74,859	47,104	26,594	15,996
Marketing and sales expense	332,592	235,035	142,774	95,552	67,862
General and administrative expense	206,129	162,328	83,222	56,491	42,072
Unrealized gain on investment in affiliated company	(13,691)	(9,683)	(4,468)		
Other income and expense, net	18,776	2,893	10,034	9,372	8,364
	676,280	465,432	278,666	188,009	134,294
Income from consolidated companies before provision for income taxes	484,539	366,847	228,065	76,536	43,782
Provision for income taxes	165,010	119,296	92,709	31,908	17,187
Income from consolidated companies	319,529	247,551	135,356	44,628	26,595
Equity in net income (loss) of affiliated company	13,771	7,691	911	(1,731)	
Net income	$ 333,300	$ 255,242	$ 136,267	$ 42,897	$ 26,595
Earnings per common and common equivalent share:					
Net income	$ 7.77	$ 6.30	$ 3.59	$ 1.52	$ .97
Assuming full dilution	7.76	6.27	3.57	1.33	.90
Total assets	2,090,389	1,589,997	901,030	377,681	311,998
Long-term debt	274,434	274,930	148,915	72,809	75,000
Stockholders' equity	1,171,635	814,554	399,532	183,302	136,608
Ratios:					
Current ratio	2.3:1	2.3:1	2.0:1	2.2:1	2.4:1
Net income as a percentage of average total assets	18.1	20.5	21.3	12.4	9.8
Net income as a percentage of average stockholders' equity	33.6	42.0	46.8	26.8	21.7

PRICE RANGE OF COMMON STOCK

The Company's Common Stock is listed on the New York Stock Exchange and trades under the symbol CPQ. The following table presents the high and low sale prices for the Company's Common Stock for each quarter of 1989 and 1988, as reported by *The Wall Street Journal.*

	High	Low
1989		
1st quarter	75⅜	60½
2nd quarter	99⅝	69¾
3rd quarter	98¾	85⅜
4th quarter	111⅛	77
1988		
1st quarter	60¾	42½
2nd quarter	65⅛	47⅜
3rd quarter	65	50¾
4th quarter	60⅞	51¾

At December 31, 1989, there were 5,914 holders of the Company's Common Stock.

Using the Compaq financial statements and the analysis techniques described in this chapter, we will respond to the requirements listed below:

REQUIRED:

1. Evaluate Compaq's profit performance over the three-year period 1987–1989, using comparative component percentage income statements.

2. Identify any structural changes in the assets, liabilities, or equity of Compaq, using component percentage balance sheets.

3. The total assets of Compaq grew by $500,392,000 between 1988 and 1989. Where did the firm secure the resources for this investment in assets?

4. Compute the 19 financial ratios for Compaq for 1989 and, where possible, for 1988. Evaluate the information provided by these ratios.

SOLUTIONS:

1. An examination of the comparative component percentage income statements in Exhibit 15–17 indicates that the revenues of Compaq grew by 39.2 percent in 1989 and 68.7 percent in 1988. Profit growth was 30.6 percent in 1989 and 87.3 percent in 1988. Profit grew less rapidly than revenues in 1989 because of the following increases in component percentages: 1.0 percentage point increase in research and development costs, .3 percentage point increase

EXHIBIT 15–17   INCOME STATEMENTS

COMPAQ COMPUTER CORPORATION
Comparative Component Percentage Statements of Income

(dollar amounts in thousands)

| | YEAR ENDED DECEMBER 31 | | | | | |
| | 1989 | | 1988 | | 1987 | |
	AMOUNT	%	AMOUNT	%	AMOUNT	%
Sales	$2,876,062	100.0	$2,065,562	100.0	$1,224,067	100.0
Cost of sales.	1,715,243	59.6	1,233,283	59.7	717,336	58.6
Gross margin.	$1,160,819	40.4	$ 832,279	40.3	$ 506,731	41.4
Research and development costs.	132,474	4.6	74,859	3.6	47,104	3.8
Marketing and sales expense	332,592	11.6	235,035	11.4	142,774	11.7
General and administrative expense. .	206,129	7.2	162,328	7.9	83,222	6.8
Income from operations	$ 489,624	17.0	$ 360,057	17.4	$ 233,631	19.1
Unrealized gain on investment	13,691	.5	9,683	.5	4,468	.4
Interest expense	(40,388)	(1.4)	(22,757)	(1.1)	(12,466)	(1.0)
Other income (expense), net.	21,612	.7	19,864	1.0	2,432	.2
Income before income taxes.	$ 484,539	16.8	$ 366,847	17.8	$ 228,065	18.6
Provision for income taxes	165,010	5.7	119,296	5.8	92,709	7.6
Income from consolidated companies	$ 319,529	11.1	$ 247,551	12.0	$ 135,356	11.1
Equity in income of affiliated company	13,771	.5	7,691	.4	911	.1
Net income	$ 333,300	11.6	$ 255,242	12.4	$ 136,267	11.1

Note: Percentages do not always add to subtotals and totals because of rounding.

EXHIBIT 15-18   BALANCE SHEETS

COMPAQ COMPUTER CORPORATION
Comparative Component Percentage Balance Sheets

(dollar amounts in thousands)	YEAR ENDED DECEMBER 31			
	1989		1988	
ASSETS	AMOUNT	%	AMOUNT	%
Current assets:				
Cash and short-term investments	$ 161,313	7.7	$ 281,179	17.7
Accounts receivable, net.....................................	530,228	25.4	428,338	26.9
Inventories	559,042	26.7	386,973	24.3
Prepaid expenses	61,916	3.0	18,152	1.2
Total current assets	$1,312,499	62.8	$1,114,642	70.1
Investment in affiliated company	58,673	2.8	35,731	2.2
Property, plant, and equipment, net......................	705,475	33.7	428,937	27.0
Other assets..	13,742	.7	10,687	.7
Total assets	$2,090,389	100.0	$1,589,997	100.0
LIABILITIES AND STOCKHOLDERS' EQUITY				
Current liabilities:				
Notes payable...	$ 30,000	1.4		
Accounts payable......................................	253,909	12.2	$ 238,634	15.0
Income taxes payable	20,100	1.0	23,135	1.5
Other current liabilities................................	259,439	12.4	218,078	13.7
Total current liabilities	$ 563,448	27.0	$ 479,847	30.2
Long-term debt..	274,434	13.1	274,930	17.3
Deferred income taxes...................................	80,872	3.9	20,666	1.3
Total liabilities	$ 918,754	44.0	$ 775,443	48.8
Stockholders' equity:				
Common stock..	$ 393	.0	$ 385	.0
Capital in excess of par value...........................	363,973	17.4	340,200	21.4
Retained earnings	807,269	38.6	473,969	29.8
Total stockholders' equity	$1,171,635	56.0	$ 814,554	51.2
Total liabilities and equity	$2,090,389	100.0	$1,589,997	100.0

Note: Percentages do not always add to subtotals and totals because of rounding.

in interest expense, and .2 percentage point increase in marketing and sales expense. Profit growth in 1988 exceeded revenue growth because of the following changes in component percentages: 1.8 percentage point decrease in provision for income taxes, .8 percentage point increase in other income, .3 percentage point increase in equity in income of affiliated company, and .2 percentage point decrease in research and development costs. The 1988 profit growth occurred despite a 1.1 percentage point increase in cost of sales.

2. An examination of the comparative component percentage balance sheets in Exhibit 15–18 indicates that the total assets of Compaq grew by 31.5 percent in 1989, a smaller increase than the increase in revenues. The current asset component percentage decreased 7.3 percent (62.8 percent in 1989 versus 70.1 percent in 1988), while the property, plant, and equipment percentage increased by 6.7 percent and the investment in affiliated company increased

by .6 percent. Among the current assets, the largest change was the 10.0 percent decrease in cash and short-term investments. In 1989, liabilities were a smaller, and equity a larger, part of total liabilities and equity. Equity increased because of an 8.8 percent increase in retained earnings partially offset by a 4.0 percent decrease in capital in excess of par value. Liabilities decreased because of decreases in the accounts payable, income taxes payable, and other current liability component percentages.

3. Exhibit 15–18 indicates that Compaq has secured resources to finance its 1989 asset growth from (1) increases in retained earnings ($807,269 in 1989 versus $473,969 in 1988), (2) increases in current liabilities ($563,448 versus $479,847), and (3) issuance of additional common stock, indicated by common stock ($393 versus $385) and capital in excess of par ($363,973 versus $340,200).

4. The financial ratios for Compaq are computed as follows. All dollar amounts, except for per-share amounts, are in thousands.

SHORT-TERM LIQUIDITY RATIOS	1989	1988
1. Current ratio		
Total current assets.....................	$1,312,499	$1,114,642
Total current liabilities.................	563,448	479,847
Current ratio	2.33	2.32
2. Quick ratio		
Quick assets*.........................	$691,541	$709,517
Total current liabilities.................	563,448	479,847
Quick ratio...........................	1.23	1.48

* Cash and short-term investments plus accounts receivable.

Compaq's short-term liquidity ratios provide mixed signals. The current ratio is essentially unchanged, while the quick ratio has decreased because quick assets declined while current liabilities increased.

DEBIT-MANAGEMENT RATIOS	1989	1988
3. Times interest earned ratio		
Net income + Interest + Taxes	$538,698	$397,295
Interest	40,388	22,757
Times interest earned ratio	13.3	17.5
4. Debt to equity ratio		
Debt in current liabilities...............	$ 30,000	$ 0
Long-term debt	274,434	274,930
Total debt............................	$304,434	$274,930
Total stockholders' equity..............	$1,171,635	$814,554
Debt to equity ratio	.26	.34
5. Debt to total assets ratio		
Total debt............................	$ 304,434	$ 274,930
Total assets..........................	2,090,389	1,589,997
Debt to total assets ratio	.15	.17

6. Long-term debt to equity ratio

Long-term debt	$ 274,434	$ 274,930
Total stockholders' equity	1,171,635	814,554
Long-term debt to equity ratio	.23	.34

7. Long-term debt to total assets ratio

Long-term debt	$ 274,434	$ 274,930
Total assets	2,090,389	1,589,997
Long-term debt to total assets ratio	.13	.17

The debt-management ratios indicate that creditors are very secure, since Compaq uses relatively little debt to finance its assets. All the ratios except for times interest earned also indicate that creditors were more secure at the end of 1989 than at the end of 1988.

OPERATING RATIOS	1989
8. Accounts receivable turnover ratio	
Sales revenue	$2,876,062
Average accounts receivable*	479,283
Accounts receivable turnover ratio	6.00
Days receivables outstanding (365/6.00) .	61
*(Beginning receivables + Ending receivables)/2.	
9. Inventory turnover ratio	
Cost of goods sold	$1,715,243
Average inventory*	473,008
Inventory turnover ratio	3.63
Days inventory on hand (365/3.63)	101
*(Beginning inventory + Ending inventory)/2.	
10. Asset turnover ratio	
Sales revenue	$2,876,062
Average total assets*	1,840,193
Asset turnover ratio	1.56
*(Beginning total assets + Ending total assets)/2.	

Because balance sheet data for 1987 was not included in the 1989 Compaq financial statements, operating ratios could be prepared only for 1989. The turnover ratios for Compaq are all smaller than those calculated for The Limited. The receivables turnover difference is likely due to the fact that Compaq sells nearly all its computers on credit while The Limited makes many of its sales for cash or on bank credit cards. Thus, one would expect receivables to be relatively larger per dollar of sales for Compaq. The inventory turnover difference is due, in part, to the fact that Compaq's inventory includes parts required to manufacture computers as well as finished product while The Limited's inventory includes only goods ready to sell to customers. Compaq's asset turnover ratio, while lower than The Limited's, is very good for a manufacturer.

PROFITABILITY RATIOS

11.–13. Gross margin, operating income, and net income ratios

	1989		1988	
	AMOUNT	PERCENT OF SALES	AMOUNT	PERCENT OF SALES
Sales revenue	$2,876,062		$2,065,562	
Cost of sales	1,715,243		1,233,283	
Gross margin	$1,160,819	40.4	$ 832,279	40.3
Research & development	132,474		74,859	
Marketing and sales .	332,592		235,035	
General and administrative	206,129		162,328	
Income from operations.	$ 489,624	17.0	$ 360,057	17.4
Unrealized gain on investment	13,691		9,683	
Interest expense	(40,388)		(22,757)	
Other income, net . . .	21,612		19,864	
Income before taxes .	$ 484,539		$ 366,847	
Provision for taxes. . .	165,010		119,296	
Income from consolidated companies. .	$ 319,529		$ 247,551	
Equity in income of affiliated company.	13,771		7,691	
Net income.	$ 333,330	11.6	$ 255,242	12.4

14. Return on assets ratio

Provision for taxes. . .	$165,010
Income before taxes .	484,539
Income tax rate	34%
Interest expense	$40,388
Interest net of tax [(1 − Tax rate)(Interest)]	26,656
Net income.	333,300
Net income + Interest net of tax .	$359,956
Average total assets* .	$1,840,193
Return on assets ratio	19.6%

* (Beginning total assets + ending total assets)/2.

15. Return on equity ratio

Net income.	$333,300
Average stockholders' equity*	993,095
Return on equity ratio	33.6%

* (Beginning equity + ending equity)/2.

Compaq's profitability ratios are all excellent. Gross margin, operating income, and net income all compare favorably with those for The Limited, a very profitable retailer. The return on assets and return on equity ratios also compare favorably with those for The Limited and, in the case of the return on assets ratio, for the food processing firms identified in Exhibit 15–15.

STOCKHOLDER RATIOS	1989	1988
16. Earnings per share ratio (EPS)		
Net income...........................	$333,300,000	$255,242,000
Average number of common shares outstanding for purposes of calculating earnings per share*.....................	42,895,753	40,514,603
Earnings per share ratio	$7.77	$6.30

* Cannot be calculated from common shares outstanding because Compaq has other securities and stock options outstanding that are considered to be the equivalent of common shares for purposes of calculating earnings per share. Numbers inferred from earnings per share reported on Compaq's income statement.

STOCKHOLDER RATIOS	1989	1988
17. Dividend yield ratio		
Cash dividends per share	$ –0–	$–0–
Market price:*		
High	$111⅛	$65⅛
Low.................................	60½	42½
Dividend yield ratio	0%	0%
18. Dividend payout ratio		
Cash dividends per share	$ –0–	$ –0–
Earnings per share	$7.77	$6.30
Dividend payout ratio	0%	0%
19. Price earnings ratio (P/E)		
Market price:*		
High	$111⅛	$65⅛
Low.................................	60½	42½
Earnings per share	$7.77	$6.30
Price earnings ratio (range)	7.8 to 14.3	6.7 to 10.3

* From a stock price table in a business newspaper.

The dividend yield and dividend payout ratios are not meaningful for Compaq because no dividends were paid. Earnings per share increased from 1988 to 1989 because of the increase in net income despite the increase in the number of shares of common stock outstanding. Compaq's stock price increased in 1989 by more than the earnings per share increase, so the price earnings ratio range increased as well. If Compaq continues to be increasingly profitable, then one would expect the stock price to continue to increase, keeping the price earnings ratio high.

SUMMARY

The role of information is to help decision makers choose among alternative courses of action. Analysis of financial statement data can provide decision makers with information that is helpful in evaluating the consequences of different choices. The first section of the chapter described some typical decision situations in which financial statement data can be helpful — granting of credit, investment, customer activities, selling activities, and employment.

Next, three techniques used to develop information from financial statements were described — examination of comparative financial statements, examination of comparative component percentage statements, and ratio analysis. Comparative financial statements are side-by-side presentations of the same statement for two or more accounting periods. Component percentage statements recast a financial statement, with each item presented as a percentage of the largest amount on the statement. Comparative component percentage statements are side-by-side presentations of consecutive component percentage statements. Both comparative and comparative component percentage statements are useful for detecting important changes in financial statement items. The use of comparative component percentage statements was illustrated with a brief analysis of the financial statements of The Limited, Inc.

The next portion of the chapter used The Limited's financial statements to explain the preparation of the five types of ratios: (1) short-term liquidity, (2) debt-management, (3) operating, (4) profitability, and (5) stockholder. Each type of ratio provides information for different decisions. Short-term liquidity ratios aid short-term creditors. Debt-management ratios help long-term creditors assess the likelihood of eventual repayment. Operating ratios help customers, creditors, stockholders, and others determine the efficiency of some parts of a firm's operations. Profitability ratios indicate the components of profit and returns to suppliers of capital. Stockholder ratios provide data on a firm's performance and returns to the stockholders.

Sources of data for comparison, the cornerstone of all financial statement analysis, were suggested and illustrated. The effect of accounting alternatives on financial statement analysis was also examined and illustrated. The chapter concluded with a review problem that illustrated the three general analysis techniques and their use in statement analysis.

KEY TERMS

ACCOUNTS RECEIVABLE TURNOVER RATIO (p. 695)

ASSET TURNOVER RATIO (p. 696)

COMPARATIVE COMPONENT PERCENTAGE STATEMENTS (p. 687)

COMPARATIVE FINANCIAL STATEMENTS (p. 683)

COMPONENT PERCENTAGE STATEMENTS (p. 687)

CURRENT RATIO (p. 690)

DEBT (p. 693)

DEBT-MANAGEMENT RATIOS (p. 692)

DEBT TO EQUITY RATIO (p. 693)

DEBT TO TOTAL ASSETS RATIO (p. 693)

DIVIDEND PAYOUT RATIO (p. 702)

DIVIDEND YIELD RATIO (p. 702)

EARNINGS PER SHARE RATIO (EPS) (p. 701)

GROSS MARGIN RATIO (p. 697)

INVENTORY TURNOVER RATIO (p. 696)

LONG-TERM DEBT TO EQUITY RATIO (p. 694)

LONG-TERM DEBT TO TOTAL ASSETS RATIO (p. 694)

NET INCOME RATIO (p. 698)

OPERATING INCOME RATIO (p. 698)

OPERATING RATIOS (EFFICIENCY RATIOS) (p. 695)

PRICE EARNINGS RATIO (P/E) (p. 702)

PROFITABILITY RATIOS (p. 697)

QUICK RATIO (p. 691)

RATIO ANALYSIS (p. 690)

RETURN ON ASSETS RATIO (p. 698)

RETURN ON EQUITY RATIO (p. 699)

SHORT-TERM LIQUIDITY RATIOS (p. 690)

STOCKHOLDER RATIOS (p. 700)

TIMES INTEREST EARNED RATIO (p. 692)

TURNOVER (p. 695)

QUESTIONS

Q15-1. What is a decision?

Q15-2. How can information alter a decision?

Q15-3. What are some common decision-making situations in which financial statement data may be helpful?

Q15-4. What are comparative financial statements? How can comparative financial statements aid in decision making?

Q15-5. What are comparative component percentage statements? What kinds of information about a firm do they help detect?

Q15-6. When are comparative component percentage statements helpful?

Q15-7. What are the five basic types of financial ratios?

Q15-8. For which kinds of decisions is each of the five types of ratios helpful?

Q15-9. Are larger amounts always preferred over smaller amounts for financial ratios? Why?

Q15-10. Why must financial statement analysis be based on comparison?

Q15-11. To which kind of data can comparisons be made in financial statement analysis?

Q15-12. In a typical retail business, which accounting alternatives would tend to increase income?

EXERCISES

E15-13. COMPARATIVE INCOME STATEMENT DATA Consolidated income statements for Toys "R" Us appear below:

TOYS "R" US, INC. AND SUBSIDIARIES
Statements of Consolidated Earnings

(in thousands)			Fiscal Year Ended
	January 29 1989	January 31 1988	February 1 1987
Net sales	$4,000,192	$3,136,568	$2,444,903
Costs and expenses:			
Cost of sales	2,766,543	2,157,017	1,668,209
Selling, advertising, general and administrative . . .	736,329	584,120	458,528
Depreciation and amortization.	54,564	43,716	33,288
Interest expense	25,812	13,849	7,890
Interest and other income.	(11,880)	(8,056)	(7,229)
	3,571,368	2,790,646	2,160,686
Earnings before taxes on income	428,824	345,922	284,217
Taxes on income.	160,800	142,000	132,000
Net earnings	$ 268,024	$ 203,922	$ 152,217

REQUIRED:

1. By what percentage did sales increase between 1987 and 1988? Between 1988 and 1989?

2. By what percentage did each of the other income statement items change?

3. Why did net earnings (net income) increase at a faster rate than sales in 1989 and 1988?

E15-14. COMPARATIVE BALANCE SHEETS   Consolidated balance sheets for Toys "R" Us appear below:

TOYS "R" US, INC. AND SUBSIDIARIES
Consolidated Balance Sheets

(in thousands)	Fiscal Year Ended	
	January 29 1989	January 31 1988
ASSETS		
Current Assets:		
Cash and short-term investments	$ 122,912	$ 45,996
Accounts receivable	68,030	62,144
Merchandise inventories	931,120	772,833
Prepaid expenses	10,822	5,050
Total Current Assets	1,132,884	886,023
Property and Equipment:		
Real estate (net)	951,788	762,082
Other (net)	436,264	351,037
Leased property under capital leases (net)	8,910	11,397
Other Assets	25,114	16,520
	$2,554,960	$2,027,059
LIABILITIES AND STOCKHOLDERS' EQUITY		
Current Liabilities:		
Short-term notes payable to banks	$ 76,133	$ 17,657
Accounts payable	505,370	403,105
Accrued expenses	240,928	169,227
Income taxes	55,839	71,003
Total Current Liabilities	878,270	660,992
Deferred income taxes	78,819	53,356
Long-term debt	174,184	177,390
Stockholders' Equity:		
Common stock, par value $.10 per share	13,164	13,053
Additional paid-in capital	305,739	252,493
Retained earnings	1,122,445	854,421
Foreign currency translation adjustment	28,049	23,586
Treasury shares at cost	(43,407)	(5,929)
Other	(2,303)	(2,303)
Total Stockholders' Equity	1,423,687	1,135,321
	$2,554,960	$2,027,059

REQUIRED:

1. By what percentage did total assets increase between 1988 and 1989?

2. By what percentage did each of the other balance sheet items change?

3. From what sources does Toys "R" Us appear to have secured the resources for its asset increase?

E15-15. USING COMPARATIVE FINANCIAL STATEMENT DATA   The consolidated 1989, 1988, and 1987 income statements for E. I. duPont de Nemours and Company appear below:

E. I. duPont de Nemours and Company
Consolidated Income Statement

(in millions)

	1989	1988	1987
Net Sales.	$35,534	$32,360	$29,931
Cost of Goods Sold.	19,604	17,900	16,613
Selling, General and Administrative Expenses	3,377	3,065	2,716
Depreciation, Depletion and Amortization.	2,530	2,216	2,225
Petroleum Exploration Expenses.	430	468	459
Research and Development Expense.	1,387	1,319	1,223
Interest Expense	623	428	435
Taxes Other Than on Income.	3,716	3,578	3,085
Total.	31,667	28,974	26,756
Other income	457	411	413
Earnings Before Income Taxes	4,324	3,797	3,588
Provision for Income Taxes	1,844	1,607	1,802
Net Income.	$ 2,480	$ 2,190	$ 1,802

REQUIRED:

1. By how much did sales; cost of goods sold; gross margin; and research and development expense increase between 1988 and 1989? Between 1987 and 1988?

2. What was duPont's tax rate in 1989, 1988, and 1987?

3. Why did net income increase by a larger percentage than sales in 1989 and 1988?

E15-16. COMPARISONS BETWEEN YEARS   The consolidated 1989 and 1988 balance sheets for E. I. duPont de Nemours and Company appear below:

E. I. duPont de Nemours and Company

Consolidated Balance Sheet

(in millions)

December 31	1989	1988
Assets		
Current Assets:		
Cash and Cash Equivalents	$ 692	$ 603
Receivables	5,298	4,815
Inventories	4,910	4,467
Prepaid Expenses	444	353
Total Current Assets	11,344	10,238
Property, Plant, and Equipment	40,812	36,879
Less: Accumulated Depreciation	21,936	19,658
	18,876	17,221
Investment in Affiliate	858	628
Other Assets	3,637	2,632
Total	$34,715	$30,719
Liabilities and Stockholders' Equity		
Current Liabilities:		
Accounts Payable	$ 2,889	$ 2,540
Short-Term Borrowings	3,839	2,075
Income Taxes Payable	387	209
Other Accrued Liabilities	2,233	1,872
Total Current Liabilities	9,348	6,696
Long-Term Borrowings	4,149	3,232
Other Liabilities	2,260	2,203
Deferred Income Taxes Payable	3,037	2,899
Total Liabilities	18,794	15,030
Minority Interest in Consolidated Subsidiary	123	109
Stockholders' Equity		
Preferred Stock	237	237
Common Stock	411	399
Additional Paid-In Capital	4,399	4,595
Reinvested Earnings	10,751	10,349
Total Stockholders' Equity	15,798	15,580
Total	$34,715	$30,719

REQUIRED:

1. By what percentage did duPont's total assets increase during 1989?

2. Have any of the asset categories experienced larger increases than others?

3. Where had duPont acquired the capital to finance its asset growth?

4. Have any of the individual liability or equity items increased at a rate different from the rate at which total liabilities and equity have increased?

E15-17.   USING COMPONENT PERCENTAGE STATEMENTS   The following comparative component percentage income statements and balance sheets are available for Bryant Products Company:

BRYANT PRODUCTS COMPANY
Comparative Component Percentage Statements of Income

| | YEAR ENDED MAY 31 | | | | | |
| | 1990 | | 1989 | | 1988 | |
	AMOUNT	%	AMOUNT	%	AMOUNT	%
Revenues....................	$901,170	100.0	$728,035	100.0	$661,850	100.0
Costs and expenses						
Cost of sales.................	$539,801	59.9	$439,005	60.3	$401,743	60.7
Selling and administrative	318,113	35.3	206,034	28.3	176,052	26.6
Interest.....................	17,122	1.9	18,201	2.5	17,208	2.6
Other expenses (income)	9,913	1.1	2,912	.4	(1,324)	(0.2)
	$884,949	98.2	$666,152	91.5	$593,679	89.7
Income before provision for income taxes	$ 16,221	1.8	$ 61,883	8.5	$ 68,171	10.3
Provision for income taxes.........	4,506	.5	22,569	3.1	23,827	3.6
Net income	$ 11,715	1.3	$ 39,314	5.4	$ 44,344	6.7

BRYANT PRODUCTS COMPANY
Comparative Component Percentage Balance Sheets

| | AS OF MAY 31 | | | | | |
| | 1990 | | 1989 | | 1988 | |
	AMOUNT	%	AMOUNT	%	AMOUNT	%
ASSETS						
Current assets....................	$147,129	31.4	$ 62,417	14.3	$ 66,927	16.1
Investment......................	30,925	6.6	95,589	21.9	91,453	22.0
Property, plant, and equipment (net)	270,831	57.8	261,015	59.8	241,519	58.1
Other assets	19,680	4.2	17,459	4.0	15,796	3.8
Total assets	$468,565	100.0	$436,480	100.0	$415,695	100.0
LIABILITIES AND STOCKHOLDERS' EQUITY						
Current liabilities..................	$ 68,410	14.6	$ 29,244	6.7	$ 28,683	6.9
Long-term debt	152,284	32.5	162,807	37.3	152,976	36.8
Total liabilities	$220,694	47.1	$192,051	44.0	$181,659	43.7
Common stock....................	$183,209	39.1	$183,322	42.0	$171,266	41.2
Retained earnings.................	64,662	13.8	61,107	14.0	62,770	15.1
Total stockholders' equity.........	$247,871	52.9	$244,429	56.0	$234,036	56.3
Total liabilities and stockholders' equity..........	$468,565	100.0	$436,480	100.0	$415,695	100.0

REQUIRED:

1. Why did income from operations decrease in 1989 and 1990 while sales increased?

2. Has the proportion of resources invested in the various asset categories changed?

3. Has the proportion of capital supplied by creditors changed?

4. From what sources did Bryant secure the capital to finance its increase in current assets in 1990?

E15-18. PREPARATION OF COMPONENT PERCENTAGE STATEMENTS   Condensed financial statements for K mart Corporation appear below.

K mart Corporation
Consolidated Statements of Income

(millions)	Fiscal Year Ended		
	January 31, 1990	January 25, 1989	January 27, 1988
Sales	$29,533	$27,301	$25,627
Cost of merchandise sold	21,745	19,914	18,564
Selling, general, and administrative expenses	6,071	5,603	5,296
Advertising	571	581	617
Interest expense	380	346	330
Other expenses (income)	251	(387)	(351)
Income before income taxes	515	1,244	1,171
Taxes on income	192	441	479
Net earnings	$ 323	$ 803	$ 692

K mart Corporation
Consolidated Statements of Income

(millions)	January 31, 1990	January 25, 1989
Assets		
Current Assets:		
Cash	$ 353	$ 948
Merchandise inventories	6,933	5,671
Accounts receivable	698	527
Total current assets	7,984	7,146
Investments in Affiliated Retail Companies	512	506
Property and Equipment—net	3,850	3,896
Other Assets and Deferred Charges	799	578
	$13,145	$12,126
Liabilities and Shareholders' Equity		
Current Liabilities:		
Long-term debt due within one year	$ 11	$ 1
Notes payable	601	—
Accounts payable	2,319	2,334
Accrued liabilities	1,152	931
Income taxes	216	226
Total current liabilities	4,299	3,492
Long-Term Debt	3,029	2,946
Other Long-Term Liabilities	745	459
Deferred Income Taxes	100	220
Shareholders' Equity:		
Common stock	205	204
Capital in excess of par value	601	588
Retained earnings	4,341	4,345
Treasury shares	(146)	(131)
Foreign currency translation adjustment	(29)	3
Total shareholders' equity	4,972	5,009
	$13,145	$12,126

REQUIRED:

1. Prepare comparative component percentage income statements for K mart for 1990, 1989, and 1988. Prepare component percentage balance sheets for K mart for 1990 and 1989.

2. Did gross margin grow as much as sales between 1988 and 1989? Between 1989 and 1990? If so, why?

3. Did the relative proportion of K mart's assets change between 1989 and 1990? If so, how?

4. Did the relative proportion of K mart's liabilities and equity change between 1989 and 1990? If so, how?

5. How does K mart appear to have financed the 8.4 percent increase in assets that occurred between 1989 and 1990?

E15-19. SHORT-TERM LIQUIDITY RATIOS   The financial statements for Eastman Kodak Company appear below:

Consolidated Statement of Earnings

Eastman Kodak Company and Subsidiary Companies

	1989	1988	1987
		(in millions)	
Sales			
Sales to: Customers in the United States.	$10,302	$ 9,554	$ 7,611
Customers outside the United States.	8,096	7,480	5,694
TOTAL SALES	18,398	17,034	13,305
Costs			
Cost of goods sold	11,075	9,727	8,037
Sales, advertising, distribution, and administrative expenses.	4,857	4,495	3,190
Restructuring costs.	875	—	—
Total costs and expenses.	16,807	14,222	11,227
Earnings			
EARNINGS FROM OPERATIONS	1,591	2,812	2,078
Investment income.	148	132	83
Interest expense	(895)	(697)	(181)
Other income (expense)	81	(11)	4
Earnings before income taxes	925	2,236	1,984
Provision for United States, foreign, and other income taxes	396	839	806
NET EARNINGS.	$ 529	$ 1,397	$ 1,178

Consolidated Statement of Financial Condition

Eastman Kodak Company and Subsidiary Companies

	Dec. 31, 1989	Dec. 25, 1988
	(in millions)	
ASSETS		
Current Assets		
Cash	$ 1,095	$ 848
Marketable securities	184	227
Receivables	4,245	4,071
Inventories	2,507	3,025
Prepaid charges (expenses)	254	241
Other current assets	306	272
Total current assets	8,591	8,684
Properties		
Land, buildings, machinery, and equipment at cost	16,774	15,667
Less: Accumulated depreciation	8,146	7,654
Net properties	8,628	8,013
Other Assets		
Unamortized goodwill	4,579	4,610
Long-term receivables and other noncurrent assets	1,854	1,657
TOTAL ASSETS	$23,652	$22,964
LIABILITIES AND SHAREOWNERS' EQUITY		
Current Liabilities		
Payables	$ 6,073	$ 5,277
Taxes—income and other	338	411
Dividends payable	162	162
Total current liabilities	6,573	5,850
Other Liabilities and Deferred Credits		
Long-term borrowings	7,376	7,779
Other long-term liabilities	1,371	990
Deferred income tax credits	1,690	1,565
Total liabilities and deferred credits	17,010	16,184
Shareowners' Equity		
Common stock, par value $2.50 per share	934	934
Additional capital paid-in or transferred from retained earnings	6	1
Retained earnings	7,802	7,922
Accumulated translation adjustment	(41)	(18)
	8,701	8,839
Less: Treasury stock at cost	2,059	2,059
Total shareowners' equity	6,642	6,780
TOTAL LIABILITIES AND SHAREOWNERS' EQUITY	$23,652	$22,964

REQUIRED:

1. Compute the current ratio for 1989 and 1988.

2. Compute the quick ratio for 1989 and 1988.

E15-20. DEBT-MANAGEMENT RATIOS   Use the Eastman Kodak financial statements in Exercise 15–19 to respond to the following requirements.

REQUIRED:

1. Compute the five debt-management ratios for 1989 and 1988.

2. Have the ratios changed? Do the ratios suggest whether Kodak is more or less risky for long-term creditors in 1989 than in 1988?

E15-21. OPERATING RATIOS   Use the Eastman Kodak financial statements in Exercise 15–19 and the following data to respond to the requirements below.

STATEMENT ITEM	1987 AMOUNT (millions)
Receivables	$ 3,144
Inventories	2,178
Total assets	14,698

REQUIRED:

1. Compute the three operating ratios for 1989 and 1988.

2. What was the length of Kodak's operating cycle in 1989 and 1988?

E15-22. PROFITABILITY RATIOS   Use the Eastman Kodak financial statements in Exercise 15-19 and the following data to respond to the requirements below.

STATEMENT ITEM	1987 AMOUNT (millions)
Total assets	$14,698
Total shareowners' equity	6,013

REQUIRED:

1. Compute the five profitability ratios for 1989 and 1988.

2. Was Kodak more profitable in 1989 or 1988?

E15-23. STOCKHOLDER RATIOS   Use the Eastman Kodak financial statements in Exercise 15–19 and the following data to respond to the requirements below.

	1989	1988
Preferred dividends.	None	None
Average number of common shares outstanding.	324.3	324.2
Dividends per share	$2.00	$1.90
Market price per share:		
High	$52¼	$53¼
Low.	$40	$40

Note: Amounts in millions except per-share amounts.

REQUIRED:

1. Compute the four stockholder ratios for 1989 and 1988.

2. Were there significant changes in these ratios between 1988 and 1989? Do the stockholder ratios suggest whether Kodak was a better investment in 1989 than it was in 1988?

PROBLEMS

P15-24. CHANGE IN EXPECTED LIFE   The 1985 annual report for Union Carbide included the following information:

> In the third quarter of 1985 Union Carbide revised, retroactive to January 1, 1985, the estimated useful lives used to depreciate the cost of machinery and equipment. Machinery and equipment lives, which formerly ranged from 10 to 20 years, were shortened to 10 to 15 years.

REQUIRED:

1. What would be the effect on 1985 income of the change in estimated lives for the depreciable assets?
2. If Union Carbide continues to invest in depreciable assets, what will be the effect of this change on future income statements?

P15-25. ACCOUNTING CHANGES AND FINANCIAL ANALYSIS   The 1987 annual report for McDermott International, Inc., contained the following information:

> Effective April 1, 1986, McDermott International changed the method of depreciation for major marine service vessels from the straight-line method to a units of production method based on the utilization of each vessel.

REQUIRED:

If McDermott's marine service vessels were idled for part of the year because of reduced demand, what would be the effect of the change in depreciation method on net income?

P15-26. ACCOUNTING ALTERNATIVES AND FINANCIAL RATIOS   The 1987 annual report for Time Incorporated included the following information on a change in the procedure for amortizing its investment in pay-TV programming:

> In the first quarter of 1986 the Company changed the rate of amortization of its pay-TV programming costs to more closely reflect audience viewing patterns. The effect of this change was to reduce programming costs by $58 million and $57 million, resulting in increased net income of $35 million and $31 million, or $.58 per share and $.49 per share, during 1987 and 1986 respectively.

REQUIRED:

1. Which financial ratios would be affected by this change?
2. Would you expect this change in amortization policy to affect the accounts by a larger or smaller amount in future years? Why?

P15-27. USING COMPARATIVE INCOME STATEMENT DATA   The 1989, 1988, and 1987 income statements for Marriott Corporation and Subsidiaries appear on the next page.

Consolidated Statement of Income

Marriott Corporation and Subsidiaries

Fiscal years ended December 29, 1989, December 30, 1988, and January 1, 1988	1989	1988	1987
	(in millions except per share amounts)		
SALES			
Lodging			
Rooms	$2,093	$1,815	$1,536
Food and beverage	1,082	997	875
Other	371	328	262
	3,546	3,140	2,673
Contract Services	3,990	3,484	3,173
	7,536	6,624	5,846
OPERATING COSTS AND EXPENSES			
Lodging			
Rooms	481	404	338
Food and beverage	816	745	646
Other operating expenses, including payments to hotel owners and, in 1989, restructuring costs of $194 million	2,117	1,693	1,425
Contract Services, including 1989 restructuring costs of $51 million	3,818	3,281	2,984
	7,232	6,123	5,393
OPERATING INCOME			
Lodging	132	298	264
Contract Services, including $231 million gain on divestiture of the airline catering division in 1989	403	203	189
	535	501	453
Corporate expenses including $11 million of restructuring costs in 1989	(107)	(93)	(75)
Interest expense	(185)	(136)	(90)
Interest income	55	40	47
INCOME FROM CONTINUING OPERATIONS BEFORE INCOME TAXES	298	312	335
Provision for income taxes	117	123	148
INCOME FROM CONTINUING OPERATIONS	181	189	187
INCOME FROM DISCONTINUED OPERATIONS	(4)	43	36
NET INCOME	$ 177	$ 232	$ 223
EARNINGS PER SHARE	$ 1.58	$ 1.95	$ 1.67

REQUIRED:

1. By how much did each of the revenues and expenses change from fiscal year 1987 to 1988 and 1988 to 1989?

2. What was the primary cause of Marriott's increase in net income in 1988 and the decrease in 1989?

P15-28. USING COMPARATIVE COMPONENT PERCENTAGE STATEMENTS   The following income statement and component percentage data are available for Robbins Audio Products:

ROBBINS AUDIO PRODUCTS
Comparative Component Percentage Statements of Income

	YEAR ENDED JUNE 30					
	1990		**1989**		**1988**	
(dollar amounts in thousands)	**AMOUNT**	**%**	**AMOUNT**	**%**	**AMOUNT**	**%**
Sales	$2,970.0	100.0	$3,465.0	100.0	$3,960.0	100.0
Other income	23.7	.8	34.6	1.0	39.6	1.0
	2,993.7	100.8	3,499.6	101.0	3,999.6	101.0
Costs and expenses:						
Cost of goods sold	1,303.8	43.9	1,566.2	45.2	1,920.6	48.5
Selling and administrative	1,571.1	52.9	1,593.9	46.0	1,564.2	39.5
Interest	62.4	2.1	65.8	1.9	59.4	1.5
	2,937.3	98.9	3,225.9	93.1	3,544.2	89.5
Income before income taxes	56.4	1.9	273.7	7.9	455.4	11.5
Income taxes expense	14.8	.5	107.4	3.1	182.2	4.6
Net income....................	$ 41.6	1.4	$ 166.3	4.8	$ 273.2	6.9

REQUIRED:

1. Suggest why net income declined from $273,200 to $41,600 while the cost of goods sold percentage decreased each year and selling and administrative expenses remained nearly constant.

2. What could cause sales to decline while the gross margin percentage increases?

P15-29. USING COMPARATIVE STATEMENTS   Logo, Inc., owns and operates a small chain of sportswear stores located near colleges and universities. Logo has experienced significant growth in recent years. The following data are available for Logo:

LOGO, INC.
Consolidated Statements of Income

	YEAR ENDED MARCH 31		
(in thousands)	**1990**	**1989**	**1988**
Sales.....................................	$51,638	$41,310	$34,425
Cost of sales	31,050	24,840	20,700
Gross margin	20,588	16,470	13,725
Other income...........................	383	426	405
	20,971	16,896	14,130
Cost and expenses:			
Selling and administrative.................	16,570	13,465	11,350
Interest..............................	1,237	765	554
	17,807	14,230	11,904
Income before income taxes................	3,164	2,666	2,226
Provision for income taxes.................	885	746	623
Net income	$ 2,279	$ 1,920	$ 1,603

LOGO, INC.
Consolidated Balance Sheets

(in thousands)	AS OF MARCH 31		
ASSETS	**1990**	**1989**	**1988**
Current assets:			
Cash	$ 360	$ 293	$ 236
Accounts receivable.......................	4,658	3,690	3,285
Inventories	6,064	4,478	3,442
Total current assets	11,082	8,461	6,963
Property, plant, and equipment (net)	4,860	3,600	2,756
Other assets................................	574	585	562
Total assets.........................	$16,516	$12,646	$10,281
LIABILITIES AND STOCKHOLDERS' EQUITY			
Current liabilities:			
Short-term notes payable...................	$ 4,230	$ 1,620	$ 450
Accounts payable	1,147	1,013	720
Total current liabilities...................	5,377	2,633	1,170
Long-term debt...........................	3,150	3,150	3,150
Total liabilities	8,527	5,783	4,320
Paid-in capital............................	4,725	4,725	4,725
Retained earnings	3,264	2,138	1,236
Total stockholders' equity................	7,989	6,863	5,961
Total liabilities and stockholders' equity ...	$16,516	$12,646	$10,281

REQUIRED:

1. By how much have Logo's sales, net income, and assets grown during these three years?

2. How has Logo financed the increase in assets?

3. Is Logo's liquidity adequate?

4. Why is interest expense growing?

5. If Logo's sales grow by 25 percent in 1991, what would you expect net income to be?

6. If Logo's assets must grow by 25 percent to support the 25 percent sales increase and if 50 percent of net income is paid in dividends, how much capital must Logo raise?

P15-30. PREPARATION OF RATIOS   Use the Logo, Inc., financial statements in Problem 15-29 to respond to the following requirements.

REQUIRED:

1. Compute operating ratios for Logo for 1990 and 1989. Has efficiency changed?

2. Has Logo's profitability changed during the three-year period 1988–1990?

3. Compute the debt-management ratios for 1990, 1989, and 1988. Are creditors as secure in 1990 as they were in 1988?

P15-31. COMPARING FINANCIAL RATIOS   Presented below are selected ratios for four firms: Albertsons (a grocery chain), Caterpillar (a heavy equipment manufacturer), Gannett (a newspaper publisher), and Kellogg (a food manufacturer).

	ALBERTSONS	CATERPILLAR	GANNETT	KELLOGG
Short-term liquidity ratio				
Current ratio	1.2	1.5	1.4	.9
Debt-management ratio				
Long-term debt to equity	.23	.51	.46	.23
Operating ratios				
Receivables turnover	169.65	3.97	7.45	12.28
Inventory turnover	11.71	4.25	27.42	6.38
Profitability ratios				
Operating income	5.8%	11.7%	26.9%	19.3%
Net income	2.6	4.5	11.3	9.1
Return on assets	11.4	4.8	10.5	12.7
Return on equity	22.7	11.6	21.0	30.7

REQUIRED:

1. Why is there little difference among the four firms in the current ratio?

2. Why would the turnover ratios vary so much among the four firms?

3. Why is the return on equity ratio larger than the return on asset ratio for all four firms?

4. Can the large differences in the return on equity ratios exist over long periods of time?

P15-32. PREPARING COMPONENT PERCENTAGE STATEMENTS   The financial statements for Nike, Inc., appear below and on the next page:

NIKE, INC.
CONSOLIDATED STATEMENT OF INCOME (in thousands)

	Year Ended May 31		
	1990	1989	1988
Revenues	$2,235,244	$1,710,803	$1,203,440
Costs and expenses:			
Cost of sales	1,384,172	1,074,831	803,380
Selling and administrative	454,521	354,825	246,583
Interest	10,457	13,949	8,004
Other (income) expense	(7,264)	(3,449)	(20,722)
	1,841,886	1,440,156	1,037,245
Income before income taxes	393,358	270,647	166,195
Income taxes	150,400	103,600	64,500
Net income	$ 242,958	$ 167,047	$ 101,695

NIKE, INC.
CONSOLIDATED BALANCE SHEET (in thousands)

	May 31	
	1990	1989
Assets		
Current assets:		
Cash	$ 90,449	$ 85,749
Accounts receivable	400,877	296,350
Inventories	309,476	222,924
Prepaid expenses	19,851	14,854
Other current assets	17,029	18,504
Total current assets	837,682	638,381
Property, plant and equipment	238,461	154,314
Less: Accumulated depreciation	78,797	64,332
	159,664	89,982
Goodwill	81,021	81,899
Other assets	16,185	15,148
	$1,094,552	$ 825,410
Liabilities and Shareholders' Equity		
Current liabilities:		
Current portion of long-term debt	$ 8,792	$ 1,884
Notes payable	31,102	39,170
Accounts payable	107,423	71,105
Accrued liabilities	94,939	76,543
Income taxes payable	30,905	27,201
Total current liabilities	273,161	215,903
Long-term debt	25,941	34,051
Deferred income taxes	10,931	13,352
Other long-term liabilities	300	300
Common shareholders' equity		
Common stock	2,874	2,871
Capital in excess of stated value	78,582	74,227
Foreign currency translation adjustment	1,035	(2,156)
Retained earnings	701,728	486,862
	784,219	561,804
	$1,094,552	$ 825,410

REQUIRED:

1. Prepare comparative component percentage income statements for Nike for 1990, 1989, and 1988.

2. Using the component percentage and comparative income statements, indicate why Nike's profit increased 45.4 percent between 1989 and 1990.

3. Prepare component percentage balance sheets for 1990 and 1989.

4. Has the proportion of dollars invested in the various categories of assets changed significantly from 1989?

5. Has the proportion of capital raised from the various liability categories and common shareholders' equity changed significantly from 1989?

6. How would you describe Nike's performance and financial position?

P15-33. PREPARATION OF RATIOS   Use the Nike financial statements in Problem 15-32 and the following data to respond to the requirements below.

	1990	1989	1988
Receivables.	$ 400,877	$296,350	$258,393
Inventories	309,476	222,924	198,470
Total assets.	1,094,552	825,410	709,095
Total common shareowners' equity	784,219	561,804	411,774
Average number of common shares outstanding.	37,834	37,572	—
Dividends per share	$.75	$.55	—
Market price per share:			
High	$83	$39¾	—
Low.	38	14	—

Note: Amounts are in thousands except per-share amounts.

REQUIRED:

1. Prepare the 19 financial ratios for Nike for 1990 and 1989.
2. Is Nike's short-term liquidity adequate?
3. Is Nike operating efficiently?
4. Is Nike profitable?
5. Should long-term creditors regard Nike as a high-risk or low-risk firm?
6. Are Nike's shareowners earning an adequate return on their investment?

P15-34. USING COMPARATIVE DATA FOR CREDIT ANALYSIS   You are the credit manager for Materials Supply Company. One of your sales staff has made a $50,000 credit sale to Stewart Electronics, a manufacturer of small computers. Your responsibility is to decide whether to approve the sale. You have the following data for the computer industry and Stewart Electronics:

FOR THE YEARS 1986–1990	INDUSTRY	STEWART ELECTRONICS
Average annual sales growth	13.4%	17.6%
Average annual operating income growth	10.8%	9.7%
Average annual net income growth	14.4%	9.9%
Average annual asset growth	10.3%	14.2%
Average debt to equity ratio.	.32	.26
Average current ratio	4.04	3.71
Average inventory turnover ratio.	2.53	2.06
Average accounts receivable turnover ratio	3.95	4.18

For Stewart Electronics, you have the following data for the year ended December 31, 1990:

Sales revenue	$3,908,000
Net income.	359,000
Total assets.	3,626,000
Current ratio	1.82
Debt to equity ratio	.37
Inventory turnover ratio.	1.79
Accounts receivable turnover ratio.	3.62

The salesperson believes that Stewart Electronics would order about $200,000 per year of materials that would provide a gross margin of $35,000 to Materials Supply if reasonable credit terms could be arranged.

REQUIRED:

State whether or not you would grant authorization for Stewart to purchase on credit. Write a short report indicating the reasons for your decision.

P15-35. USING COMPARATIVE DATA FOR INVESTMENT ANALYSIS   Assume that you are a trust officer for the West Side Bank. You are attempting to select a pharmaceutical manufacturer's stock for a client's portfolio. You have secured the following data:

	FIVE-YEAR AVERAGES				
	INDUSTRY AVERAGE	FIRM A	FIRM B	FIRM C	FIRM D
Sales growth	8.3%	9.8%	7.9%	7.2%	10.1%
Net income growth	13.0	12.0	10.7	4.2	16.6
Asset growth	5.0	6.1	4.6	4.4	6.2
	CURRENT YEAR				
Return on equity	16.2%	17.5%	17.5%	19.4%	21.6%
Return on assets	8.5	7.8	12.7	8.4	11.4
Dividend payout	43.0	40.0	23.0	31.0	31.0
Price earnings ratio	12	11	6	10	9

REQUIRED:

Select one of the securities for the portfolio and write a short report indicating why you selected that security.

P15-36. ACCOUNTING ALTERNATIVES AND FINANCIAL ANALYSIS   Shady Deal Automobile Sales Company has asked your bank for a $100,000 loan to expand its sales facility. Shady Deal provides you with the following data:

	1990	1989	1988
Sales revenue.	$6,100,000	$5,800,000	$5,400,000
Net income	119,000	112,000	106,000
Ending inventory (FIFO)*	665,000	600,000	500,000
Purchases.	5,370,000	5,105,000	4,860,000
Depreciable assets	1,240,000	1,150,000	1,090,000

* The 1987 ending inventory was $470,000 (FIFO).

Your inspection of the financial statements of other automobile sales firms indicates that most of these firms adopted the LIFO method in the late 1970s. You further note that Shady Deal has used 5 percent of depreciable asset cost when computing depreciation expense and that other automobile dealers use 10 percent. Assume that Shady Deal's effective tax rate is 25 percent of income before tax. Also assume the following:

	1990	1989	1988
Ending inventory (LIFO)*	$508,000	$495,000	$480,000

* The 1987 ending inventory was $470,000 (LIFO).

PROBLEM CONTINUES

REQUIRED:

1. Compute cost of goods sold for 1990, 1989, and 1988, using both the FIFO and the LIFO methods.

2. Compute depreciation expense for Shady Deal for 1990, 1989, and 1988, using both 5 percent and 10 percent of the cost of depreciable assets.

3. Recompute Shady Deal's net income for 1990, 1989, and 1988, using LIFO and 10 percent depreciation. (Don't forget the tax impact of the increases in cost of goods sold and depreciation expense.)

4. Does Shady Deal appear to have materially changed its financial statements by the selection of FIFO (rather than LIFO) and 5 percent (rather than 10 percent) depreciation?

P15-37. ANALYZING GROWTH   Comparative financial statements for Tandy Corporation, a manufacturer and retailer of electronic products through Radio Shack stores, follow:

Consolidated Statements of Income
Tandy Corporation and Subsidiaries

In thousands

	1988	1987	1986
Net sales and operating revenues	$3,793,767	$3,452,178	$3,035,969
Cost of products sold	1,870,429	1,700,109	1,471,310
Gross profit	1,923,338	1,752,069	1,564,659
Expenses:			
Selling, general and administrative	1,341,090	1,208,750	1,079,304
Depreciation and amortization	68,156	62,591	55,388
Interest expense (income)	(588)	21,937	42,953
	1,408,658	1,293,278	1,177,645
Income before taxes and equity in operation spun off	514,680	458,791	387,014
Provision for income taxes	198,326	213,625	186,436
Income before equity in operations spun off	316,354	245,166	200,578
Equity in net income (loss) in operations spun off	—	(2,837)	(2,919)
Net income	$ 316,354	$ 242,329	$ 197,659

Consolidated Balance Sheets
Tandy Corporation and Subsidiaries

	June 30	
In thousands	1988	1987
Assets		
Current assets:		
Cash and short-term investments	$ 188,224	$ 78,114
Receivables	462,374	197,219
Inventories	1,287,854	1,128,435
Other current assets	47,622	41,436
Total current assets	1,986,074	1,445,204
Property, plant and equipment (net)	367,264	337,154
Other assets	176,754	183,031
	$2,530,092	$1,965,389
Liabilities and Stockholders' Equity		
Current liabilities:		
Notes payable	$ 306,475	$ 31,304
Accounts payable	116,818	113,001
Accrued expenses	205,191	160,254
Income taxes payable	20,778	(1,118)
Total current liabilities	649,262	303,441
Notes payable, due after one year	153,641	168,194
Subordinated debentures, net of unamortized bond discount	26,957	26,414
Deferred income taxes	68,977	58,821
Other non-current liabilities	28,143	28,480
Total other liabilities	277,718	281,909
Stockholders' equity:		
Common stock, $1 par value	95,645	95,645
Additional paid-in capital	114,999	102,305
Retained earnings	1,609,346	1,344,394
Foreign currency translation effects	8,105	4,130
Common stock in treasury, at cost	(224,983)	(166,435)
Total stockholders' equity	1,603,112	1,380,039
	$2,530,092	$1,965,389

REQUIRED:

1. Prepare component percentage income statements for 1988 and 1987.

2. Using the component percentage and comparative income statements, indicate why Tandy's profits increased more rapidly than sales from 1986 to 1988

3. Prepare component percentage balance sheets for 1988 and 1987.

4. Did the proportion of assets invested in the various classes of assets change significantly from 1987 to 1988?

5. How has Tandy financed its growth in assets?

6. Did the income statement change as much between 1987 and 1988 as the balance sheet?

P15-38. ANALYZING GROWTH THROUGH ACQUISITIONS   Following are comparative financial statements for Stone Container Corporation, a manufacturer of wood and paper products. During 1989 Stone expanded its business primarily by acquiring other businesses in its industry.

STONE CONTAINER CORPORATION AND SUBSIDIARIES

Consolidated Statements of Income

(in millions) Year ended December 31,		1989	1988	1987
Sales	Net sales	$5,329.7	$3,742.5	$3,232.9
	Other income	67.1	34.5	11.1
		5,396.8	3,777.0	3,244.0
Costs and expenses	Cost of products sold	3,893.8	2,618.0	2,347.8
	Selling, general and administrative expenses	474.5	351.1	343.8
	Depreciation and amortization	237.1	148.1	138.7
	Interest expense	344.7	108.3	131.1
	Interest (income)	(24.1)	(1.9)	(2.0)
	Equity (income) loss from affiliates	(10.2)	3.9	1.2
		4,915.8	3,227.5	2,960.6
Income before income taxes	Income before income taxes	481.0	549.5	283.4
	Provision for income taxes	195.2	207.7	122.1
Net income	Net income	$ 285.8	$ 341.8	$ 161.3

STONE CONTAINER CORPORATION AND SUBSIDIARIES

Consolidated Balance Sheets

(in millions) Year ended December 31,		1989	1988
Assets	Current assets:		
	Cash and cash equivalents	$ 22.9	$ 8.5
	Receivables	684.8	440.6
	Inventory	767.0	367.9
	Other	212.3	48.7
	Total current assets	1,687.0	865.7
	Property, plant and equipment	3,855.1	1,859.5
	Accumulated depreciation and amortization	(877.2)	(583.5)
	Property, plant and equipment—net	2,977.9	1,276.0
	Timberlands	103.9	102.7
	Goodwill	1,089.8	29.8
	Other	395.1	120.8
	Total assets	$6,253.7	$2,395.0

	(in millions) Year ended December 31,	1989	1988
Liabilities and stockholders' equity	Current liabilities		
	Notes payable	\$ 66.4	\$ 10.0
	Current maturities of long-term debt.......................	286.0	5.8
	Accounts payable	355.9	178.9
	Income taxes...	71.1	42.2
	Accrued and other current liabilities	293.2	171.4
	Total current liabilities	1,072.6	408.3
	Long-term debt.......................................	3,536.9	765.1
	Other long-term liabilities	78.6	17.4
	Deferred taxes.......................................	185.6	140.3
	Redeemable preferred stock of consolidated affiliate	22.7	—
	Minority interest.....................................	9.7	.3
	Stockholders' equity:		
	Common stock	433.5	433.5
	Retained earnings	875.1	632.2
	Foreign currency translation adjustment....................	41.8	—
	Other..	(2.8)	(2.1)
	Total stockholders' equity	1,347.6	1,063.6
	Total liabilities and stockholders' equity	\$6,253.7	\$2,395.0

REQUIRED:

1. Evaluate Stone's operating performance in 1989.

2. How did Stone's assets change as a result of the acquisitions in 1989?

3. How did Stone finance the $3,858.7 million increase in assets in 1989?

ANALYTICAL OPPORTUNITIES

A15-39. ASSESSING THE EFFECTS OF THE "CLEAN AIR" LEGISLATION   In late 1990, Congress passed and the President signed into law legislation that will require significant reductions over a several-year period in the quantity of sulfur dioxide that electric utilities will be allowed to discharge into the air. Electric utilities most affected by this legislation will be those that generate their electricity by burning inexpensive but relatively high-sulfur coal. Some utilities have indicated that they intend to comply with this legislation by changing to coal with a lower sulfur content. Other utilities have indicated that they intend to install devices on power plant smokestacks that will remove sulfur dioxide before it is discharged into the air.

REQUIRED:

1. In what places on the financial statements of coal-dependent electric utilities do you expect to observe the effects of this legislation?

2. In what places on the financial statements of companies that mine coal do you expect to observe the effects of this legislation?

A15-40. WINNING THE "COLD" WAR Since the end of World War II, a large number of businesses have devoted the majority of their operations to the development and production of equipment for the U.S. Defense Department. As the 1990s began, political developments in Eastern Europe suggested that the United States might be able to reduce its defense spending significantly, as the threat of an armed conflict in Europe appeared to become more remote.

REQUIRED:

How would a major long-term reduction in defense spending affect the financial statements of firms supplying goods and services to the U.S. Defense Department?

A15-41. CHANGES IN THE PRICE OF FUEL FOR AIRCRAFT The cost of fuel is reported to be about 20 percent of the total operating cost for a major airline. Events in the Middle East caused jet fuel costs nearly to double during the last half of 1990.

REQUIRED:

1. If you were the CEO of a major airline, how would you suggest that the airline respond to the fuel price increase?
2. How would you expect the financial statements of major airlines to be affected by the fuel price increase and the actions that the airlines would take in response?

ACCOUNTING AND CORPORATE INCOME TAXATION

INCOME TAX: A tax based on the amount of taxable income earned by a taxpayer.

TAXABLE INCOME: Income subject to taxation, as measured according to rules established by the government that levies the tax and reported to that government on a document known as an income tax return.

INCOME TAX RETURN: A document containing a statement of taxable income and the related computation of income tax.

PRETAX ACCOUNTING INCOME: Income before taxes measured according to generally accepted accounting principles (GAAP) and reported on the income statement.

For most corporations, income tax payments to federal, state, and local governments represent a sizable expense. Corporations engaged in international operations also pay income taxes to foreign governments. An **income tax** is a tax based on the amount of taxable income earned by a taxpayer. **Taxable income,** in turn, is income that is subject to taxation, as measured according to rules established by the government that levies the tax. Taxable income and the related computation of income tax are reported on a document known as an **income tax return.** The rules for measuring taxable income and preparing tax returns are complex. A complete exposition of just the federal income tax laws and the related regulations would require thousands of pages. Tax rules also vary from one state and local government to another. To further complicate matters, tax rules are subject to frequent change. As a consequence, corporations that do business in several states or in several countries find it quite costly to prepare the documents required to support their various income tax payments.

In order to make this chapter manageable, we shall restrict our discussion to those income taxes levied on business corporations by the U.S. federal government. Thus, for the remainder of this chapter, the term *income tax* should be understood to mean the federal income tax on business corporations. (Federal income tax for individuals is described in Supplementary Topic D at the end of this book.)

The rules that are followed when computing taxable income and preparing tax returns differ from the accounting principles that are employed when determining net income and preparing financial statements. The income tax system has different objectives than does the financial reporting system. Income taxation is designed to gather funds equitably to support the activities of government and to induce taxpayers to behave in ways deemed desirable by the government. Financial reports, in contrast, are intended to communicate information about the financial position of a corporation and the results of its operations. Consequently, *taxable income* is fundamentally different from *pretax accounting income.* Taxable income is measured according to tax laws and regulations and is reported to the government on a tax return. **Pretax accounting income,** on the other hand, is measured according to generally accepted accounting principles (GAAP) and is reported to the stockholders and other statement users on the income statement, as income before taxes. Although a comprehensive discussion of the differences between the two systems is beyond the scope of this book, this chapter explains some of the major differences and shows how they influence business decision making. We begin by considering the objectives and structure of corporate income taxation and turn next to the accounting issues raised by income taxes and, finally, to the influence of income taxes on business decisions.

OBJECTIVES AND STRUCTURE OF CORPORATE INCOME TAXATION

The corporate income tax promotes various objectives of the federal government. These objectives are reflected both in the laws and regulations that must be followed when calculating taxable income and in the structure of the tax computed on taxable income. Let us begin by considering these objectives and the structure of the tax computation.

OBJECTIVES OF INCOME TAXATION

A government cannot adequately plan and control its activities without a predictable revenue flow. The primary objective of taxation is to provide governments, in an effective and equitable manner, with the resources required to finance their activities. An effective taxation system provides predictable amounts of revenues and is efficient to administer. The taxation system must be efficient to administer so that substantial governmental revenues are not spent to levy and collect the tax.

In order to secure popular support, the taxation system must be equitable as well as effective. Under an equitable system, equal economic circumstances are taxed equally; unequal circumstances are taxed differently in the appropriate degree. An income tax uses taxable income as the measure of economic circumstances. Two corporations that have equal taxable incomes must pay equal taxes, and higher taxable income implies higher tax payments.

Any provision in the tax law that confers special benefits or special penalties on a particular industry should be regarded as a departure from strict equity. For example, if the government wishes to encourage the development of new sources of energy, energy-related industries may be allowed to compute their taxable income in ways that will reduce or postpone their tax payments. The reduction or postponement of tax payments increases resources available for use in the favored industry—both directly, by reducing tax payments, and indirectly, by encouraging the flow of capital into the industry.

Some persons argue that the corporate income tax is inequitable because corporate income is taxed twice. First the corporation pays a tax on its taxable income, which is determined before the payment of dividends. Then a portion of that taxable income is distributed to stockholders as dividends, and the stockholders pay individual income taxes on the dividends. Income of sole proprietorships and partnerships is also subject to individual income tax, but sole proprietorships and partnerships[1] do not pay a separate business income tax. Defenders of the corporate income tax argue that it is justified by the fact that governments confer benefits on corporations that are not conferred on other business organizations.

---

[1] As explained in Chapter 12, the taxable income of each partner includes the partner's share of partnership net income whether or not that income has been paid to the partner. Thus partnership net income is taxed only once and at individual income tax rates. Certain small, closely held corporations, called *S corporations,* qualify to be taxed like partnerships. Since individual income tax rates in recent years have been relatively low, many such corporations have elected S-corporation treatment.

For example, laws that prescribe the rights and responsibilities of stockholders and creditors make it easier for corporations to gather capital.

Although the primary objective of taxation is to finance the activities of government, the tax law may also be used to encourage certain general economic effects that are deemed desirable by the government. For example, most income taxes are **progressive taxes,** which means that higher incomes are taxed at higher rates than lower incomes. U.S. income taxation is progressive for both corporations and individuals. The principal intent of progressive taxation for corporations is to encourage the development of new businesses. The intent of progressive income taxes for individuals is to redistribute income from high-income groups to low-income groups. Many people regard such redistribution as a desirable objective for the government. Progressive taxes are also consistent with the view that the marginal utility of income declines as income increases and that each dollar of income should be taxed to result in about the same sacrifice of utility.

PROGRESSIVE TAX: A tax paid at higher rates by persons or organizations with higher incomes.

The tax law may also be used to influence the general levels of production, employment, or inflation. Taxes reduce disposable income—the amount that corporations and individuals have available to spend or save. Tax cuts are sometimes justified as a way of increasing the amount of spending and thereby increasing production and employment. Tax increases are sometimes justified as a means to decrease spending and thereby reduce the rate of inflation. The theories and arguments that underlie these uses of income taxes are more appropriately described in economics texts. The important point for our purposes is that the taxation system serves a different set of objectives than does the financial reporting system described in earlier chapters.

STRUCTURE OF THE CORPORATE INCOME TAX

The objectives of corporate income taxation influence both the structure of the tax calculation and the laws and regulations that guide the calculation of taxable income. We begin by considering the structure of the tax calculation and then turn to the calculation of taxable income.

The corporate income tax is based on the amount of taxable income earned by a corporation. The calculation of the tax requires that taxable income be divided into two parts—capital gains and losses, and ordinary income. **Capital gains and losses** are gains and losses on the sale of capital assets. **Capital assets** are the land, depreciable property, and securities held by the firm for investment or for use in the business.[2]

CAPITAL GAINS AND LOSSES: Gains and losses on the sale of capital assets.

CAPITAL ASSETS: Land, depreciable property, and securities held by the firm for investment or for use in the business.

ORDINARY INCOME: The component of corporate taxable income measured as the excess of taxable revenues (and noncapital gains) over deductible expenses (and noncapital losses).

All corporate income other than capital gains and losses is called **ordinary income,** which is measured as the excess of taxable revenues (and noncapital gains) over deductible expenses (and noncapital losses). Ordinary income is separated from capital gains and losses to permit determination of the *excess of capital losses over capital gains.* Capital losses can be used to offset capital gains; otherwise they are not deductible in the current year but must be carried back to earlier years or forward to future years, as explained later in this chapter. Thus taxable income is the sum of ordinary income and the excess of capital gains over capital losses.

[2] Strictly speaking, property held for use in the business is not a capital asset. Rather, business property held for the long term is called Section 1231 property. However, the treatment of Section 1231 property is sufficiently similar to the treatment of capital assets that we shall not emphasize the distinction. (The principal differences are that net losses on the sale or exchange of such property are treated as ordinary losses and net gains are treated as capital gains.)

Prior to the 1986 Tax Act, capital gains were taxed at a lower rate than ordinary income. Now, however, ordinary income and any excess of capital gains over capital losses are both taxed according to the following rate schedule:

TAXABLE INCOME	TAX RATE
First $50,000	15%
Over $50,000 up to $75,000	25
Over $75,000*	34

* An additional 5 percent tax is charged on taxable income over $100,000 and up to $335,000.

To illustrate, a corporation with taxable income of $170,000 would pay an income tax of $49,550, calculated as follows:

$$
\begin{aligned}
(\$50,000)(.15) &= \$\ 7,500 \\
(\$25,000)(.25) &= \ \ \ 6,250 \\
(\$95,000)(.34) &= 32,300 \\
(\$70,000)(.05) &= \ \ \ 3,500 \\
&\ \ \ \overline{\$49,550}
\end{aligned}
$$

Of course, tax rates are subject to change from time to time as the government adjusts its policies and reassesses its need for resources.

The tax associated with a given amount of taxable income may be reduced by certain adjustments called *tax credits.* The government establishes tax credits to offset the cost to corporations of certain corporate activities. Provisions of the tax law require corporations to compute an *alternative minimum tax,* which is discussed later in this chapter. Tax due for the year is the greater of the tax due on ordinary income and capital gains (less tax credits) or the alternative minimum tax. Exhibit 16–1 shows the structure of the tax computation in a diagram. Let us consider these components: capital gains and losses, tax credits, and the alternative minimum tax.

Capital Gains

Recall that capital losses are not deductible in a given year unless they can be used to offset capital gains in that year and that taxable income is the sum of ordinary income and the *excess of capital gains over capital losses.* Determining the excess of capital gains over capital losses to be included in taxable income requires a rather lengthy calculation.

First, capital gains and losses are divided into two groups — long-term gains and losses and short-term gains and losses. **Long-term capital gains and losses** are gains and losses on the sale of capital assets held for more than one year. **Short-term capital gains and losses** are gains and losses on the sale of capital assets held for one year or less.

Second, the net long-term capital gain or loss and the net short-term capital gain or loss are calculated, according to the following formulas:

LONG-TERM CAPITAL GAINS AND LOSSES: Gains and losses on the sale of capital assets held for more than one year.

SHORT-TERM CAPITAL GAINS AND LOSSES: Gains and losses on the sale of capital assets held for one year or less.

Total of long-term capital gains	−	Total of long-term capital losses	=	Net long-term capital gain (or loss)
Total of short-term capital gains	−	Total of short-term capital losses	=	Net short-term capital gain (or loss)

EXHIBIT 16–1   THE STRUCTURE OF CORPORATE INCOME TAXATION

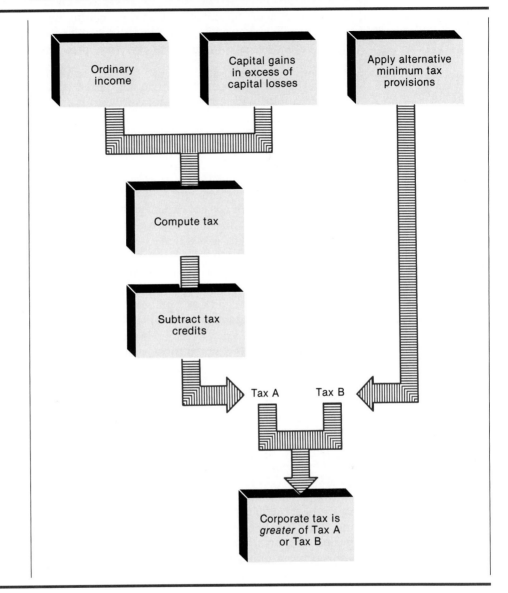

In each formula, if the total of gains exceeds the total of losses, then the difference is a net gain. On the other hand, if the total of losses exceeds the total of gains, then the difference is a net loss. As a result of these calculations, all capital gains and losses for an accounting period are summarized in two numbers—a net long-term capital gain or loss and a net short-term capital gain or loss.

The third step is to determine the *excess of capital gains over capital losses* for the year. The computation varies according to the structure of gains and losses, as follows:

1. *Taxation of two net gains:* If a period has both a net long-term capital gain and a net short-term capital gain, then both net gains are included in taxable income for the period and are taxed at the ordinary income rate.

2. *Taxation of two net losses:* If the period has both a net long-term capital loss and a net short-term capital loss, then neither net loss is included in taxable income of the period. Instead, the two net losses reduce capital gains of past or future periods according to the carryover provisions described below.

3. *Taxation of one net gain and one net loss:* Two cases can be identified — (a) a net long-term gain coupled with a net short-term loss and (b) a net short-term gain coupled with a net long-term loss. In both of these cases, the net loss is offset against the net gain. If the result is an excess of gain over loss, then the excess is added to ordinary income and tax is computed on the sum. On the other hand, if the result is an excess of loss over gain, then the excess of loss reduces capital gains of past or future periods according to the carryover provisions described below.

Therefore, except for the net capital gains that are offset by the net capital losses, capital gains are combined with ordinary income for purposes of computing income tax. All capital losses that cannot be offset against the capital gains of the current period may be carried back or forward to be offset against capital gains in past or future years. Further, under current tax rules, net short-term gains and net long-term gains are taxed at the same rates. In years past, federal tax laws have taxed net short-term gains at a higher rate to discourage short-term, speculative transactions in capital assets.

Capital losses may be carried back three years and forward five years to be offset against capital gains in those years. These provisions of tax law are called **carryover provisions.** Further, all capital losses carried back or forward are treated as short-term capital losses, whether or not they arose as short-term capital losses. This means that the short-term capital losses of years to which capital losses are carried over may be increased by the amount of such carryovers to the extent that capital gains in those years are sufficient to absorb them.

To clarify the application of these rules, consider the data from three corporations shown in Exhibit 16–2. The $38,000 net capital loss of corporation X is subject to the carryover provisions. Suppose corporation X reported long-term capital gains for each of the past three years: $50,000 last year, $20,000 two years ago, and $30,000 three years ago. The $38,000 loss can be carried back to offset the entire $30,000 gain and $8,000 of the $20,000 gain, which will result in a refund of the taxes paid on those gains. This treatment of the net capital loss is appropriate whether it represents an excess of long-term losses (as for corporation X), an excess of short-term losses, or an excess of both long-term and short-term losses. For corporation Y, the $20,000 net capital gain represents the excess of net short-term gain over net long-term loss and is added to ordinary income. For corporation Z, the $45,000 excess of net long-term gain over net short-term loss is also added to ordinary income for purposes of determining the tax. For example, suppose that Z's ordinary income is $80,000; then Z's taxable income is $125,000 [$80,000 + $45,000]. Since the entire $25,000 excess of taxable income over $100,000 is attributable to net long-term gain, the $25,000 will be taxed at 39 percent, the 34 percent rate for income over $75,000 plus the 5 percent additional tax for income between $100,000 and $335,000. To alter the example, if Z's ordinary income were $110,000, then Z's taxable income would be $155,000 [$110,000 + $45,000]. Again, the net long-term gain would incur the additional 5 percent tax and $10,000 of the excess taxable income over $100,000 would also incur the additional tax.

When the time or form of transactions can be controlled by a corporation, it is important that the corporation's management understand the tax effects of

CARRYOVER PROVI-SIONS: Provisions of the tax law that permit losses in one year to be applied against taxable income in other years, thereby reducing the amount of tax payable on income in those other years.

EXHIBIT 16–2   **CAPITAL GAINS AND LOSSES FOR THREE CORPORATIONS**

	CORPORATION X		CORPORATION Y		CORPORATION Z	
Total of long-term capital gains	$ 60,000		$ 60,000		$ 218,000	
Total of long-term capital losses	(150,000)		(150,000)		(150,000)	
Net long-term capital gain (loss)		$(90,000)		$ (90,000)		$ 68,000
Total of short-term capital gains	$ 127,000		$ 127,000		$ 127,000	
Total of short-term capital losses	(75,000)		(17,000)		(150,000)	
Net short-term capital loss (loss)		52,000		110,000		(23,000)
Net capital gain (loss)		($38,000)		$ 20,000		$ 45,000

alternative transactions. The arrangement of transactions to secure tax advantages is sometimes called *tax planning*. The following analysis shows an instance of tax planning related to the sale of an investment.

ANALYSIS
TIMING OF SHORT-
TERM CAPITAL GAINS

Oregano Products, Inc., purchased shares of stock in Fennel for $100,000 on August 1, 19X2, with the expectation of realizing a gain on its sale. The market value of the shares has increased to $108,000 by the end of 19X2 and is expected to reach $110,000 by early 19X3. Oregano has no other capital gains or losses, and ordinary incomes for 19X2 and 19X3 are expected to be $40,000 and $75,000, respectively. Assume that ordinary income is taxed at rates of 15 percent on the first $50,000 and 25 and 34 percent on successive $25,000 increments.

1. *How much will be paid in taxes if the stock is sold in 19X2?*

If the stock is sold in 19X2, an $8,000 short-term capital gain increases 19X2 ordinary income to $48,000. Taxes for 19X2 and 19X3 are computed as follows:

19X2 INCOME TAX	19X3 INCOME TAX
($48,000)(.15) = $7,200	($50,000)(.15) = $ 7,500
	($25,000)(.25) = 6,250
	$75,000 $13,750

Hence the total tax bill for 19X2 and 19X3 is $20,950 [$7,200 + $13,750].

2. *How much will be paid in taxes if the stock is sold in early 19X3?*

If the stock is sold in 19X3, a $10,000 short-term capital gain increases 19X3 ordinary income to $85,000.

19X2 INCOME TAX	19X3 INCOME TAX
($40,000)(.15) = $6,000	($50,000)(.15) = $ 7,500
	($25,000)(.25) = 6,250
	($10,000)(.34) = 3,400
	$85,000 $17,150

Hence, the total tax bill for 19X2 and 19X3 is $23,150 [$6,000 + $17,150].

3. *When should the stock be sold?*

Waiting to sell in 19X3 should result in an additional gain of $2,000 [$10,000 − $8,000] and should increase the tax bill by $2,200 [$23,150 − $20,950], which more than offsets the additional gain of $2,000. Hence, selling in 19X2 should have a $200 advantage.

Losses and Income Tax

OPERATING LOSS: An excess of deductible expenses over taxable revenue.

Whereas capital gains and ordinary income give rise to taxes, losses do not give rise to taxes. Two kinds of losses are identified for income tax purposes—capital losses and operating losses. Recall that a capital loss is an excess of capital losses over capital gains in a given period. An **operating loss** is an excess of deductible expenses over taxable revenue. The carryover provisions for capital losses have been described briefly. Under the tax law, similar carryover provisions are available for operating losses. In this way, losses in one year produce a tax benefit in a year that has taxable income by reducing the amount of tax payable on that income. The tax law permits both types of losses to be carried back three years and applied against the income of previous years, which results in a refund or credit for taxes paid on that income. The tax law also permits losses not exhausted by carrybacks to be carried forward and applied against income of subsequent years, which reduces the amount of future taxes. The paragraphs that follow describe and illustrate these provisions for capital and operating losses.

CAPITAL LOSS CARRYOVERS When a firm has a net capital loss in an accounting period, the amount of that loss can be carried back as a short-term capital loss to the previous three years' tax returns or carried forward as a short-term capital loss to the next five years' tax returns. In other words, when there are capital gains on the tax returns of any of the previous three years or the next five years, the loss carryover can be used to reduce the taxes on those gains.

OPERATING LOSS CARRYOVERS Operating losses are carried over by using a procedure nearly identical to that used for capital losses. The major differences are that the carryforward period for operating losses is 15 years, and the loss carryback or loss carryforward is applied against operating income rather than against capital gains. Let us illustrate the carryover of operating losses: Carroll, Inc., has operating income for 19X1 through 19X3 as shown in Exhibit 16–3. If Carroll has an operating loss of $110,000 in 19X4, it can elect to carry back $50,000 of the loss to 19X1 and $60,000 to 19X2. The carryback of the operating loss produces a tax refund of $19,000 ($7,500 from 19X1 and $11,500 from 19X2). Remember that the determination of a tax refund from an operating loss carryback (or carryforward) must be computed using the appropriate schedule of tax rates. The $11,500 refund from 19X2 in our example is produced by carrying back $25,000 against income taxed at 25 percent and $35,000 against income taxed at 15 percent. (Notice that the carryback is first applied against income of the earliest of the three years and against the income that was taxed at the highest rate paid.)

Tax Credits

TAX CREDITS: Governmentally authorized reductions of the amount of tax otherwise payable, to offset the cost to the corporation of certain corporate activities.

After the ordinary income and capital gains tax rates are applied and the total tax due has been calculated, a corporation may have some **tax credits,** governmentally authorized adjustments that reduce the amount of tax otherwise payable. The income tax law makes tax credits available to corporations to offset part or all of the cost of certain corporate activities. For example, tax credits are available for creation of new jobs, increases in certain research and development expenditures, investment in pollution control equipment, hiring handicapped or other employees with specified attributes, and rehabilitation expenses for certain property. Discussion of the detailed provisions of these credits can be found in a taxation text; here we will illustrate the effect of tax credits on the tax due for a year. The

EXHIBIT 16–3   SCHEDULE OF OPERATING INCOME

CARROLL, INC.
Operating Income

	19X1	19X2	19X3
Operating income.	$50,000	$75,000	$25,000
Tax on operating income	7,500	13,750	3,750

Bryant Company has only ordinary income of $100,000, which results in a tax liability of $22,250. Bryant has the following tax credits:

Investment in pollution control equipment, cost $60,000	$6,000
Hiring handicapped workers	2,000
Total credits	$8,000

Bryant's taxes due for the year thus are reduced $8,000 by the tax credits:

Tax on income of $100,000	$22,250
Less: Tax credits.	8,000
Tax due for year.	$14,250

The Alternative Minimum Tax

ALTERNATIVE MINIMUM TAX (AMT): A tax system, separate from the regular system, which is intended to ensure that profitable corporations pay a minimum amount of income tax.

The purpose of the **alternative minimum tax (AMT)** is to ensure that any profitable corporation pays some federal income tax. The AMT was created because of a perception that many corporations were not paying taxes commensurate with their profitability. Thus, in addition to computing their tax liability under the regular tax system, corporations must also compute their tax liability under an alternative system. The elements of the AMT computation are described in the following five-step process:

1. Begin with *regular taxable income.*
2. Calculate AMT adjustments for the following items:
   a) Excess of tax return depreciation over AMT depreciation
   b) Certain income deferred under the installment method
   c) Certain tax-exempt interest
   d) Certain charitable contributions of property
   e) An amount defined by the tax law intended to move effective taxable income closer to "adjusted current earnings" (an adjusted version of accounting net income)
   f) Net operating losses up to 90 percent of the AMT income
3. Adjust regular taxable income for the items listed in step 2. The result is *AMT taxable income.*
4. Impose a 20 percent tax on AMT taxable income to establish the AMT.
5. Pay the larger of the AMT or regular income tax.

The rules for determining the AMT are very complex; a more complete explanation of them is given in income tax courses.

TAXABLE INCOME AND ACCOUNTING INCOME

We have noted that the system of laws and regulations used for measuring taxable income and preparing tax returns differs from the system of accounting concepts and principles used to measure net income and prepare financial statements. The differences between taxable income and pretax accounting income take two forms, *permanent differences* and *temporary differences.* Both permanent differences and temporary differences influence the measurement of income tax expense and balance sheet items. Although a complete explanation of permanent and temporary differences is beyond the scope of this chapter, we shall consider examples of both forms of difference as a basis for illustrating the calculation of income tax expense.

PERMANENT DIFFERENCES

PERMANENT DIFFERENCES: Elements of taxable income that are permanently excluded from the determination of pretax accounting income or elements of accounting income before taxes that are permanently excluded from the determination of taxable income.

Permanent differences are elements of taxable income that are permanently excluded from the determination of pretax accounting income (exclusions from accounting income) or elements of pretax accounting income that are permanently excluded from the determination of taxable income (exclusions from taxable income). Let us consider three examples of permanent differences.

The first example is the *intercorporate dividend exclusion,* which permits corporations to exclude from taxable revenues 80 percent of the dividends received from other U.S. corporations.[3] This provision implies that only 20 percent of dividends paid by one corporation to another are subject to double taxation. Although 20 percent of dividends paid by one corporation to another are taxed both when earned and when distributed, the remaining 80 percent is taxed only when earned by the distributing corporation. Of course, all such dividends are included in revenues for purposes of calculating pretax accounting income. Consequently, income before taxes (on the income statement) will exceed taxable income (on the tax return) by 80 percent of dividends from other corporations.

Interest on most bonds and other obligations of state and local (municipal) governments is also excluded from taxable income but included in pretax accounting income. Like the dividend exclusion, the exclusion from federal taxation of interest paid by state and local governments makes pretax accounting income larger than taxable income.

A third example of a permanent difference is *depletion in excess of cost,* an exclusion from pretax accounting income. In order to encourage the development of certain natural resources, tax laws authorize the deduction of amounts for depletion of those resources that exceed the cost of the resources. Depletion in excess of cost is a deductible expense that is never subtracted in the determination of pretax accounting income. The use of depletion in excess of cost on the tax return and depletion at cost on the income statement makes pretax accounting income larger than taxable income. Accountants must distinguish between the

---

[3] The 80 percent exclusion is allowed if the taxpaying corporation owns at least 20 percent of the dividend-paying corporation. If the taxpaying corporation owns less than 20 percent of the dividend-paying corporation, then the exclusion is only 70 percent of the dividend. On the other hand, if the two corporations qualify as an "affiliated group," the dividend recipient may be able to exclude 100 percent of the dividend. In the interest of simplicity, we shall assume an 80 percent dividend exclusion in all exercises and problems.

two types of permanent difference (exclusions from accounting income and exclusions from taxable income) when calculating income tax expense.

The analysis below illustrates the effect that permanent differences can have on a firm's *effective tax rate,* the ratio of tax expense to accounting income before taxes.

ANALYSIS

UNDERSTANDING A FIRM'S EFFECTIVE TAX RATE

For most large firms (those with taxable income in excess of $335,000), the expected federal income tax rate is essentially 34 percent. However, a firm with large tax credits or large permanent differences will ordinarily have an effective tax rate less than the highest corporate tax of 34 percent. When the effective rate is substantially below (or above) 34 percent, a table must be included in the footnotes to the financial statements to explain the reasons for the difference. An example of such a table for Helmerich & Payne, Inc., a diversified, energy-oriented company, is presented below.

Analysis of Effective Income Tax Rate

	1990	1989	1988
U.S. federal income tax rate..........................	34%	34%	34%
Deduction related to dividends received from domestic corporations........................	(2)	(6)	(9)
Excess statutory depletion over cost depletion		(1)	(1)
Effect of foreign taxes	1	5	(3)
Other, net..	(2)	(2)	
Effective income tax rate.......................	31%	30%	21%

Why was Helmerich & Payne's effective tax rate less than the statutory federal tax rates?

The data in the table indicate that Helmerich & Payne's income tax rate was decreased by the exclusion of dividends from taxable income that are included in accounting income, by the deduction of depletion in excess of cost on the tax return, and by permanent differences arising from taxes paid to foreign governments. The effect of these factors has been an effective tax rate below the statutory federal rate for each of the three years.

How can this information be used by readers of the financial statements?

A statement reader should examine a table like this to estimate future effective tax rates for the company. With the possible exception of the foreign tax effect, all the factors appear to result in a lowering of the effective tax rate. Thus, although some variation might be expected, the statement reader is apt to expect effective tax rates to remain below statutory rates for this company. Of course, estimates of future effective tax rates should also take into consideration prospects for changes in the level of statutory rates.

Before we discuss the calculation of income taxes expense, let us consider temporary differences, the second form of difference between taxable income and accounting income.

TEMPORARY DIFFERENCES

TEMPORARY DIFFERENCES: Elements of income that are included in taxable income of one period and in pretax accounting income of another period.

Temporary differences are elements of income that are included in taxable income of one period and in pretax accounting income of another period. Since corporations usually prefer to put off the payment of taxes as long as possible, corporations will usually endeavor to delay taxable revenues as long as legally possible and to recognize deductible expenses as soon as legally possible. Although most elements of income must be included in taxable income and accounting income of the same period, tax laws and regulations permit a number of significant temporary differences. Let us consider three important examples of temporary differences.

Installment Sales

In general, most revenues are recorded at the same times and in the same amounts for the accounting income statement and for the tax return. However, income from sales of certain property on an installment basis (commonly called *installment sales*) may be included in accounting income of one period and in taxable income of a subsequent period.[4] As we have seen, revenue recognition and matching concepts usually require that the income (revenue less cost of property) related to a sale be included in accounting income of the period in which the sale (the delivery of property) occurs. In contrast, the tax law permits use of the installment sales method, which recognizes income from the installment sale as the cash is collected; thus, each period's taxable income includes installment sale income in proportion to the amount of cash actually collected in each period. For example, consider an installment sale that produces income of $1,000 with 40 percent of the cash collected in the first year and 30 percent in each of the next two years. The income from this sale would be recognized on the income statement and the tax return as follows (for simplicity, ignore interest on the receivable):

YEAR	INCOME STATEMENT	TAX RETURN	TEMPORARY DIFFERENCE
1	$1,000	$ 400*	$ 600
2	–0–	300†	(300)
3	–0–	300†	(300)
Totals	$1,000	$1,000	$ –0–

* (.40)($1,000) = $400
† (.30)($1,000) = $300

Depreciation Expense

ACCELERATED COST RECOVERY SYSTEM (ACRS): A segment of the federal income tax law that provides for the rapid expensing of depreciable assets.

Depreciable assets usually constitute the largest source of expense-related temporary differences. Depreciation for accounting income statements is generally measured using the straight-line method over the expected useful life of the asset. For federal income tax purposes, however, the costs of most long-lived assets are expensed using the **accelerated cost recovery system (ACRS)**. ACRS is a segment of the federal income tax law that provides for the rapid expensing of depreciable assets. The ACRS "method" assigns all depreciable assets one of eight expected lives (see Exhibit 16–4). The ACRS method assumes a zero residual value, half a

---

[4] The installment method of accounting is not available for computing taxable income arising from sales of goods or services by dealers in those goods and services (like department or appliance stores).

EXHIBIT 16–4 ACCELERATED COST RECOVERY SYSTEM

ACRS EXPECTED LIFE IN YEARS	ACRS ASSET DESCRIPTION
3	Some racehorses, equipment with useful life up to 4 years
5	Autos, light-duty trucks, research and development equipment, computers, and other assets with an expected useful life up to 10 years
7	Most other equipment, railroad track
10	Equipment with useful lives of 16 to less than 20 years
15	Sewage treatment plants and telephone plant
20	Municipal sewers
27.5	Residential real property
31.5	Nonresidential real property

EXHIBIT 16–5 ACRS FRACTION OF INSTALLED COST TO BE DEPRECIATED EACH YEAR

YEAR	3-YEAR PROPERTY	5-YEAR PROPERTY	7-YEAR PROPERTY	10-YEAR PROPERTY
1	.3333	.2000	.1429	.1000
2	.4445	.3200	.2449	.1800
3	.1481	.1920	.1749	.1440
4	.0741	.1152	.1249	.1152
5		.1152	.0893	.0922
6		.0576	.0892	.0737
7			.0893	.0655
8			.0446	.0655
9				.0656
10				.0655
11				.0328

year's depreciation in the year in which the asset is placed in service, and half a year's depreciation in the year of disposition.[5] Exhibit 16–5 presents the actual proportions of asset cost that are to be expensed for four categories for each year of the asset's life.

Under ACRS, depreciation amounts are what would be computed if the declining balance method were used, with a switch to straight-line depreciation at the point that provides the most rapid write-off of cost (with only one-half of a year's depreciation available in the first year). Using the data in Exhibit 16–5, the ACRS depreciation schedule shown in Exhibit 16–6 would be developed for an asset with a $5,000 acquisition cost and an ACRS life of five years.

[5] For buildings, the midyear rule is replaced by a mid-month rule. Although the tax law specifies this and other exceptions, we will ignore these complexities and use the midyear rule for all depreciable assets.

EXHIBIT 16-6   ACRS DEPRECIATION

YEAR	DEPRECIATION EXPENSE	ACCUMULATED DEPRECIATION	BASIS*
1	$1,000	$1,000	$4,000
2	1,600	2,600	2,400
3	960	3,560	1,440
4	576	4,136	864
5	576	4,712	288
6	288	5,000	-0-

* In the tax law, cost less accumulated depreciation is called the *basis* of depreciable property. Thus the word *basis* in tax records corresponds to *book value* in accounting records, although the two are frequently different amounts.

During the early years of an asset's life, ACRS depreciation for the income tax return is normally larger than depreciation expense for the income statement. To illustrate, assume that Clifford Corporation put a new item of equipment in service in January 19X1. The following data apply:

Acquisition cost	$49,000
Expected residual value	-0-
Expected useful life	7 years
ACRS life	5 years

The computation of depreciation expense for this asset for the tax return and for the income statement is presented in Exhibit 16-7. ACRS depreciation accelerates the depreciation in the earlier years of the asset's life. When the firm is regularly purchasing new assets, ACRS depreciation should exceed depreciation for income determination. For example, assume that the Clifford Corporation purchases new infra-red sensors each year, and that all are subject to the three-year ACRS schedule. The actual expected useful life of the sensors is four years. Residual value is assumed to be zero. As Exhibit 16-8 indicates, the use of ACRS depreciation (rather than straight-line depreciation) will produce larger depreciation for the tax return each year, as long as the total cost of new sensors purchased does not decrease for an extended period.

Warranty Expense Measurement

Another temporary difference between taxable income and pretax accounting income involves warranties. As you will recall from Chapter 10, the matching concept requires that warranty expense be estimated and recorded in the period in which goods are sold. However, for tax purposes, warranty expense cannot be recorded until resources are actually consumed to satisfy warranty claims. When sales of goods under warranty are increasing, the warranty expense on the accounting income statement is likely to be larger than the warranty expense on the tax return.

INCOME TAX EXPENSE   Recall from Chapter 10 that income taxes expense represents all taxes associated with income before tax, whether those taxes are paid in the current period or in an earlier or later period. In other words, the amount of taxes assessed on the basis of taxable income for a period may not be the same as the amount of taxes expense calculated on the basis of pretax accounting income. Taxes expense is calculated on the basis of income before taxes because the matching concept requires that

EXHIBIT 16-7   THE TAX EFFECT OF ACRS DEPRECIATION

CLIFFORD CORPORATION
Depreciation Expense

YEAR	ACRS DEPRECIATION (TAX RETURN)	STRAIGHT-LINE DEPRECIATION (INCOME STATEMENT)	EXPENSE TEMPORARY DIFFERENCE
19X1	$ 9,800	$ 7,000	$ 2,800
19X2	15,680	7,000	8,680
19X3	9,408	7,000	2,408
19X4	5,645	7,000	(1,355)
19X5	5,645	7,000	(1,355)
19X6	2,822	7,000	(4,178)
19X7	–0–	7,000	(7,000)
Total	$49,000	$49,000	$ –0–

EXHIBIT 16-8   ASSET GROWTH AND TEMPORARY DIFFERENCES

YEAR	SENSOR PURCHASES	STRAIGHT-LINE DEPRECIATION* (INCOME STATEMENT)	ACRS DEPRECIATION† (TAX RETURN)	TEMPORARY DIFFERENCE
1	$ 8,000	$ 2,000	$ 2,666	$ 666
2	12,000	5,000	7,556	2,556
3	16,000	9,000	11,852	2,852
4	20,000	14,000	16,148	2,148
5	24,000	18,000	20,148	2,148
6	28,000	22,000	24,148	2,148

* The sum of .25 times the cost of the sensors purchased this year and in each of the previous three years. In year 5, for example, (.25)($24,000 + $20,000 + $16,000 + $12,000) = $18,000.

† The sum of .3333 times the cost of the sensors purchased this year plus .4445 times the cost of the sensors purchased in the previous year plus .1481 times the cost of the sensors purchased two years ago plus .0741 times the cost of the sensors purchased three years ago. In year 5, for example, (.3333)($24,000) + (.4445)($20,000) + (.1481)($16,000) + (.0741)($12,000) = $20,148.

taxes expense be determined by the transactions recorded in the period for which the taxes expense is determined. The difference between income taxes expense and income taxes assessed gives rise to a deferred tax liability. Let us explain first the calculation of income taxes expense and then the related deferred tax liability.

Calculation of Income Taxes Expense

In order to simplify our presentation of the income taxes expense calculation, we shall focus our attention on ordinary income and ignore the additional steps introduced by capital gains and losses, carryover provisions, the alternative minimum tax, and tax credits. With these complications set aside, the calculation of income tax assessed is based on taxable income (which now equals ordinary income). The income tax that would be assessed on pretax accounting income (adjusted for permanent differences) equals the related income taxes expense.

Let us demonstrate this procedure with an example: River City Manufacturing reports 19X5 taxable income of $430,000, as shown in Exhibit 16–9. The

EXHIBIT 16–9   TAXABLE INCOME AND ACCOUNTING INCOME

RIVER CITY MANUFACTURING, INC.
19X5 Taxable Income and Pretax Accounting Income

	TAXABLE INCOME	PRETAX ACCOUNTING INCOME	DIFFERENCE
Sales revenue	$1,800,000	$1,800,000	$ –0–
Installment sales income.	140,000	270,000	(130,000)
Municipal bond interest		24,000	(24,000)
	$1,940,000	$2,094,000	$(154,000)
Cost of goods sold	(980,000)	(980,000)	–0–
Salaries expense	(240,000)	(240,000)	–0–
Depreciation expense	(275,000)	(170,000)	(105,000)
Warranty expense	(15,000)	(45,000)	30,000
Taxable income	$ 430,000		
Pretax accounting income		$ 659,000	
Taxable income minus pretax accounting income			$(229,000)

EXHIBIT 16–10   TAX ASSESSMENT COMPUTATION

RIVER CITY MANUFACTURING, INC.
Computation of 19X5 Income Tax Assessment

INCOME TAX*

$$
\begin{aligned}
(\$50,000)(.15) &= \$\ \ \ 7,500 \\
(\$25,000)(.25) &= \ \ \ 6,250 \\
(\$355,000)(.34) &= 120,700 \\
(\$235,000)(.05) &= \ \ 11,750 \\
&\ \ \ \ \$146,200
\end{aligned}
$$

* (Taxable income)(Tax rate) = Income tax.

tax assessment on this amount is calculated as shown in Exhibit 16–10 and is $146,200. Exhibit 16–9 also shows River City's pretax accounting income to be $659,000, which exceeds taxable income by $229,000 [$659,000 − $430,000] as a result of both permanent and temporary differences. Temporary differences arise from installment sales income ($130,000), depreciation expense ($105,000), and warranty expense ($30,000). In addition, a permanent difference of $24,000 is created by interest on municipal bonds held by the corporation.

The computation of River City's 19X5 income taxes expense is shown in Exhibit 16–11. Notice that income taxes expense is based on pretax accounting income, after that amount has been adjusted for permanent and temporary differences and for the tax effects of temporary differences. Municipal bond interest, the permanent difference in this example, is an element of pretax accounting income that is excluded from taxable income. It must therefore be

EXHIBIT 16–11   **TAXES EXPENSE COMPUTATION**

RIVER CITY MANUFACTURING, INC.
Computation of 19X5 Income Taxes Expense

Pretax accounting income		$659,000
Permanent difference:		
Municipal bond interest		(24,000)
Pretax accounting income adjusted for permanent		
difference......................................		$635,000
Temporary differences:		
Installment sales income.........................		(130,000)
Depreciation expense		(105,000)
Warranty expense		30,000
Pretax accounting income adjusted for permanent and		
temporary differences		$430,000
Tax on the amount of pretax accounting income		
adjusted for permanent and temporary differences		
[($430,000)(.34)]		$146,200
Tax effects of temporary differences:		
Additions to deferred tax liability		
Tax on installment sales income taxable in future		
years [($130,000)(.34)]	$44,200	
Tax on tax return depreciation to be expensed in		
future years [($105,000)(.34)]	35,700	
Reductions in deferred tax liability		
Tax on warranty expense deductible on future tax		
returns [($30,000)(.34)]......................	(10,200)	
Net addition to deferred tax liability		69,700
Income taxes expense		$215,900

---

removed from pretax accounting income before computing income tax expense. Pretax accounting income must also be adjusted to allow for permanent differences that are elements of taxable income but excluded from pretax accounting income (such as depletion in excess of cost).

Tax Effects of Temporary Differences

River City's 19X5 pretax accounting income includes three temporary differences: installment sales income, depreciation expense, and warranty expense. The installment sales temporary difference is income that appears on the 19X5 income statement but will appear on a future tax return. Therefore, the tax effect of this temporary difference is to defer tax from 19X5 to some future period. In Exhibit 16–11, the amount of the future tax effect is estimated to be $44,200, using the tax rate of 34 percent. (In this example, 34 percent is the *marginal tax rate,* which is the tax rate that would apply to the next dollar of income.) The depreciation expense temporary difference represents expense that appears on the 19X5 tax return but will appear on a future income statement. The tax effect of this temporary difference is also to defer tax from 19X5 to some future period. In Exhibit 16–11, the amount of the future tax effect is estimated to be $35,700. The effect of the warranty expense temporary difference is opposite that of the other two temporary differences. The warranty expense temporary difference is an expense that is reported on the 19X5 income statement but will appear on a future tax return. Therefore, the tax effect of this temporary difference (estimated to be $10,200) is to prepay tax in the current period that will be absorbed in future periods. Accounting rules permit the tax effects of deferrals and prepayments to be offset when determining the overall effect of temporary differences. Thus, in Exhibit 16–11, the tax effect of the temporary differences is $69,700 [$44,200 + $35,700 − $10,200].

Interperiod Tax Allocation

The difference between income taxes expense and income taxes assessed in any year represents an allocation of taxes from one year to another. This difference is accounted for as a deferred income tax liability or asset, though it is much more common for deferred taxes to be a liability. Deferred taxes liabilities (or assets) represent the accumulated tax effects of temporary differences. For example, River City Manufacturing, Inc., must record deferred income taxes payable of $69,700 by making an adjusting entry at the end of 19X5. Suppose River City Manufacturing made the advance tax payments of $135,000 during 19X5 that are summarized by the following entry:

Income taxes expense	135,000	
Cash		135,000

The year-end adjustment to record deferred taxes would take the following form:

Income taxes expense ($215,900 − $135,000)	80,900	
Deferred income tax liability		69,700
Income taxes payable ($146,200 − $135,000)		11,200

The debit to income taxes expense raises the balance of the expense account from the amount paid during the year ($135,000) to the amount of taxes expense for the year ($215,900).[6] The credit to income taxes payable ($11,200) establishes as payable the amount remaining to be paid on the tax assessment for 19X5. The credit to deferred income tax liability ($69,700) includes in taxes expense the tax effects of the temporary differences.[7]

Deferred income taxes represent the tax effects of temporary differences. Since temporary differences arise because elements of income are included in taxable income of one period and pretax accounting income of another period, the deferred tax effects eventually reverse themselves. For example, the deferred tax liability originated by an installment sale is reversed when the cash is collected and the related gross margin enters taxable income. A similar process occurs for depreciation when a deferred tax liability, originated by using ACRS depreciation for tax purposes and straight-line depreciation for financial reporting purposes, is reversed as ACRS depreciation drops below straight-line depreciation in the later years of assets' lives. Of course, if the investment in such assets grows, the addition

[6] The foregoing journal entry assumes that tax payments during the year are debited to the income taxes expense account. Alternatively, such interim tax payments could be debited to a prepaid income taxes account which would alter the foregoing entry as shown in footnote 5 of Chapter 10.

[7] The change in deferred taxes for any period would also include the effects of any tax rate changes on deferred tax amounts already recorded. The additional computations that would form the basis for such an entry are described in intermediate accounting texts.

to the deferred tax liability may always exceed the reduction. Many growing companies have accumulated large deferred tax liabilities as a result of temporary differences arising from depreciation. This phenomenon has led some accountants to object to the recording of deferred income tax liabilities because it results in the creation of a liability that will not be paid unless the firm becomes smaller or goes out of business. These accountants argue that income taxes expense should equal the amount of tax assessed in each period. However, generally accepted accounting principles require the use of deferred income tax accounts to match taxes expense with related accounting income.

As we have seen, cash outflows may or may not be necessary to satisfy a deferred income tax liability. The cash outflow requirements can affect the value of a business, as we illustrate in the following analysis of a stock purchase decision.

ANALYSIS
CONSIDERATION OF
DEFERRED TAXES IN
THE PURCHASE OF
A BUSINESS

As an investor, you are contemplating the purchase of all of the common stock of Seaside Resorts, Inc., a hotel, golf, and tennis complex, from its current owner. Seaside's most recent balance sheet provides the following data:

SEASIDE RESORTS, INC.
Balance Sheet
As of December 31, 19X8

ASSETS

Current assets...	$ 200,000
Property, plant, and equipment	3,700,000
Other assets..	100,000
Total assets..	$4,000,000

LIABILITIES

Current liabilities..	$ 150,000
Long-term debt	1,000,000
Deferred income tax liability.........................	300,000
Total liabilities...	$1,450,000

EQUITY

Common stock..............................	$1,800,000	
Retained earnings	750,000	
Total equity		2,550,000
Total liabilities and equity		$4,000,000

The current owners are asking $7,000,000 for their stock. An appraisal of Seaside's assets by a respected independent appraisal firm indicates that the current fair value of the property, plant, and equipment is $8,000,000 and that the fair value of all the other assets equals their book value.

1. *What is the significance of the deferred income tax liability?*

You inquire about the deferred taxes and the current owners indicate that deferred taxes have been growing by $30,000 per year, reflecting larger depreciation on the tax return than on the income statement.

2. *Assuming that you will continue to invest in the business, does the price asked by the current owner seem reasonable?*

If investment in property, plant, and equipment continues, then continued growth in deferred taxes should be expected. Consequently, the deferred tax liability is unlikely to require payment at any time in the foreseeable future. On this basis, the following computation is appropriate:

Fair value of assets ($8,000,000 + $200,000 + $100,000)..	$8,300,000
Less: Fair value of liabilities	1,150,000
Fair value of Seaside Resorts...........................	$7,150,000

Accordingly, you conclude that the price asked by the current owners seems reasonable.

Having described the objectives and structure of the corporate income tax and having considered its impact on financial statements, we turn now to the role of income taxes in decisions by taxpayers.

TAXATION AND DECISION MAKING

The tax law influences corporate decisions about both tax return preparation and corporate operations. A corporation's objective in preparing the corporate tax return is to minimize its tax payments by carefully choosing among alternative methods allowed under the tax law for the preparation of its tax return. This process, which is known as *tax avoidance,* is perfectly legitimate. Indeed, a great many firms employ tax specialists as consultants or as full-time members of their accounting staff to perform this complex activity. (Tax avoidance must be distinguished from *tax evasion,* which is, of course, illegal.) In addition, management must understand the effect of income tax provisions on the costs and benefits associated with their activities. To illustrate the impact of the tax laws, we will examine five common corporate decision situations. The first two situations pertain to tax return preparation and the last three to corporate operations. We will begin with an examination of the tax implications of the selection of accounting procedures.

TAX IMPLICATIONS OF ACCOUNTING PROCEDURES

Selection of accounting procedures can have significant tax implications. For example, we have seen that the use of the installment sales procedure for recognizing income and the accelerated cost recovery system for determining tax return depreciation expense defer taxable income to future periods and thus postpone tax payments. For the financial statements, most firms recognize installment sale profits in the period of the sale and use the straight-line depreciation procedure.

The use of the LIFO (last-in, first-out) procedure for determining cost of goods sold in periods of rising prices and rising or stable inventory levels increases cost of goods sold relative to other inventory costing methods, thereby reducing income before taxes and the resultant cash outflows for taxes.[8] Since the selection

[8] Use of the LIFO method for tax purposes requires that it also be used for the income statement. From a financial reporting point of view, the income effects of LIFO may not be attractive and may discourage its use.

of inventory accounting methods is an item-by-item process, LIFO is usually selected for items whose costs and inventory quantities are expected to increase, and some other method (such as FIFO or weighted average) should be used when prices or inventory quantities are expected to decline or remain stable (Chapter 7).

One difficulty with using accounting procedures as a tax minimization device is that the Internal Revenue Service (IRS) usually approves accounting policy changes for tax computations only for long-term use. Furthermore, when approval for a change is given by the IRS, the firm is presumed to have always used the new procedure and any taxes that would have resulted in the past are due immediately. For example, when a firm that has been using LIFO is permitted to switch to FIFO, the taxes that would have been paid had FIFO been used in all past periods are computed and compared with the taxes actually paid. If the FIFO taxes are larger, the difference is due when the change is effected. In other words, firms are not at liberty to change from one tax accounting procedure to another and, even if a change is allowed, retroactive adjustments to taxes may make it undesirable.

ACCOUNTING ESTIMATES AND TAXES

While selections of accounting procedures are relatively permanent decisions, corporate taxpayers have somewhat more latitude in establishing accounting estimates. Before the implementation of the ACRS system, estimates of life and residual value had a much larger influence on depreciation deductions and, therefore, on income tax payments. While these two estimates are still made independently for financial reporting purposes, ACRS specifies asset lives and residual value, thus reducing the latitude allowed taxpayers in determining them for tax purposes.

Another type of estimate is made when a firm examines its inventory to determine which items are not likely to be sold or, if sold, will produce only a fraction of their cost in revenue. As we saw in Chapter 7, the cost of inventory must be written down to market value (when market is less than cost) for the financial statements. A write-down decreases both assets and income.

A similar value estimate and write-down procedure is employed for some other assets, such as items of property, plant, and equipment. Although actual disposal is, again, often required for the write-down to be used on the tax return, firms can alter the timing of taxable profit by deciding when to include asset write-downs on the tax return. Although ACRS has reduced taxpayers' latitude in establishing estimates for depreciable property, other elements of taxable income still depend on estimates that may be chosen to secure tax advantages.

CAPITAL STRUCTURE AND TAXES

The balancing of debt and equity in the capital structure of a corporation can also influence taxes paid by the corporation. Interest payments to creditors are an expense that may be deducted from revenue when computing taxable income. Dividend payments to stockholders may not be deducted. Therefore, firms with larger proportions of debt in their capital structure will have smaller cash outflows for taxes, thus permanently increasing the cash available for reinvestment in the firm or payment to stockholders. For example, assume that there are two firms, each of which has $500,000 of assets. Firm A has secured all its capital ($500,000) from stockholders, while firm B has secured half ($250,000) its capital from creditors at an interest rate of 12 percent. Both firms pay dividends equal to 12

EXHIBIT 16–12   EFFECT OF CAPITAL STRUCTURE ON INCOME AND CASH FLOWS

	FIRM A	FIRM B
IMPACT ON INCOME		
Income from operations	$100,000	$100,000
Less: Interest expense..............................	–0–	30,000
Income before taxes	$100,000	$ 70,000
Income tax (.34)	34,000	23,800
Net income.......................................	$ 66,000	$ 46,200
IMPACT ON CASH FLOWS		
Dividends...	$ 60,000	$ 30,000
Interest	–0–	30,000
Less: Tax reduction from interest deduction		(10,200)
Net cash outflow	$ 60,000	$ 49,800

percent of equity to stockholders each year. Both firms also have income from operations of $100,000 each year. For simplicity, assume that both firms have a tax rate of 34 percent. A comparison of the impact on income of the differing capital structures of the firms is shown in Exhibit 16–12.

Remember, however, that debt is a more risky form of financing for the firm than is equity because of the requirement that principal and interest be paid at specified times without regard to the firm's profitability (see Chapters 11A, 11B, and 12). Nevertheless, debt does offer a tax advantage over equity as a source of capital. The advantages and disadvantages must be weighed when making decisions concerning capital structure.

TAX IMPLICATIONS OF ASSET ACQUISITION

Income taxes influence decisions about assets as well as decisions about debt and equity. The asset acquisition decision has two parts: (1) what assets should be acquired and (2) how the firm should arrange for the acquisition. Consideration of the issues involved in deciding what assets should be acquired can be found in a financial management or capital budgeting text. Here, we will examine the three ways in which a firm can structure an asset acquisition—as a *purchase,* a *capital lease,* or an *operating lease.*

To begin with, there are different tax implications to each of these three acquisition alternatives. When assets are purchased, the purchasing firm secures the rights to apply ACRS depreciation for the asset on its tax return. When property is acquired for use on an operating lease, the entire amount of the lease payment is an expense. However, the ACRS depreciation remains with the lessor.

The situation when assets are acquired on a capital lease is less straightforward. The lessee (the purchaser) secures the rights to ACRS depreciation for the tax return. As we have discussed, only the interest component of the cash outflows for a capital lease is an expense (see Chapters 11A and 11B). The remainder of the cash payments reduces the lease liability. The interest expense does, of course, reduce income before taxes, which in turn reduces taxes. But the interest-based tax reduction is not an exclusive advantage of leasing (compared to purchasing) because assets purchased are often financed by borrowing, which also produces interest-based tax reduction.

Whenever assets are acquired, a careful evaluation must be made of the tax implications of purchasing or leasing the asset. Often substantial cost savings can be made by using the tax implications of an asset purchase to bargain for more attractive purchase or leasing terms. The following analysis highlights some of these issues.

ANALYSIS
TAX AND CASH FLOW IMPLICATIONS OF AN ASSET ACQUISITION

Shawn Taylor, the manager of data processing services for Midwest Department Stores, and Spencer Fields, the manager of the purchasing department, have been discussing the acquisition of 20 microcomputers for the store's credit staff. The computers are to be acquired in early January 19X1, will cost $4,500 each, and will have an expected life of five years and no residual value. Shawn and Spencer ask Steve Dietsch, the firm's controller, whether there are any financial savings to be realized by leasing or by borrowing to finance the purchase.

Steve determines that the computers will be depreciable over five years. Steve says that the following three alternatives are available for acquisition of the computers:

1. An operating lease with five annual payments of $24,967, with the first payment on December 31, 19X1.

2. A capital lease with five annual payments of $24,967, with the first payment on December 31, 19X1.

3. Borrowing $90,000 on a five-year note with annual interest payments. The first interest payment is to be December 31, 19X1. The principal is to be repaid at the end of 19X5.

For alternatives 2 and 3, Steve notes that an interest rate of 12 percent is appropriate. Since their bonuses are affected by both net income and cash availability, Spencer and Shawn ask Steve to prepare the following analysis:

1. *What is the effect on 19X1 income of each alternative?*

Operating lease

Lease expense	$24,967
Tax expense reduction due to lease expense [($24,967)(.34)]*	(8,489)
Income reduction	$16,478

Capital lease

Interest expense [($90,000)(.12)(1)]	$10,800
Depreciation expense ($90,000/5)	18,000
Tax expense reduction due to expenses [($10,800 + $18,000)(.34)]* ..	(9,792)
Income reduction	$19,008

Borrowing

Interest expense [($90,000)(.12)(1)]	$10,800
Depreciation expense ($90,000/5)	18,000
Tax reduction due to expenses [($10,800 + $18,000)(.34)]*	(9,792)
Income reduction	$19,008

* The tax rate is assumed to be 34 percent.

2. *What is the effect on 19X1 cash flows of each alternative?*

Operating lease

Lease payment	$24,967
Tax reduction	(8,489)
Net cash outflow	$16,478

Capital lease

Lease payment	$24,967
Tax savings from interest expense and depreciation expense	(9,792)
Net cash outflow	$15,175

Borrowing

Interest payment	$10,800
Tax savings from interest expense and depreciation expense	(9,792)
Net cash outflow	$ 1,008

For 19X1 the operating lease has the smallest negative effect on income. Borrowing has the smallest cash flow impact in 19X1. Of course, in subsequent years both the income and cash flow effects will change for leasing and borrowing.

EMPLOYEE COMPENSATION POLICIES AND TAXES

Our final illustration of a decision affected by income taxes concerns employee compensation policy. When employee compensation is mentioned, most students think of salary. However, fringe benefits such as medical insurance and stock purchase plans are also used to compensate employees. Wage and salary payments to employees are an expense for the employer and taxable income on the employee's personal tax return. Most fringe benefits (such as medical insurance and meals and lodging) are expenses for the employer but are not taxable income to the employee. Many firms use a form of executive compensation that is neither salary nor fringe benefit—the stock option. A *stock option* is an agreement between the firm and one or more of its employees that allows each identified employee to purchase a certain number of shares of the firm's stock for a specified price within a specified period of time. If the stock price rises above the specified price, the employees may exercise the option and acquire stock for less than its then current price. If the stock price does not rise, the options are not exercised. In general, the firm does not receive a tax deduction when a stock option is granted or exercised. The employee, though, does pay income tax on the increase in the value of the stock if the option is exercised.

Because of the possible tax implications for its employees, a firm must carefully examine the forms of its employee compensation both to maximize employees' aftertax financial positions and to minimize its own compensation expense for tax purposes (within the compensation outlays budgeted).

SUMMARY

The system of rules used to compute taxable income differs from the system of accounting principles used to measure pretax accounting income. The differences between taxable income and accounting income arise from the exclusion of income elements from one of the two income calculations (permanent differences) or from the inclusion of income elements in accounting income of one period and in taxable income of another period (temporary differences). Permanent differences affect the calculation of income taxes expense. Under the requirement that income taxes be matched with related accounting income, temporary differences also influence the calculation of income taxes expense. In addition, temporary differences give rise to deferred taxes through a process called interperiod tax allocation.

In addition to these influences of the corporate income tax on accounting procedures, the chapter also considered the influence of the corporate income tax on decisions. The provisions of the income tax laws alter the aftertax costs and benefits of many business decisions and thus influence the way in which decisions are made. This fact enables the federal government to manipulate the tax laws to encourage corporations to behave in certain ways. From the corporation's viewpoint, the impact of laws on the costs and benefits associated with its activities must be well understood.

KEY TERMS

ACCELERATED COST RECOVERY SYSTEM (ACRS) (p. 766)
ALTERNATIVE MINIMUM TAX (AMT) (p. 763)
CAPITAL ASSETS (p. 757)
CAPITAL GAINS AND LOSSES (p. 757)
CARRYOVER PROVISIONS (p. 760)
INCOME TAX (p. 755)
INCOME TAX RETURN (p. 755)
LONG-TERM CAPITAL GAINS AND LOSSES (p. 758)

OPERATING LOSS (p. 762)
ORDINARY INCOME (p. 757)
PERMANENT DIFFERENCES (p. 764)
PRETAX ACCOUNTING INCOME (p. 755)
PROGRESSIVE TAX (p. 757)
SHORT-TERM CAPITAL GAINS AND LOSSES (p. 758)
TAXABLE INCOME (p. 755)
TAX CREDITS (p. 762)
TEMPORARY DIFFERENCES (p. 766)

QUESTIONS

Q16-1. Describe the objectives of the federal government in levying income taxes.

Q16-2. What are the components of corporate income for tax computations?

Q16-3. Describe the corporate tax rate structure.

Q16-4. How do short-term and long-term capital gains affect the determination of ordinary income?

Q16-5. How do permanent and temporary differences affect income taxes expense? Give an example of each.

Q16-6. Why might corporations prefer revenues from dividends and municipal bonds over revenues from other sources?

Q16-7. Describe two temporary differences between the measurement of revenue and expense for pretax accounting income and for taxable income.

Q16-8. Why might management want to accelerate the recognition of expenses and decelerate the recognition of revenues for tax computations?

Q16-9. How does interperiod tax allocation relate to the matching concept?

Q16-10. What are the circumstances that give rise to regular increases in the deferred income tax liability?

Q16-11. Describe in general terms how income taxes affect decisions by corporations.

EXERCISES

E16-12.   OBJECTIVES AND STRUCTURE OF TAXATION   Indicate whether each of the following statements is true or false. If the statement is false, explain in a sentence or two why it is false.

1. The primary objective of taxation is to provide governments, in an effective and equitable manner, with the resources required to finance their activities.

2. Equity in taxation requires that the same amount of tax be assessed on the first $10,000 of income earned by a corporation as the first $10,000 of income earned by an individual.

3. Equity in taxation requires that two corporations with equal taxable incomes pay equal amounts of tax.

4. The granting of special tax benefits to energy-related industries in the interest of encouraging development in these industries does not represent a departure from strict equity in taxation, if the nation as a whole will benefit.

5. Double taxation of corporate dividends refers to the fact that corporations pay two taxes—one on their taxable income, which does not allow a deduction for dividends paid to stockholders, and a second on distributions of that income to stockholders in the form of cash dividends.

6. The double taxation of corporate dividends can be defended by arguing that corporations enjoy privileges not conferred on other business organizations.

7. The taxable income of sole proprietorships and partnerships is taxed at corporate income tax rates.

8. The principal objective of the progressive structure of corporate income tax rates is to encourage the development of small corporations.

E16-13.   USING THE CORPORATE TAX RATE STRUCTURE   For each of the ordinary income amounts noted below, determine the amount of corporate income tax due for the year.

a) $18,000

b) $45,000

c) $166,000

d) $1,204,000

e) $2,198,000

E16-14.   THE STRUCTURE OF CORPORATE INCOME TAXES   The following data are available for Auburn Corporation for a recent year:

Tax on ordinary income	$61,400
Tax credits	3,110
Alternative minimum tax	59,920

The company had no capital gains or capital losses for the year.

REQUIRED:

Determine the amount of tax due for the year.

E16-15. CORPORATE CAPITAL GAINS   Kinzer, Inc., has had several transactions involving capital assets during 19X5. Kinzer's accountant has developed the following data:

DATE	TRANSACTION	SELLING PRICE	COST	HOLDING PERIOD
1/10	Purchased security A	$ –0–	$ 6,000	–0–
2/20	Sold security M	16,000	14,000	2 years
3/21	Sold security Q	5,000	5,600	6 months
4/15	Sold security R	12,000	13,000	7 months
6/23	Sold land	29,000	14,000	4 years
8/15	Purchased security X	–0–	11,000	–0–
9/10	Sold security A	5,000	6,000	8 months

REQUIRED:

1. What is the net short-term capital gain or loss?
2. What is the net long-term capital gain or loss?
3. What is the effect of capital asset dispositions on taxable income for 19X5?

E16-16. CORPORATE CAPITAL GAINS   In addition to ordinary income of $105,000, the Pernell Company has the following summary data for transactions involving its capital assets for 19X9:

Short-term capital gains	$18,000
Short-term capital losses	2,000
Long-term capital gains..	34,000
Long-term capital losses	11,000

REQUIRED:

1. What amount of capital gains will be a part of the ordinary income component of corporate income?
2. How will the net amounts be taxed?

E16-17. MINIMIZING TAXES   Heidenreich and Company has asked you to advise it regarding possible sales of some of its capital assets to try to minimize current taxes. Assume that Heidenreich's income before any additional sales of capital assets is $100,000 and that Heidenreich has already recorded long-term capital gains of $30,000 and $4,000 of short-term capital gains for 19X3.

SECURITY	COST	CURRENT MARKET VALUE	HOLDING PERIOD SO FAR
A	$ 5,000	$ 3,000	6 weeks
B	13,000	15,000	4 months
C	19,000	21,000	2 years
D	8,000	7,000	13 months
E	14,000	10,000	9 months

REQUIRED:

1. What will Heidenreich's taxes be on the capital gains items already recorded if it sells none of these securities?
2. Which securities should be sold to minimize current taxes on the capital gains items already recorded?
3. Why might Heidenreich want to defer the sale of some of the securities that are still in the short-term category until early next year?

E16-18. REVENUE EXCLUSIONS   Using the data below, determine the amount of revenue to be included when computing corporate taxable income.

Sales revenue (no installment sales)	$12,200,000
Dividend income	320,000
Interest revenue, corporate bonds............................	416,000
Interest revenue, municipal bonds	62,000

E16-19. DEDUCTION OF EXPENSES   Montpelier Construction Supplies, Inc., has the following expense items for the year:

Cost of goods sold	$488,300
Depreciation expense	59,100
Sales and adminstrative expenses	96,500
Depletion expense on gravel pit (based on cost)*...................	12,700
Amortization expense, patents................................	6,300

* The tax law allows a depletion deduction for the gravel pit in the amount of $14,920.

REQUIRED:

Determine what amount of these expenses should be deducted in the computation of corporate taxable income.

E16-20. REVENUES AND TAXABLE INCOME   Prospero Bank and Trust has the following revenue items for 19X3:

Interest revenue, notes	$1,740,500
Interest revenue, municipal bonds	112,000
Dividend income	297,000

REQUIRED:

1. How much revenue should Prospero include in its 19X3 income statement?

2. How much revenue should Prospero report on its 19X3 tax return?

3. Why are the two amounts different?

E16-21. DEFERRED TAX LIABILITY   During 19X2, Wilson Products, Inc., sold a tract of land under a four-year installment sale contract resulting in a gain of $160,000. The gain from this sale (exclusive of interest earned on the contract) was recognized as follows on the income statement and tax return:

YEAR	INCOME STATEMENT	TAX RETURN	DIFFERENCE
19X2	$160,000	$40,000	$120,000
19X3	–0–	40,000	(40,000)
19X4	–0–	40,000	(40,000)
19X5	–0–	40,000	(40,000)

Assume that taxes are paid at a rate of 34 percent.

REQUIRED:

1. Construct a T-account for deferred tax liability associated with this transaction. Show the balance at the end of each of the four years.

2. How will the income taxes expense related to this installment sale be reported on company income statements over the four-year period of the contract?

E16-22. CORPORATE TAX AND FINANCIAL REPORTING MEASUREMENT DIFFERENCES   Sturgis Manufacturing has the following data for its depreciable assets:

ITEM	INSTALLED COST	ECONOMIC LIFE IN YEARS	ACRS LIFE IN YEARS	YEAR-END ASSET AGE IN YEARS
Furnace	$1,360,000	10	7	1
Machine #1	60,000	5	5	2
Machine #2	35,000	7	7	3
Machine #3	43,000	8	7	4
Truck	14,000	5	5	2
R&D equipment	210,000	6	5	2

Assume that all the assets have a residual value of 10 percent of their installed cost.

REQUIRED:

1. Compute straight-line depreciation expense for the income statement.
2. Compute ACRS depreciation expense for the tax return (see Exhibit 16–5).
3. If the tax rate for Sturgis is 34 percent, by how much is the cash outflow for taxes reduced this year when ACRS depreciation is used?

E16-23. CORPORATE TAX AND DEFERRED TAXES   The controller of Gibson Corporation has asked your help in preparing the journal entry to record taxes for 19X8. He has given you the following data (all differences are temporary differences):

ITEM	INCOME STATEMENT	TAX RETURN
Sales revenue	$2,630,000	$2,440,000
Expenses:		
Cost of goods sold	1,560,000	1,560,000
Depreciation.	380,000	270,000
Administrative	110,000	110,000
Interest..................................	40,000	40,000
Warranty	30,000	10,000
Other operating	90,000	90,000

REQUIRED:

1. Compute income taxes expense.
2. Compute income taxes payable.
3. Prepare the entry to record income taxes for 19X8.

E16-24. DETERMINATION OF CORPORATE TAXES   Tolly Company had the following data available for computing its 19X1 federal income tax:

Revenues (except dividends).......................		$3,402,000
Expenses...		3,176,000
Dividend income		45,000
Long-term capital gain		28,000
Tax credits:		
Historic structures..............................	$19,000	
Pollution control equipment......................	22,000	41,000

REQUIRED:

Compute Tolly's regular federal income tax due for 19X1.

E16-25. DETERMINATION OF CORPORATE TAXES   Floyd's Wholesale Hardware had the following data for 19X3:

Sales revenue $6,400,000
Cost of goods sold 5,200,000
Operating expenses 1,000,000
Financial expenses   60,000

Tax credits of $6,000 are available to Floyd's for installation of pollution control equipment on its furnace.

REQUIRED:

Compute Floyd's Wholesale Hardware's regular federal income tax due for 19X3.

PROBLEMS

P16-26. CHARACTERISTICS OF ACCOUNTING AND TAXABLE INCOME   Match each characteristic with the appropriate subject to create a correct sentence concerning accounting net income or taxable income of corporations as determined for federal income tax purposes. Your answer should list the characteristic numbers 1 through 10 and, opposite each number, the letter of the matched subject. Thus "1.B" indicates the correct sentence "Taxable income (not accounting net income) is reported on a tax return and used, in conjunction with other information, to compute the amount of taxes owed for the period."

SUBJECTS

A. Accounting income (not taxable income)

B. Taxable income (not accounting income)

C. Both accounting income and taxable income

D. Neither accounting income nor taxable income

CHARACTERISTICS

1. Is reported on a tax return and used, in conjunction with other information, to compute the amount of taxes owed for the period.
2. Is measured according to generally accepted accounting principles.
3. Permits use of accelerated depreciation methods.
4. Includes taxes expense for the period.
5. Is measured according to rules established by the U.S. government.
6. Is affected, either directly or indirectly, by changes in rules governing the computation of taxable income.
7. Is the basis for computing income taxes expense.
8. Includes the period's short-term capital losses in excess of capital gains.
9. Includes interest revenue on municipal bonds.
10. Under certain circumstances, may include depletion in excess of cost.

P16-27. CORPORATE TAX DETERMINATION   Briggs Company has the following data available for a recent year:

Ordinary income	$1,320,000
Net long-term capital gains.	21,000
Net short-term capital loss	5,000
Tax credits	11,000

REQUIRED:

Determine the amount of tax due for the year.

P16-28. CORPORATE CAPITAL GAINS   Northam Manufacturing, Inc., had the following capital asset transactions during 19X1:

a) Sold land that cost $187,000 for $179,000 cash. The land had been purchased five months earlier for eventual use as a new factory site and was sold as a result of a change in long-term plans.

b) Sold an old factory facility for $2,400,000. Northam paid $10,000,000 for the facility 12 years ago and had accumulated depreciation for tax purposes of $7,200,000 since that time.

c) Sold a small office building to an accounting and consulting firm for $210,000 cash. The building cost Northam $150,000 several years ago and had accumulated depreciation for tax purposes of $27,000 since that time.

d) Sold unneeded land for $610,000 cash to a country club for expansion of its golf course. The land was acquired three months ago as part of the purchase of a factory facility. The separate cost of the land was $500,000.

REQUIRED:

1. Determine the short-term or long-term capital gain or loss from each of these transactions.

2. Assuming that these transactions are Northam's only capital asset dispositions during 19X1 and that ordinary income from other sources totals $972,000, calculate taxable income for 19X1.

P16-29. ALTERNATIVE MINIMUM TAX   Ellis Manufacturing, Inc., has regular taxable income of $320,000 (before AMT adjustments). The following adjustments are required for the computation of the alternative minimum tax:

Excess of tax return depreciation over AMT depreciation	$27,000
Adjustment for charitable contributions of property	10,000
Adjustment for tax-exempt interest revenue	50,000

REQUIRED:

1. Calculate the alternative minimum tax.

2. Calculate the amount of the tax liability for 19X6.

P16-30. EXCLUSION FROM TAXABLE INCOME   Granville Corporation has the following items of revenue and expense:

Sales revenue.	$2,250,000
Interest revenue, corporate bonds	40,000
Interest revenue, municipal bonds.	8,000
Dividend income.	16,000
Operating expenses	1,930,000
Interest expense.	105,000

REQUIRED:

What is the ordinary income component of taxable income for Granville Corporation for 19X2?

P16-31.   THE EFFECTIVE TAX RATE   Karen Company has the following data for 19X7:

Computed taxes at the statutory rate (.34)......................	$3,060,000
State income taxes net of federal tax benefit	54,000
Tax credits	(1,830,000)
Actual taxes expense.....................................	$1,284,000

REQUIRED:

1. What was income before taxes?

2. What was Karen's effective tax rate?

P16-32.   INSTALLMENT SALE AND TAXES   On January 1, 19X2, Fountain Square Products sold a tract of land for $40,000 under a long-term contract, resulting in a long-term capital gain of $14,000. The contract requires an initial payment of $10,000 and 10 annual payments of $5,200 each with the first payment on December 31, 19X2. Thus, a total of $62,000 (principal of $40,000 and interest of $22,000) is paid to Fountain Square under the terms of the contract. Fountain Square recognizes interest on a straight-line basis at a rate of $2,200 per year for financial statements, but uses the installment sales method for its income tax return.

REQUIRED:

1. How much income does the contract contribute to Fountain Square's income statements for 19X2 and 19X3.

2. How much income does the contract contribute to Fountain Square's corporate tax returns for 19X2 and 19X3.

3. Why does the tax law permit the installment sales method?

P16-33.   DETERMINATION OF CORPORATE TAX   Butters, Inc., sells furniture to retail customers. For 19X8 Butters has the following data:

Sales revenue	$4,300,000
Cost of goods sold..	2,540,000
Operating expenses*......................................	1,106,000
Dividend income	20,000
Interest expense	70,000
Interest revenue, corporate bonds............................	15,000
Short-term capital gains	10,000
Long-term capital gains	37,000

* Includes ACRS depreciation expense of $220,000. Depreciation expense on the income statement is $170,000.

REQUIRED:

1. Compute regular federal income tax due for Butters for 19X8.

2. Determine taxes expense for Butters's income statement if the only temporary difference is the depreciation difference noted above.

P16-34. DETERMINATION OF CORPORATE TAX Mountain Transit Service provides ground transportation from airports to ski resorts in northern Nevada. For 19X4 the following data are available from which to determine Mountain Transit's federal income tax:

Transportation service revenue	$938,000
Operating expenses	792,000
Short-term capital loss.	27,000
Long-term capital gain	38,000
Interest revenue, municipal bonds.	7,000
Interest expense.	11,000
Tax credits:	
Employment of disadvantaged persons	4,000
Investment in pollution control equipment	21,000

REQUIRED:

Compute federal income tax for Mountain Transit Service for 19X4.

P16-35. EFFECT OF TAXES ON INVESTMENT COST The Harris Company is considering two alternative investments. Both investments produce the same revenues each year. Assume that the tax rate applicable to revenues and expenses from these investments is 34 percent. The investment options are as follows:

Investment 1: The cost of this investment is $100,000 cash to be paid at the time of the purchase. The cost can be expensed for tax purposes evenly over four years (an expense of $25,000 each year for four years).

Investment 2: This investment requires a cash outflow of $120,000 to be paid at the time of the purchase. The cost can be expensed for tax purposes evenly over three years (a $40,000 expense each year for three years). This investment also provides a pollution control tax credit of $12,000 in the first year.

REQUIRED:

Determine which investment requires the larger net cash outflow in the first year. Your response should incorporate the effect of the investment options on taxes.

ANALYTICAL OPPORTUNITIES

A16-36. INCOME TAXES IN ANNUAL REPORTS Income taxes affect the financial statements and related footnotes in many ways.

REQUIRED:

1. To demonstrate this fact, secure a recent annual report for a company of your choice. (Many libraries maintain files of annual reports and some subscribe to services that provide annual reports on film. In addition, most large companies whose stock is widely traded will send a copy of their most recent annual report upon request.)

2. Examine the financial statements and footnotes of your annual report. Prepare a list of the financial statement items and footnote paragraphs that mention matters related to income taxes.

A16-37. CONCEPTUAL BASIS FOR THE DEFERRED TAX LIABILITY Some accountants have argued that recognition of a deferred tax liability is conceptually unsound because such "liabilities" do not represent legally enforceable claims against the reporting entity.

REQUIRED:

Write a paragraph in which you (1) state your agreement or disagreement with the point of view stated above and (2) support your position by reference to specific accounting concepts.

SUPPLEMENTARY TOPICS

LEARNING OBJECTIVES

Careful study of this supplementary topic will enable you to:

1. Distinguish non-business entities from business entities.
2. Define the term *fund* and explain the nature of fund accounting.
3. Distinguish modified accrual accounting from accrual accounting.
4. Record budgets and encumbrances in a fund.

BUSINESS ENTITY: An organization of people and resources established to sell goods or provide services at a profit.

NONBUSINESS ENTITY: An organization of people and resources established to sell goods or provide services without regard to profit.

ACCOUNTING FOR NONBUSINESS ENTITIES

A large segment of our nation's resources is managed by nonbusiness entities—federal, state, and local governments; public educational systems; and nonprofit organizations such as hospitals, research foundations, and social service organizations. As noted in Chapter 1, a **business entity** is established to sell goods or provide services in order to earn a profit, whereas a **nonbusiness entity** is established to sell goods or provide services without regard to profit. For example, educational systems disseminate and produce knowledge; nonprofit hospitals provide health care through training, research, and service; governments engage in diverse programs, each with its own objectives. In short, the goals of nonbusiness entities are defined in terms of the specific goods and services they provide rather than in terms of profitability.

In nonbusiness entities, the difference between inflows and outflows of resources is interpreted not as profit, but merely as evidence of a difference between the rate at which resources are obtained and the rate at which they are used. In business entities, a large excess of revenue over expense is a sign of a high level of accomplishment; but in nonbusiness entities, an excess of inflows over outflows may be associated with either high or low levels of accomplishment. For example, a state government may report a large surplus of tax collections over disbursements simply because favorable economic conditions increase tax collections. The excess may occur during a period of successful or unsuccessful operation for state programs. Indeed, the excess may merely indicate that tax rates could be reduced without impairing the operation of state programs.

We begin this supplement with a brief introduction to the fund accounting system used by nonbusiness entities. Then we turn to a discussion of two distinctive aspects of fund accounting systems. The first, which is called *modified accrual-basis accounting,* is used in the absence of revenue-producing activity in nonbusiness entities. The second distinctive aspect of fund accounting systems is the practice of recording budgets and expenditure authorizations (*encumbrances*), a practice that serves as a basis for controlling the outflow of resources. We conclude with a discussion of accounting standard setting for nonbusiness entities.

FUND ACCOUNTING SYSTEMS

The financial accounting system for a business entity produces reports that characterize the organization as a single accounting entity. In contrast, the financial accounting system for a nonbusiness entity produces reports that character-

EXHIBIT A–1   STATEMENT OF INFLOWS AND OUTFLOWS

SMALLVILLE UNIVERSITY
Statement of Inflows and Outflows for Unrestricted
and Restricted Current Funds
For the Year Ended December 31, 19X9

	UNRESTRICTED	RESTRICTED	TOTAL
INFLOWS			
Student tuition and fees	$270,000		$270,000
Governmental appropriations	209,000		209,000
Private gifts	125,000	$160,000	285,000
Total inflows.....................................	$604,000	$160,000	$764,000
OUTFLOWS			
Instruction...	$335,000	$ 53,000	$388,000
Libraries..	61,000	12,000	73,000
Student services	77,000		77,000
Operation and maintenance of plant	95,000		95,000
General administration...............................	86,000		86,000
Student aid	6,000	50,000	56,000
Total outflows....................................	$660,000	$115,000	$775,000
Net increase (decrease) in fund balance	$ (56,000)	45,000	$ (11,000)

FUND: A collection of assets, liabilities, and equity related to a specified subset of the activities of a nonbusiness organization.

FUND BALANCE: The equity in a fund representing the excess of assets over liabilities that is available for future use by the fund.

ize the organization as a collection of interrelated accounting entities called funds. A **fund** is a collection of assets, liabilities, and equity related to a specified subset of the activities of a nonbusiness organization. The equity in a fund, which is usually called the **fund balance,** is not an ownership interest but simply the excess of assets over liabilities that is available for future use by the fund. (When liabilities exceed assets, the fund balance is negative.)

Financial statements report separately the information related to each fund. Consider the statement of inflows and outflows for Smallville University shown in Exhibit A – 1. All of Smallville's resource inflows and outflows during 19X9 are recorded in two funds, each represented by a separate column in the statement. The *restricted current fund* records the inflow and outflow of resources that must be spent only in specified ways. During 19X9 inflows to the restricted fund totaled $160,000 and represented private gifts to be spent for purposes specified by the donors. The outflows from the restricted current fund included expenditures for instruction, libraries, and student aid. For example, the $53,000 outflow for instruction was made possible by cash given with the stipulation that it be spent on teaching prizes and awards for educational innovation. The *unrestricted current fund* records the inflow and outflow of resources that may be spent to meet any needs of the university. Smallville University receives unrestricted funds in the form of student tuition and fees, government appropriations of state tax revenues, and private gifts. These funds are spent for instruction, libraries, student services, operation and maintenance of plant, general administration, and student aid.

Assets, liabilities, and equity are reported in separate balance sheets for each fund. For example, the balance sheets for Smallville University's current funds

EXHIBIT A-2 BALANCE SHEET

SMALLVILLE UNIVERSITY
Balance Sheet for Unrestricted and Restricted Current Funds
As of December 31, 19X9 and 19X8

	UNRESTRICTED		RESTRICTED	
	12/31/X9	12/31/X8	12/31/X9	12/31/X8
ASSETS				
Cash..........................	$21,500	$ 30,400	$ 8,000	$3,200
Marketable securities	70,500	122,600	46,000	4,100
Total assets...................	$92,000	$153,000	$54,000	$7,300
LIABILITIES				
Accounts payable................	$ 7,000	$ 12,000	$ 2,000	$ 300
FUND EQUITY	85,000	141,000	52,000	7,000
Total liabilities and fund equity	$92,000	$153,000	$54,000	$7,300

are shown in Exhibit A-2. Notice that the $56,000 decrease in the unrestricted current fund reported in Exhibit A-1 equals the change in the unrestricted fund equity account reported in Exhibit A-2 [$85,000-$141,000]. Similarly, the $45,000 increase in the restricted current fund reported in Exhibit A-1 equals the change in the restricted fund equity account reported in Exhibit A-2 [$52,000-$7,000].

In addition to the two current funds, which account for all inflows and outflows of resources related to day-to-day operations, Smallville University has other funds to account for specific activities. Such funds include the acquisition of new buildings and equipment (buildings and equipment fund), the renewal and replacement of buildings and equipment (renewal and replacement fund), the lending of money to students (student loan fund), the investment in buildings and equipment (investment in buildings and equipment fund), and the investment in income-producing assets (endowment fund). A separate balance sheet and statement of inflows and outflows would be prepared for each of these funds and included in an extended version of the statements prepared for the current funds.

FUND ACCOUNTING SYSTEM: The collection of all funds that describes the various activities of a nonbusiness entity.

Taken together, the collection of all funds that describes the various activities of a nonbusiness entity is called a **fund accounting system.** Fund accounting systems vary significantly from one nonbusiness entity to another. Both the types of funds employed and the names attached to funds differ, reflecting differences in the nature of operations. Description of these differences is beyond the scope of this supplement. Our focus will be on the distinctive accounting procedures used by fund accounting systems. In the discussion that follows, we will use government organizations for our examples. We will begin by describing a modified form of accrual-basis accounting that is used mainly by governments for funds that are not associated with revenue-producing activity. The following section describes a method for recording budgets and expenditure authorizations in the accounting system used by many nonbusiness entities.

MODIFIED ACCRUAL-BASIS ACCOUNTING

The financial reports of business entities are prepared on the accrual basis of accounting. As explained in Chapter 1, *accrual-basis accounting,* which recognizes income when it is earned, is distinguished from *cash-basis accounting,* which recognizes income when the cash is received and paid. The accrual basis is superior to the cash basis for evaluating business performance because it ties income measurement to selling, the principal revenue-producing activity of most businesses. In contrast, cash-basis accounting for income is influenced by many factors that have little to do with the performance of the business. The accrual basis is also used by nonbusiness entities for funds established for revenue-producing organizations or programs. For example, many hospitals, universities, and city-owned public utilities use the accrual basis for financial reporting. However, when a fund is not associated with a revenue-producing activity but is established to control resources set aside for a particular purpose, then accrual-basis accounting is not applicable and an alternative basis is used. For example, when tax revenues are appropriated to support various operations of a government, a fund is established to provide a record to ensure that the tax revenues are spent for the appropriate purposes and that the appropriation is not over- or underspent.

One alternative to the accrual basis is cash-basis accounting. However, the cash basis merely records cash receipts and payments and does not consider events that give assurance of future receipts or events that obligate the fund to make future payments. Fund managers may underspend and fail to perform their function adequately if the records do not reflect amounts whose receipt in the near future is assured. Or they may inadvertently overspend by authorizing outflows in excess of appropriations if obligations to make future payments are not recorded in the accounting records.

Such shortcomings of cash-basis accounting are avoided when modified accrual-basis accounting is used. **Modified accrual-basis accounting** provides for the recognition of inflows when receipt is reasonably assured and for the recognition of outflows when a commitment is made to pay. It is called *modified* accrual-basis accounting because it permits certain departures from the accrual basis regarding the recognition of revenues and the matching of expenses with revenues. We will now examine modified accrual-basis accounting more closely. We will consider first the recognition of inflows of resources or revenues and then the recognition of outflows of resources or expenditures.

MODIFIED ACCRUAL-BASIS ACCOUNTING: The method of recognizing inflows of resources (revenues) when receipt is reasonably assured and recognizing outflows of resources (expenditures) when a commitment is made to pay.

MODIFIED ACCRUAL-BASIS REVENUE RECOGNITION

Recall that business entities recognize revenue when it is earned—that is, when substantially all the effort required to earn revenue has been performed and when the selling price is known. Modified accrual-basis accounting replaces the "substantial performance" condition with a "funds availability" condition. This means that a fund using the modified accrual basis recognizes revenue when two conditions are satisfied: (1) The amounts are *available* to satisfy obligations of the government unit that are related to the current year and (2) the amounts are *known.* If either condition is not met, the related amounts should not be recognized as revenue. For example, suppose a county government bills property taxes in the total amount of $110,000. The taxes are used to pay for the maintenance of roads and other services. The county estimates that 5 percent of this amount will never be collected. Following modified accrual-basis accounting, the county would make the following entry when the tax bills are sent:

Taxes receivable...................................	110,000	
Allowance for uncollectible taxes..................		5,500
Tax revenue		104,500

In contrast, a state government responsible for the collection of sales taxes that depend on an unknown level of retail sales would probably not establish a receivable for the sales taxes. Instead, it would record sales tax revenue on the cash basis.

MODIFIED ACCRUAL-BASIS EXPENDITURE RECOGNITION Modified accrual-basis accounting substitutes the expenditure recognition concept for the accrual concepts of expense recognition and matching. *Expenditure recognition* refers to the process by which costs are charged against fund revenues as the fund becomes obligated to pay such costs. Exhibit A–3 illustrates the difference between expenditure recognition under modified accrual-basis accounting and expense recognition under accrual-basis accounting in terms of

EXHIBIT A–3 **EXPENDITURE VERSUS EXPENSE RECOGNITION**

TRANSACTION	EXPENDITURE RECOGNITION (MODIFIED ACCRUAL)		EXPENSE RECOGNITION (ACCRUAL)	
1. 6/30/X9: Pay $1,200 for fire insurance policy providing one year of coverage	Insurance *expenditures* . 1,200 Cash 1,200		Prepaid insurance .... 1,200 Cash................ 1,200	
2. 12/31/X9: Adjusting entry for insurance	No entry		Insurance *expense*....... 600 Prepaid insurance 600	
3. 8/15/X9: Purchase supplies on account for $800	Supplies *expenditures*... 800 Accounts payable 800		Supplies inventory ...... 800 Accounts payable 800	
4. 9/10/X9: Pay $800 cash for supplies purchased on account	Accounts payable ...... 800 Cash 800		Accounts payable .... 800 Cash................ 800	
5. 11/5/X9: Use supplies costing $800	No entry		Supplies *expense* .... 800 Supplies inventory 800	
6. 1/1/X9: Purchase equipment for $5,000 cash	Equipment *expenditures* 5,000 Cash 5,000		Equipment .... 5,000 Cash................ 5,000	
7. 12/31/X9: Adjusting entry for straight-line depreciation, based on 10-year life and no residual value	No entry		Depreciation *expense* .... 500 Accumulated depreciation.............. 500	

seven transactions. The first two transactions in Exhibit A – 3 illustrate the recording of an insurance prepayment. Following expenditure recognition, the entire $1,200 premium is charged against revenue in the period in which the government unit becomes obligated to pay it rather than being divided between the two years to which the premium applies. The third, fourth, and fifth transactions in Exhibit A – 3 illustrate the different entries for the purchase and use of supplies. Following expenditure recognition, no inventory is established in the accounts and the goods are debited to an expenditure account immediately upon purchase.[1] Under accrual-basis expense recognition, the cost of supplies is held in an inventory account until the supplies are used. The last two transactions in Exhibit A – 3 illustrate the different entries for purchase and use of equipment. Expenditure recognition does not require depreciation; rather, the costs of long-lived assets are charged against revenue in the periods in which the acquisition costs are incurred. In these ways, modified accrual-basis expenditure recognition abandons the matching concept used for accrual-basis expense recognition.

We turn now to a second distinctive feature of fund accounting, the recording of budgets and expenditure authorizations in the accounting records. Coupled with expenditure recognition, the recording of budgets and expenditure authorizations is the basis for controlling the spending of amounts appropriated to a fund.

RECORDING BUDGETS AND ENCUMBRANCES

The control process begins with the preparation of a budget. Frequently, an initial budget is prepared by the government unit and submitted to the government's legislative body for possible modification, adoption, and final enactment. The control of expenditures is facilitated by two distinctive accounting procedures: (1) the recording of budgeted revenues and expenditures and (2) the recording of expenditure authorizations or encumbrances. We begin by considering the first procedure and then turn to the second.

RECORDING BUDGETED REVENUES AND EXPENDITURES

Government funds frequently record *budgeted* revenues and expenditures as well as *actual* revenues and expenditures. This dual recording makes possible a continuing comparison of actual and budgeted items throughout the year. The budgeted amounts are entered in the "budget" accounts at the beginning of the fiscal year; during the year, actual revenues and expenditures are recorded in separate accounts. The result of this dual-entry procedure is that the difference between appropriations and expenditure accounts represents the unexpended residual of budgeted expenditure and the difference between estimated revenue and revenue accounts represents the unrecognized residual of budgeted revenue.

To illustrate the journal entries to record budgeted and actual revenues and expenditures, let us take as an example the summary data for the general fund of the City of Hampshire. The general fund of a city is similar to the unrestricted

---

[1] However, government units should disclose significant inventories in statements of financial position, whether the goods are charged to revenue on the basis of their use (or other disposition) or on the basis of expenditures. Such information is necessary for purposes of budgetary control.

current fund of a university. Hampshire's general fund begins 19X1 with no assets and a budget showing estimated revenues of $100,000 and authorized expenditures of $95,000. To simplify our illustration, assume that all revenues of the fund are received in cash when recognized and that all expenditures are paid in cash when recognized. Consequently, no entries to accounts receivable or accounts payable will be required. Actual revenues and expenditures for 19X1 were $96,000 and $94,500, respectively.

Recording the Annual Budget

The 19X1 budget for Hampshire is recorded by the following entry:

a) *Entry to record annual budget*

Estimated revenues..............................	100,000	
Appropriations		95,000
Fund balance...................................		5,000

This entry, which is made at the beginning of 19X1, is shown as entry **a** in the T-accounts in Exhibit A–4. Observe that estimated revenues are recorded as a *debit* and appropriations (authorized expenditures) as a *credit.* The excess of estimated revenues over appropriations is a credit to the fund balance. The fund balance is the principal residual equity account of every fund.

Recording Actual Revenues and Expenditures

The recording of actual 19X1 revenues and expenditures for Hampshire's general fund is summarized by the following entries:

b) *Entry to summarize recording of actual revenues*

Cash...	96,000	
Revenues		96,000

c) *Entry to summarize recording of actual expenditures*

Expenditures	94,500	
Cash..		94,500

EXHIBIT A–4   **RECORDING BUDGETED AND ACTUAL REVENUES AND EXPENDITURES**

	Estimated revenues				Appropriations		
(a)	100,000	100,000	(d)	(e)	95,000	95,000	(a)

	Revenues				Expenditures		
(d)	96,000	96,000	(b)	(c)	94,500	94,500	(e)

	Cash				Fund balance		
Balance	–0–					–0–	Balance
(b)	96,000	94,500	(c)			5,000	(a)
				(d)	4,000	500	(e)
Balance	1,500					1,500	Balance

These entries, which are also shown in Exhibit A–4, summarize the recording of revenues and expenditures during the year. Throughout the year, the excess of the estimated revenues account over the revenues account represents the portion of budgeted revenues that remains to be collected. Similarly, the excess of the appropriations account over the expenditures account represents the portion of authorized expenditures that remains to be spent.

Closing Revenue and Expenditure Accounts

In order to prepare the accounts for the next year, the current year's budget must be removed from the records and the revenue accounts and expenditure accounts must be closed to the fund balance. This two-step closing process is accomplished for Hampshire's general fund by the following entries:

d) *Entry to close estimated and actual revenue accounts to fund balance*

Revenues	96,000	
Fund balance	4,000	
Estimated revenues		100,000

e) *Entry to close appropriations and expenditure accounts to fund balance*

Appropriations	95,000	
Expenditures		94,500
Fund balance		500

As a result of the closing entries **d** and **e**, the fund balance account has a year-end balance of $1,500, which equals the excess of actual revenues over actual expenditures.

ACCOUNTING FOR ENCUMBRANCES

ENCUMBRANCE: An authorization to make a future expenditure that is issued prior to incurrence of the related liability (e.g., purchase orders and purchase agreements).

Encumbrance accounting is a second accounting procedure used by governments to facilitate control of expenditures. Government units frequently issue formal expenditure authorizations as the first step in making expenditures and prior to incurrence of the related liability. Such expenditure authorizations, called **encumbrances,** take the form of purchase orders or purchase agreements for goods and services. Since encumbrances are associated with future expenditures, the amount available for future expenditure is the excess of the appropriation over the sum of both encumbrances and expenditures. In order to avoid commitments that would exceed appropriation limits, encumbrances are recorded in the expenditure subsidiary accounts as well as in the encumbrances control account.

Encumbrances lead to expenditures, but the two amounts must be distinguished from one another. An encumbrance is frequently recorded before the amount of the future expenditure is known with precision; consequently, the recording of encumbrances does not replace the recording of expenditures. As an example, let's consider a purchase of police department supplies. The 19X5 supplies budget is $1,200. On January 15, 19X5, a purchase order is issued for supplies with an estimated cost of $500 and the following entry is made:

Encumbrances (supplies)	500	
Reserve for encumbrances		500

EXHIBIT A-5   JOINT SUBSIDIARY RECORD FOR ENCUMBRANCES AND EXPENDITURES

Police Department Supplies Account

| DATE | ITEM | ENCUMBRANCES | | | EXPENDITURES | | | UNENCUMBERED BALANCE |
		DEBIT	CREDIT	BALANCE	DEBIT	CREDIT	BALANCE	
1/1/X5	Appropriation							1,200
1/15/X5	Purchase order	500		500				700
2/2/X5	Invoice		500	–0–	512		512	688

On February 2, 19X5, the supplies are received, together with an invoice giving their cost as $512, and the following entries are made to reverse the earlier encumbrance entry and to record the purchase:

Reserve for encumbrances.............................. 500
    Encumbrances....................................... 500

Supplies expenditures................................. 512
    Accounts payable.................................... 512

These entries use two control accounts—one for encumbrances and one for expenditures. The subsidiary records may be designed so that the two control accounts correspond to different segments of a joint subsidiary record, as illustrated in Exhibit A–5 for the supplies account. Observe that the joint record displays the unencumbered balance (the excess of the appropriation over the sum of *both* encumbrances and expenditures) as well as the balance of encumbrances and the balance of expenditures.[2]

We turn now to a discussion of setting accounting standards for nonbusiness entities.

ACCOUNTING STANDARDS FOR NONBUSINESS ENTITIES

No single, well-articulated set of generally accepted accounting principles exists for nonbusiness organizations. Instead, principles have been developed for special types of nonbusiness entities under the direction of various rule-making bodies and professional organizations.

Accounting for the federal government and its many agencies is ultimately the responsibility of Congress. The Congress has established two agencies that direct accounting within the federal government—the Office of Management and Budget, which assists the President in the preparation of the annual federal budget, and the General Accounting Office, which establishes and reviews the accounting systems and procedures applied in all agencies of the federal government.

[2] When expenditures are made at a fairly uniform rate per period and are subject to long-standing, continuing commitments, then the encumbrances related to such expenditures are frequently not recorded. For example, encumbrances for salaries of a government unit's personnel are not usually recorded; instead, salaries are simply recorded as expenditures when incurred. In other words, a fund may record encumbrances for some expenditures and not for others.

The principal rule-making agency for state and local governments is the Governmental Accounting Standards Board (GASB), which was established in 1984 under the general direction of the Financial Accounting Foundation, which also oversees the operations of the Financial Accounting Standards Board. The GASB sets standards for state and local governments. However, subunits of state and local governments that function like business entities (such as municipal utilities and city hospitals) are subject to standards issued by both the FASB and the GASB. Accounting for state and local governments is also subject to the rules and directives of federal, state, and local legislative bodies.

Accounting principles for nonprofit organizations have been developed by various agencies. The FASB is the primary source of standards for nonprofit organizations. The FASB issues both general accounting and reporting standards and standards tailored to the needs of specific nonprofit organizations, including hospitals, colleges and universities, health and welfare organizations, libraries, museums, political parties, private elementary and secondary schools, private foundations, professional associations, and religious organizations.

SUMMARY

Nonbusiness entities are divided into governments and nonprofit organizations. The principal difference between business and nonbusiness entities is that business entities are established to sell goods or provide services in order to earn a profit, while nonbusiness entities are established to sell goods or provide services without regard to profit. The absence of a profit motive in nonbusiness entities means that nonbusiness accounting systems need not measure the net income or profit of the entity; rather, nonbusiness accounting systems are designed to facilitate control of the entity's resources and activities. Accordingly, the accounting system of a nonbusiness entity consists of a collection of funds—each fund representing the assets, liabilities, and equity related to a subset of the entity's activities. Separate financial statements are prepared for each fund. Funds established for revenue-producing activities can be maintained on an accrual basis. However, when a fund is not associated with revenue-producing activity, the fund must be maintained on a modified accrual basis that supports an emphasis on expenditure control. Expenditure control is also facilitated by the recording of budgeted revenues and expenditures in the accounts and by the use of encumbrance accounting. The principal source of accounting standards for governments is the Governmental Accounting Standards Board (GASB), while the Financial Accounting Standards Board (FASB) is the principal source of standards for nonprofit organizations.

KEY TERMS

BUSINESS ENTITY   (p. 790)

ENCUMBRANCE   (p. 797)

FUND   (p. 791)

FUND ACCOUNTING SYSTEM   (p. 792)

FUND BALANCE   (p. 791)

MODIFIED ACCRUAL-BASIS ACCOUNTING (p. 793)

NONBUSINESS ENTITY   (p. 790)

QUESTIONS

QA-1. Describe the principal difference between business entities and nonbusiness entities.

QA-2. Name and describe the two types of nonbusiness entities.

QA-3. Define the term *fund.*

QA-4. What is a fund accounting system?

QA-5. How does revenue recognition under modified accrual-basis accounting differ from revenue recognition under accrual-basis accounting?

QA-6. How does expenditure recognition under modified accrual-basis accounting differ from expense recognition under accrual-basis accounting?

QA-7. How are budgets recorded in the records of a government, and what purpose does this recording serve?

QA-8. What are encumbrances? How are encumbrances reflected in the accounting records of a fund?

QA-9. Identify and describe the principal sources of accounting standards established for nonbusiness entities.

EXERCISES

EA-10. ACCRUAL-BASIS AND MODIFIED ACCRUAL-BASIS ACCOUNTING   An accounting entity engaged in the following activities.

a) Purchased supplies on account for $740.
b) Paid for the supplies purchased in transaction **a**.
c) Used supplies costing $513.
d) Prepaid one year's rent in the amount of $8,400.
e) Adjusting entry for eight month's of the rent prepaid in transaction **d**.
f) Purchased equipment at a cost of $36,000.
g) Adjusting entry for one full year's usage of the equipment purchased in transaction **f**. Assume a six-year life and no residual value.

REQUIRED:

1. Prepare the journal entries to record these transactions under accrual-basis accounting.

2. Prepare the journal entries to record these transactions under modified accrual-basis accounting.

EA-11. RECORDING BUDGETED REVENUES AND EXPENDITURES   The annual budget for the general fund of a small city estimates revenues of $86,000 and authorizes expenditures of $83,500. The fund uses a single expenditure account and a single revenue account supported by appropriate subsidiary records.

REQUIRED:

Prepare the journal entry to record the budget at the beginning of the year.

EA-12. RECORDING ENCUMBRANCES   The City of Tullyville plans to purchase office supplies. The estimated cost of the supplies is $760.

REQUIRED:

1. Prepare the journal entry to record an encumbrance for this planned purchase.

2. Assume that the supplies are delivered at a cost of $753. Prepare the journal entries to record removal of the encumbrance and payment for the supplies upon delivery.

EA-13. ACCRUAL-BASIS ACCOUNTING VERSUS MODIFIED ACCRUAL-BASIS ACCOUNTING   Supplies costing $300 are ordered on July 10, 19X6, received on August 5, 19X6, and paid for on August 27, 19X6.

REQUIRED:

Prepare the journal entries to record these transactions in the records of a fund using (a) accrual-basis accounting (without encumbrance recording) and (b) modified accrual-basis accounting (with encumbrance recording).

EA-14. SOLVING FOR UNKNOWN AMOUNTS   Find the missing amounts (numbered 1 through 9) for each of the three unrelated funds described below

		FUND A		FUND B		FUND C
Inflows		$350		$620		$232
Outflows		294	(4)	____	(7)	____
Increase (decrease) in fund balance	(1)	____		210	(8)	____
Assets at year-end		622		975		405
Liabilities at year-end	(2)	____		298		97
Fund balance at beginning of year		396	(5)	____		126
Fund balance at year-end	(3)	____	(6)	____	(9)	____

EA-15. MODIFIED ACCRUAL-BASIS REVENUE RECOGNITION   The County of Royer collects property taxes and sales taxes. The following events occurred during January 19X4.

a) 1/2/X4: The county commissioners approved the 19X4 budget. The budget estimates that 19X4 sales tax collections will be $12,450,000. In the past there has been considerable error in sales tax collection estimates.

b) 1/15/X4: Cash in the amount of $1,105,420 was received from merchants for December 19X3 sales taxes.

c) 1/25/X4: Property tax bills totaling $46,398,280 were sent to property owners. Taxes are due on April 15 and the county expects to receive 95 percent of the amount billed.

d) 1/31/X4: $2,140 of the April 15 amount was collected from a property owner who plans to be out of the country until June.

REQUIRED:

Prepare journal entries to record these events using modified accrual-basis accounting.

PROBLEMS

PA-16. RECORDING BUDGETED AND ACTUAL REVENUES AND EXPENDITURES   The general fund for the City of Blimp begins 19X4 with cash and a fund balance of $92,000. The 19X4 budget estimates revenues of $44,500,000 and authorizes expenditures of $43,750,000. Actual 19X4 revenues were $44,827,300 in cash. Actual expenditures for 19X4 are $44,123,735 and were all paid in cash during the year.

REQUIRED:

1. Prepare the journal entries to record Blimp's general fund budget at the beginning of the year.
2. Prepare journal entries to summarize the recording of actual revenues and expenditures. Use a single revenue account and a single expenditure account.
3. Prepare closing entries for 19X4.
4. Prepare T-accounts for cash and the fund balance showing entries for 19X4 and the balances at the end of 19X4.

PA-17. RECORDING ENCUMBRANCES   Prepare the journal entries in the general fund to record the following events. Assume that the modified accrual basis is applied and that encumbrances are recorded.

a) 3/12/X2: A purchase order is issued for the purchase of a personal computer for the bookkeeping office; the computer has an estimated cost of $4,800.

b) 4/20/X2: The personal computer ordered on March 12, 19X2, is received, together with an invoice giving its cost as $4,910.

PA-18. PREPARATION OF UNIVERSITY FINANCIAL STATEMENTS   Central University reports the following trial balances for its restricted and unrestricted current funds:

(Amounts in thousands)	UNRESTRICTED		RESTRICTED	
	DEBIT	CREDIT	DEBIT	CREDIT
Student tuition and fees.		$ 72,109		
State government appropriation		158,100		
Private gifts		1,409		$3,985
Accounts payable		378		247
Fund balance, 6/30/X3		1,720		208
Cash	$ 510		$ 62	
Marketable securities.	111		1,429	
Instructional expenditures.	137,020		195	
Library expenditures	14,218		272	
Physical plant operations expenditures	23,143			
Administration expenditures	48,307			
Student financial aid expenditures.	10,407		2,482	
Totals.	$233,716	$233,716	$4,440	$4,440

REQUIRED:

1. Prepare a statement of inflows and outflows for the unrestricted and restricted current funds for Central University for the year ended June 30, 19X4.

2. Prepare balance sheets for Central University for the unrestricted and restricted current funds as of June 30, 19X4.

ANALYTICAL OPPORTUNITY

AA-19. FORECASTING INFLOWS FOR GOVERNMENTAL ENTITIES   The process of preparing financial statements for most governmental entities is supervised by elected officials. One of the frequent issues in a political campaign is the amount of income or sales tax revenue that will be available to finance governmental expenditures. It is frequently asserted that incumbent politicians seeking reelection over-forecast tax revenues in order either to budget unsustainable amounts of politically popular expenditures or to delay recognition of the need for politically unpopular tax increases.

REQUIRED:

Assume that you are a reporter for a newspaper. What questions would you ask the candidates as the basis for preparing an article to help the public understand whether or not tax revenues have been over-forecasted?

LEARNING OBJECTIVES

Careful study of this supplementary topic will enable you to:

1. Distinguish between specific price changes and changes in the general level of prices.
2. Explain how financial statements based on the cost concept are deficient when changes occur in specific prices or in the general level of prices.
3. Describe the difference between net income and current cost operating profit.
4. Adjust nominal dollar amounts for changes in the general level of prices.

CURRENT COST CONCEPT: The concept that leads to the adjustment of costs in financial statements for changes over time in the cost of the related assets.

CONSTANT DOLLAR CONCEPT (CONSTANT PURCHASING POWER CONCEPT): The concept that leads to the adjustment of financial statement amounts for changes in the purchasing power of the dollar.

ACCOUNTING FOR CHANGING PRICES

The financial statements described in the text chapters follow the cost concept. According to this concept, assets and related expenses are measured in terms of the cash expenditures actually made for them. Although it has many advantages, the cost concept has two disadvantages when it comes to measuring the effect of pronounced price changes on the earnings and resources of business enterprises.

The first deficiency of the cost concept is its presumption that asset values do not change. Between the time an asset is acquired and its sale or use, it is likely that its value will change. Consider a car dealer whose inventory contains ten current models purchased early in the season prior to a substantial wholesale price increase. Under the cost concept, the inventory would be reported at the old cost rather than at the higher current cost of the cars. To offset this deficiency, supplementary financial statements can be prepared using the **current cost concept.** Under the current cost concept, all costs in the financial statements are adjusted for changes over time in the cost of the related assets.

The second deficiency of the cost concept is its implicit assumption that the dollar, as a unit of measure, has a constant purchasing power, even though it is generally understood that the purchasing power of the dollar has declined in recent years. An example will demonstrate the effect of reduced purchasing power on the dollar as a unit of measure: Land purchased for $5,000,000 ten years ago, when the purchasing power of the dollar was approximately twice what it is today, represents about a $10,000,000 sacrifice of purchasing power if measured in today's dollars. The effect on firms of changes in the purchasing power of the dollar as a monetary unit is measured according to the **constant dollar concept.** Under the constant dollar concept (also called the **constant purchasing power concept**), all financial statement amounts are restated in dollars of current purchasing power.

Thus, adjustment of the conventional financial statements for the current cost and constant dollar concepts leads to two alternative sets of financial statements—current cost financial statements and constant dollar financial statements. This supplement discusses both current cost and constant dollar adjustments, with particular emphasis on the effect of these adjustments on income.

Although the Financial Accounting Standards Board encourages companies to disclose such adjusted information in footnotes to its financial statements, companies are not required to do so at the present time. Since inflation has been moderate in recent years, most companies have not made such disclosures. However, some have made a brief narrative statement about the general impact of inflation in a footnote to their financial statements.

CHANGING PRICES AND THE CURRENT COST CONCEPT

The difference between the current cost and historical cost of assets held by a firm is an important indicator of the impact of inflation on the financial welfare of the enterprise. When the purchase prices for assets held by an enterprise are rapidly rising, the enterprise must pay more to replenish its inventories and to replace its plant and equipment than it paid in the past. Furthermore, to the extent that expenses are based on old historical costs, subtracting the old historical cost expenses from revenue may overstate income and encourage the payment of dividends that impair the ability of the enterprise to replace its assets and maintain its current level of productive capacity. Let us examine more closely the nature of current cost and its use in income measurement.

HISTORICAL COST AND CURRENT COST

CURRENT COST: The price that would be paid for an asset at the present time.

The *historical cost* of an asset is the price that was paid for the asset at the time of its acquisition. Historical cost provides the basis for the cost concept and for recording asset acquisitions in the primary financial records of the firm. In contrast, the **current cost** of an asset is the price that would be paid for the asset at the present time. At acquisition, the current cost of an asset equals its historical cost; but subsequently, current cost may deviate substantially from historical cost. To illustrate, consider a grocer whose inventory includes a case of imported canned salmon that was purchased last year for $50 and is currently available for $62. The current cost of the salmon is $62, which exceeds its historical cost by $12.

The current cost concept also applies to depreciable assets, as illustrated by the following example: Two years ago, Hershell Printing Company purchased a printing press for $100,000. Straight-line depreciation was recorded at a rate of $20,000 per year, using a five-year life and no residual value. At the present time, an equivalent new machine sells for $110,000 and two-year-old models sell for $68,000. The book value of the machine held by the company, based on historical cost, is $60,000 [$100,000 − (2)($20,000)]. Its current cost is $68,000 — the price that would be paid for the asset in its present condition. The market price of used assets is frequently difficult to determine because many assets are not regularly bought and sold during their useful lives. When the market price of a used asset is unknown, it may be estimated by depreciating the current cost of a new asset. For example, the current cost of Hershell's printing press could be estimated at $66,000 [$110,000 − (2)($22,000)]. Thus the current cost of a particular asset changes over time. Changes in the current cost of assets held by a firm have an impact on its net income, and it is often useful to isolate that impact.

CURRENT COST OPERATING PROFIT

Recall that net income is the difference between revenue and expense. When expense is based on historical costs, increasing prices can erode the significance of net income as a measure of the additional wealth generated by operations. As a result, unwary stockholders, creditors, and managers may believe that operations have generated more or less additional wealth than is actually the case. For example, let us examine the case of an enterprising student who sells cans of cold fruit juice outside the recreational gym. Each morning the student has been purchasing 200 cans of juice from a distributor for $.85 each, or a total of $170. During the afternoon, the student has been selling the juice for $1.25 per can, or a total of $250. Each day's sales have produced net income of $80 ($250 of revenue less $170 of expense). One morning the distributor informs the student that the fruit juice will cost $.90 per can beginning the next day. Suppose the student began that day with $170 cash, spent the $170 for fruit juice, and collected $250 cash from customers. At the end of the day, the student had $250, $80 more than in the morning. Is the student really $80 better off than at the start of the day, as the net income suggests? If the student spends the entire day's net income that evening on food, cab fare, and a movie, the cash balance will fall to $170. However, now the student will be unable to purchase the usual 200 cans of fruit juice tomorrow because the juice will cost $180 (200 cans at $.90 each). In other words, net income indicates how much the student can spend without reducing the cash balance below the starting amount, but it does not indicate how much can be spent without reducing the *level of operations* for the business.

Is there an alternative income calculation that will tell the student how much can be spent while maintaining the customary level of operations at 200 cans per day? The answer is yes; however, an additional amount must be introduced into expense to provide for the increase in the cost of the fruit juice. Since 200 cans of juice will now cost $180 ($10 more than before), income computed using the current cost of goods sold ($180) rather than the historical cost of goods sold ($170) will yield the desired result. Income computed using the current cost of goods sold is called *current cost operating profit* and is computed as follows:

Revenue	$250
Current cost of goods sold	180
Current cost operating profit	$ 70

CURRENT COST OPERATING PROFIT: The excess of revenue over total current cost expense.

In general, **current cost operating profit** is the excess of revenue over total current cost expense. In contrast, **historical cost net income** is computed as follows:

Revenue	$250
Historical cost of goods sold	170
Historical cost net income	$ 80

HISTORICAL COST NET INCOME (NET INCOME): The excess of an entity's revenue over its expense, measured using historical cost.

Observe that the current cost of goods sold, $180 (200 cans at $.90 each), causes current cost operating profit to be $10 less than net income. In other words, net income ($80) includes $10 of profit that current cost operating profit does not contain because the historical cost of goods sold is $10 less than the cost of replacing the inventory of fruit juice that was sold. This $10 difference represents the portion of net income that cannot be consumed without reducing the student's level of operations.

USES OF CURRENT COST INFORMATION

We turn now to the use of current cost information by both internal and external decision makers in assessing the impact of dividends on the level of the firm's operations. The difference between current cost operating profit and dividends is an indicator of changes in the level of operations. Current cost operating profit in excess of dividends often indicates that there can be growth in the level of operations. Current cost operating profit that falls short of dividends often indicates that the level of operations is being reduced. Because changes in the amount of outstanding long-term debt or stock also affect the level of operations, the net effect on the level of operations must include changes in debt or stock as well as the relationship between current cost operating profit and dividends. For example, an excess of current cost operating profit over dividends might be accompanied by a reduction in long-term debt rather than an increase in the operating level. In other cases, the impact of dividends in excess of current cost operating profit might be offset by an increase in outstanding debt, with the result that the level of operations is maintained. The use of current cost information to formulate dividend policy is demonstrated in the following analysis of Wayward Lumber.

ANALYSIS USING CURRENT COST DATA

Wayward Lumber, Inc., is a medium-size company that acquires, holds, and harvests tracts of timber and sells the logs to the plywood industry. Wayward's assets include 10 major timber tracts acquired at various stages of development. Some tracts were acquired early in their growth cycle and require long holding periods; others were acquired later in their cycle and require much shorter holding periods. Wayward's net income for 19X4 reached a record high level because logs sold in that year were taken from several tracts acquired early in their growth cycle. Comparable tracts today, even early in their growth cycle, would cost three times as much as those harvested and sold in 19X4. Wayward's management is contemplating an increase in the dividend in response to the increase in net income.

1. *What does current cost information imply about the source of Wayward's income?*

The excess of (historical cost) net income over current cost operating profit represents the portion of Wayward's net income attributable to changes over time in the cost of timber tracts and other assets held by Wayward. Such amounts should be distinguished from current cost operating profit, which represents the excess of revenues over the current cost of assets used to secure those revenues.

2. *How is the current cost operating profit relevant to Wayward's dividend policy?*

Wayward's 19X4 net income is substantially larger than its current cost operating profit. If Wayward is interested in maintaining its present level of operations without securing new capital, it must replace the harvested tracts with funds provided by revenues. If the dividend is raised to distribute more than the current operating profit, revenues may not support the same level of operations. Accordingly, Wayward's management would be well advised to consider its dividend policy in relation to current cost operating profit.

Current cost information also assists decision makers both inside and outside a firm in making projections of the firm's future income and cash flows. The current cost operating profit measures the effectiveness of the firm's continuing operations, whereas the change in the current cost of assets indicates the effectiveness of the firm's asset-holding activities. These measures are useful because economic events have different impacts on continuing operations and asset-holding activities. If an investor wishes to project future income or cash flows by using predictions of related economic events in conjunction with past income, then the measurement of current cost operating profit is likely to improve the quality of predictions.

Deviations of current cost from historical cost are not the only evidence of changing prices. Changing prices (specifically, inflation) also alter the significance of the dollar as a unit of measure. The constant dollar concept provides a mechanism to adjust for such changes.

UNSTABLE MONETARY UNIT AND THE CONSTANT DOLLAR CONCEPT

SPECIFIC PRICE CHANGE: A change in the price of a particular asset, which alters the current cost of that asset.

GENERAL PRICE LEVEL CHANGE: A change in a large group of prices viewed as a whole, which alters the purchasing power of the monetary unit.

STABLE MONETARY UNIT ASSUMPTION: The assumption that the purchasing power of the monetary unit is stable over time.

CONSTANT DOLLAR AMOUNTS: Dollar amounts, whether of historical cost or current cost, that have been adjusted for general price level changes.

NOMINAL DOLLAR AMOUNTS (NOMINAL AMOUNTS): Dollar amounts, whether of historical cost or current cost, that have not been adjusted for general price level changes.

From the viewpoint of economic theory, *inflation* is a persistent upward movement in the level of prices in response to forces acting on *all* prices. Accordingly, a particular price change may not be evidence of inflation. Some prices change in response to seasonal swings in the supply of, or demand for, goods and services or as a result of technological developments peculiar to specific goods and services. Accountants, as well as economists, distinguish between general price level changes and specific price changes. A **specific price change** is a change in the price of a particular asset. In other words, a specific price change alters the current cost of that asset. For example, a computer that sells (new) for $9,000 in 19X3 may sell (new) for $6,500 in 19X5. In contrast, a **general price level change** is a change in a large group of prices viewed as a whole; a general price level change alters the purchasing power of the monetary unit.

Measurements of historical cost and measurements of current cost are both prepared under the assumption that the purchasing power of the monetary unit is stable over time. This assumption is known as the **stable monetary unit assumption.** Such an assumption justifies combining, without adjustment, dollar amounts arising from transactions that occur at different times. If, however, the general price level changes, then the stable monetary unit assumption is violated. Under those circumstances, it is appropriate to adjust amounts representing purchasing power at different times before these amounts are presented together. Such adjustments are intended to correct for instability in the monetary unit as a measure of purchasing power.

Dollar amounts that have been adjusted for general price level (purchasing power) changes are called **constant dollar amounts.** Dollar amounts that have not been adjusted for general price level changes — whether such amounts are historical costs or current costs — are called **nominal dollar amounts** (or **nominal amounts**). For example, the revenue amount that is reported in the primary income statement and in the current cost income statement is a nominal dollar amount. When comparative statements present revenues from several years, the revenues from different years are not strictly comparable in terms of purchasing power. In times of inflation, the purchasing power represented by a dollar of revenue earned in an earlier year is greater than the purchasing power of a dollar of revenue earned in a later year. Accordingly, nominal amounts must be adjusted if they are to be stated in constant dollars. This adjustment of nominal amounts for general price level changes restates all components in dollar amounts of the same purchasing power. In general, all of the dollar amounts in constant dollar financial statements represent purchasing power effective on the same date — usually the date of the most recent balance sheet.

MEASUREMENT OF GENERAL PRICE LEVEL CHANGES

PRICE INDEX: A numerical summary of the history of prices for a group, or "market basket," of commodities.

General price level changes are measured by price indexes. A **price index** is a numerical summary of the history of prices for a group, or "market basket," of commodities. The construction of a price index requires two steps. The first step is to identify the group of commodities on which the index will be based. The second step is to specify the relative importance of each commodity by assigning each a weight in a standard "market basket."

To illustrate, let us construct a three-commodity price index for a market basket that contains 10 pounds of ground beef, 20 loaves of bread, and 5 gallons of

EXHIBIT B–1   PRICES AND COSTS FOR A THREE-COMMODITY MARKET BASKET

| | | GROUND BEEF | | BREAD | | MILK | | TOTAL COST OF MARKET BASKET |
	YEAR	UNIT PRICE	COST OF 10 UNITS	UNIT PRICE	COST OF 20 UNITS	UNIT PRICE	COST OF 5 UNITS	
	19X7	$1.00	$10.00	$1.10	$22.00	$1.60	$8.00	$40.00
	19X8	1.20	12.00	1.05	21.00	1.80	9.00	42.00
	19X9	1.50	15.00	1.00	20.00	1.60	8.00	43.00

milk. Fictitious price histories for these three commodities are given for three years in the unit price columns of Exhibit B–1. The unit price columns exhibit various patterns of change. The price of ground beef is rising (from $1.00 to $1.20 to $1.50), while the price of bread is falling (from $1.10 to $1.05 to $1.00). The price of milk begins by rising (from $1.60 to $1.80) and then falls (from $1.80 to $1.60). In other words, all the prices do not move together, and inspection of individual price histories does not necessarily indicate a clear pattern of movement (for example, inflation or deflation) for all prices taken as a whole. In such cases, development of a price index is necessary to form an overall impression of price level changes.

A price index measures the year-to-year movement in the price level, relative to the price level in a particular year called the base year. For the purposes of our illustration, let us designate 19X7 as the base year. Thus the price index for our market basket for each of the years in our illustration is simply the ratio of the market basket's cost in that year to its cost in the base year. The three index values relative to the 19X7 base year are calculated as shown in Exhibit B–2. Observe that the base year (19X7) index equals one. Since our index increases as time moves forward from the base year, our three-commodity market basket shows an inflationary pattern of price changes. Inflation causes the purchasing power of the dollar to decline. Consequently, the current purchasing power represented by past expenditures exceeds the nominal amount of such expenditures.

We turn now to the use of general price indexes to adjust nominal dollar amounts to reflect the current level of purchasing power.

EXHIBIT B–2   CALCULATION OF INDEXES FOR BASE YEAR 19X7

$$19X9 \text{ index} = \frac{19X9 \text{ cost}}{19X7 \text{ cost}} = \frac{\$43}{\$40} = 1.075$$

$$19X8 \text{ index} = \frac{19X8 \text{ cost}}{19X7 \text{ cost}} = \frac{\$42}{\$40} = 1.050$$

$$19X7 \text{ index} = \frac{19X7 \text{ cost}}{19X7 \text{ cost}} = \frac{\$40}{\$40} = 1.000$$

ROLL-FORWARD ADJUSTMENTS

ROLL-FORWARD ADJUSTMENT: An adjustment of nominal dollar amounts for changes in the general level of prices subsequent to the transaction date.

An adjustment of nominal dollar amounts for changes in the general level of prices subsequent to the transaction date is called a **roll-forward adjustment.** In other words, the purchasing power of the nominal dollar amount is "rolled forward" from the transaction date associated with the nominal dollar amount to the current date. The adjustment thus uses two values of the general price level index — the value of the index at the transaction date and the value of the index at the current date. A roll-forward adjustment has the following general form:

$$\frac{\text{Current index}}{\text{Transaction date index}} \times \frac{\text{Nominal dollar}}{\text{amount}} = \frac{\text{Constant dollar amount}}{\text{in current dollars}}$$

If the nominal dollar amount is a historical cost, the transaction date is the date of the related transaction. If the nominal dollar amount is a current cost, the transaction date is the date on which the current cost is determined.

To illustrate the roll-forward adjustment of a nominal dollar amount, consider revenue of $1,000 earned two years ago when the general price index was 95. The unadjusted (nominal) amount of revenue is $1,000, or 1,000 units of two-year-old purchasing power. When purchasing power changes over time, 1,000 units of two-year-old purchasing power may be equivalent to more or less than 1,000 units of current purchasing power. Continuing the example, if the general price index currently stands at 114, the 1,000 units of two-year-old purchasing power are equivalent to 1,200 units of current purchasing power [(114/95)($1,000) = (1.2)($1,000) = $1,200]. The 20 percent increase in the general price index from 95 to 114 [(114 − 95)/95 = 20 percent] indicates a 20 percent increase in the number of purchasing power units required to represent a two-year-old inflow in units of current purchasing power. In other words, $1,200 has the same purchasing power today as $1,000 had two years ago when the revenue was earned. It is important to understand that the roll-forward adjustment does not alter the historical character of the financial amounts. Both the constant dollar amounts and the nominal dollar amounts represent the same inflow or outflow of resources. The two amounts differ only as to the date of purchasing power units used to measure the inflow or ourflow.

A separate roll-forward adjustment need not be calculated for every transaction. When transactions occur at a uniform rate throughout a period of time, a shortcut roll-forward adjustment can be used. Instead of rolling forward each transaction amount separately, it is acceptable to apply a single adjustment factor to the sum of nominal dollar amounts for the period. This shortcut adjustment uses the average general price level index for the transaction period and takes the following form:

$$\frac{\text{Current index}}{\text{Average index for transaction period}} \times \frac{\text{Total nominal}}{\text{dollar amount}} = \frac{\text{Constant dollar}}{\text{amount in}}$$
$$\text{for period} \qquad \text{current dollars}$$

Suppose that revenue for 19X9 totals $100,000 and that the average general price level index for 19X9 is 112. If the December 31, 19X9, index is 115, then constant dollar revenue in current (December 31, 19X9) dollars is $102,679 [(115/112)($100,000)]. Clearly, this calculation is easier than rolling forward the amount of each sale separately. The two roll-forward adjustments — the adjustment for single transactions and the adjustment for multiple transactions occurring at a uniform rate—may be used to roll forward an entire income statement. Furthermore, in making roll-forward adjustments for accounting purposes, it is customary to simplify calculations by using only average indexes for each period. This means that the current index is taken to be the average index for the most recent year and that the transaction date index is simply the average index for the period in which the transaction occurred. In most cases, this simplification does not lead to significant errors.

USE OF CONSTANT DOLLAR INFORMATION

The principal objective of investors in a firm is to earn a return on their investments. Such returns are paid to them in the form of interest or dividends. Since investors generally are concerned with the amounts of goods and services that their cash returns will purchase, constant dollar information is useful in assessing the significance of past and current interest and dividends in terms of current purchasing power. When choosing which firms are good investments, investors use constant dollar presentations to help assess the availability of corporate resources for interest and dividends. The following analysis illustrates the use of constant dollar information by a stockholder.

ANALYSIS USING CONSTANT DOLLAR DATA

Ms. J. W. Bush owns 10 percent of the outstanding stock of the Thornbrook Corporation. Her investment in Thornbrook represents Ms. Bush's principal source of income. She pays all her living expenses from the quarterly dividend checks and invests whatever amount remains in a savings account. It is now the end of 19X6. In recent years, the amounts Ms. Bush has had available to invest in savings have been declining, and she would like to know the extent to which recent inflation is to blame. Her questions can be answered by using constant dollar information.

Have the dividends to Ms. Bush kept pace with inflation?

Rolling forward her last three years' dividends to end-of-19X6 dollars, Ms. Bush discovers the following adjusted dividend stream:

YEAR	NOMINAL AMOUNT	ADJUSTED AMOUNT
19X4	$30,000	$36,000
19X5	32,000	35,400
19X6	34,000	34,500

Although the dividend in nominal dollars has been rising, it has not kept pace with inflation. The dividend has declined in terms of general purchasing power. The 19X4 dividend could have purchased goods and services worth $36,000 at end-of-19X6 prices, but the 19X6 dividend could have purchased goods and services worth only $34,500 at those prices. Accordingly, the 19X6 dividend represents lower purchasing power than the 19X4 dividend. Of course, this conclusion requires that the general price index applied is based on purchases similar to those made by Ms. Bush. The conclusion also assumes that Ms. Bush has not changed her spending practices.

SUMMARY

Price changes can be measured either in terms of the price changes for particular goods and services or as the change in a price index, which captures the movement in all prices taken as a whole. The recognition of price changes for particular goods and services leads to the current cost concept, and the recognition of changes in a general price index leads to the constant dollar concept. The application of these two concepts produces adjusted financial information that, when interpreted in conjunction with information reported in the primary financial statements, enables us to assess the impact of changing prices on a firm.

Current cost operating profit is the excess of revenue over current cost expense—expenses adjusted for changes in current cost. Current cost expense exceeds expense from the primary financial statements whenever the current cost of related assets (that is, the specific price of related assets) increases during the period.

The constant dollar concept leads to adjustments for changes in the general level of prices, which in turn represent changes in the general purchasing power of the dollar. The purchasing power of the dollar shrinks in times of inflation, with the result that a past expenditure represents more dollars of current purchasing power than the number of dollars originally spent.

KEY TERMS

CONSTANT DOLLAR AMOUNTS (p. 807)

CONSTANT DOLLAR CONCEPT (CONSTANT PURCHASING POWER CONCEPT) (p. 803)

CURRENT COST (p. 804)

CURRENT COST CONCEPT (p. 803)

CURRENT COST OPERATING PROFIT (p. 805)

GENERAL PRICE LEVEL CHANGE (p. 807)

HISTORICAL COST NET INCOME (NET INCOME) (p. 805)

NOMINAL DOLLAR AMOUNTS (NOMINAL AMOUNTS) (p. 807)

PRICE INDEX (p. 807)

ROLL-FORWARD ADJUSTMENT (p. 809)

SPECIFIC PRICE CHANGE (p. 807)

STABLE MONETARY UNIT ASSUMPTION (p. 807)

QUESTIONS

QB-1. What are the two deficiencies in the cost concept from the standpoint of accounting for changing prices?

QB-2. Define the terms *historical cost* and *current cost*. Explain how the current and historical costs of an asset are related.

QB-3. Describe two ways to determine the current cost of an asset subject to depreciation.

QB-4. Define the term *current cost operating profit*.

QB-5. How is current cost information useful as an indicator of growth or reduction in the level of a firm's operations?

QB-6. How can current cost information assist decision makers in predicting the future income or cash flows of a firm?

QB-7. What is a general price level change? How is a general price level change measured?

QB-8. What is the stable monetary unit assumption? Under what conditions is the assumption not valid?

QB-9. How do constant dollar amounts differ from nominal dollar amounts?

QB-10. Define the term *price index*. How are price indexes constructed?

QB-11. How are price indexes related to current cost and constant dollar amounts?

EXERCISES

EB-12. CURRENT COST AND HISTORICAL COST   On July 1, Whittinghill Autos acquired 20 cars (identical models) for resale to customers by paying cash of $280,000. The same autos can be purchased for $14,600 each on August 1 and for $14,750 each on September 1.

REQUIRED:

1. What is the current cost of an auto on each of the three dates mentioned above?
2. What is the historical cost of an auto on each of the three dates mentioned above?

EB-13. CURRENT AND HISTORICAL COST   Ocala Propane Company buys, holds, and later sells propane to industrial customers and homeowners. On March 31, 19X4, Ocala bought 250,000 pounds of propane at the market price of $.18 per pound. Ocala maintained the propane in inventory until September. Market price data for propane from March 1 until August 31 are as follows:

DATE	PRICE PER POUND
April 30	$.17
May 31	.15
June 30	.16
July 31	.17
August 31	.19

On September 15, Ocala sold the 250,000 pounds of propane for $.20 per pound.

REQUIRED:

1. Calculate the current cost of the 250,000-pound propane inventory on June 30 (Ocala's fiscal year-end), based on the price history for propane.
2. Calculate the historical cost of the 250,000-pound propane inventory on June 30.
3. Calculate the current cost and the historical cost of the 250,000-pound propane inventory on the date of its sale.

EB-14. CURRENT COST OPERATING PROFIT AND NET INCOME   Calculate the missing amount or amounts for each of the following independent cases:

	CASE A	CASE B	CASE C
Revenue	$ 100	$____	$6,000
Historical cost (nominal dollar) expense	43	610	____
Current cost (nominal dollar) expense..........	65	____	____
Current cost operating profit.................	____	206	930
Net income (as reported in primary financial statements)	____	290	1,850

EB-15. CONSTRUCTION OF A PRICE INDEX   A price index for attending City University can be constructed from the prices for three commodities—textbooks, tuition, and dormitory fees—for which the following prices are available:

YEAR	COST PER TEXTBOOK	TUITION PER TERM	DORMITORY FEES PER TERM
19X1	$35	$ 900	$1,700
19X2	38	980	1,820
19X3	40	1,010	1,960

The index is constructed by assuming annual purchases of 15 textbooks and school attendance of three terms.

REQUIRED:

1. Calculate the amount of annual purchases in each year.
2. Calculate the index for each of the three years, assuming the base year is 19X1.
3. Calculate the index for each of the three years, assuming the base year is 19X3.

EB-16. ROLL-FORWARD ADJUSTMENTS FOR REVENUE   Prepare a five-year revenue summary in 19X5 constant dollars, using the following information. Comment on the change in revenue over this period.

YEAR	ANNUAL REVENUE DOLLARS)	GENERAL PRICE INDEX
19X5	$16,000	142
19X4	15,800	135
19X3	15,000	130
19X2	14,000	120
19X1	12,000	105

EB-17. ROLL-FORWARD ADJUSTMENT   Ten years ago, Missouri Manufacturing acquired a tract of land for $17,000 when the general price index was 85. The land has been used as a parking lot. During 19X3 the parking lot produced revenues of $28,000. The average price index for 19X3 was 120 and at December 31, 19X3, the index stood at 125. Apply the roll-forward adjustment to the cost of the land and to 19X3 revenue, stating both amounts in constant (December 31, 19X3) dollars.

PROBLEMS

PB-18. CURRENT COST AND LEVEL OF OPERATIONS   A vendor sells newspapers on a city street corner. Early one afternoon, the vendor buys 200 papers from his supplier for $.25 each. The vendor has just enough cash to pay for the 200 papers. The supplier tells the vendor that newspapers will cost $.30 tomorrow and every day thereafter. During the afternoon and early evening, the vendor sells all 200 papers for $.40 each.

REQUIRED:

1. Calculate the vendor's net income for the day, using historical costs.
2. Calculate the maximum personal expenditure the vendor can make without reducing his cash balance below the starting amount.
3. Calculate the maximum personal expenditure the vendor can make without reducing his level of operations.
4. Calculate the vendor's current cost operating profit for the day.

PB-19. STATEMENT OF CURRENT COST OPERATING PROFIT   Iowa Products Company prepared the following historical cost income statement for 19X4:

IOWA PRODUCTS COMPANY
Income Statement
For the Year Ended December 31, 19X4

Sales revenue		$795,300
Less: Cost of goods sold		463,100
Gross margin		$332,200
Less: Operating expenses:		
Depreciation	$ 32,700	
Rent	29,300	
Salaries and wages	193,400	255,400
Income from operations		$ 76,800
Less: Interest expense		21,300
Income before taxes		55,500
Less: Income taxes expense		10,100
Net income		$ 45,400

Current cost of goods sold and current cost depreciation expense are known to be $489,400 and $38,200, respectively. All other expenses (including income taxes) are the same amount on both a current cost and a historical cost basis.

REQUIRED:

Prepare the 19X4 statement of current cost operating profit for Iowa Products Company.

PB-20. CURRENT COST INFORMATION AND DIVIDEND POLICY   Noodles Lumber, Inc., acquires, holds, and harvests tracts of timber and sells the logs to the paper industry. Noodles's assets include 10 major timber tracts acquired at various stages of development and scheduled for harvest at various future times. Net income for 19X6 reached a record high level, with the sale of logs from a large tract acquired early in its growth cycle. A comparable tract today, even one early in its growth cycle, would cost three times as much as the tract harvested in 19X6.

REQUIRED:

1. Why did 19X6 net income reach a record high level?

2. How might the current cost information be used in formulating dividend policy for Noodles Lumber?

PB-21. USE OF CONSTANT DOLLAR INFORMATION BY A STOCKHOLDER   At the end of 19X3, Robin Jones owns 20 percent of the outstanding stock of Roth, Inc. Mr Jones pays all his living expenses from the quarterly dividend checks he receives and then invests any remainder in a savings account. In recent years, Mr. Jones's investments in savings have been declining, even though the annual dividend, which now stands at $38,000, has increased at a rate of $2,000 per year. Applying the general price index to the nominal amount of the dividend yields the following adjusted amounts in end-of-19X3 dollars:

YEAR	NOMINAL AMOUNT	ADJUSTED AMOUNT
19X1	$34,000	$42,200
19X2	36,000	41,000
19X3	38,000	39,300

Over this same period, Roth's net income has remained constant.

REQUIRED:

1. Has the dividend stream to Mr. Jones kept pace with inflation? Explain your answer and identify any assumptions you make.

2. Has inflation impaired Roth's capacity to pay dividends?

ANALYTICAL OPPORTUNITY

AB-22. MANAGING WITH CHANGING PRICES   Philadelphia Coat Company manufactures high-quality outerwear for sale under the private label of a number of department stores. Typically, Philadelphia and each customer annually negotiate one-year contracts for the number and price of coats Philadelphia is to supply. Recently Philadelphia has been approached by a major catalog retailer who wants Philadelphia to enter into a five-year contract to supply coats. The catalog retailer initially proposed a contract under which Philadelphia would supply coats at the same price for all five years. Philadelphia's accountant suggests that a five-year fixed price contract may not be advantageous for Philadelphia if costs of manufacturing the coats rise during the five-year period. The accountant notes that Philadelphia's costs change at about the same rate as the changes in the general level of prices.

REQUIRED:

What counterproposal should Philadelphia make to the catalog retailer to provide Philadelphia with some protection against cost increases during the five-year period?

Careful study of this supplementary topic will enable you to:

1. Evaluate the effects of changes in exchange rates.
2. Account for purchases and sales denominated in foreign currencies.
3. Describe the process of translating financial statements of foreign subsidiaries from local currency into the parent company's currency.
4. Explain the usefulness of international accounting standards.

C ACCOUNTING FOR INTERNATIONAL OPERATIONS

Just a few years ago, most U.S. managers and accountants thought of international operations as an obscure activity that affected only a few businesses located in U.S. border or coastal cities. Today, practically every business considers purchasing from or selling to international customers and many U.S. firms have branches or subsidiaries in foreign countries. In some industries (such as athletic shoes, cameras, and video recorders), nearly all of the products that are sold in this country are manufactured outside the United States. In other industries, important components of products are manufactured outside the United States and then assembled and sold here. In both of these circumstances, foreign companies and foreign subsidiaries of U.S. companies are involved in offshore manufacturing. Many U.S.-based companies also sell actively in foreign countries. These sales activities are executed through branch offices or subsidiaries or through arrangements with foreign corporations. In little more than 40 years, the U.S. economy has changed from having an almost exclusively internal focus to being an integral part of a worldwide network of customers and suppliers. As the 1986 and 1989 data in the table below suggest, practically all areas of American business are involved in international operations and almost all are increasing their international operations.

	NON-U.S. REVENUES		NON-U.S. ASSETS	
COMPANY	1989	1986	1989	1986
General Motors	24.6%	19.3%	24.1%	20.6%
Goodyear	44.2	37.9	38.7	33.3
Hewlett-Packard	53.3	46.3	41.7	45.8
McDonald's	36.1	23.9	38.5	27.2
Nike	21.8	26.6	28.1	27.8
Pepsi	17.9	13.2	36.3	28.3
Polaroid	42.7	39.8	40.7	40.4
Xerox	30.2	28.1	25.0	23.7

Today's managers have a dual challenge: They must be able to do business with customers, suppliers, and other managers from practically any nation; and they must understand how the international portion of their activities will be measured by their accountants.

INTERNATIONAL ECONOMIC ACTIVITY

Businesses engage in essentially the same activities internationally that they do domestically: They buy and sell, invest in assets, and secure capital. Throughout this text, we have described how businesses account for these activities. The same accounting concepts and principles apply to international operations. However, there are additional managerial and accounting concerns when international operations are involved.

Although the dollar is not a completely stable unit of measurement, its changes in value have been small enough that managers have generally not attempted to tie the terms of their transactions to changes in the value of the dollar. However, the currencies of some countries change in value by material amounts over very short periods. Managers must incorporate these unpredictable, but potentially significant, changes in currency values into their decisions as they contemplate transactions. The values of historical investments in assets and obligations to creditors located in foreign countries are also affected by the changing values of currencies. Accountants must measure the effects of changes in exchange rates and incorporate these effects in the financial statements.

EXCHANGE RATES

EXCHANGE RATE: The rate at which one unit of one nation's currency is exchanged for one unit of another nation's currency.

Today there are a number of organized markets on which the currencies of most nations are traded. The rate at which one unit of one nation's currency is exchanged for one unit of another nation's currency is an **exchange rate.** Exchange rates are an essential part of international business activity, as they allow measurement of transactions in terms of the currencies involved. Exchange rates between many foreign currencies and the U.S. dollar are published daily in the business section of most newspapers, in tables like the one that follows.

COUNTRY	CURRENCY	EXCHANGE RATE*
Britain	Pound	$1.8960
Canada	Dollar	.8678
France	Franc	.1100
Germany	Mark	.6481
Israel	Shekel	.4972
Italy	Lira	.0008628
Japan	Yen	.007326
Mexico	Peso	.0003393
South Korea	Won	.001400

* U.S. dollars per unit of foreign currency.

The numbers in the table are interpreted as follows: One British pound could be exchanged for 1.8960 U.S. dollars on this day. Therefore, a transaction that involved 10,000 British pounds would be measured at $18,960 on that day. Managers who are negotiating transactions will often call foreign exchange brokers for information about exchange rates. These brokers are actively involved in buying and selling foreign currency for clients and for speculative purposes.

CHANGES IN EXCHANGE RATES

That exchange rates change is an observable reality. The interesting questions are why they change and who wins and who loses when exchange rates change. U.S. dollars, Mexican pesos, and Japanese yen are commodities, like gold or coffee or corn or oil. The price of a commodity changes with its supply and demand. If gold were suddenly to become more plentiful, its price would fall. If the demand for coffee were suddenly to increase, one would expect its price to rise. For similar reasons, the relative prices of currencies rise and fall. Units of a nation's currency are needed to buy goods or services sold by that nation's businesses or to invest in that nation's capital markets. Therefore, changes in the demand for a nation's products or changes in the relative attractiveness of its capital markets also affect the demand for its currency. These changes in demand are reflected in the exchange rates for that currency. As this portion of this text was being written in 1991, the U.S. dollar had for some time been declining in value relative to the currencies of most of the U.S.'s major trading partners. Analysts attributed this decline to an excess of imports over exports of U.S. products and services and a chronic excess of U.S. government expenditures over tax revenues.

A second major factor affecting exchange rates is the internal inflation rate that is anticipated for a particular country. When inflation is expected to be low, currencies will purchase more and will therefore rise in value relative to the currencies of nations expecting higher internal inflation.

When a currency increases in value, businesses gain if they are holding that currency or claims on that currency (an account receivable or note receivable, for example) and businesses experience a loss if they must purchase the currency to meet obligations payable in the currency (such as an account payable or note payable). Conversely, a decline in the value of a currency produces losses for holders of the currency and gains for those who must purchase it to satisfy obligations.

A currency is observed to increase in value relative to another when one unit of it can be exchanged for more units of the other currency. The data in the table above indicated that one British pound could be exchanged for 1.8960 U.S. dollars or, conversely, that one U.S. dollar would purchase .5274 pound [1/1.8960]. If the exchange rate were to become $1.8900 per pound (or $1 per .5291 pound), one would say that the dollar had increased in value relative to the pound because it takes more pounds (.5291 versus .5274) to buy one dollar. In other words, one pound buys fewer dollars ($1.8900 versus $1.8960). Examined from the perspective of the British, the same data would suggest that the pound had decreased in value relative to the U.S. dollar.

TRANSACTIONS DENOMINATED IN FOREIGN CURRENCY

When a transaction is denominated in a foreign currency (that is, when the cash part of the exchange takes place in a foreign currency), the transaction must be measured in dollars so that it can be recorded in the U.S. firm's accounting records. When the transaction is agreed to and consummated at the same time, then the U.S. party to the transaction can measure the transaction by reference to one exchange rate. For example, assume that Schulman Photo Products purchases 1,000 cameras from a Japanese wholesaler that operates in the United States and asks to be paid in yen. The price of each camera is 21,500 yen.

Schulman calls its foreign exchange broker and is told that the current exchange rate for yen is $.007326 per yen. Schulman agrees to the proposed purchase, asks its exchange broker to secure the necessary yen, and arranges for the yen to be delivered to the seller in exchange for the cameras. Schulman would record this transaction with the following journal entry:

Camera inventory [(1,000 cameras)(21,500 yen)($.007326
    per yen)]   157,509
Cash (dollars paid to exchange broker).   157,509

PURCHASES More commonly, purchase transactions involve a passage of time between the date that a transaction is agreed to and performance by both of the parties involved. For example, assume that on June 1, Schulman agrees to purchase 200 zoom lenses from a Korean manufacturer for 16,000,000 won. On July 15, the lenses are delivered; Schulman buys 16,000,000 won from its exchange broker and pays the manufacturer. Because exchange rates change constantly, accounting rules for transactions denominated in foreign currency require Schulman to measure this transaction twice — once on the purchase date and again on the date the merchandise is delivered. Let us assume that the following data are available for the dollar-per-won exchange rates on these two dates:

DATE	EXCHANGE RATE
June 1	$.001400
July 15	.001390

Using these data, the following journal entries would be prepared by Schulman to record this transaction:

June 1

Purchases [(16,000,000 won)($.001400 per won)]   22,400
    Accounts payable.   22,400

FOREIGN EXCHANGE GAIN: A gain that arises when a firm owes foreign currency and the exchange rate falls or when a firm is to receive foreign currency and the exchange rate rises.

July 15

Accounts payable.   22,400
    Cash [(16,000,000 won)($.001390 per won)]   22,240
    Foreign exchange gain [$22,400 − $22,240]   160

FOREIGN EXCHANGE LOSS: A loss that arises when a firm owes foreign currency and the exchange rate rises or when a firm is to receive foreign currency and the exchange rate falls.

Note that the account payable was measured at $22,400 on June 1. On July 15, because the exchange rate had changed, only $22,240 was required to secure the 16,000,000 won necessary to satisfy the payable. Therefore, Schulman experienced a **foreign exchange gain** as a result of the increase in the value of the U.S. dollar relative to the won. Had the July 15 exchange rate been $.001415 per won (a decrease in the value of the U.S. dollar relative to the won), then $22,640 would have been required to purchase the 16,000,000 won [(16,000,000 won)($.001415 per won)] and Schulman would have experienced a **foreign exchange loss** of $240 [$22,400 − $22,640].

SALES Similar entries are made for businesses engaged in sales transactions denominated in foreign currency. For example, assume that Schulman sold 300 electronic flash attachments to a Canadian retailer for 22,000 Canadian dollars. If the exchange rate on September 4, the date of the sale, was $.8680 per Canadian dollar, Schulman would make the following entry:

September 4

Accounts receivable [(22,000 Canadian $)($.8680 per
    Canadian $)]   19,096
    Sales revenue   19,096

If Schulman received the 22,000 Canadian dollars on October 3, when the exchange rate was $.8660 per Canadian dollar (an increase in the value of the U.S. dollar relative to the Canadian dollar), and exchanged the Canadian dollars for U.S. dollars immediately, Schulman would make the following entry:

October 3

Cash [(22,000 Canadian $)($.8660 per Canadian $)]   19,052
Foreign exchange loss ($19,052 − $19,096)   44
    Accounts receivable.   19,096

HEDGES

HEDGE: A transaction that is designed to exactly offset any foreign exchange gains or losses that might occur.

Businesses can enter into transactions that provide protection against unfavorable changes in exchange rates. This kind of transaction is called a **hedge.** For example, consider a business that is purchasing goods. At the same time that it makes the purchase, it could hedge against changes in the exchange rate by entering into a transaction with an exchange broker to purchase the needed foreign currency at a specified price. This second transaction establishes the amount of U.S. dollars that the business will have to spend to acquire the needed foreign currency. By providing a hedge against changes in the exchange rate, this second transaction has fixed the price of the goods being purchased. Similar hedges are available for sales transactions denominated in foreign currency. Accounting for hedges is discussed at length in advanced accounting texts.

ACCOUNTING FOR FOREIGN INVESTMENTS

TRANSLATION: A process that transforms financial statements presented in a foreign currency into dollar-based statements.

The second important element of accounting for foreign operations concerns investments by U.S. corporations in assets or whole businesses that are located in other nations. The data we presented in the introduction to this supplement indicate that a substantial portion of the assets of many U.S. corporations are located outside this country. Most of those assets represent U.S. businesses' investments in foreign subsidiaries (and branches). When a U.S. parent company prepares its financial statements, the accounts of these foreign subsidiaries must be consolidated with the accounts of the U.S. parent. Because these subsidiaries maintain accounting records in their local currencies (a legal requirement in many countries) and enter into transactions denominated in these local currencies, the subsidiaries' accounts must be translated into dollars before they can be combined with those of the U.S. parent company. (It would be meaningless to add dollars, pesos, marks, and francs). In addition to **translation** from foreign currencies to dollars, accountants must accommodate any differences in accounting principles. Most countries have their own generally accepted accounting principles that must be used by all companies based there (including subsidiaries of U.S. parent companies).

TRANSLATION   Accounting rules for translations include the following:

1. Revenues and expenses must be translated at the average exchange rate for the period in which they are recognized.

2. Assets and liabilities must be translated at the exchange rate in effect on the balance sheet date.

3. Paid-in capital must be translated at the "historical" exchange rate — the rate that existed when the paid-in capital was invested.

3. Retained earnings must be translated as the sum of the translated net incomes less the sum of the translated dividends.

**CUMULATIVE TRANSLA-
TION ADJUSTMENT:** A stockholders' equity account that measures the effects of translating a foreign subsidiary's asset and liability accounts at the current exchange rate and the equity accounts at historical rates.

Because the equity elements of the balance sheet are translated at rates different from those employed for assets and liabilities, the translated balance sheet will not balance without the addition of a **cumulative translation adjustment.** This stockholders' equity account represents the cumulative effects of changes in the exchange rates on the parent company's investments in its foreign subsidiaries. The cumulative translation adjustment is a part of the parent company's stockholders' equity.

In Exhibit C‑1, we illustrate the basic elements of translation of financial statements. Realtime Security Systems installs and operates electronic security systems for homes, apartments, and small businesses. Several years ago, Realtime created a subsidiary in Britain that is engaged in the same activities, using equipment purchased locally. The condensed financial statements for 19X9, shown in Exhibit C‑1, have been prepared for Realtime Security Systems, Britain. The financial statements for the British subsidiary are presented in local currency (pounds) and translated into dollars.

The purpose of translation is to help statement users assess the returns obtained from a parent company's investment in foreign subsidiaries. The translated income statement provides some evidence about these returns. Another factor in evaluating the return on a foreign investment is the change in the translated value of the investment during the period. As exchange rates change, the translated amount of an investment in a foreign subsidiary will change. For example, assume that a U.S. parent established a Mexican subsidiary with net assets of 800,000,000 pesos when the exchange rate was $.0006800 per Mexican peso. The translated value of that investment is $544,000. Further assume that the subsidiary has operated successfully for some years within Mexico and, as a result, its net assets have grown to 1,200,000,000 pesos. However, the exchange rate has fallen to $.0003400 per Mexican peso. The translated value of the investment is now only $408,000. The U.S. parent's investment has declined in value, despite successful operation of the subsidiary in Mexico. One of the purposes of the cumulative translation gain or loss account is to help statement users identify the effects of exchange rate changes on investments in foreign subsidiaries.

INTERNATIONAL ACCOUNTING PRINCIPLES

Just as each nation has its own customs, language, and dress, we find that business practices and accounting rules also differ across countries. When U.S. accoun-

EXHIBIT C–1   **TRANSLATION OF FINANCIAL STATEMENTS**

REALTIME SECURITY SYSTEMS, BRITAIN
Condensed Financial Statements

(All amounts in thousands, except translation rates)	POUNDS	TRANSLATION RATE	DOLLARS
INCOME STATEMENT			
Revenues	£ 10,000	1.8960	$18,860
Less: Expenses	9,800	1.8960	18,581
Net income	£ 200		$ 279
STATEMENT OF CHANGES IN RETAINED EARNINGS			
Retained earnings, 12/31/X8	£ 700		$ 1,085*
Add: Net income	200		279
Retained earnings, 12/31/X9	£ 900		$ 1,364
BALANCE SHEETS			
Assets	£ 11,000	1.9100	$21,010
Liabilities	£ 5,600	1.9100	$10,696
Paid-in capital	4,500	1.7600	7,920
Retained earnings	900		1,364
Cumulative translation adjustment	—	Plug†	1,030
Total	£ 11,000		$21,010

* From last period's translation.
† A *plug* is an amount required to balance the relationship; in this case, the plug makes translated assets equal translated liabilities plus equity. (Of course, if sufficient information were available, the adjustment could be calculated directly in terms of all prior effects of exchange rate changes on the parent's investment the British subsidiary.)

tants are asked to prepare combined financial statements that include translated statements of foreign subsidiaries, a part of the translation process is to adjust the data in the non-U.S. statements for differences in accounting principles. Certainly, the accountant's task would be easier if all countries employed the same accounting principles. The International Accounting Standards Committee (IASC) is a voluntary organization, composed of representatives of professional accounting organizations and accounting regulators from a number of member countries, that seeks to develop uniform international accounting standards.[1] Compliance with IASC standards is voluntary. Some accountants question the appropriateness of uniform accounting standards. They argue that for the same reasons that it is improper to force one country's culture on another, it is also inappropriate to suggest that accounting rules that are suitable for one country must also be suitable for another. However, users of financial statements do benefit from uniformity. For example, investors or creditors who want to compare the financial results of Japanese and American automobile companies would find that task much easier if the accounting principles used to prepare financial statements for all the firms were the same. Because the effects of apply-

[1] In late 1990, the IASC had 76 members and had issued 29 standards.

ing different accounting principles are often subtle, investors or creditors could unknowingly misallocate their resources. The IASC's standards are an attempt to help statement users make meaningful cross-national financial statement comparison and, hopefully, to improve international resource allocation.

SUMMARY

International operations are an increasingly important part of the total business activity for many U.S. firms. Not only do U.S.-based businesses sell to, and buy from, foreign businesses, they also invest in branches and subsidiaries that are located outside the United States. Measuring the effects of these international activities requires that transactions denominated in foreign currencies be measured in dollars. The financial statements of foreign subsidiaries must be translated into dollars before they are combined with the statements of a U.S.-based parent. These measurements and translations are performed by using the rates of exchange between foreign currencies and the U.S. dollar. Translations must also take into account any differences between U.S. accounting principles and those employed in the country in which the subsidiary is located.

KEY TERMS

CUMULATIVE TRANSLATION ADJUSTMENT (p. 820)
EXCHANGE RATE (p. 816)
FOREIGN EXCHANGE GAIN (p. 818)

FOREIGN EXCHANGE LOSS (p. 818)
HEDGE (p. 819)
TRANSLATION (p. 819)

QUESTIONS

QC-1. Describe the kinds of international economic activity in which U.S. businesses are engaged.

QC-2. How are exchange rates used in purchase and sale transactions denominated in foreign currency?

QC-3. Explain the meaning of the statement "The dollar rose against the Japanese yen." Explain the meaning of the statement "The dollar fell against the Japanese yen."

QC-4. What is the purpose of a hedge?

QC-5. What exchange rate is used when translating each of the following: revenues, expenses, assets, liabilities, and paid-in capital?

QC-6. When might uniform international accounting standards be beneficial?

EXERCISES

EC-7. PURCHASE DENOMINATED IN FOREIGN CURRENCY Tarkington Cookware purchased 100 sets of gourmet cookware from a French manufacturer for 66,000 francs when the exchange rate was $.1910 per franc. When Tarkington paid for the cookware 60 days later, the exchange rate was $.1921 per franc.

Tarkington purchased the necessary francs from its exchange broker and then used those francs to pay the manufacturer immediately.

REQUIRED:

1. Record the purchase in Tarkington's journal.
2. Record the payment in Tarkington's journal.

EC-8. SALE DENOMINATED IN FOREIGN CURRENCY   Vermont Products sold 10,000 bottles of maple syrup to a wholesaler in Italy for 104,500,000 lire. The exchange rate at the time of the sale was $.0008628 per lira. The Italian wholesaler paid for the syrup 90 days later, when the exchange rate was $.0008651 per lira. Vermont sold the lire to its exchange broker for dollars immediately upon receipt.

REQUIRED:

1. Record the sale in Vermont's journal.
2. Record the cash collection in Vermont's journal.

EC-9. GAINS AND LOSSES FROM EXCHANGE RATE FLUCTUATIONS   Chicago Music Products imports musical instruments from manufacturers in several countries. You have the following data for four notes payable that Chicago entered into during 19X3:

AMOUNT	EXCHANGE RATE AT ISSUE	EXCHANGE RATE AT YEAR-END
100,000 British pounds	$1.8960	$1.9005
800,000 Danish kroner.	.1679	.1697
400,000 German marks	.6481	.6468
500,000 Finnish markkas.	.2701	.2690

REQUIRED:

For each note, compute the amount of gain or loss that resulted from the change in exchange rate from the time the note was issued until year-end.

PROBLEMS

PC-10. PURCHASES AND PAYMENTS DENOMINATED IN FOREIGN CURRENCY   Mountainside Ski Shop sells skiing equipment that it purchases from manufacturers in several countries. During 19X7, Mountainside engaged in the following transactions:

a) Purchased 40 downhill ski sets at a cost of 28,000 francs from a French supplier. The exchange rate was $.1105 per franc at the time of the purchase.

b) Purchased 50 pair of cross-country skis at a cost of 20,000 markkas per pair from a Finnish manufacturer. The exchange rate at the time of the purchase was $.2700 per markka.

c) Paid for the purchase in transaction a when the exchange rate was $.1067 per franc.

d) Paid for the purchase in transaction b when the exchange rate was $.2708 per markka.

REQUIRED:

Prepare the journal entries to record these transactions.

PC-11. SALES AND COLLECTIONS DENOMINATED IN FOREIGN CURRENCY   Erin Products sells dental office equipment to wholesalers throughout the United States, Europe, and Asia. The following international sales and collection transactions occurred during 19X4:

TRANSACTION	AMOUNT	EXCHANGE RATE
#461 Sale	5,100 British pounds	$1.8850
#462 Sale	13,100,000 Korean won	.001400
#461 Collection.	5,100 British pounds	1.8910
#462 Collection.	13,100,000 Korean won	.001392

REQUIRED:

1. Record the two sales in Erin's journal.

2. Assume that Erin Products exchanged foreign currency for U.S. dollars as soon as it was received from the customer. Record the two cash collections in Erin's journal.

PC-12. EFFECTS OF EXCHANGE RATES ON OPERATING CASH FLOWS CTVT is the U.S. subsidiary of a Korean manufacturer of television picture tubes. CTVT USA pays for its purchases of picture tubes in Korean won and sells the tubes for dollars to U.S. TV manufacturers. The market for picture tubes is highly competitive, so CTVT USA must meet the prices charged by U.S. competitors as well as those charged by manufacturers from other foreign countries. During 19X4 CTVT made three purchases of picture tubes from its Korean parent. Data for these transactions appear in the following table:

PURCHASE	PRICE	EXCHANGE RATE
100,000 tubes	6,200,000,000 won	$.001390
200,000	12,400,000,000	.001500
175,000	10,850,000,000	.001620

Assume that all picture tubes sold during 19X4 were sold for $100 each.

REQUIRED:

1. Compute the gross margin per unit realized from the sale of each batch of picture tubes that was purchased.

2. Explain why the gross margin per unit changed.

PC-13. TRANSLATION OF FINANCIAL STATEMENTS Sayers Products Company manufactures auto parts in the United States and Germany. The financial statements for Sayers' German subsidiary, presented in German marks, appear below.

SAYERS AUTO PARTS, GERMANY
Condensed Financial Statements

INCOME STATEMENT	MARKS
Sales revenues.	92,500,000
Less: Expenses	85,400,000
Net income.	7,100,000

STATEMENT OF CHANGES IN RETAINED EARNINGS	
Retained earnings, 12/31/X3	23,600,000
Add: Net income	7,100,000
Retained earnings, 12/31/X4	30,700,000

BALANCE SHEET	
Assets	156,200,000
Liabilities	97,400,000
Paid-in capital	28,100,000
Retained earnings.	30,700,000
Total	156,200,000

Assume that the following exchange rates are appropriate for 19X4:

	EXCHANGE RATE
Average for 19X4	$.6510
12/31/X4.	.6470

The paid-in capital for Sayers, Germany, was issued when the exchange rate was $.6130. The translated amount for retained earnings at 12/31/X3 was $14,504,000.

REQUIRED:

Prepare translated financial statements using the format presented in Exhibit C–1.

ANALYTICAL OPPORTUNITY

AC-14. HEDGING A LONG-TERM INVESTMENT   Evans Corporation plans to establish a subsidiary in Greece. The subsidiary will operate exclusively in Greece. Evans expects that $10,000,000 will be required to acquire the assets and begin subsidiary operations. Once operations begin, Evans expects that enough cash (in Greek drachmas) will be produced by the subsidiary to sustain operations and provide for appropriate growth. Evans' management observes that the carrying amount in U.S. dollars of some of Evans' other foreign investments has declined when the foreign currency of the subsidiary country declined against the dollar. Evans wants to minimize the risk that the value of its investment will be negatively affected by a decrease in the value of the Greek drachma.

REQUIRED:

How can Evans provide a hedge for this investment? (Note that hedges of the type described in the text of the supplement are effective over a maximum period of a few months.)

LEARNING OBJECTIVES

Careful study of this supplementary topic will enable you to:

1. Evaluate the alternative methods of recognizing income and deductions.
2. Identify the sources of taxpayer income, exclusions, and deductions.
3. Compute income tax using a three-bracket tax table.
4. Describe the system by which tax is paid by taxpayers.
5. Explain the usefulness of tax planning, tax avoidance, and tax shelters.

D PERSONAL INCOME TAXATION

Perhaps no single subject evokes stronger expressions of opinion among Americans than the federal income tax. Some of us curse, some complain, and some just sigh in resignation — but nearly all of us pay. The purpose of this supplement is to explain some of the major provisions of the U.S. federal income tax for individuals, so that you will be able to understand how various forms of personal income and expense are treated for tax purposes.

Federal income taxes assessed on individuals, like those assessed on corporations, are calculated under laws enacted by Congress. The Internal Revenue Service (IRS), an agency of the U.S. Treasury Department, collects federal income taxes and administers enforcement of the tax laws. In addition, both the Treasury Department and the IRS issue detailed rules that interpret the tax laws.

Congress modifies the tax law quite frequently. Modifications may be designed to increase or, rarely, decrease the amount of money raised to support government operations; to make the effect of taxes more equitable; to respond to political pressure from special interest groups; or to support various administrative or social objectives. Although such changes are frequent and may have significant impact on the amounts of taxes paid, the basic framework of the tax law has remained in place for many years.

We begin our explanation of this law with a description of the structure of the individual income tax system.

THE STRUCTURE OF INDIVIDUAL INCOME TAXATION

Basically, individual income tax is levied on most, but not all, receipts of money, property, or benefits. All or part of a taxpayer's expenditures for a relatively small number of items can be deducted from the taxpayer's earnings and other income when determining taxable income. Individual income tax is computed by using a three-bracket rate structure that assesses taxes at a higher rate in higher brackets of taxable income.

Some of the provisions of tax law apply to individuals and corporations in the same way, while others apply only to individuals or only to corporations. For example, both corporate and individual taxpayers must file an annual tax return and both must make payments by year-end that will accumulate to approximately the amount of tax due for the year. Corporations, however, are permitted to exclude from taxation a portion of dividends received from other U.S. corporations, while individuals must include all such dividends when determining taxable income.

For most individual taxpayers, the tax year runs from January 1 through December 31. Tax returns are due by April 15 of the following year. Individual income tax returns are filed on either Form 1040EZ, 1040A, or 1040. Form 1040EZ can be used only by single taxpayers and 1040A only by taxpayers who have fairly simple tax returns. Form 1040 is used by all taxpayers who cannot use either of the other two forms. Form 1040 is often supplemented by a number of schedules that document nonwage or nonsalary sources of income or provide details about deductions and exclusions.

Let us begin our explanation of individual income taxation by examining when and how various items of income and deductions are brought onto the tax return.

RECOGNITION OF INCOME AND DEDUCTIONS

As noted in Chapter 1, generally accepted accounting principles require the activities of a business entity to be recorded on the accrual basis of accounting. The accrual basis is also acceptable for determining taxable income, but individual taxpayers may elect to use the cash basis or a wide variety of other bases for determining taxable income. The principal requirement is that the basis chosen "clearly reflect income." Indeed, a taxpayer may use different bases for different sources of income, as long as the same basis is applied to an income source consistently over time.

Under federal tax regulations, cash-basis income for the period must include all revenues actually or constructively received. **Constructive receipt** occurs when a taxpayer can take possession of the income. Therefore, interest added to savings accounts is considered to be income when it is credited to the account. A salary check represents income when it is available for the employee, regardless of when the employee actually picks up the check. Thus the constructive receipt doctrine limits a taxpayer's ability to defer recognition of taxable income by merely delaying the technical receipt of cash that is readily available.

CONSTRUCTIVE RECEIPT: The point at which income is available for possession by taxpayers; income is taxable when actually or constructively received.

Accrual accounting requires that income be recorded when earned and that expenses be recorded when incurred. For most individual taxpayers, the accrual basis would be used only for income derived from a business.

Once a taxpayer has identified which basis, or bases, will be used to recognize income and deductions, he or she can proceed to identify amounts needed for the tax computation.

THE INDIVIDUAL INCOME TAX STRUCTURE

The computation of an individual taxpayer's taxable income involves five items: total income, exclusions (to arrive at gross income), deductions (to arrive at adjusted gross income), standard and itemized deductions, and personal exemptions. The organization and relationships of these five items are shown in Exhibit D–1 and each is described in the sections that follow.

Total Income

TOTAL INCOME: All income available to the taxpayer, from whatever source it is derived.

For tax purposes, **total income** includes all income available to the taxpayer, from whatever source it is derived, except for the return of amounts that had previously been invested. For example, a taxpayer who purchased stock for $1,700 and later sold it for $2,500 would have a gain of $800 [$2,500 − $1,700] to be included in taxable income. The $1,700 is considered to be a return of capital and is thus not a part of total income. Total income includes wages, interest, dividends, gains,

EXHIBIT D–1   DETERMINATION OF TAXABLE INCOME

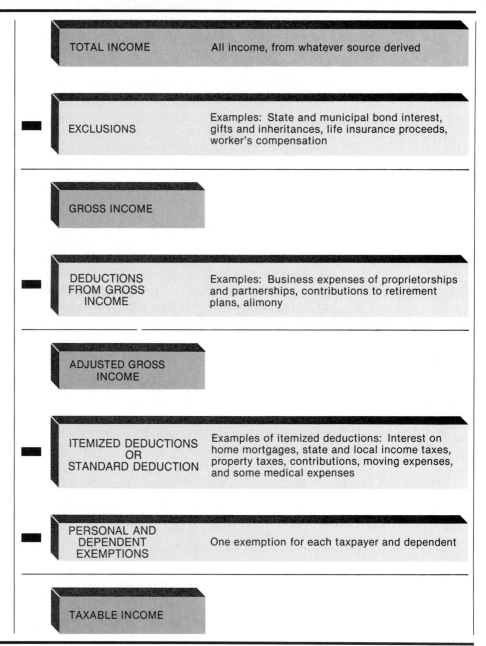

| TOTAL INCOME | All income, from whatever source derived |

| EXCLUSIONS | Examples: State and municipal bond interest, gifts and inheritances, life insurance proceeds, worker's compensation |

GROSS INCOME

| DEDUCTIONS FROM GROSS INCOME | Examples: Business expenses of proprietorships and partnerships, contributions to retirement plans, alimony |

ADJUSTED GROSS INCOME

| ITEMIZED DEDUCTIONS OR STANDARD DEDUCTION | Examples of itemized deductions: Interest on home mortgages, state and local income taxes, property taxes, contributions, moving expenses, and some medical expenses |

| PERSONAL AND DEPENDENT EXEMPTIONS | One exemption for each taxpayer and dependent |

TAXABLE INCOME

gross profits from business activity, prizes, awards, pension benefits (including social security), rents, royalties, and many services or benefits provided by employers for employees. If, for example, an employer provides a social club membership or a car for an employee, the fair value of the benefit provided is a part of the employee's total income. Income from business activity conducted as a proprietorship or partnership must be reported as income by the taxpayers involved, because proprietorships and partnerships are not taxed directly. Since corporations are taxed directly, an individual taxpayer who owns all or part of a corporation need not include corporate income in his or her individual income (unless the corporation elects to be taxed as an S corporation, as explained in Chapter 16).

Exclusions

GROSS INCOME: Total income less exclusions.

EXCLUSIONS: Sources of income excluded from taxation.

Certain items are excluded from taxation by statute. These items are subtracted from total income to produce **gross income. Exclusions**—sources of income excluded from taxation—include interest on most bonds issued by state and municipal governments, most life insurance proceeds, most disability benefits, gifts and inheritances (of course, donors may have been taxed), damage awards, and the cost of premiums for employer-provided health and accident plans and benefits provided to taxpayers under those plans.

Deductions from Gross Income

DEDUCTIONS: Outflows made by taxpayers that reduce taxable income.

Deductions are outflows that reduce taxable income; they are conceptually different from exclusions. Exclusions are inflows that are not counted as income, while deductions are outflows that reduce taxable income. Deductions fall into three categories: expenses or costs, realized losses, and depreciation. Expenses or costs may include the costs of carrying on a trade or profession, the reimbursed expenses of an employee, alimony payments, contributions to self-employment retirement plans, and contributions to some individual retirement plans. Realized losses occur when property is exchanged or sold. Depreciation is calculated in accordance with income tax rules. Deductions are subtracted from gross income to arrive at **adjusted gross income.**

ADJUSTED GROSS INCOME: Gross income less deductions from gross income.

Itemized Deductions or Standard Deduction

Individual taxpayers are also allowed to deduct certain specified items from adjusted gross income. These *itemized deductions* include charitable contributions, medical expenses, interest on home mortgages, property taxes, state and local income taxes, certain casualty losses, and moving expenses. For certain deductions, the amount deductible may be limited in various ways. For example, taxpayers with adjusted gross income over $100,000 are allowed to deduct certain items only to the extent that they exceed 3 percent of the excess of adjusted gross income over $100,000. To simplify the itemized deductions portion of the tax calculation, taxpayers are allowed to subtract a *standard deduction* (in 1991, $3,400 for single taxpayers and $5,700 for married taxpayers filing joint returns) rather than listing or "itemizing" these deductions in detail. Taxpayers whose allowable itemized deductions exceed the standard deduction pay less tax if they itemize, whereas taxpayers whose allowable itemized deductions are less than the standard deduction pay less tax if they take the standard deduction.

Personal and Dependent Exemptions

Each taxpayer is entitled to one *personal exemption* for himself or herself and one for each dependent. Taxpayers who are over 65 years of age or who are blind are entitled to an additional standard deduction if they do not itemize deductions. For 1991, exemptions are $2,150 per individual; however, the amount of the

EXHIBIT D–2   INDIVIDUAL INCOME TAX RATES FOR 1991

SINGLE TAXPAYERS	
TAXABLE INCOME	**TAX**
$0–$20,350	15% of taxable income
$20,350–$49,300	$3,052.50 + 28% of excess over $20,350
Over $49,300	$11,158.50 + 31% of excess over $49,300

MARRIED TAXPAYERS FILING JOINT RETURN	
TAXABLE INCOME	**TAX**
$0–$34,000	15% of taxable income
$34,000–$82,150	$5,000 + 28% of excess over $34,000
Over $82,150	$18,582.50 + 31% of excess over $82,150

TAXABLE INCOME (INDIVIDUAL): Adjusted gross income less itemized deductions (or the standard deduction) and exemptions.

exemption is reduced for adjusted gross incomes in excess of specified limits.[1] When itemized deductions (or the standard deduction) and exemptions are subtracted from adjusted gross income, the remainder is the taxpayer's **taxable income.**

COMPUTING THE INDIVIDUAL INCOME TAX

Once taxable income has been determined, the amount of the tax due for the year is determined by using a three-bracket rate structure. That rate structure is described in Exhibit D–2. Note that all taxpayers fall into one of three tax brackets—15 percent, 28 percent, or 31 percent. Assume, for example, that single taxpayer Jay Stance had taxable income of $54,300. Jay's income tax for the year would be $12,708.50 [$11,158.50 + (.31)($54,300 − $49,300)]. Alternatively, assume that Claudia and Rich Edwards are married taxpayers filing a joint return. Claudia and Rich have taxable income of $172,500. Claudia and Rich's income tax for the year would be $46,591 [$18,582.50 + (.31)($172,500 − $82,150)].

The tax on an individual's taxable income may be reduced by *tax credits.* For example, taxpayers who incur child care expenses, who are elderly or disabled, or who pay foreign income taxes may qualify for such credits. Tax *credits,* which reduce taxes directly, should be distinguished from tax *deductions,* which reduce taxes only indirectly; thus, a $100 tax credit reduces taxes by $100, whereas a $100 tax deduction reduces taxes by only $31 for a taxpayer in the 31 percent bracket.

SATISFYING THE TAX LIABILITY

By the end of a tax year, individual taxpayers are required to have transmitted to the Internal Revenue Service either 90 percent of the tax that will be due for the year or 100 percent of the previous year's tax, whichever is less. For taxable income arising from wages or salary, employers are required to withhold a por-

[1] For example, Mr. and Mrs. Henderson, who file a joint return, have three dependent children and adjusted gross income of $195,000. For joint returns, each exemption is reduced by $43 per $2,500 of adjusted gross income above $150,000; thus each of the Henderson's five personal exemptions will be reduced by $774 [($45,000/$2,500) ($43)] to $1,376 ($2,150 − $774).

tion of each wage or salary payment. Employers deposit these withholdings with the Internal Revenue Service as the amounts are withheld. The amount withheld is determined by the amount of wages or salary and the number of personal exemptions claimed by the taxpayer. Each employee is required to file a W-4 form with his or her employer. On the W-4 form, the employee must first identify all expected income other than wages and any substantial deductions. Then the employee modifies the number of personal exemptions claimed so that the employer will withhold an amount that approximates the tax due for the year.

Taxpayers who have substantial amounts of income from sources other than wages or salary must make **quarterly payments of estimated tax.** The sum of these quarterly payments and the employer's withholdings must equal at least 90 percent of the current year's tax or 100 percent of the previous year's tax, whichever is less. Taxpayers whose withholdings and quarterly payments of estimated tax are less than the minimum amount required by year-end must pay a penalty that is based on the amount of underpayment.

If the tax due for the year exceeds the sum of withholdings and quarterly payments of estimated tax, the remaining tax due must be paid when the tax return is submitted.

QUARTERLY PAYMENT OF ESTIMATED TAX: Tax payments made quarterly, based on a taxpayer's estimated tax due for the year.

TAX PLANNING AND TAX AVOIDANCE

Although some of the detailed provisions of the individual income tax law change frequently, the basic provisions generally remain the same for several years at a time. Therefore, it is beneficial for taxpayers to consider in advance how to structure their activities to ensure that their income tax payments will be as small as possible. The practice of evaluating the tax effects of contemplated actions or transactions is called **tax planning.** Taking actions or structuring transactions to minimize taxes is called **tax avoidance.** For example, assume that a single taxpayer with $50,000 of taxable income is employed by a corporation and wishes to spend $3,000 per year for life insurance. The taxpayer has two choices to secure the insurance: She can (1) purchase the insurance herself by spending $3,000 of aftertax dollars or (2) enroll in a program offered by her employer that allows the corporation to reduce her salary by $3,000 and then purchase group life insurance with the salary reduction. The employee in our example would find the following tax effects for these two choices:

TAX PLANNING: The practice of evaluating the tax effects of contemplated actions or transactions.

TAX AVOIDANCE: Taking actions or structuring transactions to minimize taxes.

(1) *Purchase of insurance with aftertax dollars*

Taxable income		$50,000
Less: Tax on $50,000...........................	$11,376	
Cost of life insurance.......................	3,000	14,376
Aftertax income available for consumption..........		$35,624

(2) *Purchase of insurance through salary reduction*

Taxable income	$47,000
Less: Tax on $47,000...........................	10,515
Aftertax income available for consumption..........	$36,485

The employee could avoid $861 of federal income tax and thus increase her spendable aftertax income by $861 by purchasing group life insurance through the salary reduction plan managed by her employer. (Note that group life insurance premiums paid by employers are identified above as exclusions from total income.)

Federal courts have supported the concept that taxpayers are under no obligation to pay more than the minimum tax due under the law. If taxpayers can organize their affairs so that their taxes are decreased, then they are acting both rationally and legally. However, taxpayers who knowingly misrepresent income or deductions with the objective of decreasing taxes are engaging in **tax evasion.** Tax evasion is an illegal activity that is subject to civil or criminal prosecution with possible fines, jail terms, or both upon conviction.

TAX EVASION: Knowing misrepresentation of income or deductions with the objective of reducing taxes.

TAX SHELTERS

TAX SHELTER: An arrangement requiring an expenditure of cash in the current period that (1) reduces current tax and (2) is expected to produce future tax benefits or future income in an amount greater than the current expenditure.

The primary form of tax avoidance is the use of tax shelters. A **tax shelter** is an arrangement requiring an expenditure of cash in the current period that (1) reduces current tax and (2) is expected to produce future tax benefits or future income in an amount greater than the current expenditure. The most common tax shelters include contributions to retirement programs (such as IRAs and Keogh plans) and the tax-free treatment of income earned by funds invested in these programs. Another common shelter is investment in real estate, although recent changes in the tax law have denied it to taxpayers with incomes in excess of $100,000. A taxpayer purchases property with a small down payment. The remainder of the purchase price is borrowed. The interest on the borrowed funds is a deduction, and part or all of the cost of the property can be depreciated. Therefore, an investor can secure substantial tax deductions for interest and depreciation with a relatively small investment of cash. The investor expects that rental income and appreciation on the real estate will provide future income greater than the current expenditure, as noted in the definition above.

Tax shelters arise from provisions of the tax law that were designed to provide economic incentives for certain activities. After saying that, however, we must also note that some individuals have been far too aggressive in establishing and promoting tax shelters. Some promoters have even marketed tax shelters that they knew to be in violation of tax law, taking advantage of the length of time required to detect, investigate, and secure a legal judgment against an abusive tax shelter. One of the major elements of the 1986 Tax Reform Act was a collection of provisions that made it more difficult for taxpayers to benefit from potentially abusive tax shelters, while retaining the encouragement for legitimate investment opportunities that were intended by the earlier tax law.

SUMMARY

The individual income tax system begins with an identification of total taxpayer income, from which a series of exclusions and deductions are made to arrive at taxable income. Tax is determined by applying a three-bracket rate structure to taxable income. Taxes are paid during the tax year primarily through withholdings and, for taxpayers with substantial income from sources other than wages or salaries, through quarterly payments of estimated tax. Tax planning and tax shelters allow taxpayers to avoid some tax and to minimize the amount that must be paid.

KEY TERMS

ADJUSTED GROSS INCOME (p. 829)

CONSTRUCTIVE RECEIPT (p. 827)

DEDUCTIONS (p. 829)

EXCLUSIONS (p. 829)

GROSS INCOME (p. 829)

QUARTERLY PAYMENT OF ESTIMATED TAX (p. 831)

TAXABLE INCOME (INDIVIDUAL) (p. 830)

TAX AVOIDANCE (p. 831)

TAX EVASION (p. 832)

TAX PLANNING (p. 831)

TAX SHELTER (p. 832)

TOTAL INCOME (p. 827)

QUESTIONS

QD-1. When is cash-basis income to be recognized in the tax return?

QD-2. Identify the sources of total taxpayer income.

QD-3. Identify the sources of income exclusions, deductions, and itemized deductions. Explain the difference between an exclusion and a deduction.

QD-4. Explain how taxpayers are expected to meet their tax liability for the year.

QD-5. Why might tax planning be useful?

QD-6. What is the purpose of a tax shelter?

EXERCISES

ED-7. TAX CONCEPTS AND DEFINITIONS Identify the tax concept or definition that is illustrated by each of the situations described below.

TAX CONCEPTS AND DEFINITIONS

A. Constructive receipt

B. Personal and dependent exemptions

C. Exclusions from total income

D. Adjusted gross income

E. Standard deduction

F. Itemized deductions

G. Joint return

H. Tax credits

I. Tax shelter

J. Tax planning

SITUATIONS

1. The tax rate structure confers a significant tax advantage on many individuals who are married.

2. Martha Randall's tax return shows the excess of gross income over deductions from gross income to be $57,000.

3. James Case invested $700 in a retirement fund and is not required to pay tax on the $700 or any income earned on it until the amounts are withdrawn from the fund.

4. Axel Smith, a married taxpayer with no children, was allowed to subtract $4,300 from 1991 adjusted gross income.

5. Randolf Hedges anticipates higher tax rates and higher adjusted gross income in 19X4 than in 19X3. Accordingly, Mr. Hedges defers all of his charitable contributions until 19X4.

6. Amy Jones, a cash-basis taxpayer, is paid at the end of every month but did not pick up her December 19X7 check until January 5, 19X8. Yet Amy is required to pay 19X7 tax on the December check.

7. Ambrose Johnson, a single taxpayer, was allowed to deduct $3,400 from his adjusted gross income for 1991 without regard to any actual expenditures made by him.

8. Nancy Majors is not required to pay tax on interest earned on investments in bonds issued by the City of East Lansing.

EXERCISE CONTINUES

9. Mr. and Mrs. McNally calculate their income tax for 19X5 to be $15,900, but they are able to subtract $310 from this amount as a result of child care expenses.

10. George Kellogg's tax return shows $12,600 in charitable contributions, $16,700 in state and local taxes, $14,000 in home mortgage interest, and $3,200 in property taxes.

ED-8. TAXABLE INCOME   James Gardner, a single taxpayer, had salary income of $37,000, income from a professional partnership of $15,100, interest on municipal bonds of $430, and interest on corporate bonds of $1,200. During the year, Mr. Gardner made a $8,200 contribution to his tax-sheltered retirement plan. Mr. Gardner was allowed itemized deductions totaling $4,420, or a standard deduction of $3,400.

REQUIRED:

Compute Mr. Gardner's taxable income.

ED-9. TAXABLE INCOME FOR A JOINT RETURN   Adam and Evelyn West file a joint return. The following data describe their income, exclusions, and deductions:

Evelyn's salary $49,500
Adam's self-employment income 37,200
Municipal bonds interest 900
Contributions to tax-sheltered retirement plans 7,300
Itemized deductions 9,700

Adam and Evelyn can claim two personal exemptions.

REQUIRED:

Compute taxable income for Adam and Evelyn's joint tax return.

ED-10. TAX COMPUTATION   For four taxpayers, the following information is available:

TAXPAYER	FILING STATUS	TAXABLE INCOME	TAX CREDITS
Gregory Mitchell	Single	$38,700	$ –0–
John Banker	Single	52,100	1,100
Kay and John Smith	Married, joint return	54,900	–0–
Dora and Ray Epen	Married, joint return	87,200	970

REQUIRED:

Compute the amount of income tax due for each taxpayer.

PROBLEMS

PD-11. TAXABLE INCOME AND INCOME TAX   Jane Westmore is employed as an accountant by a small software development company. Jane has the following income, exclusions, deductions, exemptions, and credits:

Jane's salary $35,000
Gift from parents 5,000
Gross income from part-time tax practice 6,300
Business expenses of part-time tax practice 1,750
Itemized deductions allowed 3,900
Tax credits 510

Jane is single.

REQUIRED:

Compute Jane's taxable income and income tax.

PD-12. TAXABLE INCOME AND INCOME FOR A JOINT RETURN   Johanna and Marshall Kelly are employed by the same corporation and file a joint return. Their joint income from salaries is $97,500. They have a small investment portfolio that produced taxable income of $310 from dividends and $275 from interest. Marshall Kelly received $10,000 of the proceeds from a life insurance policy carried by his father, who died during the year. The Kellys invested $7,600 in tax-deferred retirement funds during the year. The Kellys are allowed itemized deductions of $4,100 for moving expenses, $7,800 for mortgage interest, $1,850 for property taxes, $5,100 for state and local income taxes, and $2,300 for charitable contributions. The Kellys have four personal exemptions of $2,150 each and no tax credits.

REQUIRED:

Compute Johanna and Marshall Kelly's taxable income and income tax.

PD-13. TAXABLE INCOME AND INCOME TAX FOR A SELF-EMPLOYED TAXPAYER   Cecelia Land operates a computer software business. Cecelia evaluates software for clients, purchases software from vendors for clients, trains client personnel, and provides assistance with problems encountered by clients. Cecelia has provided you with the following data:

BUSINESS INCOME	AMOUNT
Evaluation service revenue	$ 8,100
Purchasing service revenue	2,200
Training revenue	78,900
Advisory revenue	26,300

BUSINESS EXPENSES	AMOUNT
Rent	$12,000
Utilities	3,650
Transportation	4,700
Depreciation, computing equipment	4,800
Office supplies	1,100
Miscellaneous	380

PERSONAL ITEMS	AMOUNT
Contribution to tax-deferred retirement plan	$2,000
Mortgage interest, condominium residence	9,400
Property taxes, condominium residence	1,440
State and local income tax	3,060

Cecelia is single with one personal exemption of $2,150 and no tax credits.

REQUIRED:

Compute Cecelia's taxable income and income tax.

ANALYTICAL OPPORTUNITY

AD-14. EVALUATING PROPOSED TAX LAW CHANGE   A Washington think tank has developed a proposal to change the taxation of individuals by doing away with deductions *from* adjusted gross income (itemized deductions and standard deductions) and reducing the tax rate in each bracket by a number of percentage points that is just sufficient to offset the tax revenues lost by the elimination of deductions.

REQUIRED:

Identify and explain two strengths and two weaknesses of this proposal.

LEARNING OBJECTIVES

Careful study of this supplementary topic will enable you to:

1. State the four criteria that guide the recording of transactions under accrual accounting.

2. Recognize revenue in exceptional cases when the customary time-of-sale recognition is not appropriate.

3. Understand that disclosures in footnotes to the financial statements are not subject to the recognition framework.

RECOGNITION: The act of recording transactions in the accounting system which involves determinations of whether or not events qualify to be recorded and, if they do, when they should be recorded.

MEASUREMENT: The determinations of the amount to be recorded for a transaction and the account titles to be used to describe the transaction.

RECOGNITION AND MEASUREMENT

Information reported in financial statements represents the accumulated effects of an entity's activities recorded in the accounting system. Under accrual accounting, these activities are recorded when they occur rather than when cash is received or paid. An activity may involve a sequence of transactions, each of which is recorded differently; thus the occurrence of an activity may be associated with several discrete transactions. The credit sale is a familiar two-transaction example: The delivery of goods to the customer increases revenue and accounts receivable and the subsequent collection from the customer increases cash and reduces accounts receivable. Further, some activities may be associated with continuous transactions that require partial recordings using adjusting entries (e.g., when rent revenue is increased and prepaid rent is decreased from the portion of a lease that expires within the current period). Whatever the form of business activity, recording it requires an accounting decision concerning the timing of the recognition in the accounting records and the amounts and accounts affected.

The act of recording transactions in the accounting system is called **recognition.** Recognition involves a determination of whether or not activities qualify to be recorded and, if they do, a determination of when to make an entry in the accounting records. In addition, of course, recognition involves **measurement,** a determination of the amount to be recorded for a transaction and the account titles used to describe the transaction.

The preceding chapters of this book describe the principles that govern the recognition and measurement of many different types of transactions, including revenue transactions, expense transactions, asset acquisitions, incurrences of liabilities, and so forth. These recognition and measurement principles are an extension of general concepts described in the paragraphs that follow. This supplement also illustrates the problems that can arise in applying those concepts to unusual activities and transactions.

MANAGERS, AUDITORS, AND RECOGNITION

The recognition and measurement of commonly occurring transactions—like day-to-day purchases of materials and sales of product—are routine matters. Accounting for these activities involves the application of familiar, widely accepted accounting principles and does not require involved analysis. However, when transactions are unusual or involve complex commitments by a business, the required accounting may be unfamiliar and may require a careful consideration of recognition criteria and accounting principles. Such transactions may be preceded by a lengthy planning stage during which the details of the transaction are contemplated and finally agreed to. For example, planning for the acquisition of one company by another, the construction of a new manufacturing facility, or the issuance of new stock may require several years. In some instances, transactions may be redesigned because of their anticipated impact on the accounting system, financial statements, and external perceptions of the entity. Although a transaction is not recorded during this stage, management and the company's auditors usually reach a preliminary agreement on when and how to record the transaction. The analysis section that follows illustrates this interaction between management and the auditors.

ANALYSIS
REVENUE
RECOGNITION
UNDER LONG-TERM
SALES CONTRACT

Midway Molding, Inc., is a small manufacturer of plastic parts used in the highly competitive automotive and computer industries. Midway's manufacturing processes are automated and use new flexible manufacturing technology. Midway has negotiated a five-year contract to produce a specialized part for a computer manufacturer. The contract specifies that the computer manufacturer will purchase at least 500,000 parts each year and that Midway will supply up to 500,000 additional parts each year if requested to do so. The contract also provides that the computer manufacturer may return for full credit up to 200,000 parts in any given year.

Midway has ambitious expansion plans that depend on its ability to issue additional capital stock, which in turn depends on Midway's ability to show growth in net income. The newly signed sales contract is viewed by Midway management as a signal that the time for a new stock issue has come. In fact, Midway management had pressed hard to secure the 500,000-unit guarantee provision to strengthen this signal and to support an argument for rapid recognition of some portion of the revenues. In the week following the signing of the contract, Midway management began planning for a stock offering that would double the number of its outstanding shares.

In preparing its financial statements for the current year, Midway's controller has consulted with the company's external auditor about revenue recognition for the new sales contract. Midway's management argues that the contract guarantees sales of at least 300,000 parts per year for five years and that all this revenue should be recognized when the contract is signed. When the number of parts delivered (less returns) exceeds 300,000 in any year, then revenues from the number of parts in excess of 300,000 units should also be recorded. In addition, management plans to reduce the amount of revenue recorded in any year for returns announced by the buyer.

Midway's auditors object to this revenue recognition plan. They assert that it violates generally accepted accounting principles by recognizing revenues on the basis of signing a sales agreement. Further, the auditors also object to restricting the provision for returned parts to announced returns. In a highly competitive industry, production schedules are volatile and parts requirements can change rapidly and without warning. Further, competition among parts manufacturers can undermine the entire sales contract; it may be possible for a buyer who is willing to incur legal costs and possibly legal damages to escape a purchase contract.

The auditors propose that revenue recognized in each year be based on the number of parts delivered during that year, that a realistic allowance for sales returns be established, and that the adequacy of the allowance be evaluated at the end of each year. Further, the auditors point out that if a reasonable estimate of sales returns cannot be made, then generally accepted accounting principles do not permit recognition of revenue associated with any units sold that are subject to return.

Midway's management is unhappy with the auditor's proposal, believing that it ignores the guarantee provision of the long-term sales agreement and jeopardizes the success of planned stock offering. The auditors counter that information about the details of the contract can be disclosed in documents that accompany the financial statements. Management takes slim comfort in this disclosure opportunity, believing that the stock market is much more strongly influenced by the effects of transactions recognized on the income statement than by the effects of transactions that must be inferred from supplementary disclosures.

If sufficiently unhappy with the auditor's proposal, Midway could search for an auditor that would take a different view and change auditors if a more agreeable auditor can be found. It is unlikely that Midway could find an auditor that would accept a significantly different recognition plan than the one proposed by the present auditor. Further, changes of auditor are reported to the public and may raise suspicions in the minds of potential stock buyers. Consequently, Midway is likely to reluctantly accept the auditor's revenue recognition proposal.

The experience of Midway Molding, Inc., illustrates the interest of company management in both the form of a transaction and its accounting recognition. The example shows how the recognition of important transactions may produce conflict between management and external auditors over when to recognize revenues.

Recognition decisions are made by analyzing generally accepted accounting principles, which in turn are based on concepts set forth in the FASB's conceptual framework (see especially *FASB Statement of Financial Accounting Concepts No. 5*, paragraphs 63–77). We turn now to a discussion of these concepts.

RECOGNITION CONCEPTS

RELIABLE MEASURE-MENT: A description in words and numbers that is reasonably free from error and bias and that is a faithful representation of what it purports to represent.

As noted in Chapter 3, *transactions* are events or happenings of consequence to an entity that are recorded in its accounting records. To qualify as a transaction, the effect of the underlying events on the entity must be subject to **reliable measurement.** A reliable measurement is a description in words and numbers that is reasonably free from error and bias and that is a faithful representation of what it purports to represent. The concept of reliable measurement can be stated more completely in terms of four criteria or tests that a transaction must meet to qualify for recognition:

1. *Definitional test.* The transaction must cause changes in elements of financial statements that fit the definition of assets, liabilities, equity, revenues, or expenses.

2. *Measurability test.* The transaction must be associated with an attribute or attributes that can be measured in dollars.

3. *Relevance test.* The information recorded about the transaction must be relevant, that is, capable of making a difference in the decisions of investors, creditors, or other users of the financial statements.

4. *Reliability test.* The information recorded must be reliable, which means that a user of the financial statements can rely on the information to faithfully represent the transaction that it purports to represent. This assurance to financial statement users comes from verification of the information by accounting experts. Information is *verifiable* if most accounting experts would agree on

the representation. Formal verification is not undertaken as a regular practice; however, preparers of financial statements must be able to argue convincingly that their representations are verifiable and, therefore, reliable. Theoretically, every recognition principle and procedure should result in accounting entries that meet these four recognition tests.

In addition to these four tests, recognition also requires that the transaction be *material*—that it is likely to have a significant effect on a statement user's decisions—and that its recognition be *cost-beneficial*—that the benefits of recognition exceed the costs of recognition. Although it is frequently possible to estimate the cost of producing information, assessment of the benefits is made difficult by the fact that financial statement information is available to everyone. The benefits of most commodities purchased in a marketplace are enjoyed more or less exclusively by the purchaser and thus are called *private goods* by economists. The benefits of financial statement information, however, are not confined to the managements that pay for it. Once the financial statements are issued—and in some cases even before this point—the information is available to the general public. Thus, accounting information is an example of a *public good.* Whereas private goods can be traced to particular buyers, which facilitates the measurement of benefits, public goods cannot be traced to particular buyers, which greatly complicates the assessment of their benefits. Although materiality is somewhat easier to assess, it too depends on the identity of a hypothetical user of the information, an individual whose attributes are difficult to specify in a public good environment.

Generally accepted accounting principles are continually evolving in response to new forms of transacting and deal making and in response to long-standing unresolved controversies over the form of accounting principles. The recognition concepts discussed above provide general guidance for the continuing development of accounting principles, but the detailed principles must be developed in terms of the specifics of the transactions involved. Variations in revenue recognition principles for special classes of transactions illustrate the way in which different recognition principles can be accommodated by the conceptual structure.

REVENUE AND INCOME RECOGNITION PRINCIPLES

POINT-OF-SALE METHOD: The usual method of revenue recognition under which sales revenue is recognized when goods are transferred to customers or when services are perfomed for customers.

As we discussed in Chapter 2, income is revenue when it is earned, that is, when the seller has put forth substantially all the effort required to sell goods or services and when the selling price is known. Further, following the matching concept, expenses of a period are the costs of assets given up (as in the case of inventory) or used (as in the case of labor and machines) to earn the revenue recognized in that period. Thus, the net income for a period is the revenue recognized less the product and period expenses matched with that revenue. Therefore, a decision to recognize revenue is actually an income recognition decision that recognizes first revenue and then associated expenses. Because the revenue recognition decisions dominate this income determination process, accountants refer to these joint revenue, expense, and income recognition decisions as revenue recognition.

The customary procedure for recognizing revenue is called the **point-of-sale**

method. Under this method, *sales revenue* is usually recognized when goods are transferred to customers and *service revenue* is recognized when services are performed for customers. Although the point-of-sale method is usually applicable, different revenue recognition methods are appropriate for a variety of special cases. Let us consider three such cases of revenue recognition—extended production, production for insatiable markets, and installment sales.

EXTENDED PRODUCTION

The production of some goods may require many months or even years to complete. Office buildings, factories, bridges, highways, ships, and airplanes are common examples. The growing of timber for lumber, which may require decades, is an extreme example. Use of the point-of-sale method in such cases would delay all revenue recognition until the completed product—the completed building, bridge, ship, log, or lumber—is transferred to its new owner.[1] Completed production revenue recognition would require the accumulation of substantial production costs as an asset on the balance sheet until the period of the product's completion. Further, the income statement would give no indication of the effect of company activities on its net income until the very end of that activity, too late to be of much relevance.

PERCENTAGE-OF-COM-PLETION METHOD: The method of revenue recognition that recognizes revenue and related product expense during the production period in proportion to the work completed.

Under certain conditions, an alternative method is applicable. Called the **percentage-of-completion method,** it permits recognition of revenue and related product expense during the production period in proportion to the work completed. If the product is contracted for before production, so that total revenue is known, and if total product cost and the percentage of completion are reliably estimable—conditions that satisfy measurability and reliability criteria—then generally accepted accounting principles permit the recognition of income as production proceeds. The amount of income (revenue less product expense) recognized in each year is determined by using an estimate of the percentage of the total project complete at year-end. These estimates are either supplied by an architect or engineer or calculated by accountants using actual and projected costs. The increase in the estimated percentage of completion during a year gives the percentage of income to be recognized in that year.

Let us illustrate the percentage-of-completion method using a three-year, $4,000,000 contract awarded by the State of Ohio to Sandusky Construction at the beginning of 19X3. During 19X3 Sandusky collected contract progress payments from the State of Ohio of $1,500,000 and incurred costs of $1,000,000 for the project. At the end of 19X3, engineers estimate that the project is 30 percent complete and that $2,000,000 in additional costs will be required to complete the contract. Exhibit E–1 shows how Sandusky calculates that percentage-of-completion income is $300,000 and presents journal entries used to recognize 19X3 contract activities.

During 19X4, Sandusky collected $1,500,000 in progress payments and incurred contract costs of $1,600,000. At the end of 19X4, engineers estimate that the contract is 80 percent complete and that $400,000 of costs will be required to complete the project. Exhibit E–2 shows how Sandusky calculates that 19X4 percentage-of-completion income is $500,000 and presents journal entries used to recognize 19X4 contract activities.

---

[1] A very similar revenue recognition method, the *completed-contract method,* delays all revenue recognition until the completion of the contract. Since buyers typically take possession of long-term projects shortly after their completion, this method usually produces the same result as the point-of-sale method.

EXHIBIT E–1   **FIRST-YEAR PERCENTAGE-OF-COMPLETION INCOME RECOGNITION**

Contract revenue		$4,000,000
Less: Costs incurred to date.....................	$1,000,000	
Costs to complete	2,000,000	3,000,000
Expected contract profit		1,000,000
Times: Percentage complete		× .30
19X3 percentage-of-completion income		$ 300,000

Journal entries to record 19X3 contract activities:

Entry to record collection of contract progress payments

Cash...	1,500,000	
Billings on contract		1,500,000

Entry to record incurrence of costs under contract (assumed paid in cash)

Construction in progress........................	1,000,000	
Cash.......................................		1,000,000

Entry to record recognition of percentage-of-completion income

Construction in progress........................	300,000	
Income on long-term contract..................		300,000

EXHIBIT E–2   **SECOND-YEAR PERCENTAGE-OF-COMPLETION INCOME RECOGNITION**

Contract revenue		$4,000,000
Less: Costs incurred to date.....................	$2,600,000*	
Costs to complete	400,000	3,000,000
Expected contract profit		$1,000,000
Times: Percentage complete.....................		× .80
19X4 year-end total income recognizable..........		$ 800,000
Less: Income recognized in prior years		300,000
19X4 percentage-of-completion income		$ 500,000

* $1,000,000 from 19X3 and $1,600,000 from 19X4.

Journal entries to record 19X4 contract activities:

Entry to record collection of contract progress payments

Cash...	1,500,000	
Billings on contract		1,500,000

Entry to record incurrence of costs under contract (assumed paid in cash)

Construction in progress........................	1,600,000	
Cash.......................................		1,600,000

Entry to record recognition of percentage-of-completion income

Construction in progress........................	500,000	
Income on long-term contract..................		500,000

EXHIBIT E-3   **LAST-YEAR PERCENTAGE-OF-COMPLETION INCOME RECOGNITION**

Contract revenue	$4,000,000
Less: Costs incurred.	3,160,000*
Contract profit	$ 840,000
Less: Income recognized in prior years	800,000
19X5 percentage-of-completion income	$ 40,000

* $1,000,000 from 19X3, $1,600,000 from 19X4, and $560,000 from 19X5.

Journal entries to record 19X5 contract activities:

Entry to record collection of contract progress payments

Cash	1,000,000	
Billings on contract		1,000,000

Entry to record incurrence of costs under contract (assumed paid in cash)

Construction in progress.	560,000	
Cash		560,000

Entry to record recognition of percentage-of-completion income

Construction in progress.	40,000	
Income on long-term contract.		40,000

Entry to record completion of contract and transfer of property to the State of Ohio

Billings on contract	4,000,000	
Construction in progress.		4,000,000

During 19X5, Sandusky completed the contract and collected the remaining $1,000,000 in progress payments. Contract costs required to complete the contract were $560,000. Exhibit E–3 shows how Sandusky calculates that 19X5 percentage-of-completion income is $40,000 and presents journal entries used to recognize 19X5 contract activities.

The construction in process account is an asset (inventory) whose balance represents costs incurred under the contract and income recognized to date on the contract. The billings on contract account is a contra-asset account that is offset against construction in progress in the financial statements. When the contract is complete and the constructed asset is transferred to the purchaser, construction in progress and billings on contract have the same balance and are closed against each other.

Service contracts are similar to long-term construction contracts in that productive activity occurs over a long period of time. When a service contract provides for a number of similar service engagements, it is usually appropriate to recognize revenue on partially completed engagements following a procedure much like the percentage-of-completion method. However, when the service contract provides for a final act prior to which the service commitment cannot be viewed as complete, then recognition of revenue must wait until that act is performed. For example, a consulting firm responsible for the installation of a new computer system should probably wait to recognize any part of the related revenue until the system has been tested and "debugged," an activity that takes place at the end of the contract.

Although the appropriate revenue recognition for most types of service contracts is fairly clear, there are service contracts for which the appropriate revenue recognition plan must be tailored to the circumstances of the particular contract. For example, consider a health club that offers lifetime memberships for a fixed initial fee. How should such revenues be recognized by the club? One approach would be to recognize revenues over a period equal to the average expected life of members, recognizing that members may make much heavier use of the club during the early years of their membership.

PRODUCTION FOR INSATIABLE MARKETS

Markets for most agricultural products and precious metals will accept as much production as a firm can possibly deliver and will do so at a price that can be predicted with considerable accuracy. Further, production is considered to be the critical event in the earnings process, and the costs of selling and distributing the product are either small or highly predictable. In such markets, revenue is reliably measurable once production is completed; further, revenue on completed production is relevant to readers of financial statements. It is reasonable to recognize revenue and related product expense for such markets as soon as the product is produced and available for sale, whether or not the sale has actually taken place. This method of revenue recognition is called the **completed-production method.**

COMPLETED-PRODUCTION METHOD: The method of revenue recognition that recognizes revenue and related product expense as soon as the product is available for sale.

To illustrate, consider Nevada Mining, Inc., which produces 10,000 ounces of gold in 19X5, 9,000 in 19X6, and 10,000 in 19X7. Production cost is $210 per ounce plus $1,500,000 per year for rent and depreciation. In addition, the cost of selling each ounce is $10, which is paid at the time of sale. Because there is some variation in gold prices from year to year, Nevada Mining follows the sales strategy of withholding from sale and storing all or part of production in low-price years in the hope of securing a better price in the next year, as shown in Exhibit E–4. Since the price was high in 19X5, Nevada Mining sold 10,000 ounces and had no inventory at year-end; since production equaled sales, both the point-of-sale and completed-production methods produced the same amount for 19X5 revenue. Since the price was low in 19X6, Nevada Mining made no sales and held its entire production for sale next year. Thus no revenue would be recognized under the point-of-sale method, but revenue of $3,510,000, based on the ex-

EXHIBIT E–4   **COMPLETED-PRODUCTION AND POINT-OF-SALE METHODS**

	19X5	19X6	19X7
Price during year..............................	$400	$350	$390
Year-end price estimate for next year.............	360	390	390
Inventory data:			
Inventory, 1/1	–0– oz.	–0– oz.	9,000 oz.
Production..................................	10,000	9,000	10,000
Available for sale............................	10,000	9,000	19,000
Less: Sales.................................	10,000	–0–	16,000
Inventory, 12/31	–0–	9,000	3,000
Revenue recognized:			
Completed-production method	$4,000,000	$3,510,000	$3,900,000
Point-of-sale method	4,000,000	–0–	6,240,000

EXHIBIT E–5	**INCOME STATEMENTS FOR POINT-OF-SALE AND COMPLETED-PRODUCTION METHODS**

NEVADA MINING, INC.
Income Statements

	19X5		19X6		19X7	
POINT-OF-SALE METHOD						
Sales revenue..........		$4,000,000		–0–		$6,240,000
Cost of goods sold						
Inventory, 1/1........	$ –0–		$ –0–		$3,390,000	
Production	3,600,000		3,390,000		3,600,000	
Available for sale	$3,600,000		$3,390,000		$6,990,000	
Inventory, 12/31......	–0–	3,600,000	3,390,000	3,390,000	1,080,000*	5,910,000
Gross margin		$ 400,000		–0–		$ 330,000
Selling expense........		100,000		–0–		160,000
Operating income		$ 300,000		–0–		$ 170,000

* $1,080,000 = ($3,600,000/10,000 units)(3,000 units), computed using the FIFO inventory costing method.

	19X5	19X6	19X7
COMPLETED-PRODUCTION METHOD			
Sales revenue	$4,000,000	$3,510,000	$3,900,000
Cost of goods produced	3,600,000	3,390,000	3,600,000
Gross margin	$ 400,000	$ 120,000	$ 300,000
Selling expense....................	100,000	90,000	100,000
Operating income	$ 300,000	$ 30,000	$ 200,000

pected sales next year at $390 per ounce, would be recognized under the completed-production method. In 19X7, Nevada Mining sold all but 3,000 ounces, resulting in revenue of $6,240,000 [($390)(16,000 ounces)] under the point-of-sale method. Under the completed-production method, 19X7 revenue reflects only 19X7 production [(10,000 ounces)($390) = $3,900,000]. Of course, if 19X6 production were sold for a different amount than was estimated at the end of 19X6, then an adjustment would be required in 19X7. Such an adjustment is not required in the illustration because Nevada Mining correctly estimated the 19X7 price at the end of 19X6.

Expenses are matched with sales under the point-of-sale method and with production under the completed-production method. Thus, as shown in Exhibit E–5, cost of goods sold is determined by using the number of units sold during the year and cost of goods produced is determined by using the number of units produced during the year. Similarly, selling expense corresponds to units sold when the point-of-sale method is used and to units produced when the completed-production method is used.

The completed-production method results in an unusual valuation of inventory on the balance sheet. Under the point-of-sale method, the cost of production is debited to the inventory account, where it remains until the product is sold. Thus inventory is valued at cost. Under the completed-production method, in contrast, the cost of production for each year is debited to cost of goods sold for that year, and the inventory is carried at its net realizable value, the net amount the company expects to realize from its sale. Thus the inventory becomes a kind of receivable measured by the excess of anticipated revenue over cost (whether incurred or anticipated) for units that remain to be sold. The accounting for such inventories is considered in intermediate accounting courses.

INSTALLMENT SALES

INSTALLMENT SALES METHOD: The method of revenue recognition that recognizes revenue and related product expense as cash is collected.

Our final example of an unusual revenue recognition method is the installment sales method, which is used when a credit sale is collected over a long period of time and the uncollectible accounts expense cannot be reliably estimated. Under the **installment sales method,** income or gross margin (revenue less product expense) on the credit sale is recognized as the cash is collected. To illustrate, consider Rawlins Electronics, a seller of electronic audio and video equipment on a no-money-down, 18-months-to-pay basis, which began operations in 19X2. All Rawlins' sales are at a gross margin of 40 percent. Rawlins sells to customers for whom collection is highly uncertain. Therefore, the installment sales method is appropriate. Exhibit E–6 shows information for the first three years of Rawlins' operation.

Under the installment sales method, income (gross margin) would be $12,000 in 19X2, $68,000 in 19X3, and $138,000 in 19X4. Under the point-of-sale method, gross margin would be $40,000 in 19X2, $128,000 in 19X3, and $216,000 in 19X4, with income in each year being reduced by an appropriate amount of uncollectible account expense. If uncollectible account expense can be reliably estimated, then the two methods would yield approximately the same net income; in such cases, of course, the point-of-sale method should be used. If, however, uncollectible account expense cannot be reliably estimated, then use of the point-of-sale method would involve considerable guesswork and periodic readjustment. Readers of the income statement would find the wide year-to-year variations in the uncollectible account expense difficult to interpret and might be misled by revenue amounts, large segments of which might turn out to be uncol-

---

EXHIBIT E–6   INSTALLMENT SALES METHOD

	19X2	19X3	19X4
Installment sales made during year	$100,000	$320,000	$540,000
Cash collections on installment sales:			
19X2 sales	$ 30,000	$ 55,000	$ 5,000
19X3 sales	–0–	115,000	140,000
19X4 sales	–0–	–0–	200,000
Total	$ 30,000	$170,000	$345,000
Gross margin (income) recognized:*			
Installment sales method	$ 12,000	$ 68,000	$138,000
Point-of-sale-method:			
Revenue	$100,000	$320,000	$540,000
Cost of goods sold	60,000	192,000	324,000
Gross margin	$ 40,000	$128,000	$216,000

* 40 percent of cash collections on installment sales.

lectible. In these cases, the installment sales method, which produces an easily interpretable and conservatively estimated income figure, is called for.

Use of the installment sales method results in the deferral of gross margin associated with future collections. These amounts are usually recorded in deferred gross margin accounts which are reported as current or long-term assets, as appropriate. The accounting for such assets is considered in intermediate accounting courses.

UNCERTAINTIES, CONTINGENCIES, AND RECOGNITION

CONTINGENCIES: Future events that influence the present recognition and disclosure of transactions.

The installment sales method shows that uncertainty about the course of future events can affect the recording of transactions. Future events that influence the present recognition and disclosure for transactions are called **contingencies.** Contingencies arise in many different types of transactions. Anticipated gains or losses from legal actions represent an important category of such transactions. Another category includes contracts that explicitly incorporate uncertain future events, making the performance by one of the contracting parties contingent on the occurrence of a specified future event. For example, notes receivable discounted with recourse (as discussed in Chapter 8) and warranties and pension agreements (as discussed in Chapter 10) incorporate such contingencies and give rise to contingent liabilities. Contingency provisions are also used in sales contracts that make the price contingent on some future event. For example, a baseball player's contract might be sold to another team for a price conditional on the player's performance during the next season, an office building might be sold for a price conditional on the occupancy rate during the next several years, or a business might be sold for a price conditional on its revenues during the next several years.

Under generally accepted accounting principles, proper accounting for such contingencies depends on whether occurrence of the future event in question results in a gain or a loss. If the occurrence of the future event results in a gain, the gain is usually not reported in the financial statements until the event occurs. (If cash collection is viewed as a contingency in an installment sale, then the installment sales method is consistent with this practice.) On the other hand, if the occurrence of the future event results in a loss, three accounting treatments are possible, depending on the likelihood that the future event, called a *loss contingency,* will occur. If occurrence of the loss contingency is *probable*—that is, if it is likely to occur—then the loss should be estimated and recorded. If occurrence of the loss contingency is merely *reasonably possible*—that is, if its occurrence is less than likely but more than remote—then the loss should be estimated and disclosed in a footnote but should not be recorded. In cases in which occurrence of the loss contingency is remote, neither footnote disclosure nor recording is appropriate. Of course, the determination of whether a loss contingency is probable, reasonably possible, or remote is often difficult. The willingness to recognize and report loss contingencies and the reluctance to recognize or report gain contingencies are consistent with the conservatism convention discussed in Chapter 7.

SUMMARY

Recognition, the act of recording transactions in the accounting system, is guided by accounting principles that, in turn, are developed by reference to recognition concepts. The most important aspect of the recognition concept is that the effect of events underlying a recognizable transaction must be subject to reliable measurement. A more complete statement of the recognition concept involves definitional, measurability, relevance, and reliability tests and a determination that the transaction is material and that its recording is cost-beneficial.

Variation in revenue recognition principles for special classes of transactions illustrates the way in which different recognition principles can be accommodated by the revenue recognition concept. Cases of extended or long-term production may call for the percentage-of-completion method of revenue recognition. Cases of production for insatiable markets may call for the completed-production method of revenue recognition. Installment sales may call for the installment sales method of revenue recognition.

Using a somewhat more detailed representation of the operating cycle than presented in Chapter 2, Exhibit E–7 shows the relationship among the four revenue recognition methods discussed in the foregoing supplement. The point-of-sale method falls between the completed-production method and the installment sales method when the three methods are arrayed on the operating cycle. In

EXHIBIT E–7   REVENUE RECOGNITION AND THE OPERATING CYCLE

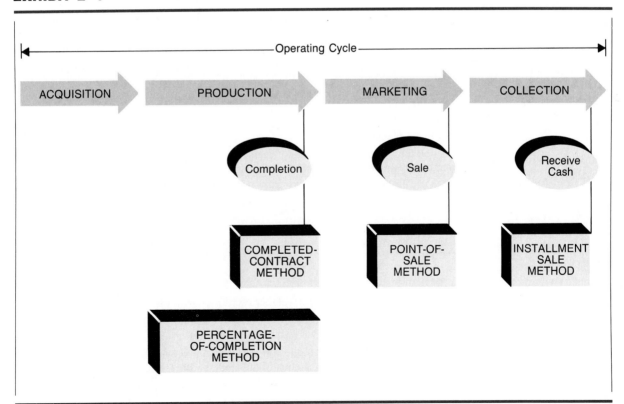

this sense, the point-of-sale method recognizes revenue sooner than the installment sales method but not as soon as either the completed-production or the percentage-of-completion method. In general, delaying the recognition of revenue improves the reliability of the accounting information but impairs its timeliness and relevance.

The chapter concludes with a discussion of *contingencies,* future events that influence the present recognition and disclosure for transactions. Under generally accepted accounting principles, contingencies associated with gains are usually not recorded until the event occurs, whereas contingencies associated with losses are subject to recognition provided that the occurrence of the event is sufficiently likely.

KEY TERMS

COMPLETED-PRODUCTION METHOD (p. 843)	PERCENTAGE-OF-COMPLETION METHOD (p. 840)
CONTINGENCIES (p. 846)	POINT-OF-SALE METHOD (p. 839)
INSTALLMENT SALES METHOD (p. 845)	RECOGNITION (p. 836)
MEASUREMENT (p. 836)	RELIABLE MEASUREMENT (p. 838)

QUESTIONS

QE-1. The definitions of recognition and measurement involve four determinations. List the four determinations.

QE-2. Why are external auditors interested in management's decisions concerning recognition?

QE-3. The concept of reliable measurement can be stated in terms of four tests and two properties of a transaction. List these six elements of the recognition concept.

QE-4. Explain the relationship between the operating cycle and the four methods of revenue recognition discussed in this supplement.

QE-5. List and describe four methods of revenue recognition. For each method, describe a situation to which it would apply and explain why it would be applicable.

QE-6. Generally accepted accounting principles for gain contingencies differ from those for loss contingencies. Explain the difference.

EXERCISES

EE-7. APPLYING THE DEFINITIONAL TEST Indicate whether each listed event meets the definitional test for recognition in the accounting system. If a proposed transaction fails any part of the definitional test, explain why it fails.

1. A major stockholder of Randolf Corporation sells her 35 percent interest in the company to a wealthy investor who is trying to take control of Randolf's operations.

2. A drought during the year just ended is expected to cause a 40 percent reduction in next year's sales by Deerman Farm Products.

EXERCISE CONTINUES

3. Merchandise held in inventory at year-end is determined to have little market value but is carried on the records at a significant amount.

4. A retailer uses office space in a building owned by the retailer.

5. A retailer uses office space in a building rented under an operating lease from another company.

6. The FASB has just adopted a new accounting standard. The standard will not be effective for the financial statements of Jefferson Laboratories, which are about to be issued to stockholders, but will be effective for the financial statement issued in one year. Jefferson estimates that it will cost $20,000 during the next year to implement the new standard.

EE-8. LONG-TERM CONSTRUCTION CONTRACT ACCOUNTING Highway Construction Company has a $8,000,000, two-year contract to build 10 miles of a new highway in New Mexico. At the time the contract is signed, Highway expects to complete 60 percent of the job in the first year and the remainder in the second year. Highway expects to incur $5,000,000 of cost in the first year and $2,500,000 of cost in the second year on this job.

REQUIRED:

Assume that Highway Construction Company records income from this contract on a percentage-of-completion basis and that its estimates for costs and completion percentages are realized. How much income will be recognized in each of the two years on this contract?

EE-9. PRODUCTION FOR INSATIABLE MARKETS Metal Products Company mines and refines platinum. The company has a contract with the U.S. government that allows it to sell to the U.S. government any amount of platinum that it can produce at the market price for platinum on the day it delivers the metal to the government. The following are data for platinum production, sales, ending inventory, and prices for two recent years:

	19X6	19X7
Production	15,000 ounces	20,000 ounces
Sales	11,000	22,000
Ending inventory	4,000	2,000
Price	$375 per ounce	$390 per ounce

REQUIRED:

Assume that Metal Products records revenue for platinum when production is complete. How much revenue will be recorded in 19X6 and 19X7 for platinum?

EE-10. INSTALLMENT SALES Rameriz Corporation sold a parcel of land to Sorbet Company for $200,000 on January 1, 19X4. The land had cost Rameriz $120,000. The terms of the transaction require Sorbet to make four $50,000 annual payments, with the first payment due one year after the sale. (The transaction also requires Sorbet to pay interest on the unpaid balance, but we will ignore that part of the transaction for this exercise.) Because Sorbet has experienced financial difficulties, Rameriz believes that the installment method of accounting for the transaction is appropriate.

REQUIRED:

Prepare a schedule that indicates the amount of income from this transaction that will be recognized in Rameriz's financial statements if Sorbet makes the payments as scheduled.

PROBLEMS

PE-11. TRANSACTION RECOGNITION Halogen Chemical Company has been particularly careful with the toxic chemical by-products of its processes. In mid-December 19X2, a large truck, owned and operated by Halogen, that was transporting 10,000 gallons of these toxic wastes to a reputable incinerator for safe disposal was involved in a traffic accident that was completely the fault of the other driver. However, the entire load of toxic waste spilled onto the ground. The particular ground was high in sand content, so the toxic waste dispersed into the soil before it could be collected. Just after the accident rain fell in the area, increasing substantially the volume of contaminated soil. Unfortunately for Halogen, the other driver involved in the accident was uninsured. Halogen's business insurance does not provide coverage for accidents involving toxic waste. By December 31, 19X2, Halogen's engineers estimate that Halogen's cost for cleaning up the toxic chemical spill will be $25,000,000, a material amount.

REQUIRED:

1. Do these events qualify as a transaction for Halogen's 19X2 financial statements?

2. Assume that Halogen spends $10,000,000 during 19X3 for cleanup activities and that its engineers estimate that the cleanup will be completed during 19X4 but that the costs to complete the cleanup will be $20,000,000. Should Halogen recognize the $5,000,000 increase in estimated cleanup costs in its 19X3 financial statements?

PE-12. PERCENTAGE-OF-COMPLETION METHOD DeBruicker Construction Company was awarded a $15,000,000 contract to build a new bridge over the Cumberland River in Nashville, Tennessee at the beginning of 19X4. At the time the contract was awarded, DeBruicker made the following estimates.

	19X4	19X5	19X6
Expected contract costs...........	$5,000,000	$6,000,000	$3,500,000
Expected collections under contract .	5,000,000	5,000,000	5,000,000
Expected percentage complete......	30%	70%	100%

REQUIRED:

1. Assume that 19X4 results were as expected. Prepare the journal entries to record 19X4 contract activities.

2. Assume that 19X5 results were as planned except that actual contract costs were $5,900,000 and that only $3,300,000 of costs are expected to be required during 19X6 to complete the contract. Prepare the journal entries to record 19X5 contract activities.

3. Assume that 19X6 results are as forecast at the end of 19X5. Prepare the journal entries to record 19X5 contract activities and the transfer of the bridge to the contracting authority at completion of the job.

PE-13. COMPLETED-PRODUCTION METHOD Doster Agricultural Products, Inc., owns a large grain farm. The following data are available for Doster's production and sale of corn for three recent years:

	19X1	19X2	19X3
Price during year (per bushel).........	$2.50	$2.60	$2.30
Year-end price estimate for next year....	2.40	2.30	2.50
Inventory data:			
Inventory, 1/1....................	10,000 bu.	–0– bu.	–0– bu.
Production	80,000	95,000	90,000
Available for sale	90,000	95,000	90,000
Less: Sales......................	90,000	95,000	15,000
Inventory, 12/31..................	–0–	–0–	75,000

Assume that Doster Agricultural Products' cost of production is $2.10 per bushel.

REQUIRED:

1. Prepare a schedule of sales revenue, cost of goods sold, and gross margin for Doster for 19X1–19X3 on a completed-production basis.

2. Prepare a schedule of sales revenue, cost of goods sold, and gross margin for Doster for 19X1–19X3 on a point-of-sale basis.

PE-14. INSTALLMENT SALES   On January 1, 19X5, Bridgewater Properties sold a small shopping center that it had constructed to Retail Properties, Inc., for $2,000,000. The shopping center cost Bridgewater $1,700,000 to construct. The terms of the transaction require Retail Properties to pay $200,000 down and three annual payments of $600,000 each, with the first annual payment due one year after the sale. The purchase/sale agreement also requires Retail Properties to pay 10 percent interest on the unpaid installment balance. Because both the interest and principal payments are to be made from rentals that Retail Properties expects to collect from shopping center tenants, Bridgewater believes that the installment method of accounting for this transaction is appropriate.

REQUIRED:

Prepare a schedule that indicates the amount of income including interest from this transaction that will be recognized in Bridgewater's financial statements if Retail Properties makes the payments as scheduled.

ANALYTICAL OPPORTUNITY

AE-15. A CLOUD ON THE HORIZON   In 19X2 Turbine Company was approached by a major aircraft manufacturer with a request that it develop a turbine engine for a new aircraft that was under development. Turbine evaluated the proposal, discussed the market with a number of airlines, and decided to develop the engine. Turbine estimates that it will be able to sell a total of 1,000 of the new engines over a 10-year period beginning in 19X4. During 19X2 and 19X3 Turbine spent $200,000,000 of its own funds to develop the engine. Turbine estimates that it will break even on the engine project if it can sell 800 engines. The first 50 operational models of the new engine were produced in 19X4. The engine met every one of its operational targets. In addition, Turbine's manufacturing costs for the engine were lower than had originally been estimated, reducing the break-even point to 750 engines.

REQUIRED:

1. In late 19X5 financial difficulties caused one of the airlines that had placed orders for the new aircraft to indicate that it did not plan to exercise options for purchases of the new aircraft beyond the quantities that it was obligated to purchase. Remaining firm orders and options suggest that at least 400 aircraft (800 engines) will eventually be sold. How should Turbine Company respond to this information?

2. In early 19X6 several additional airlines also canceled their options for additional aircraft and engine purchases. It now appears that only 250 aircraft and 500 engines will eventually be manufactured and sold. How should Turbine Company respond to this information?

GLOSSARY

Accelerated cost recovery system (ACRS): A segment of the federal income tax law that provides for the rapid expensing of depreciable assets. (Chapter 16)

Accelerated depreciation: Depreciation computed using one of several depreciation methods that allocate a larger amount of an asset's cost to the early years of its life. (Chapter 9)

Account: A place in which all the changes in one of the entity's assets, liabilities, equity, revenues, or expenses are recorded. (Chapter 3)

Accounting: The identification, measurement, recording, and communication of economic information for use in financial decision making. (Chapter 1)

Accounting cycle: The procedures for processing information about the firm's economic activities in order to produce the various financial statements. (Chapter 3)

Accounting entity: An organization that has an identity separate from that of its owners and managers and for which accounting records are kept and accounting reports are issued. (Chapter 1)

Accounting system: The methods and records used to identify, measure, record, and communicate economic information about an entity. (Chapter 5)

Account payable: A current liability representing an amount owed by the entity for goods or services. (Chapter 10)

Account receivable: Money due from another business or individual as payment for the performance of services or the sale of goods on credit. (Chapter 8)

Accounts receivable turnover ratio: Measurement of the number of times accounts receivable is turned over each year. (Chapter 15)

Accrual: An entry that recognizes revenue or expense and records the related noncash asset or liability. (Chapter 4)

Accrual-basis accounting (accrual accounting): The method of recording the activities of a business entity when the activities occur rather than when the related cash is received and paid. (Chapter 1)

Accrued payables: Liabilities recorded by adjusting entries for expenses incurred but not paid—expenses associated with partially completed continuous events. (Chapter 10)

Accumulated depreciation: The total amount of depreciation that has been recorded for an asset as of any given time. (Chapter 9)

Acquisition cost: The purchase price plus all costs necessary to ready an asset for use. (Chapter 9)

Adjusted balance: The postadjustment balance to which an account is changed by an adjusting entry. (Chapter 4)

Adjusted gross income: Gross income less deductions from gross income. (Supplementary Topic D)

Adjusted trial balance: A trial balance that incorporates the effects of adjusting entries on the unadjusted trial balance. (Chapter 5)

Adjusting entry: A journal entry made at the end of an accounting period to record the completed portion of an incomplete continuous event. (Chapters 4 and 5)

Administrative expenses: The costs of managing and administering all activities of a business entity. (Chapter 2)

Aging method: A way of determining uncollectible account expense *indirectly* by first multiplying estimated uncollectible accounts percentages by the dollar amount of accounts receivable in various age categories (to find the desired balance for the allowance for uncollectible accounts) and then computing the amount of adjustment necessary to bring the allowance to the desired balance; the amount of the adjustment is also the amount of the uncollectible account expense. (Chapter 6)

Allowance for uncollectible accounts: A contra-asset account that reduces accounts receivable to the amount estimated to be collectible; also called *allowance for bad debts.* (Chapter 6)

All-resources concept: The concept that requires that financial statements disclose information about all acquisitions and sales of assets, all issues and repayments of debt, and all issues and repurchases of capital stock, regardless of whether or not they affect cash. (Chapter 13)

Alternative minimum tax (AMT): A tax system, separate from the regular system, which is intended to ensure that profitable corporations pay a minimum amount of income tax. (Chapter 16)

Amortization: The portion of the cost of intangible operating assets recognized as an expense for each period. (Chapter 9)

Annuity: A specified number of equal cash flows occurring one interest period apart. (Chapter 10)

Assets: Economic resources representing probable future economic benefits obtained or controlled by an entity (e.g., cash, accounts receivable, inventory, land, equipment, and buildings). (Chapter 1)

Asset turnover ratio: Measurement of the intensity with which a firm's assets are used to produce sales revenue. (Chapter 15)

Audit: An examination of financial statements and the underlying accounting system, conducted by a certified public accountant who issues a written opinion as to the fairness of the financial statements. (Chapter 1)

Authorized shares: The maximum number of shares of a given class of stock that a firm may legally issue (sell). (Chapter 12)

Balance sheet: The financial statement that provides information about an entity's economic resources (assets) and the claims against those resources by creditors and owners (liabilities and equity). (Chapter 1)

Bank reconciliation: A comparison of the bank statement with the firm's own cash account. (Chapter 8)

Basket purchase: The purchase of two or more assets together in a transaction that does not indicate the separate purchase price of each. (Chapter 9)

Bond: A formal promise by the issuer (borrower) to make specified future payments to discharge a liability. (Chapters 11A, 11B)

Bond issue: A collection of bonds, all of which are issued or sold by an entity at the same time. (Chapters 11A, 11B)

Bond sinking fund: A fund that will be used to redeem a bond issue at maturity. (Chapter 11B)

Book value: The amount at which an item is currently carried in the accounting records. In the case of depreciable assets, book value is cost less accumulated depreciation. (Chapter 9)

Boot: A payment or receipt of cash that accompanies the exchange of plant assets in a trade-in. (Chapter 9)

Business entity: An organization of people and resources established to sell goods or provide services at a profit. (Supplementary Topic A)

Callable bonds: Bonds that permit the issuer to repurchase or redeem the bonds at specified times by paying the bondholder a specified amount known as the *call price.* (Chapters 11A, 11B)

Capital assets: Land, depreciable property, and securities held by the firm for investment or for use in the business. (Chapter 16)

Capital expenditure: The original expenditure made to acquire a plant asset and any subsequent asset-related expenditure on which depreciation is taken. Such expenditures are said to be *capitalized* when added to an asset account. (Chapter 9)

Capital gains and losses: Gains and losses on the sale of capital assets. (Chapter 16)

Capital lease: A lease that is in substance a purchase of the asset leased. (Chapters 11A, 11B)

Capital stock: The component of equity in a corporation contributed by owners of the entity. (Chapter 1)

Carrying amount (book value): The recorded amount of a liability or asset after subtraction of contra accounts or addition of adjunct accounts. (Chapters 11A, 11B)

Carryover provisions: Provisions of the tax law that permit losses in one year to be applied against taxable income in other years, thereby reducing the amount of tax payable on income in those other years. (Chapter 16)

Cash-basis accounting: The method of recording the activities of a business entity only when the related amounts of cash are received and paid. (Chapter 1)

Cash over and short: The account in which a firm records the difference, or discrepancy, between cash actually taken in and cash reported as received by documents of receipt. (Chapter 8)

Certified public accountant (CPA): A licensed public accountant trained to perform auditing, management consulting, and tax services. (Chapter 1)

Charter (articles of incorporation): A document that authorizes the creation of a corporation, stating its name and purpose and the names of the incorporators and describing the stock the corporation is authorized to issue. (Chapter 12)

Chart of accounts: A list of all accounts, with a specific block of numbers assigned to each category (e.g., liabilities all numbered in the 2000s). (Chapter 3)

Closing entries: Journal entries that transfer revenue, expense, and dividends account balances to retained earnings. The closing of revenue and expense accounts employs an income summary account as an intermediate step in the transfer. (Chapter 5)

Common stock: Shares of equity of a corporation that usually give stockholders both voting rights and a residual equity interest. (Chapter 12)

Comparative component percentage statements: The side-by-side presentation of consecutive component percentage statements. (Chapter 15)

Comparative financial statements: Side-by-side presentations of consecutive financial statements of the same type. (Chapter 15)

Completed-production method: The method of revenue recognition that recognizes revenue and related product expense as soon as the product is available for sale. (Supplementary Topic E)

Component percentage statements: Financial statements in which the statement items are expressed as percentages of the largest statement amount. (Chapter 15)

Compound interest: A method of computing interest and then adding interest to an account (representing money borrowed or loaned) at regular intervals. (Chapter 10)

Concept: An idea or proposition that is broadly applicable to a variety of situations or contexts. (Chapter 1)

Conceptual framework of accounting: General concepts that derive from the objectives of financial reporting and from which generally accepted accounting principles (GAAP) are derived. (Chapter 1)

Conservatism: The convention that leads accountants to select from among acceptable accounting methods and procedures the one that results in the lowest (the most conservative) net income and net assets in the current period. (Chapter 7)

Consistency: The convention that discourages changes in accounting methods from one period to another, even if acceptable alternative methods exist. (Chapter 7)

Consolidated financial statements: Accounting reports presenting combined information about several interrelated corporations that form a single accounting entity. (Chapters 2, 14)

Consolidation worksheet: A schedule on which adjustments are made that transform corporate financial statements of a parent and its subsidiary into consolidated financial statements. (Chapter 14)

Constant dollar amounts: Dollar amounts, whether of historical cost or current cost, that have been adjusted for general price level changes. (Supplementary Topic B)

Constant dollar concept (constant purchasing power concept): The concept that leads to the adjustment of financial statement amounts for changes in the purchasing power of the dollar. (Supplementary Topic B)

Constructive receipt: The point at which income is available for possession by taxpayers; income is taxable when actually or constructively received. (Supplementary Topic D)

Contingencies: Future events that influence the present recognition and disclosure of transactions. (Supplementary Topic E)

Contingent liability: An obligation whose amount, timing, or recipient depends on future events. (Chapters 8, 10)

Continuous transaction: A transaction that is ongoing throughout a period of time. (Chapter 4)

Contra asset: A balance sheet item that is subtracted from the cost of an asset (e.g., accumulated depreciation). (Chapter 2)

Control account: An account in the general ledger that reports the total of the account balances of a subsidiary ledger. (Chapter 8)

Control environment: The collection of environmental factors that influence the effectiveness of control procedures. (Chapter 5)

Control procedures: The policies and procedures established by an entity to achieve its objectives. (Chapter 5)

Correcting entry: A journal entry that corrects erroneous account balances. (Chapter 5)

Cost: The cash expended or the cash value of noncash assets, liabilities, or equity given in exchange for an asset. Cost is the basis for recording assets, liabilities, and equity. (Chapter 1)

Cost method: The method of accounting for investments that recognizes investment income as distributions (dividends and interest) are accrued and carries investments at cost, subject to a lower-of-cost-or-market adjustment. (Chapters 8, 14)

Cost of goods available for sale: The cost of beginning inventory plus the cost of goods purchased during the accounting period. (Chapter 6)

Cost of goods sold: The purchase price of goods sold to customers during the accounting period plus the cost of readying the goods for sale. Cost of goods sold is calculated as the cost of goods available for sale minus the cost of the ending inventory. (Chapters 2, 6)

Credit: A change in an account representing a decrease in an asset or an increase in a liability or equity; credits are recorded on the right side of a T-account. (Chapter 3)

Credit card: A card that authorizes the holder to make purchases up to some limit from specified retail merchants. (Chapter 8)

Credit sales method: A way of determining uncollectible account expense *directly* by multiplying an estimated uncollectible account percentage by the total dollar amount of credit sales for the period. (Chapter 6)

Cumulative dividend preference: The provision that stockholders of cumulative preferred shares are to be paid both dividends in arrears and current dividends before dividends are paid to common stockholders. (Chapter 12)

Cumulative translation adjustment: A stockholders' equity account that measures the effects of translating a foreign subsidiary's asset and liability accounts at the current exchange rate and the equity accounts at historical rates. (Supplementary Topic C)

Current asset and current liability concept: The concept that assets and liabilities that are expected to turn over within the next operating cycle or next year, whichever is longer, should be identified on the balance sheet as current assets and current liabilities. (Chapter 2)

Current assets: Cash and other assets that will be either converted into cash or used to provide goods or services within one year or one operating cycle, whichever is longer. (Chapter 2)

Current cost: The price that would be paid for an asset at the present time. (Supplementary Topic B)

Current cost concept: The concept that leads to the adjustment of costs in financial statements for changes over time in the cost of the related assets. (Supplementary Topic B)

Current cost operating profit: The excess of revenue over total current cost expense. (Supplementary Topic B)

Current dividend preference: The provision that stockholders of preferred shares are to be paid current dividends before any dividends are paid to common stockholders. (Chapter 12)

Current liabilities: Obligations to outsiders that will require the firm to pay cash or provide goods or services within one year or one operating cycle, whichever is longer. (Chapters 2, 10)

Current market value: The monetary worth attributed to an asset by the marketplace at the present time. (Chapter 2)

Current ratio: An assessment of a firm's short-term liquidity, computed by dividing current assets by current liabilities. (Chapter 15)

Data collection: The identification of transactions affecting the firm and the gathering of all related documents in preparation for transaction analysis. (Chapter 3)

Date of record: The date on which a stockholder must have owned one or more shares of stock in order to receive a dividend. (Chapter 12)

Debit: A change in an account representing an increase in an asset or a decrease in a liability or equity; debits are recorded on the left side of a T-account. (Chapter 3)

Debit card: A card that authorizes a bank to make an immediate electronic withdrawal (debit) from the holder's bank account. (Chapter 8)

Debt: The sum of long-term debt and the debtlike obligations in current liabilities (notes or short-term loans). (Chapter 15)

Debt-management ratios: Measurements of a firm's ability to meet obligations involving debt. (Chapter 15)

Debt securities: The interest-bearing debt of businesses and governments in the form of notes and bonds. (Chapter 8)

Debt to equity ratio: Measurement of the proportion of capital provided by creditors relative to that provided by stockholders. (Chapter 15)

Debt to total assets ratio: Measurement of the proportion of total capital provided by creditors; most useful when equity is small or subject to substantial changes. (Chapter 15)

Declaration date: The date on which a corporation announces its intention to pay a dividend on capital stock. (Chapter 12)

Declining balance depreciation: The accelerated depreciation method that calculates depreciation by multiplying the declining book value of an asset by a depreciation rate. (Chapter 9)

Deductions: Outflows made by taxpayers that reduce taxable income. (Supplementary Topic D)

Deferral: An entry that records an asset or liability before the related expense is recognized. Deferrals frequently lead to subsequent adjusting entries. (Chapter 4)

Deferred charges: Usually, prepaid expenses scheduled to expire after one year or one operating cycle, whichever is longer. (Chapter 2)

Deferred tax liability: A liability created when temporary differences between the income statement and the tax return produce net taxable amounts that will not be taxed until future years. (Chapters 10, 16)

Depletion: The portion of the cost of natural resources recognized as an expense for each period. (Chapter 9)

Deposit in transit: An amount received and recorded by the firm and transmitted to the bank but not yet recorded by the bank. (Chapter 8)

Depreciable cost: The excess of an asset's acquisition cost over its residual value, which also equals the total depreciation over the life of the asset. (Chapter 9)

Depreciation: The portion of the cost of tangible operating assets (other than land) recognized as expense for each period. (Chapters 2, 9)

Depreciation methods: The standardized calculations required to determine periodic depreciation for various patterns of decline in the service potential of assets. (Chapter 9)

Discounting: The sale of a note receivable before maturity to a financial institution, such as a bank, at the note's maturity amount less a discount. (Chapter 8)

Discount on bonds payable: The excess of the total face amount of bonds over the amount received from their sale (proceeds). (Chapters 11A, 11B)

Discount on note: The excess of the maturity amount of a non-interest-bearing note over the amount borrowed (the principal). (Chapter 10)

Discrete transaction: A transaction that occurs at a particular point in time. (Chapter 4)

Dividend payout ratio: Measurement of the proportion of a firm's profits that are returned to stockholders immediately as dividends. (Chapter 15)

Dividends: Amounts paid periodically by a corporation to its stockholders as a return on their invested capital. Dividends represent distribution of net income, not expense. (Chapter 1)

Dividend yield ratio: Measurement of the rate at which dividends provide a return for the stockholder. (Chapter 15)

Double-entry system: The system based on the fundamental accounting model that records a two-part effect for every transaction. (Chapter 3)

Earnings per share: A corporation's net income divided by the number of shares of capital stock held by investors. (Chapter 2)

Earnings per share ratio (EPS): Measurement of the income available for common stockholders on a per-share basis. (Chapter 15)

Effective interest amortization: The assignment of interest to each interest period over the term of the liability in accordance with compound interest principles. (Chapter 11B)

Effective interest rate (yield rate): The interest rate that, when used to compute the present value of the future cash payments specified by a bond, produces a present value equal to the amount borrowed. (Chapter 11B)

Encumbrance: An authorization to make a future expenditure that is issued prior to incurrence of the related liability (e.g., purchase orders and purchase agreements). (Supplementary Topic A)

Equity (owners' equity): The owners' claims against the assets of a business entity, which equal the residual interest in the assets that remains after deducting the liabilities. (Chapters 1, 12)

Equity method: The method of accounting for long-term investments in equity securities that recognizes investment income as it is reported by the investee, causing investments to be carried at acquisition cost plus the investor's share of investee net income less the investor's share of investee dividends. (Chapter 14)

Equity securities: Ownership shares in another corporation in the form of capital stock. (Chapter 8)

Exchange rate: The rate at which one unit of one nation's currency is exchanged for one unit of another nation's currency. (Supplementary Topic C)

Exclusions: Sources of income excluded from taxation. (Supplementary Topic D)

Expected life: The period of time over which a firm anticipates deriving benefit from the use of an asset. (Chapter 9)

Expense: The outflow or other using up of assets by an entity in order to sell goods or services. (Chapter 1)

Face amount (par value): A payment required by a bond on the maturity date of the bond. (Chapters 11A, 11B)

Factoring: The sale of accounts receivable to a financial institution. (Chapter 8)

Fair value (fair market value): The estimated amount of cash required to acquire an asset. (Chapter 9)

Financial accounting: The process by which financial statements are prepared. (Chapter 1)

Financial Accounting Standards Board (FASB): The private-sector rule-making agency whose pronouncements are a primary source of generally accepted accounting principles. (Chapter 1)

Financial statements: Summary reports on the economic performance and status of a business entity as a whole, prepared for all decision makers outside the entity. (Chapter 1)

Financing cycle: The elapsed time between the receipt of financial resources from owners or creditors and the repayment of the original amount received. (Chapter 2)

First-in, first-out (FIFO) method: The method of allocating the costs of goods available for sale between ending inventory and cost of goods sold based on the assumption that the earliest purchases are sold first. (Chapter 7)

Flows: Measurements of changes in account balances (stocks) that occur during a given period of time. (Chapter 13)

Foreign exchange gain: A gain that arises when a firm owes foreign currency and the exchange rate falls or when a firm is to receive foreign currency and the exchange rate rises. (Supplementary Topic C)

Foreign exchange loss: A loss that arises when a firm owes foreign currency and the exchange rate rises or when a firm is to receive foreign currency and the exchange rate falls. (Supplementary Topic C)

Fund: A collection of assets, liabilities, and equity related to a specified subset of the activities of a nonbusiness organization. (Supplementary Topic A)

Fund accounting system: The collection of all funds that describes the various activities of a nonbusiness entity. (Supplementary Topic A)

Fund balance: The equity in a fund representing the excess of assets over liabilities that is available for future use by the fund. (Supplementary Topic A)

Future amount: The amount to which an account will grow by a specified future time when interest is compounded. (Chapter 10)

General ledger: The accounting record that contains the accounts that appear in the financial statements. (Chapter 3)

Generally accepted accounting principles (GAAP): The basic set of rules and conventions for the accounting profession, consisting of both official pronouncements (standards) and uncodified practices and procedures. (Chapter 1)

General price level change: A change in a large group of prices viewed as a whole, which alters the purchasing power of the monetary unit. (Supplementary Topic B)

Going concern assumption: The assumption that a firm is a healthy, ongoing enterprise that will recover through normal operations the cost of assets currently held and that will replace those assets as they are used up or sold. (Chapter 2)

Goodwill: The portion of the valuation differential in excess of the revaluation increment. (Chapter 14)

Gross income: Total income less exclusions. (Supplementary Topic D)

Gross margin (gross profit): Sales revenue minus cost of goods sold. (Chapter 2)

Gross margin method: A procedure for estimating cost of goods sold and ending inventory on the basis of the estimated gross margin rate, net sales revenue, and cost of goods available for sale. (Chapter 7)

Gross margin rate: The ratio of gross margin to net sales revenue. (Chapter 7)

Gross margin ratio: Measurement of the proportion of each sales dollar that is gross margin. (Chapter 15)

Hedge: A transaction that is designed to exactly offset any foreign exchange gains or losses that might occur. (Supplementary Topic C)

Historical cost: The cash originally expended or the original cash value of noncash assets, liabilities, or equity given in exchange for an asset; often used as a synonym for cost. (Chapter 2)

Historical cost net income (net income): The excess of an entity's revenue over its expense, measured using historical cost. (Supplementary Topic B)

Income before taxes: Income from operations plus the amount of other revenues and gains less the amount of other expenses and losses. (Chapter 2)

Income from operations: Gross margin (gross profit) minus operating expenses. (Chapter 2)

Income statement: The financial statement that reports the profitability of a business entity during a specific period of time. (Chapter 1)

Income summary: A temporary account to which all revenues and expenses are transferred or closed and which is itself closed to retained earnings. (Chapter 5)

Income tax: A tax based on the amount of taxable income earned by a taxpayer. (Chapter 16)

Income taxes expense: The income tax paid or owed to federal or other governments that is related to income before taxes. (Chapter 2)

Income tax return: A document containing a statement of taxable income and the related computation of income tax. (Chapter 16)

Installment sales method: The method of revenue recognition that recognizes revenue and related product expense as cash is collected. (Supplementary Topic E)

Intangible operating assets: Assets used in the operations of a firm that have a legal rather than a physical substance (e.g., patents, trademarks, and copyrights). (Chapter 9)

Interest: The excess of the total amount paid to a lender over the amount borrowed. (Chapter 8)

Interest amortization: The assignment of interest on a liability (or asset) to the interest periods that make up the term of the liability (or asset). (Chapters 11A, 11B)

Interest period: The time interval between interest calculations. (Chapter 10)

Interest rate: The percentage multiplied by the beginning-of-period balance to yield the amount of interest for that period. (Chapter 10)

Internal control structure: All the policies and procedures established by an entity to achieve its objectives and the environment in which these policies and procedures are used. (Chapter 5)

Interperiod tax allocation: The process of deferring income taxes expense from one period to another by use of a deferred tax liability account. (Chapter 10)

Inventory costing methods: Various systematic methods of determining the cost of the ending inventory (and hence the cost of goods sold), each based on a different assumption about the composition of the ending inventory in terms of the different prices paid for goods over time. (Chapter 7)

Inventory turnover ratio: Measurement of the number of times inventory is turned over each year. (Chapter 15)

Investments: A firm's holdings of shares of ownership or debt securities of other firms or of government securities. (Chapter 2)

Involuntary conversion: Disposition of an asset as a result of theft, an act of nature, or an accident. (Chapter 9)

Issued shares: The number of shares of a given class of stock actually sold to stockholders. (Chapter 12)

Journal: A chronological record of the double-entry effects of transactions on an entity over a specific period of time. (Chapter 3)

Journal entry: A double-entry change in accounts entered in a journal to record the effects of a transaction. (Chapter 3)

Journalizing: The process of entering the effects of transactions into a journal. (Chapter 3)

Last-in, first-out (LIFO) method: The method of allocating the cost of goods available for sale between ending inventory and cost of goods sold based on the assumption that the most recent purchases are sold first. (Chapter 7)

Lease: A document that enables its holder to use property without legally owning it. (Chapters 11A, 11B)

Ledger: The record containing the accounts of an entity. (Chapter 3)

Leverage (trading on equity): A firm's use of capital secured from creditors in the hope of producing more income than that needed to cover the interest on the related liability, with the excess income accruing to the stockholders. (Chapters 11A, 11B)

Liabilities: Probable future sacrifices of economic benefits (e.g., debts owed to creditors). (Chapters 1, 10)

Liquidity of a firm: The ability of a firm to meet its financial obligations as they come due. (Chapter 8)

Liquidity of an asset: The ease with which an asset can be converted into cash. (Chapter 8)

Long-term capital gains and losses: Gains and losses on the sale of capital assets held for more than one year. (Chapter 16)

Long-term debt to equity ratio: Measurement of the proportion of capital provided by long-term creditors relative to that provided by stockholders; most useful when there is little permanent short-term debt. (Chapter 15)

Long-term debt to total assets ratio: Measurement of the proportion of total capital provided by long-term creditors; most useful when there is little short-term debt and when equity is small or subject to substantial changes. (Chapter 15)

Long-term liabilities: The firm's obligations to outsiders that will require payment beyond the next year or next operating cycle, whichever is longer. (Chapter 2)

Long-term notes payable: Notes payable with terms that extend beyond the longer of one year or one operating cycle. (Chapters 11A, 11B)

Lower-of-cost-or-market adjustment: An adjusting entry that reduces the carrying amount of an asset from its cost to its lower market value and recognizes a corresponding loss on the income statement. (Chapter 8)

Lower-of-cost-or-market principle: The principle requiring that assets be reduced from their original cost to their current market value when the market value falls below cost. (Chapter 7)

Managerial accounting: Preparation of financial information designed for use by managers and decision makers inside the business entity. (Chapter 1)

Marketable security: A security that has a determinable market value and is traded regularly in an active market. (Chapter 8)

Market value: The monetary worth attributed to an asset by the marketplace. (Chapter 1)

Matching: The process of identifying expense (the cost of assets that have been given up or used to earn revenue) with a particular accounting period. (Chapter 2)

Matching concept: The concept that the expense of a given accounting period is the cost of assets given up or used to earn the revenue recognized in that period. (Chapter 2)

Measurement: The determination of the amount to be recorded for a transaction and the account titles to be used to describe the transaction. (Supplementary Topic E)

Minority interest: The portion of a subsidiary's stockholders' equity that corresponds to shares held by minority stockholders. (Chapter 14)

Modified accrual-basis accounting: The method of recognizing inflows of resources (revenues) when receipt is reasonably assured and recognizing outflows of resources (expenditures) when a commitment is made to pay. (Supplementary Topic A)

Natural resources: Operating assets that are physically consumed as they are used by the enterprise (e.g., coalfields, oil pools, and mineral deposits). (Chapter 9)

Net income: The excess of an entity's revenue over its expense during a period of time. Net income is calculated as income before taxes minus income taxes expense. (Chapters 1, 2)

Net income ratio: Measurement of the proportion of each sales dollar that is profit; sometimes called the *profit margin.* (Chapter 15)

Net loss: The excess of an entity's expense over its revenue during a period of time. (Chapter 1)

Nominal dollar amounts (nominal amounts): Dollar amounts, whether of historical cost or current cost, that have not been adjusted for general price level changes.

Nonbusiness entity: An organization of people and resources established to sell goods or provide services without regard to profit. (Supplementary Topic A)

Nopar stock: Stock that is without a par value but not necessarily without a stated (legal) value. (Chapter 12)

Note payable: The liability of a borrower arising from a note given to a lender. (Chapter 10)

Note receivable: A legal document given by a borrower to a lender stating the time of repayment and, directly or indirectly, the amount to be repaid. (Chapter 8)

Operating assets: Long-lived assets that remain on the business's records until used by the business in the course of operations. (Chapter 9)

Operating cycle: The elapsed time between the purchase of salable goods (or the purchase of materials used to produce salable goods or services) and the collection of cash from customers. (Chapter 2)

Operating expenses: The period expenses a business incurs in selling goods or providing services and in administering the entire range of its activities. (Chapter 2)

Operating income ratio: Measurement of the profitability of a firm's operations per sales dollar. (Chapter 15)

Operating lease: A lease in which the lessor retains the risks and obligations of ownership of the leased asset. (Chapters 11A, 11B)

Operating loss: An excess of deductible expenses over taxable revenue. (Chapter 16)

Operating ratios (efficiency ratios): Measurements of a firm's intensity of use of its assets (e.g., receivables, inventory, or total assets). (Chapter 15)

Ordinary income: The component of corporate taxable income measured as the excess of taxable revenues (and noncapital gains) over deductible expenses (and noncapital losses). (Chapter 16)

Other assets: Any assets outside the standard categories, including assets no longer used and assets not yet in operation. (Chapter 2)

Other expenses and losses: Expenses from activities not related to the firm's principal operations and losses from sales of assets that were not acquired for resale. (Chapter 2)

Other revenues and gains: Revenues from activities not related to the firm's principal operations and gains from sales of assets that were not acquired for resale. (Chapter 2)

Outstanding check: A check issued and recorded by the firm but not yet presented to the firm's bank for payment. (Chapter 8)

Outstanding shares: The number of issued shares actually in the hands of stockholders. (Chapter 12)

Paid-in capital in excess of par: The excess of total paid-in capital over the total par value of common (or preferred) shares issued by a corporation. (Chapter 12)

Parent: An entity whose investment in the stock of another firm enables it to control the other firm. (Chapter 14)

Participating dividend preference: The provision that stockholders of participating preferred shares receive a share of amounts available for dividends to other classes of stock in addition to the stated dividend on the preferred stock. (Chapter 12)

Par value: A monetary amount assigned to, and printed on, each share of stock that establishes a minimum price for the stock when issued but does not determine the economic value of the stock. (Chapter 12)

Payment date: The date on which a dividend is actually paid. (Chapter 12)

Pension expense: The cost of pension benefits matched with a given period, which usually differs from both the amount of funding and the amount of benefits paid during the period. (Chapter 10)

Pension funding: The process of making payments to a pension fund established to provide for the future payment of pension benefits. (Chapter 10)

Pension liability: The liability of an employer for future payments to a pension fund. (Chapter 10)

Percentage-of-completion method: The method of revenue recognition that recognizes revenue and related product expense during the production period in proportion to the work completed. (Supplementary Topic E)

Period expenses: The cost of assets assigned to the period of their use or consumption. (Chapter 2)

Periodicity concept: The concept that financial statements should be issued sufficiently often to provide timely information, but not so often that the precision of the statements is seriously impaired. (Chapter 2)

Periodic system: An inventory accounting system that records the cost of purchases as they occur during the accounting period but records the cost of goods sold only at the end of the accounting period; the inventory account reflects the correct inventory balance only at the end of each accounting period. (Chapter 6)

Permanent differences: Elements of taxable income that are permanently excluded from the determination of pretax accounting income or elements of accounting income before taxes that are permanently excluded from the determination of taxable income. (Chapter 16)

Perpetual system: An inventory accounting system that records both the cost of purchases and the cost of goods sold as purchases and sales occur during the accounting period; the inventory account reflects the correct inventory balance throughout the accounting period. (Chapter 6)

Physical inventory: The process whereby all items in inventory on a given date are identified and counted. (Chapter 6)

Point-of-sale method: The usual method of revenue recognition under which *sales revenue* is recognized when goods are transferred to customers or when services are performed for customers. (Supplementary Topic E)

Pooling-of-interests method: A method of accounting for business combinations that uses the book value of the investee's stockholders' equity as the investor's acquisition cost; applies only to a stock-for-stock exchange. (Chapter 14)

Postclosing trial balance: A trial balance prepared from the account balances immediately after the closing entries have been posted. (Chapter 5)

Posting: The process of transferring journalized transaction data to accounts in the ledger. (Chapter 3)

Preferred stock: Shares of equity of a corporation that usually do not give voting rights to the stockholders but grant a specified dividend subject to various guarantees or preferences. (Chapter 12)

Premium on bonds payable: The excess of the amount received from the sale of bonds (proceeds) over their total face amount. (Chapters 11A, 11B)

Present value: The present liability balance that will be exactly paid off by the related future payments (or, from the lender's viewpoint, the present asset balance that will be exactly liquidated by the future cash receipts). More generally, the present value is the current value of future cash flows discounted at an appropriate interest rate. (Chapter 10)

Pretax accounting income: Income before taxes measured according to generally accepted accounting principles (GAAP) and reported on the income statement. (Chapter 16)

Price earnings ratio (P/E): Measurement of the market's risk assessment and growth expectations for a firm's net income. (Chapter 15)

Price index: A numerical summary of the history of prices for a group, or "market basket," of commodities. (Supplementary Topic B)

Principal: The amount borrowed by the payer of a note. (Chapter 8)

Principle: A proposition or rule that applies to specific situations or contexts. (Chapter 1)

Prior period adjustment: Correction of an error made in the financial statements of a prior period that is entered as a direct adjustment to retained earnings. (Chapter 12)

Product expenses: The cost of assets sold to customers in a given period. (Chapter 2)

Profitability ratios: Measurements of (1) the contribution of the elements of operations to a firm's profit or (2) the relationship of profit to total investment and stockholder investment. (Chapter 15)

Progressive tax: A tax paid at higher rates by persons or organizations with higher incomes. (Chapter 16)

Property, plant, and equipment: Tangible operating assets used by a business to produce revenues. (Chapter 2)

Purchase discount: A price reduction (usually expressed as a percentage of the purchase price) granted by the seller conditional on prompt payment by the purchaser; also called a *cash discount.* (Chapter 6)

Purchase method: A method of accounting for business combinations that uses the fair value of the consideration given up to determine the acquisition cost. (Chapter 14)

Purchase returns: The cost of merchandise returned to suppliers during the accounting period. (Chapter 6)

Purchases: The cost of goods acquired for resale received from suppliers during the accounting period. (Chapter 6)

Quarterly payment of estimated tax: Tax payments made quarterly, based on a taxpayer's estimated tax due for the year. (Supplementary Topic D)

Quick ratio: A conservative assessment of a firm's short-term liquidity, computed by dividing quick assets (cash, receivables, and marketable securities) by current liabilities. (Chapter 15)

Ratio analysis: The examination of financial statements by preparing and evaluating a series of ratios developed from financial statement data. The purpose of ratio analysis is to develop decision-relevant information about a firm. (Chapter 15)

Recognition: The act of recording transactions in the accounting system, which involves determinations of whether or not events qualify to be recorded and, if they do, when they should be recorded and how they should be measured. (Chapter 3, Supplementary Topic E)

Reliable measurement: A description in words and numbers that is reasonably free from error and bias and that is a faithful representation of what it purports to represent. (Chapter 3, Supplementary Topic E)

Residual equity interest: An interest in all retained earnings of a corporation that are not specifically reserved for parties other than common stockholders. (Chapter 12)

Residual value (salvage value): The amount of cash or trade-in consideration that a firm expects to recover on retiring a particular asset from service. (Chapter 9)

Retail method: A procedure for estimating cost of goods sold and ending inventory by using the sales value (retail price) of the ending inventory and the ratio of cost to retail for the goods available for sale during the current period. (Chapter 7)

Retained earnings: The component of equity in a corporation representing accumulated profits in excess of losses and payments to owners. (Chapter 1)

Return on assets ratio: Measurement of the profit earned by a firm through the use of all its capital. (Chapter 15)

Return on equity ratio: Measurement of the profit earned by a firm through the use of capital supplied by stockholders. (Chapter 15)

Revaluation increment: The portion of the valuation differential applicable to specific assets. (Chapter 14)

Revenue: The inflow of assets to an entity resulting from the sale of goods or services by the entity. (Chapter 1)

Revenue expenditure: An expenditure that is not subject to depreciation. Such expenditures are said to be *expensed* when added to an expense account. (Chapter 9)

Revenue recognition: The process of identifying each dollar of revenue with a particular accounting period. (Chapter 2)

Revenue recognition concept: The concept that revenue should be recognized as earned when the seller has put forth substantially all the effort required to sell the related goods or services and when the selling price is known. (Chapter 2)

Reversing entries: Journal entries made at the beginning of an accounting period to reverse the preceding period's adjusting entries for revenue earned before collection or for expense incurred before payment. (Chapter 5)

Roll-forward adjustment: An adjustment of nominal dollar amounts for changes in the general level of prices subsequent to the transaction date. (Supplementary Topic B)

Sales allowance: A price reduction granted by the seller when goods retained by the purchaser are slightly defective, are shipped late, or in some other way are rendered less valuable. (Chapter 6)

Sales discount: A price reduction (usually expressed as a percentage of the selling price) granted by the seller conditional on prompt payment by the purchaser; also called a *cash discount.* (Chapter 6)

Sales returns: Merchandise or goods returned by the purchaser to the seller. (Chapter 6)

Sales revenue: Revenue resulting from the sale of goods or services by a business. (Chapter 2)

Securities and Exchange Commission (SEC): The federal agency established by Congress to regulate securities markets and to ensure effective public disclosure of accounting information. (Chapter 1)

Selling expenses: The costs of selling goods or selling and providing services. (Chapter 2)

Service potential concept: The view that an asset's cost should be allocated over its expected life to reflect the decline in its service potential. (Chapter 9)

Share: One of a large number of equal units into which a firm's total equity is divided. (Chapter 12)

Short-term capital gains and losses: Gains and losses on the sale of capital assets held for one year or less. (Chapter 16)

Short-term liquidity ratios: Measurements of a firm's ability to meet its short-term obligations as they mature. (Chapter 15)

Source documents: Those internally or externally prepared documents that describe a transaction and the monetary amount it involves. (Chapter 3)

Specific identification method: The method of allocating the cost of goods available for sale between ending inventory and cost of goods sold based on an identification of the actual units sold and in inventory. (Chapter 7)

Specific price change: A change in the price of a particular asset, which alters the current cost of that asset. (Supplementary Topic B)

Stable monetary unit assumption: The assumption that the purchasing power of the monetary unit is stable over time. (Supplementary Topic B)

Stated capital (legal capital): The amount of capital that, under law, cannot be returned to a corporation's owners unless the corporation is liquidated. (Chapter 12)

Stated rate (coupon rate, nominal rate, face rate, or contract rate): The ratio of one year's total interest payments to the face amount of the bond. (Chapters 11A, 11B)

Statement of cash flows: The financial statement that describes the inflows (sources) and outflows (uses) of a firm's financial resources during a given period of time. (Chapters 1, 13)

Statement of changes in retained earnings: The financial statement that summarizes the factors that altered retained earnings during a given accounting period. (Chapter 1)

Stock certificate: A document that represents one or more shares of stock and is issued in exchange for cash or other assets. (Chapter 12)

Stock dividend: A dividend paid to stockholders in the form of additional shares of stock (instead of cash). (Chapter 12)

Stockholder (shareholder): The owner (holder) of one or more shares of a corporation's stock; an owner of the corporation. (Chapter 12)

Stockholder ratios: Measurements of a firm's performance and stock returns that are relevant to investors' decisions. (Chapter 15)

Stockholders' equity: A title often used to identify the equity accounts on the balance sheets of corporations. (Chapter 2)

Stocks: Account balances that measure the dollar amount of an asset, a liability, or an equity at a given time. (Chapter 13)

Stock split: A stock issue by a corporation that increases the number of outstanding shares without changing the balance of any of its equity accounts. (Chapter 12)

Straight-line depreciation: The depreciation method that allocates an equal amount of an asset's cost to each year of the asset's expected life. (Chapter 9)

Straight-line interest amortization: The assignment of an equal amount of interest to each interest period over the term of the related liability. (Chapter 11A)

Subsidiary: A firm whose operations are controlled by another entity through that entity's investment in the firm's stock. (Chapter 14)

Subsidiary ledger: A ledger that provides supporting details for a specific account in the general ledger. (Chapter 8)

Sum-of-the-years'-digits depreciation: The accelerated depreciation method that calculates depreciation by multiplying depreciable cost by a declining ratio derived from the sum of the years in expected life. (Chapter 9)

Tangible operating assets: Assets used in the operations of a firm that have a visible, physical presence in the firm (e.g., buildings, equipment, and land). (Chapter 9)

Taxable income: Income subject to taxation, as measured according to rules established by the government that levies the tax and reported to that government on a document known as an *income tax return.* (Chapter 16)

Taxable income (individual): Adjusted gross income less itemized deductions (or the standard deduction) and exemptions. (Supplementary Topic D)

Tax avoidance: Taking actions or structuring transactions to minimize taxes. (Supplementary Topic D)

Tax credits: Governmentally authorized reductions of the amount of tax otherwise payable, to offset the cost to the corporation of certain corporate activities. (Chapter 16)

Tax evasion: Knowing misrepresentation of income or deductions with the objective of reducing taxes. (Supplementary Topic D)

Tax planning: The practice of evaluating the tax effects of contemplated actions or transactions. (Supplementary Topic D)

Tax shelter: An arrangement requiring an expenditure of cash in the current period that (1) reduces current tax and (2) is expected to produce future tax benefits or future income in an amount greater than the current expenditure. (Supplementary Topic D)

Temporary differences: Elements of income that are included in taxable income of one period and in pretax accounting income of another period. (Chapter 16)

Times interest earned ratio: Measurement of the excess of income available for interest payments over the amount of interest payments. (Chapter 15)

Time value of money: A synonym for *interest*. (Chapter 10)

Total income: All income available to the taxpayer, from whatever source it is derived. (Supplementary Topic D)

Trade-in: An asset acquisition in which the consideration given includes previously used plant assets. (Chapter 9)

Trade receivable: An account receivable due from a credit customer as a result of an ordinary business transaction. (Chapter 8)

Transaction analysis: Examination of the source documents or other data for a transaction to determine the accounts affected, the monetary amount of each effect, and the resulting increases or decreases in the account balances. (Chapter 3)

Transactions: Events or happenings of consequence to an entity that are recorded in its accounting system. (Chapter 3)

Translation: A process that transforms financial statements presented in a foreign currency into dollar-based statements. (Supplementary Topic C)

Transportation-in (freight-in): The account debited for the cost to the purchaser of transporting goods from suppliers. (Chapter 6)

Treasury stock: Previously issued stock that is repurchased by the issuing corporation. (Chapter 12)

Trial balance: An ordered list of all active accounts and their balances that shows whether total debit balances equal total credit balances. (Chapter 3)

Turnover: The average length of time required for assets to be consumed or replaced. (Chapter 15)

Unadjusted trial balance: A trial balance prepared immediately before the adjusting entries are posted. (Chapter 5)

Uncollectible account expense: The amount of credit sales predicted to be uncollectible, estimated in the period of sale; also called *bad debt expense.* (Chapter 6)

Unearned revenue: A liability created by a customer paying for goods or services in advance of their delivery or performance. (Chapter 10)

Unrealized gain or loss: A change in the market value of an investment that occurs prior to its sale. (Chapter 8)

Usage depreciation: The depreciation method that allocates the cost of an asset over its expected life in direct proportion to the actual use made of the asset. (Chapter 9)

Valuation differential: The difference between the acquisition cost of stock to a long-term investor and the book value of the stock (equity) on the financial statements of the acquired firm. (Chapter 14)

Voluntary retirement: Disposition of an asset by choice of the owner when the asset has reached the end of its usefulness to the owner. (Chapter 9)

Warranty: A guarantee given by a seller to a purchaser to repair or replace defective goods or parts of goods during a limited period following the sale. (Chapter 10)

Weighted average method: The method of allocating the cost of goods available for sale between ending inventory and cost of goods sold based on a single, weighted average cost per unit. (Chapter 7)

Worksheet: A schedule that summarizes the information generated in the performance of the end-of-period steps in the accounting cycle and enables the accountant to check this information for completeness and consistency. (Chapter 5)

INDEX

Page numbers in **boldface** contain definitions.